The **Dog** ENCYCLOPEDIA

The Dog

ENCYCLOPEDIA

Adaptations:

German :
    Translations   K. Ayche, C. Belakhdar, B. Janka, A. Lucke, V. Matyssek, E. Moser, M. Neumann, B. Sallegger,
        S. Schmidt-Wussow, U. Wapler, P. Warnier-Kofler, R. Xanthopoulos.
    Layout   Magali Barrailler, Vania Soraru, Nathalie Courdent, Irina Azvedo-Tadieu, Joël Chapuis, Sabrina Monchi
    Rewriting   Kathrin Busch-Kschiewan, Nadja Hultsch, Sonja Zabel, Ursula Zabel
English :
    Translations   Diane Dinsmore, Julie Plovnick, Chari Voss, Andrene Everson.
    Layout   Catherine Naas
    Rewriting   Roy Herridge, Emmanuel Pacitto, Anne Karpoff
Brazilian :
    Translations   S. Artamonoff, B. Delevallee, M. D'Orey de Faria, L. Goncalves, B. Magne, E. Rio Branco, M. Rosemberg,
    Madame Antunes.
    Layout   Florbela Lourenço Pires, Joël Chapuis, Irina Azvedo-Tadieu, Nathalie Courdent, Sabrina Monchi
    Rewriting   Claude Mouette, Yves Micelli, Valeria Cardoso de Melo Carvalho
Chinese :   Royal Canin Chine / François Gergaud
Spanish :
    Translations   Maria-Claudia Filgueira, Carles Sanchez
    Layout   Isabelle Riener
    Rewriting   Marie-Pierre Ellie, Maria-Claudia Filgueira
Italian :
    Translations   B. Baldi, D. Benigni, G. Conollo, D. De Leo, L. De Berardinis, L. Desotgiu, V. Fucci, C. Galimberti,
        S. Guazzoni, R. Kohn,
        P. Mequin, A.-M. Negrerte, A. Sudano, C. Torossi Bovo.
    Layout   Sabrina Monchi, Vania Soraru, Irina Azvedo-Tadieu, Nathalie Courdent, Joël Chapuis
    Rewriting   Franco Rapetti, Luca Bussolati
Netherlands :
    Translations   C. Boerhigter, K. Desmarsevers, A. Detelder, C. Dijkman, A. Frehen-Asures, B. Raemaekers, A. Scherpbier,
        P. Smift, M. Van Den Berg, B. Van Oosterhout, M. Van Zanten.
    Layout   Nathalie Courdent.
    Rewriting   Muriel Jacqmin, Cécile Devroy, Bastiaan Rohrer & The team Royal Canin Nederland b.v.
Swedish :
    Translations   A. Brantley, H. Hellberg, M. Jarvelin, R. Johansson, S. Jonsson, H. Karlson, J. Lindberg, U. Lundquist,
        M. Persson, S. Petersson, B. Sandstrom, C. Wallen, M. Vikberg.
    Layout   Joël Chapuis, Irina Azvedo-Tadieu.
    Rewriting   Bo Edoff, Anne-Catherine Edoff, Susanne Hellman, Ronan Mage, Hanna Edoff, Maud Dickson, Elisabeth
        Raab-Alvarson, Carin Lyrholm, Leg. Vet. Katarina Bewig, Wilhelm Dufwa, Ninni Hjortvall,
        Siw & Charles de Windle, Leg. Vet. Monica Stavenborn

This book is also available in French.

Coordination Royal Canin: Catherine Legros
Project Editors: Diffomédia / Paris
Coordination: Béatrice Fortamps, assistée de Marie-Édith Baret
Creation and Illustrations: Agnès Pezon, Guy Rolland
Cover: Teckel, épagneul breton, Berger allemand - © F. Nicaise & Dogue Allemand - © Ch. Renner

© 2000 First edition in French

© 2005 Aniwa SA

Publisher: Aniwa Publishing
10, rue du Colisée - F.-75008 - Paris
Tél. : + 33 (0) 1 44 95 02 20 Fax : + 33 (0) 1 44 95 02 22
www.aniwa.com

ISBN : 2-7476-0010-6

Printed in EEC

Contributors

SCIENTIFIC DIRECTION

PROFESSOR DOMINIQUE GRANDJEAN
Department of Breeding and Sport Medicine (UMES)
Alfort National School of Veterinary Medicine
Main author and scientific coordinator

JOSÉE AND JEAN-PIERRE VAISSAIRE,
Doctors of Veterinary Medicine, France

AND IN ALPHABETICAL ORDER

Karine Alves, veterinarian, Department of Breeding and Sport Medicine, Alfort National School of Veterinary Medicine, France
Hélène Bacqué, Digest of Veterinary Medicine, France
René Bailly, Doctor of Veterinary Medicine, President of the National Union of Free Exercise Veterinarians
Vincent Biourge, Doctor of Veterinary Medicine, Royal Canin Research Center, France
Mark Bloomerg (=), Doctor of Veterinary Medicine, Professor at the University of Florida, Gainesville, USA
Monique Bourdin, Doctor of Veterinary Medicine, Behavior Consultant, Alfort National School of Veterinary Medicine, France
Brigitte Bullard-Cordeau, animal journalist, Editor-in-Chief of Animal Junior, France
Eliane Chatelain, Doctor of Veterinary Medicine, Professor at the School of Veterinary Medicine of Lyon, Department of Anatomy
Jean-François Courreau, Doctor of Veterinary Medicine, Professor of Zootechnology, Alfort National School of Veterinary Medicine, France
Fabrice Crépin, Doctor of Veterinary Medicine, Royal Canin
Fathi Driss, Doctor of Sciencs, Professor of Nutrition, Université René-Descartes, Paris V, France
Milette Dujardin, Royal Canin, France
Catherine Escriou, Doctor of Veterinary Medicine, Researcher at the Neurological Laboratory, Alfort National School of Veterinary Medicine, France
Jean-Louis Esquivié, Commanding General, National Gendarmerie School, France
Vanessa Fuks, Doctor of Veterinary Medicine, Department of Breeding and Sport Medicine, Alfort National School of Veterinary Medicine, France
Aude-Gaëlle Heitzman-Béné, Doctor of Veterinary Medicine, Dept of Breeding and Sport Medicine, Alfort National School of Veterinary Medicine, France
Petra Horvatic-Peer, Doctor of Veterinary Medicine, University of Vienna, Austria
Ann Hudson, Royal Canin, USA
Elen Kienzle, Doctor of Veterinary Medicine, Professor of Nutrition, University of Munich, Germany
David Kronfeld, Doctor of Veterinary Medicine, Professor of Physiology, Virginia Tech, Blacksburg, USA
Henri Lagarde, CEO, Royal Canin, France
Dominique Lebrun, Royal Canin, France
Nathalie Moquet, Veterinarian, Department of Breeding and Sport Medicine, Alfort National School of Veterinary Medicine, France
Robert Moraillon, Doctor of Veterinary Medicine, Alfort National School of Veterinary Medicine, France
Nicolas Nudelmann, Doctor of Veterinary Medicine, Professor of Reproductive Pathology, Alfort National School of Veterinary Medicine, France
Bernard Paragon, Doctor of Veterinary Medicine, Professor of Nutrition, Alfort National School of Veterinary Medicine, France
Sandrine Pawlowiecz, Veterinarian, Department of Breeding and Sport Medicine, Alfort National School of Veterinary Medicine, France
Jacques Philip, Fairbanks, Alaska, USA
Pascale Pibot, Doctor of Veterinary Medicine, Royal Canin Research Center, France
Jacques Pidoux, Royal Canin, U.K.
Philippe Pierson, Doctor of Veterinary Medicine, Royal Canin
Bruno Polack, Doctor of Veterinary Medicine, Professor of Parasitology, Alfort National School of Veterinary Medicine, France
Jean-Marc Poupard, Researcher at the Laboratoire de biosociologie animale et comparée, University of Paris-Sorbonne, France
Jean-Pierre Samaille, Doctor of Veterinary Medicine, Editor-in-Chief of L'Action vétérinaire, France
Renaud Sergheraert, Director of the Royal Canin Research Center, France
Adolfo Spektor, Doctor of Veterinary Medicine, international judge
Helena Spektor, international judge, Royal Canin, Argentina
Florence Tessier, Royal Canin, France
Anne-Karen Tourtebatte, Veterinarian, Department of Breeding and Sport Medicine, Alfort National School of Veterinary Medicine, France
Jérôme Vanek, Doctor of Veterinary Medicine, University of Minnesota, St. Paul, Minnesota, USA
Pierre Wagner, Royal Canin, USA

FROM KNOWLEDGE COMES EXPERTISE...
...FROM PASSION COMES KNOWLEDGE

"Mankind's real moral test,
a test so radical and so deep that it escapes our gaze,
is probably the one of its relations with those that are the most at its mercy: the animals".
MILAN KUNDERA

M AN'S NATURE IS SUCH that he can't help bringing everything back to himself, comparing everything with himself, with his own condition, sometimes ending up treating his dog like a human being, or even a child.
And yet, true respect for the dog, like for any human being, does not lie there!

It has to do with each of us becoming aware of the real identity of the canine species.
A morphological, biological identity and, of course, a psychological and behavioral identity, highly complex thanks to an animality that has adapted to man over the centuries.

Therefore, respecting the dog means respecting both the original prehistoric animal, and the modern animal, the fruit of a zoological evolution that has been wanted and conducted by man.

The prehistoric animal was above all a pack animal, obeying a precise hierarchy, both instinctive and imposed upon, within this pack, a source of efficiency in its struggle for survival.

The modern animal has retained, in the depth of its true nature, the same need for hierarchical integration, and it has indeed integrated, with a fantastic adaptability, into all forms of human societies and civilizations.

The dog is a social and hierarchical animal; it expects from its master the coherence, the consistency and the same respect that its ancestors found in the hierarchy of the pack.

Respecting the animal means first respecting its true biological and psychological needs.

Such an approach is possible only if it is based on the understanding, analysis and synthesis of our knowledge of the canine species.

And from knowledge comes competence, precision.

A specialist in canine high nutrition, Royal Canin pioneered the taking into account of the exceptional diversity of the canine species, and of the consequences of this diversity as regards nutrition, as early as in 1980 with the large-breed puppy food (AGR), and in a comprehensive and global manner in 1997 with Size.

Indeed, of all the animal species to be found on earth, the dog is undoubtedly one of the most diversified ones. Not only may its adult size vary from 1 to over 90 kg, but also one now knows that small, medium and large breeds have neither the same life expectancy (8/9 years in large breeds, 14/15 in small breeds), nor the same length of growth, nor the same number of puppies per litter (1 to 3 in small breeds, 8 or even 12 in large breeds). Moreover, one knows now that there are fundamental physiological differences, depending on the breeds' size and format. Thus, for instance, the digestive tract of a large breed dog accounts for only 2.8% of its total weight, as against 7% in a small-sized dog, which explains many digestive, bone, biological problems left unsolved for a long time.

This consideration led us to propose from now on, for example for Maxi Giant Breed (between 45 kg and 90 kg) (99,5-198,5 lb)a totally specific diet;

- Giant kibbles to encourage the dog to chew, salivate and slowly ingest to favor a better digestion.
- A kibble with maximum digestibility enriched with Vit. E, chondroitine, …

At the same time, the scientific advances of the last few years have led us to go beyond the two traditional roles of nutrition (on the one hand, build and maintain the body, and on the other hand, supply energy), in order to integrate a third dimension: prevention.

It's the birth of nutrition-health, which will be the nutrition of the 21st century, combining pleasure with health.

Nurtured on the considerable passion, knowledge and scientific precision of the teams at Royal Canin and at the Alfort National School of Veterinary Medecine, the edition of this encyclopedia represents a decisive step in and a radical upgrading of the approach to knowledge of the canine species: from now on, the evolution of the nutritional approach is dependent on the dog's size considered as a fundamental element.

This encyclopedia is also the expression of all the contributors' commitment to a rational and not exclusively emotional vision of the relations that must prevail between man and this fascinating animal.

It is no accident that it has been carried out under the supervision of Professor Dominique Grandjean: this is the fruit of a long and productive scientific collaboration between the Research Center of the Royal Canin company and the teams of the State Veterinary School of Alfort, especially that of the Breeding and Sports Medicine Unit (UMES).

This is also the result of a tradition of intense scientific partnership with researchers and institutes all over the world, in Europe, in the United States and in South America.

May they all be thanked.

HENRI LAGARDE
Chairman and Chief Executive Officer
Royal Canin Group

Foreword

IT TOOK more than one hundred thousand years for a wild, wandering canine to become the marvelous companion we enjoy today. For many millennia, dogs helped humans with daily tasks. Little by little, dogs worked their way into the hearts of humans, enhancing quality of life. By the nineteenth century, dogs had integrated themselves into homes, becoming well-loved members of many families.

As a result, we have become more involved in the lives of dogs, carefully breeding and training them, and providing optimal nutrition. We do this not simply so they can live, but so that through their relationship with us, they have a better quality of live. Over the centuries, types of dogs, then breeds evolved. Man often played a role in the development of dogs as he molded individual breeds for certain needs or simply for pleasure. The original dog gave birth to several hundred distinct breeds that have been defined by kennel clubs around the world. Add to those the breeds that have not yet been recognized, plus millions of dearly-loved "mutts." As a result of scientific study, there is a growing awareness of the vast biological differences and needs of different dogs. There is remarkable variation in size and body shape from one breed to the next. At the close of the twentieth century, we have learned that the food, training, and medical care provided to a small dog is not proper for a medium or large dog. This encyclopedia takes a bold step forward by providing the latest information from veterinary and biological research and applying it to the everyday care and needs of your dog. Armed with this new knowledge, you the reader will be in a position to better understand and care for your dog. Our desire was to develop a complete, up-to-the minute reference that touched on all aspects of the dog. This would not have been possible without the collaboration between the worlds of academics business—collaboration between the Royal Canin research department and the Department of Breeding and Sport Medicine of the Alfort National School of Veterinary Sciences.

Specialists from numerous European countries and the United States have contributed to this international work, which is a reflection of what the scientific world should be—an international effort, just like the dog, breaking down linguistic and cultural barriers. Many individuals have contributed to the development of this encyclopedia, making it more informative and interesting. We would like to thank in particular doctors of veterinary medicine Josée and Jean-Pierre Vaissaire, and Philippe Pierson, D.V.M., member of the Department of Breeding and Sport Medicine and a European specialist in dog breeding and its related medical field.

It is our hope that this encyclopedia, which combines up-to-date scientific data, practical information, cultural context, and high-quality illustrations, will answer questions our readers may have regarding the use, feeding, and health of their dogs, as well as a new understanding and real respect for this magnificent animal—the dog.

PROFESSOR DOMINIQUE GRANJEAN
Doctor of Veterinary Medicine
Doctor of Nutrition, HDR
Head of the Department of Breeding
and Sport Medicine
Alfort National School of Veterinary Sciences

BERNARDO GALLITELLI
Chairman and Chief Executive Officer
Aniwa S.A.

Preface

From time immemorial, aanimals, particularly dogs, have been present in art and popular traditions, which gives witness to man's devotion to and special interest in one of his oldest companions. While a dog's unique behavior has always privileged a symbiotic relationship between humans and dogs, the tie has become even stronger as dogs'traditional role as a worker has given way to his role as faithful companion. Guard dogs no longer simply guard the estate. They are now often considered part of the family.

Dogs improve quality of life in urban settings. The dog acts as a buffer against loneliness, filling a gap in society where personal relationships are often unsatisfying.

The French are often said to have a love affair with the dog. Perhaps it is true considering a country with a population of 58 million has approximately eight million dogs.

An encyclopedia attempts to provide readers with complete, detailed information about its subject matter. To do this, the authors, under the supervision of Professor Dominique Grandjean, at the Alfort School of Veterinary Medecine, have covered all aspects of cynology and dog medicine. Considerable attention is given to the dog in art and communication, demonstrating the significant role this animal species plays in a wide range of human activities. The role of the dog as a helper is discussed in depth. While most are aware of the vital role a dog plays in providing companionship for the elderly or children, many do not realize what a vital role dogs can play in helping handicapped individuals or the therapeutic benefits of the presence of a dog in hospitals or nursing homes. Detailed information about utility dogs and sporting dogs is also provided.

A scientific and technical study of the dog is undertaken, providing the reader with the essentials of dog anatomy, physiology, growth and aging processes, nutrition, and primary diseases.

In addition, practical information on maintaining a pet's health and how to prepare and train a sporting dog is presented. Veterinary professions are discussed in detail.

Prof. Grandjean is to be congratulated for his role in developing and coordinating the publication of this Encyclopedia. He has succeeded in presenting highly technical information in a manner easily understandable by a lay person.

Professor Robert Moraillon
Director of the Alfort National School
of Veterinary Medecine

Summary

List of breeds

The purpose of this work is to provide information to the reader. It should not be used as a medical reference or as a substitute for consulting or visiting a veterinary office. Please consult your veterinarian regularly.

Photo Credits

All photos in this Encyclopedia are from the Cogis photo archives:

Francais, Garguil, Gauzargues, Gehlmar, Gelhar, Gengoux, Grissey, Hermeline, Ingeborg, Labat, Lanceau, Lepage, Lili, Nicaise, Potier, Remy, Rocher, Schwartz, Seitre, Varin, Vedie, Vidal, Willy's, Zizola.

Except:
- *Photos by Yann Arthus-Bertrand appear on the following pages:*
27, 30, 33, 37, 38, 39, 47, 49, 50, 55, 58, 60, 61,62, 70, 71, 75, 77, 78, 85, 87, 88, 89, 91, 96, 98, 101, 102, 104, 105, 108, 123, 128, 129, 130, 131, 134, 137, 138, 139, 140, 141, 142, 144, 148, 154, 161, 168, 173, 176, 182, 184, 195, 205, 224, 228, 237, 238, 244, 250, 259, 260, 261, 274, 275, 277, 278, 282, 283, 291, 292, 295, 298, 300,307, 312, 313, 314, 315, 316, 317, 318, 320, 321, 322, 323, 326, 328, 329, 330, 331, 332, 333, 335, 340, 343, 347, 351.
- *Photos from the Royal Canin archives: Philippe Psaïla, Jean-Pierre Lenfant et Yves Renner*
- *Illustrations provided by museums and private institutes specializing in art or historical photos are clearly referenced in the captions of the illustrations.*
- *UMES: 386, 388, 389, 390, 391, 394, 395, 396, 397, 404, 436, 437, 438, 440, 446, 447, 448, 450, 451, 579*
- *Agence Giraudon, Paris: 1, 364, 365, 369, 371*
- *Photographie Selva, Paris: 7, 366, 368, 370, 374, 375, 377, 379, 383, 384, 408*
- *Kharbine-Tapabor, Paris: 14, 15, 353, 359, 376, 378, 382, 387, 403, 407*
- *ENVA: 581*

True **respect** of the **Dog**

As forgivable as it may be, treating the dog like a little human being is a biological error that may prove dangerous for the animal.

Respecting the dog for what it gives us and represents to us should not consist of developing an anthropomorphic approach aiming to make the dog, as we often hear, "a child, if only it could speak". Biology is such that it preferred the earthly diversity of living creatures, making each one of them the complement of the others so as to tend towards a delicate balance that Man may not alter in any way.
This anthropomorphic reflex, as forgivable as it may be, given the sometimes powerful emotions that we all feel towards our dogs, must therefore be shunned as being disrespectful of their biological and physiological functioning and, consequently, may prove to be dangerous to them.

The best examples of this reality may be found in the daily diet:

- Man can change his diet at each mealtime without problems ... but, if his digestive system were designed like that of the dog, such continuous dietary variation would give him constant problems with diarrhoea.

- Man needs cooked food, salt, sugar, appetizing smells and presentation of the food on his plate in order to enjoy his meal, but, if his senses were those of the dog, he would need only the merest hint of the latter to appreciate it completely ...

- For thousands of years, man has been able to take his time to eat his meals, without the risk of becoming the prey of a wild predator but, if he were a dog, evolution would have left him with more of that reflex of rapid consumption imprinted in the genes of all animals likely to have their food stolen by a member of its own species or be attacked by a predator ...

So, with all due deference; dogs are dogs. They must be appreciated, treated and respected as such. And, if we consider the examples already mentioned, science and observation will only support these facts.

The digestion is a typical example of the reactions and mechanisms proper to each species, any assimilation may prove to be dangerous for the dog (or for humans), the differences being so obvious and the behavior patterns so dissimilar.

The passage of food in the organism allows a better understanding of these key notions.

Generally speaking, the human digestive system represents 10% of the body weight, compared with only 2.7 to 7% for the dog (depending on its size). Hardly surprising to hear that Man is better able to digest the most varied elements.

Food appreciation: smell and taste differently involved

The dog, unlike human beings, appreciates its food first and foremost by smell. According to the breed, the surface of its nasal mucus is between 10 and 100 times greater than that of humans. The nose of a German Shepherd contains up to 200 million olfactory receptors, while the most sensitive human nose has no more than 20 million. Taste however, despite the received wisdom, is only very marginally involved in the dog's food preferences. While humans have some 9 000 "taste buds" (the cells that receive and analyse the taste of food), the dog has 6 to 8 times fewer and, once in its mouth, the food does not linger on the tongue but is sent very quickly towards the stomach.

Taste buds

9000

1700

Predigestion: *from the oral cavity to the stomach*

The dog does not chew its food. It swallows it, whereas humans ready their food for digestion by prolonged chewing, finding pleasure by releasing flavors and, by grinding the food down and mixing it with saliva, begins the first stage of digestion via the enzymes contained in the latter. For the dog, however, the stomach is the chief location where the processes of digestion are started.

Scientific reality shows us once again: the stomach represents 2/3 of the total weight of the digestive system of the canine species, compared with only 10% for humans.

The very acid stomach pH, plus the large amounts of hydrochloric acid (6 times greater than in humans), equips the dog's stomach admirably for its function as a purifier, providing it with an extraordinarily efficient natural barrier against digestive infections.

Weight of digestive tract as percentage of body weight	11%	2.7% for a giant dog and 7% for a small dog
Surface of nasal mucus	2 to 3 cm²	60 to 200 cm²
Olfactory cells	5 to 20 million	70 to 220 million
Taste buds	9 000 buds	1 700 buds
Dentition	32 teeth	42 teeth
Mastication	prolonged	very reduced
Salivary digestive enzymes	YES	NO
Duration of food intake	1 hour	1 to 3 minutes
Stomach capacity	1.3 l	0.5 to 8 l
Stomach pH	2 to 4	1 to 2
Length of small intestine	6 to 6.5 m	1.7 to 6 m
Length of large intestine	1.5 m	0.3 to 1 m
Density of intestinal flora	10 000 000 bacteria/g	10 000 bacteria/g
Duration of intestinal transit	30 hours to 5 days	12 to 30 hours
Adult carbohydrate requirement	60 to 65% of the dry matter	very low
Adult protein requirement	8 to 12% of the dry matter	20 to 40% of the dry matter
Adult lipid requirement	25 to 30% of the dry matter	10 to 65% of the dry matter
Dietary habit	**omnivore**	**semi-carnivore**

Digestive performance: *inherited in the genes*

The dog was once a pack animal that had to digest its prey quickly and be capable of deriving the maximum of nutrients. This explains why the digestive transit is very rapid in the dog compared with that of a human being (12 to 24 hours compared with 30 to 48 hours).

Unlike that of the complete omnivore that is man, who has to adapt to such varied foods as meat, vegetables, fruit… the dog's intestinal flora is very targeted. Man's bacterial intestinal flora is 1 000 denser than a dog's.

To understand these elements, which may also be considered in other biological functional aspects, is to understand the dog, and above all to accept that the dog is very different to the human, not only in its appearance or in the fact that it cannot "speak". The sometimes-extreme anthropomorphism touted in certain films, for instance, is not only scientifically regrettable, but is actually very harmful and may even reduce the life expectancy of the animal.

The differences between man and dog

*Physiological differences
and differences in basic dietary habit mean
that each has specific nutritional needs.*

Failure to recognize the real needs of the animal, combined with every owner's natural desire to "do the best", may represent a danger to our animals by projecting on to them our wishes, our lifestyles, without taking account of the essential: their animal nature.

Responsible for the domestication of the dog, man has the duty of feeding it according to its true specific needs, and not according to any human projections. The animal is an animal, and in no way a human being as regards its biology. This is the first rule of true respect of the animal. The choice of food best adapted to one's animal must therefore be guided by a dietary approach that is not influenced by one's own eating habits.

Since the dawn of time Man has been an omnivore, blessed with a sense of taste and enjoying variety to dispel boredom, whereas the organism of the dog, a carnivore, is adapted to one particular type of food. Although it is sometimes tempting to apply the rule of diversity to your dog and serve it food more closely resembling a human meal, this would be ill-adapted to its condition or its morphology. Nearly 10 000 years of domestication of the canine race have not succeeded in transforming these carnivores into omnivores.

The same applies to all those little pleasures we offer them in the image of those we treat ourselves to. Butter, a spoonful of yogurt, a piece of chocolate (a high dose is poisonous for dogs!), fish, a lump of sugar, a piece of Gruyère (the calories contained in 30 g of Gruyère correspond to one third of the whole day's energy requirement of a small dog!), cheese, a piece of bread, ... all these little "extras" disturb the perfectly balanced intake calculated by a nutritionist. Such imbalances may result in intestinal problems and slowly but surely debilitate the animal. We must remain on our guard and curb our anthropomorphic instincts that may harm the good health of our animals.

From "feeding" to "Health Nutrition"

*To enjoy life
as long as possible.*

Although death is, and will remain, an inescapable biological process, it is also true that immense progress has been made in medical science, especially on the preventive side of the equation, now ensuring our canine friends a steadily increasing life expectancy.

An extraordinary improvement in nutrition:

In the past 30 years, the foods prepared by animal feed manufacturers for domestic pets have brought about a revolutionary change in the conditions of life of our dogs, formerly fed on scraps and leftovers and bread soaked in water. It has been estimated that dogs have acquired nearly 3 years of additional life expectancy in the past 15 years alone. According to Banfield, one of the leading private chains of clinics and veterinarians in the United States, the average life of a dog will have increased by as much as 28% in 10 years.

It is quite probable that the years to come will bring even higher figures, since three major advances have been made in the past 30 years:

- until 1980, a dog was simply "fed" to stop it feeling hungry, without worrying too much about anything else.

- after 1980, Health Nutrition took its first steps by allowing for 2 parameters: the Age of the animal and its Level of Activity,

- 1997 to 2000 marks the arrival of Health Nutrition with two new dimensions: Prevention and type of Breed. Four parameters were now taken into account: not only Age and Activity, but also Breed and Physiological Condition of the animal.

The four objectives of Health Nutrition

1 - To build up/sustain the organism
2 - To provide energy
3 - Nourish and Prevent
4 - Nourish and Treat

It is now possible to formulate feeds in the light of clearly identified requirements, according to known and indexed deficiencies that have to be combated, and to specificities discovered along the way as research moves onwards. Scientists now realize that dogs do not have to be fed the same way regardless of whether they are puppies, adult or mature dogs, of small, medium-sized or large breeds.

This realization is growing daily and allows the development from the simple Feed (giving the animal something to eat) to Basic Nutrition (meeting the nutritional needs of the organism), then going on to Health Nutrition, where a distinction is made between two complementary approaches: "Nourish and Prevent" and "Nourish and Treat".

So, driven by scientific research in veterinary medicine, the traditional concept of nutrition, namely building up/sustaining the organism and providing energy, has transformed in a matter of years to include the dimensions of prevention and, under certain conditions, treatment.

Basic Nutrition (Nutritional Needs for Sustaining the Body)

1 - Building up/sustaining the body:
Amino acids, minerals, trace elements, vitamins, proteins and certain lipids meet the minimum nutritional need to build up and sustain the body.

Proteins: growth, reproduction, muscles, coat...
Minerals and trace elements: nervous system, skeleton, teeth, blood...
Vitamins: sight, reproduction, skeleton, cells...
Lipids: cell membranes

2 - Providing energy:
Lipids and carbohydrates provide the animal with the necessary energy.

Lipids: energy, appetite
Carbohydrates: energy, digestion
Non-essential amino acids

Health Nutrition

Nutrition is now - and this is at least one point of convergence between man and dogkind - a key aspect of prevention, probably even the most important; this accounts for its being considered as the first among medicines (as did Hippocrates in antiquity) … and no doubt the gentlest of them all!

3 - Nourish and prevent:
Certain nutrients are integrated in the prevention of risks such as kidney diseases, digestive problems or the effects of old age…

Bone condition: calcium, excess fatty deposits
Kidney problems: reduced phosphorus levels
Digestive problems: addition of "prebiotics", fermentable fibres encouraging good balance of the intestinal flora, proteins
Premature ageing: vitamins E-C, essential fatty acids, grape and green-tea polyphenols

4 - Nourish and treat:
To aid recovery from certain illnesses, highly specific nutrients will be included in or left out of the food as part of the therapeutic and convalescent processes.

Kidneys, allergies, heart, obesity, intestines

"Nutrients" approach
and "Ingredients" approach

The "Nutrients" approach: a "nutritional jigsaw puzzle" with fifty pieces.

This presentation of the concept of nutrition in general and health nutrition in particular thus reinforces the distinction between two approaches with regard to the formulation of products for use in animal feeding: the "Nutrients" approach and the "Ingredients" approach.

The "Nutrients" approach allows the formulation of a balanced feed by the putting together of a veritable "jigsaw puzzle" of some fifty "nutrients". Each one of them is indispensable for the health of the animal. In the right proportions, the nutrients represent a more of less large part of each piece of the puzzle. This composition makes possible the accomplishment of the four main objectives of Health Nutrition (building up and sustaining the organism,

providing energy, nourishing and preventing, nourishing and treating), taking account of the parameters of Age, Level of Activity, Breed and Physiological Condition of the Dog. It also meets the real precise and specific needs of each animal.

The "Ingredients" approach, on the other hand, is no more than a simple list of standardized elements (or primary alimentary materials if you will) used in the composition of a food preparation, sometimes even with a simple anthropomorphic vision, as if the animal had the palate and the digestive system of a human. It therefore proves to be less precise, and above all disregards the real needs of the animal.

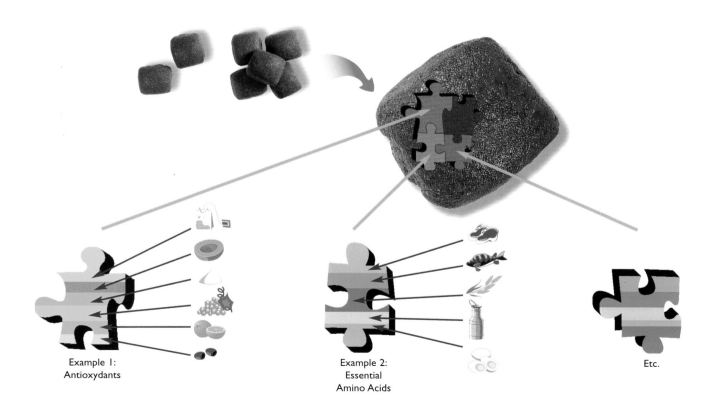

Example 1:
Antioxydants

Example 2:
Essential
Amino Acids

Etc.

Nutrients
or ingredients? The trap

"Ingredients"

25%
fresh meat

4 to 5%
of the proteins

How does a feed containing 25% of fresh meat in fact contribute only 4% to 5% of the proteins originating in the fresh meat?

Nourishing a dog properly is therefore a 2-stage operation:

1st stage: a genuine understanding of the animal, its physiology, its biology, its behavior and, therefore, the real needs of its organism

2nd stage: an equally scientific approach not only to the nutrients intended to cover these needs, but also to those intended to generate the preventive side - or, as the case may be, the curative side - of the prepared animal feed.

A genuinely nutritional feed is therefore most often a veritable jigsaw puzzle of 50 or 60 essential nutrients (proteins, minerals, vitamins, trace elements, lipids, carbohydrates, …), whereas the seduction of an eye-catching list of "Ingredients" is only very anthropomorphic and serves no real purpose beyond that of flattering the master ("chicken flavor", "lamb", "salmon").

As surprising as it may seem, the protein content of a feed claiming "25% fresh meat" is only between 4% and 5% of the total weight on the dry mat-

ter. In fact, the regulations require the pet food manufacturers to list the ingredients by descending order of weight, before cooking. Fresh meat or certain ingredients containing large amounts of water may therefore be placed at the top of the list, creating the illusion of their being the main source of nutrition.

In the case of a feed claiming to contain 25% lamb, the dry kibble will therefore contain only 4% to 5% of lamb proteins after cooking. Suppose this feed also contains 20% maize, 20% rice, 15% dried fish, 10% poultry fat and 10% vegetable oil. The manufacturer can write "Lamb" in large characters as the main ingredient but, in reality, there is only 4% to 5% lamb proteins, while the cereals are the main ingredients in the finished feed in terms of quantity

One feed, three different descriptions!

"with beef"	minimum 4% of beef
"with lamb"	minimum 4% of lamb
"with chicken"	minimum 4% of chicken
"rich in beef"	minimum 14% of beef
"rich in lamb"	minimum 14% of lamb

Dry dog food "with beef" 4% beef

Dry dog food "with lamb" 4% lamb

Dry dog food "with chicken" 4% chicken

The same ingredients... the same foodstuffs... but 3 different names and 3 different packs

Another example: the same feed containing, among other ingredients, 4% chicken, 4% lamb and 4% beef may be labelled under three different descriptions: "chicken", "lamb" or "beef". And there will always be someone there to tell you that his animal prefers the lamb version, despite the fact that the actual lamb content is exactly the same as that of the chicken version.

However, this "Ingredients" approach, which has deceived more than one owner, fails to take account of the dosage, quantity, or quality, and of the variety of origins of nutrients - essential to life and adapted to the specific needs of dogs and cats - that ensure the quality of a balanced feed. A "standard" feed may, for instance, contain some fifteen nutrients, whereas a "premium" or "nutritional" feed will usually contain up to fifty.

Royal Canin, undisputed precursor of canine health nutrition

Royal Canin: a nutrition concept that wins the day by uncompromising fidelity to its roots: "Knowledge and Respect".

Since its creation, the veterinarians and nutritional experts at Royal Canin have directed their constant efforts towards achieving major advances in terms of canine and feline nutrition. Each year brings its crop of new nutritional programs and new nutritional formulas that, besides the nutrients essential for maintaining healthy life, also incorporate natural elements to prevent certain diseases and to protect the animal.

1977
Start of the first test to determine the long-term effect of different food protein levels in dogs by Doctor Jacques Paquin and Professor Robert Moraillon (Ecole Nationale Vétérinaire d'Alfort). For the first time they consider the invalidity of the theory that states that an increased level of proteins is harmful for healthy old dogs (or cats). So, 20 years before the rest, Royal Canin foods for old dogs were the only pet foods in the world to contain high levels of quality proteins (27-28%), allowing "old dogs" to reduce the loss of muscle mass.

1980
Development and launch of AGR (Aliment Grande Race), under the guidance of Doctor Daniel Cloche, famous world specialist in canine bone problems in general and German Shepherds' bone problems in particular. During 16 years this product asserted as the only food in the world for large breeds pups ("cynotechnical" range for breeders).

1990
Formulation of RCCI (Royal Canin Cynotechnique International), "high nutrition" range of dog food for pups and adult dogs, including AGR 36 (Large Breed Puppy Food) - which went on to become a world reference - and PR27, first Small Breed dog food.

1995
Development of foods adapted to the type of effort practised by sporting or working dogs (Stress 35…).

1997
RCCI Size, the first nutritional programme in the world to take account not only of age and activity, but also the size/weight ratio of different dog breeds. In 3 years, this revolutionary concept discovered by Royal Canin was also adopted by the world's big 3 players in top-of-the-range Canine Nutrition, as well as the RC weight categories (small breeds: 1 to 10 kg, medium-sized breeds: 11 to 25 kg, large breeds: + 26 kg).

1998
Creation of Starter, the first weaning food for breeders, was designed to protect the pup from the risk of the "immunological gap" (loss of the mother's immune system defences and gradual development of its own, between the 4th and 12th week).

2000
Size Nutrition: 3 unique nutritional programmes in the world (Mini/Medium/Maxi) combining the three parameters of age, activity and size, plus a fourth - the physiological condition of the dogs - to help to prevent joint problems, heart trouble, obesity…

2001
Development of Giant, a nutritional programme specially designed with the large-breed dogs (45 to 100 kg) in mind and the 3 specific features of these breeds:
• A very low digestive capacity: the relative weight of the digestive tract in relation to their total weight is 2.7%, compared with 7% for the small breeds and … 11% for humans.
• Growth in 2 distinct stages, characteristic of large-breed dogs:
o 1 to 8 months: formation of the bones,
o 8 to 18/24 months: development of the muscle mass.
• A relatively short lifespan; cellular ageing therefore has to be prevented from the 24th month.

2001
V-Diet, to Nourish and Treat, development of 13 dietetic products for dogs and cats and, in particular:
- the hydrolysate for the hypoallergenic programs,
- the hyperprotein diet for the Obesity programs.

2002
A further advance in canine nutrition with Immunity Program, a true innovation designed to strengthen the dog's natural defences at each stage of its life.

Familiarity breeds respect

The cornerstone of the company, Knowledge of the real nutritional needs of the dog is derived from the daily experience of the partner breeders and the veterinary nutritionists and from the first-hand scientific observations of the Royal Canin Research and Development experts. An original method that allows Royal Canin, more than any other brand to be genuinely in the vanguard of nutritional innovation and to share its knowledge of the dog in reference works such as the guides to breeding, training, dog diseases and, of course, the Encyclopedia of the Dog.

ROYAL CANIN

KNOWLEDGE AND RESPECT

*Diana
The Huntress.
School of
Fontainbleau
(France). Paris,
Musée du Louvre.
Giraudon coll.*

Part 1

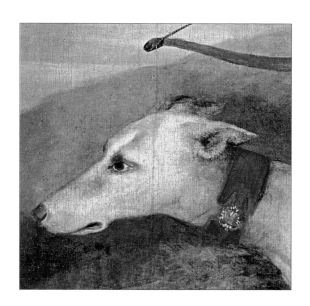

Yesterday to Today

Dog Breeds

Origin and Evolution of the Dog

When we consider that Earth is approximately 4.5 billion years old, and that the first mammals appeared one hundred million years ago, and the first dogs fifty million years ago, the appearance of early man a mere three million years ago seems quite recent. If the history of Earth were recorded on a kilometer measure, mammals would appear only on the last few meters and dogs the last few centimeters!

Origin of Canids

Canids are mammals characterized by pointed canines (developed for an omnivorous diet) and a skeleton built for a mode of walking or running called digitigrade (walking on the toes without the heels touching the ground).

They belong to the Carnivora order, which developed in the early Tertiary Era in ecological niches abandoned by large reptiles that disappeared at the end of the Mesozoic Era.

At that time, they began to spread throughout North America and diversify with the appearance of a Carnivora family—Miacidae—which resembled the modern-day weasel. Miacids (a family which included forty-two different genera) flourished forty million years ago; today, only sixteen genera remain. The modern Canid family includes three sub-families: Cuoninae (Lycaon), Otocyoninae (South African Otocyon), and Caninae (dog, wolf, fox, jackal, coyote).

Evolution of Canids

Canids gradually replaced Miacids, giving rise to the *Hesperocyon* genus, which was very common approximately thirty-five million years ago. Their skull and toes showed skeletal and dental features similar to those of modern-day wolves, dogs, and foxes, indicating a direct link to these early carnivores.

During the Miocene, the *Phlaocyon* genus appeared. It is thought to have resembled a raccoon. The teeth of the *Mesocyon* genus, which also developed at that time, were similar to those of modern dogs.

The body profile of Canids evolved through the *Cynodesmus* (which looked like a coyote), the *Tomarctus*, and the *Leptocyon*, gradually taking on the appearance of today's wolf or even Spitz-type dogs with the loosening of the curl of the tail, the lengthening of the legs and extremities, and the diminution of the fifth toe (dewclaw), which allowed the animal to run more quickly.

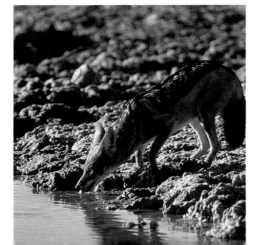

Rise of the Canis genus

Canis Canids did not appear until the end of the Tertiary Era. They crossed the Bering Strait and reached Europe during the late Eocene, but seemed to disappear during the early Oligocene as Ursids (bears) grew in numbers. In the late Miocene, *Canis lepophagus* migrated to Europe from North America. This new arrival looked much like modern dog, though was closer to the size of a coyote. During the Pliocene, these Canids spread toward Asia then Africa. Ironically, they apparently did not move into South America until much later, during the early Pleistocene.

Finally, humans introduced the genus to Australia around 500,000 years ago, during the late Pleistocene. However, there is no proof that these early Canids gave rise to the Dingo—modern-day wild dogs that were brought to Australia a mere 15,000 to 20,000 years ago.

Ancestor of the wolf, jackal, and coyote

Canis etruscus (Etruscan dog) appeared approximately one to two million years ago. Despite its smaller size, it is thought to be the ancestor of European wolves. *Canis cypio*, which lived in the Pyrenees eight million years ago, seems to be the ancestor of modern jackals and coyotes.

Importance of archeological sites in Europe and China

Several varieties of dogs have been found at European archeological sites. The largest are thought to be descended from the large northern wolves which stood as tall as the withers of today's Great Dane. They probably gave rise to Nordic dogs and large herders. The smaller dogs, morphologically similar to modern-day wild Dingos, are likely descended from smaller wolves from India or the Middle East.

Is the Wolf the Ancestor of the Dog?

The oldest dogs'skeletons ever found are approximately 30,000 years old, and therefore lived after Cro-Magnon (*Homo sapiens sapiens*) was already walking the earth. These ancient remains have always been found near human skeletons; this is why they were given the name Canis familiaris (- 10,000 years). It only seems logical that domestic dogs are descended from early wild Canids. Other possible ancestors include the wolf (*Canis lupus*), the jackal (*Canis aureus*), and the coyote (*Canis latrans*).

In addition, the oldest dog remains have been found in China, where it is believed jackals and coyotes never lived. It was also in China that the first authenticated association (dating to 150,000 years ago) between man and a small wolf variety (Canis lupus variabilis) took place. The coexistence of these two species during a period prior to their evolution, seems to corroborate the theory that the wolf is the ancestor of the domestic dog.

This hypothesis was recently reinforced following several discoveries, including the finding that some Nordic breeds are directly descended from the wolf. In addition, studies that compared the mitochondrial DNA of these species revealed similarity greater than 99.8% between the dog and the wolf, compared to only 96% between the dog and the coyote. Moreover, more than forty-five wolf sub-species have been classified; the diversity of the wolf species could explain the diversity of dog breeds. Finally, body and vocal languages are very similar and commonly understood between the two species.

Similarities between the dog and the wolf: a difficult analysis

The similarities between dogs and wolves make it difficult for paleozoologists to accurately determine whether remains are that of a wolf or a dog when remains are incomplete or the archeological context suggests that cohabitation is unlikely. Only a few minor, and highly unreliable, differences existed between primitive dogs and their ancestors. These included the length of the nose bridge, the angle of the stop, and the distance between the carnassial tooth and the upper tubercles. In addition, there were certainly fewer Canids than the animals that they preyed upon, and

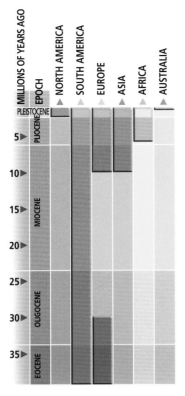

GEOGRAPHIC DISTRIBUTION OF CANIDS OVER TIME
(by F. Duranthon, SFC, 1994).

According to recent research in the United States and Sweden, the dog appeared approximately 135,000 years ago, 100,000 years earlier than previously believed. Canid remains morphologically similar to wolves that were found with human skeletal remains at sites dated at 100,000 years old.

GENUS CANIS FOSSILS
(by M. Thérin).

therefore, it is less likely that Canid remains will be uncovered. These difficulties and the possibility of dog-wolf hybridization explain why many links are missing in the chain of events that led to the development of modern dog. Perhaps one day we will discover the link between *Canis lupus variabilis* and *Canis familiaris*, and the battle of the theories will come to an end.

It is worth noting that the diffusionist theory, which suggests primitive dogs adapted to their new environs as humans migrated, does not exclude the evolutionist theory, which states that dog varieties came from different areas where the wolf was domesticated.

Domestication of the Wolf

Wolf prints and skeletal remains as much as 40,000 years old have been discovered in territories occupied by humans in Europe, though the use of dogs by *Homo sapiens* has not been validated by prehistoric cave drawings.

At that time in history, humans had not yet settled into a sedentary existence. They followed the animal that they hunted for food. Climatic changes (end of an ice age and sudden atmospheric warming) that took place approximately 10,000 years ago between the Holocene and Pleistocene Epochs changed the landscape; forests replaced tundra, and as a result, mammoths and bison became rare as deer and boar flourished. When the game they hunted became smaller, humans developed new weapons and hunting techniques. Suddenly, man was competing with wolves for the same food and using the same "pack" hunting methods using "beaters".

It is only natural that early humans felt the need to find a way to use the wolf for hunting. For the first time, they attempted to tame an animal, long before humans had settled into a sedentary life style and began raising livestock.

Therefore, primitive dogs were without a doubt hunting dogs, not herders.

Taming the wolf and domestication

Wolves were domesticated when humans passed from "predation" to "production". A few individual wolves would have been tamed in early attempts. Each time a tamed wolf died, work had to begin again to tame another; but this early work marked a first, vital step toward domesticating a species. The second step was controlled breeding.

Domestication of wolves probably began in several locations in Asia. It did not happen overnight based on the number of domestication centers discovered at archeological sites.

Several attempts were made around the world with young wolf pups from various groups. These pups irreversibly imprinted to man during their first months of life. When they rejected their wild relatives, domestication was successful. The fact that wolf pups naturally submit to the hierarchical rules of the pack undoubtedly made domestication easier. Though, occasionally, some domesticated bitches were impregnated by wild wolves, the pups were raised in proximity with humans, and therefore were far less likely to return to the wild.

From the wolf to the dog

As is always the case with any animal, the domestication of wolves led to several morphological and behavioral changes, following the evolution of humans. By studying skeletal remains, scientists have found there was a juvenile regression, called pedomorphosis, as if over the generations, the adult ani-

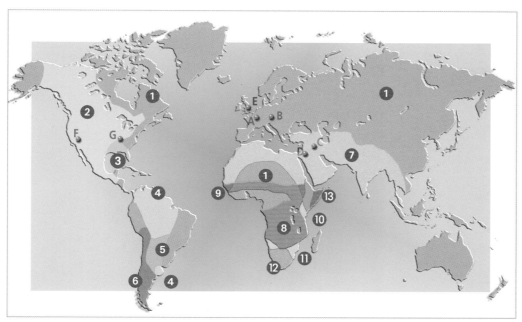

GEOGRAPHIC RANGE OF CANIS, SOUTH AMERICAN FOXES, AND REMAINS OF FIRST DOGS.

(by Y. Lignereux, I. Carrière, SFC, 1994, La Recherche, 1996.)

1	Canis lupus
2	Canis latrans
3	Canis rufus
4	Cerdocyon
5	Dusicyon (psedalopex) Cerdocyon

6	Dusicyon (psedalopex)
7	Canis avreus
8	Canis adustus
9	Canis adustus / Canis avreus

10	Canis mesomelas / C. adustus / C. avreus
11	Canis mesomelas / Canis adustus
12	Canis mesomelas
13	Canis mesomelas / Canis aureus

REMAINS OF FIRST DOGS

A Bonn-Oberkassel: -14 000
B Dobritzgniegrotte: -13 000
C Palagawra Cave: -12 000
D Matlaha (and several others): -11 000 / -12 000
E Starr car / Seamen car: -9 000 / -10 000
F Danger Cave: -9 000 / -10 000
G Koster: -8 500

mals retained certain immature characteristics and behaviors, including decreased size, shortened nose bridge, deepened stop, barking, whining, playful disposition, etc. This led some archeozoologists to believe that the dog is still undergoing speciation, that it has become stuck at adolescence and must depend on humans for survival.

Paradoxically, the phenomenon is accompanied by a shortening of the growth stage, meaning puppies reach puberty early, and therefore, are capable of reproducing at an early age. This explains why small breeds reach puberty earlier than large breeds, and why all domestic dogs reach puberty earlier than wolves, which do not mature sexually until approximately two years of age. In addition, the teeth of domestic dogs have adapted to an omnivorous diet rather than a primarily carnivorous diet, since domestic dogs could make do with table scraps rather than hunting for survival.

This type of degeneration as a result of domestication is seen in most species. Other examples are the pig (shortening of the snout) and foxes, which can take on puppylike behavior after only twenty generations of breeding. So it seems that domestication modifies natural evolution (unless humans are considered an integral part of nature's equation) and becomes a new method of selection.

Results of Selective Breeding

Though described as the greyhound in Egyptian paleontology or the Molossus in Assyrian history, different breeds are simply varieties, types of dogs, sub-species of *Canis familiaris*. Dating from antiquity, the development of individual breeds is much more recent than domestication of wild dogs.

Apart from a few breeds such as the Maltese Bichon, whose bloodline was maintained in a limited territory, most dog breeds were produced through selective breeding carried out by humans. Selective breeding only became possible after dogs were domesticated and mating could be controlled.

Man's attempts to domesticate animals failed regularly. Ancient Egyptians tried to domesticate hyenas, gazelles, wild cats, and foxes, but they only managed to tame a few individuals at best. More recently, attempts to domesticate wild Dingos also failed. Some would say domestication of cats is still a work in progress.

Adaptation of the canine species over time

Unlike undomesticated species such as crocodiles, which have hardly evolved in two hundred million years (twenty meters on our kilometer scale), the canine species adapted (or was adapted) in record time to a wide range of climates, civilizations, and geographic areas. The Siberian Husky, Mexican Hairless, Pekinese, Great Dane, Boxer and Dachshund, just a few of the four hundred breeds currently standardized by the Fédération Cynologique Internationale (FCI) which, despite their diversity, all belong to the genus *Canis familiaris*. It is interesting to note that the shape of the head, legs and spine have evolved independently from breed to breed throughout the evolution of domestic dogs.

This diversification began as humans moved from a nomadic to sedentary lifestyle, from "consumer" to "producer", in the late Stone Age. At that time in history, dogs were most likely of medium size and looked like the "Tourbières Loulou" (similar to the modern-day Spitz type) described by von den Driesch in England.

Appearance of different types

Two large types appeared in the third millenium in Mesopotamia—the Molosser dogs that protected livestock against predators (bears and ironically, its own ancestor, the wolf) and the greyhound type which was adapted for running and desert regions and which became an indispensable hunting tool for man.

In addition to these two basic types, there undoubtedly were already types that correspond to the primary groups as defined by Kennel Clubs around the world.

When humans set their minds and efforts to selective breeding, results can be achieved in a remarkably short time. For example, it took only one hundred years in Argentina to produce miniature horses, measuring only forty centimeters at the withers, from standard horses. Comparable results can be achieved in even shorter periods with dogs since they are quite fertile and gestation is much shorter.

Growing ties between dogs and humans

From antiquity, dogs have filled numerous roles and have been used in a wide variety of activities, including fighting, meat production, sled pulling in polar regions, and sacrificial rites in mythology. Later in history, the Roman Empire became the pioneer in dog breeding and was proud to call itself the "fatherland of a thousand dogs", foreshadowing the diversity of dog varieties whose primary uses would be to provide companionship, to guard farms and herds, and to help with the hunt.

It is easy to imagine how diversification increased over the centuries as human populations crossed paths through genetic mutation (probably the origin of chondrodystrophic dwarfism in modern Bassets), selective breeding, and natural or voluntary thinning. Some extreme results were achieved, such as the Bulldog originally bred for bull-baiting or the Pekinese that provided companionship to Chinese empresses.

Hunting dogs and the first standard

In the Middle Ages, different dog varieties were bred according to their aptitude for various hunting techniques. Bloodhounds and pointers were used to locate game without hunting, scent and sighthounds were used to tire deer, and bird dogs were used to flush feathered game. Barking dogs were also described as being used to pursue prey. The use of bassets for underground hunting was even mentioned. Though it is impossible to positively identify a skeleton as being that of a specific breed, some breeds are no doubt now extinct.

"Fixing" of characteristics, inextricably linked to the concept of standard, did not truly begin until the sixteenth century for hunting dogs. In the seventeenth and eighteenth centuries, an attempt was made to establish a family tree for Buffon's breeds. In the nineteenth century, interest in breeding soared after the first dog shows in London in 1861 and in Paris in 1863.

Thereafter, fanciers strove to create new morphological types from existing breeds. Each breed club has recorded the precise date of the show that officially recognized a breed which, until that point, had been classified only as a variety.

Hunting scenes. Miniature from the Treasury of Hunting, after the manuscript from Harduin de Fontaines-Garin. Selva, Paris.

Modern Dog

From Roman antiquity, dogs have been classified according to their skills. Originally, they were divided into herders, hunting dogs and house dogs. Aristotle recorded seven separate dog breeds, but made no reference to greyhounds, which had long lived in Egypt. In the eighteenth century, Buffon attempted to classify dogs by ear shape, separating them into thirty straight-eared breeds, drop or semiprick, whereas Cuvier proposed dividing the canines into hounds, mastiffs, and spaniels based on the shape of the dog's skull. In 1885, the Livre des Origines Français (French Stud Book) divided canines into twenty-nine separate sections. These sections were narrowed to eleven groups in the early twentieth century, then in 1950, reduced to the ten groups that are recognized today.

Concept of Breed, Variety and Standard

In 1984, the FCI formally approved Professor R. Triquet's proposal to establish a technical zoological definition of the concepts of dog group, breed and variety.

Species and Breed

According to Prof. Triquet, breed is "a group of individuals with common characteristics that distinguish them from other members of their species and that can be genetically passed on to the next generation". He held that, "species is determined by nature while breed is determined by the culture or fashions of the show ring". Indeed, selective breeding may produce a new breed, but will never result in the creation of a new species.

For example, Jack Russell Terriers (a breed) were created when Parson Jack Russell crossed various terriers in an attempt to create a better hunting dog. However, some dogs, such as Languedoc Sheepdogs, have never been officially recognized as separate breeds. Others, such as the Chambray, the Lévesque, or the Normand-Poitevin, slowly disappeared because of lack of numbers of interest and were permanently removed from the FCI registry. Currently, the Belgian Short-haired Pointer and the Ardennes Cattle Dog are under consideration for removal, whereas the Saint-Usuge Spaniel and the American Bulldog have been submitted to the FCI for approval. Over the past fifty years, the number of breeds recognized by the FCI has practically tripled in response to increased precision in breeding, sometimes simply in an effort to create something original.

Group, breed, variety

Group is defined as "a group of breeds have certain distinguishing characteristics in common that can be transmitted genetically". For example, Group 1 (sheepdogs) dogs have different morphology, but all instinctively strive to guard livestock.

Variety, according to Raymond Triquet, is "a subdivision within a breed wherein all specimens have a common, genetically transmittable characteristic that distinguishes them from other specimens of that breed".

For example, the Longhaired German Shepherd is a variety of the German Shepherd breed, though it is possible that the offspring of a Longhaired variety may not have long hair (the long hair characteristic being passed on by a recessive gene).

Many breeds include a number of varieties, including color and texture of the coat or ear carriage. There are three Dachshund varieties—smooth, wire and long.

Breed and standard

Standard is defined as "the group of characteristics that defines a breed". It serves as a reference point when a specimen is examined to judge its conformation to the behavioral and morphological characteristics of the breed.

Each breed has a standard which is established by the breed association of its country of origin. Only the original association may modify the standard. The standard established in the country of origin is the only one recognized by the FCI, despite the fact that some countries try to impose their own varieties. For example, English, American, and Canadian Akita varieties have been proposed to the FCI for recognition, but without success. Others are recognized only through national genealogical proceedings.

Some varieties, such as Toy and Apricot Poodles, have eventually been accepted by the country of origin as officially belonging to the Poodle breed.

Standard of beauty and sporting body-type

Some dog breeds are difficult to classify within the existing groups because they may no longer be used for their original purpose. To maintain the purity of breeds, some breed associations require natural aptitude tests, or working trials, such as field trials for pointers. This allows the dog to be judged on his skills, not just physical appearance and phenotype.

Usefulness of breeding across varieties

Dog shows, competitions, and championships allow judges and conformation experts to promote breeding of dogs that will "improve" a breed, since it has been judged to display desired working or appearance traits. This practice of judging dogs keeps selection in line with breed-club goals. As a result, however, there is a risk that specimens of exaggerated type will be created which do not reflect the original standard for the breed. Different varieties could even gradually appear if working qualities are incompatible with appearance standards. In order to avoid this trend to create new varieties, which threatens the integrity and standard of a breed, the best specimens of each variety of the breed must be crossed regularly to preserve working and appearance qualities unique to that breed.

An excellent example is that of the Belgian Sheepdog, which has four distinct

Some breeds are no longer used for their original purpose. For example, few Yorkshire Terriers are used as earth dogs; most are now kept as house pets. The same is true of Labrador Retrievers, which were used for hunting with pointers. Today it is rare that they are bred for their working abilities.

varieties. Inter-variety mating between Groenendaels and Tervuerens is done regularly, maintaining a degree of homogeneity, while Malinois and other breeds are crossed to improve working abilities (bite, indifference to gunfire), which could threaten the integrity of this variety.

Intra-breed selection aimed only at developing working abilities may then result in the creation of a specimen that does not conform to standard, as is true for the English Setter. In addition, morphological characteristics are lost much more rapidly than working abilities are acquired.

Rootstock, Line, Family

Each breed has its own rootstock which gives rise to different lines with each litter.

Even if the genetic input of the sire and the dam to the first generation of puppies is the same, we refer to maternal rootstock and paternal rootstock when several generations of the pedigree are studied.

There are always more descendants of an elite stud than of a champion brood bitch, which is physiologically limited to fewer than two litters per year.

Confirmation and recommendation of a stud is therefore always given considerable weight since the male has a much greater impact on the breed than the female.

Family and inbreeding

A dog's origin is revealed by examining its pedigree. The pedigree will also indicate the degree of inbreeding in a particular line (or strain). Parallel breeding of several related lines ("blood relatives") is the most common method used for dog breeding. The breeder ends the line several generations later after fixing the sought-after characteristics. This line then constitutes a family that can be recognized by an expert fancier. A family is a group of related individuals that have similar characteristics and come from the same breeding lines. Each line is identified by name.

The need to introduce new blood

However, excessive inbreeding within the same family can result in a decrease of occurrence and variation of genetic traits. In this case, the breeder may choose to introduce new blood. With modern technology, it is even possible to preserve semen and therefore the hereditary material of certain family lines possessing qualities worth reintroducing at a later date.

What About Mutts?

Unlike mixed breed dogs that are the product of a cross between two dogs of different breed or a purebred dog and one of undetermined heritage, mutts are impossible to classify accurately since there is no rhyme or reason to their bloodlines. Mutts are the result of a cross between two dogs of unknown breed. Experts estimate that as much as 60% of all dogs in France are mutts or mixed breeds, though it is difficult to determine precisely how many exist.

Working abilities and rusticity

Though far from beautiful, mutts are greatly respected by their owners for their working abilities and rusticity.

Mutts typically have "wild dog" coloration (the dominant colors of the coat are gray or fawn) and are generally of medium size. Instinctively self-reliant, they are excellent hunting dogs, and their natural coloration acts as camouflage so they blend in with their surroundings. Only ten percent of hunting dogs in France have a pedigree.

Thanks to their colorful backgrounds, mutts have an extremely rich genetic heritage. Undesirable genes (often recessive) are likely to be dominated by desirable genes.

Unknowns of genetic diversity

The unfortunate side effect of this genetic diversity is that there is no guarantee that desirable characteristics will be passed on to the next generations. It is also very difficult to anticipate the morphological and psychological characteristics of puppies born to mutt parents, even if both parents present the desired characteristics.

Though it is often said that mutts are lively, intelligent, hardy and game, it is, in fact, impossible to make this broad statement since only the most lucky and skilled products of this genetic roulette find a place in society. The truth is, mutts account for the vast majority of dogs in shelters and pounds.

We have seen that quantitative characteristics such as working ability, that depend on the action of numerous genes, are less inheritable than morphological characteristics such as color or coat texture, that are passed on through a more limited number of genes. Mutt devotees are often hunters and will admit that it is difficult to raise mutts in the hopes of fixing their traits. However, since they have no market value and they are so numerous, hunters often have no qualms about starting over with their stock.

Dingo: Scientists know that the Australian Dingo reached Australia 15,000 to 20,000 years ago when crossing to the continent on land was still possible. However, they do not know if the Dingo was a domesticated dog that returned to the wild or a distinct species. If it was a domesticated dog, it should be called Canis familiaris dingo, but if it was a separate wild species, it would be called Canis dingo. Until its origins can be clarified, the dingo will not have a scientific name.

Do Wild Dogs Still Exist?

Even today it is still difficult to classify some Canids such as the Abyssinian Wolf *Canis simensis* (500 still exist in Ethiopia) among wolves, foxes or wild dogs.

Whatever the case, if we exclude wolves from the wild dog group, there are still some wild dogs, including the singing dogs of New Guinea, Indian and African Pariah dogs, the Congo Basenji (many have been domesticated and recognized by the FCI), Carolina dogs, and Australian Dingos. All wild dogs have similar morphology.

We know that dogs are descended from wolves. So if dogs were left in the wild, would they revert to wolves?

Starting from the principal that evolution never backtracks, researchers at the University of Rome studied colonies of wild dogs living in the Abruzzes in central Italy. They noticed that these dogs of the forest lived like wolves, in packs with clearly defined territories, unlike stray village dogs that generally looked out only for their own interests. However, wild dogs do not look like wolves. They are smaller and of an amber-brown color, indicating that they have permanently lost some alleles, undoubtedly as the result of a period of domestication in their history.

Dogs of the Future

By studying the annual statistics gathered by the French Kennel Club, we can identify current breeding trends and, from this information, try to determine what dogs will look like in the future. Registered births by breed indicate a trend away from the most well known breeds in favor of increasingly more original breeds.

Exaggerated type

This quest for originality and extreme types is a selection technology that has been developed primarily in the United States and England. The result is the creation of specimens with exaggerated type, such as Bull Dogs, whose faces are now so pushed in that they must be born by cesarean and can breathe only if their mouth is open. Labradors are predisposed to obesity. Dachshunds are getting longer. Shar-Pei's have more natural folds in the skin. German Shepherds have increasingly sloped croups. Small breeds are getting smaller and are now referred to as Toys and Miniatures. On the other hand, large breeds are growing increasingly large. These trends seem to leave only mutts in the medium size category. We see a tendency to push the extremes and ignore those that fall in the middle.

Genetic influence for custom dogs

Morphing is a computer technique that could perhaps serve as an analogy to demonstrate how we can predict these trends, taking into account changes in lifestyles and progress in genetic manipulation. Lifestyle changes follow urban development. A decrease in the number of farm dogs can be anticipated with a corresponding increase in the number of pets, as a result of telecommuting becoming more commonplace and improved connectivity. However, it is difficult to predict what dogs will look like since people's preferences change as fashion evolves.

If current trends continue, we can expect an increase in the number of breeds. Future dogs will be anything but average! Coat color and texture genetics are advancing by leaps and bounds; therefore it will likely be possible to "genetically color" dogs. The mechanics of genetics will be more fully understood. In fact, we estimate a canine genome map will be achieved within twenty years. As a result, it will be possible to eliminate genetic faults and reduce chance in breeding, meeting demand for increasingly original breeds.

The development of artificial insemination, using refrigerated or frozen sperm, will eliminate the need to bring animals together. Borders and quarantine will disappear as two animals selected from a catalog on the Internet are "virtually" mated. The semen of a prime stud dog could even be preserved to impregnate a brood bitch after the death of the stud. However, these techniques will never be as successful in dogs as they have been in cattle since the concentration of sperm in canine ejaculate is much lower than in that of steers.

It is possible fewer dogs will be abandoned in the future. But these "made-to-order" dogs of the future will look less and less like wild dogs. Future dogs may look so different that their wild cousins may no longer even recognize them!

Fédération Cynologique Internationale (FCI)

Though the FCI stemmed from the French SCC and the Belgian Société Royale Saint-Hubert, it is no longer officially linked to either organization. The FCI is an international organization based in Thuin, Belgium. It is responsible for:

• Establishing the criteria for recognition of stud books of member countries (more than fifty are currently members, including most European countries and many Asian, Latin American, and African countries);

• Standardizing international dog show rules (organization, judging, international working or beauty championship titles);

• Promoting the sharing of breed standards established by the country of origin. These standards are regularly published in the French Official Dog Fancier's Review;

• Monitoring member countries to ensure that each country holds a minimum of four international championships each year.

Dog Fancy around the World

Three independent organizations work closely with the FCI, without being subordinated to it —the Kennel Club (KC) of the United Kingdom, the American Kennel Club (AKC) of the USA, and the Canadian Kennel Club (CKC) of Canada. Several other kennel clubs promote dog fancy throughout the world as well. They include:

The Kennel Club

Created in 1873, earlier than the French SCC, the Kennel Club is the oldest organization devoted to purebred dogs. For the first one hundred years of its existence, only men could be members of the Kennel Club. It was not until 1979 that women were admitted.

Poster E.E. Doisneau (1902)
Coll. Kharbine-Tapabor, Paris

The Official Cynology

The function of the Kennel Club is similar to that of the French SCC. The KC organizes approximately 6,000 dog shows each year. The most prestigious on the international stage is undoubtedly Crufts, which assembles more than 26,000 dogs over four days of competition.

The American Kennel Club

Formed in 1884, the AKC was created around the same time as the French SCC. The AKC is made up of breed clubs and associations, but also admits multi-breed clubs. The AKC's staff works in offices in North Carolina and New York. The AKC organizes more than 13,000 dog shows each year and also contributes in several other fields, such as the creation of a training institute for judges and a foundation for research in the field of dog health.

The Bermuda Kennel Club

The youngest of all the federations, the BKC was founded in 1955 and is still affiliated with the FCI. The BKC organizes two annual shows, one in fall and one in spring.

Australian National Kennel Council (ANKC)

The ANKC was founded in 1911 as an affiliate of the FCI. It maintains the same standards, but judging of the 153 breeds it recognizes differs slightly. The ANKC's committee is made up of two delegates from each of eight Member States. The committee meets two times per year for four days.

Judges are chosen by the General Council of each Member State from candidates who must have at least ten years of experience. There are currently 876 judges recognized in Australia, 233 of which are approved to judge all breeds.

The Canadian Kennel Club

Based in Toronto, the CKC was formed in 1888. The CKC has approximately 25,000 individual active members represented by twelve delegates elected by the different regions. In 1995, the CKC organized 1,961 dog shows, with a seemingly higher registration than in previous years.

Dog Breeds

Each international registering body has established different groupings to classify the breeds that it recognizes: the Société Centrale Canine of France – 10; the FCI (Fédération Cynologique Internationale) – 10; the Kennel Club of England – 6; the American Kennel Club – 7; the Canadian Kennel Club – 7; the Svenska Fennel Klubben of Sweden – 8; the Real Sociedad Canina of Spain – 5; the Australian National Kennel Council – 6; and the Bermuda Kennel Club – 6. The breed names listed in this encyclopedia are those proposed by the FCI and approved by the FCI General Assembly held in Jerusalem from June 23-34, 1987, and updated in March 1999.

Groups

For the reader's convenience, the dog breeds in this book have been presented by group and by section. Dogs within the same group and section are listed in alphabetical order, not by country of origin.

The groups and sections are the following:

Group 1:
Sheepdogs (Section 1) and Cattledogs (Section 2), except Swiss Cattledogs.

Group 2:
Pinschers and Schnauzers (Section 1), Molossians (Section 2), and Swiss Cattledogs (Section 2).

Group 3:
Terriers.

Group 4:
Dachshunds.

Group 5:
Spitz and primitive types: Nordic breeds (Section 1); European Spitz (Section 2); Asian Spitz and related breeds (Section 3); primitive types (Section 4); primitive hunting dogs (Section 5).

Group 6:
Scenthounds (section 1); Leash (scent) Hounds (section 2) and related breeds (section 3)

Group 7:
Continental pointing dogs (Section 1) and British and Irish Pointers and Setters (Section 2).

Group 8:
Flushing dogs (Section 1), Retrievers (Section 2), and Water Dogs (Section 3).

Group 9:
Companion and toy dogs, divided into twelve sections: Bichons and related breeds (Section 1); Poodles (Section 2); small Belgian dogs (Section 3); hairless dogs (Section 4); Tibetan breeds (Section 5); Chihuahuas (Section 6); Dalmatians (Section 7); English toy spaniels (Section 8); Japanese Chin and Pekingese (Section 9); Continental toy spaniels (Section 10); Kromfohrländer (Section 11); small Molossian type dogs (Section 12).

Group 10:
Sighthounds and related breeds.

Miscellaneous rare breeds are mentioned at the end of the chapter.

Standards

The FCI classification, original name, other common names, and varieties (if applicable) are listed for each breed. Information regarding behavior, personality, training, use and standard is also provided.

The standard covers the origin of the breed, accepted varieties, general appearance, and a description of the head, neck, body, legs and tail, followed by disqualifying faults. When such faults are present, the dog is not considered a desirable candidate for breeding to carry on or improve the breed, since it is presumed that such a dog would pass on a hereditary fault. If a dog is descended from two purebred parents, he can be registered as a purebred. Dogs with particularly impressive bloodlines can be pedigreed and will be in high demand to be mated with the best of their breed.

Standards are modified over the years. Some standards established at the turn of the century have been updated as the breed has evolved.

Vocabulary

A highly specialized vocabulary has evolved to describe dog breeds and their standards. The reader will find the key terms defined in the following glossary useful (from M. Luquet and R. Triquet).

Small Breeds under 10 kg (20 lb)

Medium Breeds between 10 and 25 kg (20-55 lb)

Large Breeds between 25 and 45 kg (55-100 lb)

Giant Breeds over 45 kg (over 100 lb)

The outlines at right are used to indicate the size category of a given breed. This outline is used throughout the book and is particularly relevant in the chapters on health and nutrition.

SMALL BREEDS
MEDIUM BREEDS
LARGE BREEDS
GIANT BREEDS

The weight and height of domestic dogs vary dramatically from one breed to the next, perhaps more than any other species in the animal kingdom. The Chihuahua weighs only one kilogram, yet the Great Dane can weigh more than one hundred kilograms. Compare this to humans or domestic cats, whose largest members are only 2 to 2-1/2 times the size of the smallest. These great variations in size result in differing morphology, physiology, metabolism, behavior and interaction with humans. A dog also has different health and nutritional needs depending on its size. Based on their weight and height at full maturity, dogs are divided into four general categories: small breeds, medium breeds, large breeds and giant breeds.

Active: Describes a dog that is always alert, in action, on the lookout, moving, hunting.

Aggressive: The tendency to attack without being provoked. This behavior is unacceptable in all standards.

Albino: Describes a white coat caused by lack of pigment in the hairs.

Aquiline: Having a curved shape.

Arched loin: Arched curvature of the back.

Balanced: Said of a well-proportioned dog whose individual parts appear in correct ratio to one another.

Bare patch: An area lacking pigment.

Barrel: Describes a round thoracic region, or well-arched in cobby breeds.

Basset: A type of dog having the body of a larger dog from which it is descended, supported by short legs. These are low-stationed dogs.

Bay: The sound a hunting hound makes when it barks; good voice.

Beagle: A medium-sized hound bred with excellent results from a larger breed. Smaller than the breed from which it is descended, larger than the Basset.

Belton: A white coat with ticking or roaning (orange, lemon).

Bi-color: Said of a coat composed of two distinct colors.

Bichon: An abbreviation for the Barbichon descended from the Barbet. Toy breed with a long or short, silky, stand-off coat.

Black and Tan: Refers to a black dog with tan or sable markings.

Blaze: A narrow white band running up the center of the face.

Blood: Breed. To inject new blood, to cross a dog with a bitch of another breed.

Bloodhound: A dog specialized in searching out large wounded game—a practice called "blood hunting" because the dog follows the blood trail. (Group VI dog breeds)

Blotch: Color covering a large area on a white background.

Blue: The dilution of black coat color.

Blunt muzzle: A short, flat muzzle.

Bobtail: A dog with a naturally short tail.

Brachet: A short-haired, medium-sized hound from the Middle Ages.

Pointer

Close-coupled type

Dish-faced

Domed

Brachycephalic skull: A short, wide, round skull (Bulldog, Pug).

Breast: The chest.

Brick-shaped: Describes a dog whose shape resembles a rectangle, the longest side of the rectangle generally being the length of the dog.

Brindle: Refers to a coat with more or less vertical dark streaking on a lighter color.

Brisket: The chest, thoracic cavity.

Broad: Said of a wide, powerful chest.

Brown: Chocolate and liver are shades of brown. tan and beige are obtained by the dilution of brown.

Brush: A tail that resembles that of a fox.

Cape: The long, thick hair covering the neck and shoulders.

Cat foot: Round.

Chestnut: Fawn with a red or orange cast.

Chippendale Front: A dog with a Chippendale front has forelegs out at the elbows, pasterns close and feet turned out.

Chiseled: Clean-cut head and muzzle. Well-defined, precise lines.

Chocolate: A dark, reddish brown. A chocolate or liver coat is brown.

Cloddy: Said of a dog that is short, compact and thickset.

Close-coupled: Describes a dog that is comparatively short from the last rib to the commencement of the hindquarters.

Close-lying: Said of straight hair that falls flat against the skin.

Coat: Refers to the hair and its color; sometimes refers simply to the color of the hair.

Cobby: Said of a thick-set, compact dog with relatively short, strong, bowed legs. The Pug is cobby.

Coin-sized: The size and shape of a coin, like the spots on Dalmatians.

Collar: White markings around the neck. Hairs around the neck.

Collarette: A ruff formation around the neck.

Corky: Said of a lively, active dog that is constantly in motion.

Cropped: Refers to very short hair close against the body. Some cropped hair is called short in official standards.

Crossbreeding: The mating of a dog of one breed with a bitch of another for one generation to avoid inbreeding. Crossing of dogs of the same breed, but from different lineage or parentage.

Croup: The region of the pelvic girdle formed by the sacrum and surrounding tissue. When the croup is very sloped, it is referred to as goose rump.

Breeching: Long, thick hairs covering the thighs. Sometimes a fringe on the back of the upper thighs.

Dense: Describes very thick hair.

Dewlap: The fold of skin under the neck at the throat; can extend down to the chest.

Dish-faced: Said of a dog with a concave profile having slightly depressed frontal bones. Example: Bulldog, Boxer, Pug.

Dolichocephalic: Having a long, narrow skull, as in that of the Greyhound.

Domed: Describes the skull of a dog with a convex profile, having arched frontal bones. Example: Bedlington Terrier.

Dwarfism: A balanced decrease in size of all body parts of a normal-sized specimen.

Ear: Depending on the breed, ears can be erect or pricked, pendulous, drop, semi-prick. The rose ear is a small drop ear that folds over and back, revealing the burr. In the button ear, the ear flap folds forward, barely away from the head, with the tip lying close to the skull.

Eye: Spaniels have oval eyes; Bulldogs have round eyes; Greyhounds have almond eyes.

Fallow: The result of the dilution of brown, a variation of tan.

Fawn: A color ranging from tan to red. Tan markings are fawn. The dilution of the fawn color produces a tawny color.

Fawn: Fawn red; fawn coat ranging from red to rust.

Fearlessness: The quality of a dog that fears nothing and may bite.

Feathering: Long hairs forming a fringe on the external ear, back of the legs, the tail and the chest.

Filled-up: Refers to a filled-up face: finely chiseled, smooth skin over the bones, flat muscles.

Flare: A white stripe on the forehead that often continues along the head.

Flashings: Irregular white markings on the face and chest.

Flecked: Said of a variegated coat with spotted markings (small dark spots on a white background).

Flushing Dog: A dog, such as the spaniel, that flushes game, that is, forces the game out in the open without pursuing it like hounds and without indicating its presence like pointers.

Forehead: The portion of the head above the muzzle.

Forequarters: The region from the shoulder blades down to the feet.

Gait: The pattern of the footsteps. Natural gaits—walk, trot, gallop. Free gait—easy, untiring movement. Frictionless gait—made with no apparent effort. Balanced gait—uniform speed and stride.

Griffon: A medium- or long-haired pointer or hound with tousled, wiry or shaggy hair.

Hare foot: Long and narrow.

Harlequin: Refers to a multicolored coat with patched or pied coloration on gray or blue; spots of black on white (patches of black on white, as in Great Danes).

Harsh: Describes hard, coarse, weather-resistant hair.

Hedge hunter: A dog that hunts in the brush. A dog that flushes game, but does not point or retrieve. (Synonym of springer)

Height: The height of the body measured by a vertical line running from the withers to the ground when the animal is in a relaxed standing position. Size can range from 0.2 to 1 meter.

Herder: A dog used to herd stock.

High-Standing: Said of a tall dog with plenty of leg, like the Greyhound.

Hindquarters: The region including the croup and hind legs.

Hollow: Said of an area of the body with a convex profile.

Hound: A dog with drop ears that takes to the trail and tracks while giving tongue, eventually running down the animal being hunted. (Group VI dog breeds).

Interbreeding: The mating of two dogs of different breeds.

Isabella: A fawn or light bay color.

Kissing spot: A round spot of color on the head of the King Charles and the Cavalier King Charles Spaniels. A tan or fawn mark above and between the eyes on black and tan dogs.

Large: Said of dogs that are larger than average (such as the Great Dane).

Leashhound: A hunting dog with a refined sense of smell that tracks silently on a leash.

Leggy: Describes a dog with long legs and giving the impression of being high off the ground.

Line: All the descendants of a common ancestor.

Liver: Brown.

Loin: The lumbar region posterior to the ribs and anterior to the croup.

Long back: Describes the back when the distance from the withers to the rump exceeds the height at the withers.

Low to ground: Said of dogs with relatively short legs and well let down chest. (Dachshund).

Mantle: A dark portion of the coat on the back that differs in color from the rest of the coat.

Marking: A white or other color marking on different colored background.

Mask: A dark shading on the face.

Mastiff: A large-headed, thick-set guard dog with strong jaws. Short-haired Molossian types are mastiffs.

Medium: Describes an average-sized dog.

Merle: A coat with dark, irregular blotches against a lighter, often gray, background. French dogs with this coat are called harlequin; British dogs are called blue merle.

Mesomorph: A dog having a well-proportioned, muscular body. Example: setters, pointers, French Shepherd, Belgian Shepherd.

Mismarks: Self color with any area of white hairs.

Molossian type: A large thick-muscled guard dog with a large head and powerful body. Mastiffs are Molossian types.

Morphology: P. Megnin (1932) classified dog breeds into four main morphological groups:

Braccoids: Fairly long muzzle. Marked stop. Hanging ears. Pointers, Spaniels, Setters and Dalmatians belong to this group.

Graioids: Long-bodied dogs with an elongated conical head. Straight skull. Small ears. Long muzzle. Indistinct stop. Tight-lipped. Slender body, thin legs, abdomen well tucked up. The Greyhound belongs to this group.

Lupoids: Wolf-like. Prick ears, long muzzle, short, tight lips. Example: Belgian shepherds.

Molossoids: Massive, round head. Pronounced stop. Short, powerful muzzle. Drop ears. Thick lips. Massive body low to ground. Loose skin. Heavy-boned.

Mottled: Describes a coat with blotches of dark hairs on a lighter background of the same color. Example: Australian Cattle Dog.

Multi-color: A coat of several colors. The juxtaposition of colored spots or patches.

Mute: Refers to a dog that does not bark or bay while trailing.

Muzzle: The facial region comprising the stop, the nose, and the jaws. Only the dorsal portion of the stop is included in the muzzle.

Griffon

Long-limbed type

Mesomorph

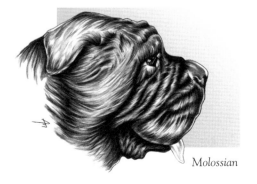

Molossian

Pips

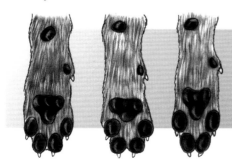

Foot shape :

Normal foot   Cat foot   Hare foot

Note: In the almond-shaped eye, the tissue surrounding the eye is longer than the eye. The eye itself, of course, is round.

Nuance: A variation in the intensity of a color.

Pace: A gait in which the left foreleg and left hind leg advance together, followed by the right foreleg and right hind leg.

Pack: An organized group of hounds that hunt larger animals.

Pad: The foot's shock-absorber located under and behind the toes. The pads are covered by calloused, hard, rough, irregularly patterned, highly pigmented skin.

Parti-color: Describes a variegated coat with two or more colors.

Patch: A limited area of color or white in the coat.

Pear-shaped: Having the shape of a pear.

Pendulous: A long, hanging ear.

Pied: Refers to a coat with large patches of white and another color. Example: Pied-Black (white is dominant); Black-Pied (black is dominant).

Pig Dog: A dog used for hunting boar.

Pigmented: Colored by pigments.

Pips: The tan (fawn) spots above each eye giving the impression that the dog has four eyes. This is the typical pattern in black and tan breeds.

Plume: A long fringe of hair on the tail.

Point: The action or position of a dog that has found game. The dog freezes to indicate the presence of game.

Pointer: A dog that assumes an immovable stance when it scents a bird nearby. It "points out" the bird. (Group 7 dog breeds)

Pointer: A short-haired hunter that indicates the presence of game by pointing in the direction of the game with its nose.

Primitive: Related to the most ancient breeds closest to the ancestral wolf (Nordic breeds).

Proportions: The body parts in relation to each other. Each part considered separate as compared to the whole. There are many terms to describe a dog's proportions: close-coupled, low-stationed, off-square, etc.

Puce: Dark brown, brown.

Red-Roan: Describes a coat with a uniform mixture of white and orange or fawn hairs.

Red: One extreme of fawn (from fallow to red).

Retriever: A hunting dog trained to find and bring wounded or killed game back to the handler.

Roan: A coat in which white blotches have a fine mixture of white and fawn hairs or a mixture of three colors (white, red, black or brown).

Robust: Describes a strong, hardy, heavy-boned dog.

Rolling: A transversal movement of the body with each step. A dog can have a "rolling gait".

Ruby: Bright red.

Rustic: A dog adapted to living outdoors in all kinds of weather without special care.

Sable: Describes a coat having black-tipped hairs on a background of fawn.

Saddle: A small blanket.

Sedge: A color between fallow and red in the range of fawn shades.

Self-Color: A one-color coat (except for lighter shadings), without white spots or hairs.

Self-Marked: Refers to a coat with white markings on a whole colored dog.

Setter: A bird dog trained for net hunting in which the net is dropped over both the crouched dog and the bird.

Setter: A pointer from the British Isles. Like the ancient "crouchers", he sets by crouching or half crouching.

Shaded: A light coat with dark areas.

Skeleton: The bones of the body and legs.

Skewbald: Describes a white coat with brindle markings (French Bulldog).

Smoky: A fairly light-colored coat (fawn, sable) tipped with black, brown or blue.

Socks: White markings on the feet.

Sole: An improper term used to describe the surface of the paw pads.

Spaniel: A hunting dog with long- or medium-length (often silky) hair, rectangular body outline, medium size. A mesomorph. Continental Spaniels are pointers. British Spaniels are called spaniels or hedge hunters.

Spaniel: From the French word espaigneul designating spaniels of British, Irish or American origin.

Speck: A small light spot (fawn) on white background.

Speckled: Refers to a coat with small flecks or dapple.

Splashed: Refers to a white coat with patches of color or a colored coat with patches of white.

Spot: Any area of color that differs from that of the background. The spot can be white or colored. Spots have different names depending on size: fleck (small spot), patch (large spot), blotch (very large spot). If a coat has several juxtaposed colored spots, it is a multi-color coat.

Spotted: Describes a coat covered with small spots, including dappled and mottled.

Square body outline: Describes a dog whose height at the withers is equal to the length from the point of the shoulder to the point of the rump.

Standard: A description of the ideal dog. The first dog standard, written in 1876, was that of the Bulldog. Standards are often imprecise.

Stop: The facial indentation between the forehead and the muzzle where the nasal bones and cranium meet. Bulldogs have distinct stops; Greyhounds have almost no stop; Pointers have moderate stops.

Straight: Describes the lines of the body. Example: straight back, straight front, straight in pastern.

Strain: The ancestor from which a family descends. A group of animals breeding amongst themselves for several generations without the introduction of new blood.

Svelte: Thin, supple, slender.

Tail: The guide mark for tail length is the hock. The tail is of medium length if it reaches the hock, short if it does not reach the hock, and long if it extends beyond the hock. The tail carriage can be described in many ways: horizontal, saber, gay, sickle, scimitar, tightly curled (Shar-Pei), double curl (Pug), snap (Akita), docked (German Short-Haired Pointer), etc.

Tan: The fawn or tawny markings on black and tan dogs.

Tawny: Light fawn color resulting from the dilution of fawn.

Terrier: From the French word terre (earth). A hunting dog that roots animals from burrows, that "hunts underground".

Thick: Said of an abundant coat.

Thorax: The length of the thorax is measured horizontally from the chest at the last rib. It is well let down when the brisket reaches slightly below the knees. (Depth and length of – example, a long, deep chest.)

Tight-lipped: Having thin, firm lips.

Tongue: The baying of hounds on the trail. Hounds "give tongue", they do not bark.

Toy: A very small companion dog (Toy Poodle).

Track: A succession of footfalls, footprints (the imprint left by the foot as it strikes the ground).

Track: Action of a dog hunting for game.

Trail: The route followed by an animal; the print or scent left along its path.

Trousers: Long hair on the thighs, longer than the culotte. For Poodles, the hair left on the legs during grooming – English Saddle clip (also called the Lion Clip).

Tufted tail: A tail with a tuft of hair at the end.

Turn-up: Describes a short, uplifted muzzle.

Undercoat: The fine, soft, dense hair under the outer coat.

Undershot Jaw: This term usually applies only when the lower jaw projects beyond the upper jaw. This can be a fault or a characteristic of a breed.

Variety: A subdivision of breed; dogs possessing the distinctive characteristics of the breed, yet having at least one common hereditary trait that distinguishes them from other varieties (size, length and texture of coat, coat color, ear carriage).

Walleye: An eye that lacks pigment. The unpigmented portion of the eye appears to be a light gray-blue, sometimes whitish (Pearl Eye). Can affect one or both eyes. Acceptable in some breeds. Note: Not to be confused with heterochromatic eyes, where each eye is of a different color.

Washed out: Said of a very light color appearing as though it has been highly diluted with water.

Waterdog: A dog that hunts in marshy areas for waterfowl; particularly a retriever. (Group 8 dog breeds)

Wedge-shaped: In the form of a wedge, v-shaped, tapering.

Well-knit: Describes body sections that are firmly joined by well-developed (but not over-developed) muscles.

Well-muscled thighs: Thighs that are well-developed with rounded musculature.

Wheaten: A pale fallow or fawn color.

Whip tail: A tail carried stiffly at back level, like that of hunting dogs.

Wire-haired: A very hard coat, rough to the touch.

Wire-haired: Describes a dog with hard, wiry hair.

Wise: Describes a dog that is calm, docile and even-tempered, but that will not be intimidated.

Withers: A point between the neck and the back. Height at the withers determines the size of the dog.

Wolf gray: A smoky fawn or sable coat.

Jack Russell Terrier

Poitevin Hound

St. Bernard

English Cocker Spaniel

Guidelines for Understanding

Background and Discussion of the Breed

Complete Name of the Breed

Dog Profile (1)

Group Color (2)

Group Number (3)

Section Number (4)

Section Color (5)

Extract from FCI Standard

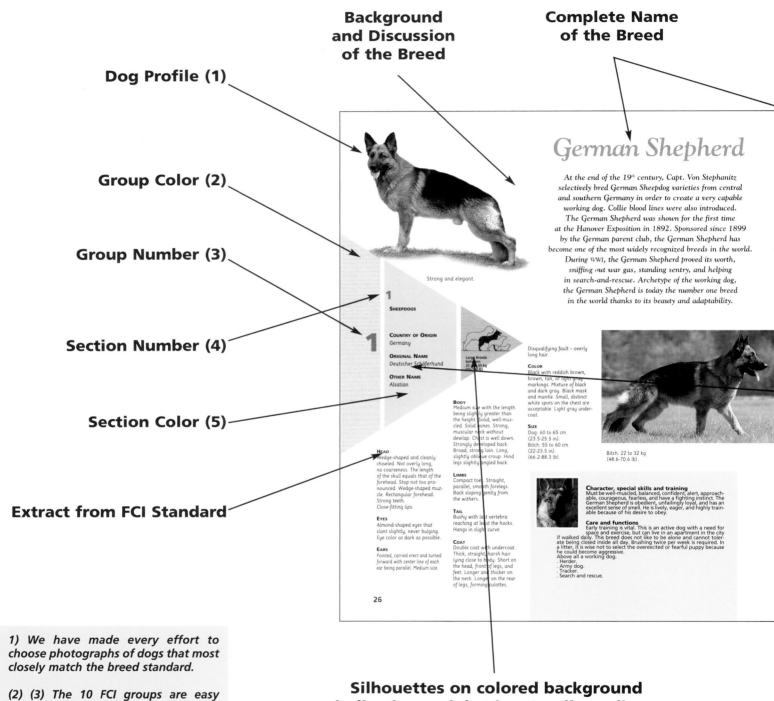

German Shepherd

At the end of the 19th century, Capt. Von Stephanitz selectively bred German Sheepdog varieties from central and southern Germany in order to create a very capable working dog. Collie blood lines were also introduced. The German Shepherd was shown for the first time at the Hanover Exposition in 1892. Sponsored since 1899 by the German parent club, the German Shepherd has become one of the most widely recognized breeds in the world. During WWI, the German Shepherd proved its worth, sniffing out war gas, standing sentry, and helping in search-and-rescue. Archetype of the working dog, the German Shepherd is today the number one breed in the world thanks to its beauty and adaptability.

Strong and elegant.

1
SHEEPDOGS

1

COUNTRY OF ORIGIN
Germany

ORIGINAL NAME
Deutscher Schäferhund

OTHER NAME
Alsatian

Large Breeds between 25 and 45 kg (55-99.2 lb)

Disqualifying fault – overly long hair.

COLOR
Black with reddish brown, brown, tan, or light gray markings. Mixture of black and dark gray. Black mask and mantle. Small, distinct white spots on the chest are acceptable. Light gray undercoat.

SIZE
Dog: 60 to 65 cm (23.5-25.5 in).
Bitch: 55 to 60 cm (22-23.5 in).
(66.2-88.3 lb).

Bitch: 22 to 32 kg (48.6-70.6 lb).

BODY
Medium size with the length being slightly greater than the height. Solid, well-muscled. Solid bones. Strong, muscular neck without dewlap. Chest is well down. Strongly developed back. Broad, strong loin. Long, slightly oblique croup. Hind legs slightly angled back.

LIMBS
Compact toes. Straight, parallel, smooth forelegs. Back sloping gently from the withers.

TAIL
Bushy with last vertebra reaching at least the hocks. Hangs in slight curve.

COAT
Double coat with undercoat. Thick, straight, harsh hair lying close to body. Short on the head, front of legs, and feet. Longer and thicker on the neck. Longer on the rear of legs, forming culottes.

HEAD
Wedge-shaped and cleanly chiseled. Not overly long, no coarseness. The length of the skull equals that of the forehead. Stop not too pronounced. Wedge-shaped muzzle. Rectangular forehead. Strong teeth. Close-fitting lips.

EYES
Almond-shaped eyes that slant slightly, never bulging. Eye color as dark as possible.

EARS
Pointed, carried erect and turned forward with center line of each ear being parallel. Medium size.

Character, special skills and training
Must be well-muscled, balanced, confident, alert, approachable, courageous, fearless, and have a fighting instinct. The German Shepherd is obedient, unfailingly loyal, and has an excellent sense of smell. He is lively, eager, and highly trainable because of his desire to obey.

Care and functions
Early training is vital. This is an active dog with a need for space and exercise, but can live in an apartment in the city if walked daily. This breed does not like to be alone and cannot tolerate being closed inside all day. Brushing twice per week is required. In a litter, it is wise not to select the overexcited or fearful puppy because he could become aggressive.
Above all a working dog.
. Herder.
. Army dog.
. Tracker.
. Search and rescue.

26

Silhouettes on colored background indicating weight/size: Small, medium, large and giants breeds (see page 17)

1) We have made every effort to choose photographs of dogs that most closely match the breed standard.

(2) (3) The 10 FCI groups are easy to locate because they are presented in a different color (background and lettering).

(4) (5) FCI sections have also been presented in a different color (background and lettering).

the Breed Descriptions

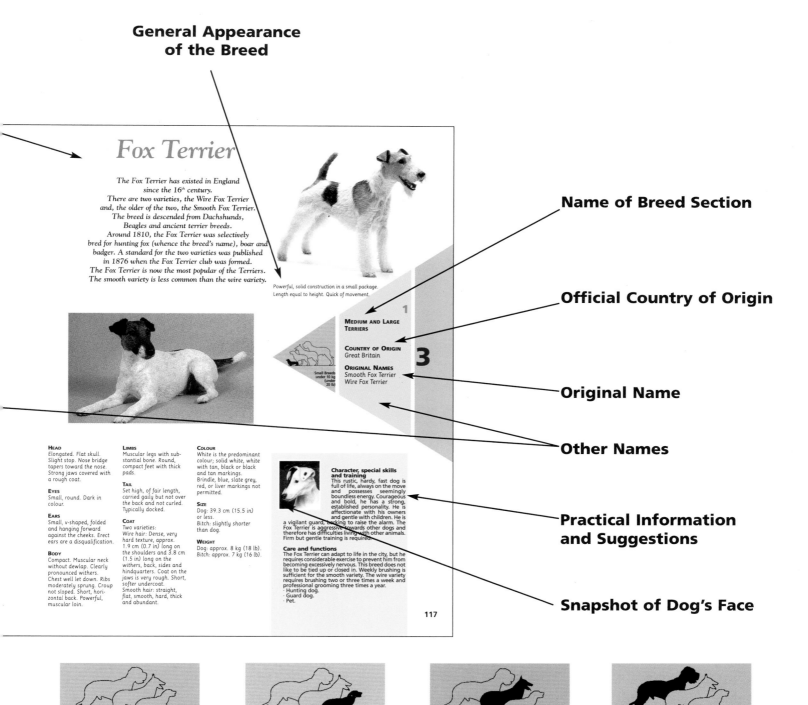

General Appearance of the Breed

Fox Terrier

The Fox Terrier has existed in England since the 16th century.
There are two varieties, the Wire Fox Terrier and, the older of the two, the Smooth Fox Terrier.
The breed is descended from Dachshunds, Beagles and ancient terrier breeds.
Around 1810, the Fox Terrier was selectively bred for hunting fox (whence the breed's name), boar and badger. A standard for the two varieties was published in 1876 when the Fox Terrier club was formed.
The Fox Terrier is now the most popular of the Terriers.
The smooth variety is less common than the wire variety.

Powerful, solid construction in a small package.
Length equal to height. Quick of movement.

Name of Breed Section

1

MEDIUM AND LARGE TERRIERS

Official Country of Origin

COUNTRY OF ORIGIN
Great Britain

3

ORIGINAL NAMES
Smooth Fox Terrier
Wire Fox Terrier

Small Breeds under 10 kg (under 20 lb)

Original Name

Other Names

HEAD
Elongated. Flat skull. Slight stop. Nose bridge tapers toward the nose. Strong jaws covered with a rough coat.

EYES
Small, round. Dark in colour.

EARS
Small, v-shaped, folded and hanging forward against the cheeks. Erect ears are a disqualification.

BODY
Compact. Muscular neck without dewlap. Clearly pronounced withers. Chest well let down. Ribs moderately sprung. Croup not sloped. Short, horizontal back. Powerful, muscular loin.

LIMBS
Muscular legs with substantial bone. Round, compact feet with thick pads.

TAIL
Set high, of fair length, carried gaily but not over the back and not curled. Typically docked.

COAT
Two varieties:
Wire hair: Dense, very hard texture, approx. 1.9 cm (0.7 in) long on the shoulders and 3.8 cm (1.5 in) long on the withers, back, sides and hindquarters. Coat on the jaws is very rough. Short, softer undercoat.
Smooth hair: straight, flat, smooth, hard, thick and abundant.

COLOUR
White is the predominant colour; solid white, white with tan, black or black and tan markings. Brindle, blue, slate grey, red, or liver markings not permitted.

SIZE
Dog: 39.3 cm (15.5 in) or less.
Bitch: slightly shorter than dog.

WEIGHT
Dog: approx. 8 kg (18 lb).
Bitch: approx. 7 kg (16 lb).

Character, special skills and training
This rustic, hardy, fast dog is full of life, always on the move and possesses seemingly boundless energy. Courageous and bold, he has a strong, established personality. He is affectionate with his owners and gentle with children. He is a vigilant guard, barking to raise the alarm. The Fox Terrier is aggressive towards other dogs and therefore has difficulties living with other animals. Firm but gentle training is required.

Care and functions
The Fox Terrier can adapt to life in the city, but he requires considerable exercise to prevent him from becoming excessively nervous. This breed does not like to be tied up or closed in. Weekly brushing is sufficient for the smooth variety. The wire variety requires brushing two or three times a week and professional grooming three times a year.
· Hunting dog.
· Guard dog.
· Pet.

117

Practical Information and Suggestions

Snapshot of Dog's Face

| Small Breeds under 10 kg (20 lb) | Medium Breeds between 10 and 25 kg (20-55 lb) | Large Breeds between 25 and 45 kg (55-100 lb) | Giant Breeds over 45 kg (over 100 lb) |

The outlines at right are used to indicate the size category of a given breed. This outline is used throughout the book and is particularly relevant in the chapters on health and nutrition.

Group
1

SECTION 1

GERMAN SHEPHERD
AUSTRALIAN SHEPHERD
BERGER DE BEAUCE
BERGAMASCO
BRIARD
MAREMMA SHEEPDOG
PICARDY SHEEPDOG
PYRENEAN SHEPHERD DOG
SOUTHERN RUSSIAN SHEEPDOG
SHETLAND SHEEPDOG
OLD ENGLISH SHEEPDOG
BORDER COLLIE
BELGIAN SHEEPDOG:
    MALINOIS
    LAEKENOIS
    GROENENDAEL
    TERVUREN
CATALAN SHEEPDOG
CROATIAN SHEEPDOG
DUTCH SHEPHERD
PERRO DE PASTOR MALLORQUIN
POLISH LOWLAND SHEEPDOG

PORTUGUESE SHEEPDOG
POLISH MOUNTAIN DOG
SAARLOOS WOLFHOND
CZECHOSLOVAKIAN WOLFDOG
COLLIE:
    SMOOTH COLLIE
    ROUGH COLLIE
BEARDED COLLIE
KELPIE
KOMONDOR
KUVASZ
MUDI
PULI
PUMI
SCHAPENDOES
SCHIPPERKE
SLOVAK CUVAC
WELSH CORGI

SECTION 2

AUSTRALIAN CATTLE DOG
BELGIAN CATTLE DO

Belgian Sheepdog Malinois

25

German Shepherd

Strong and elegant.

At the end of the 19th century, Capt. Von Stephanitz selectively bred German Sheepdog varieties from central and southern Germany in order to create a very capable working dog. Collie blood lines were also introduced. The German Shepherd was shown for the first time at the Hanover Exposition in 1892. Sponsored since 1899 by the German parent club, the German Shepherd has become one of the most widely recognized breeds in the world. During WWI, the German Shepherd proved its worth, sniffing out war gas, standing sentry, and helping in search-and-rescue. Archetype of the working dog, the German Shepherd is today the number one breed in the world thanks to its beauty and adaptability.

1
SHEEPDOGS

COUNTRY OF ORIGIN
Germany

ORIGINAL NAME
Deutscher Schäferhund

OTHER NAME
Alsatian

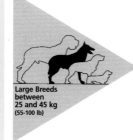

Large Breeds
between
25 and 45 kg
(55-100 lb)

HEAD
Wedge-shaped and cleanly chiseled. Not overly long, no coarseness. The length of the skull equals that of the forehead. Stop not too pronounced. Wedge-shaped muzzle. Rectangular forehead. Strong teeth. Close-fitting lips.

EYES
Almond-shaped eyes that slant slightly, never bulging. Eye color as dark as possible.

EARS
Pointed, carried erect and turned forward with center line of each ear being parallel. Medium size.

BODY
Medium size with the length being slightly greater than the height. Solid, well-muscled. Solid bones. Strong, muscular neck without dewlap. Chest is well down. Strongly developed back. Broad, strong loin. Long, slightly oblique croup. Hind legs slightly angled back.

LIMBS
Compact toes. Straight, parallel, smooth forelegs. Back sloping gently from the withers.

TAIL
Bushy with last vertebra reaching at least the hocks. Hangs in slight curve.

COAT
Double coat with undercoat. Thick, straight, harsh hair lying close to body. Short on the head, front of legs, and feet. Longer and thicker on the neck. Longer on the rear of legs, forming culottes.

Disqualifying fault – overly long hair.

COLOR
Black with reddish brown, brown, tan, or light gray markings. Mixture of black and dark gray. Black mask and mantle. Small, distinct white spots on the chest are acceptable. Light gray undercoat.

SIZE
Dog: 60 to 65 cm (23.5-25.5 in).
Bitch: 55 to 60 cm (22-23.5 in).

WEIGHT
Dog: 30 to 40 kg (66.2-88.3 lb).

Bitch: 22 to 32 kg (48.6-70.6 lb).

Character, special skills and training
Must be well-muscled, balanced, confident, alert, approachable, courageous, fearless, and have a fighting instinct. The German Shepherd is obedient, unfailingly loyal, and has an excellent sense of smell. He is lively, eager, and highly trainable because of his desire to obey.

Care and functions
Early training is vital. This is an active dog with a need for space and exercise, but can live in an apartment in the city if walked daily. This breed does not like to be alone and cannot tolerate being closed inside all day. Brushing twice per week is required. In a litter, it is wise not to select the overexcited or fearful puppy because he could become aggressive.
Above all a working dog.
. Herder.
. Army dog.
. Tracker.
. Search and rescue.
. Guard dog.
. Guide dog.
. A loyal, affectionate pet.

Australian Shepherd

In the twentieth century, the Australian Shepherd was developed in California from Australian sheepdogs. Californian farmers and ranchers used the breed as a working dog.

Well-balanced. Slightly longer than tall. Solidly constructed. Of medium size and bone. Lithe, agile. Smooth, relaxed, easy gait.

1

SHEEPDOGS

COUNTRY OF ORIGIN
United States

ORIGINAL NAME
Australian Shepherd

Medium Breeds between 10 and 25 kg (20-55 lb)

HEAD
Clean-cut, strong, and dry. Length equal to width. Moderate, well-defined stop. Black or brown nose in harmony with coat color.

EYES
Almond shape. Brown, blue, amber, or any variation or combination thereof.

EARS
Set on high. Triangular. Moderate size. Break forward or to the side when dog is alert. Prick or hanging ears are severe faults.

BODY
Strong neck. Straight, strong topline. Deep chest. Ribs well sprung. Moderately sloped croup.

LIMBS
Legs strong of bone. Oval, compact feet.

TAIL
Straight, naturally short or docked (may not exceed 10 cm (4 in).

COAT
Of medium length and texture. Straight and wavy. Moderate mane, frill, and breeching.

COLOR
Blue merle, black, red merle. All of these colors with or without white markings, with or without tan (copper). White color must not extend beyond the withers. White permitted at the neck, on the chest, legs, and muzzle underparts, with a blaze on the head. Eyes must be fully surrounded by color.

SIZE
Dog: 51 to 58 cm (20-23 in).
Bitch: 46 to 53 cm (18-21 in).

WEIGHT
20 to 25 kg (44-55 lb).

Character, special skills, and training:
The Australian Shepherd is extremely active, hardy, and fast. This intelligent dog can cover up to 60 km per day while tending large herds. This exceptional herder also guards the farm. Affectionate, gentle, good-natured, and very loyal, the Australian Shepherd makes a good pet.

Care and fonctions
This dog of almost unlimited energy is made for wide-open spaces. He should not be kept in enclosed spaces and is not made for life indoors. Regular brushing is sufficient to maintain the coat.
· Herder.
· Guard dog.
· Pet.

Well-balanced. Wolf-like. Well-built. Free, relaxed gait (stretched out trot).

Berger de Beauce

The Berger de Beauce is descended from the "Plains Dogs" that guarded the flocks near Paris. At the end of the 19th century, the short-haired "Plains Dogs" were named Beaucerons; long-haired varieties were named Briards. E. Boulet (best known for his Griffons) introduced the breed and helped set up the French Shepherd club in 1896. In 1911, the Friends of the Beauceron Club was founded. The name "Bas Rouge" was given to the Beauceron because of the tan markings on its legs, that look like socks (bas). Breed selection has vacillated between working dogs, show dogs and dogs bred to compete in guard and defense events. Nevertheless, the Berger de Beauce is, above all, a herder. Very popular in France, this breed is almost unknown in other countries, except Belgium.

1

SHEEPDOGS

COUNTRY OF ORIGIN
France

OTHER NAMES
Beauceron,
Bas rouge,
French Shorthaired Shepherd

Large Breeds between 25 and 45 kg (55-100 lb)

HEAD
Long (2/5 of height), chiseled, with a flat skull. Stop not pronounced. Slightly convex forehead. Muzzle neither straight nor pointed.

EYES
Round, dark color. Frank regard.

EARS
Set on high. Naturally drop, short and flat, but not close against the head. Carried erect if cropped.

BODY
Solid, powerful, well-developed and muscled, but not heavy. Muscular neck. Broad, deep chest. Straight back. Croup barely sloped Broad loin

LIMBS
Two dewclaws on the inside of each hind leg, close to the foot. Leg held slightly back. Round, strong feet

TAIL
Carried straight down reaching the hocks and forming a slight J-hook. Slightly bushy.

COAT
Flat on the head. Heavy and dense, lying close to the body (3 to 4 cm (1.5 in) long). Slight fringing on thighs and along underline. Very short, fine, dense, soft undercoat preferably of slate color.

COLOR
Black and tan (bi-color), bas rouge (most common). Glossy black. Tan is squirrel red. Tan markings: spots above the eyes, on sides of muzzle, throat, and under the tail. Tan extends down legs to feet and wrists (coloration pattern forms a "sock", whence the name

Bas Rouge, or Red Socks). Harlequin: gray, black and tan (tri-color): even amounts of gray and black in spots with the same characteristic tan spots.

SIZE
Dog: 65 to 70 cm (25.5-27.5 in). Bitch: 61 to 68 cm (24-27 in).

WEIGHT
27 to 37 kg (60-80 lb).

Character, special skills and training
This breed is forthright, courageous, fast, hardy and alert, and has amazing dissuasive powers. He is wary with strangers and not easily won over.
This dog is loyal to his owner and gentle with children. He bonds to the entire family, but is guarded when strangers are present. Owners are warned that this breed openly exerts its dominance over other male dogs. His well-developed sense of smell is used to sniff out truffles. A wise breed, he is forthright, dynamic and courageous when working, yet is obedient and easy to handle.

Care and functions
This hardy "country gentleman" needs space to run and is not suited to apartment living. Do not leave him leashed; he cannot tolerate being closed in. This dog needs firm training, discipline, and lots of exercise to burn off energy. He matures late. Two to three brushings per month are sufficient. Dewclaws must be trimmed regularly.
· Herder (Sheep and Cattle), guard dog, defense dog, army dog, tracker, search and rescue.
· Pet.

Bergamasco

This ancient Sheepdog spread throughout the Alps region of Italy, but was most concentrated in the Bergamo area where sheep farming was particularly developed. Some believe the Bergamasco is descended from the Briard. Others hypothesize that the Bergamasco came to Italy from Asia, stating that sheepdogs of this type arrived in Western Europe during the Mongol invasions.

Medium size. Well proportioned. Solid skeleton. Muscular. Fast, easy gait.

SHEEPDOGS

Large Breeds between 25 and 45 kg (55-100 lb)

1

1

COUNTRY OF ORIGIN
Italy

ORIGINAL NAME
Cane de Pastore Bergamasco

OTHER NAME
Bergamese Shepherd

HEAD
Large appearance. Capacious skull. Pronounced superciliary arches. Marked stop. Fairly short, blunt muzzle. Large nose.

EYES
Large and oval. Brown color. Darkness of shade varies with color of coat. Black rims. Long fall covering the eyes.

EARS
Soft, triangular drop ears. Thin leather.

BODY
Square body outline. No dewlap on the neck. Full brisket. Short, powerful loin. Straight, well-muscled back. Broad, sloping, solid, well-muscled croup

TAIL
Thick and strong at the base tapering toward the tip. Covered in slightly wavy, shaggy hair. Hangs in the shape of a saber when relaxed.

COAT
Very long and wiry (goat hair) on the front portion of the body. Corded over the rest of the body. Short, dense, soft undercoat.

LIMBS
Forelegs: oval, compact feet. Strong, oval hare feet. Compact, arched toes. Solid-boned, well-muscled hind legs

COLOR
Gray flecked with black, tan, or white. Uniform black coat is acceptable, though uniform white is not. White spots covering no more than 1/5 of the body are permitted.

SIZE
Dog: 58 to 62 cm (23-24.5 in).
Bitch: 54 to 58 cm (21-23 in).

WEIGHT
Dog: 32 to 38 kg (70-84 lb).
Bitch: 26 to 32 (57.5-70 lb).

Character, special skills and training
Alert, keen and well-balanced, this dog has an ideal personality for flock guarding. This breed's friendly disposition, gentleness and patience also make him an excellent pet. His impressive size makes him a good guard dog. This often stubborn dog requires early, firm training.

Care and functions
This is not a city dweller. He needs space and a lot of exercise. Groom the coat by running your fingers through the hairs to separate the cords.
· Sheepdog.
· Guard dog, search-and-rescue (avalanches, natural disasters).
· Pet.

Briard

Like the Berger de Beauce, the Briard descended from "Plains Dogs" from the region around Paris. The name Chien de berger de Brie describing long-haired sheepdogs was first used in 1809 at the Agriculture Show at the Rozier Abby. In 1863 at the first dog show in Paris, a bitch resembling a Briard placed Best in Show. In 1888, P. Mégnin wrote in L'Eleveur (Breeder), "The Briard is a cross of the Barbet with the Berger de Beauce, the Briard's distinguishing trait being his long, wooly coat." The Briard was registered for the first time in 1885 with the LOF. The first standard was written by the French Shepherd dog club in 1897, describing a variety with wooly hair and another with goat hair. The goat hair variety won out and is the breed described in the current 1988 FCI standard.

During WWI, the Briard was used as a guard dog. Cropping this breed's ears is an old practice. Originally, the ears were cropped so there would be fewer exposed areas where other dogs or wolves attempting to attack the flock could get a grip.

Slightly longer than tall.
Well-proportioned.
Lively, bright gait.

1

SHEEPDOGS

COUNTRY OF ORIGIN
France

ORIGINAL NAME
Berger de Brie

Large Breeds
between
25 and 45 kg
(55-100 lb)

HEAD
Strong and long. Pronounced stop. Rectangular forehead. Squarish nose. Head covered in hairs forming a beard and mustache with fall shading the eyes.

EYES
Set horizontally. Large and of dark color. Long fall covering the eyes.

EARS
Set on high. Preferably cropped and carried erect.

BODY
Solid, muscular, well constructed and of good length. Broad, deep chest. Muscular loin. Slightly sloped croup. Straight back

LIMBS
Two dewclaws close to ground Strong, round feet. Compact toes. Muscular legs strong in bone

TAIL
Not docked. Well-feathered, forming a hook at the tip. Carried low, not falling to the right or left.

COAT
Coarse, dry (goat hair), light undercoat no more than 7 cm (3 in) long.

COLOR
All uniform colors (except white), brown, mahogany and bi-color. Dark colors are preferred.

SIZE
Dog: 62 to 68 cm (24.5-27 in).
Bitch: 56 to 64 cm (22-25 in).

WEIGHT
30 to 40 kg (66-88 lb).

Character, special skills and training
Though he looks a bit like a teddy bear, this dog is a proud, powerful athlete. He is agile, well-balanced, courageous, wise and vigorous. Underneath his hard exterior lies a heart of gold. The Briard is very affectionate, loyal and playful. He is very attached to his owner and plays well with children. He is reserved with strangers. The male is dominant. Strict training from a very young age is required for this somewhat stubborn, independent dog. He does not reach full maturity until the age of two or three.

Care and functions
This robust, active, powerful dog needs lots of space and exercise. He is not a city-dweller. His coat should be brushed and combed regularly to keep it mat-free: two to three times per week if he is an outdoor dog; once per week if he is an indoor dog.
· Sheepdog.
· Handsome pet.

Maremma Sheepdog

It is believed that the Maremma Sheepdog is an ancient breed. The Roman agronomist Varro mentions a breed of white dogs in his writings as early as 100 BC. Like most European Molossian types, this breed's roots can be traced to the Shepherd dogs of central Asia that arrived in Western Europe with the Mongols. Until 1950/1960, the Maremma Sheepdog (short-haired) was distinguished from the longer-haired Abruzzes Sheepdog. It was determined that this distinction had been made only because of the fact that this dog worked from June to October in the Abruzzes and from October to June in the region of Maremma. Approximately twenty-five years ago, Prof. G. Solaro wrote one standard for the breed and the names were joined.

Large, majestic breed. Powerfully built. Rustic appearance. Fairly thick skin. Gaits: extended walk and trot.

SHEEPDOGS

Large Breeds between 25 and 45 kg (55-100 lb)

1

1

COUNTRY OF ORIGIN
Italy

ORIGINAL NAME
Cane da Pastore Maremmano-Abruzzese

OTHER NAME
Pastore Abruzzese

HEAD
Large, flat, wedge-shaped; similar to that of the polar bear. Stop not pronounced.

EYES
Almond-shaped, relatively small in relation to the rest of the body. Ocher or dark brown color.

EARS
Set on high. Relatively small, drop, triangular (V-shaped). Cropped ears acceptable for working dogs.

BODY
Length greater than height. Large, strong neck. Deep chest is well open. Well-sprung ribs. Powerful, muscular, slightly sloped croup. Rectangular back

LIMBS
Large feet, almost round. Toes covered with thick, short hair.

TAIL
Covered with thick hair. Set on low. Carried down when relaxed; when alert, carried at the level of the back with the tip curved up.

COAT
Thick, long (8 cm (3 in) on the body), harsh to the touch. Short on the head. Collarette and fringes on the back of the legs. Heavy undercoat in winter.

COLOR
Solid white. Ivory, pale orange or lemon nuances are permitted.

SIZE
Dog: 65 to 73 cm (25.6-28.7 in).
Bitch: 60 to 68 cm (23.6-26.8 in).

WEIGHT
Dog: 35 to 45 kg (77-99 lb).
Bitch: 30 to 40 kg (66-88 lb).

Character, special skills and training
Calm, reflective, proud, and not likely to be submissive, this dog needs firm training. He is devoted to his owner, is good with children, and makes a good companion. Very distrustful of strangers, he is a reliable, dedicated guardian.

Care and functions
This breed is not suited for apartment living. He needs space and a lot of exercise. This robust dog does not handle heat well. Regular brushing is required.
· Sheepdog.
· Guard dog.
· Pet.

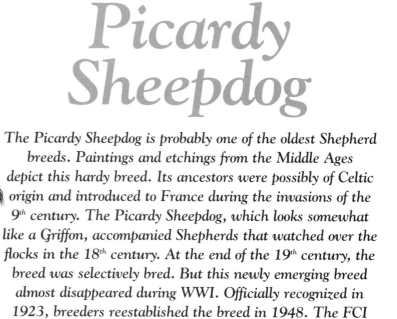

Picardy Sheepdog

The Picardy Sheepdog is probably one of the oldest Shepherd breeds. Paintings and etchings from the Middle Ages depict this hardy breed. Its ancestors were possibly of Celtic origin and introduced to France during the invasions of the 9th century. The Picardy Sheepdog, which looks somewhat like a Griffon, accompanied Shepherds that watched over the flocks in the 18th century. At the end of the 19th century, the breed was selectively bred. But this newly emerging breed almost disappeared during WWI. Officially recognized in 1923, breeders reestablished the breed in 1948. The FCI approved a standard for the Berger de Picardie in 1964.

Average size. Rustic, yet elegant, appearance.

1

SHEEPDOGS

COUNTRY OF ORIGIN
France

ORIGINAL NAMES
Berger de Picardie,
Berger Picard

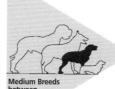

Medium Breeds
between
10 and 25 kg
(20-55 lb)

HEAD
Good proportion to overall size. Hair 4 in long. Prominent brow. Slight stop. Strong muzzle, but not overly long. Mustache and beard.

EYES
Dark color, medium size. Light colors or walleyes are objectionable.

EARS
Medium size, wide at the base with points slightly rounded. Carried erect.

BODY
Muscular and well-construct-ed. Strong, muscular neck. Deep chest. Long through the shoulders and thighs. Chest slightly up. Straight back. Strong loin.

LIMBS
Strong, sound legs. Arched, short, compact feet. Dark nails. No dewclaw.

TAIL
Hangs straight down, reaching the hocks and forming a slight hook at the tip.

COAT
Wiry, of medium length (5 to 6 cm (2-2.4 in), neither curly nor flat. Rough and crisp to the touch.

COLOR
Gray, gray-black, gray-blue, rusty gray, light or dark fawn. Large white markings are undesirable.

SIZE
Dog: 60 to 65 cm (23.5-25.5 in).
Bitch: 55 to 60 cm (22-24 in).

WEIGHT
19 to 23 kg (42-51 lb).

Character, special skills and training
This quicksilver, courageous dog is well-balanced and stable. Adapted to life in the country, he is very hard and has a penchant for hard work. The Picardy Sheepdog thrives in a family setting and is gentle with children.

Care and functions
This dog is not a city-dweller. He needs space and room to run. Regular, vigorous brushing is required.
· Sheepdog.
· Guard dog.
· Pet.

Pyrenean Shepherd Dog

The history of the smallest French Sheepdog traces back many years. It is thought that he descended from local breeds and never left the high valleys of the Pyrenees mountains until the late 19th century. During WWI, the Pyrenean Shepherd Dog was used as a lookout and messenger dog and to search for wounded. The breed was standardized in 1936. This breed was called by various names, which reflected its region of origin, such as the Labrit, the Landes Shepherd, the Bagnères Shepherd, the Auzun Shepherd, the Arbazzi Shepherd, etc. The Labrit, the largest and most rustic looking, measuring 50 to 55 in at the withers, was almost recognized as a separate breed in 1935. Today, the Labrit no longer exists; it is considered a Pyrenean Shepherd dog. There are two varieties of this breed, the very common long-haired variety and the rarer smooth-muzzled variety, which has short hair on the head and has a shorter body than the long-haired variety.

Bushy coat. Elegant gait. Smallest of the french Sheepdogs.

1

SHEEPDOGS

COUNTRY OF ORIGIN
France

ORIGINAL NAME
Berger des Pyrénées

Up to 25 kg (55 lb)

1

HEAD
Wedge-shaped, like that of the brown bear. Stop not accentuated. Long-haired variety has a fairly short muzzle. Smooth-muzzled variety has a longer muzzle.

EYES
Dark brown color. Black rims. Walleyes are permitted in dogs with harlequin or slate-gray coat.

EARS
Short, generally cropped. Carried three-fourths erect with tips breaking forward or to the side.

BODY
The body of the smooth-muzzled variety is slightly shorter than that of the long-haired variety. Strong neck. Deep, broad chest. Oblique croup. Long back.

LIMBS
Two dewclaws on hind legs.

Well-knit hind legs. The feet of the smooth-muzzled variety are more compact and arched than those of the long-haired variety.

TAIL
Long-haired variety: not too long, full fringe, attached low and forming a hook at the tip; often docked. Smooth-muzzled variety: fairly long, thick hair forming a flag, carried low; hook at the tip; tail circles over the back making a wheel when dog is alerted.

COAT
Long-haired variety: long- or medium-length, thick, almost flat or slightly wavy; more wooly on the croup and thighs; hair on muzzle and cheeks falls forward. Smooth-muzzled variety: thick, flat, fairly long and flexible; longer on the tail

and around the neck; head covered with short, fine hair; short hair on legs and breeching on the thighs.

COLOR
Long-haired variety: dark fawn with or without a mixture of black hairs, occasionally with white spots on the chest and feet; light gray with white on the head, chest and legs; shades of harlequin. White coat is a disqualification. Smooth-muzzled variety: white or white with gray (badger), pale yellow, wolf gray or tan spots on the head, ears and base of the tail. Badger coat preferred.

SIZE
Long-haired variety
Dog: 40 to 48 cm (16-19 in).
Bitch: 38 to 46 (15-18 in).
Smooth-muzzled variety
Dog: 40 to 54 cm (16-21 in).
Bitch: 40 to 52 cm
(16-20.5 in).

WEIGHT
Both varieties: 8 to 15 Kg
(17.5-33 lb).

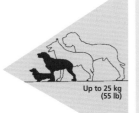

Character, special skills and training
The smooth-muzzled pyrenean Shepherd dog is a less nervous, more trainable dog than the long-haired variety. Hyperactive and energetic, with an excessively nervous disposition, this dog needs constant exercise. This is not an easy breed. This courageous dog is rather vocal, is wary of anything unknown, and is constantly on guard. He needs a strong-minded owner.

Care and functions
This dog is not suited to apartment living. If left alone, he will destroy everything within reach. If not given enough exercise, he will become aggressive. Weekly brushing is adequate.
· Sheepdog.
· Guard dog.
· Pet.
· Utility dog: search-and-rescue (in wreckage), drug and explosives dog.

Southern Russian Sheepdog

This breed is descended from Asian Molossian types and was later crossed with Borzois to give it a more streamlined silhouette. The breed was officially recognized in the USSR in 1952 and was the first Russian breed to be recognized by the FCI. The red army used this dog as a sentry. This breed is still rare outside of its country of origin.

1

SHEEPDOGS

1

COUNTRY OF ORIGIN
Russia

ORIGINAL NAME
Yuznarusskaya Ovtcharka

OTHER NAMES
Southern Russian Owtcharka
Ovtcharka de Russie
Meridionale

Robust constitution. Muscular. Natural gaits: lumbering trot and gallop.

Medium Breeds between 10 and 25 kg (20-55 lb)

HEAD
Elongated, with a moderately wide forehead. Slight stop. Large nose.

EYES
Dark color, oval. Set horizontally in the skull.

EARS
Fairly small, drop, triangular.

BODY
Very muscular. No dewlap. Fairly deep, broad chest, slightly flattened on the sides. Belly moderately tucked up. Strong, straight back. Short, broad, rounded loin.

LIMBS
Legs with plenty of bone. Strong, oval feet with well-arched toes.

TAIL
Long.

COAT
Long (10 to 15 cm) (4-6 in), rough, thick, bushy, slightly wavy. Heavy undercoat.

COLOR
White, white and yellow, straw, gray, dark gray. White with small gray markings or flecked with gray.

SIZE
Dog: less than 65 cm (25.6 in).
Bitch: less than 62 cm (24.5 in).

WEIGHT
Approx. 25 kg (55 lb).

Character, special skills and training
This active dog is robust, strong and well-balanced. He is well-known for his courage and is distrustful of strangers. This dominant dog is very protective of his owner. Though he can be aggressive, he can be a good companion with proper training.

Care and functions
This dog needs a lot of exercise. Regular brushing is required.
· Sheepdog.
· Guard and defense dog.
· Pet.

Shetland Sheepdog

The Shetland Sheepdog's name indicates where this breed originated – the Shetland Islands off the northern coast of Scotland. He is thought to have been the result of crosses between Scottish collies, the "Yakki" dogs of Greenland whalers, and the Spitz that accompanied Scandinavian fishers. Others believe the Shetland Sheepdog is descended from the King Charles Spaniel. Called "Sheltie" for short, this breed looks like a miniature, long-haired collie. A Shetland Sheepdog club was formed in the Shetlands in 1908. The breed was introduced in England in the late 19th century but was not officially recognized until 1914.

Miniature version of the collie.
Balanced body.
Free action.

1

SHEEPDOGS

COUNTRY OF ORIGIN
United Kingdom

OTHER NAME
Sheltie

WEIGHT
5 to 10 kg
(11-22 lb).

Small Breeds
under 10 kg
(under 20 lb)

1

HEAD
Long and wedge-shaped. Flat, straight skull. Slight stop.

EYES
Set obliquely in skull, almond-shaped. Dark brown color, though blue or merle eyes are permitted for some merle varieties.

EARS
Small, carried three-fourths erect breaking forward at the tip.

BODY
Length slightly greater than height. Muscular and well-balanced. Deep chest with well-sprung ribs. Straight back.

LIMBS
Oval feet. Thick pads. Compact, knuckled-up toes. Strong-boned legs.

TAIL
Carried low. Abundantly feathered. Raised when dog is alert, but never carried above the level of the back.

COAT
Long, straight, harsh. Abundant, short, soft undercoat. Very full mane and frill giving the dog a majestic air. Hind legs are heavily feathered.

COLOR
Shades of sable – from golden through mahogany; tricolor – jet black with tan and white markings; blue merle – silvery blue, mottling, merled with black; black and white; black and tan.

SIZE
Dog: 36 to 40 cm (14-16 in).
Bitch: 34 to 38 cm (13-15 in).

Character, special skills and training
This active, alert, happy and easy-going dog is affectionate, gentle and easy to train. He is reserved toward strangers, but never fearful. This dog is vocal.

Care and functions
Brushing two times per week is required, more often during periods of seasonal shedding. Do not bathe this breed more than once per month. Daily walks are necessary.
· Sheepdog.
· Pet.

Old English Sheepdog

The ancestry of the Bobtail is disputed. Some believe this breed descended long ago from Sheepdogs, including the Italian Mastiff (extinct), introduced by the Romans. Others believe the Bobtail is the result of crossing continental and English Sheepdogs, such as the Puli and the Briard. Wherever he came from, the Bobtail has been around for centuries. A 1771 Gainsborough painting depicts this breed. The Old English Sheepdog was shown for the first time at the 1873 dog show in Birmingham. Officially recognized in the United Kingdom in 1888, the first Old English Sheepdog club was formed in the United States in 1900.

1

SHEEPDOGS

1

COUNTRY OF ORIGIN
United Kingdom

OTHER NAME
Bobtail

Cobby, muscular and short-bodied. Body high on the legs. Square body outline. Characteristic rolling, elastic gallop.

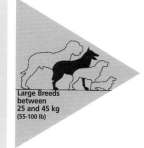

Large Breeds between 25 and 45 kg (55-100 lb)

HEAD
Strong and blocky. Capacious skull. Well-defined stop. Square, strong, truncated muzzle. Large nose.

EYES
Wide-set. Dark color or walleye. Blue eyes are acceptable.

EARS
Small, carried flat against the head.

BODY
Short and compact. Deep, full chest with well-sprung ribs. Shoulders well laid back. Legs with plenty of bone. Gently arched, stout loin. Withers lower than the loin. Long neck.

LIMBS
Small, round feet with well-arched toes. Thick, hard pads.

TAIL
Bobtailed or docked.

COAT
Profuse, hard texture, shaggy, free from curl. Thicker on the hindquarters than on the rest of the body. Soft, dense undercoat.

COLOR
Any shade of gray, grizzle, or blue. The body and hindquarters are of uniform color, with or without small white markings on the feet (socks). The head, neck, legs and underbody must be white. Any brown markings are faults.

SIZE
Dog: minimum of 61 cm (24 in).
Bitch: minimum of 56 cm (22 in).

WEIGHT
25 to 30 kg (55-66 lb).

Character, special skills and training
The old english Sheepdog is a vigorous, playful animal. He is neither fearful nor aggressive. This affectionate breed is calm and even-tempered. Nicknamed the "nanny dog", he always looks out for the children. Though he has the heart of a guardian, he is not aggressive and will not bite. Besides, with his teddy bear appearance and "broken" bark, he does not look particularly threatening.

Care and functions
The old english Sheepdog can adapt to city life in an apartment if he is always with his owner and can have time to run each day. He does not bear the heat well. This intelligent dog has a mind of his own, and therefore needs firm training. Daily brushing is very important to keep his profuse, shaggy coat from knotting.
. Sheepdog (now rarely used as a Sheepdog).
. Pet.

Border Collie

It is thought that the Border Collie's ancestors are Nordic breeds that guarded reindeer herds. When they arrived on the British Isles with the Vikings, they were crossed with local sheepdogs. The Border Collie was named after the region where the breed was developed, the hilly border country between England and Scotland. The most common of the Collies, the Border Collie still has the same duties today as he did in the eighteenth century—guarding the herd. The breed was not standardized until the nineteenth century. It was recognized by the Kennel Club of England in 1976 and by the Canadian Kennel Club in 1985.

Agile and elegant. Moves with minimal lift of the feet.

1

SHEEPDOGS

COUNTRY OF ORIGIN
Great Britain

Medium Breeds between 10 and 25 kg (20-55 lb)

1

HEAD
Moderately long skull. Strong, relatively short muzzle. Distinct stop. Black, brown, or dark gray nose, according to coat color.

EYES
Oval, set well apart. Brown color except for merles, which may have blue eyes.

EARS
Medium size, set well apart, and carried erect or semi-erect.

BODY
Well-balanced and athletic. Strong neck. Ribs well sprung. Muscular loin. Moderately broad chest, well let down.

LIMBS

Oval feet. Compact, arched toes.

TAIL
Moderately long. Set low, curving up slightly at the tip.

COAT
There are two varieties, the rough coat, which has a mane, culottes and fox tail (brush), and the smooth coat. In both varieties, the coat is dense and of medium texture; dense, soft undercoat.

COLOR
Generally pied, with white collar, blaze and socks, with the remainder of the coat being black. All colors permissible, but white must not be the dominant color.

SIZE
Dog: 50 to 55 cm (20-22 in).
Bitch: 47 to 52 cm (18.5-20.5 in).

WEIGHT
15 to 20 kg (33-44 lb).

Character, special skills and training
This energetic, eager dog is very gentle by nature, though is a tenacious worker. He is exceptionally devoted to his owner and is easy to train because he is alert and highly intelligent. The Border Collie is reserved toward strangers, but is not shy or aggressive. This breed has a keen sense of smell, but it is best known for its ability to "eye", a skill that he uses to will sheep to move and turn. While working with his owner, the dog crouches a short distance from a sheep and stares intently into its eyes, seeming to hypnotize it; he then slowly creeps up like a hunting dog. The Border Collie is the best represented breed at herding trials.

Care and functions
This dog is a sheepdog through and through and must remain as such. His training begins around the age of six months and can last one or two years. He does not adapt well to urban living, though can adapt rather easily to life as a family pet. This tireless sheepdog requires daily exercise. No special grooming or other care is required.
. Sheepdog. This dog's inborn skills and breeding make it the ideal herder, which it should remain.

Belgian

BELGIAN SHEEPDOG, MALINOIS

The four varieties of the large Belgian Sheepdog are thought to be descended from herders from central Europe or from interbreeding of local breeds of Mastiff and Deerhound brought over from England in the 13th century. In the 19th century, there were many Sheepdog-looking native dogs of varied coloration and hair type. The first breeds were recognized around 1885. The Belgian Shepherd Club was formed in 1891 after A. Reul, a professor of animal breeding, cataloged four distinct varieties.

1

SHEEPDOGS

COUNTRY OF ORIGIN
Belgium

ORIGINAL NAMES
Groenendael, Groenendaler, Lakense, Mechelaar, Tervurense, Tervuren

OTHER NAMES
Groenendael, Laekense, Malinois, Tervuren

Balanced proportions. Square body.
Wolf-like. Well-balanced.
Elegant solidity without bulkiness.

Large Breeds
between
25 and 45 kg
(55-100 lb)

BELGIAN SHEEPDOG, TERVUREN
The second most popular of the Belgian Sheepdogs (following the Malinois).

Sheepdog

BELGIAN SHEEPDOG, GROENENDAEL
Named after the castle of the variety's primary breeder, N. Rose.

In 1898, the long-haired black Belgian Sheepdog was given the name Groenendael. At the same time, at the Royal Castle of Laeken, the wire-haired, fawn Belgian Sheepdog was named the Laekenois. This last variety is now very rare. Most short-haired Belgian Sheepdogs from the area of Malines were named Malinois. A brewer near Tervuren bred long-haired, fawn Belgian Sheepdogs and produced what came to be called the Tervuren.

BELGIAN SHEEPDOG, LAEKENOIS
The rarest of the Belgian Sheepdogs.

HEAD
Long, filled-up, and finely chiseled. The muzzle tapers gradually. Straight forehead. Moderate, though marked, stop. Lips well closed. Smooth, flat cheeks.

EYES
Medium size, almondlike. Browncolor. Black rims.

EARS
Set on high, straight, rigid, triangular.

BODY
Powerful without being bulky. Long neck. The chest is not broad. Tight, strong musculature. Proud carriage of the head. Straight, broad, powerful back. Slight sloping of the croup

LIMBS
Round, compact toes. Powerful hind legs, not bulky

TAIL
Medium length, strong at the base. Carried down when relaxed; does not form a hook or curve.

COAT
Always abundant and dense. Wooly undercoat. Collarette, culottes on the thighs. Long-haired (short on the head) – Groenendael and Tervuren. Short-haired (flat on the head) – Malinois. Wire-haired (harsh, dry, shaggy, 6 cm (2,4 in) long – Laekenois.

COLOR
the mask must cover the face with a solid area of black. Tervuren: warm fawn well-filled with black (preferred). Malinois: only fawn tinged with black, with black mask. Groenendael: only solid black. Laekenois: fawn with flecks of black on the muzzle and tail.

SIZE
Dog: 60 to 66 cm (23.5-26 in).
Bitch: 56 to 62 cm (22-24.5 in).

WEIGHT
28 to 35 kg (61.5-77 lb).

Character, special skills and training
Nervous, sensitive and impulsive, this breed is extremely lively in his response to stimuli. Watchful, attentive, with a strong personality, he is remarkably devoted to his owner and is occasionally aggressive toward strangers. He is very energetic, active and dynamic, and needs a lot of exercise. The Belgian Sheepdog will not accept a leash. The Malinois, which was chosen for guard dog and sporting activities at the end of the 19th century, is more assertive and has a stronger personality than the other calmer varieties because of its true sheepdog origins. These very sensitive dogs cannot tolerate harsh treatment. Training must be firm, but gentle, and undertaken with the greatest patience.

Care and functions
This breed needs peaceful surroundings and regular exercise to blossom. Long-haired varieties require weekly brushing.
. Sheepdog.
. Guard dog, police dog, good trackers, search-and-rescue, customs.
. Pet (very attached to his owner and environment).

Catalan Sheepdog

This breed came from Catalonia, Spain. It is presumed that he is descended from the ancient Pyrenees Sheepdogs. During the Spanish Civil War, the Catalan Sheepdog served as messenger and sentry.

Medium breed. Slightly longer than tall. Dark, thick skin. Normal gait: short trot.

1

SHEEPDOGS

1

COUNTRY OF ORIGIN
Spain

ORIGINAL NAMES
Gos d'Atura Catala
Perro de Pastor Catalan

OTHER NAME
Catalonian Shepherd

Medium Breeds
between
10 and 25 kg
(20-55 lb)

HEAD
Strong, slightly convex. Pronounced stop. Straight, short forehead. Cone-shaped muzzle.

EYES
Round. Dark amber eyes. Black rims.

EARS
Set on high. Fine leather. Drop, triangular ending in a point. Cropped ears are acceptable for working dogs.

BODY
Strong with length being slightly greater than height. Deep chest. Ribs well sprung. Straight back Powerful, slightly sloped croup

LIMBS
Oval feet. Black nails and pads. Strong legs. Two dewclaws on hind legs

TAIL
Attached low. Long or short (maximum length 10 cm (4 in). Some varieties are naturally tailless. Docked tail is permitted for working dogs. Hangs in a hook when relaxed. Richly clad with hair.

COAT
Long, flat and rough. Thick undercoat. Full beard, mustache, forelock and fall. Seasonal shedding occurs in two stages, beginning with the front half of the body, followed by the back half of the body.

COLOR
Color created by a mixture of hairs of various shades – fawn, reddish-brown, gray, black and white. The base colors are fawn, gray and sable.

SIZE
Dog: 47 to 55 cm (18.5-22 in).

Bitch: 45 to 53 cm (18-21 in).

WEIGHT
Dog: approx. 18 kg (40 lb).
Bitch: approx. 16 kg (35 lb).

Character, special skills and training
The Catalan Sheepdog is courageous, intelligent and energetic. His greatest traits shine through when herding; not only is he obedient to the commands of his handler, but he often takes the initiative, directing the sheep with remarkable ease. This brave, alert breed also makes an excellent guard dog. As a pet, he is loyal and gentle with children. This breed is well adapted to living outdoors.

Care and functions
While this dog can live indoors, he needs a lot of exercise. Daily brushing is required.
. Sheepdog (guard and herder)·
. Guard dog, police dog.
. Pet.

Croatian Sheepdog

This dog of eastern origin is almost unknown outside his home country, where he has guarded farms and herds for centuries. The breed is thought to be descended from northern Croatian sheepdogs.

Rectangular body outline. Fine-boned.
Preferred gait: Trot.

1

SHEEPDOGS

COUNTRY OF ORIGIN
Croat Republic

ORIGINAL NAME
Hrvatski Ovcar

Medium Breeds
between
10 and 25 kg
(20-55 lb)

1

HEAD
Fine, wedge-shaped (approx. 20 cm (7,9 in) long), dry overall. Eyebrows not pronounced. Cheeks filled out. Stop not pronounced. Straight nose bridge.

EYES
Chestnut to black color. Medium size. Almond shape. Dark rims.

EARS
Triangular, erect or semi-erect. Moderate length. Attached toward the sides of the head. Erect ears are preferred and must not be cropped.

BODY
Slightly longer than tall. Short, muscular back is very muscular in the short lumbar region. Chest not prominent. Ribs well sprung. Solid, well-filled out flanks. Croup slightly sloped.

LIMBS
Muscular legs. Small, slightly oval feet.

TAIL
Set on moderately high. Long, bushy hair. Carried below the line of the back at rest, above when alert.

COAT
Relatively soft. Wavy or curly. Never wooly. Short on the face. Long (7 to 14 cm) (2.8-5.5 in) on the back. Feathering and culottes on the legs. Bushy undercoat.

COLOR
Black background. Some white markings on the throat, forechest, and chest are permissible. White markings on the feet and toes are tolerated, but not desirable.

SIZE
Approx. 40 to 50 cm (16-20 in).

WEIGHT
15 to 20 kg (33-44 lb).

Character, special skills and training
Lively, attentive, and of uncommon endurance, the Croatian Sheepdog is easy to train.

Care and functions
This dog requires exercise and room to run.
· Herder.
· Guard dog.

Dutch Shepherd

This breed, developed in the Netherlands in the 19th century, is a cross between local Sheepdogs and the Belgian Malinois. The varieties (short-, long- and rough-haired) have been introduced over the years at dog shows.

Medium size. Lupoid. Powerfully built. Free, relaxed gait.

1

SHEEPDOGS

COUNTRY OF ORIGIN
Netherlands

ORIGINAL NAMES
Hollandse Herder
Hollandse Herdershond

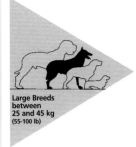

Large Breeds between 25 and 45 kg (55-100 lb)

HEAD
Clean, long, not massive. The rough-haired variety has a slightly more blocky head. Straight forehead. Stop barely perceptible. The muzzle is slightly longer than the skull.

EYES
Almond-shaped, of medium size. Dark color.

EARS
Small, erect, held forward. Rounded ears are not permitted.

BODY
Solid and well-balanced. No dewlap. Deep chest. Ribs are slightly sprung. Solid loin. Straight, short, powerful back.

LIMBS
Well-muscled, strong legs with solid bones. Round feet with compact, arched toes. Black nails and pads.

TAIL
Attached low, hanging in a slight curve. Reaches the hocks when relaxed; carried high when in motion.

COAT
The most common variety has short hair over all of the body, with a wooly undercoat. Collarette, culottes and flag tail. Long-haired variety has long hair over all of the body lying close to the body. Straight, harsh, not wavy or curly, with a wooly undercoat. Tail is covered with long, thick hair. The rough-haired variety has thick, wiry hair over all of the body, held away from the body by a thick, wooly undercoat. Dense, long hair on tail and long breeching.

COLOR
Short- and long-haired varieties: shades of brindle on a brown or gray background. Black mask preferred. Rough-haired variety: blue-gray, salt and pepper, gold or silver brindle.

SIZE
Dog: 57 to 62 cm (22.5-24.5 in).

Bitch: 55 to 60 cm (22-24 in).

WEIGHT
Approx. 30 kg (66 lb).

. Sheepdog.
. Guard dog.
. Pet.

Character, special skills and training
This lively, rustic breed has great endurance and is an excellent jumper. He is affectionate, calm, loyal, gentle with children and very attached to his owner. The Dutch Shepherd is fairly aggressive toward other dogs. A guard dog to the core, he makes an excellent army or police dog.

Care and functions
This dog needs heavy physical activity on a daily basis. The three hair-types require weekly brushing.

Perro de Pastor Mallorquin

This ancient breed originating on the Balearic Islands is used as a guard dog and herder for flocks of sheep and goats.

Solid, rustic appearance. Well-balanced. Light gray skin. Swift, elegant, confident gallop.

Large Breeds between 25 and 45 kg (55-100 lb)

1

SHEEPDOGS

COUNTRY OF ORIGIN
Spain

ORIGINAL NAMES
Perro de Pastor Mallorquin
Ca de Bestiar

1

HEAD
Massive. Gently sloped stop. Broad muzzle. Black lips.

EYES
Slightly almond-shaped, set obliquely. Light or dark color. Black rims.

EARS
Drop, triangular, set on high. Thick.

BODY
Large, sturdy and well-proportioned. Solid neck. Full chest with well-sprung ribs. Broad, powerful loin. Broad, square croup. Horizontal back.

LIMBS
Hare-like feet. Sound legs.

TAIL
Fairly long, curves up in the shape of a saber when dog is alert.

COAT
Short-haired (most common) variety – 1.5 to 3 cm (0.6-1.2 in) on the back. Very fine undercoat. Long-haired variety – slightly wavy on the back (approx. 7 cm) (2.8 in). Fairly light undercoat. Both varieties have soft, fine, weather-resistant hair.

COLOR
Black, white markings acceptable only on the breast and the feet. Jet black is preferred.

SIZE
Dog: 66 to 73 cm (26-29 in). Bitch: 62 to 68 cm (24-26.8 in).

WEIGHT
Approx. 40 kg (88 lb).

Character, special skills and training
This fleet-footed, robust breed is agile, brave and extremely territorial. The Perro de Pastor Mallorquin is calm, affectionate and loyal. He bonds only to his owner and is wary by instinct around strangers.

Care and functions
This breed needs to be brushed occasionally and requires room to run and exercise.
. Herder.
. Guard and defense dog.
. Pet.

Polish Lowland Sheepdog

The Polish Lowland Sheepdog was bred from the Hungarian Puli and other Asian Sheepdogs, such as the Tibetan Terrier. This relative of the Old English Sheepdog (and possibly the Bearded Collie) is a good guardian of the flock. The breed almost disappeared after WWII, but in 1971, it was recognized by the FCI.

Medium breed. Rectangular silhouette. Relaxed, extended gait (pace).

1

SHEEPDOGS

1

COUNTRY OF ORIGIN
Poland

ORIGINAL NAME
Polski Owczarek Nizinny

OTHER NAME
Valee Sheepdog

Medium Breeds
between
10 and 25 kg
(20-55 lb)

HEAD
Medium size. Domed skull. Distinct stop. Large nose. Long, tousled hair on the forehead, cheeks and chin, giving the face a soft look.

EYES
Oval, hazel color, with dark rims.

EARS
Medium size, drop, set on fairly high.

BODY
Stocky, strong and muscular. Strong neck. Deep chest. Broad loin. Very muscular back. Short croup.

LIMBS
Oval, compact feet.

TAIL
Naturally short; docked if necessary.

COAT
Coarse, dense, thick and abundant. Soft undercoat. Long fall over the eyes is characteristic of the breed.

COLOR
All colors acceptable, including piebald.

SIZE
Dog: 45 to 50 cm (17.5-20 in).
Bitch: 42 to 47 cm (16.5-18.5 in).

WEIGHT
15 to 20 kg (33-44 lb).

Character, special skills and training
This is an alert, courageous, rustic breed that is well-adapted to living outdoors in harsh weather conditions. The Polish Lowland Sheepdog is intelligent, dominant, vocal and strong-willed. This dog requires firm training. Very distrustful of strangers, he is an excellent guard dog. Unfailingly loyal, this happy dog adores his owner and children, making him a good pet.

Care and functions
This sheepdog can adjust to city living if he is given a lot of exercise. Brushing once or twice per week is required.
· Sheepdog.
· Guard dog.
· Pet.

Portuguese Sheepdog

Some experts believe today's Portuguese Sheepdog is descended from a pair of Briards imported by the Conde de Castro Cuimaraes in the early 20th century. But today's breed has its own distinct characteristics. It is very similar to the Pyrenean Shepherd Dog, which leads us to believe a branch of this breed already existed and breeders tried to improve the breed by crossing it with the Briard.

Medium size. Monkey-like appearance and behavior.

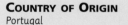

1

SHEEPDOGS

COUNTRY OF ORIGIN
Portugal

ORIGINAL NAME
Cao da Serra de Aires

OTHER NAME
"Monkey Dog"

Medium Breeds
between
10 and 25 kg
(20-55 lb)

HEAD
Strong and broad. Domed skull. Occipital protuberance is visible. Marked stop. Rectangular, slightly hollow forehead. Well set off, slightly turned up nose.

EYES
Dark color, round, set horizontally, full of life. Black rims.

EARS
Set on high, drop (without folds). Cropped: carried erect, triangular, medium length, finely textured and smooth.

BODY
Length greater than height.

No dewlap. Broad, prominent chest. Muscular thighs. Deep chest is well let down. Long back. Short, arched loin.

LIMBS
Round feet, not flat. Long toes covered with hair that is darker in color than the rest of the coat. Thick, tough pads. Strong legs.

TAIL
Set on high. Pointed. Reaches the hocks curving at tip when relaxed, curling up slightly when the dog is in motion.

COAT
Long, straight or slightly

wavy, forming a long beard and mustache.

COLOR
Shades of yellow, brown, gray, fawn, wolf gray and black, marked with tan, with or without a mixture of white hairs.

SIZE
Dog: 45 to 55 cm (17.5-21.5 in).
Bitch: 42 to 52 cm (16.5-20.5 in).

WEIGHT
12 to 18 kg (26.5-39.8 lb).

Character, special skills and training
Rustic, serious and very active, the portuguese Sheepdog is extremely devoted to his owner and the animals that he guards. He is always hostile toward strangers.

Care and functions
This is not a city-dweller. This dog needs space and exercise. Weekly brushing is adequate.
· Sheepdog.
· Guard dog.
· Pet.

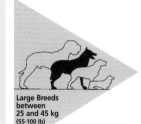

Strong, compact build. Rectangular body ouline.

Polish Mountain Dog

Like many European Molossian types, the Polish Mountain Dog may be descended from Tibetan Sheepdogs that arrived during the massive invasions from the East. Related to the Hungarian Kuvasz, this dog guards the flocks in the high valleys of the Tatra range (the highest peaks of the Carpathians), protecting them from bears and wolves. Almost wiped out during WWII, this breed was recognized by the FCI in 1967.
A very popular breed in its country of origin.

1

SHEEPDOGS

COUNTRY OF ORIGIN
Poland

ORIGINAL NAME
Owerzarek Podkalanski

OTHER NAMES
Tatra Mountain Sheepdog
Owczarek Tatrzanski

Large Breeds between 25 and 45 kg (55-100 lb)

HEAD
Clean and broad. Marked stop. Large muzzle. Broad forehead.

EYES
Medium size, set slightly oblique. Dark brown color. Dark rims.

EARS
Medium size, drop, set on high. Triangular, fairly thick.

BODY
Long, sturdy and muscular. No dewlap. Deep chest. Broad, well-knit loin. Ribs sloping and rather flat. Belly moderately tucked up. Sloping croup. Straight, broad back.

LIMBS
Strong-boned legs. Oval, strong feet. Strong, hard pads.

TAIL
Set on low. Carried below the topline, curving slightly at the tip. Covered with thick hair forming a flag.

COAT
Short and thick on the head and front of the forelegs. Long, thick and straight on the neck and body. Thick mane. Heavy undercoat.

COLOR
Uniform white. Cream markings are not desirable.

SIZE
Dog: 65 to 70 cm (25.6-27.5 in).
Bitch: 60 to 65 cm (23.6-25.6 in).

WEIGHT
30 to 45 kg (66-99 lb).

· Guard dog.
· Pet.

Character, special skills and training
This hardy breed is courageous, lively and alert. He is an agile, swift runner. He is naturally gentle and calm and must never be treated harshly. Loyal to his owner and affectionate with children, he watches over his territory and family.

Care and functions
This dog must not live in an apartment. He needs considerable space and exercise. Weekly brushing is sufficient. During seasonal shedding, stripping the coat is recommended.
· Sheepdog.

Saarloos Wolfhond

Around 1930 in Rotterdam, L. Saarloos crossed a German Shepherd with a Russian wolf in an attempt to increase the German Shepherd's endurance and hardiness. In 1975, the Saarloos Wolfhond was recognized in the Netherlands. In 1981, the FCI officially recognized the breed. The Saarloos Wolfhond is rare outside its country of origin.

Lupoid. Balanced construction. Gait resembles that of the wolf.

1

SHEEPDOGS

COUNTRY OF ORIGIN
Netherlands

ORIGINAL NAME
Saarloos Wolfhound

Large Breeds
between
25 and 45 kg
(55-100 lb)

1

HEAD
Wolflike, well-balanced in relation to the rest of the body. Wide, flat skull. Slight stop. Broad muzzle. Black or liver nose, depending on the color of the coat. Tight-lipped jaws.

EYES
Medium size, almond. Preferably yellow color.

EARS
Medium size. Thick, pointed, held erect.

BODY
Powerful. Slightly longer than tall. Smooth, muscular neck. Ribs well sprung. Powerful, muscular rump. Slightly sloped croup. Straight, massive back.

LIMBS
Oval, very compact feet Long, strong-boned legs.

TAIL
At rest, carried in the shape of a saber.

COAT
Harsh and straight (in the shape of a baton). Thick, wooly undercoat.

COLOR
Light to dark black (wolf gray), light to dark brown, cream to white. Any other color is a disqualification.

SIZE
Dog: 65 to 75 cm (25.6-29.5 in).
Bitch: 60 to 70 cm (23.6-27.5 in).

WEIGHT
30 to 35 kg (66-77 lb).

Character, special skills and training
This attentive, affectionate dog is reserved toward strangers. When with other dogs, his pack instinct is still strong. Independent and stubborn, this dog needs a handler capable of dominating him mentally without resorting to physical blows. It is vital to socialize this dog well during the first two years of his life.

Care and functions
The saarloos wolfhond is not suited for urban life. Even in the country, he needs regular walks. The coat does not require any special care.
· Guide dog.
· Rescue dog.
· Pet.

Czechoslovakian Wolfdog

In 1955, german shepherds and carpathian wolves were crossed in Czechoslovakia. In 1965, a project to selectively breed this animal was undertaken in the hope of combining the best of the wolf and the dog. In 1982, the Cesky Vlcak was recognized as a national breed by the Czechoslovakian committee of breeder associations. In 1994, the FCI recognized the breed.

1

SHEEPDOGS

1

COUNTRY OF ORIGIN
Czech Republic

ORIGINAL NAME
Cesky Vlcak

Wolflike (gait, coat, mask).
Robust constitution. Gait: smooth, relaxed, trot with good reach.

Large Breeds between 25 and 45 kg (55-100 lb)

HEAD
Obtuse cone-shape. Slightly domed forehead. Stop moderately pronounced. Rectangular nose bridge. Oval nose.

EYES
Narrow, set obliquely in the skull. Amber color.

EARS
Held erect. Narrow, short, triangular.

BODY
Robust. Rectangular body outline. Smooth, muscular neck. Full chest. Short, muscular loin. Short, slightly sloped croup. Rectangular back.

LIMBS
Powerful hind legs. Solid forelegs with dry joints. Large front feet turned slightly out.

TAIL
Set on high, hanging straight down at rest. Sickle tail when in action.

COAT
Straight, close-lying. Undercoat is abundant in winter.

COLOR
Wolf coloring or silvery gray with characteristic light mask. Light hairs at the base of the neck and on the chest. Dark gray mask is tolerated.

SIZE
Dog: at least 65 cm (25.5 in).
Bitch: at least 60 cm (23.5 in).

WEIGHT
Dog: at least 26 kg (57.5 lb).
Bitch: at least 20 kg (44 lb).

Character, special skills and training
This eager, extremely active dog has great endurance and quick reflexes. He is bold and courageous. While he is exceptionally loyal to his owner, he is distant and wary around strangers (men in particular). His sense of smell is considerably more developed than that of most dogs. With his powers of dissuasion, perhaps this breed should be trained as a guard and defense dog.

Care and functions
The cesky vlcak should be owned only by individuals who have an excellent understanding of animal behavior.
· Guard and defense dog.

Collie

The Collie is descended from Scottish herding dogs. When the Romans invaded, their dogs were crossed with native Scottish dogs. Early shepherds began crossing the short-tailed and long-tailed shepherd dogs, and the result was the superb animal with an aristocratic bearing that we know today. The origin of this breed's name is disputed. Some believe the name comes from the word "colley", an early variety of Scottish sheep with a black mask and tail. Others believe the breed is named for its beautiful collar. The smooth Collie is much less common than the Rough Collie.

Extremely beautiful. Dignified carriage.

1

SHEEPDOGS

Between 10 and 45 kg (20-100 lb)

COUNTRY OF ORIGIN
Great Britain

ORIGINAL NAMES
Two varieties:
Smooth Collie
Rough Collie

OTHER NAME
Scotch Collie

HEAD
Long, clean, wedge-shaped. Size in proportion to body. Flat skull. Slight stop.

EYES
Medium size, almond, set obliquely in the skull. Dark brown color, except blue merles that often have blue or blue flecked eyes.

EARS
Medium size, fairly wide set. Carried forward and semi-erect.

BODY
Medium size, longer than tall. Powerful neck. Deep chest. Ribs well sprung. Straight back with a slightly arched loin.

LIMBS
Oval feet. Compact, arched toes. Muscular legs with a fair amount of bone.

TAIL
Long, reaching the hocks. Generally carried low. Profuse covering of hair.

COAT
Rough Collie: straight, harsh, long and dense; soft, dense undercoat; abundant on the mane and frill; feathering on the legs. Smooth collie: flat and harsh; dense undercoat.

COLOR
Three colors are recognized: sable – from light gold to dark mahogany. Tricolor – predominantly black with tan shadings on the head and legs and white markings. Blue merle (marbled) – blue-gray marbled or mottled with black.

SIZE
Dog: 56 to 61 cm (22-24 in).
Bitch: 51 to 56 cm (20-22 in).

WEIGHT
Dog: 20 to 29 kg (44-64 lb)
Bitch: 18 to 25 kg (39.5-55 lb).

Character, special skills and training
This active, lively dog is typically well-balanced, but can be anxious and timid. This gentle, sensitive lassie dog is a faithful companion. The Collie is reserved toward strangers, but not aggressive. He should receive firm, but gentle training.

Care and functions
The Collie can live in the city but he will be happier with a yard and space to run. Regular exercise is required. Brushing two times per week is adequate.
· Sheepdog.
· Police dog, guide dog.
· Pet.

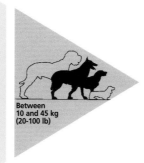

Solid construction. Free, supple gait.

Bearded Collie

Some writers believe the Bearded Collie's oldest ancestor is the Magyar Komondor of central Europe. Others contest that this breed is the result of a cross between a Scottish sheepdog and the Polski Owczarek Nizinny, a Polish sheepdog, and was developed in the Highlands of Scotland. This breed almost disappeared in the 20th century, replaced by the Old English Sheepdog. But thanks to the efforts of a Scottish breeder, the breed began a comeback in 1950 and continues to flourish today.

1

SHEEPDOGS

COUNTRY OF ORIGIN
Great Britain

OTHER NAMES
Highland Collie
Beardie

Between
10 and 45 kg
(20-100 lb)

HEAD
Wide and flat. Strong muzzle. Moderate stop. Large, squarish nose.

EYES
Large and wide-set. Color varies according to coat color. Eyebrows arched to the sides, framing the head.

EARS
Medium size, hanging close to the head.

BODY
Long. Deep chest. Ribs well sprung. Strong loin Straight back Underline fairly high off the ground.

LIMBS
Oval feet. Compact, arched toes. Thick pads. Legs with substantial bone.

TAIL
Set low and covered with abundant hair. Not kinked or twisted. Carried low and curving up slightly at the tip.

COAT
Long, flat, harsh, strong and shaggy. Sometimes wavy. Coat increases in length at the cheeks and chin, forming the characteristic beard.

COLOR
Slate, dark fawn, black, blue, any shade of gray, with or without white markings. Coat does not take on its definitive color until the age of three, lightening and darkening several times over the first three years.

SIZE
Dog: 53 to 56 cm (21-22 in).
Bitch: 51 to 53 cm (20-21 in).

WEIGHT
20 to 30 kg (44-66 lb).

Character, special skills and training
This well-balanced, lively dog is neither shy nor aggressive. He is self-confident, affectionate, and always ready to play. The bearded Collie, which becomes very attached to his owner and adores children, does not like to be left alone. Though he barks a lot, he does not make a very good guard dog. His good sense of smell is put to use searching for truffles. Early, firm (though not harsh) training is required.

Care and functions
The bearded Collie can adapt to being a house dog if he has many opportunities to go out and is not left alone. Regular brushing, at least twice per week, is required to keep his coat tangle-free. Otherwise, it will be impossible to brush out all of the knots.
· Pet.

Kelpie

This breed is probably the result of a cross between the Dingo (an Australia wild dog) and the short-haired Scottish Collie brought to Australia in the late 1860s. The breed's name is said to have been taken from a novel by R.L. Stevenson in which a devil river called Kelpie is mentioned. Thought not very well-known in Europe, the Kelpie is the primary working dog used on Australia and New Zealand ranches.

Hardy. Solid. Flexible

HEAD
LOng, narrow, fox-like. Slightly domed skull. Pronounced stop. Tight, clean lips.

EYES
Almond-shaped. Brown, in harmony with coat color.

EARS
Carried erect, coming to a fine point at the tip. Thin ear leather. Interior of the earflap is well-clad with hairs.

BODY
Moderately long neck without dewlap. Full collarette. Topline is strong and horizontal. Chest well let down, deeper than broad. Ribs well sprung. Strong, muscular loin. Rather long, sloped croup.

LIMBS
Muscular legs strong of bone. Round, strong feet. Thick pads. Compact, arched toes. Short, strong nails.

TAIL
Hangs down in a slight curve reaching the hocks. Well-clad, brush.

COAT
Thick, straight, hard, close-lying, short (2-3 cm) (0.8-1.2 in). Longer on the underbody and back of the legs. Collarette at the neck. Short, dense undercoat.

COLOR
Black, black and tan, red, red and tan, chocolate (brown), and smoky blue.

SIZE
Dog: 46 to 51 cm (18-20 in).
Bitch: 43 to 48 cm (17-19 in).

Medium Breeds between 10 and 25 kg (20-55 lb)

1

SHEEPDOGS

COUNTRY OF ORIGIN
Australia

ORIGINAL NAME
Australian Kelpie

OTHER NAME
Bard

WEIGHT
11 to 20 kg (24-44 lb).

1

Character, special skills and training
This tireless working dog is extremely active and full of life. The Kelpie is naturally gentle and calm and is a very loyal, devoted dog. The breed has a natural instinct for working sheep, whether in open fields or in the farmyard.

Care and functions
The Kelpie needs exercise and room to run. Weekly brushing is sufficient.
· Herder.

Komondor

This breed is a native sheepdog brought to hungary around 1,000 years ago by the nomadic magyars. The komondor is descended from various asian sheepdogs, including the tibetan Mastiff. This dog has long been used to protect the flocks from wolves and bears and to chase away other pests.

Imposing stature. Noble, dignified gait. Highly pigmented skin. Relaxed gait: walk and stretched out trot.

1

SHEEPDOGS

COUNTRY OF ORIGIN
Hungary

ORIGINAL NAMES
Komondor
kiraly

Giants Breeds
over 45 kg
(over 100 lb)

HEAD
Broad. Size in proportion to the rest of the body. Covered with abundant hair. Domed skull. Pronounced stop. Bridge of nose is straight. Very broad muzzle.

EYES
Oval. Dark color.

EARS
Long and hanging, u-shaped.

BODY
Slightly longer than tall. No dewlap. Broad breast. Deep, barrel chest. Broad loin.Slightly sloping croup. Short back.

LIMBS
Large, round feet. Thick pads. Strong, slate-colored

nails. Front legs look like vertical pillars, with massive bone.

TAIL
Carried hanging down at rest and at the level of the back when in action.

COAT
Long - 20 to 27 cm (8-10.5 in) on the rump; 15 to 22 cm (6-8.7 in) on the back, chest and shoulders; 10 to 18 cm (3.9-7 in) on the head, neck and legs. Hair is harsh, corded and bushy, with a fine, wooly undercoat. At birth, a puppy's coat is made up of soft, fine, curly or wavy white hairs.

COLOR
White.

SIZE
Dog: approx. 80 cm (32 in).
Bitch: approx. 70 cm (28 in).

WEIGHT
Dog: 50 to 60 kg (110-132 lb).
Bitch: 40 to 50 kg (88-110 lb).

Character, special skills and training
This dog is not very affectionate, but is loyal and devoted to his owner and gentle with children. The komondor is a rustic breed that needs vigorous exercise. He is a superb guard dog, protecting the flock and the home with unfailing courage and daring. This dog will fight to the death to protect his owner. When he attacks, it is in determined silence. Particularly firm training is required for this breed.

Care and functions
This dog is not suitable as a house dog; he needs space and a lot of exercise. Komondors are never brushed. Instead, begin separating the cords with your fingers once the dog reaches the age of eight months. The komondor should be bathed only once or twice per year.
· Sheepdog.
· Guard dog.
· Pet.

Kuvasz

Some writers believe the Kuvasz was imported by primitive Hungarians, while others contest that it was brought to the Carpathians by the Kumans, nomadic shepherds of Turkish origin that came to Hungary in the thirteenth century as they tried to escape the invading Mongols. What is certain is that this breed is descended from Asian sheepdogs. In the fifteenth century, King Mathias I used Kuvasz for hunting big game, though this breed is more skilled at guarding flocks than hunting wild boar. Until the nineteenth century, the Kuvasz was used as a flock guard. Later, he was used almost exclusively to guard large estates. This breed is not common outside of its native Hungary, though it is bred in the United States.

Noble and powerful. Almost square body outline. Muscular without bulkiness. Strong-boned. Slow, heavy walk. Swaying trot.

1

SHEEPDOGS

COUNTRY OF ORIGIN
Hungary

Giants Breeds
over 45 kg
(over 100 lb)

1

HEAD
Nobel and strong. Long (but not pointed) skull. The longitudinal midline of the forehead is pronounced. Moderate stop. Nose bridge is broad and long. Straight muzzle. Lips closely cover the teeth.

EYES
Set obliquely in the skull, almond shape. Dark brown color.

EARS
relatively small, set on high. Drop, v-shaped. Held slightly away from the head.

BODY
Solidly built and muscular. Powerful neck. Deep chest. Shoulders broad and sloping. Croup slightly sloped. Short loin Straight back. Deep brisket. Highly pigmented skin (slate gray).

LIMBS
Round, compact feet. Strong, slate-colored nails.

TAIL
Bushy, set fairly low. Reaches the hocks, curving up slightly at the tip.

COAT
Strong, wavy and long on the body. Mane on the neck and feathering on the back of the legs. Short, straight hair on the head and front of the legs. Wooly undercoat.

COLOR
White. Ivory is tolerated.

SIZE
Dog: 71 to 75 cm (28-30 in).
Bitch: 66 to 70 cm 26-28 in).

WEIGHT
Dog: 40 to 52 kg (88-115 lb).
Bitch: 30 to 42 kg (66-93 lb).

Character, special skills and training
This loyal dog meets any challenge head on. He is hardy and serious and not overly demonstrative. The kuvasz has a keen sense of smell, which he used in the past to hunt wolf and wild boar.

Care and functions
This dog is not a city-dweller. He needs space and exercise. Daily brushing is required to keep the coat from knotting.
· Sheepdog.
· Guard dog, police dog.
· Pet.

Mudi

This breed is thought to have been developed in the late nineteenth and early twentieth centuries. Some believe it is the result of a cross between a Puli and a Spitz-type breed. The Mudi has always been used to guard and herd sheep and cattle, as well as to hunt wild boar.

Medium size. Pigmented skin. Jerky gait.

1

SHEEPDOGS

COUNTRY OF ORIGIN
Hungary

1

Up to 25 kg
(55 lb)

HEAD
Long and snippy. Slightly domed skull. Straight muzzle. Pointed nose.

EYES
Oval, set slightly oblique. Dark brown color.

EARS
Held erect, pointed, in the shape of an upside-down "v".

BODY
Oblong. Short straight back. Short, sloping croup. Topline sloping from rump to withers. Long, deep chest.

LIMBS
Round, compact feet. Strong, slate nails. Dewclaws not desirable.
Legs plants slightly back.

TAIL
Short or docked at the length of two or three fingers.

COAT
Straight, short and smooth on the head and front of the legs. Longer (5 to 7 cm) (2-3 in), thick, wavy and glossy on the rest of the body.

COLOR
Black, white, or black and white pied, with spots of medium size over all the body. Color of the feet is always that of the dominant coat color.

SIZE
35 to 47 cm (14-18.5 in).

WEIGHT
8 to 13 kg (18-29 lb).

Character, special skills and training
This rustic, hardy, lively, vigorous dog is always on the alert, rather vocal and has a seemingly unlimited supply of energy. Docile and affectionate, the mudi bonds to only one person and must receive firm training. He needs someone in control who can give him a mission or a job to do. Having a tendency to bite, this dog is respected for its ability to guard the herd and the home. His keen sense of smell makes him a good dog for hunting boar.

Care and functions
This dog is not made for living indoors. He needs space and exercise. Daily brushing is required.
· Herder (cattle).
· Hunting dog (large game).
· Guard dog.
· Pet.

Puli

The Puli is very much like the Tibetan Terrier. He is thought to be descended from the Persian sheepdog or ancient Asian sheepdogs. The Puli arrived on the Hungarian Plains when the nomadic Magyars invaded in the eleventh century. The Puli has always been used as a herder. As the breed became rarer, its role began to change to that of guard dog, protecting the farm. The puli has even been used for police work. In 1930, the puli was introduced in the United States, then recognized by the American Kennel Club six years later. The standard for the Puli was established in 1955.

Square body outline. Cobby. Skin is of slate color. Quick-stepping, light-footed.

1

SHEEPDOGS

COUNTRY OF ORIGIN
Hungary

OTHER NAME
Hungarian sheepdog

Medium Breeds between 10 and 25 kg (20-55 lb)

1

HEAD
Small and fine. Round skull. Pronounced stop. Short muzzle. Large nose. Pronounced superciliary arches.

EYES
Round. Dark brown color. Partially obscured by long fall. Black rims.

EARS
Hanging, v-shaped, broad and rounded.

BODY
Square. Powerful neck. Deep brisket. Short loin. Croup slightly sloping. Medium length back

LIMBS
Hind legs have well-bent stiples, dry hocks. Strong, straight front legs. Front feet short, round and compact. Slate nails.

TAIL
Medium length, carried curved over the rump, blending into the backline because its long hairs intermingle with those of the croup.

COAT
Bushy, wavy, with a tendency to become feltlike. Wooly undercoat. The corded coat is made up of long hairs that clump together. Longest hair (8 to 18 cm) (3-7 in) is on the croup, loin and thighs. Shortest hair is on the head and feet.

COLOR
Solid color, rusty black. Shades of gray and white are common.

SIZE
Dog: 40 to 44 cm (16-17 in).
Bitch: 37 to 41 cm (14.5-16 in).

WEIGHT
Dog: 13 to 15 kg (29-33 lb).
Bitch: 10 to 13 kg (22-29 lb).

Character, special skills and training
This rustic, lively breed is very agile and a good jumper. The puli is a happy, affectionate, loyal dog. Both independent and possessive, he needs his family to be near. The puli is excellent with children. Suspicious of strangers, the puli is always on the alert and ready to raise the alarm with his throaty bark. Training should begin early and be done gently.

Care and functions
This dog can adapt to living indoors, but he needs exercise. His corded coat should not be brushed or combed. Once his coat starts to grow around the age of eight to twelve months, groom the coat regularly by running your fingers through the cords from the skin the tips of the cords. This dog should be bathed when he is dirty. Extra attention is required for the cords on the flews and around the anus to keep the hair from clumping.
· Excellent herder (sheep, cattle, goats).
· Hunting dog (retriever) (ducks).
· Guard dog.
· Pet.

Square body outline. Smooth gait. Light-footed gallop. Topline sloping toward the croup.

Pumi

The Pumi, developed in the seventeenth and eighteenth centuries, was bred from prick-ear sheepdogs imported from France and Germany and crossed with the Puli. For many years, the Pumi and the Puli were not considered separate breeds. It was not until around 1920 that the Pumi was officially recognized as a breed separate from the Puli and the standard was written for the breed.

1

SHEEPDOGS

COUNTRY OF ORIGIN
Hungary

Up to 25 kg
(55 lb)

HEAD
Long with a long bridge. Domed forehead. Indistinct stop. Straight muzzle. Long, pointed nose.

EYES
Set slightly oblique. Dark brown color.

EARS
Set on high. V-shaped. Held erect with tips breaking forward slightly. Medium size, well-proportioned.

BODY
Medium size. Sturdy. Pronounced withers. Short back. Ribs relatively flat. Deep, broad, long chest. Short, slightly sloping crop.

LIMBS
Round, compact feet. Dewclaws not desirable. Hard, slate nails.

TAIL
Set high, carried horizontally or slightly above the level of the back. One-third of the tail is removed.

COAT
Medium length with undercoat. Curly, forming ringlets, but not cords. Never feltlike. Short hair on the legs.

COLOR
Solid colors preferred. Any shade of gray (slate, silvery gray). Black, reddish brown, white. Brindle not permitted.

SIZE
35 to 44 cm (14-17 in).

WEIGHT
8 to 13 kg (18-29 lb).

Character, special skills and training
This high-spirited, energetic dog is remarkably daring. Suspicious of strangers, he barks at even the most innocent sound. He is affectionate with his owner and has a keen sense of smell.

Care and functions
Regular brushing is required. The pumi needs exercise and room to run.
· Herder.
· Hunting dog, hunter of vermin.
· Guard dog.
· Pet.

Schapendoes

At the turn of the century, the Schapendoes was well-known in the Netherlands, particularly in the northern province of Drenthe where he worked large sheep flocks. The Schapendoes is related to the Bearded Collie, the Puli, the Polski Owczarek Nizinny, the Old English Sheepdog, the Briard, the Bergamasco and others. The dog fancier P.M.C. Toepoel was responsible for preserving this breed. After the ravages of World War II, he used the few remaining Schapendoes to resurrect the breed. The Schapendoes club was created in 1947 and a standard was written in 1954, though it was not officially approved until 1971. The FCI recognized the breed in 1989.

Light structure. Light, elastic gait. Remarkable jumper.

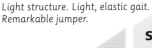

1

SHEEPDOGS

Medium Breeds between 10 and 25 kg (20-55 lb)

COUNTRY OF ORIGIN
Netherlands

ORIGINAL NAME
Nederlandse Schapendoes

OTHER NAME
Dutch Sheepdog

1

HEAD
Covered by abundant hair making it look larger than it is. Nearly flat skull. Marked stop. Moderately short muzzle. Full mustache and beard.

EYES
Round, moderately large. Brown color.

EARS
Set on relatively high. Medium size. Drop.

BODY
Slightly longer than tall. Belly slightly tucked up. Chest well let down. Ribs well sprung. Powerful neck.

LIMBS
Wide, oval feet. Compact toes. Dewclaws on hind legs permitted. Legs lightly boned.

TAIL
Long, hanging down at rest. Carried at the level of the back when at a gallop. Elevated at attention. Feathering.

COAT
Long, fine, dry, slightly wavy, tending to have a tufted, tousled look, particularly on the hindquarters. Must not be curly. Abundant undercoat.

COLOR
All colors acceptable. Blue gray to black preferred.

SIZE
Dog: 43 to 50 cm (17-20 in). Bitch: 40 to 47 cm (16-18.5 in).

WEIGHT
10 to 18 kg (22-40 lb).

Character, special skills and training
This rustic, lively, tireless dog is courageous. He is never nervous or aggressive. He is affectionate, cheerful, playful and loyal, but rather independent and stubborn. The owner that does not assert his authority over this dog will quickly find himself with an out-of-control dog.

Care and functions
This dog can live in the city if he can get out to expend his energy every day. A good brushing once or twice per week is sufficient.
· Herder.
· Pet.

Schipperke

The Schipperke, which looks rather like spitz dogs and Belgian sheepdogs, is thought by some to be descended from the Leauvenaar, a small sheepdog from Louvain in the Flemish provinces of Belgium. Others think that he is descended from northern spitz dogs. This tailless dog, the most popular guard dog in Belgium, guarded the canals. He was also a much loved companion. Shown for the first time in 1880, the breed was officially recognized by the Royal Schipperkes Club of Brussels in 1888. An official standard was written in 1904. Today, the Schipperke is a popular breed in England and South Africa.

The smallest sheepdog. Bouncy step.

1

SHEEPDOGS

COUNTRY OF ORIGIN
Belgium

OTHER NAME
Schip

1

Small Breeds
under 10 kg
(under 20 lb)

HEAD
Resembles that of a fox. Moderately broad forehead, slightly rounded skull. Distinct, but not pronounced stop. Tapered muzzle. Small nose.

EYES
Ideally oval. Dark brown color.

EARS
Placed high on the head. Small, triangular. Held erect, very mobile.

BODY
Short and thickset. Deep, broad chest. Belly moderately tucked up. Broad loin. Straight, horizontal back.

LIMBS
Fine-boned legs.

Small, round, compact feet. Strong, straight, short nails.

TAIL
Tailless or docked.

COAT
Abundant and dense. Short on the head, body and front of legs. Longer on the neck (ruff), shoulders, chest (apron) and back of legs (breeching).

COLOR
Solid black.

SIZE
32 to 36 cm (12.5-14 in).

WEIGHT
3 to 8 kg (6.5-18 lb), depending on size.

Character, special skills and training
This perky, cheerful, seemingly tireless dog is constantly alert, always in motion. He raises the alarm with his piercing bark at the slightest provocation. Loyal and gentle with his owners and children, he is reserved with strangers. He is highly trainable.

Care and functions
This is an ideal house dog, though he does require regular exercise. He should be brushed and combed two or three times per week.
· ratter and vermin hunter.
· guard dog.
· pet.

Slovak Cuvac

Originating in the Carpathian mountains, this large sheepdog looks much like the Hungarian Kuvasz. Characteristics for this breed were fixed in the 1960s based on native Sheepdogs.

1

SHEEPDOGS

COUNTRY OF ORIGIN
Slovakia

OTHER NAME
Slovensky Tchouvatch

Large Breeds
between
25 and 45 kg
(55-100 lb)

1

HEAD
Broad skull. Nose bridge is straight. Fairly broad muzzle.

EYES
Oval. Dark color.

EARS
Set on high. Drop, with rounded lower border reaching the level of the mouth. Covered in fine hair.

BODY
Broad forechest. Solid, relatively broad, muscular rump.

TAIL
Set low. Richly clad. Hangs down when at rest; carried in an arch at the level of the croup when in action.

COAT
5 to 10 cm (2-4 in) long. Thicker and harsher on the neck. Slightly wavy on the back and hindquarters. Short on the head and ears. Mane at the neck.

COLOR
White. A small amount of yellow on the ears and neck is permissible.

SIZE
Dog: 60 to 70 cm (23.5-27.5 in).
Bitch: 55 to 65 cm (21.5-25.5 in).

WEIGHT
Dog: 35 to 45 kg (77-99 lb).
Bitch: 30 to 40 kg (66-88 lb).

Character, special skills and training
This impressive dog is courageous, vigorous and always alert. He is an obedient, gentle, affectionate and loyal companion. With his solid constitution, the slovak cuvac effectively defends his flock against wolves and bears.

Care and functions
The slovak cuvac needs space and exercise. Weekly brushing is required.
· Sheepdog.
· Guard dog.
· Pet.

Welsh Corgi

The two Welsh Corgi varieties have similar origins. However, some writers hold that their history differs. The Cardigan is thought to have been introduced in Wales by the Celts, then crossed with Nordic breeds and British sheepdogs. The Pembroke, on the other hand, is said to have been introduced by Flemish weavers during the Middle Ages and may be related to some Nordic breeds. The two varieties were crossed in the 19th century, making them more similar in appearance. Since 1934, each variety has had its own standard. The pembroke, the most common variety, owes his royal connections to King George VI who introduced the breed to the court when he gave a Pembroke to his daughter, Queen Elizabeth II.

Sturdily built and strong. Relaxed gait.

1

SHEEPDOGS

COUNTRY OF ORIGIN
Great Britain

ORIGINAL NAMES
Two varieties:
Cardigan Welsh Corgi
Pembroke Welsh Corgi

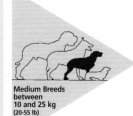

Medium Breeds
between
10 and 25 kg
(20-55 lb)

HEAD
Foxy in shape and appearance. Broad, flat skull. Stop not pronounced. Tapered muzzle.

EYES
Medium size, round. Variations of brown in harmony with the coat color.

EARS
Held erect. Moderately long, rounded at the tips.

BODY
The cardigan is larger than the pembroke, but his chest is not as broad. Belly slightly tucked up. Straight back.

LIMBS
Large, round, compact feet. Forelegs turned slightly outward.

TAIL
Cardigan: relatively long, richly clad, carried low at rest. Pembroke: naturally short or docked at birth.

COAT
Cardigan: short or medium length, harsh and straight; short, thick undercoat. Pembroke: medium length, straight, thick, neither harsh nor soft; dense undercoat.

COLOR
Cardigan: all colors acceptable, with or without white markings, but white must not be dominant color. Pembroke: self colors—red, sable, fawn, tan—with or without white markings on the legs, forechest, neck and head.

SIZE
Cardigan: approx. 30 cm (12 in).
Pembroke: 25 to 30 cm (10-12 in).

WEIGHT
Cardigan: 12 to 15 kg (26.5-33 lb).

Pembroke:
Dog: 12 to 15 kg (26.5-33 lb).
Bitch 10 to 11 kg (22-24 lb).

Character, special skills and training
This robust, lively, tireless dog is very active, always alert and a hard worker. He is loyal, very gentle with children and not shy or aggressive. This breed requires firm but gentle training.

Care and functions
This dog adapts readily to living indoors provided he receives regular exercise and room to run. The cardigan requires daily brushing; the pembroke requires weekly brushing.
· Herder.
· Utility dog: assistant, drug search, rescue.
· Guard dog.
· Pet.

Australian Cattle Dog

This breed is thought to be the result of crossbreeding of the now extinct Smithfield (closely related to the Old English Sheepdog), the Dingo, the Collie and the Bull terrier. Around 1840, Dalmatian and Kelpie blood may have been introduced. The Australian Cattle Dog is also called the heeler for his ability to nip at the heels of cattle without being injured. The breed was recognized around 1890, but it was not introduced in the United States and Europe until the 1970s.

Conveys the impression of great agility, strength and endurance. True, free, supple action.

CATTLE DOGS 2

1

Medium Breeds between 10 and 25 kg (20-55 lb)

COUNTRY OF ORIGIN
Australia

OTHER NAMES
Blue Heeler
Australian Queensland Heeler

HEAD
Strong. Broad, slightly convex skull. Slight stop. Muscular cheeks. Powerful, medium-length nose bridge. Tight, clean lips.

EYES
Oval, medium size. Dark brown color.

EARS
Moderately small, pointed, broad at the base, muscular. Held erect.

BODY
Longer than tall. Compact, balanced construction. Exceptionally strong neck without dewlap. Strong back. Chest well let down and muscular. Ribs well sprung. Shoulders strong, sloping and muscular. Deep flanks. Horizontal topline. Broad, strong, muscular loin.

LIMBS
Round feet. Short, strong, arched, compact toes. Strong legs.

TAIL
Hangs down forming a slight curve at rest. Richly clad (brush).

COAT
Weather-resistant. Short (2,5 to 4 cm) (1 to 1,5 in), straight, smooth, close-lying, dense, harsh. Double coat. Longer on the back of the legs and on the underbody. Short, dense undercoat.

COLOR
Blue: blue, blue-mottled or speckled, with or without black, blue or tan markings on the head. Red speckle: small, even red speckle all over the body.

SIZE
Dog: 46 to 51 cm (18-20 in).
Bitch: 43 to 48 cm (17 to 19 in).

WEIGHT
15 to 20 kg (33-44 lb).

Character, special skills and training
This dynamic dog is always on the alert. Courageous and vigilant, he was born to the life of herding and guarding cattle. This hardy, remarkably agile dog works in almost complete silence. When he does bark, it is said that he sounds like a hooting owl. The australian cattle dog is indispensable to the australian farmers who work extremely large ranches in a hot climate. A loyal companion, this dog becomes attached to his owner and the family. Being suspicious of strangers, he makes an excellent guard dog for the home.

Care and functions
This dog is not a city dweller. If forced to live indoors, he will get into mischief for lack of space or adequate activity. The australian cattle dog needs considerable exercise every day. Regular brushing is sufficient.
· Herder, herd guard, cattle dog.
· Guard dog.

Molossian type. Cobby. Square body outline.
Normal gaits: walk and trot.

Belgian Cattle Dog

Originating in Flanders, the Belgian Cattle Dog was produced by crossing several breeds in order to produce an ideal working dog for the farm. Some believe this breed was brought to Flanders by Spanish invaders. Others think large barbets, Mastiffs and Picardy Shepherds were crossed to produce the breed, or perhaps that he is descended from the Beauceron and the Griffon. During World War I, the Belgian Cattle Dog was almost eliminated. Flemish breeders rebuilt the breed from the few survivors. Its standard was established by the FCI in 1965.

2

CATTLE DOGS

1

COUNTRY OF ORIGIN
Belgium

ORIGINAL NAME
Vlaamse Koehond

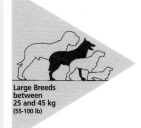

**Large Breeds
between
25 and 45 kg
(55-100 lb)**

HEAD
Massive, chiseled, size in proportion to the body. Stop not pronounced. Broad, powerful, well filled out muzzle, tapering toward the nose. Flat, clean cheeks. Pronounced superciliary arches.

EYES
Medium size, slightly oval in shape. Dark color.

EARS
Held erect, set on high. Triangular if cropped. Naturally drop.

BODY
Short and thickset. Strong, muscular neck. Broad, deep forechest. Deep brisket. Short flanks. Croup almost

horizontal. Short, broad back. Broad, muscular loin.

LIMBS
Strong, muscular legs. Short, round, solid feet. Compact toes. Strong, black nails.

TAIL
Docked, leaving two or three vertebrae (approx. 4 in). Carried gaily in action. Some dogs born tailless.

COAT
Medium length (2 in). Harsh, dry, dull and tousled. Shorter on the head. Full mustache and beard. Fine, dense undercoat.

COLOR
Black to fawn, often brindle or pepper and salt passing through gray. White star on the chest is allowed. Light, washed out coats not desirable.

SIZE
Dog: 62 to 68 cm
(24.5-27 in).
Bitch: 59 to 65 cm
(23-25.5 in).

WEIGHT
Dog: 35 to 40 kg (77-88 lb).
Bitch: 27 to 35 kg (60-77 lb).

Character, special skills and training
This rustic, energetic, bold breed is dominant and bonds to only one person. He is calm, wise and steady. He is alert, well behaved and docile, though can be a bit surly. This active dog has energy to spare. He must receive firm, consistent training. Strangers will find his forbidding countenance very dissuasive. This dog has always worked on the farm, guarding and herding the cattle as sled dog and even turning a wheel in the butter-churning process. His superb sense of smell makes him useful for police work.

Care and functions
This breed must be brushed once or twice per week and taken to a professional groomer three or four time per year for stripping. This is not a house dog. He requires considerable space and exercise.
· Herder.
· Police dog (tracking, messenger).
· Guard dog.
· Pet.

Tibetan Mastiff

Group
2

SECTION 1

AFFENPINSCHER
DOBERMANN PINSCHER
PINSCHER
AUSTRIAN SHORTHAIRED PINSCHER
SCHNAUZER
DUTCH SMOUSHOND
BLACK RUSSIAN TERRIER

SECTION 2

AIDI
BOXER
DANISH BROHOLMER
BULLDOG
BULLMASTIFF
CANE CORSO
ANATOLIAN SHEPHERD DOG
CENTRAL ASIAN SHEEPDOG
CAUCASIAN SHEEPDOG
KARST SHEEPDOG
CAO DE CASTRO LABOREIRO
GREAT PYRENEES
ESTRELA MOUNTAIN DOG
GREAT DANE
ARGENTINEAN MASTIFF

FRENCH MASTIFF
MALLORQUIN BULLDOG
TIBETAN MASTIFF
FILA BRASILEIRO
HOVAWART
LANDSER
LEONBERG
MASTIFF
SPANISH MASTIFF
NEAPOLITAN MASTIFF
PYRENEAN MASTIFF
RAFEIRO DO ALENTEJO
ROTTWEILER
ST. BERNARD
SARPLANINAC
SHAR-PEI
NEWFOUNDLAND
TOSA

SECTION 3

APPENZELLER
BERNES MOUNTAIN DOG
ENTELBUCHER
GREATER SWISS MOUNTAIN DOG

65

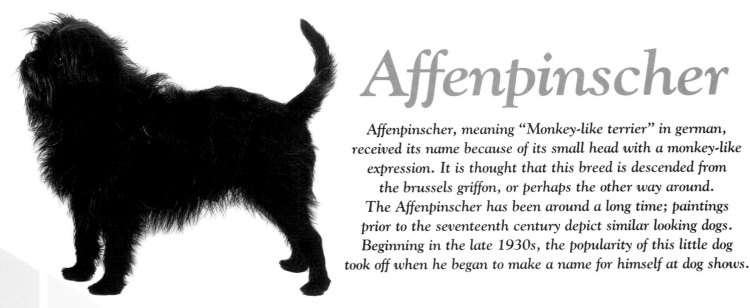

Affenpinscher

Affenpinscher, meaning "Monkey-like terrier" in german, received its name because of its small head with a monkey-like expression. It is thought that this breed is descended from the brussels griffon, or perhaps the other way around. The Affenpinscher has been around a long time; paintings prior to the seventeenth century depict similar looking dogs. Beginning in the late 1930s, the popularity of this little dog took off when he began to make a name for himself at dog shows.

Small and compact.

1

PINSCHERS

2

COUNTRY OF ORIGIN
Germany

OTHER NAME
Diabletin moustachu
(mustached little devil)

Small Breeds
under 10 kg
(under 20 lb)

Character, special skills and training
This dog exhibits a mixture of exuberance and serenity. He is lively, alert, loyal, affectionate, bold, and rather obstinate. The affenpinscher is a hunter of vermin and an excellent guard dog that will bark a warning to alert his owner.

Care and functions
This breed can make a good house dog. Daily brushing and combing is required.
· Guard dog.
· Hunter of vermin.
· Pet.

HEAD
Round. Monkey-like expression. Short muzzle. Slightly undershot bite. Black lips.

EYES
Round. Dark color.

EARS
Small, set on high. If cropped, held erect and forward. If natural, v-shaped, drop or held erect.

BODY
Square body outline. Short neck. Ribs slightly sprung. Well developed breast. Underline slightly tucked up

at the loin. Straight short back sloping slightly from withers to croup.

LIMBS
Small, round feet. Compact, arched toes. Hard pads.

TAIL
Docked to approximately three vertebrae. Set high and carried erect.

COAT
Harsh and dense on the body. Less harsh on the head, standing off and framing the face. Bushy eyebrows, full beard.

COLOR
Preferably black. Brown or gray markings or nuances permissible.

SIZE
25 to 30 cm (10-12 in).

WEIGHT
4 kg (9 lb) or less.

Doberman Pinscher

This breed's history begins in Apolda, a small German village in the province of Thueringen. F. L. Doberman developed this fearless guard dog to protect him as he made his rounds collecting taxes. Around 1870, he crossed a number of aggressive breeds (many ancestors of the Rottweiler), including local black and tan Sheepdogs, the German Pinscher, the German Shepherd, the Beauceron, and the Rottweiller. The result was a vigilant working dog, farm dog, guard dog and police dog. For hunting, the Doberman was used to fight off predators. Later, new blood was added, notably the Black and Tan Terrier and probably the greyhound. In 1910, the standard for the doberman was established.

Mesomorph. Elegant, pure lines. Solidly built and muscular without bulkiness. Highly pigmented skin. Elastic, supple, relaxed gait.

1A

PINSCHERS

COUNTRY OF ORIGIN
Germany

2

Large Breeds between 25 and 45 kg (55-100 lb)

During World War I, the Doberman served as a patrol, as a sentry at military bases and as a guide dog for soldiers blinded during the fighting.

HEAD
Long and dry. Strong, blunt wedge-shape. Stop not pronounced. Muzzle line almost at level with topline of skull. Powerful, broad jaws. Lips smooth, lying close to the jaws.

EYES
Medium size. Oval. Dark color.

EARS
Set on high. Cropped, erect, length in proportion to length of the head. If not cropped, semi-drop with the front edge lying alongside the cheek.

BODY
Square body outline. Dry, well muscled neck. Powerful forechest. Clearly defined

hocks. Well developed chest with slightly sprung ribs. Belly well tucked up. Rounded croup. Solid, short back

LIMBS
Solid legs. Short feet with compact, arched toes. Black nails.

TAIL
Set high, short, docked after the second caudal vertebra.

COAT
Short, hard, thick, smooth and close-lying. No undercoat.

COLOR
Black or brown with clearly defined tan markings on the muzzle, cheeks, throat, forechest, legs and feet.

SIZE
Dog: 68 to 72 cm (27-28 in).
Bitch: 63 to 68 kg (25-27 in).

WEIGHT
Dog: 40 to 45 kg (88-99 lb).
Bitch: 32 to 35 kg (70-77 lb).

Character, special skills and training
Lively, courageous, vigilant and energetic, the doberman has a slightly disquieting, resolute expression. This proud, determined, impulsive breed must be stable, composed and sociable. This is not a dog for everyone. He requires an authoritative owner who is fair, calm and will assert himself with patience and gentleness. The doberman is blindly loyal and devoted to his owner and can be trusted with children. He is a born guardian and is extremely wary of strangers. Fundamentally peace-loving, the doberman is an emotionally sensitive dog and does not like conflict.

Care and functions
This dog needs space and exercise to burn off energy. He will not tolerate being tied up. Regular brushing is required.
· Working dog: police dog, army dog.
· Guard and defense dog.
· Pet.

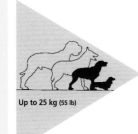

Pinscher

The origin of the Pinscher is not clear. Some writers believe it is descended from a very old german breed related to the schnauzers, which is descended from the black and tan terrier. The blood of the standard pinscher contributed to the development of the Doberman Pinscher. The breed was recognized in 1879 and the Pinscher Club was created in 1895. The standard Pinscher is less common than the miniature Pinscher.

Well-balanced construction.
Square body outline.

1A

PINSCHERS

2

COUNTRY OF ORIGIN
Germany

OTHER NAMES
Standard (German) Pinscher
Miniature Pinscher
(Zwergpinscher)

Up to 25 kg (55 lb)

HEAD
Robust, long. Slight stop. Rectangular nose bridge. Blunt, wedge-shaped muzzle. Lips smooth, lying close to jaws.

EYES
Medium size. Oval. Dark color.

EARS
If cropped, prick. If natural, drop, v-shaped.

BODY
Compact. Dry neck. Moderately broad chest. Ribs slightly sprung. Well developed forechest. Belly moderately tucked up. Short back. Heavily muscled legs.

LIMBS
Short, round feet. Compact, arched toes.

TAIL
Docked to approximately three vertebrae. Set high, carried erect.

COAT
Short, thick, smooth and close-lying.

COLOR
Solid color: fawn or shades of brown to stag red. Bi-color: black with tan, red, or lighter markings above the eyes, on the neck, forechest, lower legs, feet, inside of hind legs and around the anus. Markings also on the cheeks, flews and lower jaw in the miniature pinscher.

SIZE
43 to 58 cm (17-23 in).
Miniature Pinscher:
25 to 30 cm (10-12 in).

WEIGHT
12 to 16 kg (26.5-35 lb).
Miniature Pinscher:
2 to 4 kg (4.5 to 9 lb).

Character, special skills and training
This spirited, courageous, playful dog is vigilant, well-balanced and good-tempered. Very fond of family, the pinscher is a good playmate for children provided the dog is not man handled. The miniature pinscher is more high-strung and has a stronger personality than the standard pinscher. They need firm, consistent training.

Care and functions
This is a very clean breed. The pinscher can live in the city if he receives a fair amount of exercise. Regular brushing is required.
· Guard dog (standard pinscher); excellent ratter.
· Pet.

Austrian Shorthaired Pinscher

The origins of this breed are not known. It is closely related to the standard Pinscher, but the Austrian Shorthaired Pinscher was raised to be a good farm dog rather than a pet. This breed is rare outside of its native Austria.

Austrian shorthaired Pinscher.
Cobby. Elegant.

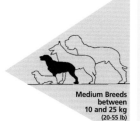

1A

PINSCHERS

COUNTRY OF ORIGIN
Austria

ORIGINAL NAMES
Osterreichischer
Kurzhaariger Pinscher

2

Medium Breeds
between
10 and 25 kg
(20-55 lb)

HEAD
Pear-shaped. Broad skull. Pronounced stop. Strong, short muzzle. Large nose. Lips smooth, lying close to jaws.

EYES
Large. Dark color.

EARS
Rose or v-shaped. Held erect or semi-erect.

BODY
Thickset. Powerful neck. Long, deep, barrel chest.

Long, broad loin. Short, broad back and loin. Broad chest.

LIMBS
Compact feet with well arched toes.

TAIL
Set high. Typically carried curved over the back. May be docked.

COAT
Short, flat, straight, with undercoat.

COLOR
Most common are yellow, golden brown, fawn, reddish-brown, black, black and tan, brindle, almost always with large white markings on the throat, forechest, legs and head (flare).

SIZE
35 to 50 cm (14-20 in).

WEIGHT
12 to 18 kg (26.5-40 lb).

Character, special skills and training
This spirited, hardy, active animal makes a remarkable guard dog. He is cheerful, kind and very open to training. His terrier instinct drives him to chase rabbits and foxes.

Care and functions
This breed needs space and plenty of exercise. Weekly brushing is sufficient.
· Guard dog.
· Pet.

Schnauzer

Square body outline. Robust, yet elegant. Sound gait.

1B

SCHNAUZERS

COUNTRY OF ORIGIN
Germany

OTHER OAMES
Giant Schnauzer
Standard Schnauzer
Miniature Schnauzer

2

Up to 45 kg
(100 lb)

GIANT SCHNAUZER

HEAD
Strong, elongated. Pronounced stop. Rectangular nose bridge. Shaggy muzzle ending in a blunt wedge. Black lips.

EYES
Oval. Dark color.

EARS
If cropped, carried erect. If natural, v-shaped, breaking at skull level or small and held erect.

BODY
Square outline. Arched neck. Medium width chest with moderately sprung ribs. Belly moderately tucked up. Short back sloping gently toward the croup

LIMBS
Short, round feet. Compact, arched toes. Dark nails. Muscular legs.

TAIL
Set high and carried erect. Docked to three vertebrae.

COAT
Hard, wiry, thick. Dense undercoat. Wiry beard on the muzzle; eyes slightly hidden by bushy eyebrows.

"Schnauze" means "muzzle" in German, so this breed was named for its characteristic shaggy muzzle. Up to the nineteenth century, Schnauzers were considered rough-haired Pinschers. There are three schnauzer varieties. The Standard Schnauzer's ancestry is unknown since it has been around for a very long time. Perhaps its roots can be traced to the Biberhund and a rough-haired ratter, or shepherd breeds. The Standard Schnauzer was primarily used to clear vermin. The Giant Schnauzer is thought to be the result of crossbreeding of the Standard Schnauzer, the Great Dane and the Belgian Cattle Dog. Of course, the Giant Schnauzer may simply be an enlarged model of the Standard Schnauzer. Depicted in one of artist Albrecht Dürer's works, the Giant Schnauzer was probably developed in the Wurtemberg region. These dogs guarded farm carts and kept stables free of vermin.
The Miniature Schnauzer was developed around 1880 by selectively breeding small Standard Schnauzers. In Europe, the Giant Schnauzer is the most popular variety, but in English-speaking countries, the Miniature Schnauzer is more common.

MINIATURE SCHNAUZER

STANDARD SCHNAUZER

COLOR
Solid black or pepper and salt. Dark mask. White markings are not desirable.

SIZE
Giant Schnauzer:
60 to 70 cm (23.5-27.5 in).
Standard Schnauzer:
45 to 50 cm (18 to 20 in).
Miniature Schnauzer:
30 to 35 cm (12-14 in).

WEIGHT
Giant Schnauzer:
30 to 40 kg (66-88 lb).
Standard Schnauzer:
approx. 15 kg (33 lb).
Miniature Schnauzer:
4 to 7 kg (9-15.5 lb).

Character, special skills and training
The schnauzer is high-spirited, energetic, impetuous (though stable), hardy, proud and dominant. The Giant Schnauzer is calmer than the spunky miniature. This devoted, affectionate dog loves children and makes an excellent pet. Constantly alert, wary of strangers and very reliable, the Standard and Giant Schnauzers are excellent guard dogs. This breed requires firm authority and a lot of attention.

Care and functions
Schnauzers should not be confined indoors. They are active dogs and need space and considerable exercise to stay fit and maintain their mental health. Daily brushing and professional grooming once every three months is required.
· Guard dog, defense dog, military dog.
· Pet.

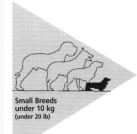

Dutch Smoushond

The Smoushondje, which means dog of the jews in Dutch, were very common in the Netherlands in the past. The Dutch Smoushond was considered a stable dog. He kept the stable clear of rats and accompanied horses and drivers.

Square body outline

1C

SMOUSHOND

2

COUNTRY OF ORIGIN
Denmark

ORIGINAL NAMES
Hollandse Smoushound
Hollandse Smoushondje

Small Breeds under 10 kg (under 20 lb)

Character, special skills and training
This affectionate, cheerful, well-balanced dog makes an excellent family pet.

Care and functions
Weekly brushing is required. · Pet.

HEAD
Short and broad. Domed skull. Distinct stop. Moderately short jaws. Fine lips.

EYES
Large, round. Dark color. Dark rims.

EARS
Small, fine, set on high, falling forward along the cheeks.

BODY
Sturdy. Short neck. Broad chest. Well sprung ribs. Muscular croup. Belly very slightly drawn up. Straight, broad back.

LIMBS
Round feet. Black nails. Legs with strong bone.

TAIL
Natural or cropped to one third its length. If natural, relatively short length, carried gaily.

COAT
Body: 4 to 7 cm (1.5 to 3 in) long; harsh, straight, slightly shaggy, not wavy or curly; adequate undercoat. Legs: medium length. Tail: bushy, without feathering. Head: short on the skull and long on the cheeks; mustaches, beard and long eyebrows.

COLOR
Any shade of solid yellow. Preferably dark straw color. Ears, mustaches, beard and eyebrows are darker than the rest of the coat.

SIZE
Dog: 37 to 42 cm (14.5-16.5 in).
Bitch: 35 to 40.5 cm (14-16 in).

WEIGHT
9 to 10 kg (20-22 lb).

Black Russian Terrier

The Black Russian Terrier was created in Russia in the early twentieth century by crossing the Airedale Terrier with the Giant Schnauzer and the Rottweiller. The breed was used to guard military installations. The largest of all terriers, the Black Russian Terrier is rare outside of Russia. The breed was recognized by the FCI in 1984.

Massive skeleton and musculature. Relaxed, graceful gait.

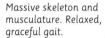

Large Breeds between 25 and 45 kg (55-100 lb)

COUNTRY OF ORIGIN
Russia

OTHER NAME
Chiornyi

HEAD
Long. Flat skull. Pronounced stop. Massive muzzle. Thick, fleshy lips.

EYES
Small, oval, set obliquely in the skull. Dark color. Coarse, bushy eyebrows.

EARS
Set on high, small, triangular, drop.

BODY
Massive. Long, dry neck. Broad, deep chest. Short, broad, muscular loin. Belly is tucked up. Broad, muscular croup sloping slightly to the tail. Broad, straight, muscular back.

LIMBS
Muscular legs. Large, round feet.

TAIL
Thick, set high. Docked short, leaving three or four vertebrae.

COAT
Harsh, hard, 2 to 4 in long, with mustaches, beard and mane. Thick, well developed undercoat.

COLOR
Black or pepper and salt.

SIZE
Dog: 66 to 72 cm (26-28 in).
Bitch: 64 to 70 cm (25- 27.5 in).

WEIGHT
Approx. 40 kg (88 lb).

Character, special skills and training
This sturdy, rustic, hardy dog has a strong, steady personality. The Russian Black Terrier is very devoted to his owner. An excellent guard dog, the breed is suspicious of strangers, has an active defense reaction and will bite. Firm training is a necessity.

Care and functions
This breed can adapt to life in the city if born to it. Long daily walks are required. Regular brushing and professional grooming are needed.
· Guard dog.

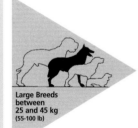

Aidi

No sheepdog breed exists in the Atlas mountains. This Moroccan dog, probably originating in the Sahara, lives in the mountains and defends his owner and property from wildcats, but he has never worked as a flock guard. This explains why his 1963 standard, which was published under the name Atlas Sheepdog, was nullified in 1969.

2B
MOUNTAIN TYPE MOLOSSIANS

2

COUNTRY OF ORIGIN
Morocco

ORIGINAL NAMES
Kabyle Dog
Chien de l'Atlas

Strong construction. Muscular.

Large Breeds between 25 and 45 kg (55-100 lb)

Character, special skills, and training
This very rustic breed has remarkable power and agility. He is always on the alert and ready for action. He will protect his owner and loved ones from predators and strangers with great courage. This breed can even sniff out snakes. The sensitive, lively Aidi must receive firm, but kindly, training.

Care and functions
The Aidi can live indoors provided he gets exercise every day. Weekly brushing is required.
· Guard dog.
· Pet.

HEAD
Like that of a bear. Dry. Size in proportion to the body. Flat, broad skull. Stop not pronounced. Tapered muzzle. Black or brown nose, matching coat color. Strong jaws. Black or brown tight lips.

EYES
Medium size. Dark color. Dark, slightly oblique rims.

EARS
Medium size with rounded tips, semi-drop.

BODY
Powerful. Muscular neck without dewlap. Broad, very

deep chest. Ribs slightly sprung. Powerful, arched loin. Belly tucked up.

LIMBS
Slightly rounded feet with strong nails (color of coat). Broad, muscular back. Solid, fairly muscular legs.

TAIL
Long, carried down, reaching the hock joint, in the form of a scimitar at rest. Very thick fur (plume).

COAT
Very thick, slightly long (6 cm) (2,5 in) except on the head and ears where it is very short and not as thick.

Mane at the neck (particularly impressive in dogs).

COLOR
Wide range of colors: white, tawny, fawn, red, black and white, fawn and white, shades of gray, tri-color, etc.

SIZE
52 to 62 cm (20.5 to 24.5 in).

WEIGHT
Approx. 30 kg (66 lb).

Boxer

Like all Mastiffs, the Boxer's ancestors included eastern Molossians, breeds used for fighting and defending their charges against wild animals. The German Bullenbeisser (now extinct) was crossed with the English Bulldog to create the modern Boxer in 1890. The Boxer was first shown in 1896 in Munich and a standard was established some ten years later. This breed was used by the German army during World War I. The Boxer is very popular as a pet and guard dog.

Sturdy appearance. Well developed muscles. Tight-fitting coat without wrinkles. Lively, noble, powerful gait.

2A

MASTIFF TYPE MOLOSSIAN

COUNTRY OF ORIGIN
Germany

2

Large Breeds between 25 and 45 kg (55-100 lb)

HEAD
Harmonious proportions. Clean and square. Domed skull. Distinct stop. Muzzle as broad and powerful as possible. Lower jaw protrudes beyond the upper jaw and curves slightly upward (prognathism).

EYES
Not too small, not protruding. Dark brown color. Dark rims.

EARS
Set on high. Not too broad. Cropped to a point, held erect.

BODY
Square. Round, powerful neck. Broad, deep forechest. Deep brisket. Well sprung ribs. Short, muscular loin. Straight, muscular back.

LIMBS
Straight, sturdy legs with plentiful bone. Small, round feet.

TAIL
Set high. Docked and carried erect.

COAT
Short and lying close to the body, hard, thick and shiny.

COLOR
Fawn or brindle. Shades of fawn from light tan to mahogany, preferably golden-red. Black mask. Brindle coat has dark or black streaking on a fawn background. White markings are permissible.

SIZE
Dog: 57 to 64 cm (22.5-25 in).
Bitch: 53 to 60 cm (21-23.5 in).

WEIGHT
25 to 30 kg (55-66 lb).

Character, special skills and training
This is an energetic, impetuous, dominant, self-assured breed. The boxer must be calm, well-balanced and sociable. He forms a strong bond with his family and remains loyal at all cost. Alert and wary toward strangers, he demonstrates fearless courage in his role as protector and guard. Training should start at a very young age.

Care and functions
The boxer can make a good house dog, but he must be given a considerable amount of exercise. His short coat requires little care.
· Guard and defense dog.
· Utility dog: police dog, guide dog.
· Pet.

Danish Broholmer

This Molossian-looking shepherd dog belongs to an old Danish breed, which was the result of crossings between Mastiffs and German dogs of undetermined breeds. The breed appeared in Denmark in the 19th century, although it really spread out during the two World Wars. It is almost unknown in France.

Large. Very powerful.
Mastiff-type square body.

2

2A

MASTIFF TYPE MOLOSSIANS

COUNTRY OF ORIGIN
Denmark

Giants Breeds
over 45 kg
(over 100 lb)

Character, special skills and training
This is a steadfast, peace-loving, well-balanced, good-natured breed. The broholmer is well known for his even temper and courage. Firm training is required to temper any aggressive tendencies he may have toward strangers.

Care and functions
This dog needs space and a lot of exercise. Weekly brushing is sufficient.
· Herder.
· Guard dog.
· Pet.

HEAD
Strong and broad. Carried slightly down. Relatively short muzzle. Pendulous lips.

EYES
Round. Black or dark amber color.

EARS
Small. Set on moderately high.

BODY
Square body outline. Thick neck. Broad forechest. Long back. Croup slightly sloping.

LIMBS
Strong, thick, solid feet. Powerful legs.

TAIL
Medium length, thick. Carried low at rest, saber when in action.

COAT
Short, thick, weather-resistant.

COLOR
Fawn (light yellow, golden) with black mask; black. White markings on the forechest, feet and tip of the tail are permissible.

SIZE
Dog: at least 75 cm (30 in).
Bitch: at least 70 cm (28 in).

WEIGHT
50 to 60 kg
(110-132 lb).

Bulldog

The Bulldog is thought to be descended from ancient Mastiffs of asiatic blood, combat dogs that were introduced in Great Britain by early phoenician navigators. Its name reflects its original purpose; the Bulldog was used for bull-baiting. Organized dog fights were also the rule of the day. In 1835, the cruel practice of bull-baiting was outlawed in England. In 1875, the first Bulldog standard was published. Selective breeding since that time has turned the Bulldog into a loving family pet.

Thickset. Low-swung. Broad, powerful and compact. Heavy gait.

2A

MASTIFF TYPE MOLOSSIANS

COUNTRY OF ORIGIN
Great britain

OTHER NAME
English Bulldog

Medium Breeds between 10 and 25 kg (20-55 lb)

2

HEAD
Kassive. Short face. Broad skull. Loose, wrinkled skin. Deep stop. Well developed cheeks. Short, broad, upturned muzzle. Broad nostrils. Thick, pendulous flews. Broad, square jaws. Lower jaw protrudes beyond the upper jaw and curves slightly upward.

EYES
Very wide set. Medium size, round. Very dark color.

EARS
Ket on high and placed wide apart. Small and thin. Rose ear, in which the ear folds in such a way as to show the inside of the burr.

BODY
Short, well-knit. Very thick neck with dewlap. Shoulders broad and slanting outward. Capacious, round brisket. Ribs well sprung. Elevated, strong hindquarters. Belly tucked up. Short, strong back. Arched loin.

LIMBS
Round, compact feet. Slightly out-turned. Forelegs set wide apart. Strong, muscular legs.

TAIL
Set low, round, moderate length. Carried low, hanging straight, not curving up.

COAT
Fine, short, smooth and thick.

COLOR
Uniform color with black mask or muzzle. Uniform colors: red, fawn. Brindle, white, or piebald (white with the above colors). Liver, black and tan are undesirable.

SIZE
30 to 40 cm (12-16 in).

WEIGHT
Dog: 24 to 25 kg (53-55 lb). Bitch: 22 to 23 kg (48-51 lb).

Character, special skills and training
The Bulldog is vigorous, courageous, hardy, uniform and dignified. Despite his frightening appearance, he is an affectionate, calm, quiet dog of excellent character. He makes a marvelous playmate for children and develops a strong bond with his owner. Firm training is required.

Care and functions
The Bulldog can adapt to city living provided he exercises regularly. He does not tolerate heat well. Daily brushing is required. Special attention must be given to the folds on his to ward off possible skin irritation.
· Guard dog.
· Police dog, army dog.
· Pet.

Bullmastiff

Created by crossing the Bulldog and a Mastiff, the Bullmastiff is fast and active like the Bulldog, large and heavy like a Mastiff. This breed was developed in the nineteenth century to guard large estates. The breed was recognized in 1924.

Powerful. Harmonious build. Powerfully built without bulkiness.

2A

MASTIFF TYPE MOLOSSIANS

2

COUNTRY OF ORIGIN
Great britain

Giants Breeds between over 45 kg (over 100 lb)

HEAD
Broad. Strong, square skull. Skin on face is wrinkled when dog is alert. Distinct stop. Well developed cheeks. Short, broad muzzle. Flews must not be pendulous.

EYES
Medium size. Dark or hazel color.

EARS
Small, v-shaped, set on high and placed wide apart. Darker color than the rest of the coat.

BODY
Powerful. Very muscular neck. Broad chest. Muscular shoulders. Broad loin. Short, straight back.

LIMBS
Strong, muscular legs with plenty of bone. Small, round cat feet with rounded, well-arched toes. Dark nails.

TAIL
Set high, strong at the base and tapering to the tip. Carried straight or curved and reaching the hocks.

COAT
short, hard, close-lying.

COLOR
Any shade of brindle, red or fawn. White spot on the chest is acceptable. Black mask on the muzzle. Dark markings around the eyes.

SIZE
Dog: 63 to 68 cm (25 to 27 in).
Bitch: 61 to 66 cm (24-26 in).

WEIGHT
Dog: 50 to 59 kg (110 to 130 lb).
Bitch: 41 to 50 kg (90.5 to 110.5 lb).

Character, special skills and training
Active, agile, showing great endurance and of solid build, the Bullmastiff has a symmetrical appearance. He is earnest, courageous and alert, making him an excellent guard dog. He is also loyal and gentle, an excellent playmate for children. The Bullmastiff has a very keen sense of smell and a dominant personality. Early, firm (though gentle) training is required.

Care and functions
The Bullmastiff is not a good house dog. He needs a lot of space and exercise. Regular brushing of the coat and cleaning of his folds are required.
· Guard and defense dog
· Police and army dog
· Pet.

Cane Corso

The Corso is the direct descendant of the ancient Roman molosser dogs. In the past, the breed was common throughout Italy, but it is now found only in the southern Italian province of Puglia and neighboring regions. The name is derived from the Latin word Cohors (farmyard or enclosure) meaning protector, guarder of farms, courtyards, and enclosed property. The breed first appeared in the sixteenth century and was used for hunting and guard duties.

Solid. Powerfully muscled. Elegant. Agile. Rather thick skin. Preferred gait: Trot.

2

MOUNTAIN TYPE MOLOSSIANS

2

COUNTRY OF ORIGIN
Italy

ORIGINAL NAME
Cane Corso Italiano

Giants Breeds between over 45 kg (over 100 lb)

HEAD
Broad, like that of molossians. Pronounced stop. Strong, square muzzle is shorter than the skull. Straight nose bridge. Very broad, thick jaws.

EYES
Medium size. Almost oval shape. Darkest colors preferred; in harmony with coat color.

EARS
Triangular, broad at the base, hanging. Often cropped to an equilateral triangle.

BODY
Slightly longer than tall.

Sturdy neck. Withers higher than croup. Straight, very muscular back. Prominent chest. Solid, short loin. Long, broad, slightly sloped loin.

LIMBS
Powerful legs. Hind feet are round and more compact than forefeet.

TAIL
Set on high. Very thick at the root. Docked at the fourth vertebra.

COAT
Short, very thick. Thin undercoat.

COLOR
Black, lead gray, slate gray, light gray, light fawn, fawn

red, dark fawn, brindle (streaks on fawn or gray background of various nuances). Fawn and brindle subjects have a black or gray mask. Small white spot on the chest, on the tip of the feet, and on the nose bridge is permissible.

SIZE
Dog: 64 to 68 cm (25-27 in).
Bitch: 60 to 64 cm (23.5-25 in).

WEIGHT
Dog: 45 to 50 kg (99-110 lb).
Bitch: 40 to 45 kg (88-99 lb).

Character, special skills and training
This rustic, hardy dog is full of energy and is extremely courageous. The Corso is proud and well-balanced, gentle and affectionate with his owner. This breed tolerates children well and is playful with them. The Corso is wary of strangers. This breed is easy to train.

Care and fonctions
The Corso needs exercise and room to run. Weekly brushing is sufficient.
· Guard and defense dog.
· Herder.
· Hunting dog.
· Pet.

Anatolian Shepherd Dog

Descended from molossus of Asian origin, the Anatolian Shepherd Dog's roots can be traced to the high plateaus and mountains of Turkey. This breed was used to guard sheep and protect them from predators, such as wolves. The Anatolian Shepherd Dog is also used as a hunting dog and army dog.

Powerful. Tall. Relatively streamlined. Supple, stretched out gait, like that of a cat.

2B

MOUNTAIN TYPE MOLOSSIANS

2

COUNTRY OF ORIGIN
Turkey

ORIGINAL NAME
Goban Kopegi

OTHER NAME
Anatolian Karabash Dog

Giants Breeds
between
over 45 kg
(over 100 lb)

Character, special skills and training
His habit of living and working outdoors in all weather conditions and his rugged past make this a sturdy, hardy breed. The Anatolian Shepherd Dog has a strong personality and is often stubborn and requires an owner with an alpha personality. While he is loyal and gentle with his owner and children, this dog is very distrustful of strangers, making him a superb guard dog.

Care and functions
The Anatolian Shepherd Dog should live in the country where he can get the vigorous daily exercise that he requires. Regular brushing is sufficient.
· Flock guard.
· Guard dog.
· Pet.

HEAD
Strong and broad. Slightly domed skull. Slight stop. Muzzle is slightly shorter than the skull. Black lips.

EYES
Small. Golden to brown color depending on coat color.

EARS
Medium size, drop, triangular with rounded tips.

BODY
Powerful. Thick, muscular neck. Deep chest. Belly well tucked up. Chest well let down. Ribs well sprung.

LIMBS
Solid, muscular legs. Solid, oval feet with arched toes.

TAIL
Long, carried low and slightly curled.

COAT
Thick, short or moderately long. Thick undercoat. Longer on the neck, shoulders and thighs.

COLOR
All colors permissible. Preferred colors are tawny and fawn with black mask and ears.

SIZE
Dog: 74 to 81 cm (29-32 in).
Bitch: 71 to 79 cm (28-31 in).

WEIGHT
Dog: 50 to 65 kg (110-143 lb).
Bitch: 40 to 55 kg (88-121 lb).

Central Asian Sheepdog

This breed is most likely descended from the Asian molussus. The Central Asian Sheepdog is found in all Central Asian republics and in some neighboring regions. The dog is used to defend herds from wolves and thieves.

HEAD
Massive, broad. Flat forehead. Very slight stop. Large black or brown nose.

EYES
Wide set, round. Dark color.

EARS
Set on low, small, triangular, drop. Often cropped.

BODY
Powerful. Short neck. Deep, broad brisket. Rounded ribs. Short, broad, slightly arched loin. Belly moderately tucked up. Broad, muscular, almost horizontal croup. Strong, straight, broad back.

LIMBS
Strong, oval, compact feet.

TAIL
Docked. Set high, carried down in the shape of a saber.

COAT
Harsh, straight and coarse. Long-haired variety: 7 to 8 cm (2.5-3 in) in length; Short-haired variety: 3 to 5 cm (1-2 in) in length, smooth. Thick undercoat.

COLOR
White, gray, black, straw, reddish-brown, tiger, pied or mottled.

SIZE
Dog: at least 65 cm (26 in).
Bitch: at least 60 cm (24 in).

WEIGHT
40 to 50 kg (88-110 lb).

Rugged construction. Massive bone structure. Powerfully muscled. Thick skin. Gait: slow, collected trot and gallop are most common.

2B

MOUNTAIN TYPE MOLOSSIANS

COUNTRY OF ORIGIN
Asia
Russia

ORIGINAL NAME
Sredneasiatskaya Ovtcharka

2

Large Breeds between 25 and 45 kg (55-100 lb)

Character, special skills and training
This rustic breed requires little care and adapts easily to all climates. The Central Asian Sheepdog is well-balanced and peaceable. Nevertheless, he is bold and suspicious of strangers and will react instantaneously to defend his charges with valor. Firm training is required.

Care and functions
The Central Asian Sheepdog is not a house dog. He needs exercise and room to run. Weekly brushing is sufficient.
· Flock guard
· Guard dog

Caucasian Sheepdog

Originating in the Caucasus, this large sheepdog is most likely one of the most direct descendants of the Tibetan Mastiff, which was introduced in Russia during the Asian invasions. This dog can be found throughout most of the former Soviet Union. The Caucasian Sheepdog of the steppes is taller and rangier than the Caucasian Sheepdog found in mountainous regions.

Large. Robust. Rugged construction. Massive bone structure. Heavily muscled. Gait: Lumbering gallop and clipped trot.

2B

MOUNTAIN TYPE MOLOSSIANS

2

COUNTRY OF ORIGIN
Russia

ORIGINAL NAME
Kavkazskaya Ovtcharka

OTHER NAME
Caucasian Owtcharka

Giants Breeds
over 45 kg
(over 100 lb)

Character, special skills and training
This very rustic breed requires little care and adapts easily to all climates. The Caucasian Sheepdog is well-balanced, active and even-tempered. However, he is suspicious of strangers and may bite. Firm training is required.

Care and functions
The Caucasian Sheepdog requires space and exercise. Weekly brushing is sufficient.
· Flock guard
· Guard and defense dog.
· Pet.

HEAD
Massive and broad. Distinct stop. Relatively short muzzle with large black or brown nose. Thick, though tight, lips.

EYES
Small, oval. Dark color.

EARS
Set on high, drop, cropped short.

BODY
Slightly longer than tall. Powerful, short neck. Deep, broad, slightly rounded chest. Short loin. Belly moderately tucked up. Broad, muscular back. Broad, muscular, almost horizontal croup.

LIMBS
Large, oval, compact feet. Solid legs.

TAIL
Set high, hanging down in the shape of a sickle, hook or ring. Docked tails are permitted.

COAT
Straight and coarse. Shorter on the head and front of the legs. Extremely thick undercoat of lighter color.
Three types:
- Long hair with mane, feathering, breeching and plume.
- Short hair without mane, feathering, etc.
- Medium length hair, long, but without mane, feathering, breeching or plume.

COLOR
Gray in patches with a variety of nuances, normally light and tending toward red, white, reddish-brown, brindle and piebald and speckled.

SIZE
Dog: at least 65 cm (26 in).
Bitch: at least 62 cm (24 in).

WEIGHT
45 to 65 kg (99-143 lb).

Karst Sheepdog

This sheepdog lives in the mountainous region of Karst (or Kras). He is a tireless defender of the herd. This breed was mentioned for the first time in 1689 and was officially recognized in 1939 under the name of Illyrian Sheepdog, which also included the future Sarplaninac. The Karst Sheepdog and the Sarplaninac were separated in 1968.

Medium size. Robust. Dark-colored skin. Preferred gait: trot.

Large Breeds between 25 and 45 kg (55-100 lb)

2

MOUNTAIN TYPE MOLOSSIANS

COUNTRY OF ORIGIN
Slovenia

ORIGINAL NAME
Kraski ovcar

2

HEAD
Broad and noble. Slightly convex skull. Stop not accentuated. Straight, broad forehead.

EYES
Almond-shaped eyes set slightly oblique. Chestnut or dark brown color.

EARS
Lie flat against the head in a V.

BODY
Strong, slightly rectangular, and well-muscled. Broad, muscular neck. The deep chest long is well let down. Sloped croup.

LIMBS
Forelegs oval, compact feet. Hind legs round, compact feet. Arched toes.

TAIL
Set on high, of medium length. Saber tail. Richly clad with long hair.

COAT
Short on the head and front of legs. Long and abundant over the rest of the body. Lies flat. Mane at neck; flag tail. Feathering on the hind legs.

COLOR
Iron gray, dark nuances desirable, particularly on the withers, the abdomen, and the feet. Dark mask on the head.

SIZE
Dog: 57 to 63 cm (22.5-25 in).
Bitch: 54 to 60 cm (21-23.5 in).

WEIGHT
Dog: 30 to 42 kg (66-93 lb).
Bitch: 25 to 37 kg (55-82 lb).

Character, special skills, and training
This dog is brave and courageous, but not fearless. He is of excellent character and easy-going. Devoted to his owner, he makes an excellent pet. Wary of strangers and not easily won over, he is a good guard dog and will protect his owner. Firm, but not harsh training is appropriate for this breed.

Care and functions
This breed needs space and exercise. Regular brushing is required.
· Sheepdog.
· Guard dog.
· Pet.

Cao de Castro Laboreiro

*The Cao de Castro Laboreiro is one of the oldest breeds on the Iberian peninsula.
Springing from the village Castro Laboreiro, this typical Portuguese breed is widespread in the region
bordered by the Minho and Limia rivers between the Peneda and Suajo mountain
chains in northern Portugal. The Cao de Castro Laboreiro, a mastiff, protects herds from wolves.
He is also used as a guard dog and police dog.*

Lupoid Mastiff. Rustic. Noble bearing.
Very relaxed gait. Threatening bark.

2B

**MOUNTAIN TYPE
MOLOSSIANS**

2

COUNTRY OF ORIGIN
Portugal

ORIGINAL NAME
Cao de Castro Laboreiro

OTHER NAME
Portuguese Cattle Dog

Large Breeds
between
25 and 45 kg
(55-100 lb)

Character, special skills and training
This robust, loyal, docile breed is affectionate, calm
and even-tempered. Constantly on the alert, this dog's
great courage and wariness of strangers make him a
superb guard dog. Firm training is required.

Care and functions
The Cao de Castro Laboreiro needs exercise and room
to run. Regular brushing is required.
· Flock guard.
· Guard dog. Police dog.
· Pet.

HEAD
Medium size, dry, no wrinkles. Stop not pronounced.
Long, strong, straight nose
bridge. Powerful jaws.

EYES
Set obliquely in the skull.
Medium size. Light brown
color in light-coated varieties
and dark brown in dark-coated varieties.

EARS
Medium size, slightly thick,
almost triangular with
rounded tips, drop.

BODY
Rectangular. Short neck
without dewlap. Broad, deep
chest. Narrow through the

belly. Broad, short, strong,
muscular loin. Croup slightly
sloped.

LIMBS
Muscular legs with substantial bone. Almost round feet
with thick toes and black or
dark gray nails.

TAIL
Thick and bushy, carried in
the shape of a saber, reaching the hock joint.

COAT
Thick, coarse, short
(5 cm) (2 in), harsh, close-lying and smooth.

COLOR
Wolf gray most common.

Any shade of gray, with or
without a black mask;
brindle.

SIZE
Dog: 55 to 60 cm
(21,5-23,5 in).
Bitch: 52 to 57 cm
(20.5 to 22.5 in).

WEIGHT
Dog: 30 to 40 kg
(66 to 88 lb).
Bitch: 20 to 30 kg
(44-66 lb).

Great Pyrenees

Like many Molossians, the Great Pyrenees' distant ancestor may be Tibetan Mastiff, which was introduced in Europe during Asian invasions. Identified as early as the 12th century, the Great Pyrenees protected the shepherd and his flock from wolves and bears, guarded homes and castles, and even sat in the royal court of Louis XIV. The Argeles and Cauterets clubs, founded in 1907, established the first standard for this breed. This standard was officially accepted in the 1960s. The Great Pyrenees is one of the few French breeds that is common outside of France. The breed is particularly popular in the United States and Japan.

Majestic. Powerfully built. Elegant.

2B

MOUNTAIN TYPE MOLOSSIANS

Giants Breeds between over 45 kg (over 100 lb)

COUNTRY OF ORIGIN
France

ORIGINAL NAME
Montagne des Pyrénées

OTHER NAME
Pyrenean Mountain Dog

2

Broad, straight, level back. Slightly elongated, compact feet with arched toes.

LIMBS
Solid legs with feathering. Double dewclaw on hind legs.

TAIL
Fairly long and bushy (plume). Carried low at rest and carried over the back making a wheel when alert.

COAT
Long, flat, resistant and thick. Longer on the tail, thighs and neck, where it may be slightly wavy. Thick, wooly undercoat.

COLOR
White with or without gray spots (badger coat) or pale yellow or orange on the head, ears and root of the tail. Badger coat is preferred. A few body spots are permissible.

SIZE
Dog: 70 to 80 cm (27.5-31,5 in).
Bitch: 65 to 72 cm (25.5-28 in).

WEIGHT
Dog: approx. 60 kg (132 lb).
Bitch: approx. 45 kg (99 lb).

Character, special skills and training
The Great Pyrenees has a rather independent nature and is proud, dominant and fairly strong-willed. Firm training from a very young age is required to bring this dog under control. This dog is tolerant, affectionate, gentle with children and very protective, making him an excellent pet. Reserved around strangers, this dog is a born protector. His size and demeanor can make him appear fearsome indeed.

Care and functions
This dog is not suited to city living. He needs exercise and room to run, or he will develop behavioral problems. He does not like to be shut in. Brushing three times per week and bathing several times per year are required.
· Flock guard.
· Guard dog.
· Pet.

HEAD
Size in proportion to body. Slightly domed skull. Stop not pronounced. Broad muzzle tapering toward the nose. Black, very slightly drooping lips.

EYES
Fairly small. Dark amber color. Black rims.

EARS
Small and triangular with rounded tips, hanging flat against the head.

BODY
Powerful. Strong, moderately short neck. Deep, broad brisket. Ribs slightly sprung. Belly slightly tucked up. Croup slightly sloped.

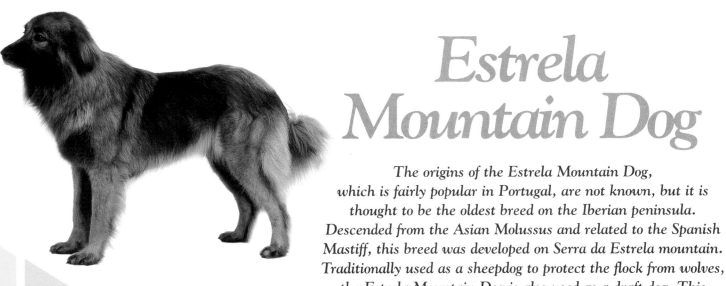

Estrela Mountain Dog

Molossian. Mastiff type. Well balanced body proportions. Rustic.

The origins of the Estrela Mountain Dog, which is fairly popular in Portugal, are not known, but it is thought to be the oldest breed on the Iberian peninsula. Descended from the Asian Molussus and related to the Spanish Mastiff, this breed was developed on Serra da Estrela mountain. Traditionally used as a sheepdog to protect the flock from wolves, the Estrela Mountain Dog is also used as a draft dog. This breed's standard was established in 1934. The Estrela Mountain Dog is still quite uncommon outside of Portugal.

2B

MOUNTAIN TYPE MOLOSSIANS

2

COUNTRY OF ORIGIN
Portugal

ORIGINAL NAME
Cao da Serra da Estrela

OTHER NAME
Portuguese Sheepdog

Large Breeds between 25 and 45 kg (55-100 lb)

HEAD
Strong and capacious. Convex profile to the skull. Stop not pronounced. Powerful jaws. Elongated nose bridge.

EYES
Medium size, oval. Dark amber color preferred. Black rims.

EARS
Small, narrow, triangular with rounded tips, drop. Cropped ears are permissible.

BODY
Compact. Short, thick neck. Deep, broad, rounded brisket. Short, broad loin. Short back. Croup slightly sloped.

LIMBS
Muscular legs with substantial bone and dry joints. Feet neither too long nor too round. Thick, compact toes. Dark or black nails.

TAIL
Long, carried down reaching the tip of the hock joint. Richly clad (feathering in long-haired variety).

COAT
Thick, slightly coarse, rather goatlike, smooth or slightly wavy. Two varieties exist; the long-haired variety is the most common, while the short-haired variety has almost disappeared.

COLOR
Only shades of fawn, wolf gray and yellow, solid color or parti-color.

SIZE
Dog: 65 to 72 cm (25.5 to 28 in).
Bitch: 62 to 68 (24.5 to 27 in).

WEIGHT
Dog: 40 to 50 kg (88-110,4 lb).
Bitch: 30 to 40 kg (66 to 88 lb).

Character, special skills and training
This impassive dog has quick reflexes. He is extremely hardy, energetic and courageous. The Estrela Mountain Dog is devoted to protecting the flock and works hard as a defense dog and draft dog. His exceptional sense of smell makes him a good hunter. Distrustful of strangers and even aggressive, he is known as an excellent guard dog. Docile and calm with his owners, he makes an excellent family pet. Firm, but gentle, training must be started at a very early age.

Care and functions
This dog is not suited to city living. He needs exercise and room to run to expend his energy. Regular brushing is required for the long-haired variety.
· Flock guard.
· Guard dog, police dog, army dog.
· Pet.

Great Dane

This large Mastiff is thought to be descended from the tibetan Mastiff introduced in europe by the phoenicians, then by the nomadic persian alans. In the middle ages, there were two varieties of this Mastiff: a smaller alaunt, powerful, agile, streamlined dogs that hunted in packs for boar, wolf and bear and a heavier, more compact alaunt used for guard duties. The immediat ancestors are the Bullenbeisser (now extinct) crossed with large hunting dogs descended from the more streamlined alaunt.

Later, names such as Ulm Dog, Great Dane, and Siberian Dog were used to indicate the different types of this breed. In 1878, all varieties were placed under the one name, Great Dane. The standard was written around 1890 in Germany.

Large. Powerful. Harmonious build. Robust, strong, elegant, regal. The Apollo of dogs. Proud. Pigmented skin. Harmonious, supple gait.

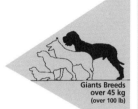

2A

MASTIFF TYPE MOLOSSIANS

Giants Breeds over 45 kg (over 100 lb)

COUNTRY OF ORIGIN
Germany

ORIGINAL NAME
Deutsche Dogge

OTHER NAME
German Mastiff

2

HEAD
Finely chiseled. Elongated, narrow. Very expressive. Always carried high. Strongly pronounced stop. Well developed superciliary arches. Broad nose bridge. Deep, rectangular muzzle. Black nose (lighter in the harlequin).

EYES
Medium size. Round. As dark as possible. Lighter eyes permissible in blue danes. Lighter eyes or eyes of different color permissible in harlequin danes.

EARS
Set on high, naturally drop. Cropped to a point, carried rigid and erect.

BODY
Square outline. Long, dry, muscular, well arched neck. Prominent forechest. Ribs well sprung. Wide croup sloping slightly. Belly well tucked up. Short, almost rectangular back. Broad, slightly arched loin

LIMBS
Strong, muscular legs Round cat feet. Very compact, arched toes.

TAIL
Medium length reaching the hocks. Set high, broad at the root tapering to a narrow tip. Curved slightly in the form of a saber when in action.

COAT
Very short, thick, smooth, shiny, lying close to the skin.

COLOR
Brindle: background color is light to dark yellow gold always with strong, black cross stripes; a black mask is preferred.
Fawn: light to dark yellow gold; a black mask is preferred.
Black: glossy black; white

markings are permissible. Blue: pure steel blue; white markings on the chest and feet are permissible. Harlequin: pure white background with glossy black torn patches of differing sizes well distributed over the entire body.

SIZE
Dog: at least 80 cm (31,5 in).
Bitch: at least 72 cm (28 in).

WEIGHT
50 to 70 kg
(110.5-154.5 lb).

Character, special skills and training
The great dane may be the most peace-loving of all the Mastiffs. He is a gentle, tender, kind, sensitive and affectionate dog, particularly with children. This stable, calm dog rarely barks and is never aggressive unless the situation warrants. He is alert, protective of his territory and his owner's property, wary around strangers and not easily swayed. His formidable size is enough to dissuade almost anyone. Training must start early. It should be firm, but undertaken with patience.

Care and functions
The great dane can be content living in an apartment, but he must get out daily to stretch his long legs. This athletic dog needs space and exercise. However, he should not exercise too vigorously until he has stopped growing, or he may damage his joints and ligaments. This dog has a short life expectancy of only eight years.
· Guard dog.
· Pet.

Argentinean Mastiff

This breed was created in Argentina by the Martinez brothers in the early twentieth century. The root stock was the Fighting Dog of Cordoba, a ferocious Mastiff. As the breed was developed it was crossed with the Spanish Mastiff, the Great Pyrenees, the Great Dane, the Boxer, Mastiffs, the Bulldog, Pointers, and the Irish Wolfhound. The result was a versatile breed that could be used for hunting, fighting, guard duties and more. The first standard was written in 1928 and approved by the Argentina Kennel Club in 1965. In 1973, the FCI established a standard for the breed and, in 1975, officially recognized the first and only breed ever developed in argentina.

Molossian type. Imposing, solid, elegant.

2A

MASTIFF TYPE MOLOSSIANS

2

COUNTRY OF ORIGIN
Argentina

ORIGINAL NAME
Dogo argentino

OTHER NAME
Dogo

Giants Breeds between over 45 kg (over 100 lb)

Character, special skills and training
This is a very robust, active, energetic, agile, courageous breed. The dogo argentino is calm, peaceful, affectionate and docile. He is very sociable and needs to stay close to his owner. He rarely barks. This breed is aggressive and dominant with other dogs and is fearsome indeed when defending his owner's property. Firm training is required, but be gentle with this sensitive dog.

Care and functions
The argentinean Mastiff can adjust to life in an apartment if he can get out two or three times each day and get plenty of exercise. He should be outdoors as much as possible. Brushing once or twice per week and bathing two or three times per year is recommended. It is necessary to clean his eyes regularly to avoid streaks.
· Hunting dog (large game – boar, puma, etc.)
· Utility dog: police dog, army dog, customs, search and rescue, guide dog.
· Guard dog.
· Pet.

HEAD
Molossian appearance. Strong, well chiseled. Capacious, convex skull. Deep wrinkles on forehead. Slightly hollow muzzle. Powerful jaws.

EYES
Dark or hazel color.

EARS
Set on high. Held erect or semi-erect, v-shaped. Generally cropped.

BODY
Powerful without bulkiness. Arched, strong neck. Deep, full chest. Solid back.

LIMBS
Very muscular hind legs. Long, straight forelegs. Mod-erately oval feet with arched toes.

TAIL
Long and thick, naturally hanging down.

COAT
Short, thick, lying close to the skin.

COLOR
White. Any color marking is a disqualification.

SIZE
Dog: 62 to 65 cm (24.5-26.5 in).
Bitch: 57 to 60 cm (22.5-23.5 in).

WEIGHT
40 to 50 kg (88-110.5 lb).

French Mastiff

The Dogue de Bordeaux, one of the oldest breeds in France, is the only Mastiff of French origin. This dog may be descended from the Roman Molossus, the Spanish Mastiff and others. During the middle ages, the breed was used for hunting and dog fighting. In the eighteenth century, Buffon described it as the Dogue d'Aquitaine. This breed was long known as the "Butcher dog" because butchers often selected this breed to protect their homes. He has also been known as the "Turk dog" in reference to his asian ancestors. An official standard was recognized in 1926 after the breed had been crossed several times with Mastiffs.

Brachycephalic molossian type. Very muscular. Built fairly low to the ground. Compact, athletic build. Imposing and proud.

2A

Giants Breeds over 45 kg (over 100 lb)

MASTIFF TYPE MOLOSSIANS

COUNTRY OF ORIGIN
France

ORIGINAL NAME
Dogue de Bordeaux

OTHER NAME
Dogue d'Aquitaine

2

HEAD
Extremely capacious, angular, broad, relatively short. Viewed from the side, it has the shape of a trapezoid. The skull (perimeter equaling dog's height) is slightly convex. Strong stop. Forehead, which is wider than high, dominates the face. Deep, symmetrical wrinkles. Powerful, thick, moderately short, slightly hollow muzzle. Broad nose. Extremely powerful jaws. Undershot jaw (lower jaw protruding 0.2 to 1 in). Thick flews.

EYES
Oval, moderately wide set. Hazel to dark brown color in dogs with a black mask, lighter color permissible in dogs with a red mask.

EARS
Small, slightly darker than the rest of the coat. Drop close to head along the cheeks.

BODY
Powerful. Very strong, almost cylindrical neck with dewlap. Powerful, deep, broad chest. Ribs well sprung. Broad, muscular back. Belly tucked up. Powerful chest. Slightly sloping croup.

LIMBS
Round, strong feet with compact toes. Dark nails. Muscular legs with a lot of bone.

TAIL
Very thick, carried low with the tip reaching no further than the hocks.

COAT
Fine, short, smooth and soft.

COLOR
Fawn or dark auburn with a red or black mask. Good pigmentation preferred. Small white markings on the forechest and feet are permissible.

SIZE
Dog: 60 to 68 cm (23,5-27 in).
Bitch: 58 to 66 cm (23-26 in).

WEIGHT
Dog: at least 50 kg (110 lb).
Bitch: at least 45 kg (99 lb).

Character, special skills and training
This former fighting dog is an excellent guard dog that vigilantly protects the home with courage, though not aggression. The french Mastiff does not like to socialize with other dogs. This gentle, calm, sensitive dog forms a strong bond with his owner and is very affectionate with children. He rarely barks. This breed detests solitude and lack of activity. This dog must be exceptionally well-trained in order to keep him under control.

Care and functions
The french Mastiff is not suitable as a house dog. He needs space and exercise. No special care of the coat is required.
· Guard and defense dog.
· Pet.

Mallorquin Bulldog

Originating on the island of Majorca, the mallorquin Bulldog was developed for bull-baiting and dog-fighting, like the english Bulldog. When this practice came to an end, the very existence of the Mallorquin Bulldog came into question. The breed was saved by spanish breeders, but is still very rare.

Mastiff. Medium size. Powerful, muscular build.

2A

MASTIFF TYPE MOLOSSIANS

2

COUNTRY OF ORIGIN
Balearic Island of Majorca, Spain

ORIGINAL NAME
Perro de Presa Mallorquin

OTHER NAME
Ca de Bou

Large Breeds between 25 and 45 kg (55-100 lb)

Character, special skills and training
This extremely courageous, independent dog has a combative personality. This breed must receive strict training.

Care and functions
This breed needs space and a lot of exercise. Regular brushing is required.
· Guard and defense dog.
· Pet.

HEAD
Massive. Broad, square skull. Broad, flat forehead. Deep stop. Broad muzzle. Very strong, bulging jaw muscles.

EYES
Large, bulging slightly and slightly out of round. Very dark color.

EARS
Short and thin. Set on high. Rose ears folded back exposing the burr.

BODY
Massive. Long, very powerful neck. Deep, cylindrical chest.

Short loin and flanks. Belly drawn up. Croup slightly higher than the withers.

LIMBS
Round, medium size, compact feet. Forelegs shorter than hind legs. Dewclaws on hind legs.

TAIL
Strong at the base and tapering to a point reaching the hocks.

COAT
Short, harsh, smooth, lying close to the skin.

COLOR
Fawn, brindle, dark striped with white markings.

SIZE
56 to 58 cm (22-23 in).

WEIGHT
Approx. 40 kg (88 lb).

Tibetan Mastiff

This Mastiff is the direct descendent of the ancient Greater Tibetan Mastiff. Originating in the high plateaus of central Asia, the breed migrated into the rest of central Asia, into Asia Minor, eastern Europe and finally central Europe. Many modern-day mastiffs are descended from this breed, which can be found on the steppes and in the foothills of the Himalayas guarding flocks and villages alike with great ferocity. This breed was much larger in the past than today's version. In fact, the Tibetan Mastiff used to be so big that Marco Polo claimed the dog was "as big as a donkey"! Almost extinct by the nineteenth century, the Tibetan Mastiff was saved by British fanciers.

Formidable. Powerful. Massive. Well constructed. Beautiful expression. Gait: Light, elastic movement. Slow, measured walk.

2B

MOUNTAIN TYPE MOLOSSIANS

Giants Breeds over 45 kg (over 100 lb)

COUNTRY OF ORIGIN
Tibet
Sponsored by Great Britain

ORIGINAL NAME
Do-Kyi (meaning "dog that can be tied up")

2

HEAD
Thick and strong. Massive skull. Pronounced stop. Square muzzle. Strong jaws. Broad nose. Thick lips.

EYES
Medium size, oval, set slightly oblique and well apart. Any shade of brown.

EARS
Medium size, drop, triangular.

BODY
Strong, with length being slightly greater than height. Strong, arched neck without dewlap and with a thick mane. Deep forechest. Moderately deep and broad brisket. Straight back. Croup almost imperceptible.

LIMBS
Strong, round, compact feet. Heavy-boned legs.

TAIL
Medium to long length, not reaching beyond the hock joint. Richly clad and curling over the back.

COAT
Fairly long, thick, straight and harsh. Never silky, curly or wavy. Dense, thick, rather wooly undercoat.

COLOR
Jet black, black and tan, brown, shades of gold or gray, gray with gold markings. Tan and gold markings above the eyes, on the lower legs and the tip of the tail. White spot on the chest is permissible. Small white markings on the feet are tolerated, though not preferred.

SIZE
Dog: approx. 66 cm (26 in).
Bitch: approx. 61 cm (24 in).

WEIGHT
55 to 80 kg
(121.5-176.5 lb).

Character, special skills and training
This rustic, hardy, even-tempered dog is affectionate, but not demonstrative and can have a stubborn streak. He is very distant with strangers and can even become aggressive. A guard dog to the core, he is particularly vigilant at night. His loud bark can strike fear in the heart of even the hardiest soul. Firm, patient training must start very early. The Tibetan Mastiff does not reach full maturity until the age of three or four and the bitch cycles only once per year.

Care and functions
This breed should not be kept as a house dog. The Tibetan Mastiff needs exercise and room to run. Weekly brushing is required.
· Flock guard.
· Guard dog. · Pet.

Fila Brasileiro

Spanish and Portuguese conquistadors brought Mastiffs, Scenthounds and Bloodhounds to Brazil in the seventeenth century. These breeds were crossed with Brazilian dogs to create the Fila Brasileiro. The Fila was originally used to track escaped slaves. Later, the breed was used as a guard and to drive cattle. The Fila Brasileiro was recognized in 1950.

Molossian type. Rectangular, compact build. Harmonious proportions. Great agility. Relaxed trot. Powerful gallop. Camel pace.

2A

MASTIFF TYPE MOLOSSIANS

2

COUNTRY OF ORIGIN
Brazil

OTHER NAMES
Brazilian Mastiff, Brazilian molosser

Giants Breeds over 45 kg (over 100 lb)

Character, special skills and training
This valiant, courageous, fiery, resolute breed can be calm, self-assured, obedient and tolerant of children. However, firm training is required to achieve these traits. The fila brasileiro is distrustful of strangers.

Care and functions
This breed does not adapt well to urban living. He needs wide open spaces and plenty of exercise.
· Cattle driver.
· Guard dog, hunting dog (large game).
· Pet.

HEAD
Large, square, capacious. Broad skull. Stop not pronounced. Strong, broad, deep muzzle. Broad nose.

EYES
Medium size, almond. Deep chestnut to yellow color. Lids are often drooping.

EARS
Large, thick, v-shaped, drop.

BODY
Strong, longer than tall. Very strong neck with dewlap. Chest broad and well let down. Thick, loose skin. Broad, long, sloping croup. Withers slightly lower than croup.

LIMBS
Legs with plenty of bone. Strong feet with arched toes. Black nails.

TAIL
Thick at the base and tapering to a point reaching the hock joint.

COAT
Short, thick, soft, lying close to the skin.

COLOR
Any solid color (except white, mouse-gray, black and tan, or blue), brindle with moderately dark streaking. With or without a black mask. White markings on the feet, chest and tip of the tail are permissible provided they cover no more than a quarter of the body.

SIZE
Dog: 65 to 75 cm (25.5 to 29.5 in). Bitch: 60 to 70 cm (23.5 to 27.5 in).

WEIGHT
Dog: at least 50 kg (110 lb). Bitch: at least 40 kg (88 lb).

Hovawart

This old breed's name comes from the German word *Hofewart*, meaning estate dog, revealing his traditional role as guard dog for German farms in the thirteenth century. His distant ancestors were probably Asian Mastiffs. Over the centuries, the breed was gradually abandoned. It wasn't until the 1920s that the breed was resurrected by crossing German Shepherds, Leonbergers, Newfoundlands and others. The breed was recognized in 1936 and established as a utility dog by the FCI in 1964. Today, the Hovawart is quite popular in Germany and Scandinavian countries.

Medium size without bulkiness. Longer than tall.

2B

MOUNTAIN TYPE MOLOSSIANS

COUNTRY OF ORIGIN
Germany

Between 10 and 45 kg (20-100 lb)

2

HEAD
Robust. Broad, arched forehead. Pronounced stop. Long muzzle. Black lips.

EYES
Dark color.

EARS
Triangular, pendulous, hanging flat against the head.

BODY
Muscular and streamlined. Powerful neck without dewlap. Broad, deep brisket. Croup slightly sloped. Straight, solid back.

LIMBS
Robust, very muscular legs. Solid, oval feet.

TAIL
Long, richly clad, reaching just below the hocks. Carried low at rest.

COAT
Long with slightly wooly undercoat. Coarse with slight wave. Short on the head and front of the legs. No streaking or curl.

COLOR
Fawn (blond) becoming lighter on the legs and abdomen. Black. Black and tan (most common) with fawn markings (above the eyes, on the chest, legs and under the root of the tail). Each of the three varieties allows one small white spot on the forechest and mixture of a few lighter colored hairs, particularly on the tip of the tail.

SIZE
Dog: 63 to 70 cm (25 to 27.5 in).
Bitch: 58 to 65 cm (23 to 25.5 in).

WEIGHT
25 to 40 kg (55 to 88 lb).

Character, special skills and training
This weatherproof, hardy, energetic dog loves to swim and is an excellent runner and jumper. He also has a keen sense of smell. The Hovawart is always on the alert, but is never aggressive without cause. This breed can fill several roles. The Hovawart is calm, even-tempered, affectionate with his owners and gentle with children. He is highly trainable, but training must be firm and undertaken with patience. He rarely barks, but when he does, his bark is loud, deep and resonant. This breed reaches full maturity around two years of age.

Care and functions
While this dog can adapt to city living, he needs exercise and room to run. Weekly brushing is sufficient to maintain the coat.
· Flock guard.
· Utility dog: rescue (avalanches), tracker (drugs), guide dog.
· Guard dog.
· Pet.

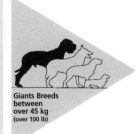

Large. Robust. Harmonious proportions.
Longer legs and more powerfully built
than the Newfoundland.

Landseer

Bred from the Newfoundland, the Landseer
was named after the artist Sir Edwin Landseer who depicted
the breed in paintings around 1837. He has been wrongly
considered a black and white version of the Newfoundland, a
variety British and Americans called the Landseer
Newfoundland. The breed almost disappeared in the early
twentieth century, but was saved by German breeders
who introduced mountain dog blood, including that of the
Great Pyrenees. In 1960, the FCI recognized the Landseer
as a separate breed, distinct from the Newfoundland.

2B

**MOUNTAIN TYPE
MOLOSSIANS**

2

COUNTRY OF ORIGIN
Germany

Giants Breeds
between
over 45 kg
(over 100 lb)

· Hunting dog.
· Rescue dog.
· Guard dog.
· Pet.

**Character, special
skills and training**
This alert, courageous dog
loves the water. He is affectionate and gentle.

Care and functions
This breed does not like to be
closed in. He needs exercise
and room to run. Daily brushing is required.

HEAD
Broad and massive. Skin on
the head is not wrinkled.
Covered with short, fine
hairs. Distinct stop, but less
pronounced than that of the
St. Bernard. Firm flews.

EYES
Medium size. Brown to dark
brown color.

EARS
Medium size, triangular, set
on close to the eyes and
hanging close against the
head. Covered with short,
fine hairs.

BODY
Powerful. Muscular neck.
Deep, broad brisket. Ribs
well sprung. Straight, broad,
robust back. Broad, rounded
croup.

LIMBS
Round feet. Muscular legs
with substantial bone.

TAIL
Strong, bushy, carried down
and reaching the hocks.

COAT
Long, smooth, fine to the
touch, the thicker the better.
Undercoat is not as thick as
that of the Newfoundland.

COLOR
Clear white with distinct
black spots on the body and
croup. The neck, forechest,
underbelly, legs and tail
must be white. The head is
black with a white muzzle.

SIZE
Dog: 72 to 80 cm (28-31.5 in).
Bitch: 67 to 72 cm (26.5-28 in).

WEIGHT
50 to 70 kg (110-154 lb).

Leonberger

This breed is named after a town in Wurtemberg, Germany where it is thought to have existed for many years, or perhaps after the town of Löwenberg in Switzerland. Some experts believe it is descended from the Tibetan Mastiff, while others believe that H. Essig, from the town of Leonberg, crossed Newfoundlands, St. Bernards and Great Pyrenees in 1846. However, it is more likely that this breed is the last descendant of the Greater Swiss Mountain Dog, a breed distinct from the St. Bernard. The first standard was established in 1895 and the FCI established a standard in 1973.

Well proportioned. Powerfully built. Elegant. Light-footed.

2B

MOUNTAIN TYPE MOLOSSIANS

COUNTRY OF ORIGIN
Germany

ORIGINAL NAME
Leonberger

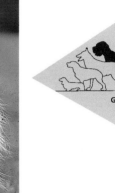

Giants Breeds between over 45 kg (over 100 lb)

2

HEAD
Fairly narrow, longer than wide. Moderately domed skull. Moderate stop. Slightly aquiline nose bridge (like that of a ram). The muzzle is never pointed. Black, tight lips.

EYES
Medium size. Light to dark brown color.

EARS
Set on high, drop, falling flat against the head.

BODY
Slightly longer than tall. Powerful neck. Deep chest. Robust loin. Strong back.

LIMBS
Strong, muscular legs with plenty of bone. Rounded feet with compact toes and black pads.

TAIL
Very richly clad (brush). Carried half down, never too high or curled over the back.

COAT
Medium fine to coarse, thick, long, smooth, lying close to the skin. Presence of undercoat. Beautiful mane on the neck and forechest.

COLOR
Lion-colored: fawn, gold yellow or reddish-brown with black mask. A small white spot on the forechest is permissible. Sable with a black overlay is also permissible. The collarettes, trousers (feathering on the back of the legs), culottes and feathering on the tail may be lighter in color than the rest of the coat.

SIZE
Dog: 72 to 80 cm (28-31.5 in).
Bitch: 65 to 75 cm (26-30 in).

WEIGHT
60 to 80 kg
(132-176 lb).

Character, special skills and training
The "weatherproof" Leonberger an excellent swimmer. He is lively, calm and self-assured. He will only bark to warn of danger. This breed is loyal, docile, very loving with his owner and extremely gentle with children. Though he can appear formidable indeed to strangers, he generally will not bite. Due to his size, early training is required to teach this dog to be gentle. The Leonberger reaches full maturity at the age of three.

Care and functions
The Leonberger needs exercise and room to run. He does not like to be tied up or left alone. Weekly brushing is sufficient, except during the twice-yearly seasonal shedding, when more frequent brushing is required.
· Flock guard.
· Rescue dog (mountain rescues and drowning accidents).
· Pet.

Mastiff

The Mastiff, which is of British origin, is descended from Assyrian mastiffs (descended from the Tibetan Mastiff imported to Europe by the Phoenicians), through the Roman Molossus. Originally bred as a fighting dog, the Mastiff later was used as a guard dog for English Seigneurs' herds and estates and as a hunting dog for large game. This breed was given the name Mastiff toward the end of the fourteenth century. The first Old English Mastiff standard was published in 1883. During World War II, this mighty breed almost disappeared, but was saved and restored from a few remaining Mastiffs that were imported into the United States.

2A

MASTIFF TYPE MOLOSSIANS

2

COUNTRY OF ORIGIN
Great Britain

OTHER NAME
Old English Mastiff

Massive. Powerful. Well-balanced proportions. Well constructed. A combination of grandeur and courage.

Giants Breeds
over 45 kg
(over 100 lb)

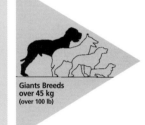

Character, special skills and training

This peaceable, gentle dog is affectionate with his owner and children. Courageous and not easily swayed, he is a guard dog through and through. This breed requires rigorous training because he can present a danger to strangers.

Care and functions
The Mastiff needs a lot of space and exercise. Regular brushing is required.
· Guard dog.
· Pet.

HEAD
Square. Broad skull. Flat forehead with distinct wrinkles when at attention. Pronounced stop. Short, blunt muzzle (squarish). Slightly pendulous flews.

EYES
Small, set wide apart. Hazel color (the darker the better).

EARS
Small, thin, wide set and set on high. Hang flat against the cheeks.

BODY
Massive, broad and tall. Slightly arched, very muscular neck. Ribs well sprung.

Broad, muscular back and loin. Deep flanks. Broad, well let down chest.

LIMBS
Large, round feet with arched toes and black nails. Heavy boned legs set wide apart.

TAIL
Set high. Broad at the root and tapering toward the tip. Carried straight down at rest and hanging to the hock joint.

COAT
Short, lying very close to the body. Not too fine on the shoulders, neck and back.

COLOR
Fawn, apricot, silvery fawn or fawn-brindle. All have black mask, ears and nose. Eyes surrounded by black.

SIZE
Dog: 75 to 82 cm (29.5-32 in).
Bitch: at least 66 cm (26 in).

WEIGHT
70 to 90 kg
(154-198 lb).

Spanish Mastiff

Developed in Extremadura in southwestern Spain, the Spanish Mastiff is possibly descended from the Mastiff and Roman Molossus. In the past, this breed was used for dog fighting, in war and for hunting boar and other large game.

Tall. Very large. Balanced proportions. Solid construction. Very powerful and muscular. Compact bone structure. Thick, pink skin with darkly pigmented areas.
Preferred gait: Trot.

2B

MOUNTAIN TYPE MOLOSSIANS

Giants Breeds over 45 kg (over 100 lb)

COUNTRY OF ORIGIN
Spain

ORIGINAL NAME
Mastin Español

OTHER NAMES
Mastin de Extremadura
Mastin de Leon
Mastin de la Mancha

2

HEAD
Solid, massive, size in proportion to the body. Moderately domed skull. Stop not pronounced. Rectangular muzzle. Large nose.

EYES
Small, almond. Dark color preferred (hazel). Black rims.

EARS
Medium size, triangular, drop, hanging against the cheeks.

BODY
Massive, elongated (longer than tall). Solid, tapered neck. Thick, double dewlap.

Withers slightly pronounced. Deep, broad brisket. Ribs well sprung. Long, broad loin. Broad, sloped croup. Powerful, muscular back.

LIMBS
Powerful, muscular legs. Dewclaws sometimes present on hind legs. Round cat feet with compact toes.

TAIL
Thick at the root and tapering to the tip. Hair on the tail is longer than on the rest of the body. Carried low at rest, reaching the hocks.

COAT
Heavy, thick, moderately

long, smooth. Shorter on the legs.

COLOR
Any color. Solid colors are preferred: yellow, fawn, red, black, wolf gray and piebald.

SIZE
Dog: at least 77 cm (30 in).
Bitch: at least 72 cm (28 in).

WEIGHT
50 to 65 kg (110-143.5 lb).

Character, special skills and training
This rustic, lively, self-confident breed has a noble bearing. He is calm, affectionate, gentle with children and forms a close bond with his owner. The Spanish Mastiff holds his ground with predators and strangers. His bark is deep, resonant, husky and powerful.

Care and functions
The Spanish Mastiff needs a lot of exercise and room to run. Regular brushing is required.
· Flock guard.
· Hunting dog (boar).
· Guard and defense dog.
· Pet.

Heavy. Massive. Noble. Majestic.
Thick, abundant, loose skin.
Gait: walk is slow and bearlike. Rarely gallops.

Neapolitan Mastiff

The Neapolitan Mastiff is descended from the Tibetan Mastiff through the large Roman Molossus described by agronomist Columella in the first century. This breed fought with the Roman legions and was spread throughout Europe during the Roman invasions. The Neapolitan Mastiff has also been used as a circus dog. This breed was the progenitor of many mastiff breeds in other European countries. The breed survived for many centuries. Spanish Mastiff blood was later introduced. The breed has been selectively bred since 1947.

2A

MASTIFF TYPE MOLOSSIANS

2

COUNTRY OF ORIGIN
Italy

ORIGINAL NAME
Mastino Napoletano

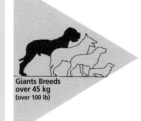

Giants Breeds
over 45 kg
(over 100 lb)

Character, special skills and training
This calm, loyal, devoted dog is very affectionate with his owners and gentle with children. Dominant with other dogs, he is courageous and suspicious of strangers. This breed is not aggressive and will not bite without cause. Formidable in appearance, he is even more fearsome if provoked. Early, firm training is vital. The Neapolitan Mastiff should not be trained to attack, because he could become overly aggressive and dangerous.

Care and functions
This breed needs wide open spaces and a lot of exercise. The Neapolitan Mastiff should not be allowed to sleep on hard surfaces or unsightly calluses may form on his elbows and knees. Regular brushing is required. Special attention should be given to the folds in the skin and drooping eyelids.
· Guard dog.
· Police dog.
· Pet.

HEAD
Short, massive, imposing. Broad, flat skull. Loose skin with wrinkles and folds. Pronounced stop. Broad, deep muzzle. Powerful jaws. Large nose. Thick, fleshy, pendulous lips.

EYES
Wide set, round, of a darker color than that of the coat.

EARS
Small, triangular, flat, lying against the cheeks. If cropped, they are the shape of an equilateral triangle.

BODY
Massive, longer than tall. Tapered neck with double dewlap. Broad withers (not pronounced). Large brisket. Ribs well sprung. Broad back. Broad, powerful, sloping croup.

LIMBS
Heavy boned legs. Round, large feet with arched, compact toes.

TAIL
Broad and thick at the root, tapering slightly toward the tip. If left natural, tail hangs down reaching the hock joint. Typically, one-third of the tail is removed.

COAT
Short, harsh, hard, thick and smooth (maximum length (1.5 cm) (0.6 in).

COLOR
Preferred colors: gray, lead gray and black, brown, fawn, stag-red, sometimes with small white spots on the chest and feet. All colors may be brindle.

SIZE
Dog: 65 to 75 cm (25.5-29.5 in).

Bitch: 60 to 68 cm (23.5-27 in).

WEIGHT
Dog: 50 to 70 kg (110 to 154 lb).
Bitch: 50 to 60 kg (110 to 132 lb).

Pyrenean Mastiff

The Pyrenean Mastiff was developed on the southern slopes of the Pyrenees Mountains in Spain. It is not to be confused with a closely related French breed, the Great Pyrenees. Some experts believe the Pyrenean Mastiff is the product of a cross between the Great Pyrenees and the Spanish Mastiff. Over the centuries, they guarded flocks during the Transhumante, the formal mass migration of the flocks up and down the mountainside with the change of the seasons. The breed was recognized in the late nineteenth century.

Tall. Massive proportions. Balanced construction. Balanced proportions. Very powerful and muscular. Compact skeleton. Thick, pink skin with spots of darker pigmentation.

Giants Breeds over 45 kg (over 100 lb)

2B

MOUNTAIN TYPE MOLOSSIANS

COUNTRY OF ORIGIN
Spain

ORIGINAL NAME
Perro Mastin de los Pirineos

OTHER NAMES
Mastin d'Aragon
Mastin de Navarre

2

WEIGHT
55 to 70 kg
(121-154 lb).

HEAD
Large and solid. Broad, slightly rounded skull. Stop not pronounced. Rectangular muzzle tapering toward the large nose.

EYES
Small, almond. Hazel, preferably dark, color. Black rims. Mild droop of lower lid slightly revealing the conjunctiva.

EARS
Medium size, triangular, dropping flat against the cheeks.

BODY
Slightly longer than tall. Very strong and robust. Tapering neck with double dewlap. Withers slightly pronounced. Broad, deep brisket. Ribs well sprung. Belly moderately tucked up.

Powerful, muscular back. Broad, solid, sloped croup.

LIMBS
Round, compact cat feet with arched toes. Muscular legs.

TAIL
Thick at the root, supple, richly clad with fur (plume). Carried low at rest reaching the hocks, with the last third always curving up.

COAT
Stiff, thick, dense. Moderate length (6 to 9 cm) (2,4-3,5 in). Longer on the shoulders, neck, underbelly and back of the legs.

COLOR
White with a well-defined mask. Sometimes the body has distinct markings of the same color as the mask. Ears are always dark. Tri-colors and solid white coats not preferred. Tip of the tail and feet must be white. Mask clearly visible, with a light-colored back-ground. Preferred colors are white (solid white or snow white with medium gray or bright golden yellow markings), brown, black, silvery gray, light beige, yellowish sable, mottled.

SIZE
Dog: at least 77 cm (30 in).
Bitch: at least 72 cm (28 in).

Character, special skills and training
This breed is affectionate and calm and has a noble bearing. But he is also courageous and can be formidable with strangers, never backing down if property, owner, or animals under his charge are threatened. The Great Pyrenean has a deep, loud bark. His temperament is benign with other dogs. Firm training should start early.

Care and functions
This dog is not made for city living. He does not like to be closed in. Brushing once or twice per week is required.
· Flock guard.
· Guard and defense dog.
· Pet.

Rafeiro do Alentejo

The Rafeiro do Alentejo was developed from local breeds
in the Alentejo region, an area in southern Portugal with a continental climate.
A good herder, this breed is now used as a flock guard.
The Rafeiro do Alentejo is the largest dog of its type in Portugal.

Large. Strong. Long back. Massive head.

2B

MOUNTAIN TYPE MOLOSSIANS

2

COUNTRY OF ORIGIN
Portugal

ORIGINAL NAME
Rafeiro do Alentejo

Large Breeds
between
25 and 45 kg
(55-100 lb)

Character, special skills and training
This rustic, powerful, hard-working dog is courageous and dedicated. He is loyal and affectionate
with his owner. The Rafeiro do Alentejo is aggressive
toward strangers, as with predators. Firm training is
required.

Care and functions
This dog is not suited to city living. He needs exercise
and room to run. Weekly brushing is sufficient.
· Flock guard.
· Guard and defense dog.
· Pet.

HEAD
Bearlike. Broad, domed
skull. Slight stop. Domed
nose bridge. Strong jaws.
Oval nose. Thin lips.

EYES
Small, oval. Dark color.
Dark rims.

EARS
Small, folded, triangular,
drop.

BODY
Strong and long. Strong,
short neck. Deep, broad
chest. Broad loin. Straight

back. Broad, slightly sloped
croup.

LIMBS
Strong, compact feet with
long toes

TAIL
Long, thick, carried down
and curving slightly.

COAT
Short or medium length
(preferred), smooth, coarse
and thick.

COLOR
Black, wolf gray, fawn or
yellow, with or without

white; or white with spots,
stripes or brindle.

SIZE
Dog: 66 to 74 cm (26-29 in).
Bitch: 64 to 70 cm (25 to
27.5 in).

WEIGHT
Dog: 40 to 50 kg
(88 to 110,5 lb).
Bitch: 35 to 45 kg
(77-99 lb).

Rottweiler

Some writers believe this very German dog is descended from the Bavarois Bouvier. Others contest that it is descended from Roman Molosser dogs brought to Germany during the Roman invasions. By the Middle Ages, this powerful, courageous dog was already guarding the herd and defending cattle merchants against bandits in the village of Rottweil in Wurtemberg, Germany. Butchers commonly kept this dog and as a result, the breed became known as the "butcher dog". The first Rottweiler club was formed in 1907. During World War I, the Rottweiler served in the German army. The breed was officially recognized in 1966 and it became well-known worldwide around 1970.

Compact. Powerful. Harmonious proportions. Power and agility. Gait: Trot.

2A

MASTIFF TYPE MOLOSSIANS

COUNTRY OF ORIGIN
Germany

ORIGINAL NAME
Rottweiler

OTHER NAMES
Rottweiler Metzgerhund
(Butcher dog)
Rottie

Giants Breeds
over 45 kg
(over 100 lb)

2

touch, dense and lying flat. Presence of undercoat.

COLOR
Black with distinct tan markings on the cheeks, above the eyes, on the muzzle, on the underside of the neck, on the forechest, legs and under the root of the tail.

SIZE
Dog: 61 to 68 cm
(24 to 27 in).
Bitch: 56 to 63 cm
(22 to 25 in).

WEIGHT
Dog: approx. 50 kg (110 lb).
Bitch: approx. 42 kg (93 lb).

HEAD
Strong. Broad, moderately convex skull. Pronounced stop. Rectangular nose bridge. Large nose. Powerful jaws. Black, tight lips.

EYES
Medium size, almond. Dark brown color.

EARS
Set on high, medium size, triangular, very wide set. Drop, hanging forward tightly against the head.

BODY
Compact. Powerful neck

without loose skin (no dewlap). Well pronounced forechest. Roomy chest. Ribs well sprung. Short loin. Straight, powerful back. Broad, slightly rounded croup.

LIMBS
Round feet with arched, compact toes and black nails. Muscular legs.

TAIL
Docked (to one or two vertebrae) or natural.

COAT
Medium length, coarse to the

Character, special skills and training
Exhibiting great endurance, the Rottweiler is hardy, well-balanced and peaceable, though he has a very strong personality and is an alpha dog to the core (particularly the male). He must give the appearance of contained power. He never barks without cause. The Rottweiler forms a strong bond and is devoted to his owner and patient with children. This fearless dog is an excellent guard dog, particularly with his menacing appearance. The Rottweiler may exhibit aggressiveness toward strangers. Early, very firm (but gentle) training is required to ensure that this dog will obey without fail. The Rottweiler reflects the personality of his owner. If treated cruelly, he can develop into a ferocious weapon.

Care and functions
The Rottweiler requires considerable space and exercise. He does not like to be closed in or tied up. This breed does not tolerate heat well. Daily brushing is required.
· Guard dog.
· Police and army dog.

Heavy. Powerful. Harmonious proportions.

St. Bernard

The St. Bernard is thought to be descended from ancient Molosser dogs that crossed the Alps with the Roman legions. This breed's roots can be traced to Switzerland where monks at the Grand Saint Bernard Hospice (founded in the Middle Ages) developed the breed around the twelfth century. The St. Bernard quickly developed a reputation as a mountain rescue dog. The most famous St. Bernard in history, Barry, born in 1800, saved forty people over a period of ten years. Prior to 1830, St. Bernards had short coats. They were later crossed with the Newfoundland and the long-haired variety was created. It is the long-haired variety that is now most common. Called at different times in history the Mountain Dog, the Alpine Mastiff and the Barry Dog, this breed was officially recognized as the St. Bernard in 1880. The Swiss St. Bernard club was formed in Basel in 1884, and the St. Bernard's standard was fixed in Bern as of 1887.

2B

MOUNTAIN TYPE MOLOSSIANS

2

COUNTRY OF ORIGIN
Switzerland

ORIGINAL NAME
Bernhardiner

Giants Breeds
over 45 kg
(over 100 lb)

Character, special skills and training
This tranquil, calm, gentle, friendly dog is very sociable, devoted to his owners and adores children. Wary around strangers, the St. Bernard can be aggressive if the situation warrants. Firm training is required.

Care and functions
This breed requires considerable space and long walks every day. Energetic daily brushing is required. The St. Bernard does not tolerate heat well.
· Guard dog.
· Mountain rescue dog.
· Pet.

HEAD
Powerful and imposing. Broad, slightly domed skull. Straight nose bridge. Short muzzle. Large nose.

EYES
Fairly large. Dark brown color. Dark rims.

EARS
Medium size, set on high, triangular, drop.

BODY
Imposing. Powerful neck. Withers strongly pronounced. Ribs well sprung. Broad back.

LIMBS
Well-developed hindquarters with powerful, muscu-larthigs. Large, straight, compact, solid feet with high knuckles. Dewclaws are permissible on the back legs.

TAIL
Long, heavy, hanging down and reaching the hocks.

COAT
Two varieties:
- Short-haired: Dense, tough, lying smooth; abundant undercoat.
- Long-haired: Straight. Breeching, feathering, bushy tail. Short on the face and ears. Abundant undercoat.

COLOR
White with moderately large reddish-brown markings.

Reddish-brown brindle is permissible. Dark shadings on the head are favored.

SIZE
Dog: at least 70 cm (27.5 in).
Bitch: at least 65 cm (25.5 in).

WEIGHT
55 to 100 kg (121.5 to 221 lb).

Newfoundland

Experts speculate that this breed may be descended from the Scandinavian "bear dogs" brought over from Norway in the sixteenth century, or perhaps from the Labrador, or Molosser dogs introduced by the Vikings, or the Leonberger, or the St. Bernard, or the Great Pyrenees introduced by Basque fisherman. In reality, it is not know how the ancestors of the Newfoundland found their way to Newfoundland in Canada. In the nineteenth century, French cod fisherman brought the Newfoundland to France. In England, the breed was lauded by Byron and immortalized in Landseer's paintings.

Noble. Majestic. Powerful. Massive bone structure. Relaxed, slightly rolling gait.

Giants Breeds over 45 kg (over 100 lb)

2B
MOUNTAIN TYPE MOLOSSIANS

COUNTRY OF ORIGIN
Canada – Newfoundland Scandinavian Countries Great Britain, etc.

OTHER NAME
Newfie

2

HEAD
Broad and massive. Stop not too pronounced. Short, rather squarish muzzle.

EYES
Small and wide set. Dark brown color.

EARS
Small, lying close to the head.

BODY
Massive. Strong neck. Chest well let down. Broad back. Strong, muscular loin.

LIMBS
Large, webbed feet.

TAIL
Thick at the root. Moderately long, reaching slightly past the hocks and carried down forming a slight curve.

COAT
Long, straight, coarse. Oily feel, water-resistant. Feathering on the legs. Soft, wooly undercoat.

COLOR
Acceptable colors: black (dull jet black), brown (chocolate or bronze), Landseer (British-American type, only black and white permissible).

SIZE
Dog: average of 71 cm (28 in).
Bitch: average of 66 cm (26 in).

WEIGHT
Dog: 64 to 69 kg (141 to 152 lb).
Bitch: 50 to 54.5 kg (110-120 lb).

Character, special skills and training
This gentle, friendly, extraordinarily loyal dog is even-tempered and affectionate. He loves children. While his appearance may be formidable, the Newfoundland is not a guard dog. By instinct, he is a rescue dog. Because of his willingness to dive into the water and swim for hours to save a drowning victim, he has been called the "St. Bernard of the sea." Training must be firm, but under-taken with patience because this gentle giant does not reach emotional maturity until two years of age.

Care and functions
The Newfoundland can adapt to life as a housedog provided he is not left alone too often. He needs room to romp. This breed does not tolerate heat well. Brushing twice per week is sufficient.
· Water rescue dog.
. Pet.

Large. Robust conformation.
Imposing bearing. Energetic, powerful gait.

Tosa

*This Japanese fighting dog was developed
in the late nineteenth and early twentieth centuries.
The breed was created by crossing the native Kochi,
the Bull Terrier, the Bulldog, the Great Dane
and the Saint Bernard, creating a truly imposing specimen.*

2A

**MASTIFF TYPE
MOLOSSIANS**

2

COUNTRY OF ORIGIN
Japan

OTHER NAME
Tosa Inu

Giants Breeds
over 45 kg
(over 100 lb)

Character, special skills and training
This breed is remarkably patient, calm, courageous and bold. The Tosa forms a strong bond with his owners but is distrustful of strangers. He can be a formidable adversary if necessary. Firm training is required.

Care and functions
Brushing once per week is required. This breed needs space and exercise.
· Guard dog.
· Pet.

HEAD
Strong. Broad skull. Fairly abrupt stop. Straight nose bridge. Square muzzle. Solid jaws. Large nose.

EYES
Moderately small. Dark brown color.

EARS
Relatively small, thin, set on high, falling along the cheeks.

BODY
Powerful. Muscular neck

with dewlap. Elevated withers. Deep, broad chest. Broad, muscular loin. Belly well tucked up. Straight back.

LIMBS
Solid legs. Slightly arched loin. Compact feet. Hard, dark nails.

TAIL
Set high. Strong at the root tapering toward the tip. Carried low reaching the hock joint.

COLOR
Solid red is preferred. All shades of fawn permissible. White and red markings are tolerated.

SIZE
Dog: at least 60.5 cm (24 in).
Bitch: at least 54.5 cm (22 in).

WEIGHT
Approx. 40 kg (88 lb).

Appenzeller

*Originating in Appenzell canton in eastern Switzerland,
the Appenzeller was first described in an early work as a
"quite vocal, multi-colored, short-haired drover of medium size".
The breed is thought to be descended from Tibetan Molosser dogs
and Nordic breeds. The Appenzeller was established as
a distinct breed in 1898. Max Siever, a great promoter
of the Appenzeller, worked on the first standard for the breed.
The Swiss Appenzeller club was created in 1906.
The breed is rare outside of its native Switzerland.*

Compact. Balanced proportions.
Not massive. Gait: Long strides.

3

**MOUNTAIN TYPE
MOLOSSIANS**

Medium Breeds
between
10 and 25 kg
(20-55 lb)

2

COUNTRY OF ORIGIN
Switzerland

ORIGINAL NAME
Appenzeller Sennenhund

OTHER NAME
Appenzell Mountain Dog

HEAD
Slightly wedge-shaped. Stop not pronounced. Rectangular nose bridge. Black or brown nose. Tight lips.

EYES
Small, almond. Dark brown to chestnut color.

EARS
Set on high, triangular, drop, lying against the head.

BODY
Robust, compact. Strong, dry neck. Broad chest is well let down. Prominent forechest. Belly slightly tucked up.

Muscular legs. Short croup.

LIMBS
Straight, solid back. Short, well-arched, compact feet.

TAIL
Set high, strong, moderately long, bushy. In action, carried curled over the croup, falling to the side or along the midline.

COAT
Short, thick, lying close to the skin. Thick undercoat.

COLOR
Black or tan background

with symmetrical tan or white markings. Tan markings above the eyes and on the cheeks, forechest and legs. White flare, white patch from chin to forechest. White markings on the feet and tip of the tail.

SIZE
Dog: 50 to 58 cm (20-23 in).
Bitch: 48 to 56 cm (19-22 in).

WEIGHT
22 to 25 kg (49-55 lb).

Caracter, special skills and training
This courageous, robust, self-confident dog is energetic and has a lively temperament. The Appenzeller fills many roles. This affectionate, gentle breed makes a good pet. Wary of strangers and possessing the defense instinct, he is also a good guard dog. The breed is also used as a draft dog and rescue dog.

Care and functions
The Appenzeller is not suited to city living. He needs a lot of exercise and room to run. Regular brushing is required.

· Herder (rounds up cattle).
· Draft dog (pulls milk carts).
· Utility dog: (rescue: avalanches, earthquakes, etc.).
· Guard dog.
· Pet.

107

Powerful. Supple. Balanced proportions.

3

**MOUNTAIN TYPE
MOLOSSIANS**

2

COUNTRY OF ORIGIN
Switzerland

ORIGINAL NAME
Berner Sennenhund

Giants Breeds
over 45 kg
(over 100 lb)

Bernese Mountain Dog

This ancient breed was developed near Bern, primarily in Duerrbach and Burgdorf. The Bernese Mountain Dog is descended from the Roman molussus fighting dog brought with the Roman legions and later used to guard the flock. This breed began appearing in dog shows in 1902 and a standard was published in 1907. In 1949, Newfoundland blood was introduced. The Bernese Mountain Dog is now the most common of the Swiss mountain dogs. In 1990, the Bernese Mountain Dog was crossed with the Labrador, creating the still experimental Boulab.

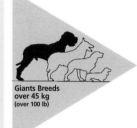

Character, special skills and training
This hardy, well-balanced, peaceable dog naturally has a sweet, happy temperament. He is loyal and affectionate with his owners, but is wary around strangers and will courageously defend his owners and their property if necessary, though he is not aggressive and does not bark often. This breed despises being left alone. Firm, but gentle, training must be undertaken with patience because the breed does not reach emotional maturity until eighteen months to two years of age.

Care and functions
The Bernese Mountain Dog does not like to be locked up in a house. He loves wide open spaces and exercise. Weekly brushing is sufficient.
· Herder (large animals).
· Guard dog, police dog, draft dog (light carts).
· Pet.

HEAD
Powerful. Slightly domed skull. Well-defined stop.

EYES
Almond shape. Dark brown color.

EARS
Set on high, triangular, drop when at rest.

BODY
Thickset. Broad chest is well let down. Belly not tucked up. Straight, solid back. Slightly rounded croup.

LIMBS
Short, rounded, compact feet. Strong legs with substantial bone.

TAIL
Bushy, carried low at rest.

COAT
Long, straight or slightly wavy.

COLOR
Tri-color. Black background with tan (rich rust) markings on the checks, above the eyes and on the legs and chest. White markings on the head (flare), on the neck extending down the forechest, on the feet and tip of the tail.

SIZE
Dog: 64 to 70 cm (25-27.5 in).
Bitch: 58 to 66 cm (23-26 in).

WEIGHT
40 to 50 kg (88-110 lb).

Entelbucher

This small Swiss mountain dog is closely related to the Appenzeller. He is named after the region where he originated, Entlebuch in the canton of Lucerne. Bred to guard and drive cattle, the Entelbucher was very popular in the past. The breed almost disappeared, but then began a comeback in 1913.

Well proportioned. Agile. Harmonious construction. Friendly expression.

3

MOUNTAIN TYPE MOLOSSIANS

COUNTRY OF ORIGIN
Switzerland

ORIGINAL NAME
Entlebucher Sennenhund

2

Medium Breeds between 10 and 25 kg (20-55 lb)

HEAD
Well proportioned. Flat forehead. Slight stop. Powerful jaws.

EYES
Fairly small. Brown color. Lively expression.

EARS
Set on high, not overly large, hanging flat against the head. Tip of ear well rounded.

BODY
Slightly longer than tall.

Short, compact neck. Broad, deep chest. Strong legs. Strong, straight back.

LIMBS
Strong, compact feet. Dewclaws not desireable.

TAIL
Docked at birth.

COAT
Short, thick, hard, shiny, lying close to the skin.

COLOR
Black with markings ranging from yellow to rust above the eyes, on the cheeks and on all four legs. Symmetrical markings on the head (flare), neck, forechest and feet. Yellow to rust markings must always appear between the black and white.

SIZE
Dog: 40 to 50 cm (16-20 in).

WEIGHT
15 to 25 kg (33-55 lb).

Character, special skills and training
This robust, agile, stable dog is an excellent guard, both of cattle and its owner's property. The friendly Entelbucher also makes an excellent pet. The breed is used to transport milk and cheese. Naturally good tempered, the Entelbucher is easy to train.

Care and functions
This breed needs exercise and room to run. Regular brushing is required.
· Cattle drover.
· Guard dog.
· Pet.

Greater Swiss Mountain Dog

The ancestors of the Greater Swiss Mountain Dog are the powerful tri-color dogs referred to as "butcher mastiffs." In the latter Middle Ages, this breed went to battle with Swiss soldiers. In 1908, two "Short-haired Bernese Mountain Dogs" were exhibited at a show. Dr. Albert Heim was present at the show and recognized them as survivors of the large butcher mastiffs that were on the verge of extinction. In 1909, the Swiss registry recognized the variety as a distinct breed. The Swiss Greater Swiss Mountain Dog club, created in 1912, implemented a breeding program to restore the breed. The standard for the Greater Swiss Mountain Dog was published for the first time by the FCI in 1939.

Robust. Sturdy skeletal structure. Extremely muscular. Agile. Long stride.

3

MOUNTAIN MOLOSSIANS

2

COUNTRY OF ORIGIN
Switzerland

ORIGINAL NAME
Grosser Schweizersennenhund

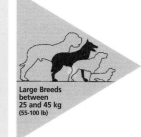

Large Breeds between 25 and 45 kg (55-100 lb)

Character, special skills and training
This attentive, alert dog has remarkable endurance. He is easy to train and serves many purposes, such as guard dog protecting cattle, farms and homes, draft dog and rescue dog searching out victims buried in avalanches. As a pet, he is loyal and gentle and very fond of children.

Care and functions
The Greater Swiss Mountain Dog is not suitable as a house dog. He needs a lot of exercise and room to run. Regular brushing is required.
· Cattle drover.
· Draft dog.
· Guard dog.
· Rescue dog.
· Pet.

HEAD
Powerful without bulkiness. Broad, flat skull. Stop not pronounced. Powerful muzzle. Black lips.

EYES
Medium size, almond shape. Hazelnut or chestnut color.

EARS
Medium size, set on moderately high, triangular, hanging flat against the cheeks.

BODY
Powerful but not massive. Powerful, thick neck without dewlap. Broad, well let down chest. Broad forechest. Belly and flanks slightly tucked up. Long, broad croup. Straight, solid back.

LIMBS
Solid legs. Solid, compact feet with arched toes.

TAIL
Thick, hanging down and reaching the hocks at rest.

COAT
Medium length, dense. Thick undercoat.

COLOR
Black background with symmetrical rich rust and white markings. Rust markings between the black and white markings on the cheeks, above the eyes, inside the ears, on each side of the chest, on all four legs and under the tail. White blaze and muzzle; white markings on forechest, feet and tip of the tail.

SIZE
Dog: 65 to 72 cm (25.5-28 in).
Bitch: 60 to 68 cm (23.5-27 in).

WEIGHT
Dog: approx. 40 kg (88 lb).
Bitch: approx. 35 kg (77 lb).

Group

3

Scottish Terrier

Airedale Terrier

The Airedale Terrier, "King of Terriers", was created around 1850 by breeders in Yorkshire in the valley of Aire who crossed the Otterhound with the Old English Black and Tan Terrier (now extinct). The goal was to produce a dog capable of hunting otter and rodents. The Airedale Terrier was recognized by The Kennel Club in 1886. During World War I, the breed was enlisted as a messenger, attack dog and sentinel.

Muscular. Powerful. Cobby. Noble gait.

1

MEDIUM AND LARGE TERRIERS

3

COUNTRY OF ORIGIN
Great Britain

OTHER NAMES
Working Terrier
Waterside Terrier
Bingley Terrier

Medium Breeds
between
10 and 25 kg
(20-55 lb)

Character, special skills and training
This rustic breed is strong, energetic and full of life. Possessing legendary courage, the speedy Airedale Terrier is always on the alert. He forms a close bond with his owner and is gentle with children. The breed can be dominant, even aggressive with other dogs. The Airedale Terrier has many skills. He is a strong swimmer and is used to hunt ducks and otter as well as boar and deer. He will also valiantly protect his owner and his property. As a working dog, this breed serves in the army and works with police as well as search and rescue teams.

Care and functions
If the Airedale Terrier is to be kept as a house dog, he must have long walks every day. Brushing two times per week is required. This breed should be professionally groomed three times per year.
· Hunting dog, ratter.
· Guard dog.
· Utility dog: police dog, tracker, guide dog, army dog.
· Pet.

HEAD
Well proportioned, without wrinkles. Long, flat skull. Stop hardly visible. Flat cheeks. Powerful jaws. Tight lips.

EYES
Small, dark color. Very lively expression.

EARS
Small, v-shaped, carried to the side of the head. Topline of folded ear should be slightly above level of the skull.

BODY
Must not be too long. Muscular neck without dewlap. Chest well let down. Ribs well sprung. Muscular loin.

LIMBS
Small, round, compact feet with moderately arched toes. Short, strong, straight back. Muscular legs with plenty of bone.

TAIL
Set high, carried gaily, but not curled over the back. Typically docked.

COAT
Hard, dense, wiry, not so long as to appear shaggy. Hair is straight, dense and lies close to the skin. Undercoat is shorter and softer.

COLOR
Saddle and top of the neck and tail are black or grizzle. All other areas are tan. Ears are often darker tan and a black mixture is often found around the neck and sides of the head. Some white hairs on the front feet are permissible.

SIZE
Dog: approx. 58 to 61 cm (23-24 in).
Bitch: approx. 56 to 59 cm (22-23 in).

WEIGHT
Approx. 20 kg (44 lb).

Bedlington Terrier

The Bedlington Terrier was developed in England in the thirteenth century in Bedlington, a small village near Rothbury in Northumberland. Its ancestors include the Dandie Dinmont Terrier, the Otterhound and the Whippet. This breed was first used to hunt vermin and fox. Later, they worked in the mines clearing rats from the galleries. The Bedlington Terrier was recognized by The Kennel Club in 1873.

Strongly constructed. Arched head like that of a sheep. Graceful. Supple. Muscular. Capable of galloping at great speed.

1

MEDIUM AND LARGE TERRIERS

COUNTRY OF ORIGIN
Great Britain

OTHER NAME
Rothbury Terrier

3

Small Breeds under 10 kg (under 20 lb)

HEAD
Pear-shaped or wedge-shaped. Narrow, deep and rounded, covered with abundant silky, almost white hair. No stop. Long, tapering jaws.

EYES
Small, triangular appearance. Blues have dark eyes; Blue and tans are less dark with amber lights; browns and sandies have hazelnut color eyes.

EARS
Moderate size, set on low and hanging flat against the cheeks. Thin leather, velvety texture; covered with short, fine hair, with a silky, white tassel at the tip.

BODY
Slightly longer than tall.

Muscular and flexible. Long neck without dewlap. Deep, fairly broad chest. Flat-ribbed. Arched loin. Back arching over the loin.

LIMBS
Long, hare-like feet with thick, compact pads. Hind legs are longer than forelegs.

TAIL
Set low, moderate length; thick at the root and tapering toward the gently curved tip. Never carried over the back.

COAT
Thick, crisp but not wiry. Tendency to curl, particularly on the head and face.

COLOR
Blue, liver or sandy with or without tan. Darkest colors

are preferred. Blues and blue and tans must have a black nose. Livers and sandies must have a brown nose.

SIZE
Approx. 40 cm (16 in).

WEIGHT
8 to 10.5 kg (18-23 lb).

Character, special skills and training
This robust, fast, energetic, courageous dog has a strong personality. Happy and affectionate with his owners, he is gentle and playful with children. The Bedlington Terrior can be aggressive toward other dogs if attacked. Firm but gentle training is required.

Care and functions
The Bedlington Terrier makes a good house dog, but he must be walked daily. Weekly brushing is required. This breed should be professionally groomed two or three times per year.
· Ratter.
· Guard dog.
· Pet.

Stocky. Low-slung. Thick skin. Relaxed gait.

Border Terrier

As its name suggests, the Border Terrier originated in the Border country in southern Scotland. The breed is thought to be descended from an ancient type of Bedlington crossed with the Lakeland Terrier and the Dandie Dinmont Terrier. The breed received the name Border Terrier in 1880 and a Border Terrier club was formed in 1920. The breed was initially used to hunt fox and accompany hound packs.

1

MEDIUM AND LARGE TERRIERS

3

COUNTRY OF ORIGIN
Great Britain

Small Breeds under 10 kg (under 20 lb)

HEAD
Similar to that of an otter. Moderately broad skull. Strong, short muzzle.

EYES
Dark color.

EARS
Small, v-shaped, hanging forward along the cheeks.

BODY
Tall, narrow, fairly long. Neck of moderate length. Deep ribs carried well back. Strong loin

LIMBS
Legs of medium bone. Small feet with thick pads

TAIL
Moderately short. Fairly thick at the root and tape-

ring toward the tip. Carried gaily but not over the back.

COAT
Hard, dense. Thick undercoat.

COLOR
Red, wheaten, grizzle and tan, blue and tan.

SIZE
Dog: no more than 40 cm (16 in).
Bitch: no more than 36 cm (14 in).

WEIGHT
Dog: 5.9 to 7.1 kg (13-16 lb).
Bitch: 5.1 to 6.4 kg (11-14 lb).

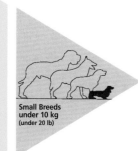

Character, special skills and training
This rustic, courageous, strong, lively, dog possesses a seemingly boundless supply of energy. In fact, he is capable of keeping pace with a horse. While the Border Terrier has a strong personality, he also has a happy disposition. He forms a strong bond with his owners and adores children. This breed is often aggressive when first meeting other dogs. Firm training is required.

Care and functions
The Border Terrier can adapt to living indoors if he frequently gets out for long walks. Occasional brushing is all that is required to maintain the coat. Professional grooming is not required.
· Hunting dog (hound type).
· Pet.

116

Fox Terrier

The Fox Terrier has existed in England since the sixteenth century. There are two varieties, the Wire Fox Terrier and, the older of the two, the Smooth Fox Terrier. The breed is descended from dachshunds, beagles and ancient terrier breeds. Around 1810, the Fox Terrier was selectively bred for hunting fox (whence the breed's name), boar and badger. A standard for the two varieties was published in 1876 when the Fox Terrier club was formed. The Fox Terrier is now the most popular of the Terriers. The smooth variety is less common than the wire variety.

Powerful, solid construction in a small package. Length equal to height. Quick of movement.

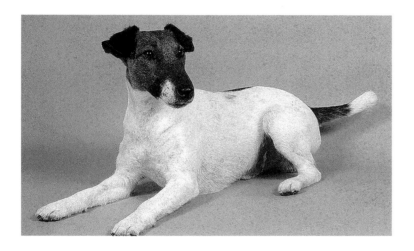

1

MEDIUM AND LARGE TERRIERS

COUNTRY OF ORIGIN
Great Britain

ORIGINAL NAMES
Smooth Fox Terrier
Wire Fox Terrier

Small Breeds under 10 kg (under 20 lb)

3

HEAD
Elongated. Flat skull. Slight stop. Nose bridge tapers toward the nose. Strong jaws covered with a rough coat.

EYES
Small, round. Dark color.

EARS
Small, v-shaped, folded and hanging forward against the cheeks. Erect ear is a disqualification.

BODY
Compact. Muscular neck without dewlap. Clearly pronounced withers. Chest well let down. Ribs moderately sprung. Croup not sloped. Short, horizontal back. Powerful, muscular loin.

LIMBS
Muscular legs with substantial bone. Round, compact feet with thick pads.

TAIL
Set high, of fair length, carried gaily but not over the back and not curled. Typically docked.

COAT
Two varieties:
Wire hair: Dense, very hard texture, approx. 1.9 cm (0.7 in) long on the shoulders and 3.8 cm (1.5 in) long on the withers, back, sides and hindquarters. Coat on the jaws is very rough. Short, softer undercoat.
Smooth hair: straight, flat, smooth, hard, thick and abundant.

COLOR
White is the predominant color; solid white, white with tan, black or black and tan markings. Brindle, blue, slate gray, red, or liver markings not permitted.

SIZE
Dog: 39.3 cm (15.5 in) or less.
Bitch: slightly shorter than dog.

WEIGHT
Dog: approx. 8 kg (18 lb).
Bitch: approx. 7 kg (16 lb).

Character, special skills and training
This rustic, hardy, fast dog is full of life, always on the move and possesses seemingly boundless energy. Courageous and bold, he has a strong, established personality. He is affectionate with his owners and gentle with children. He is a vigilant guard, barking to raise the alarm. The Fox Terrier is aggressive toward other dogs and therefore has difficulties living with other animals. Firm but gentle training is required.

Care and functions
The Fox Terrier can adapt to life in the city, but he requires considerable exercise to prevent him from becoming excessively nervous. This breed does not like to be tied up or closed in. Weekly brushing is sufficient for the smooth variety. The wire variety requires brushing two or three times per week and professional grooming three times per year.
· Hunting dog.
· Guard dog.
· Pet.

Glen of Imaal Terrier

This Irish Terrier has been bred for centuries in the Imaal valley in the county of Wicklow near Dublin. It has been used for hunting fox, badger and other vermin. The breed was recognized by the Irish Kennel Club in 1933, imported to the United States in 1968. However, it is still quite rare outside of Ireland.

Strong. Agile. Longer than tall (rectangular). Relaxed gait.

1

MEDIUM AND LARGE TERRIERS

3

COUNTRY OF ORIGIN
Ireland

OTHER NAME
Glen

Medium Breeds between 10 and 25 kg (20-55 lb)

Character, special skills and training
This robust, rustic, active, courageous, spirited dog is agile and very playful. Glens are excellent companions for children and adults alike. While his demeanor is that of a guard dog, his size makes him far from formidable. However, he is quarrelsome with other dogs. This breed has retained a strong hunting instinct.

Care and functions
The Glen Terrier can adapt to life in the city if he receives enough exercise. Daily brushing is required.
· Hunting dog.
· Pet.

HEAD
Fairly broad and long. Relatively broad skull. Pronounced stop. Muzzles tapers toward the tip. Powerful jaws.

EYES
Medium size, round and wide set. Brown color.

EARS
Small, rose, or semi-prick when dog is alert.

BODY
Longer than tall. Very muscular neck. Broad, strong chest. Ribs well sprung. Strong loin. Straight back.

LIMBS
Strong, compact feet. Hind feet turn out slightly. Muscular legs with plenty of bone.

TAIL
Docked. Strong at the root, carried gaily.

COAT
Medium length, harsh exture. Soft undercoat.

COLOR
Blue brindle, but not tending to black. Light wheaten with golden red tones. Ink blue mask. Blue strip along the back, on the tail and the ears is acceptable.

SIZE
33 to 35 cm (13-14 in).

WEIGHT
14 to 16 kg (31-35 lb).

Soft-Coated Wheaten Terrier

*Originating in the county of Munster,
the Soft-Coated Wheaten Terrier is one of the oldest Irish breeds.
He is thought to be the ancestor of the Kerry Blue Terrier
and the Irish Terrier. He was used on Irish farms
to guard livestock and the farm and to hunt vermin.
The breed was not recognized by The Kennel Club until 1943.*

Well constructed. Powerful appearance.
Free, lively gait.

1

MEDIUM AND LARGE TERRIERS

COUNTRY OF ORIGIN
Ireland

3

Medium Breeds
between
10 and 25 kg
(20-55 lb)

HEAD
Long and powerful. Flat skull, not too wide. Pronounced stop. Powerful, "fearsome" jaws.

EYES
Not too large. Dark hazelnut or dark color.

EARS
Small to medium size. Carried forward, breaking level with the skull.

BODY
Short, compact. Strong neck without dewlap. Deep forechest. Ribs well sprung. Short, powerful loin. Straight topline.

LIMBS
Muscular legs with plenty of bone. Small, compact feet.

TAIL
Not too thick; carried gaily. Docked to one-third its natural length (after the sixth vertebra).

COAT
Abundant, soft texture, silky, wavy or loose curls. Must not exceed 12,7 cm (5 in) at greatest length.

COLOR
Any shade from light wheaten to golden-reddish. The texture and color of the puppy's coat passes through several stages before attaining its permanent color at one and one-half to two and one-half years of age.

SIZE
Dog: 46 to 48 cm (18-19 in). Bitch: 43 to 47 cm (17-18.5 in).

WEIGHT
Dog: 15,7 to 18 kg (35-40 lb). Bitch: 13 to 15 kg (29-33 lb).

Character, special skills, and training
This rustic, energetic, courageous, and bold dog is rather independent and stubborn. He is very affectionate, devoted to his owner, and is a playful, gentle, happy pet. Wary of strangers, this good guard dog threatens with his bark but is not aggressive. Strict training is required.

Care and functions
This dog is not a good choice as a house dog. He needs considerable space and exercise to maintain his mental health. Regular brushing is required. Grooming may be required from time to time.
· Livestock guard.
· Hunting dog.
· Guard dog.
· Pet.

Irish Terrier

This terrier is thought to have existed in Ireland for centuries, but its origins have been obscured by time. The Irish Terrier could be descended from the old breed of wire-haired black and tan terrier and a larger variety of the Wheaten Terrier, which is said to have lived in the county of Cork. This breed's modern type was fixed in 1875. Before type was fixed, the breed's coloring could be red, black and tan, or even brindle. An Irish Terrier club was formed in 1879 and the first standard for the breed was established in 1880. During World War I, the Irish Terrier served side-by-side with English soldiers.

1

MEDIUM AND LARGE TERRIERS

3

COUNTRY OF ORIGIN
Ireland

OTHER NAMES
Irish Red Terrier
"Daredevil"

Square build.
Silhouette with racy lines.

Medium Breeds
between
10 and 25 kg
(20-55 lb)

Character, special skills and training

This robust, fast dog has great endurance and plenty of spirit. He is independent, combative and stubborn. The Irish Terrier is affectionate, cheerful and devoted to his owner, making him a good pet. This hunting dog, at home on land and in the water, is used to hunt hare, vermin and otter. As a guard dog he can be ferocious if attacked and will fight to the death. The Irish Terrier is aggressive with other dogs. Firm but gentle training is required.

Care and functions

This dog can adapt to life as a house dog, but he requires considerable space and exercise. Brushing once or twice per week is required. This breed should be groomed two times per year.
· Hunting dog (shooting and with hounds).
· Guard dog.
· Pet.

HEAD
Long. Flat, fairly narrow skull. Stop hardly visible. Strong jaws. Close, well-fitting lips.

EYES
Small. Dark color.

EARS
Small, v-shaped, falling forward along the cheeks.

BODY
Neither too long nor too short. No dewlap on neck. Deep, muscular chest. Muscular, very slightly arched loin. Strong, straight back.

LIMBS
Very muscular legs with substantial bone. Strong, round feet with arched toes and black nails.

TAIL
Set on fairly high. Carried gaily but not over the back or curled. Typically docked to three-quarters its normal length.

COAT
Dense, very compact, wiry, with broken appearance but still lying close to the body. Must not be curly or form tufts. Hair on the face is short (0.6 cm) (0.25 in). The only long hair that is acceptable is a slight beard.

COLOR
Whole-colored. Preferred colors are bright red, red wheaten and golden red. White markings on the forechest and feet are permissible.

SIZE
Approx. 45 cm (18 in).

WEIGHT
Dog: 12.2 kg (27 lb).
Bitch: 11.4 kg (25 lb).

German Hunt Terrier

Descended from English terriers, the German Hunt Terrier was selectively bred in Germany in the nineteenth century. The breed is thought to be the result of crosses between the Fox Terrier, the Welsh Terrier and the Old English Terrier. It is possible that dachshund and pinscher blood was also introduced. This remarkable hunter is considered to be one of the best terriers (unearthing fox and badger). He also hunts boar and hare in small packs, retrieves small land or water game, and is an excellent scenthound.

Solid. Well constructed.

MEDIUM AND LARGE TERRIERS

1

COUNTRY OF ORIGIN
Germany

ORIGINAL NAME
Deutscher Jagdterrier

3

Small Breeds under 10 kg (under 20 lb)

HEAD
Elongated. Broad, flat skull. Stop not pronounced. Robust muzzle. Rounded cheeks. Powerful jaws.

EYES
Small, deep set, oval. Dark color.

EARS
Set on high, not overly small, v-shaped, carried lightly against the sides of the head.

BODY
Slightly longer than tall. Robust neck. Deep, rounded chest. Powerfully muscled loin. Strong, straight back. Powerfully muscled croup.

LIMBS
Compact feet. Front feet are often wider than hind feet. Muscular legs with substantial bone.

TAIL
Docked to about one third its natural length. Carried somewhat high, but not gaily.

COAT
Fairly short, hard, dense, harsh, stiff, lying very close to the skin.

COLOR
Black is predominant color, gray and black mixture, or dark brown, with relatively light tan markings above the eyes, on the muzzle, checks, feet and anus. Light or dark mask and small white markings on the forechest and feet are permissible.

SIZE
33 to 40 cm (13-15.7 in).

WEIGHT
Dog: 9 to 10 kg (20-22 lb). Bitch: 7.5 to 8.5 kg (16.5 to 19 lb).

Character, special skills and training
This lively, cantankerous, fearless, courageous "killer" has a difficult personality. Suspicious of strangers, he is a vigilant guard dog. The German Hunt Terrier is aggressive toward other dogs. Though he can be affectionate with his owners, the German Hunt Terrier is one of the few terriers that is not suitable as a pet. Very firm training is required. This dog will obey only his owner.

Care and functions
This is not a house dog. If he lives indoors, he will become excessively nervous. This breed requires regular outings. Brushing once per week is required.
· Hunting dog.

121

Well knit. Balanced proportions. Sculpted appearance.

Kerry Blue Terrier

Many years ago in the county of Kerry in southwestern Ireland, the Blue Kerry Terrier hunted badger, fox and otter. His ancestors probably include the Bedlington Terrier, the Bull Terrier, the Irish Terrier and the Wolfhound. The Blue Kerry Terrier is the largest of the Irish terriers. He was first exhibited at a dog show in 1887. The breed's standard was fixed by the Irish registry in 1920 and today the Kerry Blue Terrier has become a national symbol in Ireland. In 1923, the breed was recognized by The Kennel Club.

1

MEDIUM AND LARGE TERRIERS

3

COUNTRY OF ORIGIN
Ireland

OTHER NAME
Irish Blue Terrier

Medium Breeds
between
10 and 25 kg
(20-55 lb)

HEAD
Strong, with abundant hair. Slight stop. Powerful, muscular, "fearsome" jaws. Gums and palate of dark color.

Character, special skills and training
This hardy, fiery dog is stubborn but relatively calm. He is very friendly with his owners and gentle with children. Dominant and cantankerous, he is aggressive toward other dogs and pets. An excellent guard dog, he is courageous and will bite. This strong swimmer is used to attack otter in deep waters. As a ratter, he has no equal. Training should be firm, but not harsh or unkind.

Care and functions
The Kerry Blue Terrier can adapt to life indoors but he requires plenty of daily exercise. Regular brushing is required. This breed should be professionally groomed three or four times per year.
· Hunting dog (rabbit, vermin, etc.).
· Guard dog.`
· Utility dog: police dog.
· Pet.

EYES
Medium size. Dark hazelnut or dark color.

EARS
Small, thin leather, carried forward or falling forward against the sides of the head.

BODY
Compact and muscular. Moderately long neck. Broad, high forechest. Chest well let down. Ribs well sprung. Straight back. Short loin.

LIMBS
Compact feet with black nails. Muscular legs with substantial bone.

TAIL
Thin. Set on high and carried gaily erect.

COAT
Soft, dense and wavy.

COLOR
Any shade of blue, with or without black on the extremities. Black or fawn permissible up to the age of eighteen months.
The Kerry is born black and the coat gradually lightens to blue around fifteen to eighteen months of age.

SIZE
Dog: 45.5 to 49.5 cm (18-19.5 in).
Bitch: 44.5 to 48 cm (17.5-19 in).

WEIGHT
Dog: 15 to 18 Kg (33-40 lb).
Bitch: proportionally lighter.

Lakeland Terrier

The Lakeland Terrier originated in the counties of Cumberland and Westmoreland in northern England. The breed is thought to be the result of crosses between various terriers, including the Border Terrier, the Bedlington Terrier, the Dandie Dinmont Terrier, the Fox Terrier and the Old English Terrier (now extinct). The Lakeland Terrier looks like a miniature Airedale Terrier. This working dog protects the flock, primarily from fox. The first Lakeland Terrier club was formed in 1912. The breed was recognized by The Kennel Club in 1921.

Sturdy. Balanced proportions.

1

MEDIUM AND LARGE TERRIERS

Small Breeds under 10 kg (under 20 lb)

COUNTRY OF ORIGIN
Great Britain

OTHER NAMES
Patterdale Terrier
Fell Terrier

3

HEAD
Harmonious proportions. Flat skull. Broad muzzle. Powerful jaws. Black or brown nose.

EYES
Hazelnut or dark color.

EARS
Small, v-shaped, hanging close to the head.

BODY
Compact. Long neck without dewlap. Moderately narrow chest. Strong, short back.

LIMBS
Small, round, compact feet. Strong legs with plenty of bone.

TAIL
Set high; carried gaily but not curled over the back. Typically docked.

COAT
Medium length, dense, weather-resistant, hard. Thick undercoat.

COLOR
Black and tan, blue and tan, red, wheaten, red grizzle, liver, blue or black. Small spots of white on the feet and forechest are permissible.

SIZE
34 to 37 cm (13.5-14.5 in).

WEIGHT
6.7 to 7.7 kg (15-17 lb).

Character, special skills and training

This robust, lively, courageous, obstinate dog is as at home in the water hunting ottes as he is on land hunting fox and badger. The Lakeland Terrier forms a strong bond with his owner. He has a happy disposition, is gentle with children and an excellent companion. Wary of strangers, he is an excellent, albeit small, guard dog. Gentle training is required.

Care and functions
This breed can adapt to life in the city, but requires considerable exercise. Daily brushing is required. This breed should be professionally groomed three times per year.
· Hunting dog.
· Pet.

123

Compact. Sturdy. Elegant.
Relaxed gait.

1

MEDIUM AND LARGE TERRIERS

3

COUNTRY OF ORIGIN
Great Britain

OTHER NAME
Black and Tan Terrier

Small Breeds
under 10 kg
(under 20 lb)

Manchester Terrier

The Manchester Terrier is the modern version of a ratter called the Old Black and Tan Terrier, a breed that was very common in northwest England in the past. The Manchester Terrier is thought to be the result of a cross between the Old Black and Tan Terrier, the Whippet and the West Highland White Terrier. A smaller variety, the Toy Manchester Terrier, was created around 1850. The first Manchester Terrier club was founded in 1879. The breed almost disappeared during World War II and is still quite rare outside of England.

Character, special skills and training
This robust, hardy, courageous dog is eager, fast and rather obstinate, though he is a cheerful, affectionate pet. The Manchester Terrier requires firm training.

Care and functions
The Manchester Terrier adjusts well to life as a house dog. Daily brushing is required. This breed is a good ratter.
· Guard dog.
· Pet.

HEAD
Long and tight skinned. Flat, narrow, wedge-shaped skull. Muzzle tapers toward the nose. Tight lips.

EYES
Small, almond. Dark color.

EARS
Small, v-shaped, carried well above the level of the head and falling forward toward the eyes.

BODY
Short. Fairly long neck without dewlap. Chest is narrow between the legs and deep in the brisket.

Ribs well sprung. Belly tucked up.

LIMBS
Strong, muscular legs. Small, strong feet, between cat and hare foot

TAIL
Short, thick at the root and tapering toward the tip. Carried slightly below the level of the back.

COAT
Short, smooth, dense; not soft.

COLOR
Jet black and rich mahogany tan. Separation of colors

must be clearly demarcated. Muzzle, jaws, throat, body extremities and inside of the forelegs are tan. Small tan spot on each cheek and above each eye. The nasal bone, body and feet must be jet black.

SIZE
Dog: 39 to 42 cm (15.5-16.5 in).
Bitch: 37 to 40 cm (14,5-16 in).

WEIGHT
7.5 to 8 kg (16.5-17.5 lb).

Brazilian Terrier

The Brazilian Terrier's ancestors were European terriers imported to Brazil in the nineteenth and early twentieth centuries. In Brazil, they were crossed with Pinschers and indigenous dogs, including the Chihuahua. The new breed resembled a Fox Terrier with its rounded shapes and smooth coat.

Medium size. Solid construction without excessive heaviness. Square body outline. Rounded lines. Svelte. Relaxed gait.

1

3

MEDIUM AND LARGE TERRIERS

Small Breeds under 10 kg (under 20 lb)

COUNTRY OF ORIGIN
Brazil

ORIGINAL NAME
Terrier Brasileiro

SIZE
Dog: 35 to 40 cm (14-16 in).
Bitch: 35 to 38 cm (14-16 in).

WEIGHT
max. 10 kg (22 lb).

HEAD
Triangular in shape when viewed from above. Domed skull. Pronounced stop. Strong muzzle. Dry, tight lips.

EYES
Wide set, large, round. Darker colors preferred. Gray-blue in blues; brown, green, or blue in browns. Prominent eyebrows.

EARS
Wide set, triangular. Carried semi-erect with the tip breaking toward the outer corner of the eye.

BODY
Well-balanced. Dry, moderately long neck. Prominent withers. Topline drops slightly to the croup. Moderately broad forechest. Ribs well sprung. Back and loin short and strong. Slightly sloped croup.

LIMBS
Muscular legs. Hare foot.

TAIL
Set on low. Naturally short. Carried high. Docked between the second and third vertebrae.

COAT
Short, smooth, fine, close-lying.

COLOR
White background marked with black, brown, or blue. Standard markings: Tan above the eyes, on the sides of the muzzle, and inside and along the edge of the ears. The head must have black, brown, or blue markings on the forehead and ears. White blaze and white spots along the midline of the forehead and sides of the muzzle permitted.

Character, special skills and training
This active, lively dog is always on the move. He has a true Terrier personality. The Brazilian Terrier is loving toward those he is close to and may form a strong bond with only one person. Firm training is required.

Care and fonctions
The Brazilian Terrier can adjust to life as a housedog provided he is taken for walks regularly. Weekly brushing is sufficient. No professional grooming is required.
· Hunting dog (small game).
· Guard dog.
· Pet.

Jack Russell Terrier

This dog was named after Parson Jack Russell who lived in the county of Devon, England in the nineteenth century. The Parson developed this breed from old wire hair terriers to obtain a dog capable of forcing fox, rabbit and boar to go to ground. Though the breed is very popular in England, it was not recognized until 1990. The FCI recognized the breed in 1994.

Built for speed and endurance. Longer than tall. Thick, loose skin. Relaxed, lively gait.

1

MEDIUM AND LARGE TERRIERS

3

COUNTRY OF ORIGIN
Great Britain

OTHER NAME
Parson Terrier

Small Breeds under 10 kg (under 20 lb)

HEAD
Strong bone structure. Flat skull. Stop not pronounced. Powerful jaws.

EYES
Almond shape. Dark color.

EARS
Small, v-shaped, dropping forward and carried against the head.

BODY
Fairly long. Muscular neck. Chest is moderately well let down. Straight, solid back. Slightly arched loin.

LIMBS
Strong, muscular legs. Compact feet.

TAIL
Set high, strong, straight.

Typically docked to a length just long enough to grasp with the hand.

COAT
Rough, thick, dense; smooth or broken.

COLOR
All white or white with tan, lemon, or black markings, preferably only on the head and root of the tail.

SIZE
Dog: 35 cm (14 in).
Bitch: 33 cm (13 in).

WEIGHT
6 to 7 kg (13-15.5 lb).

Character, special skills and training
This rustic, lively, fearless dog is independent, somewhat stubborn and has a strong personality. He makes a devoted, affectionate pet and is easy to train.

Care and functions
The Jack Russell Terrier can adjust to life as a house dog provided he gets a lot of much needed exercise. The coat requires little care.
· Hunting dog.
· Pet.

Welsh Terrier

The Welsh Terrier is probably descended from the now extinct Old English Black and Tan Terrier (also called Old English Broken Haired Terrier) and the Fox Terrier. The breed was used in Wales working in packs to hunt fox, badger and otter, like other terriers and waterdogs. The breed was recognized by The Kennel Club in 1886 and its standard was fixed in 1947.

Square build. Distinguished air.

1

MEDIUM AND LARGE TERRIERS

Small Breeds under 10 kg (under 20 lb)

COUNTRY OF ORIGIN
Great Britain
Wales

OTHER NAME
Welshie

3

HEAD
Elongated. Flat skull. Slight stop. Powerful jaws.

EYES
Small. Dark color.

EARS
Set on fairly high. Small, v-shaped, folded, carried forward close to the cheeks.

BODY
Compact. Slightly arched neck of moderate length. Chest well let down. Strong forequarters. Short back. Strong loin.

LIMBS
Small, round cat feet. Robust, muscular legs with plenty of bone.

TAIL
Typically docked. Not carried too gaily.

COAT
Hard, wiry, very dense and abundant. Absence of undercoat is a fault.

COLOR
Black and tan is preferred. Black grizzle and tan

without black markings on the feet.

SIZE
39 cm (15.5 in) or less.

WEIGHT
9 to 9.5 kg (20-21 lb).

Character, special skills and training
This robust, hardy, rustic, tenacious, spirited breed has a strong, dominant personality. The Welsh Terrier forms a strong bond with his owners and is affectionate, playful and cheerful. Wary of strangers, though not aggressive, he makes a good guard dog. Firm training must start at a young age.

Care and functions
The Welsh Terrier can adapt to life in the city provided he can go for long walks every day. Brushing once or twice per week is required. This breed should be professionally groomed two to four times per year.
· Hunting dog.
· Pet.

127

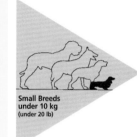

Long, low-swung. Relaxed, elastic gait.

Australian Terrier

Descended from British breeds, the Australian Terrier was shown for the first time in Sidney in 1899. The breed's ancestors include the Cairn Terrier, the Irish Terrier, the Scottish Terrier and, of course, the Yorkshire Terrier, which looks much like its Australian descendant. The breed was developed for hunting rabbit and rats. The Australian Terrier Club was founded in 1921 and the first standard was published the same year. The Australian Terrier was recognized by The Kennel Club in 1936.

2

SMALL TERRIERS

3

COUNTRY OF ORIGIN
Australia

OTHER NAME
Aussie

Small Breeds
under 10 kg
(under 20 lb)

Character, special skills and training
This lively, courageous dog is affectionate and cheerful, but has a true terrier personality. Firm training is necessary.

Care and functions
This active dog needs plenty of exercise. Daily brushing is required.
· Hunting dog.
· Pet.

HEAD
Long. Flat skull. Slight stop. Strong, powerful muzzle. Strong jaws.

EYES
Small, oval, wide set. Dark brown color.

EARS
Small, pointed. Held erect.

BODY
Long, solidly built. Strong, slightly arched neck. Well developed forechest. Deep, moderately broad chest. Ribs well sprung. Strong loin. Horizontal topline.

LIMBS
Short legs of strong bone. Small, round, compact feet.

TAIL
Docked. Carried gaily but not over the back.

COAT
Approx. 6 cm (2,4 in) long; straight, rough and dense. Short, soft undercoat. The muzzle, lower legs and feet are free of long hair.

COLOR
Blue, steel blue, or dark gray-blue with rich tan markings on the face, ears, underbelly, lower legs, feet and around the anus. Sandy or red.

SIZE
Approx. 25 cm (9.8 in).

WEIGHT
3.6 to 6.3 kg (8-14 lb).

Cairn Terrier

The Cairn Terrier, one of the oldest Scottish terriers,
is mentioned in writings from the fifteenth century.
The breed was named for its ability to move about in the cairns
(piles of stones where the dog hunted rabbit and fox).
The breed was developed in the western highlands
and the Isle of Skye west of Scotland. The Cairn Terrier is
an ancestor of the Scottish Terrier and the West Highland White
Terrier. The Kennel Club recognized the breed in 1912.

Compact. Solid skeleton.
Very proud bearing. Very relaxed gait.

2

SMALL TERRIERS

COUNTRY OF ORIGIN
Great Britain
Scotland

OTHER NAME
Short-haired Skye

Small Breeds
under 10 kg
(under 20 lb)

3

HEAD
Small. Broad skull. Pronounced stop. Powerful muzzle. Strong jaws.

EYES
Medium size, wide set. Dark color. Bushy eyebrows.

EARS
Small, pointed. Held erect.

BODY
Long. Strongly coupled neck. Ribs well sprung. Solid hindquarters. Straight back. Strong, supple loin.

LIMBS
Short legs of good bone. Front feet are larger than

hind feet and may turn out slightly.

TAIL
Short, richly clad, but without brush. Carried gaily but not curling up toward the back.

COAT
Long, coarse, abundant. Short, soft, thick undercoat.

COLOR
Cream, wheaten, red, gray, or near black. All brindle colors acceptable. Pure black, white, or black and tan are not permitted. Darker extremities, such as the ears and muzzle, are typical.

SIZE
Dog: 28 to 31 cm (11-12 in).
Bitch: 25 to 30 cm (10 to 12 in).

WEIGHT
6 to 7.5 kg (14-16.5 lb).

Character, special skills and training
This rustic, lively, spirited, game dog has a dominant personality. His is a cheerful, mischievous pet. The Cairn Terrier makes a good guard dog, coming alert at the least noise, barking to raise the alarm, but not becoming aggressive. This excellent swimmer hunts otter and vermin. Very firm training is required.

Care and functions
Though the Cairn Terrier is more at home in the country than in the city, he can adapt well to any environment. This small dog needs regular outings and plenty of exercise. Brushing two or three times per week is required. No professional grooming is required.
· Hunting dog.
· Pet.

129

Basset terrier. Long, short body, like that of a weasel. Supple, relaxed, free action.

Dandie Dinmont Terrier

The first record of the Dandie Dinmont Terrier appears in the eighteenth century. The breed was probably the result of a cross between an old Scottish terrier and the Bedlington Terrier (and possibly the Otterhound). The breed gained widespread fame in Walter Scott's 1815 Guy Mannering, in which the hero, a farmer named Dandie Dinmont, kept a pack of Basset Terriers. The farmer's name was given to the breed, which has been known as the Dandie Dinmont Terrier ever since. Around 1820, a Scottish farmer named James Davidson selectively bred the Dandie. The first Dandie club was formed in 1875. An excellent ratter by profession, the Dandie is a loving pet.

2

SMALL TERRIERS

COUNTRY OF ORIGIN
Great Britain

3

Small Breeds
under 10 kg
(under 20 lb)

Character, special skills and training
This robust, lively, courageous, tireless dog has a strong personality. He is independent, tenacious and sometimes stubborn. He is a loving, cheerful pet. The Dandie Dinmont hunts vermin (rodents, badger, polecat, weasel, etc.). He is also an excellent guard dog with a loud bark. Firm training is called for.

Care and functions
The Dandie Dinmont can adapt to life as a house dog provided he gets long daily walks. Brushing two or three times per week is required. This breed should be professionally groomed two times per year.
· Hunting dog.
· Pet.

HEAD
Solidly built, strong. Broad skull. Domed forehead. Deep, strong muzzle. Strong jaws. Muscles covering the foreface are particularly well developed.

EYES
Large, round, wide set. Dark hazelnut color.

EARS
Set on low, hanging close to the cheeks. Length varies between 7,6 to 10,2 cm (3 -4 in). Color must blend with coat color. Ears are dark in peppers and dark mustard in mustards.

BODY
Long and short. Very strong,

muscular neck. Ribs well sprung. Topline rather low at the shoulder. Both sides of backbone are well muscled.

LIMBS
Short, very muscular legs with plenty of bone. Front legs are slightly longer than the hind legs.

TAIL
Rather short (20 to 26 cm) (8-10 in), fairly thick at the root and tapering toward the tip. Carried in a curve like a scimitar.

COAT
Long, hard, giving a crisp texture. Hind legs are feathered. Undercoat is soft, like linen.

COLOR
Pepper – ranging from dark bluish black to silvery gray with legs ranging from rich tan to pale fawn.
Mustard – ranging from reddish brown to pale fawn with legs and feet of a darker shade than the head.

SIZE
25 to 30 cm (9.8-11.8 in).

WEIGHT
8 to 11 kg (17.6 to 24.3 lb).

Norfolk Terrier

This breed was developed in the county of Norfolk. It was originally considered a variety of the Norwich Terrier from which it is descended, since it differed only in the carriage of its ears. In 1932, The Kennel Club recognized the Norwich Terrier. The Norfolk Terrier was not recognized until 1964.

Stocky. Sturdy, with good substance. True, low and driving gait

2

SMALL TERRIERS

COUNTRY OF ORIGIN
Great Britain

Small Breeds
under 10 kg
(under 20 lb)

3

HEAD
Round. Broad, slightly domed skull. Distinct stop. Strong, wedge-shaped muzzle. Strong jaws. Tight lips.

EYES
Oval. Dark chestnut or black color.

EARS
Medium size, v-shaped, slightly rounded tips, falling forward against the cheeks.

BODY
Compact, strong neck. Horizontal topline. Ribs well sprung. Short back.

LIMBS
Short, powerful legs with plenty of bone. Round feet.

TAIL
Medium docked, carried erect. Medium length, thick at the root and tapering to the tip. Carried straight and proudly.

COAT
Hard, wiry, straight, lying close to the skin. Longer and bushier on the neck and shoulders.

COLOR
All shades of red, wheaten, black and tan or grizzle. White markings or patches are not permissible.

SIZE
25 to 26 cm (9.8 to 10.2 in).

WEIGHT
Approx. 5 kg (11 lb).

Character, special skills and training
This rustic, hardy, alert, bold dog is essentially calm, friendly and gentle with children. He is an ardent hunter that forces prey from burrows, hunts vermin and is capable of hunting in a pack. The Norfolk is also an excellent guard dog. Firm training is required.

Care and functions
The Norfolk can live in a city if he gets out often to burn off excess energy. Daily brushing is required. This breed should be professionally groomed two to four times per year.
· Hunting dog.
· Pet.

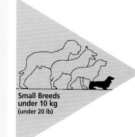

Stocky. Sturdy.

2

SMALL TERRIERS

3

COUNTRY OF ORIGIN
Great Britain

OTHER NAME
Trumpington Terrier

Small Breeds
under 10 kg
(under 20 lb)

Norwich Terrier

The Norwich Terrier originated in Norwich, the capital of Norfolk, in 1870. The breed was the result of crossing red terriers with black and tan or gray terriers. The Norwich Terrier is identical to the Norfolk, except that the Norwich carries his ears erect rather than along the head like the Norfolk. For many years, the two were simply considered separate varieties of the same breed. By 1914, the Norwich Terrier had almost disappeared, but the breed was reconstructed from a few remaining specimens crossed with perhaps the Staffordshire Bull Terrier, the Bull Terrier and the Bedlington Terrier. The Norwich Terrier was recognized by The Kennel Club in 1932. This mascot of Cambridge University is less common than the Norfolk Terrier.

Character, special skills and training
This robust, exceptionally energetic dog is eager and bold and has a strong personality. He does not bark often. This breed is an excellent bolter and hunter of vermin, though the Norwich Terrier is also a good pet. Firm training is necessary.

Care and functions
The Norfolk can live in a city if he gets plenty of exercise. Brushing and combing three times per week is required. This breed should be professionally groomed two to four times per year.
· Hunting dog.
· Pet.

HEAD
Round. Broad, slightly domed skull. Distinct stop. Wedge-shaped muzzle. Strong jaws. Tight lips.

EYES
Small, oval. Dark color.

EARS
Medium size, set well apart. Held erect.

BODY
Compact. Strong neck. Chest well let down. Broad, strong hindquarters. Short loin. Short back.

LIMBS
Short, muscular legs. Round feet.

TAIL
Medium docked; carried gaily. Medium length; thick at the root and tapering to the tip; should be as straight as possible and carried high.

COAT
Harsh, wiry, straight, lying close to the skin. Longer and bushier on the neck, forming a collarette. Thick undercoat.

COLOR
All shades of red, wheaten, black and tan, or grizzle. White markings or patches are not desirable.

SIZE
25 to 26 cm (10-10.5 in).

WEIGHT
Approx. 5 kg (11 lb).

Scottish Terrier

This old breed was developed in the highlands of northern Scotland. Thanks to the work of breeders in Aberdeen (whence the breed's first name, Aberdeen Terrier), the Scottish Terrier took its current form in the early nineteenth century. The first Scottish Terrier Club was founded in 1882 and a standard was published in 1889. Originally used to hunt badger and fox, the Scottish Terrier is now typically kept as a pet.

Thickset. Powerfully muscled. Lively, trotting gait.

SMALL TERRIERS

2

3

COUNTRY OF ORIGIN
Scotland

OTHER NAME
Scottie

Small Breeds
under 10 kg
(under 20 lb)

HEAD
Long. Almost flat skull. Slight stop. Solid, deep muzzle. Large nose. Thick mustache.

EYES
Almond shape, wide set. Dark brown color. Long eyebrows.

EARS
Small, set on high, pointed. Held erect. Covered with velvety short hair.

BODY
Compact. Muscular neck of moderate length. Chest is well let down. Ribs well sprung. Remarkably powerful hindquarters. Short, very muscular back. Deep, muscular loin

LIMBS
Large, compact, arched feet. Short legs are heavy in bone

TAIL
Moderate length (7 in), thick at the root and tapering to the tip. Carried straight or slightly curved.

COAT
Long, rough, wiry, dense, lying close against the skin. Short, dense, soft undercoat.

COLOR
Black, wheaten or brindle of any color.

SIZE
25 to 28 cm (10-11 in).

WEIGHT
8.5 to 10.5 kg (18-23 lb).

Character, special skills and training
The Scottish Terrier is a very robust, feisty, hardy, agile and courageous breed. He has a strong personality and is rather independent, proud and obstinate. This dog forms a strong bond with his owner, is cheerful and affectionate, but not overly demonstrative. The Scottie is wary of strangers and not easily swayed, making him a good guard dog that is always ready to attack any and all potential "enemies". He rarely barks. Firm, consistent training must start at a young age or he will become difficult to live with.

Care and functions
The Scottie can adapt to life as a house dog provided he gets out for daily walks to burn off his abundant energy. Frequent brushing is required. This breed should be professionally groomed three to five times per year.
· Hunting dog.
· Pet.

133

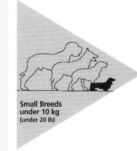

A lot of dog in a small package.
Lively, energetic, powerful gait.

Sealhyham Terrier

This breed was developed in the nineteenth century in the village of Sealyham in Wales. Beginning in 1850, Captain J. Edwards began crossing various terriers, including the Fox Terrier, the West Highland White Terrier, the Dandie Dinmont Terrier and perhaps the Welsh Corgi. The result was the Sealyham Terrier. This breed was used in the past to hunt otter and polecat. The Sealyham Terrier Club was founded in 1908 and the breed was recognized by The Kennel Club in 1911.

2

SMALL TERRIERS

COUNTRY OF ORIGIN
Great Britain

3

Small Breeds
under 10 kg
(under 20 lb)

Character, special skills and training
This robust, active, lively, bold, courageous dog is cheerful, calm and stable. As a pet, the Sealyham Terrier is affectionate and gentle with children. Ever vigilant, he will bark a loud warning if a stranger comes near. Firm training is required.

Care and functions
The Sealyham Terrier can adapt to life as a house dog if he is exercised every day. Daily brushing and combing are required. Professional grooming is necessary.
· Hunting dog.
· Pet.

HEAD
Strong and elongated. Broad, slightly domed skull. Square, powerful jaws. Thick beard.

EYES
Medium size, round. Dark color. Dark rims are preferred.

EARS
Medium size, hanging close to the cheeks.

BODY
Longer than tall. Thick neck. Deep, broad chest is well let down. Ribs well sprung.

Exceptionally powerful hindquarters. Horizontal back.

LIMBS
Short, strong legs. Round feet with thick pads.

TAIL
Carried straight. Typically docked.

COAT
Long, hard, wiry. Weather-resistant undercoat.

COLOR
All white or white with lemon, chestnut, blue or badger markings on the head and ears.

SIZE
Less than 31 cm (12 in).

WEIGHT
Dog: 9 kg (20 lb)
Bitch: 8 kg (17.5 lb).

Skye Terrier

This breed originated on the Isle of Skye. Type has been fixed for many years. The Skye Terrier is thought to be descended from long-haired bassets. This breed is highly skilled at unearthing prey and is used to control fox and other vermin. Queen Victoria owned a Skye Terrier and the breed was first shown in 1864.

The longest and shortest of all the terriers. Length is equal to twice his height. Elegant. Dignified bearing.

2

SMALL TERRIERS

COUNTRY OF ORIGIN
Scotland

3

Medium Breeds between 10 and 25 kg (20-55 lb)

HEAD
Long and powerful. Slight stop. Powerful muzzle. Strong jaws.

EYES
Medium size, close set. Brown color.

EARS
Small, carried erect, feathered. Drop ears are larger in size.

BODY
Long and short. Oval rib cage is long and well let down. Straight back.

Short loin.

LIMBS
Short, muscular legs. Forefeet are larger than hind feet.

TAIL
Carried down or in line with the back. Feathered.

COAT
Long, hard, straight, flat, without curl. Short, softer hair on the head veils the face and eyes. Short, dense, soft, wooly undercoat.

COLOR
Black, light or dark gray, fawn, cream, with black extremities. Any solid color coat is acceptable. A small white spot on the chest is permissible.

SIZE
25 to 26 cm (10-10.5 in).

WEIGHT
10 to 12 kg (22-26.5 lb).

Character, special skills and training
This rustic, self-confident dog has a strong personality. He is rather obstinate and stubborn, but is extremely loyal and completely devoted to his owner. He is wary of strangers. Firm training is required.

Care and functions
The Skye Terrier loves the great outdoors, but he can adapt to life in the city if he goes for long walks every day. This breed does not like to be closed in or tied up. Regular brushing and combing are required. No professional grooming is necessary.
· Pet.

135

Japanese Terrier

The Japanese Terrier was developed in the eighteenth century in the region around Kobe and Yokohama from Terriers (particularly the Smooth Fox Terrier) that had been imported from England. The Smooth Fox Terrier was crossed with local breeds, producing a breed with finer lines. Type was fixed around 1930 and the breed was recognized in Japan in 1940. The Japanese Terrier almost disappeared during World War II, and today is rare outside of Japan.

Square body outline. Distinguished appearance. Light, agile movements.

2

SMALL TERRIERS

3

COUNTRY OF ORIGIN
Japan

ORIGINAL NAME
Nihon Teria

OTHER NAME
Nippon Terrier

Small Breeds under 10 kg (under 20 lb)

Character, special skills and training
This vigilant, lively, cheerful dog is a very affectionate pet.

Care and functions
The Japanese Terrier can adapt to life in the city but needs plenty of exercise. The breed does not handle cold well. Regular brushing is required.
· Pet.

HEAD
Small. Flat skull. Stop not pronounced. Straight nose bridge. Tight, thin lips.

EYES
Medium size, oval. Dark color.

EARS
Set on high, small, thin leather, v-shaped, dropping forward.

BODY
Compact. Strong neck without dewlap. Chest well let down. Ribs well sprung.

Strong loin. Belly well tucked up. Short, firm back. Strong, slightly sloped croup.

LIMBS
Compact feet. Legs with fairly light bone

TAIL
Moderately thin, docked to the third or fourth vertebrae.

COAT
Very short (2 mm) (0.008 in), smooth and thick.

COLOR
Tri-color: tan and white with black head; white with black markings and black and tan spots on the body.

SIZE
Approx. 30 to 33 cm (12 -13 in).

WEIGHT
3 to 4 kg (6.5 -9 lb).

Czesky Terrier

This breed was created in the 1930s by Czech breeder F. Horak, who crossbred the Scottish and Sealyham Terriers. The Czesky Terrier hunts small game and vermin, but is now often kept as guard dog and pet. The breed was recognized by the FCI in 1963.

Robust. Supple.

1

SMALL TERRIERS

COUNTRY OF ORIGIN
Czech Republic

OTHER NAME
Bohemian Terrier

3

Small Breeds
under 10 kg
(under 20 lb)

HEAD
Long. Large nose. Thick beard. Powerful jaws.

EYES
Light or dark chestnut color. Bushy eyebrows.

EARS
Folded above the level of the head and hanging against the cheeks.

BODY
Long and compact. Very muscular hindquarters. Back slightly arched

LIMBS
Short, sturdy legs

TAIL
Approx. 20 cm (8 in) long, carried straight out in line with the back when in action.

COAT
Silky, abundant.

COLOR
Gray-blue or light coffee. Puppies are born black and attain their final color around two years of age.

SIZE
27 to 35 cm (10.5-14 in).

WEIGHT
6 to 9 kg (13-20 lb).

Character, special skills and training
This hardy, obstinate dog has a strong personality, but is a very gentle, playful pet. He is of strangers, but lives peacefully with other domestic animals.

Care and functions
The Czesky Terrier requires considerable exercise. Regular brushing is required. This breed should be professionally groomed every two to three months.
· Guard dog.
· Hunting dog.
· Pet.

West Highland White Terrier

Originating in the mountains of western Scotland, the West Highland White Terrier was probably a white Cairn Terrier that the Colonel Malcolm de Poltalloch family bred selectively to produce this new white breed. The standard for the breed was established in 1906 by the first West Highland White Terrier Club. The breed became fashionable and is now quite popular.

Square body outline. Sturdy build. Strength and activity.

2

SMALL TERRIERS

COUNTRY OF ORIGIN
Great Britain
Scotland

OTHER NAME
Westie

3

Small Breeds
under 10 kg
(under 20 lb)

Character, special skills and training
This rustic, lively, courageous, independent, stubborn dog has a strong personality. He is an affectionate, cheerful pet that loves children. This excellent little guard dog also sounds the alarm at the least provocation. The Westie is a skilled hunter whose prey is fox, badger and other vermin. If he receives proper, firm training, the Westie makes an excellent addition to the household.

Care and functions
This little dog adjusts well to life as a house dog provided he gets long walks. Daily brushing is required. Maintaining the white coat requires special care. Professional grooming is unnecessary unless the dog spends a lot of time outdoors.
· Hunting dog.
· Pet.

HEAD
Round. Slightly domed skull. Pronounced stop. Nose bridge narrows toward the nose. Heavy eyebrows. Strong jaws.

EYES
Medium size, wide set, not round. Color as dark as possible.

EARS
Small, carried tightly erect. Terminate in a sharp point.

BODY
Compact. Muscular neck. Chest is well let down.

Ribs well sprung. Powerful hindquarters. Straight back. Broad, strong loin.

LIMBS
Strong, round feet. Short, muscular, sinewy legs.

TAIL
12.5 to 15 cm (5 to 6 in) long, covered with hard hair. As straight as possible. Carried proudly but not gaily and not curving over the back.

COAT
Approx. 5 cm (2 in) long, straight and hard.

Undercoat is short, soft and dense.

COLOR
White.

SIZE
28 cm (11 in).

WEIGHT
6 to 8 kg (13-17.5 lb).

American Staffordshire Terrier

*Descended from the Staffordshire Bull Terrier
(an English fighting dog), the American Staffordshire Terrier
is a larger and more powerful, highly prized "pit bull".
First recognized by the American Kennel Club in 1935
as the Staffordshire Terrier, he was officially given the name
American Staffordshire Terrier in 1972.
The English Bull Terrier and the American Staffordshire Terrier
are recognized as two distinct breeds. The aggressive tendencies
of the American Staffordshire Terrier should never
be encouraged because the dog could become dangerous.*

Larger, more massive, more imposing than its english cousin. Innate power. Elastic gait.

3

BULL TYPE TERRIERS

Medium Breeds between 10 and 25 kg (20-55 lb)

COUNTRY OF ORIGIN
United States

OTHER NAMES
Pit Bull Terrier
Pit Dog

3

HEAD
Moderate length. Broad skull. Distinct stop. Pronounced cheek muscles. Powerful, strong lower jaw. Lips close and even, with no looseness.

EYES
Round, wide set. Dark color.

EARS
Cropped or uncropped. Short, rose or half-prick uncropped ears are preferred.

BODY
Compact. Thick, arched neck without dewlap. Slight sloping from withers to rump. Croup slightly sloped. Ribs well sprung. Chest is broad and well let down. Slightly sloped croup. Rather short back.

LIMBS
Muscular, heavy-boned legs. Compact feet with well arched toes.

TAIL
Set low, short and tapering to a fine point. Not curled or carried over the back.

COAT
Short, dense and hard.

COLOR
Any color, solid, parti or patched is permissible, but coats more than 80% white, black and tan and liver (brown) are not to be encouraged.

SIZE
Dog: 46 to 48 cm (18-19 in). Bitch: 43 to 46 cm (17-18 in).

WEIGHT
17 to 20 kg (37.5-44 lb).

Character, special skills and training
This strong-willed, independent breed combines the power of a bulldog and the agility of a terrier. The breed is tough, tenacious and well known for its remarkable courage. The American Staffordshire Terrier is a loyal, affectionate pet. This remarkable guard dog is aggressive toward other dogs. Firm, consistent though gentle discipline must start at a very young age. It is necessary to socialize this breed well and not develop its aggressive, biting tendencies or the result will be a fearsome "weapon".

Care and functions
Life as a house dog is not ideal for this breed, which requires considerable exercise and space to maintain mental health. Brushing once or twice per week is all that is required to maintain the coat.
· Guard dog.
· Pet.

Bull Terrier

Very muscular. Compact. Powerfully built.

The Bull Terrier was bred from crosses of Bulldogs with terriers to create the "gladiator of the dog race". The new breed was first used for bull-baiting then for dog fighting. In 1835, this practice was outlawed. The Bull Terrier's silhouette was refined and around 1860. A white variety was selectively bred, giving birth to the modern breed. The Bull Terrier was recognized by The Kennel Club in 1933.

3

BULL TYPE TERRIERS

3

COUNTRY OF ORIGIN
Great Britain

OTHER NAME
English Bull Terrier

Medium Breeds
between
10 and 25 kg
(20-55 lb)

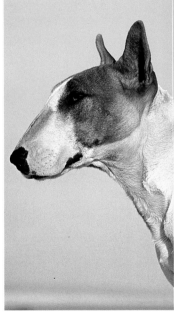

Character, special skills and training
This very robust, eager, courageous dog is stable and well-balanced, but rather obstinate. He is an affectionate, playful pet that does not bark often. Strict, firm but gentle training is necessary.

Care and functions
This breed adapts well to life as a house dog but does not like to be left alone and requires plenty of exercise. Weekly brushing is required.
· Guard dog.
· Pet.

HEAD
Long, strong, oval (egg-shaped). Top of skull is almost flat. No stop. Strong lower jaw.

EYES
Appear narrow, set obliquely in the skull, triangular. Black or very dark brown color (the darker the better).

EARS
Small, thin leather, close set. Held erect.

BODY
Massive. Very muscular neck. Broad, deep chest. Ribs well sprung. Broad, heavily muscled loin. Short, extremely muscular back.

LIMBS
Muscular, heavy-boned legs. Round, compact feet with arched toes.

TAIL
Short, set low, carried horizontally. Thick at the root and tapering to a thin tip.

COAT
Short, flat, hard with tight-fitting skin. Soft undercoat in winter.

COLOR
Whites have solid white coat; pigmentation of the skin and markings on the head are not faults. In colored varieties, color must be dominant over the white.

Black brindle, red, fawn and tri-color are acceptable.

SIZE
No limit.

WEIGHT
No limit
Miniature Bull Terriers must measure 35.5 cm (14 in) or less and weigh 9 kg (20 lb) or less. The head is foxlike, with a slightly domed, broad skull. The stop is pronounced and the muzzle is chiseled. Tight lips.

Staffordshire Bull Terrier

This breed was created in the nineteenth century in Staffordshire by crossing the Bulldog with various terriers. The Staffordshire Bull Terrier was first used for bull-baiting then for pit fighting, earning it the name Half Pit Dog. The Staffie became a fashionable dog to own in the United States between the two World Wars and later became popular in Great Britain and Europe. Recognized in 1935, the Staffordshire Bull Terrier is much less common than its descendant, the American Staffordshire Terrier.

Strong, muscular, agile. Balanced proportions. Relaxed, supple movement.

3

BULL TYPE TERRIERS

COUNTRY OF ORIGIN
Great Britain

OTHER NAME
Staffie

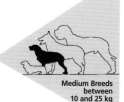
Medium Breeds between 10 and 25 kg (20-55 lb)

3

HEAD
Short, deep through. Broad skull. Distinct stop. Short nose bridge. Very pronounced cheek muscles. Strong jaws. Tight lips.

EYES
Medium size, round. Dark color. Dark rims.

EARS
Rose or half-prick.

BODY
Compact and powerful. Muscular, moderately short neck. Broad forechest. Chest is well let down. Ribs well sprung. Horizontal topline.

LIMBS
Strong feet with black nails. Front legs well muscled and set rather far apart.

TAIL
Medium length, set low and tapering toward the tip. Carried moderately low.

COAT
Short, smooth, dense.

COLOR
Red, fawn, white, black or blue or any of these colors with white. Any shade of brindle with or without white.

SIZE
35 to 40 cm (14 to 15.5 in).

WEIGHT
Dog: 12.7 to 17.2 kg 28-38 lb).
Bitch: 10.8 to 15.4 kg (24-34 lb).

Character, special skills and training
This vigorous, courageous, highly tenacious, bold, strong-willed dog is, in fact, calm and stable. If trained properly, he is gentle and affectionate with his owners, though is a formidable, aggressive guard dog as required. The Staffie is quite aggressive toward other dogs.

Care and functions
The Staffordshire Bull Terrier can adapt to life as a house dog if he gets plenty of exercise. Regular brushing is required.
· Guard dog.
· Pet.

Silky Terrier

The Silky Terrier was bred by crossing Yorkshire and Australian Terriers. The breed first appeared in the late nineteenth century when silky-coated puppies began to be born to Australian Terriers. Skye Terrier and Cairn Terrier blood was probably introduced as well. The breed was recognized by the Sidney Kennel Club in 1933 and later exported to Great Britain and the United States.

Stocky. Compact. Moderately low-set. Toy size.

4

TOY TERRIERS

3

COUNTRY OF ORIGIN
Australia

OTHER NAME
Sidney Silky

Small Breeds
under 10 kg
(under 20 lb)

Character, special skills and training
This robust little dog is spunky, eager and stable. A cheerful companion, he forms a strong bond with his owner and loves children. His terrier instinct makes him an excellent ratter. Firm training is required.

Care and functions
This very clean breed is well suited for life as a house dog provided he gets out often for long walks. Regular brushing and combing are required.
· Hunting dog.
· Pet.

HEAD
Strong and of moderate length. Flat skull. Strong jaws. Tight lips.

EYES
Small, round. Color as dark as possible.

EARS
Small, V-shaped, thin leather. Set high on the head and carried erect.

BODY
Moderately long. Deep, moderately wide chest. Strong loin. Straight back.

LIMBS
Small, round, compact feet with black nails. Legs of round bone structure.

TAIL
Cropped and carried straight.

COAT
Fine and silky. 13 to 15 cm (5-6 in) long from behind the ears to the base of the tail. Lower legs are free of long hair.

COLOR
Blue and tan or gray-blue and tan. Blue on the tail must be dark. Gray-blue has tan tufts at the base of the ear, on the muzzle and sides of the face. Blue extends from the base of the skull to the tip of the tail and down the legs to the knees and hocks. Tan markings on the feet and under the tail.

SIZE
Approx. 22.5 cm (9 in).

WEIGHT
3.5 to 4.5 kg (8-10 lb).

Toy Manchester Terrier

The Toy Manchester Terrier was bred from small Manchester Terriers, creating a diminutive version of the original. The breed was decreased in size even more in the nineteenth century, when it was fashionable for women to tuck toy dogs in their sleeves. Beginning in the twentieth century, breeders returned to the more robust, stronger miniature.

Balanced proportions. Elegant. Compact. Gait is similar to a stretched out horse gallop.

Small Breeds under 10 kg (under 20 lb)

4

TOY TERRIERS

COUNTRY OF ORIGIN
Great Britain

OTHER NAMES
English Toy Terrier
Black and Tan Toy Terrier

3

HEAD
Long. Narrow, flat skull. Slight stop. Muzzle tapers slightly toward the nose. Strong jaws.

EYES
Small, almond, set obliquely in the skull. Dark to black color.

EARS
Long and erect. Wider at the base and tapering toward the slightly pointed tip. Set well up on the skull and relatively close together.

BODY
Compact. Long, graceful, slightly arched neck. Straight, deep chest.

TAIL
Set low. Thick at the root and tapering to a point, not reaching beyond the hocks. Slight arch over the loin. Slightly arched back.

LIMBS
Compact feet. Fine-boned legs.

COAT
Short, dense, thick.

COLOR
Black and tan (black with tan markings). Jet black and rich mahogany tan. Clear, well defined lines of color. Tan markings on the muzzle, lower jaw, throat and front of forelegs. Tan spot above each eye and on each cheek.

SIZE
25 to 30 cm (10-12 in).

WEIGHT
2.7 to 3.6 kg (6-8 lb).

Character, special skills and training
This energetic, lively, hardy little dog has a true terrier personality. He is a cheerful, affectionate companion. Wary of strangers, he also guards the home, raising the alarm with his shrill bark. Firm training is needed.

Care and functions
This breed is well suited to indoor living. The Toy Manchester Terrier needs little exercise. Daily brushing is required.
· Pet.

143

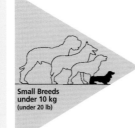

Miniature beauty queen.
Refined beauty and dignity.

Yorkshire Terrier

The Yorkshire Terrier is descended from Clydesdale and/or Paisley Terriers and the Waterside Terriers which migrated to the area around Glasgow, in the county of York, in the early nineteenth century. They were later crossed with other breeds, including the Broken-Haired Terrier (now extinct), the Cairn Terrier, the Maltese Bichon and others.
In 1886, the breed was officially named by The Kennel Club and its first standard was published in 1898.
The Yorkie was originally used to keep mines clear of rats and as a hunting dog to unearth prey. The breed later became a fashionable pet. The breed was promoted in the United States and Europe where it was bred for decreased size beginning in 1930. The Yorkie is now reputed to be the most popular miniature breed in the world.

4

TOY TERRIERS

3

COUNTRY OF ORIGIN
Great Britain

OTHER NAME
Yorkie

Small Breeds
under 10 kg
(under 20 lb)

Character, special skills and training
This impulsive, lively, spunky dog is courageous but strong-willed. This pampered dog does not do well with active children. The Yorkshire Terrier will bark at almost anything. With his dominant personality, the Yorkie will not hesitate to attack another dog, even larger ones. Very strict training is required to bring this dog under control.

Care and functions
The Yorkie is well suited to indoor living, but this sporting dog requires exercise. Daily brushing and combing are required. This breed should be professionally groomed monthly.
· Pet.

HEAD
Rather small and flat. Skull not too prominent or round. Muzzle not too long.

EYES
Medium size. Dark color. Dark rims.

EARS
Small, v-shaped, not too wide set. Carried erect. Solid fawn color.

BODY
Compact, stocky. Elegant neck. Ribs moderately sprung. Height of shoulder same as rump. Straight back.

LIMBS
Straight legs. Round feet with black nails.

TAIL
Typically docked to a moderate length. Carried slightly above the line of the back. Covered in long, thick hair of darker blue color than on the rest of the body.

COAT
Moderately long on the body. Perfectly straight, fine, silky texture. Long on the head and of rich golden fawn color. Hair falls perfectly straight on each side of the body and is parted in the middle from the nose to the tip of the tail. Feet are of a golden fawn color.

COLOR
Dark steel blue (not silver blue) extending from the eyes to the base of the tail, never mixed with fawn, bronze or darker hairs. Hair on the forechest is rich fawn. All fawn hairs are darker at the root and lighten along their length. Puppies are born with black coats that change to steel gray several months later.

SIZE
Approx. 20 cm (8 in).

WEIGHT
Up to 3.1 kg (6. 7 lb).

Group
4

DACHSHUNDS

Dachshund

Dachshund

The FCI has dedicated an entire group (Group 4) to this hunting dog. There are three varieties of Dachshunds: Standard, Miniature and Rabbit. Each variety is divided into three types according to coat: Smooth (Kurzhaar), Longhaired (Langhaar), and Wirehaired (Rauhhaar).

The origins of the dachshund have been obscured by time. The smooth variety is the oldest and is thought to have been produced by crossing a short Jura Bruno with a pinscher. The Smooth Dachshund gave rise to the other two varieties. Type was fixed for the longhaired variety in the seventeenth century. The wirehaired variety was created in the late nineteenth century by crossing the Smooth Dachshund, the Schnauzer, the Dandie Dinmont Terrier and perhaps the Scottish Terrier. The first standard for the breed was written in 1879. The Deutscher Teckel Club (German Dachshund Club) was formed in 1888. The standard variety (particularly the wirehaired standard) is used as a scenthound for large game, hare and rabbit, as well as an earth dog for fox and badger. The Kaninchen (Rabbit Dachshund) was created specifically for hunting rabbit. In the early twentieth century, fanciers preferred the smooth variety, then later turned their favor to the longhaired variety. Today, the Wirehaired Dachshund is the most popular.

SHORTHAIRED

1A

KANINCHEN (RABBIT DACHSHUND)

COUNTRY OF ORIGIN
Germany

ORIGINAL NAME
Dachshund
(meaning badger dog)

OTHER NAMES
Standard Dachshund
(Normalgrösse)
Miniature Dachshund
(Zwerg)
Rabbit Dachshund
(Kaninchen)

4

Standard Dachshund. Low-set. Long, compact body. Head carried proudly.

Small Breeds under 10 kg (under 20 lb)

HEAD
Fine lines, elongated and narrowing toward the nose. Slightly arched skull. Stop not pronounced. Slightly arched, narrow muzzle. Finely chiseled nose of black or brown color depending on coat color. Very well developed jaw bones. Tight lips.

EYES
Medium size, oval. Reddish brown to black-brown color. Walleyes permitted in grays and harlequins.

EARS
Set on high. Rounded at the tips and hanging against the cheeks.

BODY
Long. Muscular, dry neck without dewlap. Powerful, fairly prominent sternum. Deep, broad chest. When viewed from the front, rib cage is oval. Fairly flat ribs. Belly well tucked up. Long, rounded, compact croup slopes very slightly to the root of the tail. Low-set, long, compact body. Short, rigid back
Short, broad, firm, slightly arched loin.

LIMBS
Broad, round feet are slightly turned out. Compact, well arched toes. Short, muscular legs.

TAIL
Not too curved and not carried too gaily.

COAT
Smooth variety: flat and smooth.
Wirehaired variety: dense with undercoat. Mustache, bushy eyebrows, smooth and short, flat on the ears. Longhaired: soft, flat, slightly wavy (like an Irish Setter). Longer on the throat,
body, ears, upper legs and tail (feathering).

COLOR
– Smooth variety: Single color – red, golden red, golden with or without mixture of black hairs. Bi-color – Black, brown, gray, white on extremities, tan with markings above the eyes, on the sides of the muzzle, on the forechest, upper legs and feet, etc. Harlequin – Light brown, light gray, or white background with irregular dark brown, golden, golden red, or black spots.
– Wirehaired variety: All colors permissible.
– Longhaired variety: Same as smooth variety.

SIZE
26 to 37 cm (10-14.5 in), depending on variety.

WEIGHT
Standard: less than 9 kg (20 lb); ideally 6.5 to 7 kg (14.5-15.5 lb).
Miniature: less than 4 kg (9 lb) at eighteen months. Diameter of chest less than 35 cm (14 in).
Kaninchen: less than 3.5 kg (7 lb). Diameter of chest less than 30 cm (12 in).

LONGHAIRED

WIREHAIRED

Character, special skills and training

This robust, courageous dog has great endurance, but does not always have a good disposition. The Dachshund is independent, belligerent, has a tendency to bite and tries to exert his dominance over other dogs. His habit of barking at the least noise makes him a good guard dog. The Dachshund is affectionate and cheerful, but tends to be possessive and is often jealous. The smooth variety is the most energetic, while the wirehaired variety is the most rustic and has the greatest hunting instinct. The longhaired variety is the calmest of the three. All dachshunds must receive firm but gentle training from a very young age.

Care and functions

The Dachshund is well-suited to life as a house dog, particularly the longhaired variety. However, this small dog needs plenty of exercise to maintain his mental health. The wirehaired and longhaired varieties require regular brushing and combing.
· Hunting dog.
· Guard dog.
· Pet.

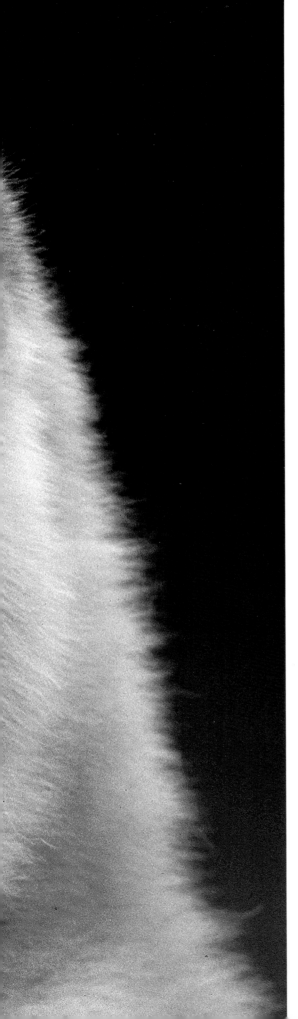

Group 5

Akita

Alaskan Malamute

For centuries, the Alaskan Malamute was indispensable to the native peoples of Alaska. He was named for the Mahlemuts, an Inuit tribe that developed this breed and used it for hunting caribou and guarding the camp. Though not as fast as the Husky, the Alaskan Malamute can pull heavier loads, earning it the reputation as the "snow train" of the north. The breed was recognized by the American Kennel Club in 1935.

Largest and most powerful of the sled dogs. Proud, tall bearing. Distinct wolflike appearance. Supple movement.

1

NORDIC SLED DOGS

COUNTRY OF ORIGIN
United States

5

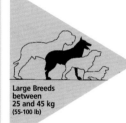

Large Breeds between 25 and 45 kg (55-100 lb)

Character, special skills and training

This robust, calm, steady dog has great endurance. Though quite independent, he is not as feisty as the Husky. He is playful, affectionate and gentle with children, making him an excellent pet. The Alaskan Malamute makes a poor guard dog because he rarely barks, is not aggressive and is very sociable. His pack instinct is still strong and he is rather dominant with other dogs. Firm training must begin at a very young age.

Care and functions

The Alaskan Malamute could possibly adapt to life in the city, but this dog does not like to be left alone and hates inactivity. If closed in, he will destroy a house. To maintain mental and physical health, this dog must take long, frequent walks and, if possible, be allowed to pull loads. This breed does not tolerate heat well. Brushing twice per week is required. A curry comb is needed during seasonal shedding.
· Sled dog (heavy loads over long distances).
· Pet.

HEAD
Broad and strong. Broad skull. Slight stop. Strong, massive muzzle. Black or brown nose in red dogs. Close fitting lips.

EYES
Almond shape, set obliquely in the skull. Brown color. Blue eyes are a disqualifying fault.

EARS
Medium size, triangular, wide set. Held erect.

BODY
Compact and well muscled. Strong neck. Well developed chest. Straight back. Solid, muscular loin.

LIMBS
Large, compact, thick feet. Powerful, heavy-boned legs.

TAIL
Richly clad. Carried over the back, but not in a tight curl.

COAT
Thick, harsh; never long or soft. Hair is longer on the shoulders, neck, length of the back, croup, thighs and tail. Dense, wooly, oily undercoat is 2.5 to 5 cm (1-2 in) long.

COLOR
Light gray through intermediate shadings to black or shadings of sable to red. Color combinations are acceptable in undercoat.

The only solid color allowed is white. White is always the predominant color on the underbody, feet and parts of leg and face markings.

SIZE
Dog: 65 cm (25.5 in).
Bitch: 58 cm (23 in).

WEIGHT
Dog: 38 kg (84 lb).
Bitch: 34 kg (75 lb).

Greenland Dog

This polar spitz breed undoubtedly has northern wolf blood. Originating in the arctic, this pure breed was selectively bred for thousands of years by Eskimos for its energy and power. Paul-Emile Victor introduced the breed to the world in 1936 when he brought back the dogs he used for his polar expeditions.

Slighty longer than tall.
Built for endurance. Energetic, powerful appearance.

1

NORDIC SLED DOGS

COUNTRY OF ORIGIN
Scandinavian Countries

ORIGINAL NAME
Grønlandshund

Large Breeds between 25 and 45 kg (55-100 lb)

5

HEAD
Wolflike. Broad, slightly domed skull. Pronounced stop. Straight, broad nose bridge. Wedge-shaped muzzle. Nose must be black in summer but may be flesh colored in winter. Thin, tight lips.

EYES
Set obliquely in the skull. Preferably of a dark color.

EARS
Rather small, triangular, rounded at the tips. Held erect.

BODY
Strong and muscular. Very strong, rather short neck. Very wide chest. Straight back. Croup slightly sloped.

LIMBS
Strong, round, rather wide feet. Muscular, heavy-boned legs.

TAIL
Thick and rather short. Set high and carried curled over the back.

COAT
Dense, straight, harsh. Short on the head and legs, longer on the body. Thick and long on the underside of the tail. Dense, soft undercoat.

COLOR
Any color, solid or parti-color, is acceptable, except albinos.

SIZE
Dog: at least 60 cm (23.5 in).
Bitch: at least 55 cm (22 in).

WEIGHT
Approx. 30 kg (66 lb).

Character, special skills and training
This rustic, exceptionally vigorous dog has remarkable endurance and can withstand even the lowest temperatures. The Greenland Dog is intelligent, lively, affectionate and sociable, making him a good pet. While he makes a good guard dog, he is not aggressive. The breed communicates emotion by making various sounds: whining to express submission, emitting a rumbling groan to express aggression, barking to express excitement and howling to express his unity with the greater pack. The Greenland Dog is aggressive with other dogs. Firm training is required.

Care and functions
This dog is not suited to indoor living, nor to hot climates. This sled dog requires abundant exercise. Regular brushing is required.
· Hunting dog (seals and bear).
· Sled dog.
· Guard dog.
· Pet.

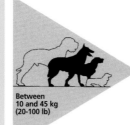

Samoyed

This Arctic spitz is directly descended from the breed that accompanied Samoyed tribes on their migrations. The Samoyed belongs to one of the oldest Siberian breeds. The Samoyeds used these dogs to guard herds and to hunt bear and walrus. The first Samoyeds arrived in Great Britain around 1890. Robert Scott, an early polar explorer, brought the breed to the attention of the world, demonstrating its ability to pull heavy loads over long distances. At that time, the breed began to spread around the globe.

Spitz type. Square body outline. Powerful. Elegant. Dignified. Trotter. Relaxed, energetic gait.

1

NORDIC SLED DOGS

COUNTRY OF ORIGIN
Scandinavian countries

5

ORIGINAL NAME
Samoiedskaya Sabaka

Between 10 and 45 kg (20-100 lb)

Character, special skills and training
Rustic, robust, energetic and active, the Samoyed is independent, self-assured and calm. This breed makes an affectionate, gentle pet. The Samoyed barks a lot, making him a good guard dog. Training must be firm, but undertaken with patience and loving attention.

Care and functions
The Samoyed must not be closed up indoors. He needs space and room to run. Daily brushing is required. A curry comb is necessary during seasonal shedding.
· Hunting dog (walrus, etc.).
· Sled dog.
· Guard dog.
· Pet.

HEAD
Strong. Wedge-shaped skull. Straight nose bridge. Strong, deep muzzle tapering toward the nose. Tight, black lips. Lips curve up at the corners producing the "Samoyed smile".

EYES
Almond shape, set obliquely in the skull, wide set. Dark brown color. Black rims.

EARS
Set on high, relatively small, triangular, mobile and carried erect.

BODY
Robust, compact, muscular. Strong neck carried erect. Broad chest is well let down.

Belly moderately tucked up. Strong, muscular, slightly sloped croup. Straight, muscular back.

LIMBS
Oval feet with slightly splayed, arched toes. Muscular legs with substantial bone.

TAIL
Carried curved over the back along the midline or to the side. Can be carried down. Richly clad.

COAT
Profuse, heavy, dense, flexible. Forms ruff around the neck and shoulders (particularly prominent

in the dog). Shorter on the head and front of the legs. Dense, soft, short, compact undercoat.

COLOR
White, cream, or white and biscuit (white background with light biscuit markings).

SIZE
Dog: approx. 57 cm (22.5 in). Bitch: approx. 53 cm (21 in).

WEIGHT
Dog: 20 to 30 kg (44-66 lb). Bitch: 17 to 25 kg (37.5-55) lb.

Siberian Husky

In Canada, a Husky is any sled dog with a husky bark. Originating in northern Siberia, the Siberian Husky, which is probably descended from the wolf, was developed by the native Chukchi tribe. In 1909, the breed was introduced in Canada to be used in sled dog races. The first standard was published in 1930 and the first American Siberian Husky Club was formed in 1938. The breed arrived in Europe in 1950 and was recognized by the FCI in 1966.

Smallest and lightest of the nordic breeds. Fastest. Elegant purebred appearance. Balanced proportions. Quick and light in action.

NORDIC SLED DOGS 1

COUNTRY OF ORIGIN
North America

OTHER NAME
Arctic Husky

Between 10 and 45 kg (20-100 lb)

5

HEAD
Not heavy. Skull slightly rounded on the top. Very pronounced stop. Muzzle of moderate length. Dark lips. Nose blends with coat color.

EYES
Almond shape, set slightly oblique. Brown or blue color. One eye of each color or parti-colored eyes permissible.

EARS
Medium size, triangular. Carried erect, set high and close together. Thick and well furred.

BODY
Moderately compact. Arched neck carried proudly erect when dog is standing. When trotting, neck is extended forward so that head is carried slightly forward. Deep and strong, but not too broad. Taut, lean loin. Sloped croup, though never steeply sloped. Straight, solid, moderately long back.

LIMBS
Muscular legs of substantial bone. Compact, oval (not long) feet with hard pads.

TAIL
Richly clad, carried above the level of the back in a sickle curve.

COAT
Medium length, straight and somewhat smooth-lying. Never harsh. Dense, soft undercoat.

COLOR
Any color from black to solid white is acceptable. A variety of markings and striking patterns is common.

SIZE
Dog: 54 to 60 cm (21-23.5 in). Bitch: 51 to 56 cm (20-22 in).

WEIGHT
Dog: 20.5 to 28 kg (45-60 lb). Bitch: 15.5 to 23 kg (35-50) lb.

Character, special skills and training
This rustic dog of great endurance is very independent and tends to roam. As a pet, he is affectionate and sociable. The Siberian Husky does not make a good guard dog because he is not wary of strangers. This breed is not aggressive with other dogs. The Siberian Husky's hunting instinct is extremely strong, so he requires a strong, high enclosure. Through firm training, the owner must establish his position as pack leader.

Care and functions
This breed is made for the great outdoors and will be very unhappy if kept indoors. The Siberian Husky needs intense exercise to maintain mental health. Weekly brushing is required. Currying is required during seasonal shedding.
· Sled dog (light loads at moderate speeds over great distances).
· Pet.

155

Spitz type.
Very well constructed.

2

NORDIC HUNTING DOGS

COUNTRY OF ORIGIN
Norway

ORIGINAL NAMES
Norsk Elghund Grä (Gray Norwegian Elkhound)
Norsk Elghund Sort (Black Norwegian Elkhound)

Medium Breeds between 10 and 25 kg (20-55 lb)

Norwegian Elkhound

Originating in Norway, the very old Norwegian Elkhound already existed at the time of the Vikings. This mighty hunter attacks large game (deer, elk, bear, wolves) without a moment's hesitation. The breed was shown for the first time in 1877 and recognized by The Kennel Club in 1901. There are two varieties: the Gray Norwegian Elkhound and the Black Norwegian Elkhound.

Character, special skills and training
This sporting, courageous dog has great endurance. Though the Norwegian Elkhound is rather independent, he is very friendly and calm. He is affectionate and loving with his owner and very gentle with children, making him an excellent pet. With his remarkable sense of smell, he can sniff out an elk from several kilometers away. The Norwegian Elkhound uses a broad range of barks to communicate. This very alert dog makes a good guard dog. He can be aggressive toward other dogs. Firm but gentle training is appropriate.

Care and functions
The Norwegian Elkhound is not suited to life in the city. He needs a lot of room to run and burn off his energy, preferably in the forest. Daily brushing and combing are required.
· Herder.
· Sled dog.
· Utility dog: Army dog.
· Pet.

HEAD
Broad between the eyes. Skull almost flat. Clearly marked stop. Straight nose bridge. Moderately long muzzle. Strong jaw. Tightly closed lips.

EYES
Brown color, as dark as possible.

EARS
Set on high. Firm and erect. Pointed tips.

BODY
Short and compact. Strong, muscular neck without dewlap. Broad, deep chest. Ribs well sprung. Belly very slightly tucked up. Broad, straight back. Muscular loin.

LIMBS
Oval, compact feet with tightly closed toes. Powerful legs with substantial bone.

TAIL
Set high. Thick. Carried curled tightly over the back.

COAT
Harsh, thick, abundant. Short on the head and front of the legs. Longer on the chest, neck (collarette), back of the legs and thighs. Long on the extremities. Wooly, lighter undercoat in grays. Blacks have black undercoat.

COLOR
Gray variety: shades of gray with black tips on the longest hairs; lighter on the chest,
belly, legs and under the tail. Black variety: brilliant black. A small amount of white on the chest, front legs and feet is permissible.

SIZE
Gray variety: dog: approx. 52 cm (20.5 in); bitch: approx. 49 cm (19.5 in). Black variety: dog: 45 to 50 cm (18-20 in); bitch: 42 to 47 cm (16.5-18.5 in).

WEIGHT
Gray variety: approx. 25 kg (55 lb).
Black variety: approx. 20 kg (44 lb).

Swedish Elkhound

This ancient breed hunts elk and bear, pulls sledges and guards livestock. Its type was fixed in 1953, and the breed is rare outside Sweden.

Lupoid. Balanced proportions. Relaxed, easy gait.

Large Breeds between 25 and 45 kg (55-100 lb)

2

NORDIC HUNTING DOGS

COUNTRY OF ORIGIN
Sweden

ORIGINAL NAME
Jämthund

5

HEAD
Long, dry, relatively broad. Slightly domed skull. Pronounced stop. Straight nose bridge. Tightly closed lips.

EYES
Slightly oval and fairly small. Dark brown color.

EARS
Set on high. Relatively small. Carried erect. Pointed tips.

BODY
Compact, sturdy and dry. Long, strong neck without dewlap. Broad chest. Powerful loin. Belly slightly tucked up. Broad croup is very slightly sloped. Straight back slopes gently from withers to croup.

LIMBS
Strong, compact, slightly oval feet.

TAIL
Set high. Moderate length. Thick and strong. Carried curled over the back.

COAT
Long and hard with dark tips. Short and smooth on the head and front of the legs. Longer on the neck, chest, tail and back of the legs. Shorter, soft, lighter (preferably white) undercoat.

COLOR
From dark to light gray. Light gray or cream on the muzzle, cheeks and throat is typical.

SIZE
Dog: 58 to 63 cm (23-25 in).
Bitch: 53 to 58 cm (21-23 in).

WEIGHT
Approx. 30 kg (66.2 lb).

Character, special skills and training
This hardy, courageous, bold dog is stable and calm. He is friendly and gentle with children, making him a good pet. He is also a good guard dog. The Swedish Elkhound is slightly dominant with other dogs.

Care and functions
The Swedish Elkhound is not suited to life in the city. He needs a lot of room to run and considerable exercise. Daily brushing and combing are required.
· Herder.
· Utility dog: Army dog.
· Sled dog.
· Hunting dog: elk, bear, small game (marten, ermine, etc.).
· Pet.

Lundehund

The Lundehund originated on Vaeroy Island, one of the Lofoten Islands off the northern coast of Norway. The breed is thought to have been developed in the village of Mostad. In the past, the Lundehund was used for hunting web-footed birds and puffins (Lunde in Norwegian) on cliffs and for guarding livestock. When this work was abandoned, the breed almost disappeared. It was not reestablished until after 1960. This breed is esteemed for its special skills and the fact that its anatomical structure is very similar to that of primitive dogs. It is now kept as a pet.

Spitz type. Supple, fairly light. Elastic gait with forelegs circling outward slightly.

2

NORDIC HUNTING DOGS

5

COUNTRY OF ORIGIN
Norway

ORIGINAL NAME
Norsk Lundehund

OTHER NAME
Norwegian Puffin Dog

Small Breeds under 10 kg (under 20 lb)

Character, special skills and training

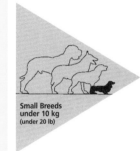

This vigorous, energetic, alert, lively dog has an independent streak, but is not aggressive. He is a cheerful, affectionate pet. The breed is remarkably agile and flexible. In fact, Lundehund can turn his forelegs straight out at 90-degree angles and his neck is so flexible, he can touch his back with his head. Firm training is required.

Care and functions
This dog cannot be confined indoors. He needs space and considerable exercise. Regular brushing and combing are required.
· Hunting dog.
· Pet.

HEAD
Medium width, conical shape. Slightly domed skull. Pronounced stop. Slightly arched nose bridge.

EYES
Slightly almond shaped. Yellowish-brown color.

EARS
Medium size, triangular. Broad at the base. Very mobile, carried erect. When the dog is underwater, the ear folds back sealing the ear canal.

BODY
Rectangular outline. Strong. Fairly strong neck with collarette. Long chest is well let down. Slightly tucked up belly. Slightly sloped croup. Straight back.

LIMBS
Strong legs. Oval feet are turned out slightly. There are six toes on each foot, eight pads on the forelegs and seven pads on the hind legs.

TAIL
Set high. Moderate length. Richly clad. Carried either in a ring, slightly curled over the back, or hanging.

COAT
Dense and heavy. Short on the head and front of the legs. Longer on the neck, back of the thighs and tail. Soft undercoat.

COLOR
Color always in combination with white: chestnut to fawn sprinkled with black-tipped hairs; gray; white with dark spots.

SIZE
Dog: 35 to 38 cm (14-15 in).
Bitch: 32 to 35 cm (12.5-14 in).

WEIGHT
Dog: approx. 7 kg (15.5 lb).
Bitch: approx. 6 kg (13.2 lb).

Karelian Bear Dog

Closely related to the Laika, the Karelian Bear Dog is descended from an old Finnish breed to which Russian breeders introduced Utchak Sheepdog blood. The Karelian Bear Dog originated in Karelia, the territory extending from north of St. Petersburg to Finland. The Karelian Bear Dog was originally used to hunt elk, then later to hunt bear and large game. The breed was recognized by the FCI in 1946.

Sturdy constitution.
Slightly longer than tall.

Medium Breeds
between
10 and 25 kg
(20-55 lb)

NORDIC HUNTING DOGS 2

COUNTRY OF ORIGIN
Finland

ORIGINAL NAME
Karjalankarhukoïra

5

HEAD
Triangular when viewed from the front. Broad skull. Slightly convex forehead. Distinct stop. Deep muzzle. Large nose. Thin, tightly closed lips.

EYES
Small. Brown color.

EARS
Carried erect. Slightly rounded tips.

BODY
Solid. Strong, arched neck. Capacious chest. Straight, supple back. Broad, slightly sloped croup.

LIMBS
Compact, fairly round feet. Strong legs.

TAIL
Set high. Moderate length. Carried curled over the back.

COAT
Stiff and harsh. Longer on the neck, back and back of the thighs. Soft, dense undercoat.

COLOR
Black with dull brownish cast caused by the normally chestnut undercoat. White spots or markings on the head, neck, chest, underbelly and legs.

SIZE
Dog: 57 cm (22.5 in) (ideal).
Bitch: 52 cm (20.5 in) (ideal).

WEIGHT
Approx. 25 kg (55 lb).

Character, special skills and training
This very rustic, hardy dog is courageous and eager. Though stable, the breed is independent and a bit anti-social. He is gentle with his family, though his personality is not like that of most pets. He uses his keen sense of smell for hunting large game. The Karelian Bear Dog is a good guard dog, but is not a herder or sled dog. Given his latent aggressive nature, this dog should never be trained to attack. Firm training is a must.

Care and functions
This dog must not be closed up indoors. He needs a lot of space and considerable exercise to burn off energy. Daily brushing is required.
· Hunting dog (large game).
· Pet.

Sturdy constitution
Thick skin.

Laika

The Laika belongs to the spitz family. There are three varieties. The Russo-European Laika is descended from the hunting Laikas and originated in northern Russia. This variety is now common in the central region of the country. The Western Siberian Laika originated in the northern Urals and is the result of crossing Laikas and hunting dogs. The Eastern Siberian Laika originated in the large forests in the east. It is the result of crosses of various Laikas. This variety is used for hunting large northern game. This breed is famous because a Laika became the "first living ambassador from Earth" when he was hurtled into space aboard Sputnik II on November 3, 1957.

2

NORDIC HUNTING DOGS

5

COUNTRY OF ORIGIN
Russia

ORIGINAL NAMES
Three varieties:
Rusko Evropeiskaya Laika (Russo-European Laika)
Zapadno Sibirskaya Laika (Western Siberian Laika)
Vostotchno Sibirskaya Laika (Eastern Siberian Laika)

Between 10 and 45 kg (20-100 lb)

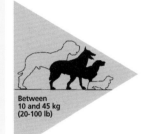

Character, special skills and training
This lively, alert dog has a strong, stable personality. He barks a lot (laika means "barker"). The Laika is very devoted to his owner and suspicious of strangers. Firm training is a must.

Care and functions
This dog is not suited for life as a house dog. He needs space and considerable exercise.
· Hunting dog.
· Sled dog.
· Guard dog.
· Pet.

HEAD
Not heavy. Skull is the shape of an isosceles triangle. Stop not pronounced. Clean muzzle. Tight lips.

EYES
Not large. Oval. Set obliquely in the skull. Dark color.

EARS
Triangular, carried erect. Mobile. Pointed tips.

BODY
Strong. Pronounced withers. Full chest is well let down. Broad, slightly sloped croup. Belly is tucked up. Short, slightly sloped loin. Solid, muscular back.

LIMBS
Strong legs with substantial bone. Oval, compact feet.

TAIL
Carried in a sickle or curled over the back or the back of the thighs.

COAT
Russo-European and Western Siberian Laikas: Hard, straight, short on the head and ears. Longer on the neck, withers and shoulders. Feathering on the back of the legs. Full undercoat. Eastern Siberian Laika: Long, coarse, dense, straight. Male has a mane and collarette. Dense, supple undercoat.

COLOR
Russo-European Laika: black, gray, white, pepper and salt, dark with white markings or white with dark markings. Western Siberian Laika:

white, pepper and salt, red and shades of gray; black is permissible.
Eastern Siberian Laika: pepper and salt, white, gray, black, shades of red or brown; spotted or mottled.

SIZE
Russo-European Laika: dog: 52 to 58 cm (20.5-22.8 in), bitch: 50 to 56 cm 19.7-22 in).
Western Siberian Laika: dog: 54 to 60 cm (21-23.5 in), bitch: 52 to 58 cm (20.5-22.8 in).
Eastern Siberian Laika: dog: 55 to 63 cm (22-25 in), bitch: 53 to 61 cm (21-24 in).

WEIGHT
20 to 30 kg (44-66 lb).

Finnish Spitz

The Finnish Spitz was probably brought to Finland by nomadic Asian tribes and is related to the Russian Laika. In days of old, the Finnish Spitz was used by the Lapps to track elk and bear. Today, the breed is used to hunt birds like grouse. The first standard was written in 1892 and the breed was recognized by The Kennel Club in 1935.

Bold carriage. Noble gait.

2

NORDIC HUNTING DOGS

COUNTRY OF ORIGIN
Finland

ORIGINAL NAME
Suomenpystikorva
("dog with pointed ears")

OTHER NAMES
Loulou Finnois
Finsk Spets

Between 10 and 45 kg (20-100 lb)

5

HEAD
Moderate size, dry, foxlike. Slightly arched forehead. Pronounced stop. Tight, thin lips.

EYES
Medium size. Dark color.

EARS
Mobile, carried erect. Pointed tips. Covered with fine hair.

BODY
Almost square. Deep chest. Belly slightly tucked up. Strong, straight back.

LIMBS
Round feet. Strong legs.

TAIL
Carried curled over the loin and pointing toward the thigh.

COAT
Short on the head and front of the legs. Longer and straight on the body, back of the legs and tail. Much longer on the shoulders, particularly in dogs. Short, soft, dense, lighter-colored undercoat.

COLOR
Reddish-brown or golden-red on the back. Lighter shade on the cheeks, under the muzzle, on the chest, abdomen, inside of the legs, back of the thighs and under the tail. White markings on the feet and a narrow white stripe on the forechest are permitted, as are black hairs on the lips and along the back.

SIZE
Dog: 44 to 50 cm (16,5-20 in).
Bitch: 39 to 45 cm (15.5-18 in).

WEIGHT
23 to 27 kg (51-59.5 lb).

Character, special skills and training
This lively, courageous, happy dog is well loved as a pet. His hunting instinct is put to use for finding flocks of birds. The breed is very "vocal" and expresses itself with a wide range of sounds, including "yodeling". His distrust of strangers makes him an excellent guard dog. This sensitive dog requires firm yet gentle training.

Care and functions
The Finnish Spitz can adapt easily to life as a house dog provided he gets plenty of outdoor exercise and is not left alone for extended periods. This breed is very clean. Daily brushing is required, but professional grooming is not.
· Hunting dog.
· Guard dog.
· Pet.

Norbottenspets

This very old breed is directly descended from the peat dogs. He is used as a hunting dog (hare and rabbit) and as a sled dog.

Spitz type. Cobby. Well built. Free, even gait.

2

NORDIC HUNTING DOGS

5

COUNTRY OF ORIGIN
Sweden

OTHER NAME
Nordic Spitz

Small Breeds under 10 kg (under 20 lb)

Character, special skills, and training
This courageous, lively, hardy breed is very active and has great endurance. He has a balanced personality and is never nervous or aggressive. This affectionate breed gets along well with children. He is also a good guard dog.

Care and functions
The Norbottenspets can adapt to life in the city provided he gets long, frequent walks. Regular brushing is required.
· Hunting dog.
· Guard dog.
· Pet.

HEAD
Dry, strong, wedge-shaped. Moderately broad, rather flat skull. Slightly domed forehead. Stop not pronounced. Straight nose bridge. Very pointed muzzle. Fine, dry lips.

EYES
Medium size, almond, set obliquely in the skull. Dark color.

EARS
Set on high. Held stiffly erect.

BODY
Square body outline. Dry neck is carried proudly.

Pronounced forechest. Chest is moderately deep. Muscular, slightly sloped croup. Belly is moderately tucked up. Broad, short loin. Short, strong, muscular neck.

LIMBS
Muscular legs. Small, solid, very compact feet.

TAIL
Set high and carried in a large circle curling loosely over the back with the tip touching the side of the thigh.

COAT
Short, hard, dense. Short

hair on the head and front of the legs. Longer on the body, back of the thighs, and under the tail. Fine, dense undercoat.

COLOR
All colors permitted. Ideal coat color is a black background with yellow orange markings.

SIZE
Dog: approx. 45 cm (18 in). Bitch: approx. 42 cm (16.5 in).

WEIGHT
Approx. 10 kg (22 lb).

Lapland Reindeer Dog

The Lapland Reindeer Dog was used for centuries to guard reindeer herds and defend them from bears and wolves. The breed is thought to be the result of a cross between the Swedish Lapphund and the German Shepherd.

Solid bone and muscle.

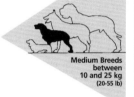

3

NORDIC GUARD AND SHEEPDOGS

Medium Breeds between 10 and 25 kg (20-55 lb)

COUNTRY OF ORIGIN
Finland

ORIGINAL NAME
Lapinporokoïra

OTHER NAMES
Lapponian Herder
Lapponian Vallhund

5

HEAD
Moderate length, slightly domed skull. Distinct stop. Straight muzzle. Tight lips.

EYES
Fairly wide set. Dark color.

EARS
Fairly short. Held erect and forward.

BODY
Longer than tall. Dry, powerful neck. Deep, broad chest. Belly is slightly tucked up. Slightly sloped croup. Straight, strong back

LIMBS
Strong legs. Compact feet. Dewclaws not desirable

TAIL
Moderate length, thick. Not curled, but instead hangs down in a curve.

COAT
Moderate length, straight, coarse, somewhat stand off. Thicker and longer on the neck, chest, and thighs. Soft, dense undercoat.

COLOR
Shades of black with tan markings. White "double eyes" are common. Lighter coloring (grayish or brownish preferred) on the cheeks, underbody and legs. White markings on the neck, chest and legs are permissible.

SIZE
Dog: 49 to 55 cm (19-22 in). Bitch: 43 to 49 cm (17-19 in).

WEIGHT
Approx. 25 kg (55 lb).

· Herder.
· Guard dog.
· Pet.

Character, special skills, and training
This energetic, calm dog makes a nice pet. He barks easily, making him a good guard dog.

Care and functions
The Lapland Reindeer Dog needs considerable space and exercise to burn off energy. Daily brushing is required.

163

Typical spitz. Light construction.
Square body outline.

3

NORDIC GUARD AND SHEEPDOGS

5

COUNTRY OF ORIGIN
Norway

ORIGINAL NAMES
Norsk Buhund
Norwegian Buhund

OTHER NAME
Norwegian Sheepdog

Medium Breeds
between
10 and 25 kg
(20-55 lb)

Norwegian Buhund

Bu means homestead in Norwegian and buhund means sheepdog. This very old breed was used to herd livestock and as a guard dog. The breed was introduced in Iceland where it contributed to the development of the Iceland Dog. The Norwegian Buhund is rare outside of Norway. The breed was recognized by The Kennel Club in 1968.

Character, special skills and training

This rustic, very energetic, courageous dog is quite independent. He is stable, friendly and cheerful, making him an excellent pet. Aggressive if the situation warrants, he is a good guard dog. The Norwegian Buhund is blessed with a remarkable sense of smell, which he uses to hunt wild birds.

Care and functions

The Norwegian Buhund can adapt to life in the city provided he has plenty of space and is allowed to get a lot of exercise. Regular brushing and combing is required.
· Herder (reindeer, sheep).
· Guard dog.
· Versatile utility dog.
· Pet.

HEAD
Conical shape, dry. Skull is almost flat. Distinct stop. Straight nose bridge. Short muzzle tapers toward the nose. Very tight lips.

EYES
As dark as possible and in harmony with coat color.

EARS
Pointed. Held stiffly erect.

BODY
Short, compact. Dry, fairly short neck. Chest is well let down. Ribs well sprung. Strong loin. Straight, strong back.

LIMBS
Dry, muscular legs with plenty of bone. Compact, oval feet.

TAIL
Set high and carried curled tightly over the back. Richly clad.

COAT
Dense, abundant, hard, close-lying. Short on the head and front of the legs. Longer on the neck and forechest. Soft, thick, wooly undercoat.

COLOR
Wheaten: solid color ranging from light to golden red;

mask permissible.
Black: solid color with white flashing on the head; white markings on the forechest, narrow white collar around the neck and white on the feet are permissible.

SIZE
Dog: 43 to 47 cm (17-18.5 in).
Bitch: 41 to 45 cm (16-18 in).

WEIGHT
Dog: 14 to 18 kg (31-40 lb).
Bitch: 12 to 16 kg (26.5-35 lb).

Iceland Dog

This breed is probably descended from the Norwegian Buhund which was crossed with local Icelandic breeds. The Iceland Dog was used to guard sheep and horses. In the nineteenth century, the breed was almost wiped out by distemper, but was saved by breeders in Iceland and England.

Light Spitz type

3

NORDIC GUARD AND SHEEPDOGS

Up to 25 kg (55 lb)

COUNTRY OF ORIGIN
Iceland - England

5

ORIGINAL NAME
Islandsk Färehond

OTHER NAMES
Icelandic Sheepdog
Iceland Spitz

HEAD
Light and fairly broad. Distinct stop. Fairly short muzzle. Tight lips.

EYES
Small, round. Dark color.

EARS
Broad at the base. Triangular with pointed tips. Carried very erect.

BODY
Strong, fairly short. Not heavy. Strong neck. Broad, deep chest. Belly is well tucked up.

LIMBS
Oval feet. Very muscular legs.

TAIL
Moderate length. Thick. Carried curled over the back.

COAT
Hard, moderately long. Longer on the neck, thighs and under the tail. Short on the head and legs. Lies flat on the body.

COLOR
White with fawn, golden or light fawn markings with black tips.

SIZE
Dog: 42 to 48 cm (16.5-19 in).
Bitch: 38 to 44 cm (15-17 in).

WEIGHT
10 to 15 kg (22-33 lb).

Character, special skills and training
This sturdy, hardy dog has a strong personality. He is affectionate and very friendly with people. This alert dog likes to bark, making him a good guard dog. Firm training is required.

Care and functions
This breed is accustomed to living in the great outdoors, therefore keeping him as a house dog is not recommended. The Iceland Dog needs room to run. Regular brushing is required.
· Herder.
· Guard dog.
· Pet.

Finnish Lapphund

This breed was developed by the Lapps for hunting and guarding their reindeer herds. It is rare outside of its native Finland.

Type Spitz. Medium size.

3

NORDIC GUARD DOGS AND HERDERS

5

COUNTRY OF ORIGIN
Finland

ORIGINAL NAME
Lapinkoïra

Medium Breeds between 10 and 25 kg (20-55 lb)

Character, special skills and training
This rustic, energetic, lively dog is always alert, but is still calm and obedient. Wary of strangers, the Finnish Lapphund barks easily. Firm training is required.

Care and functions
The Finnish Lapphund needs space and plenty of exercise. Regular brushing is required.
· Herder.
· Hunting dog.
· Pet.

HEAD
Fairly short. Broad skull. Distinct stop. Slender, tapering muzzle. Tight lips.

EYES
Fairly wide set. Dark color.

EARS
Held erect and forward. Rather wide set.

BODY
Slightly longer than tall. Dry, strong neck. Deep chest. Belly is slightly tucked up. Straight, broad back.

LIMBS
Strong, muscular legs. Compact feet.

TAIL
Moderate length. Thick and carried curled loosely over the back.

COAT
Moderate length. Straight, rather stand-off and coarse. Dense, soft, thick undercoat.

COLOR
Shades of gray-black, fawn with other color markings.

Ideal is black with reddish nuances.

SIZE
Dog: 46 to 52 cm (18-20.5 in).
Bitch: 40 to 46 cm (16-18 in).

WEIGHT
Approx. 25 kg (55 lb).

Swedish Lapphund

Originating in Finland, the Swedish Lapphund may be descended from the arctic wolf and the 7,000-year-old Varanger Dog, which was discovered in northern Norway. If this is true, the Swedish Lapphund may be the common ancestor of all spitz dogs. The Lapphund has always been used to guard livestock and pull sleds. The breed has been popular in Sweden for centuries but was not recognized by the FCI until 1944.

Large Spitz

3

5

NORDIC GUARD AND SHEEPDOGS

Medium Breeds between 10 and 25 kg (20-55 lb)

COUNTRY OF ORIGIN
Finland

ORIGINAL NAME
Lapplandska Spetz

OTHER NAME
Swedish Spitz

HEAD
Strong lines. Domed skull. Pronounced stop. Straight muzzle. Tight lips.

EYES
Dark color.

EARS
Short, broad at the base, wide set, very mobile. Held erect.

BODY
Long. Moderately long neck. Ribs well sprung. Belly very slightly tucked up. Straight back.

LIMBS
Oval, compact feet. Powerful legs that appear short.

TAIL
Moderate length or short. Thick. Often carried over the loin.

COAT
Long, straight, dense. Shorter on the head and front of the legs. Collarette at the neck. Soft, thick undercoat.

COLOR
Solid or pied black or liver.

SIZE
Dog: 45 to 50 cm (18-20 in).
Bitch: 40 to 45 cm (16-18 in).

WEIGHT
15 to 20 kg (33-44 lb).

Character, special skills and training
This hardy, alert, calm dog has remarkable courage. He is very loyal to his owner and has found his place as an affectionate pet. Suspicious of strangers, this guard dog is always on alert. Firm training is needed.

Care and functions
The Swedish Spitz needs a lot of exercise and room to run. Regular brushing and combing are required.
· Herder.
· Utility dog: army security dog.
· Guard dog.
· Pet.

Swedish Vallhund

Long, low on leg. Powerful. Beautiful movements.

An indigenous Swedish breed, the Swedish Vallhund
is a spitz type dog, despite the fact that he looks similar
to the Pembroke Welsh Corgi. In the past, the Swedish Vallhund
was used for cattle droving and guarding horses. Count Bjorn von
Rosen worked on behalf of the breed, getting it recognized
and registered with the Swedish Kennel Club in 1948.
In 1974, a few specimens were sent to Great Britain,
but the breed is still rare outside its native Sweden.

3

NORDIC GUARD AND SHEEPDOGS

5

COUNTRY OF ORIGIN
Sweden

ORIGINAL NAME
Väsgôtaspets

OTHER NAME
Swedish Cattledog

Up to 25 kg
(55 lb)

Character, special skills and training
This rustic, extremely courageous, lively dog is energetic, always on the alert and quite independent. He has earned his place as an affection pet that is gentle with children. His vigilance has gained him the reputation of a good guard dog. Firm training is required.

Care and functions
This sporting dog is not suited for life indoors. He needs to work off his abundant energy daily. Regular brushing is required.
· Cattle dog.
· Guard dog.
· Pet.

HEAD
Fairly long and foxlike. Skull is almost flat. Distinct stop. Square muzzle profile. Tightly closed lips.

EYES
Medium size, oval. Dark brown color.

EARS
Medium size, pointed tips. Held erect.

BODY
Long. Long, muscular neck is held high. Long chest is well let down. Ribs well sprung. Broad, slightly sloped croup. Belly slightly tucked up. Strong, short loin. Horizontal, muscular back.

LIMBS
Short, muscular legs with plenty of bone. Short, oval feet with strong pads.

TAIL
Two types: long or naturally very short. Carried straight out at back level. Many puppies are born tailless.

COAT
Moderate length. Hard, compact and weatherproof. Short on the front of the legs. Slightly longer on the neck, chest and back of the legs. Dense, soft undercoat.

COLOR
Preferred colors are gray, grayish brown, grayish gold and reddish brown, with darker hairs on the back, neck and sides of the body. Lighter hairs on the muzzle, throat, chest, underbelly, thighs, hocks and feet. Lightest coloring on the shoulders ("harness markings") is desirable. Small white markings are permissible, such as a narrow flare, a spot on the neck or a slight collar.

SIZE
Dog: 33 cm (13 in).
Bitch: 31 cm (12 in).

WEIGHT
9 to 14 kg (20-31 lb).

WOLFSPITZ

GIANT SPITZ

4

EUROPEAN SPITZ

5

COUNTRY OF ORIGIN
Germany

ORIGINAL NAME
Deutscher Spitz

Up to 25 kg
(55 lb)

Compact, Sturdy
and thickset. Elegant
silhouette. Thick, fluffy coat.
Light, elastic gait.

German Spitz

*Spitz dogs are descended from Stone Age peat dogs
(Canis familiaris palustris), through Neolithic lacustrine
spitz dogs. They are, therefore, one of the oldest domestic breeds,
descended from lupoid dogs. There are numerous spitz varieties:
- Wolfspitz, also known as the Keeshond, is the largest
variety measuring 45 to 55 cm (18-22 in).
- Giant Spitz (Grosspitz) measuring 42 to 50 cm (16,5-20 in).
- Standard Spitz (Mittlespitz) measuring 30 to 38 cm (12-15 in).
- Small Spitz (Kleinspitz) measuring 23 to 29 cm (9-11,5 in).
- Toy Spitz (Zwergspitz) measuring 18 to 22 cm (7-9 in).
The Wolfspitz first became popular in the Netherlands
where it was named the Keeshond after W. Kees, the Dutch
leader who revolted in the seventeenth century against
the House of Orange. The Keeshond later became popular
in the United States. The Small and Toy Spitz have been called
Pomeranian Loulous after the Baltic region where some spitz
were developed. The first Spitz club, called the French
Pomeranian Loulou Club, was created in France in 1935. In
1960, the club changed its name to the French Spitz Club.
The small and toy varieties are the most common spitz.*

WHITE STANDARD SPITZ

TOY SPITZ

ORANGE TOY SPITZ

ORANGE SMALL SPITZ

HEAD
Medium size, foxlike. Wedge-shaped skull tapering to a pointed nose (spitz means "pointed"). Moderate stop. Muzzle is not overly long. Black lips except in brown coated spitz.

EYES
Medium size, slightly oval and set slightly obliquely in the skull. Dark color.

EARS
Small, close set, triangular, pointed tips. Always held erect.

BODY
Square body outline. Moderately long neck without dewlap and with a thick collarette. Chest is well let down. Broad, short, powerful loin. Belly slightly tucked up. Short, horizontal back. Broad, short croup is not sloped.

LIMBS
Round, compact feet with thick pads. Muscular legs with plenty of bone.

TAIL
Very bushy. Carried forward curled tightly over the back.

COAT
Long, straight, stand-off. The head, ears, front of the legs and feet are covered with dense, short hair. The rest of the body is covered with long, abundant hair. Not wavy, curly or shaggy. Thick main, feathering and breeching. Short, thick, wooly undercoat.

COLOR
- Wolfspitz: wolf gray only (shaded gray, silvery charcoal gray with black on the tips of the hairs).
- Standard Spitz: Black, brown, white orange, wolf gray and other colors, including blue, cream, beaver or color on white background.
- Toy Spitz: black, brown, white orange, wolf gray and other colors.

SIZE
According to variety:
18 to 55 cm (7-22 in).

WEIGHT
Wolfspitz: approx. 20 kg (44 lb).
Toy Spitz: less than 3.5 kg (8 lb).

Character, special skills and training
This robust, lively, alert dog is calm and independent by nature. He forms a strong bond with his owner and makes an affectionate, though sometimes jealous, pet. Courageous, vigilant and wary of strangers, the Wolfspitz in particular is an excellent guard dog. The spitz tends to be aggressive with other dogs. Firm, patient training is required.

Care and functions
Small spitz adjust to city living better than larger varieties. Brushing twice per week is required.
· Guard dog.
· Pet.

171

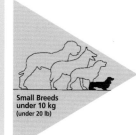

Volpino Italiano

The Volpino Italiano is descended from European Spitz that developed in central Italy during the Bronze Age. This ancient breed is esteemed for natural guard dog instinct. The Volpino Italiano looks similar to the German Spitz and the Pomeranian Loulou. The Volpino was loved by palace lords; Michealangelo himself even kept a Volpino. Cart drivers in Tuscany and Latium also favored this fluffy companion.

Small and very compact. Balanced proportions. Gait: long strides.

4

EUROPEAN SPITZ

5

COUNTRY OF ORIGIN
Italy

ORIGINAL NAME
Volpino italiano
(volpino means "small fox" in Italian)

OTHER NAMES
Fiorentine Spitz
Cane de Quirinale

Small Breeds
under 10 kg
(under 20 lb)

Character, special skills and training
This lively, cheerful, playful dog has a strong personality. The Volpino is affectionate and a good playmate for children. Wary of strangers, this dog does not hesitate to bark, making him a reliable guard dog. Firm training is required.

Care and functions
The Volpino italiano adapts easily to life as a house dog. Regular brushing is required. This breed should not be bathed too often.
· Guard dog.
· Pet.

HEAD
Pyramid shape. Egg-shaped, round skull. Marked stop. Straight nose bridge. Pointed muzzle. Black lips.

EYES
Average size, wide open. Dark ochre color. Black rims.

EARS
Short and triangular. Held erect.

BODY
Square construction. Chest extends to the elbow. Ribs well sprung. Belly very slightly tucked up. Croup extends the line of the loin. Straight back.

LIMBS
Oval feet with black pads and nails. Light-boned legs.

TAIL
Always carried curled over the back. Covered with very long hair.

COAT
Bushy, very long and stand-off. Harsh texture. Medium-long on the skull. Short on the muzzle. Feathering on the backs of the legs.

COLOR
Solid white, solid red (rare). Champagne is permissible.

SIZE
Dog: 27 to 30 cm (10.5-12 in).
Bitch: 25 to 28 cm (10-11 in).

WEIGHT
Approx. 5 kg (11 lb).

Akita

The Akita was developed in Akita Province on Honshu Island. Originally called the Akita Matagi (dog that hunts bears), this breed is a medium size hunting dog. The ancestors of the Akita may have been Chinese breeds which were later crossed with a mastiff and the Tosa. The Akita was long used as a large game hunting dog and for dog fighting. The breed began to decline, but made an astonishing comeback when it was designated as part of Japan's natural heritage. The Akita, the largest Japanese spitz type, is now kept almost exclusively as a pet. This large spitz is also prized in Europe and the United States where a larger variety has been developed that weighs approximately 50 kg (110 lb).

Sturdy construction. Balanced proportions. Powerful. Noble, dignified bearing. Powerful, elastic gait.

5

ASIAN SPITZ AND RELATED BREEDS

COUNTRY OF ORIGIN
Japan

ORIGINAL NAME
Akita Inu

OTHER NAME
Japanese Akita

Large Breeds between 25 and 45 kg (55-100 lb)

5

HEAD
Strong. Broad forehead. Marked stop with distinctly visible furrow extends up the forehead. Straight nose bridge. Fairly long, strong muzzle. Tight lips.

EYES
Small, almost triangular. Dark brown color.

EARS
Small, thick, triangular, with slightly rounded tips. Held erect and forward.

BODY
Elongated. Thick, muscular neck without dewlap. Deep chest. Ribs are moderately well sprung. Belly well tucked up. Broad, muscular loin. Straight, solid back.

LIMBS
Thick, round, compact, arched feet. Heavy-boned, powerful legs.

TAIL
Set high. Thick. Carried curled tightly over the back.

COAT
Short, hard, straight. Longer on the withers and croup. Even longer on the tail. Dense, soft undercoat.

COLOR
Red, sesame, brindle and white. All except whites must be urajiro (whitish hair on the sides of the muzzle, on the cheeks, under the jaw, on the throat, forechest, underbody, bottom of the tail and inside of the legs).

SIZE
Dog: 67 cm (26.5 in), (64 to 70 cm) (25-27.5 in). Bitch: 61 cm (24 in), (58 to 64 cm) (23-25 in).

WEIGHT
30 to 50 kg (66-110 lb).

Character, special skills and training
This robust, vigorous, very courageous dog is independent and proud, but calm. He is docile, making him an excellent pet that is easy to live with. This exceptional guard dog is wary of strangers and always on alert, but he rarely barks. The Akita has an alpha personality and therefore has difficulty living with other dogs. Firm though gentle training is required.

Care and functions
This very sporting breed can adapt to life as a house dog only if he gets a lot of exercise every day. Daily brushing is required. A curry brush is recommended during seasonal shedding.
· Guard dog.
· Utility dog: police dog, guide dog.
· Pet.

Chow Chow

The Chow Chow (named Chou, "hunting dog" in its native land) has been popular in China for more than two thousand years. The Huns, Mongols and Tartars used the breed in war, for hunting and as a draft and guard dog. This furry dog was sometimes eaten (chow means "food") and its fur was used for clothing. The breed first appeared in Europe in 1865 when Queen Victoria was given a magnificent specimen. Selective breeding began in England in 1887 in an attempt to develop a more sociable Chow. The breed was recognized by the Kennel Club in 1894. This breed is now considered a luxury pet.

Compact, powerful, lionlike. Proud, dignified bearing. Short and stilted.

5

ASIAN SPITZ AND RELATED BREEDS

5

COUNTRY OF ORIGIN
China
Sponsored by Great Britain

ORIGINAL NAME
Chou

Medium Breeds between 10 and 25 kg (20-55 lb)

Character, special skills and training

This sturdy, courageous, independent, calm dog has a strong, aloof personality. The Chow Chow rarely barks and is not particularly active. He forms a strong bond with his owner, but is rather distant and not demonstrative. Extremely suspicious of strangers, the Chow Chow is an excellent guard dog. He is aggressive with other dogs. Firm but patient, gentle training must start at a very young age.

Care and functions

The Chow Chow can adapt to life in the city provided he gets out for long daily walks. Daily brushing and combing are required for this very clean dog. A curry brush is needed during seasonal shedding. The Chow Chow despises being tied up and does not tolerate heat well.
· Hunting dog.
· Draft dog.
· Herder.
· Pet.

HEAD
Large. Flat, broad skull. Stop not pronounced. Broad muzzle. Large nose matches coat color. Tongue, palate and lips are blue-black. Black gums.

EYES
Almond shape, fairly small. Dark color. Blue and fawns may have eyes the color of their coat.

EARS
Small, thick, wide set. Held rigidly erect and forward, giving the face its characteristic scowl.

BODY
Balanced proportions. Strong, full neck. Broad chest. Powerful loin. Short, horizontal, strong back.

LIMBS
Muscular, heavy-boned legs. Stifle joint shows little angulation, causing the characterstic stilted gait. Small, round feet.

TAIL
Set high and carried well over the back.

COAT
Rough-coated variety: very abundant, dense, straight, harsh and stand-off; particularly thick around the neck (mane or collarette) and on the back of the thighs (culottes). Soft, wooly undercoat.
Smooth-coated variety: abundant, dense, straight and smooth.

COLOR
Solid black, red, blue, fawn, cream or white, often nuanced but never spotted or parti-color. Underside of the tail and rump are often lighter in color.

SIZE
Dog: 48 to 56 cm (19-22 in). Bitch: 46 to 51 cm (18-20 in).

WEIGHT
Dog: 20 to 25 kg (44-55 lb). Bitch: 18 to 20 kg (40-44 lb).

Eurasian

Professor Julius Wipfel created this dog around 1950
by crossing the Chow Chow and the Wolfspitz.
Samoyed blood was later introduced.
In 1973, the breed was recognized by the FCI.

Balanced proportions. Slightly longer than tall.
Dark skin.

5

ASIAN SPITZ AND RELATED BREEDS

COUNTRY OF ORIGIN
Germany

ORIGINAL NAME
Wolf-Chow

OTHER NAME
Eurasier

Between
10 and 45 kg
(20-100 lb)

5

HEAD
Triangular. Wedge-shaped skull is not overly broad. Stop not pronounced. Muzzle tapers to the nose. Strong jaws. Black lips.

EYES
Medium size, set slightly obliquely in the skull. Dark color. Black rims.

EARS
Medium size, triangular, slightly rounded tips. Held erect.

BODY
Solid, not overly short. Muscular neck. Pronounced withers. Prominent fore-chest. Oval rib cage.

Straight, broad croup. Straight, muscular back.

LIMBS
Muscular legs with moderately heavy bone. Oval, compact feet.

TAIL
Straight, round and solid at the root, tapering to the tip. Carried forward over the back, slightly curved over the side of the loin or curled.

COAT
Moderately long. Not truly stand-off, but not lying close to the skin. Short on the face and front of the legs. Longer on the neck, tail and back of the legs (feathering and culottes). Dense undercoat.

COLOR
All colors and combinations are permissible except pure white, pinto or brown.

SIZE
Dog: 52 to 60 cm (20.5-23.5 in).
Bitch: 48 to 56 cm (19-22 in).

WEIGHT
Dog: 23 to 32 kg (50.5-70 lb).
Bitch: 18 to 26 kg (40-57.5 lb).

Character, special skills and training
This very vigorous dog is good-natured, friendly, calm and stable, though he does tend to be a bit noisy. The Eurasian forms a strong bond with his owners and is gentle with children. Though reserved with strangers, he will never attack. The Eurasian is a vigilant guard dog. Rigorous though gentle training is required.

Care and functions
If this dog is to live indoors, he must get out for daily walks. The Eurasian hates to be left alone or tied up. This very clean dog must be brushed regularly.
· Guard dog.
· Pet.

Ainu Dog

Dating back to 1,000 BC, the Ainu Dog is one of the oldest Japanese breeds. The Ainu originated in the mountainous regions of Hokkaido Island and was brought to Japan by the ancient Ainus. This hardy dog was used for hunting large game.

Sturdy construction. Dignified bearing. Quick, light, lively gait.

5

ASIAN SPITZ AND RELATED BREEDS

5

COUNTRY OF ORIGIN
Japan

ORIGINAL NAME
Ainu-Ken

OTHER NAME
Hokkaido Dog

Medium Breeds between 10 and 25 kg (20-55 lb)

Character, special skills and training
This courageous, self-confident, very alert dog is docile and affectionate with his owners. The Ainu Dog has a remarkable sense of direction. Firm training is required.

Care and functions
The Ainu Dog requires considerable space and exercise. Regular brushing is necessary.
· Sled dog.
· Hunting dog (large game).
· Guard dog.
· Pet.

HEAD
Triangular, foxlike. Broad, flat skull and forehead. Distinct stop. Straight nose bridge. Wedge-shaped muzzle. Black nose (flesh color in whites). Tight lips.

EYES
Small, triangular, wide set. Dark brown color.

EARS
Small, triangular. Held erect and slightly forward.

BODY
Strongly constructed. Powerful neck without dewlap. Pronounced

withers. Moderately wide loin. Prominent forechest. Deep chest. Belly is well tucked up. Straight, solid back. Nicely sloped croup.

LIMBS
Very compact, wel! arched feet. Muscular legs with substantial bone.

TAIL
Set high. Thick. Carried over the back, tightly curled or in the form of a sickle.

COAT
Short, harsh, straight. Slightly longer on the tail. Soft, compact undercoat.

COLOR
Brindle (black, red, white, etc.). Black, red or brown.

SIZE
Dog: 48.5 to 52 cm (19-20.5 in).
Bitch: 45.5 to 48.5 cm (18-19 in).

WEIGHT
Approx. 25 kg (55 lb).

Kai Dog

*The Kai Dog is descended from extinct medium-size
Japanese breeds and was developed in the Kai district.
The Kai was used for hunting boar and deer.
The breed was named as a "Natural Monument" in 1934.*

Sturdy construction. Balanced proportions.
Light, elastic gait.

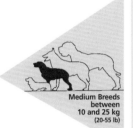

Medium Breeds
between
10 and 25 kg
(20-55 lb)

5

ASIAN SPITZ AND RELATED BREEDS

COUNTRY OF ORIGIN
Japan

ORIGINAL NAME
Tora

OTHER NAME
Tiger Dog

5

HEAD
Strong. Broad forehead.
Abrupt stop. Straight nose
bridge. Pointed muzzle.
Tight lips.

EYES
Small, almost triangular.
Dark brown color.

EARS
Medium size, triangular.
Held erect and slightly for-
ward.

BODY
Solidly constructed. Thick,
powerful, muscular neck.
Pronounced withers. Chest
is well let down. Ribs mode-

rately sprung. Belly well
tucked up. Broad, muscular
loin. Straight, short back.

LIMBS
Very muscular legs with
substantial bone.

TAIL
Set high. Thick. Carried
tightly curled or curved
over the back in the shape
of a sickle.

COAT
Short, hard, straight.
Longer on the tail.
Dense, soft undercoat.

COLOR
Black brindle, red bridle or

brindle. Puppies are born
solid color.

SIZE
Dog: 50 to 56 cm
(20-22 in).
Bitch: 46 to 50 cm
(18-20 in).

WEIGHT
Approx. 25 kg (55 lb).

Character, special skills and training
This courageous, eager, vigilant dog is always on alert.
He is also very agile.

Care and functions
The Kai Dog requires considerable space and exercise.
Weekly brushing is necessary.
· Hunting dog (large game).
· Pet.

Kishu

The Kishu is thought to have originated on the large island of Kyushu located south of Japan. This multi-talented breed is very old. The Kishu was used for hunting, fishing and guarding livestock and property. It was also kept as a pet.

Noble, dignified bearing. Balanced proportions. Muscular. Light, elastic gait.

5

ASIAN SPITZ AND RELATED BREEDS

5

COUNTRY OF ORIGIN
Japan

Medium Breeds
between
10 and 25 kg
(20-55 lb)

Character, special skills and training
The Kishu has remarkable endurance. This alert dog is docile, calm, affectionate and gentle.

Care and functions
The Kishu requires considerable space and exercise. Regular brushing is necessary.

· Hunting dog.
· Guard dog.
· Herder.
· Pet.

HEAD
Broad forehead. Rather abrupt stop. Straight nose bridge. Thick, wedge-shaped muzzle. Black nose (flesh color in whites). Tight lips.

EYES
Small, slightly triangular, wide set. Dark brown color.

EARS
Small, triangular. Held erect and slightly forward.

BODY
Compact. Thick, muscular neck. Pronounced withers.

Deep chest. Belly well tucked up. Broad, muscular loin. Straight, short back.

LIMBS
Muscular legs with substantial bone. Compact feet with dark nails.

TAIL
Set high. Thick. Carried tightly curled or curved over the back in the shape of a sickle.

COAT
Short, harsh, straight. Slightly longer on the cheeks

and tail. Soft, compact undercoat.

COLOR
White, red or brindle.

SIZE
Dog: 51.5 cm (20.5 in).
Bitch: 45.5 cm (18 in).

WEIGHT
20 to 25 kg (44-55 lb).

Korean Jindo Dog

This breed is thought to have existed for several centuries on Jindo Island, located off the extreme south-west point of the Korean Peninsula. The Jindo probably arrived from Korea where Jindo Dogs were called Jindo-Kae or Jindo-Kyon ("Kyon" means "dog" in Korean).

Medium size. Well-proportioned. Strong. Dignified.

Medium Breeds between 10 and 25 kg (20-55 lb)

5

ASIAN SPITZ AND RELATED BREEDS

COUNTRY OF ORIGIN
Korea

OTHEL NAME
Korean Jindo

5

HEAD
Viewed from above, blunt triangle. Slightly domed skull. Distinct stop. Muzzle neither massive nor turned up. Well-developed, dry cheeks. Thin, tight lips.

EYES
Small, triangular. Dark brown color.

EARS
Medium size, triangular, thick, erect and pointing slightly forward.

BODY
Longer than tall. Thick neck without dewlap. Strong, straight back. Strong, moderately high chest. Ribs well sprung. Muscular, taut loin.

LIMBS
Well developed. Round, compact toes.

TAIL
Set on fairly high. Carried in the form of a sickle or curled with the tip touching the back or flank. Richly clad.

COAT
Straight, short on the head, legs, and ears. Longer at the neck, body, tail, and back of the legs. Soft, thick, light-colored undercoat.

COLOR
Most common colors are fawn and white. Black, black and tan, wolf-gray, and brindle also exist.

SIZE
Dog: 50 to 55 cm (20-22 in).
Bitch: 45 to 50 cm (18-20 in).

WEIGHT
Dog: 18 to 23 kg (39.7-50.8 lb).
Bitch 15 to 19 kg (33-42 lb).

Character, special skills, and training
This hardy, brave, alert dog is extremely loyal to his owner. He is wary of strangers and rather aggressive toward other dogs. Firm training is required.

Care and functions
This dog needs exercise and room to run. Regular brushing is required.
. Hunting dog

179

Shiba Inu

This ancient, indigenous breed developed on Honshu Island. The Shiba Inu (Shiba meaning "small" and Inu meaning "dog"), thought to have Chow and Kishu blood, was crossed with English setters and pointers that had been imported to Japan. Therefore, by the early twentieth century, pure Shibas had become rare. Around 1928, measures were taken to maintain pure blood lines. A standard was published in 1934 and the Shiba Inu was declared a "Natural Monument" in 1937. The breed almost disappeared during World War II. Today, the Shiba is one of the most popular breeds in Japan.

Balanced proportions, solid construction. Light, lively gait.

5

ASIAN SPITZ AND RELATED BREEDS

5

COUNTRY OF ORIGIN
Japan

OTHER NAME
Shiba

Up to 25 kg (55 lb)

Character, special skills and training
This robust, hardy, lively, alert dog is calm, independent and reserved. He is an affectionate, playful, loving pet. The courageous Shiba is always on the alert and raises the alarm with his easy bark. Firm though gentle training is required.

Care and functions
The Shiba Inu adapts well to life as a house pet. However, this is a sporting breed and therefore requires long, frequent walks. Daily brushing is needed for this very clean dog.
· Hunting dog (birds and small game).
· Guard dog.
· Pet.

HEAD
Foxlike. Broad skull. Distinct stop. Straight nose bridge. Muzzle tapers to the nose. Full cheeks. Tight lips.

EYES
Fairly small, triangular. Dark brown color.

EARS
Small, triangular. Held erect and slightly forward.

BODY
Moderately short. Thick neck. Deep chest. Ribs moderately sprung. Belly well tucked up. Straight back. Broad, muscular loin.

LIMBS
Compact, well-arched feet. Muscular legs with substantial bone.

TAIL
Set high. Thick. Carried curled or curved in the shape of a sickle.

COAT
Short, hard, straight. Longer on the tail. Soft, dense undercoat.

COLOR
Red, sesame (hint of black on rich, dark red background), black sesame, red sesame, black and tan, brindle, white, light red, light gray. All colors except whites must be urajiro (whitish hair on the sides of the muzzle, on the cheeks, under the jaw, on the throat, forechest, underbody, bottom of the tail and inside of the legs).

SIZE
Dog: 38 to 41 cm (15-16 in). Bitch: 35 to 38 cm (14-15 in).

WEIGHT
6 to 12 kg (13-26.5 lb).

Japanese Spitz

The Japanese Spitz is probably not related to the Miniature American Eskimo. Some experts think it is related to the Samoyed, but most believe the Japanese Spitz is decended from the White Giant German Spitz, which was introduced in Japan around 1920 after passing through Siberia and China. White Giant Spitz were imported from Canada, the United States and China. In 1948, the Japanese Kennel Club published a standard for the breed. This little breed is growing in popularity in Europe.

Balanced proportions. Dignified, elegant bearing. Lively, active movement.

5

ASIAN SPITZ AND RELATED BREEDS

COUNTRY OF ORIGIN
Japan

ORIGINAL NAME
Nihon Supittsu

Small Breeds under 10 kg (under 20 lb)

5

HEAD
Moderately wide and rounded. Distinct stop. Pointed muzzle. Small nose. Tight, preferably black lips.

EYES
Moderately large, almond shape, set slightly obliquely in the skull. Dark color. Black rims.

EARS
Set on high, small, triangular. Held erect and turned forward.

BODY
Sturdy construction. Muscular neck. Pronounced withers. Broad chest is well let down. Ribs well sprung. Belly well tucked up. Straight, short back. Broad loin.

LIMBS
Round feet with thick pads. Muscular legs.

TAIL
Set high, moderately long. Carried over the back.

COAT
Straight, stand-off. Short on the face, ears and front of the legs. Long and abundant on the rest of the body. Apron on the forechest and plume on the tail. Soft, dense undercoat.

COLOR
Pure white.

SIZE
Dog: 30 to 38 cm (12-15 in)
Bitch: 30 to 35 cm (12-14 in).

WEIGHT
Approx. 10 kg (22 lb).

Character, special skills and training
This sturdy, supple, lively dog is cheerful, bold and clever. He is an affectionate pet. The Japanese Spitz is extremely wary of strangers and barks easily, making him a good "early warning" guard dog. Firm training is required.

Care and functions
The Japanese Spitz is well suited to life as a house dog. Regular brushing and combing are required.
· Pet.

181

Aristocrat. Light construction. Elegant. Graceful. Pliant skin. Relaxed, lively gait.

6

PRIMITIVE TYPES

5

COUNTRY OF ORIGIN
Africa (Congo)
Sponsored by Great Britain

OTHER NAME
Congo Dog

Up to 25 kg
(55 lb)

Basenji

Originating in the Congo, the Basenji is one of the oldest breeds in the world. It was named for a native pygmy tribe whose name meant "bushman". The Basenji's ancestors, the Tesem and the Egyptian Hound, were depicted on the tombstones of the Pharaohs. Its body looks like a miniature version of its cousin, the Ibizan Hound. In Africa, the Basenji is used as a bush or forest guide, for hunting small game and to guard villages. The breed was imported to Great Britain around 1930 and to the United States around 1940. The Basenji is now very popular in the USA, and has become increasingly popular.

HEAD
Flat and well chiseled. Slight stop. Fine wrinkles on the forehead. Strong jaws.

EYES
Almond shape, set obliquely in the skull. Dark color.

EARS
Small, pointed and slightly hooded. Thin leather. Carried erect.

BODY
Balanced proportions. Strong, well arched neck. Chest is well let down. Ribs moderately sprung. Definite waist. Straight, short back. Short loin

LIMBS
Long, fine-boned legs. Small, narrow, compact feet with well-arched toes

TAIL
Set high. Carried tightly curled against the croup.

COAT
Short, shiny, dense, very fine.

COLOR
Pure black and white, red and white, black and tan and white with tan markings above the eyes and tan muzzle, fawn and white. White on the feet, forechest and tip of the tail.

SIZE
Dog: 43 cm (17 in), (ideal).
Bitch: 40 cm (16 in), (ideal).

WEIGHT
Dog: 11 kg (24 lb), (ideal).
Bitch: 9.5 kg (21 lb), (ideal).

Character, special skills and training
This sturdy, lively, independent, stable dog has a strong personality. He is an affectionate, playful pet and is good with children. The Basenji is aloof with strangers. Blessed with an excellent sense of smell, the Basenji is used as a scenthound. Like cats, he likes high perches. This breed does not bark. Instead, it "yodels" when happy. Firm but gentle, loving training is required.

Care and functions
The Basenji can adapt to city living provided he gets out daily for a walk. This breed does not like to be alone. If left in the house alone, he may become destructive. This very clean breed cleans itself like a cat and has no body odor. A glove should be used daily to groom the coat.
· Hunting dog (small game).
· Utility dog: bush guide.
· Guard dog.
· Pet..

Canaan Dog

This very ancient breed originated in Canaan (modern day Israel). It was the result of crosses of various half-wild pariah dogs from regions of Northern Africa and the Near East. Selective breeding of the Canaan Dog began in the 1930s. It has been used as a messenger and rescue dog in the army. The Canaan Dog was only recently recognized by the American Kennel Club. The breed is also being developed in Europe.

Balanced proportions. Short, quick trot.

6

PRIMITIVE TYPES

COUNTRY OF ORIGIN
Israel

ORIGINAL NAME
Kelef K'naani

Medium Breeds between 10 and 25 kg (20-55 lb)

5

HEAD
Moderate length. Skull neither domed nor flat. Stop not pronounced. Muzzle of moderate length and width. Powerful jaws. Tight lips.

EYES
Almond shape. As dark as possible. Dark rims.

EARS
Short, fairly wide, slightly rounded tips. Wide, set low on the head. Carried erect.

BODY
Square body outline. Straight neck. Pronounced withers. Moderately broad chest. Ribs well sprung. Belly well tucked up. Arched loin

LIMBS
Rather long legs. Round feet

TAIL
Medium length. Bushy. Carried over the back.

COAT
Short to moderately long. Straight, harsh texture. Dog has a ruff. Undercoat varies with the seasons.

COLOR
Tawny to reddish brown, white or black, black, white and brown, with or without mask.

SIZE
50 to 60 cm (20-24 in).

WEIGHT
18 to 25 kg (39.5-55 lb).

Character, special skills and training
This rustic, lively dog has great endurance. He forms a strong bond with his owner and is very gentle with children. The Canaan Dog is extremely vigilant and wary of strangers. He is a good defense dog, though is not naturally aggressive toward humans. This breed is aggressive with other dogs. Firm training is required.

Care and functions
The Canaan Dog needs exercise and room to run. Regular brushing is required.
· Herder.
· Guard dog.
· Utility dog: army dog, guide dog.
· Pet.

183

Pharaoh Hound

The Pharaoh Hound looks like the prick-ear hounds depicted in paintings on ancient Egyptian tombs. From Egypt, the breed spread to Europe through Spain and was maintained in the Balearic Islands.

Noble bearing. Graceful but powerful. Relaxed, free gait.

6

PRIMITIVE TYPE

5

COUNTRY OF ORIGIN
Malta

ORIGINAL NAME
Kelb-tal Fenek

Large Breeds between 25 and 45 kg (55-100 lb)

Character, special skills and training
This active, very swift, supple dog is an excellent jumper and eager hunter (rabbit, hare, pheasant, etc.). He is a loving, affectionate, playful pet.

Care and functions
The Pharaoh Hound is not suited to life as a house dog. He needs frequent exercise. Regular brushing is required.
· Hunting dog.
· Pet.

HEAD
Blunt wedge shape. Long, dry, finely chiseled skull. Slight stop. Nose bridge slightly longer than the skull. Flesh color nose. Powerful jaws.

EYES
Oval shape. Amber color matching the coat.

EARS
Large. Thin leather. Broad at the base. Carried erect but very mobile.

BODY
Supple, almost square. Long, dry, muscular neck without dewlap. Chest is well let down. Ribs well sprung. Topline is almost straight.

LIMBS
Fine-boned legs. Strong, firm feet.

TAIL
Fairly thick at the root and tapering to the tip. Hangs down just past the hocks when at rest. Carried high and curved when in action.

COAT
Short, smooth, glossy, ranging from fine and close to slightly harsh.

COLOR
Self-color fawn with white markings on the tip of the tail (strongly desired), on the forechest (star) and on the toes. Narrow white stripe on the face is permissible.

SIZE
Dog: 56 to 63.5 cm (22-25 in).
Bitch: 53 to 61 cm (21-24 in).

WEIGHT
Approx. 28 kg (62 lb).

Mexican Hairless Dog

The Mexican Hairless Dog is one of the world's oldest breeds. He might have been brought to Mexico from northeastern Asia by the nomadic ancestors of the Aztecs. The Toltecs, the first inhabitants of Mexico, kept Chihuahuas in their temples. When the Aztecs conquered the land, they introduced the Mexican Hairless Dog. Some believe that these two breeds were crossed to produce the Chinese Crested Dog. The name Xoloitzcuintle comes from the ancient Aztec god Xolotl, who accompanied souls to the afterworld. Despite this godly name, native peoples ate these dogs and kept them for protection and healing purposes. The first descriptions of the Mexican Hairless Dog date to the seventeenth century. The American Kennel Club published a standard in 1933. The breed is rare in Europe.

Well-balanced. Graceful. Well-proportioned. Skin smooth, soft to the touch.

6

HAIRLESS DOGS

COUNTRY OF ORIGIN
Mexico

ORIGINAL NAMES
Xoloitzcuintle
Tepeizeuintle

OTHER NAME
Xolo

Up to 25 kg
(55 lb)

5

HEAD
Long. Fairly broad skull. Minimal stop. Long, slender muzzle. Tight-lipped. Nose dark pink or brown, depending on coat color.

EYES
Medium-sized, slightly almond-shaped, preferably dark, ranging from yellow to black.

EARS
Large (up to 10 in), thin. Held stiff and slanted in action.

BODY
Fairly long. Neck carried high, slightly arched, graceful, without dewlap. Chest

deep but fairly narrow. Tuck-up. Straight back. Well-rounded croup.

LIMBS
Slender legs. Hare feet with retracted toes and black or clear nails.

TAIL
Set on low, smooth, fairly long.

COAT
Tuft of short, stiff hair on the skull. Crisp hair on the tip of the tail. The complete absence of hair is not penalized.

COLOR
Preferably solid dark bronze,

elephant grey, greyish-black or black. Unpigmented areas with pink or brown patches are acceptable. Hair on the head and tail must be black in dark varieties. In light varieties, it can be any color that blends with the overall appearance.

SIZE
30 to 50 cm (12-20 in).

WEIGHT
Varies according to size.

Character, special skills and training
Lively but calm, merry, very affectionate and good-natured, the Mexican Hairless Dog is a delightful pet. He is reserved toward strangers, making him a good watchdog.

Care and functions
He needs minimal exercise. Because of his delicate skin, he must be bathed regularly and rubbed with a moisturizer. He cannot tolerate cold or bright sun.
· Companion dog.
· Watchdog.

Peruvian Hairless Dog

The origins of this very ancient breed are hotly debated. The Peruvian Hairless Dog may have been brought to Peru by Chinese immigrants or by groups migrating from Asia to the Americas via the Bering Strait. Others believe he comes from Africa. Nevertheless, there is irrefutable evidence – including representations of the dog on pottery – that the breed has inhabited Peru for many centuries and existed even before the Incas. The Peruvian Hairless Dog was once the favorite pet of Incan royalty. He is now rare in his native country. The breed comes in three sizes with fairly similar body structure.

6

HAIRLESS DOGS

5

COUNTRY OF ORIGIN
Peru

ORIGINAL NAME
Perro sin Pelo del Perú

OTHER NAME
Inca Hairless Dog

Dignified. Elegant. Svelte. Gait is fairly short but quick.

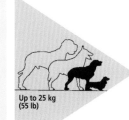

Up to 25 kg (55 lb)

HEAD
Lupoid in structure. Broad skull. Stop not very pronounced. Straight nosebridge. Tight-lipped. Dentition almost always incomplete (missing one or all premolars and molars). Nose matches coat color.

EYES
Medium-sized, slightly almond-shaped. Ranging from black to brown to yellow, depending on coat color.

EARS
Medium in length, nearly pointed at the tips. Erect in action. Lying back against the head at rest.

BODY
Medium-sized. Domed topline. Withers not very pronounced. Chest of good width. Ribs slightly wellsprung. Straight back. Rounded, solid croup.

LIMBS
Slender legs. Prehensile hare feet with tough pads, able to grip objects.

TAIL
Set on low. Fairly thick at the base, tapering toward the tip. In action, raised in a curve above the topline but not curled. At rest, hanging down with a slight upward hook at the tip.

COAT
Vestiges of hair allowed on the head, lower legs and tip of the tail. Sparse hair on the back also allowed.

COLOR
Hair is black in the black variety. In other varieties, hair is slate black, elephant grey, bluish-grey, any other shade of grey, or dark brown to light blond. All colors solid or with pinkish spots anywhere on the body.

SIZE
Large: 50 to 60 cm (19.7-23.6 in).
Medium: 40 to 50 cm (15.7-19.7 in).
Small: 25 to 40 cm (9.8-15.7 in).

WEIGHT
Large: 12 to 23 kg (26.5-50.5 lb).
Medium: 8 to 12 kg (17.5-26.5 lb).
Small: 4 to 8 kg (9-17.5 lb).

Character, special skills and training
Lively, alert and fast, this calm, intelligent, affectionate dog is a good pet. He is distrusting of strangers and therefore makes a good watchdog.

Care and functions
An indoor dog, he cannot tolerate bright sunlight and cold temperatures. His skin must be rubbed with a moisturizer.
· Companion dog.
· Watchdog.

Ibizan Hound

The Ibizan Hound originated on the islands of Majorca, Ibiza and Minorca. Descended from the Pharaoh Hounds, the Ibizan was probably brought to the islands by the Phoenicians, the Carthaginians and, eventually, the Romans. One of the oldest known breeds, the Ibizan is a very primitive, vigorous dog. At one point, the breed was called the French Hound because it was common in the nineteenth century in the regions of Langedoc, Roussillon and Provence in France. It became very rare around the 1880s, when use of the Ibizan for hunting hare was outlawed.

Clean-cut lines. Strong without appearing heavily muscled. Fast gallop.

7

PRIMITIVE TYPE HUNTING DOGS

Medium Breeds between 10 and 25 kg (20-55 lb)

COUNTRY OF ORIGIN
Spain

5

ORIGINAL NAMES
Podenco Ibicenco
Ca Eivissencs

OTHER NAME
Charnigue

HEAD
Long, narrow, extremely dry. Long, flat skull. Narrow forehead. Stop not pronounced. Long, narrow, slightly Roman convex muzzle. Flesh color nose.

EYES
Small, set obliquely in the skull. Clear amber color (caramel color).

EARS
Medium size. Thin leather. Very mobile and always held rigidly erect. Pointed forward or up.

BODY
Slightly longer than tall. Very dry, muscular, slightly arched neck. Shoulder blades are well laid back. Deep, narrow, long chest. Flat ribs. Arched, powerful loin. Belly is tucked up. Slightly arched, powerfully muscled loin. Long, straight, flexible back.

LIMBS
Long, dry legs. Long, compact feet. Nails are typically white.

TAIL
Set low, tapers to the tip. Carried in a well curved saber position.

COAT
Smooth, hard, long. Shorthair must be smooth, rather hard, not silky. Wire hair must be hard, coarse, thick and short on the head. Beard is desirable. Longest hair is the softest, very abundant on the head and at least 5 in long.

COLOR
Preferably white and red, or solid white or red. Fawn permissible in shorthaired only if the dog is an exceptional specimen.

SIZE
Dog: 66 to 72 cm (26-28 in).
Bitch: 60 to 67 cm (23.5-26.5 in).

WEIGHT
Dog: approx. 23 kg (50,5 lb).
Bitch: approx. 19 kg (42 lb).

Character, special skills and training
This tireless, fast, very agile dog is an excellent jumper. He uses his keen sense of smell for sniffing out partridge and his excellent eyesight to spot rabbit as well as hare and large game. He is a good retriever. The Ibizan Hound forms a strong bond with his owner, but he is strong-willed. He is wary of strangers and aggressive with other dogs. Firm training is required.

Care and functions
It is not recommended that this breed be kept as a house dog. The Ibizan Hound needs considerable exercise and room to run. Regular brushing is required.
· Hunting dog.
· Pet.

Portuguese Hound

Muscular. Balanced proportions. Solid skeleton. Strong. Rapid, light gait.

7

PRIMITIVE TYPE HUNTING DOGS

5

COUNTRY OF ORIGIN
Portugal

ORIGINAL NAME
Podengo Purtugueso

Up to 45 kg (100 lb)

The Portuguese Hound, descended from large-eared hounds, is very common in northern Portugal where it is used as a hunter and pet. There are three varieties:
- *The Large Portuguese Hound (Podengo grande), a very rare breed used for hunting large game;*
- *The Medium Portuguese Hound (Podengo medio), which hunts rabbit in packs or alone and looks very much like the Ibizan Hound;*
- *The Small Portuguese Hound (Podengo pequeno), which hunts rabbit underground and looks much like the Chihuahua.*

Character, special skills and training
This rustic, extremely lively dog is used for hunting, but also makes an excellent pet and loyal guard dog. Firm training is required.

Care and functions
The Portuguese Hound requires a lot of exercise and room to run. Daily brushing is required.
· Hunting dog.
· Guard dog.
· Pet.

HEAD
Dry. Shape of the head is like that of a four-sided pyramid, with a broad base and pointed tip. Flat skull. Stop not pronounced. Straight nose bridge. Thin nose. Tight, fine lips.

EYES
Small, set obliquely in the skull. Honey or chestnut color.

EARS
Broad at the base, triangular, thin leather. Held perfectly erect or tilting slightly forward.

BODY
Long. Strong, long neck without dewlap. Narrow forechest. Chest is well let down. Ribs are rather flat. Broad, muscular loin. Long, straight back. Broad, muscular, very slightly sloped croup.

LIMBS
Round feet with long, strong toes. Dry, muscular legs with plenty of bone.

TAIL
Strong, thick, pointed. Moderate length. Carried horizontal and slightly arched when in action.

COAT
Two varieties: short, smooth and dense; or long and hard. Moderately coarse. The Small Portuguese Hound has the shortest coat.

COLOR
Predominant colors: yellow and fawn with lighter and darker shades and a black tint. Solid color or pied.

SIZE
Large Hound: 55 to 70 cm (21.5-27.5 in).
Medium Hound: 40 to 55 cm (15.5-21.5 in).
Small Hound: 20 to 30 cm (8-11 in).

WEIGHT
Large Hound: 20 to 30 kg (44-66 lb).
Medium Hound: 15 to 20 kg (33-44 lb).
Small Hound: 4 to 5 kg (9-11 lb).

Cirneco dell'Etna

Some experts believe the Cirneco was brought to Sicily by the Phoenicians and that it is descended from the Pharaoh Hound. According to current thinking, however, the Cirneco is an indigenous breed that originated around the Sicilian volcano Mount Etna as early as the fourth century BC. The breed closely resembles the dog depicted in bas-reliefs on Egyptian tombstones. The Cirneco was used to hunt rabbit, pheasant and partridge on rough terrain. The first standard for the breed was written in 1939.

Long lines. Balanced proportions: streamlined, light bone structure. Elegant. Fine, taut skin. Trotlike gallop.

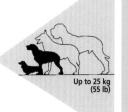

7

PRIMITIVE TYPE HUNTING DOGS

COUNTRY OF ORIGIN
Italy

OTHER NAME
Sicilian Greyhound

5

Up to 25 kg (55 lb)

HEAD
Long. Skull is almost flat. Distinct stop. Straight nose bridge. Pointed muzzle. Flat cheeks. Fine, thin, tight lips.

EYES
Small, almond shape. Ocher (not too dark), amber or gray color.

EARS
Set high and close together. Triangular with narrow, pointed tips. Held rigidly erect and forward.

BODY
Square body outline. Top profile of neck is well arched. Tapered neck. Rather narrow chest. Ribs barely sprung.

Straight back. Dry, sloped croup.

LIMBS
Compact, arched oval feet with brown or pinkish-ochre nails. Long, light-boned legs with well-defined, taut muscles.

TAIL
Set low. Rather thick and long. Carried in the shape of a saber at rest and curving up to the back when in action.

COAT
Stiff like horse hair. Short on the head, ears and legs. Longer (3 cm)(1.2 in), smooth and close-lying on the body and tail.

COLOR
Solid fawn, either bright or diluted (Isabella, tawny). Fawn with white markings. Solid white with orange markings is permissible, but not desirable.

SIZE
Dog: 46 to 50 cm (18-20 in).
Bitch: 42 to 46 cm (16.5-18 in).

WEIGHT
Dog: 10 to 12 kg (22-26.5 lb).
Bitch: 8 to 10 kg (17.5-22 lb).

Character, special skills and training
This very rustic, hardy, lively, agile, powerful dog has a strong personality, but a good temperament. He is an affectionate, cheerful, gentle pet. Reserved toward strangers, but not aggressive, the Cirneco makes a good guard dog. This sighthound specializes in rabbit hunting. Early, firm training is required.

Care and functions
The Cirneco adapts easily to city living. However, he needs constant exercise. Regular brushing is required.
· Hunting dog.
· Guard dog.
· Pet.

Thai Ridgeback Dog

This breed, developed in Thailand, is used primarily in eastern Thailand for hunting. It has also been used to escort carts and as a guard dog. Since the Thai Ridgeback has never been crossed with other breeds, it has not deviated from its original type. The breed was recognized by the FCI in 1993.

Streamlined. Elegant. Muscular.

8

PRIMITIVE TYPE HUNTING DOG WITH A RIDGE ON THE BACK

5

COUNTRY OF ORIGIN
Thailand

ORIGINAL NAME
Thai Ridgeback Dog

Large Breeds
between
25 and 45 kg
(55-100 lb)

Character, special skills and training
This hardy, active, vigorous dog is an excellent jumper and a vigilant guard dog. Firm training is vital.

Care and functions
The Thai Ridgeback requires exercise and room to run. Regular brushing is required.
· Hunting dog.
· Guard dog.

HEAD
Rather large, flat skull. Moderate stop. Straight, long nose bridge. Wedge-shaped muzzle. Strong jaws. Black mark on the tongue. Tight lips.

EYES
Medium size. Almond shape. Dark brown color. Amber if the coat is blue or silver.

EARS
Rather large. Triangular. Carried erect and tilted forward.

BODY
Long. Chest well let down.

Solid back. Broad, strong loin. Slightly rounded croup. Belly tucked up.

LIMBS
Solid with plenty of bone. Nails black or of a lighter color.

TAIL
Thick at the root and tapering gradually to the tip. Carried vertical or curved in the shape of a sickle.

COAT
Short and smooth. A ridge, or linear tuft, is formed along the back by individual hairs pushing against the

grain of the rest of the coat.

COLOR
Chestnut red, light-colored, solid black, silver, and blue. Fawns have a black mask.

SIZE
Dog: 56 to 61 cm (22-26 in).
Bitch: 51 to 56 cm (20-22 in).

WEIGHT:
Approx. 30 kg (66 lb).

Group 6

Saint Hubert Hound

Anglo-French Hound

The Anglo-French Hound is the result of crossing English and French hounds. The first crosses most certainly occurred in the sixteenth century. By the late nineteenth century, huntmasters highly prized this all-terrain dog as a multi-purpose pack hound for hunting deer, wild boar and fox.

Anglo-French Hounds come in various sizes and coat colors, based on the breeds used in their development:
- The Great Anglo-French Hound, descended mainly from the Poitevin and crosses between the Gascon Saintongeois and the Foxhound;
- The Great Anglo-French Tricolor Hound, the variety with the most English blood;
- The Great Anglo-French White and Orange Hound (now very rare), the product of crosses between the Billy and the Foxhound;
- The Great Anglo-French White and Black Hound, descended from the Gascon Saintongeois; and
- The Small Game Anglo-French Hound, developed recently by crossing the Harrier with the Poitevin, the Porcelaine, the Small Gascon Saintongeois and the Small Blue Gascony Hound. Initially called the Small Anglo-French Hound, this variety was recognized as the Small Game Anglo-French Hound in 1978. Today, Anglo-French Hounds are used in most large game hunting packs.

1

SCENT HOUNDS

ORIGINAL NAME
Chien Anglo-Français

6

Large Breeds between 25 and 45 kg (55-100 lb)

Most powerful scenthound.
Robust. Elegant - Dignified. Strong build.
Easy gait.

Small Game Anglo-French Hound
Solidly built, not heavy.
Smooth skin with no wrinkles.

HEAD
Fairly short in the Great Anglo-French Hound, longer in the Small Game Anglo-French Hound. Broad, flat skull. Slight occipital peak. Pronounced stop. Nose-bridge approximately as long as skull.

EYES
Large, dark brown.

EARS
Set on at least at eye level, short, flat, slightly folded toward the tip. Set on low in the Small Game Anglo-French Hound.

BODY
Balanced and well-proportioned. Strong neck with a slight dewlap in the Great Anglo-French Hound. Broad, well let-down chest. Curved ribs. Broad, short loin. Straight, level back. Fairly long, sloping croup.

LIMBS
Strong, muscular, well-boned legs. Fairly round feet with tight toes.

TAIL
Thick at the base, fairly long, well covered with hair.

COAT
Lying flat against the body and fairly thick. Short, dense and smooth in the Small Game Anglo-French Hound. Skin white with black or orange patches, depending on variety.

COLOR
- White and black: large mantle, black spots of varying size, sometimes with black or steel-grey flecks (or tan flecks, only on the legs). Pale spots above the eyes (pips), light tan markings on the cheeks, below the eyes and ears and at the base of the tail.
- White and orange: white and lemon or white and fairly light orange.
- Tricolor: usually with a black mantle or spots of varying size. Rich or coppery tan, not smoky. A mixed wolf grey coat is not a fault.

SIZE
Great Anglo-French Hound: 60 to 70 cm (23.5-27.5 in). Small Game Anglo-French Hound: 48 to 56 cm (19-22 in).

WEIGHT
Great Anglo-French Hound: 30 to 35 kg (66-77 lb). Small Game Anglo-French Hound: approx. 25 kg (55 lb).

Character, special skills and training
Some of the finest breeds were used in developing the Anglo-French Hound. English blood, in particular, gave him his build, bone structure and vigor, while French blood gave him a keen nose and resonant voice. Hardy, strong, quick, courageous and tenacious, the Anglo-French Hound adores hunting. He hunts large and small game on all types of terrain. He requires firm training.

Care and functions
Anglo-French Hounds are not suited to city life. They are kept in kennels in packs. They need space and exercise and require regular brushing and attention to the ears.
· Hunting dog.

Ariégeois

This dog from Ariège in southern France, sometimes called "the Bastard Hound", was produced by crossing medium-sized French hounds with the Blue Gascony Hound and the Gascon Saintongeois (both pack hounds). The Ariégeois has the typical characteristics of a pack hound but is shorter, smaller and lighter in weight. The breed was recognized in 1907 by France's Gaston Phœbus Club. It almost disappeared after World War II but was successfully revived by 1970.

1

SHENT HOUNDS

COUNTRY OF ORIGIN
France

6

Solidity built. Small version of the Gascon Saintongeois. Slender. Lightweight. Elegant. Dignified. Thin skin without folds or wrinkles. Flexible, easy gait.

Large Breeds between 25 and 45 kg (55-100 lb)

Character, special skills and training
Hardy, tenacious, energetic and not very fast, the Ariégeois is merry, docile, friendly and calm. With his keen sense of smell, superb voice and determination, he excels at launching the hunt, staying focused and showing initiative. As a small game hound, he is especially skilled on hare but is also used in tracking deer and wild boar. He is very comfortable on the rocky, dry terrain of southern France and he is easy to train.

Care and functions
The Ariégeois is not suited to city life and does not like being confined in an apartment. He needs daily exercise. He must be brushed once or twice a week and his ears should be checked regularly.
· Hunting dog.

HEAD
Long and chiseled. Slightly domed skull. Slightly pronounced occipital peak. Slight stop. Bridge of nose straight or slightly curved, equal in length to skull. Well-developed nose. Cleanly cut cheeks. Tight, thin lips.

EYES
Wide, brown.

EARS
Set on low. Long, thin, supple and curled.

BODY
Long. Neck lightly boned, long, slightly arched. Chest long, moderately wide. Ribs moderately curved. Solidly attached, slightly arched loin. Flat flank. Slight tuck-up. Very muscular, level back. Fairly level croup.

LIMBS
Solid legs. Long, oval hare feet with tight toes and black pads and nails.

TAIL
Hanging down to the hock. Thin at the tip, carried gaily in saber fashion.

COAT
Short, fine, dense.

COLOR
White with well-defined black spots or flecks. Pale tan markings on the cheeks and above the eyes, forming pips.

SIZE
Dog: 52 to 58 cm (20,5-23 in).
Bitch: 50 to 56 cm (18-22 in).

WEIGHT
Approx. 30 kg (66 lb).

Artesian Norman Basset

The Artesian Norman Basset was produced in the nineteenth century by two famous breeders, Louis Lane and Count Le Coulteux de Canteleu, from the Norman Basset (or Lane Basset). The Norman Basset had bandy forelegs and was heavier, slower and less active than the Artois Basset, a descendent of the old Great Artois Hound. The Artesian Norman Basset was introduced successfully to Great Britain and the United States as the breed was becoming popular in France. The first standard was written in 1898 and modified in 1910 and 1924. A Norman Basset Hound club was created in 1927. For a long time, the breed was the most popular of the bassets, but today it seems less popular as a hunting dog than as a companion dog.

The smallest of the french Scenthounds. Well-planted. Compact. Dignified. Elegant. Thin, supple skin. Smooth, fairly easy gait.

1

SCENT HOUNDS

COUNTRY OF ORIGIN
France

ORIGINAL NAME
Basset Artésien Normand

Medium Breeds between 10 and 25 kg (20-55 lb)

6

HEAD
Bony appearance. Domed skull with pronounced occipital peak. Pronounced stop. Slightly curved nosebridge. Cheeks with one or two folds. Upper lip almost completely covering lower lip.

EYES
Large, oval, dark. Conjunctiva of lower eyelid sometimes showing. Calm, gentle expression.

EARS
Set on as low as possible, narrow at the base, well-twisted, very long, supple, thin and ending in a point.

BODY
Long for its height. Neck fairly long with slight dewlap. Long chest, oval in cross-section. Loin slightly clean-flanked. Full loin. Short, half-bandy front legs with folds of skin on the wrists.

LIMBS
Broad, level back. Rounded croup.

TAIL
Fairly long, thick at the base and tapering toward the tip. Carried in saber fashion, never falling onto the back.

COAT
Close-lying, short and dense, but not too fine.

COLOR
- Tricolor: fawn with white and black mantle. Head mostly covered with reddish-fawn. - Bicolor: fawn and white.

SIZE
30 to 36 cm (12-14 in).

WEIGHT
15 to 20 kg (33-44 lb).

Character, special skills and training
This hardy, courageous dog with a great deal of endurance is active and resourceful. He can penetrate the densest vegetation, but terrain that is too rugged should be avoided because of his short legs. With his very keen nose and magnificent voice, he tracks and launches the hunt very confidently, without hurrying. He hunts small game alone or in packs. He excels on rabbit and hare and can also work on fox and wild boar. Calm, merry, gentle and affectionate, he is a pleasant companion. He needs firm training because he is tenacious and obstinate.

Care and functions
The Artesian Norman Basset is one of the rare scenthounds who can live in an apartment, but he still needs space and exercise. He also requires regular brushing and attention to the ears.
· Hunting dog.
· Companion dog.

Basset Hound

*English breeders crossed French bassets
(the Artesian Norman Basset, the Artois Basset
and the Ardennes Basset) to arrive at the Basset Hound.
The breed was shown for the first time in Paris in 1863
and in England in 1875, where it was developed. A Basset
Hound club was founded in England in 1883 and the first
standard was published in 1887. Basset Hounds were brought
to the United States as early as 1883 and were very popular.*

The heaviest Basset.
Massive. Well-proportioned. Dignified.
Loose skin. Relaxed, smooth gait.

1

SCENT HOUNDS

COUNTRY OF ORIGIN
Great Britain

6

Large Breeds
between
25 and 45 kg
(55-100 lb)

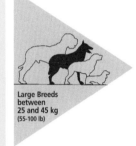

Character, special skills and training

The tenacious Basset Hound hunts with his nose, works instinctively in packs, has a deep, melodious voice and is not afraid of brambles. He has great endurance and is placid, never aggressive—his strong will and stubbornness are legendary. He is a skilled pack hound, trailing small and medium-sized game (including rabbit, hare, wild boar and deer). Affectionate and gentle, he is a prized family friend. He needs firm training.

Care and functions

This athlete needs space and lots of exercise. He does not tolerate solitude or heat very well. He requires regular brushing and attention to the ears and eyes.
· Hunting dog.
· Companion dog.

HEAD
Large, massive. Domed skull. Prominent occipital peak. Moderate stop. Bridge of nose slightly longer than skull. Cleanly cut muzzle. Strong jaws. Skin loose enough to form wrinkles. Flews cover most of lower lip.

EYES
Diamond-shaped. Dark to medium-brown in variety with light-colored coat. Conjunctiva of lower eyelid showing.

EARS
Set on low, very long, longer than tip of muzzle when outstretched. Very supple, thin, narrow and well-curled.

BODY
Long and deep. Muscular neck with dewlap. Prominent sternum. Broad chest. Well-rounded ribs. Very muscular, well-sprung hindquarters. Fairly broad back.

LIMBS
Short, powerful, well-boned legs with folds of skin on the shins. Massive, compact feet.

TAIL
Fairly long, thick at the base and tapering toward the tip. In action, carried raised, curved loosely in saber fashion.

COAT
Short, smooth, dense, but not too fine.

COLOR
Generally tricolor (black, tan and white); bicolor (lemon and white), but all hound colors are allowed.

SIZE
33 to 38 cm (13-15 in).

WEIGHT
25 to 30 kg (55-66 lb).

Westphalian Dachsbracke

This very ancient breed from Westphalia was a favorite of German royalty. It is believed to be the product of crosses between medium-sized scenthounds and bassets (dachshunds, etc.). The first standard for the breed was established in 1910.

Smaller version of the German Hound. But more compact and powerful.

1

6

SCENT HOUNDS

Medium Breeds between 10 and 25 kg (20-55 lb)

COUNTRY OF ORIGIN
Germany

ORIGINAL NAME
Westfälische Dachsbracke

OTHER NAME
Dachsbracke

HEAD
Narrow, long, dignified. Stop not pronounced. Bridge of nose slightly curved. Lips moderately pendulous. Pale band on middle of nose. Extremely strong teeth.

EYES
Almond-shaped, dark.

EARS
Medium in length, wide, lying flat against the head, curved bluntly at tips.

BODY
Long. Moderately long neck without dewlap. Long chest, narrower than in the Dachshund. Broad, well-developed loin. Slight tuck-up. Slightly arched back with slight dip behind withers. Sloping croup.

LIMBS
Well-knit, solidly boned legs. Solid feet with short, tight toes.

TAIL
Well set-on, ending in a tufted tip without feathering, thick brush of hair on underside. Carried erect in saber fashion or hanging down.

COAT
Harsh, very dense. Short on the head, ears and lower legs. Longer on the neck, back and underside of tail.

COLOR
Red to yellow with a black saddle or mantle, plus typical white hound markings: flare or blaze, white around muzzle, white collar, white on chest, legs and tip of the tail. Bicolor is undesirable, as are black markings on the head. Chocolate markings are a fault.

SIZE
30 to 38 cm (12-15 in).

WEIGHT
Approx. 15 kg (33 lb).

Character, special skills and training
The Westphalian Dachsbracke is obstinate and has a very keen sense of smell, a fighting spirit and great endurance. Nimble and flexible, he can follow trails and penetrate burrows. He hunts hare, fox and also large game (including deer and wild boar). Affectionate and obedient, he is a good companion. He needs firm training.

Care and functions
He needs space and lots of exercise and requires regular brushing.
· Hunting dog.
· Companion dog.

Beagle

This very ancient English breed was mentioned in the third century by the Scottish bard Ossian. Beagles were highly favored under the reigns of King Henry VIII and Queen Elizabeth I. At that time, three varieties were described:
- The Southern Beagle, the largest (45 cm tall, white and black coat);
- The Northern Beagle, of medium size; and
- The Small Beagle, less than 35 cm tall, including the Elizabeth Beagle (under 20 cm tall), also known as the "Singing Beagle" because of his melodious voice. Beagles were first introduced to France around 1860 and a French Beagle club was founded in 1914. A dog for all kinds of owners, he has become the most popular hound worldwide. People appreciate his small size, even temper, versatility, effectiveness and speed.

The smallest english Scenthoud. Close-coupled. Cobby. Elegant. Well-proportioned. Brisk gait.

1

SCENT HOUNDS

6

COUNTRY OF ORIGIN
Great Britain

Medium Breeds
between
10 and 25 kg
(20-55 lb)

Character, special skills and training

According to his standard, the Beagle is a merry, brave dog who is highly active, energetic and determined. He is quick, intelligent and even-tempered. He is also courageous, hardy and very fast, with a hard-hitting voice and a keen nose. He is enthusiastic and effective on the trail, giving tongue often. He can work alone, in pairs, or in packs. This small, versatile pack hound hunts hare, rabbit, fox, deer and wild boar. In England, he is used exclusively for beagling, or hunting hare. Affectionate and good-natured, he is a great family pet. He needs firm training.

Care and functions

The Beagle can adapt to city life but needs lots of space to let off steam. He must be brushed once or twice weekly and his ears need regular attention.
· Hunting dog.
· Companion dog.

HEAD
Powerful but not heavy, without wrinkles or puckering. Slightly domed skull. Slight occipital peak. Well-pronounced stop. Straight nosebridge. Strong jaws. Fairly short muzzle. Lips moderately pendulous. Wide nose.

EYES
Dark brown or hazel, fairly large, well spaced with a gentle expression.

EARS
Set on low, long, thin. Rounded tips. Hang against the cheeks.

BODY
Compact, exuding dignity without heaviness. Fairly long neck with slight dewlap. Broad, deep chest. Well-curved ribs. Short, powerful loin. Slight tuck-up. Straight forelegs well-placed under the body, rounded bone structure. Flat, muscular back.

LIMBS
Well-muscled, powerful thighs. Round or slightly elongated feet with firm, tight toes and compact pads.

TAIL
Thick, moderately long, set on high and carried gaily. Well-covered with hair, especially at the tip (tufted).

COAT
Short, dense, strong.

COLOR
All recognized hound colors except liver. - Tricolor (white, black and rich fawn): white muzzle and tip of the tail. - Bicolor: white and rich fawn, lemon and tan.

SIZE
33 to 40 cm (13-16 in).

WEIGHT
15 to 20 kg (33-44 lb).

Beagle Harrier

The Beagle Harrier is a recent creation developed in France in the late nineteenth century by Baron Gérard. The breed is a cross between the Beagle and the Harrier and probably received blood from medium-sized breeds indigenous to southwestern France. Larger and faster than the Beagle, the Beagle Harrier is excellent in small game hunting (hare, fox, deer, and wild boar). Attempts by breeders to upset the balance in favor of the Beagle or the Harrier were unsuccessful. Today's breeders have stabilized the breed, which is neither a large Beagle nor a small Harrier. The standard was officially registered with the FCI in 1974 and is gaining popularity in France.

Mesomorph. Well-balanced. Well-proportioned. Dignified. Clean, lively, flexible gait.

1

SCENT HOUNDS

COUNTRY OF ORIGIN
France

6

Medium Breeds between 10 and 25 kg (20-55 lb)

HEAD
Moderately heavy. Fairly broad skull. Stop not pronounced. Bridge of nose straight. Tapering muzzle. Well-developed nose.

EYES
Wide, dark in color.

EARS
Fairly short and medium-sized. Slightly folded in the mid-section. Hanging flat against the skull and turning slightly at the bottom edge.

BODY
Well-built. Neck open. Chest well let-down but not too flat. Abdomen fairly full, tuck-up never excessive. Short, level, muscular back. Heavy, muscular loin, may be slightly clean-flanked.

LIMBS
Solid, muscular legs. Feet tight and not too long, with tough pads.

TAIL
Moderately long, fairly heavy.

COAT
Not too short, fairly thick, flat.

COLOR
Tricolor (fawn to black and white): mantle not too pronounced. Pale to deep tan or smoky markings. There are grey Harriers and grey Tricolor Beagle Harriers.

SIZE
45 to 50 cm (16-20 in).

WEIGHT
Approx. 20 kg (44 lb).

Character, special skills and training
The Beagle Harrier is hardy, vigorous, fast, agile, and courageous but less powerful than the Harrier. With his determination and keen sense of smell, he works well in packs and is not afraid to enter even the thickest brambles. This easygoing, straightforward dog is a pleasant companion.

Care and functions
He needs space and exercise, as well as regular brushing.
· Hunting dog.
· Companion dog.

201

Billy

The Billy is the final descendant of the Chien Blanc du Roy, a large scenthound popular with royalty from King François I to King Louis XIV. The breed was developed in the nineteenth century in Poitou, France, by Mr. Hublot du Rivault. He crossed several breeds that no longer exist: the Céris, a hunter of hare and wolf, the Montembœuf, a hunter of wild boar and the keen-nosed Larye. He named the new breed the Haut-Poitou Hound, after the region where he grew up. The standard for the breed was established in 1886. The Billy is one of the most popular pack hounds for large game hunting.

Strong. Light-weight. Dignified. Forequarters larger than hindquarters. White skin, sometimes with dark brown spots. Easy gallop.

1

SCENT HOUNDS

6

COUNTRY OF ORIGIN
France

Large Breeds between 25 and 45 kg (55-100 lb)

Character, special skills and training
This remarkable large game hunting dog is hardy and very fast. He excels on deer and has a melodic voice. He may be contentious with pack mates.

Care and functions
The Billy does not adapt well to city life. He needs wide open spaces.
· Hunting dog.

HEAD
Fairly thin, chiseled. Slightly domed skull, not very broad. Pronounced stop. Nose-bridge straight, slightly domed. Angular nose of medium length. Black or orangish-brown nose. Flews slight or absent.

EYES
Large, dark, edged with black or brown.

EARS
Medium-sized, fairly flat, turning slightly at the tip.

BODY
Solidly built. Fairly long, powerful neck with slight dewlap. Chest very deep and narrow. Flat ribs. Fairly broad, strong, slightly convex back. Loin broad, fairly clean-flanked.

LIMBS
Long, powerful legs. Tight, fairly round feet.

TAIL
Long, strong, sometimes slightly velvety.

COAT
Lying close to the body, hard to the touch, often rather thick.

COLOR
Completely white, white with coffee-brown markings, or white with spots. Mantle light orange or lemon.

SIZE
Dog: 60 to 70 cm (24-27.5 in).
Bitch: 58 to 62 cm (23-24.5 in).

WEIGHT
Approx. 35 kg (77 lb).

Blue Gascony Hound

The Blue Gascony Hound, a very ancient breed, is thought to be derived from the Saint Hubert Hound imported from the Ardennes to Gascony in the fourteenth century by Gaston Phoebus, Count of Foix and crossed with scenthounds. Henri IV had a pack of these dogs for hunting wolf and wild boar. The Blue Gascony Hound exists in several varieties or sub-breeds:
- The Great Blue Gascony Hound, produced from the common strain of Blue Gascony Hounds. This breed is becoming more and more common;
- The Small Blue Gascony Hound, the result crossing a medium-sized Blue Gascony Hound with a coarse-haired griffon (the Vendée Griffon). The standard for this variety was established in 1919. After nearly disappearing, this variety is currently gaining popularity; and
- The Blue Gascony Basset, a variety whose origin is hotly debated. Some believe this breed is the result of a mutation in the Great Blue Gascony Hound. Others say it was produced by crossing the Saintongeois Basset with the Blue Gascony Hound. Later, Great Vendée Bassets and even Artesian Norman Bassets were commonly used. Once quite rare, the Blue Gascony Basset has been gaining popularity over the past twenty years.

1

SCENT HOUNDS

COUNTRY OF ORIGIN
France

6

ORIGINAL NAME
Chien Bleu de Gascogne

Blue Gascony Basset
Typical basset. Dignified. Well-balanced. Fairly full-bodied but not heavy. Skin black or white marbled with black blotches. Smooth, easy gait.

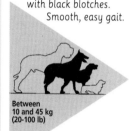

Between
10 and 45 kg
(20-100 lb)

HEAD
Fairly large and long. Slightly domed skull, not too broad. Slight stop. Pronounced occipital peak. Nosebridge straight or slightly curved. Cheeks cleanly cut, lips fairly pendulous. Wide nose.

EYES
Oval. Brown or dark brown.

EARS
Thin and supple, curled, slightly pointed at the tip.

BODY
Powerful. Neck fairly broad and slightly arched. Pro-
nounced dewlap in the Great Blue Gascony Hound. Well-developed chest. Curved ribs. Muscular loin. Fairly long back. Slightly sloping croup. Long back.

LIMBS
Well-muscled, solidly boned legs. Feet slightly oval with well-knit, tight toes. Powerful forelegs, slight to half-bandy legs allowed. Short, oval feet with black pads and nails.

TAIL
Well set-on and fairly covered with hair, carried in saber fashion.

COAT
Short, fairly thick and very dense. In the Griffon, hard, harsh and dense. Slightly shorter on the head, with fairly thick eyebrows.

COLOR
Completely spotted (black and white), creating a slate-blue cast. May be marked with black spots of varying size. Two black spots generally located on either side of the head, covering the ears and eyes and ending at the cheeks. These spots do not meet at the top of the skull but are separated by a white space, often with a small,
black, oval spot in the center, characteristic of the breed. Two tan spots of varying richness above the eyebrows, forming pips. Tan markings on the cheeks, flews, inside surface of the ears, the legs and underside of the tail.

SIZE
Great Blue Gascony Hound: dog: 65 to 72 cm (25.5-28 in); bitch: 62 to 68 cm (24.5-27 in). Small Blue Gascony Hound: dog: 52 to 60 cm (20.5-23.5 in); bitch: 50 to 56 cm (20-22 in). Blue Gascony Basset: 34 to 38 cm (13.5-15 in).

WEIGHT
Great Blue Gascony Hound: approx. 35 kg (77 lb). Small Blue Gascony Hound: approx. 25 kg (55 lb). Blue Gascony Basset: approx. 17 kg (37.5 lb).

Powerful.
Exudes calm strength and dignity.
Fairly thick, supple skin is either black or
richly marbled with black spots.
Smooth, easy gait.
Small: short; well-built. Black skin.

Griffon. Rustic appearance. Well-balanced. Solidly built.
Skin is thick, black or black marbled. Flexible, brisk gait.

Character, special skills and training

Whatever the variety, the Blue Gascony Hound is a gifted hunter with a keen sense of smell and a beautiful voice. Enthusiastic and hardy, he works well in packs.
- The Great Blue Gascony Hound has a very keen sense of smell and a resonant, deep voice. He is massive and slow but maintains a steady pace on the trail and is very determined. He hunts instinctively in packs but also individually as a bloodhound. He works on large game (deer and wild boar) and also on hare. He is used in the crossbreeding of large game hounds.
- The Small Blue Gascony Hound, lively and active, can hunt most game and is used especially in shooting. Hare is his favorite quarry.
- The Blue Gascony Griffon combines the superb nose and voice of the Blue Gascony Hound with the tenacity of the Griffon. This very versatile breed is excellent on wild boar and is also used on hare. He hunts well in packs and is highly prized for his work on difficult terrain.
- The Blue Gascony Basset, like the Basset Hound, is active, nimble and gifted with that booming Basset howl. He works like a charm in packs and is used on rabbit and hare.
These dogs are gentle, affectionate and very attached to their owner. They require firm training.

Care and functions

They are not suited to city life. They must live in the country, in a kennel if they are part of a pack. They need exercise and space, as well as regular brushing and attention to the ears.
· Hunting dog.

Hardy. Low to the ground. Well-muscled. Skin without folds. Preferred gait: trot.

1

SCENT HOUNDS

6

COUNTRY OF ORIGIN
Germany

ORIGINAL NAME
Deutsche Bracke

Medium Breeds
between
10 and 25 kg
(20-55 lb)

German Hound

This ancient breed comes from the Sauerland region of northwestern Germany. Its standard was not written until 1955.

Character, special skills and training

The very hardy and enthusiastic German Hound hunts hare in the mountains and tracks wounded large game. His calmness and even temper make him a good companion dog. He needs firm training.

Care and functions

He needs space and exercise and requires regular brushing.
· Hunting dog.
· Companion dog.

HEAD
Lightweight. Slightly domed skull. Pronounced stop. Straight nosebridge. Darkly pigmented lips.

EYES
Medium in size. Dark brown. Edge of eyelids pigmented.

EARS
Set on fairly far back, wide, long, hanging flat.

BODY
Robust. Muscular neck. Long, broad chest. Moderate tuck-up. Straight, well-muscled back. Croup not too long, slightly sloping.

LIMBS
Muscular, solidly boned legs; hind legs longer than forelegs. Round feet with very tight toes and firm pads.

TAIL
Long, covered with dense hair (brush), hanging loosely.

COAT
3 to 5 cm (1.2-2 in) long, straight, firm, very dense. Dense undercoat.

COLOR
Dark reddish-fawn, may be slightly smoky (black tips), or black and tan. Also allowed: light reddish-fawn or black with limited or indistinct tan markings. White spots undesirable.

SIZE
Dog: 37 to 38 cm (14.5-15 in).
Bitch: 36 to 37 cm (14-14.5 in).

WEIGHT
Approx. 20 kg (44 lb).

Austrian Black and Tan Hound

The Austrian Black and Tan Hound
(with pips) is considered a true descendent
of Celtic hounds. Similar to Swiss hounds,
he hunts primarily in the mountains.
It is not well-known outside his native land.

1

SCENT HOUNDS

COUNTRY OF ORIGIN
Austria

ORIGINAL NAME
Ostreichische Glathaarige
Brache

6

Medium Breeds
between
10 and 25 kg
(20-55 lb)

HEAD
Broad skull. Straight nose-bridge. Strong muzzle.

EYES
Dark brown.

EARS
Set on high, medium in length, not too broad, hanging flat against the cheeks.

BODY
Long. Strong neck. Well-pronounced withers. Chest broad, well let-down. Long back. Slightly sloping croup. Slight tuck-up.

LIMBS
Strong, round, arched feet.

TAIL
Long, gradually tapering, slightly curved. Brush on underside.

COAT
Smooth, very close-lying, dense, tight, about 2 in in length.

COLOR
Black with minimal, clearly defined tan markings ranging from light to dark fawn. Tan pips above the eyes are required.

SIZE
Dog: 50 to 56 cm (20-22 in).
Bitch: 48 to 54 cm (19-21 in).

WEIGHT
Approx. 20 kg (44 lb).

Character, special skills and training
Solidly built and with a very keen nose, he is an excellent, elegant runner, has a lovely voice, and tracks hare but is used on all sorts of game. He is good-natured and makes a fine pet.

Care and functions
He is not a city dweller. He needs daily exercise and regular brushing.
. Hunting dog

Polish Hound

This ancient breed is indigenous to Poland, but some say it is descended from Austrian or German strains.

Compact and solidly built. Exudes power. Slow, heavy trot. Heavy gallop.

1

SCENT HOUNDS

6

COUNTRY OF ORIGIN
Poland

ORIGINAL NAME
Ogar Polski

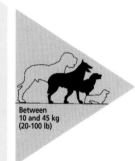

Between
10 and 45 kg
(20-100 lb)

HEAD
Fairly heavy, elegantly chiseled. Skull as long as nosebridge. Pronounced stop. Well-developed brow bones. Very wrinkled forehead. Long muzzle. Strong jaws. Thick, pendulous flews. Large, wide nose.

EYES
Slanted, dark brown.

Character, special skills and training
This tenacious dog with more endurance than speed has a very keen sense of smell and a resonant voice. He can work on all kinds of terrain, in any kind of weather. He is affectionate and a good companion.

Care and functions
He is not at all suited to city life. He needs space and exercise and requires regular brushing.
· Hunting dog.

EARS
Set on low, fairly long, hanging freely, slightly rounded at the tip.

BODY
Massive. Strong, muscular neck with folded dewlap. Broad chest. Large, broad brisket. Well-curved ribs. Broad abdomen. Flank level. Long, broad, muscular back. Broad, level croup.

LIMBS
Well-muscled, solidly boned legs. Feet have very tight toes with strong nails.

TAIL
Set on fairly low, large, hanging lower than the hock, slightly pendulous.

COAT
Medium in length, thick. Slightly longer on the spine, the backs of the hind legs and the lower tail. Thick undercoat.

COLOR
Fawn and black. Tan head, ears, legs, sternum and thighs. Body black or dark grey, with a black mantle. White hair tolerated as flashings or a flare or on the chest, lower legs and tip of the tail.

SIZE
Dog: 56 to 65 cm (22-25.5 in).
Bitch: 55 to 60 cm (22-23.5 in).

WEIGHT
Dog: 25 to 32 kg (55-70.5 lb).
Bitch: 20 to 26 kg (44-57.5 lb).

Tyrolean Hound

The Tyrolean Hound is descended from Celtic hounds. Emperor Maximilian I used this brachet in Tyrol as early as about 1500. The first standard was established in 1896 and the breed was officially recognized in 1908.

Stocky. Long. Well-balanced. Maintains a swift gait.

1

SCENT HOUNDS

6

COUNTRY OF ORIGIN
Austria

ORIGINAL NAME
Tiroler Bracke

OTHER NAME
Austrian Brachet

Medium Breeds between 10 and 25 kg (20-55 lb)

Character, special skills and training
This versatile scenthound hunts hare and fox and is used as a bloodhound. He is well-suited to hunting in the forest or the mountains. He has a very keen nose, a good voice and an even temper. He is an affectionate companion.

Care and functions
The Tyrolean Hound needs space and exercise and requires regular brushing.
· Hunting dog.

HEAD
Wide. Broad, slightly domed skull. Pronounced stop. Straight muzzle. Short lips.

EYES
Round, dark brown.

EARS
Set on high, wide, rounded at the tips.

BODY
Slightly longer than it is tall. Well-knit neck without dewlap. Pronounced withers. Well-domed, moderately wide, well let-down chest. Slight tuck-up. Broad, long, moderately sloping croup. Firm, straight back.

LIMBS
Well-muscled legs. Large feet with tight toes.

TAIL
Set on high, long. Carried high in action. A brush tail with dense hair is prized.

COAT
Fairly thick, lying close to the body. Pronounced culottes on the thighs. Undercoat.

COLOR
Fawn or black and tan, tricolor. Fawn (red to yellowish-red) or black and tan (black mantle) varieties have well-defined reddish-tan markings on the legs, chest, abdomen and head. Both varieties may have white markings (collar, chest, legs and feet).

SIZE
Dog: 44 to 50 cm (17-20 in).
Bitch: 42 to 48 cm (16.5-19 in).

WEIGHT
Approx. 20 kg (44 lb).

Spanish Hound

This shorthaired, medium-sized hound is an ancient breed indigenous to Spain. It comes in two varieties:
- The Great Spanish Hound (tipo grande); and
- The Small or Lightweight Spanish Hound (tipo ligero).
He is known for hunting hare but works on all sorts of quarry.

Solid. Agile. Fairly thick skin.

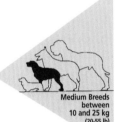

1

6

SCENT HOUNDS

COUNTRY OF ORIGIN
Spain

ORIGINAL NAME
Sabueso Español

Medium Breeds
between
10 and 25 kg
(20-55 lb)

HEAD
Long. Domed skull. Wrinkled forehead. Long, slightly domed muzzle. Thin lips.

EYES
Brown. Well-pigmented eyelids.

EARS
Very long, thin and supple.

BODY
Powerful, long. Strong neck with dewlap. Broad, deep chest. Well-arched ribs. Loin fairly short. Tuck-up. Straight back

LIMBS
Long feet. Strong legs.

TAIL
Thick. Hanging down at rest.

COAT
Short, fine and glossy.

COLOR
Great Spanish Hound: white with large, rounded orange or black spots of varying intensity.
Small Spanish Hound: white with red or black spots, sometimes large enough to completely cover the body except for the neck, muzzle, chest and lower legs.

SIZE
Great Spanish Hound
Dog: 51 to 56 cm (20-22 in).
Bitch: 49 to 52 cm (19-20.5).
Small Spanish Hound
Dog: under 51 cm (20 in).
Bitch: under 49 cm (19 in).

WEIGHT
Great Spanish Hound: approx. 25 kg (55 lb).
Small Spanish Hound: approx. 20 kg (44 lb).

Character, special skills and training
The lively, even-tempered Spanish Hound has considerable stamina. He is independent and stubborn. Though loyal and affectionate, he is not really a companion dog. He needs firm training.

Care and functions
He needs space and lots of exercise and requires regular brushing.
· Hunting dog.
· Utility dog: police dog and watchdog.

211

Finnish Hound

This breed similar to the Harrier was created by Tammelin, a Finnish metalsmith, by crossing German, Swiss, English and Scandinavian hounds. The Finnish Hound is believed to have existed since 1700 and is known for hunting fox, hare, elk and lynx.

Solidly built but lightweight.
Light, springy gait.

SCENT HOUNDS

COUNTRY OF ORIGIN
Finland

ORIGINAL NAME
Suomenajokoïra

OTHER NAME
Finskstövare

6

1

Medium Breeds
between
10 and 25 kg
(20-55 lb)

Character, special skills and training
Fast, energetic, calm and even-tempered, the Finnish Hound is independent and has a great deal of stamina. He is a pleasant companion in winter when he is not hunting. He needs a firm owner.

Care and functions
He needs space and lots of exercise and requires regular brushing.
· Hunting dog.
· Companion dog.

HEAD
Dignified, fairly cleanly cut. Slightly domed skull. Pronounced occipital peak. Stop not very pronounced. Long muzzle. Well-developed nose. Strong jaws.

EYES
Dark.

EARS
Moderately long, pendulous.

BODY
Longer than it is tall. Neck well-knit, medium in length. Deep chest. Fairly arched ribs. Slight tuck-up. Moderately long, straight, muscular back. Well-developed, powerful croup.

LIMBS
Well-muscled legs.

TAIL
Long and tapering toward the tip. Usually carried level with the back or slightly lower.

COAT
Moderately long, straight and fairly stiff.

COLOR
Black mantle. Tan markings on the head, abdomen, shoulders, thighs and elsewhere on the legs. Usually white markings on the head, neck, chest, lower legs and tip of the tail.

SIZE
Dog: 55 to 61 cm (22.5-24 in).
Bitch: 52 to 58 cm (20.5-23 in).

WEIGHT
Approx. 25 kg (55 lb).

212

Halden Hound

This breed was named after the town of Halden in southeastern Norway. He is believed to be the product of crosses between local, Swedish, German, and English scenthounds. The standard for the Halden Hound was established in the 1950s. He is virtually unknown outside his native country.

Medium-size. Solid. Long. Built to hunt.

1

SCENT HOUNDS

COUNTRY OF ORIGIN
Norway

ORIGINAL NAME
Haldenstövare

Medium Breeds between 10 and 25 kg (20-55 lb)

6

HEAD
Medium-sized, finely chiseled. Slightly domed skull. Pronounced stop. Straight nosebridge. Lips not too pendulous. Flat cheeks.

EYES
Medium-sized, dark brown.

EARS
Curled, pendulous, must reach mid-muzzle when outstretched.

BODY
Rectangular. Neck fairly long, arched, well-knit, without dewlap. Deep chest. Well-sprung ribs. Broad loin. Straight, solid back. Well-

developed, rounded, slightly sloping croup.

LIMBS
Muscular, solidly boned, well-knit legs. Feet preferably oval, with tight toes and tough pads.

TAIL
Hanging nearly to hocks, fairly thick, carried low.

COAT
Smooth, very dense, neither too fine nor too short.

COLOR
White with black spots or brown shading on the head and legs and between black and white markings. Small

black or brown spots are considered a fault. Black should not be predominant. Any other color or pattern is cause for disqualification.

SIZE
Dog: 47 to 55 cm (18.5-21.5 in). Bitch: 44 to 52 cm (17-20.5 in).

WEIGHT
Approx. 20 kg (44 lb).

Character, special skills and training
The Halden Hound can withstand cold and is a fast hunter able to chase quarry for long periods at a quick pace. He is not a pack hound. He hunts hare and other plains quarry. Kind and affectionate, he makes a good pet.

Care and functions
He needs space and exercise for his well-being. He requires regular brushing.
· Hunting dog.

213

Hamilton Hound

The Hamilton Hound is named after the founder of Sweden's Kennel Club, who developed the breed by crossing German hounds (the Hanoverian Hound, the Hölsteiner Hound, etc.) with the English Foxhound.

Well-balanced structure.
Exudes power and grace.

1

SCENT HOUNDS

6

COUNTRY OF ORIGIN
Sweden

ORIGINAL NAME
Hamiltonstövare

OTHER NAME
Swedish Foxhound

Medium Breeds
between
10 and 25 kg
(20-55 lb)

Character, special skills and training
With his endurance and resistance to the cold, this courageous dog usually hunts alone for large game (including deer and wild boar).

Care and functions
He needs a great deal of exercise and requires regular brushing.
· Hunting dog.

HEAD
Long, slender, chiseled. Slightly domed, moderately wide skull. Fairly pronounced stop. Well-developed nose.

EYES
Dark brown.

EARS
Set on high, pendulous.

BODY
Rectangular. Long, solid neck. Powerful loin. Straight back. Broad, muscular croup.

LIMBS
Well-knit legs.

TAIL
Set on high, thick at the base, carried straight or loosely in saber fashion.

COAT
Short, hard, dense. Undercoat short, thick, fine.

COLOR
Tricolor. Black markings on the top of the neck, on the back, sides of the body and underside of the tail. Brown markings on the head, legs and the sides of the lower neck, trunk and tail. White band on the neck extending from the chin to the chest. The tip of the tail and the feet are also white.

SIZE
Dog: 50 to 60 cm (19.5-23.5 in).
Bitch: 46 to 57 cm (18-22.5 in).

WEIGHT
Approx. 25 kg (55 lb).

Hygen Hound

This superb hunting dog was named after Hygen, the man who developed the breed in the nineteenth century by crossing the German Hölsteiner Hound with other scenthounds. The breed was then crossed with the more lightweight Norwegian Hound. The Hygen Hound is rare outside his native country.

Solid

SCENT HOUNDS 1

COUNTRY OF ORIGIN
Norway

ORIGINAL NAME
Hygenhund

6

Medium Breeds
between
10 and 25 kg
(20-55 lb)

HEAD
Neither heavy nor long, a bit broad. Slightly domed skull. Very pronounced stop. Straight nosebridge. Broad, fairly short muzzle. Tight lips.

EYES
Medium-sized, dark or hazel.

EARS
Wide, fairly short, moderately thick. Front edge lying against the cheek.

BODY
Compact. Strong neck, slight dewlap. Deep, long chest. Loin strong and muscular. No tuck-up. Short, straight, strong back. Long, broad, slightly rounded croup.

LIMBS
Feet with tight toes and tough pads. Solid, clean-cut legs, not too heavy.

TAIL
Thick at the base, tapering toward the tip. Carried gaily, but not curled over the back.

COAT
Short, dense, glossy, slightly harsh to the touch.

COLOR
Brown or yellowish-red, with or without black shading. Black and tan. The two colors may be combined with white. White with tan and yellow markings or white with black and tan markings. All these colors are of equal value.

SIZE
Dog: 47 to 55 cm.
Bitch: slightly smaller.

WEIGHT
20 to 25 kg.

Character, special skills and training
This lively breed with great stamina is a distance runner. He can follow a trail to find wounded game. He hunts all sorts of quarry on, all kinds of terrain, in all types of weather. A fine watchdog, he is also a good companion.

Care and functions
He needs space and lots of exercise.
· Hunting dog.

Istrian Hound

This very ancient breed has always been prized in Istria. The breed's mysterious origins probably match those of Italian hounds. The two varieties of Istrian Hound are the Wirehaired Istrian Hound (Istarski Ostrodlaki Gonic) and the more popular Smoothhaired Istrian Hound (Istarski Kratkolaki Gonic), also known as the Istrian Pointer.

Solidly built. Reddish skin without wrinkles. Flexible, springy gait.

1

SCENT HOUNDS

6

COUNTRY OF ORIGIN
Yugoslavia

ORIGINAL NAME
Istarski Gonic

Medium Breeds between 10 and 25 kg (20-55 lb)

Character, special skills and training
The Istrian Hound is calm, has a powerful voice, excels on hare and fox and is a very good bloodhound. He is affectionate and makes a good companion.

Care and functions
He needs space and lots of exercise and requires regular brushing.
· Hunting dog.

HEAD
Long, not very lightweight. Slightly domed skull. Fairly broad forehead. Stop not very pronounced. Strong, rectangular muzzle. Well-joined lips. Visible mucosas are dark.

EYES
Large, dark. Eyebrows very bushy and thick in the wire-haired variety.

EARS
Long, hanging against the cheeks.

BODY
Robust, slightly longer than it is tall. Neck has no dewlap. Broad chest. Rounded ribs. Slight tuck-up. Broad, slightly sloping croup. Straight, broad back.

LIMBS
Muscular, solidly boned legs. Round feet with tight toes and tough pads.

TAIL
Thick at the base, tapering toward the tip. Carried low, curved slightly upward.

COAT
Wirehaired: 5 to 10 cm (2-4 in) long, standing on end. Thick, short undercoat. Smoothhaired: fine, dense and glossy.

COLOR
White. Ears usually orangish or covered with orangish flecks. Orange flashings on the forehead. Orangish spots and flecks may also appear on the body.

SIZE
44 to 58 cm (17-23 in).

WEIGHT
18 to 20 kg (40-44 lb).

Italian Hound

The Italian Hound's origins are quite distant. The descendant of Egyptian scenthounds, he is believed to have been imported to Greece and then Italy, where he might have been crossed with the Roman Molossus. Images of this scenthound can be found in ancient statuary, as well as in Renaissance paintings. By the late nineteenth century, the breed had branched into several varieties, including the Lomellina Hound and Alpine Hound, which were used to develop today's breed. An Italian Hound won the first European Cup in 1993 in France.

Well-proportioned. Skin is slightly thick. Preferred gait: gallop.

1

6

SCENT HOUNDS

COUNTRY OF oORIGIN
Italy

ORIGINAL NAME
Segugio Italiano

Between
10 and 45 kg
(20-100 lb)

HEAD
Long. Slightly domed skull. Stop not very pronounced. Large nose. Long, domed nosebridge.

EYES
Large, dark ocher-colored.

EARS
Triangular, flat, pendulous, pointed at the tips.

BODY
Can be inscribed inside a square. Very well-knit neck without dewlap. Moderately wide chest. Well-muscled loin. No tuck-up. Straight, muscular back. Level, well-muscled croup.

LIMBS
Oval feet with tight, arched toes and black nails. Long, well-knit legs.

TAIL
Set on high, hanging in saber fashion. Carried no higher than the back in action.

COAT
Medium in length (under 5 cm), harsh except for on the head, legs and tail. A short-haired variety with smooth hair also exists.

COLOR
Solid fawn, ranging from dark smoky reddish-fawn to light fawn and black and tan. Fawn may be accompanied by white markings on the muzzle, skull, neck, lower legs and tip of the tail and white flashings on the chest.

SIZE
Dog: 52 to 60 cm (20.5-23.5 in).
Bitch: 50 to 58 cm (20-23 in).

WEIGHT
Dog: 20 to 28 kg (44-62 lb).
Bitch: 18 to 26 kg (40-57.5 lb).

Character, special skills and training
This robust, very hardy, fast, lively, enthusiastic dog with a superb nose works alone or in packs. He is perfectly adapted to the most rugged terrain and hunts hare, fox and wild boar. He has a resonant, harmonious voice. Although the Italian Hound is independent and not very outgoing, he can be a companion animal. He needs firm training.

Care and functions
He needs space and lots of exercise and requires regular brushing.
· Hunting dog.
· Companion dog.

Norwegian Hound

To develop this breed, able to hunt rabbit by scent instead of sight, the Norwegian breeder W. Dunker is believed to have crossed a Russian Harlequin Hound with various keen-nosed hounds. The Norwegian Hound is popular in Scandinavia.

1

SCENT HOUNDS

COUNTRY OF ORIGIN
Norway

ORIGINAL NAME
Dunker

6

Rectangular body. Solid but not heavy.

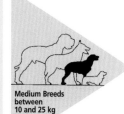

Medium Breeds between 10 and 25 kg (20-55 lb)

Character, special skills and training
Very robust and able to adapt to all types of weather and terrain, the Norwegian Hound is built for long-distance running rather than sprinting. He hunts hare. Even-tempered and kind, he makes a good companion.

Care and functions
He needs space and exercise, as well as regular brushing.
· Hunting dog.
· Companion dog.

HEAD
Cleanly cut, long, without loose skin. Slightly domed skull. Pronounced stop. Straight nosebridge. Long muzzle.

EYES
Fairly large, dark. Heterochromatic eyes are tolerated in the blue marbled (harlequin) variety.

EARS
Medium in length, slightly rounded at the tips. Carried flat against the head.

BODY
Longer than it is tall. Fairly long neck without dewlap. Spacious chest with well-rounded ribs. Broad, muscular loin. Well-muscled, slightly sloping croup.

LIMBS
Solidly boned legs. Compact feet with well-arched toes.

TAIL
Thick at the base, tapering toward the tip. Must be set on level with the topline.

COAT
Short, dense, straight, not too soft.

COLOR
Black or blue marbled (harlequin), with fawn and white markings.

SIZE
Dog: 50 to 55 cm (20-22 in).
Bitch: 48 to 53 cm (19-21 in).

WEIGHT
20 to 25 kg (44-55 lb).

Posavatz Hound

This dog was named after Posavina, a plains region in northern Bosnia. The breed was registered with the FCI in 1955 as the Kras Posavac Basin Hound. In today's standard, he is known as the Posavatz Hound. His origins are uncertain and he is virtually unknown outside his native country.

Mesomorph. Solidly built. Supple skin without folds. Fluid, moderately lively gait.

1

SCENT HOUNDS

COUNTRY OF ORIGIN
Yugoslavia

ORIGINAL NAME
Posavaski Gonic

OTHER NAME
Kras Posavac Basin Hound

6

Medium Breeds between 10 and 25 kg (20-55 lb)

HEAD
Long and narrow. Forehead slightly domed. Pronounced frontal furrow. Stop not very pronounced. Slightly domed nosebridge. Fairly long muzzle. Wide nose, black or dark chestnut in color. Tight-lipped.

EYES
Large, dark in color.

EARS
Flat, thin, with rounded tips, hanging against the cheeks.

BODY
Longer than it is tall. Muscular neck without dewlap. Pronounced withers. Long, broad, deep chest. Rounded ribs. Tuck-up. Robust, muscular, broad back. Moderately sloping, rounded croup.

LIMBS
Muscular, sturdy legs. Round, tight feet with strong nails.

TAIL
Moderately long, thick at the base, carried in saber fashion, covered with thick hair.

COAT
2 to 3 cm (0.8-1.2 in) long, stiff, dense and flat. Hair slightly longer on the lower abdomen, backs of the legs and lower part of the tail.

COLOR
All shades of reddish-wheaten. Should never be brown or chocolate. White markings on the head, neck, chest, abdomen, lower legs and tip of the tail.

SIZE
46 to 58 cm (18-23 in).

WEIGHT
Approx. 25 kg (55 lb).

Character, special skills and training
This fast, hardy, lively dog with a high, resonant voice has a good sense of smell and can hunt on any kind of terrain, mainly for hare and deer. He is very affectionate with his owner and has a good character.

Care and functions
He is very active and needs space and lots of exercise. He also requires regular brushing.
· Hunting dog.

219

Schiller Hound

This breed has been known since the Middle Ages. The standard was fixed and recognized in 1952, thanks to P. Schiller, the breeder from whom this dog takes his name. Schiller crossed Swedish scenthounds with Swiss, German and Austrian bloodhounds. The breed is rare outside his native land.

Robust. Lightweight. Well-balanced. Dignified.

1

SCENT HOUNDS

6

COUNTRY OF ORIGIN
Sweden

ORIGINAL NAME
Schillerstövare

Medium Breeds
between
10 and 25 kg
(20-55 lb)

Character, special skills and training
Robust, energetic and lively, he is the fastest Swedish hound. He hunts hare and fox alone in the snow. He makes a good companion and needs firm training.

Care and functions
He needs space and lots of exercise, as well as regular brushing.
· Hunting dog.

HEAD
Long, cone-shaped. Well-pronounced stop. Well-developed nose. Lips not pendulous.

EYES
Hazel.

EARS
Pendulous, soft to the touch.

BODY
Long, powerful. Deep chest. Slightly curved ribs. Strong loin. Slightly sloping croup. Straight back.

LIMBS
Long legs. Compact feet with flexible toes and tough pads.

TAIL
Carried straight or loosely in saber fashion.

COAT
Short, strong, glossy. Thick undercoat.

COLOR
Black and tan. Black neck, shoulders, flanks and base of the tail.

SIZE
Dog: 50 to 60 cm (19.5-23,5 in).
Bitch: 46 to 57 cm (18-22.5 in).

WEIGHT
18 to 25 kg (39.5-55 lb).

Slovakian Hound

This very old breed is believed to be descended from the scent-thounds who inhabited eastern Europe in ancient times. In 1996, there were about two hundred Slovakian Hounds in France.

Lightweight. Rectangular body. Dark brown to black skin. Lively, smooth gait.

1

SCENT HOUNDS

COUNTRY OF ORIGIN
Slovakia

ORIGINAL NAME
Slovensky Kopov

6

Medium Breeds
between
10 and 25 kg
(20-55 lb)

HEAD
Slightly domed skull. Pronounced brow bones and frontal furrow. Straight, long nosebridge. Tight-lipped.

EYES
Almond-shaped, dark. Eyelids edged with black.

EARS
Moderately long, rounded at the tip, lying flat against the head.

BODY
Longer than it is tall. Short, muscular neck without dewlap. Wide brisket. Broad, long chest. Curved ribs. Fairly broad, solid loin. Moderate tuck-up. Straight, moderately long back. Moderately wide, rounded croup.

LIMBS
Muscular, solidly boned legs. Oval feet with well-arched toes and black nails.

TAIL
Set on low, tapering to a point. Hanging at rest. Carried curved in saber fashion in action.

COAT
2 to 5 cm long, moderately thick, lying flat, dense. Longer on the back, neck and tail. Dense undercoat.

COLOR
Black with brown to mahogany markings on legs.

SIZE
Dog: 45 to 50 cm (17.5-19.5).
Bitch: 40 to 45 cm (15.5-17.5).

WEIGHT
15 to 20 kg (33-44 lb).

Character, special skills and training
This hardy, very courageous dog can follow a scent for hours on end. He has a top-notch nose, is known for his drive and has a highly developed sense of direction. He hunts wild boar alone. Lively, very independent and strong-willed, he makes a good guard dog. Although he is affectionate, he is not very well-suited to being a pet. He needs firm training.

Care and functions
He needs space and lots of exercise and requires regular brushing.
· Hunting dog.

221

Smälands Hound

This breed comes from Smålands in southern Sweden. It is the oldest Swedish scenthound breed. It was recognized by the Swedish Kennel Club in 1921, but the standard was not definitively established until 1952.

Robust but lightweight. Elegant. Dignified.

1

SCENT HOUNDS

6

COUNTRY OF ORIGIN
Sweden

ORIGINAL NAME
Smålandsstövare

Medium Breeds
between
10 and 25 kg
(20-55 lb)

Character, special skills and training
Vigorous, obstinate and gifted with a superlative nose, the Smålands Hound is used primarily on fox and hare. He can work in all kinds of weather and makes a good companion.

Care and functions
He needs space and lots of exercise, as well as regular brushing.
· Hunting dog.
· Companion dog.

HEAD
Narrow, cleanly cut. Straight nosebridge. Well-developed muzzle. Wide nostrils.

EYES
Dark.

EARS
Set on high, fairly flat, hanging flat against the head.

BODY
Compact. Neck of medium length, powerful. Deep chest. Powerful loin. Muscular abdomen with tuck-up.

Slightly sunken, short back. Long, broad croup.

LIMBS
Muscular, well-boned legs. Large feet with well-arched toes.

TAIL
Long, hanging to hocks or docked at birth. Carried high.

COAT
Short, thick, smooth and glossy.

COLOR
Black with tan markings above the eyes, around the flews and on the chest and lower legs.

SIZE
Dog: 45 to 54 cm (17.5-21 in).
Bitch: 42 to 50 cm (16.5-19.5 in).

WEIGHT
15 to 20 kg (33-44 lb).

Swiss Hounds

JURA HOUND

The Swiss hound has very ancient origins. He reportedly lived in Helvetia during the Roman Empire and he has been prized by dog fanciers since the fifteenth century. Unlike French Hounds, Swiss Hounds have no English blood in their veins. In 1882, a standard was established for each of the five "forms" of Swiss Hound.

In 1909, the Thurgovian Hound (from eastern Switzerland) became extinct. In 1933, a single standard was written for the four remaining varieties:
- The Bernese Hound (Berner Laufhund);
- The Jura Hound (Aargovian Hound);
- The Lucerne Hound (Luzerner Laufhund); and
- The Schwyz Hound (Schwyzer Laufhund).

The ancient Jura Hound, a type similar to the Saint Hubert, has virtually disappeared. Each of the four varieties also comes in a smaller model, the result of crosses between normal-sized Swiss Hounds and bassets.

Medium-sized. Elongated body. Thin, tight skin of a different color in each of the four varieties. Gait: long strides.

1

SCENT HOUNDS

COUNTRY OF ORIGIN
Switzerland

6

ORIGINAL NAME
Schweizerischer Laufhund

Medium Breeds
between
10 and 25 kg
(20-55 lb)

HEAD
Long, cleanly cut. Narrow, finely chiseled, domed skull. Pronounced stop. Bridge of nose straight or very slightly curved. Narrow, long muzzle. Solid jaws. Cleanly cut cheeks. Well-developed nose.

EYES
Slightly oval, a shade of brown.

EARS
Set on low, narrow, pendulous, folded and twisted, rounded at the tip.

BODY
Longer than it is tall. Long, muscular neck with slight dewlap. Chest deeper than it is wide. Slightly curved ribs. Muscular loin. Slight tuck-up. Compact, straight back. Long, slightly sloping croup.

LIMBS
Very muscular, solidly boned legs. Rounded feet with tight toes and tough pads.

TAIL
Medium in length, tapering to the tip. Hanging naturally at rest. Carried above the topline in action.

COAT
Short, smooth, dense, very fine on the head and ears. The Lucerne Hound always has close-lying hair.

COLOR
- Bernese Hound: white with black spots or a black saddle, fawn marking above the eyes, on the cheeks, on the inside surface of the ears and around the anus.
- Jura Hound: fawn with a black, sometimes smoky mantle, or black with fawn markings above the eyes, on the cheeks and on the legs. Sometimes a white spot on the chest.
- Lucerne Hound: blue, resulting from a combination of black and white hairs, strongly flecked, with black spots or a black saddle, fawn markings above the eyes, on the cheeks, chest, legs and around the anus. Black mantle is allowed.
- Schwyz Hound: white with orangish-fawn spots or an orangish-fawn saddle, sometimes very lightly speckled. Orangish-fawn mantle is allowed.

SIZE
30 to 55 cm (12-21.5).

WEIGHT
15 to 20 kg (33-44 lb).

LUCERNE HOUND

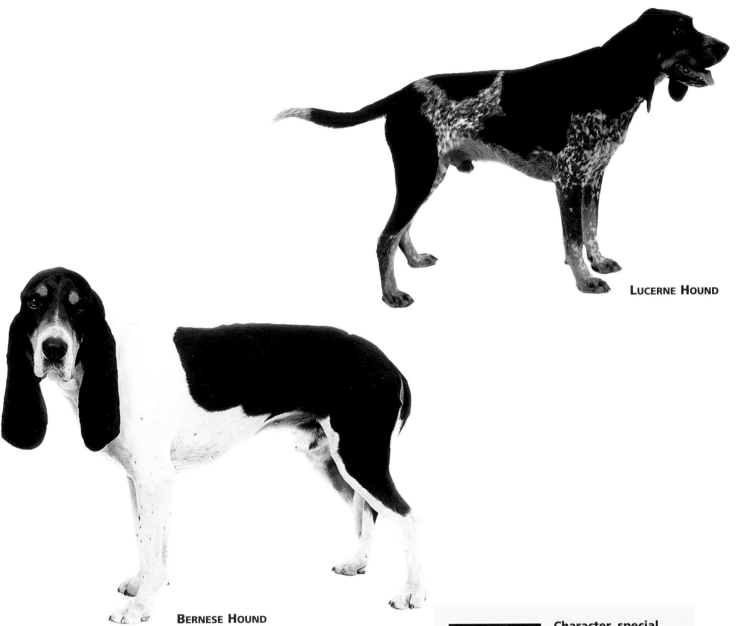

LUCERNE HOUND

BERNESE HOUND

SCHWYZ HOUND

Character, special skills and training

Swiss Hounds are hardy, vigorous, calm dogs with a great deal of stamina, a discerning nose and a powerful voice. The hard-driving, gloriously voiced Bernese Hound ("the Howler of Jura") is used especially on hare. The Jura Hound, an excellent tracker, is more commonly used on wild boar and deer. The active, enthusiastic Lucerne Hound is similar to the Small Blue Gascony Hound and works on deer. The Schwyz Hound, less popular in France, is reserved for rabbit and hare. Gentle, docile and very attached to their owner, Swiss Hounds are pleasant companions. Firm training is helpful.

Care and functions

For their well-being, they need space and lots of exercise. They require regular brushing.
· Hunting dog.
· Companion dog.

225

Transylvanian Hound

The Transylvanian Hound originated in the ninth century, when the Magyars brought in hounds and crossed them with local breeds and Polish hounds. He was used in hunting wolf and bear and comes in two varieties:
- Short-legged, used on fox and hare; and
- Long legged, specializing in wild boar, deer and lynx.

Medium-sized. Darkly pigmented skin. Pace is not fast. Marvelously smooth gallop.

1

SCENT HOUNDS

6

COUNTRY OF ORIGIN
Hungary

ORIGINAL NAME
Erdelyi Kopo

Large Breeds between 25 and 45 kg (55-100 lb)

Character, special skills and training
Tireless, bold and determined, the Transylvanian Hound has a very keen sense of smell and an acute sense of direction. A versatile hunting dog, he is obedient and docile. He needs firm training.

Care and functions
He needs lots of exercise and regular brushing.
· Hunting dog.

HEAD
Fairly long. Slightly domed skull. Stop not pronounced. Straight nosebridge. Tight-lipped.

EYES
Medium-sized, oval, slightly slanted, dark brown.

EARS
Hanging without wrinkles, wider in the center, rounded tips.

BODY
Nearly square. Muscular neck of medium length. Pronounced withers. Long, broad chest. Slight tuck-up. Straight back. Moderately sloping croup.

LIMBS
Round, well-knit feet with strong, black nails. Solid, muscular legs.

TAIL
Set on low. Hanging at rest. Curled level with the topline in action.

COAT
Short-legged variety: short, straight, dense hair.
Long-legged variety: longer, denser, harsher hair. Undercoat.

COLOR
Short-legged variety: reddish-brown toward the abdomen and legs.

Long-legged variety: black. Red spots on the eyebrows, muzzle and legs.
Both varieties often have white spots on the forehead, chest, feet and tip of the tail.

SIZE
Short-legged variety: 45 to 50 cm (18-20 in).
Long-legged variety: 55 to 65 cm (22-25 in).

WEIGHT
30 to 35 kg (66-77 lb).

Yugoslavian Hound

Considered an indigenous breed, the Yugoslavian Hound is found in the southern region of the former Yugoslavia. He comes in two varieties:
- The Yugoslavian Mountain Hound (Jugoslovenski Planinski Gonic or Planinski) and
- The Yugoslavian Tricolor Hound (Jugoslovenski Trobojni Gonic).
These dogs are not well known outside their native land.

Mesomorph. Rectangular body. Tight skin without folds. Gait: long strides.

Medium Breeds between 10 and 25 kg (20-55 lb)

1

SCENT HOUNDS

COUNTRY OF ORIGIN
Yugoslavia

ORIGINAL NAME
Jugoslovenski Gonic

6

HEAD
Long. Slightly domed skull. Pronounced brow bones. Stop not pronounced. Straight nosebridge. Solid, wedge-shaped muzzle. Tight black lips.

EYES
Dark.

EARS
Pendulous and without folds. Rounded tips.

BODY
Slightly longer than it is tall. Muscular neck without dewlap. Broad brisket. Wide, deep chest. Tuck-up. Broad, muscular, slightly sloping croup. Broad, muscular back.

LIMBS
Solid, muscular legs. Round feet with tight toes.

TAIL
Straight or curved loosely in saber fashion.

COAT
Short, dense. Thick undercoat in the Planinski.

COLOR
Yugoslavian Mountain Hound: black and tan, with characteristic tan markings above the eyes. Yugoslavian Tricolor Hound: fox-red or wheaten-red covering most of the body or with a black saddle. White markings on the head (flare), neck (collar), chest, lower legs and tip of the tail.

SIZE
45 to 55 cm (18-22 in).

WEIGHT
20 to 25 kg (44-55 lb).

Character, special skills and training
This very hardy, bold, persistent hunter with a very keen sense of smell is particularly skilled on rough terrain. He hunts hare, fox, deer and other quarry. Gentle, calm and good-natured, he makes a pleasant companion.

Care and functions
He needs wide open spaces and lots of exercise, as well as regular brushing.
· Hunting dog.
· Companion dog.

227

Artois Hound

This very old, medium-sized pack hound was nearly extinct by the early twentieth century. It has made a comeback, but is still rare. It was first mentioned in the fifteenth century and is believed to have been used by royalty for deer hunting. The result of crosses between scenthounds and pointers, the Artois Hound was also popular throughout the centuries as a hare-hunting dog. His ancestor is the Great Artois Hound, himself descended from the Saint Hubert. A splash of English blood modified the breed.

Well-built. Muscular. Not too long. Fairly thick skin. Flexible, clean, calm gait.

1

SCENT HOUNDS

6

COUNTRY OF ORIGIN
France

OTHER NAME
Briquet d'Artois

Large Breeds
between
25 and 45 kg
(55-100 lb)

Character, special skills and training
Hardy, robust and courageous, the Artois Hound has great stamina and is even-tempered and calm. This medium-sized hound combines the qualities of pointers and scenthounds: a strong sense of direction, a very keen nose, precise pointing, speed and drive. A hare hunter, he is also used on deer, wild boar and fox. He needs a firm owner.

Care and functions
He needs space and exercise and requires regular brushing.
· Hunting dog.

HEAD
Heavy, broad, fairly short. Slightly domed skull. Stop not pronounced. Bridge of nose broad and straight, not very long. Well-developed nose. Lips somewhat thick.

EYES
Large, prominent, very wide.

EARS
Set on at eye level, large, thick, nearly flat and fairly long.

BODY
Massive. Neck fairly long, powerful. Very slight dewlap. Wide brisket. Fairly broad, well let-down chest. Ribs fairly rounded. Loin broad and muscular. Flank let-down and very full. Broad, slightly sloping croup. Well-muscled, moderately long back.

LIMBS
Strong legs. Large, well-knit, moderately long, tight feet with black pads.

TAIL
Fairly long, tufted and carried in sickle fashion.

COAT
Lying close to the body, thick, fairly strong.

COLOR
Tricolor: white, dark fawn to hare or even badger grey, with mantle or large black spots. Head usually fawn, sometimes smoky.

SIZE
52 to 58 cm (20,5-23 in).

WEIGHT
25 to 30 kg (55-66 lb).

Otterhound

This large, shaggy breed is believed to be descended from the Saint Hubert Hound and French griffons (the Griffon Vendée and the Griffon Nivernais) imported to England before 1870 after receiving Harrier and Wirehaired Terrier blood. Otterhounds were developed to hunt otter, pursuing it even underwater. After otter hunting was banned in England around 1970, the breed became rare.

Large. Strong. Robust. Flexible gait.

1

SCENT HOUNDS

COUNTRY OF ORIGIN
Great Britain

6

Large Breeds between 25 and 45 kg (55-100 lb)

HEAD
Taller than it is wide. Well-domed skull. Stop not pronounced. Strong, high-set muzzle. Abundant flews. Slight beard and mustache. Strong, large jaws.

EYES
Color depends on coat color.

EARS
Long and pendulous, with feathering and a characteristic fold. Front edge folded or rolled inward.

BODY
Solid. Long, powerful neck. Chest well let-down. Broad back. Short, strong loin.

LIMBS
Straight, solidly boned legs. Feet large, round, compact.

TAIL
Thick at the base, tapering toward the tip. Carried high in action.

COAT
4 to 8 cm long, dense, thick, hard and waterproof. Oily, woolly undercoat.

COLOR
All recognized hound colors allowed: whole-colored, grizzled, sable, red, wheaten and blue. May have slight white markings on the head, chest, feet and tip of the tail. White dogs may have slight lemon, blue, or badger grey markings.

SIZE
Dog: approx. 67 cm (26.5 in).
Bitch: approx. 60 cm (23.5 in).

WEIGHT
approx. 32 kg (70.5 lb).

Character, special skills and training
Otterhounds are courageous, tenacious and stubborn. They are very resistant to cold, love water and are excellent swimmers. They can spend an entire day hunting in the water but can also gallop about on dry land. Kind, even-tempered, affectionate and playful, they make wonderful companions. Otterhounds require firm training.

Care and functions
Otterhounds need lots of exercise and weekly brushing.
· Hunting dog.
· Companion dog.

Saint Hubert Hound

Heavy. Massive. Majestic.
The most impressive scenthound. Imposing, slow gait.

1

SCENT HOUNDS

6

COUNTRY OF ORIGIN
Belgium

ORIGINAL NAME
Chien de Saint-Hubert

OTHER NAMES
Bloodhound
Flanders Hound
Ardennes Hound

Giants Breeds
over 45 kg
(over 100 lb)

This large-sized hound from a very ancient strain was improved beginning in the ninth century by the monks of the Saint Hubert Monastery in the Ardennes (Saint Hubert is the patron saint of hunters). The breed was maintained there until 1790. When William the Conqueror brought it to Great Britain in the eleventh century, it was called the Bloodhound because of his ability to follow blood-trails but perhaps also because it was used in manhunts. In Germany it was called the Leithund, or leashound. The Saint Hubert Hound is the famous forefather of today's scenthound breeds that retain more or less the same head features as their ancestor.

The Saint Hubert was used in royal packs until the reign of Saint Louis. At that time, a white Saint Hubert was crossed with an Italian Pointer, producing the Chien Blanc du Roy. This breed replaced the Saint Hubert and formed the great packs of the kings of France from François I to Louis XIV.

HEAD
Large in all dimensions except width. Very tall, pointed skull with highly prominent occipital peak. Very wrinkled skin on the forehead and cheeks. Flews very long and pendulous. Jaws very long and wide.

EYES
Relatively small, dark hazel. Very pendulous lower eyelid revealing dark red conjunctiva.

EARS
Set on low, very long, hanging forward against the jaws in delicate folds.

BODY
Wide and long. Long, well-muscled neck. Well-developed dewlap. Broad, deep chest. Slight tuck-up. Broad, very strong back. Solid loin.

LIMBS
Round feet. Muscular, well-boned legs.

TAIL
Carried in an elegant curve above the topline but not touching the back.

COAT
Short and fairly hard on the body. Soft and silky on the ears and skull.

COLOR
Black and tan (most prized), solid tan, brown and tan. Black markings should form a saddle on the back and appear on the flanks, above the neck and on the top of the head. White is not tolerated.

SIZE
Dog: approx. 67 cm (26.5 in).
Bitch: approx. 60 cm (23.5 in).

WEIGHT
40 to 48 kg (88-106 lb).

Character, special skills and training
First used on large game, the Saint Hubert hunted wild boar and deer. When he was no longer used in packs, he became the bloodhound par excellence used to launch the hunt. He is skilled in tracking wounded game. In fact, his exceptionally keen nose makes him the very best tracking dog. He is courageous, persevering, hardy, determined and very confident. He makes an excellent scenthound. He may not be very fast, but no other dog stays so stubbornly fixed on his quarry. Wise and obedient, he has a magnificent voice. Affectionate, calm and very gentle, he has become a pleasant companion. He is wary of strangers but is not aggressive, making him an excellent watchdog. He needs gentle but firm training. Treating him harshly may make him hostile and even dangerous.

Care and functions
Despite his size, he can adapt to city life, but he needs lots of exercise. He also requires regular brushing.
· Hunting dog.
· Utility dog: manhunts (police).
· Companion dog.

Black and Tan Coonhound

The Black and Tan Coonhound was developed by crossing the Bloodhound with the Foxhound. This champion raccoon hunter also tracks bear and opossum. The breed was recognized by the American Kennel Club in 1945. Other Coonhound varieties include the Redbone (solid red coat), the Bluetick (tricolor coat) and the Treeing Walker (tricolor or bicolor coat). These varieties are not officially recognized.

Powerful. Agile. Well-muscled croup

1

SCENT HOUNDS

6

COUNTRY OF ORIGIN
United States

Large Breeds between 25 and 45 kg (55-100 lb)

Character, special skills and training
Very hardy, alert and lively, Coonhounds are vigilant and aggressive hunters. They require firm training.

Care and functions
They are not suited to apartment life and require regular brushing.
· Hunting dog.

HEAD
Finely chiseled, similar to that of the Saint Hubert Hound. Long, square muzzle. Flews pendulous. Wide nostrils.

EYES
Round, hazel-colored.

EARS
Long and pendulous, framing the face with delicate folds.

BODY
Well-proportioned. Powerful chest.

LIMBS
Strong legs, black toenails.

TAIL
Robust, carried gaily.

COAT
Short, thick.

COLOR
Black with tan markings

above the eyes, on the muzzle, chest and lower legs.

SIZE
58 to 68 cm (23-27 in).

WEIGHT
35 kg (77 lb).

Drever

This very ancient breed is quite similar to the Westphalian Basset, since it is a cross between the Westphalian Basset and local hound breeds. Some believe the Dachshund was used. The Drever was officially recognized by the Swedish Kennel Club in 1947 and by the FCI in 1953. The first standard was established in 1953. The Drever is not very well known outside his native country.

Compact. Well-balanced. Well-muscled. Flexible. Agile.

1

6

SCENT HOUNDS

COUNTRY OF ORIGIN
Sweden

OTHER NAMES
Swedish Dachsbracke
Swedish Pointer

Medium Breeds
between
10 and 25 kg
(20-55 lb)

HEAD
Relatively large and long. Slightly pronounced stop. Straight or slightly curved nosebridge. Strong, very angular muzzle. Large nose.

EYES
Dark brown. Thin lids.

EARS
Medium in length, wide with rounded tips, hanging flat against head.

BODY
Can be inscribed inside a rectangle. Long, fairly strong neck without dewlap. Well-developed chest. Base of sternum below elbows. Powerful, relatively short loin. Slight tuck-up. Straight, strong back. Broad, strong, slightly sloping croup.

LIMBS
Sturdy feet with tight, well-arched toes and tough pads. Short, strong, muscular legs.

TAIL
Long, thick at the base, carried hanging down.

COAT
Dense, straight. Relatively short on the head, lower legs and underside of the tail. Longer on the neck, back and backs of the thighs. Forming a brush at the tip of the tail.

COLOR
All colors allowed but white markings highly visible on all sides are required. White flare and collar very desirable, as are white markings on the tip of the tail and feet. Colors must be pure.

SIZE
Dog: 32 to 40 cm 12.5-15.5 in).
Bitch: 30 to 38 cm (11.8-15 in).

WEIGHT
Approx. 15 kg (33 lb).

Character, special skills and training
Tenacious, courageous and alert, the Drever has an exceptional nose and a loud voice. He hunts alone or in packs for hare, fox and even wild boar. He makes a pleasant companion and needs a firm owner.

Care and functions
He needs space and exercise for his well-being. He also requires regular brushing.
· Hunting dog.

Brittany Fawn

Bony. Muscular. Exude vigor and hardiness.
The shortest basset. Somewhat compact
overall. Lively gait.

1

SCENTHOUNDS

6

COUNTRY OF ORIGIN
France

ORIGINAL NAME
Fauve de Bretagne

Medium Breeds
between
10 and 25 kg
(20-55 lb)

The Great Brittany Fawn, which currently comes
in two varieties—the Brittany Fawn Griffon and the Brittany
Fawn Basset—is a very ancient breed. It was once used
in famous large packs, such as that of Anne de Beaujeu,
the daughter of King Louis XI. These spirited, strong-willed,
yellowish- and reddish-fawn dogs standing 60 to 65 cm
(23.5-25.5 in) tall were the best wolf hunters around. The breed
nearly went extinct in the late nineteenth century, when wolves
became scarce. Crossbreeding produced a more lightweight
hound, the Brittany Fawn Basset, for which the first standard
was established in 1921. The Brittany Fawn Griffon
—a medium-sized version of the Great Brittany Fawn—
was declared extinct in 1928. But after World War II in 1949,
a Medium-sized Brittany Fawn club was created. In 1981,
the club saved the breed when it decided to include the Brittany
Fawn Griffon (now the breed's official name), standing 48
to 56 cm (19-22 in) tall at the withers and the Brittany Fawn
Basset, standing 32 to 38 cm (12.5-15 in) tall.
The rapidly increasing popularity of these varieties,
especially the basset, is encouraging.

HEAD

Fairly long skull, never flat. Pronounced occipital peak. Long, straight or slightly curved nosebridge. Stop not very pronounced in the Brittany Fawn Griffon, more pronounced in the Brittany Fawn Basset. Nose black or dark brown.

EYES

Dark brown.

EARS

Set on at eye level, nearly reaching the muzzle when outstretched, turning slightly and with a pointed tip. Covered with close-lying hair.

BODY

Vigorous. Compact in the Brittany Fawn Basset. Fairly short, muscular neck. Tall, broad chest. Fairly rounded ribs. Slight tuck-up. Short, broad back. Broad, well-muscled loin.
Brittany Fawn Basset: broad, well-muscled, powerful loin. Short, broad back.

LIMBS

Solid legs. Compact feet with tight toes.
Brittany Fawn Basset: slightly bandy or nearly straight hind legs. Compact feet with tight toes.

TAIL

Carried loosely in sickle fashion, medium in length. Thick at the base, tapering toward the tip, often tufted.

COAT

Very hard, crisp, fairly short, never woolly or frizzy.

Foreface should never be bushy.

COLOR

Fawn. The best shades are wheaten gold and brick red, sometimes with flashings on the chest.

SIZE

Brittany Fawn Griffon.
Dog: 50 to 56 cm (19.7-22 in).
Bitch: 48 to 52 cm (19-20.5 in).
Brittany Fawn Basset.
32 to 38 cm (12.5-15 in).

WEIGHT

Brittany Fawn Griffon.
Approx. 23 kg (51 lb).
Brittany Fawn Basset.
Approx. 15 kg (33 lb).

Character, special skills and training

The Great Brittany Fawn gave its modern-day descendents its hardiness, courage, vigor, spirit, speed, keen nose, strong will and independent personality. The Brittany Fawn Basset, with his difficult character and stubbornness (crosses with the Vendée Griffon Basset have calmed him down), hunts alone, in pairs, in small groups, or in packs. He works in thickets and rabbit is his specialty. When well-trained, he makes a good bloodhound. The Brittany Fawn Griffon is a very courageous, excellent pack leader with a glorious voice. He excels at wild boar and fox. Some also use him on hare and deer. Both varieties are calm and affectionate with their owner. These strong-willed hounds need firm training.

Care and functions

The Brittany Fawn Griffon, raised chiefly in packs, is usually kept in a kennel. The Brittany Fawn Basset can live with his owner inside the house or in an outdoor run. Both need space and lots of exercise, as well as regular brushing and attention to the ears.
· Hunting dog.

American Foxhound

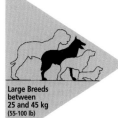

Slender profile. Lightly boned.

English Foxhounds were imported to the United States around 1650 by the British breeder R. Brooke. The breed was crossed with English, French and Irish hounds. American Foxhounds, probably the oldest American hounds, come in many varieties and hunt fox and large game. Recognized by the American Kennel Club in 1894, the breed is not very common.

1

SCENT HOUNDS

COUNTRY OF ORIGIN
United States

6

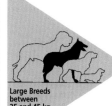

Large Breeds between 25 and 45 kg (55-100 lb)

Character, special skills and training
American Foxhounds are smaller and faster than English Foxhounds and have a keener sense of smell. They have a melodic voice and hunt fox and wild boar. They make excellent companions.

Care and functions
American Foxhounds need lots of exercise and regular brushing.
· Hunting dog.
· Companion dog.

HEAD
Fairly long. Broad, slightly domed skull. Moderate stop. Straight, square muzzle.

EYES
Large, well-spaced. Brown or hazel.

EARS
Long, thin, fairly wide, hanging close to the head.

BODY
Long. Neck open, strong, without dewlap. Chest deep and narrower than in the English Foxhound. Well-sprung ribs. Strong, muscular back. Broad, slightly arched loin.

LIMBS
Long, muscular legs. Round feet with well-arched toes and tough pads.

TAIL
Carried gaily, slightly curved but not hanging over the back. Slight brush.

COAT
Medium in length, dense, harsh.

COLOR
All colors are tolerated.

SIZE
Dog: 56 to 64 cm (22-25 in).
Bitch: 53.3 to 61 cm (21-24 in).

WEIGHT
Approx. 30 kg (66 lb).

236

English Foxhound

The origins of the English Foxhound, the only large game hunting breed from England, are under debate. He is believed to have been developed in Great Britain around the fifteenth century for fox hunting from Staghounds, deer-hunting bloodhounds. Hunters wanted smaller, much faster, hardier dogs and were less concerned with voice and sense of smell. Fox hunting reached its peak in England in the first half of the nineteenth century. The English Foxhound was a favorite of Napoleon III. By the seventeenth century, the breed was used in the United States to develop the American Foxhound. Because of his bone structure, vigor and hardiness, the English Foxhound was also used in France to develop pack hounds for large game hunting.

Mesomorph. Solid. Well-built. Relaxed gait.

1

SCENT HOUNDS

COUNTRY OF ORIGIN
Great Britain

OTHER NAME
Foxhound

6

Large Breeds between 25 and 45 kg (55-100 lb)

HEAD
Well-developed, with a broad skull. Slight stop. Muzzle relatively long.

EYES
Round, brown.

EARS
Set-on high. Medium, wide, hanging flat.

BODY
Built for speed and endurance. Neck long but not thick. Shoulders not heavy. Deep chest and rounded ribs. Well-muscled hindquarters. Fairly long loin. Broad back.

LIMBS
Long, well-boned legs. Round feet with tight toes.

TAIL
Long, curving slightly inward.

COAT
Short, dense, hard, glossy.

COLOR
Tricolor: white and fawn with a black mantle. Bicolor: white and orangish-fawn.

SIZE
Dog: 58 to 64 cm (23-25 in).
Bitch: 53 to 61 cm (21-24 in).

WEIGHT
30 to 35 kg.

Character, special skills and training
This robust, courageous, tireless, speedy dog has a fighting spirit and can cover 6.5 km (4 miles) in 8 minutes and maintain a swift gallop for hours on end. With a relatively weak nose and voice, the English Foxhound always stays in sight of his quarry. His unique specialty in England is fox, but in France he hunts wild boar and deer. He is very skilled in the water. He is not really a companion dog. He needs a firm owner he can accept as the leader of the pack.

Care and functions
For a pack of dogs in the country, kennel life is best. Apartment life is not ideal. The English Foxhound does not like to be alone or idle. He requires regular brushing.
· Hunting dog.

Dignified. Solidly built. Flexible, extended gallop.

French Hound

The French Hound, descended from ancient French breeds, comes in several varieties that differ in coat color:
- The French White and Black Hound, descended from two breeds from southern France, the Saintongeois and the Blue Gascony Hound, with a splash of Foxhound blood. The variety was officially recognized in 1957;
- The French Tricolor Hound, a recent creation (1957) produced by crossing the Anglo-French Tricolor Hound with the French Hound. Crosses were made with the Poitevin, the Billy, and possibly the Blue Gascony Hound. The French Tricolor Hound is sturdier and not quite as fast as the Poitevin. The standard for this variety was officially recognized in 1965;
The French White and Orange Hound, very rare, was developed in 1978 through crosses with the Billy.

HEAD
Fairly large and long. Slightly domed skull. Slight stop

Character, special skills, and training
These dogs are hardy, brave, and able to maintain a swift pace for several hours. With a good voice and keen sense of smell, they hunt confidently in packs. Their work is meticulous. They specialize in deer. They require a firm owner they can accept as the leader of the pack.

Care and functions
French Hounds live in kennels. They need space and exercise. They require regular brushing and attention to the ears.
· Hunting dog.

(pronounced in the French Tricolor Hound and the French White and Orange Hound). Nosebridge slightly curved. Flews covering the lower lip. Nose black or orangish-brown in the White and Orange.

EYES
Dark.

EARS
Turning slightly, reaching almost to the base of the nose when outstretched.

BODY
Powerful. Neck fairly long and strong. Chest taller than it is wide. Slightly rounded ribs. Slight tuck-up. Back fairly long and level. Loin muscular and solidly attached.

LIMBS
Strong legs.

TAIL
Fairly thick at the base and fairly long, carried gracefully.

COAT
Lying close to the body, fairly thick and dense. Finer in the Tricolor.

COLOR
- White and Black: must be white and black with a large mantle or fairly large black spots. Black, steel-grey, or even tan flecks only on the legs. Pale spot above each eye and pale tan markings on the cheeks, below the eyes, under the ears and at the base of the tail. As in the Gascon Saintongeois, "deer markings" on the thigh are fairly common. Skin is white under white hair and black under black hair, sometimes with blue or pale blue blotches on the abdomen and inner thighs.
- Tricolor: white and fawn rich or even coppery tan) with black mantle. Wolf grey hair is tolerated.
- White and Orange: white and lemon or white and orange, as long as orange is not too dark or reddish. Skin white with yellow or orange spots.

SIZE
White and Black: dog: 65 to 72 cm (25.5-28 in); bitch: 62 to 68 cm (24.5-27 in).
Tricolor: dog 62 to 72 cm (24.5-28 in); bitch: 60 to 68 cm (23.5-27 in).
White and Orange:
62 to 70 cm (24.5-27.5 in).

WEIGHT
Approx. 30 kg (66 lb).

Gascon Saintongeois Hound

In the mid-nineteenth century, Count J. de Carayon-Latour wanted to revive the declining Saintonge Hound population. To do this, he crossed the last specimens of the breed with Baron de Ruble's Blue Gascony Hounds, thereby creating the Gascon Saintongeois, or the Virelade Hound, named after his chateau. This was the end of the Saintonge Hound, descended from the Saint Hubert and sporting a white coat with black spots and tan markings.

The Gascon Saintongeois is a pack hound that comes in two varieties:
- The Great Gascon Saintongeois Hound, used in shooting and sometimes in large game hunting. This variety is becoming extinct and is used in the crossbreeding of other hunting breeds; and
- The Small Gascon Saintongeois Hound, used mainly in hare hunting. This variety was developed in the early twentieth century when hunters in southwestern France selected the smallest dogs from Great Gascon Saintongeois litters.

Elegant. Strong. Well-built. White skin with black spots. Smooth, easy gait.

1

6

SCENT HOUNDS

COUNTRY OF RIGIN
France

ORIGINAL NAME
Gascon-Saintongeois

OTHER NAME
Virelade Hound

Between 10 and 45 kg (20-100 lb)

HEAD
Chiseled, long. Fairly narrow, domed skull. Slight stop. Bridge of nose large and slightly curved. Cleanly cut cheeks. Well-developed nose.

EYES
Oval, dark brown.

EARS
Set on below the eyes, long and thin, curled, pendulous.

BODY
Long. Neck of medium length and thickness, slightly arched, with slight dewlap. Deep, broad chest. Slightly rounded ribs. Loin

slightly arched. Fairly long flank. Very level back . Broad, fairly level croup.

LIMBS
Not very long, oval feet with tight toes and black nails. Strong, solidly boned legs.

TAIL
Well-set on and very slender at the tip. Carried in saber fashion.

COAT
Short and dense.

COLOR
White background with black spots, sometimes flecked. Two black spots usually appear on either side of

the head, covering the ears and eyes and ending at the cheeks. Cheeks are tan, preferably pale in color. Two tan markings above the eyebrows form pips. Tan markings on the inside surface of the ears. Tan speckling on the legs. Sometimes, a dead foliage "deer marking" appears on the lower thigh.

SIZE
Great Gascony Saintongeois: dog: 65 to 72 cm; bitch: 62 to 68 cm (25.5-28 in). Small Gascony Saintongeois: dog: 52 to 60 cm (24.5-27 in); bitch: 50 to 56 cm (20-22 in).

WEIGHT
Great Gascony Saintongeois: approx. 35 kg (77 lb). Small Gascony Saintongeois: approx. 25 kg (55 lb).

Character, special skills and training
This pack hound par excellence is very fast and has a keen nose and resonant howl. He is considered the best hare tracker. Very versatile, he is also used for large game hunting. He needs a firm owner.

Care and functions
The Gascon Saintongeois Hound is best suited to kennel life. He needs space and exercise, as well as regular brushing.
· Hunting dog.

Nivernais Griffon

The Nivernais Griffon is one of the very old hound breeds used on wolves. His ancestors include the Chien Gris de Saint Louis, as well as Foxhounds and breeds from Auvergne, Vendée and Bresse. Today's Nivernais Griffon was developed in the Morvan and Nièvre regions of France. A club for this breed was founded in 1925. After a critical period, the Nivernais Griffon has made a comeback and careful selection is improving the breed's structure, speed and character.

Powerful. Well-built. Shaggy coat characteristic of griffons and similar to that of primitive scenthounds. Flexible, springy gait.

1

SCENT HOUNDS

6

COUNTRY OF ORIGIN
France

ORIGINAL NAME
Griffon Nivernais

Medium Breeds
between
10 and 25 kg
(20-55 lb)

HEAD
Bony, fairly long, lightly boned but not small. Skull nearly flat. Slight stop. Straight nosebridge. Brow bones accentuated by bushy eyebrows. Beard on the chin. Very prominent nose.

EYES
Preferably dark.

EARS
Supple, moderately wide and long, slightly curled toward the tip.

BODY
Long. Neck fairly lightly boned, well-knit, without dewlap. Brisket not broad. Chest let down to elbow. Slight tuck-up. Level loin. Long back.

LIMBS
Well-knit, muscular legs. Slightly elongated feet.

TAIL
Not very long, carried in saber fashion, more tufted in the middle.

COAT
Long, thick, bushy, fairly strong and hard. Neither woolly nor frizzy.

COLOR
Preferably wolf grey or bluish-grey, boar grey, faded black, or salt and pepper, with tan markings on the cheeks, above the eyes, on the inner and lower legs, or fawn with a mixture of black and white hairs, creating a dark cast.

SIZE
Dog: 55 to 60 cm (21.5-23.5 in).
Bitch: 53 to 58 cm (21-23 in).

WEIGHT
Approx. 25 kg (55 lb).

Character, special skills and training
This wolf tracker of yore is still a hardy, independent, enthusiastic hunter. Although the breed is now calmer and faster, it is still just as robust. The Nivernais Griffon's superb nose and remarkable voice also explain why he is so popular with hunters. He can be affectionate and a good companion, but he needs a firm owner.

Care and functions
The Nivernais Griffon is not a city dweller. He is happy only in the country, where he can get lots of exercise. He does not tolerate heat well and requires regular brushing and attention to the ears.
· Hunting dog.

Vendée Griffon

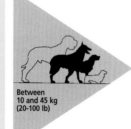

Between
10 and 45 kg
(20-100 lb)

The Vendée Griffon comes in four varieties or sub-breeds:
- The Great Vendée Griffon, initially the only variety. It is believed to be descended from the Chien Blanc du Roy (or Greffier), the Brittany Fawn Griffon, the Chien Gris de Saint Louis and the Bresse Griffon. Hunters used this variety to track wolf and wild boar. The Vendée Griffon club was founded in 1907. By 1946, the "breed" was virtually extinct. It was revived under the guidance of M. A. Dézamy, the club's president. A new standard was published in 1969. Crosses with the Billy and the Great Anglo-French Hound made the breed more lightweight, faster and more disciplined;
- The Medium Vendée Griffon, touted as "a well-balanced and improved version of the Great Vendée Griffon". This variety was developed in the early twentieth century by the Count of Elva. After World War II, it was crossed with the Grey Porcelaine Harrier;
- The Large Vendée Griffon Basset, descended from the Great Vendée Griffon. P. Dézamy was aiming for a typical basset with straight legs; and
- The Small Vendée Griffon Basset, more compact and angular, also the smallest and most popular variety. Bandy or half-bandy forelegs are tolerated. Together with the Beagle and the Brittany Fawn Basset Hound, this variety is the most commonly used small game pack hound.

– Great Vendée Griffon
Distinguished structure and gait. Well-proportioned. Robust without heaviness. Flexible gait.

– Medium Vendée Griffon
Distinguished in structure and gait. Short build. Well-proportioned. Flexible gait.

– Large Vendée Griffon Basset
Slightly elongated body. Fairly thick skin, often marbled in tricolor and white and black varieties. Easy gait.

– Small Vendée Griffon Basset
Fairly long back. Well-balanced. Elegant. Very relaxed, easy gait.

HEAD

Long, not too broad. Fairly short in the Medium Vendée Griffon. Fairly domed skull. Pronounced stop. Nose-bridge straight or slightly curved. Thick mustache. Shorter muzzle in the Small Vendée Griffon Basset.

EYES

Fairly large, dark.

EARS

Set on low. Supple, narrow, thin, covered with long hair. Turning considerably inward.

BODY

Strong. Long in the Large Vendée Griffon Basset, not as long in the Small Vendée Griffon Basset. Fairly long neck without dewlap. Chest deep and not very broad. Fairly rounded ribs. Solid loin. Great Vendée Griffon: well-muscled loin. Solid, straight back. Medium Vendée Griffon: Loin straight and muscular. Solid, short back. Large Vendée Griffon Basset: very muscular, broad croup. Long, broad, straight back.

Small Vendée Griffon Basset: well-muscled, fairly broad croup. Muscular, straight loin.

LIMBS

Great Vendée Griffon: muscular legs. Feet not too large, with tight toes and tough pads. Medium Vendée Griffon: muscular, well-boned legs. Feet not too large, with tough pads. Large Vendée Griffon Basset: straight legs. Large, tight, well-knit feet. Small Vendée Griffon Basset: solidly boned legs. Feet not too large, with tough pads.

TAIL

Set on high, fairly long, thick at the base, tufted, tapering toward the tip. Carried in saber fashion.

COAT

Not excessively long, harsh to the touch, neither silky nor woolly. Thick undercoat. Eyebrows well pronounced in the Great Vendée Griffon, sometimes bushy in the Medium Vendée Griffon. Moderate feathering in the Vendée Griffon Bassets.

COLOR

Solid-color: a shade of fawn, hare, whitish-grey. Bicolor: white and orange, white and black, white and grey, white and tan. Tricolor: white, black and tan. Whitish hare. White, grey and tan.

SIZE

Great Vendée Griffon: 60 to 65 cm (23.5-25.5 in). Medium Vendée Griffon: 48 to 55 cm (19-22 in). Large Vendée Griffon Basset: 38 to 42 cm (15-16.5 in). Small Vendée Griffon Basset: 34 to 38 cm (13.5-15 in).

WEIGHT

Great Vendée Griffon: approx. 35 kg (77 lb). Medium Vendée Griffon: approx. 29 kg (64 lb). Large Vendée Griffon Basset: approx. 18 kg (39.7 lb). Small Vendée Griffon Basset: approx. 15 kg (33 lb).

Character, special skills and training

The Vendée Griffon is known for his solidity, hardiness, vigor and stubbornness. He is often independent and strong-willed, rather than obedient.

With his good voice and keen nose, the Great Vendée Griffon is a pack hound once used on wolf. He is not afraid of rough terrain and water. In large game hunting, faster and more obedient pack hounds are preferred. In shooting, he competes with the Medium Vendée Griffon. The Great Vendée Griffon hunts deer and especially wild boar.

The Medium Vendée Griffon hunts nearly all game except rabbit. He is used especially on deer and wild boar.

The Large Vendée Griffon Basset, the fastest of all the bassets, is determined, can maintain a quick pace and penetrates even the thorniest thickets. This variety was developed for hare hunting and shooting.

The Small Vendée Griffon Basset is energetic, bold and very lively. He is remarkable at launching the hunt. Hunting individually or in pairs, he is the ideal rabbit dog. He is widely used on pheasant.

Calm, affectionate and friendly, Vendée Griffons make good companions. Most Small Vendée Griffon Bassets are companion dogs. They need firm training.

Care and functions

Vendée Griffons are not city dwellers. They are better suited to country life, because they need space and lots of exercise. They require regular brushing and attention to the ears.

· Hunting dog.

Harrier

The Harrier is an ancient breed born in southern England and developed for hunting hare. He is a close cousin of other old English scenthounds, including the Talbot Hound (white, close-lying coat) and the Old Southern Hound (white with blue spots), himself descended from a strain of Gascon Saintongeois. He is also believed to have a splash of Foxhound blood and contributed to improving the Small Game Anglo-French Hound.

1
SCENT HOUNDS

6

COUNTRY OF ORIGIN
Great Britain

OTHER NAME
Harehound

Solid and lightweight. Less powerful than the Foxhound. Skin white with black spots. Gait flexible and confident.

Large Breeds between 25 and 45 kg (55-100 lb)

Character, special skills and training
The Harrier is lively, quick and keen-nosed, with great endurance and a very resonant voice. This little pack hound works well with other dogs and is easy to lead. He is ideal on hare and, in England, also runs fox. He is also used in shooting deer and wild boar. He needs firm training.

Care and functions
He needs space and exercise, as well as regular brushing.
· Hunting dog.

HEAD
Moderately wide, fairly long. Flat skull. Slight stop. Fairly long, pointed muzzle. Flews covering the lower jaw.

EYES
Medium-sized, oval, always dark.

EARS
Set on high, V-shaped, nearly flat, fairly short.

BODY
Powerful. Long, open neck. Chest taller than it is wide. Ribs not very rounded. Flank neither too full nor tucked up. Straight, muscular back. Strong, slightly arched loin.

LIMBS
Muscular legs. Feet neither too tight nor too round.

TAIL
Medium in length, slightly tufted and carried proudly.

COAT
Not too short and flat.

COLOR
Usually white with black to orange shading. In France, generally tricolor with a black mantle covering the upper back.

SIZE
48 to 55 cm (19-22 in).

WEIGHT
Approx. 25 kg (55 lb).

Poitevin Hound

The Poitevin Hound was developed as the "Haut-Poitou Hound" in 1692 by Marquis F. de Larye. The breed's most notable ancestors are the Chien Céris and the Montembœuf, descendants of the famous Chien Blanc du Roy and of Irish scenthounds and English greyhounds. Crosses were made with the Foxhound and the Saintongeois. Known as an excellent wolf hunter in the nineteenth century, he is now prized for his skill on hare and deer. In 1957, the breed's name was changed to the "Poitevin Hound" Stet of the French Pack Hound Club in 1977, this breed has steadily gained popularity.

Sighthound with the Head of a scenthound. Strength. Power. Dignity. Slenderness. Easy, spirited gallop.

Large Breeds between 25 and 45 kg (55-100 lb)

1

6

SCENT HOUNDS

COUNTRY OF ORIGIN
France

ORIGINAL NAME
Haut-Poitou Hound

HEAD
Long and slender, bony, not very broad. Fairly flat skull, sloping slightly downward into curved, moderately long nosebridge. Slightly tapering muzzle. Large, broad, prominent nose.

EYES
Large, brown, edged with black.

EARS
Set on fairly low, slender and medium in width and length, loosely folded.

BODY
Long. Neck long and thin, without dewlap. Very deep chest, taller than it is wide. Long ribs. Slight tuck-up. Muscular loin. Well-muscled back.

LIMBS
Well-muscled, well-knit, strong legs. Fairly long, very tough wolf feet.

TAIL
Medium in length, slender, without tuft. Carried gracefully in a loose curve.

COAT
Short and glossy.

COLOR
Tricolor, with a black mantle or large spots, sometimes white and orange. Wolf grey coloring common.

SIZE
Dog: 62 to 72 cm (24.5-28.3 in).
Bitch: 60 to 70 cm (23.5-27.5 in).

WEIGHT
Approx. 35 kg (77 lb).

Character, special skills and training
This very active, hardy, speedy, spirited dog can pursue quarry all day long. He is not afraid of thickets and brambles. With his keen nose, powerful voice and great skill as a pack hound, he excels on deer. Like all pack hounds, he is not well-suited to family life. He must be trained not to abandon the trail of one animal to pursue another.

Care and functions
He is not a city dweller and does not like to be left alone. A natural pack hound, he is well-suited to kennel life. He needs daily exercise and requires regular brushing and attention to the ears.
· Hunting dog.

245

Porcelaine

The Porcelaine, one of the oldest French hunting breeds, is believed to be the descendent of the Chien Blanc du Roy or a white variety of the Saint Hubert (the Saint Hubert Blanc de Lorraine). Porcelaines were kept at the monasteries in Cluny and Luxeuil and by the Choiseul family in eastern France. Crosses were made with the Somerset Grey Harrier, the Gascon Saintongeois and the Billy. The Porcelaine's bright white, glossy coat earned him his name. The Porcelaine Club, founded in 1971, helped revive this elegant breed.

Elegant. Dignified. Thin, supple skin marbled with many black spots. Merry, lively gait. Light gallop.

1

SCENT HOUNDS

6

COUNTRY OF ORIGIN
France

OTHER NAMES
Lunéville Hound
Franche-Comté Hound

Large Breeds
between
25 and 45 kg
(55-100 lb)

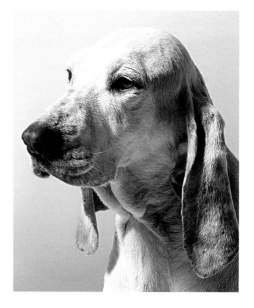

Character, special skills and training
Hardy and robust, the Porcelaine is quick, impulsive and enthusiastic. With his keen nose and resonant voice, he is a hard-driving hunter who works well in a pack. He specializes in small game and is remarkable on hare, but also excels on deer and wild boar. Serene and gentle, he is a pleasant companion. He needs a firm owner.

Care and functions
Nothing should keep the Porcelaine from living with his owner. A kennel is recommended for more than one dog in the country. He needs regular brushing and attention to the ears.
· Hunting dog.
· Companion dog.

HEAD
Cleanly cut, finely chiseled, fairly long. Broad skull with rounded occipital peak. Flat forehead with pronounced median furrow and stop. Nosebridge straight at the base and slightly curved at the tip. Well-developed, dark black nose.

EYES
Dark.

EARS
Long, thin, well-curled, pointed at the tip. Must be set on below eye level.

BODY
Long. Neck fairly long and lightly boned. Chest moderately wide, well let-down.

Flank raised but full. Hips sloping slightly. Broad, very muscular loin. Broad, straight back.

LIMBS
Feet with long, thin, tight toes and tough pads. Long, well-knit, lightly boned legs.

TAIL
Fairly thick at the base, tapering toward the tip, medium in length, never tufted, carried curved slightly inward.

COAT
Lying close to the body, fine, dense and glossy.

COLOR
Bright white with round

orange spots never forming a mantle. These spots normally cover black spots on the skin. Orange flecks on the ears are very characteristic of the breed.

SIZE
Dog: 55 to 58 cm (21.5-23 in).
Bitch: 53 to 56 cm (21-22 in).

WEIGHT
Approx. 28 kg (61.5 lb).

Alpine Basset Hound

Similar to the Dachshund, the Alpine Basset Hound is an intermediate form between the pure basset and the long-legged pointer. In fact, in 1896 the breed was named the Basset Pointer. It was officially recognized in 1975.

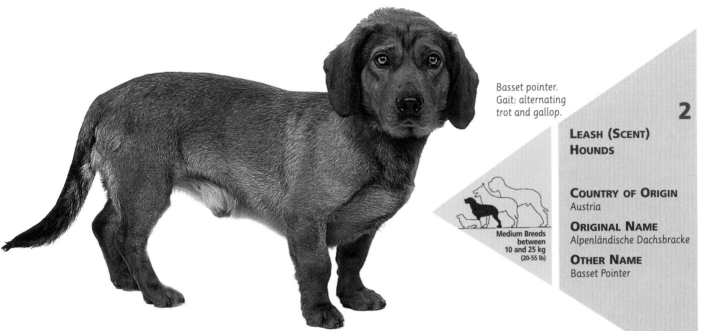

Basset pointer.
Gait: alternating trot and gallop.

Medium Breeds between 10 and 25 kg (20-55 lb)

2

LEASH (SCENT) HOUNDS

COUNTRY OF ORIGIN
Austria

ORIGINAL NAME
Alpenländische Dachsbracke

OTHER NAME
Basset Pointer

6

HEAD
Long. Slightly domed skull. Slight stop. Straight nose-bridge. Muzzle fairly broad. Thin, well joined flews.

EYES
Medium in size, round, dark or light brown.

EARS
Medium in length, wide, rounded, hanging straight against head.

BODY
Long. Muscular neck without dewlap. Pronounced withers. Well-curved chest. Full loin. Pronounced tuck-up. Round, sloping croup. Straight, firm, long back.

LIMBS
Short, sturdy, muscular, well-boned legs. Forefeet stockier than hind feet.

TAIL
Medium in length, thick at the base, usually hanging or raised in a loose curve. Hair forms a brush.

COAT
Short, very thick, lying flat against the body, hard. Sparse undercoat. Long and harsh on the back, abdomen and backs of the thighs.

COLOR
Black and red: dark black with rust markings. Brown: brown with lighter markings, brown nose. Red: reddish-fawn, rust, reddish-yellow with lighter markings. White: spotted with several colors (West-phalian): all colors allowed for red combined with white. Markings below the eyes, on the muzzle, legs and chest.

SIZE
34 to 42 cm (13.4-16.5 in).

WEIGHT
Approx. 18 kg (39.7 lb).

Character, special skills and training
This hardy, obstinate, agile dog has great stamina, a fighting spirit, a good voice and a very keen sense of smell. He does not hunt in packs. He is used in hunting hare, fox and wild boar, retrieving feathered game (wild goose, etc.) and tracking wounded game. He makes a very affectionate pet. He needs firm training.

Care and functions
He needs space and exercise and requires regular brushing.
· Hunting dog.

247

Bavarian Mountain Hound

All bloodhounds are descended from primitive hunting dogs (brachet scenthounds). Hunters chose the most loyal dogs of the pack and used them to track game wounded in the hunt. From these dogs, breeders developed bloodhounds (Schweisshunde) used uniquely for trailing wounded game. Crosses were also made with local mountain hound breeds (the Ticoler Bracken, the Brandlbracken and the Dachsbracken). In 1912, the Bavarian Bloodhound Club was founded. The breed is rare.

Well-balanced. Long and lightweight. Tight-fitting skin. Gait: long strides.

2
LEASH (SCENT) HOUNDS

6

COUNTRY OF ORIGIN
Germany

ORIGINAL NAME
Bayerischer Gebirgsschweisshund

Medium Breeds between 10 and 25 kg (20-55 lb)

Solid jaws. Lips fully covering mouth. Black or dark red nose. Wide nostrils.

EYES
Neither too large nor too round. Dark brown or somewhat lighter. Pigmented eyelids.

EARS
Set on high, medium in length, wide at the base, rounded at the tips, heavy, hanging flat against the head.

HEAD
Strong and elongated. Relatively broad, slightly domed skull. Pronounced stop. Slightly curved nosebridge. Sufficiently broad muzzle.

BODY
Slightly longer than it is tall. Slightly raised at the rump. Neck medium in length, strong, with a slight dewlap. Topline sloping slightly upward from withers to hindquarters. Chest well-developed, long, moderately wide and well let-down. Slight tuck-up. Long, fairly straight croup. Solid back.

LIMBS
Fairly short, well-muscled, solidly boned legs. Spoon-shaped feet with well-arched, tight toes and tough, pigmented pads.

TAIL
Set on high, medium in length, hanging to the hock. Carried level to the ground or hanging down.

COAT
Short, dense, lying very flat against the body, moderately harsh. Finer on the head and ears, harsher and longer on the abdomen, legs and tail.

COLOR
Fawn, red, reddish-fawn, dark fawn (reddish-brown), light fawn (pale yellow) to sable fawn; fawn grey like a deer's winter coat, also brindled or ticked with black. The background color on the back is usually more intense. Dark muzzle and ears. Tail generally ticked with black. Small, light-colored markings on the chest (flashings) are allowed.

SIZE
Dog: 47 to 52 cm (18.5-20.5 in).
Bitch: 44 to 48 cm (17-19 in).

WEIGHT
20 to 25 kg (44-55 lb).

Character, special skills and training
Courageous, spirited, fast and agile, the Bavarian Mountain Hound is at ease on rugged terrain. With his superb nose and powerful hunting instinct, he was originally used on chamois but can hunt all other game. Calm, even-tempered, docile and attached to his owner, he is a good companion. As with any bloodhound, he needs a patient, experienced trainer.

Care and functions
The Bavarian Mountain Hound is not suited to city life. He needs space and exercise. He also requires regular brushing.
· Hunting dog.

Hanoverian Hound

The Hanoverian Hound, descended from the large bloodhounds of the Middle Ages and consequently from the Saint Hubert Hound, was developed in the seventeenth century and improved in the nineteenth century through crosses with scenthounds including the Heidebracke. Introduced to France in the 1980s, the Hanoverian Hound is very rare.

Well-muscled. Soldly boned. Energetic, flexible gait with long strides.

Large Breeds between 25 and 45 kg (55-100 lb)

2

LEASH (SCENT) HOUNDS

COUNTRY OF ORIGIN
Germany

ORIGINAL NAME
Hannoverischer Schweisshund

6

HEAD
Large, long. Broad, slightly domed skull. Prominent brow bones. Pronounced stop. Slightly curved nosebridge. Solid, broad muzzle. Powerful jaws. Wide nose.

EYES
Dark brown.

EARS
Set on high, medium in length, rounded at the tips, hanging very flat against the head, not curled.

BODY
Long. Long, sturdy neck. Chest deeper than it is broad. Loin slightly domed,

broad. Slight tuck-up. Powerful back. Broad, long croup sloping slightly toward the tail.

LIMBS
Solid, round, tight feet with well-arched toes. Well-muscled, fairly short legs.

TAIL
Set on high, long, thick at the base, tapering toward the tip, slightly curved.

COAT
Short, dense, hard to harsh on the trunk. Longer and harsher on the backs of the thighs and underside of the tail.

COLOR
Light to dark reddish-fawn, more or less strongly brindled. With or without mask. A small white spot on the chest is tolerated.

SIZE
Dog: 50 to 55 cm (20-21.5 in).
Bitch: 48 to 53 cm (19-21 in).

WEIGHT
30 to 35 kg (66-77 lb).

Character, special skills and training
Hardy, vigorous and powerful, the Hanoverian Hound has a keen nose. He is a remarkable tracker, hard-driving and very determined on the trail. He is often used on deer and wild boar. He works alone or in pairs. Obedient and affectionate, he makes a good companion. He needs firm, patient training.

Care and functions
He is not a city dweller. He needs space and lots of exercise. He also requires regular brushing and attention to the ears.
· Hunting dog.

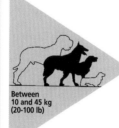

Dalmatian

The Dalmatian is believed to have originated in the Mediterranean region. He was named after Dalmatia either because it was his birthplace or because he was used in this region during the Balkan war. The Dalmatian is thought to be descended from the now extinct Bengal Pointer crossed with the Bull Terrier and the English Pointer. In the seventeenth century, the Dalmatian was popular at the Vatican. In eighteenth-century England, he was kept by the aristocracy to escort horse-drawn carriages, thus earning the nickname "coach dog". In the United States, the Dalmatian was adopted by firefighters as their mascot. The Disney movie 101 Dalmatians (1961) helped popularize the breed.

Well-proportioned. Well-balanced. Very relaxed gait.

3

RELATED BREEDS

COUNTRY OF ORIGIN
Central Mediterranean Basin

6

Between 10 and 45 kg (20-100 lb)

Character, special skills and training
Tough and athletic, the Dalmatian has great stamina and was first used as a draft dog and an escort for horse-drawn carriages. Calm, docile, affectionate and very gentle with children, the Dalmatian is a wonderful pet. He rarely barks, is not aggressive and is somewhat distant toward strangers, making him a good watchdog. He needs firm and early training.

Care and functions
He can live in an apartment as long as he gets enough exercise. He needs regular brushing. Puppies are born all white; spots appear gradually and are not fully developed until the dog is one year old.
. Companion dog.
. Seeing-eye dog.
. Watchdog.

HEAD
Long. Flat skull. Well-pronounced stop. Muzzle long and powerful, not tapering. Powerful jaws. Tight-lipped.

EYES
Medium-sized, well-spaced, round. Dark in the variety with medium-brown spots, ranging to amber in the variety with liver spots.

EARS
Set on high, medium-sized, carried against the head. Rounded tips. Thin, smooth, covered with coin-sized spots.

BODY
Square build. Neck moderately long, well-arched, with-out dewlap. High, wide chest. Well-sprung ribs. Well-defined withers. Powerful, straight back. Well-muscled, slightly clean-flanked loin.

LIMBS
Muscular, solidly boned legs. Round, firm feet with tough pads.

TAIL
Thick at the base, tapering gradually to the tip. Carried curved loosely upward but never curled.

COAT
Short, hard, dense, smooth.

COLOR
Pure white ground. Black variety has dark black coin-sized spots; brown variety has liver brown coin-sized spots. Spots should not blend together but instead be round, well-defined, well-distributed and 2 to 3 cm (0,8-1,2 in) diameter. Spots on the head, tail and extremities should be smaller.

SIZE
Dog: 56 to 61 cm (22-24 in).
Bitch: 54 to 59 cm (21-23 in).

WEIGHT
Dog: approx. 27 kg (59.5 lb).
Bitch: approx. 24 kg (53 lb).

Rhodesian Ridgeback

This South African dog was named for the ridge of hairs on his back. He is thought to be descended from a dog once used by the Hottentots and crossed with dogs imported by the first colonists from Europe in the seventeenth century, particularly mastiffs and the Bloodhound. The Rhodesian Ridgeback was developed by the Boers and the standard for the breed was set in 1922 in the former Rhodesia. He is highly prized in the United States and Canada, where he hunts bear.

Well-balanced. Strong. Muscular. Relaxed, energetic gait.

Large Breeds between 25 and 45 kg (55-100 lb)

3

6

RELATED BREEDS

COUNTRY OF ORIGIN
South Africa

OTHER NAMES
Lion Dog
African Lion Hound

HEAD
Of good length. Flat, fairly broad skull. Pronounced stop. Long, powerful muzzle. Strong jaws. Well-joined lips. Nose black or brown, depending on coat color.

EYES
Round, matching coat color.

EARS
Set on fairly high, medium in size with rounded tips, carried close to the head.

BODY
Powerful. Strong neck without dewlap. Chest not too broad, well let-down and ample. Moderately well-sprung ribs. Strong, muscular loin. Crest on the back, running from behind the shoulders to the hips, formed by hair growing in the opposite direction from the rest of the coat. Powerful back.

LIMBS
Solid, well-boned legs. Compact feet with well-arched toes.

TAIL
Thick at the base, tapering toward the tip. Carried in a loose upward curve.

COAT
Short, dense, smooth, neither woolly nor silky.

COLOR
Pale wheaten to reddish-fawn. Head, trunk, legs and tail must be the same color. Minimal white markings on the chest and toes is allowed.

SIZE
Dog: 63.5 to 68.5 cm (25-27 in).
Bitch: 61 to 66 cm (24-26 in).

WEIGHT
Approx. 35 kg (77 lb).

Character, special skills and training
Hardy, solid, very fast and courageous, this dog with great endurance and a keen nose hunts wild beasts (such as lion). Working in a pack, he can bring down large cats. Not friendly toward strangers, he makes a reliable dissuasive watchdog. He is aggressive toward other dogs. He is calm, barks rarely and can be an affectionate pet. He needs rigorous training.

Care and functions
He is not suited to city life. He needs lots of exercise. He is resistant to heat and cold and can tolerate a lack of water or food. He should be brushed twice a week.
· Hunting dog.
· Watchdog, police dog.
· Companion dog.

Group 7

French Spaniel

Old Danish Pointing Dog

The Old Danish Pointing Dog is a product of Italian or Spanish pointers imported around the seventeenth century and crossed with several Danish hunting dogs. The breed's standard was recognized in 1962 by the Danish Kennel Club. He is very popular in his native country.

Solid. Elegant. Flexible, springy gait.
More of a trotter than a galloper.

1

CONTINENTAL POINTING DOGS

7

COUNTRY OF ORIGIN
Denmark

ORIGINAL NAME
Gammel Dansk Honsehund

OTHER NAMES
Gammel Dansk
Danish Pointer

Medium Breeds
between
10 and 25 kg
(20-55 lb)

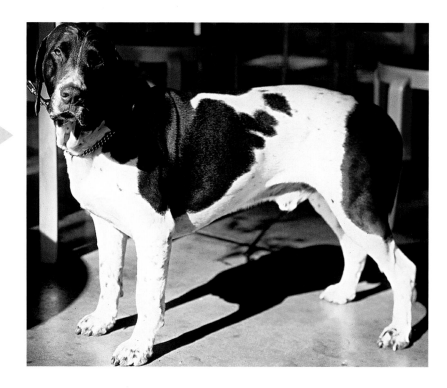

Character, special skills and training
Very hardy, vigorous, courageous and tenacious, this multi-purpose hunting dog can work on all types of terrain. He makes a gentle and affectionate pet.

Care and functions
He needs space and exercise, as well as regular brushing and checking of the ears.
· Hunting dog.
· Companion dog.

HEAD
Fairly short. Broad muzzle. Liver-colored nose. Flews slightly pendulous.

EYES
Light or dark hazel.

EARS
Long, rounded at the tips, pendulous.

BODY
Long. Muscular neck with traces of a dewlap. Deep, broad chest. Strong loin.

LIMBS
Solid legs. Round feet with tight toes and tough pads.

TAIL
Medium in length. Thick at the base, tapering toward the tip, hanging down.

COAT
Short, dense, thick.

COLOR
White with dark to light brownish-liver spots.

SIZE
Dog: 52 to 58 cm
(20.5-22.8 in).
Bitch: 48 to 54 cm
(19-21.5 in).

WEIGHT
18 to 24 kg (39.5-53 lb).

Bohemian Wirehaired Pointing Griffon

For centuries, a wirehaired dog once used by nobility for hunting lived in Bohemia. The first standard was written in 1887, but later the breed nearly went extinct. After World War II, it was revived through crosses with German pointers, including the Stichelhaar. A Cesky Fousek club was founded in 1924. Very popular in Czechoslovakia, the Bohemian Wirehaired Pointing Griffon ranks second among today's hunting dogs.

Bohemian Wirehaired Pointing Griffon. Well-balanced, dignified appearance noble. Very smooth gait.

Between 10 and 45 kg (20-100 lb)

1

7

CONTINENTAL GRIFFON TYPE POINTING DOGS

COUNTRY OF ORIGIN
Czechoslovakia

ORIGINAL NAME
Cesky Fousek

OTHER NAMES
Czech Coarsehaired Pointer
Slovakian Wirehaired Pointer

HEAD
Chiseled, fairly narrow, and long. Domed skull. Pronounced brow bones. Moderate stop. Nosebridge slightly curved, a bit longer than the skull. Muzzle tapering toward the nose. Powerful jaws. Typical beard on the cheeks and flews. Wide, dark brown nose.

EYES
Almond-shaped, dark amber to chestnut-brown. Eyebrows standing at a slant.

EARS
Set on very high, tapering toward the tip. Lying very flat against the head.

BODY
Compact. Neck medium in length, well-muscled, cleanly cut. Well-developed brisket.

Oval chest. Well-sprung ribs. Short loin. Slight tuck-up. Short, stocky back sloping toward the croup. Fairly broad, slightly sloping croup.

LIMBS
Well-muscled, solidly boned legs. Compact feet with tight toes and nails ranging from dark grey to black.

TAIL
Medium-sized. Carried level to the ground or slightly raised. Docked by three-fifths its length.

COAT
Three types of hair. Fairly hard, heavy guard hairs 3 to 4 cm (1.6 in) long, lying very flat against the body. Long, hard, straight, bristles 5 to 7 cm (2-2.8 in) long,

absent from the chest, topline, groin, and shoulders. Soft, dense undercoat 1.5 cm (0.6 in) long, shed almost completely in summer. Hair shorter and harder on the fronts of the legs. Feathering on the backs of the legs. Short and hard on the top of the head. Short and soft on the ears.

COLOR
Colors allowed: dark roan with or without brown blotches, brown with ticking on the chest and lower legs, or solid brown with no markings.

SIZE
Dog: 60 to 66 cm (23.6-26 in).
Bitch: 58 to 62 cm (22.8-24.5 in).

WEIGHT
Dog: 28 to 34 kg (62-75 lb).
Bitch: 22 to 28 kg (48.5-61.8 lb).

Character, special skills, and training
Very tough and hardy, the Bohemian Wirehaired Pointing Griffon has great endurance and is a multi-purpose dog. He can hunt in the woods and in swampland, where his thick coat protects him from bitter cold. He commonly hunts at a gallop and is a firm pointer and reliable retriever. He excels at locating wounded game. He is very attached to his owner and needs firm training.

Care and functions
He needs wide open spaces and lots of exercise, as well as regular brushing and attention to the ears.
· Hunting dog.

German Pointing Dog

The German Pointing Dog is believed to be descended from the strain common to all pointers: the Chien d'Oysel, later called the Chien de Rêts, used for netting birds and for hawking. These pointers attained the courts of German royalty by way of France, Spain and Flanders. A splash of foreign blood was added through crosses with Spanish, English and Italian pointers. Today's model has existed since 1880. This breed is the most popular pointer in Germany and the most widely used pointer in the world.

Dignified. Well-balanced. Very well-bred. Elegant. Dignified demeanor. Skin without folds. Relaxed gait with long strides.

1

CONTINENTAL POINTING

7

COUNTRY OF ORIGIN
Germany

ORIGINAL NAMES
Deutscher Kurzhaariger
Vorstehhund

OTHER NAME
Stichelhaar

Large Breeds
between
25 and 45 kg
(55-100 lb)

Character, special skills and training
The German Pointing Dog is a vigorous, strong, fast distance galloper with great endurance, who is not afraid of the cold and can hunt on any terrain. He is a hunting dog par excellence, a pointer above all. He specializes in feathered quarry in the field or in the woods and can also be used to track wounded game. Bursting with energy but even-tempered and obedient, he is strong-willed and can be stubborn. He is attached to his owner and loves children, making him a good companion. He is a good watchdog but not aggressive. He needs firm training.

Care and functions
He can adapt to city life but needs space and exercise, including long daily outings. He also needs regular brushing and checking of the ears.
· Hunting dog.
· Companion dog.

HEAD
Cleanly cut, neither too lightweight nor too heavy. Fairly large, slightly domed skull. Moderately pronounced stop. Slightly convex nosebridge. Long, broad, thick and powerful muzzle. Nose brown or flesh colored in white-coated variety. Powerful jaws. Tight, well-pigmented lips.

EYES
Medium in size, dark brown.

EARS
Set on high, medium in length, rounded at the tip, pendulous but not twisted, flat against the sides of the head.

BODY
Slightly elongated. Muscular neck without dewlap. Pronounced withers. Chest taller than it is broad. Well-curved ribs. Short, broad, muscular loin. Broad, well-muscled, sufficiently long, slightly sloping croup. Firm, well-muscled back.

LIMBS
Muscular, solidly boned legs. Rounded feet with very tight toes and tough pads.

TAIL
Set on high, thick at the base, tapering gradually. Docked by about half for hunting. At rest, hanging down. In action, carried level to the ground.

COAT
Short (kurzhaar means "short hair"), dense, crisp, hard to the touch.

COLOR
Chestnut without markings. Chestnut with white spots or flecks on the chest and legs. Dark chestnut-roan with chestnut head and chestnut blotches or spots (very good camouflage for hunting). Light chestnut-roan with chestnut head and chestnut spots, with or without chestnut blotches. White with chestnut markings on the head and chestnut blotches or spots. Black with the same shades as for chestnut or roan. Tan markings are allowed. A white flare or blaze with spotted lips are allowed.

SIZE
Dog: 62 to 66 cm (24.5-26 in).
Bitch: 58 to 63 cm (23-25 in).

WEIGHT
25 to 32 kg (55-70.5 lb).

256

German Wirehaired Pointing Dog

In the late nineteenth century, German breeders desiring a multi-purpose pointer crossed the German Shorthaired Pointing Dog, the Poodle, the Pudelpointer, pointing griffons, and the Airedale Terrier. The Stichelhaar, a broken-coated old German pointer, might also have been used. The German Wirehaired Pointing Dog inherited amazing potential from his ancestors. He is named for his hard, bristly coat (drahthaarig means "wirehaired"). A breed club was founded in 1902 in Germany, and the Kennel Club recognized the breed in 1955. Very popular in Germany.

Mesomorph. Dignified. Chiseled appearance. Tight skin. Energetic, wide, easy, smooth gait.

1

CONTINENTAL POINTING DOGS

7

COUNTRY OF ORIGIN
Germany

ORIGINAL NAMES
Deutscher Drahthaariger Vorstehhund

OTHER NAMES
Drahthaar
German Wirehaired Pointer

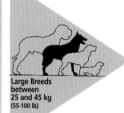

Large Breeds between 25 and 45 kg (55-100 lb)

Character, special skills, and training
This hardy, courageous, energetic, spirited dog with lightning speed and great endurance works on all types of game on all kinds of terrain and in all weather. With his highly acute nose, he tracks steadily and persistently and points precisely. He is both a pointer and a hunter of hare, fox, and wild boar. He is also a remarkable blood trailer of wounded large game. Very loyal, even-tempered, and gentle, he is a good pet. Given his strong will, possible stubbornness, and jealousy of other dogs, he needs firm but flexible training.

Care and Functions
He can live in the city, though not ideal, as long as he gets two long walks a day. He also requires brushing several times a week and attention to the ears.
. Hunting dog.
. Companion dog.

HEAD
Broad. Foreface has an energetic expression. Slightly domed skull. Moderate stop. Long, broad, powerful muzzle. No pendulous flews. Dark brown nose. Thick beard.

EYES
Oval, the darker the better. Bushy eyebrows.

EARS
Set on high, medium in width, not curled.

BODY
Square build. Neck medium in length, curved. Withers high, well-muscled. Broad, well let-down chest. Well-sprung ribs.

Short, straight back. Muscular loin. Broad hips. Long, broad, gently sloping croup. Slight tuck-up. Short flanks.

LIMBS
Vigorous, well-knit legs. Round feet with tight toes and thick, firm pads

TAIL
Not too thick. Docked for hunting. Carried as straight and level with the ground as possible.

COAT
Hard, wirehaired, lying flat, dense. Good protection from bad weather and injury; 2 to 4 cm (0.8-1.6 in) in length. Shorter below the chest and

abdomen and on the head and ears. Dense undercoat.

COLOR
Dark to medium brown (brown mixed with white or light brown, and grizzled. Mixed with black and white hairs, with or without patches of color).

SIZE
Dog: 60 to 67 cm (23.5-26.5 in).
Bitch: 56 to 62 cm (22-24.5 in).

WEIGHT
27 to 32 kg (60-70.5 lb).

Ariège Pointer

The Ariège Pointer is the result of nineteenth-century crosses of the old French Pointing Dog with white- and orange-coated pointers from southern France and perhaps the Saint Germain Pointer for added lightness and vigor. Hunters and breeders in Ariège, France, are dedicated to the survival of the breed.

Mesomorph. Braccoid type. Elegant. Dignified. Powerfully built but not heavy. Gait: steady trot alternating with gallop.

Large Breeds between 25 and 45 kg (55-100 lb)

1

7

CONTINENTAL POINTING DOGS

COUNTRY OF ORIGIN
France

ORIGINAL NAME
Braque de l'Ariège

OTHER NAMES
Braque de Toulouse
Braque du Midi

HEAD
Long, angular, narrow. Slightly domed skull. Fairly pronounced occipital peak. Slight stop. Long, straight, sometimes slightly convex nosebridge. Fairly thin lips. Pink, reddish (flesh-colored), or chestnut lips, depending on coat color.

EYES
Slightly oval, dark amber or brown.

EARS
Long, thin, curled, not flat against the head.

BODY
Svelte. Neck not very long, fairly strong, slight dewlap. Pronounced withers. Chest broad, high, well let-down. Rounded ribs. Slight tuck-up. Slightly sloping croup. Back straight and somewhat long.

LIMBS
Cleanly cut, muscular, solidly boned legs. Compact, nearly round feet with tight toes.

TAIL
Thick at the base, tapering toward the tip. Docked by about half. Should not be raised higher than the topline.

COAT
Short, dense, glossy. Finer and lying closer to the body on the head and ears.

COLOR
Light orangish fawn or sometimes chestnut with predominant white patching (speckles or flecks). Some dogs are even white with speckles or flecks.

SIZE
Dog: 60 to 67 cm (23.5-26.5 in).
Bitch: 56 to 65 cm (22-25.5 in).

WEIGHT
25 to 30 kg (55-66 lb).

Character, special skills and training
This hardy, very energetic dog with an excellent sense of smell is a skilled retriever suited to all kinds of hunting. He is used particularly on partridge and quail. Quick and independent, he needs firm training.

Care and functions
He needs space and exercise, as well as regular brushing.
· Hunting dog.

Auvergne Pointing Dog

The Auvergne Pointing Dog is thought to be descended from dogs imported to Auvergne, France, in the late eighteenth century by the Knights Templars or the Knights of Malta. Some believe it is more likely that the breed came from the old strain of the French Pointing Dog. Auvergne Pointing Dogs were first bred in Cantal, France. A splash of English Pointer blood was added, and the first standard was written in 1913. The population of Auvergne Pointing Dogs remains small but stable.

Powerful. Somewhat light in build. Elegant. Fairly loose skin speckled black and white.

1

CONTINENTAL POINTING DOGS

7

COUNTRY OF ORIGIN
France

ORIGINAL NAME
Braque d'Auvergne

OTHER NAME
Bleu d'Auvergne

Medium Breeds between 10 and 25 kg (20-55 lb)

Character, special skills, and training

Known for his incredible hardiness, energy, and speed, this active dog can adapt to almost any environment. He has an excellent nose and is a good pointer and retriever. Prized for woodcock hunting, he also specializes in partridge. He is kind and easygoing, although a bit stubborn, and makes a gentle, affectionate companion. He needs firm but gentle training.

Care and functions

He can adapt to city life as long as he gets a daily walk. He needs regular brushing and checking of the ears.
· Hunting dog.
· Companion dog.

HEAD
Long. Broad, slightly domed skull. Stop not very pronounced. Fairly long, straight nosebridge. Fairly large lips.

EYES
Medium in size, dark hazel. Black eyelids.

EARS
Set on low, fairly long and curled, framing the head well.

BODY
Well-built, can be inscribed inside a square. Neck fairly long and strong, slightly arched with a slight dewlap. Chest well let-down. Rounded ribs. Short, slightly arched, and well-muscled loin. Short, straight back. Broad, bony croup, minimally sloping.

LIMBS
Feet fairly short and compact, with tight toes and tough pads. Muscular, solidly boned legs.

TAIL
Of medium thickness, carried level to the ground. Docked by about two-thirds.

COAT
Short, not too fine, never hard, glossy.

COLOR
- Light: white with black blotches and a fair amount of spots.
- Dark: called "smoky", produced by a mixture of white and black, with the more abundant black giving a smoky grey cast to the coat. The color to seek is white with bluish-black blotches, fairly numerous black spots. The head should have regular black markings such that both eyes are surrounded by black. White or blue flare.

SIZE
Dog: 57 to 63 cm (22.5-25 in).
Bitch: 55 to 60 cm (21.5-23.5 in).

WEIGHT
22 to 25 kg (48.5-55 lb).

Bourbonnais Pointing Dog

The Bourbonnais Pointing Dog was already known in the sixteenth century as a skilled quail hunter. He was described as hardy, born with a short tail and sporting a white coat speckled with fawn or covered or dotted with pale chestnut spots. The breed was fairly popular in the early twentieth century, but the two World Wars nearly spelled its end. A breed club was founded in 1925. Currently, breeders are working toward the survival of the breed.

Mesomorph. Braccoide type. Smaller and more compact than other pointers. Exudes hardiness and strength. A certain elegance. Gait: medium-sized strides. Steady, flexible gallop.

CONTINENTAL POINTING DOGS

1

7

COUNTRY OF ORIGIN
France

ORIGINAL NAME
Braque du Bourbonnais

Medium Breeds between 10 and 25 kg (20-55 lb)

HEAD
Solid. Rounded skull. Slightly pronounced stop. Straight or slightly curved nosebridge. Strong, cone-shaped muzzle. Solid jaws. Nose the same color as the coat.

EYES
Large, hazel or dark amber, depending on coat color.

EARS
Hanging along cheeks, minimally curled, reaching slightly past the throat when outstretched.

BODY
Can be inscribed inside a square. Very open, muscular neck, slight dewlap tolerated. Pronounced withers. Broad, long, tall chest. Well-

curved ribs. Loin short and broad. Flank flat, slight tuck-up. Back short, fairly level. Rounded, moderately sloping croup.

LIMBS
Very muscular, well-boned legs. Feet with tight toes, hard pads.

TAIL
Set on fairly low, naturally short. Tail should be either absent or short (no longer than 15 cm) (6 in).

COAT
Short, fine, dense. Somewhat thicker and sometimes longer on the back.

COLOR
- Chestnut with patching,

heavily to moderately spotted, hairs relatively mixed. As a whole, the coat may have a pale lilac cast.
- Fawn with patching, heavily to moderately speckled, hairs closely mixed. As a whole, the coat may have a pale peach cast. Colored markings on the head, whether symmetrical or not, are allowed only if they are unobtrusive and if both eyes are not in the same spot.

SIZE
Dog: 51 to 57 cm (20-22.5 in).
Bitch: 48 to 55 cm (19-22 in).

WEIGHT
Dog: 18 to 25 kg (40-55 lb).
Bitch: 16 to 22 kg (35-48.5 lb).

Character, special skills and training
Hardy, not very fast and with a keen nose, the Bourbonnais Pointing Dog adapts easily to any terrain and to a wide variety of quarry. An excellent tracker, he points precisely and is known as a specialist in partridge and woodcock. Gentle and affectionate, he is a wonderful companion. He needs firm but gentle training.

Care and functions
He needs space and exercise. If he lives in the city, he needs several daily outings. He requires regular brushing and checking of the ears.
· Hunting dog.
· Companion dog.

Burgos Pointing Dog

Descended from the old Spanish Pointing Dog, the Burgos Pointing Dog is an old breed that has remained very pure. He was once very popular among the Spanish pointers but is now becoming extinct.

Mesomorph. Exudes strength. Thick pink skin. Gait: fluid, powerful trot.

1

CONTINENTAL POINTING DOGS

7

COUNTRY OF ORIGIN
Spain

ORIGINAL NAME
Perdiguero de Burgos

Large Breeds between 25 and 45 kg (55-100 lb)

Character, special skills and training
Hardy and adapted to all types of terrain, with a superb nose, the Burgos Pointing Dog points and retrieves like a charm. He is equally skilled on quarry with feathers and fur. He needs firm training.

Care and functions
He needs space and exercise, as well as regular brushing.
· Hunting dog.

HEAD
Large, broad. Wide skull. Arched forehead. Prominent brow bones. Slight stop. Muzzle almost square. Thick lips, not too pendulous.

EYES
Almond-shaped, fawn or dark in color.

EARS
Set on high, large, long, folding from base to pointed tip, very supple.

BODY
Compact, strong. Round, strong neck with slight folds on the jabot. Slightly pronounced withers. Broad chest. Well-rounded ribs. Moderate tuck-up. Powerful, muscular back. Well-rounded, low, broad croup.

LIMBS
Long, solid, well-muscled legs. Short, round feet with arched toes.

TAIL
Thick at the base, tapering toward the tip, docked to one-third its length, carried gaily.

COAT
Short, dense, smooth.

COLOR
Predominately white with liver spots or flecks or a shade of liver with white flecks.

SIZE
Dog: 65 to 75 cm (25.6-29.5 in).
Bitch: slightly smaller.

WEIGHT
Approx. 30 kg (66 lb).

French Pointing Dog

Descended from the continental pointer of the Middle Ages, the Italian Cane da Rete, or the Spanish Pointing Dog, the French Pointing Dog was known in France by the seventeenth century and later called the Charles X Pointer. He is believed to be the ancestor of many continental pointers. The breed is divided into two types of different sizes:
- The Gascony type, solidly built and calm. This type is losing popularity.
- The Pyrenees type, smaller and lighter but very muscular. This type is very popular.

Gascony type: mesomorph. Braccoid. Dignified appearance. Powerful but not heavy. Fairly loose skin.
Pyrenees type: mesomorph. Braccoid. Hardy but not heavy. Tight skin.

Between 10 and 45 kg (20-100 lb)

CONTINENTAL POINTING DOGS

COUNTRY OF ORIGIN
France

ORIGINAL NAME
Braque Français

OTHER NAME
Charles X Pointer

1

7

HEAD
Fairly large, not too heavy. Skull nearly flat. Slight stop. Wide nosebridge, sometimes slightly convex. Flews well let-down except in the Pyrenees type.

EYES
Brown or dark yellow.

EARS
Medium in length, very loosely folded, framing the head well. Rounded tips touch the base of the nose when outstretched.

BODY
Strong. Fairly long neck, slightly arched with slight or no dewlap. Broad, long chest. Rounded ribs. Short,

muscular, slightly clean-flanked loin. Flat flanks. Slight tuck-up. Broad, straight, very level back. Slightly sloping croup.

LIMBS
Muscular legs. Round, compact feet with tight toes.

TAIL
Long or docked. In the Pyrenees type, short at birth or docked.

COAT
Short. Fairly thick and dense. Finer on the head and ears. Finer and shorter in the Pyrenees type.

COLOR
Chestnut. Chestnut and

white, either with abundant spotting or with chestnut marked with fawn (above the eyes, on the flews and legs).

SIZE
– Gascony type:
Dog: 58 to 69 cm (23-27 in); Bitch: 56 to 68 cm (22-27 in).
Pyrenees type:
Dog: 47 to 58 cm (18.5-22.8 in); Bitch: 47 to 56 cm (18.5-22 in).

WEIGHT:
– Gascony type: 25 to 32 kg (55-70.5 lb).
– Pyrenees type: 17 to 25 kg (37.5-55 lb).

Character, special skills and training
Very hardy and resistant to heat, this dog with an excellent sense of smell is as comfortable in the swamps as he is in the woods and fields. The Gascony type trots on the hunt, methodically exploring the terrain. The faster Pyrenees type has a wider search range. He confidently points quarry with fur and feathers. Even-tempered, gentle, sensitive and very attached to his owner, he makes a pleasant companion. He needs firm but fair training.

Care and functions
He can adapt to the city but needs daily exercise. He also requires regular brushing and attention to the ears.
· Hunting dog.
· Companion dog.

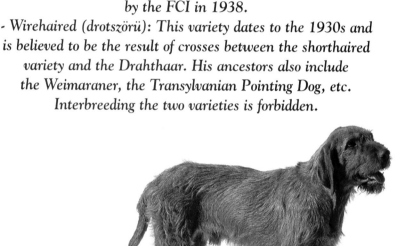

Hungarian Pointing Dog

The Hungarian Pointing Dog comes in two varieties:
- Shorthaired (rövidszörü): This is the older variety. Its ancestors include the Hungarian Pointing Dog, the Turkish Yellow Dog and the Sloughi. The first specimens with the current comformation appeared by the early eighteenth century. The variety received blood from other hunting dogs, including the German Pointing Dog. The Shorthaired Hungarian Pointing Dog is the more popular variety in France and was recognized by the FCI in 1938.
- Wirehaired (drotszörü): This variety dates to the 1930s and is believed to be the result of crosses between the shorthaired variety and the Drahthaar. His ancestors also include the Weimaraner, the Transylvanian Pointing Dog, etc. Interbreeding the two varieties is forbidden.

Shorthaired Hungarian Pointing Dog: lightweight build. Well-proportioned. Elegant. Tight, pigmented skin. Vigorous, easy gait. Sustained gallop. Wirehaired Hungarian Pointing Dog: powerful build. More massive and more solidly boned than the shorthaired variety. Pigmented skin. Vigorous gait.

1
CONTINENTAL POINTING DOGS

7

COUNTRY OF ORIGIN
Hungary

ORIGINAL NAME
Magyar Vizsla

OTHER NAME
Vizsla

Between 10 and 45 kg (20-100 lb)

HEAD
Chiseled, dignified. Moderately wide, slightly domed skull. Moderate stop. Straight nosebridge. Broad muzzle. Well-developed nose. Chestnut, fairly tight lips.

EYES
Slightly oval, the darker the better, matching coat color. Brown eyelids.

EARS
Medium in length, hanging flat against the cheeks.

BODY
Slightly elongated but powerful. Neck medium in length, well-muscled, slightly curved, without dewlap. Pronounced withers. Chest moderately wide, well let-down. Moderately curved ribs. Level loin. Straight, short back. Slightly rounded croup.

LIMBS
Long, well-muscled, solidly boned legs. Feet slightly oval with strong, tight toes and slate-grey pads.

TAIL
Set on fairly low, moderately thick. Tip curving slightly upward. Usually docked by one-fourth. Docked by one-third in wirehaired variety.

Character, special skills and training
This lively, very adaptable dog with an excellent nose is skilled on rough terrain and tolerates heat well. He does not search widely, preferring to hunt near his owner. He points precisely, retrieves well and is a good swimmer. The shorthaired variety has a swifter gallop and is thus preferred in flat areas. The wirehaired variety excels on small quarry, including woodcock and is used in tracking wounded large game. Both are even-tempered and very comfortable in a family. They need firm but not harsh training.

Care and functions
He needs space and exercise, as well as regular brushing and checking of the ears.
· Hunting dog.
· Companion dog.

COAT
Short, dense, straight, harsh. Lying flat and silkier on the ears. Beard on the chin. Short and crisp on the head. Thick, hard eyebrows. Hard and dense on the neck and trunk, 2 to 4 cm (0.8-1.6 in) long. Dense undercoat. Longer on the backs of the legs. Dense and thick on the tail.

COLOR
Dark golden or a shade of sable fawn. Tiny white spots on the chest and feet. Dotting is not a fault.

SIZE
– Shorthaired variety
Dog: 56 to 61 cm (22-24 in).
Bitch: 52 to 57 cm (20.5-22.5 in).
– Wirehaired variety
Dog: 58 to 62 cm (22.8-24,5 in).
Bitch: 54 to 58 cm (21-22.8 in).

WEIGHT
Shorthaired variety
22 to 30 kg (48.5-66 lb).
Wirehaired variety
25 to 32 kg (55-70.5 lb).

Italian Pointing Dog

Solid build. Well-balanced. Dignified.
Supple skin. Gait: extended, rapid trot.

Like the Chien d'Oysel, this ancient Italian breed was used in the Middle Ages for netting birds. Fourteenth-century frescoes bear witness to the Italian Pointing Dog's unquestionable popularity over the centuries. Later, he was adapted to shooting, making him the oldest of the European pointers. All the kings of Europe had an Italian Pointing Dog. The breed was later improved by adding English Pointer blood, making him lighter and faster.

Two sub-breeds were developed: the Great Italian Pointing Dog, standing 66 to 70 cm (26-27,5 in) tall at the withers and weighing 35 to 40 kg (77-88 lb) and the faster and slimmer Lightweight Italian Pointing Dog (25 to 28 kg) (55-62 lb). In 1926, these two varieties were grouped under a single standard.

1

CONTINENTAL POINTING DOGS

COUNTRY OF ORIGIN
Italy

ORIGINAL NAME
Bracco Italiano

Large Breeds between 25 and 45 kg (55-100 lb)

7

HEAD
Angular, narrow. Slightly domed skull. Pronounced occipital crest. Slight stop. Straight or slightly curved nosebridge, of the same length as the skull. Very large nose, chestnut to pink or flesh-colored, depending on coat color. Cleanly cut cheeks. Thin lips.

EYES
Oval, a shade of ocher or brown, depending on coat color.

EARS
Long, supple, with slightly rounded tips. Front edge lying against the cheek.

BODY
Can be inscribed inside a square. Powerful neck with slight dewlap. Very pronounced withers. Broad, deep, well let-down chest. Well-curved ribs. Slight tuck-up. Broad, muscular back. Long, broad croup sloping at a 30-degree angle.

LIMBS
Well-knit legs with prominent muscles. Oval feet with tight toes, hard pads and dewclaws.

TAIL
Thick at the base, straight. Carried level to the ground in action. Docked to a length of 15 to 25 cm (6-9,8 in).

COAT
Short, dense, glossy, finer and lying flatter on the head, ears, feet and backs of the legs.

COLOR
White. White with orange or amber spots of varying size and shade. White with chestnut spots of varying size. White with pale orange spots (speckled). White with chestnut spots (chestnut roan). Mask preferably symmetrical.

SIZE
Dog: 58 to 67 cm (28-26.5 in).
Bitch: 55 to 62 cm (22-24.5 in).

WEIGHT
25 to 40 kg (55-88 lb).

Character, special skills and training
This hardy, vigorous dog with a keen nose is skilled at all kinds of hunting. He searches for quarry actively, head held high, at an extended trot. He is a good retriever and adapts easily to family life. He needs firm training.

Care and functions
He needs wide open spaces and lots of exercise, as well as regular brushing and checking of the ears.
· Hunting dog.
· Companion dog.

265

Saint Germain Pointing Dog

The Saint Germain Pointing Dog was developed around 1830 from French pointers descended from the royal packs of King Louis XV and the English Pointer, brought to France by Mr. de Girardin, a master huntsman for King Charles X. The products of this cross were bred by the keepers of Saint-Germain-en-Laye Forest, for which the breed was named. This English-French blend is the most elegant of the French pointers. Although very common in the early twentieth century, the breed is now relatively rare because it is not very widespread and it competes with the English Pointer, a dog similar in appearance and aptitudes.

Mesomorph. Elegant. Dignified. Thin, supple skin. Heavier gallop than that of the English Pointer.

1
CONTINENTAL POINTING DOGS

7

COUNTRY OF ORIGIN
France

ORIGINAL NAME
Braque Saint-Germain

Medium Breeds between 10 and 25 kg (20-55 lb)

Character, special skills, and training
The enthusiastic, swift, sometimes obstinate Saint Germain Pointing Dog excels in the fields and woods and even in swampland, although the cold season should be avoided. More predictable than the English Pointer but faster than the French Pointing Dog, he is a good runner with a wide search range. He is used especially on pheasant and rabbit. Gentle, affectionate, and very attached to his owner, he makes a good pet. He needs firm but gentle training.

Care and functions
If he lives in the city, he needs long, daily walks. He tolerates heat well. He needs regular brushing and attention to the ears.
· Hunting dog.
· Companion dog.

HEAD
Finely chiseled. Broad skull. Prominent occipital peak. Pronounced stop. Nose-bridge long and straight or slightly domed. Thin, pink lips. Wide, dark pink nose.

EYES
Fairly large, golden yellow.

EARS
Pendulous, longer than in the English Pointer, supple, standing well out from the head.

BODY
Well-proportioned. Solid, fairly long neck. Broad, deep chest let-down to the elbow. Powerful, fairly short, slightly arched loin. Short, straight back. Bony, slightly sloping croup.

LIMBS
Strong, muscular legs. Elongated feet with tight toes and tough pads.

TAIL
Thick at the base, very thin at the tip. Carried level to the ground. This is the only pointer whose tail does not have to be docked.

COAT
Short, not too fine, but never hard.

COLOR
Dull white with bright orange spots. Orange may be mixed with some white hairs. Some spotting is tolerated.

SIZE
Dog: 56 to 62 cm (20-24.5 in).
Bitch: 54 to 59 cm (21-23 in).

WEIGHT
18 to 26 kg (40-57.5 lb).

Weimaraner

Some believe the Weimaraner is of French origin, descended from the Chien Gris de Saint Louis used in royal packs. But by the early nineteenth century, the Weimaraner—more likely descended from grey German Hounds—was bred as a blood trailer in the court of the Duke of Weimar. Crosses were made with the Chien d'Oysel, the equivalent of today's spaniel, the Saint Hubert and the English Pointer. In the early twentieth century, the more popular Shorthaired Weimaraner was joined by a longhaired variety that is not very widespread. Raised as a purebred for over one hundred years, the Weimaraner is the oldest of the German pointers. The Weimaraner Club was founded in 1897 and the first standard was written in 1925. The breed is very popular in the United States, where it is nicknamed "the grey ghost".

Shapely. Well-muscled. Chiseled. Firm, tight-fitting skin. All gaits: great ease and long strides.

1

CONTINENTAL POINTING DOGS

COUNTRY OF ORIGIN
Germany

ORIGINAL NAME
Weimaraner Vorstehhund

Large Breeds between 25 and 45 kg (55-100 lb)

7

HEAD
Chiseled, in proportion to body size. Very slight stop. Straight nosebridge, often slightly curved. Long, powerful muzzle. Large, flesh-colored nose, darkly pigmented. Powerful jaws. Well-muscled cheeks.

EYES
Round, very slightly slanted. Light to dark amber. Puppies have light blue eyes.

EARS
Set on high, fairly long, slightly rounded at the tip. Turned slightly forward and folded when the dog is alert.

BODY
Slightly elongated. Nobly carried, muscular, well-knit neck. Well pronounced with-

ers. Powerful, well let-down, long chest. Well-curved ribs. Firm, muscular, somewhat long back. Long, moderately sloping croup.

LIMBS
Long, well-knit, well-muscled legs. Powerful, round feet with tight toes.

TAIL
Set on fairly low, powerful, covered with abundant hair. Hanging down at rest. Carried level to the ground in action. Docked by between one-half and two-thirds its length.

COAT
- Shorthaired variety: short, dense, very thick, lying flat. No or very little undercoat. - Longhaired variety (rare):

supple, with or without undercoat. Smooth and slightly wavy. Culotte and feathering. Handsome plume on the tail.

COLOR
Silvery grey, brownish-grey, mouse grey, or any intermediate shade. Head and ears generally lighter in color. Minimal white spotting is allowed on the chest and toes. Sometimes there is a more or less pronounced dark stripe down the middle of the back known as an "eel stripe".

SIZE
Dog: 59 to 70 cm (23-27.5 in). Bitch: 57 to 65 cm (22.5-25.5 in).

WEIGHT
Dog: 30 to 40 kg (66-88 lb). Bitch: 25 to 35 kg (55-77 lb).

Character, special skills and training
This enthusiastic dog with a remarkable nose was originally a hound but became a pointer in the nineteenth century. He is a diligent, systematic tracker, though a bit slow and a confident pointer and water dog. He can track wounded game and retrieve all sorts of quarry. He has a strong predisposition toward guarding and defending. He is a very pleasant companion and needs firm training.

Care and functions
He can adapt to apartment life but needs daily walks. He also requires regular brushing and checking of the ears.
· Hunting dog.
· Watchdog and defense dog.
· Companion dog.

Stout. Muscular. Elegant. Dignified expression. Lively gait.

1

CONTINENTAL SPANIEL TYPE POINTING DOGS

7

COUNTRY OF ORIGIN
Germany

ORIGINAL NAME
Deutscher Langhaariger Vorstehhund

OTHER NAME
Langhaar

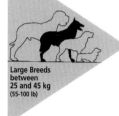

Large Breeds between 25 and 45 kg (55-100 lb)

German Longhaired Pointing Dog

The origins of the German Longhaired Pointing Dog are not well known. Some believe that this spaniel is the result of crosses between the German Spaniel (Deutscher Wachtelhund) and French spaniels. Splashes of Irish Setter and Gordon Setter blood may have been added. Despite his attributes, the German Longhaired Pointing Dog is uncommon both in Germany and France.

Character, special skills and training
With his effective nose, he can adapt to any style of hunting. He searches actively and has an ample range. He is obedient and very easy-going.

Care and functions
He needs space and exercise, as well as regular brushing.
. Hunting dog.

HEAD
Long, chiseled. Slightly domed skull. Sloping stop. Slightly domed nosebridge. Nose a shade of brown.

EYES
As dark as possible.

EARS
Set on high, wide with rounded tips, lying very flat against the head. Slightly wavy hair hanging down from the tips.

BODY
Stout, square build. Solid neck. Deep chest. Well-developed loin. Solid, straight, short back. Slightly sloping croup.

LIMBS
Muscular legs. Feet moderately rounded and medium in length.

TAIL
Well set-on, carried level with the ground or curving loosely upward. Handsome plume.

COAT
Long, lying very flat. 3 to 5 cm (1.2-2 in) on the back and sides of the trunk. Short on the head. Longer on the throat, chest, and abdomen. Well-feathered feet.

COLOR
Brown.

SIZE
63 to 70 cm (25-27.5 in).

WEIGHT
30 to 35 kg (66-77 lb).

Stabyhoun

This Dutch breed native to the Friesland province of Holland has been known since the early nineteenth century. He may be descended from spaniels imported to the Netherlands by the Spanish and possibly crossed with the Drentse Partridge Dog. The Stabyhoun is not very well known outside his native land.

Powerfully built.

1

CONTINENTAL SPANIEL TYPE POINTING DOGS

COUNTRY OF ORIGIN
The Netherlands

7

Medium Breeds between 10 and 25 kg (20-55 lb)

HEAD
Chiseled, longer than it is wide. Slightly domed skull. Moderate stop. Straight nosebridge. Powerful muzzle, equal in length to skull. Nose wide, black or brown, depending on coat color. Lips not pendulous.

EYES
Medium in size, round, dark brown in black-coated variety and light brown in brown-coated variety.

EARS
Set on low, medium in length, hanging close to the head without twisting. Hair fairly long near the base, shorter toward the tip.

BODY
Powerful, rectangular build. Short, round neck without dewlap. Chest wider than it is deep, such that forelegs are spread fairly widely apart. Well-sprung ribs. Moderate tuck-up. Straight, fairly long back. Croup nearly level.

LIMBS
Strong legs. Slightly oval or round feet with thick pads.

TAIL
Long, reaching the hock, carried low with the last third curving loosely upward. Covered with long hair.

COAT
Long and flat on the trunk, slightly wavy on the croup. Short on the head. Thick on the backs of the legs.

COLOR
Black, brown, or orange with white markings. Spotting and mixing of colors is allowed in the white areas.

SIZE
Approx. 50 cm (20 in).

WEIGHT
15 to 20 kg (33-44 lb).

Character, special skills, and training
The Stabyhoun is a good tracker, a firm pointer, and a good retriever. Calm and gentle, he is an affectionate pet.

Care and functions
He needs space and lots of exercise, as well as regular brushing and attention to the ears.
. Hunting dog.
. Companion dog.

Italian Wirehaired Pointing Dog

The Italian Wirehaired Pointing Dog is considered one of the oldest griffon type pointers. Some believe he is strictly Italian in origin, descended from wirehaired Italian pointers or hounds (segugios). Others think he descended from the Bresse Griffon and was brought to the Piedmont region of northwestern Italy. Crosses with German pointers, the Porcelaine, the Barbet, and the Korthals Griffon might also have contributed to the breed's development.

Stout, hardly, vigorous structure.
Skin thick, tight, well-fitting.
Extended, swift trot.

1

CONTINENTAL GRIFFON TYPE POINTING DOGS

7

COUNTRY OF ORIGIN
Italy

ORIGINAL NAME
Spinone Italiano

OTHER NAME
Italian Griffon

Large Breeds between 25 and 45 kg (55-100 lb)

Character, special skills, and training
This tough, very hardy, vigorous dog can hunt on all types of terrain in any weather. He fears neither water nor brambles (spinone means "thorn"). With his fairly short muzzle, he searches methodically and is an excellent retriever with hound-like tendencies. Calm, friendly, and affectionate, he makes a good pet. He needs firm training.

Care and functions
He needs wide open spaces and lots of exercise, as well as regular brushing and attention to the ears.
· Hunting dog.
· Companion dog.

HEAD
Strong, heavy. Viewed from the front, the skull is shaped like a double-eaved roof and has a very prominent occipital peak. Barely pronounced stop. Straight or slightly curved nosebridge. Muzzle equal in length to skull. Powerful jaws. Enormous nose, flesh-pink in the white-coated variety and brown in the roan brown variety. Bushy mustache and beard.

EYES
Large, round, a shade of ocher. Long, stiff eyebrows.

EARS
Long, triangular, pendulous. Front edge lying against the cheek, not twisted.

BODY
Square build. Powerful, muscular neck. Slight dewlap. Broad, deep chest. Well-sprung ribs. Slightly domed loin. Straight back. Broad, long, well-muscled, sloping croup.

LIMBS
Well-muscled, solidly boned legs. Compact, round feet with tight toes and hard pads.

TAIL
Thick at the base, carried level to the ground or hanging down. No feathering. Docked to a length of 15 to 25 cm (6-10 in).

COAT
4 to 6 cm (1.5-2.5 in) long, stiff, hard, dense. No undercoat. Shorter on the head, ears, and fronts of the legs. Feathering on the backs of the legs.

COLOR
Pure white, white with orange spots, white flecked with orange, white with brown, roan or roan brown spots. Tricolor coat, tan markings, and any shade or combination of black markings not allowed.

SIZE
Dog: 60 to 70 cm (23.5-27.5 in).
Bitch: 58 to 65 cm (23-25.5 in).

WEIGHT
Dog: 32 to 37 kg (70.5-82 lb).
Bitch: 28 to 30 kg (62-66 lb).

Portuguese Pointing Dog

The Portuguese Pointing Dog's origins are unknown. He may have come from the East, but he is now considered indigenous to Portugal. Pointing dogs have lived on the Iberian peninsula since the fourteenth century. The Portuguese Pointing Dog is not very well known outside his native country.

Mesomorph. Braccoid. Well-balanced overall. Solidly built. Great flexibility.

Between 10 and 45 kg (20-100 lb)

1

CONTINENTAL POINTING DOGS

COUNTRY OF ORIGIN
Portugal

ORIGINAL NAME
Perdigueiro Portugues

OTHER NAME
Portuguese Pointer

7

HEAD
Somewhat heavy, covered with flaccid, thin skin. Square from the front, straight in profile. Slightly domed skull. Pronounced brow bones. Pronounced stop. Straight nosebridge. Pendulous upper lip.

EYES
Large, oval, in different shades of brown, preferably dark.

EARS
Medium in length, thin, supple, wide at the base, rounded at the tip. Hanging flat.

BODY
Can be inscribed inside a square. Straight, long neck with short dewlap. High, broad chest. Short, broad, well-muscled loin. Short, full flanks. Short, broad, straight back. Broad, minimally sloping croup.

LIMBS
Muscular legs. Fairly round feet with tight, solid toes.

TAIL
Thick at the base, tapering toward the tip. Hanging naturally against the thighs. In action, raised level to the ground. Usually docked by one-third.

COAT
Short, thick, lying very flat against the body, not very soft. Fine and close-lying on the head and ears. No undercoat.

COLOR
Yellow or chestnut, whole-colored or with white spots.

SIZE
Dog: 52 to 60 cm (20.5-23.5 in).
Bitch: 48 to 56 cm (19-22 in).

WEIGHT
Dog: 20 to 27 kg (44-59.5 lb).
Bitch 16 to 22 kg (35-48.5 lb).

Character, special skills and training
Tenacious, active, strong-willed, lively and fast, this dog has a very good sense of smell. Initially used in hunting feathered quarry (perdigueiro = "partridge"), he has become a multi-purpose hunting dog able to work on any terrain. He tracks with enthusiasm and retrieves very well. He is calm and very affectionate and friendly, making him a good companion. He needs firm training.

Care and functions
He needs space and exercise, as well as regular brushing and checking of the ears.
· Hunting dog.
· Companion dog.

Blue Picardy Spaniel

The Blue Picardy Spaniel is believed to be the product of crosses between black and grey Picardy Spaniels and English or Gordon Setters. The breed was recognized in 1938 and would have disappeared if not for the efforts of breeders and hunters. Unable to compete with foreign breeds (like the Labrador Retriever), the Blue Picardy Spaniel remains confined to the Somme region of France.

Powerful. Standing fairly low to the ground. Built for working.

1

CONTINENTAL SPANIEL TYPE POINTING DOGS

7

COUNTRY OF ORIGIN
France

ORIGINAL NAME
Épagneul Bleu de Picardie

OTHER NAME
Bleu Picard

Medium Breeds between 10 and 25 kg (20-55 lb)

Character, special skills, and training
The hardy, courageous, active Blue Picardy Spaniel has a subtle nose and is a good hunter on all types of terrain, particularly swampland. His specialty is woodcock. Sweet and affectionate, he makes a good pet. He needs gentle training.

Care and functions
He needs space and exercise for his well-being. He does not like being left alone. He requires regular brushing and attention to the ears.
· Hunting dog.
· Companion dog.

HEAD
Fairly large. Relatively broad, oval skull. Pronounced stop. Long, fairly broad nosebridge. Wide nose. Flews large, very pendulous.

EYES
Large, dark.

EARS
Set on slightly above eye level. Fairly thick, framing the head. Covered with silky waves of hair.

BODY
Strong. Neck with very slight dewlap allowed. Chest sufficiently deep. Well-arched ribs. Loin not too heavy. Back not too long. Slightly sloping croup.

LIMBS
Strong, well-muscled legs. Round, somewhat wide feet.

TAIL
Not much longer than the hock. Never hooked.

COAT
Flat or slightly wavy. Feathering on the legs and tail.

COLOR
Flecked grey or black, creating a bluish cast, with black spots.

SIZE
Dog: 57 to 60 cm (22.5-23.5 in).
Bitch: slightly less.

WEIGHT
Approx. 20 kg (44 lb).

Brittany Spaniel

The Brittany Spaniel is one of the descendents of the Chien d'Oysel, a breed trained in the Middle Ages for netting game birds. He is the product of the initially accidental 19th century crossbreeding of Brittany farm dogs – short, broad-backed, hardy, and used on woodcock – with English Setters, English Pointers, and English Springer Spaniels left in France during the off-season by British hunters in order to improve the new breed's nose and speed. The Brittany Spaniel became increasingly popular. Mr. de Pontavic and Mr. de Combouz presented the breed in 1896 in Paris, and a breed club was founded in 1907 in Londéac. The first standard was adopted in 1908 and revised in 1938. The Brittany Spaniel is the second most popular dog in France, and the most popular French breed abroad. He is one of the most common pointers in the United States.

Close coupled. Cobby. Stocky. Broad-backed. Elegant. Thin, fairly loose skin. Energetic gait.

1

7

CONTINENTAL SPANIEL TYPE POINTING DOGS

COUNTRY OF ORIGIN
France

ORIGINAL NAME
Épagneul Breton

Medium Breeds between 10 and 25 kg (20-55 lb)

HEAD
Round. Rounded skull. Gently sloping stop. Straight nosebridge. Thin lips.

EYES
Dark amber, matching coat color.

EARS
Set on high, fairly short, slightly rounded, covered with wavy hair.

BODY
Square build. Neck medium in length. Deep chest. Fairly rounded ribs. Short, broad loin. Tuck-up. Short back. Slightly receding croup.

LIMBS
Slender, muscular legs. Feet have tight toes.

TAIL
Straight or hanging down (unless the animal is tail-less). Always short, about 10 cm (4 in) in length. Often slightly twisted with a tuft at the tip.

COAT
Not too fine, fairly flat or very slightly wavy, never curly.

COLOR
White and orange. White and brown. White and black. Tricolor (white, black, and tan) or roan (colored hair mixed with white).

SIZE
Dog: 48 to 50 cm (19-20 in). Bitch: 47 to 49 cm (18.5-19 in).

WEIGHT
Dog: 15 to 18 kg (33-40 lb). Bitch: 14 to 15 kg (31-37.5 lb).

Character, special skills, and training
This hardy, enthusiastic, tireless dog with a fighting spirit can hunt on any type of terrain. "Maximum quality for minimum size" could be the motto of the breed club for this lightweight dog. With an excellent nose, he tracks rapidly, points firmly, and is a very good waterfowl retriever. A multi-purpose dog, he hunts game birds, preferring woodcock and snipe. Even-tempered, gentle, intelligent, and good-natured, he is a delightful pet. He needs gentle training.

Care and functions
He can adapt to apartment life as long as he gets long, daily walks to let off steam. He requires brushing once or twice a week, as well as regular attention to the ears.
· Hunting dog.
· Companion dog.

French Spaniel

Like all the other spaniels who became the first pointers, the French Spaniel is a distant descendant of the longhaired Chien d'Oysel "setter" of the Middle Ages. By the sixteenth century, the French Spaniel was widely used by game bird hunters. After a decrease in population due to competition with English breeds, the French Spaniel was revived in the nineteenth century by Father Fournier. The first standard, written in 1891 by J. de Connick, describes the breed as larger and more powerful than the Brittany Spaniel. The French Spaniel is virtually unknown abroad, and the breed's population in France is low, despite renewed popularity.

Mesomorph. Braccoid. Well-proportioned. Dignified. Well muscled. Supple, tight-fitting skin. Easy, elegant gait.

1

CONTINENTAL SPANIEL TYPE POINTING DOGS

7

COUNTRY OF ORIGIN
France

ORIGINAL NAME
Épagneul Français

Medium Breeds
between
10 and 25 kg
(20-55 lb)

Character, special skills, and training
Hardy, courageous, persistent, and enthusiastic, the French Spaniel is appreciated for his work on rugged terrain. He is a flusher and excels at work in the water. With an excellent nose but less speed and a more limited search range than the Brittany Spaniel, he hunts at a gallop or extended trot. He points very precisely and is one of the best retrievers. Calm, even-tempered, intelligent, very attached to his owner, and gentle with children, he is a great pet. He needs firm but gentle training.

Care and functions
The French Spaniel is built for country life. He does not like being left alone and needs to run every day. He requires brushing twice weekly and regular attention to the ears.
· Hunting dog.
· Companion dog.

HEAD
Of medium length and width. Well-chiseled, but not excessively. Pronounced brow bones. Sloping stop. Slightly domed nosebridge a bit shorter than the skull. Brown nose. Upper lip does not cover lower lip.

EYES
Fairly large, oval, dark amber.

EARS
Well set-on, covered to rounded tips with wavy, silky hair.

BODY
Slightly elongated. Slightly arched neck without dewlap. Cleanly cut, pronounced withers. Broad, spacious chest. Loin broad, not too long. Tuck-up. Horizontal, level back. Broad, rounded croup.

LIMBS
Well-knit, muscular, solidly boned legs. Oval feet with tight toes and dark pads.

TAIL
Reaching to the hock, carried sloping or curved loosely in an S. Covered with long, wavy hair.

COAT
Long and wavy on the ears, backs of the legs, and tail. Flat, silky, and dense on the body, with some waviness behind the neck and on the upper chest. Close-lying and fine on the head.

COLOR
White and brown with moderate patching. Sometimes heavily marked with irregular patches with slight to moderate spotting or moderately spotted and roan. Brown ranges from cinnamon to dark liver. White flare on the head desirable.

SIZE
Dog: 56 to 61 cm (22-24 in).
Bitch: 55 to 59 cm (21.5-23).

WEIGHT
Approx. 25 kg (55 lb).

Münsterländer

Among the Münsterländer's nineteenth-century ancestors are longhaired German pointers, the French Spaniel, the English Setter, and the English Pointer. In the early twentieth century, two varieties were developed in the Münster region of Westphalia, Germany:
- The Small Münsterländer (Kleiner Münsterländer Vorstehhund), the more popular variety, and
- The Large Münsterländer (Grosser Münsterländer Vorstehhund). The first standard was written in 1936. The Small Münsterländer first appeared in France in the late 1960s.

Powerful. Clean lines. Springy, long strides.

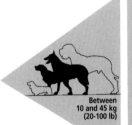

1

CONTINENTAL SPANIEL TYPE POINTING DOGS

COUNTRY OF ORIGIN
Germany

ORIGINAL NAME
Münsterländer Vorstehhund

OTHER NAMES
Münster Spaniel
Large Münsterländer
Small Münsterländer

Between 10 and 45 kg (20-100 lb)

7

HEAD
Long, cleanly cut, dignified. Skull not too broad. Slightly pronounced stop. Straight nosebridge. Powerful, long muzzle. Lips not pendulous. Nose black in the Large Münsterländer, brown in the Small Münsterländer.

EYES
As dark as possible.

EARS
Set on fairly high, wide, rounded at the tips, hanging close to the skull.

BODY
Square build. Powerful, well-muscled neck. Long withers. Chest broad, well let-down. Short flanks. Slight tuck-up. Short, firm, straight back. Long, broad, well-muscled, moderately sloping croup.

LIMBS
Very muscular, powerful legs. Feet medium in length with tight toes (feet round in the Small Münsterländer).

TAIL
Medium in length, carried level to the ground.

COAT
Long, dense, smooth. Feathering on the backs of the legs and on the ears and tail. Short and very close-lying on the head. Medium in length, smooth, dense, slightly wavy in the Small Münsterländer.

COLOR
– Large Münsterländer: white with black patches and spots or grizzled hairs. Black on the head, sometimes with a small white spot or flare.
– Small Münsterländer: brown and white, spotted brown and white. Fawn markings on the muzzle and ears allowed.

SIZE
Large Münsterländer dog: 60 to 65 cm (23.5-25.5 in); bitch: 58 to 63 cm (23-25 in). Small Münsterländer: dog: 50 to 56 cm (20-22 in); bitch: 48 to 54 cm (19-21 in).

WEIGHT
– Large Münsterländer: approx. 30 kg (66 lb).
– Small Münsterländer: 18 to 23 kg (40-51 lb).

Character, special skills, and training
The lively Münsterländer has an excellent nose and is as skilled in the fields and forests as he is in the water. He tracks fairly close to his owner, points very firmly, and is a good retriever. He hunts either small or large game, depending on the variety, and is sometimes used in packs. He is a wonderful pet. This breed needs firm training, especially the Small Münsterländer.

Care and functions
He is poorly suited to apartment life. He needs space and lots of exercise. He requires brushing twice weekly and regular attention to the ears.
· Hunting dog.
· Companion dog.

Drentse Partridge Dog

Known for centuries, the Drentse Partridge Dog was developed in Drentse, a province of northeastern Holland. He is thought to be descended from the same strain as spaniels and setters. He is not very well known, even in his native country.

Solidly built. Well-proportioned.

1

CONTINENTAL SPANIEL TYPE POINTING DOGS

7

COUNTRY OF ORIGIN
The Netherlands

ORIGINAL NAME
Drentsche Patrijshond

OTHER NAME
Dutch Partridge Dog

Medium Breeds
between
10 and 25 kg
(20-55 lb)

HEAD
Broad and flat. Slight stop. Straight nosebridge. Wedge-shaped muzzle. Brown nose.

EYES
Amber.

EARS
Covered with long hair, hanging flat against the cheeks.

BODY
Compact. Deep chest. Long ribs. Broad loin. Powerful back. Fairly long, slightly sloping croup.

LIMBS
Strong legs. Rounded feet with tight toes and thick pads.

TAIL
Long, hanging down at rest, raised in action.

COAT
Thick, medium in length on the body. Feathering on the ears, legs, and tail.

COLOR
White with brown or orangish spots.

SIZE
Dog: 57 to 63 cm (22.5-28 in).
Bitch: slightly less.

WEIGHT
20 to 25 kg (44-55 lb).

Character, special skills, and training
Quite persistent and gifted with a very subtle nose, the Drentse Partridge Dog is just as comfortable in the field as he is in swampland. He hunts all game birds (patrijshond means "partridge dog") and ground game. He points precisely and is an excellent retriever. This good-natured dog makes a nice pet.

Care and functions
He needs space and exercise, as well as daily brushing.
· Hunting dog.
· Companion dog.

Picardy Spaniel

The Picardy Spaniel has long been known in France's Somme Valley.
Like the French Spaniel, he is descended from the old, longhaired Chien d'Oysel
"setter" used to point game birds in the Middle Ages. Some believe the Picardy
Spaniel is a cousin to the setters. After a decline in popularity in the late
nineteenth century, the breed was shown in Paris in 1904, renewing
the interest of hunters. The first standard was written in 1908.
The Picardy Spaniel has never been common outside his native region.

Very stocky. Beautifully developed forequarters. Fairly thin skin.

1

CONTINENTAL SPANIEL TYPE POINTING DOGS

COUNTRY OF ORIGIN
France

ORIGINAL NAME
Épagneul Picard

7

Medium Breeds between 10 and 25 kg (20-55 lb)

HEAD
Strong. Broad, rounded skull. Pronounced occipital peak. Sloping stop. Broad, long nosebridge. Lips not too pendulous. Brown nose.

EYES
Dark amber.

EARS
Set on fairly low, framing the head well, covered with silky, wavy hair.

BODY
Athletic. Well-muscled neck. Deep, fairly broad chest let down to elbow. Loin very straight, broad, and thick.

Hips slightly lower than withers. Flat flanks. Moderate tuck-up. Moderately long back. Croup rounded, very slightly sloping.

LIMBS
Well-muscled, strong legs. Round, wide, tight feet.

TAIL
Forming two loose curves inward and outward, not too long. Covered with silky hair.

COAT
Medium in length, thick, not very silky. Fine on the head. Slightly wavy on the body.

COLOR
Grey, spotted, with brown blotches on various parts of the body and the base of the tail, usually with tan markings on the head and legs.

SIZE
55 to 60 cm (22-23.5 in).

WEIGHT
20 to 25 kg (44-55 lb).

Character, special skills, and training
This hardy dog with great endurance and a remarkable nose works well on any kind of terrain, especially swampland. He is a persistent hunter, a perfect pointer, and an excellent retriever. He works well on duck and woodcock, as well as rabbit and hare. Merry, gentle, friendly, and good-natured, he makes a delightful pet.

Care and functions
He is very poorly suited to apartment life. He needs space and regular exercise, as well as weekly combing and brushing and regular attention to the ears.
· Hunting dog.
· Companion dog.

277

Pont-Audemer Spaniel

Developed in the nineteenth century, the Pont-Audemer Spaniel is believed to be descended from an old spaniel breed native to Pont-Audemer, in the Eure region of France, crossed with the Irish Water Spaniel. The Picardy Spaniel and the Barbet may also have contributed to the breed. The Pont-Audemer Spaniel has been represented by the Picardy Spaniel Club since 1980. Already fairly rare by the early twentieth century, the Pont-Audemer Spaniel is still quite limited in number.

Well-built. Stocky.

1

CONTINENTAL SPANIEL TYPE POINTING DOGS

7

COUNTRY OF ORIGIN
France

ORIGINAL NAME
Épagneul de Pont-Audemer

Medium Breeds between 10 and 25 kg (20-55 lb)

Character, special skills and training
Tough, hardy and vigorous, the Pont-Audemer Spaniel is remarkably resistant to cold and bad weather. A flusher, he plows through thickets, but water is his element. He was bred to hunt waterfowl, including duck. Skilled at tracking a wide variety of game, he is a firm pointer and a perfect retriever. Affectionate, gentle with children and very attached to his owner, he makes a good pet. His training need not be too rigorous.

Care and functions
He can adapt to city life but needs lots of exercise. He also requires weekly brushing.
· Hunting dog.
· Companion dog.

HEAD
Slender. Round skull with a very curly topknot. Prominent occipital peak. Pronounced stop. Long nosebridge with a bump in the middle. Lips thin, not very pendulous. Pointed, brown nose.

EYES
Fairly small, dark amber or hazel.

EARS
Set on fairly low, flat, moderately thick, long and covered with long, silky, very curly hair that blends with the topknot, framing the head.

BODY
Well-proportioned. Neck slightly arched, cleanly cut, well-muscled. Deep, broad chest. Long, well-sprung ribs. Fairly short, solid, muscular loin. Flat flanks. Slight tuck-up. Straight or slightly domed back. Very slightly sloping croup.

LIMBS
Strong, muscular legs. Round feet with curly hair between the toes.

TAIL
Carried fairly straight. Usually docked to one-third its length, thickly covered with curly hair. If not docked, it should be medium in length and slightly curved.

COAT
Curly and slightly rough. Very dense.

COLOR
Brown, preferably mottled brown and grey, with dead foliage highlights.

SIZE
52 to 58 cm (20.5-23 in).

WEIGHT
Approx. 20 kg (44 lb).

French Wirehaired Pointing Griffon

The French Wirehaired Pointing Griffon was developed by E. Korthals, a Dutch kennel master in Germany's grand duchy of Hesse. Beginning in 1860, he decided to revive the old Wirehaired Griffon through selection, inbreeding, and crossbreeding. To do this, he crossed his own French and German griffons with pointers, spaniels, and the Barbet. The new breed was first shown in 1870, and the first standard was published in 1887. The French Wirehaired Pointing Griffon is recognized as a French breed by the FCI and is well-represented in France.

Mesomorph. Solidly built.

1

CONTINENTAL GRIFFON TYPE POINTING DOGS

Medium Breeds between 10 and 25 kg (20-55 lb)

COUNTRY OF ORIGIN
France

ORIGINAL NAME
Korthals

OTHER NAMES
Wirehaired Griffon
Korthals Pointing Griffon

7

HEAD
Large, long. Skull not too broad. Stop not very pronounced. Slightly curved nosebridge. Long, angular muzzle. Brown nose. Prominent mustache and eyebrows.

EYES
Large, rounded, yellow or brown.

EARS
Medium in size, lying flat, not curled.

BODY
Long. Fairly long neck without dewlap. Chest not too broad. Ribs slightly curved. Broad loin. Sturdy back.

LIMBS
Strong legs. Round, stocky feet with tight toes.

TAIL
Carried level to the ground. Bushy hair but no plume. Usually docked by one-third or one-fourth.

COAT
Hard and harsh, much like a boar's bristles. Bushy but not too long. Never curly or woolly. Fine, dense undercoat.

COLOR
Preferably steel grey with brown markings or solid brown, often reddish-brown or roan. White and brown or white and orange also allowed.

SIZE
Dog: 55 to 60 cm (21.5-23,5 in).
Bitch: 50 to 55 cm (19.5-21.5 in).

WEIGHT
20 to 25 kg (44-55 lb).

Character, special skills and training
Vigorous, hardy and enthusiastic, the French Wirehaired Pointing Griffon has a very subtle nose and can maintain a steady gallop. He is a multipurpose pointer for all game, all types of terrain (from thickets to swampland) and any kind of weather. He is a good tracker, a firm pointer and a good retriever. He is perfect on woodcock. Gentle, kind and very attached to his owner, he is a good pet. However, he is strong-willed and a bit restless. He needs firm but not harsh training.

Care and functions
The French Wirehaired Pointing Griffon is not well-suited to city life. He does not like being left alone or tied up. He needs lots of exercise every day, as well as brushing several times a week and regular attention to the ears.
· Hunting dog.
· Companion dog.

Slovakian Wirehaired Pointer

The Slovakian Wirehaired Pointer is believed to be the result of crossing the Czech Griffon with the German Wirehaired Pointing Dog, with added blood from the Weimaraner. A recent creation, the Slovakian Wirehaired Pointer was not bred until after World War II. The breed was recognized in 1975 and registered by the FCI in 1983.

Dignified. Solidly built. Not heavy. Grey skin without folds. Well-balanced, lively gait.

1

CONTINENTAL POINTING DOGS

7

COUNTRY OF ORIGIN
Slovakia

ORIGINAL NAMES
Slovensky Hrubosrsty Stavac (Ohar)

Large Breeds between 25 and 45 kg (55-100 lb)

Character, special skills and training
This hunting dog is skilled in fields and forests, as well as in the water. He tracks and retrieves wounded game. He is obedient and easy to train.

Care and functions
He needs space and exercise, as well as regular brushing. . Hunting dog.

HEAD
Long, chiseled, without folds. Rectangular skull. Moderate stop. Straight nosebridge. High, broad muzzle. Dark nose. Tight-lipped.

EYES
Almond-shaped, amber. Azure in puppies.

EARS
Set on above eye level, rounded at the tips.

BODY
Slightly elongated. Cleanly cut, well-muscled neck. Pronounced withers. Long, broad, oval chest. Well-sprung ribs. Moderate tuck-up. Straight, well-muscled back. Broad, sufficiently long, level croup.

LIMBS
Strong, well-muscled legs. Feet rounded with tight toes.

TAIL
Set on fairly high, moderately large, hanging down at rest. Carried level to the ground in action. Well-furnished with hair. Docked to half its length.

COAT
Approximately 4 cm (1.6 in) long, hard, straight, lying flat. Mustache on the muzzle. Eyebrows standing at a slant. Soft and short on the head and ears.

COLOR
A shade of sable with brown shadowing (called "grey"), with or without white markings on the legs and chest.

SIZE
Dog: 62 to 68 cm (24.5-27 lb).
Bitch: 57 to 64 cm (22.5-25 in).

WEIGHT
25 to 35 kg (55-77 lb).

Pudelpointer

The Pudelpointer was developed by Germany's Baron von Zedlitz in the late nineteenth century. He crossed the Poodle (Pudel), descended from the Barbet, with the English Pointer in an attempt to create a tracking, pointing and retrieving dog. Still today, the breed is not very stable. The Pudelpointer is popular neither in Germany, where he competes with the German Wirehaired Pointing Dog, nor abroad. The breed is quite rare.

Built like a heavy English Pointer.

CONTINENTAL POINTING DOGS

COUNTRY OF ORIGIN
Germany

Large Breeds between 25 and 45 kg (55-100 lb)

1

7

HEAD
Medium in length, broad, with bristly hair (beard and bushy eyebrows). Abrupt stop creates a slightly dish-faced appearance. Curved nosebridge like that of the English Pointer. Broad, long muzzle.

EYES
Large, round, yellow to yellowish-brown.

EARS
Medium in length, more pointed than rounded, well-furnished with hair, hanging very flat against the cheeks.

BODY
Fairly solid. Neck medium in length, cleanly cut, arched, muscular. High, long withers. Chest moderately broad, very deep. Well-arched ribs. Very muscular loin. Tuck-up. Short flanks. Short, straight back. Long, well-muscled, moderately sloping croup.

LIMBS
Muscular legs. Round feet with tight toes and firm pads.

TAIL
Lightweight, very straight, with hard hair. Docked.

COAT
Hard, medium in length, harsh and dense. Short on the lower legs.

COLOR
Dead foliage or brown. White, black, too pale or bridled markings are not allowed.

SIZE
Approx. 60 to 65 cm (23.5-25.5 in).

WEIGHT
25 to 30 kg (55-66 lb).

Character, special skills and training
The energetic Pudelpointer can hunt on all types of terrain (fields, woods and swampland). From the English Pointer he inherited his keen nose, spiritedness and speed; from the Poodle he got his cleverness and love of water. He tracks energetically and is a very good retriever. He is good-natured and needs firm training.

Care and functions
He needs space and exercise, as well as regular brushing and attention to the ears.
. Hunting dog.

English Pointer

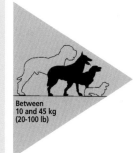

Some say the old English Pointer originated in Portugal, the home of a quick, tireless pointer who hunted with his nose held high. It is uncertain exactly when this dog arrived in England. Yet in the eighteenth century, British breeders crossed a shorthaired pointer from Portugal with various other breeds to arrive at today's English Pointer. They probably used foxhounds, the Bloodhound, the Greyhound, etc. In the nineteenth century, the new breed apparently received a great deal of French and Italian pointer blood. The English Pointer breed club was founded in 1891. English Pointers are widespread in Europe, where the breed competes with the German Pointing Dog as the most popular shorthaired or wirehaired pointer.

Dignified. The "Thoroughbred" of Pointers. Mesomorph. Well-built. Well-balanced. Strong. Flexible. Smooth gait. Extended gallop.

2

7

BRITISH AND IRISH POINTERS

COUNTRY OF ORIGIN
Great Britain

OTHER NAME
Pointer

Between 10 and 45 kg (20-100 lb)

HEAD
Slender. Skull medium in length, flat. Pronounced stop. Pronounced occipital peak. Angular, slightly concave muzzle. Strong jaws. Thin lips. Wide nose.

EYES
Round, hazel or brown, depending on coat color.

EARS
Set on fairly high. Medium in length, thin, lying flat against the head, slightly pointed at the tips.

BODY
Square build. Long, muscular, slightly arched, without dewlap. Shoulder blades close together. Chest broad, well let-down. Well-sprung ribs. Solid, short, muscular, slightly clean-flanked loin. Straight back. Long croup.

LIMBS
Muscular, well-boned legs. Oval feet with very tight toes.

TAIL
Medium in length, thick at the base and tapering toward the tip. Carried level with the topline without curving upward. In action, wagged from side to side.

COAT
Fine, short, hard, smooth, straight and very glossy.

COLOR
Usual colors are lemon and white orange and white, liver (brown) and white and black and white. Whole-color and tricolor coats also allowed.

SIZE
Dog: 63 to 69 cm (25-27 in).
Bitch: 61 to 66 cm (24-26 in).

WEIGHT
20 to 30 kg (44-66 lb).

Character, special skills and training
This hardy, active, quick and agile athlete with great endurance has two main attributes: his speed and his extraordinary, peerless nose. He excels in flat, open fields. His hunt is energetic, avid, steady and extensive. His pointing (a "pointer" is a shorthaired dog that indicates the presence of game by standing still) is spectacular, confident and steady. He appears almost sculpted, standing frozen with his body rigid, muscles tensed, head raised and tail stiff and level with the topline. He is the most highly skilled pointer but not as good a retriever. He excels on woodcock, quail, pheasant and partridge and will also tackle ground game. Easygoing and good-natured, the English Pointer is a very affectionate pet. He can be a watchdog. He needs firm but patient, gentle training.

Care and functions
He is not suited to city life. He needs wide open spaces and lots of exercise. He is sensitive to cold and dampness. He requires weekly brushing and regular attention to the ears.
· Hunting dog.
· Companion dog.

English Setter

The English Setter is the oldest British setter type dog.
In the 16th century, he was used in netting game birds.
He was named the Laverack Setter after E. Laverack,
a breeder from Shropshire County who modified and improved
the breed beginning in 1825 through inbreeding and selection.
Laverack continued his efforts for fifty years. He is believed
to have used pointers (including the English Pointer)
and spaniels. The new breed was recognized by the Kennel Club
by 1873. The first English Setters were imported to France
in 1879 and the first breed club was founded in 1891.
Together with the Brittany Spaniel, the English Setter
is the best known and most common setter type breed.

Well-balanced. Clean lines. Elegant.
Clean, well-balanced gait.

2

BRITISH AND IRISH SETTERS

COUNTRY OF ORIGIN
Great Britain

OTHER NAME
Laverack Setter

Large Breeds
between
25 and 45 kg
(55-100 lb)

7

HEAD
Long, cleanly cut, carried high. Oval skull. Prominent occipital peak. Pronounced stop. Fairly square muzzle. Strong jaws. Nose black or liver, depending on coat colour. Lips not too pendulous.

EYES
Hazel to dark brown.

EARS
Set low, medium in length, falling in well-defined folds against the cheeks.

BODY
Moderately long. Neck fairly long, muscular, cleanly cut, slightly curved, without dewlap. Chest well let-down, deep, high, broad.

Well-sprung ribs. Loin broad, strong, slightly clean-flanked. Short, level back.

LIMBS
Compact feet with tight, well-arched toes. Very muscular legs.

TAIL
Medium in length, curved loosely inwards or carried in sickle fashion. Long feathering.

COAT
Starting from the back of the head behind ears, slightly wavy but not curly, long and silky. Feathering on the legs.

COLOUR
Black and white (blue belton), orange and white (orange belton), lemon and white (lemon belton), brown and white (liver belton) or tricolour (black, white and tan or brown). All patterns without heavy patching on the body. An entirely flecked coat is preferable.

SIZE
Dog: 65 to 68 cm (25.5-27 in).
Bitch: 61 to 65 cm (24-25.5 in).

WEIGHT
25 to 30 kg (55-66 lb).

Character, special skills and training
Hardy, enthusiastic, lively and fast, the English Setter can hunt on all types of terrain but is best suited to wetlands and swamps, rather than dry terrain. With his excellent nose, he has a wide search range and skims over the ground at a fluid trot, approaching game much like a cat. He sets (points game) either half-crouched or flat on the ground. Woodcock is one of his specialties. Very friendly, gentle, affectionate and good-natured, he is often kept as a pet. He needs firm but gentle, patient training.

Care and functions
He needs space and exercise. He does not like being confined. He requires brushing twice a week, as well as regular attention to the ears.
· Hunting dog.
· Companion dog.

Gordon Setter

The Gordon Setter was developed in the mid-sixteenth century in Scotland. By the late eighteenth century, the Duke of Gordon had arrived at a breed resembling that of today. Some believe that English and Irish Setters, the Collie and the Bloodhound were used in developing the Gordon Setter. The first so-called "Black and Tan Scottish Spaniels" were imported to France by 1860. In 1923, a Gordon Setter club was founded. The Gordon Setter is less common than other setters.

The most majestic and massive Setter. Well-balanced. Powerful. Smooth, relaxed, clean gait.

2

BRITISH AND IRISH SETTERS

7

COUNTRY OF ORIGIN
Great Britain

OTHER NAMES
Scottish Setter
Black and Tan Setter

Large Breeds between 25 and 45 kg (55-100 lb)

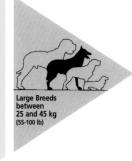

Character, special skills and training
Tough and extremely hardy, the Gordon Setter can adapt to all kinds of terrain. He has an excellent nose and differs from the English Setter in his heavier structure, less impressive gallop and standing point. His search range is more limited than that of other setters. He is a remarkable swimmer, tracks all sorts of game and can retrieve. His specialties include woodcock and snipe. Calm, docile and affectionate, he makes a wonderful pet. He needs firm but patient and gentle training.

Care and functions
He adapts fairly well to city life. He needs space and lots of exercise, as well as regular brushing and attention to the ears.
· Hunting dog.
· Companion dog.

HEAD
Taller than it is wide, chiseled. Slightly domed skull. Pronounced stop. Long muzzle. Strong jaws. Lips not pendulous. Pink nose.

EYES
Dark brown.

EARS
Set on low, medium in size, thin, hanging against the head. Long, silky feathering at the tops of the ears.

BODY
Medium in length. Brisket not too wide. Chest well letdown. Well-sprung ribs. Short back. Broad, slightly arched loin.

LIMBS
Strong legs. Oval feet with tight, well-arched toes.

TAIL
Thick at the base, tapering to thin tip. Straight or curved loosely in sickle fashion, carried level to the ground. Long, straight feathering (or fringe).

COAT
Short and fine on the head and fronts of the legs. Medium in length on the rest of the body. Long, fine, flat feathering on the backs of the legs. Feathering on the abdomen.

COLOR
Rich, glossy, smoky black without traces of rust, with tan markings of a bright reddish-chestnut. Black pencil marks on the toes are allowed, as are black stripes below the jaw. Tan markings: two spots above the eyes, on either side of the muzzle. Two large spots on the chest. Markings on the insides of the hind legs. On the forelegs, tan markings from the feet to the elbows. Markings around the anus. A small white spot on the chest is allowed.

SIZE
Dog: approx. 66 cm (26 in).
Bitch: approx. 62 cm (24.5 in).

WEIGHT
Dog: approx. 30 kg (66 lb).
Bitch: approx. 25 kg (55 lb).

Irish Setter

The Irish setter comes in two varieties: solid red and red and white. By about the nineteenth century, the solid red variety had virtually eclipsed the red and white variety, which became so rare that some considered it extinct. In the 1920s, an attempt was made to revive it, sparking renewed interest. The first standard for the Irish Setter was published in 1885. Founded in 1906, the Irish Setter Club (Red Club) oversees the breed in France. The beautiful Irish Setter is so popular as a pet that people often forget his skill as a hunter.

The "Thoroughbred" of Setters. Beautiful. Strong. Powerful. Well-balanced. Fairly long-backed.

2

7

BRITISH AND IRISH SETTERS

COUNTRY OF ORIGIN
Ireland

OTHER NAME
Irish Red Setter

Medium Breeds between 10 and 25 kg (20-55 lb)

WEIGHT
20 to 25 kg (44-55 lb).

HEAD
Long, cleanly cut, without heaviness. Oval skull. Pronounced occipital peak. Pronounced stop. Muzzle fairly angular. Flews not pendulous. Nose mahogany, brown or black. Head slightly broader in the red and white variety.

EYES
Not too big, dark (hazel or brown).

EARS
Set on low, medium-sized, thin, hanging with a fold flat against the head. Set on at eye level in the red and white variety.

BODY
Well-proportioned. Neck very muscular, not too thick, without dewlap. Chest narrow when viewed from the front, as deep as possible.

Rounded ribs. Muscular, slightly arched loin. Straight, well-muscled back. Broad, powerful croup.

LIMBS
Long, well-muscled, wiry, well-boned legs. Small, very firm feet with abundant hair between strong, tight, arched toes.

TAIL
Set on fairly low, medium in length, thick at the base, tapering to a thin point. Carried level with the topline or lower. Beautiful feathering.

COAT
Short on the head and fronts of the legs. Elsewhere, hair is medium in length, flat, neither wavy nor curly. Feathering long and silky at the tops of the ears, long and fine on the backs of the legs.

Beautiful feathering on the abdomen.

COLOR
Mahogany setter: golden mahogany, never smoky. White markings on the chest, throat or toes, small flashings on the forehead or a narrow flare on the nose-bridge or head are tolerated.

SIZE
Red and white:
Dog: 62 to 66 cm (24.5-26 in);
Bitch: 57 to 61 cm (22.5-24 in).
Red:
Dog: 57 to 70 cm (22.5-27.5 in);
Bitch: 54 to 67 cm (21-26.5 in).

Character, special skills and training
The Irish Setter is energetic, spirited and independent. He has a highly developed sense of smell and works rapidly, but his search range is smaller than that of the English Pointer. He is flexible and points firmly. He specializes in woodcock and partridge. Very affectionate, Irish Setters make wonderful pets. They need firm but gentle training.

Care and functions
To live in the city, he needs lots of exercise for his physical and emotional well-being. He requires daily brushing and regular attention to the ears.
· Hunting dog.
· Companion dog.

Group 8

English Cocker Spaniel

Golden Retriever

The Golden Retriever most likely descended from the same strain as the Labrador and was improved through various crosses (of the yellow Flat-coated Retriever from Newfoundland with Scottish water spaniels and other breeds). The breed was stabilized in England in the nineteenth century. Some believe that the Golden Retriever was created by crossing the Bloodhound with yellow dogs from the Caucasus Mountains – Russian Yellow Retrievers – used in Scotland to retrieve wounded game. The Golden Retriever was recognized by the Kennel Club in 1913. In the United States, the Golden is a very popular pet.

Well-balanced. Well-proportionned. Energetic gait.

1

RETRIEVERS

8

COUNTRY OF ORIGIN
Great Britain

OTHER NAME
Flat-coated Golden

Large Breeds between 25 and 45 kg (55-100 lb)

Character, special skills and training
Hardy, vigorous and active, the Golden Retriever has an excellent nose and works both in water and in thickets. He is a tenacious tracker, although less methodical than the Labrador. He excels at retrieving waterfowl and has a remarkable memory. Lacking aggressiveness, he rarely barks and is not a watchdog. Very gentle, intelligent, calm and even-tempered, he makes a wonderful pet. He needs firm but gentle training.

Care and functions
He is not suited to apartment life because he needs lots of exercise. He hates being left alone. He requires brushing once or twice weekly, as well as combing during the shedding season.
· Hunting dog.
· Utility dog: guide dog, wreckage search dog, drug detection dog.
· Companion dog.

HEAD
Well-proportioned, finely chiseled. Broad skull. Pronounced stop. Powerful muzzle. Black nose. Strong jaws.

EYES
Widely spaced, dark brown. Dark edges of eyelids.

EARS
Set on at about eye level, medium in size.

BODY
Powerful, well-balanced. Neck moderately long, cleanly cut and muscular. Chest well let-down. Well-sprung ribs. Short, strong back

LIMBS
Round feet. Muscular, well-boned legs.

TAIL
Set on and carried level with the topline. Reaching to the hock. Does not curl at the tip.

COAT
Flat or wavy with abundant feathering. Dense, waterproof undercoat.

COLOR
Any shade of golden or cream. Should not be red or mahogany. Sparse white hairs allowed only on the chest.

SIZE
Dog: 56 to 61 cm (22-24 in).
Bitch: 51 to 56 cm (20-22 in).

WEIGHT
Dog: 26 to 31.5 kg (57.5-69.5 lb).
Bitch: 25 to 27 kg (55-59.5 lb).

Labrador Retriever

A native of Canada, the Labrador Retriever is thought to be descended from the Saint Jones Dog that inhabited the island of Newfoundland in the eighteenth century. The breed was definitively set in the early twentieth century in England, where it was imported after being crossed with the English Pointer, in particular. The most popular retriever owes his success to his exceptionally even-tempered personality, which explains why he is first and foremost a companion animal.

Powerful structure. Solidly built. Relaxed gait.

RETRIEVERS

COUNTRY OF ORIGIN
Great Britain

OTHER NAME
Saint Jones Dog

Large Breeds between 25 and 45 kg (55-100 lb)

1

8

HEAD
Broad and round. Broad skull. Pronounced stop. Powerful jaws. Wide nose.

EYES
Medium-sized, brown or hazel.

EARS
Set fairly far back, neither large nor heavy, falling against the head.

BODY
Powerful, rounded build. Powerful, cleanly cut neck. Chest broad, well let-down with well-sprung ribs. Short, broad, powerful loin.

LIMBS
Round, compact feet. Muscular, well-boned legs.

TAIL
Very thick at the base, tapering toward the tip. Medium in length with no feathering but completely covered with short, thick, dense hair, giving it a rounded, "otter tail" appearance. May be carried gaily but must not curve over the back.

COAT
Short and dense, without waves or feathering. Weather-resistant undercoat.

COLOR
Solid black, yellow or brown (liver-chocolate). Yellow ranging from pale cream to reddish-brown (fox red). A small white spot on the chest is allowed.

SIZE
Dog: 56 to 57 cm (22-22,5 in).
Bitch: 54 to 56 cm (21-22 in).

WEIGHT
25 to 30 kg (55-66 lb).

Character, special skills and training
This king of retrievers is highly active, agile, confident and tenacious. Sometimes called the "pointer of retrievers", he has a remarkably keen nose and is an excellent swimmer. He can retrieve all sorts of game on land and in the water. With his vast visual memory, he can recall the locations of several fallen birds. A tenacious tracker, he is a good bloodhound on the trail of wounded large game. Very even-tempered and never aggressive, he has a delightful personality that makes him a wonderful pet. He needs firm and gentle training.

Care and functions
He does not like being left alone. He needs lots of exercise to curb his restlessness. He must be brushed two to three times per week and combed during shedding season.
· Hunting dog.
· Utility dog: canine assistant (guide dog), drug detection dog.
· Companion dog.

Curly-coated Retriever

The Curly-coated Retriever, the oldest of the English retrievers, is believed to be descended from a cross between the Newfoundland and the Irish Water Spaniel. The Poodle and the Labrador may also have contributed to the breed. He was shown for the first time in 1860. A breed club was founded in 1896 and the standard was established in 1913. In the mid-nineteenth century in England, he was more popular as a pet than as a hunting dog. Today, the breed is very limited in number except in a few countries, including New Zealand.

1

RETRIEVERS

COUNTRY OF ORIGIN
Great Britain

8

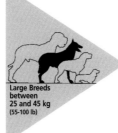

Large Breeds
between
25 and 45 kg
(55-100 lb)

Character, special skills and training
Tough, strong, active and courageous, the Curly-coated retriever has great endurance and a very subtle nose. He is an excellent swimmer and a very good retriever. He hunts duck in swampland. He is calm, poised and affectionate but very independent. He needs firm but patient and gentle training.

Care and functions
He is not suited to city life because he needs lots of exercise. He does not like being confined or left alone. He must be brushed twice weekly.
· Hunting dog.

HEAD
Long. Skull flat and long. Strong jaws. Wide nostrils. Nose black or brown (liver). Lips not pendulous.

EYES
Large. Black or dark brown.

EARS
Set on low, small, lying flat against the head, covered with short curls of hair.

BODY
Rectangular build. Neck moderately long, without dewlap. Chest well let-down. Well-sprung ribs. Short loin.

LIMBS
Strong, muscular legs. Round, compact feet.

TAIL
Moderately short, carried straight, covered with curly hair, tapering toward the tip, never carried gaily or curled.

COAT
A mass of crisp, tight curls covering entire body.

COLOR
Black or brown (liver).

SIZE
Dog: 68.5 cm (27 in).
Bitch: 63.5 cm (25 in).

WEIGHT
30 to 35 kg (66-77.5 lb).

Flat-coated Retriever

Of English origin, the Flat-coated Retriever existed by the early nineteenth century as the Wavy-coated Retriever. The Irish Setter, the Newfoundland and the English Pointer are thought to have contributed to the breed; breeders also added a splash of Labrador blood. The Flat-coated Retriever was first shown in 1860. He was commonly used as a utility dog during World War I and was recognized by the FCI in 1935.

Powerful but not heavy. Elegant. Strong. Relaxed, easy gait.

RETRIEVERS

COUNTRY OF ORIGIN
Great Britain

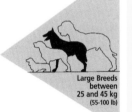

Large Breeds between 25 and 45 kg (55-100 lb)

8

HEAD
Long. Flat, moderately broad skull. Slight stop. Long, strong jaws.

EYES
Medium-sized, dark brown or hazel. Round eyes are not tolerated.

EARS
Small, lying flat against the head.

BODY
Short and rounded. Neck without dewlap. Chest well let-down, fairly broad. Short, angular loin.

LIMBS
Round, strong feet with tight toes. Muscular, well-boned legs.

TAIL
Short, straight, well set-on, carried gaily but never much higher than the topline.

COAT
Dense, moderately fine, as flat as possible. Abundant feathering on the legs and tail.

COLOR
Solid black or brown (liver).

SIZE
Dog: 58 to 61 cm (23-24 in).
Bitch: 56 to 59 cm (22-23 in).

WEIGHT
Dog: 27 to 36 kg (59.5-79.5 lb).
Bitch: 25 to 32 kg (55-70.5 lb).

Character, special skills and training
Very hardy, tough, lively, swift and energetic, the Flat-coated Retriever could be called the "Formula 1 of retrievers". He has exceptional drive and a very subtle nose and he can swim like an otter. Apart from hunting in fields and woods, he specializes in tracking and retrieving waterfowl. Intelligent, affectionate, merry, gentle and good-natured, he makes a good pet. He needs gentle but firm training.

Care and functions
He is not a city dweller. He needs space and exercise, as well as brushing twice weekly and regular attention to the ears.
· Hunting dog.
· Utility dog: guide dog, drug detection dog.
· Companion dog.

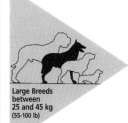

Chesapeake Bay Retriever

This breed was developed in the northeastern United States, in the Chesapeake Bay region of Maryland, where he is used for his exceptional hunting skill in swampland. He is thought to have been developed by crossing the canine survivors of a shipwreck off the coast of Maryland in 1807 with the Curly-coated Retriever, the Flat-coated Retriever, the Otterhound, the Irish Setter and Irish water dogs. He was first shown in Baltimore in 1876. The first standard was written in 1890 and a breed club was founded in 1918. He is rare in Europe, despite being a fairly old breed.

Powerful. Well-proportionned.

1

RETRIEVERS

COUNTRY OF ORIGIN
United States

8

Large Breeds
between
25 and 45 kg
(55-100 lb)

Character, special skills and training
Tough, very hardy, tireless, courageous and lively, the Chesapeake Bay Retriever is a remarkable swimmer, even in icy waters. He is used on duck. Calm and devoted to his owner, he is rough-mannered but never brutal. He makes a good watchdog. He needs very firm training.

Care and functions
He needs space and lots of exercise, as well as regular brushing.
· Hunting dog.

HEAD
Broad and round. Wide, domed skull. Moderate stop. Short, pointed muzzle. Lips thin, not pendulous.

EYES
Medium-sized, very pale yellowish.

EARS
Small, hanging loosely.

BODY
Medium in length (not cobby). Neck medium in length. Deep, broad chest. Tuck-up.

LIMBS
Strong, muscular, well-boned legs. Long feet with tight toes.

TAIL
Medium in length, 27 to 37 cm (10.5-14.5 in) long. Fairly thick at the base. Feathering allowed.

COAT
Thick, short, under 3.7 cm (1,5 in) long. Very short on the foreface and legs. Top-coat and oily undercoat are virtually waterproof.

COLOR
From dark brown to pale tan or deadgrass ranging from tan to straw. Small white spots on the chest and toes are allowed.

SIZE
Dog: 58 to 66 cm (23-26 in).
Bitch: 53 to 61 cm (21-24 in).

WEIGHT
Dog: 29 to 34 kg (64-75 lb)
Bitch: 25 to 29 kg (55-64 lb).

Nova Scotia Duck Tolling Retriever

The smallest of the retrievers comes from the Canadian province of Nova Scotia. He may have been developed by crossing the Chesapeake Bay Retriever with the Golden Retriever. With his fox-like appearance, he tricks curious ducks by luring them toward hunters. The breed was recognized by the FCI in 1982.

Powerful. Compact.

1

RETRIEVERS

COUNTRY OF ORIGIN
Canada

Medium Breeds
between
10 and 25 kg
(20-55 lb)

8

HEAD
Broad. Slightly domed skull. Pronounced stop. Brown nose.

EYES
Almond-shaped, widely spaced, amber or brown.

EARS
Set on high, triangular.

BODY
Strong. Deep chest.

LIMBS
Powerful, solidly boned legs

TAIL
Well-feathered.

COAT
Medium in length, somewhat wavy, slightly oily, water-proof. Undercoat. Feathering on the backs of the legs.

COLOR
Rust with white markings on the chest, feet, tip of the tail and sometimes the foreface.

SIZE
Dog: 49 to 55 cm (19-21.5 in).

Bitch: 43 to 49 cm (17-19.5 in).

WEIGHT
Approx. 25 kg (55 lb).

Character, special skills and training
This very lively, active swimmer with great endurance excels at retrieving duck. Because he is strong-willed and difficult to dis-cipline, he needs rigorous training.

Care and functions
He needs space and exercise for his well-being, as well as regular brushing and combing.
· Hunting dog.

German Spaniel

Known in German as the Wachtelhund, meaning "quail dog", because of his favorite game, the German Spaniel was developed around 1890 in Germany by the breeder F. Roberth. Several breeds were used in creating this spaniel, particularly an old German breed called the Stöber and various longhaired water dogs. The German Spaniel is not well-known outside his native land.

Very long body. Small in size.

2

FLUSHING DOGS

8

COUNTRY OF ORIGIN
Germany

ORIGINAL NAMES
Wachtelhund
Deutscher Wachtelhund

OTHER NAME
German Quail Dog

Medium Breeds
between
10 and 25 kg
(20-55 lb)

Character, special skills and training
Tough and courageous, the German Spaniel can work on all kinds of terrain, mainly woods and swampland. This active tracker and flusher uses his voice on the trail and hunts all small game but also pests (fox) and large game. He is a good retriever as well as a bloodhound able to track wounded game. He is affectionate and makes a good pet. He needs firm training.

Care and functions
He needs space and exercise, as well as daily brushing and regular attention to the ears.
· Hunting dog.
· Companion dog.

HEAD
Chiseled. Skull flat, not too broad. Very slight stop. Curved nosebridge. Muzzle equal in length to the skull. Thin lips. Large, brown nose.

EYES
Medium-sized, almond-shaped, slanting, preferably dark brown.

EARS
Set on high, flat, not curled, not too long or thick, hanging just behind the eyes. Covered with long, often curly hair.

BODY
Long. Solid neck without dewlap. High, long withers. Chest deep, well let-down. Short, broad, deep loin. Moderate tuck-up. Very short, solid back. Flat, long croup.

LIMBS
Powerful, well-muscled, well-boned legs. Spoon-shaped feet with very tight toes.

TAIL
Set on high, carried straight or hanging down, wagged energetically in the presence of game. Docked by one-third its length. Well-feathered.

COAT
Long, tough, dense, wavy. Slightly curly (like Astrakhan lamb's wool) or flat. Often curly on the neck, ears and croup. Short on the head. Backs of the legs well-feathered.

COLOR
- Solid dark brown with white spots on the chest and toes or with tan markings (red to yellow) above the eyes and on the muzzle, legs and around the anus. Whole-colored in shades of fox red or fawn red.
- Roan-brown: roan background (white and brown hairs closely mixed), often with a brown head and brown blotches or a brown mantle covering the entire body.
- Spotted brown and white (with a white background).
- Harlequin (white background with brown spots and flecks and brown blotches). Tricolor (roan, spotted or harlequin with tan markings as in the solid-colored variety).

SIZE
Dog: 48 to 54 cm (19-21.3 in).
Bitch: 45 to 51 cm (17.5-20 in).

WEIGHT
Approx. 20 kg (44 lb).

Clumber Spaniel

The Clumber Spaniel, the largest of the spaniels, is thought to be of French origin. In the eighteenth century, the Duke of Noailles apparently gave a pair of these dogs to the Duke of Newcastle, who lived in the Clumber Park castle near Nottingham. Uncommon in England, the breed is quite rare in Europe.

Imposing. Strong. Powerful. Well proportioned. The heaviest of the English hunting spaniels. Rolling gait.

FLUSHING DOGS

2

COUNTRY OF ORIGIN
Great Britain

8

Large Breeds
between
25 and 45 kg
(55-100 lb)

HEAD
Angular, massive. Broad skull. Pronounced occipital peak. Heavy brow bones. Strongly pronounced stop. Heavy, angular muzzle. Strong jaws.

EYES
Dark amber. Conjunctiva slightly visible.

EARS
Large, shaped like grape leaves, hanging slightly forward. Feathering.

BODY
Massive, long, close to the ground. Thick, powerful neck. Chest well let-down. Well-sprung ribs. Flanks well let-down. Very powerful

hindquarters. Muscular loin. Straight, long, broad back.

LIMBS
Short, very powerful, well-boned legs. Large, round feet.

TAIL
Set on low, carried level with the topline. Well-feathered.

COAT
Thick, dense, silky and straight. Feathering on the legs and chest.

COLOR
White with lemon markings, orange is allowed. Light markings on the head and flecks on the muzzle.

SIZE
Dog: approx. 48 cm (19 in).
Bitch: approx. 46 cm (18 in).

WEIGHT
Ideal:
Dog: 34 kg (75 lb),
Bitch: 29.5 kg (65 lb).

Character, special skills and training
The Clumber Spaniel has an excellent nose and his search is slow, silent and limited in range but persistent. He is a good flusher of rabbit, woodcock and pheasant. He is a good retriever, fearing neither brambles nor water. In England he is used in packs on pheasant hunts. He is less friendly than other spaniels but calm, playful and kind, making him a good pet. He has no aggressive tendencies. He needs firm, patient training.

Care and functions
Preferably, he should live in the country. He needs space and exercise, as well as frequent brushing and regular attention to the ears.
· Hunting dog.
· Companion dog.

American Cocker Spaniel

The American Cocker Spaniel is a direct descendent of the English Cocker Spaniel. In 1882 he was introduced to the United States, where breeders wanted to develop a small companion dog with a marvelous coat. Recognized by the American Kennel Club in 1946, the American Cocker Spaniel has become the most popular dog in the US.

2

FLUSHING DOGS

COUNTRY OF ORIGIN
United States

8

OTHER NAMES
Cocker Spaniel
Cocker

Medium Breeds
between
10 and 25 kg
(20-55 lb)

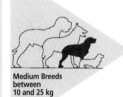

Character, special skills and training
Solid, fast, easygoing, even-tempered and merry, the American Cocker Spaniel is a good companion. He is a show dog and a pet, rather than a hunting dog. A bit stubborn, he needs firm training.

Care and functions
He can adapt to apartment life, as long as he is taken on daily walks. He requires daily brushing and combing, bimonthly bathing and monthly grooming. His ears need regular attention.
· Companion dog.

HEAD
Finely chiseled. Rounded skull. Clearly pronounced brow bones. Pronounced stop. Broad, high muzzle. Black or brown nose, depending on coat color.

EYES
Slightly almond-shaped, brown, as dark as possible, with an irresistible pleading expression.

EARS
Long, thin, well-feathered.

BODY
Short, compact. Fairly long, muscular neck without dewlap. High, broad chest. Well-sprung ribs. Strong back. Broad croup.

LIMBS
Strong legs. Compact, large, round feet with tough pads.

TAIL
Set on and carried level with the topline or slightly higher. Docked. Wagging in action.

COAT
Short and fine on the head. Medium in length on the body. Ears, chest, abdomen and legs well-feathered. Hair is silky, flat or slightly wavy. Undercoat.

COLOR
Solid black. Black with tan tips. A small amount of white on the chest and/or throat is allowed. Any solid color other than black. Particolor: two or more well-broken, well-distributed colors, one of which must be white. Roans are classified as particolors. Tan markings range from the lightest cream to the darkest red and should cover no more than 10% of the coat. Tan markings above each eye, on the sides of the muzzle and cheeks, on the underside of the ears, on all feet and/or legs, on the chest and under the tail.

SIZE
Dog: 36 to 39 cm (14-15.5 in).
Bitch: 34 to 36 cm (13.5-14 in).

WEIGHT
10 to 13 kg (22-28.5 lb).

English Cocker Spaniel

The English Cocker Spaniel is descended from the spaniel that inhabited Great Britain since the fourteenth century and was used for netting game birds ("spaniel" comes from the word espainholz, derived from the Old French term epaignir, meaning "to lie down", which is exactly what setters did in order not to disturb the hunter as he threw his net over game). The English Cocker Spaniel was developed by British breeders. In the eighteenth century, he was used on woodcock ("cocking"). A splash of English toy spaniel was added and the new breed was officially recognized in 1883. He was first imported to France and the United States at about the same time. The Spaniel Club was founded in 1898. Today, this very popular breed (the best known and most common of the spaniels) is considered above all as a model pet.

Strong. Elegant. Well-balanced. Compact overall. Clean gait.

2

8

FLUSHING DOGS

Medium Breeds between 10 and 25 kg (20-55 lb)

COUNTRY OF ORIGIN
Great Britain

OTHER NAMES
Cocker Spaniel
Cocker

Character, special skills and training
Vigorous, very active, tenacious and lively, the English Cocker is a great hunter of fowl and ground game on rugged terrain. He does not fear brambles. With his very keen sense of smell, he tracks ten or fifteen meters away from the hunter. His search is hard-driving. After pointing, he snaps at any game and uses his voice as he flushes it. He has been used widely on rabbit. He is a good retriever but sometimes has difficulty carrying a duck in his mouth in deep water. Merry, playful, exuberant and bursting with life, he is strong-willed and independent but also affectionate and gentle. He is a charming pet.

Care and functions
He can live in an apartment, but long, daily walks are necessary. He requires brushing and combing twice weekly and grooming twice or three times per year. His ears must be checked regularly.
· Hunting dog.
· Companion dog.

HEAD
Long. Well-developed, chiseled skull. Pronounced stop. Very angular muzzle. Strong jaws. Wide nose.

EYES
Brown or hazel, depending on coat color.

EARS
Set on low, lobe-shaped, thin. Long, straight, silky feathering.

BODY
Stocky, square build. Neck moderately long, muscular, without dewlap. Well-developed chest. Well-sprung ribs. Short, broad loin. Broad, well-muscled croup.

LIMBS
Short, well-boned legs. Round, firm feet with thick pads.

TAIL
Set on low, carried level to the ground, never raised. Usually docked. Constant wagging of the tail in action is typical.

COAT
Flat, silky, never wirehaired or wavy, not too thick and never curly. Feathering on the legs and body.

COLOR
Various colors. In the whole-colored variety, white is allowed only on the chest.

SIZE
Dog: 39 to 41 cm (15.5-16 in).
Bitch: 38 to 39 cm (15-15.5 in).

WEIGHT
12 to 14.5 kg (26.5-32 lb).

Field Spaniel

The Field Spaniel has the same origins as the English Cocker Spaniel but is larger, falling midway between the English Cocker Spaniel and the English Springer Spaniel in size. The Sussex Spaniel, the English Springer Spaniel, the English Cocker Spaniel and perhaps even the Basset Hound were used in developing the breed, which is very rare.

Dignified. Proud. Elegant. Well-proportioned. Long strides.

2

FLUSHING DOGS

8

COUNTRY OF ORIGIN
Great Britain

Medium Breeds between 10 and 25 kg (20-55 lb)

Character, special skills and training

Very hardy, tough, active, agile and powerful but not heavy like the Clumber Spaniel, the Field Spaniel is effective on all types of terrain, from water to thickets. He hunts in a very determined, methodical manner, never losing contact with his owner. After locating game, he flushes it into the air. He is a good retriever, bringing in even large specimens. He is very vigilant and mistrusting of strangers, but he rarely barks. Intelligent, even-tempered and affectionate, he is one of the most delightful spaniels. He needs patient, flexible training.

Care and functions

He is entirely unsuited to city life. If he must live in the city, he will need lots of exercise for his well-being. He also needs brushing once or twice weekly, as well as regular attention to the ears.
· Hunting dog.
· Companion dog.

HEAD
Dignified, finely chiseled, cleanly cut below the eyes. Pronounced occipital peak. Moderate stop. Long, cleanly cut muzzle. Strong jaws. Well-developed nose.

EYES
Almond-shaped. Dark hazel.

EARS
Set on low. Moderately long and wide, well-feathered.

BODY
Long. Long, strong, muscular neck. High, well-developed chest. Moderately well-sprung ribs. Strong, straight, muscular loin. Strong hindquarters. Strong, straight, muscular back.

LIMBS
Short, muscular legs. Round, tight feet with strong pads.

TAIL
Set on low, never carried above the topline. Nicely feathered. Usually docked by one-third.

COAT
Long, flat, glossy, silky. Never curly, short or hard. Dense and weather-resistant. Abundant feathering on the chest, the underside of the body and the backs of the legs.

COLOR
Solid black, brown (liver) or roan or one of these colors with tan markings.

SIZE
Approx. 45 cm (17.5 in).

WEIGHT
18 to 25 kg (39.5-55 lb).

Small Dutch Waterfowl Dog

This small spaniel of a fairly old Dutch breed was recognized in 1966. In Dutch, his name means "Kooiker's dog", a kooiker being the person in charge of the lures and decoys on a waterfowl hunt. A yearly "Kooikerhondje Day" has helped popularize this hunting breed.

Gait: Well-balanced and springy.

2

FLUSHING DOGS

COUNTRY OF ORIGIN
The Netherlands

ORIGINAL NAME
Kooikerhondje

OTHER NAME
Kooiker Dog

8

Medium Breeds between 10 and 25 kg (20-55 lb)

HEAD
Carried high. Fairly broad, moderately domed skull. Stop not very pronounced. Muzzle the same length as the skull. Lips not pendulous.

EYES
Almond-shaped, dark brown.

EARS
Medium-sized, hanging flat against the cheeks, covered with long hair.

BODY
Square build. Straight, well-muscled neck. Chest well let-down with moderately well-sprung ribs. Solid back.

LIMBS
Small feet with tight toes.

TAIL
Carried level to the ground or somewhat merrily, never curled. Well-feathered.

COAT
Medium in length, smooth, slightly wavy, not curly or too fine. Thick undercoat.

COLOR
Patches ranging from orange to red distributed over a white background such that the color is dominant. Black with white patches and tricolor patterns are not allowed.

SIZE
35 to 40 cm (14-16 in).

WEIGHT
10 to 15 kg (22-33 lb).

Character, special skills and training
This hardy dog can withstand cold and damp weather. With his very keen nose, he is a good flusher and retriever of waterfowl. Affectionate and attentive, he makes a good pet. He needs firm but gentle training.

Care and functions
He needs space and lots of exercise, as well as daily brushing.
· Hunting dog.

English Spriŋger Spaniel

The English Springer Spaniel is one of the oldest hunting dog breeds. His ancestors are thought to be the spaniel of the Middle Ages, as well as the Norfolk Spaniel. British breeders made numerous crosses, particularly with the old Water Spaniel. With a head similar to that of the French Spaniel, the English Springer is the father of all spaniels except the Clumber Spaniel. The breed was officially recognized in 1902 and became the most popular hunting dog in the British Isles.

Well-balanced. Compact. Strong. The "thoroughbred" of spaniels. Balanced, easy, clean gate. He can move at an ambling pace.

2

FLUSHING DOGS

COUNTRY OF ORIGIN
Great Britain

8

Medium Breeds between 10 and 25 kg (20-55 lb)

Rounded, compact feet with tough pads.

TAIL
Set on low, never carried higher than the topline. Well-feathered. Usually docked.

COAT
Dense, straight, weather-resistant, never harsh. Feathering on the ears, body and legs.

COLOR
Liver and white, black and white, or one of these combinations with tan markings.

SIZE
Approx. 51 cm (20 in).

WEIGHT
Approx. 22.5 kg (50 lb).

HEAD
Long. Skull fairly broad, slightly domed. Pronounced stop. Broad, high muzzle. Strong jaws. Flat cheeks. Flews well let-down.

EYES
Almond-shaped, dark.

EARS
Set on at eye level, fairly long, hanging close to the head. Nice feathering.

BODY
Rectangular build. Neck strong and muscular, without dewlap. Well let-down, well-developed chest. Well-sprung ribs. Muscular, strong loin.

LIMBS
Strong, well-boned legs.

Character, special skills and training
This hardy, tough, vigorous, energetic, swift dog with a keen nose fears neither thickets nor wet ground. He is stronger and more driven than the English Cocker Spaniel. He tracks actively and persistently, snapping vigorously at game. He lunges into thickets, causing game to spring out in a panic (as the name suggests, a "springer" is a dog who lunges and flushes game). The English Springer Spaniel excels on rabbit, pheasant, woodcock, and waterfowl. He is also a remarkable retriever, especially in the water. A bit rambunctious and strong-tempered, he needs firm training. He can be a good pet, but he's no lap dog!

Care and functions
He is not at all suited to apartment life. He needs space and lots of exercise, as well as brushing twice weekly and regular checking of the ears.
· Hunting dog.

Welsh Springer Spaniel

This Welsh dog has very distant origins. For a long time, the English Springer and the Welsh Springer were one and the same. Not until the early twentieth century was a distinction made between the two breeds. Some believe the Welsh Springer Spaniel is the product of a cross between the English Springer and the Clumber Spaniel. Note, however, that the Welsh Springer, whose head is similar to that of the Brittany Spaniel, is more lightweight than the English Springer. The Welsh Springer is rare.

Well-balanced. Compact. Smooth, powerful gait.

2

FLUSHING DOGS

COUNTRY OF ORIGIN
Great Britain

OTHER NAME
Welsh Springer

8

Medium Breeds
between
10 and 25 kg
(20-55 lb)

HEAD
Well-chiseled, fairly long. Slightly domed skull. Pronounced stop. Muzzle of medium length, straight, fairly angular. Brown or dark brown nose. Strong jaws.

EYES
Medium-sized, hazel or dark in color.

EARS
Set on fairly low, hanging close to cheeks.

BODY
Strong, not long. Neck long, muscular, without dewlap. Well-sprung ribs. Short back.

Muscular, slightly clean-flanked loin.

LIMBS
Moderately long, well-boned legs. Round feet with thick pads.

TAIL
Set on low, never carried above the topline. Usually docked.

COAT
Straight and flat, silky, dense, never hard or wavy. Light feathering on the legs, ears and tail.

COLOR
Bright red and white. No other colors allowed.

SIZE
Dog: approx. 48 cm (19 in).
Bitch: approx. 46 cm (18 in).

WEIGHT
17 to 20 kg (37.5-44 lb).

Character, special skills and training
Tough, lively, active, fast and very enthusiastic, this high-energy dog has a very keen nose and is more comfortable in the water than the English Springer but less of a flusher. He has a medium search range, covering terrain thoroughly and methodically. He uses his voice on the trail of rabbit and hare. He also excels on woodcock. Merry and kind but strong-willed and stubborn, he is not at all aggressive and makes a fairly good pet. He needs firm but gentle training.

Care and functions
He is not suited to apartment life. He needs space and lots of exercise, as well as brushing twice weekly and regular checking of the ears.
· Hunting dog.

Sussex Spaniel

The Sussex Spaniel was created in the nineteenth century in Sussex. He is the product of crosses between various spaniels, including the English Springer and later the Clumber Spaniel. The Sussex Spaniel is smaller and less stocky than the Clumber Spaniel. Shown for the first time in London in 1862, the breed was officially recognized in 1895. He is very rare in France, where he is not commonly used in hunting. The survival of the Sussex Spaniel appears threatened.

Massive. Solidly built. Relaxed gait with a characteristic roll.

2

FLUSHING DOGS

COUNTRY OF ORIGIN
Great Britain

8

Medium Breeds between 10 and 25 kg (20-55 lb)

Character, special skills and training
Tough, energetic, active and tenacious, this keen-nosed dog tracks calmly and slowly, using his voice at the sight of fleeing game. He is the most vocal of all the spaniels. He hunts pheasant and partridge, in particular. His calmness and good nature make him an affectionate pet. He needs gentle training.

Care and functions
He needs space and exercise, as well as daily brushing and combing and regular checking of the ears.
· Hunting dog.
· Companion dog.

HEAD
Large. Broad, slightly domed skull. Pronounced stop. Brown nose. Strong jaws.

EYES
Fairly large, hazel.

EARS
Set on fairly low, fairly large, thick, hanging against the head.

BODY
Massive, long. Long, strong neck with slight dewlap. Chest well let-down and well-developed. Broad, muscular back. Broad, thick loin.

LIMBS
Short, muscular, well-boned legs. Round feet.

TAIL
Set on low, never carried above the topline. Usually docked to 12 to 17 cm (4.5-6.5 in) in length. No feathering.

COAT
Abundant, flat. Moderate feathering on the legs. Very dense undercoat.

COLOR
Rich, golden brown (liver) to golden at the tips. Golden color is dominant.

SIZE
38 to 41 cm (15-16 in).

WEIGHT
Approx. 22 kg (48.5 lb).

Barbet

The Barbet has existed in Europe since the Middle Ages, when he was known simply as the Waterdog. Mentioned in sixteenth century writings and represented in several drawings from the same period, the breed was used on duck and swan. Buffon mentioned the breed in Natural History and Spallanzani used it to conduct the first successful artificial insemination in 1779. The Barbet nearly went extinct in the late nineteenth century, when he was used for hunting only by poachers and country folk. He may be considered the ancestor of all breeds with long, woolly or curly hair (including bichons and the Poodle) and a direct cousin to sheepdogs like the Briard, with whom he has many similarities. The standard for the Barbet was updated in 1986. Still fairly rare, his survival is threatened.

Mesomorph. Thick skin.

3

WATER DOGS

COUNTRY OF ORIGIN
France

OTHER NAME
Barbillot

8

Medium Breeds
between
10 and 25 kg
(20-55 lb)

HEAD
Round. Broad, round skull. Pronounced stop. Short nosebridge. Very angular muzzle. Thick, pigmented lips.

EYES
Round, preferably dark brown. Hidden by hair on the skull and nosebridge.

EARS
Set on low, long, flat, furnished with long hair forming tufts.

BODY
Powerful. Strong, short neck. Broad, well-developed chest.

Curved ribs. Short, flat, arched loin. Very slightly domed back. Rounded croup.

LIMBS
Strong, muscular, well-boned legs. Round, wide feet.

TAIL
Set on low, raised but not as high as the topline, slightly hooked at the tip.

COAT
Long, woolly, wavy, sometimes curly, forming tufts. This thick fleece is good protection from cold and damp weather. Hair on head should hang down to the

nosebridge, hiding the eyes. Long beard, bushy mustache.

COLOR
Black, grey, brown, fawn, sable, or white with no markings or with a certain degree of patching. All shades of fawn and sable are allowed.

SIZE
Dog: at least 54 cm (21 in). Bitch: at least 50 cm (20 in).

WEIGHT
20 to 25 kg (44-55 lb).

Character, special skills and training
Very powerful, tough and vigorous, the Barbet is resistant to cold and dampness. He loves the water and swims very well. With a good nose and slow gait, he is used by waterfowl hunters. He is a very good retriever and has also been employed as a sheepdog to guide herds. Even-tempered, gentle and never aggressive, he is an affectionate pet.

Care and functions
He can live in the city but must not be confined alone for long periods. He needs regular walks. Because of his thick coat, he does not tolerate heat well. Without regular dematting, his hair can become tangled.
· Hunting dog.
· Companion dog.

American Water Spaniel

This fairly recent breed was developed in Wisconsin. He is thought to be descended from the Irish Water Dog but is smaller. The Curly-coated Retriever and the Field Spaniel were used in developing the breed. The American Water Spaniel was recognized by the American Kennel Club in 1940.

3

WATER DOGS

COUNTRY OF ORIGIN
United States

8

Solidly built. Well-balanced. Distinguished.

Medium Breeds
between
10 and 25 kg
(20-55 lb)

Character, special skills and training
Tough and energetic, this dog has great endurance and is an enthusiastic hunter of game birds (quail, duck, pheasant, etc.). He is a very good swimmer and is also used as a retriever. He is an affectionate pet.

Care and functions
He needs space and lots of exercise, as well as daily combing and brushing.
· Hunting dog.
· Companion dog.

HEAD
Broad. Skull fairly broad. Stop not very pronounced. Angular muzzle. Nose black or dark brown. Tight-lipped.

EYES
Medium-sized, ranging from light yellowish brown to hazel brown or dark, depending on coat color.

EARS
Long, wide.

BODY
Stocky, slightly longer than it is tall. Round, strong, muscular neck without dewlap.

Chest well-developed, not too broad. Well-sprung ribs. No tuck-up. Solid loin.

LIMBS
Muscular, well-boned legs. Feet have tight toes.

TAIL
Moderately long. Carried level with the back. Moderate feathering.

COAT
From uniform waves to tight curls. The degree of waviness and curliness may vary over the body. Undercoat. Moderate feathering on the legs.

COLOR
Solid liver, brown, or dark chocolate. Minimal white markings on the toes and chest are allowed.

SIZE
36 to 46 cm (14-18 in).

WEIGHT
Dog: 13.5 to 20.5 kg (30-45 in).
Bitch: 11.5 to 18 kg (25.5-39.5 lb).

Spanish Water Dog

His origins are thought to match those of the old Barbet. The Spanish Water Dog has been found on the Iberian Peninsula for centuries. He is common especially in Andalusia, where he is used as a sheepdog. He is also known as the Turkish Dog. Currently, he is not commonly bred.

Well-balanced. Fairly long-backed. Supple, thin, sometimes pigmented skin. Preferred gait: trot. Short, springy gallop.

Medium Breeds between 10 and 25 kg (20-55 lb)

3

WATER DOGS

COUNTRY OF ORIGIN
Spain

ORIGINAL NAME
Perro de Agua Español

OTHER NAME
Turkish Dog

8

HEAD
Powerful. Flat skull. Stop not very pronounced. Nose color matches that of the coat.

EYES
Slightly slanted, ranging from hazel to brown.

EARS
Triangular and pendulous.

BODY
Stocky. Short, well-muscled neck without dewlap. Withers not very pronounced. Chest broad, well let-down. Well-sprung ribs. Slight tuck-up. Slightly sloping croup. Straight, powerful back.

LIMBS
Solid legs. Rounded feet with tight toes.

TAIL
Docked to the second to fourth caudal vertebra. Sometimes short at birth.

COAT
Always curly with a woolly texture. Wavy or curly when short. May form thick cords when long.

COLOR
Solid color: a shade of white, black, or brown. Added hairs: any shade of white

and black or white and brown (patching).

SIZE
Dog: 40 to 50 cm 15.5-19.5 in).
Bitch: 38 to 45 cm (15-17.5 in).

WEIGHT
Dog: 16 to 20 kg (35-44 lb).
Bitch: 12 to 16 kg (26.5-35 lb).

· Hunting dog.
· Sheepdog.
· Companion dog.

Character, special skills and training
This tough, courageous dog with a well-developed sense of smell is a great aid to fishermen and waterfowl hunters. Merry and even-tempered, he is a good pet.

Care and functions
He needs space and exercise, as well as regular brushing.

Frisian Water Dog

A native to the Dutch Frisian Islands, the Frisian Water Dog has been known for centuries and is thought to be descended from the Otterhound. This water dog (Wetterhoun) was officially recognized in 1942.

Solidly built. Compact. Skin without folds.

3

WATER DOGS

8

COUNTRY OF ORIGIN
The Netherlands

ORIGINAL NAME
Wetterhoun

OTHER NAMES
Frisian Spaniel
Dutch Water Dog

Medium Breeds
between
10 and 25 kg
(20-55 lb)

Character, special skills and training
Tough, hardy and solid, the Frisian Water Dog is a fine hunter of water game, especially otter. However, because the otter is a protected species in many countries, the Frisian Water Dog is used for all types of work. Reserved toward strangers and slightly aggressive, he makes a good watchdog. Calm but stubborn, he needs firm training.

Care and functions
He is not a city dog. He needs space and lots exercise, as well as regular brushing and combing.
· Hunting dog.
· Companion dog.

HEAD
Strong, powerful, cleanly cut. Broad, slightly domed skull. Stop not very pronounced. Straight nose-bridge. Strong muzzle. Nose well-developed, black or brown, depending on coat color. Lips not pendulous.

EYES
Medium-sized, oval, slightly slanted. Dark brown or brown, depending on coat color.

EARS
Set on fairly low. Medium in length, carried against the head, not twisted. Covered with curly hair that is fairly long at the base.

BODY
Very sturdy. Square build. Neck short, strong, without dewlap. Broad chest. Well-sprung ribs. Strong loin. Moderate tuck-up. Short, straight back. Fairly level croup.

LIMBS
Strong legs. Round feet with thick pads.

TAIL
Long and curled, carried above the croup or on the side.

COAT
Except for the head and legs, the entire body is covered with thick curls of stiff, thick hair that is fairly harsh and oily to the touch.

COLOR
Solid black or brown, black with white spots, or brown with white spots. A combination coat and patches are allowed.

SIZE
Ideal
Dog: 59 cm (23 in).
Bitch: 55 cm (22 in).

WEIGHT
Approx. 25 kg (55 lb).

Irish Water Spaniel

The Irish Water Spaniel, the largest of the spaniels, was developed in the nineteenth century from the Poodle, the Irish Setter and perhaps the Barbet. Some believe he is a close cousin to the Portuguese Water Dog. The Irish Water Spaniel was first shown in 1862 in Birmingham. The first club was founded in 1890. After a fruitful period between the two World Wars when he was exported to France, the United States and Canada, he is now rare and in danger of extinction.

Solidly built.

3

WATER DOGS

COUNTRY OF ORIGIN
Great Britain

8

Medium Breeds between 10 and 25 kg (20-55 lb)

HEAD
Large but long. Domed skull covered with long curls forming a topknot. Gradual stop. Long, strong, angular muzzle. Dark liver nose.

EYES
Medium to dark brown.

EARS
Set on low, very long, hanging against the cheeks, covered with long curls.

BODY
Compact. Sturdy, fairly long neck. Broad chest. Ribs set well back. Short, broad back. Deep, broad loin.

LIMBS
Well-boned legs. Large, nearly round feet.

TAIL
Set on low, short, straight, thick at the base and tapering toward the tip. Carried straight, below the topline. A well-defined band extending 8 to 10 cm (3-4 in) from the base must be covered with tight curls. The rest of the tail is hairless or covered with fine, straight hair.

COAT
Thick, tight, crisp curls. Oily hair. Feathering on the legs.

COLOR
Dark liver with a bluish or velvety cast specific to the breed and sometimes called "puce".

SIZE
Dog: 53 to 58 cm (21-23 in).
Bitch: 51 to 56 cm (20-22 in).

WEIGHT
22 to 26 kg (28.5-57.5 lb).

Character, special skills and training
Dynamic, active, enthusiastic and tenacious, the Irish Water Spaniel has great endurance and a very discerning nose. He specializes in wild birds (including duck). He is a good flusher and well-adapted to working in the water. His search is hard-driving and quick and he is silent on the trail. Adorable and courageous, according to some, he is often difficult. He needs firm training.

Care and functions
He needs wide open spaces and lots of exercise, as well as combing twice weekly and regular checking of the ears.
· Hunting dog.

Portuguese Water Dog

This miniature Newfoundland is native to the Algarve province of Portugal. Some believe he is the result of crosses between the Barbet and various local breeds. He has traditionally aided fishermen on the boat and in port.

3

WATER DOGS

8

COUNTRY OF ORIGIN
Portugal

ORIGINAL NAME
Cão de Agua

Mesomorph. Braccoid. Well-balanced. Very muscular. Relaxed gait.

Medium Breeds
between
10 and 25 kg
(20-55 lb)

Character, special skills and training

This energetic, impetuous, tough dog with great endurance and a good nose is an extraordinary swimmer and diver, making him very good on water game. He can be a watchdog and makes a delightful pet. He needs firm training.

Care and functions

He needs space and lots of exercise, as well as frequent combing and brushing. For competition, the hair on the hindquarters must be clipped from the last rib to two-thirds of the way down the tail.
· Hunting dog.
· Watchdog.
· Companion dog.

HEAD
Strong and broad. Domed skull. Prominent brow bones. Pronounced stop. Muzzle narrower at the nose than at the base. Strong jaws. Nose wide, matching coat color. Thick lips.

EYES
Medium-sized, round, slightly slanted. Eyelids edged with black.

EARS
Set on high, thin, hanging flat against the head with the back edge standing out slightly.

BODY
Strong. Short, rounded neck without dewlap. Broad withers. Chest broad, well let-down. Well-sprung ribs. Small abdomen. Straight back. Slightly sloping croup.

LIMBS
Strong legs. Round feet.

TAIL
Thick at the base, tapering toward the tip. In action, curled in a circle. The tail is a valuable tool for swimming and diving.

COAT
Tough. No undercoat. Two varieties: long and wavy, or in short tufts. Wavy hair on the head (crisp hair in the second variety) forming a sort of topknot.

COLOR
Solid or a combination of colors. Solid white, black, or brown. A combination of black or brown with white.

SIZE
Dog: 54 cm (21.3 in).
Bitch: 46 cm (18 in).

WEIGHT
Dog: 19 to 25 kg (42-55 lb).
Bitch: 16 to 22 kg (35-48.5 lb).

Romagna Water Dog

The Romagna Water Dog is an old breed of waterfowl retriever from the lowlands of Comacchio and the swamps of Ravenna. Over the centuries, the large swamps were drained. Subsequently, the Romagna Water Dog became an excellent truffle hunter, used in the plains and hills of Romagna. The breed was recognized by the FCI in 1995.

Well-balanced. Compact. Thin skin without folds.

3

WATER DOGS

COUNTRY OF ORIGIN
Italy

ORIGINAL NAME
Lagotto Romagnolo

Medium Breeds between 10 and 25 kg (20-55 lb)

8

HEAD
Moderately large. Skull broad, longer than the muzzle, slightly domed. Pronounced brow bones. Straight nosebridge. Strong jaws. Flat cheeks. Large nose.

EYES
Fairly large, rounded. Dark brown or a shade of ocher or hazel, depending on coat color.

EARS
Medium-sized, triangular, rounded at the tips, pendulous.

BODY
Compact, strong. Strong, muscular, cleanly cut neck. Prominent withers. Well-developed chest. Short, very solid loin. Straight, very muscular back. Long, broad, slightly sloping croup.

LIMBS
Muscular, well-boned legs. Slightly rounded, compact feet with pigmented pads.

TAIL
Tapering toward the tip. At rest, carried in saber fashion. In action, carried much higher.

COAT
Dense, curly, woolly, forming very tight ringlets. Curls distributed over the entire body except the head, where the hair forms eyebrows, a mustache and a thick beard. Waterproof topcoat and undercoat. If the coat is not clipped, it tends to become matted.

COLOR
Solid white, white with brown or orange markings, roan brown, solid brown (any shade), solid orange.

SIZE
Dog: 43 to 48 cm (17-19 in).
Bitch: 41 to 46 cm (16-18 in).

WEIGHT
Dog: 13 to 16 kg (28.5-35 lb).
Bitch: 11 to 14 kg (24.5-31 lb).

Character, special skills and training
The Romagna Water Dog has lost his hunting instinct but retains his very keen nose, making him highly effective at finding truffles. With his vigilance and tendency to bark, he makes a good watchdog. Docile, affectionate and very attached to his owner, he is a good pet. He needs firm training.

Care and functions
He needs space and exercise. To prevent matting, he must be clipped completely at least once a year.
· Truffle-hunting dog.
· Companion dog.

Group
9

Tibetan Spaniel

Bolognese

The Bolognese's origins are commingled with those of the Maltese, its close cousin. Their distant ancestors were the small dogs Aristotle called canes melitenses. Throughout Roman times, the Bolognese was a precious gift given among those in power. Italians believe the breed was born in the city of Bologna. A favorite of the Medicis family during the Renaissance, he was popular until the late eighteenth century, when the Poodle took his place. Today, he is rarely found outside his native land.

Small. Compact. Head carried proudly. Dignified. Relaxed, energetic gait.

1

BICHONS

9

COUNTRY OF ORIGIN
Italy

OTHER NAME
Bichon Bolognese

Small Breeds
under 10 kg
(under 20 lb)

Character, special skills and training

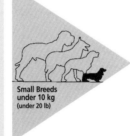

Lively, merry, docile and very affectionate, the Bolognese is eager to please his owner and makes a wonderful pet. Never rambunctious, he is less restless than other bichons. He needs gentle training.

Care and functions

The Bolognese is an apartment dog. He needs moderate exercise and does not like being left alone. He requires daily dematting and combing and does not shed. He is very clean and needs bathing only once a month. For showing, he must be groomed.
· Companion dog.

HEAD
Round. Skull fairly flat. Pronounced stop. Straight nosebridge. Front of muzzle nearly square. Large, black nose.

EYES
Large, round, dark ocher. Edge of eyelids black.

EARS
Set on high, long, pendulous. Upper pinna standing out from skull.

BODY
Square build. Neck without dewlap. Broad chest. Well-sprung ribs. Very slight tuck-up. Straight back. Very broad, nearly level croup.

LIMBS
Short, well-positioned limbs. Oval feet with dark pads and black nails.

TAIL
Curved over the back.

COAT
Long on entire body. Shorter on the nosebridge. Fairly woolly, standing off the body in tufts. No feathering.

COLOR
Pure white with no spots. No other shades of white.

SIZE
Dog: 27 to 30 cm (10.5-12 in).
Bitch: 25 to 28 cm (10-11 in).

WEIGHT
2.5 to 4 kg (5.5-9 lb).

Havanese

The Havanese, possibly descended from the Bolognese, comes from the western Mediterranean region and was developed along the Spanish and Italian coasts. Some believe that the Havanese was brought to Cuba early in his development by Spanish conquistadors or Italian explorers. Others believe he arrived in Cuba after being brought to Argentina and crossed with small Poodles. The main coat color of this breed, Havana brown (reddish-tan), inspired the myth that the Havanese comes from Havana, Cuba's capital city. The old Havanese strain in Cuba is now extinct. A few descendents were smuggled off the island to the United States, where the breed became quite popular.

Small. Vigorous dog. Lively, springy gait.

1

BICHONS

COUNTRY OF ORIGIN
Western Mediterranean Basin
Cuba

OTHER NAME
Havana Silk Dog

Small Breeds
under 10 kg
(under 20 lb)

9

HEAD
Moderately long. Flat, broad skull. Moderate stop. Gradually tapering muzzle. Tight-lipped. Flat cheeks.

EYES
Fairly large, almond-shaped, dark brown.

EARS
Set on high, hanging against the cheeks with a subtle fold. Covered with long feathering.

BODY
Slightly long. Moderately long neck. Well-sprung ribs. Pronounced tuck-up. Straight back. Strongly sloping croup.

LIMBS
Short, well-boned legs. Feet slightly elongated, small, compact.

TAIL
Raised either in snap fashion or, preferably, curled on the back. Long, silky feathering.

COAT
Very long (12 to 18 cm) (4,5-7 in), soft, flat or wavy. May form curly tufts. Undercoat woolly, sparse or absent.

COLOR
Two varieties: - completely pure white (rare), pale fawn to Havana brown (reddish-tan tobacco color), spotting in these colors, some smokiness allowed. - coat colors and spotting as above (white, light fawn to Havana brown) with black spots, black coat.

SIZE
21 to 29 cm (8-11.5 in).

WEIGHT
No more than 6 kg (13 lb).

Character, special skills and training
Intelligent, extremely affectionate and gentle with children, the Havanese is a charming pet. Very alert, he makes a good watchdog. He needs firm training.

Care and functions
This apartment dog does not need lots of exercise. He requires daily brushing and combing. Any kind of grooming, trimming, or stripping is not allowed.
· Companion dog.

Maltese

The Maltese is a very old breed with hotly debated origins. This little dog's ancestors hunted pests in the ports and maritime cities of the central Mediterranean. It is certain that this dog or a similar breed existed in ancient Egypt and Greece and later in Rome. The ancient Greek geographer Strabon reported that the Sicilian city of Melita exported dogs called canes meliteris. Even though the Maltese is named after Malta, there is no proof that he is a native of this island. Prized by nobility, he was a favorite of England's royal court under Queen Elizabeth I. Today, the breed is not very common.

Very elegant. Head held proudly and with dignity. Skin pigmented with dark spots like wine stains. Skimming, relaxed gait. Distinctive trot makes the dog appear to be on wheels.

1

BICHONS

9

COUNTRY OF ORIGIN
Central Mediterranean Basin
Italy

OTHER NAMES
Straight-haired Bichon
Maltese Terrier

Small Breeds under 10 kg (under 20 lb)

Character, special skills and training
Tough and tireless, the Maltese has the liveliness one would expect of a renowned ratter. He is merry, playful and animated. Affectionate and very calm, he rarely barks and makes an adorable pet. He needs rigorous training.

Care and functions
He can live in an apartment and needs limited exercise. He does not like being left alone. He requires daily dematting and brushing, as well as regular baths and grooming twice a year. His ears and eyes should be checked regularly.
· Companion dog.

HEAD
Fairly broad. Flat skull. Very pronounced stop. Straight nosebridge. Thin lips. Large nose.

EYES
Fairly large, dark ocher. Edge of eyelids black.

EARS
Set on high, pendulous, hanging against the sides of the head.

BODY
Long. Withers protruding slightly from the topline. Chest well let-down. Straight back. Very broad and long, nearly level croup.

LIMBS
Short, well-boned legs. Round feet with tight, arched toes.

TAIL
Thick at the base and thin at the tip. Forming a single large curve with the tip hanging between the hips and touching the croup.

COAT
Very long on the entire body, completely straight, without waves or curls. Silky. Hair on the trunk should be longer than the height at the withers and fall heavily to the ground. No undercoat. Very long on the head. Hair on the tail hangs on only one side of the trunk.

COLOR
Pure white. Pale ivory allowed. Traces of pale orange highlights are tolerated, as long as they resemble soiled hairs, but they are a flaw.

SIZE
Dog: 21 to 25 cm (8-10 in).
Bitch: 20 to 23 cm (8-9 in).

WEIGHT
3 to 4 kg (6.5-9 lb).

Bichon Frisé

The Bichon Frisé was once thought to be a Spanish breed introduced to the Canary Islands in the fourteenth century. For this reason, he was long called the Tenerife Dog or the Bichon Tenerife, after the capital of the islands. The Bichon Frisé was developed during the Italian Renaissance by crossing the Maltese with other small Barbets and Poodles. His name comes from the French diminutive barbichon. He was introduced to France during the reign of King François I and he must have been all the rage under King Henry III, since he was this king's favorite breed. He was brought to Belgium during the Spanish occupation of Flanders. He strutted through the literary salons of the seventeenth century and of France's Second Empire and Belle Époque. Recognized in France in 1933, he became a French-Belgian breed in 1960. The Bichon Frisé is enjoying renewed popularity after a brief decline in the 1970s.

Small barbet. Graceful. Head raised high and carried proudly. Lively gait.

1

9

BICHONS

COUNTRY OF ORIGIN
France - Belgium

ORIGINAL NAME
Bichon à Poil Frisé

OTHER NAMES
Tenerife Dog
Bichon Tenerife

Small Breeds
under 10 kg
(under 20 lb)

HEAD
In proportion to the body. Skull fairly flat, longer than the muzzle. Stop not very pronounced. Flat cheeks. Thin lips. Black nose.

EYES
Rounded, dark. Edges of eyelids dark.

EARS
Pendulous, furnished with long, finely curled hair. When alert, carried fairly forward.

BODY
Slightly elongated. Neck fairly long, raised high and carried proudly. Well-developed chest. Broad, muscular, slightly domed loin. Slightly rounded croup.

LIMBS
Muscular, fine-boned legs. Round feet, nails preferably black.

TAIL
Raised and curving gracefully without curling onto the back.

COAT
7 to 10 cm (2.8-4 in) long, fine, silky, curly, very loose, similar to that of the Mongolian goat, neither flat nor wavy.

COLOR
Pure white.

SIZE
25 to 30 cm (10-12 in).

WEIGHT
2.5 to 3 kg (5.5-6.5 in).

Character, special skills and training
Stout, lively, exuberant and very merry, the Bichon Frisé is quite strong-willed. Very adaptable, intelligent and gentle, he is a charming pet. He needs firm training.

Care and functions
He does well in an apartment but needs long walks and does not like being left alone. He requires daily brushing and monthly baths. The hair on his feet and muzzle should be lightly trimmed and he should be groomed every three months. He hardly sheds and is very clean. His ears and eyes require regular attention.
· Companion dog.

Coton de Tuléar

The Coton de Tuléar, named for his cottony coat, is a bichon breed. His ancestors were ratters brought to Madagascar by French troops. These ratters gave rise to the Coton de Réunion on the island by that name. Now extinct, this breed was modified in Madagascar through crosses with the Maltese, in particular. The new breed was named after Madagascar's city of Tuléar. The Coton de Tuléar was popularized by French nobility living on islands in the Indian Ocean during colonial times. In 1970 the breed was recognized by the FCI.

Thin skin without folds possible spotting in various shades of grey.
Preferred gait: trot.

1

BICHONS AND RELATED BREEDS

9

COUNTRY OF ORIGIN
Madagascar

Small Breeds under 10 kg (under 20 lb)

Character, special skills and training
The stout, hardy, very lively Coton de Tuléar likes to swim. In Madagascar, he was used as a terrier, watchdog and eliminator of pests. He is restless, rambunctious and strong-willed but very affectionate and devoted to his owner. He may be aggressive toward other dogs and barks often. He needs firm, early training.

Care and functions
He can adapt to apartment life. This athlete needs long walks and hates being left alone. He requires daily dematting, brushing and combing, as well as regular baths and grooming three or four times a year.
· Companion dog.

HEAD
Short, triangular when viewed from the top. Domed skull. Stop not very pronounced. Straight nose-bridge. Thin lips. Black or dark reddish-tan nose.

EYES
Round, dark, widely spaced.

EARS
Set on high, pendulous, thin, triangular. Covered with white or colored hair (yellow spots, a combination of yellow and black, or a few black hairs).

BODY
Long. Muscular neck without dewlap. Well-developed chest. Loin very slightly arched, well-muscled. Standing low to the ground. Very slightly arched, well-muscled back. Rounded, broad croup.

LIMBS
Muscular, well-boned legs. Round, small feet with tight toes.

TAIL
Set on low, approximately 18 cm (7 in) long, thick at the base, thin at the tip. At rest hanging below the hock with the tip raised.

COAT
Approximately 8 cm (3 in) long, thin, slightly wavy, cottony.

COLOR
White. Some yellow spots, particularly on the ears, are allowed.

SIZE
Dog: 25 to 32 cm (10-12.5 in).
Bitch: 22 to 28 cm (8.5-11 in).

WEIGHT
Dog: 4 to 6 kg (10-13 in).
Bitch: 3.5 to 5 kg (7.5-11 lb).

Little Lion Dog

This bichon is believed have originated in the Mediterranean Basin. Present in France and Spain since the late sixteenth century and recognized as a French breed, he was probably developed from the Maltese, toy spaniels and small Barbets. Once highly prized by nobility, the Little Lion Dog is now rare.

Well proportioned. Lively gait.

1

9

BICHONS AND RELATED BREEDS

Small Breeds under 10 kg (under 20 lb)

COUNTRY OF ORIGIN
France

ORIGINAL NAME
Petit Chien Lion

OTHER NAME
Löwchen

HEAD
Short. Fairly broad skull. Black nose.

EYES
Round, dark.

EARS
Long, pendulous, with feathering.

BODY
Short, well-proportioned.

LIMBS
Fairly tall, slender legs. Small, round feet.

TAIL
Medium in length, clipped. Tuft at the tip forming a plume.

COAT
Fairly long, wavy but not curly.

COLOR
All colors, solid or spotted, are allowed except shades of brown (chocolate, liver).

SIZE
25 to 32 cm (10-12.5 in).

WEIGHT
4 to 8 kg (9-17.5 lb).

Character, special skills and training
Hardy, very stout, full of energy and merry, the Little Lion Dog is affectionate and gentle with children. He is a good watchdog. He needs firm, gentle training.

Care and functions
He adapts well to apartment life, as long as he is walked daily. He also needs daily brushing. For shows, he should be groomed every two months with a Continental (or Lion) clip like that of the Poodle. Sporting this clip, he truly lives up to the name Löwchen, meaning "little lion".
· Companion dog.

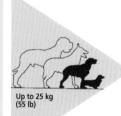

Poodle

This French breed once used to hunt waterfowl was originally named the Caniche, from the nickname chien à cane or canichon (duck dog). "Poodle" is short for Pudelhund, from the Low German pudeln (to splash) and Hund (dog). According to Buffon, the Poodle comes from Africa: He is descended from the Barbet of northern Africa, brought by the Arabs to the Iberian Peninsula, where he was apparently crossed with the Portuguese Water Dog. From Iberia the breed spread throughout Europe, after setting down roots in France. As a result, in 1936 the FCI officially recognized France as the birthplace of the Poodle. A standard was published the same year and a Poodle club was founded in Paris in 1922. Initially used on waterfowl, the Poodle was kept by noble ladies under Louis XIV, was a lapdog under Louis XV and was miniaturized under Louis XVI. The Poodle comes in four varieties according to size, but the Standard Poodle has been cast aside in favor of smaller versions (Miniature and Toy). The popularity of the breed peaked in the nineteenth and twentieth centuries. Able to adapt to any lifestyle (whether hunting, performing or providing companionship), the Poodle soon became the world's most popular pet. Unfortunately, this craze led to overbreeding to the detriment of quality. For this reason, potential Poodle owners should be wary.

2

POODLE

COUNTRY OF ORIGIN
France

ORIGINAL NAME
Caniche

9

Up to 25 kg
(55 lb)

White Standard Poodle. Mesomorph. Well-balanced. Elegant. Supple, pigmented skin. Bouncy, light-footed gait.

HEAD
Dignified, straight, in proportion to body. Slightly domed skull. Pronounced occipital peak. Stop not very pronounced. Straight nose-bridge. Fairly tight-lipped. Nose matches coat color.

EYES
Almond-shaped, slightly slanted. Black or very dark brown to dark amber, depending on coat color.

EARS
Fairly long, hanging against the cheeks, tips reaching to the commissure of the lips when outstretched. Covered with wavy, very long hair.

BODY
Longer than height at the withers. Solid, slightly arched neck. No dewlap. Chest well let-down. Firm, muscular loin. Tuck-up. Back short, neither arched nor hollow. Croup rounded but not sloping.

LIMBS
Muscular, well-boned legs.

Small, short, oval feet with arched toes and nails of varying color.

TAIL
Set on high, docked by one-third or one-half in curly-coated variety. Left natural in corded variety. Raised to a slant in action.

COAT
Curly: abundant, fine, woolly, very curly. Thick, well-furnished, of uniform length, forming regular curls. Corded: abundant, fine,

woolly, dense, forming small, well-defined cords of uniform length. Must be at least 20 cm (8 in) long.

COLOR
Black, white, brown, grey and apricot. Brown, grey and apricot must be solid.

SIZE
Standard Poodle:
45 to 60 cm (17.5-23.5 in).
Medium-sized Poodle:
35 to 45 cm (14-17.5 in).
Miniature Poodle:
28 to 35 cm (11-14 in).

Toy Poodle: less than 28 cm (11 in).

WEIGHT
Standard Poodle:
approx. 22 kg (48.5 lb).
Medium-sized Poodle:
approx. 12 kg (26.5 lb).
Miniature Poodle:
approx. 7 kg (15.5 in).
Toy Poodle: less than 7 kg (15.5 lb).

Character, special skills and training
Active, athletic, merry, very alert and intelligent, the friendly Poodle delights in life. His loyalty is legendary, but he can be possessive. Highly adaptable, outgoing and good-natured, he make a wonderful pet. Still a hunter like his ancestors, he is quite a good swimmer with a very keen nose. If he does not receive firm training, he can become difficult.

Care and functions
He is just as happy in the country as in the city. He hates being left alone. He is very clean and needs daily brushing and combing, as well as one or two baths per month. His ears must be checked regularly and he requires grooming every two months. There are several different clips: the Continental (or Lion) clip, the Kennel clip (in which the hair is trimmed to the same length on the entire body), the English Saddle clip (with leg bracelets) and the Puppy clip (Continental clip with trousers). Poodles do not shed.
· Companion dog.

Small Belgian Dogs

BELGIAN GRIFFON

3

SMALL BELGIAN DOGS

9

COUNTRY OF ORIGIN
Belgium

ORIGINAL NAME
Griffontjes van België

Small Breeds
under 10 kg
(under 20 lb)

There are three varieties of small Belgian dogs
that differ only in coat type and color:
- The Brussels Griffon (Brussels Griffontje)
has hair of medium length
- The Belgian Griffon (Belgische Griffontje)
also has hair of medium length; and
- The Small Brabant (Kleine Brabandere) has short hair.

- The Brussels Griffon, the oldest variety, is descended
from the Barbet (Belgian kennels). Selection
and improvement of the variety began by 1880 in Brussels. Numerous crosses were made with the Barbet (Belgian kennels), griffons (Belgian kennels), the Affenpinscher the Yorkshire Terrier, the Pug and the solid ruby (reddish-brown) King Charles Spaniel.
The Brussels Griffon was first shown in Brussels in 1880.
The first standard was published in 1883 and
modified in 1904. Belgium's Royale Saint-Hubert
recognizes the Brussels Griffon and its two varieties, the
Belgian Griffon and the Small Brabant. Specimens were
first shown in France in 1889, in the city of Roubaix.
In 1894, the Central Canine Society created a class for
Brussels Terriers. Breeding was interrupted by
the two World Wars. Great Britain is the country
with the highest population of small griffons.
In France, the population remains very limited.

- The Belgian Griffon was developed by crossing the Brussels Griffon with the Pug and perhaps with toy terriers.
The type was set in 1905 and the Central Canine Society
recognized it as a distinct "breed" in 1908. The Belgian
Griffon nearly went extinct during World War I. Breeding
was begun again in 1928, but the Belgian Griffon is the
least common of the small Belgian dogs.

- The Small Brabant is also descended from a cross
between griffons (Belgian kennels) and other breeds, particularly the Pug. The Small Brabant is very uncommon.

SMALL BRABANT

BRUSSELS GRIFFON

HEAD
Broad and round. Well-domed forehead. Prominent chin. Lower incisors cover upper incisors in an underbite. Hard, tousled hair, long around the eyes, nose, cheeks and chin. Wide, black nose.

EYES
Very large, round, black. Eyelids edged with black.

EARS
Very straight, always cropped to a point.

BODY
Square build. Chest fairly broad and deep.

LIMBS
Short, round, compact feet with black pads and nails. Legs of medium length

TAIL
Raised, docked by one-third.

COAT
- Brussels and Belgian Griffons: medium in length, hard, tousled, dense.
- Small Brabant: short.

COLOR
- Brussels Griffon: Reddish-brown. Minimal black markings on the mustache and chin are tolerated.
- Belgian Griffon: Black, black and tan and a combination of black and reddish-brown are the only colors allowed.
- Small Brabant: reddish-brown and black and tan are the only colors allowed. A black mask is not a fault.

SIZE
- Large variety:
approx. 28 cm (11 in).
- Small variety:
approx. 24 cm (9.5 in).

WEIGHT
- Large
Dog: less than 4.5 kg (10 in);
Bitch: less than 5 kg (11 in).
- Small
Dog: less than 3 kg (6.5 in);
Bitch: less than 3 kg (6.5 in).

Character, special skills and training
Brussels Griffon: Tough, energetic, lively and merry, this dog is very attached to his owner. He rarely barks, but his vigilance makes him a good little watchdog.
Belgian Griffon: This lively, merry, even-tempered dog is quite tough and vigorous and makes a very good pet. Vigilant and vocal, he makes a good watchdog. He is also a good eliminator of pests.
Small Brabant: This very confident, lively, strong-willed dog is quite intelligent and makes a good pet.
These dogs need firm training.

Care and functions
The Brussels Griffon is well-suited to apartment life but does not like being left alone. This very clean dog requires regular brushing and must be groomed every three months to maintain his handsome appearance. He does not tolerate heat well. His eyes must be checked regularly.
The Belgian Griffon can live in an apartment, as long as he gets regular walks. He requires daily brushing and regular grooming. His eyes and the folds on his face must be checked regularly.
The Small Brabant is a very clean city dog. Regular brushing is enough to maintain his wiry coat.
· Companion dog.

Chinese Crested Dog

Archaeologists have found ten thousand-year-old remains of a Chinese hairless dog. The Chinese Crested Dog could be the ancestor of the Mexican Hairless Dog, or he could be the result of a cross between the Mexican Hairless Dog and the Chihuahua. The Chinese Crested Dog was first shown in the West in 1885 in New York and appeared in France in 1975. He is most common in the United States and England. There are two varieties: hairless and powder puff with veil coat. Two different body types are also described: a fine-boned "deer type" and a more solidly boned "cobby type".

4

HAIRLESS DOGS

9

COUNTRY OF ORIGIN
China - Great Britain

OTHER NAME
Chinese Hairless Dog

Graceful. Svelte. Fine-grained skin becomes pigmented in summer. Extended, relaxed, elegant gait.

Small Breeds
under 10 kg
(under 20 lb)

HEAD
Graceful, smooth, without wrinkles. Slightly rounded and elongated skull. Slightly pronounced stop. Muzzle tapering gradually to prominent nose. Cleanly cut, flat cheeks. Strong jaws. Thin lips. Crest of long hair beginning at the stop and ending on the neck.

EYES
Medium-sized, very widely spaced. So dark they appear black.

EARS
Set on low, large, erect, with or without feathering. Drop ears allowed in powder puff variety.

BODY
Long. Neck long, slender, without dewlap. Chest well let-down. Strong loin. Moderate tuck-up.

LIMBS
Well-rounded, muscular croup. Long, fine-boned to fairly solidly boned legs, depending on body type. Very elongated, narrow feet with very long toes.

TAIL
Set on high, long, slender, very straight. Hanging down at rest. Long, supple feathering limited to the last third.

COAT
No large hairy patches anywhere on the body. Coat of powder puff variety consists of an undercoat of long, fine hair forming a veil.

COLOR
All colors and all combinations of colors are allowed.

SIZE
Dog: 28 to 33 cm (11-13 in).
Bitch: 23 to 30 cm (9-12 in).

WEIGHT
Variable, but under 5.5 kg (12 lb).

Character, special skills and training
Lively, alert and energetic, the Chinese Crested Dog is very affectionate and intelligent, making him an excellent pet. He is wary of strangers but not aggressive. He needs firm but gentle training beginning when he is still very young.

Care and functions
He should live inside but needs daily walks. He is sensitive to the cold and does not like being left alone. He needs regular baths.
· Companion dog.

322

Tibetan Spaniel

The origins of this very ancient breed are unclear. Dogs were traded between Tibet and China so long ago that the Shih Tzu and the Pekingese may have contributed to the Tibetan Spaniel's development. Alternately, the Tibetan Spaniel crossed with the Pug may have produced the Pekingese. The Tibetan Spaniel has always been a favorite of Tibetan monks, who kept the breed in their monasteries and used him to turn praying wheels. Tibetan Spaniels were brought to Europe by missionaries in the fifteenth century. While the first specimens were brought to Great Britain in 1905, the breed was not developed there until after World War II.

Well proportioned. Lively, relaxed, energetic gait.

TIBETAN BREEDS

5

COUNTRY OF ORIGIN
Tibet

9

Small Breeds under 10 kg (under 20 lb)

HEAD
Small. Slightly domed skull. Slight stop. Short muzzle. Chin fairly high and wide. Complete dentition is preferable.

EYES
Medium-sized, oval, fairly widely spaced. Dark brown. Eyelids edged in black.

EARS
Set on fairly high, medium-sized, pendulous, standing slightly away from skull, well-feathered.

BODY
Fairly long. Neck fairly short, strong, well set-on, covered with a mane (or "shawl") of longer hair, especially in the male. Well-sprung ribs. Straight back. Strong hindquarters.

LIMBS
Legs short, medium build. Small hare feet.

TAIL
Set on high, carried curled gaily over the back in action. Well-furnished with hair.

COAT
Medium in length, silky, smooth on the foreface and fronts of the legs. Feathering on the ears and backs of the legs. Fine, dense undercoat.

COLOR
All colors and combinations of colors are allowed.

SIZE
Dog: approx. 27 cm (10.5 in).
Bitch: approx. 24 cm (9.5 in).

WEIGHT
4 to 7 kg (9-15.5 lb).

Character, special skills and training
Lively, energetic, fast and agile, the Tibetan Spaniel is good-natured, affectionate and gentle. He is calm, intelligent, fairly quiet and unaggressive, but his mistrust of strangers makes him a good watchdog. He needs gentle training.

Care and functions
He is well-suited to apartment life, as long as he is walked daily. He needs regular brushing.
· Companion dog.
· Watchdog.

Lhasa Apso

The Lhasa Apso has existed in Tibet for thousands of years. A sacred animal, he was kept in temples and palaces, and the finest specimens lived with the Dalai Lama. Apso means "Tibetan goat". The Lhasa Apso did not appear in the West (England) until around 1930, because exporting the breed was forbidden. The first official standard was defined in 1934.

Well-balanced. Stout. Relaxed, lively gait.

5

TIBETAN BREEDS

9

COUNTRY OF ORIGIN
Tibet

Small Breeds
under 10 kg
(under 20 lb)

Character, special skills and training

Hardy, lively, courageous and always on the alert, the Lhasa Apso is very trong-willed, confident and somewhat stubborn. Calm, affectionate, intelligent and gentle with children, he makes a good pet. He is an excellent watchdog, since he is mistrusting of strangers and has a keen sense of hearing and a sharp voice. He needs firm training.

Care and functions

He can live in an apartment, but he loves to walk. He does not like being left alone. He requires daily dematting, brushing and combing, as well as monthly bathing and regular attention to the eyes.
· Companion dog.
· Watchdog.

HEAD
Round. Skull moderately narrow, not entirely flat. Moderate stop. Straight nosebridge. Muzzle not angular. Complete dentition desirable.

EYES
Medium-sized, dark.

EARS
Pendulous, with abundant feathering.

BODY
Long and compact. Neck strong, well-arched. Well-sprung ribs. Well-developed hindquarters. Strong loin. Straight back.

LIMBS
Short, well-muscled legs. Round cat feet with tough pads.

TAIL
Set on high, carried well over the back. Well-furnished with hair.

COAT
Long, abundant, straight and hard, neither woolly nor silky. Moderate undercoat. Abundant topknot hanging over the eyes. Well-furnished mustache.

COLOR
Golden, sable, honey, dark grey, slate grey, smoky grey or parti-color (several distinct colors, black, white or brown).

SIZE
Dog: approx. 25 cm (10 in). Bitch: slightly smaller.

WEIGHT
4 to 7 kg (9-15.5 lb).

Shih Tzu

The Shih Tzu is most certainly the product of crossing the Lhasa Apso from Tibet with the Pekingese from China. In 1643, the Dalai Lama presented the Manchurian dynasty with a gift of small "lion dogs" (shih tzu). The breed was long appreciated by the royal court and China's last empress kept them in her palace until 1908. In 1923, a kennel club was founded in Beijing. In 1930, Lady Browning brought the first specimens to England. The British Kennel Club recognized the breed in 1946. In France that same year, the Countess of Anjou founded a kennel and registered the first litters with the Central Canine Society in 1953. The FCI recognized the breed in 1954. The Shih Tzu is less common than the Pekingese and the Lhasa Apso.

Stout. Graceful carriage. Sumptuous coat. Smooth, balanced gait.

5

TIBETAN BREEDS

COUNTRY OF ORIGIN
Tibet
Sponsorship: Great Britain

OTHER NAME
Chrysanthemum Dog

9

Small Breeds
under 10 kg
(under 20 lb)

HEAD
Broad and round. Pronounced stop. Nosebridge 2.5 cm (1 in) long. Broad, angular, short muzzle. Tousled topknot with hair falling over the eyes. Well-furnished mustache and beard. Hair growing upward on the muzzle resembles a chrysanthemum flower.

EYES
Large, round, dark or light, depending on coat color.

EARS
Large, with long pinnae. Carried hanging down. So well-furnished with hair that they blend with the hair of the neck.

BODY
Fairly long, stout. Chest broad, well let-down. Loin well set-on, solid. Straight back. Strong hindquarters

LIMBS
Short, muscular, well-boned legs. Rounded, firm feet with tough pads.

TAIL
Set on high, carried gaily well over the back, forming an abundant plume.

COAT
Long and dense but not curly. Slightly wavy hair is allowed. Fairly thick undercoat.

COLOR
All colors are allowed, but a white flare on the forehead and white markings on the tip of the tail are highly prized in the multi-color variety.

SIZE
No more than 26 cm (10 in)

WEIGHT
4.5 to 8 kg (10-17.5 lb).

Character, special skills and training
Lively, very active and independent, this calm, gentle, merry dog needs lots of love and attention. He is the most outgoing of the Asian breeds. He is indifferent toward strangers and barks to announce their presence. He needs firm and gentle training.

Care and functions
He was meant for the city but needs exercise, including daily walks. He does not like being left alone. He requires daily brushing and combing. It is strongly recommended that the hair on his head be tied back out of his eyes. He needs a monthly bath and regular checking of the eyes. He cannot tolerate intense heat.
· Companion dog.
· Watchdog.

Tibetan Terrier

This very ancient breed resembling both a miniature Old English Sheepdog and a Lhasa Apso comes from Tibet, where he was once kept by monks. He was actually worshiped as a sacred animal and a guardian of temples. Around 1920, a Tibetan princess gave Dr. Greig, her British doctor, a pair of Tibetan Terriers as a gift. He brought them back to England, where they were used to develop the European strain. The breed was officially recognized in 1930. The Tibetan Terrier is still very uncommon in Europe.

Very stout. Powerful. Looks like a miniature Old English Sheepdog. Smooth gait. Powerful movement.

5

TIBETAN BREEDS

9

COUNTRY OF ORIGIN
Tibet
Sponsorship: Great Britain

ORIGINAL NAME
Dhokhi Apso

OTHER NAME
Phassa Terrier

Up to 25 kg
(55 lb)

Character, special skills and training

This tough, weather-resistant, vigorous, courageous, lively dog was once used to drive herds. He is not a true terrier, since he was never used in hunting. He is bursting with energy, spirited, independent and a bit stubborn. He is exceptionally attached to his owner and gentle with children. Vigilant and distrusting of strangers, he can be a watchdog but rarely barks. He needs firm training.

Care and functions

He can live in an apartment. He is athletic and needs exercise. He also requires daily brushing and combing.
· Companion dog.
· Watchdog.

HEAD
Medium in length. Skull not completely flat. Pronounced stop. Strong muzzle. Well-developed lower jaw with a slight beard. Black nose.

EYES
Large, round, dark brown. Veiled with long hair.

EARS
Not too large, forming a V. Pendulous but not too close to the head, with heavy feathering.

BODY
Square build, compact, muscular. Well-developed neck. Short, slightly arched loin. Level croup. Straight back.

LIMBS
Large, round feet with unarched toes. Well-muscled legs.

TAIL
Set on fairly high, medium in length, carried gaily, curled over the back. Very well-furnished with hair.

COAT
Long and fine but neither silky nor woolly. Straight or wavy, but not curly. Fine, woolly undercoat.

COLOR
White, golden, cream, grey or smoky, black, parti-color and tricolor. Chocolate and liver (brown) are undesirable.

SIZE
Dog: 35 to 40 cm (14-15.5 in).
Bitch: slightly smaller.

WEIGHT
8 to 13 kg (17.5-28.5 lb).

Chihuahua

This ancient breed was named after the region in northern Mexico where it might have originated. The Chihuahua's origins are uncertain. He might have been brought to Mexico by the Chinese; yet it is more likely that he descended from various Aztec ancestors, including the Techichi. The Chihuahua was a favorite sacred animal of the Aztecs, who consumed the dogs as holy food and sacrificed them to the gods. The Chihuahua also brought good luck to the home. Several specimens are thought to have been brought to Spain during the Spanish conquest. The Chihuahua was first bred in the United States in the nineteenth century. The breed soon became highly prized and was recognized by the American Kennel Club in 1904. He arrived in Europe after World War II. In 1995, the FCI recognized a new standard with a weight range of 0.5 to 3 kg (1-6.5 lb), but a weight between 1 and 2 kg (2.2-4.5 lb) is still preferred.

The smallest dog in the world. Svelte. Graceful. Light-footed gait.

6

CHIHUAHUA

COUNTRY OF ORIGIN
Mexico

9

Small Breeds under 10 kg (under 20 lb)

HEAD
Well-rounded "apple-dome" skull. Parietal fontanelle remaining. Pronounced stop. Nose fairly short and slightly pointed. Thin cheeks. Slight prognathism may be allowed. Nose dark black or lighter, depending on coat color.

EYES
Well spaced, not greatly protruding. Luminous black, brown, blue or ruby.

EARS
Large, very widely spaced. Carried erect in action. Carried at a 45° angle at rest.

BODY
Cylindrical, compact, longer than it is tall. Round, well-proportioned neck. Slender shoulders. Muscular hindquarters.

LIMBS
Fairly short, slender legs Small feet with well-spaced toes.

TAIL
Moderately long. Carried curled over the back or hanging loosely to the side. Well-furnished with hair; hairless is also allowed.

COAT
Long, wavy (rare variety). Short, dense, glossy. A small collar on the neck is prized.

COLOR
All colors and combinations are allowed. The most common and most prized colors are fawn or brown, chocolate, brindle fawn or brown, white, cream, silver fawn, silver grey, black and tan and black.

SIZE
16 to 20 cm (6.5-8 in).

WEIGHT
0.9 to 3.5 kg (2-7.5 lb).

Character, special skills and training
Stout, quite hardy, bold and very lively, the Chihuahua is fairly independent, courageous, proud and strong-willed. He is very attached to his owner, even possessive. He is not very good with children. Quite vocal and sometimes aggressive toward strangers, he makes a good watchdog. He needs firm training.

Care and functions
He is an apartment dog who needs daily walks. He is sensitive to the cold. His eyes need regular attention and his teeth should be checked regularly for tartar build-up. He needs regular brushing.
· Companion dog.

327

Cavalier King Charles Spaniel

Well-balanced. Graceful. Moves with grace and flexibility. Powerful hindquarters.

7

ENGLISH TOY SPANIELS

9

COUNTRY OF ORIGIN
Great Britain

OTHER NAME
English Toy Spaniel

Small Breeds under 10 kg (under 20 lb)

This dog's history is both recent and ancient, since the breed existed by the sixteenth and seventeenth centuries. In 1926, an American dog fancier noticed that today's King Charles differs from the spaniel depicted in tapestries of yore. British breeders then re-created the ancient toy spaniel that was once a favorite of British kings and princes.

Crosses with the King Charles Spaniel, the Pekingese and the Pug established the first strains of the Cavalier King Charles Spaniel, officially recognized as a breed in 1945. The Cavalier King Charles is stockier and has a longer muzzle than the King Charles Spaniel. The Cavalier King Charles, which has eclipsed the King Charles, is becoming increasingly popular.

Character, special skills and training
Tough, lively, athletic, energetic and very spirited, this mini-spaniel was a hunting dog who tracked game by scent and sight. Very good-natured, intelligent and gentle, he is a great companion. He does not bark excessively and is not a watchdog. He needs firm but gentle training.

Care and functions
He adapts well to city life but needs long walks. He does not like being left alone and he cannot tolerate cold and dampness. He requires brushing and combing two or three times a week, but no grooming. His ears and eyes must be checked regularly.
. Companion dog.

HEAD
Round. Skull nearly flat. Stop not very pronounced. Cone-shaped muzzle. Strong jaws. Lips not pendulous. Well-developed, black nose.

EYES
Large, round, not protruding, dark.

EARS
Set on high, long. Abundant feathering.

BODY
Long. Neck moderately long, slightly arched. Medium-sized chest. Well-sprung ribs. Straight back. Short loin.

LIMBS
Compact feet with tough pads. Short, moderately well-boned legs

TAIL
Carried gaily but never much above the topline. Natural or docked by more than one-third.

COAT
Long, silky, not curly. Slightly wavy. Abundant feathering.

COLOR
Black and tan (King Charles): raven-black with tan markings above the eyes, on the cheeks, insides of the ears, chest, legs and underside of the tail. White markings not allowed. Ruby (the rarest variety): solid, rich red. White markings not allowed. Blenheim: rich chestnut markings well-distributed over a pearly white ground. Markings should be divided evenly on the head, with a characteristic kissing spot between the ears.
Tricolor (Prince Charles): well-spaced and well-distributed black and white markings with tan markings above the eyes and on the cheeks, insides of the ears, inner legs and underside of the tail.

SIZE
25 to 34 cm (10-13.5 in).

WEIGHT
5 to 9 kg (11-20 lb).

King Charles Spaniel

Originally from Asia or Spain, King Charles Spaniels existed in sixteenth-century England. The ladies of Queen Elizabeth I's court used to hide them beneath their skirts. The breed was very popular with King Charles II, who took a special liking to this spaniel named in his honor. The breed suffered a slow decline and came close to extinction in the early 1950s.

Refined. Compact. Cobby.

7

ENGLISH TOY SPANIELS

COUNTRY OF ORIGIN
Great Britain

ORIGINAL NAMES
English Toy Spaniel
King Charles

Small Breeds
under 10 kg
(under 20 lb)

9

HEAD
Round. Voluminous, well-domed skull. Well-pronounced stop. Angular, wide muzzle. Very short, turned-up nose. Wide lower jaw. Slight underbite. Tight-lipped.

EYES
Very large, dark, well-spaced.

EARS
Set on low, hanging flat against the cheeks. Very long and feathered.

BODY
Short. Neck moderately long. Chest wide, well let-down. Strong hindquarters. Short, straight back.

LIMBS
Short, muscular legs.

Compact, round feet with tough pads.

TAIL
Carried neither on the back nor above the topline. Well-feathered. Docking not obligatory.

COAT
Long, silky, straight, never curly. Slight waviness allowed. Abundant feathering on the legs, ears and tail.

COLOR
Black and tan: rich, glossy black with tan and mahogany markings above the eyes and on the muzzle, legs, chest, insides of the ears and underside of the tail. A white chest is not allowed.
Tricolor: pearly white ground

with well-distributed black spots and rich tan markings on the cheeks, insides of the ears and underside of the tail. Small tan spots above the eyes. Wide, white flare between the eyes and white blaze on the head.
Blenheim: pearly white ground with well-distributed chestnut-red markings. Wide, very distinct, white blaze (kissing spot) on the center of the skull with distinct chestnut-red markings.
Ruby: solid, rich chestnut-red. White chest is a serious fault.

SIZE
26 to 32 cm (10-12.5 in).

WEIGHT
3.6 to 6.3 kg (8-14 lb).

Character, special skills and training
Adorable, loyal, affectionate, reserved and even-tempered, the King Charles Spaniel has a heart of gold. He is merry and enjoys playing with children. He rarely barks and has a remarkable sense of smell. He needs gentle training.

Care and functions
He is an apartment dog and requires little exercise. He needs daily brushing and combing and his eyes and ears should be checked regularly.
. Companion dog.

329

Japanese Chin

Ancestors of the Japanese Chin were given to the Japanese court in 732 A.D. by Korean royalty. In the following century, many of these dogs were brought to Japan. In the nineteenth century, Japanese Chins were exported to the United States and England, where Queen Victoria owned one. In 1882, several Japanese Chins were shown in New York. Currently, this little companion dog is very widespread.

Elegant. Graceful. Light-footed, proud gait.

8

9

JAPANESE SPANIELS

COUNTRY OF ORIGIN
Japan

OTHER NAMES
Japanese Spaniel
Chin

Small Breeds
under 10 kg
(under 20 lb)

Character, special skills and training
Very tough, lively, alert and somewhat rambunctious, the Japanese Chin is very attached to his owner. Merry, affectionate and gentle, he rarely barks and is a pleasant companion. He is mistrusting of strangers but not surly. He needs rigorous training.

Care and functions
He is a very clean apartment dog. He requires daily brushing and cannot tolerate intense heat. His ears and eyes must be checked regularly.
. Companion dog.

HEAD
Relatively large, broad and flat. Broad, rounded skull. Pronounced stop. Very short, wide nosebridge. Nose at eye level.

EYES
Large, round, well-spaced, shiny black.

EARS
Long, triangular, pendulous, covered with long hair.

BODY
Square build. Neck fairly short, carried high. Moderately wide chest. Slightly well-sprung ribs. Pro-

nounced tuck-up. Broad, slightly rounded croup. Short, straight back.

LIMBS
Small, elongated feet. Fairly long, slender legs.

TAIL
Carried on the back, covered with long, abundant hair.

COAT
Long, straight, silky. The entire body except the foreface is covered with abundant hair. Abundant feathering on the ears, neck, thighs and tail.

COLOR
White with black or red markings. Preferably, markings are distributed symmetrically around the eyes and on the ears and over the entire body. A wide, white flare from the muzzle to the top of the head is especially prized.

SIZE
Approx. 25 cm (10 in).

WEIGHT
2 to 6 kg (4.5-13 lb).

Pekingese

This dog of Chinese origin is one of the world's oldest breeds. He is depicted on bronze objects over 4,000 years old. For centuries, the Pekingese was bred, maintained and honored in China's Imperial palace. Believed to protect the emperor in the afterlife, the Pekingese was sacrificed at the emperor's death. After seizing Peking and pillaging the Summer Palace in 1860, British soldiers brought Pekingese dogs back to England. There, they were given to Queen Victoria, the Duchess of Wellington and the Duchess of Richmond, who established the first strain of "sun dog" from Imperial China. A breed club was founded in France in 1924. The Pekingese became very popular between World Wars I and II. Although limited, the breed's population remains stable.

Basset build. Stocky. Lionlike appearance. Well-balanced. Dignified. Rolling gait.

8

JAPANESE SPANIELS AND PEKONGESE

COUNTRY OF ORIGIN
China
Sponsorship: Great Britain

OTHER NAME
Pekingese Spaniel

9

Small Breeds under 10 kg (under 20 lb)

HEAD
Massive, wider than it is tall, flat. Wide, flat skull. Pronounced stop. Short, wide nose. Tight-lipped.

EYES
Large, round, dark. Edges of eyelids are black.

EARS
Heart-shaped, carried flat against the head. Long, abundant feathering.

BODY
Wide forequarters, narrower near the abdomen, short. Thick, very short neck. Wide

chest. Well-sprung ribs. Pronounced flank. Straight back.

LIMBS
Feet large, flat, not round; forefeet turned slightly outward. Short, solid, well-boned legs.

TAIL
Set on high, carried firmly, curved loosely on one side of the back. Long feathering.

COAT
Long, straight, with an abundant mane forming a collarette around the neck.

Long, abundant hair on the ears, backs of the legs, tail and feet. Dense undercoat.

COLOR
All colors and markings are allowed and equal in value, except albino and brown (liver). In the multi-color variety, markings are evenly distributed.

SIZE
15 to 25 cm (6-10 in).

WEIGHT
2.5 to 5.5 kg (5.5-12 lb).

Character, special skills and training
This lively, independent, strong-willed dog is very attached to his owner and does not always tolerate children. Distant toward strangers, the Pekingese barks often and is a good watchdog. He needs firm but gentle training.

Care and functions
He is happy living in an apartment. Not highly athletic, he needs only short daily walks. He requires daily brushing and combing and his eyes and the folds on his face must be checked regularly. . Companion dog.

331

Well balanced. Graceful. Proud gait. Easy, elegant movement.

9

CONTINENTAL TOY SPANIELS

9

COUNTRY OF ORIGIN
France - Belgium

Small Breeds
under 10 kg
(under 20 lb)

Continental Toy Spaniel

All of today's Continental Toy Spaniels are thought to be descended from a strain maintained by French and Flemish kennels. This explains the breed's mixed French and Belgian origins. An ideal pet, the Continental Toy Spaniel was a favorite guest of royal courts and salons of the aristocracy. There were once several varieties, but only two remain:
- The Phalene Continental Toy Spaniel (with hanging ears, named after a moth with folded wings) was popular and then suffered a decline before regaining popularity; and
- The Papillon Continental Toy Spaniel (with erect ears) appeared in the late nineteenth century and is probably descended from a cross with the Toy German Spitz.
The standard was accepted by the FCI in 1937.

Character, special skills and training
Tough, hardy, lively, enthusiastic and quick, the even-tempered Continental Toy Spaniel is very intelligent and charming but sometimes jealous. He is always distant toward strangers, making him a good watchdog. He needs firm but gentle training.

Care and functions
He adapts well to city life. He is very clean and requires daily brushing and combing. He cannot tolerate intense heat. His drop ears need regular checking.
. Companion dog.

HEAD

Slightly rounded. Skull not very rounded. Fairly pronounced stop. Straight nose-bridge. Muzzle tapering, shorter than the skull. Thin, tight, pigmented lips. Small, black nose.

EYES

Fairly large, almond-shaped, dark. Well-pigmented eyelids.

EARS

Set on fairly far back.
- Drop-eared variety or Phalene.
- Prick-eared variety or Papillon, with ears slanted at a 45° angle.
Crossing the two varieties often produces semi-erect ears with droping tips. This mixed version is a serious fault.

BODY

Slightly elongated. Neck of medium length. Topline neither arched nor hollow. Chest wide, fairly well let-down. Slight tuck-up. Solid, slightly arched loin. Straight back.

LIMBS

Fairly slender legs. Elongated hare feet with strong nails of varying color.

TAIL

Set on fairly high, rather long, thickly feathered, forming a lovely plume. Carried raised, in line with the spine and curving inward. Tip may touch the back.

COAT

Abundant, wavy. Short on the foreface, muzzle and fronts of the legs. Medium in length on the body, ears and backs of the forelegs. Ample breeching on the backs of the hind legs. Hair 7.5 cm (3 in) long on the withers. Feathering 15 cm (6 in) long on the tail.

COLOR

All colors allowed on white ground. White on the body and legs must dominate colored markings. White on the head extending into a fairly broad flare is prized. White is allowed on the lower part of the head, but dominant white markings on the head are a fault.

SIZE

28 cm maximum (11 in).

WEIGHT

One category under 2.5 kg (5.5 lb) . One category over 5 kg (11 lb).

Kromfohrländer

Developed in the eighteenth century, this reddish, griffon-type dog is believed to have been crossed with a terrier after World War II to produce the current version. The breed was recognized in Germany in 1953 and by the FCI shortly thereafter. The Kromfohrländer is not very well-known outside his native country.

Well-balanced. Elegant. Powerful build.
Firm, pigmented skin without wrinkles.

10

9

KROMFOHRLÄNDER

COUNTRY OF ORIGIN
Germany

Medium Breeds
between
10 and 25 kg
(20-55 lb)

Character, special skills and training
Tough, lively and alert, this sharp-eared hunting dog clearly has terrier blood. Affectionate and obedient, he makes a delightful pet. He is also a very good watchdog.

Care and functions
He can adapt to apartment life but needs lots of exercise. He must be brushed and combed twice a week.
. Hunting dog.
. Watchdog.
. Companion dog.

HEAD
Long, wedge-shaped. Flat skull. Well-pronounced stop. Straight nosebridge. Muzzle fairly rounded near the nose.

EYES
Medium-sized, oval, slightly slanting. Dark, ranging to dark brown.

EARS
Set on high, triangular with rounded tips, flat, carried flat against the head.

BODY
Very slightly elongated. Neck carried high, without dewlap. Moderately wide, deep chest. Slightly well-sprung ribs. Tuck-up. Power-

ful back. Moderately wide, very muscular, slightly sloping croup.

LIMBS
Elongated feet. Muscular, well-boned legs.

TAIL
Medium in length, thick, carried loosely curved.

COAT
Two varieties: one with rough, wiry hair (more common variety) and one with long, stiff hair. In both varieties, hair is preferably medium in length.

COLOR
White ground with light

brown markings (various shades of tan).

SIZE
38 to 46 cm (15-18 in).

WEIGHT
Approx. 15 kg (33 lb).

French Bulldog

The French Bulldog is thought to be descended from the Tibetan or Asian Mastiff. After giving rise to the Macedonian Mastiff, the Asian Mastiff was probably imported to England by the Phoenicians. Crosses with various terriers gradually reduced the breed's size. When the breed appeared in France around 1850, it already had certain similarities to today's French Bulldog. Subsequent crosses with the Pug and other breeds contributed to today's model. Prized ratters, French Bulldogs were kept by the butchers of La Villette in Paris and served as bodyguards to Pantin's bums (Paris's suburbs). The standard for the breed was set around 1898. After a period of decline, the French Bulldog is now regaining popularity.

Close-coupled. Powerful for his small size. Cloddy in all proportions. Compact structure. Solidly boned. Relaxed gait.

11

SMALL MOLOSSIAN TYPE DOGS

Up to 25 kg (55 lb)

COUNTRY OF ORIGIN
France

ORIGINAL NAME
Bouledogue Français

9

HEAD
Very strong, wide, angular with folds and wrinkles. Wide, nearly flat skull. Well-domed foreface. Very pronounced stop. Short, blunt foreface. Nosebridge with concentric folds. Wide, turned-up nose. Thick, black lips. Wide, angular, powerful jaws. Moderate underbite.

EYES
Round, fairly large, slightly protruding, dark. Edge of eyelids is black.

EARS
Straight, medium-sized, broad at the base and rounded at the tip (bat ears).

BODY
Compact, very muscular. Topline rising gradually to the loin. Short neck without dewlap. Slightly open, cylindrical brisket. Barrel-shaped ribs. Short loin. Tuck-up. Slanting croup. Broad back.

LIMBS
Hind legs slightly longer than forelegs. Forelegs stocky and short.. Round cat feet turning slightly outward.

TAIL
Naturally short, thick at the base, screw or straight, tapering toward the tip.

COAT
Close-lying, dense, glossy and soft.

COLOR
Brindle: fawn with vertical black stripes or streaks. A combination of black and chestnut hairs. A minimal amount of white on the chest and head is allowed. White and brindle or skewbald: brindle with predominant patching. White ground with brindle markings. A solid white coat is categorized as skewbald.

SIZE
25 to 35 cm (10-14 in).

WEIGHT
8 to 14 kg (17.5-31 lb).

Character, special skills and training
Active, bold, strong-willed and tough, the French Bulldog is a good watchdog. Very affectionate, intelligent and good-natured, he makes a delightful pet who needs lots of love and attention. He is gentle with children but fairly aggressive with other dogs. He requires firm and early but gentle, persuasive training.

Care and functions
The ideal city dog, he adapts well to apartment life. During walks, he must be taught not to pull on the leash or he may develop a poor gait. He hates being separated from his owner. Because of his overly short nose, he may have difficulty breathing, especially in hot weather. He needs daily brushing during the shedding season, as well as a bath every two months. His eyes and the folds on his face need regular attention.
. Companion dog.
. Watchdog.

335

Pug

The Pug is a very ancient breed believed to be from China and thought to have the same origins as the Tibetan Mastiff. He arrived in Europe via Holland in the 16th century and was developed in England during the 17th century. The British created two varieties—the fawn-coated Morisson Pug and the black-and-coffee-brown Willoughby Pug. These two varieties became one in 1866 and the breed was crossed with small spaniels to produce the now extinct Alicante Dog. In the 18th century, Pugs were brought to France, where Marie Antoinette and later Joséphine de Beauharnais (the first wife of Napoleon I) kept them as pets. The Pug is named for his stubby nose. He is known in Germany as the Mops (from the German word meaning "to grumble") and in France as the Carlin (after the 18th century Italian actor Carlo "Carlino" Bertinazzi, who wore a black mask as Harlequin). After a period of decline and then notoriety thanks to the Duke of Windsor, the breed is gaining popularity.

Mini-Mastiff. Molossian type. Small molossian, stocky, compact, solid. "A lot of dog in a small space". Gait: slight roll in the hindquarters.

11

SMALL MOLOSSIAN TYPE DOGS

9

COUNTRY OF ORIGIN
Great Britain

OTHER NAMES
Carlin
Mops

Small Breeds
under 10 kg
(under 20 lb)

Character, special skills and training
Affectionate, intelligent and gentle, this little lap dog is a good-natured pet but can be exclusive and touchy. He does not tolerate children well. The rambunctious Pug puppy becomes a calm, poised adult. He seldom barks and is not a watchdog, despite being reserved toward strangers. He needs firm, very early training.

Care and functions
He is perfectly suited to apartment life. Not an athlete, he can survive on short walks. He hates being left alone or separated from his owner. He should be kept out of intense heat since, like all brachycephalic dogs, he is susceptible to respiratory blockage. His eyes are sensitive to dust and need regular checking, as do the wrinkles on his face. He must be brushed twice or three times a week.
. Companion dog.

HEAD
Strong, round. Skull without furrows. Pronounced stop. Muzzle short, angular, not turned up. Distinct wrinkles. Slight underbite. Lower incisors set in nearly a straight line.

EYES
Very large, globular, dark, shiny.

EARS
Thin, small, soft. Two shapes allowed: - rose: small, drop ears folding back to expose the external canal; - button (preferred): falling forward with the tip against the head and the canal covered.

BODY
Compact, square build, cobby. Neck slightly arched, strong, thick. Wide chest. Straight back

LIMBS
Very strong legs of medium length
Feet neither round nor very long, with very tight toes

TAIL
Set on high ("spire"), curled as tightly as possible over the hip. Double curl is prized.

COAT
Thin, smooth, soft, short and glossy. Neither hard nor woolly.

COLOR
Silver, apricot, fawn or black. Each color very distinct, creating a complete contrast between coat, trace (black stripe from the occiput to the tail) and mask color. Markings are well-defined. Black markings are as dark as possible on the muzzle or mask, ears, moles on the cheeks, thumb mark or diamond on the forehead and trace.

SIZE
Approx. 30 cm (12 in).

WEIGHT
6.3 to 8.1 kg (14-18 lb).

Boston Terrier

The Boston Terrier was created by American breeders around 1870 for Boston's traditional dog fights. To develop the breed, they crossed the Bulldog and the Bull Terrier in order to maximize the fighting skill of both breeds. Additional crosses were made with the French Bulldog. The Boston Terrier was first shown in Boston in 1870. In 1891, the Boston Terrier Club of America was founded. The breed is not very widespread in Europe.

Square build. Solid. Compact. Well-proportioned. Graceful and strong. Smooth, easy gait.

11

SMALL MOLOSSIAN TYPE DOG

COUNTRY OF ORIGIN
United States

OTHER NAME
Boston Bull Terrier

9

Small Breeds
under 10 kg
(under 20 lb)

HEAD
Angular, short. Skull angular, flat, without wrinkles. Well-pronounced stop. Short, angular, broad, high muzzle. Broad, angular jaws. Wide, black nose.

EYES
Large, round, well-spaced, dark.

EARS
Set on high, small, carried erect, either natural or cropped.

BODY
Fairly short. Neck slightly arched. Broad brisket. Chest well let-down. Well-sprung ribs. Fairly short back. Slightly sloping, somewhat curved croup.

LIMBS
Strong, well-muscled legs. Small, round, compact feet with well-arched toes.

TAIL
Set on low, short, slender. Straight or screw. Should not be carried above the topline.

COAT
Short, smooth, fine.

COLOR
Brindle, seal color (black with chestnut highlights) or black with evenly spaced white markings. Required markings: white band around the muzzle, white flare between the eyes, white on the brisket. Forelegs entirely or partially white. White markings below the hocks on the hind legs are prized.

SIZE
25 to 40 cm (10-15.5 in).

WEIGHT
7 to 11 kg (15.5-24.5 lb).

Character, special skills and training
Tough, solid and very lively, this ratter trained for dog fights seldom barks. He is very good-natured and has a big heart, making him a wonderful pet. He has even been nicknamed the "American Gentleman". He is a vigilant little watchdog but is not aggressive. He needs firm training.

Care and functions
He can adapt to apartment life but needs regular exercise. He is clean and needs daily brushing. His eyes and the folds of his face must be cleaned. . Companion dog.

Group 10

Borzoi

Borzoi

The Borzoi might be the product of crossing the Asian Greyhound with the northern Laika or the Saluki with a Russian sheepdog or the Arabian Greyhound with a longhaired indigenous dog. The breed is believed to have been set in Russia in the sixteenth century. The Borzoi was long the favorite pet of large Russian families who used the dog in wolf hunting. Borzois were sent to England in 1842 as gifts to Princess Alexandra. The breed was introduced to western Europe around 1850 and to the United States in 1889. The Russian Revolution of 1917 put an end to breeding by the Russian aristocrats. European breeders worked to protect the Borzoi and breeding was later renewed in Russia.

The most long-backed of the sighthounds. Flattened profile. Well-balanced structure. Exceedingly elegant. Dignified. Thin, tight, well-pigmented skin. Rapid gallop with long, flexible strides.

1

LONGHAIRED OR FRINGED SIGHTHOUNDS

10

COUNTRY OF ORIGIN
Russia

ORIGINAL NAME
Sowaya Barzaya

OTHER NAME
Russian Wolfhound

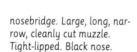

Large Breeds between 25 and 45 kg (55-100 lb)

Character, special skills and training
The very noble, seemingly impassive Borzoi was an excellent hunter of hare, fox and wolf. Powerful, enthusiastic and bold, this blue-blood has great stamina and is often attached exclusively to his owner. Not very patient with children, he is indifferent and even hostile toward strangers. He makes a good watchdog but rarely barks. He may bite other dogs. He needs firm but gentle training since he cannot tolerate harsh treatment.

Care and functions
It is better not to keep him in an apartment or leave him alone for long periods. He needs a great deal of space and exercise. He must be kept on a leash on walks, because he may try to chase cats and other animals. He requires brushing two or three times a week.
. Hunting dog.
. Watchdog.
. Companion dog.

HEAD
Long, narrow, cleanly cut, finely chiseled. Flat, very narrow skull. Stop practically absent. Slightly curved nosebridge. Large, long, narrow, cleanly cut muzzle. Tight-lipped. Black nose.

EYES
Large, almond-shaped, dark brown. Opening of the eyelids is edged in black and slightly slanted.

EARS
Set on high and well back, relatively small, thin, narrow and ending in a point. Carried back against the neck at rest (rose-shaped).

BODY
Elongated. Neck long, well-muscled, flattened sideways, without dewlap. Brisket not very pronounced. Long, deep, narrow, flat chest. Pronounced tuck-up. Very muscular back forming an arch especially in males; highest point is at the last rib. Long, broad, muscular croup

LIMBS
Long, cleanly cut, muscular legs. Narrow, oval feet with tight, well-arched toes.

TAIL
Set on low, long, forming a sickle. Abundant hair. Carried low at rest. Carried raised but not above the topline in action.

COAT
Long, silky, wavy, but not in large curls. Very thick around the neck, on the lower chest, backs of the legs and tail. Short on the head, ears and fronts of the legs.

COLOR
White, any shade of gold; silvery gold; gold-shaded; black-shaded tan with dark muzzle and legs; grey; gold, tan or grey brindle with long stripes of a darker shade; tan; black. Tan markings are allowed but not desirable. Dark-coated specimens have a characteristic black mask. All colors solid or spotted on a white ground.

SIZE
Dog: 70 to 82 cm (27.5-32.5 in).
Bitch: 65 to 77 cm (25.5-30.5 in).

WEIGHT
35 to 45 kg (77.5-100 lb).

Afghan Hound

The Afghan Hound's origins are practically unknown. A cousin of the Saluki (Persian Greyhound), his ancestors are thought to have been brought from Persia (Iran) to Afghanistan, where they might have developed their long coat. A favorite of Afghan royalty, Afghan Hounds were brought to England by British soldiers around 1890, after the second Afghan War. The first specimens shown in London in 1907 were a big hit. An English breed club was founded in 1926. Afghan Hounds were a huge fad in the 1980s.

Long-backed. Strong. Powerful. Flexible. Dignified. Noble gait. Flexible, springy stride.

1

LONGHAIRED OR FRINGED SIGHTHOUNDS

COUNTRY OF ORIGIN
Afghanistan

10

OTHER NAMES
Tazi
Afghan
Balkh Hound
Barutzy Hound
Baluchi Hound
Kabul Hound

Large Breeds between 25 and 45 kg (55-100 lb)

HEAD
Long. Skull long, not too narrow. Prominent occipital peak. Slight stop. Long muzzle. Powerful jaws.

EYES
Nearly triangular, slightly slanted, preferably dark, but a golden shade is not a fault.

EARS
Set on low, carried very flat against the head, covered with long, silky hair.

BODY
Long. Long, strong neck. Deep chest. Well-sprung ribs. Prominent, fairly widely spaced hip bones. Flat, muscular back sloping slightly

toward the hip. Straight, strong, fairly short loin.

LIMBS
Long, muscular legs. Large, broad feet.

TAIL
Not too short, forming a ring at the tip, sparsely covered with hair, carried high in action.

COAT
Very long, silky, fine hair covering the forequarters, hindquarters and entire body except the back from the withers to the base of the tail, where the hair is short and dense. Long, silky forelock starting on the forehead. Short and dense on

the foreface. Ears and legs covered with long, abundant hair.

COLOR
All colors are allowed.

SIZE
Dog: 69 to 74 cm (27-29 in).
Bitch: 62 to 69 cm (24.5-27 in).

WEIGHT
25 to 30 kg (55-66 lb).

Character, special skills and training
Tough, hardy and not as fast as the Greyhound, the Afghan Hound was used in his native land as a watchdog and hunter of antelope, wolf, jackal and other game. The British Army used the Afghan Hound as a messenger dog in India. Calm, often dominant, sensitive and not very demonstrative, he does not like to be bothered. Affectionate and very attached to his owner, he is distant and even haughty toward strangers. He needs firm but not harsh training.

Care and functions
He can adapt to apartment life as long as he has space and lots of exercise. He requires daily brushing and combing, as well as a monthly bath and grooming two or three times a year.
. Hunting dog.
. Companion dog.

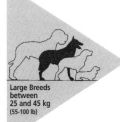

Polish Greyhound

The Polish Greyhound is descended from the Asian Greyhound. He is used in Poland's harsh climate for hunting hare, fox, roe deer and wolf.

Powerful. Stronger and less fine-boned than the other shorthaired sighthound. Solidly boned. Fluid, energetic gait.

1

SHORTHAIRED SIGHTHOUNDS

10

COUNTRY OF ORIGIN
Poland

ORIGINAL NAME
Chart Polski

Large Breeds between 25 and 45 kg (55-100 lb)

Character, special skills and training
Tough and hardy, this hunting dog makes a pleasant pet. He needs firm training.

Care and functions
He needs space and lots of exercise, as well as regular brushing.
. Hunting dog.
. Companion dog.

HEAD
Strong, cleanly cut, long. Flat skull. Stop not very pronounced. Strong muzzle and jaws. Lips not pendulous. Nose black or dark in color, depending on coat color.

EYES
Fairly large, almond-shaped, dark (ranging from dark brown to amber). Edge of eyelids black or dark in color.

EARS
Medium-sized, fairly narrow. Tips easily reach the inside corners of the eyes when outstretched.

BODY
Long. Long, muscular, powerful neck. Pronounced withers. Spacious chest. Wide, muscular loin. Tuck-up. Straight back. Gradually sloping, long, muscular, broad croup.

LIMBS
Long, cleanly cut, well-muscled legs. Oval feet with tight, well-arched toes.

TAIL
Long, thick at the base, carried low at rest. Tip must form an upward-curving sickle or a complete ring.

COAT
Fairly hard, neither wire-haired nor silky. Variable in length. Longer on the withers and shorter on the sides of the trunk. Longer on the hindquarters and underside of the tail, forming breeching and brush.

COLOR
All colors are allowed.

SIZE
Dog: 70 to 80 cm (27,5-31,5 in).
Bitch: 68 to 75 cm (27-29,5 in).

WEIGHT
Approx. 40 kg (88 lb).

Saluki

The name "Saluki" is most likely derived from "Seleucidae", a Hellenistic Dynasty. These kings are believed to have promoted the breeding of fringed sighthounds. The Saluki is thought to have been introduced to Europe by the Celts, who used the breed in hunting. By the second century B.C., the Romans brought the Saluki to Italy after conquering Greece. Related to the Afghan Hound and a close cousin to the Arabian Greyhound, the Saluki was highly prized by Arab peoples for his ability to follow their horses and his skill at hunting gazelle with falcons. The first Saluki imported to England in 1840 was called a "Persian Greyhound". The Kennel Club recognized the breed in 1923. The Saluki's numbers remain low.

Elegant. Well-bred. Easy, light-footed, very flexible gait.

1

LONGHAIRED OR FRINGED SIGHTHOUNDS

COUNTRY OF ORIGIN
Middle East - Iran

OTHER NAME
Persian Greyhound

10

Between 10 and 45 kg (20-100 lb)

HEAD
Long, narrow, cleanly cut. Skull moderately wide, not domed. Stop not very pronounced. Black or liver nose.

EYES
Large, dark to hazel.

EARS
Set on high, long, very mobile, carried flat against the cheeks. In the fringed variety, the ears are covered with silky hair of varying length.

BODY
Long. Long, flexible, well-muscled neck. Long, high,

fairly narrow chest. Slightly arched, sufficiently long loin. Pronounced tuck-up. Fairly broad back. Long, slightly sloping croup.

LIMBS
Long, muscular legs. Large feet with long, well-arched toes.

TAIL
Set on low, long. Carried curved in a natural extension of the topline. Underside has fairly long, silky feathering.

COAT
Smooth, silky. More or less abundant feathering on the

backs of the legs. Possible feathering on the throat. Short, without feathering.

COLOR
All colors and combinations of colors are the same for both varieties.

SIZE
Dog: 58 to 71 cm (23-28 in). Bitch: slightly smaller.

WEIGHT
15 to 30 kg (33-66 lb).

Character, special skills and training
The tough, hardy Saluki is a skilled hunter on sandy or rocky terrain. With his lightning acceleration, he can outrun gazelles. Calm intelligent and affectionate, he is a delightful pet who adores children. Very reserved toward strangers, he makes an effective watchdog. He is a quick learner and must be trained gently.

Care and functions
He can live in an apartment but needs long, daily walks and frequent opportunities to run. He is clean and requires brushing twice a week.
. Hunting dog.
. Companion dog.

343

Deerhound

The Deerhound has long existed in Scotland, where he might have arrived with Phoenician merchants or Celtic invaders. The breed quickly became a favorite of clan leaders. He received his name because he was once used to hunt fallow deer. When fallow deer became scarce, Deerhound breeding was nearly abandoned. British breeders worked to preserve and improve the Deerhound and the first standard was written in 1892. A Deerhound and Irish Wolfhound breed club was founded in 1974.

Powerful. Larger and stronger than the greyhound. Relaxed, energetic, natural gait.

2

COARSEHAIRED SIGHTHOUNDS

10

COUNTRY OF ORIGIN
Great Britain

OTHER NAME
Scottish Deerhound

Large Breeds between 25 and 45 kg (55-100 lb)

Character, special skills and training
Very hardy, active and not as fast as the Greyhound, the Deerhound seldom barks and is gentle, calm, good-natured and a devoted pet. He loves children and is neither mistrusting nor aggressive. He needs firm training.

Care and functions
He is not suited to apartment life. He prefers to live outdoors, where he can get lots of exercise. He does not tolerate heat well and he requires regular brushing.
. Companion dog.

HEAD
Long. Skull fairly flat, covered with hair of medium length and softer than on the rest of the body. No stop. Muzzle tapering toward the nose. Tight-lipped. Strong jaws.

EYES
Dark, either dark brown or hazel. Edge of eyelids black.

EARS
Set on high, small, folded back at rest. Black or dark in color.

BODY
Like that of a Greyhound, but larger. Neck very strong, without dewlap. Chest taller than it is wide. Well-arched loin. Broad, powerful croup

LIMBS
Long, muscular legs. Compact feet.

TAIL
Long, thick at the base and tapering toward the tip. Curved in action but never raised above the topline. Well-furnished with hair. Underside covered with very hard, wiry hair.

COAT
Shaggy, thick, close-lying, uneven, rough or crisp. Hard, wiry hair 7 to 10 cm (3-4 in) long on the body, neck and hindquarters. Much softer on the head, chest and abdomen. Light feathering on the inner legs.

COLOR
Dark blue-grey; darker and lighter shades of grey; brindle and yellow; sand or reddish-fawn with black extremities; white chest and toes and a small white spot on the tip of the tail are allowed.

SIZE
Dog: at least 76 cm (30 in).
Bitch: at least 71 cm (28 in).

WEIGHT
Dog: approx. 45.5 kg (100.5 lb).
Bitch: approx. 36.5 kg (80.5 lb).

Irish Wolfhound

The Irish Wolfhound, the world's largest sighthound, may be descended from dogs brought to Ireland by the Celts or from an old breed indigenous to Ireland. Some believe he is the product of crossing Irish sheepdogs with Arabian Greyhounds. Others believe the Deerhound was used in creating the breed, developed to hunt and kill wolf. The Irish Wolfhound nearly went extinct around 1800, at the same time as the wolf. In 1860, Captain G. Graham decided to revive the breed by crossing the last specimens with the Deerhound and perhaps the Great Dane, the Borzoi and other breeds. The Irish Wolfhound was recognized by the Kennel Club in 1897.

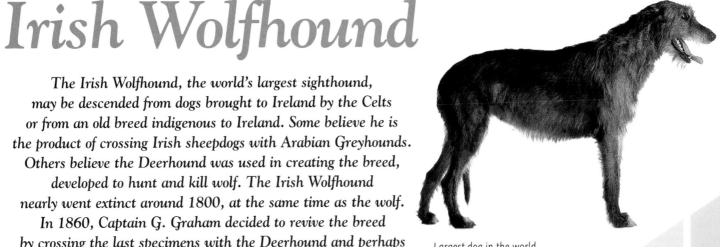

Largest dog in the world, record size 106 cm (41 in), together with the Great Dane. Powerful. Strong. Very muscular. Shaggy. Relaxed, lively gait.

2

COARSEHAIRED SIGHTHOUNDS

COUNTRY OF ORIGIN
Ireland

OTHER NAME
Wolfhound

Giants Breeds between over 45 kg (over 100 lb)

10

HEAD
Long. Skull not too wide. Long, moderately pointed muzzle.

EYES
Dark.

EARS
Small, carried like those of the Greyhound.

BODY
Powerful, elongated. Neck fairly long, very strong and muscular, well-arched, without dewlap. Wide, very deep chest. Arched loin. Pronounced tuck-up. Fairly long back

LIMBS
Strong legs. Fairly large, round feet with well-arched, tight toes.

TAIL
Long, slightly curved, moderately thick and well-furnished with hair.

COAT
Harsh and rough on the body, legs and head. Especially hard and long above the eyes and below the jaw.

COLOR
Grey, brindle, chestnut, black, pure white or any other color appearing in the Deerhound.

SIZE
Dog: at least 79 cm (31 in) (preferably 81 to 86 cm) (32-34 in).
Bitch: at least 71 cm (28 in).

WEIGHT
Dog: at least 54 kg (119 lb).
Bitch: at least 40.5 kg (89.5 lb).

Character, special skills and training
This very bold dog with incredible stamina and strength may be gentle when petted but can be ferocious when provoked. He hunts wolf and wild boar and also makes an effective, dissuasive watchdog. He should not be trained as a defense and attack dog, since he could be very dangerous. Calm and gentle with children, he is very attached to his owner. Firm training is necessary to keep him under control.

Care and functions
He should not live in the city. He needs to run often in wide open spaces. He must be brushed weekly.
. Hunting dog.
. Companion dog.

Azawakh

This African sighthound comes from the middle Nigerian Basin in the Azawakh Valley on the border of Mali. The breed was developed by the Tuaregs of the southern Sahara to trip gazelles so that horsemen could catch them. The Azawakh was also used in ceremonies and kept as a pet. He is a close cousin to the Arabian Greyhound and the Saluki. The first Azawakhs were imported to Europe in the early 1970s. The breed was officially recognized by the FCI in 1981 and a standard was published in 1982.

Long-backed. Slender. Elegant. Very refined. Bone and muscle structure show through thin, taut skin. Thin, tight skin. Very flexible gait. Bounding gallop. Very lightweight appearance.

3

SHORTHAIRED SIGHTHOUNDS

10

COUNTRY OF ORIGIN
Mali

OTHER NAMES
Tuareg Greyhound
Tuareg Sloughi
South Saharan Greyhound

Medium Breeds
between
10 and 25 kg
(20-55 lb)

Character, special skills and training
Tough, very hardy and lively, the Azawakh hunts by sight and is a bounder, chasing after antelope and catching birds in flight. Very reserved toward strangers, vigilant and ferocious, he makes a good watchdog for nomad camps. Very strong-willed and independent, he is affectionate toward a select few. He needs early and rigorous but patient training.

Care and functions
He should not be confined to an apartment. He needs space and lots of exercise, as well as weekly brushing.
. Hunting dog.
. Companion dog.

HEAD
Long, narrow, slender, cleanly cut, chiseled. Skull nearly flat, fairly long. Prominent occipital peak. Stop not very pronounced. Long, straight muzzle. Long, strong jaws. Flat cheeks. Black or brown nose.

EYES
Fairly large, almond-shaped. Dark or amber-colored. Pigmented eyelids.

EARS
Set on high. Thin, pendulous, lying flat against the head, never rose-shaped.

BODY
Long. Neck long, slender, muscular, slightly arched, without dewlap. Prominent withers. Brisket not very wide. Chest long, high, not very broad. Long, visible ribs. Short, cleanly cut, slightly arched loin. Prominent hips slightly higher than the withers. Pronounced tuck-up. Short, straight back. Croup slanted but not sloping.

LIMBS
Long, cleanly cut legs. Rounded feet with thin, tight toes.

TAIL
Set on low, long, thin, cleanly cut and tapering. Hanging with the tip slightly raised. May be carried above the topline in action.

COAT
Close-lying, fine, sparse to absent on the abdomen.

COLOR
Fawn with limited patching on the extremities. All shades are allowed, from light sand to dark fawn. Possible black mask on the head and very uneven flare. White chest and white tuft at the tip of the tail. White stockings required on each leg, at least as a trace on the feet. Black streaks are allowed.

SIZE
Dog: 64 to 74 cm (25-29 in).
Bitch: 60 to 70 cm (23.5-27.5 in).

WEIGHT
Dog: 20 to 25 kg (44-55 lb).
Bitch: 15 to 20 kg (33-44 lb).

Greyhound

Like the Arabian Greyhound and the Saluki, the Greyhound is thought to be descended from the Tesem, an ancient Egyptian sighthound featured on the tombs of the pharaohs. He arrived in Europe via Greece and was brought to Britain by the Phoenicians. "Greyhound" is thought to be derived from "Greek Hound". The Spanish Greyhound imported to England is thought to have contributed to the breed, developed during the reign of King Henry VIII for hunting hare or coursing. At the request of Queen Elizabeth I, the Duke of Norfolk established guidelines for judging sighthounds in outdoor hare coursing. By 1927, the Greyhound was used in artificial hare coursing at dog race tracks. Built to race, the Greyhound is to sighthounds what the thoroughbred is to horses – a magnificent running machine.

Solidly built. Sturdy stance. Well-balanced. Powerful muscles. Very powerful movement. Dignified. Elegant.

3

SHORTHAIRED SIGHTHOUNDS

Large Breeds between 25 and 45 kg (55-100 lb)

COUNTRY OF ORIGIN
Great Britain

OTHER NAME
English Greyhound

10

HEAD
Long, moderately wide. Flat skull. Slight stop. Long muzzle. Powerful jaws. Black, pointed nose.

EYES
Oval, set at a slant. Preferably dark.

EARS
Small, thin, rose-shaped.

BODY
Generously proportioned. Neck long, arched, without dewlap. High, ample chest. Long, well-sprung ribs.

Powerful, arched loin. Pronounced tuck-up. Fairly long, broad, square back. Powerful hindquarters.

LIMBS
Long, well-muscled, solidly boned legs. Compact feet.

TAIL
Set on fairly low, long, thick at the base and tapering toward the tip. Carried low and curving slightly inward.

COAT
Close-lying or short, fine and dense.

COLOR
Black, white, red, blue, fawn, pale fawn, brindle or any of these colors with white patches.

SIZE
Dog: 71 to 76 cm (28-30 in). Bitch: 68 to 71 cm (27-28 in).

WEIGHT
Approx. 30 kg (66 lb).

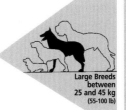

Character, special skills and training
Lively, vigorous and bold, the Greyhound has great stamina and is known as the world's fastest sighthound, able to reach speeds of 70 km/h (43,5 miles/h). With his excellent eyesight, he is a first-rate hunter and courser. At the dog track, the Greyhound is the Formula 1 of the canine world. He is affectionate, gentle, calm, intelligent and good-natured. He is indifferent toward strangers and needs firm training.

Care and functions
He needs space and must run every single day. He requires daily brushing.
. Hunting dog.
. Racing dog.
. Companion dog.

Spanish Greyhound

This sighthound was kept by the Romans in ancient times but brought to Spain even earlier. Some believe the Spanish Greyhound (galgo means "greyhound" in Spanish) might be descended from the Arabian Greyhound, introduced to Spain by the Moors in the ninth century. The Spanish Greyhound was prized by Spanish nobility and used primarily in racing. In order to obtain faster dogs, many crosses were made with the Greyhound, creating an English-Spanish variety. Many Spanish Greyhounds were exported to Ireland and England, in particular, during the sixteenth, 17th and 18th centuries. It is still commonly used by Spanish hunters.

Symmetrical build. Fairly long-backed. Solid. Elegant. Very well-balanced. Very muscular. Compact bone structure, tough, supple, pink skin. Typical gait: gallop. Extended, skimming trot.

3

SHORTHAIRED SIGHTHOUNDS

10

COUNTRY OF ORIGIN
Spain

ORIGINAL NAME
Galgo Español

Large Breeds between 25 and 45 kg (55-100 lb)

HEAD
Long, narrow, cleanly cut. Skull not very broad, subconvex. Very slight stop. Slightly curved nosebridge. Long, narrow muzzle. Very tight-lipped. Small, black nose.

Character, special skills and training
The tough, active, very hardy Spanish Greyhound specializes in hare but also hunts fox and wild boar. He has a rather mediocre nose. Gentle and very attached to his owner, he is the most affectionate and demonstrative of all the sighthounds. He needs gentle training.

Care and functions
He cannot live in an apartment and does not like being confined. He needs lots of exercise, including frequent runs. He must be brushed regularly.
. Hunting dog.
. Companion dog.

EYES
Small, almond-shaped, slanted. Dark hazel. Dark eyelids.

EARS
Set on high, wide at the base, triangular, with rounded tips. Rose-shaped and lying flat against the head at rest.

BODY
Strong, slightly rectangular build. Neck long, strong, oval in cross-section. Chest not very broad but ample. Ribs highly visible. Long, strong, arched loin. Pronounced tuck-up (high-standing). Straight, long back. Long, powerful, arched croup.

LIMBS
Powerful, well-muscled hind legs. Slender forelegs. Hare feet with tight toes and tough pads.

TAIL
Set on low, very long, flexible, thick at the base and tapering toward the tip. At rest, hanging in sickle fashion with an inward-curving hook at the tip.

COAT
Short, very fine, smooth, dense. Slightly longer on the backs of the thighs. In the wirehaired variety, medium in length and forming a light beard, mustache, eyebrows and topknot.

COLOR
All colors are allowed. The most typical, in order of preference, are a shade of well-pigmented fawn and brindle. Black. Spotted black, dark and light. Burnt chestnut. Cinnamon. Yellow. Red. White.

SIZE
Dog: 62 to 70 cm (24.5-27.5 in).
Bitch: 60 to 68 cm (23.5-27 in).

WEIGHT
Dog: 25 to 30 kg (55-66 lb).
Bitch: 20 to 25 kg (44-55 lb).

Hungarian Greyhound

The Hungarian Greyhound is believed to be descended from Asian Greyhounds brought to Hungary in the ninth century by the Magyars and probably crossed with local hounds. In the nineteenth century, crosses were made with the Greyhound to make the breed faster. Originally named the Magyar Agar (agar means "greyhound" in Hungarian).

Slender but strong.

3

SHORTHAIRED SIGHTHOUNDS

COUNTRY OF ORIGIN
Hungary

ORIGINAL NAME
Magyar Agar

10

Large Breeds between 25 and 45 kg (55-100 lb)

HEAD
From the top and sides, resembles a long triangle. Relatively broad skull. Slight stop. Powerful muzzle. Strong jaws. Strong cheeks.

EYES
Medium-sized, preferably brown.

EARS
Set on fairly high, medium-sized, not too thin, semi-pendulous, V-shaped.

BODY
Long, muscular. Neck not very long, well-muscled. Rel-atively wide brisket. Chest deep, not too flat. Slightly curved loin. Slight tuck-up. Firm, fairly broad, straight back. Broad, slightly sloping croup.

LIMBS
Long, cleanly cut, powerful, well-muscled, well-boned legs.

TAIL
Long, not too thin, slightly curved at the tip, always carried below the topline.

COAT
Close-lying, not too fine. Thick in winter.

COLOR
All colors are allowed, solid, spotted or brindle.

SIZE
Dog: 65 to 70 cm (25.5-27.5 in).
Bitch: slightly smaller.

WEIGHT
Dog: approx. 30 kg (66 lb).
Bitch: approx. 25 kg (55 lb).

Character, special skills and training
Tough, active, persistent and bold, the Hungarian Greyhound is not as fast as the Greyhound but is hardier and is a tireless tracker. In Hungary, he is used to catch and kill hare and fox. He has a mediocre nose. Gentle, affectionate, calm and loyal, he is a delightful pet. He is fairly independent but even-tempered. He needs firm training.

Care and functions
He can live in the city but needs regular opportunities to run. As with other sighthounds, he should be kept away from cattle. He cannot tolerate cold and must be brushed twice a week.
. Hunting dog.
. Companion dog.

Italian Greyhound

This very ancient breed – possibly a mutated Egyptian Greyhound – was brought to Italy via Greece as early as the fifth century B.C., as evidenced by numerous representations on vases and mixing bowls. The Italian Greyhound was very common in the Roman Empire and throughout the Middle Ages but was most popular with the nobility of Renaissance times. This dog was commonly painted by the grand masters of Italy and abroad. The Italian Greyhound charmed the elite of this period, from King François I to Frederick the Great. Then interest in the dog waned, due to a decline in the breed caused by miniaturization. After World War II, the breed was revived and its earlier traits were restored. A standard was established in 1968.

The smallest sighthound. Miniature greyhound or arabian greyhound. Very refined. A model of grace, dignity and elegance. Thin, tight skin. Bouncy gait. Quick, clean gallop.

3

SHORTHAIRED SIGHTHOUNDS

10

COUNTRY OF ORIGIN
Italy

ORIGINAL NAME
Piccolo Levriero Italiano

Small Breeds under 10 kg (under 20 lb)

HEAD
Long, narrow. Flat skull. Stop not very pronounced. Pointed muzzle. Cleanly cut cheeks. Thin lips.

EYES
Large, dark. Edge of eyelids pigmented.

EARS
Set on high, small. Folded back on themselves and carried against the upper neck.

BODY
Square build. Neck shaped like a short cone, without dewlap. Fairly pronounced withers. Chest deep, well let-down, narrow. Arched back. Very sloping, broad, muscular croup.

LIMBS
Slender, cleanly cut legs. Small, nearly oval feet with tight, arched toes and pigmented pads.

TAIL
Set on low, thin even at the base, tapering gradually toward the tip. First half carried low and straight; remainder curving.

COAT
Close-lying and fine on entire body.

COLOR
Solid or any shade of black, grey, slate grey, slate or yellow. White is tolerated only on the chest and feet.

SIZE
32 to 38 cm (12.5-15 in).

WEIGHT
Up to 5 kg (11 lb).

Character, special skills and training
This tiny Greyhound or miniature Arabian Greyhound often quivers with excitement. Despite his dainty and fragile appearance, he is lively, energetic, hardy and agile. He likes to hunt small game (including rabbit and hare). Affectionate, intelligent, very loving, merry and playful, he is a charming pet. He is quiet, reserved and distant toward strangers. He needs gentle but firm training.

Care and functions
He can adapt to city life but needs exercise. He does not like being left alone and cannot tolerate cold weather and rain. He requires regular brushing.
. Companion dog.

Arabian Greyhound

The Arabian Greyhound is probably descended from the large Egyptian Greyhound and is associated with the Arab peoples who inhabited northern Africa. Named after a city in Tunisia, he is common especially in Morocco, where he is used to hunt hare and gazelle. French soldiers brought the first Arabian Greyhounds to France around 1860, after the war in Algeria. Currently, the Arabian Greyhound is one of the rarest sighthound breeds in the West.

Dignified. Very well-bred. Cleanly cut. Muscular. Very fine skin without wrinkles or dewlap.

3

SHORTHAIRED SIGHTHOUNDS

COUNTRY OF ORIGIN
Morocco

ORIGINAL NAME
Sloughi

Large Breeds between 25 and 45 kg (55-100 lb)

10

HEAD
Long, elegant, slender, but fairly large. Skull flat, fairly broad, rounded at the back. Very slightly pronounced stop. Straight nosebridge. Muzzle shaped like an elongated wedge. Strong jaws. Thin, supple lips.

EYES
Large. Eyelids slightly slanted. Dark or amber if the coat is light-colored.

EARS
Set on high, pendulous, lying very flat against the head, not too large, triangular, slightly rounded at the tip.

BODY
Square build. Neck long, without dewlap. Chest deep, not too broad. Flat ribs. Pronounced tuck-up. Bony, slanting croup. Short, nearly level back.

LIMBS
Long, slender, muscular legs. Thin, elongated oval feet.

TAIL
Thin, bony, carried above the topline.

COAT
Very close-lying, dense, fine.

COLOR
Sand. Light sand with or without black mask. Chestnut-sand with or without black mantle. Smoky sand. Brindle.

SIZE
Dog: 66 to 72 cm (26-28.5 in).
Bitch: 61 to 68 cm (24-27 in).

WEIGHT
30 to 32 kg (66-70.5 lb).

Character, special skills and training
Very tough and active, the Arabian Greyhound has great stamina, is an excellent runner and hunts gazelle by sight. Independent, strong-willed and skittish, he is very attached to his owner but subtle in showing affection. He seldom barks but is very reserved toward strangers and perhaps one of the most mistrusting sighthounds. He makes a good watchdog. He needs firm training.

Care and functions
He can adapt to city life, as long as he gets long, daily walks. He cannot tolerate cold weather. He must be brushed two to three times a week.
. Hunting dog.
. Watchdog.
. Companion dog.

Graceful. Elegant. Powerful. Muscular.
Skims over the ground with long strides.

3

SHORTHAIRED SIGHTHOUNDS

10

COUNTRY OF ORIGIN
Great Britain

ORIGINAL NAME
Miniature Greyhound

Small Breeds
under 10 kg
(under 20 lb)

Whippet

The Whippet was developed in northern England about a century ago to replace the Fox Terrier in hunting hare. He is believed to be the product of crosses between various terriers (Fox, Bedlington), the Italian Greyhound and the Greyhound. He was used in competitions staged by miners. This miniature Greyhound's name is derived from "whip up" or "whip it". The breed was recognized in England in 1902 and became quite common in other countries. After being ignored for some time, the Whippet is enjoying renewed popularity.

Character, special skills and training

The tough, hardy Whippet was used on hare. One of the world's swiftest sighthounds, he is very fast for his weight and is more adept than the Greyhound. He truly shines in races and lure coursing events. Very affectionate and intelligent, gentle with children, calm and quiet, the Whippet makes a wonderful pet. He is not a watchdog. His training must not be harsh.

Care and functions

He can adapt to the city but needs lots of exercise for his well-being. He does not like being left alone and cannot tolerate the cold. He is very clean and needs brushing once or twice a week.
. Racing dog.
. Companion dog.

HEAD
Long, thin. Long, flat skull. Slight stop. Powerful jaws. Nose matches coat color.

EYES
Oval, shiny.

EARS
Small, thin, rose-shaped.

BODY
Square build. Neck long, muscular, delicately arching. Very high chest. Well-sprung ribs. Strong hindquarters.

Tuck-up. Well-arched loin. Broad, fairly long back.

LIMBS
Cleanly cut, muscular legs. Cleanly cut feet with well-separated toes and thick pads.

TAIL
Long, tapering, carried below the topline.

COAT
Short, fine and dense.

COLOR
Any color or combination of colors.

SIZE
Dog: 47 to 51 cm (18.5-20 in).
Bitch: 44 to 47 cm (17.5-18.5 in).

WEIGHT
Approx. 10 kg (22 lb).

Special Breeds

HUNDE I.

Etching from J. Bungartz.
German encyclopedia.
Late nineteenth century.
Jonas/Kharbine Tapabor collection, Paris.

Some breeds registered with the International Canine Federation remain very restricted or are represented by only a few rare specimens. Others have become more common but are not yet accepted by the FCI. These "new", or more specifically, "neoform" (Y. Surget) breeds are often varieties of existing breeds.

Rare Breeds

BOUVIER DES ARDENNES

Some believe that the Bouvier des Ardennes was the result of a cross between the Belgian Cattle Dog and the Picardy Shepherd. Others hold that it is a native breed, probably developed around the eighteenth century by crossing several local sheepdog breeds.

GROUP 1 - SECTION 2
CATTLE DOGS

COUNTRY OF ORIGIN: Belgium
OTHER NAME: Ardennes Cattle Dog

HEAD
Massive, relatively short. Stop not pronounced. Short, broad muzzle with goatlike beard. Tight-lipped jaws.

EYES
Dark color. Gold color or walleyes not permissible.

EARS
Not cropped. Flat ears are not permissible. Erect ears breaking forward and semi-prick folding to the side are permitted.

BODY
Medium size. Short, thick neck. Broad forechest. Broad, deep chest. Ribs well sprung. Belly not tucked up. Topline (back, loin, croup) powerful, broad and horizontal.

LIMBS
Strong legs. Round feet with compact toes. Dewclaws not permitted on hind legs.

TAIL
Naturally tailless or docked to one vertebra.

COAT
Rough, mussed, 5 cm (2 in) long. Must be shorter on the head and legs. Very thick undercoat.

COLOR
All colors permitted.

SIZE
Approx. 60 cm (23.5 in).

WEIGHTT
22 to 25 kg (48-55 lb).

Character, special skills and training
This rustic breed is accustomed to living outdoors, tough guard work and herding cattle, at which it excels. This tough, hard-working dog is always on the alert and is wory of strangers. He is affectionate with his owner and very obedient.

Care and functions
This dog is not made for city living. He needs space and a lot of exercise. Regular brushing is required.
· Herder.
· Guard dog.
· Pet.

CANARY WARREN HOUND

This dog of Egyptian origin was probably brought to the Canary Islands by the Phoenicians, the Greeks, the Carthaginians and the Egyptians themselves. The Canary Warren Hound is one of the oldest breeds—its remains have been found in the tombs of the pharaohs. He is used on rabbit.

GROUP 5 - SECTION 7
PRIMITIVE TYPE - HUNTING DOGS

COUNTRY OF ORIGIN: Spain
OTHER NAME: Podenco Canario

HEAD
Long, shaped like a blunt cone. Parallel cranio-facial wrinkles. Skull flat, longer than it is wide. Stop not very pronounced. Broad muzzle. Flesh-colored nose. Tight-lipped.

EYES
Almond-shaped, small, slanted. A shade of amber.

EARS
Fairly large, erect, wide at the base and pointed at the tip.

BODY
Slightly longer than it is tall. Neck well-muscled, without dewlap. Well-developed chest. Oval ribs. Tuck-up. Strong back. Solidly boned croup.

LIMBS
Round feet with firm pads.

TAIL
Round, hanging down or raised in sickle fashion. Usually white.

COAT
Short, smooth, dense.

COLOR
Preferably red and white, with red ranging from orange to dark red (mahogany). All combinations of colors.

SIZE
Dog: 54 to 64 cm (21-25 in).
Bitch: 53 to 60 cm (21-23.5 in).

WEIGHT
Approx. 25 kg (55 lb).

Character, special skills and training
Long-backed and slender, he is extremely hardy, bold and energetic. He moves at an extended, very light-footed trot. He is eager, fast and active. He is a pleasant, peaceful pet but not a watchdog. His marvelous nose makes him an excellent tracker.

Care and functions
He needs space and exercise, as well as regular brushing.

BOSNIAN ROUGHHAIRED HOUND

This breed created in the nineteenth century sports a coat similar to that of the Griffon Nivernais and has griffon blood; some believe he was also developed from molossian breeds. Initially known as the Illyrian hound, the breed was recognized in 1965 as the Bosnian Roughhaired Hound.

GROUP 6 - SECTION 1
SCENT HOUNDS

COUNTRY OF ORIGIN: Bosnia
OTHER NAME: Bosanski Ostrodlaki Gonic Barak

HEAD
Long, moderately broad. Slightly domed forehead. Very pronounced brow bones. Gently sloping stop. Straight nosebridge. Strong, long, rectangular muzzle covered with a bushy mustache and beard. Broad nose. Tight, thick lips.

EYES
Large, oval, chestnut-colored.

EARS
Moderately long, broad. Pendulous, somewhat thick.

BODY
Slightly longer than it is tall. Muscular neck. Moderately pronounced withers. Chest long, moderately broad. Ribs not very rounded. Very slight tuck-up. Broad, muscular back. Broad, slightly sloping croup. Supple, tight, well-pigmented skin.

LIMBS
Muscular, strong legs. Cat feet with very tight toes.

TAIL
Thick at the base, tapering toward the tip. Carried in sickle fashion in a loose, upward curve. Well-furnished with hair.

COAT
Long, hard, shaggy, disheveled. Thick undercoat.

COLOR
Wheaten yellow, reddish-yellow, earth grey, or blackish ground. White markings often appear on the head and brisket, under the throat and neck, beneath the chest and on the lower legs and tip of the tail. Colors may be combined in a bicolor or tricolor pattern.

SIZE
46 to 56 cm (18-22 in).

WEIGHT
16 to 25 kg (35-55 lb).

Character, special skills and training
Stocky and powerful, this solidly boned dog is hardy, persistent, bold and spirited. With his sonorous, deep voice and long, confident strides, he excels on all sorts of game on all kinds of terrain.

Care and functions
Affectionate, gentle and calm, he makes a good pet but needs a firm owner and lots of space and exercise. He also requires daily brushing.

HELLENIC HOUND

This very ancient breed indigenous to Greece is believed to be descended from hounds brought from Egypt by the Phoenicians. The Hellenic Hound is not very well-known outside his native land.

GROUP 6 - SECTION 1
SCENT HOUNDS

COUNTRY OF ORIGIN: *Greece*
ORIGINAL NAME: *Hellinikos Ichnilatis*

HEAD
Long. Flat skull. Stop not very pronounced. Straight or slightly curved nosebridge. Strong jaws. Fairly developed lips.

EYES
Normal in size, brown.

EARS
Medium-sized, set on high, flat, rounded at the tip, pendulous.

BODY
Slightly longer than it is tall. Mesomorph. Neck powerful, muscular, without dewlap. Well-developed chest. Slightly circular ribs. Slightly arched, short, strong, well-muscled loin. Slight tuck-up. Long, straight back. Croup long, broad, nearly level.

LIMBS
Muscular, stocky legs.

Rounded, compact feet with large, tight toes.

TAIL
Short, thick at the base and tapering slightly toward the tip. In action, carried in saber fashion.

COAT
Close-lying, dense, somewhat hard.

COLOR
Black and tan. A small white spot on the chest is tolerated. Visible mucosa, nose and nails are black.

SIZE
Dog: 47 to 55 cm (18.5-21.5 in).
Bitch: 45 to 53 cm (17.5-21 in).

WEIGHT
17 to 20 kg (37-44 lb).

Character, special skills and training
Very hardy, vigorous and lively, the Hellenic Hound has a subtle nose and a far-reaching, melodic voice. Skilled in hunting on rugged terrain, he is a speedy and light-footed tracker of all game alone or in small packs. He is not well-suited to being a pet. He needs firm training.

Care and functions
Needs space and exercise.
. Hunting dog.

STYRIAN ROUGHHAIRED MOUNTAIN DOG

C. Peintinger, a manufacturer in the Austrian province of Styria, created the Styrian Roughhaired Mountain Dog in 1870 by crossing a red Hanoverian Hound with a roughhaired Istrian Hound.

GROUP 6 - SECTION 1
SCENT HOUNDS

COUNTRY OF ORIGIN: *Austria*
ORIGINAL NAMES: *Steirische Rauhhaarbracke, Steirische Rauhhaarige, Hochgebirgsbracke*

HEAD
Slightly domed skull. Pronounced stop. Solid, straight muzzle. Fairly tight-lipped.

EYES
Brown.

EARS
Not too large, lying flat against the cheeks, covered with fine hair.

BODY
Solid. Neck strong, not too long. Chest well let-down, broad. Straight, broad back. Sloping croup. Moderate tuck-up.

LIMBS
Well-muscled, solid legs. Feet with very tight, arched toes and tough pads.

TAIL
Medium in length, thick at the base, well-furnished with hair, never curled, carried raised loosely in sickle fashion. Brush on underside.

COAT
Harsh, hard, rough. Shorter on the head than on the rest of the body.

COLOR
Red and pale yellow. White flashings on the chest are allowed.

SIZE
Dog: 47 to 53 cm (18.5-21 in).
Bitch: 45 to 51 cm (17.5-20 in).

WEIGHT
Approx. 18 kg (40 lb).

Character, special skills and training
This tough-looking dog with a flexible gait and considerable stamina is hardy, active and resistant to bad weather. With a strong voice, he is used to force small game but also specializes in blood trailing over rugged, mountainous terrain.

Care and functions
He is affectionate and gentle but is not a companion dog. He needs a firm owner, as well as space, exercise and daily brushing.
. Hunting dog.

BALKAN HOUND

According to legend, the ancestors of the Balkan Hound came from Egypt and were brought to Europe by the Phoenicians around 1000 B.C.

GROUP 6 - SECTION 1
SCENT HOUNDS

COUNTRY OF ORIGIN: Yugoslavia
ORIGINAL NAME: Balkanski Gonic

HEAD
Long. Skull moderately wide. Forehead slightly domed. Well-pronounced brow bones. Slight stop. Straight nosebridge. Long muzzle. Well-developed, tight black lips.

EYES
Oval, brown with black eyelids.

EARS
Medium in length, flat, lying against the cheeks, fairly large.

BODY
Longer than it is tall. Neck slightly arched, very strong, without dewlap. Withers not very pronounced. Broad, long chest. Rounded ribs. Slight tuck-up. Long, broad back. Long, powerful, slightly sloping croup.

LIMBS
Well-muscled, powerful legs. Round feet with arched, tight toes.

TAIL
Thick at the base, tapering toward the tip. Held low and loosely in saber fashion.

COAT
Short, thick, slightly rough, glossy. Undercoat.

COLOR
Background fox-red or wheaten-red with black mantle or saddle. Black coloring extends to the head.

SIZE
Dog: 46 to 54 cm (18-21 in).
Bitch: 44 to 52 cm (17.5-20.5 in).

WEIGHT
Up to 20 kg (44 lb).

Character, special skills and training
A tireless, tenacious, lively hunter, the Balkan Hound has a fiery temper but is good-natured and docile. He has a high, sometimes booming voice and hunts hare, deer and wild boar. He is an energetic tracker of wounded animals. He needs a firm owner.

Care and functions
He needs space and lots of exercise and requires regular brushing.
· Hunting dog.

GERMAN BROKEN-COATED POINTING DOG

Born in Frankfurt-on-Main in the early twentieth century, the German Broken-coated Pointing Dog, now fairly rare, was produced by crossing griffons with pointers. Some believe he is the ancestor of the German Wirehaired Pointing Dog. He resembles a miniature Wirehaired Pointing Griffon.

GROUP 7 - SECTION 1
CONTINENTAL POINTING DOGS

COUNTRY OF ORIGIN: Germany
ORIGINAL NAMES: Deutscher Stichelhaariger Vorstehhund

HEAD
Medium-sized, not too heavy. Slight stop. Long nosebridge. Mustache on the muzzle.

EYES
Slightly oval, medium-sized, brown or lighter in color. Well-furnished, bushy eyebrows.

EARS
Set on high, medium in length, rounded at the tips, pendulous.

BODY
Strong. Powerful neck. Deep chest. Broad, short loin. Moderate tuck-up. Broad, straight back. Croup not too short, nearly level.

LIMBS
Muscular legs. Round feet with tough pads.

TAIL
Medium in length. Straight or curving slightly upward. May be lightly docked. Well-furnished with hair.

COAT
About 4 cm (1,5 in) long, hard and stiff on the body. A bit longer on the withers and lower the body. Thick undercoat in winter. Feathering on the backs of the legs.

COLOR
Brown and white, apparently a mixed greyish-brown or with isolated, fairly large brown spots.

SIZE
Dog: 60 to 66 cm (23.5-26 in).
Bitch: slightly smaller.

WEIGHT
25 to 30 kg (55-66 lb).

Character, special skills and training
The German Broken-coated Pointing Dog excels on all kinds of terrain and on all sorts of game. He is powerful, but not heavy and is a good tracker of wounded game (bloodhound). He accepts only one leader and may be aggressive toward strangers.

Care and functions
He needs firm training, space and exercise, as well as regular brushing.
. Hunting dog

DUPUY POINTING DOG

This very ancient breed, known since the eighteenth century and named after the French breeder from Poitou who created it. The Dupuy Pointing Dog is thought to be descended from a cross between the Poitou Pointing Dog and the English Pointer or between the old French Pointing Dog and the Greyhound or Arabian Greyhound. The breed was very common in the Poitou region and in western France in the early twentieth century. Today, it is practically extinct.

GROUP 7 - SECTION 1
CONTINENTAL POINTING DOGS

COUNTRY OF ORIGIN: *France*
OTHER NAME: *Pointing Greyhound*

HEAD
Long, narrow, slender, cleanly cut. Narrow, long, domed skull. Very pronounced occipital peak. No stop. Long, narrow, curved nose-bridge. Dark brown, broad nose. Tight-lipped.

EYES
Golden or brown.

EARS
Fairly long, narrow, very thin and supple, very pendulous and carried loosely back.

BODY
Slender. Neck very long, lightly boned, thin, without dewlap. Very open withers. Chest high, well let-down, deep. Flat ribs. Very developed sternum. Flanks slightly hollow, tuck-up. Level back. Slightly clean-flanked, powerful, fairly short loin.

LIMBS
Strong, bony legs. Long, very cleanly cut feet with tight toes.

TAIL
Of medium thickness, fairly long, carried low or very loosely curved. Fairly well-furnished with hair.

COAT
Fairly short, always smooth. Close-lying and very fine on the head and ears. Rough on the back and loin.

COLOR
White and dark brown. Lovely white ground with brown spots of varying size or brown mantle with or without spots, brown mottling mainly on the forelegs. Very thin skin.

SIZE
Dog: 67 to 68 cm (26.5 in).
Bitch: 65 to 66 cm (25.5 in).

WEIGHT
Approx. 30 kg (66 lb).

Character, special skills and training
The Dupuy Pointing Dog is large, slender and dignified. Quick, light-footed, flexible and keen-nosed, this firm pointer was used for hunting in the plains.

Care and functions
He needs space and exercise
. Hunting dog

POINTING GRIFFON

This griffon developed by E. Boulet in the nineteenth century is a longhaired pointer resembling a smooth-coated Barbet. The French Woolly-haired Pointing Griffon, which some believe is descended from the Barbet, has long existed in northern France. Boulet improved the breed around 1880 by crossing it, according to some, with pointers, the Poodle, sheep-dogs and other breeds. Now very rare in France.

GROUP 7 - SECTION 1
CONTINENTAL POINTING DOGS

COUNTRY OF ORIGIN: *France*
OTHER NAME: *Boulet Griffon*

HEAD
Bushy appearance. Long, broad, angular muzzle with thick mustache. Blond or brown nose.

EYES
Yellow. Thick eyebrows may lightly veil the eyes.

EARS
Set on fairly low, pendulous, loosely curled, covered with smooth or wavy hair.

BODY
Compact. Neck fairly long. Chest broad and deep. Strong loin.

LIMBS
Strong, muscular legs. Slightly elongated feet.

TAIL
Straight, well-carried, without plume.

COAT
Long, fairly silky, smooth or wavy, never curly.

COLOR
Dead foliage with or without white markings, but never with large white spots.

SIZE
Dog: 55 to 60 cm (21.5-23.5 in).
Bitch: 50 to 55 cm (19.5-21.5 in).

WEIGHT
20 to 25 kg (44-55 lb).

Character, special skills and training
Very hardy and somewhat heavy in appearance, the French Woolly-haired Pointing Griffon has a very keen nose and excels in woods and swamps. His coat is perfect protection from cold and harsh weather. He has a limited search range, tracking slowly but methodically.

Care and functions
He is a delightful pet who needs space and exercise, as well as regular brushing and attention to the ears.
. Hunting dog.
. Companion dog.

HUNDE II (JAGDHUNDE).

Etching from J. Bungartz.
German encyclopedia.
Late nineteenth century.
Jonas/Kharbine Tapabor collection, Paris.

Provisionally Accepted Breeds

SHEEPDOGS

ALAPAHA BLUE BLOOD BULLDOG (UNITED STATES)
Descended from the English Bulldog and bred in Georgia, the Alapaha Blue Blood Bulldog measures 51 to 63 cm (20-25 in) tall, weighs 23 to 40 kg (50-88 lb), has a short coat in a variety of colors and is both a watchdog and a pet.

WHITE SHEPHERD (UNITED STATES)
This German Shepherd variety has been developed with a white coat. Measuring 55 to 65 cm (21.5-25.5 in) tall and weighing approximately 40 kg (88 lb), the White Shepherd has become a companion dog. A French breed club exists.

NORTH AMERICAN SHEPERD (UNITED STATES)
This breed resembling a miniature Australian Shepherd measures 33 to 46 cm (13-18 in) tall, weighs 7 to 13.5 kg (15-30 lb) and has a coat of medium length in a variety of colors. The North American Shepherd has also become a companion dog.

LANCASHIRE HEELER (OMSKIRK TERRIER)
Produced by crossing the Welsh Corgi and the Manchester Terrier, the Lancashire Heeler is native to Britain. He stands low to the ground, has a long body, measures 25 to 30 cm (10-12 in) tall, weighs 3.5 to 7 kg (7.5-15.5 lb) and has a short, black and tan coat. This cattledog who nips at herd members' heels is kept in his native Lancashire County and is also a ratter and rabbit hunter. A provisional standard was published in 1986. He is rare outside Great Britain.

DANISH FARM DOG (DENMARK)
The result of crossing various breeds living in Denmark, the Danish Farm Dog measures 26 to 30 cm (10-12 in) tall, weighs 12 to 14 cm (26-31 lb) and has a close-lying coat in a variety of colors.

NEW ZEALAND HUNTAWAY
This sheepdog stands 51 to 61 cm (20-24 in) tall, weighs 18 to 30 kg (40-66 lb), has semi-erect ears, a thick, feathered tail and a black coat with tan markings.

CORSICAN DOG
This ancient mesomorph breed measures 41 to 58 cm (16-23 in) tall, weighs 20 to 30 cm (44-66 lb) and has a short or medium-length brindle fawn or smoky fawn coat, often with a black mask. An association was founded in 1989 to preserve the breed.

AKBASH (COBAN KOPEGI)
This sheepdog of Turkish origin is used in the United States. Measuring 71 to 86 cm (28-34 in) tall, weighing 40 to 50 kg (88-110 lb) and sporting a thick coat, he is thought to be descended from the Komondor, the Kuvasz and the Tatra Mountain Sheepdog.

HIMALAYAN SHEEPDOG (INDIA)
This dog of unknown origin stands 51 to 66 cm (20-26 in) tall, weighs 23 to 41 kg (50.5-90.5 lb) and has a thick coat in a variety of colors.

White shepherd (United States)

Danish Farm Dog (Denmark)

Kyiapo
(Bearded Tibetan Mastiff)

WATCHDOGS

Canary Dog (Perro de Presa Canario)

Boerbull (South Africa)

OLD ENGLISH BULLDOG (UNITED STATES)

In the interest of reviving the ancient English Bulldog, this breed was produced in the twentieth century by crossing the English Bulldog, the Bull Mastiff and the American Pit Bull. Standing 51 to 64 cm (20-25 in) tall and weighing 29 to 48 kg (64-105 lb), the Old English Bulldog has a massive head, a solidly built, mastiff-type body, rose ears and a close-lying coat in a variety of colors. This bold, determined dog may be aggressive.

BULL BOXER (GREAT BRITAIN)

This recent creation was produced by crossing the Boxer with the Staffordshire Bull Terrier. Standing 41 to 53 cm (16-21 in) tall and weighing 17 to 24 kg (37.5-53 lb), the Bull Boxer has a powerful body, cropped ears and a close-lying coat in a variety of colors. He is a delightful pet.

CANARY DOG (*PERRO DE PRESA CANARIO*)

This ancient Spanish fighting dog is thought to be descended from a cross between the English Mastiff and a now extinct local breed, the Bardino Majero. The powerful Canary Dog stands 55 to 65 cm (21.5-25.5 in) tall and weighs 38 to 48 kg (83-105 lb). He has an angular head, close-lying hair and fairly loose skin. His coat is fawn, red brindle, or black brindle, with possible white markings. Bold and determined, he is a good watchdog and a delightful pet.

BOERBULL (SOUTH AFRICA)

This powerful molossian breed is descended from the ancestor of the Boxer, the English Mastiff and the English Bull Mastiff imported to South Africa. Specimens were brought to Holland in 1994. The Boerbull measures up to 70 cm (28 in) tall and weighs 60 to 70 (130-155 lb). He has pendulous ears and a short brindle, yellow, grey, reddish-brown, or brown coat. He is a defense dog.

SANSHU (JAPAN)

The Sanshu was created in the early twentieth century from a cross between the Chow and the old Aichi from Japan. He weighs 20 to 25 cm (44-55 lb) and stands 45 to 55 cm (17.5-21.5 in) tall. He has a short, stocky body, a broad head, almond-shaped eyes, straight ears and a curved tail. His hair is medium in length, hard and rough and his coat is rust-colored, black and tan, light brown, salt and pepper, white, etc. Bold and hardy, he makes a good watchdog and an affectionate companion.

KYIAPO (*BEARDED TIBETAN MASTIFF*)

The ancestors of this very ancient breed protected Tibetan nomads and their herds of sheep. He stands 63 to 71 cm (25-28 in) tall and weighs 32 to 41 kg (70-90 lb). He has long hair and a curved, well-feathered tail.

HUNTING DOGS

AMERICAN STAGHOUND (UNITED STATES)

this cross between the Deerhound, the Greyhound and the Irish Wolfhound specializes in deer.

BLUETICK COONHOUND (UNITED STATES)

this variety of Black and Tan Coonhound stands 51 to 69 cm (20-27 in) tall, weighs 20 to 36 kg (44-79 lb) and has a close-lying, tricolor coat consisting of a white ground with dark blue spots and fawn markings. Developed in the nineteenth century, the Bluetick Coonhound hunts raccoon.

CATAHOULA (*CATAHOULA LEOPARD DOG*)

a symbol of the state of Louisiana, the Catahoula has obscure origins. He measures 51 to 66 cm (20-26 in) tall, weighs 18 to 30 kg (40-66 lb), has pendulous ears and may have heterochromatic eyes. He wears a close-lying, grey coat with uneven black markings and fawn coloring on the head and legs. This hound is as skilled on large game (bear) as he is on raccoon. He is used as a sheepdog and makes a good watchdog.

PLOTT HOUND (UNITED STATES)

This breed is descended from dogs imported from Germany to the United States by the Plott family in the eighteenth century and crossed with English hounds. The Plott Hound hunts wolf, puma, coyote, wildcat, deer, bear and wild boar. Measuring 53 to 64 cm (21-25 in) tall and weighing 18 to 29 cm (40-64 lb), he has pendulous ears, short hair and a tricolor coat (white and tan with a black saddle).

REDBONE COONHOUND (UNITED STATES)

This variety of Black and Tan Coonhound stands 53 to 66 cm (21-26 in) tall and weighs 23 to 32 kg (50-70 lb). He has short hair and a solid red coat. He hunts raccoon.

REDTICK COONHOUND (UNITED STATES)

This close cousin to the Bluetick Coonhound measures 51 to 69 cm (20-27 in) tall and weighs 20 to 36 kg (44-79 lb). He has pendulous ears, short hair and a heavily spotted, reddish-chestnut coat. He hunts raccoon and fox and is also a good watchdog.

TREEING WALKER COONHOUND (UNITED STATES)

Another variety of Black and Tan Coonhound, the Treeing Walker is gifted at treeing, or forcing game up a tree and holding it there until the hunters arrive. He hunts raccoon and opossum. He stands 51 to 69 cm (20-27 in) tall and weighs 23 to 32 kg (50-70 lb). He has a solid head, pendulous ears, close-lying hair and a tricolor (black, white and tan) or bicolor (white and tan) coat.

TRIGG HOUND (UNITED STATES):

This variety of American Fox Hound stands 51 to 61 cm (20-24 in) tall, weighs 20 to 25 kg (44-55 lb) and has fine hair. All coat colors are allowed. He is hardy and has a subtle nose.

MAJESTIC TREE HOUND (UNITED STATES)

This recently created bloodhound developed by crossing the Saint Hubert Hound with other hounds is used on big cats and large game. He has an excellent nose and a lovely voice. Large and massive, he has a wrinkled foreface, short hair and a solid or mixed coat.

MOUNTAIN CUR (UNITED STATES)

The product of crossing European dogs introduced by colonists with local pariahs, this powerful, stocky dog resembles the Cur, an extinct English cattledog. A good tracker who seldom barks, the Mountain Cur is hardy and bold.

LUCAS TERRIER (GREAT BRITAIN)

The Lucas Terrier was created in the 1950s by crossing the Sealyham Terrier with the Norfolk Terrier. He stands 25 to 30 cm (10-12 in) tall and weighs 4.5 to 6 kg (10-13 lb). He hunts in packs.

LURCHER (GREAT BRITAIN)

This Irish breed resembling a small sighthound was produced by crossing Collie-type dogs with sighthounds (including the Greyhound and the Deerhound). The Lurcher measures 69 to 76 cm (27-30 in) tall and weighs 27 to 32 kg (59.5-70.5 lb). He has a long, narrow head, a long body, hard or close-lying hair and often a bicolor coat (white with a dark mantle and spots). This hunting dog is very popular, particularly with poachers and is virtually unknown outside of Ireland.

PLUMMER TERRIER (GREAT BRITAIN)

B. Plummer created this breed by crossing the Fell-type Terrier (a variety of Patterdale Terrier) with the Parson Jack Russell Terrier, an American Beagle and the Bull Terrier. The Plummer Terrier stands 29 to 34 cm (11.5-13.5 in) tall, weighs 5.5 to 7 kg (12-15.5 lb), has pendulous ears and is an excellent ratter.

PATTERDALE TERRIER (GREAT BRITAIN)

A native of northern England, this breed was named after the town of Patterdale in Cumberland, where he was very popular. He stands 30 cm (12 in) tall and weighs 5 to 6 kg (11-13 lb). The stocky, well-built Patterdale Terrier has folded ears, close-lying hair and a black, black and tan, brown, or red coat. Bold and tenacious, he hunts rabbit.

KERRY BEAGLE (POCADAN)

Descended from a deer-hunting dog of southern Ireland, the Kerry Beagle was used on hare. In the twentieth century, he was introduced to the United States, where he was used to develop American hound breeds. Larger than the Beagle, he stands 56 to 66 cm (22-26 in) tall and weighs 20 to 27 kg (44-59.5 lb). He has a broad head, pendulous ears and short hair. His coat can be white and tan, blue and tan, black and tan, or tricolor.

ALANO (SPAIN)

This breed was created by crossing the descendents of Celtic hounds with mastiffs. The Alano, believed to be an ancestor of the Argentinean Mastiff, has a massive head, pendulous ears and a fairly short body. He has short hair and a red coat with a black muzzle. He hunts wild boar.

BRAZILIAN TRACKER (RASTREADOR BRASILEIRO)

This breed is descended from crosses between the American Fox Hound, the Black and Tan Coonhound, the Treeing Walker Coonhound and the Bluetick Coonhound. He measures approximately 65 cm (25.5 in) tall and weighs approximately 25 kg (55 lb). He has pendulous ears and short hair. His coat is black and tan, tricolor, etc. Strong, lively and bold, he has great stamina and hunts jaguar.

RAMPUR DOG (INDIA)

This dog's origins are uncertain. He is believed to be related to the Afghan Hound and the Arabian Greyhound. A splash of Greyhound blood was added in the nineteenth century. He stands 56 to 76 cm (22-30 in) tall and weighs 23 to 32 kg (50.5-70.5 lb). He has close-lying hair and is not very well-known outside his native land.

SAINT USUGE SPANIEL (FRANCE)

A standard existed in 1936 for this very ancient spaniel separated from the French Spaniel by a regional differentiation in Burgundy and Franche-Comté. This breed may soon be officially recognized.

Redbone Coonhound (United States)

Lurcher (Great Britain)

Patterdale Terrier (Great Britain)

Catahoula (Catahoula Leopard Dog)

COMPANION DOGS

CAROLINA DOG (UNITED STATES)

Discovered in South Carolina, this dog is believed to be Asian in origin. He stands 56 cm (22 in) tall and weighs 13 to 18 kg (28.5-39.5 lb). He has a long head, large, erect ears, short, dense hair and a golden yellow coat. Originally a sheepdog and a hunting dog, the Carolina Dog has become a companion animal despite his wild instincts.

TOY AMERICAN ESKIMO

This small dog is descended from the Spitz. He measures 28 to 31 cm (11-12 in) tall and weighs 3 to 5 kg (6.5-11 lb). He has erect ears and his head resembles that of a fox. His tail has a lovely plume and is carried curved over the back. The Toy American Eskimo has long, thick hair and a pure white coat. He is vigorous and athletic.

KYI LEO

Developed in California in the 1970s, the Kyi Leo is the product of a cross between the Lhasa Apso and the Maltese. Measuring 23 to 28 cm (9-11 in) tall and weighing 6 to 7 kg (13-15.5 lb), he has pendulous ears, long, slightly wavy hair and usually a bicolor coat (black and white). He makes an adorable pet.

Kyi Leo

SHILOH SHEPERD (UNITED STATES)

Created in the 1980s, the Shiloh Shepherd stands 66 to 70 cm (26-27.5 in) tall and weighs 36 to 50 kg (79-110 lb). He has erect ears.

TOY FOX TERRIER, AMERTOY

Developed in the 1930s, the Toy Fox Terrier is the result of crossing the Toy Smooth Fox Terrier, the English Toy Terrier and the Chihuahua. He measures 25 cm (10 in) tall and weighs 2 to 3 kg (4.5-6.5 lb). He has a domed skull and a well-pronounced stop. He has erect ears and his tail is usually docked. He has round, dark eyes and a close-lying, tricolor (white with black and tan markings) or bicolor (white and tan, white and black) coat. Lively and alert, he is a ratter and is also trained as a service dog for the handicapped.

Toy Fox-Terrier, Amertoy

PRAZSKY KRYSAVICK (CZECH REPUBLIC)

This small dog was developed some twenty years ago. He stands 20 cm (8 in) tall and weighs 1 to 3 kg (2-6.5 lb). He has a delicate head with a narrow muzzle. His hair is close-lying and fine.

BICHON-YORKIE (GREAT BRITAIN)

Developed by crossing the Bichon Frisé with the Yorkshire Terrier, the Bichon-Yorkie stands 23 to 31 cm (9-12 in) tall and weighs 3 to 6 kg (6.5-13 lb). His hair is dense and soft.

NEW GUINEA SINGING DOG

Known in the nineteenth century, this breed became extinct in the twentieth century. Pairs found in the 1950s and 1970s were used in an attempt to revive the breed. Similar to the Dingo, the New Guinea Singing Dog stands 35 to 38 cm (13.5-15 in) tall and weighs 8 to 10 kg (17.5-22 lb). He has a short coat consisting of various shades of red with white markings.

He often lives in the wild and has a melodious howl. Distant and unpredictable, he may not be the perfect pet!

CACKERPOO

The Cackerpoo was created in the United States by crossing Miniature Poodles and American Cockers. The Cackerpoo weighs 9 to 11 kg and measures 35 to 38 cm at the withers. Coat colors are similar to those of Poodles.

INCA HAIRLESS DOG (MOONFLOWER DOG)

Discovered by the Spanish conquistadors in the sixteenth century, this breed was kept by the Indios until the early twentieth century. He has been introduced to the United States and Europe. His is bare except for a tuft of hair on his head. He measures 50 to 65 cm (19.5-22.5 in) and weighs 12 to 23 kg (26.5-50.5 lb).

DINGO (HALIKI, WARRIGAL, NOGGUM, BOOLOMO)

This pariah-type dog is thought to have migrated to Australia over 20,000 years ago, at the same time as the Aborigines. He was kept as a hunting dog and a pet. Resistant to domestication, the Dingo has returned to the wild. He stands up to 53 cm (20 in) tall and weighs 10 to 20 kg (22-44 lb). His eyes are yellow or orange. He has close-lying hair and a coat in a variety of colors, often yellow, chestnut, black and white. He can be trained if started very young.

UTILITY DOGS

BOULAB (ST. PIERRE)

Of Canadian origin, the Boulab was created in 1990 by crossing the Labrador Retriever with the Bernese Mountain Dog to obtain a dog with the Labrador's liveliness and the Bernese Mountain Dog's obedience. The Boulab is slightly larger than the Labrador but has a similar coat. He is trained as a seeing-eye dog.

LABRADOODLE (AUSTRALIA)

The Labradoodle was created in 1989 by crossing the Standard Poodle and the Labrador Retriever. He stands 54 to 65 cm (21-25.5 in) tall and weighs 25 to 35 kg (55-77 lb). He has a curly coat in a variety of colors. He makes a good pet and is often trained as a seeing-eye dog.

SLED DOGS

ALASKAN HUSKY (ALASKA, UNITED STATES)

Created in the early twentieth century by alaskan mushers, by crossing siberian huskies, indian dogs, and various sporting breeds. The Alaskan Husky is definitly the most performing sled dogs and represents worldwide 90 % of the racing dogs population. He stands 45 to 60 cm (17.5-23.5 in) in tall and weighs 18 to 26 kg (39-58 lb), and looks like a nordic dog.

CHINOOK (UNITED STATES)

Created in the early twentieth century by crossing the Eskimo Dog, the Saint Bernard and the Belgian Sheepdog, the Chinook is very rare, even endangered. He weighs 30 to 40 kg (66-88 lb) and measures 53 to 61 cm (21-24 in) tall. He gives the impression of great strength. His ears are pendulous or cropped. He has an abundant, thick, fawn-colored coat. He is both a watchdog and a pet.

ESKIMO DOG (CANADA)

This very ancient lupoid breed stands 51 to 68 cm (20-27 in) tall and weighs 27 to 48 kg (59-105 lb). His ears are erect and his hair is thick and dense. His tufted tail is carried curled on the back. All coat colors are allowed.

GREYSTER (NORWAY)

This breed, still very rare, is the product of crossing the German Pointing Dog and the Greyhound. The Greyster measures 68 to 75 cm (26.5-29.5 in) tall and weighs 25 to 35 kg (55-77 lb). He has a short, black or brown brindle coat. He is a sprinter but not a distance runner.

Alaskan Husky

Part 2

Dogs in Art

Fresco by Andrea Mantegna (1431-1506), Italy.
The couple's bedroom. Leaving for hunting.
Detail: Lower segment (after restoration).
Gal. E. Museo Di Palazzo Ducale, Mantoue.
Alinari-Giraudon Collection, Paris.

Dogs in Art and History

*Thèbes: Bibân el Molouk.
Vases, furniture, and various subjects painted
in the tombs of kings, Anubis, god of the dead,
bending over the mummy of the Pharaoh.
Selva Collection, Paris.*

Since the beginning of history, humans have created images of the animals around them. Cave art, archeology, sculpture and paintings illustrate the important role dogs have played in both daily life and imagination. Watchdog, hunting dog or companion, guardian of the dead or protector of the gates of hell, symbol of vigilance, loyalty and obedience, the dog was also cursed and associated with death and evil. He is often featured on coats of arms, coins and, more recently, postage stamps.

Dogs in Archeology

Dogs account for a large number of the animal representations that have been discovered by archeologists. These representations give evidence of the dog's status in society - from slave to god, depending on place and time. The oldest is a cave painting in Spain's Cueva Vieja from about 10,000 B.C. In it, a dog is apparently blocking a deer's path to safety - the hunt is on!

Deified Dogs

The best known example of the deified dog in Egypt is Anubis, the half-dog, half-jackal god found beginning in the 19th Dynasty (around 1200 B.C.). Because dogs were often seen lurking around cemeteries at night, Anubis was the god of the dead. He presided over funerals and burial rites, particularly embalming.

In Greek mythology, the dog was a creature forged by Hephaestus, the god of fire and blacksmith to the other gods. The dog's divine origin earned him a place of privilege among the animals.

Working Dogs and Warrior Dogs

Since the beginning of time, humans have relied on dogs as helpmates. Used as slaves in Asia Minor (the ideogram for "dog" is the same as that for "slave" in cuneiform writing from around 2000 B.C.!), dogs gradually gained a respected role in human work.

Nearly all early hunting scenes show dogs alongside humans. For example, paintings on the walls surrounding Çatal Hüyük, a Neolithic settlement in Asia Minor, depict humans using hounds to hunt big cats. Prior to the 18th Dynasty in Egypt, dogs helped humans hunt antelope and gazelle. By about 1500 B.C., dog breeding and breed specialization had produced greyhounds, which were faster than earlier dogs. In ancient Greece and Rome, just as in Egypt, dogs helped in the hunt and were often represented in art.

They also began serving as watchdogs, like Cerberus, known in Greek mythology for guarding the entrance to the underworld or Hades. In the Far East, toy dogs were the guardians of eunuchs (3470 B.C.). In ancient Rome (first century A.D.), dogs on leashes guarded homes (thus the inscription *cave canem* - beware of dog - on a mosaic from Pompei).

Dogs also aided soldiers at war. In the Far East around 1000 B.C., Mesopotamian dogs, especially hounds, were highly sought after for tracking down humans, such as escaped slaves. Sculptures of the mastiffs used in wars decorate a door of a Buddhist temple in Sanshi-Tope, India. Warrior dogs in ancient Rome had various specialties. Defense dogs protected the back lines, attack dogs were sent to the front lines and liaison dogs ensured communication between army posts. Liaison dogs were perhaps the worst off: They were forced to swallow messages and sacrificed upon arrival.

Mosaic, Tunisian Dog, 3rd century.
Cogis, Paris

Dogs in the Home

Although dogs seem to have held a less-than-desirable position in ancient times, evidence shows that they were sometimes treated with kindness and respect. In the New Dynasty in Egypt, dogs were so highly regarded that to mistreat or kill one was punishable by law. Ancient Greek artists depicted dogs as animals who had earned the privilege of human company. The sculptors of Assourbanipal in Mesopotamia evoke this privilege in Jeune satyre au repos [Young Satyr at Rest], a piece held by the Louvre Museum in Paris. But the first sign that dogs were truly a part of family life is an earthenware piece from Gaul depicting a couple embracing in a bed with a dog sleeping soundly at their feet. Surprisingly, this sculpture portraying an entirely modern notion of "love" for dogs dates to around 50 A.D.

Dogs in Paintings

Since the dawn of civilization, paintings of dogs have hinted that the dog is "man's best friend". The first cave paintings of dogs date as far back as prehistoric times, around 4500 B.C. Although dogs appear less frequently in cave paintings than game animals - the main inspiration for this art - they are nevertheless present as hunting dogs unlike any currently known breed. More recent paintings from ancient Egypt show breeds similar to those of today.

Roman Empire: Watchdogs

In the Roman Empire, the status of dogs in society was changing. In fact, dogs were fully accepted as domestic animals who also protected the home and were a precious resource for hunting. They were constant companions, loyal and completely devoted to their owners. The dogs of the Roman Empire were essentially regal yet ferocious mastiffs who defended their home from strangers.

Jean le Bon surrounded by the nobles.
Selva Collection, Paris.

Middle Ages: Primarily Hunting Dogs

From the fall of the Roman Empire to the Middle Ages, dogs are nearly absent in art, perhaps because painters of the time feared stray dogs as aggressive, dangerous beasts who hungrily devoured carcasses. In Islam, dogs were seen as cursed symbols of death and the force of evil.

The use of dogs in hunting helped change public opinion. Still, in the early Middle Ages, dogs were valued only for their aggressiveness. Dogs reappear in paintings of this time usually in packs, rather than alone. Some paintings show kings hunting with their dogs, sometimes in packs of a thousand.

Over time, the portrayal of dogs in art became closer and closer to reality. Still, it is not always easy to determine exactly which breed is depicted in a piece, since subjects may be the result of crossbreeding. Nevertheless, each type of dog had his own specialty. Scenthounds are shown hunting only mammalian game, tracking it by its scent. These breeds with a similar appearance but different coat colors include the French Chien de Saint-Hubert, Chien Blanc du Roy, Fauve de Bretagne and Gris de Saint-Louis. Their names show quite clearly to whom they belonged or where they came from. Pointers are shown with falcons, hunting large game. These dogs were used to kill prey before the invention of rifles.

Renaissance: Dogs Are Domesticated

Companion dogs begin to appear in paintings in the late Middle Ages. Renaissance ladies are shown with small dogs on their lap or at their feet. These greyhounds and other small breeds seem to enchant their mistresses, who show them a great deal of affection. Renaissance artists used dogs as subjects much more frequently than their predecessors. All sorts of breeds appear in sixteenth-century paintings, from the small companion dogs of ladies and damsels to dignified greyhounds to the larger dogs who accompanied lords.

In Renaissance times, dogs became closer to humans. Dogs are shown lying under the table at banquets, savoring the tidbits tossed by guests. They finally became full-fledged companion animals. Artists from many different countries used dogs as subjects: In Venice, for example, artists painted toy dogs reclining on cushions, being doted on by their mistresses during a gondola ride. Yet dogs were still indispensable hunting companions. Painters began to make a clearer distinction between the different kinds of hunting dogs (scenthounds, pointers, etc.).

Seventeenth Century to Today: Breeds Diversify

Starting in the seventeenth century, the number of breeds began to grow, once again because of hunting, at least at first. As hunting techniques and game diversified, so did hunting dog breeds.

Pol Limobourg
(15th century).
"Très riches heures
du Duc de Berry".
Calendar, January:
The Duke of Berry dining
(with zodiac).
Chantilly, Musée Condé,
France.
Giraudon Collection,
Paris.

Detail: Two dwarf dogs
on the table.

369

Nevertheless, by the late seventeenth century, the focus had switched to smaller dogs like the King Charles, a favorite of royalty.

Little by little, dogs began to appear in paintings alone or at least as the focal point. Some artists began to specialize in animal subjects, including François Desportes (1661-1743, the official painter of King Louis XIV), Paul de Vos (1596-1678), and Jean-Baptiste Oudry (1686-1755).

Dogs were depicted with striking realism, both in terms of anatomy and expression. The postures and expressions characteristic to each breed were copied directly from reality. In some pieces, it seems as though the artist included a dog only to immortalize him!

More recently, in the nineteenth and twentieth centuries, artists—and contemporary society as a whole - began to show a growing interest in dogs. In paintings, the packs of large hunting dogs that once served royalty are replaced almost entirely by domestic breeds and, in some cases, by sheepdogs and watchdogs. The painters of this period give an almost sentimental image of these dogs.

Soon the style became abstract. Dogs began to be portrayed as symbols, making it impossible to determine which breed had inspired a particular piece. Still today, dogs continue to be a source of endless admiration and inspiration, appreciated by all.

Saint-Hubert.
Miniature by Jean Bourdichon, copy of
"Heures d'Anne de Bretagne", 15th century.
Selva Collection, Paris.

Dogs in Sculpture

As humans evolved, they invented art to express their feelings about the world around them. They began by drawing what they saw on cave walls, using pigments on engravings in stone. Later, they discovered pottery and sculpture. Animals naturally became artistic subjects. They also became religious symbols, either feared or respected.

Prehistoric Times: Figurative Art

The first sculptures of dogs are earthenware objects in a very simple style. This purely figurative art is based primarily on the form of the animal seen as a companion in hunting, herding, and everyday life. Some pieces show evidence of claw and tooth marks. These early sculptures depict animals with oversized bellies and short legs.

Precolumbian art is also very simple. Dogs are depicted not realistically, but with the qualities of the god with whom they were associated. Precolumbian sculpture became an expression of the spiritual and mystical world, a trend that reached its peak in ancient times.

Egypt: Dogs as Stylized Symbols

Ancient Egyptians worshiped all sorts of animals, including the dog, considered the earthly incarnation of the god Anubis and sometimes Thot. In their very elaborate and stylized sculptures, Egyptian artists sought to evoke one of the dog's characteristics while retaining the animal's form, generally based on that of the desert greyhound. The limestone dog at the Louvre Museum in Paris - depicting a sheepdog wearing a collar - is a perfect example of this. Egyptian bas-reliefs often show dog racing or hunting scenes including dogs.

Ancient Egyptians also used dogs to decorate tombs and cemeteries. The sarcophagus of Madja from the 18th Dynasty clearly shows a dog with a fox's tail in a reclining position. Two statues of dogs stand guard at the entrance to all Egyptian temples as a symbol of the sovereign's watchfulness over his people.

Asia: Lion-Dogs

The dog occupies a very unique position in Asia, where he has been considered either a god or a delicacy, earning either respect or scorn. At the entrance to most Chinese temples and palaces stand two "lion-dogs" with clear similarities to the mastiff breeds native to the region. Even in everyday sculpted objects, dogs are depicted with exaggerated features and embellished with ornaments of various sizes.

Assyria: Fine Animal Sculpture

The animal art of Assyria is abundant and of very high quality. In this civilization, art was inspired by religion and the worship of royalty. Dogs are generally depicted alone in incredible detail, in hunting scenes, or alongside their master.

Ancient Greece and Rome: Geometric Style

Closer to modern times, the art of ancient Greece and Rome is primarily geometric in style, with clean lines. Like human sculpture, animal sculpture became more refined, to the point of near perfect realism. Very few statues of dogs have been found from this period. This is not surprising, since in these cultures dogs were no longer seen as gods.

Middle Ages: Imaginative Representations

In the Middle Ages, art became focused on the imagination and on symbolic representation. Next to religion, good and evil were the main sources of inspiration. Dogs played a limited, mainly decorative, role in art.

In Renaissance times, artists focused on anatomical and morphological studies in an effort to find the ideal proportions. Horses were the main subjects; dogs apparently had limited appeal.

Seventeenth Century to Today: Popular Subjects

Following the Renaissance, the dog was a subject more for experimental sculpture than for true art. But beginning in the nineteenth century, true animal artists started to use dogs as primary subjects. For example, Antoine Louis Barye (1796-1875) created anatomically accurate bronze sculptures based on dissections. Hunting breeds were his favorite.

Diana the Huntress.
Ceramic dish.
"L'œuvre de Bernard Palissy"
by C. Delange and C. Borneman,
Paris, 1869.

371

The Dog: Myths and Symbols

Humans have always used objects and creatures from daily life to represent the invisible and the mystical. For nearly fifteen thousand years, dogs have lived alongside humans. Therefore, it is only natural that dogs are an important element in mythical and symbolic art. The dog's appearance and especially his behavior have been used to symbolize situations, special powers, and even divinities.

Guardian of the Gates of Hell

Dogs watch over the home, howl at the moon, and often hunt at night. For these reasons, many cultures have associated dogs with death. Both Cerberus, the three-headed black dog of Greek mythology, and Garm, the guardian of Niefheim in Germanic civilization, protected the gates of hell, maintaining the separation between the living and the dead.

Guide to the Spirits of the Dead

Dogs were seen as everyday companions in life as in death. They symbolized the force that guided spirits in their journey to the kingdom of the dead. The best known dog-guide is Anubis, an ancient Egyptian god with the head of a jackal. His role was to oversee the embalming of the dead before leading them to the place where spirits were judged. At the judgment, Anubis weighed the heart of the dead against the feather of truth.

Anubis' counterpart in ancient Mexican civilization is the god Xolotl, a lion-colored dog who accompanied the sun god in his journey to the underworld. Traditionally, a dog of the Xoloitzcuintli breed, with a yellow coat like the sun, was sacrificed at funerals. The dog of the deceased person might also be sacrificed, to ensure that his owner would be protected until arriving at the gates of death. In Guatemala, dog figurines were traditionally placed at the four corners of the tomb, a practice still observed today.

In Eastern cultures, the dead and dying were entrusted to dogs who might guide them to heaven, the seat of the divine.

Messenger between the Living and the Afterworld

Dogs have also been seen as a link between the world of the living and the afterworld. Two variations on this theme can be found: Some Sudanese cultures and the Bantus of the former Zaire believed that dogs delivered messages to a sorcerer in a trance. Other Sudanese tribes and the Iroquois of North America believed that dogs themselves carried messages to the dead after being sacrificed.

From these examples, it is easy to understand how the dog's association with death, combined with his nocturnal hunting habits, might have fueled rumors of sorcery and evil spells with regard to dogs.

Dual Symbol

Islam adopted this negative view of dogs, considering them impure creatures, like pigs. Dogs were seen as carcass eaters who frightened the angels and heralded death with their barking. People were to avoid dogs, and anyone who killed one became as impure as the dog himself. However, Muslims believed they could protect themselves from evil spells by eating the flesh of a puppy, and they appreciated a dog's loyalty to his owner. Paradoxically, Muslims revered the greyhound as a noble animal and a symbol of goodness and luck.

Dogs can also be found as dual symbols in the cultures of the Far East. In China, the dog was seen either as the destroyer - the huge, hairy beast T'ien K'uan - or the loyal companion who escorted immortals to heaven. The philosopher Lao Tzu portrays the dog as an ephemeral creature, describing the ancient Chinese custom of burning straw effigies of dogs to ward off evil spells. On the contrary, in Japanese culture the dog was a good animal who protected children and mothers. In Tibet, dogs were symbols of sexuality and fertility, providing the spark of life. This leads to another aspect in the symbolism of dogs, that of fire.

Dogs on Fire

Strangely, in most cases the dog did not symbolize fire itself but instead was seen as the creature who transmitted fire to humans. The dog was therefore is the equivalent of Prometheus in certain African and Native American tribes. On the South Sea Islands, the dog was the master of fire, growling and sleeping beside the flames. For the Aztecs he was fire itself, while for the Mayas he was simply the guardian of the sun at night.

Alternately, dogs could symbolize war and victory, as for the Celts. In Celtic culture, the dog was praised, and being compared to a dog was an honor.

Ambiguous Symbol

Over time, the dog became an important symbol. Yet the symbolism of dogs throughout history shows the apparent ambiguity with which different cultures regarded them. Protector and watchdog for some, evildoer and demon for others, the symbolism of dogs changed constantly before being completely forgotten by modern civilization.

Dogs do still appear in current expressions but, paradoxically, nearly always with negative connotations. Used as an attribute, "dog" yields "to have a dog's life", "to be dog-tired", and "to have a dog's chance". Used in the comparative sense, "dog" expresses scorn, degradation, and dissention, as in the phrases "to treat someone like a dog", "to work like a dog", "to be as ugly as a dog", "to be as sick as a dog", and "to fight like cats and dogs". Other negative expressions include "going to the dogs" and "it's a dog-eat-dog world". Expressions in which "dog" is used in a positive sense are rare: "Dog is man's best friend".

Who knows? Given the growing importance of dogs in our lives, perhaps future generations will create a more respectable cultural image of our four-legged friend.

Other Representations of Dogs in Art

Images of dogs have been used for various purposes on coats of arms, coins, and, more recently, postage stamps.

Dogs in Heraldry

Coats of arms were used beginning in the eleventh century, during the Crusades. Because lords had trouble recognizing one another in their heavy armor, they decided to wear a personalized sign that all could identify. The coat of arms was born. Nobility in France and abroad, especially in England, used highly imaginative designs to express the qualities they wished to represent. At first, imaginary animals were used most often. Gradually, they were replaced by real animals.

THE FRENCH GENDARMERIE'S COAT OF ARMS

Each different section of the French Army has a coat of arms. The School of Non-commissioned Officers of the Gendarmerie (Police Force) Training Center for Dog Handlers in Gramat is no exception. Its insignia was created by heraldry expert Robert Louis in 1948 and approved December 10, 1948.

The coat of arms is combined with the gendarmerie's characteristic insignia: a fifteenth-century plumed helmet in a three-quarters view atop a shield with a sword and a civic crown. On the shield below the helmet's throat-piece is the gendarmerie's grenade ornament. The plumed helmet is specific to this army corps. It evokes the origins of the gendarmerie, established in the fifteenth century by the High Provost Marshal as the Compagnie de la Connétablie et de la Maréchalerie [Company of the Constabulary and of the Field Marshal]. The shield features an unsheathed sword pointing straight upward as a symbol of justice over force. The circular civic crown of oak branches was bestowed upon soldiers in Rome who had risked their life to save others. The silver field is specific to specialized training centers. The entire grouping represents the mission of protecting citizens and helping those in danger. It also represents the gendarmerie's military origins and its military and civilian activities.
The coat of arms itself is specific to the training center in Gramat. In the language of heraldry, the field consists of azure and sable sections with an argent grenade ornament charger. Blue and black are the gendarmerie's traditional colors, and the grenade ornament is its traditional badge. In the center of the grenade ornament is a dog standing in front of red flames, signifying that dogs fear nothing, even fire.

Coats of Arms - Charrière, "Armorial Général de l'Empire français" by H. Simon, 1812. Selva Collection, Paris.

Images of dogs were used from the very beginning. They symbolized hunting, an exclusive privilege of the nobility. Beginning in the ninth century, specific breeds of hunting and fighting dogs appeared. By the twelfth century, hounds and mastiffs adorned the coats of arms of English, Scottish, and Irish lords. Since that time, coats of arms have also been adopted as emblems of large institutions, such as the French Army.

On coats of arms, dogs symbolize the protective instinct, as well as vigilance, loyalty, obedience, and gratitude. Dogs are depicted in various postures: on the hind legs (with the back facing the edge of the insignia), in profile, passant (in heraldry, facing and walking toward the viewer's right with one foreleg raised), running, sitting, couchant (lying down with the head raised), and rampant (rearing on the left hind leg with the forelegs elevated). The colors and metals used - black, red (gules, in heraldry), green (vert), blue (azure), gold (or), and silver (argent) - form a code: a silver dog on a black field signifies a loyal, steadfast knight; a gold dog on a red field signifies a knight willing to die for his lord; and a black dog on a gold field signifies a knight in mourning for his lord. Dogs might also be used as supporters, the figures appearing on either side of a coat of arms.

Dogs on Coins

Coins from all eras feature dogs either as the dominant subject of a side, as an element in a more complex scene, or as a purely decorative symbol. Dogs are found more frequently on ancient coins than on modern ones.

The first known coins with images of dogs are in silver or bronze. On these coins from 480-440 B.C., dogs are the symbol of Segesta. The mythical origin of this city is attributed to Acestes, son of the nymph Segesta and the river god Crimisus, who took the form of a dog at their wedding. A dog appears on the reverse side of various coins featuring Segesta's head on the obverse side. In the same period, heavy bronze coins were used in certain Italic regions. In the Latium-Campania series, a dog is shown running toward the left; in the Tuder-Umbrian series (the origin of the lira) a dog is shown lying down.

After dogs were featured on several small bronze coins of the Rome-Campania series minted around 210 B.C., they appeared on the Roman Republic's silver denarius. This coin, minted extensively in Rome for economic and commercial reasons, is one of the most important, for it uses a variety of subjects to illustrate many aspects of the social, economic, historic, and religious life of the period.

Dogs are depicted on many coins from feudal times, mainly pieces of lesser value. A dog reclining with his head to the left appears on the reverse side of some coins from Tuscany, a dog tied to a tree appears on the lira from Milan under Philippe II of Spain (1556-1598), and a dog is shown as a winged figure on some smaller coins from Verona (1375-1381). The Gonzaga family showed the greatest interest in dogs, depicting the animal crawling, lying down, and climbing. Their coins are characterized by an inscription surrounding the central dog figure and reading *"Infensus feris tantum"* ("Enemy of none but the big cats"). This inscription echoes nicely the highest praise of dogs as "man's best friend".

EXAMPLES OF ROMAN COINS:

- In 82 B.C., Magistrate Caius Manilius Limetanus evokes the touching scene in which the elderly Argos recognizes his master Ulysses.
- In 69 B.C., a dog is shown running between the legs of the deer pulling Diana's chariot.
- In 64 B.C., a sprinting greyhound covers the entire reverse side of a denarius from the period of Caius Postumus.
- In 60 B.C., a hunting scene is depicted in which a dog attacks an injured wild boar.
- In 45 B.C. on a silver sesterce, Titus Crisius shows a dog running toward the right, while on a denarius from the period of Augustus, a dog appears at the feet of the goddess Diana carrying her bow and arrows.

Dogs on Stamps

Dogs are an integral part of a country's art and daily life. It is therefore only normal to find dogs on postage stamps, to the thrill of many collectors. Whether as the main figure or as a simple detail that only an expert collector would spot, dogs are one of the most coveted themes in stamp collecting (including individual stamps, books of stamps, and postal logos and slogans). In fact, there are so many dog stamps that philatelic organizations recommend that collectors limit themselves to a subgroup (a breed or specialty) to keep things under control.

Dogs first appeared on stamps from their country of origin. In 1887, for example, the first "philatelic dog", a magnificent Newfoundland, was featured on a stamp from the island by that name. The Belgian

Noblemen strolling in
"Très riches heures du duc
de Berry"
French stamp, 1965.
Selva Collection, Paris.

Sheepdog appeared on Belgian stamps, and sled dogs were featured on stamps from Scandinavian countries. Since dogs seemed to "sell" stamps, they began to appear on stamps from many countries, regardless of the origins of a particular breed. For example, an English Springer Spaniel can be found on a Nicaraguan stamp. The postal service may also use dogs for purely promotional purposes, as in France's postal logo reading, "La voix de son maître" ("His Master's Voice") for Pathé-Marconi.

Dogs may appear on stamps with cultural subject matter, as when a painting with a dog is used on a stamp or when a dog is associated with a book or comic strip.

Dogs are also featured on stamps commemorating important events. For example, the former Soviet Union published numerous stamps with Laika, the first canine cosmonaut. Sometimes, community education is the focus, as in the Parisian postal slogan, *"Apprenez-leur le caniveau"* ("Curb your dog").

True philatelic fanatics are also interested in the history of dogs in the postal service. They know, for example, that in the 1940s mail in Alaska was carried from town to town by sled dog teams; there is a post office on the Île aux Chiens (Island of Dogs), a neighbor of Saint Pierre and Miquelon in the North Atlantic Ocean; and during World War I, military kennels in France received a special "postage paid" stamp.

Dogs in Literature and the Media

Since the beginning of civilization, dogs have lived alongside humans. It's only natural, then, that these animals appear in literature throughout the centuries. In fiction, fables and fantasy, dogs generally play the same roles they occupy in real life. More recently, dog heroes from the comics have been brought to movies and television. Dogs have also appeared in the press and in advertisements that take advantage of the dog's considerable influence on people.

White Fang; Ill. André Toutain - 1926. Jonas/Kharbine - Tapabor Collection, Paris.

Robinson Crusoe. Jonas/Kharbine. Tapabor Collection, Paris.

Dogs in Literature

The dog's main role in literature mirrors the dog's role in everyday life - that of guardian angel and loyal companion.

Friend and Guardian

In Homer's classic *Odyssey*, Ulysses' dog Argos has an important role. Argos is the only character who recognizes Ulysses after his perilous voyage. Dogs in children's literature generally act as protectors and are often the main character. This is the case in *Belle et Sébastien* (Belle and Sebastian), a story by French author Cécile Aubry about the alpine adventures of a Pyrenean Mountain Dog and his young owner. The same is true of Eric Knight's *Lassie*, the story of a faithful Collie and her young owner, Joe. Both books have the same general theme: A child in trouble is saved by a big, loyal dog. The dog breeds featured in these stories have become so popular that in France, for example, many people call Collies "Lassies".

In other books, dogs appear in supporting roles, rather than as main characters. In the writings of Jules Verne (1828-1905), including *Journey to the Center of the Earth*, *A Two Years' Vacation* and *Mysterious Island*, a little dog accompanies the characters in their travels and helps them out of difficult situations using his sense of smell.

Still other stories feature dogs in a purely symbolic or even exaggerated role, sometimes helping reveal a situation or emotion. Although these depictions of dogs are brief, they are far from insignificant. In *Of Mice and Men*, John Steinbeck illustrates human selfishness, injustice and loneliness through his description of the slow death of an old dog, the hapless companion of a poor day laborer who cannot bear the loss of his friend.

Dogs and Wolves

Wolves, wild cousins to dogs, also appear frequently in literature. While dogs represent loyalty and respectfully serve their master, wolves represent freedom, the wilderness and the refusal of all constraint, even at the risk of death. As in Jean de la Fontaine's fable *The Wolf and the Dog*, wolves would rather live free than be confined.

The opposition between dogs and wolves illustrates the innate human conflict between being a "good" slave and resisting slavery at the risk of death. This is a favorite theme of Jack London, a fervent humanist who lived during the 1891 Gold Rush in Alaska. While London defends animals against man's brutality, he does not give a definite answer to the question of which path to choose: that of White Fang, a wolf-dog who chooses to live among humans, or that of Buck in *Call of the Wild*, a pet dog who goes to live among wolves. Perhaps this means that we each are a bit dog and a bit wolf, depending on the circumstances.

Wild Beast

Anubis was an Egyptian god, but Cerberus guarded the underworld in Roman mythology. This dark side of the dog has inspired many writers. Poets and novelists describe the prowling beast, a frantic, demonic creature who devours dead bodies or small children. Sir Arthur Conan Doyle even uses a dog in the title of one of Sherlock Holmes' best known adventures, *The Hound of the Baskervilles*, in which a huge dog devours the inhabitants of a dreary Scottish moor.

In the poem *"Carrion"* from the collection *Flowers of Evil*, Baudelaire also evokes the dog's dark side:

> Around the rocks a restless bitch was eyeing
> Us with a look of one forsaken,
> As if from the living skeleton she were spying
> The flesh that from it had been taken.

(Baudelaire, Prose and Poetry. Translated by Arthur Symons. Albert & Charles Boni, New York, 1926.)

Within these lines is a hidden metaphor: The "restless bitch" is actually man, the dog's thinking alter ego.

What the Future Holds?

The fate of man and dog seems forever closely linked and science fiction writers often evoke this connection. For example, in his novel Pet Cemetery, Stephen King uses the description of a dog who returns from the dead to foreshadow the fate of the dog's owner.

Science fiction author Frank Herbert devotes an entire short story to dogs. In it, an epidemic decimates the canine population, causing mass hysteria and disaster for humans and dogs. In this dark depiction of the future, man and dog share the same terrible fate.

Whether as friend or foe, our canine companion continues to appear in literature as an innocent reflection of human shame, misery and loneliness so deep that even in books we need the company of our four-legged friend.

Portrait of Colette and her dog Toby.
"Vu", July 3, 1929.
Selva Collection, Paris.

THE DOG, THE ROOSTER AND THE FOX

A dog and a rooster who were friends were walking along together. At nightfall, the rooster climbed into a tree to sleep and the dog lay down at the base of the tree, which was hollow. At daybreak, the rooster crowed, as was his habit. Upon hearing him, a fox ran to the base of the tree and asked the rooster to climb down, so that he might kiss the animal who had such a lovely voice. The rooster told the fox to wake the gatekeeper sleeping at the base of the tree and he would climb down after the gatekeeper had answered. But when the fox went to find the gatekeeper, the dog leapt forth and tore him to shreds. The moral of the story is that when enemies attack, wise people put them off by leading them to someone stronger.

Aesop, Fables. Translated from Greek by
Émile Chambry, Histoire des chiens
(History of Dogs), Sortilèges, Paris.

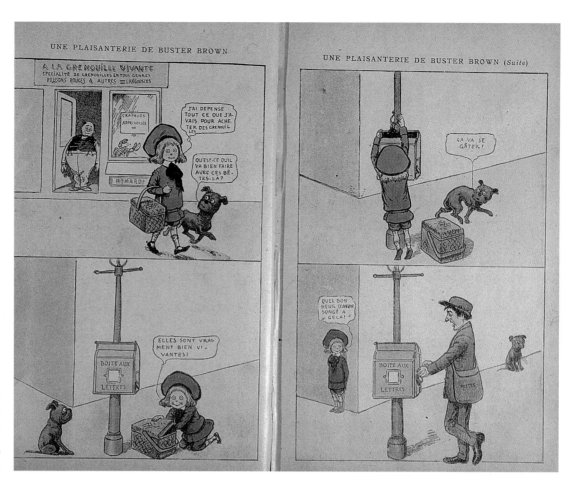

Comic strip by Richard Outcault, appeared in the New York Times in 1903 - "My Newspaper", October 26, 1907. Jonas/Kharbine - Tapabor Collection, Paris

Dogs in Comics and Cartoons

Dogs have always appeared in the favorite comic strips and cartoons of children (and adults!). The very first comic strip, published in a New York daily in the early twentieth century, takes place at a dog show. This was the beginning of fame for dogs, who later became the heroes of cartoons. Since then, they have appeared in roles of growing importance, sometimes as the main character of the story.

Everyday Hero

Some comic strip dogs remain true dogs, used essentially to help develop the main character. The first was Pluto, who later appeared in cartoons. Apart from being Mickey's companion, Pluto is the source of both disasters and happy endings. A similar character to Pluto is the Fox Terrier Milou, the faithful companion of Tintin. Milou expresses himself not through speech, but by barking at his master and through thought bubbles when he wants to communicate with the reader. He is so famous in France that his adventures have been made into cartoons and even animated films. Other dogs play a similar role in French comic strips: Rantanplan, a supporting character to cowboy Lucky Luke, is not too smart and follows his master without speaking to him. Although Rantanplan does sometimes have thoughts, the other characters are not aware of them. In this aspect, Rantanplan is similar to Jolly Jumper, the thinking horse. Another French comic strip dog, Idefix, is a tiny mutt who is inseparable from his master, the imposing Obelix. This little dog with a big heart is very loveable because he never causes trouble. The canine characters mentioned above have an important role among humans, yet retain their doglike qualities.

Almost Human

In other cases, dogs are depicted as more or less human. This is usually true when the dog is the main character of the story. Some comic strip dogs, like Charlie Brown's Snoopy, have philosophical thoughts, just like humans. But Snoopy is still a dog: He sleeps in - or on - his doghouse, eats dog food and lives like other dogs. The wise Cubitus walks on his hind legs and speaks, like the other characters in the French comic strip. He also teaches lessons. With all his good sense, Cubitus could be human, except that he looks like an Old English Sheepdog.

In the French comic *Boule et Bill* [Boule and Bill], Bill the Cocker Spaniel - probably the first purebred comic strip canine - acts like a human around other dogs but like a playful puppy at home. Still, on walks he flirts with attractive female dogs and fights off rivals, mimicking his owners and other humans.

Some comic strip dogs are hardly dogs at all. For example, the perpetually sad-faced Gai Luron, created by Gotlib, gets caught up in the events of the world around him.

Animated Films

Some comic strip dogs have become so popular that their adventures have been made into animated films. One such character is Dingo, a dog who stands on two legs like a human but has a dog's head with long, droopy ears. He has often appeared as a "spokesdog" for educational purposes, including car safety campaigns targeting young children. Sad-looking Droopy, the dog in Tex Avery's cartoons, repeatedly announces his presence with the famous line, *"You know what? I'm happy!"* He is the cartoon equivalent of Gai Luron, a French comic strip dog.

Album cover, "Pluto" by Walt Disney, Albums Roses Collection, Hachette. Selva Collection, Paris.

Other cartoon dogs live with humans, just like real pets or watchdogs. This is true of Lady and the Tramp, who live with their owners but share a romantic dinner and lead their own lives among other dogs. When Lady's owners bring home a new baby, they ignore her and humiliate her by forcing her to wear a muzzle. This serves as a brutal reminder that she is "only" a dog.

Perdita and Pongo, the leading dogs in *101 Dalmatians*, perhaps the most famous cartoon canines, are also companion animals to humans. But they become romantically involved with each other, just like their owners.

Nana the Saint Bernard protects the children in *Peter Pan* while leading a life like that of other dogs.

Sometimes, the dogs in animated features are almost caricatures in their appearance and actions. They may look generally like dogs, but one of their physical characteristics is exaggerated. Rarely the main character, they are more likely to serve as a watchdog for their owner or for another animal. Cartoons featuring a cat and mouse often include a big, burly, unfriendly dog who sits around licking his chops. In *Tom and Jerry*, for example, a bulldog defends Jerry by getting Tom into trouble. Dogs appear frequently in Disney cartoons. Disney's *Beagle Boys* are members of an international crime ring. All have the same physical features, are clumsy and not too smart and are constantly planning evil schemes to steal money.

By giving dogs many human qualities, both good and bad, the creators of comic strips and cartoons seem to use canine characters to represent our changing society.

Dogs in Movies

Dogs have appeared in movies almost since the birth of cinema. In the early twentieth century, dogs played small parts in several silent films. One of the most memorable was Charlie Chaplin's canine companion in misery in *The Kid* in 1921. Not until *Hollywood's Rin Tin Tin*, released in 1922, did a dog play the starring role in a movie.

Rin Tin Tin and Lassie

What could be more natural than acting for a dog whose past was far from the peaceful existence of a farm dog? Rin Tin Tin served as a messenger to the Germans during World War I and was found by an American aviator who brought him back to the United States after the war. When the American veteran discovered how quickly his canine companion could learn, he decided to make him a show dog. From 1922 to 1932, Rin Tin Tin appeared in twenty-two films, always in the role of an honorable and fearless hero who would do anything to defend the innocent. His popularity spread all over the world, making him a true movie star. He had his own dressing room, "signed" his own contracts and chose his own co-stars! When he died, his character was played by his pups and grandpups; his fourth-generation descendants brought Rin Tin Tin to television.

Another dog superstar was the famous Lassie. Purchased for five dollars by an animal trainer, this Collie launched her career in 1943 in *Lassie Come Home*. While Rin Tin Tin tore after the bad guys and leapt across chasms, Lassie exemplified the loyalty and unconditional love of a dog for her master, preferably a child. Like Rin Tin Tin, Lassie enjoyed worldwide popularity. Her trainer and agent demanded astronomical salaries for her - fifty thousand dollars a year and four thousand dollars per commercial appearance - as well as a dressing room, a private secretary and even paid holidays! Through the third generation, Lassie's descendants made films; then her legacy was brought to television.
The stories of Rin Tin Tin and Lassie are unique in the history of cinema. Both dogs had talented trainers who helped them gain recognition as true actors and who had the business sense to manage their career and earnings.

Friend and Guardian

Following these successes, the presence of dogs in cinema declined. Before the 1980s, a few books by Jack London were made into movies, but none featured dogs as developed characters. Instead, dogs usually served as sidekicks for their co-stars, as in *Call of the Wild* with Charlton Heston.

Not until the 1970s did Walt Disney Studios make another push for canine films. They needed to find a nice dog who was, of course, extremely loyal and had a friendly face with star quality - in short, a kid's best friend. Into the studios trotted Benji, a little Pyrenean Shepherd mix. For the first time, casting directors chose not a big, proud Sheepdog but a spunky ball of fur. Disney made five movies about Benji's wacky adventures before launching a televised series. With an annual salary of a million and a half dollars by 1974, Benji was certainly expensive to produce! Several movies pairing the police with dogs were also released but had little success. Since 1990, the new dog hero for kids is a big, fat Saint Bernard named Beethoven, whose movies have been successful worldwide. In addition, a new screen adaptation of Jack London's White Fang was produced recently by Disney.

Dogs Who Think and Talk

The current trend in movies involves dogs who think and talk, like human actors. For example, *Charly au pays des kangourous* [Charlie in the Land of the Kangaroos] follows the adventures of a Labrador puppy in Australia and Disney's *Incredible Journey* (1994) features two dogs and a cat who comb the United States in search of their young master.

Specialized Training Schools

Today's dog actors are graduates of professional training schools where they learn everything from barking on command to playing dead to whining - a true theater arts program! The result of all this effort does pay off for the trainer; only one of his students needs to be picked for him to make a fortune.

For some twenty years, film production has been monitored by animal protection organizations to ensure the well-being of canine actors.

As long as movies with dogs are successful, Hollywood will continue to make them. Of course, not all aspects of this success have been positive. Certain movies that feature a specific breed have triggered a considerable demand for the breed and the subsequent overbreeding of puppies of lower and lower quality. Hopefully, someday movies will show dogs for what they really are, not as mere caricatures of the almost human "nice doggy".

Dogs on Television

Dogs have had a television presence since the early days of this medium. First as extras and later as true characters, dogs quickly gained a permanent place on television.

In silent films, dogs often appeared as loyal, indispensable companions but also as a comic element (with Charlie Chaplin, for example). This was the beginning of dogs in acting. Dogs were featured more and more in televised series, playing roles of greater and greater significance.

Leading Dog

Soon, dogs were playing leading roles. Breeds were not chosen haphazardly. Larger breeds were favored for adventure and police shows and smaller breeds for comedies. Nevertheless, the focal point for all breeds on television has remained the dog's loyalty in his work and to his owner. There are many examples of this, from Belle, the Pyrenean Mountain Dog who protects Sebastian, to Lassie, the wandering Collie who is always ready to help those in need, to Rin Tin Tin, the German Shepherd police dog, to White Fang. Of course, one cannot forget Pollux, the most "British" of them all, who has touched the lives of so many children and adults. These examples show that the role of dogs on television (and in everyday life) is far from trivial.

Dog and Master

More and more, shows focus on the relationship between dog and master and prove the theory that dogs resemble their masters and vice versa. For example, in the French series *La loi est la loi* [The Law's the Law], the similarities between Max, a British Bulldog and the prosecutor are not mere coincidence. The same is true of Columbo's dog. More recently, dogs have appeared in numerous sitcoms. In some series, not only does a dog play a leading role, but he is also able to communicate with humans.

Dog Care Shows

More and more shows focusing on dog care have been produced. These shows discuss the dog's habits, the characteristics of each breed and the details of dog grooming, raising and training puppies and canine nutrition—all the practical tips an owner needs to live happily with his four-legged friend. Often, these shows end by showing a listing of dogs of all ages and breeds available for adoption.

Currently, the purpose of dog care shows seems to be to shed light on a particular dog or his owner by discussing the main characteristic of a breed. This appears to be successful, since trends in dog breeds closely follow television. Of course, some breeds, such as German Shepherds and Labradors, are unavoidable. More and more, these shows emphasize communication between dog and owner. Dogs try to understand their owner and communicate through specific behaviors. When we listen to a dog's habits and behaviors, we give him the ability to "talk" to us.

Dogs in Toys

Dogs are so important in our society that they have even inspired toys which provide children with a reliable friend. There are all kinds of toys involving dogs, from stuffed animals to educational materials.

Dog pull-toys for children.
Kharbine - Tapabor
Collection, Paris

Children's toys have been around much longer than movies, television and comic strips. Toys contribute to a child's emotional and creative development. The first toys based on images of dogs were made with clay, dough, or wood. At first, they were mounted on slabs of wood with wheels for children to pull. Later, they were jointed—with a mouth that opened, a tail that wagged—to make them more realistic.

Next to the bear, the dog is one of the only animals whose appeal in toys has lasted for centuries. Still today, dogs have a privileged place in children's playtime activities. Dogs are used to decorate the rooms of little and big kids, where they take the form of armchairs, clothes racks, lamps and all sorts of stuffed animals. For infants, a soft, cuddly stuffed animal friend is trustworthy, protective and, most importantly, just the right size. As in movies and television, breed is important in toys. Most often, stuffed animals are based on a character from the latest animated feature (like 101 Dalmatians), but the irresistible German Shepherd and Saint Bernard also have their place.

In the interest of early childhood education, many wood, fabric and plastic toys are created each year to enhance the development of children three months to two years old. The results include discovery mats and toys that make the noise of a dog barking. In these toys, the dog plays an instrumental role in teaching and raising the young.

Children's toys involving dogs may be so popular because real dogs require time, space and a great deal of responsibility. Wooden and stuffed dog toys give children a playmate, a friend who's just the right size and a gentle teacher who, most importantly, requires no parental attention!

Dogs in Advertising

Over some fifty years, advertising has become a vital element in our consumer society. It is no longer used simply to promote products, but also to spark trends. Advertisers began using images of dogs very early on, in an effort to please the consumer. In fact, the role of the dog in advertising has grown significantly in the past few decades. What is it about dogs that make them so popular with advertisers?

Dogs and Brand Names

Dogs were first used as selling points in the early 1900s. Perhaps one of the best known examples is Nipper, the dog shown listening intently to a Pathé-Marconi gramophone with the slogan "His Master's Voice". In this ad, Nipper thinks he hears his dead master's real voice when it is actually just a reproduction. The ad compares Nipper's loyalty to his master to the fidelity of the gramophone: If a dog is unable to tell whether the voice is real, then the gramophone's quality must be excellent! Advertisers

Development of commerce and industry: Commercial ties between Egyptians and neighboring countries.
Liebig Chromolithograph.
Selva Collection, Paris.

383

for Black and White Whiskey chose two Scottish Terriers for the product's logo, evoking this breed's loyalty to its native land. The larger breeds favored in ads for cars evoke power and safety: A Boxer is used for Kléber tires and a mythical six-legged dog appears in the ad for Agip oil. Big dogs like the Saint Bernard give consumers a feeling of comfort and security, while mutts give ads a humorous tone.

Today, dogs are part of the family. They play with children and keep the elderly company. For these reasons, dogs commonly appear in ads portraying the typical modern family. Dogs complete the picture and create a casual atmosphere.

Unlike the private, introverted cat, the dog is an extrovert. He evokes images of freedom and the great outdoors. In ads, dogs are generally shown inside only if they've made a mess or knocked something over—the perfect situation for advertising household products. These items might include a heavy-duty floor cleaner that eliminates the traces of the puppy's "mistakes" or a new vacuum cleaner guaranteed to remove Fluffy's long hair from the carpet.

Certain breeds, including the Afghan Hound and the Dalmatian, are a symbol of elegance. These breeds appear in ads for Chanel and other cosmetics.

Marketing Tool

Whether they're shown as real dogs or given human qualities, the dogs in the preceding examples are not the advertiser's target. They are merely marketing tools often adopted at the same time by advertising agencies that may also use the same breeds. This can create harmful trends for a particular breed.

Dogs as "Consumers"

Unlike in many ads targeting humans, dogs are the focal point in ads for pet food. Dogs are the consumers of the products in these ads, at least with the help of their owner. Different brands take different approaches. France's Royal Canin portrays dogs as animals to be respected for what they are. For this reason, its ads feature puppies exploring their surroundings and a German Shepherd running across a field to his owner. This company never uses an anthropomorphic approach. Waltham's ads feature breeders discussing its product and Canigou focuses on the dog's hardiness and energy. Ads for Fido dog food show different breeds who have "tasted and approved" the product. Friskies and Frolic take a humorous approach with skits in which the actors are obviously dogs. These ads appear in all kinds of magazines and especially on television, a better medium for showing the dog in motion.

The advertising scope of veterinary medicines is much more limited. Ads for these products are generally placed only in specialized publications on animals, where they may appear side by side with ads for pet foods. Some ads for veterinary medicines strictly target medical professionals by describing a product's effectiveness and safety. Ads for veterinary medicines are quite rare compared to those for animal care products, including everything from flea powder and worm pills to grooming accessories. These ads appear more widely, sometimes as television commercials. This recent phenomenon shows the growing importance of dogs in our society. These ads commonly use humor, even mockery, to play down the "medical" aspect of the products.

In conclusion, over time dogs have become selling points either because of the qualities they represent or as potential "consumers". Dogs have been used to sell almost everything, not only products designed specifically for them. This has created the risk of media hype, which could make dogs a thing of fashion, regardless of the consequences for dogs in general.

Part 3

Dogs Helping Humans

Dogs Who Save Lives

Canine Heroes

In certain situations, a dog's loyalty to humans may cause him to go beyond his limits in order to save lives. Dogs of various breeds have thus become legends, proving through their actions just how capable they are at rescue work.

Togo and Balto: Sled Dogs

Ever since dogs were domesticated, they have been helping humans in all areas of work, from hunting to guarding to herding. Over the years, dogs have also done much more: Canine heroes have helped find missing people and save lives after avalanches, all kinds of disasters, and accidents at sea.

In February 1925 in Alaska, a diphtheria epidemic broke out and threatened to spread to Nome, a distant city on the state's west coast. At that time of year, no plane could reach Alaska from Seattle to deliver the necessary serum. Thus, the decision was made to use the train and then sled dogs for the remaining 1,000 kilometers. Leonhard Seppala, considered one of the United States' fastest sled drivers since 1920, was called in.

As the epidemic intensified, a team of mushers took turns day and night to speed the arrival of the remedy. In a raging blizzard, Seppala was forced to take incredible risks. His two lead dogs, Togo and Balto, proved their extraordinary stamina and determination, thanks to Seppala's tenacity.

Thanks to the dogs and their drivers, the serum arrived in time. It was delivered in only 127 hours and thirty minutes, with Seppala and his dogs alone covering 500 kilometers, a significant contribution to this amazing achievement!
Since then, the Iditarod—one of today's greatest northern races—is held every year to commemorate this journey.

Barry: Alpine Rescue Dog

Saint Bernards have long been used to rescue people lost in the mountains. The Cenobite monks of the Grand-Saint-Bernard Hospice in Switzerland have raised Saint Bernards since the eleventh century and, since the seventeenth century, they have trained the dogs to rescue people in the mountains.

The Saint Bernard Barry was born in the early nineteenth century. His name, meaning "bear" has traditionally been bestowed upon the finest dog in the hospice's kennel. Barry alone saved over forty people, thus becoming a legend. A statue in his honor stands in the animal cemetery in Paris. A plaque there explains that he was killed by the last person he found, who mistook him for a bear. Actually, Barry died of old age in 1814, and his body is kept at a museum in Berne. According to a popular myth, Saint Bernard rescue dogs carry a little barrel of liquor around their neck. This is as false as the story about Barry being killed by a person, since alcohol can be fatal to people suffering from hypothermia.

Rudy: Earthquake Rescue Dog

On December 11, 1988, an earthquake measuring 7.2 on the Richter scale rattled Armenia. Because of the extent of the damage—two cities were completely destroyed—international aid was requested. France took part by sending Civilian Safety Instruction and Intervention Units (UIISC) to Armenia about twenty-four hours after the disaster occurred. These units included disaster search and rescue-dogs and their handlers, such as First Class Firefighter Deguerville and his dog Rudy, a four- or five-year-old Siberian Husky and German Shepherd mix. The weather was far from ideal: The temperature hovered near –3 or –4 °C during the day and dipped as low as –20°C at night. The teams of dogs and handlers worked in shifts, covering twenty-four hours a day for the first two days, then in six- to eight-hour shifts followed by a three-hour break. Inhabitants helped the search teams by showing them where victims might be caught. On the fourth day, an inhabitant led First Class Firefighter Deguerville to an elementary school, but no survivors were found there. Then he was brought to a nearby shoe factory. After several hours of searching, Rudy "marked" an area, that is, he showed his handler that he had detected a victim. When the wreckage was cleared, a woman was found alive and evacuated. She had spent several days caught beneath the wreckage with no food or water and a severely injured leg. Thanks to intensive medical care, she survived with her leg intact and recovered fully.

Rudy became a canine hero, like many other dogs who have helped save people trapped beneath the debris of earthquakes in Iran and Mexico.

Avalanche Rescue Dogs

What could be more gorgeous than the mountains in winter, when the snow sparkling in the brilliant sun attracts hordes of hikers and skiers . . . who sometimes forget that the mountains can be danger-ous. Even when weather conditions seem favorable, there is always the chance of an avalanche. For this reason, ski lodges have the sup-port of considerable safety resources, including teams of rescuers and trackers, rescue dogs and their handlers, experts who provide information and guidance to people who want to explore the moun-tains, and an effective weather detection system.

Search-And-Rescue Dogs

Prevention is critical, but sometimes accidents cannot be avoided. That's when the rescue teams, including search-and-rescue dogs, are called in.

Avalanche searches are a rare area of rescue work in which dogs are used imme-diately because of their speed, their determination, and, above all, their excep-tional sense of smell. Avalanche search dogs are part of a team that also includes depth sounders and shovelers. While team members work simultane-ously, the dogs are at the forefront from the start.

The dogs are important mostly because of time, an essential factor in rescuing avalanche victims, since the faster an area is explored, the more likely it is that

victims will be found alive. This is where the major advantage of using dogs becomes clear: In equal (or even more difficult) work, dogs cover terrain faster. For example, a painstaking investigation executed by twenty people requires twenty hours to complete, while a dog could complete the task in two hours and cover an area of about one hectare.

Choosing Dogs and Handlers

In France, dog rescue teams are provided by the Army, the gendarmerie, the CRS (Compagnies Républicaines de Sécurité [Republic Safety Companies] national police forces), ski lodges, and private organizations. Teams fall under two categories: Army and gendarmerie teams are trained by gendarmerie instructors, while the rest come under the domain of civilian safety. Most handlers are accustomed to the hardships of mountain life and are highly skilled skiers on all types of terrain.

The two most commonly used breeds are the Malinois Belgian Sheepdog and the German Shepherd. These breeds are popular in all types of search work, and it is easy to see why. Thanks to their large size and considerable weight, Malinois Belgian Sheepdogs and German Shepherds do not struggle through the snow, and they are tireless hard workers. Dogs are chosen based on their physical traits, personality, and overall health. Interestingly, the animals chosen adapt very quickly to their new environment. In several days, their undercoat grows thicker and retains heat better; the hair between their toes wears away less, widening the paw into a "snowshoe"; and the skin on their paw pads becomes tougher and more resistant to cold and to the salts spread on roadways to reduce slipping. Only the dogs' eyes must be protected from the sun's ultraviolet rays: During training or prolonged work outdoors, handlers administer protective eye drops.

Search Dog Teams: Training and Practice

Alpine search dogs receive several weeks of training in the mountains. This training is based on a program developed by Swiss rescue workers to teach dogs and handlers the basics.

During training, dogs gradually learn to understand what they are being asked to do, and handlers learn to "read" their dog, that is, determine the precise moment when the dog marks a location. After they complete this training, the rescue teams are ready for work.

To maintain a high level of proficiency, teams participate in regular training exercises during the winter that also give handlers the opportunity to meet and discuss their experiences.

Tracking Dogs

Tracking consists of locating people based on a number of olfactory clues (footprints, objects, possible evidence).
The goal of this work is to find one or more persons, to locate any objects or materials lost or hidden on or near the trail, or simply to indicate the direction taken.

Choosing Dogs and Handlers

In theory, all dogs have a sufficiently developed sense of smell to follow a trail left by a person. But because tracking is a complex task requiring special training to which not all dogs are receptive, animals are selected according to specific criteria.

Dogs are chosen based on the following qualities: energy, stamina, ruggedness, hardiness, a particularly well-developed sense of smell, the ability to concentrate and not become distracted by unrelated

THE TRAIL

The human body constantly emits tiny odor molecules. Tracking dogs are faced with a blend of different factors, including specific odors (of people, groups, species), chemical odors (leather, fat, clothing), broken terrain (plants that have been crushed, bacteria released through a crack in the ground, etc.), the environment (woods, prairie, fields of alfalfa or other crops, etc.), and atmospheric conditions.

Certain factors can modify a dog's sense of smell. When these factors coincide at different moments in time, tracking becomes more difficult. These factors include:

Environmental Factors

Temperature. This factor can have a favorable effect (cold weather slows the diffusion of odor molecules) or an unfavorable effect (high temperatures speed the diffusion of odors, dry mucous membranes, and decrease the resistance to fatigue).

Wind. This factor can change the direction of the trail, dry the mucous membranes, and cause considerable diffusion of odor molecules.

Precipitation. Precipitation can affect the trail favorably or unfavorably, depending on heaviness. Slight humidity, such as frost or a light snowfall, preserves the trail. Heavy precipitation "washes away" the trail and diminishes the sense of smell when water droplets or snowflakes are inhaled over the mucous membranes lining the nose. This makes tracking impossible.

Terrain. The nature of the terrain greatly affects the quality of the trail. Terrain falls under the following categories:
• Hard, dry terrain (sand, pebbles, rock, roadways, etc.), on which odors don't "stick";
• Loose and/or damp terrain (prairies, undergrowth, etc.), which retains odors for long periods (sometimes over twenty-four hours); and
• Cultivated terrain, which retains odors when the weather is cloudy or humid but loses odors quickly when the weather is dry and hot.

Electromagnetic field. Stormy weather and nearby power lines generally interfere with tracking.

Dog-Specific Factors

Breed. German Shepherds are the most commonly used breed. They are known for their exceptional sense of smell.

Gender. Dogs are greatly disturbed by the odor of another animal of their species, especially that of a bitch in heat.

Health. Dogs track well only when they are in good health.

Fatigue. Tracking takes a great deal of energy and exacts a heavy toll on the nervous system. Regular, step-by-step training delays the onset of fatigue and increases the quality of tracking.

Nutrition. Any lack in food quality or quantity affects the dog's general condition and can alter his sense of smell.

Trail-Specific Factors

Length Dogs cannot detect a body odor unless the reference (an object, such as an article of clothing) is of sufficient quality and freshness and the trail is sufficiently long before presenting difficulties. A single footprint is not enough for a dog to establish an odor; as he follows the trail, tiny amounts of body odors accumulate over time, and the dog can eventually identify the odor of the person who left the trail.

Age. Odor molecules disperse and fade into the environment. The intensity of an odor decreases gradually until it disappears completely.

Route. The route a trail follows affects tracking. Obviously, a simple, straight trail is much easier to follow than a trail with many twists and turns.

The Handler's Influence

Handlers must remain as neutral as possible, or a dog will quickly lose his effectiveness.

odors and the environment (focus and accuracy on the trail), and courage and indifference to gunfire.

Handlers must be physically fit, calm, and level-headed. In tracking, great distances must sometimes be covered at a quick and even pace. Handlers must also be observant and good at interpreting and acting on a dog's most subtle reactions.

Area-Searching Dogs

The goal of detection is to find people who are lost. This makes area search very similar to tracking.

However, in the area search a dog is given no reference object or potential point of departure. He is let go without a harness or leash, and his job is to search for a specific odor in a defined area, as is the case in searches in disaster areas or in an avalanche.

Water Rescue Dogs

As in any area of rescue work, the dog's physical abilities and determination make him an important member of water rescue teams.

Choice of Breed : the Newfoundland

Newfoundlands possess many characteristics that make them suited for water rescue:

THE NEWFOUNDLAND'S FUNCTIONS

The Dog Alone
The Newfoundland comes to the rescue in almost any situation. He can help conscious or semi-conscious victims, tow boats or equipment, extend safety ropes in floods or other disasters, and bring boats to shallow areas or areas with exposed rocks.

The Handler And His Newfy
Newfoundlands also help human rescue workers. When a worker finds a struggling victim, he can focus on keeping the victim under control while the dog does the pulling. The dog can also pull boats away from shore or out of a dangerous area. He helps people whose boat has capsized or been damaged. In area searches, the Newfy tows the divers' Zodiac, following their trail of air bubbles.

Areas Of Activity
Newfoundlands perform water rescue work in all sorts of environments.
• **Oceans:** Responding on call or upon witnessing an accident from a rescue station; ensuring the safety of hard-to-reach areas. Restriction: assistance on beaches with large waves.
• **Rivers:** Responding on call, as a back-up to existing rescue squads; providing immediate, rapid intervention regardless of obstacles, thanks to car transport. Restriction: assistance in areas upstream from lock spillways.
• **Lakes and stretches of smooth water:** Responding on call at the request of a witness or upon witnessing an accident; helping with lifeguard duty in tourist areas. Restriction: assistance in areas upstream from dams.
• **Floods:** Responding as needed, as a back-up to transport teams; recovering equipment, carrying food or lifeboats to victims, extending support ropes.
• **Disasters:** Assisting victims, performing the same activities as in floods.
• **Nautical events:** Providing support at regattas, triathlons, and other water sports events requiring short-term surveillance; responding when an accident is sighted.

- Strength: They can tow several people or a boat weighing several tons.
- Stamina: They can swim great distances, for several hours straight.
- Resistance to the cold: This means they are ready at a moment's notice, unlike a diver, who needs about five minutes to prepare his equipment.
- Calmness: The Newfy's incredible calmness in all kinds of circumstances can be very reassuring to victims.
- Determination: Newfies never abandon their mission.
- Availability: Newfies can dive in at a moment's notice, since they need no special equipment.

Choosing a Rescue Dog

A good water rescue dog needs thorough training and must be physically and psychologically suited to the work. A lack of instinct or swimming ability are the main disqualifications. But the most problematic is hip dysplasia.

Puppies are chosen as potential water rescue dogs based on their energy, strength, and healthy bone structure. A puppy's parents are systematically x-rayed to determine his susceptibility to hip dysplasia.

Raising a Rescue Dog

Whether training a puppy or an adult dog, the key phrase is "easy does it". Adult dogs must adapt to their new job. Their muscles and joints may become overstressed if training is administered too quickly. Adult dogs must progress gradually in such activities as swimming, climbing, and running. In addition, their already developed character may have to be toned down.

Like any other breed, the young Newfy must be trained gradually, in a series of short exercises based on his attention span. In addition, training should be administered at different times of the day and in different places, to prevent habits from forming.

THE NEWFY IN TRAINING

All training begins with a play session to allow the dog to let off steam and prepare for work. The actual training takes place both on land and in the water. It is always preceded by obedience lessons. From the time they are several months old, puppies are taught to heel, stay, and come when called. Later, the commands become more complicated (voice commands, gesture commands at a distance, etc.), and exercises are done on slippery or steep terrain similar to the conditions found in rescue situations. In addition to obedience training, puppies are socialized to the outside world: crowds, traffic noises, elevators, etc.

Training in the water is divided into two parts:

- The dog learns to retrieve objects and tow his handler, then strangers, and finally sailboards and boats; and

- The handler and the dog work as a team to build trust and develop cooperation. When the dog reaches fifteen months, true rescue training begins: Exercises become more difficult, the dog must climb to reach the water, he must tow heavier and heavier craft, and he may sometimes be submerged by large waves.

The frequency of training varies according to the dog's motivation and physical effort. However, basic obedience is reviewed every day.

The dog and handler must progress at the same pace. Establishing trust and cooperation between the two is fundamental. But this is possible only when the handler listens to his dog and can read him like an open book, to the point of anticipating his reactions.

The handler uses a different tone of voice, depending on whether he wants the dog to stop working or get back to work: The command to stop is issued in an abrupt, sharp voice. Encouragement to continue working is given in a lively, playful manner.

The most important thing to remember in training is that if a Newfoundland succeeds at an exercise, it is his own doing; if he fails, it is his handler's fault.

The Risks of Training

A dog may experience psychological and physiological problems during training. Overtraining (jumping, climbing, swimming, etc.) when puppies are too young can cause loose ligaments and aggravate existing dysplasia.
In addition, forcing a young dog to perform moves that frighten him can create permanent inhibitions. It would be unfortunate for a Newfy to fear water because he was forced to jump in as a puppy.

It might take several months to rebuild the confidence of a dog who has become discouraged during training. Through play, the handler can encourage the dog to perform an exercise he is refusing. Play helps eliminate a dog's timidity, reserve, apprehension, and fear. A dog can be raised to overcome the inhibitions related to his character, upbringing, or habits, and any genetic imbalance can be compensated.

Disaster Search and Rescue Dogs

A vital resource

Search dogs are used not only after major earthquakes. They may also be called to the scene of landslides; collapsed buildings, worksites, or mines; fires; train or airplane accidents; etc. Unfortunately, there is no shortage of such circumstances.

Geophonic sensors that can detect very slight noises like heartbeats are also used to detect disaster victims. However, unlike dogs, these devices work only in complete silence, which is seldom possible in areas where wreckage is being cleared. A properly trained dog can work on any type of terrain—even in dark basements—together with human rescue workers, despite the noise of the machines used to clear wreckage (cranes, sledgehammers, bulldozers). Moreover, sensors cannot detect dead bodies, while dogs not only find bodies, they also have different ways of "marking" them, depending on whether they are dead or alive. This helps rescuers plan their response time. Professionals agree that rescue dogs are an indispensable aid in any kind of rescue work dealing with wreckage.

Teamwork

As in any work involving both dogs and humans, there must be deep trust and cooperation between the handler and his dog. The handler must know his dog thoroughly and be able to "read" him as he

Dogs were first used to find people buried beneath wreckage after Great Britain was bombed during World War II.

As early as 1954, search dog training centers were established in the United States, Germany, and Switzerland. Swiss dogs were the first to gain international attention after the 1976 earthquake in Friuli, Italy, where twelve search dogs found forty-two survivors and 510 bodies. In 1977 in Romania, ten dogs found fifteen survivors and ninety-seven bodies.

In 1980, the first French search and rescue dogs were brought to El Asam, Algeria, where they found ten survivors and five hundred bodies. Today, search dogs are used after all major earthquakes (Iran, Mexico, Armenia). The dogs of the world were in the spotlight once again following the earthquakes in Turkey in 1999. Thanks to search and rescue dogs, several hundred buried victims were rescued.

Canine search-and-rescue team of the Fire Department of Paris searching through ruins.

works through the disaster area, anticipating his every move. Similarly, the dog must be able to trust his handler to follow him everywhere, regardless of the difficulties of the terrain.

This high degree of cooperation requires extensive training. After socialization and basic training (positions, heeling, etc.), the focus turns to actual search work. Various techniques are used. In general, the handler relies on the dog's attachment to him and to a particular play thing (a ball or chew toy). First the handler, then one, then several other people hide with the dog's toy. When the dog finds the victims, he "marks" them by barking and scratching at the ground. The dog's attachment to the toy helps develop this marking behavior, an essential skill for a good wreckage search dog.

When the dog is able to locate several victims who hide without him seeing, he is certified according to terms and conditions of the particular country. The handler and his dog are then registered at the national level as a civilian or military rescue team.

Canine Candidates

Good candidates for disaster search training have a keen sense of smell and are calm, poised, and energetic. They are also sociable, both toward humans and toward other dogs, since more than one dog may work in an area. In addition, playfulness is essential in training.

The most commonly used breeds are sheepdogs, particularly German Shepherds and Belgian Sheepdogs. The little Pyrenean Shepherd , the Doberman, and the Beauceron have also been trained as successful disaster search and rescue dogs.

Dogs for the Handicapped

Service Dogs for the Handicapped

For most of us, dogs are just pets. But for some people, dogs are constant companions who provide valuable help. These exceptional animals work as service dogs for the handicapped, the deaf or the hearing impaired and as guide dogs for the blind. They are trained thanks to private organizations established by dedicated, generous people.

The French organization ANECAH (Association nationale pour l'éducation des chiens d'assistance aux handicapés [National Association for the Training of Service Dogs for the Handicapped]) was established in 1989. It trains dogs used in rehabilitating people who have lost all or part of their mobility. Since its creation, ANECAH has trained more and more dogs each year, including about fifty in 1996. These dogs are either Labradors or Golden Retrievers, breeds known for their calmness, docility and ability to learn commands. Training is divided into several phases. First, puppies are placed in families who raise them. Then, dogs are trained by the association to respond to about fifty different commands.

The host family plays a vital role and influences the rest of the dog's training. As soon as puppies are three months old, they are "pretrained" or socialized, by the host family, who teaches them basic obedience. Every three weeks, the dogs and their temporary owners meet at a center where the puppies are monitored. The center staff may give advice on raising the puppy and, in some cases, decide to discharge dogs who show evidence of a character fault that disqualifies them from service work. This pretraining phase lasts until the dog is eighteen months old. Then he is trained specifically to help a person with restricted mobility. During this phase of approximately six months, he lives full-time at the center. In the last two weeks of training, dogs and potential owners are matched based on mutual affinity. Training is administered daily, with a trainer spending about a half hour with the dog each day. After twenty-four months, one-third of the dogs are discharged for behavioral or physical reasons (poor hip formation, etc.). The main goal is to find the perfect match between dog and owner, with a high degree of mutual understanding and a good use of the dog by the handicapped person. The potential owner participates in a relatively demanding, two-week program to learn how to care for his dog and give commands. He must take written and oral tests and complete a final exam. The complete training of one dog costs about 10,000 Euros. This limits the number of people able to take the program and especially the number of dogs who can be trained.

After this training period, dogs can respond to about fifty different commands. They can pick up fallen objects, fetch things (like the telephone), open and close doors, turn lights on and off, maneuver a wheelchair through tight spots, etc.

Service dogs perform many tasks that their owners cannot. But they also have a therapeutic effect on people—especially children—who suffer from various illnesses. In these cases, the dogs act almost like doctors. Apart from the tasks these dogs were trained to perform, they provide stimulation to handicapped children, who find comfort in their new friend, gain self-confidence andbecome more open toward others. They may even do things they never thought they could. The dog's help encourages them to test their limits. Research on the therapeutic effects of animals has been conducted, particularly in the field of autism, a disease with no known cause and no current treatment.

Service dogs also make it easier for people to approach the handicapped and develop a positive view toward them.

Guide Dogs for the Blind

Training schools for guide dogs for the blind have existed in France since 1952 and in England since 1930. These dogs receive roughly the same training as service dogs for the handicapped, but guide dog training is much more extensive, both in terms of the number of animals trained and the number of training schools.

One-third of the dogs used are German Shepherds and the remaining two-thirds are Golden Retrievers and Labradors. These breeds are chosen because of their obedience and learning ability. Puppies are bred specifically for guide dog training at a research center that supplies the schools. This research center focuses on genetic selection in dogs to eliminate character faults and bone and joint deformities (like hip dysplasia). The center staff are advised by veterinarians who teach at

national veterinary schools. As soon as the puppies are weaned, they are placed in host families who raise them, then distributed to the various training schools. Bitches return to the center regularly for whelping, so that the reproduction of breeding dogs may be monitored. The goal is to produce about twenty puppies per year, given that France currently has only about a thousand owner-guide dog teams.

Guide dog training occurs over four months divided into several periods during which dogs learn obedience first and foremost. Obedience training consists of simple exercises in which the dog must hold certain positions, retrieve objects, get used to wearing a harness and heel correctly. This phase lasts one week and is administered exclusively by a trainer. In the next phase, the dog learns to avoid all sorts of obstacles and indicate them to his owner. This is the pivotal point of the entire training program. The trainer is involved during the first month, then the dog is given to a blind person who must get used to the dog and let the dog guide him over various routes. At this point a close bond develops between dog and owner. The trainer serves as a link between the two and is also responsible for "training" the owner.

After four months at the guide dog school, the owner-guide dog team is ready to face daily life and work together for many years. The dog allows the blind person to re-enter society and pursue an occupation compatible with his handicap.

All over the world, similar guide dog training associations are being established to provide more handicapped and blind people with dogs who receive training of higher and higher quality.

Dogs Who Help the Deaf

In our society, being deaf or hearing impaired is a handicap that can quickly lead to isolation. Dogs are used to help remedy this problem.

A number of centers train so-called "hearing-ear" dogs worldwide, particularly in the United States, England and especially Holland (in France, such associations no longer exist). Established in 1984, the Soho Foundation near Nimegue in Herpen, Holland purchases dogs and trains them to help handicapped or deaf people. It works in cooperation with organizations in England, where most of its dogs are purchased. Most are Golden Retrievers, but some Welsh Corgis and Bearded Collies are also used.

From the age of eight weeks to one year, the dogs live with Dutch families, preferably with children, where they receive basic obedience training and learn to adapt to various surroundings (the city, the supermarket, the woods, etc.). Then they return to the foundation and begin real training for their future function. This is where the choice of breed becomes vital, since the dog's intelligence is truly put to the test: He must learn over seventy verbal commands and twenty gestures. Additional training is required because the voice of a deaf or hearing impaired person is quite different, both in terms of intonation and diction. And dogs who help deaf-mutes receive two years of training instead of one.

"Hearing-ear" dogs are trained above all to react to certain noises and communicate them to their owner. For example, the dog may jump onto the bed when the alarm goes off, tug on his owner's pant leg when someone knocks at the door or delicately take his owner's hand to alert him to an ill-timed visit. However, what owners appreciate most is that their new friend helps end their loneliness and isolation.

Statistically speaking, the training of one dog costs about 10,000 Euros. At the Dutch foundation mentioned above, 80% of the dogs successfully complete training. In 1987, Holland required forty-five service dogs, including fifteen for the deaf or hearing impaired.

Security Dogs

Dogs in the Army

Soldier Dogs

As early as the thirteenth century B.C., dogs served as full-fledged soldiers in the wars waged by humans. These mastiffs were fearsome weapons, subjugating the enemy with their vicious bites. They were of a breed originally from Asia and similar to today's Tibetan Mastiff but larger, standing 75 to 80 cm (29.5-31.5 in) tall at the withers, while today's dog measures 70 cm (27.5 in) at the withers. Fiercer than the sighthounds used in hunting by the pharaohs of Egypt, these mastiffs became popular in Egypt, then in Greece. They finally reached the Roman Empire after the Greek conquests. Meanwhile, the Gauls, Celts and Germans developed a breed derived from the Great Dane. In the first century B.C., soldier dogs were pitted against Roman and Gallic warriors in famous fights.

The training of soldier dogs was simple: Their role was to exterminate the men and horses of enemy armies. Over the centuries, these dogs were outfitted with spiked collars, armor with sharp spikes or blades on top and even leather coats covered with a highly flammable substance. Thus transformed into true war machines, dogs were sent in to scatter frightened or brutally wounded horses and foot soldiers. The use of such dogs ended in the nineteenth century, with the significant development of firearms.

Sentry Dogs

With their excellent sense of smell and instinctive tendency to defend and guard their owner, dogs were used as sentries at many forts, citadels, village squares and walled cities.

Plutarch told the story of the sentry dog Soter: Corinth was protected by a garrison aided by fifty mastiffs sleeping on the beach. One night, enemy armies arrived by sea. After a night of revelry, the Corinthian soldiers had become lax. But their dogs were not—they fought the enemy, though largely outnumbered. Forty-nine mastiffs were killed. Only one, Soter, was able to escape and sound the alert by barking. The Corinthian soldiers donned their arms and managed to ward off the assailants. To reward Soter for his courage, they gave him an elegant collar with the inscription, "To Soter, defender and savior of Corinth." Mastiffs like Soter were commonly used in the Middle Ages to defend vast expanses like Mont Saint Michel. Beginning in 1155, twenty-four English Mastiffs were released each night in the fortified city of Saint Malo to protect the ships from pirates. This practice ended in 1770, when the dogs attacked and devoured a young officer walking on the beach. Today, dogs still work as sentries in high-security facilities.

The role of security dogs has changed over the centuries with advances in weaponry and armies. They have served as canine soldiers dressed in lethal armor, as sentries, trackers, patrol dogs, message-carrying dogs and first aid dogs. Today, they play an important role in the detection of hydrocarbons, explosives and narcotics. In these new roles, their great loyalty, generosity and abilities still help ensure the security of men and society as a whole.

Tracking Dogs

Many dogs have been trained to follow the trail left by humans. When Christopher Columbus landed in North America, dogs were trained to find and kill Native Americans. At La Vega, thousands of Native Americans were put to flight by only 150 foot soldiers, thirty horsemen and some twenty soldier dogs. Later, Spanish plantation owners in South America used dogs to track runaway slaves. These dogs received minimal training: They were shown black mannequins stuffed with blood and entrails. Excited by the odor, the dogs quickly made the connection between these mannequins, given to them as food, and slaves. The slaves they found had little chance of escaping alive.

During the war in Algeria, tracking dogs were used to find enemy troops who had penetrated security points. One of these dogs was Gamin, a German Shepherd from the military kennel at Beni-Messous. When he first arrived in Algeria, he was so vicious that no one could get near him… no one except Gendarmerie Officer Gilbert Godefroid. On March 29, 1958, Officer Godefroid was awoken suddenly early in the morning when an estimated two hundred men broke through the electric fence at the Tunisian border. Gamin and his master were flown in by helicopter and immediately began a search, accompanied by the parachutists of the First Foreign Regiment. It was easy to find the fresh trail, but as soon as he released Gamin, Godefroid was hit by a barrage of automatic gunfire and fatally wounded. Though injured himself, Gamin lunged at the gunman and tore his throat.

Then he crawled back to his master and lay down on top of him to protect him. It took six men and a tent cloth to bring Gamin under control. He was brought back to the base camp and treated, but once again no one could approach him or give him commands. Military authorities decided to give Gamin a peaceful retirement at the gendarmerie's central kennel in Gramat, Lot where, according to the secretary's message, Gamin was to "receive attentive care until his death." But Gamin died of a broken heart only two weeks after his arrival. His ashes are still kept at the gendarmerie's National Training Center for Dog Handlers in Gramat and a monument was dedicated in his honor.

The Americans used tracking dogs in Vietnam. In this guerilla war, dogs were trained to silently follow the soldiers in order to locate and surround withdrawal zones and Viet Cong camps.

Message-carrying Dogs

Getting the latest news from advanced detachments and communicating with fixed points on the frontline is vital to executing or modifying military attack or defense strategies. Before the advent of telecommunications, dogs were widely used as messengers.

In ancient times, mastiffs were forced to swallow messages and were sacrificed upon arrival so that the precious documents could be recovered. This atrocious practice did not last long, not because of its cruelty, but because of the expense.

In the eighteenth century, Frederick II The Great of Prussia revived this practice for the delivery of inter-army mail in his kingdom. His message-carrying dogs were so popular during the Seven Years'War that an entire line of transmission and liaison dogs was developed.

Beginning in World War I, so-called "courier dogs" were developed. These dogs were selected based on very strict criteria: They had to stand 40 to 70 cm (15.5-27.5 in) tall at the withers; have a neutral-colored coat; be calm, intelligent, obedient and in perfect health; and have a keen sense of smell, eyesight and hearing. According to the Military Manual, these dogs also had to be between two and five years old, to ensure that they were at the height of their abilities and hardy enough to withstand bad weather, hardship and fatigue.

Their important role consisted of linking points several kilometers apart, often in difficult weather conditions. Courier dogs could reportedly cover five kilometers in twelve minutes during bombing. Paradoxically, the messages these dogs carried were clear and easily decipherable by enemy troops. But courier dogs were still very effective, since they were rarely captured.

Pack Dogs and Draft Dogs

Dogs can carry objects weighing up to 7 kilograms (15,5 lb). For this reason, they were commonly used in wars to carry munitions, supplies and even arms to the frontlines. During World War I, German dogs were captured carrying light machine guns. Two types of pack dogs were developed during this war: telegraph dogs and pigeon dogs. Telegraph dogs carried a spool of telephone wire that unrolled as they crossed a perilous route through trenches, amid gunfire, through barbed-wire fences, etc., in an effort to reestablish the lines of communication severed during combat. Pigeon dogs were trained to bring carrier pigeons to outposts.

The use of draft dogs dates to 1911, when the Belgians attached powerful dogs to machine guns on wheels. They used dogs instead of horses because dogs have greater stamina and can more easily follow men through the undergrowth. Dogs were also attached to supply carts and stretchers for transporting the wounded. The Germans even used dogs to pull sleds on the eastern front. Due to considerable debate over a dog's ability to pull an object on wheels, only the Belgian, German and Russian armies truly used draft dogs (the Germans for a limited time).

Patrol Dogs

With their highly developed protective and defensive instincts, dogs soon became popular in patrol work. Used to expel enemies hidden in the woods or in underbrush, they helped patrols upset ambushes and signaled the presence of enemy troops. Patrol dogs were also used to keep watch over prisoners on escort. Very few of these dogs made a name for themselves in history, but they helped many patrols clear out enemies and find their way.

First Aid Dogs

The Egyptians were the first to train dogs to find the wounded. After combat, dogs were released onto the battlefield to search for the injured, whom they licked and signaled to rescue workers.

First aid dogs next appeared in the late nineteenth century. They were trained to locate the wounded and indicate their presence by bringing back a personal object, often a soldier's helmet. After thus alerting the rescue workers, the dogs went back to search for more victims. First aid dogs were essential: The wounded could be transported only by dark, so the dogs helped guide the searches. The first Society of First Aid Dogs was founded in 1885 by Van de Putte from Belgium. This was followed by a German organization, founded by Bungartz, an animal painter. Not until 1908 did France begin using first aid dogs.

There are many stories of the activities of first aid dogs. A soldier from Le Mans, France injured on November 2, 1915 reported, "I had been hit in the arm by a shell and in the jaw by a bullet and a saber wound had detached part of my scalp. Half buried beneath the bodies of several mates, I felt someone caressing my forehead. It was a first aid dog licking my face. Despite my severe pain, I managed to hoist myself up a bit. I knew that dogs were trained to bring the caps of the wounded back to camp, but I had lost mine. The poor dog hesitated, so I told him, "Go on, boy, go back to the guys at camp". He understood me and crawled back to the camp. There he made such a fuss—barking, tugging on one person's cap and then another—that he attracted the attention of two stretcher-bearers. They followed him back to me and I was saved."

Dangerous Missions

Dogs have sometimes been used in difficult situations and in unusual conditions.

During the war in Indochina, the terrain and vegetation caused many problems for the French troops conducting operations there. In the first months of the campaign, they discovered the dangers that parachutists dropped in enemy territory might face. Only dogs could help speed the soldiers' painstaking but necessary trench digging work. Dogs were therefore parachuted experimentally at the parachute school in Meucon on September 5 and 6, 1949.

The difficulties encountered during parachute training centered on the dog's jump from the plane and his landing. Lighter than humans, the dogs reached the ground far later and at a considerable distance from their handlers. This greatly increased the time necessary to find the dog and put him to work. Equipping the dogs with a lighter parachute solved this problem, ensuring that the dogs landed at the same time as their handler and in the same area.

Unfortunately, some dogs lost their lives in wars. With the German armies approaching, Soviet General Panfilon decided to have dogs trained to look for food beneath armored vehicles. The dogs were starved for one or two days before the attack, mines were attached to their back and they were released to run toward their horrible fate. Although terribly cruel, this practice did wreak havoc on the German troops.

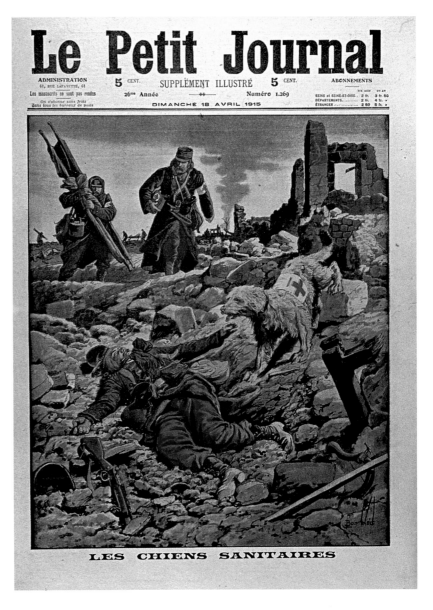

First aid dogs. Petit Journal pictorial paper, April 18, 1915.

There are four stages to training an effective drug detection dog. The length of each stage varies, depending on the dog.

Stage One

The substance to which the dog should react is placed inside a PVC tube pierced with holes. It is too dangerous for a dog in training to be in direct contact with heroin or cocaine. For this reason, small rags that have touched these substances and absorbed their odor are used instead.

For several days, the trainer plays with the dog using the tube, until the tube becomes the dog's favorite toy. During this stage, the dog learns to associate his toy with the odor of the substance he smells through the holes in the tube.

Stage Two

When the trainer considers the dog sufficiently attached to the toy, he hides it in plain sight in an easily accessible place. The dog still must use his sense of smell to find it.

Then the trainer hides the tube in places that are more and more difficult to find, even impossible to reach.

During this stage, the dog also learns to scratch when the trainer buries the tube in sand. The loose ground incites the dog to dig for his toy.

Stage Three

The tube is hidden out of plain sight without the dog seeing. The trainer leads the dog into the room, briefly encourages him to find his toy and then releases him on the command "Search"! When the dog locates his unreachable toy, he must scratch to get the trainer to give it to him.

Stage Four

In the final stage, the trainer eliminates the tube so that the dog learns to search only for the drug, which he now associates with his toy.

Canine Activities Today

While dogs have always had the same aptitudes, over the years they have been trained to face conflicts in different places, using different techniques. Dogs have had a variety of functions over the centuries. First they were trained as parachutists and entrusted with carrier pigeons; later they learned to detect mines and gas, etc. Today, dogs are trained for other types of work: They are taught to detect explosives and narcotics, thereby helping humans face the increase in bomb threats and counter the spread of drugs.

All these dogs are trained at the Ring III level, since their handlers must be in complete control of their every move.

Drug Detection Dogs

The ideal drug detection dog is playful, energetic, medium-sized and flexible enough to squeeze through tight spaces and climb over or through obstacles. He also needs a great deal of stamina, since he may be required to conduct several searches in one day. Currently, Malinois Belgian Sheepdogs are the preferred breed because they are smaller and more lively than German Shepherds.

These dogs are also trained to attack, since in drug detection work handlers must sometimes search for dealers, who may aggressively resist arrest.

Drug detection work with dogs is conducted primarily inside buildings, where dogs are used to sniff out hidden drugs (heroin, cocaine, cannabis, marijuana, etc.) and thus speed the process when a meticulous search is necessary.

It is important to note that drug detection dogs are not drugged themselves. While dogs can suffer from withdrawal, this condition would not enable a dog to find hidden substances more quickly. On the contrary, dogs suffering from withdrawal would conduct disorderly, superficial searches and become aggressive toward people, even their handler.

Explosives Detection Dogs

Explosives detection dogs are chosen based on the same criteria as drug detection dogs. But dogs trained to detect explosives must be calmer and able to conduct searches without becoming excited.

The most popular breeds for explosives detection work are therefore Malinois Belgian Sheepdogs and German Shepherds.

Hydrocarbons Detection Dogs

This specialty exists chiefly in North America and is currently being developed in Europe. Dogs trained to recognize various hydrocarbons are brought to the scene of fires to detect the chemicals used by arsonists. They may also be used in preventing fires in forests at risk or after fires of criminal origin. Hydrocarbons detection dogs mark by scratching. Flammable chemicals are then removed from the site, or samples are taken from the places the dog scratches at the scene of a fire.

Hydrocarbons detection dogs work in conditions that put many demands on their sense of smell: They must cover areas that may people have passed through. In addition, fires destroy certain odors but release many others that may be toxic and are always unpleasant and accompanied by smoke.

A dog's willingness to search comes from his desire to find his toy and play with his handler. To the dog, drugs, explosives and hydrocarbons are only markers that he must discover to get to his favorite toy.

Guard Dogs and Patrol Dogs

A guard or patrol dog protects or follows a person indicated by his handler. In this line of work, the dog's vigilance and obedience are key. The dog must remain detached and show aggression only if the person begins to struggle. Guard and patrol dogs may also be entrusted with objects, such as cars.

TRAINING EXPLOSIVES DETECTION DOGS

The four stages of training are based on the same skills needed by drug detection dogs, but with several differences. Explosives searches are conducted both inside and outside for substances including dynamite, TNT, formex, nitrate, fuel oil, hexolite, tetryl, etc.

Explosives detection dogs mark by sitting or lying down, depending on the location of the substance. Sitting indicates high positions and lying down indicates substances that are on the ground or buried.

These dogs must show no aggression (such as barking or scratching), due to the highly sensitive mechanisms in the explosive systems used by terrorists (obviously, dogs practice and are trained only with the raw materials listed above).

In the first three stages of training, the dog learns to associate a toy with the explosive materials. The trainer places the toy first in plain sight, then in plain sight but in an unreachable location and finally in a completely hidden location. The toy is always accompanied by an explosive material.

In training, the dog's toy is hidden in "hot spots" corresponding to the possible hiding spots for explosives.

Dogs are never trained to bite, since the goal of explosives detection work is simply to pinpoint the location of charges (as a preventive measure or during a bomb alert). The dog and his handler work alone in the areas to be explored. Once a charge is detected, the area is evacuated and mine clearance teams take over.

DOGS IN FRANCE'S GENDARMERIE

France's Gendarmerie has used detection dogs since 1943. Currently, the organization has 388 dog-handler teams (one dog, one handler) trained in all areas of activity, including:

- manhunts (tracking) and defense = 209 teams, including twenty qualified for avalanche search;
- drug detection = 80 teams;
- explosives detection = 43 teams; and
- guard and patrol work = 36 teams.

These teams are spread over the country and based with gendarmerie units, forming a network to ensure rapid intervention in all regions.

Handlers are selected from among officers who volunteer.

The dogs, either German Shepherds or Malinois Belgian Sheepdogs, are purchased as adults (at about eighteen months old). They are assigned to a unit when they reach about two years old, after completing a training program with their handler at the Gendarmerie's National Dog Training Center in Gramat (Lot). When the dogs become too old to serve in the Gendarmerie (generally when they reach eight to ten years old, or after five to seven years of service), they are given to their handler free of charge. They can thus spend a well-deserved retirement with an old friend.

Gendarmerie dogs are trained daily.

Each year, they are involved in close to 40,000 cases, including about 1,500 manhunts, over 300 of which are successful.

That means that almost every day, someone is found by a dog or with a dog's help.

In the mountains, five to fifteen people are found in avalanches each year.

In France it has been said—and even written—that drug detection dogs are drugged themselves. This is completely false. If it were true, how would explosives detection dogs be made to do their job?

All work is based on the dog's attachment to his handler and on the reward. The dog is actually looking for his toy.

Both dog and handler are motivated by mutual respect and admiration. Their motto is "You and me for them".

General Jean-Louis Esquivié,
Commander of the Schools
of the National Gendarmerie.

Other Ways Dogs Help Humans

Dogs have always amazed us with the many qualities that make them so helpful. In the nineteenth century, they showed their acting skill in street shows and circuses. In the early twentieth century, dogs in the country still pulled small carts loaded with wood, bottles of milk, women, or children. Today, they use their sense of smell to help people find truffles, detect minerals, and, of course, hunt wild game.

Hunting Dogs

Hunting is a popular sport, a passion—an art for many—involving over a million dogs and their owners. Hunting is a sport for dog and owner alike, since it requires excellent physical condition to work long hours in all kinds of weather, as well as a strong character, determination and a keen eye. Of course, a good hunting dog must also have a superb sense of smell.

Hunting is strictly regulated. In France, for example, the season begins with waterfowl hunting in the second week of July, continues with pointers in September and ends with hounds and woodcock hunting in late February. Without the dog, a hunter's best friend, there is no hunt, since hunting is actually a sort of competition that the dog must win. Through instinct, knowledge of the territory and sheer cleverness, the hunted animal must beat its canine adversary, who has the advantages of intelligence, a keen sense of smell, poise, vigor and the skills specific to the particular type of hunt. Dogs specialize in hunting certain game—waterfowl, small and large mammals and birds—as well as in specific parts of the hunt, such as digging up foxholes. These specialized hunting dogs are classified in several of the groups established by the FCI.

Natural Skills and Training

All hunting dogs possess considerable natural skill as a result of careful selection by expert breeders over decades. Of all the characteristics required for hunting, intelligence is the most important. It is not enough for a dog to have a good nose, he must also know how to use it.

Training is necessary to make the most of this natural skill. It is a tricky job that takes patience and has no hard-and-fast rules, since techniques vary according to the dog, his reactions and, of course, the specific goal. Training is necessary, but it is also time-consuming and often does not progress as fast as one would like. Only an expert can train a dog well in two or three months. Usually, training requires six months of daily work.

Training must include obedience, retrieval and positions (like the famous "down"). The dog must also learn to use his nose. The sensitivity of an animal's sense of smell depends on species; in dogs it depends on breed. After a hunting dog has been trained, he must be able to sort through the scents carried by the wind to avoid making mistakes. Pointers must be able to search a particular area and remain motionless while marking, in order not to frighten off game. They must also retrieve dead game and bring it to the hunter. Hunting dogs must be taught all this with as little force as possible.

In principal and by nature, hunting dogs are not apartment animals or simple pets. If owners try to resist their dog's hunting instinct, it will come back to haunt them. Non-hunting owners of a hunting breed must be sure to give their dog daily opportunities to run and play. City life is often unsuitable for such dogs.

406

Pointing Dog Field Trial In U.S.A.

Field trials are a cult sport, pursued by a small fraterniy of fanatics. They started in England about 1850. The first American one was at Memphis in 1874 - that area is known as the Cradle of Field Trials, and the National Bird Dog Championship is held at Grand Junction each February.

A field trial is a contest for pointing dogs seeking upland game birds by scent quail in the South, pheasants in the Midwest, prairie chicken, sharp-tail grouse, Hungarian partridge on the prairies, ruffed grouse and woodcock in the Lake States, Pennsylvania and New England, chukar partridge in the Northwest. The sport is bloodless, fort the pointed birds are not shot. Field trialers are ardent conservationists.

A field trial is also a show a trial dog is a performer, and so is its handler. «Gun dog's a yeoman, trial dog's a showman», the saying goes.

As in baseball, there are levels of the game. The top trials are called the major circuit, about thirty trials held at the same time each year, starting in August on the Northern Prairies, then moving south, with quail trials in December and January in the Deep South, and the finale in mid-February the National Championship at Grand Junction, Tennessee.

The adult dogs on the major circuit are called all-age dogs. Like major-league baseball players, they are world-class athletes. Handled and watched from horseback, they can take your breath away with the speed and grace of their running, the statuesque majesty of their points (bird dogs instinctively freeze - become a statue - when they detect the scent of game birds. This instinctive reaction is called a «point».

Like racecars, all-age dogs perform on the edge - a hair's breadth from out of control, driven by a consuming instinct to find game. And like racecars, trial dogs often suffer «wrecks» when in their exuberance they forget their manners or get away from their handlers.

The dogs compete two at a time, drawn by lot as bracemates. They hunt a prescribed time (usually an hour) over a prescribed course. Huge grounds are required, for the bird dog can hunt through five miles of country in one hour. After all entries have run their braces, the judges declare the winners: a champion and sometimes a runner up-or first, second and third in nonchampionship stakes. Judging in field trials is entirely subjective. The dog that points the most birds is not necessarily named winner. The dog's hunting technique, rather than the quantity of its points, is key. The dog's perfomance is called his «race» - a race to find and point birds.

Before dogs reach full maturity at about age three, the compete in puppy and derby stakes. All stakes are open or amateur, depending on the handler's status (not the dog's - the same dog often runs its owner's direction and in open stakes with its professional handler in charge). Purses are modest - a few hundred to a few thousand dollars.

Clubs sponsor the trials, some as old as the sport. The grounds are quail plantations, state wildlife-management areas, western rangelands. The Northern Prairies are the training and testing ground for the dogs. From mid-July through mid-September, trainers from all over the country work their strings on native game birds in the plains country.

The Triple A league in field trials is called the shooting-dog major circuit. The dogs competing here don't range quite as far all-age dogs, but they are wide-going and splendid athletes too. They are also handled from horseback. Then come on-foot-handler trials, the fastet growing segment, including wild-bird trials in the North on grouse and woodcolk.

How does a dog win in field trial? It must hunt at extreme range with extreme speed, making bold, independent casts for far-off objectives or along edges on the course likely to hold to game birds. When the dog scents birds, it points with lofty style and awaits discovery by its handler or his assistant, called the scout. The handler then flushes the quarry under scrutiny of mounted judges. As the bird flies to safety, the handler fires a blank.The dog must remain a statue. If the dog will do all this with aplomb, it is called «broke». Being «broke» is a great compliment to the dog, the big distinction between the field-trial dog and the ordinary hunting dog (Hunting dogs are usually just «country broke» - that is, they remain staunch untill the birds fly, but then they chase). Getting a dog «broke» and keeping it so is the daunting task of the handler. The dog points by instinct but it chases flying birds by instinct too. Teaching the dog to subdue the strong chasing instinct is a never-ending challenge.

Field-trial dogs guide the genetics of alle working bird dogs. As with racehorses, a few great sires dominate pointer and setter bloodlines. The lineage of all bird dogs goes back through field-trial winners to a handful of foundation sires from the turn of the last century.

A boy can save enough from a paper route to buy a weanling son or daughter of a National Champion, that makes the sport democratic, at least at the start. Campaigning on the major circuit is beyond the paperboy's reach, but many a great champion has been started by a farm boy. Fans follow the sport through a weekly journal, the American Field, founded in 1874, the oldest sporting magazine in America. The field also maintains the registry for working bird dogs and sanctions open stakes. An umbrella organization, the Amateur Field Trial Clubs of America, sanctions amateur championships and loosely regulates the sport. But the basic rules, set by tradition, have remained unchanged for a hundred twenty years.

The sport is intensely competitive, at alles levels. Participants, open or amateur, approach the games with deadly seriousness; all play to win. Their ultimate quest is the National

Truffle-Hunting Dogs

The search for truffles - underground mushrooms so rare they are known to some as "black gold" - has traditionally been conducted using various animals with a keen sense of smell, including goats, sheep, pigs and, most recently, dogs, who are the easiest to train and transport. Any breed of dog can be used for this activity after receiving the training necessary for professional truffle hunting (in artificial truffle-beds) or amateur truffle hunting (in natural truffle-beds).

Raising a Truffle-Hunting Dog

In the traditional method of training a dog to hunt truffles, a litter of puppies is selected for this activity even before birth. As soon as they are born, the owner surrounds them with the odor of truffles by brushing truffle juice on the mother's teats and later adding truffle juice to their food at every meal. The dogs soon learn to associate the odor of truffles with eating and will systematically seek out this odor, especially when they have not eaten in some time. Owners must be careful not to add too much truffle juice because it can dull the appetite.

In the "treat" method, the dog is trained to hunt for a treat (such as Swiss cheese or ham) which is buried alongside the truffle. Soon, only the truffle is buried and the treat is given to the dog as a reward for discovering the truffle.

In the "play" method, specifically suited to puppies and young dogs, training is made into a game. A truffle is hidden in a sock or a plastic tube that the owner uses as a toy for his dog. After the dog has developed a strong attachment to the toy, the owner hides it and encourages the dog to find it. When dog discovers the object, thanks the odor of the truffle, he has also found his favorite toy. Soon, the truffle is hidden alone and the toy is given to the dog as a reward for discovering the truffle.

Hunting in Natural and Artificial Truffle-Beds

At first, the owner guides his dog on a leash to areas known to be rich in truffles. Soon the dog becomes accustomed to finding these areas himself, first on a leash and then without one.

Mineral Detection Dogs

Dogs were first involved in mineral detection work in 1962 in Finland, where they were used to find sulphurous rocks for prospecting. The same practice has been used successfully in Sweden, the former Soviet Union and Canada.

In other countries, dogs are now used to detect deposits of nickel and copper, even though these minerals are more difficult to find than sulphurous rocks, which emit a strong odor.

Mineral detection dogs are trained using play, the same technique used for training drug and explosives detection dogs. According to reports from eastern and Scandinavian countries, good mineral detection dogs can discover deposits up to fifteen meters underground. If this is true, perhaps dogs will soon be trained to detect gold or diamonds!

Circus Dogs

Nowadays, there are very few circuses and shows featuring dogs. However, this was not always the case, especially in the nineteenth century.

Canine actors made their debut in the streets of large cities, where they performed dressed as humans, standing on their hind legs. They later appeared with troupes of traveling acrobats who used primarily "mongrels", as these dogs were once called.

In 1896 at the Olympia in Paris, Miss Dore presented the first tightrope-walking Poodles. By 1850, people were being entertained by show dogs, including Munito, the famous Poodle who answered questions by choosing cards with letters on them!

From then on, progress was made very quickly and trainers realized that dogs had a lot more to offer in a trusting environment where they were rewarded, rather than frightened. They soon noticed that dogs learned to "ham it up" all by themselves during shows, that they adored applause and that they became sad and despondent when isolated.

Whatever the field, dogs learn well only if they are interested, can have fun and are allowed to work with their owner as a team.

November 3, 1957: preparation of the dog Laïka for the journey on board Sputnik II. She was the first animal in space.

As French author Alain Dupont mentions in his book about dogs, each trainer had his favorites: David Rosaire had his Pekingese, the Ybès had their Tenerife Dogs, Barbara Hochegger had her Borzois, Ewa Oppeltowa had Collies, Fredy Knie Jr. had Fox Terriers and Gabriella had a group of various breeds (Saint Bernards, Greyhounds, Pinschers, Papillons, Spitz, Afghans and Fox Terriers). The Fischers had a German Shepherd jockey, Lupescu Schoberto had soccer-playing dogs, Philippe Gruss had a canine tramp called Max, Old Regnas had acting dogs, the Palacys featured canine trapeze artists and Eric Baddington presented tightrope-walking dogs. Meanwhile, show dogs became increasingly popular. Most spectators were unaware that these dogs'mathematical skill and predictions were nothing but clever tricks.

It is important to realize that nineteenth-century dog "training" methods were rarely based on any knowledge of canine psychology and behavior. Cruel methods including force, brutality and even starvation were used to frighten poor animals into exhibiting a certain behavior.

In London in 1929, these conditions led to the establishment of the Jack London Club, which aimed to eliminate any show or exhibit using animals, especially dogs.

Bruxelles. — Laitières.

TEACH YOUR DOG TO COUNT!

Alain Dupont, a well-known French dog fancier, created this relatively simple method for training dogs to count.

Most importantly, you must be able to make your dog bark by making a specific gesture that looks insignificant but is actually a command to the dog. To do this, the next time you give your dog a treat or a meal, raise your hand while giving the command to bark. As soon as he barks, reward him and lower your hand, with your palm toward him, while giving the command to stop. Soon, you'll be able to make him bark by simply raising your arm (as when you fix his collar) and stop his barking by lowering your arm. Then, the next time you have company, you can casually ask them to give your dog a simple math problem (addition or subtraction). Ask the dog the question and discreetly raise your arm, causing him to bark. When he has barked a number of times equivalent to the answer to the problem, discreetly lower your arm to stop his barking. Now, all you have to do is reward him. Just remember that in order for this trick to work, you must know how to count!

Part 4

Dogs in Sports and Recreation

Dogs in Sports and Recreation

By participating in shows, competitions and working trials, dogs can earn qualifications for their aptitudes. Most of the qualifications awarded in these events appear on the pedigree. Sports and recreational trials also enable dogs to participate in selective trials. In any kind of trial, a dog's performance is always a reflection of the trust and cooperation between dog and master for their mutual benefit. Without this relationship, competition and winning would not exist.

Dog Shows

Dog shows are local, national or international events during which dogs of different breeds are evaluated on their physical characteristics or performance by judges and conformation experts.

In France the SCC (Société Centrale Canine [Central Canine Society]) is involved in training show examiners, who are nominated by the various breed clubs to which they belong.

The candidates, often recruited from among recognized breeders, begin by evaluating breed standards in club shows and working trials. Candidates then take a test administered by the club to receive certification and become eligible for a one-week course given jointly by the SCC and the animal husbandry department of a veterinary school. Upon completing this course, candidates must take another exam to be eligible to work as student judges under the supervision of training judges. After acquiring experience as student judges, they can become apprentice judges and then qualified judges able to work at championships with increasingly higher stakes.

As true delegations of the SCC, the sixty-four Regional Canine Societies (SCR) promote breed standards and breeding within a given region, particularly by organizing events (shows and utility trials). These organizations federate all the utility (or working) dog clubs.

These clubs, of which there are six hundred in France, belong to Regional Canine Societies but cannot organize work and agility trials or shows. They focus on dog training and owner education.

Concerning breed associations or clubs, they are authorized by the SCC to improve a particular breed, promote it publicly and establish and modify breed standards. They also oversee part of the training of judges and conformation experts and approve conformation, thereby helping to shape selection policies.

Each association focuses on only one breed, unless a breed is waiting for official representation, in which case an established association can represent it temporarily. The same is true of judges - rarely are they allowed to judge more than one breed.

Judges assign points to various sires and dams, from one point for those who are merely conformed to six points for pedigreed sires or dams. Points are given according to appearance but also, in the case of the most highly ranked animals, according to ancestors, litter mates and progeny.

STANDARD CHAMPIONSHIPS

Since the word "beauty" might be confusing, beauty championships are now called "standard championships". In these competitions, dogs are presented in various classes.

Puppy Class "hopefuls"

Only dogs who have not yet reached the required age for conformation (generally one year old) are allowed to participate in this class. The ratings given in Puppy Class (fairly promising, promising and very promising) help owners predict the future of a puppy but should not be taken as definitive. Ratings indicate whether or not it is reasonable to put a dog on a champion track by subsequently presenting him in the Junior Class.

Junior Class

This class is reserved for conformed dogs one to two years old. It allows dogs to complete the conformation exam (measuring the degree to which they match the breed standard) through a qualitative rating of whether the dog can improve the breed or simply not harm it. After judging, a card is issued with the rating insufficient (rejudge), satisfactory (yellow), good (green), very good (blue) or excellent (red).

Open Class

As its name indicates, this class is open to all conformed dogs, including those in the Puppy Class. The same ratings are delivered. The best of the excellents receives the CACS (Certificate of Aptitude for Standard Champion), while the runner up receives the RCACS (Reserve CACS). Several dozen CACS are awarded in France each year.

"Working" Class

This class is reserved for working breeds. Organized by utility clubs according to SCC regulations, work trials focus on demonstrating the natural aptitudes specific to each breed through work or training. A dog's progress can be traced in an individual work log listing the ratings he has received. Working trials are open to all purebred dogs, even unconformed ones. Still, to receive the title of Working Class Champion, a dog must present a minimum degree of conformity. However, certain breeds like the Border Collie may require the TAN (Test of Natural Aptitude) for conformation. This is not necessary for all breeds because the later a puppy takes the TAN, the more difficult it becomes to make an objective distinction between natural aptitude and training.

"Champion" Class

This class is open only to dogs who have already received the CACS or the RCACS, given that a dog must obtain at least four CACS (including one in an international show and one in a national breed show) to qualify for the CACIB (Certificate of Aptitude for International Beauty or Standard Champion). In this competition, a candidate is selected for the rating Champion of France, usually awarded during the Longchamp show organized by the SCC and attended by over 6,000 dogs. During these shows, the best of each breed is chosen to compete against other champions. The all-breeds winner receives the honorary title Best in Show. Some thirty CACIB are awarded each year in France. To be eligible for the title of International Champion, a dog must obtain three CACIB in the same year in different countries, each from a different judge.

"Group" Class

In certain "pack" or "breed group" competitions, dogs are judged as teams, rather than as individuals. Awards in this class are given for the uniformity of the breeder's selection and the quality of his dogs' training.

THE MAIN WORKING TRIALS

The main events in which dogs can compete according to breed are sheepdog trials (herding), field trials (pointers), hunting trials (hounds), tracking trials, terrier trials, truffle-hunting trials (truffle-hunting dogs), rescue or water working trials (Newfoundlands, in particular) and dog racing (Whippets and Greyhounds).

In addition to these events, the current popularity of so-called "utility" dogs over strictly "companion" dogs has led to the development of canine sports, including agility trials and the RCI (defense and attack trials). Because these events are purely recreational, they are an excellent opportunity for socialization and training, thereby helping to integrate the dog in our society.

Agility trials, approved in France only since 1988, are open to all dogs, regardless of size, breed and age. In these events, dogs run with their owner over a course similar to a US Marine obstacle course or driver training range. This discipline requires incredible focus by dog and owner alike.

The RCI is a trial involving so many different skills (obedience, tracking, defense, motivation, etc.) that it could be called "utility dog university". The levels of RCI range from one to three, depending on the degree of difficulty of the course and trials.

Working Trials

Working trials make it possible to evaluate a dog's natural and trained aptitudes through the Test of Natural Aptitude (TAN). The main working trials are discussed below.

Sheepdog Trials

Established to encourage shepherds to train their dogs, these trials require a high level of obedience by the dog and true partnership between dog and owner. These trials are an impressive display of training. There are two types of trials: Border Collie special trials and interbreed trials.

The first sheepdog trials, organized by Lloyd Rice in 1873 and held in Bala, Wales, were a great success. By 1876, this event had become the springboard for many competitions in Wales and abroad.

The first international trials for Border Collies were held in Scotland in 1906 after regulations were developed by breed clubs. Today, similar competitions are held in France. They are open to all Border Collies registered in the LOF and led by their owner.

In sheepdog trials, dogs work a group of five sheep. In a specific amount of time, they must drive the sheep through a gate into a pen and then isolate two sheep. This is one of the most difficult exercises, since the dog must work a small herd. Dogs also herd two groups of ten sheep separately and then together, over the same course used for a single group of five sheep. In trials with a pair of dogs, six sheep are used. The two dogs are not allowed to cross paths and must drive the sheep to the shepherd in two groups of equal size. Then each dog must move his group into a separate enclosure.

JUDGING DOGS

"What criteria does a judge use to choose a winner, especially when dogs of different breeds are presented?"
First, the judge compares each dog to the official standard describing the ideal individual of that breed. These standards, based on appearance and personality, are established by large breed associations (the International Cynological Federation, the American Kennel Club, the Kennel Club of England, etc.). The judge selects dogs that best match their respective standard.

"If dogs are judged based on a single standard, why do the same dogs receive different ratings from different judges?"
There are several factors that cause this. First, an individual judge has his own interpretation of the standard based on his experiences, preferences and the weight he gives certain criteria over others. The second factor is dog-owner interaction. A dog may actually show better with one person than another, since presenters may not have the same level of fitness and outdoor temperature affects some breeds more than others.
A judge also expects presenters to behave a certain way. They must be punctual. A judge's pace must not be interrupted, since this could break his concentration and cause him to lose sight of the dogs as an overall group. Presenters must know what to do once they are on the track. Each judge has a preferred style, although the variations are slight. For this reason, it is often helpful for presenters to observe the judge to whom they will be presenting, in order to get a better idea of his preferences and expectations. Presenters must also accept graciously the final result of the competition, even if their dog does not receive the rating they expected.

In addition, the dog must be presented quickly and simply, such that the judge can see his teeth, head and, more generally, whatever he is evaluating, whether the dog is on the table, in "stay", or walking. Puppies are given a bit more leeway. Dogs should be clean and, if possible, groomed. This is considered a sign of respect.

"What criteria are used to evaluate the quality of a purebred dog?"
These criteria can be summarized as follows:
The dog's specific type. This means all the characteristics that distinguish him from other breeds. People often say that type is all in the head, but you must also consider coat color, gait, etc.

Harmony and balance. For example, a dog's head may be quite lovely but not the required size for the breed, particularly in proportion to the body.

Personality. Character is essential, as much for companion dogs as for show dogs and working dogs. If a dog is shy, aggressive, or lazy, he won't be able to complete the task he is given. Attitude is also important.

Structure. The correct bone structure and muscle mass are extremely important and are thoroughly examined when the dog is still and when he's moving (walking or trotting).

General presentation. Coat, weight, grooming, cleanliness.

Training. A well-trained dog can show his qualities better and faster during the few minutes of judging than an untrained dog.

A "good" dog could be defined as follows: a dog who presents the greatest number of characteristics common to his gender and breed, is even-tempered, is in good presentation condition and is well-trained enough to show his qualities quickly.

Héléna Mentasti de Spektor, International Judge.

Adolfo Spektor, Veterinary Doctor, International Judge

Ever since it was founded, France's sheepdog club has had organized sheepdog trials. The first was held in 1886 in Chartres, the second in 1897 in Angerville. These interbreed trials were held on a vast meadow surrounded by tall trees. There was an S-shaped plow track 6 meters (20 ft) wide and about 400 meters (1,310 feet) long. On the track were three obstacles - a ditch, a chute and a bank. Two groups of sheep were put in pens at one end of the meadow. The shepherds and their dogs had to move the sheep over the track and into the pens at the opposite end of the meadow.

France's National Sheepdog Utility Society was founded in 1911 to promote the breeding and training of sheepdogs for herding. In 1961, the Ovine Federation and the SCC established official regulations for sheepdog trials and rules for obtaining the working qualification and then the Certificate of Aptitude for Working Champion.

The courses used in sheepdog trials are carefully designed in order to best simulate normal working conditions. These trials are open to all breeds.

To participate, dogs must be at least one year old. They are led by a professional shepherd or sheep breeder and must guide the herd (120 to 150 sheep) into a pen, lead them through a chute, cross a road with passing cars and move along the edge of a cultivated field over approximately 400 meters.

Today, thanks to the efforts of breed clubs, these competitions are held in conditions very close to those in real life. In fact, it is preferable to have a dog who takes initiative, rather than one who is completely "guided". These competitions also allow people to see sheepdogs at work and encourage breeders to make selections based on performance rather than appearance. In some trials, dogs move herds of cattle or geese.

Field Trials

Field trials are highly popular sporting events for hunting dogs, pointers in particular.

There are three types of field trials:

- Spring trials, the most difficult, are held on flat grassland with pairs of wild partridges;
- Summer trials have the same rules and are also run with pairs of partridges. Some breed clubs organize special, high-altitude field trials with grouse, common capercaillies or rock partridges; and
- Fall trials, held at the beginning of France's shooting season. In these trials, dogs must retrieve shot game.
In field trials, dogs have fifteen minutes to demonstrate their hunting abilities. They must explore the designated territory rapidly with the head held high, passing in loops in front of the leader. Each of these passes must be made at a distance equivalent to what judges call "shooting range". The search range on each side of the leader varies according to each breed's characteristic search range.

In these competitions, European breeds (pointers, spaniels and griffons), are not judged in the same trials as English breeds (setters and pointers). European breeds usually compete individually, while English breeds can compete individually or in a brace (pair). Some dogs at a very high level can participate in France's Grande Quête [Great Hunt].

The Grande Quête involves only English breeds. This extremely difficult competition is reserved for very strong-willed dogs only. It could be described as a race in loops sometimes reaching a diameter of nearly 100 meters (328 ft). Dogs participate only in braces and must have an excellent nose and a high level of fitness.

The so-called Quête à la Française [French Hunt] is less complex. It is similar to spring trials and is organized in four categories: English individual, English brace, European individual and European brace.

Whatever the trial, dogs are always judged on their speed, training, sense of smell, enthusiasm, range, carriage and style, according to a very precise scale of points. Only five faults constitute grounds for elimination: insufficient overall quality; abandoning the hunt by moving away from the leader and disobeying his come-in signal; pursuing game, regardless of whether or not it has been marked; considerable skittishness when the pistol is fired; and flushing game accidentally without realizing it.

In all these trials, winners receive "working" awards based on the guidelines set by official organizations. The highest award is the CACIT (Certificate of Aptitude for International Working Champion).

The competitions described above show how an activity as ancient and instinctive for dogs as hunting has sparked the development of increasingly popular canine sporting events.

Other Competitions for Hunting Dogs

Since pointers are far from being the only hunting dogs, various trials and competitions have been organized for judging the quality of other breeds. In working trials for retrievers, retrieving ability is evaluated. At the judge's signal, the dog is released to locate and retrieve game and is assessed on his skill.

For small game hounds, there are roe deer and hare hunting trials. Packs of three to nine dogs compete in these trials, depending on the particular event.

For terriers and dachshunds (dachshunds to a lesser extent), there are trials on artificial fox or badger holes, as well as events involving tracking hare and following a blood trail, as in tracking wounded game.

Truffle-Hunting Competitions

Truffle-hunting competitions have been organized since 1969 as a means to evaluate the ability of truffle-hunting dogs. In these competitions, a dog must find and mark with his paw the ground above six truffles buried in an area measuring 25 square meters. He must work as quickly as possible, without marking the same spot twice (penalty) or digging up and eating the truffle (elimination).

There are two categories in truffle-hunting competitions. In the beginners category (dogs may participate as beginners up to three consecutive times), the owner is allowed to stay with his leashed dog inside the search area. In the second category, for more experienced dogs, the owner may enter the search area only to dig up the truffle, hand it to the judge and set his dog back to work.

Training for the second category is the same as for the first, but the dog must also be taught to moderate his digging and stay within the boundaries of the search area.

Dog Racing

Racing sighthounds is probably one of the oldest canine sports. The first sighthounds are described as early as 6000 B.C. In the first century B.C. in Treatise for the Hunt, Arrien describes organized competitions using live game. Celtic civilizations continued this tradition.

Dog racing on artificial terrain or dog race tracks began in the late nineteenth century. The first race (360 meters)(394 yards) was held in 1876 in Hendon, Britain on a horse race track. When the first American dog race track was built in Tuscon, Arizona in 1909, the sport took off. Today it is concentrated in Ireland, Great Britain and the southern United States.

In principle, dog racing is quite simple: Six dogs are released from a starting box onto an oval sand or grass track to chase an artificial hare moved by a cable or motor around the track's inner rail.

Dog races drew large crowds in the 1930s. Some canine athletes became celebrities, including Mick the Miller, with a record of nineteen consecutive wins and two victories at the Greyhound Derby, in 1929 and 1930. These races were popular because they were short (350, 480 or 760 meters) (380, 525, 830 yards) and provided an opportunity for serious betting.

THE PEDIGREE AND WORKING TRIALS

Apart from listing a dog's ancestors, the pedigree provides information on the titles, awards and qualifications his ancestors received during their careers. This information helps owners and breeders better understand an individual dog's characteristics.

The pedigree is the definitive certificate of registration in the LOF (French Stud Books) delivered by the SCC. When complete, it shows a dog's origins over three generations, whether he is from France or another country recognized by the FCI.

The pedigree includes the name of the dog, the breeder and the kennel the dog is from, as well as the dog's breed and gender, birth date, tattoo number, LOF registration number (birth rank by breed followed by conformation rank) and information on fourteen of the dog's ancestors (seven on the sire's side and seven on the dam's). Information on coat type, weight and height for breed varieties is also given.

The breed clubs belonging to the SCC have a growing pool of additional information on show and working trial results, including valuable data on the winners.

A Research Center for Racing Dogs

Greyhound racing is one of Florida's main cultural activities. These unique canine athletes, able to cover a 480-meter (1,575 feet) course in twenty-five seconds at speeds exceeding 70 kilometers (44 miles) per hour, require a very specialized approach to their preparation (training and nutrition) and medical care (true sports medicine). This approach involves concepts new to the everyday veterinarian. In the spirit of progress, the University of Florida in Gainesville recently established the Research Center for Canine Sports Medicine, focused entirely on the Greyhound. This center has its own training course for the practical observation of problems specific to the breed.

Professor Mark Bloomberg, University of Florida, Gainesville (United States).

In English-speaking countries, dog racing attracts a truly professional crowd, much like horse racing. The circuit includes breeders, trainers and race associations like the National Greyhound Racing Club, which has organized and regulated races in England since 1972. There are more than ten dog race tracks in the city of London alone!

Dog races with pari-mutual betting are held in Ireland, Great Britain, the United States, Australia, Spain and Morocco. These events, involving primarily elite canine athletes, are usually run on a 400-yard course. These dogs receive special care at training centers and specialized clinics. In Great Britain, 20,000 Greyhound births are recorded per year and races draw over 6,000 spectators. American champions can win considerable sums of money - up to 125,000 dollars for a single race. In other countries, other breeds participate in races, particularly Whippets and Afghan Hounds.

Hare coursing, founded by Queen Elizabeth I, is an age-old variation of dog racing. In hare coursing, a pair of sighthounds is set on a live hare. A judge on horseback compares the dogs' skill and speed. Even though the hare is rarely killed, animal protection leagues fiercely oppose the practice of using a live lure. An artificial lure may be used instead. All sighthound breeds are eligible to participate in this event, since the purpose is to maintain the conditioning of animals not selected for racing.

Ring, Tracking and Country Trials

Ring trials and their practical application, country trials, are a series of training events that put a dog's natural aptitudes to the test in obstacle jumping, obedience, defense and attack and tracking. Since the dogs in these events - sheepdogs and guard dogs - are chosen for their basic athletic ability, liveliness, obedience, poise and courage, the events are recognized as beneficial to the dog species. In light of this, the results are entered on the dog's pedigree, helping breeders to determine which studs might be used to improve the stock.

Origins

The first ring trials were held in Belgium as early as 1896. In 1903, the first country trials were held in Lierre, near Malines, Belgium. In the 1930s in France, three men - Mr. Dretzen, president of the Beauceron Club; Paul Megnin, an Alsatian fancier and editor of the review L'Éleveur [The Breeder]; and Joseph Couplet, president of the Belgian Kennel Club - established the first regulations for France's ring, country and anti-poaching trials.

Today, thousands of dogs participate in these trials after qualifying as defense dogs, making them eligible for ring Category I and later Categories II and III. Dogs in any of these categories can also qualify for country trials, 350-point country trials and finally 500-point country trials. When a dog reaches ring Category III, he must earn a minimum number of points in several preliminary stages and then participate in three trials to be allowed into the Championship of France, an event for the twenty-five best dogs out of nearly 250 that compete at the national level.

The country trials championship is held in a single day to prevent owners from training their dog on the course after the first candidate has completed it (courses are always different). Dogs are selected based on the highest number of points for the year's trials.

Organization

Ring trials are held in enclosed areas measuring 2,500 square meters, often those belonging to the 650 French clubs practicing mainly this discipline. Traditional trials are held on local fairgrounds, where audiences are always impressed by the spectacular show.

Country trials are held in open areas on a circuit course presenting a variety of practical challenges in which dogs must show courage and initiative. Chateau grounds are the most frequently used venues, yet it might be interesting to use industrial areas or abandoned towns. The difficulties dogs might face in urban surroundings would better correspond to the current functions dogs fulfill in various organizations. Tracking and blood trailing trials are held on surrounding farm land.

Participating Breeds

Almost all breeds in FCI Groups 1 and 2 (sheepdogs and cattledogs, pinschers and schnauzers, etc.) are working dogs of sufficient size. These groups include French sheepdogs (the Beauceron, the Briard, the Picardy Shepherd and the Pyrenean Shepherd), Belgian sheepdogs (the Groenendael, the Tervuren, the Malinois and the Laekenois), the Bouvier des Flandres, the Rottweiler, the German Shepherd and other German utility breeds (the Giant Schnauzer, the Boxer and the Doberman) and, less frequently, the Dutch Shepherd Dog, sheepdogs from the former Eastern bloc countries and the Airedale Terrier.

Currently, the two most popular breeds in utility trials are the German Shepherd and the Malinois Belgian Sheepdog. In a period of about fifteen years, the incredible Malinois Belgian Sheepdog has worked his way to the top of various sport and utility trials. This breed might truly be "the utility dog of the twenty-first century".

Training for Ring and Country Trials

Training a dog for ring or country trials begins when he is about three months old and continues until the end of his active life, generally when he reaches eight or nine years old. Category III ring trials begin when a dog is about three years old and require an average of four one-hour training sessions per week for a dog to be competitive at this level. An exceptional animal - usually the product of many years of genetic selection - therefore needs over five hundred hours of training or forty-five minutes to an hour of intense work and exposure to various situations that test his sensory and athletic skills, as well as his obedience, initiative and fighting spirit.

From three to six months, puppies are introduced to tracking and jaw holds. They are taught the basics of practical obedience, mainly the call to attention. They are taken on walks to expose them to various aspects of city life.

From six to nine months, the dog is introduced to the exercises of the program. He learns to bite the roll, then the leg pad, then the pant leg of the attack suit, developing his speed and holding technique and changing holds from the left to the right leg. He resists threats with the stick and learns to tolerate the attacker's gunshots.

When the dog is about nine months old, he begins the exercises that will continue until he is two to two and a half. The final months before competition are used to harden the dog to the rapid, discerning work of attackers. In trials, the dog must assimilate all the difficulties of the environment he will face in utility work.

Fundamental training begins as soon as the dog has stopped growing, at about twelve to fourteen months. This stage focuses on obtaining optimum performance from the dog. The breeds used are guard dogs and, more frequently, sheepdogs. These dogs developed their natural, back-and-forth trot in their ancestral work moving flocks.

In ring trials, dogs participate in events of increasing difficulty: a series of jumps, a 2.3-meter (7.5 ft) run to the fence and back, a run to the 1.2-meter (4 ft) hedge in front of a 1.5-meter (5 ft) ditch and back and a jump up to 4.5 meters (14.7 ft) long. Next comes a rest during the obedience event and then back to work, with attacks from 40 meters (130 ft) with fifteen-second holds.

The physical training currently administered by competitors and administrations is based on these two events and includes distance runs twice a week on courses 4 to 12 kilometers (2.5-7.5 miles) in length with alternating splits, as well as speed work with the retrieval of tennis balls thrown from a ramp, either as a warm-up before work or a replacement for distance splits. Next, natural obstacle courses are added, including swimming if there is a body of water nearby.

Paradoxically, dogs like the Boxer, the Doberman, the Rottweiler and the Giant Schnauzer need this sort of training the most, even though their appearance would lead one to believe otherwise. Most sheepdogs are very hardy, but not all can maintain a strong working pace, especially in intense heat. The Briard and the Bouvier des Flandres are sometimes bothered by their coat. To perform effectively in the ring and in herding, a dog should stand no taller than 65 centimeters (25.5 in) and weigh no more than 35 kilograms (77 lb), with rare exceptions.

Training Exercises

There are three elements in jumping and climbing: high jump, long jump and climbing.

While playing, young dogs are encouraged to jump small natural hedges 0.8 to 1 meter (2.6-3.3 ft) high. In so doing, the young dog becomes aware of his physical potential. For ring trials, as soon as the dog knows how to stay, he is taught to jump a barrier with no ditch and to judge where to start his jump. The barrier is progressively raised then placed in front of a regulation ditch. After several months, the dog is able to jump 1.2 meters (4 ft). Some remarkable specimens can jump 1.4 meters (4.6 ft). For country trials, the dog is trained to jump as many natural hedges as possible.

Long jump training begins by placing a hurdle in front of the ditch by the barrier the dog has already learned to jump. Once the dog can jump 3 meters (9.8 ft), the hurdle is placed in the middle of the ditch (3 meters long) (9.8 ft) working the dog up to a jump of 4.5 meters (14.7 ft). The unofficial record for long jump stands at 7 meters (23 ft).

Unlike the hedge and ditch, climbing requires the dog to find footholds on the A-frame and maintain his balance. Therefore, this is the last jump taught so that the dog does not get into the habit of stepping on the barrier or hedge to aid his jump. The current record stands at 3.4 meters (11.15 ft)on an incline. In country trials, dogs must cross lower walls (2 meters) (6.5 ft), but take-off is often more difficult than in 2.3 meter (7.5 ft) barriers.

Obedience Trials

There are many elements to obedience trials. These include: heel on leash or heel free with muzzle; retrieving thrown objects, building on required sight retrieving (an object falls from the trainer's pocket) and retrieving on command (the trainer commands the dog to retrieve an object when he notices a personal belonging has been lost). The dog also learns to hold the object in his mouth, move about without dropping it, take it back to the trainer and drop it on command. In country trials, dogs must know how to swim because water retrieval is required. Trainers teach dogs to swim in summer in shallow pools. "Forward" is yet another skill, which is taught by using an object or cloth bag as a toy to motivate the

dog to move forward on command. Dogs are also trained to hold various positions as commanded by the trainer who is standing at distance. This training is first done in a controlled area. The dog is placed on a small table so that he cannot move forward. On command, he must assume different positions, sit, down, up, before going back to the standing position. The same applies to stay. The dog remains sitting or lying down for one or two minutes while the trainer is not present. In training for country trials, an attempt may be made to distract the dog from his task. He must refuse several treats (meat, cheese, etc.) offered to him and not pick up treats placed around the grounds. Fighting and attack training follows.

It is difficult to cover all ring and country working techniques in just a few pages. Nevertheless, a scientific approach to this sport is difficult, yet fascinating given what it involves - weaving together psychological components with physical needs and abilities as the trainer teaches the exercises to the dog. These highly skilled dogs are the fruit of strict selective breeding using stringent criteria for competition ability. These practices have existed for more than a century now.

ASSERTIVENESS AND ATTACK WORK

Following initial training, the dog's assertiveness and attack skills are developed for various ring and country trials. These exercises highlight the sheepdog's natural aptitudes; his ability to take the initiative, control his nerves, move quickly and make decisions for himself, all of which make the sheepdog an excellent worker. These are the same qualities sought in dogs used for tracking, avalanche search and rescue, wreckage search and rescue and other work.

Search, Barking and Controlling the Wrongdoer

The dog must search out the wrongdoer (a well-padded individual hidden in one of six covers in the ring) as quickly as possible. When he finds him, he barks to alert his trainer. After the trainer arrives, the wrongdoer flees and fires two shots with a 9-mm revolver. The dog then guides the person for a few dozen meters. As he does so, the person will try to escape twice to verify the dog's vigilance and the swiftness of his response. In country trials, the search is much longer and the dog must rely on his sense of smell to track the wrongdoer for several hundred meters.

Defense of the Owner

The handler walks toward the attacker with the dog at heel. He shakes hands with the attacker and starts up a conversation. At the close of the conversation, the attacker walks away, then comes back to attack the handler. As the man attacks, the dog energetically defends his owner and holds the attacker at bay before being ordered back to heel. In country trials, the defense of the owner takes place in a wide range of scenarios and surroundings (in the farmyard, in a building, etc.).

The dog undergoes a second defense test while muzzled to verify the dog's true ability to defend

his owner. This is because some dogs become accustomed to the padded suit the attacker wears and many will not defend their owner in real-life situations.

Attacks

There are many types of attack. The attacker can be facing the dog or fleeing, protecting himself with a gun or baton (a cut bamboo stick that makes considerable noise and is threatening, but will not harm the dog). When the attack is over, the dog is either brought to heel or continues to hold the attacker and stops the wrongdoer when he tries to escape. In the ring, the dog faces the attacker who holds a baton, chases the fleeing wrongdoer who holds a baton, or holds the wrongdoer who has a gun.

In country trials, all combinations are used and the attacker may defend himself with various weapons, including a broom, a watering can, a branch, etc.

The technical work of attack is complex. Briefly, it includes decision-making, impact and hold techniques.

A dog is taught to make decisions by progressively and methodically training him to bite right or left pivot leg (both legs in case the other leg is pulled free). The dog is then trained to grasp the arm if the baton is swung in front of the legs and then to grasp the inside of the arm close to the body if the attacker stoops down. The training is the same as that taught in the martial arts. The dog gets his hold when the attacker lets down his defenses. The dog's inborn traits determine his impact, which allows him to force his way through even the most intense defense after the attacker has tried to side step the initial attack.

A dog's tendency to go for a throat hold is also genetic. Young dogs receiving their initial training are trained to attack a large pad, developing a strong, sure hold on the protective clothing.

Only stable, kind dogs with good nerves can learn these techniques. An aggressive dog would not tolerate the level of pressure required for this training and would rarely get through baton or other attacks in country trials.

Called-off Attacks

This spectacular event demonstrates the handler's total control over the animal. When the dog is less than one meter from the attacker, he literally throws himself down on his side at the sound of a whistle. To train a dog for this event, the handler leaves the dog at the normal attack range of twenty meters and stands next to the attacker. The handler orders the dog to attack and then forcefully calls him off three meters before the attack. The handler then alternates attack and call-off training, then progressively moves back toward the normal attack distance to join the dog. Teaching the dog to break off an attack is done last, only after the dog has learned the other skills well.

In country trials, there are two called-off attacks. One with the attacker facing the dog and one with the attacker fleeing.

Guarding an Object

This is the most complex exercise demanded of a dog in guard and police dog tests.

In ring trials, the dog guards a basket that the attacker tries to steal as he walks by two or three times.

In country trials, the object is always larger. It may be a bicycle, a caddy, a baby carriage, a wheelbarrow or some other everyday object. Fireworks are used to distract the dog. All dogs receive the following training, but progress at different rates. The dog learns to place his back legs on a small wooden box and pivot on the box to follow the wrongdoer who circles at a distance brandishing a baton. He makes the dog turn to the right, then to the left and tightens his circles. One meter from the object, he faces the dogs, which mounts a defense of the object. As soon as the dog has attacked, the handler calls him off and commands him to put his feet back on the object. The handler progressively loosens his hold on the leash, then stands next to the circling attacker to regulate the distance of the attacks. If this training is started at the age of seven months, the puppy will most likely develop into an excellent guard dog within two years.

Utility Tracking Competitions

There are two types of tracking competitions: traditional tracking courses and utility tracking. In utility tracking, the person to be tracked "hides" in surroundings similar to those that could be expected if searching for a missing person. This discipline could be a departure point for real-life searches for missing persons. There are three trials. Classes 1 and 2 prepare for the certificate and class three is the final exam. After completing all three, the team receives the utility tracking certificate.

Tracking Trials

The trail is laid by highly experienced trail layers who try to avoid a certain number of difficulties, such as making sharp turns, skirting a tarred route or walking in water for distances greater than those established for each class, artificially introducing a scent to the object other than that of the trail layer, crossing obstacles more than 1.5 meters (5 ft) high when there is no way to get around the obstacle, crossing a heavily-trafficked road, going through a town or returning to the departure point.

Objects placed along the track are everyday items, such as a wallet, handkerchief, glove, pen, scarf, pack of cigarettes or pocketknife. The items are placed randomly, dropped as if accidentally lost as the trail layer walks.

The handler is free to lead or help his dog at any point in the tracking. He may remove the dog's leash if necessary (to clear obstacles), put him back on the trail, or order him to search to pick the trail up again. The handler may also pick up objects, question people along the trail, or let his dog rest.

TEST SEQUENCE

A sketch lays out the sequence for the various tests. Here are some concrete examples.

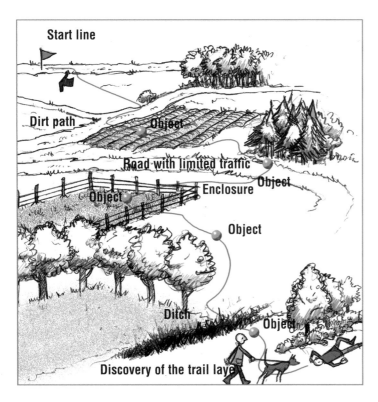

Start line

Dirt path

Object

Road with limited traffic

Object

Enclosure

Object

Object

Object

Ditch

Object

Discovery of the trail layer

CLASS 1 TRACKING TRIAL

Age of the trail: two hours

Length of the trail: approximately two kilometers (1.25 miles)

Time allowed to find the trail layer: approximately one hour

Attitude of trail layer while laying the trail: walking

Objects along the trail: first personal object dropped ten paces from the start of the trail. Five objects dropped along the trail at intervals of 500 paces.

Difficulties encountered: dirt path and grass. Electric fence for cows. Barbed wire. Walking alongside then crossing a road with limited traffic. Ditches to cross.

Position of the trail layer when found: lying down or hidden in a ditch, under a shelter, or behind a hedge or section of a wall.

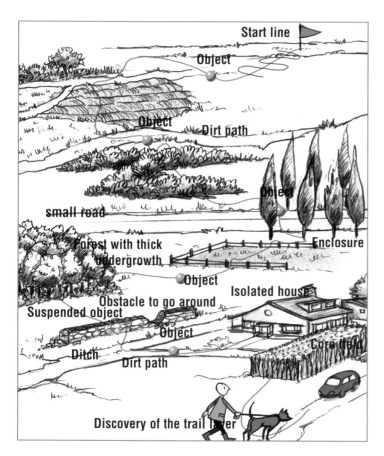

CLASS 2 TRACKING TRIAL

Age of the trail: three hours

Length of the trail: approximately two kilometers (1.25 miles)

Time allowed to find the trail layer: approximately one and one half hours

Attitude of trail layer while laying the trail: Walking

Objects along the trail: first object dropped 150 paces from the start of the trail. A reference object, enclosed in a plastic bag, is given to the handler before the start. Five objects dropped along the track at intervals of 500 paces.

Difficulties encountered: a stranger will introduce his scent at the starting line half an hour before the tracker is brought to the line. Dirt path and grass. Electric fences for cows. Barbed wire. Walking alongside, then crossing a road with little traffic (distance of 50 steps). Ditches, thick hedges, forest with thick undergrowth. 1.5 meter (5 ft) obstacle to go around. Pass by an isolated house.

Position of the trail layer when found: Lying down or hidden in a ditch, under a shelter, or behind a hedge or section of a wall, in a parked vehicle or a vehicle stopped alongside a road.

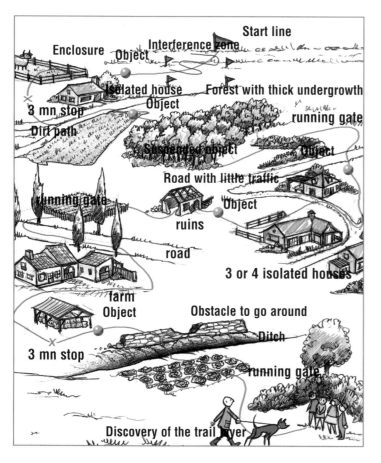

OWNER/DOG UTILITY TRACKING CERTIFICATE

Age of the trail: six hours

Length of the trail: approximately three kilometers (2 miles)

Time allowed to find the trail layer: approximately two hours

Attitude of trail layer while laying the trail: walking, with some areas crossed at a run and one or two three minute stops.

Objects along the trail: first personal object dropped 150 paces from the start of the trail. Five objects dropped along the trail at intervals of 625 paces, of which one may be attached 1.5 meters (5 ft) above the ground.

Difficulties encountered: a stranger will introduce his scent at the starting line fifteen minutes before the tracker is brought to the line. Dirt path and grass. Electric fences for cows. Barbed wire. One or more roads to walk alongside and cross. Ditches, thick hedges, forest with thick undergrowth. 1.5 meter (5 ft) obstacle to go around. Pass by an isolated house. Walk on a road for approximately 100 steps. Go through ruins and a farmyard. Pass by a small group of three or four isolated country houses.

Position of the trail layer when found: lying down or hidden in a ditch, under a shelter, in a parked vehicle or a vehicle stopped alongside a road, in a room, in a tree, in a farmyard, with a group of people, or behind a hedge or section of a wall.

Sport and Leisure Competitions

New dog sports emerged in the 1980s. Agility trials and sled dog racing are now the most popular. Sled dog racing combines the pleasure of working as a team with the pack, exploring wide-open spaces and competition. However, special skills are required for this sport. The musher must work with his dogs daily and be in good physical condition. In addition, considerable funds are required to maintain the pack and cover travel expenses. Therefore, this is a sport accessible to only a few devoted individuals.

Agility competitions differ in that they are primarily a leisure activity, a pastime. The owner is able to learn how to train his dog more effectively and have fun while he's at it. Even young children can get involved in agility training and competition. Moreover, though the owner and dog work as a team, the owner is not required to expend himself physically.

Less complex sports such as canicross and flyball have also been developed.

Canicross

In this sport, the owner runs alongside his dog on a groomed natural surface. Essentially, this competition has turned the Sunday jog with the dog into an official sport in which many people can participate.

AGILITY OBSTACLES

• Tunnel: The dog must pass through a collapsed or pipe tunnel of varying length while the owner remains outside.
• A-frame: This obstacle is made up of two inclined ramps that the dog must climb up and then down, without jumping.
• Dog walk: A board is placed several feet off the ground and the dog must cross it alone while the owner remains alongside on the ground.
• Weave poles: This exercise is made up of several stakes placed at regular intervals. The dog must go through the weave poles alone.
• Long jump: Several boards are placed one after the other establishing a minimum jump distance. The distance varies according to the difficulty of the course.
• See-saw: The see-saw is made up of a board that tips once the dog passes the mid-point.
• Pause table: The dog must jump up on the table and execute several commands, such as sit, lie down and stand.
• Pause box: The dog must stop into the pause box before continuing the course.

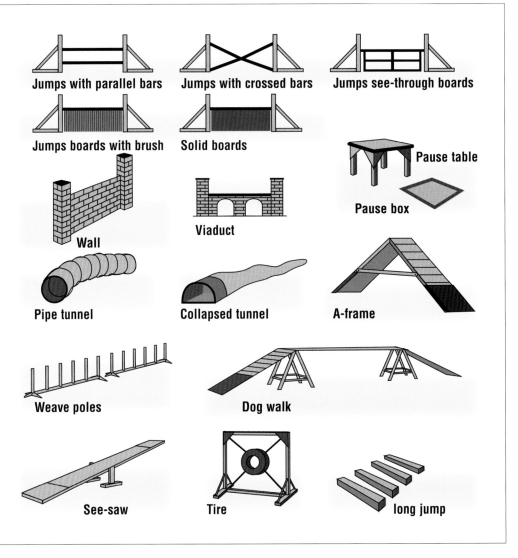

Jumps with parallel bars
Jumps with crossed bars
Jumps see-through boards
Jumps boards with brush
Solid boards
Pause table
Pause box
Wall
Viaduct
Pipe tunnel
Collapsed tunnel
A-frame
Weave poles
Dog walk
See-saw
Tire
long jump

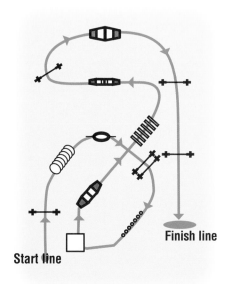

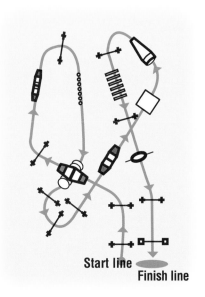

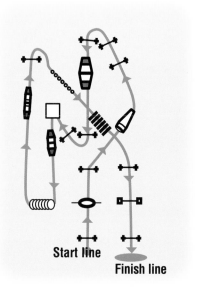

Example of an open class agility course

Royal Canin 1st Master France Agility 1st Round. Length: 170 m (186 yards). Speed: 2.5 m/second. Total course time: 68 seconds

Royal Canin 2nd Master France Agility 2nd Round. Length: 200 m (218 yards). Speed: 2.70 m/second. Total course time: 70 seconds

The rules state that the dog and owner must cover a distance of seven kilometers without stopping or handing off to another handler. The owner is attached to his dog (or the other way around if you prefer) with a regulation rope or leash tied at the waist. Judges along the route watch to verify that the owner never passes his dog nor drags him along behind—grounds for immediate disqualification. Canicross is a true team sport.

One of the unique aspects of this sport is that the size, breed, or age (within reasonable limits, of course) of the dog and the age of the runner are of no importance. Team competitions were recently introduced.

The number of canicross competitions is increasing throughout Europe. Increasing numbers of people are getting involved as participants or spectators. Given that this sport requires little training and is a good way to have fun and stay fit, we can be sure it will become even more popular in the coming years.

Agility

This recently introduced canine sport is becoming increasingly popular. It is considered a play discipline in which a dog, without a leash or a collar, negotiates a number of obstacles laid out on a course.

This sport, introduced in England by John Varley in 1978, is a derivation of equestrian jumping competitions. During a reception, Varley laid out a new form of competition restricted to dogs. His innovation quickly caught on and spread throughout Europe. In 1987, the French Central Canine Society accepted agility trials as a regulation sport and established three rules: Competition is open to all breeds; dogs with or without papers may participate; the sport is intended for relaxation, exercise and education.

The sport was made official in France in 1988 and agility championships are now held, including the annual European Masters competition. In 1989, when the sport was introduced to the world, numerous countries joined the fourteen European countries that already recognized the sport. These included, Japan, countries in South America and northern Africa and many eastern block countries.

The FCI imposed its own competition rules: Dogs must be fifteen months or older to participate in competition; dogs measuring less than forty centimeters at the withers may participate only in "mini agility" trials.

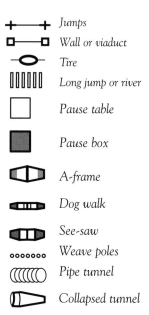

Jumps

Wall or viaduct

Tire

Long jump or river

Pause table

Pause box

A-frame

Dog walk

See-saw

Weave poles

Pipe tunnel

Collapsed tunnel

An agility course includes many elements. As is the case in equestrian jumping competitions, all obstacles must be cleared successfully. Jumps include hedges or walls, but can also include more complex tests. A dog must receive rigorous training in order to succeed, but the competition is based solely on playfulness and confidence. This makes agility competitions particularly attractive since both the dog and the owner are involved. Some owners work so well with their dogs that the dog runs the course entirely on his own. The owner simply stands at the center of the course and indicates the order of the jumps.

Though the sport is open to all, there are many clubs offering activities for beginners to advanced participants. You don't have to be a dog-lover to enjoy a day at the agility competitions where the best dogs and owners demonstrate their remarkable skills.

Leisure sport: flyball

The sport of flyball offers a way to relax, have fun and get exercise, while playing with your dog. Flyball is simply a canine version of Frisbee competitions.

The human version of this sport began in 1871 when a cake company, the Frisbie Pie Company, tossed a new product onto the American market - flat, round pie plates. American young people started using the pie plates as toys, throwing them to one another. In 1946, Walter Morrisson came up with the idea of manufacturing a resin flying disk, the Pluto Platter. And so began the Frisbee. In 1967, the first Frisbee world championships were held in Pasadena, California. Frisbee is now played around the world.

Given the dog's natural aptitude for fetch, it was inevitable that the animal and the flying pie plate would one day meet. In the 1960s, the first flyball demonstrations were held and official competitions began, primarily in Anglo-Saxon countries.

The rules are fairly simple. The owner throws a regulation disk within the regulation perimeter, which is approximately five meters in diameter. The dog must catch the Frisbee as quickly as possible and bring it back to the thrower. Dogs typically demonstrate amazing acrobatics, a behavior that is encouraged by the owner. Other Frisbee competitions include best catch, most original catch, etc.

There was only one step from Frisbee to flyball…to replace the disc by a ball, and the human throher by an automatic device controlled by the dog itself.

What is special about the canine version of this sport is the fact that any age dog or thrower can participate… and win! The size of the dog is not important. In fact, it is not uncommon to see small dogs of indeterminate breed win the most prestigious competitions.

Moreover, even handicapped persons can play flyball. And unlike other sports, all players participate in the same competitions.

Flyball is an ideal sport for dog owners who want to have fun, get a little exercise and compete without having to impose strict training on their best friend. Of course, you won't be very successful if your dog decides it would be more fun to eat the Frisbee!

Sled Dog Racing and Ski-Pulka

The first evidence of sled dog racing dates back 4,000 years to eastern Siberia. However, sled dog racing and ski-pulka were not recognized as sports until the beginning of the twentieth century. During the Gold Rush in Alaska, sled dog racing enthusiasts organized out of a desire to test their teams'strength and speed. It wasn't long before the sport of sled dog racing was born.

Alaska's first races

Mushers and gold diggers passionately debated the merits of their respective teams. Out of these debates was born the famous Nome Kennel Club, which was founded in Nome in 1907. The purpose of the club was to strictly define the rules of the race and set up well-managed official races.

One year after the club was formed, Albert Kink, a Nome lawyer, organized the first competition - the All Alaska Sweepstake. The rules were as follows:

- All mushers must be members of the Nome Kennel Club;
- All dogs must be registered with the Club;
- The musher may have as many dogs as desired, but all dogs that leave the starting line must cross the finish line, either in the harness or on the sled;
- Dogs will be identified and marked at the start line to prevent the substitution of a dog during the race;
- If two teams are in close proximity (one behind the other), the team being overtaken must immediately stop to let the overtaking team go by, then wait for a certain period of time before starting up again.

JACQUES PHILIP:
TWENTY YEARS AT THE TOP OF A MARVELOUS SPORT

Dog Sled Racing began in France in 1978-79 when only fifty individuals or so formed the CPTC. The lucky members had five dogs. I only had two.

I first really got interested in the sport during the first sled dog racing training camp organized by Thierry Bloch, the president of the club. The fantastic images brought back by Ernst Muller from his trip to Alaska piqued my interest, so I made my first trip to Alaska in 1980. I stayed with Earl and Nathalie Norris. While in Alaska, I learned the rudiments of the sport with Huskies, Malamutes and Canadian Eskimo dogs.

After returning to France, I won three French sprint championships from 1982 to 1984. In 1985, the lure of the sport got the better of me. Thanks to Joe Redington, the spiritual leader of this race, I headed to Alaska for a unique adventure - the Iditarod. I ran the race five more times from 1987 to 1991.

My partnership with the Royal Canin Company also began in 1987 and continues to this day. In 1988, a new sport - Alpirod - was introduced. This new type of race has 30 to 80 kilometer (19-50 miles) legs each day.

My specialty is the Alpirod. I won the title from 1992 to 1994. Another important moment in my career was when I ascended Mount McKinley with a team of five dogs in 1990. At 6,194 meters, Mount McKinley is the highest peak in North America. Only one other musher, Joe Redington, has ever succeeded in making it to the summit.

Currently, my wife Magali and I live near Fairbanks, Alaska where we raise eighty Alaskan Huskies.

After winning the 1997 Alaska Come Back Race, a stage race of in 800 kilometer (500 miles) legs, we are now preparing for the International Rocky Mountain Stage Stop Race, the equivalent of the Alpirod, run in the Rocky Mountains.

And the adventures continue.

With these rules in mind, the mushers began the race. The route from Nome to Candle and back to Nome covered 408 miles (approximately 650 kilometer).

The musher is the driver of the team. The term comes from the French word "marche" (meaning "to walk"), the command used by French-speaking Canadians to get their team in motion. English-speakers began to use the word and like many adopted words, the pronunciation changed - to mush. Interestingly, the term "mush", a bastardized English version of a French word, is now used in France.
Five days after the start of the race, the first teams reached Nome and a legend was born.

On this trail of "ice, high mountains, frozen rivers, tundra, forests, glaciers…". Leonard Seppala, a young Norwegian immigrant, marked his place in the history of the sport. Leonard Seppala and his Siberian Husky team won the All Alaska Sweepstake in 1915, 1916 and 1917.

One of Seppala's rivals wrote of him, "He is a superman. He passed me every day of the race even though I wasn't dawdling. I never saw him driving his dogs, yet they pulled like I've never seen any other dogs pull before. There was something between him and his dogs that is difficult to explain, something supernatural, almost an hypnotic state…".
Dog teams made great strides from 1908 to 1915. The first Huskies imported from Siberia set a new record of 74 hours, 14 minutes and 37 seconds in the 1910 with Iron Man John Johnson as the musher.
In 1911, in a horrific blizzard, Allan Scotty Allan won the race in about 80 hours with his team of Alaskan crosses (Malamutes crossed with Setters). Scotty Allan, another well-known name in the world of dog sled racing, ran in eight All Alaska Sweepstakes. He won three times, took second place three times and third place twice.

And what can be said about Leonard Seppala? This remarkable man put his stamp on the sport of dog sled racing. His best lead dog, Togo, is known to mushers throughout the world. He won many races in New England, where he met a young veterinary student named Roland Lombard, another great name in the sport. Both a veterinarian and a musher, "Doc" Lambord lent his professional skills to dramatically further the sport in North America. He won more titles at the Anchorage World Championship than any other musher before or since and was the first president of the International Sled Dog Racing Association (ISDRA).

One more name must be added to the list - George Attla, an Athabascan Indian, who won it all. His book Everything I know about Training and Racing Sled Dogs, published by Arner of New York, is considered the musher's bible. Spirit of the Wind, an excellent, though sadly not well-known, film released in France tells the story of George Attla, a man of limitless courage who accomplished his amazing feats on only one leg, his other leg having been stricken with tuberculosis of the bone.

Present-day Racing in the United States

The number of races in the United States and Canada has increased since the beginning of the twentieth century, expanding beyond the birthplace of dog sled racing - Alaska. New England became a second bastion of the sport in 1924 when the New England Sled Dog Club was formed. In 1932, the Olympic Winter Games at Lake Placid permitted demonstrations of dog sled racing, giving the sport its first big boost on the world stage.

Competitions slowed during World War II, but following the war, dog sled racing came back stronger than ever and clubs popped up everywhere. It was at that time that the Sierra Nevada Dog Drivers club was formed. Robert Levorson, the head of the club, was the president of the ISDRA from 1971 to 1974. In 1971, the State of Alaska officially proclaimed sled dog racing to be a national sport, marking another great milestone in the history of the sport.

Today, it is almost impossible to name all of the individual competitions that take place each winter in North America. The biggest races include: Fur Rendez-vous World Championship in Anchorage, Alaska; World Championship Sled Dog Derby in Laconia, New Hampshire; World Championship Dog Derby in La Pas, Manitoba; North American Championship in Fairbanks, Alaska; Alaska State Championship in Kenai-Soldotna, Alaska; Race of Champions in Tok, Alaska; Surdough Rendez-vous in Whitehorse, Yukon Territory; U.S. Pacific Coast Championship in Priest Lake, Idaho; All American Championship in Ely, Minnesota; Midwest International in Lalkaska, Michigan; Quebec International Course de chiens in Quebec City, Quebec.

All of these races are annual events. Thousands of spectators line the race route, which is made up of three legs of 25 to 70 kilometers each, depending on the category. The races begin on Friday and end on Sunday. Much or all of the race course runs right through city streets. Longer races have also been developed. The most well-known are: The Beargrease Sled Dog Marathon that runs for 500 miles in Minnesota; the Iditarod, the longest (1,049 miles in theory, but actually a bit longer), hardest, and most prestigious dog sled race; the Yukon Quest which follows the Yukon River from Canada to Fairbanks, Alaska for almost 1,300 kilometers; and the Alaska Come Back, a stage race of 800 km held in March in the Nenana region. This last race was won by the French musher Jacques Philip in 1997.

Other famous names in the dog sled racing world are Joe Redington Senior, Earl Norris (musher and the world's most famous breeder of Siberian Huskies), Eddy Streeper (Champion of the World 1985), Harris Dunlap, Rick Swenson (probably the best competitor today), and Lebbie Riddles (winner of the Iditarod in 1986, 1987, and 1988). Lebbie drove her team to an altitude of more than 6,000 meters to the summit of Mount McKinley, a feat matched by Jacques Philip in 1991. All these names are part of the legend of dog sled racing and are dear to the heart of every musher.

SPEED RACE CATEGORIES

CATEGORY C
3 to 4 dogs
7.5 km per leg (4,5 miles)

CATEGORY B
4 to 6 dogs
12 km per leg (7,5 miles)

CATEGORY A
6 to 8 dogs
18 km per leg (11,2 miles)

CATEGORY O
More than 8 dogs
25 km per leg (15,6 miles)

SHORT PULKA
1 to 3 dogs
10 km per leg (6,2 miles)

LONG PULKA
1 to 3 dogs
20 km per leg (12,4 miles)

Development of the sport in Scandinavia

Scandinavia (Denmark, Sweden, Norway, and Finland) is also a dog sled racing stronghold. However, Pulka, which combines cross-country skiing and mushing, is much more popular than traditional mushing. In this sport, the cross-country skier is attached to the dog team by a rope. The team, an average of one to three dogs, pulls a loaded sled.

Scandinavians prefer to use hunting dogs, including hounds, pointers, and setters, since they can cover short distances (7 to 12 kilometers) more quickly than other breeds and are better adapted mentally to working alone.

In the European Championships of 1988, the first direct competition between European countries, the Norwegians proved themselves to be the fastest Europeans over short distances. Since that time, only one Frenchman, François Mermet, has taken the world championship title.

Introduction and development of the sport in non-scandinavian countries

Founded in 1959 through the devotion of Dr. Thomas Althaus and the late Judge Paul Nicoud, the Swiss Nordic Dog Club set a goal for itself to promote the breeding and development of Nordic dog breeds. Not surprisingly, dog sled races soon followed. In 1964, the first competition, the Camp de traîneau suisse, was held. The race gave the few active European mushers a chance to get a real feel for the sport as it is practiced in North America.

Soon, a winter circuit of races was set up in Switzerland - in Lenk, Saint-Cergue, Saingnelégier, Sils-Saint-Moritz and other cities). In Germany, races were held in Todtmoos, Bernau and other regions. The first national competition in France was held in February 26, 1979 on the slopes of Schlucht in the Vosges mountains. The Club de la Pulka et du Traîneau à Chiens (CPTC – Pulka and Dog Sled Racing Club) was founded the same year by Thierry Bloch, Monique Bené and Yannick and Gilles Malaterre.

The number of races and dog teams is increasing rapidly. Racing structures under the auspices of ESDRA (European Sled Dog Racing Association) have been set up in each country. The Trail Club of Europe, a European club, was formed in 1973. The club adheres to the basic rules and regulations established in the United States by ISDRA (International Sled Dog Racing Association). For the first time in 1994, the Trail Club organized a championship in Switzerland and a European championship in Germany. These competitions continue today.

Only ESDRA oversees all of the national structures. ESDRA is responsible for the annual organization of championships in Europe, which were held in Saint-Moritz, Switzerland in 1984, Todmoos, Germany in 1985, Fourgs, France in 1986, Winterberg, Germany in 1987, Bruneck, Italy in 1988 and Bad Minterdorf, Austria in 1989 and 1990. National representatives compete in each category.

In 1988, the largest European race, the Alpirod-Royal Canin, was run for the first time. The stages are spread out over twelve days in January and February covering a total distance of more than 1,000 kilometers. This competition was the first of its kind and allowed Alaskan dog teams to participate in a course that passed through Italy, France, Germany, Switzerland and Austria. And they won! Joe Runyan took the title in 1988, Kathy Swenson in 1989 and Roxy Wright in 1990.

In 1990, the first world speed championships combining pulka and dog sled racing (six-dog, eight-dog and ten-dog teams) were held in Saint-Moritz under the auspices of the International Federation for Sled Dog Sport (IFSS). The race is now held annually. The IFSS is a member of the General Association of International Sporting Federations, so it is possible that the International Olympic Committee may someday approve this sport for the Winter Olympic Games.

Pulka and dog sled racing are the glory sports of the dog world. Powerful organizations and federations have negotiated this sport into the international arena. Exchanges across the Atlantic are becoming more common. The Savoie trophy, organized at the opening of the 1992 Olympic Games and the demonstrations at Lillehammer in 1994 may be indications that this sport may soon be recognized for the ultimate competition.

Training Canine Athletes

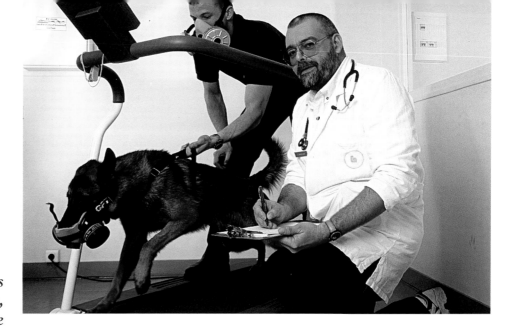

Dogs have been our companions for thousands of years. At first, they simply helped with the tasks of day-to-day living. Then, gradually, they began to give us pleasure. Finally, in the nineteenth century, they came to share in our leisure activities. Gradually, humans became increasingly involved in their dogs lives and sought to breed them selectively, raise them and train them, and feed them the best possible diet, so that humans and dogs could share the good life. So from their origins as mere instinctive hunters, guards, and pack animals, dogs became first human companions, then participants in field trials, pulka-style racing, and ring trials; herding dogs; and sled dogs. And, humans being what they are, people invented rules and competitions, so that recreation could become sport and the companion an athlete. Thus was born the world of dog sports. Four factors affect canine athletic performance: genetic selection, the psychological relationship between the dog and its handler, training (based on knowledge of the dogs physiological characteristics when working), and nutrition. Each must be taken into consideration.

The Physiology of Physical Activity

Hard work and competition give rise to both organic and psychological stress in dogs, just as they do in humans. A general knowledge of the main physiological changes induced by physical effort can help the owner or handler to better understand this, and so to better prepare the dog for competition, by choosing the best way to avoid any pathological conditions that might arise.

Cardiovascular and Respiratory Adaptations

The cardiovascular and respiratory systems are adapted for two purposes: they provide the necessary oxygen and nutrients to the muscles, and they eliminate the wastes produced by muscular metabolism, namely carbon dioxide and heat. These adaptations are essential, not only for good athletic performance, but also for any activity that continues longer than a few seconds. The body shows two different responses to muscular effort:
- an immediate response that provides for the animals needs at the moment, and thus occurs at the same time as the effort, and
- a long-term response that anticipates the animals needs and causes the animal to adapt.

During physical exercise

Changes in the circulatory system during work have the essential function of increasing blood flow and thus oxygen flow to tissues having an increased metabolic rate, particularly muscles. To accomplish this, cardiac output is increased and blood is sent to active areas and away from less-active areas. The bloods ability to carry oxygen also increases when the spleen contracts, releasing a significant number of red blood cells into the bloodstream, thus increasing the hematocrit and the amount of hemoglobin present.

Cardiac output can increase considerably, reaching ten times its resting level. The heart rate rises significantly: Depending on the intensity of the effort, it can reach 300 beats per minute in hunting hounds, or 200 beats per minute in sled dogs. Vasodilation occurs in the working muscles, thus increasing their internal blood flow:

- During the first three to four seconds of effort, the respiratory rate increases sharply.
- After a few seconds, a second, more gradual increase begins.
- A plateau is reached, which lasts until the effort is over.
- During the recovery phase, there is a slow decrease in respiratory frequency from about 200 breaths per minute to about thirty.

The training effect

After four to five weeks of daily training, the dogs cardiovascular and respiratory systems show significant changes. Changes to the heart and circulatory system resulting from repeated physical exercise tend to minimize the energy needed for the heart to work, and to develop the hearts pumping ability. Dogs in training have a lower resting heart rate than sedentary dogs and their respiratory arrhythmia is more pronounced; their plasma volume is higher; and they have better venous blood return, all of which increase overall cardiac output.

Intensive training sometimes leads to cardiac hypertrophy. For example, in the Greyhound, six months of intense daily training lead to a fifty-percent increase in the thickness of the heart wall and a thirty-percent increase in the volume of the left ventricular cavity. Training also causes the number and density of the muscle capillaries to increase. Finally, contrary to popular belief, regular physical exercise changes the respiratory tract very little or not at all in healthy dogs. It is actually the bodys overall ability to use oxygen (VO2max, or maximum oxygen consumption) that increases considerably through endurance training. These changes can occur optimally only in individuals that are in good overall health. Any change or insufficiency in these functions will limit the dogs ability to adapt to physical effort, and so limit its sport or work performance.

Monitoring oxygen consumption while the dog is active.

Effects of biological stress due to effort

In sport dogs, stress induced by environmental conditions or physical effort can cause behavioral changes (barking, lack of motivation, etc.), changes in the autonomic nervous system (salivation, tachycardia, mydriasis, etc.), digestive problems (vomiting, diarriasis, gastric ulcers), and anemia. Many of these symptoms, often reported by dog handlers to have occurred in the middle of a competition, can be attributed to this type of physiopathological process.

Overtraining is often a major cause of such changes, but the fact that the dog can easily differentiate between training and competitive or real situations on a psychological level should not be ignored. Generally speaking, stressful situations often cause distress in animals that then exteriorize it through behaviors characteristic of their species. In dogs, signs of distress or fear include the well-known actions of elimination (urination, repeated defecation), vocalization (barking, howling), and other stereotypical behaviors such as biting objects or the cage, digging in the dirt, etc.

For these reasons, behavioral, autonomic, digestive, and other reactions can inarguably be considered to be induced by stress. Among these reactions, it is quite evident that in the context of physical tests, which often place high demands on the metabolism, digestive problems are among the most harmful to physical condition, particularly when added to loss of water and electrolytic minerals, or to insufficient consumption of food and water.

An appropriate and reasonable training program, a calm and normal psychological environment, and particularly the proper type of food are key elements for preventing problems related to stress arising from physical activity or overtraining.

Metabolic changes

While muscular effort very directly influences the type and magnitude of energy needs, it also equally affects the bodys overall balance.

Energy Sources

The chemical energy used in muscle contraction arises solely from the high-energy phosphate bonds found in a very important molecule known as adenosine triphosphate, or ATP. During muscular effort, the concentration of ATP in the muscle cell decreases and must instantly be raised so that the animal can continue to run or work. There are three ways in which the level is increased, and the role of each process and its relative importance are determined by the type of effort required of the dog.

437

RELATIVE IMPORTANCE OF EACH METABOLIC ENERGY PATHWAY IN THE DOG DURING MUSCULAR EFFORT

Type of Sport	Non-lactic Anaerobiosis	Lactic Anaerobiosis	Aerobiosis
Jumping	+++	+	0
Brief Attack	++	++	+
Racing	+	+++++	++
Agility	0	++++	++
Ring Trials	0	+++	+++
Field Trials	0	++	+++
Water/ Working Trials	0	+	++++
Tracking /Country Trials	0	0	++++
Herding	0	0	+++
Hunting	0	0	++++
Sled Racing	0	0*	+++++

* Except + to ++ for speed races

Non-lactic anaerobiosis

During a very brief and very intense effort (lasting a few seconds), ATP is replaced from muscle reserves of phosphocreatine, with no need for oxygen (hence anaerobic) and no production of lactic acid (hence non-lactic).

Lactic anaerobiosis

For intense efforts lasting at least two minutes (racing, agility, face attack, etc.), the energy is replaced from glycogen stored in the muscle and from glucose in the blood. No oxygen is consumed in this case, either, but lactic acid, a metabolic waste, is produced and accumulates. Very generally speaking, it is often the accumulation of lactic acid that causes muscle fatigue and cramps.

Aerobiosis

This metabolic process covers the dogs energy needs when endurance is required (the effort is less intense but lasts from several minutes to several hours). First, the red blood cells carry oxygen to the muscles, where it oxidizes glucose from the blood. Then, very quickly (in contrast to the process in humans), fats become the dogs preferred energy source.

Without going into detail and writing an entire treatise on canine sports medicine, we can point out that the dogs training schedule and diet will be affected by knowledge of these specific metabolic processes.

Genetic Selection of Sport Dogs

Unlike other important species of domestic animals, dogs have not yet been affected by the revolution in the methods and technologies of genetic improvement. This is due mainly to the fact that the socioeconomic status of the dog is fundamentally opposite to the status of commercial livestock in our developed societies. This explains how the main genetic direction of dogs, which is characterized by an intentional diversity of form and oriented mainly toward esthetic considerations, has been determined. Nevertheless, selective breeding has at the same time affected certain physical abilities and behaviors, creating the well-known genetic divergence between show and work dogs and giving rise to the various work breeds from which the sport breeds were derived.

The importance of success

Today, as in the past, a primary criterion for sport dog breeders is the dogs success in its work. The geneticists goal is to make the best possible comparison between the candidates for breeding to determine what transmissible genetic potential (additive genetic values) is present by studying the dogs performance (phenotype). Such an approach can be taken only within the context of sport trials with very specific rules. This said, however, it must be noted and without in any way underestimating the skills and experience of expert breeders that the current state of the art still does not allow ranking of dogs within a breed according to their genetic value. It follows that the choice of the best sport dogs for breeding is still somewhat a matter of chance, and often is still too empirical.

Consequently, much remains to be done to develop effective tools for genetic selection of sport, work, and utility dogs. In a direct selection scheme (attempt to improve a particular trait), the first obstacle for sport performance is that it is frequently difficult to measure accurately (or objectively) with the required precision and reliability (reproducibility).

Timing of racing dogs is an example of an ideal situation, but even in such a case, several selection criteria can be considered, including
- the best time in the different races of a meet, and
- average time over all the races.

SIZE: THE BIGGER THE BETTER?

Dog sizes often vary with the current fashion, and the relationship between size and the quality of the dog is far from obvious. In France, the notion of respect for the breed standard wins out.

Mother Nature offers something for everyone, and there are unconditional lovers of both small- and large-breed dogs, whose enthusiasm is often based on reasons that have nothing whatsoever to do with the dogs practical use. It is certainly true that the hunters that developed the breeds we know today were much more practical-minded. The size differences were based on the specific work performed by each breed a concept that remains equally valid today, particularly among hunters that specialize. There are fashions in all things. Some are timeless, some are not; some have value, some do not. When a particular dog is in fashion due to its success in field trials, for example, it will be mated many times, thus having an influence on its breed. If the dog was very popular, and its puppies tend to be small, the average height of the breed will necessarily decrease within a few years.

If the puppies follow in their fathers footsteps they may be mated just as often, and have just as many offspring. Then the fashion may change, leading the breed to become taller. Such pendulum effects often occur as the morphology of a breed changes.

Differences among breeds

Crawling under brambles to chase a rabbit, or flushing practically impregnable woodcocks in an impenetrable fir forest, have nothing in common with killing and bringing back a fox or killing a wounded roe-deer. This is why the English created the Cocker Spaniel and the Germans created the German Roughhaired Pointer. All dogs are versatile, of course, but within the limits of their abilities. The original selection that led to the various breeds we know today took into account hunting situations that are not necessarily the same as those faced now. Thus, certain breeds created with a specific goal in mind are now used for other purposes, and a size criterion that was important for the original selection may no longer be technically important. In such cases, conformity to the breed standard allows the typical morphology of the breed to be preserved, even when the current use of the dog in the field is not necessarily related to the original size. Conversely, unquestioning conformity to an exact standard with the justification that the initial morphology of a breed must not change can lead to failure to adapt, leading in turn to the disappearance of the breed.

For Work or For Show?

When dog enthusiasts cannot find common ground with regard to the previous point, breeds end up with two differentiated types: show dogs and work dogs, which differ in size and morphology. It is revealing to note that the height and weight of working dogs are usually less than those of their show-ring counterparts, which goes to show that the physical characteristics needed for hunting do not necessarily include extra height or weight. In breeds that are officially separated into working and show varieties, as in English-speaking countries, it is generally true that the smaller dogs are the best in the field. In France, where there is only one club per breed, looks win out over performance, with a clear respect for the breed standard and, within this context, for the maintenance or better yet, the improvement of hunting abilities. Thus, some dogs that do not meet the standard because they are too large or small are not officially allowed to reproduce, even if they are intelligent and have good hunting ability. Is this good or bad for the breed? No one knows, but the fact that the dog does not happen to fit within the size range prescribed by the club does not mean that it will be a poor hunter. Even within the standards, there are large and small individuals in any breed, and the size difference may appear by chance, or it may result from selection for specialized activities.

A Matter of Specialization

Within a breed, size differences regularly appear among dogs of different origin, depending on the selection practiced by each breeder, even within the limitations of the breed standard. Working dog champions appear to be more agile than show-ring champions. This is not a matter of the dictates of fashion, but rather one of specialization. To be even more specific, we can also find small and large puppies within the same litter. Does this influence the abilities of one puppy compared with another? Perhaps if, again, the breeder is looking for a specialized dog for an activity to which a larger or smaller dog would be better adapted. Otherwise, there is no obvious relationship between size and quality. For example, my two best bird-dog setters are a small male and a large female, and my two best bird-dog pointers are a large male and a female at the lower end of the size range, barely 53 cm (21 in) tall. Each pair was chosen from a single litter at the age of eight weeks. Since it is impossible to predict a puppys future abilities at the age of two months, the first pair was chosen for coat color: light yellow, so as to be visible in the forest; and the other two, both blue beltons, were chosen because they had their mothers flair. A setter enthusiast recently came by to pick out his male puppy, and he chose the smallest one. Apparently, he has always had good luck with small dogs. Perhaps he was lucky… or did he simply reap the benefits of a natural selection having the effect that the smallest puppy in a litter has to keep up with the larger puppies, and so must necessarily be resourceful and intelligent? Some people believe that a dogs size affects its ability, and we will not try to make them change their minds starting out with a firm conviction is not always a bad thing in life.

J.-P. Koumchasky
Le Chasseur Français

In ring trials, the choice of parameters is even greater:
- The dog can be graded based on the judges scale or some other scale;
- Placing;
- Extra points based on the level of the competition and performance (this system is used for horses).

Indirect selection criteria (affecting performance) can also be considered. For example, the results of performance tests given under standard conditions; the leg length of a racing dog insofar as leg length is positively correlated with speed; or even the angle of the joints during the competition.

In fact, the current approach taken in studies such as those by Jean-François Courreau, a canine geneticist at the Veterinary College in Alfort, France, is to create a genetic selection index on the basis of several performances by the dog. These indices are then subjected to sophisticated mathematical analysis. Preliminary results have already been obtained for racing Whippets and for Malinois Sheepdogs that work in ring trials. Such methods will allow future adaptation of the methods of modern genetics to sport dogs.

Training Sport Dogs

Given that people talk about canine sports, and that for certain performances, dogs behave like true athletes, it is natural to talk about training programs for sport dogs. It is obvious to most people that human athletes undergo specific physical training depending on their sport and level of competition. The situation is identical for dogs if they are to perform well and be healthy and happy.

Basic principles of training

Training means physical, technical and strategic, intellectual, and attitudinal preparation of the athlete through physical exercises. When applied to dogs, this means that the owner or handler creates a series of physical exercises required of the dog in an environment that preserves a playful atmosphere to motivate the dog.

Workload

The concept of workload is fundamental. The work should last long enough and be of sufficient intensity so that the physical activity can be called training. The workload should increase as the desired performance improves, without becoming nerve-wracking or tedious for the dog, which would then lose all motivation.

Characteristics of the workload

The workload should be applied gradually, especially for beginner dogs (for an animal that is already well trained, some stages can be accelerated), and continuously (to be effective, training sessions should be regular).The workload should vary with time. Indeed, it is impossible to keep a dog at the same level of fitness year-round, so a distinction is made between preparation, competition, and training periods.

The content of the workload should also vary. Within a single discipline, many physical demands are made on the dog: power, speed, endurance, and coordination. These demands require different adaptations of the dogs body, with a different recovery period for each adaptation. If an effort is requested of the dog while it is recuperating from a different type of effort, the former does not affect recovery from the latter.

In fact, it can maximize it, and a system of alternating workloads saves time and yields better performance. For example, while the dog recovers from a run, it can be asked to do a very different exercise, such as a muscle stretching exercise.

The sequence of workloads should have an exact order within a single workout session, with exercises requiring explosive force, speed, and coordination generally given at the beginning of the training period, followed by exercises based on incomplete recovery, then by endurance exercises.

Training methods

Training the muscles

It is possible to increase the work and muscular force without increasing oxygen consumption or triggering anaerobic catabolism (lactic fermentation) by using very intense, very brief efforts followed by short recovery periods. This is the underlying principle of all pure force exercises, with weight-pulling competitions being the best example.

Training for anaerobic power

Anaerobic power allows the muscle to work hard when no oxygen is present, as when running quickly (Greyhounds, ring attack trials). In practice, to develop this power, very short, intense exercises (ten-second to one-minute sprints) alternate with recovery periods (two to four minutes). This type of training is very physically and psychologically demanding for the dog. It should be used only as the date of the competition approaches.

Training for aerobic power

Aerobic power is used for long efforts requiring improved transport and utilization of oxygen, as in the type of effort required of hounds and sled dogs. Long-distance running at a moderate pace or a series of short runs (three to five minutes) at a slightly faster pace followed by periods of light exercise (walk or jog) are recommended to increase aerobic power.

The relative amounts of the different types of training will vary depending on the discipline. The best indicators of the trainings effectiveness are the experience of the dog and how well it listens.

Training and competition

Warmup

All athletes warm up before a competition in order to activate the enzyme and oxygenation systems (which will furnish the energy they need) and reduce the reaction time for muscle contraction.

For dogs, the warmup can consist of a series of muscle stretches and flexes, followed by a game intended to warm up both the dogs muscles and its motivation. If the warmup is done well, it will improve the dogs neuromuscular coordination, avoid tears and contractions, and guarantee an optimum physiological and psychological state for the beginning of the competition.

BASIC PRINCIPLES OF SPORT DOG TRAINING

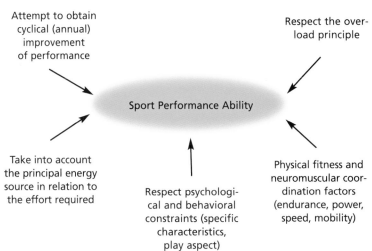

Attempt to obtain cyclical (annual) improvement of performance

Respect the overload principle

Sport Performance Ability

Take into account the principal energy source in relation to the effort required

Respect psychological and behavioral constraints (specific characteristics, play aspect)

Physical fitness and neuromuscular coordination factors (endurance, power, speed, mobility)

PRINCIPLES OF TRAINING CYCLE PROGRAMMING

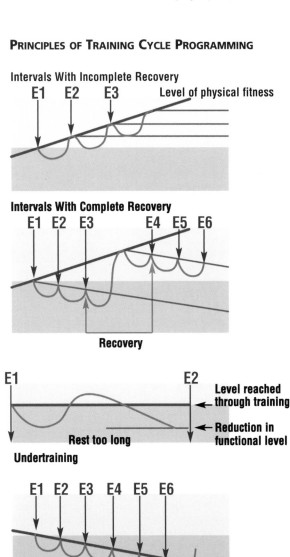

Intervals With Incomplete Recovery
E1 E2 E3   Level of physical fitness

Intervals With Complete Recovery
E1 E2 E3   E4 E5 E6

Recovery

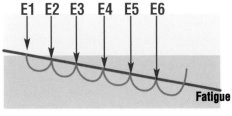

E1   E2
                        Level reached through training
Rest too long   Reduction in functional level
Undertraining

E1 E2 E3 E4 E5 E6

Fatigue
Overtraining

Generally speaking, relationships in a small-group context can be of three types: authoritarian, democratic, or laissez-faire (non-interference). In a work situation, the dog performs a task at the request of its handler. The handler has dominant status, and the dog is dominated (alpha-omega-type social structure). In this context, the non-interference type of relationship is to be avoided, as it will not allow for completion of the task. Thus, the choice of handler-dog relationship should be between the authoritarian and democratic types. One goal of the Licancabur-Chiens des Cimes expedition in Chile in April, 1996, was to study the behavior of wreckage-search dogs at high altitude. During this expedition, we were able to compare the influence of different relationship types on the behavior of dogs under extreme conditions.

In the authoritarian relationship, the dog has very little freedom. The search for victims is directed entirely by the handler, who decides which search technique should be used. The dog is in constant visual contact with the handler, and does not indicate the victims location until the handler encourages it to do so. The members of the pair have complementary functions. The dog can be considered to be the nose of the handler, who as the brain makes the decision.

In the democratic relationship, the dog and the handler go through the search area separately. The dog indicates the victims location as a result of a confrontational process between the dog and the handler. The search is accomplished through synergy between the partners.

As far as the work itself is concerned, the two relationship types are about equally effective. The victims are found in both cases. However, under extreme conditions, when the dogs were experiencing significant physiological suffering, the democratic relationship seemed to be superior.

Dogs in the democratic pairs continued to work longer under difficult conditions. It seemed that, with the encouragement of their handlers, they were able to accept and tolerate a higher level of suffering.

Dogs in the authoritarian pairs refused to follow their handler as soon as they began to suffer in a way that could have endangered them. This rebellion even extended to aggressive behavior toward the handler.

The type of relationship between the handler and the dog is a decisive factor in the accomplishment of a task under extreme conditions. The more the relationship within the pair is based on mutual exchanges, the greater the dogs acceptance of suffering seems to be. It would therefore seem advantageous to use democratic-type relationships in handler/dog work teams, and to encourage collective decision-making involving both partners.

Jean-Marc Poupard, Researcher
Laboratory for Animal and Human Biosociology
University of Paris V Sorbonne - René Descartes

Cooling down

The handler should not neglect to cool the dog down after the competition. This will help make future competitions successful, among other things. A series of light exercises will keep the level of circulation in the muscles high enough to carry off the wastes produced and accumulated during the effort (lactic acid, toxins, etc.). A light massage also helps eliminate toxins and calm the animal. Then the dog will experience much less muscle fatigue and lameness, and will be more physically and mentally fit for future events.

Tapering off

The trainer is strongly cautioned against suddenly and completely ending the training program at the end of the competition season. The animal will quickly lose any benefits acquired from the training, and will be mentally destabilized. It is better to gradually decrease the workload while increasingly directing physical activity into play.

Recovery and overtraining

After a period of intense effort, such as a competition, the dog will naturally be physiologically fatigued for a period of time. If the dog is properly fed and trained, its body will recover from this fatigue, and even overcompensate for it, i.e., for a short time following complete recovery, the dog will be in better shape than before the competition. This is the ideal time to require another significant effort.

However, if the time interval is not observed and another effort is required during the recovery period, the body will exceed its limits and will not be able to recover normally. In this case, an overtraining syndrome develops. The dog loses its appetite and loses weight, becomes more sensitive, and is easily fatigued.

SEARCH SEQUENCE AS A FUNCTION OF RELATIONSHIP TYPE

Democratic Pairs

1. Visual survey of the search area
The dog immediately heads toward a limited area where the victims are located.

2. Exploration of the search area and surroundings
The dog moves through the area.
Scent information is collected where the victims are found.
The exploration is widened to the surrounding area.
Movements are more rapid. The dog may be recalled by the handler if it goes too far outside the area.
During this exploratory phase, the dog and handler work more or less independently. The dog and the handler are relatively far apart.

3. Discovery of the victim.
The dog returns to previously-explored areas that were recognized as probable locations of buried victims.
The dog sniffs more insistently.
The dog waits for its handler to approach.
The dog establishes visual contact with its handler. As soon as it is encouraged to do so by the handler, the dog marks the location of the victims.

The process unfolds as if there were a confrontation between the deductions of the dog and those of the handler.

Authoritarian Pairs

1. The dog is taken to the search area.
The dog follows the handler into the search area.

2. Exploration of the search area and surroundings
The dog walks at the handlers side.
The dog periodically looks at the handler.
During this time, the dog and the handler work together. The dog is always under the handlers authority.

3. Discovery of the victim.
During the exploratory phase, the dog stops at the probable location of a buried victim.
The dog sniffs.
The dog makes visual contact with the handler. As soon as it is encouraged to do so by the handler, the dog marks the location of the victims.
The process unfolds as if the dog were awaiting the handlers consent to mark the victims location.

To guarantee a balanced competition season, the dogs recovery period must be respected and the owner must understand its biological clock.

By properly training the dog, the owner can guarantee it good health, muscles of steel and a will of iron throughout the year. In this way he shows respect for the dogs work, and strives to ensure that the animal can continue to work as long as possible given its physical and mental abilities. A good trainer is characterized by experience, willingness to take advice from experts, and by listening to and respecting.

Feeding a Sport Dog

Generally speaking, three types of factors affect the nutritional needs of a sport dog:

- the energy expended can vary greatly but it is extremely important to take the quality of the energy source into account,
- stress, insofar as stress caused by training and competition requires nutritional changes in the diet,
- dehydration, which to a great extent can be prevented by proper nutrition.

With these factors in mind, we can see that a food adapted for sport dogs should…

- supply an adequate amount of a high-quality energy source,
- minimize the volume and weight of intestinal digesta as much as possible,
- help maintain proper hydration,
- if possible, have a buffer effect on the metabolic acidification caused by running,
- contribute to optimal results of properly-conducted training, and
- make up for any physiological deficits caused by stress.

Feeding a racing Greyhound the same as a hunting dog, or a search dog like a sled dog, would not be at all appropriate for the trainer who wants to see a dog give its best performance and to prevent medical or traumatological problems.

Nutritional specifics

First, the amount of energy a dog requires is affected by the intensity and duration of the effort. Generally speaking, a trainers goal should be to keep the dog at its fit weight, weighing it weekly if possible and adapting the quantity of the daily food ration to maintain a stable fit weight.

Scientific data allow us to be specific about the approach in certain scenarios: thus, we know that for a Greyhound, running a race requires only five percent more energy than a maintenance diet, whereas under extreme conditions (such as the Iditarod sled race in Alaska, where dogs race 150 km (100 miles) per day in a temperature of -50°C (-45°F)), a twenty-kilogram sled dog can consume up to 12,000 kcal per day (seven times its maintenance requirement!).

Even more generally, one hour of work leads to an increase of about ten percent in the maintenance energy requirement, which means that the daily ration should be increased by forty or fifty percent to cover the needs of a day of work or sport. Changes in ambient temperature should also be taken into account: to fight the effects of cold or heat outside of its neutral temperature zone (about 20°C)(68°F), a dog needs extra energy.

The quality of the energy provided to the dog is extremely important, and so has led to a definition of optimal energy criteria for sport dogs. Two overall quality considerations should be taken into account, in addition to the nature of the foods given:

- The energy should be readily available where it is needed (muscle cell), and
- The energy-providing ingredients should be balanced in such a way that their combustion produces a minimum of wastes, maximum efficiency, and no risk of metabolic blockage.

THE PROS AND CONS OF CHANGING DIETARY FAT

In 1970, a team of competitive sled dogs was brought to me at the small-animal hospital at the University of Pennsylvania. The dogs were becoming fatigued too early, only a few kilometers into the race, and the best of the Universitys medical specialists could find nothing wrong with them.

Although I was specializing in cows milk at the time, I visited the place where the dogs were kept and collected some detailed information. I saw dogs eating their own excrement, and determined that the food was too rich in starch. I also took blood and urine samples.

Just to see, the dogs diet was changed to whole chickens, which made the problem disappear. A few weeks later, the dogs that were eating whole fat chickens were able to run faster and longer than the others.

This is where the idea of changing the fat content in the diet got started. We later developed it scientifically for sled dogs, as did Professor Arleigh Reynolds in the U.S. and Dominique Grandjean in France. These sled dogs, so well adapted for consumption of fats, also served as a model for the research studies I have been conducting for several years on horses at Virginia Tech. Like the sled dogs (but with a lower proportion of fats in the diet), a horse adapted to fat consumption uses less glycogen when it runs and so has more endurance but also is calmer and, paradoxically, weighs less (less undigested food remains in the digestive tract). For this reason, the classic muscular problem known as exertional rhabdomyolysis (destruction of muscle fibers related to the accumulation of lactic acid) disappears in animals adapted to fat consumption. However, paradoxically, other muscle problems appear (the cons), because dietary fats cause decreased antioxidant protection in the body. In the 1980s, I found that levels of vitamins E and C (antioxidants) in the blood dropped sharply during periods of physical activity in sled dogs. Research by the teams mentioned above is now focusing on this problem, to determine the proper and effective levels of nutritional supplementation for antioxidants.

Professor David S. Kronfeld
Doctor of Veterinary Medicine,
Doctor of Sciences
Diplomate of the American colleges
of nutrition and internal medicine
Virginia Polytechnic Institute and
State University, Blacksburg, U.S.

COMPOSITION OF A DIET SPECIALIZED FOR SHORT-DURATION EFFORT IN DOGS

Specialized Complete Dry Food
650 grams (28oz)/day for a 30-kg (66lb) dog

Proteins	≅	30%
Fats	≅	16 to 20%
Fiber	≅	2%
NFE	≅	43%
Calcium	≅	1.4%
Phosphorus	≅	1%
Energy	≅	4100 to 4300 kcal ME

plus other minerals, trace minerals, vitamins
Special recommendations

Homemade Specialized Daily Ration
1200 grams (42oz)/day for a 30-kg (66lb) dog

Red meat	≅	60%	
Cereal flakes	≅	30%	Proteins -> 33%
Soy oil	≅	2%	Fats -> 14%
Copra oil	≅	2%	NFE -> 45%
Fish oil	≅	2%	Energy -> 2250 kcal ME/kg

Specific vitamin/4% mineral supplement

SAMPLE DAILY RATION FOR A 30-KG (66LB) RACING GREYHOUND

Lean meat	≅	750 g
Cooked rice	≅	450 g
Bone meal	≅	2 teaspoons
Corn oil	≅	1 teaspoon
Liver	≅	30-60 g

Vitamin and trace mineral supplements

Maintenance Diet for Sport Dogs

Complete dry maintenance food
500 grams (18oz)/day for a 30-kg (66lb) dog

Proteins	≅	25 - 27%
Fats	≅	12 - 16%
Fiber	≅	3%
NFE	≅	55%
Calcium	≅	1.2%
Phosphorus	≅	1%
Energy	≅	3700 to 4100 kcal ME

plus other minerals, trace minerals, vitamins
Maintenance recommendations

Homemade Daily Maintenance Ration
1370 grams(48 oz)/day for a 30-kg(66lb) dog

Red meat	≅	450 g
Cereal flakes	≅	750 g
Soy oil	≅	120 g
Copra oil	≅	10 g
Fish oil	≅	10 g
Energy–	≅	1340 kcal ME/kg

Specific vitamin/mineral supplement

So the longer the effort expected, the greater the fat content of the food should be, ranging from between sixteen and twenty percent for a dog of which short-term effort is required, to thirty-five percent for a dog needing endurance. For an intermediate effort, twenty to twenty-five percent is an optimal fat content.

To make the energy readily available, so it can be used quickly by the working body, it seems essential to choose highly-digestible, specialized, complete dry foods (called premium or super-premium by the manufacturers) that result in a small volume of digesta and feces. This can easily be evaluated by comparing the fecal volume with the amount ingested. For a sport dog, the optimum ratio is forty-five to fifty grams of fecal matter per hundred grams of dry matter ingested.

Effort stresses the body and gives rise to specific nutritional needs that can be summarized as follows:
- Increased protein content, which should be between thirty-two and forty percent of the foods dry weight, depending on the intensity of the effort;
- Increased content of B-vitamins (especially B1, B6 and B12), antioxidant nutrients (vitamin E, selenium), and omega 3 fatty acids (these acids, from fish, improve red-blood-cell flow and oxygen exchange and decrease exercise-related inflammatory phenomena);
- Additional nutritional supplements for nutrients not present in the complete food selected: L-carnitine (essential for proper use of fatty acids by the cells and for recovery), ascorbic acid (vitamin C, which is not usually an essential nutrient for dogs), probiotics (lactic-acid bacteria, which improve digestion of food), etc.

EFFECTIVENESS IN DOGS OF VARIOUS ENERGY-PRODUCING NUTRITIONAL AIDS AVAILABLE ON THE MARKET

Substance	Activity				Daily Dose (per kg)	Safe
	Short Effort	Intermediate Effort	Long Effort	Recovery		
L-carnitine	+	++	++++	++	50 mg	yes
Aspartic acid	0	+?	+?	?	?	?
Arginine	0	+?	+?	?	?	?
Sodium bicarbonate	+	0	0	?	400 mg	yes
Dimethylglycine	++	+	0	?	1.5 mg	yes
Inosine	0	0	0	++	10 mg	yes
L-tryptophan	+?	+?	+?	0	5 mg	?
Ascorbic acid	+	++	++++	+	100 mg	yes
Methylsulfonyl methan	0	0	0	0	-	?
Superoxide dismutase	++	++	++	++	?	-
Probiotics	+?	+?	+?	?	?	?
Octacosanol	0?	0?	0?	?	?	?
Gamma oryzanol	?	?	?	?	?	?
Bioflavonoids	?	?	?	?	?	?

A practical approach to feeding

Practically speaking, the sport dogs daily ration should be
- nutritionally balanced,
- concentrated and highly digestible, and
- properly served to and eaten by the dog.

The owner should consider sport-dog foods as a series of adaptations, with the following three criteria in mind:
- Does the food meet maintenance requirements?
- Does the food have higher energy and essential nutrient content, which will reduce the volume of fecal matter?
- Is the food enriched in fat, to meet the energy needs associated with physical effort, and in proteins and vitamins, to meet the needs associated with stress?

It is clear that in such a context, there is room only for complete, dry commercial foods (with homemade foods becoming anecdotal and canned foods being completely excluded), which can be supplemented depending on the needs associated with the sport.

Once the proper food has been chosen, an annual feeding program should be drawn up so that feeding is closely adapted to the training regimen.

- During the annual rest period, the dog should be fed a very high-quality maintenance food.
- During the training period, the food should gradually be switched to a food for working dogs (with a one-week transition period for each change), or gradually-increasing amounts of dietary supplement for working dogs should be added to the maintenance food.
- During the competition period, the additional stress from the work may require supplemental dietary changes; the amount fed each day should change in relation to the animals weight.
- During the tapering-off period, there should be a gradual return to the maintenance diet.
As far as the feeding schedule is concerned, sport and utility dogs should not have to work on an empty stomach. This is an old and stupid belief that is detrimental to the dogs performance and well-being. The dog should receive one-quarter of its daily ration in the morning, at least four hours before working, with plenty of water. The rest of the meal should be given in the evening, at the same time every day.

Sport dogs should always have water available, particularly immediately following the effort, to avoid dehydration.

COMPOSITION OF DAILY RATION OF HOMEMADE FOOD FOR WORKING HUNTING DOGS (IN GRAMS)

Ingredient	Ration 1 (2300 kcal ME per kg)	Ration 2 (2350 kcal ME per kg)
Meat for animals	700	
Lean meat		600
Moist cooked rice	100	100
Vegetables	100	100
Lard	100	
Vitamin and mineral supplement*	100	100

* 1/3 brewers yeast, 1/3 sunflower oil, 1/3 mixture of calcium carbonate, dicalcium phosphate, and trace-mineral and vitamin complex

DAILY RATIONS OF HOMEMADE FOOD FOR WORKING HUNTING DOGS (FOOD COMPOSITION GIVEN ABOVE)

Weight of Dog (kg)*	Ration 1 (g)	Ration 2 (g)
5	380	370
6	440	430
7	490	480
8	550	530
9	600	580
10	640	630
11	690	680
12	740	720
13	780	770
14	830	810
15	870	860
16	920	900
17	960	940
18	1000	980
19	1040	1020
20	1080	1060
21	1120	1100
22	1160	1140
23	1200	1180
24	1240	1220
25	1280	1260
26	1320	1290
27	1360	1330
28	1400	1370
29	1430	1400
30	1470	1440
31	1510	1470
32	1540	1510
33	1580	1540
34	1620	1580
35	1650	1620

* 1 kg = 2,2 lb

COMPOSITION OF A FOOD ADAPTED TO SPORT DOGS
(as percent of dry matter)

Constituent	Sprint (Greyhound)	Intermediate Distance (Other Sports)	Long Distance (Sled Dogs)
Proteins	30 to 35	30 to 35	30 to 40
Fats	16 to 20	20 to 25	30 to 40
Glucides	50	35 to 40	15
Fiber	1 to 3	1 to 3	1 to 3
Calcium	1.2 to 1.5	1.2 to 1.5	1.5 to 1.8
Phosphorus	0.9 to 1.1	0.9 to 1.1	1 to 1.2
Sodium chloride	1.1	1.1	1.1
Magnesium	0.1	0.1	0.2

Double amounts of trace minerals (iron, copper, zinc, manganese, iodine, selenium) and vitamins A and B. Triple amounts of vitamins E, B1, B2, B6, B12.

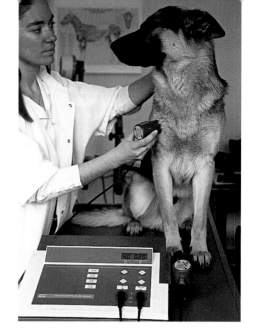

Elements of Canine Sports Medicine

The continual development of canine sports, and the greater number and higher level of competitions, have led to the emergence of canine sports medicine, in order to confront the problems arising from a very specific sports pathology.

- It is obvious that a working or sport dogs musculoskeletal system must be intact. Limping would cause pain and adversely affect performance.

Limping can be caused by problems with the footpads or spaces between the toes arising from the fact that these are the only places a dog sweats. Such problems are very familiar to hunters and mushers, and can be prevented by hardening the pads using a spray hardener, and application of grease (a mixture of lanolin and pine tar) or, better yet, of a balm made with hyperoxygenated fatty acids (which have strong anti-inflammatory properties) between the toes. In some cases (sled dogs), the use of protective boots is also highly recommended.

Moving up the limbs, it would be easy to list dozens of bone, joint, tendon, and ligament problems specific to a given sport. Like humans, sport and work dogs are subject to such classic disorders as sprains and dislocations, even fractures. Similarly, active muscles can be affected by problems ranging from simple contractures (charley horse), through strains and pulls to tears, or by inflammatory conditions such as tendinitis or myositis. Sophisticated diagnostic methods such as ultrasound or thermography (visualization of hot or cold areas using a thermal camera) are now used and allow the best-adapted therapies to be applied. Physical therapy methods are also used for the retraining phase.

In the area of canine traumatology, an ounce of prevention is worth a pound of cure. The following are essential elements of preventive medicine.

- Physical training should be well-planned and regular so that it brings the dog to its peak potential during the competition season.
- The dog should be trained so that good form appropriate to the required effort becomes automatic: The dog should be accustomed to working in various environments so that it can optimally position its feet.
- The dog should be warmed up before training sessions or competitions and cooled down afterwards.
- Water should always be available so that no dehydration, however minimal, occurs and damages the muscle.
- The type of food fed should be adapted to the type of effort required, and the amount fed should maintain the dogs fit weight.

CANINE SPORTS MEDICINE

Canine sports are continuing to develop. Some are slowly winning their Olympic laurels (in contests where handler and dog combine their efforts what could be a more logical candidate than the pulka or dogsled?), others are an extraordinary way to educate both dogs and children through play (to be convinced of this, all you need to do is attend an agility trial), and herding dogs display some of Mother Natures finest ancestral qualities.

As awareness of these sports increases and the level of professionalism rises, the number of sport dogs is increasing as well. In response, the first international day-long conference for the study of canine sports medicine was held at the Ecole Nationale Vétérinaire veterinary college in Alfort, France, in 1985. With time, what was once a mere concept led to the 1996 opening of the Unité de Médecine de l'Elevage et du Sport (Breeding and Sports Medicine Department), a clinic and research unit. This department provides services to professionals who work with dogs. In its Sports Medicine unit, the innovative veterinary-school program (which has no equivalent except at two American universities: Auburn and the University of Florida) has clinic hours three times a week, physical and occupational therapy facilities, and a research laboratory (for research on physiopathology of lipids and free radicals) that studies the biological and cellular effects of physical effort in dogs. The UMES also has a presence in the field, as its veterinarians are present in an official capacity at canine sport competitions, including on an international level. Canine sports medicine, a discipline created only a few years ago, is gradually becoming a recognized specialization, in response to a real need on the part of canine sports aficionados and covering areas ranging from preparation of the dog to specific pathological conditions or the war against doping.

CLINICAL EVALUATION OF DEHYDRATION IN DOGS

Percentage of Dehydration	Clinical Symptoms	Action
< 5	No change	Give water to drink
6	Slight persistence of cutaneous fold (a)	Oral rehydration
8	Significant persistence of cutaneous fold Capillary refill time 2-3 seconds (b) Slight endophthalmitis Dryness of the mucous membranes in the mouth	Perfusion
10-12	Severe persistence of cutaneous fold Capillary refill time greater than 3 seconds Pronounced endophthalmitis ñ cold extremities Muscle spasms, occasional tachycardia	Perfusion
12-15	State of shock Imminent death	Emergency treatment

(a) Evaluate the cutaneous fold along the topline in the lumbar region. Avoid the neck, where the skin is naturally loose.
(b) Normal capillary refill time is between 1 and 1.5 seconds.

THE 1996 LICANCABUR CHIENS DES CIMES SCIENTIFIC EXPEDITION

Objective: To study the biological and nutritional effects of high-altitude work on dogs searching for buried victims.

This study was done in 1996 in northern Chile, at the summit of the Licancabur volcano (5980 m). The purpose of the expedition was to study the biological effects of work performed at high altitudes (where there is less oxygen and the barometric pressure is lower) by dogs searching for buried victims. In fact, search dogs are frequently called upon to rescue victims of earthquakes or landslides at high altitudes (in the Andean cordillera, Asia, etc.), or victims of mountain avalanches. In such emergency situations, human and animal rescuers have no opportunity to adapt to the altitude gradually.

Men and dogs from the Paris Fire Department and Chiles Riflemen participated in a field experiment to make them better prepared to carry out their duties under these difficult conditions without suffering from the well-known effects of altitude sickness. Without prior acclimatization, they searched for buried victims in the Inca ruins located along the vents of the Licancabur volcano. The scientific results of this expedition clearly demonstrated the importance of optimal nutritional preparation, based on consumption of a high-energy, high-protein complete dry dog food by the dogs. The food was also supplemented with antioxidant vitamins (E and C) and omega 3 essential fatty acids (fish oil). At the same time, a similar comparative study was conducted in the men, and additional expeditions of this type will be undertaken in the future in cooperation with the Ecole Nationale VÈtÈrinaire veterinary colleges Breeding and Sports Medicine Department and the Royal Canin companys research center.

Doctor Fathi Driss
Paris-West University Hospital

SLED DOGS HAVE THEIR OWN INTERNATIONAL VETERINARY ASSOCIATION

The International Sled Dog Veterinary Medical Association (ISDVMA) is a professional veterinarians organization with more than 400 members on five continents, from countries ranging from New Zealand and Greenland to Japan and South Africa. The ISDVMA was founded in 1991 to actively promote and encourage actions contributing to the well-being and good health of sled dogs, and to carry out scientific research leading to a better understanding of these extraordinary dogs. The ISDVMA organizes an annual symposium, as well as meetings all over the world, to inform veterinarians of the latest scientific advances in this area. It also regularly publishes a journal and other works providing for continual interchange of information. It maintains an annually-updated database of all scientific and technical publications relating to sled dogs, offers training to educate mushers about their dogs, and provides international federations and organizations with specialist veterinarians who oversee some 4500 sled dog races per year all over the world. It also furnishes study and research scholarships for the many veterinary students interested in this subject.

Professor Jerome A. Vanek
University of Minnesota
St. Paul, MN

Physical and Occupational Therapy

Physical therapy is a medical discipline that attempts to reestablish normal function in a body part by using various non-invasive treatments, for example, heat treatments (usually ultrasound), passive mobilization of a limb, neuromuscular stimulation, or simple re-education exercises. The use of scientific physical therapy methods to improve recuperation in canine athletes or in dogs recovering from bone or muscle surgery is a recent development in veterinary medicine linked to the creation of the Breeding and Sports Medicine Department at the Veterinary College in Alfort, France. Use of these methods to improve recovery in canine athletes is still in its infancy.

The benefits of physical therapy

The goal of physical therapy is to reestablish normal function to the injured body part (or animal). In fact, surgical treatment of a torn muscle, tendon, or ligament, or stabilization of a fracture, is often only the first step of the animals rehabilitation. When there is no adequate follow-up, the animals physical abilities invariably decrease and its athletic performance suffers. The benefits of physical therapy for the canine patient include the following:

1. increased flow of blood and lymph,
2. early regression of inflammation,
3. increased production of replacement tissue,
4. prevention of contractures around the joints,
5. promotion of return to normal function by the injured part,
6. prevention of muscle atrophy.

One of the not insignificant benefits of physical therapy methods is that they include the animals owner in the treatment. The owner then becomes partially responsible for the dogs successful recovery.

Heat treatments

Heat is the oldest method of treatment and is often very effective. Heat has the following beneficial effects:

- reduces the severity of the inflammatory response (heat, pain, swelling, muscle spasms),
- increases the metabolic rate of the heated tissues,
- makes fibrous scar tissue more supple,
- increases blood flow,
- decreases pain.

Heat treatments can be superficial (instant heat packs, heat lamps, hot water), e.g., for a toe injury, or can rely on heat conduction, as in ultrasound or microwave treatments. Heat treatments can also be applied to serious injuries by utilizing the same ultrasound equipment widely used by kinesiologists.

Passive mobilization and massage

Passive mobilization is motion imposed by the therapist to try to recover the range of joint motion or to correct a lack of flexibility or elasticity in the soft tissues. It is an important tool applied after trauma to prevent tissue adhesions, maintain normal motion of the joint, improve blood and lymph drainage, and prevent muscle contractures and freezing of the joints. This type of treatment should begin the same day as surgery and continue for two or three weeks. Massage can be used when there is no muscle injury to reduce pain and improve blood circulation.

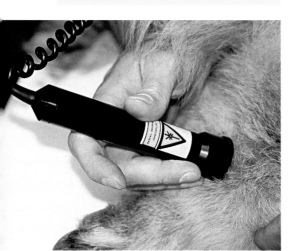

THE USE OF LASERS TO TREAT SPORTS DOG INJURIES

Various types of lasers can be used to treat sport dogs, to aid recovery from muscle problems or tendinitis. Their effectiveness depends on their technical characteristics. Usually, in dogs, low-powered lasers are used for acupuncture, medium-powered lasers for muscle and joint problems, and high-powered lasers for surgery. The therapeutic effects of lasers help reduce inflammation, edema, and pain (analgesic effect). They also accelerate the scarring process in cases of injury or tearing.

The future therapy of choice for non-invasive treatment of sport dogs, lasers can already be found among the equipment of specialized veterinarians, even though the cost remains rather high.

Doctor Petra Horvatic-Peer
Veterinarian, University of Vienna

Swimming

Swimming allows the joints to be extended and the muscles worked without placing too great a weight load on them. It also allows a wide range of joint motion and can be started very soon after surgery.

Electrostimulation

Small independent units for neuromuscular electrostimulation are used through the skin to make the principle muscle groups contract rhythmically. This prevents muscle atrophy arising from forced rest or prolonged partial immobilization.

Low-energy laser

Low-energy lasers and pulsed electromagnetic fields are also used with seemingly good results for muscle and tendon problems.

A good physical therapy program is an essential part of the dogs full recovery. By using the methods discussed above, the veterinarian and owner can cooperate to create an effective ìoccupational therapyî program that lasts several weeks and is very similar to programs designed for humans.

EXAMPLES OF PHYSICAL THERAPY PROTOCOLS

Case 1

A Greyhound had orthopedic surgery to repair a fracture of the tarsus.

Weeks 1 and 2
Immobilization by plaster cast
Passive mobilization of the hip and stifle
Stimulation of the quadriceps muscle

Weeks 3 and 4
Immobilization by plaster cast
Passive mobilization of the hip and stifle

Week 5
Removal of plaster cast
X-ray of fracture
Passive mobilization of the hip, stifle, tibio-talar joint
Stimulation of the gastrocnemius and cranial tibial muscles
Daily swim (for a few minutes)
Confinement to cage, with brief walks on a short leash so the dog can relieve itself

Week 6
Brief walks on a short leash
Daily swim
Passive mobilization of the tibio-talar joint

Week 7
Short runs off leash
Daily swim
Long slow walks

Weeks 8 and 9
Gradual increase in time and intensity of walking, trotting, running

Week 10
Training resumes

Case 2

A Greyhound had a closed fracture of the femur, which was treated surgically by setting the fracture and inserting a plate.

Week 1
Passive mobilization of the hip and stifle
Massage of the leg
Application of ice packs to the scar area to prevent inflammation and edema
Electrostimulation of thigh muscles (particularly the quadriceps)

Week 2
Ablation of structures
Passive mobilization
Massage
If necessary, application of cold compresses
Electrostimulation

Week 3
Muscle diathermy
Passive mobilization
Electrostimulation
Swim (one minute three times per week)
Walks on short leash

Week 4
Muscle diathermy
Passive mobilization
Swim (one to two minutes five times per week)
Walks on leash

Weeks 5 and 6
Walks on leash
Swim

Weeks 7 and 8
Owner performs physical therapy
Walks on leash, including slopes, ramps, or stairs

In all cases where physical therapy methods are used, it is very important to document the animals progress daily.

In a program lasting for several weeks, the dog should not advance to the next step until the previous weeks objectives have been met.

The owner cannot finish the treatment until the animals stance returns to normal.

It must be possible to tell one dog from the other during competition. Identifying dogs with an electronic transponder is cerrently the most reliable method.

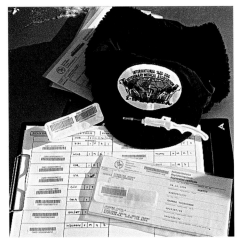

Required documents.

The War Against Doping

Given the constant development of the various canine sports and the high stakes associated with some, respect for the animals and for sportsmanship demands drug testing of sport dogs. Greyhound racing (U.S., Australia, Europe) and pulka and sled dog races (U.S., Europe) are in the forefront, having already had international rules and regular drug-testing for years.

Doping has nothing to do with the physiological preparation of the canine athlete, which is essential and must be carried out under the supervision of a veterinarian. Doping is the use of any substance or means that artificially enhances performance during a competition. It is an attack on sportsmanship and on the dogs physical and mental well-being.

Although extremely rare, cases of doping do exist in the world of dog sports,
- to win, when the stakes are high
- to lose, when a bet has been placed (Greyhound racing),
- to make others lose in this case, the goal is to administer a prohibited substance to (a) rival dog(s). This goes beyond mere fraud!

Existing rules refer to lists of prohibited substances, such as the list compiled for sled dogs by the International Federation for Sled-dog Sport (IFSS). This particular list prohibits the following:
- analgesic substances,
- steroidal or non-steroidal anti-inflammatory drugs,
- antiprostoglandins
- central nervous system stimulants
- antitussives
- sedatives and anesthetics
- diuretics

- anabolic steroids
- muscle relaxants
- anticholinergic substances
- antihistamines
- blood injections.

Drug-test samples are taken from the dog's saliva, blood, or urine, with no danger to the animal and in accordance with very strict rules (contradictory samples are coded for anonymity, placed under lock and key, and sent to the laboratory for analysis under strict security).

Aside from all the rules and tests, it is important for every owner to know that doping is dangerous to the dog. Anabolic steroids, stimulants, tranquilizers, anti-inflammatory drugs, diuretics, and beta-blockers are all medications that have harmful side effects when used for such purposes.

Thus, while it concerns only a tiny minority of thoughtless individuals, the war on doping is a necessary dissuasive force that should increasingly become the object of a serious educational and preventive campaign in the world of canine sports.

Maintaining the chain of evidence: samples are numbered and stored under lock and key.

Part 5

The Dog and His Owner

Dog Behavior and Training

Spontaneous Behavior of Pack Dogs

Due to their living conditions, domestic dogs do not form groups large enough to establish hierarchical systems that are as complex as those of wolves. Among wolves, the pack forms a social unit in which hierarchy, play and solidarity all help to maintain group cohesion, increase the chances of survival and facilitate reproduction.

Packs of wild dogs defend their territory but may also co-opt new members from other groups of stray or wild dogs.

Stray dogs and Wild Dogs

In the United States and in certain European countries, there are numerous stray dogs that only rarely have contact with humans or that have become completely wild. These dogs stick to the outskirts of big cities, public places or freely-accessible areas that are out of immediate human view, as well as to agricultural or forest regions.

These dogs, known as "free ranging dogs" (FRD), are defined as dogs that may or may not belong to an owner. Among these dogs are those that are left to roam freely by their owners for long periods of time and those that are lost or have been abandoned and therefore no longer have an owner.

Sharing Food According to the Hierarchy

There is a complex hierarchy within a pack of dogs. The feeding mode of wild canines is such that they can consume large quantities of food in a short amount of time after capturing their prey.

They do not necessarily eat every day because the hunt is not always successful. They must find their prey, but prey does not keep and there is competition from other animals.

Once the prey is captured, the dominant dogs eat first. Submissive dogs must keep a certain distance and wait until the dominant dogs have finished their meal before they have their chance at the food.

Waste Elimination Behavior: a Personal Identity Card

In wild canines, waste elimination plays more than a physiological role. It is also a means of olfactory communication, which is primarily conveyed through pheromones found in urine, feces and vaginal secretions. These pheromones provide information about the sex, identity, physiological condition and hierarchical position of the dog producing them.

Throughout the centuries, domestication has led to not only physical or physiological changes in dogs, but also behavioral changes. Today, at the end of the 20th century, the status of dogs has become one of companion animal, even though they are also used for hunting, guarding and work.

Dominant – Submissive Relationship

Within a pack of dogs, the dominant dog controls how the pack occupies space while at rest and the movement of his subjects. The dominant dogs sleep together in the middle of a circle formed by the pack. The space is divided into concentric circles for the various level of the hierarchy. The closer a dog is to the leader, the higher his rank in the hierarchy.

The dominant dog controls sexuality within the group. Only the dominant dog may express his sexuality in front of the other members of the pack. Submissive dogs may only mate in areas shielded from his view. City dogs never live in a true pack environment, but country dogs may.

Evolution of Behavior through Domestication

The exact date when dogs were first domesticated *(Canis familiaris)* is unknown. Domestication most likely occurred in diverse civilizations and regions of the world and, according to certain authors, is thought to have begun at the end of the Paleolithic period. The dog is often said to have originated from the gray wolf *(Canis lupus)*. For a long time, authors did not all agree. According to some, the golden jackal or even the coyote are the ancestors of the dog. They believe dogs came about as a result of successive crossbreeding between these animals. However, recent DNA studies seem to corroborate the wolf theory.

Dogs are the First Species to have been Domesticated..

Several hypotheses have been advanced as to the reasons why dogs were domesticated. It is currently thought that young wolf cubs were brought back to campsites and were cared for by the women. These wolf cubs were kept for various reasons: emotional or religious reasons, or for food. Their utility as guard or hunting dogs was not discovered until later.

There are numerous known subspecies of wolves that are distinguished by their size. They are thought to have played a role in the ancestry of the dog to varying degrees since it seems that the domestication process occurred in several places. The great diversity in the subspecies used is precisely what explains, at least in part, the polymorphism of the canine species and the large number of different breeds.

Throughout the centuries, dogs have been used for hunting and in some cases, to guard houses. In the Middle Ages, numerous hunting dog breeds began to appear in response to the substantial development of hunting with hounds.

The Evolution of Domestication

Because of domestication and human intervention, the 20th century dog is a far cry from his ancestors. Humans have selected dogs, their build, size, color, coat and ears (wild dogs all have erect ears by the time they reach adulthood).

In terms of physiology, sexual maturity is reached earlier in dogs. It has gone from the age of two years in wolves to six to ten months in the average-sized dog (10 – 25 kg) (22-55 lb). Moreover, the following have been observed: the reproductive cycle of dogs has doubled, the anal and perianal glands have become smaller and the morphology of the breeds has become more diverse. In addition, domestic dogs emit more sounds than wild dogs. Human-trained puppies are more vocal than dogs that live in packs. Numerous behavioral modifications have also developed such as docility and socialization to other animal species and to humans, which have thus eliminated predatory behaviors.

Negative Consequences of Domestication

Domestication does not only have positive effects. In cases of bad breeding practices or poor training by the owner, some dogs may develop behavioral problems such as noise or people phobias, or may become aggressive and bite.

Since humans furnish food and shelter, predation and the search for shelter are no longer necessary. They provide health care, which increases longevity and may in turn lead to aging-related problems. Humans regulate reproduction by sterilizing certain animals and by choosing to breed others. Humans seek to avoid confrontations between different dogs and in so doing, may modify the dom-

Pheromones are chemical substances secreted by an individual to the exterior of the body, which can be detected through smell by another individual and which trigger a behavioral or physiological response in that individual. These pheromones are produced in various organs: the anal glands, the circumanal glands, interdigitate glands and glands in the back and tail. When a dog meets another dog, he sniffs the zones of the body with the highest concentration glands.

inant/submissive relationship. If several dogs live in a human household, the dominant/submissive relationship may manifest itself among the dogs. Owners should bear this in mind and should never interfere when the dogs fight. By separating the dogs, owners in fact cause the conflict to be aggravated or prolonged because the fight cannot be pursued until one of the dogs submits.

Whelping and First Contacts

A bitch whelps after a gestation period of 57-72 days. It is important to note that during the prenatal period, the fetus begins to respond to all tactile stimulation starting from the 45th day of gestation. When the bitch's stomach is stroked, motor movements by the fetus can be observed. These movements progressively diminish after several days of handling. Puppies born to a mother who has been handled during gestation will have a higher level of tactile sensitivity and will be easier to handle. The puppies are also capable of reacting to any emotional reaction by the mother. Consequently, it is important to protect the pregnant mother from situations that cause fear and stress.

Solitary Birth

In principle, humans do not need to intervene in the natural act of birth. The bitch will choose her own spot to nest - generally a quiet place. The puppy comes out surrounded by the placenta sac and the mother cuts the umbilical cord with her teeth, opens the sac and eats it. This act is essential because this membrane contains a hormone that encourages the onset of lactation. The mother then licks her young one, which stimulates respiration. Puppies are born at intervals varying between 10 and 60 minutes. Generally, the entire whelping process is concluded in less than 12 hours, however, it may last longer with primipara. The number of puppies per litter varies from one to more than 15.

Once whelping is complete, it is best not to intervene and to leave the mother alone. In some bitches the mechanism that triggers the maternal instincts is not developed. Sometimes, in the case of a primiparous bitch (first birth), she does not display her maternal instincts and it is necessary to cut the puppy's umbilical cord, remove the fetal covering, rub the puppy down and place it next to its mother's breasts. Ideally, the mother should be left to deal with her babies herself even if they end up starving to death, in order to stimulate maturation of the maternal instinct. The degree of wakefulness of the bitch at the time of birth is important. If the mother's sensory abilities are numbed, the development of attachment may be altered. This is observed in dogs that are given a general anesthesia or dogs that give birth under the influence of tranquilizers. The puppy is born deaf, blind and anosmic.

Puppy Activity

Sleeping is the main activity of puppies. Almost 90% of the nyctohemeral period is devoted to sleeping, of which 95% is paradoxical sleep during which the puppies show movements of the face, lips, ears and limbs.

When they are not sleeping, they are nursing. Feeding appears to be on a rather regular schedule at about every three to four hours. They occur at the same time for the entire litter. When the puppy's muzzle touches the mother or another puppy, the puppy stops and searches around for the breast. This is the burrowing effect. Once the puppy finds the breast, he kneads it with his two forepaws in an alternating rhythm in order to release the flow of milk. Contact with the breast induces sucking. This is known as the labial effect.

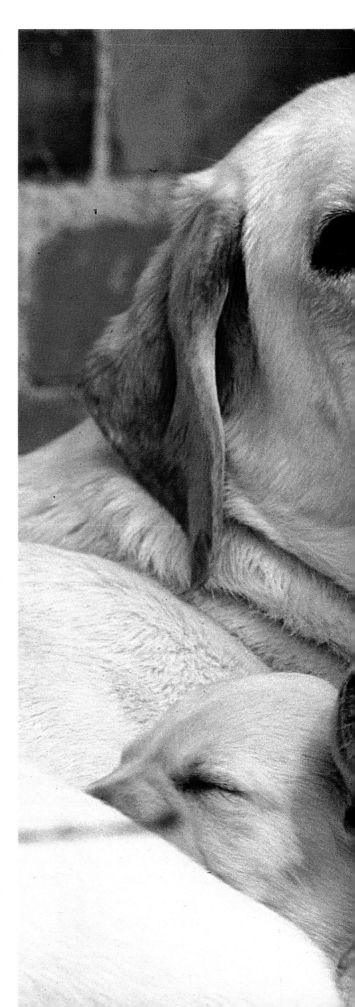

Contact with the Mother is Indispensable

The puppy moves around by crawling. Due to his limited motor skills, he cannot stand up. If the puppy finds himself out of contact range with the rest of the litter, he will become extremely agitated and emit vocal sounds that will not stop until he reestablishes contact. When the mother hears his whining, she heads toward the puppy and brings him back to the litter.

At the end of the meal, she turns her puppies over and grooms them. She licks the perineal region of her puppies to stimulate them to defecate and urinate, which she then consumes. This is called the perineal reflex. Then the puppies huddle together again and go to sleep. During this neonatal period, the puppy's tactile sensitivity is well developed, as is his sense of taste and he demonstrates basic responses to taste. During this period, the mother bonds with her puppies and anything that limits her contact with them will cause her great distress. She bonds specifically with her own puppies, even though a breastfeeding mother can sometimes be made to adopt other puppies. However, only her own puppies can appease her.

Puppy Socialization

Socialization is a lengthy learning phase during which the puppy acquires all the behaviors needed for life in the pack. This stage begins at the age of six weeks and ends arbitrarily around the age of four months. Mistakes in rearing or training during this period are possible and may jeopardize a happy and balanced relationship between the owner and his companion.

The puppy is born into the world not knowing to which species he belongs. He has to identify with his species. He will acquire this information in a unique, almost irreversible learning process, which is called "imprinting." A poorly imprinted animal is a lost cause for the species.

This learning process occurs through games with his brothers and sisters and his mother. As an adult, this will enable him to recognize his sexual partner and to avoid rejection or flight with other members of his own species.

If, however, a puppy is raised with other species (humans, cats, rabbits, even a stuffed animal), he may end up identifying with the species with which he lived. If there is a complete absence of other dogs between three and more or less sixteen weeks, the puppy will identify with the nearest species (human, cat, rabbit), or even a decoy (stuffed animal). As an adult, this will lead to social preferences as well as courting behavior and attempts to mate with the species he identifies with and aggressive behavior towards his own species. In order to avoid this type of situation, the puppy must be raised in a group, with its mother, until he is at least eight weeks old.

Dogs are not programmed to interact socially with a foreign species (cat, human, rabbit). They must be socialized to other species, as well as to humans. Thus, if a puppy is raised with cats, it will not ultimately attack them.

The breeder must therefore put the puppy in contact with other species if possible and especially with different types of people (men, women, children). This interaction must continue until after two months of age. Interaction with other species during this phase will not prevent identification with his own species. The interactive presence of other species will lead to inter-specific socialization and attachment that goes against predatory behavior.

EDUCATING THE PUPPY

Acquiring a dog implies a certain number of obligations as well as knowledge of how to train the dog so as to avoid bothersome problems that in the future can result in unfortunate abandonment, even euthanasia. A puppy must be trained in order for a harmonious relationship to prevail between him and his owners. Training involves several areas such as house-training and obeying orders.

How Do You House-Train a Puppy?

It is first necessary to understand the various learning stages in elimination behavior. From birth, the mother stimulates urination or defecation by licking the perineal region and then she ingests all the feces emitted. When the puppy starts to leave the litter, his mother continues to lick him under his tail, which stimulates urination or defecation. Ultimately, these reflexes disappear and stimulation by licking is no longer necessary. The puppy leaves the litter and eliminates his waste further away. Starting from the age of six weeks, he sniffs out the spots where he previously defecated and relieves himself in the same places. When a puppy is brought into a home, he is generally not house-trained. He does not eliminate in the place where he sleeps, but that is about it.

A House-Trained Dog is the Result of Training

Starting from the age of two months, that is, after the puppy's first vaccinations, the puppy should be taken outside. He should be taken out every five to six hours when he first wakes up and after meals until the age of four months. At first, choose a place or even a newspaper that is saturated with the puppy's own odor. A newspaper that is placed into the gutter can be removed after some time. In the beginning, as soon as the puppy relieves himself at the desired place, he should be systematically rewarded either through voice or by petting. Despite the best-intentioned efforts of the owners, there will always be

some accidents as the puppy is learning. If the owner finds stains in the house, he should never punish his dog (unless he catches him in the act). The technique of using newspaper inside the house should be banished because the dog will associate this with the place of elimination and stick to it. Even if he goes out, he will wait until he goes back inside the house to take care of his needs. When out walking, never end the walk as soon as the dog has taken care of his needs, because he will quickly learn to associate needs with the end of the walk.

The Dog Must Also Be Trained to Obey. How? By Reward or Punishment?

In order to be effective, the reward method must adhere to several principles. The reward should be significant for the dog. In other words, the owner should praise the dog through contact and abundant caresses and speak to him warmly. It should be exceptional in nature, such as giving unusual treats. Finally, when practiced systematically, it will become aleatory and the dog will no longer be motivated. Rewarding is, a posteriori, an ethological nonsense.

As for punishment, in order to be effective, it should be used when the dog is caught in the act and should be given out at the same time. It must be unpleasant in nature for the dog and must be meted out systematically for every punishable act, which is sometimes very difficult since the owners do not always catch the dog in the act. Punishment after-the-fact will cause anxiety and will aggravate the situation. Punishment can be direct, for example, grabbing the dog by the skin of his neck, which replicates the maternal behavior and shaking him by lifting him up slightly. Contrary to popular opinion, it is possible to give the dog a slap of the hand. The dog is perfectly capable of distinguishing between the hand that pets him and the hand that hits. It is also possible to punish a dog from a distance by throwing a non-dangerous object that will make noise at him. Learning by reward requires more time than punishment, but on the other hand, it sticks longer. When punishing a dog, it is necessary to recognize the submission position because at that very instant, punishment must immediately stop. If the owner continues, the punishment will cause anxiety and will cease to be effective. Equipped with this information, the owner is now ready to begin training.

Teaching Obedience (Sit, Lay, etc.) is Easy

The first thing to remember when giving a dog a command is to refrain from making speeches because the dog does not understand human speech. A simple, hearty "no" will suffice. Early on, the dog should become accustomed to wearing a collar and then a normal leash. Walking the dog on a leash can be started at home and performed several times a day, always for short periods. If the dog pulls, give a quick snap to the leash. Do not forget to reward the dog when he has done well.

Some dogs do not come when they are called. They come to within a few meters of their owner and stop. As soon as the owner approaches the dog to catch him, the dog runs away again. Above all, remain calm. Do not become annoyed and certainly do not punish the animal. You should never get angry. Even if the dog takes his time, you should not punish him when he returns. This is undoubtedly the most frequently committed mistake. The dog will associate punishment with having come back to his owner. On the contrary, when he comes back, you should praise him, pet him and above all, you should not immediately put him back on the leash. Instead, let him go back to playing. If every time he is called it means putting the leash on and going back inside, it will be a punishment for him. If you

want him to come back, you must adopt a welcoming and calm attitude and you should definitely not run after him. You will never be able to catch him! Rather, you should pretend to leave and turn around and walk away when he returns.

Dogs must be taught to come when they are called and the ideal age to start is four to five months. Here again, you must be patient. This training can start inside the home. Call the dog with a short command and praise him when he comes to you. Once obedience is mastered inside the home, continue in a closed space if possible and finally, end up in an open space. Be aware that sometimes the dog will revert backwards once outside because there will be a lot of distractions. Do not get angry but start the sessions again inside. The sessions need to be short because puppies tire quickly. He must also be taught to stay out of mischief (tearing up curtains, chewing on table and chair legs, tearing shoes to shreds, etc.).

Each time he is caught in the act, scold him with a hearty "no" and even give him a little slap. Even better, take him by the nape of his neck if possible and shake him. This will remind him of his mother.

The Need to Be "Detached"

When a puppy is brought into a home, he becomes attached to a person and vice versa. By the age of four to five months, owners must prompt separation. If this is not done, as soon as the puppy is separated from the person to whom he is attached, he will become panicked and distressed. He will look for his owners and disaster issues: ruined furniture, accidents on the carpet and howling! The dog is not trying to take "vengeance", he is simply anxious. He must learn to stay alone and to be detached from his owners. Start ignoring him 30 minutes prior to departure. When you return, if the dog jumps all over you, push him away and do not respond. As soon as he is calm, then act happy to see him and pet him. If he has caused damage, act as though you do not see him, even though you may want to punish him. The dog must learn to be separated from his owners and the only way to achieve this is to refrain from responding to his requests to play and to be petted. You must push him away. Owners must take the initiative in the relationship.

He Must Learn the Rules of Living with Others

He must eat alone. His food should be given in the kitchen. He should not be allowed to beg at the table, but he should have the right to be present when his owners eat. He should not be allowed to jump up on beds or the sofa without permission from his owners. He should quickly be given his own place to sleep, which should not be a high-traffic area or a strategic point where he is able to survey the comings and goings of the pack, i.e. his owners. His sleeping area should be located in a quiet spot where he can rest. If he nips at hands, you should stop him from doing so (if he is a big dog, nipping will ultimately hurt) and firmly push him away. You should also avoid tug-of-war type games (with a toy, a piece of stick, a rag) because this encourages biting, which is far from desirable for a future companion animal. You should not pet a puppy on demand. As with play, it is up to the master to decide when to play and to initiate contact and petting.

Learning the Hierarchy

Because dogs are born to live in a society, they must learn the rules of the hierarchy. In other words, they must learn to control their desires according to the rules in place within the pack. Learning the hierarchical structure is accomplished by learning the rules governing feeding, the control of territory and sexuality. Within the pack, the dominant dog eats first and controls the comings and goings of his subjects. In addition, he alone has the right to express his sexuality in front of the other members of the pack.

Until they are weaned, the young pups feed at the breast and do not follow any rules governing access to the teats. As they are being weaned, the mother leads them to the sources of available food in the pack. When they approach the food, they are violently shoved away by the adults. They must learn to wait their turn, that is, until after the pack leaders have eaten, before they can eat. If the dog attempts to approach the food, the leader will growl at him and may even bite him if he persists.

Around the age of five to six months in males and around the second estrous cycle in females, the dogs will be chased away from the zones frequented by the pack leaders and by the females. The mothers have less and less tolerance for their young and so the young dogs are forced to find a sleeping place on the outskirts of the pack territory. Finally, in this stage dogs gain control over their sexual behaviors. Only dominant dogs have the right to express their sexuality in front of the other members of the pack. Subordinate males and the adolescents must hide. Their sexual behavior is inhibited in the presence of dominant males.

Controling the Bite

The socialization period is when the puppy learns not to hurt by biting. He learns to control his bite partly through forms of play, which begin as early as three months and partly from his mother. He thus learns to repress his bite. During combat games, puppies bite each other and if one bites another too hard, the latter will howl. The mother steps in, picks up her young pup by the nape of his neck, shakes him vigorously and then places him back on the floor. This causes the puppy to cry out and assume a submissive posture, which then obliges him to stop biting. Thus, the mother teaches him to control both the intensity of his bite and his motor skills in general. If the puppy lives with a family, the owners should not tolerate biting. The puppy is not "teething." This will help prevent serious bites later on when the dog becomes stronger. The intensity of the bite varies according to the individual, the breed and lineage. Some breeds such as the Labrador can tolerate extremely intense bites. Finally, during this socialization period, the mother teaches the puppies to be less attached to her.

The Detachment Period

Around the age of about four to five months, the bitch begins to have less and less tolerance for her puppies, especially the males. She shows less affection towards them, she plays less and they have to find their own place to sleep. Females, however, stay with their mother longer. Detachment will occur more slowly and will occur around the second heat. In human packs, if detachment does not occur, the result may be prolonged attachment, even over-attachment, which will then be the source of behavioral problems such as mass destruction, inopportune urination or defecation and being vocal when the person who is the object of attachment is absent.

THE RULES OF THE GAME

When puppies play "loser takes all", they are learning about hierarchy. The puppy adopts many postures with his brothers and sisters. Rolling, "move over and let me in", etc. At the age of one month, his body is in constant motion. Even his mask is expressive – no more stiff baby puppy face! He curls up his lips, flaps his ears and moves his facial muscles. So many visible signs in the life of the group. Lying on one's back is the best way to get attention: the whole gang runs over, ready for trouble. At five weeks, the puppies start to play little war games. They chew on each other's ears, grab each other by the nape of the neck and nibble on each other's muzzle (the mouth is truly a multi-purpose receptacle). Not only are the puppies being initiated into combat games, they are also learning the rules of life in a pack. The puppy tests attitudes of domination and submission. If he lies flat on his back with his hind paws spread apart, it means he lost the battle! What a feeling! Games that involve pushing and hard struggle reveal the first signs of sexual activity (the young male thrusting his pelvis).

At three months there is a change of partner. Now the puppy wants to play with humans. He invites them to share in his delirious fun. He has ways and means to convince them. He looks up reverently, his eyes riveted on his owner's and wiggles around as though doing a belly dance. His lips drawn back, jaw slightly open – mimicking a smile – he uses every means of seduction. He skips about, wriggles his body, runs, jumps, leaps, etc. When at last he wins, he gets to play ball. He catches it and brings it back. A stick is thrown to him. He catches it between his teeth, runs off with it and does not let it go.

Play, which lays the foundation for the hierarchy between dogs, helps prevent fights involving serious biting, soften aggressive tendencies and strengthen ties with the owner. This is a life-long pleasure since in dogs, the desire to play increases with age.

Brigitte Bullard-Cordeau

Aggressive Behavior

In ethological terms, aggression is defined as a "physical act or threatening action that one individual commits against another, thereby limiting his very freedom and genetic potential." Several different types of aggressive behavior can be distinguished: predatory aggression, hierarchical aggression, frustration-induced aggression, territorial and maternal aggression and fear-induced aggression. Save for predatory aggression and fear-induced aggression, it is important to look at the entire behavioral sequence.
A behavioral sequence has three phases.

First, there is a threat or intimidation phase (growling, hackles raised, tail and ears erect, teeth bared), then an attack phase in which the dog charges its adversary and attempts to grab him by the skin of his neck, his breast or his fore legs. He tries to make his adversary fall and pins him down until he adopts a submissive posture.

Finally, there is the appeasement phase. The triumphant dog either bites the vanquished dog on the top of the head, or he places his paw on the withers, or he straddles him. The attack varies according to the hierarchical relationship that already exists between the two dogs. If the attacking dog is dominant, the bite will be inflicted quickly and will be followed by a second round of intimidation.

If, however, the attacking dog is in competition, he will maintain his hold until his adversary submits. If the sequence is complete, it is known as reactional aggression. If the threat or appeasement phases are not carried out, it is known as instrumentalized aggression or secondary hyper-aggression.

MAN, A TRUSTWORTHY FRIEND

By three months old, the young dog knows one thing for sure: man is his friend. But this does not come by instinct!

Ever since the beginning of domestication, man, as always, has been the one to take the first step. Used to taking the lead, he holds out his hand toward the newborn puppy who has a heightened sense of smell and is already equipped with tactile and sucking abilities. The young canine sniffs the human hand, sizes up the contact and licks the skin to see how it tastes. He seeks out the warmth it emits (he will not acquire his definitive body temperature until he is ten days old). By surrendering himself completely to the palm or nestling into the hollow of the hand, he imagines himself next to the body of one of his brothers or sisters. Until three weeks old, puppies know no fear of humans and trust them completely. The hand is the very first link established between dogs and humans. Each day as he is weighed, he breathes in this peculiar odor while searching around with his nose just like he does with the mother's breast. However, the human hand is not his only discovery. He also discovers the voice of his owner, which he begins to hear at twenty-one days, when socialization begins. A complete sound and light show! He is seventeen days old when he sees the color and shape of this soft, warm hand.
This is precisely the age when his conditioned reflexes trigger communication. He acts with his owner like he does with his mother. Still under the effects of neoteny for quite some time (i.e. he keeps baby ways), he uses his voice. He barks at ten days, but he is not heard yelping until three weeks – to make his owner aware of his minor hurts. He whines and the person feels summoned. This is the first weapon of seduction.
And as for the mouth? Although he licks his mother with the corners of his lips to make her regurgitate food for him, this is also a sign of submission and a sign of appeasement. The human who is licked on the face in this manner takes it to be a declaration of friendship.
As the puppy assimilates the rules of pack life more and more (between four and seven weeks), he applies the same communication codes with humans and follows the same dominant-submissive hierarchy.
At six weeks, however, the bond must be renewed. The battle is not over. Fear of man sets in. This reaction can already be sensed at twenty-five days when the young canine pulls back from an unknown hand.
De-socialization may occur. The game has not been won yet. This is when man must really understand psychology in order to win the dog over to him. Raising your voice is out of the question! Be careful not to make abrupt movements! The hand that made the first contact must now lavish caresses. The fate of the dog is in the hands of the owner. This is when, after distancing himself from humans, he will cease to have doubts about them. The dog is now between ten and twelve weeks old. His friendship with humans becomes unshakable.

Brigitte Bullard-Cordeau

Is Barking an Ordinary Cry?

Barking involves as many sounds as it represents messages to decipher. A young puppy whines for a multitude of reasons: he is cold, he is hungry, he is hurt, he is all alone, or he needs to defecate. Around his mother, to whom he constantly cries out for help, he sends out distress calls and, as if to vary his repertory, he mews. Sometimes, he howls a shrill cry and then growls with satisfaction!

As soon as he knows how to yelp, at less than eight days old, he makes noise, complains, cries and protests. Dogs know the word. The noise reaches its peak at nine days, but what a change by the next day! The young dog begins to bark for the first time.

The older he gets, the more he bays. He varies the tone by playing with the duration, frequency, volume and rhythm. Panting and teeth chattering are superimposed to make the classic ruff, ruff. Whining, growling, meowing, yelping, snarling, howling, coughing… what a repertory! Not to mention barking, which is the product of clever mixing of growling, howling and yelping.

This concert is not a motiveless act. It is not an ordinary cry or a threat, as one might believe. When the dog barks at the arrival of a stranger, both as a warning sign as well as to intimidate and to force himself not to be afraid, he has one desire: that other dogs come to his side as happens in the wild. As for the howling, this serves as a point of reference. At any rate, it is a highly contagious mode of expression. When a dog howls at death, winter or twilight, it is because he wants to be reassured. When another dog a few hundred meters away responds to his call, the dialogue is never-ending. The feeling of loneliness or calls for help are well understood by our canine friends.

In the company of his owner, the dog has other reasons to bark: to greet him when he opens the door, to invite him to play, because he is happy or when nothing in his dog life is going well. It's up to the owner to decipher his call.

Brigitte Bullard-Cordeau

Predatory Aggression

Predatory aggression is generally triggered by hunger. The dog pounces on his prey with his feet together, his tail and ears erect, his hackles raised and drops his two front legs on the prey. Then, he locks his jaws around him and shakes him vigorously, causing a fractured rachis. Predatory aggression is also observed in dogs that are not hungry. Such is the case of the dog that steals into the hen house and eats all the chickens, or the dog that kills cattle. These are psychological behaviors and there is no effective way to inhibit this type of aggression. From time to time, cases of predatory aggression against humans are reported. These predatory acts are committed by stray dogs organized in packs. Humans are considered to be prey because these dogs have not been socialized toward people. Sometimes companion dogs may display this type of predatory aggression toward toddlers who are not yet walking. The dogs in these cases have not had contact with children of this age.

Hierarchical Aggression

Hierarchical aggression occurs both between dogs and between dogs and humans. Hierarchical aggression is triggered in situations when the dog feels that his prerogatives as a leader are being challenged, either in the pack of dogs or in the dog-human pack. A dominant animal is an individual who ensures cohesion in the social group by inhibiting aggression by the other members of the pack. The dominant dog eats first, eats slowly and enjoys being watched by his subjects. He controls the occupation of territory and space, as well as the movement of his subjects. Consequently, he is often in a strategic place where he can monitor everything. He controls reproduction and oversees the sexual activity of the group. A dominant male or bitch may mate in front of the other members of the pack.

Within the human pack (the family, for example), this may be exacerbated in the presence of a same-sex owner. A subordinate dog, on the other hand, may not mate in front of the other dominant dogs, much less in front of the dominant owners. He will be inhibited in the presence of a same-sex owner. Dominant owners should not watch their animal mate. The dominant dog will mount his congeners, persons of the same sex, even cushions, in front of everybody. This is not a homosexual act, but an act of dominance. Any challenge to his prerogatives as the leader can be the source of hierarchical aggression involving a typical behavioral sequence (threat, bite and appeasement) that is directed at other dogs or humans.

Appeasement happens in the same way with humans as with dogs. Sometimes the dog will come over to lick the bitten limb held out to him by his owner and the owner then thinks that the dog has come to ask forgiveness. Frustration-induced aggression is triggered by frustrations such as hunger, pain, or prolonged physical contact initiated by a subordinate (such as the case of an owner who wants to pet or brush his dog). Territorial aggression is triggered when there is an invasion of the area of seclusion or the pack's territory. As for maternal aggression, the presence of puppies is a must in order for it to be triggered. However a toy, stuffed animal, even a slipper may also trigger it.

Fear-Induced Aggression

Fear-induced aggression occurs in situations where the dog is trapped and attempts to flee are impossible. He will then attack either the other dogs or humans, but there will be no threat phase. The attack is direct and unpredictable. Violent wounds are inflicted because he does not control his bite.

One of the phases (threat or appeasement), may also be left out as a result of a type of learning known as effective conditioning. Looking at the example of hierarchical aggression, dogs are known to manifest aggressive episodes when certain leader prerogatives are challenged.

At the beginning, the aggression sequence is complete, with all three phases. However, if the conflict repeats itself and the human-dog relationship is not modified, the dog will progressively alter his sequence of aggression. The owner's "flight" reaction after being bit becomes the element of reinforcement needed for the development of effective conditioning. The appeasement phase diminishes, then disappears. The intimidation phase will be modified and will become almost synchronous with the biting. Then it too will disappear. The bite becomes serious and unpredictable.

The dog has now become a dangerous animal.

Submission

The posture of submission stems from the ritualization of the urination process by the mother.

At the end of the meal, the mother turns the puppies over and grooms them. This same posture is also seen in adults. During a fight, the subordinate dog lies on his back, which serves to stop the aggression of the adversary. However, other forms of submission can also be observed such as the cry a puppy makes when he is grabbed by the skin of his neck. Pressure exerted in this region is associated with hierarchical fights.

The submissive position is a ritual. It has a cohesive function in the social group. It helps prevent attacks.

Some dogs are unable to acquire the ability to submit (absence of submissive posture) and are dangerous because they are very aggressive. And since they do not submit, the other dog becomes aggressive. Other signs of submission are also observed such as averting the eyes in an indirect look to avoid the eyes of the dominant dog, tail dropped low, lateral decubitus position with one hind leg lifted and flight. In a human-dog pack, the owner must learn to recognize the submissive posture of his dog because continuing to be aggressive toward the dog when the dog has already submitted may lead to behavioral problems.

Marking Territory

Marking behavior is common in all dogs, regardless of their sex or age. It is a means of communication that varies greatly depending on the social status of the dog. Developing communication systems is an absolute necessity, especially for social species like domestic carnivores. Marking is primarily accomplished by depositing urine or feces. It is both visual and olfactory because of the pheromones.

Olfactory communication uses chemical messages called pheromones. Pheromones are defined as hormones that transmit information between individuals of the same species. They trigger a behavioral or psychological response in the receiver. These substances are emitted by the anal glands, the perianal glands, the facial glands, the glands found in the interdigital spaces of the footpads and by the supra-caudal gland. They are also found in saliva, feces and especially in urine. These pheromones, especially those found in urine and feces, are released in social contexts such as with sexual and territorial behaviors. They serve as a means of communication and information exchange. Pheromones associated with defending territory are podalic and urinary in origin. They are released during the intimidation phase of territorial aggression. The dog scratches the ground with his fore legs and urinates on this spot by lifting his one of his hind legs.

When a subordinate dog smells a urine deposit left by a dominant dog, he tends to show signs of submission and urinate on the ground. The pheromones released in urine seem to convey hierarchical information. During a human-dog conflict there may be episodes when the dog urinates inside, which is actually a form of hierarchical urination. Dogs urinate in places that are strategic and of social importance (table legs, legs of the bed, front door, hallway, etc.). Some dogs will even defecate on a bed or the arm of the sofa, i.e. always in highly visible places. The feces is always very wet.

Sexual Behavior

The male dog reaches puberty somewhere between the age of seven to ten months, depending on his breed. Small breeds are more precocious than medium-sized dogs and even more so than large-sized breeds. The extremes on either end are six months and three years. With bitches, sexual maturity or puberty corresponds to the first heat, which occurs between six and twelve months. The bitch has two estrous cycles per year. The onset of estrous does not seem to depend on the season, but there is greater frequency in autumn and spring.

The dog will be "in heat" for approximately three weeks. Pro-estrous corresponds to the first half of the heat. During this period, the bitch is not receptive to mounting, even though she is attracting males. Owners may observe a swelling of the vulva and loss of blood. Estrous occurs during the second half. The bitch becomes agitated and agrees to be mounted. She is most likely to allow the male to mount her from the 10th to the 12th day. Ovulation occurs around the 11th or 12th day. It occurs spontaneously and is triggered by the release of the luteinizing hormone or LH. Some dogs, however, can still be impregnated two or more weeks after heat. The male's spermatozoids are highly resilient and fertilization can be achieved in a female mounted at the end of pro-estrous. Bitches always ovulate several times. If several births occur, the puppies could be from different fathers. Bitches are in heat for an especially long period of time - two to three weeks on average. Once her heat is over, the cycle continues with a phase called metoestrus. Metoestrus lasts approximately four months. Sometimes a pseudo-gestation is observed, accompanied by a change in mood, the production of milk, etc. Anoestrus follows, which is a period of rest. It lasts one to two months. The average cycle length is six months (though it can last up to ten to twelve months without necessarily indicating the presence of a disease). Thus, the bitch is in heat twice a year.

The male detects a female in season by the scent of her urine, which contains metabolites of estrogens. During the estrous cycle, the female actively seeks out the male. When the two meet up, they explore each other through smell. Often, invitations to play are observed. If the female is in her pro-estrous cycle, she will not stand still long enough. She moves, turns around, lies down, stands back up, sits and the male is unable to mount her. During estrous, however, she will stand still long enough for the male to mount her. It is easier for the male to mount the bitch in a familiar environment that is permeated with his scent. This is why the female usually comes to the male. A subordinate male or female may not mate in front of a dominant member. The dominant owner should never watch his male or female dog mate.

It is possible to prevent the female from going into heat through the use of hormonal contraceptives that temporarily suppress the cycle. The contraceptive can be administered either orally or through an injection. In either case, these products must be administered during a period of sexual quiescence, or anoestrus, which means two months before the estimated onset of the heat to be suppressed.

Contraception does have side effects. Among others, it may increase the risk of uterine infections. If the bitch is not intended for breeding, it is better to choose a more definitive solution, i.e. surgical sterilization through spaying. During this procedure, the bitch's ovaries are removed, which means she will no longer have a sexual cycle. It is advisable to spay before the onset of puberty in order to reduce the risks of genital and mammary diseases.

Feeding Behavior

Wild dogs devote a lot of time and energy to finding, chasing and capturing their prey. Their predatory behavior is motivated by hunger. The prey has the following characteristics: it is not aggressive, the dog has not been saturated with it and it is associated with the acquisition of food. The wild dog's diet is composed of small prey such as mice, lizards and insects. Sometimes, however, it may also include medium-sized prey such as rabbits and even large prey such as deer. Hunting is done either alone, in small groups or in packs.

In the case of domestic dogs, their diet must meet their needs for growth and maintenance, work and gestation based on their size, age, life style and physiological state (e.g. nursing dog).
In order to avoid possible hierarchical problems that could lead to biting, it is advisable to respect

the rules of training. The dog should eat after his owners or more than one hour before the owners dine. Owners should never give the dog food from the table. The dog's food dish should always be placed in the same spot in a room other than the one where the owners eat. The dog should be left alone when eating and should not be observed.

Coprophagy

Some puppies have the annoying habit of eating their own feces (coprophagy). This behavior should disappear by about the age of three to four months. If it persists, the cause needs to be determined. The natural attraction dogs have to their excrement and that of others is undeniable. Several etiologies explain why the dog eats his feces. Often this behavior stems from the problem of the dog not being house-trained. The owners punish the dog for relieving himself inside the house or in an inappropriate place. This punishment, especially if it is not meted out right when the act is committed, but after-the-fact once the owners return, will lead the dog to defecate more and more in the absence of his owners and then remove the evidence by eating his excrement. This behavior may also be caused when owners reinforce the attitude in their puppies. When they see that the puppy is eating his excrement, they rush over to stop him and clean it up. It then becomes a competition between the two and the dog consumes his excrement to ensure that it is not taken from him.

Sometimes, if the dog does not digest his food properly, food odors may linger in the feces, which may cause the dog to eat his excrement. Reference has also been made to the aromatic substances added to industrial food to make it more appetizing. These substances pass through undigested into the fecal matter and cause dogs to consume their excrement or that of others. Inappropriate defecation should be ignored. Do not rub the dog's nose in the excrement (since it is not repugnant to him anyway) and above all, do not clean up the excrement in front of the dog because in so doing, a crouched position is assumed, which is an invitation to play.

Behavioral Problems

Behavioral problems are frequently observed in dogs. Some of these problems can be prevented from the time when the puppy is purchased and owners can avoid others through proper training.

Some problems appear as early as infancy or adolescence such as phobias, i.e. noise, car, people phobias. These dogs will not be able to adapt to life in an urban environment. It will be very difficult, even impossible, to take them out. If they are not put on a leash, they might run away and be run over. Other dogs pull on the leash in order to go back, some dig in their paws to slow down only to then rush forward and some bound forward in a series of leaps. Still others, who are not house-trained, might wait to come back inside the house to relieve themselves even if they have been outside for several hours. They can only relieve themselves in a calm environment that they control. Often, they are afraid of people and may attack out of fear.

Expose the Puppy to Different Kinds of Sounds and Experiences early on

A puppy's brain is not fully developed at birth, but continues to develop for several weeks. Consequently, the puppy needs to be raised in a stimulating environment with a variety of people and sounds. If the puppy is raised in the country, the environment often lacks noise and different people and the dog will not be able to handle city noises and people later on. Some breeders understand this concept and they expose their puppies to various noises and have them fed and handled by different people. In general, however, a puppy purchased from a breeder for life in an urban setting will be unable to manage this new environment.

Although the breeder is partly responsible for this, the future owner may also contribute if he is not knowledgeable about training puppies. Very early on, the puppy should have many experiences: walks along the street, trips in cars, contact with other animals and people and different noises. Currently, vaccinations are available that protect the puppy against early-age diseases, which means the puppy can be taken out as early as eight weeks old, though this is nonetheless not advised.

Other dogs are insufferable. They cannot stay still in one place, they jump, run after everything that moves (joggers, bikes, birds, leaves) and play constantly. They are tireless and often cause damage in the home. They bite all the time, especially if the owners allow this, thinking that the puppy is "teething."

These puppies, in fact, are either born to mothers who are too young and do not know how to raise their puppies, or they are born in such a large litter that the mother is so overburdened that she cannot raise her puppies properly. In other instances, the puppies have been separated from their mother too soon (younger than eight weeks), purchased too young, or their mother is deceased. These puppies have not learned to control motor functions or to control their jaws. They are still rough and lack self-control.

Separation Anxiety

Another disorder, for which professional advice is frequently sought, is separation anxiety. The dogs are brought in because they have caused a lot of destruction, urinated or defecated all over the house or wherever the dog has access, or even because the dog cries when left alone (barking, howling, whimpering). These behaviors are caused by attachment, even over-attachment, to a person. Attachment is a learned mechanism that allows the subject to identify the mother as the object of attachment and a reassuring point of reference. Attachment is absolutely necessary for proper imprinting and for the healthy psychological, motor, cognitive and social development of the animal. During the neonatal period, the bitch bonds with her young ones and anything that stands in the way of contact between her and her puppies will cause great distress. During the transition period, the young pups bond to their mother. She alone will be capable of pacifying her puppies. She becomes the reassuring point of reference around which exploratory behavior develops. Attachment is therefore reciprocal. Any attempt to prevent contact causes a state of distress, expressed by vocal sounds and a state of agitation both on the part of the mother and the puppies. But where there is attachment, there must be detachment. This is an important event in the socialization process of the puppy. Once the male puppies reach the age of four to five months, the mother no longer tolerates contact with them and forbids them from approaching her. They must sleep elsewhere. This episode causes the puppies to be marginalized. As for young females, the process is slower and begins during their first or second heat.

The Object of Attachment

The dog in fact goes from exclusive attachment to its mother to attachment to the social group. When the puppy is brought into a home, he bonds to a person and vice versa. He generally becomes attached to the person who feeds him, pets him, etc. Around the age of four to five months, owners should encourage detachment. If this is not done, which is almost always the case, the puppy will fall into a state of panic and distress as soon as he is separated from the person to whom he is attached. He looks for the person and in the process causes damage, sometimes mass destruction coupled with emotional urinating and defecating, even howling so loud that it causes the neighbors to complain. The dog must learn to be detached from his owners and the only way to accomplish this is to not respond to his invitations to play and not pet him when he begs for it. He should be pushed away. It is up to the owners to take the initiative in the relationship. The dog should also be given a place to sleep that is not in the bedroom.

DEPRESSION IN DOGS

Some behavioral problems can be described as a state of depression. Depression is defined as an emotional disorder characterized by insomnia, psychomotor inhibition and withdrawal. The animal looses its ability to adapt to variations in its environment. The depression can be acute or chronic. On a behavioral level, acute depression is marked by inhibited action or apathy (inhibition of exploratory behavior). The dog is indifferent to his environment and loses interest in his normal activities. He eats less, or does not eat at all (anorexia) and sleeps a lot (hypersomnia).

There are many causes such as a violent attack (traffic accident), or the abrupt loss of a social-emotional reference point (abandonment, death of an owner or even another animal to whom he was attached). Sometimes, puppies prematurely rejected by their mother do not later enjoy a strong bond with either a person or another animal. In chronic depression, the dog displays sudden emotional responses when exposed to very intense stimuli.

Behavioral functions are altered. The dog loses interest in all his normal activities (play, social relationships). Problems sleeping and eliminating inside are reported. Chronic depression can evolve from untreated acute depression or it may also be the result of endogenous disorders such as endocrine problems (malfunction of the thyroid or adrenal gland), or even diencephalon tumors.

Biting

The number one reason why dogs are brought in for behavioral problems is biting. Like all social mammals, dogs organize their pack life around certain rules of hierarchy (access to food, control of territory and reproduction). During puberty, the dog tries to position himself within the human pack. He asserts his dominance and defends his hierarchical prerogatives. Conflicts and aggression, even urinating in the house (hierarchical urination) arise if any of his prerogatives are taken away. The prerogatives of a dominant dog are as follows: the dominant dog eats first, eats slowly and enjoys being watched by his subjects. He controls how the territory and space are occupied, as well as the movement of other members of the pack. Therefore, he is often in a strategic place (bedroom, landing, hallway) where he can monitor everything. He controls reproduction and sexual activity of the group. Any challenge to the dominant dog's prerogatives can be the source of hierarchical trouble, expressed by sequences of aggression including threats (growling) and biting, both within the dog pack and within the human pack.

Behavioral problems can be easily avoided. In order to prevent a certain number of problems, it is advisable to carefully choose the breed. Go to the breeder, ask to see the mother and the other puppies and the way they were raised, fed, etc. Do not buy a dog under ten weeks old and find out whether the puppy was separated from its mother too soon (before two months). When the puppy is brought into its future family, a certain number of rules need to be followed in order to live in perfect harmony.

Instinct and Intelligence

The concept of instinct has greatly evolved. Behavioral development requires a complex interaction of genetic predisposition and experience. To say that an animal behaves instinctively may be erroneous because this implies that behavior was not influenced by experience.

It is difficult to conclude that a form of behavior was mainly determined by genetics and that it cannot be shaped by experience. Once the principle has been established that animals can be guided by something other than instinct, the next step is to say that they are intelligent. Are they indeed truly intelligent? Is the dog who opens the door by pushing on the latch intelligent, or the dog who looks for his leash when he wants to go out, or the dog who brings his ball in order to play? There is no question that dogs do amazing things, but all these successful tricks are learned behaviors. Compare two puppies raised differently, for example. One has a mother who took care of him and was exposed to a lot of sensory stimuli and the other was raised without a mother or with a bad mother and without sensory stimuli. The first dog will be more "intelligent" than the second. In fact, the first dog will be better able to adapt to new situations because the development of his interneurons was more highly stimulated during the critical period, which in dogs, is between three and sixteen weeks. The dog who brings his ball over to play or his leash to go out, is a dog who considers himself to be dominant within the human-dog pack. He initiates contact, games, etc. This is not intelligence, but hierarchy.

Man - a Dog's Best Friend

Like Owner, Like Dog

In the eighties, a French weekly for professional veterinarians took this saying, turned it around and used it for a humor column entitled "Like Dog, Like Owner." Pictured in the photograph was a nervous, twitching dog standing alongside his equally nervous owner with a few tics of his own. Also pictured were an enormous hairball of a dog standing next to a tubby man, and a small, aggressive little pooch at the feet of a most unpleasant shrew. They were all captured in this thumbnail sketch and every veterinarian saw in this picture, with a sense of mischievousness or spite, some of his clients, or even himself with his own dog.

The Advantages of Owning a Dog

"There is a non-negligible educational factor in holding a familiar animal, which becomes increasingly important as urban man strays further and further from nature".

Konrad Lorenz
Nobel Prize 1973

While dogs make wonderful companions in an increasingly urbanized society, they do, however, present some constraints that humans must assume. The following are some of the positive aspects of having a dog in the house:
- added social stimulation within the family. Talking about the dog, taking care of him, playing with him and being interested in him are all positive for the group;
- companionship from the dog, which is especially important for persons living alone;
- relaxation that comes from walking the dog, playing with him and petting him (some studies have even shown that a person's heart rate decreases when petting a dog);
- the sense of protection that the entire family feels in the presence of a dog who guards the house;
- friendship and sense of companionship, even emotional attachment that is sometimes very intense and that bonds the owner with his faithful four-legged friend;
- the responsibility that comes with buying or adopting a puppy;
- the undeniable support role a dog plays in raising children. Moreover, dogs are widely used by psychologists to assist in reintegrating problem or delinquent children or adolescents;
- the understanding and sympathy from this animal, which at times are apt to transform human beings;
- the feeling of value and achievement that some people have when they are accompanied by their dog and can show him off;
- facilitation of social contacts in a society in which people hardly ever talk to strangers and in which walking one's dog provides a way to talk with other people walking their dogs;
- finally, the feeling of prestige that some people have in owning a certain breed of dog. Objectively speaking, however, it is questionable whether this is actually a positive virtue since a dog is not like a sports car.

Constraints and Obligations

Having a dog in the home is not only positive and serious thought should be given to the matter before making the decision to acquire one. It is necessary to be aware of the constraints linked to the presence of a dog:

- limited freedom since the dog needs to be cared for, even on weekends and vacations (many people realize this too late and abandon their animal during this period!);
- the financial costs involved in owning an animal that has to be identified, vaccinated, dewormed, maintained, fed and cared for when he is sick;
- the time that must be devoted to him;
- the notions of hygiene that must be adopted and especially imposed on the dog in a family environment;
- the problems with neighbors that are so classic that every dog owner is confronted with one at least once in his life;
- the family problems that arise during separation, death, divorce or sometimes a simple illness;
- the risks to others in that sometimes other people are afraid of dogs, or conversely, they pet the dog without taking the proper precautions and the dog may bite even if he is not mean, but simply because he was startled.

THE RISKS FOR MAN

Like any living being, including humans, dogs may present certain risks for man, for example, the risk of bite wounds or the risk of catching a disease transmitted by dogs. This, however, is rare.

Risk of being bitten

A dog's mouth serves as a means of expression, but it is also his only means of defense. Consequently, any dog that feels threatened or afraid is apt to bite, even if he is the nicest dog in the world under other circumstances. Therefore, owners need to take the basic precautions with their dogs, especially in the presence of unknown children, who, through no fault of either their own or the dog, may startle the dog, causing him to give a little bite without intending to do harm. The problems that exist in urban settings and certain cities due to the increase in populations of large, ferocious dogs or dogs originally intended for combat (pit bull terriers, Boer bull, etc.) cannot be ignored. In this respect, however, it is important to make the public understand that the dog itself, no matter what breed, is not the problem. Rather, the problem is the use that these dogs are being trained for by ill-intentioned owners. This is what needs to be curbed, even penalized. No matter what health laws are involved, a dog that bites should be placed under health surveillance by a veterinarian for two weeks.

Risk of zoonoses

By definition, zoonoses are infectious or parasitical diseases that can be transmitted from animals to humans. They may involve bacteria, viruses, fungi or parasites. It is important to know them because of their health implications. The dog's mouth is a carrier of *Pasteurella* (bacteria). When the dog bites, these bacteria will infect the wound and if the wound is deep enough, they will cause severe and painful inflammation, which will turn into an abscess with an acute ganglionic reaction. Because of this risk, which is associated with the now all-but-nonexistent risk of rabies, a person who has been bitten should clean the wound(s) with soap and water, followed by a generous dose of antiseptic. Follow-up treatment with antibiotics is advised as a precaution. Much more rare, though still possible, is the risk of transmission of *Staphylococcus* and other diseases such as leptospirosis (every dog should be vaccinated against this), tuberculosis, brucellosis and even leishmaniasis in the Mediterranean region.

Although benign, tenia can be transmitted from a dog to a person. Tinea is a skin disease linked to the growth of a microscopic fungus, which causes non-itching, circular lesions that require a lengthy and painful treatment for both dog and owner.

Finally, the possibility of transmitting digestive parasites to humans through dog excrement should also be noted. This is why dogs should be strictly forbidden from areas where young children play (sandboxes, for example).

Profile of an Owner

It is therefore incumbent upon a future owner to take all these elements – positive and negative – into consideration before making a decision. Moreover, it is interesting to note that there are many ways to "categorize" an individual's relationship with a dog, taking into account sociological and psychological factors. One such classification, for example, sets forth four types of possible attitudes towards a companion animal:

- the humanist, who has great interest in and strong emotional attachment to companion animals;
- the moralist, whose main concern is how well or poorly animals are treated and reacts violently to animal cruelty or exploitation;
- the utilitarian, who is especially interested in the material and practical value of the animal;
- the negativist, who rejects animals out of fear and disgust.

Parallel to this categorization, which could seem somewhat technical and cursory, another classification, or rather grouping, of dog owners based on more detailed analysis of human typology, was recently proposed following an international investigation conducted by a private firm in the companion animal industry. The approach was defined according to a twofold theme:
- animal-object (the dog can serve a purely material purpose, or on the contrary, may be considered as a means for man to reach a certain ideal);
- animal-socializer (the dog in this case enables the person to affirm himself, or ensures a certain level of social integration).

THE DEATH OF YOUR DOG

In general, a dog does not live as long as his owner does, so you should be prepared to shed a few tears when he dies (not to mention the great sorrow children feel when faced with the death of a dog!).

In the best case scenario, death will be sudden. Sometimes, however, in the case of a painful disease, you must summon up the courage to end the dog's suffering by placing your companion in the hands of a veterinarian who will inoculate him with a substance that will slowly put him to sleep definitively, thereby sparing him further pain and fright.

With respect to death, some technical details need to be considered.

It is mandatory to officially declare the death in the cases of dogs registered in the LOF – Livre officiel français (Official French Book), dogs obtained from an animal protection society or those who are used by businesses as guard dogs. Note that beyond sentimental value, dogs who have market value (show dogs, rescue dogs, etc.) may, under certain circumstances, have a life insurance policy with an insurance company.

Of course, it is strictly forbidden to dispose of the dog's remains in a public place or in the household trash (Health department regulation, article 98).

On the other hand, depending on a person's convictions and financial resources, several options are available.
- Bury the dog in the yard, but in order to comply with the sanitary regulations of this allowance, the dog must be buried at least 35m (115 ft) away from homes, wells or springs and must be covered with quick lime and at least 35cm (14 in) of soil.
- Bury the dog in a pet cemetery. Prices vary widely for these cemeteries (which are becoming more and more numerous). A full range of services are offered: cement or marble tombstones, vaults, caskets, grave markers, etc. One of the most famous is L'île des Ravageurs in Asnières (France), which is a listed site where more than 100,000 dogs are buried (over 40,000 tombs) including Rin Tin Tin, the dogs of Sacha Guitry and Courteline, and Barry, the famous rescue dog of the Saint-Bernard Hospice.
- In the countryside, or areas with fewer than 10,000 inhabitants, the body can be taken to the city pound, the veterinarian or a knacker (though it is difficult for most owners to even bear the thought of industrial processing to extract the fat and skin). In Paris, there is a prefecture pound service under the police department that takes care of removing the body from the home.
- Use of cremation, which offers the possibility of recuperating the ashes in an urn if individual incineration was requested.
While there is no shame in feeling great sorrow at the death of the animal, there are various solutions available that allow everyone to part with the animal in a fitting manner, without nevertheless going to extremes and erecting monuments!

Eight different groups of owners were highlighted and defined based on the dog's role: "the entertainer", the "old friend", the "fashion plate", the "child's pal", the "guardian of material goods", the "wild thing", the "clear conscience", and the "symbol of established order".

Another, not so colorful, but undoubtedly more realistic study resulted in a quantitative grouping of dog owners based on their behavior vis-à-vis the animal. Starting from the realm of the rational and ending on an emotional note, the results were as follows:
- 18% of owners claim they are totally indifferent to the current and future life of their dog;
- 15% feel that the dog only serves a strictly utilitarian purpose;
- 18%, taking into account only the "health" aspect, consider that the good health of their dog is of utmost importance;
- 8% support having a dog "in his place", in good health, living with the family, but respected as a dog without any anthropomorphism;
- 12% see their dog as an important element in their self-development;
- 14% truly love their dog and consider the dog to be equal to any human member of the family;
- finally, 18% confess that they truly adore their dog and place the dog higher than humans on their emotional value scale.

This study shows that more than one out of every three dog owners places himself in a category of extreme behavior, from ultra-rationalism to hyper-affectivity, in other words, at the two extremes of what in reality should be the place of the dog in the mind and life of someone.
Being a good owner undoubtedly lies somewhere in between these two extremes. The owner must integrate the rules of behavior, hygiene, lifestyle, nutrition and good health and respect the animal in the role he has been given on this planet. A dog is dog and not a little person. While he lacks the words and nature of humans, he does, however, have other means of expression that are just as effective. Humans must adopt an attitude towards the dog that the dog understands and above all, should not treat the dog as a child. He who has understood that the wealth of life on this earth comes from respecting the diversity of animal species, will find happiness when his dog looks at him, without his dog feeling the need to share his owners' bed!

WHERE WOULD MAN BE WITHOUT DOGS?

Where would man be without dogs? One dares not even consider the possibility. Dogs being man's best friend, man would have no more friends. The blind would grope along in vain, unable to cross the street; the lost traveler would perish in the snow on the slopes of Mount Saint Bernard without the rum-filled casket. We would no longer see dog acts at the circus, read the paper or count to twelve. The children, in their disoriented state, would be forced to tie their saucepans to the tail of the Bengal tiger; the poor cousins would shamelessly enter the villas of their rich cousins. There would be no more wholesome forms of entertainment, no more peace, no more police, no more joking, no more friendship.

Alexandre Vialatte
Chronique of dog
In Et, c'est ainsi qu'Allah est grand; Julliard, Paris, Ed.

Dogs in Everyday Life

Choosing a Puppy

Dogs have always symbolized the notion of loyalty to man. For many people, therefore, owning a dog means owning a domestic animal par excellence. Upon making the carefully thought out decision to acquire a dog, several principles need to be respected.

Which Breed?

Living with a dog in your home is not something to be taken lightly. On average, dogs live for more than ten years. Therefore, you must not only choose a good dog, but you must also learn to live with him.

It is true that certain breeds are known for their dominant trait – German shepherds are obedient, Labrador retrievers like children, Greyhounds are independent, etc. In spite of their innate character, however, dogs cannot be classified in such a categorical manner. Moreover, reputations for being hardy or fragile should be carefully scrutinized. Exceptions are always possible - from the Chihuahua, which is reputed to be fragile, to the fox terrier, which is said to be resilient.

In reality, it is best to choose a breed based on the role you want the dog to play in relationship to his weight and height. Indeed, choosing a Yorkshire as a guard dog would be just as inappropriate as keeping a German mastiff or a Pyrenees shepherd shut up inside an apartment all day. Generally speaking, although smaller breeds may be more high strung, they require less living space than medium breeds. Large and giant breeds always require a lot of living space.

The cost of the young dog will also be a factor in the owner's choice. Cost varies according to the pedigree and the relative rarity of the breed. Some people in fact clearly cannot afford to adopt a purebred and will choose instead a "mongrel" whose weight and height will be difficult to predict when acquired as a puppy. No matter which breed is chosen, always bear in mind that each dog needs attention from its owner throughout the entire day.

Dog or Bitch?

Bitches are generally calmer and gentler than dogs. Their standard is also smaller than that of dogs. Another advantage is that they receive preferential treatment from males in any encounter. Males often become mellower and less aggressive in their presence.

The main disadvantage, however, is the biannual period of heat, which generally occurs in spring and fall. They always attract groups of males and their tenacious desire. However, an ovariohysterectomy surgery, even before the first heat, can remedy this and prevent the bitch from becoming pregnant before the owner wants her to. The decision, however, is irreversible!

Males, who are known to run off more than bitches, may discover that their nature changes completely in the presence of a bitch in heat. A normally calm dog may act nervous and aggressive and may provoke fights with his congeners that are sometimes quite dramatic.

Owning several dogs may relieve the boredom of a dog living alone. In this case, you need to pay a lot of attention to each one and have a lot of space! Owning more than two dogs seems to be difficult – you have to be very strong to become the leader of a pack of three or four dogs. Having a couple – male and female – is a good solution, but you have to think about how easy it will be to place future puppies in homes and you practically have to have a breeder's mentality!

Having two males should be prohibited. As soon as they reach sexual maturity, they will quickly become rivals. On the other hand, two females generally get along well together.

In any case, the owner needs to be aware of the difficulties that may arise from having two dogs.

Where to Acquire a Dog

There are several options for the potential buyer. From the country market in particular, to specialized pet stores and breeders, the choices seem to be abundant. A few options, however, can be ruled out. At the markets, there is no guarantee in terms of the dog's history and it will be difficult to find the vendors again if the dog has any defects.

Pet stores should also be avoided for the most part. The puppies sold here are not always bred in the most scrupulous manner and may therefore have some health problems. Furthermore, their living conditions are often mediocre. The cages are sometimes ill adapted and at any rate, the puppies are not taken out and do not follow the normal behavioral growth patterns that the rest of their congeners do. They will most likely experience behavioral problems in the future. However, some pet stores now offer guarantees and can provide official proof of the original breeder of the puppy.

If the breed does not matter, or if the fact that the puppy does not have papers is not a problem, it is always possible to contact a neighbor whose bitch is pregnant and keep one of the puppies.

If a specific breed is chosen, however, it is preferable to obtain the dog from a breeder. A list of breeders can be furnished by dog associations, veterinarians and purebred clubs.

What is the Ideal Age?

A good breeder must know all of his breeding stock. Verify the living conditions of the puppies. The more they are in contact with humans of all ages, the fewer problems they will have with children. This holds true for other animals as well.

During the first visit to the breeder, it is possible that he will not have any puppies available, which proves he is a reliable breeder. His breeding bitches are not constantly pregnant and even if there are visible litters, it means the puppies are not old enough yet.

The puppy must go through certain stages before he can be placed with a family. By and large, he needs to have lived long enough with his mother who teaches him to assume his identity as a dog. Contact with humans is also important. This can happen as soon as the mother accepts the presence of a foreign person and the puppies leave the maternal nest. The puppy will be about seven weeks old by the time he reaches the end of these two stages. However, he is still fragile and it is possible that the breeder will not agree to sell his puppies until they reach a minimum of three months old. Buying a puppy less than six weeks old is a mistake.

TRUE RESPECT FOR A DOG

Dogs are living creatures, a source of interplay and coaction with their owners and their entourage.

Living harmoniously with one's dog entails getting to know him, training him, loving him and respecting him.

Knowing him means learning his innate character and being able to predict his reactions.

Training him means showing him his territory where he can grow and develop and what he does and, especially, does not have the right to do.

Loving him means being committed to providing him with care and love throughout his life.

Respecting him means taking into consideration his animality.

A dog is not a person. He does not live like a person, he does not eat like a person and he has his own nutritional needs.

A proper diet for a dog should account for specific needs based on his size/breed, age, how active he is, and his physiological stage. The anthropomorphism that occurs when human characteristics and/or feeding or other behaviors are attributed to dogs can only be harmful to the dog's health and/or his ability to fit in well with people and society.

**The dog in his place,
everything in its place,
and only in its place.**

*Milette Dujardin
Royal Canin France*

Which Puppy in the Litter?

Two aspects are interesting to explore: the health and the character of the dog. The puppy must have his papers (covering contract, birth certificate), his vaccination card, tattoo card and a bill of sale. All these papers guarantee the prior history and good health of the puppy and allow you to register the puppy in the book of origins.

The breeder should show all the puppies from the same litter and their mother. The mother may be a bit thin and have over-sensitive breasts, but she should still look content and well cared for and seem affectionate. As for the puppy, he should not have an unpleasant odor. His feces should be well shaped without any traces of blood. His eyes should be bright and his nose clean. His ears should be clean and his coat should not be dull or brittle. In addition, he should be happy and playful, both with other puppies in the litter and with humans. After acquiring the puppy, it is best to consult a veterinarian, who can confirm that the puppy is in good health and can perform what is called a "purchase consultation". Furthermore, you should check to see what kind of living space the puppy has. The thought of moving to a new dwelling place is less than inviting to a puppy, but if he was in a confined space before, with no possibility of going out, it will be even more difficult for him to adapt to his new environment.

Choosing from all the dogs present and in good health can sometimes be difficult. The best method is to conduct the temperament test developed by an American ethologist named Campbell. The test should be performed on puppies at the age of seven weeks. Before seven weeks, the puppy is too influenced by his mother and after seven weeks, he goes through a period of emotional fragility.

The tests should be carried out in an enclosed and calm space that is unfamiliar to the puppy. The person conducting the test should be neutral and consequently, should not show joy, anger or irritation during the test.

CAMPBELL TESTS

The Campbell tests help determine the main personality traits of the puppy. Bear in mind, however, that even if innate traits are dominant, the new owner can modify them through the way in which he cares for the dog. He can, in effect, reinforce certain personality traits and discourage others.

Attraction test

This test can be performed with a puppy at about seven weeks old.

After carefully placing the puppy on the ground, step back a few meters, clap your hands softly and observe the behavior of the animal:

1. He immediately runs to you with his tail held high, jumps on you and licks your hands.
2. He immediately runs to you with his tail held high and scratches your hands with his paws.
3. He immediately runs to you, wagging his tail.
4. He comes hesitantly with his tail down.
5. He does not come.

Test to see how well the puppy accepts domination

A person unknown to the puppy should perform this test.

With the puppy lying in a sphinx position, pet him, applying pressure to his head and back:

1. He struggles by scratching, turns over, growls and bites.
2. He struggles and turns over to scratch you.
3. He struggles at first and then calms down and licks your hands.
4. He turns over onto his back and licks your hands.
5. He moves away.

Test for ability to follow

This test should be performed on one puppy at a time without using your voice.

Stand up and move slowly away, staying within view of the puppy:

1. He follows you immediately with his tail held high, biting at your feet.
2. He does the same without biting.
3. He follows you immediately with his tail down.
4. He follows you hesitantly with his tail down.
5. He does not follow you and moves away.

Standing position test

A person unknown to the puppy should perform this test.

Place your hands under the chest of the puppy and stand him up. Hold him in this position for 30 seconds:

1. He struggles forcefully, growls and bites.
2. He struggles forcefully.
3. He struggles at first and then calms down and licks your hand.
4. He does not struggle and licks your hands.
5. He does not struggle

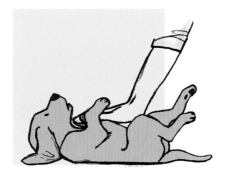

Test to see how well the puppy accepts constraint

A person unknown to the puppy should perform this test.

Lay the puppy on his back and hold him in this position for 30 seconds by placing your hand on his chest:

1. He struggles forcefully and bites.
2. He struggles until he is free.
3. He struggles at first and then calms down.
4. He does not struggle and licks your hand.
5. He does not struggle

RESULTS

Majority of answers are 1:
dominant-aggressive. Not recommended as a pet. Could be a good work or guard dog if properly trained.

Majority of answers are 2:
headstrong. Work dog that requires strict training.

Majority of answers are 3:
stable and adaptable.

Majority of answers are 4:
submissive. Animal ill-suited for work.

Majority of answers are 5:
inhibited. Poorly socialized dog, unpredictable.

The results may appear to be contradictory. If so, it advisable to redo the tests as the setting may not have been exactly right (puppy too young, meals, stress, sleep, etc.).

UNDERSTANDING YOUR DOG BETTER IN ORDER TO BETTER LIVE WITH YOUR DOG

When it comes to training a dog, it is often said, "You have to train the owner before you can train the dog". As far as I am concerned, I believe you have to be sure to inform the owner and teach him how his dog works and what the dog's possible reactions may be in a given situation so as to enable him to anticipate and prevent any negative action. He must also be taught to communicate with his dog, to understand his dog and to make himself understood by his dog. Most problems, even conflicts, stem from a lack of understanding and reciprocal ignorance of the rules and the social behavior of the other species. Owners and dogs must learn to live together.

The owner therefore will have to invent a veritable language made up of signals that his dog understands.

Domestic training of the dog cannot begin until this communication code has been established. The goal of this domestic training is to define the hierarchical position of the dog and the house rules by which he must absolutely abide in his new "domestic pack".

Very early on, his motivation for an object (ball or tube) needs to be developed. This object will be very useful later on during the various learning phases.

At the beginning, it is more a question of discipline than obedience. The rules are laid down: no food at the table, access to certain rooms forbidden, and choice of zones where the dog may relieve himself.

Using the object motivation, you can develop and quickly achieve through play a certain degree of discipline: heel, sit and down commands, recall, fetch, etc.

Once the dog has mastered basic discipline (which does not occur before eight months), you can then teach him obedience exercises such as heeling with or without a leash, changing direction, changing pace, positions (stand, down, sit), staying, recall (very important), wearing a muzzle in the case of large dogs (if need be) and group work to develop sociability towards people and other dogs.

In order to maintain balance, dogs need authority as a point of reference. Nonetheless, while the dog should obey you, he should not fear you. Not submission and not excessive rigor, which should be banished, but freely granted obedience. It is necessary to establish a climate of trust that encourages positive growth of the owner/dog relationship. This will help the dog to overcome his natural apprehensions in any circumstance.

Certain rules must therefore be respected:
- Maintain a consistent attitude, always react in the same way in a given situation. This will enable the dog to quickly discern what he is and is not allowed to do.
An inconsistent attitude = lack of understanding and defiance.

- Since dogs have a keen sense of equity, you will merit and win their trust, the basic foundation for all communication, through an attitude of fairness.

- Know how to display your feelings. Accentuate the "yes" if the dog has performed well and use a crisp, authoritarian "no" if the dog has done something wrong. The dog will soon learn to gage the satisfaction or discontent of his owner.

- Be patient and above all, very attentive, and know how to detect fatigue, excitement, questioning or fear. This will help you anticipate and avoid incidents.

- Finally, act like a good "pack leader" with all the authority and responsibility that entails.

These are a few pieces of advice that should be given to dog owners. At the same time owners should be reminded that first and foremost, the dog should be a source of pleasure and joy in the life of the owner. The owners should be able to appreciate the dog's company, and not simply put up with it, which sadly, is all too often the case.

J.-P. Petitdidier, Éducation du chien education of dog and owner, SFC, Paris, 1977.

The Dog at Home

Whether it is an adult dog or a puppy newly separated from his mother, certain rules must be followed from the very start. The dog is part of our day-to-day lives. He is undeniably a plus. But he can also be a true source of problems. This is why adopting a dog is not something to be taken lightly. Good training will prevent a lot of trouble.

The Basic Rules to Follow

First of all, as soon as the dog arrives, he needs time to become acquainted with his new home. He will explore the members of the family and the environment in which he will live from here on out. In general, one or two days are required for this adaptation. He will quickly choose the places where he feels most comfortable. However, he should not be allowed to do anything he pleases on the pretext that he is young, or if he is older, that he needs to get his bearings. The dog in fact quickly learns the difference between what is and is not permissible. For example, if he is allowed to lie on the sofa or bed at the beginning, it will be difficult, practically impossible, to dislodge him when the little fur ball turns into a huge, sixty-kilogram dog. Do not think that it is any different with a little Yorkshire or a Dachshund. They may be small, but they can cause considerable damage in a short period of time.

This is the reason why it is important to show the dog who the master of the home is by forbidding him from jumping up on beds and by giving him his own toys. You should also choose a spot where he will eat and forbid him from begging for food. Furthermore, he should eat after his owners, as happens in the pack when the leader eats first. He must also have his own place to sleep - a rug or a crate – that is located away from doors and windows so that he does not have the impression that he is controlling the comings and goings in the house.

These simple few rules will help restore the dog back to his rightful place as a pack animal. He must understand that he is subordinate and that you are dominant. It is stability within the hierarchy that allows the dog to find balance.

This rule holds true for all dogs, no matter what their size. It prevents a dachshund from becoming the household tyrant and baring his teeth whenever someone approaches his sofa or biting the calves of visitors passing through. What is important, is to always maintain consistent behavior. Do not allow the dog to do something one day that is normally forbidden. You must be firm, without being excessively so. This is how the relationship of trust established between the dog and his owner is preserved over time.

In order to establish his authority, the owner should start training his puppy by the age of three months. Choose simple commands at first, using simple words.

IDENTIFYING THE DOG

Given the rising population and the fact that people are more mobile, which increases the risk of losing a domestic animal, all dogs should be properly identified so that they can be reunited with their owner as quickly as possible.

Tatooing

A good example is France, where any carnivore whose ownership is transferred, either free-of-charge or at a price, must be tattooed. This regulation does not apply so much to breeders of purebreds because they are required to have already identified the puppies when they register the dogs in the Book of Origins.

For other dogs, tattooing is not yet mandatory, except in départements (counties) infected with rabies, the list of which varies each year. Unfortunately, this means that some owners choose not to spend the money on a means of identification that is nevertheless one of the most useful. Note, however, that a dog left at a day care or kennel for more than two weeks must by law be identified.

Only a veterinarian or a tattooer certified by the Ministry of Agriculture can give a tattoo. Applications for certification are first sent to the Société centrale canine - SCC (Central Dog Association) and then forwarded to the Ministry of Agriculture and are renewed every two years. The tattoo is placed on the ear or the inner flank. The dog's tattoo card is then registered in the central database of the SCC and can be accessed by veterinarians via Internet, which enables them to quickly locate the owner of a lost dog.

Electronic identification

Since tattooing is not always reliable (it can be falsified or rendered illegible as it deteriorates over time), a new identification system, which entails implanting an electronic microchip under the skin by means of a simple syringe, is being used more and more frequently in Europe. The electronic chip, called a "transponder", can then be read from a distance (10 - 20 cm) (4-8 in) by a "scanner", a transmitter-receiver device that picks up radio waves carrying an individual numeric code and sends it to a reader device. Implemented in 1989 for the major international dog-sled races, this system, called "Indexel" is already being used to permanently identify several million dogs in various European countries. This new system is indelible, impossible to falsify, painless and passive and should

quickly become widespread throughout the world. On January 13, 1996, an international standard was approved by the ISO (International Organization for Standardization), which was ratified by the national standardization bodies on March 7, 1996. Two standards (ISO 11784 and ISO 11785) govern the implanted chips and the reading of these chips, respectively. Consequently, each dog has an identification number that is unique throughout the world. This identification system is already mandatory when entering countries such as Norway, Sweden, United Kingdom, or New Zealand. Future generations of these chips will allow for information to be stored and read in the same way, including information on the owner's address, the dog's vaccination records and any treatment that the dog may be undergoing for a chronic disease.

René Bailly
Veterinarian
Chairman, French National Union of
Veterinary Practitioners

ELECTRONIC IDENTIFICATION OF THE DOG:
The process by which an "electronic chip" or transponder, carrying a unique numeric code is implanted under the skin of an animal just under the cutaneous and connective tissue layers is called electronic animal identification or radio frequency identification.
The implanted transponder then allows the animal to be identified by a reading device.

THE INJECTION:
The injection is made with a trocar that contains the transponder and an ejector that helps push the chip under the skin.

THE TRANSPONDER (OR ELECTRONIC CHIP):
This is an electronic device contained in a biocompatible capsule. This device is capable of storing and providing information on demand, in particular, a numeric code that serves to individually identify the animal wearing the device.

THE READING DEVICE:
This is an electronic device that contains a computerized reading program. It emits an electromagnetic wave in the direction of the chip, which activates the internal components of the chip. It then transforms these signals and imprints them on a liquid crystal screen.

Two methods are generally recommended:

- Either the initiative is left to the puppy: for example, as soon as the puppy sits, give the command "Sit" and praise the dog. The same for "Down" or "Stand". The dog will progressively associate the command with the action and with the owner's satisfaction.

-Or, the owner forces the dog into the position while giving the command. For "Sit", place one hand on the puppy's head and with the other hand, push on the puppy's rump. These combined forces will naturally force the dog to sit. For "Down", the movement is continued by pulling the forequarters forward. Repeating the session for several minutes each day will generally produce good results. Likewise, the dog should be praised when he executes the command.

The "Stay" command is harder to achieve. It requires more attention. Therefore, wait until the puppy is older before asking this of him. First, order the puppy to "Sit" and then place an object (such as his collar) on his head or nose. Command him to "Stay" and if the puppy lowers his nose and lets the object fall, show displeasure. If, however, he holds it for a few seconds, he should of course be praised. Progressively require the dog to stay still for longer periods. Finally, command the dog to stay while you walk away and to come to heel on command.

Daily Life

The future owner should prepare a little "kit" that contains all the items the dog will need, starting with a collar and a leash as well as two bowls – one for food and one for water. Easy-to-clean bowls in stainless steel or glass are preferable because some dogs have skin allergies to plastic. Be sure that the dog always has fresh water available and that the dishes are always clean. To care for the dog's coat, regular brushing several times a week will be necessary, depending on the type of dog. Brushing is more than simple hygienic care. It allows the owner to see whether the dog has any wounds or parasites, and also helps strengthen the bonds of trust needed for good balance in the hierarchy. Food distribution is an essential part of the day. Give the dog food that is appropriate to his size, age and degree of activity. The number of meals should be decreased from four to two between three and eight months of age and leveled off to one or two per day for adults. In large breeds, two meals are preferable in order to prevent stretching the stomach. Avoid competition between several dogs during meals.

Since the dog is subordinate in the hierarchy, he must accept the owner touching his bowl without growling. This is especially important if the family has children. Also, from the start, you should for example, interrupt the meal by picking up the bowl, make the puppy sit and then put the food back down. The puppy may only touch it when the owner gives the command. This training requires a lot of time given the ferocious appetite of these little wild beasts, but it is essential to guaranteeing the hierarchy. It is the pack leader who decides. In addition to this, no food should be given outside fixed meal times. This, of course, requires everyone's participation.

The dog is a sociable animal and because of this, he needs to meet other living beings and explore new territory. Be it an apartment or a house, he will not be content to be taken out for five minutes after the movie to relieve himself, or even to stay locked up in the yard. A one-hour minimum walk per day will allow him to expend his extra energy and consequently, spare the furniture in the house. It will also allow him to integrate himself into a pseudo-pack with the other dogs in the neighborhood. Of course, if you have chosen an athletic dog like the husky, your companion will require much more daily exercise for proper growth.

From a legal point of view, a dog walked in town must be held on a leash or be within voice range and arm's reach so that the owner always has him under control. Thus, if by some misfortune, a dog that is not on a leash is run over by a car, the owner will be held responsible for the damage caused. The same holds true if the dog bites another dog or a person. These annoyances can be avoided by teaching the dog to walk on a leash and to heel without protest, and by socializing the dog at an early stage. Running freely should be reserved for parks or the countryside.

HAVING A SECOND ANIMAL AT HOME

When a new dog is brought into the home, the goal is to encourage the animals to live together in the best possible conditions.

Bear in mind that the first pet is already king of the castle and he should be treated as such. The new resident should not disturb his habits and should integrate himself into the family as discretely as possible.
It is important that the first pet maintain dominance. To this end, he should be given the most attention. He should be the first to be petted, the first to receive his bowl of food, etc. Of course, close supervision will help prevent untimely and aggressive fights. What is of essence is to help the animals get to know each other and live together.

The first pet could be a dog. In this case, cohabitation will not take long and the two animals will quickly become playmates.

It could also be a cat. If one of the two is still very young, there will be very few problems (either they will get along well, or they will keep their distance). If not, the expression "to fight like cats and dogs" will take on its full meaning and life in this instance may be quite turbulent. It is better in this case to distance yourself from one of the two. This second scenario is relatively rare, however, because usually each one will stake out his territory and avoid the territory of the other.

INSURANCE

Third-party liability

Your dog can escape, wander off and cause damage once he is far from your vigilant eye. As an owner, you are liable. In general, homeowners third-party insurance compensates injured parties on your behalf. This liability is included in the "multi-risk – homeowners" or the "multi-coverage – head of household" policies. Be aware, however, that although this insurance covers damage to third parties, it does not cover any damage to you and your family that your dog may cause in your home. That will require extended coverage. If you often leave your dog in the care of someone else, you should also consider taking out an extended policy for that person. If there is slightest doubt, consult your insurance provider.

Specific liability

A third-party insurance policy may not include all the coverage you would like. It is in you interest to discuss the third-party liability clauses for dog owners or "dog caretakers" with your insurer. The beneficiary with this type of insurance is the subscriber – you, the owner – or any other person caring for your dog at no charge.

The policy protects the insured against the financial liability he may incur as a result of damage caused by his dog to a third party.

Damages include bodily, material and immaterial damage, such as untimely barking, for example.

The advantage of this type of policy is that specific coverage can be included that corresponds to specific situations such as watchdogs, hunting dogs or dogs used professionally.

In the case of an accident, remember to inform your insurance company immediately and to provide all the specific details:
- place and date of accident;
- cause and circumstances;
- names and addresses of victims;
- estimated amount of damage;
- names and addresses of witnesses.

Cost of health care

Health insurance for your dog does exist. This insurance guarantees your companion's welfare and helps you maintain your pet's vital health. The purpose of this insurance is to cover health care costs when the "hard blows" in terms of health problems start to quickly add up. Basic policies cover accidents and surgery. More comprehensive policies with some insurance companies even cover vaccinations, illness and boarding costs.

Study in detail the coverage plan your insurer proposes as the risks covered can vary greatly from company to company. Although many of the items excluded from coverage are common to all insurance companies (congenital defects and diseases, mistreatment, wounds sustained as a result of organized fights, whelping, castration, aesthetic surgery, diseases for which vaccines exist, descaling teeth, tattoos, food, antiparasitics, pre-existing diseases or accidents prior to the coverage date, etc.), some companies have added vaccines and boarding costs to their list.

CITY DOGS

Walking a dog in the city has nothing in common with walks in the countryside. Certain rules must be followed out of respect for society and concern for hygiene. Remember that not everyone appreciates our four-legged friends.

Of capital importance, the dog's vaccinations must absolutely be up-to-date and the owner (or person walking the dog) should carry the vaccination card, especially in counties primarily in the northwest of France that have been declared rabies zones. Be sure also that the dog is not carrying a disease that can be transmitted to humans or that is highly contagious to other dogs, so as to avoid the risk of epidemics.

Walking a dog in the city means that the dog must be kept on a leash with a collar or harness, both of which should be adapted to the size and nature of the dog (a choker collar can be used on highly excitable dogs).

Going out is the time for dogs to relieve themselves. If you were to calculate the number of stray dogs and the number of dogs being walked, you can well imagine the volume of canine excrement. Consequently, it is important to take the dog to a place reserved for this purpose and the sidewalk is not one of these places. In 1995, two people per day were taken to the emergency

room in Paris because they slipped on dog feces. Complete dry food labeled "premium" can help prevent this kind of problem because the dog's excrement will be rather hard and smaller in quantity. It will therefore be easy to push it into the gutter with the tip of your shoe, or better yet, scoop it up in a small plastic sack!

Not all dog breeds are allowed in cities and this is true throughout the world. Consequently, it is worthwhile to gather information from city hall about the following breeds: Pit Bull Terrier, Rottweiler, American Staffordshire Terrier and Bull Terrier. Indeed, serious accidents have demonstrated that in the wrong hands, these dogs can prove to be excessively dangerous to society.

The same precautions apply when traveling with your dog. See the section on "Tips for Traveling with Your Dog" in the practical guide at the end of the book.

Walking on a leash can be taught at a very young age. Even when little, the puppy tends to follow his owner. Take advantage of every occasion to ask him to heel. Then put him on a leash. A little time to adapt is of course indispensable. The puppy will tend to lag behind. Then, progressively, he will take the lead. Be careful never to let him pull on the leash. This bad habit is unpleasant and could prove to be dangerous in certain circumstances. To rectify this, simply stop and pull in the opposite direction. The puppy will loose his balance and after a few tumbles, will refrain from pulling ahead. Once this step is mastered, follow up with walking without a leash.

The house is your companion's territory. Driven by an instinct that is more pronounced in some breeds than in others, he guards the house, barking to make his presence known. Barking can also express boredom when the dog is left alone all day. Sometimes, however, this mode of communication becomes a source of agony for the neighbors. Good training is the key to good relations with the neighbors. Teaching the dog to bark and to stop barking upon command is simple. First of all, give the command "Bark" and praise the dog when he executes it. Later on, only give the command once the dog is silent by saying "Stop" with a firm tone.

If the dog is in a yard, be sure that he cannot escape. A good fence that is sufficiently high and well anchored in the ground (remember, dogs dig!) is essential. Know that if he escapes, you will be responsible for any damage he causes.

In fact, civil liability insurance should always be taken out, no matter what the dog.

Outings

No matter what the size, a dog needs to be taken out at least twice a day. For small breeds, half-hour outings will suffice. Large and giant dogs need to be out much longer (approximately one hour). This allows the dog to relieve himself and to release pent up energy. You need to be able to walk the dog in places that are not too dangerous for him (far from traffic for example) and where he is allowed to be off the leash. A long, two-hour walk every weekend will give the dog a chance to break up his daily routine. Take him to parks or wooded areas where he will be exposed to a new environment and encounter other dogs!

Exercise of course needs to be adjusted to the age of the dog. A young puppy will need to be taken out many times a day for short periods, whereas older or sick dogs will be content with two constitutional walks a day.

Upon return, the dog should be systematically inspected.

Paws

In the summer, it is important to inspect the footpads for injuries from thorny or sharp objects (burrs, shards of glass, etc.). Also check to see if any grass seeds have become lodged in the interdigital space. They are found in grasses, hence in the majority of prairie plants, and are shaped like microscopic harpoons. When they come in contact with tissue, they get lodged in and cause serious lesions. In the winter, if the dog has been walking in places covered in snow, he has a greater risk of having cracked pads due to the abrasiveness of the salts used on the road. Rinse the feet with warm water.

Ears

Grass seeds are partial to ears. Use eyebrow tweezers to remove them from the auditory canal (if they have gotten that far). This is a delicate, and sometimes painful operation and may require a visit to the veterinarian.

Care of the coat

In the summer, if the dog likes to swim, he needs to be rinsed afterwards. Be it a stream or the sea, particles collect on the dog's coat and can cause irritation. Careful rinsing will eliminate these particles. If the dog has gotten tar on his coat, do not attempt to remove it with oil-based products, as they are highly toxic. Simply apply vegetable oil to the tar spots, allow a few minutes for the oil to dissolve the tar particles and then bathe the dog.

In the winter, it is possible to cover the dog with a sweater if he is too cold. However, most dogs tolerate the rigors of winter quite well (except for shaved dogs), and if they grow too accustomed to being covered, they will not be able to handle going out without the sweater.

Coat brushing

SHEDDING

No matter what type of coat a dog has, hair dies and new hair grows in its place. Outdoor dogs shed their coat twice a year (spring and fall) which corresponds to the changes in daylight. Indoor dogs are not as exposed to changes in light, so they shed hair throughout the year, with two periods of increased shedding in spring and fall.
Regular brushing and bathing will help remove dead hair. The frequency and the type of equipment used will vary depending on the nature of the coat.

SHORT COATS

Although short coats do not require regular grooming, brushing once or twice a week is necessary. Using a rubber brush and working against the line of the coat will loosen dead skin and hair.
To remove this debris, use a bristle brush and work with the line of the coat, brushing the dog's entire body. Finish off by polishing with a damp chamois cloth to add sheen to the coat.

SHORT, COARSE COAT

Because of the coat density (both an undercoat and a topcoat), the dog should be brushed every other day. Use a slicker brush and work against the line of the coat to loosen as much dead skin and cells as possible and then strip the undercoat.
Use a bristle brush and work with the normal lay of the hair to remove the loosened debris.
A wide-toothed comb can be used on the hair on the tail and paws.
Dogs with wiry hair need to have their coats stripped four to five times a year using a stripping knife. This allows dead hair caught between the knife and the skin to be removed. Stripping is not painful if performed correctly, working with the lay of the coat.

LONG HAIR

Long-haired dogs are superb, but they require daily brushing. In the case of Afghan hounds, for example, brushing can take up to an hour per day.
Use a slicker brush to brush along the normal lay of the coat to remove tangles and mats. Because the hair is so long, the skin may be pulled when attempting to untangle knots. Proceed delicately in order to avoid hurting the dog.
For dogs with silky coats (Yorkshire terrier, Afghan hound, etc.), using a bristle brush will add sheen to the coat.
For dogs with a lot of hair (Scottish terriers, etc.) debris can be removed with a wire brush.
A wide-toothed comb can be used to finish untangling the hair behind the hocks. Use scissors to even out the coat length and to trim away hair that is likely to become tangled or trap debris (hocks, breast, interdigital spaces and the footpads).
Clean and store the grooming tools in a dry place after each use. To keep wire brushes from rusting, wipe them thoroughly and rub a cloth coated in vegetable oil over them.

BATHING

The frequency of baths will vary according to the coat texture. Shaved coats only need to be washed when they are dirty. Short-haired dogs need to be bathed twice a year on average and long-haired dogs need to be bathed approximately every three months.
Small dogs can be washed in a basin or a baby bathtub and large dogs in the bathtub or outdoors (weather permitting).
A rubber mat will prevent uncontrolled slipping, which could cause injury or permanently frighten the dog.
Lukewarm water should be used, along with a special shampoo for dogs. Human products (including food) are too acidic and irritate the skin.

BATHING YOUR DOG

Before bathing the dog, brush out the coat to remove any tangles. Then wet the dog's entire body. Lather up the shampoo, being careful not to get any in the ears or eyes. Allow the shampoo to work for a few minutes and then rinse thoroughly. It is best to rinse the head last or the dog may want to shake. Wipe the dog down vigorously and leave him in a warm room. In the summer, the dog can be let outside or taken for a walk as long as he does not have a tendency to roll around in everything. If the dog will tolerate it, a hair dryer may be used to dry him. Be careful not to burn him and be sure to brush him out while drying.

DAILY CARE OF THE DOG

Dogs require a certain amount of care on a daily basis in order to promote good hygiene and to help the owner detect early warning signs of disease.

Daily hygiene

There are several, very simple ways to check whether the various external organs are functioning properly and to maintain them.

Nose

The nose should be moist and fresh at all times throughout the day. However, it may become dry when the dog sleeps, but it should become moist again when the dog awakes.
No special care is required. Any signs of severe or mucopurulent crustiness, cracking or discharge are signs of infections and should be examined by a veterinarian.

Oral cavity

The flews should be clean and relatively impenetrable. They may sag more in some breeds than in others. Watch for signs of cracking or redness (especially in German shepherds as they have fragile skin).

The teeth should be white and should not have tartar buildup. Dogs are rarely cooperative when it comes to handling their mouth. It is wise to start when they are puppies so they grow accustomed to such handling. The gums should be pink. Red marks around the teeth are signs of disease and indicate painful swelling that can result in decreased appetite because the dog will not be able to pick up or chew food.
It is therefore necessary to clean the dog's teeth. This may be done in several ways. The most efficient way is to use a toothbrush and toothpaste specially designed for dogs. The dog's teeth should be brushed several times a week. There are also palatable pills available that release active ingredients when the dog chews. These are good for dogs that do not tolerate brushing. Finally, it is always possible to give the dog objects made out of buffalo skin or cartilage. This natural "chewing gum" slows the formation of tartar through its mechanical action on the teeth when the dog chews.
However, at a certain point, these methods are no longer effective. The only way to halt a budding infection and end unpleasant tartar buildup at this point is for the veterinarian to remove the plaque from the teeth and apply an antibiotic treatment.

Eyes

The dog's eyes should be clear and moist and the mucous membrane should be pink. There should be no visible discharge in the inner corner of the eye.
The dog's eyes can be cleaned on a daily basis with an eyewash. To do so, lift the dog's head, open the upper eyelid and place a few drops in his eye. Use a compress to catch the overflow. Two precautions should be taken. First, to avoid frightening the dog, approach the eye with the bottle from behind. Second, check the expiration date on the solution as well as the shelf life. These solutions can, in fact, be easily contaminated and thereby be rendered ineffective.

Ears

Dogs' ears come in two forms: either they are long and floppy or they are erect. Long ears need to be inspected more frequently. Since the external auditory canal is covered by the pinna, the ear canal is not well ventilated. The nature of the hair growing on the ear (long, curly, short, etc.) is also an important factor.
The external auditory canal should therefore be kept very clean and free of any hair.
Ears should be cleaned regularly – once or twice a week for long-eared dogs and once every two weeks for short-eared dogs. To clean the ears, use a solution adapted to the dog's ears. The procedure is as follows. Push the tip of the bottle into the canal (there is no risk of piercing the eardrum because the canal is L-shaped), squeeze out a steady stream of solution, pull out the tip, massage the base of the ear for thirty seconds and

finally, use a piece of cotton or a compress to wipe the canal without pushing it into the ear. Long-haired dogs often have tufts of hair lodged in their ears. This hair usually blocks the earwax from draining properly and must be removed from the ears.

Genital organs and the anus

Male and female genitalia should be inspected regularly for cleanliness. Any sign of discharge should be referred to a veterinarian.
The anus should be clean and there should be no traces of diarrhea.

Nails

Dogs have two types of nails: toenails and dewclaws. Nails grow continually and they will be worn down naturally in the daily activities of the dog. If not, they need to be trimmed with nail clippers (you will know because the nails will click on the floor when the dog walks). Be sure to avoid cutting the quick at the nail bed. The quick is visible in clear nails as a pink triangle. In dark nails, the quick can be detected by looking for traces on the underside of the nails. In both cases, trim below the marks.

The nail may bleed. If so, apply hydrogen peroxide or a styptic pencil. A small bandage can protect the wound for an hour.
The technique is the same for the dewclaws. These nails are often covered with hair. Do not forget to trim them because if they become ingrown, they will be painful and cause wounds.

Grooming

The first groomers or more precisely, the first "shearers" came onto the scene during the Second Empire. The poodle craze among the bourgeoisie at the time had much to do with it. In fact, the "lion" or, Continental clip, still used today dates back to this period. Back then the shearers set up shop in the streets with wooden boxes to provide more extensive services than the superficial grooming that is part of the general care of the dog.
Ever since then, professionals with specialized equipment have been providing grooming services. Grooming in fact is no longer considered to be a luxury, but a necessity for certain breeds.

The first thing you notice about a dog is his coat. The health of the animal is reflected in his coat. Therefore, it is very important to take good care of it. However, everyday grooming performed by the owner in the interest of cleanliness is not to be confused with aesthetic grooming. This type of grooming is what highlights the morphology and the character of a breed, and covers blemishes so as to give the perfect shape. For professionals, grooming is good when it is not noticeable and when it respects the animal.

In fact, country dogs rarely need to be groomed (except for certain breeds such as poodles, for example), unless it is for the personal pleasure of the owner. Professional grooming is required, on the other hand, for show dogs that are carefully scrutinized by the trained eye. In this case, the animal represents his breed and must be perfect.
Clearly, a dog must be in good health in order to be groomed. He cannot suffer from any contagious diseases or dermatosis and must have up-to-date vaccinations (especially the rabies shot in case he bites).

Equipment

Grooming equipment includes a high table with straps that attach to the collar so as to prevent any untimely movements, especially when scissors are being used. It also includes a pair of clippers with several combs - a must for poodles; a large-toothed comb for long or curly hair; several pairs of scissors: trimming, curved and thinning shears; a hand comb to puff up hair and a stripping knife.

The Technique

Having the equipment is not enough. You must know how to use it. The technique has evolved greatly over the centuries. Today, grooming is done in three phases:

-a mild shampoo suitable for the dog's coat type is applied in order to remove dirt and skin debris that can dull the color of the coat.
- the clip is done in several stages:
- clipping, which is often reserved only for poodles, requires a certain degree of precision in order to avoid leaving comb marks and to ensure that the hair grows back in evenly over the whole clipped area;
- stripping, which entails plucking hair either by hand or with a stripping knife. This step is essentially performed on dogs with coarse hair so as to remove the longest hairs and make the coat more uniform;
- trimming, or shaping the coat with a stripping knife or a comb.

In addition, the groomer provides the other grooming care normally performed by the owner: cleaning the eyes, remove unwanted hair from ears (to prevent thorns in the summer and to facilitate ear cleaning), scaling teeth if necessary, trimming nails and checking the integrity of the foot pads.
This is the normal grooming procedure. Of course, each dog is groomed differently. The following are a few examples:

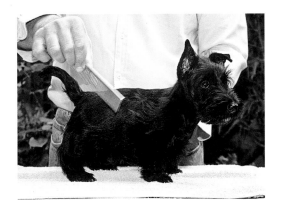

For dogs with coarse hair (such as dalmatians or labradors), dematting is useless. If need be during a molting period, a simple, stiff bristle brush will suffice. In order to give the dog the shiny coat that is characteristic of these breeds, use a leather glove followed by a chamois cloth to add "sheen" to the coat.

For a long or semi-long coat (German shepherd, Spitz, Spaniel), avoid pulling out healthy hair or breaking hairs by using a brush that is too hard. Using a currycomb is much more appropriate.

Dogs with long hair, either straight or curly (Afghan, Chow-Chow, Maltese), must have their coats dematted in order to remove dead hair. On a chow-chow, the final touch consists in adding volume to the coat by brushing it up against the lay of the coat. On fox terriers, the beard is trimmed to "square up" the head.

Finally, the Poodle is by far the most complicated case. Several clips are allowed, in particular the lion trim (known in the United States as the Continental clip) (topknot, leg bracelets, pompom), the English Saddle clip (hair combed back and held in place by a ribbon, shaved muzzle), and the Zazou clip (paws and body shaved, topknot, muzzle and ears shaved).
The range of cuts and grooming styles is therefore extremely vast. This is why in order to become a groomer, a person must be very knowledgeable about canine breeds, and especially their morphology and general character, in order to be able to adapt the grooming style to the criteria of each breed. This can be learned at school, but schooling is often not sufficient and professionals agree that the bulk of learning occurs through on-the-job experience. Indeed, a groomer's role also includes covering up defects in the dog. For example, if a dog is too tall, the hair on the paws will be cut longer to give the impression that the dog is shorter on his paws. Likewise, if the limbs are curved, one side will be cut more than the other to rectify the general shape of the paw.

The skills a good groomer needs include a mastery of the techniques, knowledge about the breed criteria, as well as patience, tact and the right touch, not to mention a good dose of psychology.

Part 6

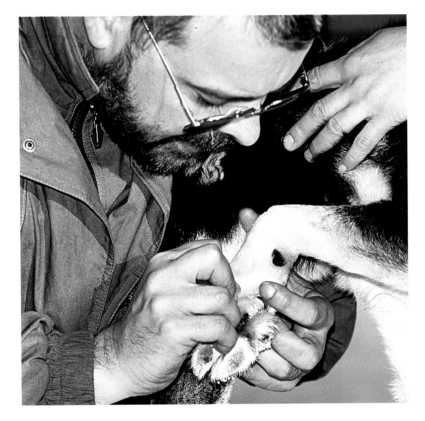

Shar-Pei

Know Your Dog

Canine Morphology

According to the system devised by Pierre Mégnin in 1896, dogs can be classified as one of the following types:

Lupoid, having a triangular head and prick ears (such as the Belgian Shepherd);

Braccoid, with hanging ears, a wide muzzle and well-defined stop (Dalmatian);

Molossoid, usually large with small hanging ears, a massive round or squared head and a short muzzle (mastiff, Pyrenean Mountain Dog);

Graioid, with small ears turned backward, a wide, fine head with an indistinct stop and thin limbs.

Four sizes of dogs are also defined, on the basis of height and weight.

Small dogs are less than 46 cm (18 in) tall, while medium dogs are between 46 (18 in) and 61 cm (24 in) tall and large and giant dogs are over 61 cm (24 in) in height.

In terms of weight, small dogs weigh less than 10 kg (22 lb), medium dogs weigh from 10 (24,3 lb) to 25 kg (55 lb), large dogs weigh from 25 kg (55 lb) and giant dogs weigh more than 45 kg (55 lb).

Regions of the body have the same names for all dogs.

The forequarters:
include the head, neck and forelegs;

the body:
includes the back, loins, ribcage and abdomen; and

the hindquarters:
include the croup, hind legs and tail.

Hair and coats: come in many different colors and textures.

Hair and coat types

A dog's coat gets its texture from two types of hair. The outermost hairs or guard hairs, are stiff, thick and longer than the secondary hairs forming the short, woolly, protective undercoat. Not all breeds have an undercoat, although a thick undercoat is important in the Nordic breeds. The coat has an aesthetic and protective role and reflects the dog's general health. Coat color is determined both by the distribution of colors on the hairs and by the pigmentation of the nose and skin. Coats can be described as whole color or variegated.

Whole-Color Coats

• Black and white dogs do exist, although these are not the most favored colors for a whole-colored dog.

• Gray is a mixture of black and white and there are many shades, including mouse-gray, slate (Yorkshire), wolf gray (yellowish gray with black tips) and silver-gray (an obvious dilution of black, although puppies are blue at birth).

• Fawn is a yellowish color with red, orange or golden highlights (as in apricot-colored Poodles). When very diluted, it appears tawny, as in the Labrador. Smoky fawn (fawn hairs with black overlay) is found in the Tervuren and a blackened sand color (often described as gray or pepper and salt) can be seen in the Giant Schnauzer.

• Brown (plain brown or liver) can be light, dark or sometimes reddish-brown. Poodles of this color are a uniform dark brown. Newfoundlands are chocolate with bronze highlights.

Variegated Coats

• Black and tan coats are found on the Gordon Setter and the Beauceron, with well-defined borders at the lips, eyelids, chest, front of the stifle and the ends of the limbs. In the German Shepherd, however, the colors are mixed.

• Mottled coats such as merle and harlequin consist of diluted spots. Australian Shepherds and Shelties can have merle coats (spots on a light background), while harlequin (gray background with black and white spots) is seen in the Great Dane. The gene responsible for this color is also associated with hearing and vision abnormalities.

• Brindle refers to a coat with dark streaking on a fawn background, as in the Boxer.

• Hounds' coats often contain three colors (fawn, black and white).

• Pied coats have black, brown or blue spots on a white background.

• Skewbald coats have brindled spots on a white background.

• Red roan is an even mixture of white and light red hairs.

• Reddish-brown. It is found in some wild dogs.

• Some Picardy Spaniels are a rare roan color made up of white, black and fawn hairs.

Notwithstanding the above definitions, coats can vary in appearance. A coat with a mantle has the same color on the back and sides, as in the German Shepherd and the Airedale. A whole-colored dog with white markings is said to have a self-marked coat. A coat can be splashed (white hairs on a brown background), flecked or speckled (fawn flecks). It can also have highlights of various colors or be diluted or grizzled. In dogs with blue merle coats, bare patches caused by a reduction in the amount of pigment present can be observed around the nose and eyes.

ZOOLOGICAL CLASSIFICATION OF THE DOG

Class: Mammalia
Subclass: Eutheria
Order: Carnivora
Suborder: Fissipeda
Family: Canidae
Genus: Canis
Species: Canis familiaris, the domestic dog
(2n = 78 chromosomes)

CHARACTERISTICS OF THE HAIR

Hair is a horny, flexible, elastic filament. The part visible above the skin is actually the dead portion. Just as there are different breeds of dogs, there are different textures and distributions of hair. The length, diameter and texture of hair varies, as does its form (straight, flexible, wavy or curly). The location of hair on the dog varies as well. There can be a forelock on the head or a mane on the neck (as in the Chow Chow). A feathered coat has long feathers on the backs of the limbs, under the belly and on the tail; while in a tufted coat the hairs of the tail are longer than those on the rest of the body.

Many factors influence hair characteristics, including age. In some breeds, a puppy's coat differs from the adult's. For example, *markings can appear as the dog ages (as in the Auvergne Hound) and many Dalmatians do not have spots when they are born. Yorkshire Terriers are completely black at birth.*

As a dog ages, its hair turns gray, especially on the head, beginning with the muzzle. An undernourished dog or one in poor health, has dull, brittle hair. Sunlight can also make the hair brittle and cause it to redden or turn brown. After a dog has been clipped, the color of its hair is noticeably lighter and purer.

A dog's hair grows continuously. Hairs are replaced by shedding, which usually happens during a period of four to six weeks in the spring and fall. However, shedding is essentially constant in dogs that live indoors.

Mexican Hairless

Pinscher

HAIR LENGTH

Hairless dogs, such as the Mexican Hairless and Chinese Hairless, have hair on their head and tail. Their skin is fine, soft and warm, with heavy black pigmentation.

Flat or straight hair is 5 to 15 mm (0,2-0,6 in) long. It can be very fine, as in Pinschers; fine and short, as in the Whippet; or thicker, as in pointers.

Short hair is from 15 mm to 4 cm (0,6-1,6 in) long. It can be straight, stiff and harsh as in the German Shepherd. When it is shorter, as in the Beagle, it is said to be coarse.

Medium-length hair is from 4 to 7 cm (1,6-2,8 in) long, while long hair is more than 7 cm (2,8 in) long. It can be fine, silky and wavy as in setters. It can be longer than the height of the withers, as in the Yorkshire Terrier. It can be curly, as in the Barbet; woolly, as in spitz breeds; or corded, as in the Puli and the Komondor

German Shepherd

Puli

Picardy Sheepdog

Dandie Dinmont Terrier

HAIR CHARACTERISTICS

Harsh hair is wiry to the touch. The coat is tousled and traps a layer of air. Picardy sheepdogs have this type of hair (medium-length coat), as does the Basset Griffon Vendéen.

Mixed hard and soft hair (pily coat) is a mixture of about 2/3 fairly harsh hair and 1/3 softer fur-like hair, as in the Dandie Dinmont Terrier.

Smooth hair looks shiny and neat, as in the Great Dane and the Rottweiler.

Silky hair is very fine, flexible and soft as in setters. Woolly hair is less shiny and looks thicker, as in the Poodle.

Great Dane

Poodle

Regions of the Body

A dog's body can be described as 52 regions, each corresponding to a specific anatomical area. These regions allow expert judges of conformation or show judges to evaluate individual dogs and explain their decisions to the owners.

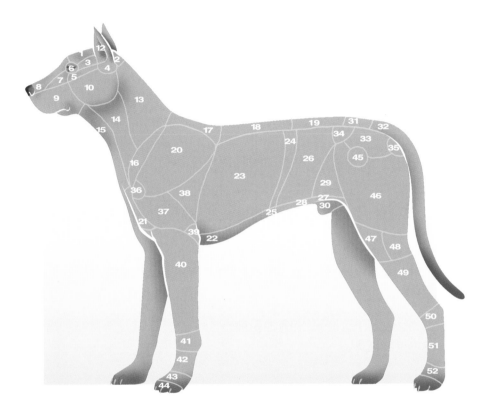

HEAD
1. Frontal region
2. Parietal region
3. Temporal region
4. Pinna
5. Zygomatic region
6. Orbital region
7. Infraorbital region
8. Nasal region
9. Buccal region
10. Masseteric region

NECK
11. Laryngeal region
12. Parotid region
13. Dorsal region of neck
14. Lateral region of neck
15. Ventral region of neck (tracheal region)
16. Prescapular region

THORACIC REGION
17. Interscapular region
18. Back
19. Loins
20. Shoulder
21. Presternal region
22. Sternal region
23. Costal region
24. Hypochondriac region

ABDOMINAL REGION
25. Xiphoid region
26. Flank
27. Umbilical region
28. Hypogastric region
29. Inguinal region
30. Preputial region

PELVIC REGION
31. Sacral region
32. Coccygeal region (caudal region)
33. Gluteal region
34. Coxal tuber region
35. Ischeal tuber region (point of hip)

FORELIMB
36. Shoulder joint
37. Upper arm
38. Biceps
39. Elbow
40. Forearm
41. Carpal region
42. Metacarpal region
43. Fetlock
44. Nails

HIND LIMBS
45. Hip joint
46. Thigh
47. Knee
48. Popliteal region
49. Leg
50. Tarsal region
51. Metatarsal region
52. Fetlock

The topskull (cranial and frontal region) can be rounded (Beagle, Cocker Spaniel), arched (Boxer), flat (Dalmatian), oval (Poodle) or broad (Rottweiler).

The stop extends from the forehead to the bridge of the nose, is visible from the side and can be more or less definite. It can form an angle between 90° (in dogs with short muzzles) and 180° (in dogs with long muzzles). It is essentially absent in hounds.

The muzzle or **bridge of the nose**, contains the nasal cavities, which are large in pointers (e.g., setters) but small in, for example, the Bulldog, which has a pushed-in muzzle. Complete flattening of the face (as in the Pekingese) can lead to abnormalities in the alignment of the jaws (undershot jaw, overlapping teeth) and to respiratory problems.

The nose has two nostrils which should be quite flared and a median fissure. If a dog is healthy, its nose is pliable, wet and cold.

The lips should meet and should not be flaccid. They should be highly pigmented and covered with hairs and vibrissae or whiskers (sturdy hairs having sensory receptors at their bases). The inside of the lips should be a shade of pink (or blue in Chow Chows).

The ears can be of different shapes and lengths and their carriage and attachment also varies. They can be pointed (Belgian Shepherd), somewhat rounded (German Shepherd), quite rounded (Bulldog) or rather fine and covered with fairly long hair (Cocker Spaniel). The ears play a fundamental role in hearing. Prick ears effectively capture sound waves, while bloodhounds often have drop ears that protect the inside of the ear from vegetation and prevent foreign objects from entering the ear canal. Terriers have short ears that will not get in their way when they enter burrows. The ears can be cropped, a practice still observed in many countries, except Great Britain. The trend in many countries is to abolish ear cropping.

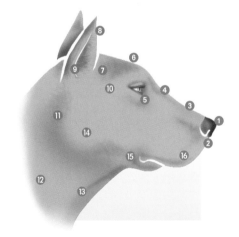

THE HEAD
1. Nose
2. Nostri
3. Bridge of nose
4. Stop
5. Eye and orbital region
6. Forehead, frontal region
7. Parietal region or cranium
8. Ear (pinna, leather)
9. Ear
10. Temples, temporal region
11. Parotid region
12. Neck
13. Throat
14. Masseteric region (flat area of the cheek)
15. Commissure of lips
16. Upper lip.

THE HEAD, NECK AND FORELIMBS

The head may be round (Cavalier King Charles Spaniel), long (sight hounds) or square. It plays an important role in balance. Long-headed dogs tend to have a pointed nose, while square-headed dogs have short, muscular jaws. (The latter applies mainly to breeds developed for fighting.)

The head has two main regions: At the back of the head is the cranium (skull), which contains the brain; and at the front is the face, where the nasal cavities are located. The area separating these two regions is centered on the two orbits. The different proportions between the cranium and the face are described by the terms dolichocephalic (having an elongated muzzle), brachycephalic (having a short, pushed-in muzzle) and mesocephalic (intermediate between the previous two).

• The head also encompasses other, less well-defined regions. The temples are located on the sides of the head, behind the eyes, bounded by the zygomatic arches, which are connected to the cranium and are quite important to the head's structure.

The parotid region is found below the ears, behind the masseteric region, which is behind the cheek. Because dogs can open their mouths very wide, their cheeks are quite small. The crest is somewhat prominent in the back, at the neck and the throat may have folds of skin known as dewlaps.

• The neck is cylindrical in shape, with a greater diameter at the thoracic end than at the head end. It ends at the withers and forms a rather open angle with the back.
The neck is important when judging a dog's beauty. It influences head carriage and balance, because it determines the position of the center of gravity. The head-neck axis thus acts as a counterweight that balances the rest of the spinal column and helps the dog to move. (When a dog's head and neck are held down on the ground, the dog cannot rise.) The neck runs into the shoulders, withers and chest. Its position changes with gait: Upright during the propulsion phase, it is extended during the footfall.

• The forelimbs are generally long and somewhat flattened. The shoulder slants from bottom to top, back to front and is slightly convex. The upper arm lies between the shoulder (above) and the elbow (below) and is attached to the chest wall. The two medial digits are longer and stronger than the two lateral digits. The footpads (a thick horny layer plus fat) are prominent and slightly convex. The nails, found on the ends of the digits, are curved and horny and should not touch the ground when the dog is standing.

• The chest or anterior portion of the thoracic region, varies in depth, width and position in relation to the forelimbs. In the French Bulldog, it forms a perfect square, while in the Bulldog it forms an arch.

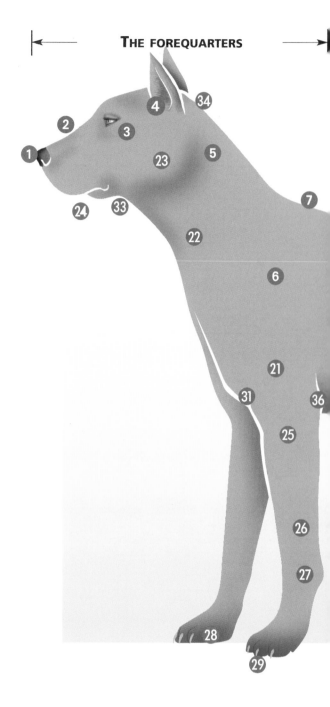

THE FOREQUARTERS

1. Nose
2. Bridge of the nose
3. Eye
4. Ear (pinna, leather)
5. Neck (dorsal region)
6. Shoulder
7. Withers
8. Back
9. Loin
10. Croup
11. Tail

21. Upper arm
22. Neck (ventral region)
23. Cheek
24. Mouth
25. Elbow
26. Forearm
27. Carpus
28. Forefoot (toes)
29. Nail
30. Sternum
31. Point of shoulder

494

THE TOPLINE, RIBCAGE AND ABDOMEN

• The topline includes the back and loins. It is nearly horizontal in mesomorphs, hollow in young dogs (saddle back) and rising in camped dogs. The back has a straight (horizontal) line and may fall slightly toward the rear. In long-backed dogs, it is arched (dipped). The loins are the posterior extension of the back and are usually slightly wider. The croup is included as part of the loins. It is slanted, with varying degrees of roundness, but always rectangular as seen from above. It ends at the root of the tail.

• The rib cage includes the chest, a very convex region formed by the 13 ribs. A deep chest is long (from the point of the shoulder to the last rib) and should represent 2/3 of the dog's total length. The sternum forms an arch (sternal arch) with a large radius. This region contains the cardiac area, which must be quite large in physically active dogs.

• The abdomen is the cavity posterior to the diaphragm. It contains a number of essential organs (the urogenital tract, spleen and digestive tract). The coupling or flank, is a slightly concave region that varies in length depending on the size of the dog. The end of the flank runs into the belly and is difficult to distinguish in dogs. In bitches, the nipples are located on the lower side of the coupling. In dogs, the posterior area of the coupling supports the sheath.

THE HINDQUARTERS AND TAIL

• The hind limbs are longer and more massive than the forelimbs and have less acute angles. The thighs are usually well muscled. The stifle separates the thigh from the upper end of the leg, which is long and slanted. The hock marks the beginning of the lower leg, the cannon bone, which is slanted toward the front and sometimes has a dewclaw on the inner side. The hind foot is generally slightly shorter than the front foot.

• Different breeds have different tails, which can vary in length, size and carriage. They can be screw tails (as in spitz breeds), long plume tails (as in setters) or short tails (as in terriers). Dogs that are born with no tail are called tailless dogs, while those with a very short tail are called bobtailed dogs. Tails can also be shortened by docking according to strict rules. Tail docking is closely regulated in many countries. The carriage of the tail can be straight, horizontal or curved.

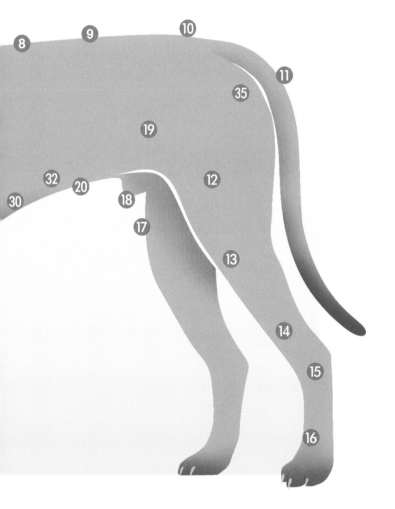

12. Thigh
13. Stifle (knee)
14. Leg
15. Hock (tarsus)
16. Metatarsus
17. Inguinal region (groin)
18. Prepuce
19. Coupling (flank)
20. Belly

32. Throat
33. Crest
34. Elbow.
35. Ribs
36. Point of rump.

STANCE

Stance refers to the direction of the limbs with respect to a horizontal surface. A dog's stance greatly influences its topline, and therefore its general appearance, as well as its sporting ability. The stance provides a good base and the proper distribution of weight on the joints and feet. For correct limb position, the limb's main axis usually must be vertical. Positions other than vertical overload the joints and the sole of the foot (on the side where the departure from vertical occurs). This leads to premature fatigue in the joints, tendons and various ligaments (a particularly severe handicap for working dogs). Stance is thus of more than purely theoretical and aesthetic interest.

When a dog is camped, the dorso-lumbar topline sags and the back slants. If the forelimbs also sag, the dog is said to be saddle-backed. In a collected dog, the loins dip and the back curves upwards. Turned-out feet are frequently seen on the hind legs, which is a natural tendency. Pigeon toes are more of a problem, however.

STANCES IN DOGS - SIDE VIEW

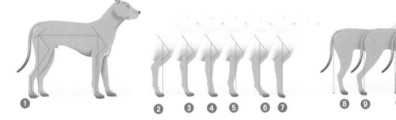

1 - Normal Stance
2 - Back at Knee
3 - Down in Pastern
4 - Knuckled Over
5 - Receding Wrist
6 - Long in Pastern
7 - Upright Pastern
8 - Camped Forward
9 - Camped Out
10 - Hyperextended Hock
11 - Stands Under

STANCE: FOREQUARTERS

Side view: A vertical line through the center of the arm passes through the center of the foot and forms a tangent with the wrist (the anterior side of the carpus). If the vertical line is in front of the center of the foot, the dog is back at the knee; if it is to the rear of the center, the dog is camped. If the wrist is in front of the line, it is said to be knuckled over and the dog has a fetlock deformity; if it is behind the line, the wrist is receding. If the vertical line falls distant from the footpads, the dog is long in the pastern, and if it nearly touches them, the dog has an upright pastern.

Front view: A vertical line dropped from the point of the shoulder should evenly divide the forearm, wrist, cannon bone, and foot. The two limbs should lie within parallel planes.

Pigeon-toed: The wrists and elbows are turned outwards; the cannon bones and feet are turned inwards.

Turned-out (east-west) feet: The elbows are too close to the body, the cannon bones and feet are outside the vertical. Pigeon toes and turned-out feet can begin at any point on the leg.

Base narrow or base wide in front: The front limbs are slanted and their extremities converge or diverge. This is not to be confused with a narrow or wide front, where the legs are parallel. If only the wrists are inside the vertical, the dog is knock-kneed. If the wrists are curved in but lie outside the vertical, the dog is said to be bandy-legged. A stance called the Chippendale front or fiddle front also exists, where the legs curve outward.

STANCE: HINDQUARTERS

Side view: The cannon bone should be vertical with respect to the ground. A vertical line dropped from the hip joint should pass through the middle of the foot.

Camped forward, stands under: Most of the limb is in front of the vertical line. If it is behind the line, it is camped out (stretched), which is not really a fault as this is a natural position. If the hock joint is too sharply angled, the dog is said to stand under; in the opposite case, the hock is hyperextended.

Rear View: A vertical line passing through the point of the rump and the hock should divide the cannon bone equally. The dog may be too narrow or wide of base, which is defined by the convergence or divergence of the limbs'extremities. This should not be confused with a narrow or wide rear. When the limb is rotated outward from the hip joint, turned-out limbs result. In this case, the stifles and feet diverge, while the hocks converge. When the limb is rotated inward, pigeon toes result. The stifles and ends of the feet converge while the hocks diverge.

STANCES IN DOGS

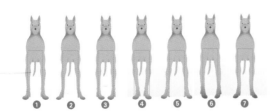

1 - Normal stance
2 - Turned-out feet
3 - Turned-in feet
4 - Base narrow
5 - Base wide
6 - Spread knees, pigeon toes
7 - East-West front
8 - Pigeon-toed
9 - East-West feet

FRONT VIEW

1 - Normal Stance
2 - Base Narrow
3 - Base Wide
4 - Turned-out Feet
5 - Pigeon-toed
6 - Cow-hocked
7 - Barrel-hocked, Spread Hocks

REAR VIEW

The Eyes

The distance between the eyes varies greatly from breed to breed. Widely-spaced eyes allow a dog to see to the sides. The eyeball is generally sunken (globular in the pug). The opening for the eye can be round, as in the pointer, or almond-shaped (doe eyes) as in sheepdogs and Nordic races. A dog's expression is conveyed mainly by its gaze, which should be lively, frank and mild.

Dogs have two visible eyelids, the upper and lower eyelids, which should be delicate, well separated, and highly pigmented, with abundant lashes. The outer part consists of skin covered with hair, and the inner part is the conjunctiva, a pink membrane. The lacrimal gland is located beneath the upper eyelid. It produces tears to moisten the cornea. The lacrimal duct, at the inner corner of the eyelids, opens into the nasal fossa.

Dogs also have a third eyelid, the nictitating membrane, which is mostly hidden beneath the lower eyelid. It functions as a windshield-wiper for the eye and removes foreign bodies.

Eye color depends on the pigmentation of the iris. Usually, a dark color (brown) is desired. In fact, this is a sign of good health. The brown can be of any shade, up through black. Eyes that are too light in color (bird of prey eyes) are not desirable, and detract from even the most handsome dog.

Eye color is not necessarily related to coat color. A dog with a very light coat may have very dark eyes, as in the Samoyed, which is required have dark eyes. In silver-gray dogs such as the Weimaraner, or blue pied or blue brindle dogs, the eyes may be light colored. The coloration may also change during the course of the dog's life.

Two eyes of different colors are called heterochromatic eyes. While not rare, this phenomenon is undesirable, although tolerated in the Siberian Husky.

Sometimes an eye lacks pigmentation in the iris and appears partially or totally whitish. This condition (walleye) is a frequent fault among dogs with ternary or mottled coats, and can affect one or both eyes. The Siberian Husky's blue eyes should not be confused with walleyes. Dogs with walleyes should be removed from the breeding pool.

Other defects of the eye include cataracts (opacity of the crystalline lens), entropion (turning in of the eyelids), glaucoma (the result of increased pressure inside the eye without expansion of the eye) and strabismus (the visual axes do not converge).

Teeth

Adult dogs have 42 teeth, 20 in the upper jaw and 22 in the lower jaw. The arrangement of the teeth is known as the dentition. The eruption of the teeth at various stages of life is also known as dentition.

The teeth are hard, with a bony appearance. They are used to grasp, tear and grind the food, an important functional role. Dogs are heterodont mammals, which means that their teeth are differentiated for specialized uses. The molars are permanent teeth, while the incisors, canines and premolars are deciduous.

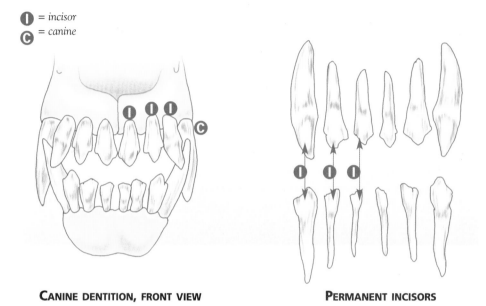

CANINE DENTITION, FRONT VIEW

PERMANENT INCISORS

The dental formula for each side of the jaws is: incisors (I) 3/3; canines (C) 1/1; premolars (PM) 4/4; and molars (M) 2/3. This formula varies in different breeds (depending on whether they have a short or long face). The incisors are larger in the upper jaw than in the lower. Beginning at the center, they are called central or nipper incisors, divider incisors, and corner incisors. The canine teeth are conical in shape, although they are narrower and more spindly in puppies. Molars and premolars are described as precarnassial, carnassial or post-carnassial.

PROGNATHISM

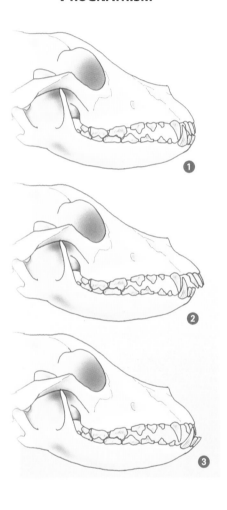

1 - *Properly-aligned jaws*
2 - *Prognathism of the upper jaw ("overshot jaw")*
3 - *Prognathism of the lower jaw ("undershot jaw")*

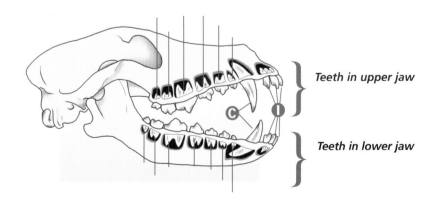

Teeth in upper jaw

Teeth in lower jaw

CANINE DENTITION, SIDE VIEW
(with the roots of the teeth exposed)

A puppy's dental formula is as follows: I 3/3, C 1/1, PM 4/4. Puppies have no teeth at birth. They acquire milk teeth beginning at the age of 20 days. Teeth appear at the following intervals (in medium-sized dogs): Canines appear at three weeks, then the premolars (PM3, PM4) and corner incisors at three to four weeks of age, followed at four to six weeks by the divider and nipper incisors and PM2. PM1 appears at about four months of age and remains in the adult. Then all the teeth are replaced between three and five months of age. The roots of the milk teeth are reabsorbed, the teeth fall out and are replaced by permanent teeth. Molars, incisors and canines come in at four to five months of age, lower M2 at five months, upper M2 and PM at five to six months, and the last molars at six to seven months.

Teeth erupt at different times in different breeds. Abnormalities in the number of teeth can also occur. Extra teeth are rare. Fewer teeth than normal are grounds for refusal of conformation. In fact, the absence of certain molars is common. The functional importance of the teeth increases from front to back of the jaw, and the first premolar is frequently absent. One or two incisors may also be missing in small breeds.

The dental arcades of the upper and lower jaws fit together, and there should be no lateral movement. The upper incisors partially cover the lower incisors. If the lower jaw is prognathous, the lower maxillary bone extends beyond the upper and the dog is said to have an undershot jaw. If the upper teeth extend beyond the lower, i.e., the upper jaw is prognathous, the dog has an overshot jaw.

Teeth play an important part in the determination of a dog's age. The top of the incisors has a three-lobed shape. As the dog ages, the incisor first becomes smooth (the medial lobe is leveled), and then is worn down (the three lobes disappear). This fact allows the dog's age to be determined from a dental table.

Dental diseases also exist. Tartar, consisting of calcified salts from saliva, accumulates at the base of the tooth. It causes gingivitis and tooth loss. Older dogs or seriously ill dogs under antibiotic treatment may have yellow teeth. Decalcification of teeth by plaque is caused by certain diseases. Dental caries ("cavities") is rare, because the enamel is very hard. Dental fistulas are caused by necrosis of the alveolar wall, leading to abscesses. Persistence of deciduous teeth can hinder the development and eruption of permanent teeth.

① = incisor   **❶** Precarnassial Premolars
C = canine   **❷** Carnassial Teeth
   ❸ Post-carnassial Molars

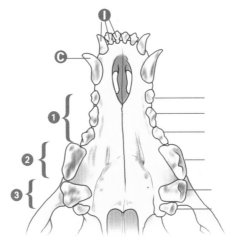

THE UPPER DENTAL ARCADE

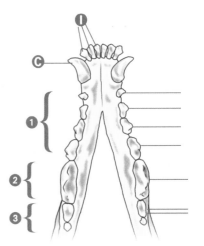

THE LOWER DENTAL ARCADE

TEETH	ERUPTION	REPLACEMENT
① nippers	30 days	4 months
① dividers	28 days	4-1/2 months
① corner incisors	25 days	5 months
C canine teeth	21 days	5 months
PM1	3-4 months	Remains in adult
PM2	4-5 weeks	6 months
PM3	3-4 weeks	6 months
PM4	3-4 weeks	5-6 months
M1	4 months	
M2 (upper jaw)	5-6 months	
M2 (lower jaw)	4-1/2 to 5 months	
M3	6-7 months	

CHANGES TO THE DENTITION AS A DOG AGES

1 month   *3 months*   *4 months*   *5 months*   *7 months*

1-and-1/2 years   *2-and-1/2 years*   *3-and-1/2 years*   *4 years and older*

Canine Physiology

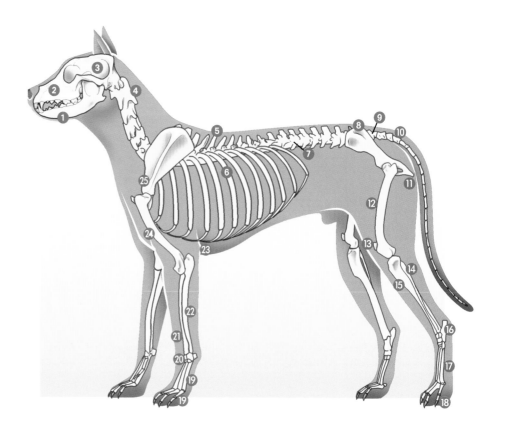

SIDE VIEW OF THE SKULL

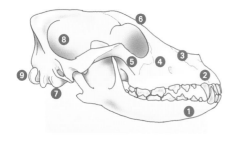

The Musculoskeletal System

A dog's framework is its skeleton, consisting of bones connected to each other by joints. Different types of joints allow varying ranges of motion: some joints are immovable (as between the bones of the skull), while others allow a full range of motion in three dimensions (as the joint between the skull and the vertebral column).
Striated muscle, which is attached to the bones by tendons, moves the skeleton. Contraction of the muscles moves the bones relative to each other, with motions such as flexion and extension. Muscular contraction is governed by nerves through the intermediary of the central nervous system: the cerebrum and cerebellum control voluntary movements, while the spinal cord controls reflexes. Neurons involved in controlling movement are called motor neurons, to distinguish them from the sensory neurons that carry information to the brain.
A dog can move at four different gaits, the walk, trot, gallop and pace, which may be more or less developed in different breeds. Dogs are good jumpers and fair swimmers, again, depending on the breed.

The Skeleton and Bones

• The skeleton. The axis of the skeleton is the spine, or vertebral column, made up of different types of vertebrae. Attached to the spinal column are 13 ribs, ten of which are connected by the sternum to form the rib cage. The skull is joined to the first cervical vertebra, the atlas, which is in turn joined to the next vertebra with a pivoting joint that allows the head to turn in every direction about the axis formed by these two vertebrae.

• The hind limbs. The hind limbs provide power for locomotion. They are attached to the pelvis at the hip joint. The pelvis is connected to the vertebral column by a complex system of ligaments. The forelegs, which play a less important role in locomotion, are attached to the vertebral column by the scapula and its adjacent muscles.

• The bones. The bones consist of a calcified fibrous structure. Calcification occurs progressively during fetal development and growth. Since the growth period is very long for large-breed puppies, careful attention should be paid to calcium supplements in the food, in order to avoid deficiencies or over-consumption. Throughout a dog's life, the calcium in its bones provides a calcium reserve that increases or decreases according to the amount of calcium in the blood, which remains constant.

The center of the bones contains bone marrow, a spongy tissue that produces red corpuscles.

The Joints and Muscles

• Joints differ according to the movements they allow. Sutures (as in the skull) allow no movement at all. Symphyses (as the pubic symphysis) allow very slight movement between the two bony structures. True joints have surfaces that are covered with hyaline cartilage and an articular capsule shared by the two bones.
The capsule defines a cavity filled with a viscous liquid known as synovial fluid, which both nourishes and lubricates the cartilage. Cartilage is a very fragile tissue. Once destroyed it does not regenerate, which is why the dual role of the protective synovial fluid is so important. The capsule is often surrounded by a fibrous casing and a number of ligaments that brace the joints. If the ends of two bones do not match exactly, a cartilaginous disk known as a meniscus may be found between the two surfaces of the joint (as in the knee).

• Muscles are made up of a number of contractile cells connected by membranes into a bundle called a fascia. Fasciae are joined at the ends, where they form fibrous tendons that attach to the bones at insertions. The contractile cells have the ability to shorten, which produces muscular contraction. This requires energy, which is supplied by the blood, then stored and metabolized at the cellular level.

Muscle contraction is controlled by nerves. The point where the nerve cell attaches to the muscle cell is known as the motor endplate, which is a complex system that converts information from the nerve into a muscle contraction. The muscular system is thus very closely associated with the circulatory and nervous systems, so changes to either of the latter two systems have swift repercussions on the musculoskeletal system.

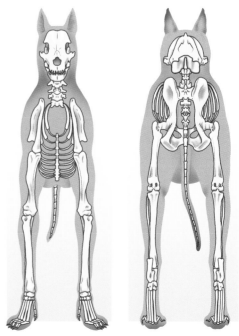

SKELETON (FRONT AND BACK VIEWS)

SUPERFICIAL LAYER OF MUSCLES

1. Parotid gland
2. Mandibular salivary gland
3. Brachiocephalic muscle
4. Sternocephalic muscle
5. Trapezius
6. Latissimus dorsi
7. Abdominal muscles
   (oblique outer muscle of the abdomen)
8. Gluteal muscle
9. Tail muscles
10. Tensor fasciae latae
11. Biceps femoris
12. Semitendinosus
13. Gastrocnemius
14. Flexor digitorum muscles
15. Common calcaneal tendon (Achilles tendon)
16. Extensor digitorum longus
17. Cranial tibial muscle
18. External intercostal muscles
19. Deep pectoral muscle
20. Flexor carpi
21. Extensor carpi radialis
22. Extensor digitorum muscles
23. Extensor carpi
24. Biceps brachii
25. Pectoral muscles
26. Triceps brachii
27. Deltoideus
28. Omohyoideus
29. Orbicularis oris
30. Zygomaticus
31. Levator muscle of upper lip and nose
32. Masseter
33. Orbicularis oculi
34. Temporalis.

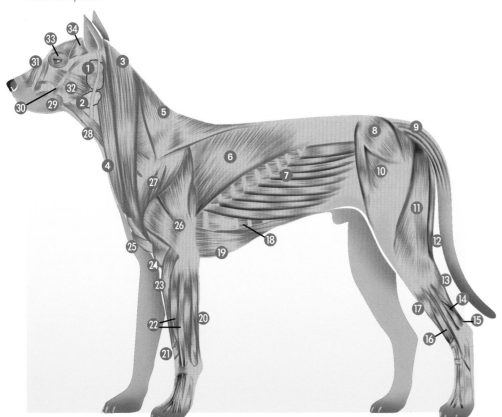

The Skin

In the broadest sense of the word, skin is the boundary between an organism and the outside world. It includes two structures: skin in the strict sense (a keratin structure) and its associated structures (hair, glands, etc.).

The Skin is a Keratinous Structure

The skin has three layers.

• **The epidermis** has several layers. A basal layer contains dividing cells and cells that produce melanin (the pigment responsible for skin color). Above this, in the nose and the foot pads, there is a very thick, clear layer (two to three cells deep). This layer includes cells arising from the division of cells in the basal layer, as well as macrophages (which dispose of any foreign matter). This is followed by a granulated layer of flattened cells and then the horny cell layer, made up of very flat cells having no nuclei. The flattened cells contain large amounts of keratin. Finally, there is an outer layer of cells in the process of flaking off.

• **The dermis,** separated from the epidermis by a basement membrane, is a relatively thick portion of the skin—1.3 mm thick on the back and 2.5 mm thick on the pads. It contains the elastic fibers and collagen that give the skin its toughness and pliability.

• **The panniculus** (subcutaneous fat) is the deepest layer. It contains large numbers of adipocytes (fat cells).

Only the dermis and the panniculus contain blood vessels and nerves. The latter transmit information from both outside and inside the body.

The functions of the skin

• **The skin serves as a barrier.** It prevents certain substances such as water, ions and macromolecules from leaving the body, and, conversely, prevents water, some molecules and bacteria from entering the body. It is possible for epidermal cells to become swollen with water, at which time they allow some molecules to enter. This fact is used in the application of wet dressings. The barrier is also a mechanical one, protecting against such harmful agents as infrared radiation (here the superficial layers play a role), ultraviolet radiation (stopped by the hair and pigmentation) and biological agents.

• **The skin plays a role in exchanges through its secretions,** sweat and sebum. Apocrine and eccrine glands produce sweat (eccrine glands are found only on the nose and metacarpal pads). In dogs, sweat seems to serve only for local cooling of the skin. Sebum is produced by the sebaceous glands, which are attached to the hair follicles. It plays a protective role by destroying bacteria.
The skin can also absorb medication or toxic agents, such as alcohol, as well as fat-soluble vitamins, sex hormones, etc.
Finally, the skin can transfer heat when the temperature changes.

• **The skin plays a role in metabolism** by storing fat in the adipocytes of the panniculus. It is also very marginally involved in vitamin D3 production, which occurs when ultraviolet rays reach the superficial layers of the skin.

• **The skin has a sensory function:** Through nerve endings located in the dermis and panniculus, it can sense temperature, pressure, pain and contact with an object.

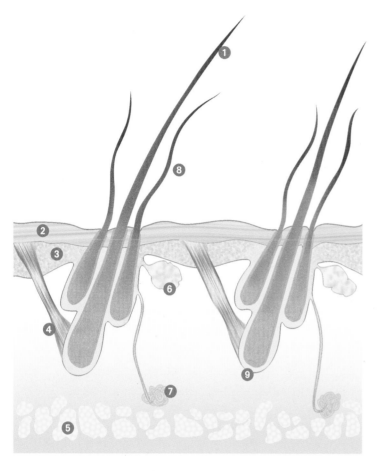

THE SKIN

1. Primary (guard) hair
2. Epidermis
3. Dermis
4. Arrector pili
5. Subcutaneous fat
6. Sebaceous gland
7. Sweat gland
8. Secondary hair (undercoat)
9. Papilla

Structures Associated with the Skin

• **Hair follicles** are made up of hairs and their pores, a sebaceous gland and the arrector pili, a muscle responsible for making the hair stand on end.
• There are two types of **sweat glands**. Apocrine glands are located deep in the dermis throughout the body and open below the sebaceous gland. Exocrine glands are located where the deep dermis and panniculus meet, but only on the nose and the metacarpal pads. They open onto the epidermis, independently of the hair follicle.
• **Other glands** include the anal glands, used to mark territory and the tail glands, located above the base of the tail.

Hair Structure

A dog's hair follicles are arranged in groups consisting of a central primary hair surrounded by thinner, shorter secondary hairs. (Puppies have no secondary hairs.)

The density of the hairs depends on the breed and age of the dog. The softer the hair, the more dense it is. For example, German Shepherds have between 100 and 300 follicle groups/cm2 (650-2000 inch², while a softer-haired dog can have from 400 to 600 groups/cm2 (2600-4000 inch²). The number of follicle groups a dog will have is already established at birth. However, in young dogs, only one type of hair (either primary or undercoat hair) is present, which is what gives puppies their well-known softness. As the dog grows, the angle of the hair with respect to the skin decreases, reaching about 45° in the adult.

Hair color is genetically determined, with certain colors being dominant over others. This explains the wide range of coat colors in dogs, as well as the specific types of spots and patches characteristic of certain breeds. For example, a Beagle's spots are not related to those of a German Shepherd.

Practically everyone has had the experience of having to pick up a large ball of hair from the rug in early summer. In fact, dog hair does not last forever. There is a cyclical loss of hair known as shedding. Like wild animals, dogs shed twice a year, resulting in a summer coat and a winter coat. These seasonal coats can be explained by the three stages of activity of the hair follicles:

Anagen phase is a period of growth for the hair and its follicle, which grows down into the dermis. It lasts about 130 days in the average dog and can be as long as 18 months in the Afghan Hound. **Catagen phase** is a resting phase. Growth stops and the follicle shrinks.

During the **telogen** phase, the follicle shrinks all the way to the orifice of the sebaceous gland. The base of the hair shrinks to a cone shape and the hair falls out. Another hair begins to grow, starting with the anagen phase and growing in the same follicle as its predecessor.

Of course, the hairs do not all fall out at the same time. Shedding begins at the rear of the dog and progresses toward the front. The winter coat is much thicker than the summer coat and protects the dog from severe cold.

These changes in the coat do not happen by chance. The most important factor governing shedding seems to be the photoperiod (the duration of daylight in relation to darkness). The lengthening day triggers shedding in the spring and the decreasing amount of daylight triggers shedding in the fall. Temperature changes affect only the density of the coat and the speed with which the hairs are replaced and are not a major factor causing shedding.

Although individual hairs are replaced, a dog's coat keeps its color, in spite of the appearance of gray hairs on the muzzles of elderly dogs. Remember, a dog's coat should be groomed regularly to avoid disease.

VIEW OF UNDERSIDE OF FRONT PAW.

1. Carpal pad
2. Metacarpal pad
3. Digital pads
4. Nail
5. Dewclaw

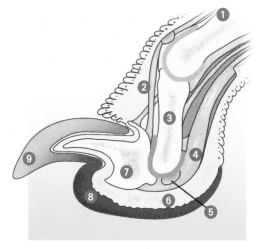

MEDIAL SECTION OF A NAIL

1. Proximal phalanx
2. Tendon of the extensor digitorum muscle
3. Median phalanx
4. Tendon of the flexor digitorum muscle
5. Sesamoid distal bone
6. Subcutaneous tissue
7. Distal phalanx
8. Epidermis
9. Nail.

503

Digestion

Food molecules ingested by the dog are generally too complex to allow them to be absorbed in the intestine or used by the cells. Digestion provides the dog with nutrients, simpler molecules that can be used by the cells.

To this end, the canine digestive tract is devoted entirely to breaking down food molecules (glucides, lipids and proteins) and absorbing nutrients. Anatomically speaking, it can be divided into three sections. The first section, where ingestion takes place, includes the tongue, teeth, salivary glands, pharynx and esophagus. The second, responsible for digestion, comprises the stomach, small and large intestines and their associated glands (the liver and pancreas). The third, dedicated to elimination, is made up of the lower end of the large intestine and the anal canal.

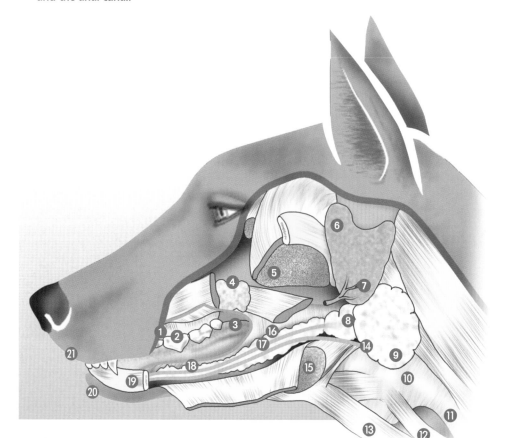

THE ORAL CAVITY

1. Mouth cavity
2. Carnassial tooth
3. Dorsal surface of tongue
4. Zygomatic gland
5. Section of temporalis muscle
6. Parotid gland
7. Parotid duct
8. Sublingual gland
9. Mandibular salivary gland
10. Pharynx
11. Esophagus
12. Sternothyroid muscle
13. Sternohyoid muscle
14. Mandibular duct
15. Section of digastric muscle
16. Sublingual gland
17. Duct of the sublingual gland
18. Sublingual gland
19. Mandible
20. Lower lip
21. Upper lip.

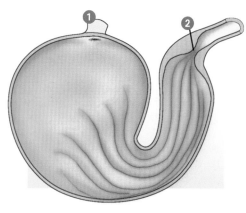

INTERNAL CONFIGURATION OF THE STOMACH

1. Cardia
2. Pylorus

Ingestion of Food

• **The mouth.** A dog ingests its food through its mouth. As in all carnivores, the teeth of canines are specialized for their different roles in chewing. These days, however, whether dogs eat household food or commercial dog food, they usually just gobble it down with hardly any chewing, which means there is little or no mechanical pre-digestion.

The paired salivary glands secrete saliva into the mouth cavity. The liquid and mucosal components of saliva moisten the food and help it to pass through the esophagus. When the food is swallowed, the tongue pushes the food into the oropharynx, the epiglottis closes (preventing the food from entering the trachea) and the food is directed into the esophagus.

• **The esophagus.** The arrival of the rest of the meal, along with the muscular contractions of the esophagus, pushes the food through the thoracic cavity and the diaphragm to the entrance of the stomach, known as the cardia.

Digestion of Nutrients

Food is made up of three types of molecules: glucides, proteins and lipids. Each is digested in a different part of the digestive tract, through different processes involving different enzymes. It is interesting to note the differences in this respect between dogs of different sizes: While a small dog's digestive tract represents 7% of its body weight, a large dog's digestive tract represents only 3% of its body weight, so the large dog is more susceptible overall to digestive problems.

• **The stomach** is on the dog's left side behind the chest wall, extending slightly beyond the sternum. It has a large volume compared to the intestines, due to the dog's meat-based diet. When a dog eats, the volume increases even more: The totally distended stomach can occupy half of the abdominal cavity. In the stomach, food is subjected to both mechanical and chemical digestion. Contraction of the tunica muscularis (muscular tissues surrounding the stomach) mix the food so that it combines with gastric juices. There is a significant amount of chemical digestion.

• **The small intestine.** The chyme (partially digested food) then passes through the pylorus into the duodenum, the first portion of the small intestine. Because the intestine is delicate, the stomach empties into it slowly, a process controlled by both the pylorus and the first part of the duodenum.

• **The digestive glands.** The digested food than passes through the small intestine, where chemical digestion continues by means of secretions from the pancreas and liver, which pass into the duodenum through ducts.

• **The pancreas** is V-shaped in carnivores. This very elongated gland is made up of groups of cells called acini that produce digestive enzymes and secrete them into the pancreatic duct as pancreatic juice. Secretion occurs only after the dog has eaten.

The enzymes are secreted in an inactive form (so they do not destroy the organs through which they must pass) and are activated by chemical processes in the intestine. They are thus precursors of proteases, lipases and amylases. Pancreatic juice also contains bicarbonates that neutralize the intestine's contents, which were acidified in their passage through the stomach.

• **The liver** has many functions, including digestion. It is found behind the diaphragm, on the dog's right side. Liver cells are organized into hepatic lobules that continuously secrete bile into the bile ducts. The ducts carry the bile to the gall bladder, where it is stored between meals. When the chyme arrives in the duodenum, the gall bladder contracts and releases the bile. The bile then comes in contact with the partially-digested food in the duodenum.

Bile contains water, mineral salts, bile pigments and bile salts. Bile pigments have no digestive function (they are products of the breakdown of hemoglobin) and are in fact eliminated by the digestive tract. Bile salts, on the other hand, play a fundamental role in the digestion of lipids.

GENERAL STRUCTURE OF THE DIGESTIVE TRACT

1. Anus
2. Rectum
3. Descending colon
4. Stomach
5. Liver
6. Cardia
7. Esophagus
8. Mandibular salviary gland
9. Parotid gland
10. Molars
11. Canine teeth
12. Tongue
13. Trachea
14. Diaphragm
15. Pylorus
16. Small intestine
17. Duodenum.

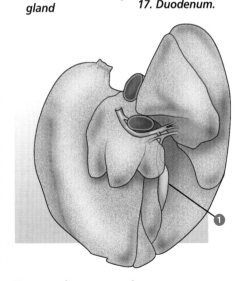

THE LIVER (VISCERAL SIDE)

1. Lobes and gall bladder

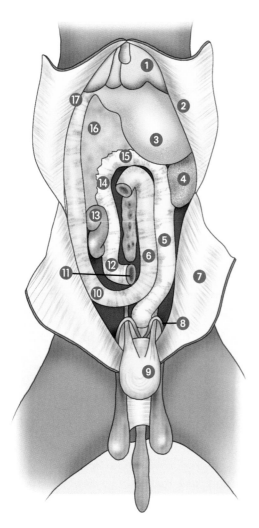

**THE ABDOMINAL CAVITY
(DORSAL DECUBITUS POSITION)**

*1. Liver
2. Costal arch
3. Stomach
4. Spleen
5. Descending colon
6. Duodenum
7. Abdominal wall
8. Vas deferens
9. Bladder
10. Transverse portion of duodenum
11. Jejunum
12. Ileum
13. Cecum
14. Ascending colon
15. Transverse colon
16. Pancreas
17. Descending portion of duodenum.*

• **Microorganisms.** A dog's intestines, like those of other animal species, contain a large population of microorganisms (mainly bacteria) that actively participate in digestion. The intestinal flora is highly sensitive to changes in the type of food. This means that unlike humans (omnivores), dogs (carnivores) cannot eat different foods at every meal. This would destroy the intestinal flora and cause diarrhea.

This phenomenon explains why:
- it is imperative to have an eight-day transition period when changing a dog's food;
- certain lactic acid bacteria found have highly beneficial ("probiotic") effects on canine digestion when mixed with the food.

• **Digestion of glucides.** Glucides are present in foods in many forms of varying complexity, which consist of chains of simpler base molecules named with a form ending in "-ose", e.g., glucose and fructose. Starch, for example, is a huge molecule made up of many glucose molecules.

Digestion breaks glucides down into smaller molecules so they can be absorbed. A number of enzymes are involved in this chemical reaction. These enzymes, known as amylases, are produced by the salivary glands (in small quantities) and the pancreas. Most breakdown of glucides occurs in the small intestine.

• **Digestion of lipids.** Lipids (fats) are broken down into triglycerides through the action of pancreatic lipase (an enzyme specific to lipids) and biliary salts from the liver. The biliary salts form an emulsion with the triglycerides, thus increasing contact with the lipases. The lipases partially hydrolyze the lipids, resulting in tiny lipid droplets known as micelles.

• **Digestion of proteins.** Proteins are made up of large or small chains of amino acids. Only amino acids can be absorbed, so proteins are broken down by enzymes under specific conditions.

Digestion is begun in the stomach by the acids and proteases (enzymes specific to proteins) of the gastric juice. It is continued in the small intestine by pancreatic proteases.

Absorption of Nutrients

• **The intestine** is responsible for most digestion and absorption of nutrients. Six times longer than the dog's body, it forms loops that are folded up in the abdomen. All of the abdominal viscera are enclosed by the greater omentum, or epiploon, which holds the organs in position.

The inside surface of the small intestine is also folded, which increases the surface area available for absorption. The cells that make up the villi (the smallest folds of the intestinal wall, at the cellular level) have different functions. The lower cells primarily secrete mucus, while the upper cells absorb digested nutrients. Dead cells also release other types of enzymes as they break down. The absorption process differs depending on the type of digested matter present.

• **Absorption of glucides.** It is mainly the basic forms of glucides, the "-oses", that are present in the small intestine and are absorbed by the intestinal cells, whereupon they enter the small intestine's numerous blood vessels.

• **Absorption of lipids.** The micelles are absorbed by the intestinal cells, which alter their various components to reconstitute triglycerides. The triglycerides are attached to proteins and other molecules and are taken up by the small intestine's lymphatic vessels.

• **Absorption of proteins.** Amino acids are absorbed by the intestinal cells in a complex process. Other peptides consisting of amino-acid chains of various lengths are also present in the intestinal lumen. The shortest, chains of two or three amino acids, can be absorbed by an active-transport system. They are then hydrolyzed by enzymes within the cells to form the amino acids that pass into the bloodstream.

Absorption of Other Nutrients

Water and mineral salts are also absorbed in the intestine. Water is only partially absorbed in the small intestine by means of a mechanism involving sodium ions and glucose molecules or amino acids. Mineral salts are absorbed in various parts of the intestine, through differing mechanisms. For example, calcium is absorbed in the duodenum by means of a transport protein.

The intestine's blood vessels join to form the portal vein, which leads to the liver, where nutrients are stored.

Elimination of Feces

Digested matter then passes through the various portions of the large intestine: the cecum, the colon, the rectum and the anal canal. The total length of the large intestine is about 70 cm (28 in) in dogs.

• **The cecum and colon.** The cecum, which is very short, has the same function as the colon, which is dorsally located in the loins. The cecum and the colon absorb any nutrients that were not absorbed by the small intestine (particularly water). The remaining material is partially digested by the intestinal microbial flora, but this is a secondary function in dogs. The resulting nutrients are absorbed as in the small intestine.

The large intestine also forms, stores and evacuates fecal material: the stools.

• **The rectum and anal canal** are located in the pelvic cavity. As in all carnivores, they store and evacuate fecal matter.

• **Defecation.** Fecal material is eliminated in three steps. First, in an essentially behavioral step, the dog "looks for a place". Dogs tend to leave their living area to defecate. Next, there is a stage of mechanical preparation: the dog assumes a particular attitude through contraction of various muscles. Finally, evacuation per se occurs when the large intestine contracts forcefully.

Respiration

Respiration is the function that allows an organism to take in oxygen and eliminate carbon dioxide. A dog's respiratory system can be divided into two parts: the upper respiratory tract and the lower respiratory tract.

The Upper Respiratory Tract

The upper respiratory tract consists of the nasal cavities, the nasopharynx, the larynx and the trachea. The nasal cavities are located in the bridge of the nose and in the forehead and are open to the outside world via the nostrils, which open from the nose. The nostrils have a cartilaginous structure and are mostly open to allow air to enter.

• **The nasal cavities and nasopharynx.** The nasal cavities include turbinate bones and nasal sinuses and are separated by a median bony partition. The turbinate bones spiral in on themselves to form a cone shape. For this reason, the mucous membrane that covers them has an extensive surface area, richly furnished with blood vessels, which enhances its role of warming the air and saturating it with water vapor.
The nasal glands contained within the nasal cavities secrete mucus, which traps noxious particles from the air (dust, microbes, etc.). Another portion of the mucous membrane has an olfactory function, allowing the dog to smell.

Body temperature: 38.5 to 39°C (101,3-102,2°F)
Average heart rate (beats per minute): 70 to 120
Arterial blood pressure: 12/6
Average rate of respiration (breaths per minute): 15 to 20

507

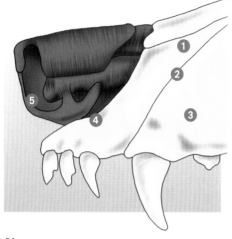

NASAL CAVITIES

1. *Nasal bone*
2. *Premaxilla*
3. *Maxillary bone*
4. *Lateral cartilage*
5. *Nasal septum.*

After leaving the nasal cavities, the air passes through the posterior nares into the nasopharynx in the back of the mouth. At this point, it is nearly at body temperature and impurities have been removed.

• **The larynx.** The air continues its passage to the lungs through the larynx and trachea. The larynx is composed of four cartilage structures (the cricoid cartilage, thyroid cartilage, arytenoid cartilage and epiglottis) and is attached to the bones of the skull by the hyoid bone. A number of muscles are responsible for moving the cartilage structures in relation to each other so that the larynx is open during respiration but closes when the dog swallows, thus avoiding entry of food into the trachea if it is swallowed the wrong way. The larynx controls the flow of air by opening or closing. It also contains the vocal cords, which vibrate when air passes through them, allowing the dog to make sounds (for example, growling and barking).

• **The trachea** is a long tube formed of about 40 cartilaginous rings closed by tracheal muscle. It carries the air from the larynx (in the throat) to the bronchi (in the thoracic cavity). Tracheal muscle contracts the trachea, reducing its diameter and so regulating the flow of air: It also prevents excessive dilation, e.g., when the dog coughs.

The Lower Respiratory Tract

The lower respiratory tract includes the bronchi and the lungs, located inside the thoracic cavity and separated from it by the pleurae. The dog's thoracic cavity is defined by the ribs on the sides and by the diaphragm at the rear. The lungs are separated from the chest wall by the pleurae, which define the pleural cavity. Thus, the lungs always remain filled with air. A dog's lungs have seven pulmonary lobes: The left lung has three (cranial, middle and caudal) and the right lung has four (cranial, middle, caudal and accessory).

The bronchi branch and carry the air to the pulmonary alveolae: There are as many bronchi as there are pulmonary lobes. After reaching the lobes, the bronchi again branch into bronchioles of decreasing diameter.

The lungs are also richly supplied with blood vessels, which allow the exchange of oxygen and carbon dioxide (oxygenation) over a large surface area.

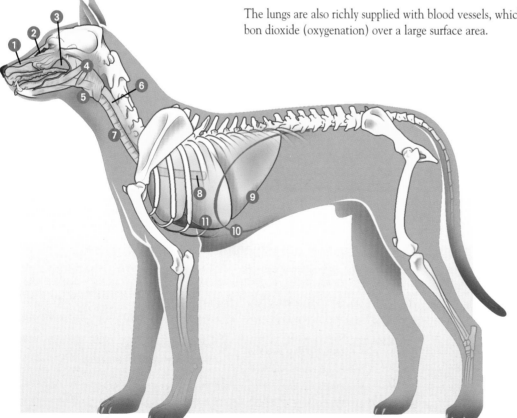

OVERVIEW OF THE RESPIRATORY TRACT

1. *Nasal cavity*
2. *Frontal sinus*
3. *Naris*
4. *Pharynx*
5. *Larynx*
6. *Esophagus*
7. *Trachea*
8. *End of trachea*
9. *Basal margin of left lung*
10. *Projection of the diaphragm*
11. *Left lung.*

Respiratory Phenomena

Respiration is a complex phenomenon involving both muscle action and the circulatory system.

• Exchange of gases between the air in the alveoli and the blood helps determine the partial pressures of oxygen and carbon dioxide on each side of the capillary wall. Gases move from areas of high partial pressure to areas of low partial pressure.

Carbon dioxide thus passes from the capillaries to the air in the lungs and oxygen travels in the opposite direction. To allow for constant oxygenation of blood, the air and the blood are continually replaced. The heart acts as a pump and causes the blood to circulate.

• Pulmonary ventilation replaces the air in the alveoli. It has two stages: inspiration (inhalation), which brings new air into the lungs and expiration (exhalation), which flushes out the contaminated air. Inspiration results mainly from the contraction of the diaphragm and intercostal muscles and the relaxation of the abdominal muscles. These muscle contractions enlarge the volume of the thoracic cavity, thus drawing air into the lungs, which inflate like a balloon. During expiration, the contracted muscles relax and the volume of the thoracic cavity decreases due to its elasticity.

The normal respiratory frequency in dogs is between 10 and 30 breaths per minute. It varies depending on the dog's size (small dogs breathe more often than large ones), physical condition, excitability, etc.

• Regulation of the respiratory system. The nervous system controls the entire process of respiration in a mainly unconscious process. In exceptional cases of forced movement (where inspiration or expiration exceeds the tidal volume, such as in a sigh), it becomes conscious. According to various physiological data, dogs can change their frequency of respiration and/or respiratory volume. For example, during strenuous effort, a dog pants, that is, breathes more rapidly through the mouth and increases the tidal volume. This is because muscle activity requires increased oxygen consumption and heats up the dog's body. The dog increases its respiratory rate to allow increased perfusion of the cells with oxygen (because the heart beats faster); and to cool its body by loss of water vapor from the lungs, since a dog sweats essentially not at all, except on its footpads. Similarly, breathing through the mouth brings cool air from the trachea in contact with the warm blood vessels, thus cooling them.

Another type of regulation depends on the characteristics of the air inhaled (the partial pressure of oxygen decreases with altitude). This system regulates the partial pressures of oxygen and carbon dioxide in the blood as a function of the blood's pH, which affects the partial pressure of carbon dioxide.

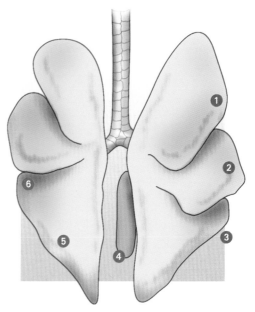

LUNGS - (DORSAL VIEW)

1. *Right cranial lobe*
2. *Middle lobe*
3. *Right caudal lobe*
4. *Accessory lobe*
5. *Left caudal lobe*
6. *Left cranial lobe.*

The Circulatory and Lymphatic Systems

Study of the circulatory system includes the blood vessels (veins and arteries) and the heart in both anatomical and physiological contexts. Adult and fetal circulation differ and so will be studied separately. Lymphatic circulation is the "drainage system" for the entire circulatory system.

Fetal Circulation

The blood vessels begin forming when the embryo can no longer be adequately nourished by simple diffusion between cells. The development of internal organs requires that nutrients be carried directly to the cells involved. In contrast, the heart has a much more complicated origin. It is formed from the embryo's outer cells and remains outside the embryo at first. Later, it is incorporated into the embryo and reaches its final position in the thoracic region. At first, the heart is rectangular (an evolutionary vestigial form). Later, it curves in, rotates and acquires its familiar form.

THE HEART

1. Third rib
2. Sixth rib
3. Aortic orifice
4. Pulmonary orifice
5. Left atrioventricular orifice (mitral valve)
6. Apex of heart
7. Elbow
8. Tricuspid valve
9. Aortic orifice
10. Third rib.

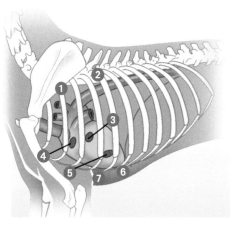

I. Side View, Left

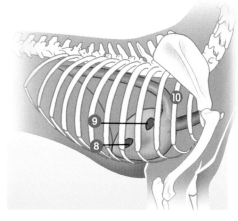

II. Side View, Right

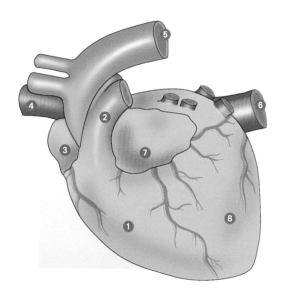

THE HEART (AURICULAR SIDE)

1. Right ventricle
2. Pulmonary trunk
3. Right auricle
4. Cranial vena cava
5. Aorta
6. Caudal vena cava
7. Left auricle
8. Left ventricle

Fetal lungs are not functional, as oxygen is received from the umbilical veins coming from the mother, while carbon dioxide is eliminated through the umbilical arteries. Thus, a major part of the circulation is "shunted" through the foramen ovale, an opening between the two sides of the heart and through the ductus arteriosus, a canal linking the aorta (the main artery leaving the left side of the heart) to the pulmonary trunk (which exits from the right side of the heart). The chambers of the heart are not separate until the end of gestation and the first hours after birth. In contrast, the ductus arteriosus does not close until after birth, once the lungs have started functioning.

This developmental phenomenon can lead to anomalies such as a defect in the septum of the heart, persistence of the ductus arteriosus, or an improperly-placed heart.

The Adult Circulatory System

In a dog that has developed normally, the heart's axis is placed obliquely in relation to the body's axis. The heart is more to the left side of the body than to the right (with 4/7 being on the left) and is flattened crosswise, which means that the right side of the heart is positioned cranially (toward the head) and the left side caudally (towards the tail). Thus, the base of the heart, where the blood vessels are located, is located cranially and dorsally, while the apex is positioned caudally and ventrally. The heart is located between the third and sixth ribs and its weight varies greatly depending on the breed.

• **The heart** is divided into four main parts: the **right atrium** receives deoxygenated blood and sends it to the **right ventricle**, which pumps it to the lungs; the **left atrium** receives the oxygenated blood from the lungs and sends it to the **left ventricle**, which in turn pumps it out to the various parts of the body. In the adult, the two halves of the heart are completely separate and the oxygenated and deoxygenated blood never mix. The blood passes from one compartment to another through valves forming a system of "portals".

Physiologically speaking, the heart has a regular cycle known as the cardiac cycle. The chambers of the heart, which have contractile properties, pump in two phases known as systole (the contraction phase) and diastole (the relaxation phase). These phases are not synchronized among all the chambers, so the atria contract before the ventricles. The number of cycles per minute is called the heart rate. In dogs, the heart rate varies from 70 to 160 depending on size (small breeds have a higher heart rate than large and giant breeds) and activity. Purely physiological phenomena also lead to bradycardia (a reduction in heart rate) during sleep and tachycardia (an increase in heart rate) when effort is exerted or there is significant stress (as with a visit to the veterinarian).

• **The cardiac cycle** functions according to a very precise rhythm. The slight return pressure in the veins and the opening of the atrioventricular valves cause the ventricles to fill passively (with the arterial valves closed). Filling is completed by the contraction of the atria during the atrial systole. Then the ventricular systole begins. The ventricle fills to capacity and the intraventricular pressure increases, which closes the atrioventricular valves as the ventricles begin to contract. This contraction becomes stronger as the ventricular pressure exceeds the arterial pressure, which causes the arterial valves to open. Finally, the heart muscles relax, allowing the arterial valves to close during the relaxation phase. The atria refill and the process repeats.

During a stethoscopic auscultation, the clinician hears only the sounds of these different phases. In dogs, the cardiac cycle produces two sounds: "lubb" (brief silence), "dupp" (long silence). The "lubb" is a long sound of multiple origin: It is caused by the closure of the atrioventricular valves, the increased pressure of the blood in the ventricles and the turbulent outrushing of blood into the large arterial trunks. The "dupp" is a shorter sound because it has only a single cause: the closing of the arterial valves. Any extraneous noises can be considered as pathological in dogs.

Thanks to the use of modern procedures such as electrocardiography and echocardiography, the entire cardiac cycle can be studied in great detail. However, the interpretation of such studies is complicated and should be left to specialists.

Another interesting question with regard to the heart is how its cyclical activity arises. In the muscle walls there are three areas of tissue, known as nodal tissue, composed of cells that can spontaneously and slowly depolarize. This gives rise to an action potential that travels through all the heart's cells, causing the heart to contract. The nodal tissue, located in the atria, imposes its rhythm, thus acting as the heart's pacemaker.

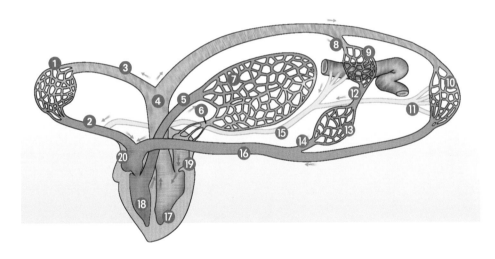

The cardiac cycle can change due to various factors, both external (seeing a stressful object) and internal, by acting on nerve pathways consisting of accelerator or inhibitory nerve fibers. The lungs and blood gases also influence the heart rate through baroreceptors located on the aortic arch. Excess oxygen slows the heart, while excess carbon dioxide causes it to accelerate.

• **Arteries and veins.** The heart merely acts as a pump. It is the blood vessels that actually carry the blood to the organs. Anatomically speaking, the blood vessels leaving the heart are called arteries (whether the blood is oxygenated or deoxygenated) and those returning to the heart are known as veins. Veins contain small valves that keep the blood under slight pressure, which is necessary for circulation to occur. This is why when an artery is cut, the blood flows in spurts, but if a vein is cut, the flow of blood is continuous.

The aorta, a large artery that carries oxygenated blood, exits from the left side of the heart toward the front of the dog. It soon curves, forming the aortic arch and leads toward the rear. Just before it curves, the brachiocephalic trunk branches off. (The brachiocephalic trunk carries blood to the head and forelimbs.) The subclavian artery also branches off and heads toward the thoracic region. Then the aorta

THE VEINS

1. Caudal vein
2. Internal iliac vein
3. Lateral sacral vein
4. Testicular vein
5. Renal vein
6. Hepatic portal vein
7. Intercostal vein
8. Cranial vena cava
9. Costocranial vein
10. Deep cervical vein
11. Vertebral vein
12. Internal jugular vein
13. Auricular vein
14. Parotid gland
15. Veins of the eyes, nose and lips
16. Mandibular salivary gland
17. Facial vein

18. External jugular vein
19. Axillary vein
20. Cardiac vein
21. Internal thoracic vein
22. Superficial vein in the forearm
23. Metacarpal vein
24. Caudal vena cava
25. Hepatic veins
26. Hepatic portal vein
27. Epigastric vein
28. Dorsal vein of the glans penis
29. Internal saphenous vein
30. Metatarsal veins
31. Lateral saphenous vein
32. Popliteal vein
33. Femoral vein
34. External iliac vein
35. Internal pudendal vein.

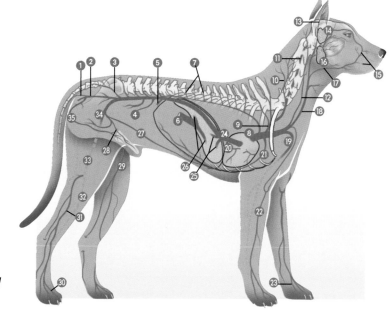

THE ARTERIES

1. Temporal artery
2. Auricular artery
3. Cervical artery
4. Dorsal scapular artery
5. Thoracic aorta
6. Intercostal artery
7. Celiac artery
8. Cranial mesenteric artery
9. Lumbar artery
10. External iliac artery
11. Internal iliac artery
12. Sacral artery
13. Internal pudendal artery

14. Tibial artery
15. Saphenous artery
16. Femoral artery
17. Median artery
18. Antebrachial artery
19. Brachial artery
20-21. Thoracic arteries
22. Axillary artery
23. Costocervical trunk
24. Thyroid artery
25. Common carotid artery
26. Vertebral artery
27. External carotid artery
28. Facial artery.

THE LYMPHATIC SYSTEM

1. Lumbar trunks
2. Visceral trunk
3. Tracheal trunk
4. Thoracic trunk
5. Bronchiomediostial trunk.

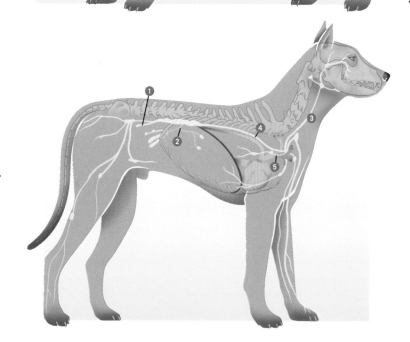

enters the abdominal region and supplies blood to all of the organs and to the hind limbs by branching into arteries of smaller diameter. When it reaches a muscle or an organ, the artery branches into a bundle of arterioles that allow the distribution of oxygen and the uptake of carbon dioxide. The blood is then carried by venules converging toward a small-diameter vein. These small veins join with the cranial vena cava in the anterior portion of the body or with the caudal vena cava in the posterior portion of the body. These two large veins return the blood to the right side of the heart, which pumps it to the lungs through the pulmonary trunk. In the lungs, the blood releases its carbon dioxide, then returns to the heart through the pulmonary veins to complete the cycle.

Lymphatic Circulation

The lymphatic system is a drainage system that removes lymph from the bloodstream. Lymph vessels contain valves and converge into two large main trunks, the thoracic duct and the right lymph duct. The vessels are not very visible, but the lymph nodes (or ganglia), which filter all of the lymph from one area, can easily be detected. There is a relatively large number of lymph nodes. Some are superficial and can be felt, others are deep (in the large cavities of the body) and are visible only with X-rays or ultrasound. Hypertrophy of the lymph nodes usually indicates inflammation in the drainage area, which is why it is important to palpate them during a clinical examination. The lymph nodes are also a preferred site where cancerous cells pass from one organ to another. This is why the ganglia are removed at the same time as tumors, in order to limit the spread of the disease.

The Urinary System

The same organs are responsible for creating and eliminating urine in dogs of either sex. In order, they are: the **kidneys**, from which two **ureters** lead to the **bladder**. A single tube, the **urethra**, carries the urine from the bladder to the outside world.

All of these organs are located in the abdomen. The bean-shaped kidneys are found beneath the lumbar arch, near the first lumbar vertebrae. The left kidney is slightly more caudal than the right. The two ureters are attached to the bladder's dorsal side and the bladder is located just in front of the pelvis. The urethra follows a different path in males and females. In bitches, it is shorter and usually wider. It opens into the vestibule of the vagina through the small urethral papilla.

In male dogs, the urethra is longer and narrower and consists of three parts: the prostatic, membranous and penile sections.

The Structure of the Kidneys

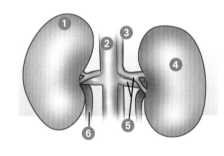

THE KIDNEYS: VENTRAL VIEW

1. Right kidney
2. Caudal vena cava
3. Abdominal aorta
4. Left kidney
5. Renal artery and vein
6. Ureter.

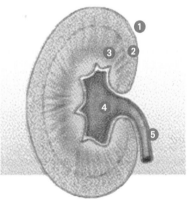

THE KIDNEY: LONGITUDINAL SECTION

1. Fibrous capsule
2. Cortex
3. Medulla
4. Renal pelvis
5. Ureter.

The kidney consists of an outer cortex; the medulla, which is inside; and the renal pelvis, a collecting pocket that extends into the ureter.
The nephrons are the kidney's basic functional units. They consist of fairly long tubules that empty into collecting tubules. They have several parts, as follows: A mass of **capillaries** passes into Bowman's capsule (the glomerular capsule). A **convoluted portion** (proximal tubule) leads from the capsule to a **straight portion**, through an **intermediate tubule** and then to a distal tubule having two sections, a **straight portion** and a **distal convoluted portion**. Each distal tubule empties into a **collecting tubule** through a short **connecting tubule**. To simplify, the nephrons' glomerular capsules and the convoluted portions of the tubules can be said to be grouped in the renal cortex, while the straight portions, forming the loop of Henle, comprise the medulla.

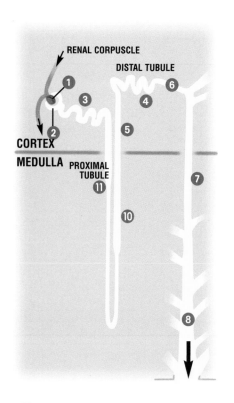

The structure of a nephron and renal corpuscle (Malpighian corpuscle)

1. Glomerulus (arterioles)
2. Bowman's capsule (glomerular capsule)
3. Convoluted portion
4. Distal convoluted portion
5. Straight portion
6. Connecting tubule
7. Collecting tubule (cortex)
8. Collecting tubule (medulla)
9. Loop of Henle
10. Ascending limb
11. Descending limb

Urine Formation

Urine is made in the kidneys, namely in the nephrons, in a multi-step process allowing part of the organism's waste matter to be eliminated. The kidney also has other functions related to various regulatory systems, notably regulation of ions, acids and bases.

Diuresis is the process by which urine is formed. It includes several steps. First, filtration of the blood forms the glomerular filtrate, a "preliminary" form of urine. The blood passes through fenestrated capillaries (tiny arteries having walls perforated by pores) in the renal tubules. Molecules that are sufficiently small can pass through the capillary walls, due to a significant difference in the pressure on either side and collect in the renal tubules.

The resulting filtrate can be called a "preliminary" form of urine because its composition will be modified before it is eliminated. At this stage, the filtrate is very similar to plasma.

Following filtration, **reabsorption** occurs in the convoluted portion of the tubules, particularly in the proximal tubule. It allows molecules and ions needed by the organism to return to the bloodstream. Transport of these substances requires the expenditure of energy by cells and is often accompanied by reabsorption of water, which is a passive process.

Chloride, sodium and potassium are the main ions reabsorbed. Molecules reabsorbed by the convoluted portions of the tubules include all glucose and proteins, as well as some amino acids and organic acids.

Finally, some substances occur in the urine as a result of **secretion**, which also occurs in the convoluted portion of the proximal tubule. This mechanism affects both substances present in the blood (such as contrast media used in medical examinations, or medications such as penicillin) and substances created in the tubule's epithelium (such as ammonia). Here, again, both active and passive mechanisms are involved, as well as exchanges.

In the last part of the nephron, the collecting tubule, urine attains its final form. Regulatory mechanisms come into play to concentrate the urine and acidify it even more.

Side view of abdominal and pelvic cavity in the bitch

1. Anus
2. Perineum
3. Vestibule of the vagina
4. Vulva
5. Rectum
6. Body of the uterus
7. Bladder
8. Left uterine horn
9. Broad ligament
10. Descending colon
11. Left uterine horn
12. Left ovary
13. Left kidney
14. Suspensory ligament of ovary.

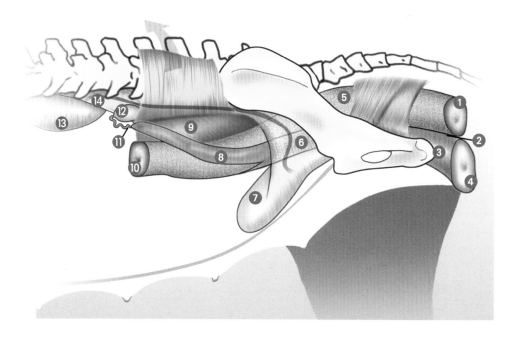

Storage and Elimination of Urine

The urine, in its final form, flows from the collecting tubules into the renal pelvis, a small pocket emptying into the urethra. The urethra carries it to the leak-proof and highly expandable bladder, where it is stored between urinations. A sphincter between the bladder and the urethra prevents urinary incontinence. When the bladder is sufficiently full, urination (miction) can occur. The bladder, which is composed of many smooth muscle fibers, contracts and the urethral sphincter relaxes. The urine is then forced out by the pressure.

Urination is regulated by the nervous system, with the brain providing voluntary and conscious control. Nerves originating in the lumbar, sacral and pelvic regions cause contraction of the bladder and relaxation of the sphincter.

Regulation

The urinary function is regulated mainly through control of the kidneys on various levels. It can be affected by factors outside the kidneys, particularly circulatory factors. In fact, the amount of urine formed by the kidneys depends heavily on the amount of blood filtered. When an organism's blood volume decreases, less urine is produced and vice versa.

The nervous system also plays a role, both by influencing renal function and by affecting urination, i.e., the bladder. Many nerves innervate the kidneys and affect the renal blood vessels. They can rapidly decrease the rate of renal perfusion, resulting in a decreased volume of urine produced.

Finally, hormones have the greatest regulatory effect. Many hormones are involved in controlling the elimination of water and ions. Most of them, however, have an effect only in pathological situations. The most important of these hormones is vasopressin, also called antidiuretic hormone. Vasopressin is secreted by the pituitary gland (hypophysis) located at the base of the brain. This hormone acts on the ends of the nephrons, namely on the end of the convoluted portion of the distal tubule and on the collecting tubule. Secretion is triggered by increased osmotic pressure in the blood., i.e., a decrease in the amount of water relative to the other molecules in the blood; or by a decrease in arterial pressure. Other stimuli may have an effect as well. Stress, a decrease in ambient temperature, or physical exercise can trigger secretion of antidiuretic hormone.

Vasopressin is captured by receptors on the cells of the collecting tubule's surface. Increased reabsorption of water in the nephron results. This mechanism allows the animal to conserve some of the water contained in its cells.

URINE
Daily volume produced: 25 to 40 ml per kg live weight.
pH: 5 to 7.
Urea: 300 to 800 mg per kg live weight per day.

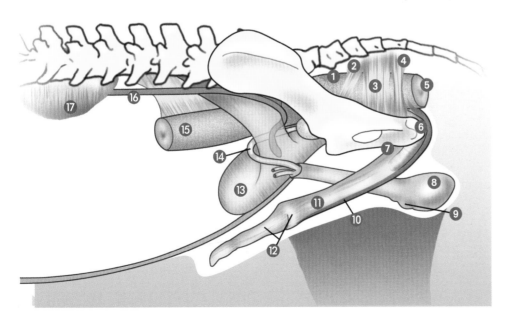

SIDE VIEW OF ABDOMINAL AND PELVIC CAVITY IN THE DOG

1. Rectum
2. Coccygeal muscle
3. Ani levator muscle
4. Sphincter ani muscle
5. Anus
6. Bulbocavernous muscle
7. Ischiocavernosus muscle
8. Left testicle
9. Left epididymis
10. Retractor muscle of penis
11. Body of penis
12. Glans penis
13. Bladder
14. Left vas deferens
15. Descending colon
16. Left ureter
17. Left kidney.

515

The Five Senses

The Eye and Vision

• **Vision in dogs**. Although this subject has been extensively debated, it is currently accepted that dogs have better night vision than humans. Their retinal cells are better at concentrating incoming light, which means they have good vision under twilight conditions. This allows them to hunt at night.

Dogs can perceive distant motion very well, but have difficulty distinguishing fixed objects at the same distance. This phenomenon is also an adaptation to the visual hunting done by dogs.

The visual angle differs among breeds, depending on the type of work the breed was developed to perform. Herding dogs, for example, need the maximum possible field of view for the best view of the livestock. Their eyes are mostly on the sides of head, giving a large visual field. In order to locate prey, hunting dogs need depth perception, with a narrower field of view, so their eyes are on the front part of the head.

• **The eye and related structures**. The eye sits in an orbit, a cavity of the skull. It is held in place by muscles that work in different directions. The muscles move the eye and aim it.

The eye is protected by surrounding structures, the eyelids and glands. Each eye has three eyelids. The upper and lower eyelids are mucus-lined folds of skin. Their edges are protected by eyelashes, which keep dust from falling into the eyes. The third eyelid is merely a membrane in the inside corner of the eye. Normally invisible, the third eyelid covers the eye when the eye is closed or irritated, or when nerve problems occur.

The eye is exposed to the dry external environment, but the exposed part (the cornea) is protected by tears, an aqueous medium secreted by the lacrimal glands. The tears then collect in the spaces between the eyelids and the eyes and are carried away by a narrow duct that begins in the inside corner of the eye and ends in the nostrils. When tears are produced in excess, or the duct is obstructed, the tears flow out onto the eyelids, where they oxidize into red streaks on the hair that resemble blood.

The eye itself has two parts:

• **The anterior portion** consists of the cornea, the iris and the crystalline lens. This part of the eye focuses light, in somewhat the same manner as a camera's objective lens. The cornea and the crystalline lens are transparent and act as optic lenses. The iris acts as a diaphragm to regulate the amount of light that enters through the hole it surrounds, the pupil.

• **The posterior portion** includes the vitreous body, the choroid and the retina. It changes the optic signals received as light into nerve signals that are transmitted to the brain by the optic nerve. To continue the camera analogy, the posterior portion of the eye serves as the film and the brain develops the picture.

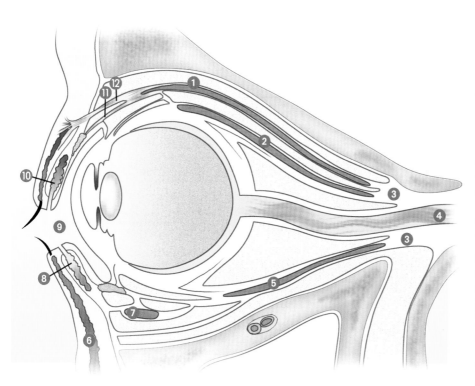

LONGITUDINAL SECTION OF THE EYE

1. Levator palpebrae superioris muscle
2. Superior rectus muscle
3. Tendons of the muscles that move the eye
4. Optic nerve
5. Inferior rectus muscle
6. Orbicularis oculi muscle
7. Inferior oblique muscle
8. Lower tarsal plate
9. Palpebral fissure
10. Upper tarsal plate
11-12. Tendons of the levator palpebrae superioris muscle.

The Sense of Hearing

Dogs hear twice as well as humans. They are able to perceive frequencies up to two and a half times higher than those heard by humans. Dogs can even hear ultrasound, which explains the effectiveness of dog whistles. They are very good at distinguishing between sounds and so can easily distinguish between words spoken by their handlers, although in this respect, tone of voice and gestures are also very important.

• **The ear.** The external ear is a cartilaginous structure covered by muscles and skin and forms the mobile pinna that aims toward the source of a sound like a radar antenna. The pinna opens into the external auditory canal, a cartilaginous tube covered with very fine skin, which is vertical at first and then horizontal. The canal ends at the very thin tympanic membrane, or eardrum. The external ear serves to collect sounds for the middle ear.

The middle ear is a resonance chamber. Sound waves strike the eardrum and cause it to vibrate, thus causing the ossicles - the malleus ("hammer"), stapes ("stirrup") and incus ("anvil") - to vibrate in the tympanic cavity through the action of a lever. This mechanism transmits sounds to the inner ear, amplifying them while damping the severe vibrations, since the ossicles have only a limited range of motion.

The two parts of the inner ear have very different functions. The cochlea changes sound waves into nerve signals and transmits the signals to the brain through the auditory nerve. The semicircular canals contain tiny hairs that perceive the position of the head and play a role in the body's overall sense of balance.

There are many nerves in the pinna of the ear, including the vagus nerve, which slows the heart. When the ears are cropped, this nerve is stimulated and can cause problems under anesthesia. Many countries have prohibited ear cropping, which is no longer required for shows or to conform to pedigree standards.

The Nose and Sense of Smell

• **The sense of smell is highly developed** in dogs and can be considered a dog's primary sense. Dogs use their sense of smell for hunting, for learning where they are, for communicating with each other and for indicating food preferences. They recognize their owners and their homes more by smell than by sight. Smell is also important for locating and tasting food and even has an effect on taste: if a dog does not like the smell of his food, he will refuse to eat it.

A dog's sense of smell is a million times more sensitive than a human's and dogs have 40 times as many of the brain cells involved in deciphering odors. This high level of olfactory sensitivity can also be attributed to the olfactory mucous membrane, a receptor surface that occupies a volume of 150 cm³ (9,2 in³) in dogs, compared with only 3 cm³ in humans (0,2 in³).

• **The perception of odors.** The mucous membrane overlies the turbinate bones in the dog's nostrils. The turbinate bones are irregular in shape and are separated by sinuses into which the inhaled air flows, thus trapping odors. Another olfactory organ, the ethmoid bone, is also made up of sensory cells and is located at the back of the nasal cavity.

When odors come into contact with these sensory cells, they trigger chemical changes that cause a nerve signal to be sent via the olfactory nerve to the area of the brain responsible for processing olfactory information.

Perception of odors varies depending on the odor's chemical composition, the ambient humidity and the molecular weight of the scent molecules. Heavy molecules that are somewhat soluble in water are more easily smelled. These are the principles underlying the work of dogs trained to recognize human scents (rescue and tracking dogs) or objects (drug- and explosive-sniffing dogs).

The Sense of Taste

• **Taste is a very subjective sense.** The sense of taste is closely linked to the sense of smell and both work together to determine food preferences. Dogs do not tire of their food: A dog can eat a food it likes every day - which, in fact, is recommended.

• **The perception of taste.** The sense of taste depends on the taste buds present in the mucous membranes of the tongue, palate and pharynx. Dogs have about 12 times fewer of these taste sensors than do humans. The glossopharyngeal and lingual nerves originate in the taste buds and carry nerve signals to the brain. As with smell, this gustatory information arises from the interaction of chemical substances in food that are dissolved in the saliva and taste cells.

The Sense of Touch

• **Sensitivity.** Certain stimuli, including thermal, tactile and painful stimuli, are sensed by the skin through a very dense network of nerve endings connected to the spinal cord and the brain. These nerve endings are irregularly distributed throughout the body.

• **Heat and Cold.** The sensation of cold is more intense than the sensation of heat. These sensations lead to reflex reactions: cold causes the hair to stand on end, while heat causes the respiration rate to increase so that more water will evaporate from the tongue.

• **Touch.** The same type of nerve network exists for the sense of touch and is concentrated at the base of the hairs. Not all hairs are equally sensitive. The vibrissae (whiskers), long hairs on the muzzle, eyebrows and chin, are particularly rich in nerve endings.

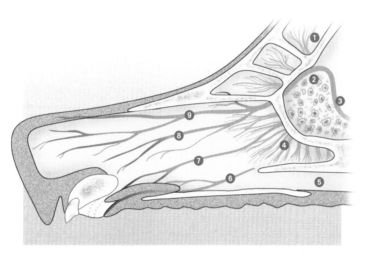

OLFACTORY SURFACES: PARASAGITTAL SECTION OF NASAL CAVITIES (WITH TURBINATE BONES REMOVED)

1. Frontal sinus
2. Sievelike portion of the ethmoid bone
3. Ethmoidal nerve
4. Olfactory nerves
5. Nasal portion of pharyngeal cavity
6. Caudal nasal nerve
7. Vomeronasal nerve
8-9. Nasal branches of ethmoidal nerve.

The Nervous System

The nervous system collects stimuli - both information from the outside world and information originating within the animal. It creates nerve impulses that cause voluntary or involuntary muscles to contract (including skeletal muscles that control movement, as well as visceral muscles and the muscles involved in glandular secretion).

The nervous system is composed of nerve cells, known as neurons and their supporting structures, which form the neuroglia.

Neurons can act as receptors, when they receive a stimulus; as transmitters, when they send nerve impulses; and as associative neurons, when they serve as a connection between two different neurons.

Nerve fibers have different levels of excitability and conductivity. The speed of nerve conduction from peripheral areas of the body to the brain (or vice versa) is about 30 m/second.

A reflex is the conversion of external sensory information received by the general nervous system directly into motor, secretory or inhibitory information and the transmission of this information from the nervous system to the organ involved, all within a relatively short time.

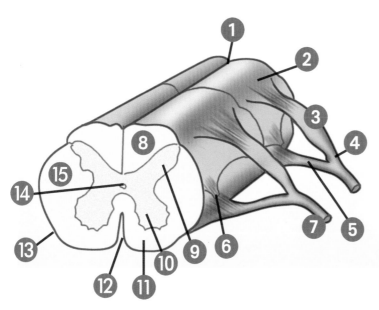

The Central Nervous System

The central nervous system includes the cerebrum, cerebellum, medulla oblongata (in the cranial cavity) and the spinal cord (in the spinal column). In addition to the bones that surround it, the central nervous system is covered by three membranes: the dura mater, which is in contact with the bone; the arachnoid membrane; and the pia mater, which is in direct contact with the nerve tissue. These membranes protect against both physical shocks and internal attack (there is a barrier between the blood and the meninges, known as the blood-brain barrier, which is resistant to various substances). It is needed because neurons are cells that do not regenerate, so any damage is irreparable.

• **The cerebrum** contains motor, sensory, visual, auditory, olfactory (smell) and gustatory (taste) centers. It is also the seat of memory and association.
• **The cerebellum** controls balance and coordination.
• **The spinal column** is an important reflex center, as is the medulla oblongata, which controls vomiting, salivation, etc., as well as automatic functions such as respiration, heartbeat and constriction/dilation of blood vessels.

The Peripheral Nervous System

The peripheral nervous system is constituted of nerve fibers grouped into nerves that branch symmetrically throughout the body. Sensory nerves carry sensory information from the peripheral areas of the body to the central nervous system's collecting centers. Motor nerves carry nerve impulses generated by the central nervous system to the targeted organ. Many nerves carry out both functions and contain both sensory and motor fibers.

The Autonomic Nervous System

The autonomic nervous system is centered in ganglia on either side of the spinal column. It controls an organism's involuntary functions (those that are not controlled by the central or peripheral nervous systems). It is subdivided into the sympathetic and parasympathetic systems, which have opposing effects in activating or inhibiting the functions of an organ. For example, the parasympathetic system stimulates intestinal activity, while the sympathetic system decreases it.

The nervous system is involved in many diseases and interactions between medications. Various illnesses can arise, requiring a thorough knowledge of the subject.

(I)

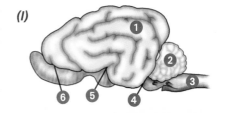

(II)

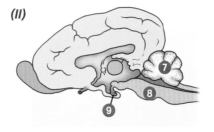

Part 7

The Stages
of a Dog's Life

The Stages of a Dog's Life

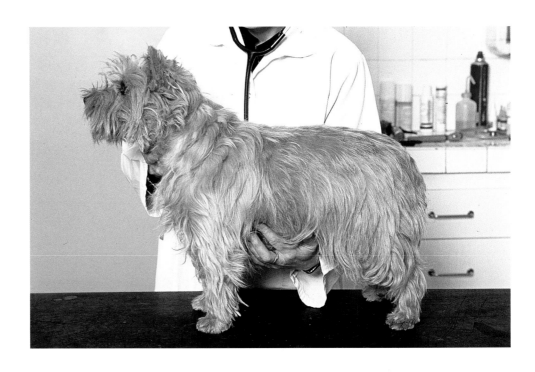

The foregoing review of anatomy, physiology and feeding will contribute to an understanding of the following discussion of the major stages of a dog's life, from mating and gestation through birth, nursing through weaning, and growth in puppies. The consequences of old age are also explained. The adult stage of a dog's life is not specifically dealt with in this section, as it is treated throughout the book.

The Reproductive Stage

While the goal of reproduction is to produce puppies, the means to this end differ substantially among private owners and breeders. The owner of a pet or utility dog will occasionally allow a bitch to reproduce in order to obtain offspring having her characteristics - although, contrary to popular belief, reproduction is not an absolute requirement for a dog's psychological or physiological health. In nature, access to reproduction in packs of wild dogs is highly dependent on an individual's status in the hierarchy, since the act of mounting is an indication of dominance. This can sometimes explain why mating occurs between dogs of incompatible temperaments.

In contrast, breeders choose their sires and dams based on origin, progeny and genetic characteristics. The breeder often overcomes hierarchical obstacles by assisting and directing the mating between the selected dogs. If the dogs refuse to cooperate, he may even resort to artificial insemination to achieve his goal.

Puberty in Dogs

Puberty in males

The age at puberty depends essentially on the adult size of the breed. It can range from six months in miniature dogs to eighteen months in the giant breeds. In the male, it corresponds to production of the first fertile spermatozoa. Since fertility declines with age, and large breeds age earlier than small breeds (a phenomenon probably linked to the aging of the thyroid gland), large dogs have a correspondingly shorter fertile period. In giant breeds, the fertility of the sperm sometimes begins to decline as early as the age of seven years.

Puberty in females

As in males, puberty is later in large-breed females than in small-breed females (also between six and eighteen months). The first heat periods are relatively unobtrusive and may pass unnoticed. In bitches, there is a difference between puberty (the ability to ovulate) and nubility (the ability to carry a pregnancy to term and to whelp), which is why it is not recommended to breed from a bitch at her first heat, when her birth canal is not yet fully developed.

Beginning at puberty, the female genital tract adopts a cyclical rhythm that is generally expressed as two heat periods per year.

The Bitch in Heat

The bitch's sexual cycle

A bitch's sexual cycle is monestrus (only one ovulation per cycle) with spontaneous ovulation (which

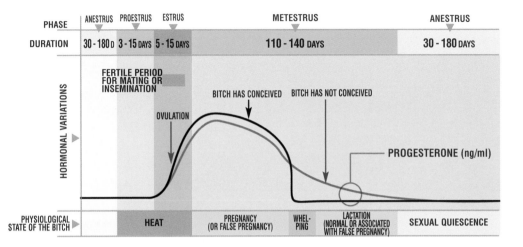

means that ovulation cannot be triggered by mating, as in the cat). It comprises four successive stages:
- proestrus, a preparatory stage before ovulation;
- estrus, or ovulation proper;
- metestrus, corresponding to the duration of gestation and lactation; and
- anestrus, or sexual quiescence.

The length of each phase of the cycle is variable. Only the metestrus (or diestrus) phase is of relatively constant length (120 ± 20 days). The bitch is "in heat" or "in season" during the proestrus and estrus phases of the cycle, a period lasting an average of three weeks, but the duration depends on the date of ovulation, which varies among bitches and in the same bitch from one cycle to another. The fact that a bitch ovulates 12 days after the first blood flow in one cycle does not mean that ovulation will occur after the same interval in the following cycle.

The phases of the cycle

During proestrus, the hypophysis (pituitary gland) causes the growing ovarian follicles to secrete hormones known as estrogens that are responsible for behavioral modifications (the bitch attracts males, seeks affection, licks her vulva) and physical changes in the bitch. The vulva becomes congested and a bloody discharge appears, which attracts males. However, the bitch will not yet allow mating to take place.

The period during which a male will be accepted corresponds in a general way to estrus. Often, a postural reflex will appear that causes the tail to be held to the side when the vulva is stimulated. However, this sign should be interpreted with caution; some bitches will accept dogs when they are not in their period of ovulation. During estrus, the vaginal discharge becomes clear and changes into mucus, which facilitates mating.

During this phase, the still-immature ova are released during their oocyte phase. They usually do not become fertile for another forty-eight hours.

Unlike those of many species, the ovaries of a bitch begin secreting progesterone several days before ovulation. Progesterone levels in the blood thus increase gradually, whether or not the ova are fertilized. Thus, in dogs, progesterone levels are an indicator of ovulation but not of gestation.

Progesterone secretion then levels off, but lasts through the rest of metestrus due to secretion by the corpora lutea of the ovaries, from which the ova were released. This hormone prepares the uterus for implantation of the embryo(s) and for pregnancy. Progesterone production falls drastically two months after ovulation, which allows lactation and uterine involution to occur until the sexual organs are completely quiescent (anestrus).

Mating or Insemination

The ideal moment

Given the length of time spermatozoa remain fertile (about forty-eight hours in the female genital tract), it is possible to optimize the chances of fertilization by making sure that sperm meets egg when both are at the height of their fecundity, to ensure the best fertility and optimal litter size. Ideally, mating or insemination should occur within the forty-eight hours following release of the oocytes, so that most of the eggs and sperm can reach the rendezvous point (in the oviducts). The ova remain capable of being fertilized for two days after maturation (in some breeds they even seem to remain fertile for up to four days), which explains why superfecundation by two different males can occur in dogs.

EVOLUTION OF HEATS

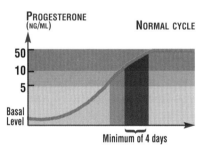

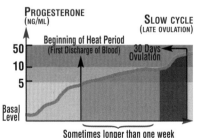

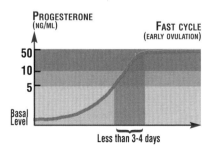

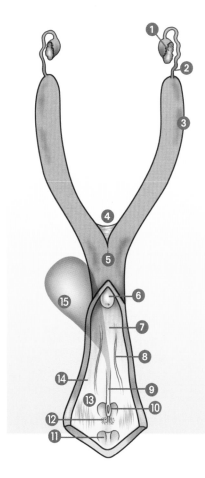

1. Ovary
2. Oviduct
3. Uterine horn
4. Intercornual ligament
5. Body of the uterus
6. Cervix
7. Vagina
8. Vaginal folds
9. Urethra
10. External orifice of urethra
11. Clitoral fossa
12. Vestibular glands
13. Vestibule of vagina
14. Hymen
15. Bladder.

The most difficult part of the process is observing the biological signs of ovulation as accurately as possible. Several complementary tools, of varying precision, are available to breeders for this purpose.

• Clearing of the vaginal discharge generally signals the end of proestrus, although it is not a reliable indicator of ovulation. Some bitches, such as Chow Chows, may show discharge until the end of estrus.

• Systematically mating the bitch about twelve days after the first bloody discharge, then again two days later, is a practical technique if the first discharge is accurately noted. This remains an imprecise method, however, as some bitches (about twenty percent) do not ovulate during this period, and so do not conceive or conceive only a few puppies.

• Acceptance of the male or teaser dog and appearance of the tail reflex are not indicative of ovulation. For example, bitches have been observed that allowed mounting from the beginning of proestrus, although they did not ovulate until later (thirty days later in the most extreme cases).

Many bitches also allow mounting during the false heats before whelping, when urinary infections are present, or when estrogen secretion by follicular cysts leads to nymphomania.

• Use of a galvanometer to measure the electrical resistivity of vaginal mucus can lead to a reasonably precise evaluation of the fluidity of vaginal secretions. This parameter usually decreases just after ovulation, signifying the end of the period of estrogen saturation and thus the rapid replacement of vaginal cells. However, this diagnostic measurement comes too late for breeding purposes, since predicting imminent ovulation is more useful than knowing that it has just occurred.

• Reagent strips that reveal biochemical changes in the vaginal mucus are difficult to introduce far enough into the vagina to avoid contamination by the urine. The results are usually imprecise (since the color change is seen within the three days preceding or following ovulation) and therefore not very reliable.

• Depending on the stain used, vaginal smears allow direct observation of changes in the vaginal cells related to hormonal variations (particularly of estrogen). This simple, economical technique is now routinely used by veterinarians and breeders to obtain a preliminary evaluation of which phase of the sexual cycle a bitch is in.

• Procedure for a vaginal smear.
First, examine the swelling of the vulva. Pull the vulvular commissure downwards and introduce the swab vertically along the caudal wall of the vagina. Avoid bumping the clitoral fossa. When the swab has reached the roof of the vagina, pivot the swab until it is horizontal and push it in as far as possible without forcing. Collect exfoliated cells and secretions from the cervix by using circular movements.

The swab will usually look red at the beginning of the heat period, pink or colorless at the end of proestrus, and purulent if vaginal or uterine infection is present.

Roll the tip of the swab delicately on a previously cleaned slide. Avoid touching the same place twice, so that there will be no clumps of cells.

Fix the sample using a fixing agent. It can then be taken to the veterinarian or stained for immediate examination.

Interpreting the smear

Vaginal smears provide a great deal of information in addition to the estimated time of ovulation.

When a bitch has run away, or if mismating has occurred through the kennel fence (!), the veterinarian can determine how long the spermatozoa remain in the vagina (up to six hours after coitus). He can also estimate the chances that fertilization has occurred, depending on the observed stage of the sexual cycle. For example, if the bitch is found to be in anestrus, the beginning of proestrus, or metestrus, the risk of pregnancy is minimal, and certainly less than the risk associated with an early abortion performed for convenience.

Vaginal smears also allow certain treatments to be performed during anestrus that would be contraindicated during periods of sexual activity. This includes most hormonal treatments.

Finally, along with hormone levels, they also help to diagnose certain causes of infertility (silent or anovular heats, persistence of a secreting corpus luteum, vaginal infection, etc.).

Thanks to their ease of execution, speed, low cost and the information they provide, vaginal smears are very useful in the field of canine reproduction. However, in certain cases when the interpretation of the smear is not certain, or does not match clinical symptoms, or if the costs of moving or inseminating the bitch are high, the owner can supplement this analysis with a more accurate tool: a measurement of progesterone levels in the blood.

Near the time when the bitch ovulates, the concentration of progesterone in the blood plasma normally rises over several days (five days, on the average) from its basal level (less than two nanograms per milliliter) to more than forty nanograms per milliliter. This rise takes place more quickly in some bitches than in others, and even varies from cycle to cycle in the same bitch. While eighty percent of bitches ovulate on about the twelfth day of their heat period, it is not rare to observe earlier or later ovulation, especially in breeds with this tendency (such as Dobermans and German Shepherds).

Traditionally, ovulation has been considered to have occurred when the concentration of progesterone exceeds

15 ng/ml (although variations due to different measurement methods in different laboratories must be taken into consideration). Mating or insemination should take place within 48 hours of this result, taking into consideration the time required for the oocytes to mature and to allow time for a second mating two days after the first.

This relatively accurate indication of ovulation not only increases the number of successful matings and inseminations, but also improves fertility. In fact, small litters, which are frequently blamed on the age of the bitch or an insufficient number of ova, are often simply a result of a poor choice of mating date.

By judicious use of both vaginal smears and measurements of progesterone levels in the blood, with due attention to careful methods, the heat periods can be tracked in a way that is both highly satisfactory and economically sound: fertility and litter size increase, unnecessary travel for unproductive matings is reduced, etc.

Diagnosing an infertile bitch

Before infertility in bitches can be treated, it must be very accurately diagnosed. For example, regular measurements of progesterone and other hormone levels, along with clinical examination, can distinguish between an anovular cycle, embryonic resorption due to involution of the corpus luteum, sexual immaturity and androgen saturation, which all have radically different treatments.

Cesarean sections

Most brachycephalic breeds (breeds with short faces), such as Bulldogs and Pugs, have whelping problems (dystocia) that cause the veterinarian to plan to deliver the puppies by Cesarean section. If a Cesarean is done too early, the puppies are premature, and usually die within a few hours after birth due to respiratory insufficiency. If the Cesarean is performed too late, the puppies suffer from cerebral anoxia due to the long wait in the birth canal. Viability of the fetus in dogs is linked to the late development of the lung surfactant that determines the respiratory capacity of puppies at birth.

In fact, the lungs mature at the same time that progesterone levels fall during the days prior to the ideal whelping date. So the measurement of the bitch's progesterone level gives the veterinarian an excellent tool for accurately determining whether the puppies are ready to survive if a Cesarean is done. This technique has considerably increased the survival rate of puppies born by Cesarean section, particularly in Bulldogs, where 90% of births are by Cesarean section.

Luteinizing hormone levels in the blood

Luteinizing hormone (LH) changes the oocyte's nourishing matrix into a corpus luteum that secretes progesterone. It is secreted by the hypophysis, and triggers ovulation. Thus, determination of the time of this hormone's maximum secretion predicts ovulation ahead of time, instead of merely revealing that it has occurred, as does an increased level of progesterone. This measurement is not yet routinely used by veterinarians when diagnosing infertility, except in a few very specific cases.

Mating

After selecting the parents and estimating the time of ovulation, the owner presents the bitch to the dog to be served. For health reasons, it is best to check ahead of time to make sure that neither dog has any genital lesions. This reduces the risk of transmission of venereal diseases (namely canine

GENITALIA OF THE MALE DOG
(ISOLATED AND FLATTENED)

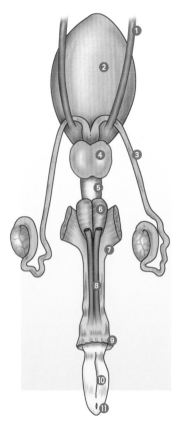

1. Ureter
2. Bladder
3. Vas deferens
4. Prostate
5. Ureter muscle
6. Bulb of penis
7. Ischiocavernosus muscle
8. Retractor muscle of penis
9. Inside of prepuce
10. Elongated portion of glans penis
11. External orifice of urethra.

1. Urethra
2. Anus
3. Retractor muscle of penis
4. Bulb of penis
5. Corpus cavernosus
6. Ischiocavernosus muscle
7. Tail of the epididymis
8. Scrotum
9. Testicle
10. Head of the epididymis
11. Prepuce
12. External orifice of urethra
13. Elongated portion of glans penis
14. Bulbourethral gland
15. Penis
16. Inguinal canal
17. Vas deferens
18. Bladder
19. Ureter.

GENITALIA OF THE DOG (SIDE VIEW)

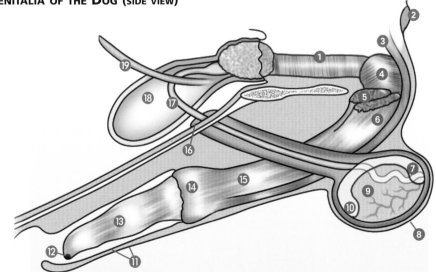

herpesvirus). Preventive prophylaxis (regular washing of the sheath, clean floors) and regular serological tests are preferable to last-minute use of antiseptics, which are often spermicidal and so prevent fertilization.

In longhaired breeds, smoothing, pulling back, or shaving the hair in the bitch's perivulvular area will facilitate the mating.

Mating begins with a brief courting and sniffing phase that excites both dogs. Erection, caused by the rigidity of the os penis and the flow of blood into erectile tissues, then allows intromission of the penis, which causes vaginal contractions in the bitch. These contractions help the sperm to ascend the reproductive tract, help maintain erection, and cause the tie during ejaculation. This phase should last at least five minutes, but may last more than a half-hour if the bitch's movements maintain the constriction around the erectile bulbs.

In most cases, if the timing is right, the dogs will get along very well by themselves and need not be disturbed. Discreet observation from a distance (or by video camera) is all that is required to verify mutual acceptance and that the tie has indeed occurred. Note that even if the tie does not occur, mating may be successful, although litter size is often reduced.

In spite of advancements made in determining the time of ovulation, it is still wise to systematically provide for a second mating forty-eight hours after the first. If the bitch's ovulation has been correctly determined, more than two matings should not be necessary.
Although there is less risk of superfecundation (fertilization by more than one male) in bitches than in queens (female cats), it is recommended that the bitch be isolated from other males until all signs of estrus have disappeared. Superfetation (mating during gestation that results in fertilization) does not occur in dogs.

Some owners sign a mating contract, then take their bitch to the stud dog's home and leave her for a few days. The contract can be based on the international rules adopted by the FCI (Fédération Cynologique Internationale) in June 1979, to replace the Monaco custom. A lease agreement governs the conditions by which a breeder releases a bitch to a third party on the condition that the breeder will own the weaned puppies.

If natural mating between the selected dogs turns out to be impossible (for any one of a variety of reasons), the breeder must resort to artificial insemination.

Artificial Insemination

Artificial insemination is any reproductive technique that makes reproduction possible when it would be impossible without human assistance. By this definition, even "assisted mating"—the simple technique of removing semen from the male and immediately introducing it into the female genital tract—is an artificial insemination technique known as "insemination with fresh semen."

Artificial insemination with fresh semen

This technique is used when sexual intercourse is impossible due to

• incompatible temperaments,

• the inexperience of one or both partners,

• constriction of the genital tract (atresia of the vulva, malformation of the vagina or vulva, vaginal prolapse due to estrogen saturation during the heat period, etc.),

• pain during mating (due to problems with the spine or hind legs, the penis, the vagina, etc.),

• lack of libido.

After verifying that the bitch is receptive, the veterinarian obtains a semen sample from the stud dog in the presence of a bitch in heat (not necessarily the bitch that is to be inseminated.) The semen is collected as follows:

• The erectile bulbs should be exteriorized (brought outside the sheath) before taking the sample, so swelling will not prevent total exteriorization.

• The erectile bulbs are massaged until spontaneous pelvic movements begin.

• Constriction behind the bulbs will help maintain the erection during the three phases of ejaculation. If necessary, the perineum can be massaged to aid ejaculation. As a rule, it is not necessary to collect all of the ejaculate from the third (prostatic) phase, except for large breeds, in which a certain fluid volume is necessary to compensate for the length of the female genital tract.

Once the semen has been obtained, a sperm count is performed using a microscope with a heated stage, to verify the number, condition and motility of the sperm. If the semen is satisfactory, it is introduced into the bitch's vagina (using an "Osiris" type vaginal probe) or the uterus (using a uterine probe).

After insemination, the bitch should be held with the hind limbs elevated for about ten minutes to aid the progress of the sperm and limit reflux. For the same reason, the female should not be allowed to urinate for several minutes after insemination.

It should be emphasized that through all of these steps, precautions must be taken to avoid any thermal, mechanical or chemical stress that would affect the sperm.

If such precautions are taken, this technique should be just as effective as natural mating (pregnancy rate of about eighty percent).

Artificial insemination with chilled semen

This procedure is used primarily to overcome the obstacle of distance between partners, by saving the bitch's owner any travel and kennel costs that would be incurred to take the bitch to the stud dog.

A licensed veterinarian obtains and inspects the semen sample, then refrigerates the sperm, which is diluted in a protective and nourishing solution, at 4°C. Then the sample is sent in a cold package (vacuum bottle sent via overnight mail) to the receiving veterinarian, who performs the insemination after checking the semen for spoilage and ascertaining the bitch's availability.

This must all take place within forty-eight hours after the sample is obtained, which requires perfect synchronization among all the players (availability of the stud dog, properly equipped and trained veterinarians, close attention to the stage of the bitch's heat, rapid transportation). This technique is thus appropriate for animals separated by a medium distance.

The results are comparable to those observed for natural mating, although the sperm's vitality diminishes each time it is handled.

Artificial insemination with frozen semen

The semen is obtained as above. The quality and number of spermatozoa are carefully measured to ensure that the sperm to be frozen contains more than 150 million motile spermatozoa and less than thirty percent abnormal spermatozoa.

The semen is then diluted in a cryoprotectant, packaged in labeled straws, and stored in containers dipped in liquid nitrogen at –196°C for an indefinite period. (The Center for Study of Assisted Reproduction at the Alfort (France) veterinary college has had some straws for more than sixteen years!)

The straws may not be used without the consent of the stud dog's owner, who can set a price with the bitch's owner on the basis of supply and demand. The sperm bank acts only as a service provider in these transactions.

Currently, in France, canine sperm may be frozen only by a licensed establishment. Inseminations, however, can be performed by any veterinarian trained in the technique. The sperm can be sent to them in special containers so that they can thaw it and perform the insemination at the appropriate time.

It is best to take advantage of the stud dog's period of maximum vitality to freeze his semen, and not wait until the dog reaches old age, is threatened with illness, or must be neutered for medical reasons.

This technique has a number of advantages in terms of animal husbandry.

• It makes possible genetic exchanges between two countries separated by a sanitary barrier or by significant distances. For example, a bitch cannot be sent to be mated to a dog living in England without having to endure a six-month quarantine, but it is possible to have the stud dog's semen sent to the bitch.

• It allows the genetic heritage of a good stud dog to be

preserved indefinitely and to be used even when the stud dog is not available or is no longer living.

• It allows breeders to take a step backwards when selective breeding as prescribed by breed clubs arrives at a dead end. For example, the extreme types with highly flattened faces often obtained these days in Bulldogs would benefit from a re-infusion of genes from the less brachycephalic stud dogs of the past, which might reduce the frequency of dystocia.

• It allows disappearing breeds to be saved, and makes recombination possible in breeds represented by only a few individuals.

Gestation

Confirmation of pregnancy

The fertilization of an ovum by a spermatozoon forms an egg that must undergo several divisions and travel to the uterus before becoming implanted in the uterine mucosa. In bitches, implantation does not occur until 17 days after fertilization, and results in the formation of embryonic vesicles that cannot be detected by ultrasound until the third week of pregnancy (18 days at the earliest).

After the third week, careful palpation of the abdomen can reveal beading of the uterus, if the bitch is not too fat and the abdominal wall is relaxed. Between the fifth and sixth weeks, the diameter of the uterus reaches the size of an intestinal loop. During this period, it is difficult to distinguish between a gravid uterus and a loop of intestine containing hard stools.

There is no point in taking X-rays until the end of pregnancy, since the fetus's skeleton does not become calcified (and thus, opaque to X-rays) until after the forty-fifth day.

Other techniques for diagnosing pregnancy occur too late or are too uncertain to be reliable. These include behavioral changes, detection of fetal heartbeats (audible in some bitches during the last two weeks of pregnancy) by auscultation, changes in the blood (sedimentation rate, hematocrit), or mammary development.

Currently, the earliest diagnosis of pregnancy is provided by ultrasound, which allows the owner to be certain of pregnancy when sending the certification of service to the National Kennel Club within the four-week deadline.

The stages of pregnancy

Gestation in dogs lasts from 58 to 68 days (63 days on average). Differences observed among bitches are linked to the difference between the mating date and the actual date of fertilization.

In fact, spermatozoa can live for up to five days in the female genital tract until the ova become fertile.

After fertilization, the eggs become embryos, which travel from the oviducts to the uterus and space themselves out through the two uterine horns. Implantation of the embryo in the uterine mucosa does not occur until sometime between the seventeenth and nineteenth days after fertilization, so confirmation of pregnancy by ultrasound is impossible before that time.

Transformation of the embryo into a fetus, and subsequent fetal growth, are possible thanks to nutrients brought by the placenta and to the development of other membranes (the amnion and the allantois) that surround and protect the fetus.

Fetal growth does not become externally visible until the second half of pregnancy.

CHRONOLOGY OF PRENATAL OBSERVATIONS

Technique allowing the chronology of the pregnancy to be determined	No. of days after fertilization	Notes (medium-sized breed)
Ultrasound	18	embryonic vesicles
	22	visible embryos
	28	heartbeats
	30 to 35	differentiation of head and torso
	43	vertebrae
	47	skull and ribs
	45	mineralization of bones begins (skull, spinal column, and ribs)
X-rays	50	shoulder, humerus, femur
	54	radius, tibia
	56	pelvis

FETAL MEMBRANES

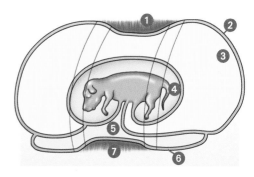

1. Chorionic villi
2. Chorion
3. Allantois
4. Amnion
5. Umbilical vesicle
6. Margin of placenta
7. zonary placenta (endothelial/chorion type)

PROBLEM	ORIGIN	SYMPTOMS	PRATICAL CONSEQUENCES
	Hormonal problems during growth Treatments to prevent estrus administered before puberty	Late first heat, sometimes accompanied by abnormal genital development and stature	Exclusion from reproduction
	True obesity	Absent or unobserved heat	Dog must lose weight
	Hormonal problems in adult	Loss of hair with no regrowth, pigmented skin, obesity, apathy, excessive thirst	Testing of hormonal levels (thyroid, adrenal gland, ovary) with eventual treatment
ABNORMAL OVUM PRODUCTION	Certain medications (androgens, progesterones, cortisone, anabolic growth stimulants, etc.)	Symptoms not obvious (sometimes hypertrophy of the clitoris with androgens)	Pay careful attention to the indications for hormone treatments and their doses and risks (side effects are often irreversible)
	Old age Cyst Tumor	Reduced fertility Abnormal heat (prolonged, nymphomania)	Retirement Ultrasound of ovaries. Hormonal treatments, possibly surgery
	Ovarian problem Insufficient hormones	No heat or cycle with late or no ovulation	Vaginal smears, progesterone treatment. Attempts to stimulate maturation and release of ova.
MATING PROBLEMS	Lesions on the vulva or vagina Genital or joint pain Breed tendency Female aggression Indifference Clumsiness Male or female too large or small	Refusal to allow mating	Assisted mating or artificial insemination
FERTILIZATION PROBLEMS	Poor synchronization of ovulation and mating	Mating does not take	Careful attention to the heat cycle, repeated inseminations, or artificial induction of ovulation
	Obstacles to fertilization	Mating does not take (infection, etc.)	Check that the genital tract is not blocked and is free from infection

Causes of infertility in the bitch

No species has a one hundred percent fertility rate. The maximum fertility observed in dog-breeding establishments under optimal conditions does not exceed eighty-five percent. It is recommended that a bitch be allowed to pass a heat period without being mated at least once every two years.

Only after a bitch has passed two consecutive heat periods without becoming pregnant should infertility be suspected. After the first failed mating, the veterinarian can begin trying to pin down the cause of the failure.

It is easy to eliminate the stud dog as a cause by check-ing the semen (several sperm analyses) and checking for recently-sired puppies. If the infertility is due to the male, there is usually little that can be done and it is best to switch to another stud dog.

Once the male has been ruled out as a cause of infertility, the many possible causes in the bitch can be explored. A thorough investigation includes a review of the bitch's history (previous cycles), any treatments that may have been given (particularly hormone treatments), the mating date, how the mating proceeded, any discharges from the vulva, etc. Such facts should lead to identification of the cause of infertility: problems with the production of ova, with fertilization, with implantation or with gestation.

Abnormal ovum production

These abnormalities can be:

• linked to late or no development of oocytes in the ovary (oocytes do not ripen). In this case, the heat period is absent, silent or irregular.

• due to blockage of oocyte release as sometimes evidenced by nymphomania (permanent or prolonged heat).

• caused by infection (herpes, notably canine herpes virus) or, more rarely, by a dietary problem (energy content of food is too low).

• linked to the persistence of a corpus luteum from the previous cycle that continues to secrete progesterone, which inhibits follicular development for the next cycle. This phenomenon is rare in dogs.

• a result of hormone treatments (anabolic growth stimulants, progesterones, corticosteroids) or excessive sport training (leading to an excess of male hormones in bitches used for sport).

• caused by hormonal dysfunction (thyroid or adrenal problems, obesity, etc.)

Since, in dogs, all of these problems are hormonal in origin, the veterinarian will need to supplement his examination by hormone-level measurements. Obviously, treatment for these fertility problems will depend on their origin. For example, sexual immaturity (absence of puberty) and androgen saturation will not be treated in the same way, although the problem to be solved (failure of the follicle to mature) is the same in each case.

Treatments depend on hormones, which are used to stimulate underactive glands or replace hormones that are lacking. The veterinarian will always use care when treating with hormones, since they can cause temporary or permanent shutdown of the glands that are supposed to produce them naturally. For example, use of progesterones in a sexually immature bitch to delay the onset of her first heat can slow growth later and lead to temporary or permanent cessation of her cycles.

The lesson here is that it is imperative to avoid using hormones as a preventive or curative measure unless the cause of infertility has been diagnosed with certainty, and to avoid using them at all unless all other possible treatments have already failed.

Fertilization problems

Most failed matings are a result of choosing the wrong date for the mating or insemination. Once this cause has been ruled out, the veterinarian can investigate possible obstacles preventing an encounter between the gametes. Vaginal, uterine, urinary tract or even prostate infections can destroy spermatozoa or disrupt their movements before fertilization. Similarly, an obstruction of the oviducts following a case of salpingitis (inflammation of the oviduct) can obstruct the passage of the ova.

Implantation problems

Once the ova have been fertilized, the eggs divide several times but continue to float free in the horns of the uterus for a time before implanting in the uterine mucosa. The uterus must be ready to receive them so that placentas can form and provide the nutrients needed by the developing fetus. Many obstacles (infection, cystic endometrial hyperplasia, etc.) can disrupt the process at this stage.
Furthermore, if a bitch has heat periods that are too close together, the uterus does not have sufficient time to return to its initial state and so is not ready to receive the embryos. In such bitches, treatment with progesterone imposes a compensatory rest period on the uterus, giving it the time required for proper maturation.

Some dietary deficiencies (vitamins A and E) could be implicated at this stage, but usually cause highly apparent symptoms of malnutrition long before this point.

Problems with gestation

During the first days of puppy development, the stage known as embryogenesis, tissue differentiation occurs. We can easily understand why the fetuses are particularly sensitive to any diseases or toxic agents affecting their mother during this period.

It is recommended that no medication be given during the first twenty days of gestation, to avoid any risk of mortality (resorption of the embryo, abortion) or physical defects (teratogenesis).

Many other factors can also interrupt gestation:

• genetic incompatibility between a male and female each possessing a lethal recessive trait that would make homozygotic embryos non-viable.

• some chromosome abnormalities.

• any number of abortive or teratogenic organisms:
- viruses: herpes, canine distemper virus
- parasites: Toxoplasma
- bacteria: Salmonella, Pasteurella
- some of these organisms seem to be epizootic, such as canine brucellosis in the U. S.

• any physical or psychological trauma, which may cause complete or partial abortion. (In a partial abortion, only part of the litter is aborted and the pregnancy continues to term.)

• involution of the corpus luteum, which in dogs secretes the progesterone required for pregnancy throughout gestation.

Nutrition for Pregnant Bitches

Given the same number of fetuses, pregnancy is much harder on small-breed bitches than on large-breed bitches. To be convinced of this, one need only compare the birth weight of the puppies to the mother's weight. This ratio is four times greater in the Yorkshire Terrier than in the Saint Bernard!

Birth weight is a good indicator of the fetal-maternal exchanges that occur during gestation. In humans, slowing of growth in utero is linked to maternal causes such as hypertension or malnutrition. Similarly, a study of 1848 piglets at the Guernévez pig farm (Caugant and Guéblez, 1993) showed that the viability of piglets prior to weaning was significantly related to their birth weights. In dogs, comparable observations have been made, and puppies that have grown slowly (for any reason) are often abandoned by their mother.

When feeding a pregnant bitch, both the quality and the quantity of the food ration should be adjusted to meet gestational needs, which are estimated according to the number of puppies in the litter and their daily weight gain.

Nutrition and infertility

While food does not affect fertility much, litter size, or the beginning of gestation in bitches, it becomes a primary factor in the health of the puppies at the end of gestation, and particularly afterwards during lactation.

NUTRITIONAL PROFILE OF A FOOD FOR A LATE-TERM PREGNANT BITCH (IN TERMS OF DRY MATTER)

Proteins	25 to 35%
Fats	10 to 30%
Crude fiber	1 to 4%
Calcium	1.1 to 1.2%
Phosphorus	0.8 to 0.9%
Vitamin A	5,000 to 10,000 IU/kg
Energy	4,000 to 5,000 Kcal/kg
Protein/Energy ratio	65 to 70 g/1,000 Kcal

No nutritional deficiency has ever been directly implicated in infertility in dogs, when the bitch is in apparent good health.

The technique of "flushing" consists of increasing the energy content of a bitch's food during the period preceding ovulation to stimulate release of oocytes. This method is widespread in commercial livestock (sheep, cattle), but its effectiveness has never been proven in dogs.

Nevertheless, it is recommended that during this period, the diet should be adapted to the hormonal changes characteristic of this stage of the sexual cycle (cholesterol, iodine, vitamins A and E, zinc, etc.). Commercial foods generally contain a generous supply.

In contrast, infertility problems are frequently observed in bitches that are obviously too thin or fat.

In this case, the owner should take advantage of anestrus to adjust the diet and allow the dog to return to her healthy weight before being bred. Practically speaking, an underweight bitch should be given about ten percent extra food during the month preceding estrus, and an overweight bitch's diet should be reduced by ten percent during the same period, by reducing the energy content (number of calories) of the food.

Energy needs

Even though a bitch's appetite increases beginning with the third week of pregnancy, her qualitative and quantitative nutritional needs remain relatively stable during the first five weeks. The fetuses are not growing much, mineralization of their skeletons has not yet begun, and their development has not yet compressed the mother's stomach.

At about the fifth week, a temporary reduction in appetite is sometimes observed, and is often considered to be a confirmation of pregnancy. At this time, the weight and skeletal development of the fetuses begins to increase exponentially, leading to a gradual increase in the protein, energy (and to a lesser extent, mineral) requirements of the mother, at the same time her appetite and stomach capacity are decreasing.

The food's energy content must therefore take into account the reduced stomach volume near the end of gestation and allow the creation of glycogen reserves in the puppies, without causing fat deposits in the mother's birth canal. In order for glycogen reserves to be created in the puppies' livers at the end of gestation, the proportion of glucides in the mother's food must be increased, or the puppies may be hypoglycemic at birth. Although it is theoretically possible to feed a dog food containing no glucides (which are not essential, since carnivores can synthesize them from lipids or proteins), experimentally feeding pregnant bitches such a diet has led to an increase in the mortality rate of the puppies due to hypoglycemia in the days following birth.

The total energy needs of a pregnant bitch include the energy needed for her own maintenance plus the energy needed for fetal growth and maintenance. For example, the energy needs of a medium-sized bitch, such as a Cocker Spaniel weighing twelve kilograms and carrying six puppies, will increase by about forty percent at the end of pregnancy.

At the end of gestation, a bitch should be given an appetizing food (to compensate for loss of appetite) with a high energy content and good digestibility, preferably in the form of several small meals spread throughout the day. Free access to food is not recommended except for underweight bitches.

Protein adjustment

Analysis reveals that, on the average, the canine fetus is 82% water, 13-15% protein (that is, about 80% of the dry matter is protein), 1.5% fat and about 2% minerals. Given the high proportion of protein in the body composition of puppies, gestation requires a protein reserve, and therefore an increase in the protein in the mother's food (about 2.8 times the maintenance requirement in the case of the Cocker Spaniel bitch in the previous example).

While some authors suspect that any excess protein in the maternal diet may be responsible for the appearance of "swimmers" in susceptible breeds, this hypothesis has never been verified. In fact, usually only one puppy in a litter is affected by flat pup syndrome. In addition, comparative pathology reveals that maternal diet is not a cause of splaylegs in piglets, a malady similar to flat pup syndrome in dogs.

Vitamins and minerals

Particular attention should be paid to the vitamin A content of the mother's food, as this vitamin diffuses across the placenta and thus provides good protection to the puppy's epithelial tissues from birth onwards.

For this reason, vitamin A consumption should be about 10,000 IU per kg (about double the amount recommended for a maintenance diet). Care should be taken to avoid overdoses (more than four times this amount), which can cause hare lip; malformation of the tail, ears and spine; fetal mummification, and neonatal mortality in the puppies. The period of greatest susceptibility is between the seventeenth and twenty-second days of gestation.

Overconsumption of vitamin D can lead to calcification of soft tissues, stenosis of the heart valves and premature closure of the fontanelles.

Bitches given excessive calcium supplements early in

TYPICAL DAILY HOME-MADE RATION FOR A PREGNANT BITCH

Formula (in grams) for 1040 kcal metabolizable energy per kg

Lean beef	300
Cooked rice	400
Green beans	100
Carrots	300
Bone meal	20

Percentage of dry matter

Crude protein	24.5%
Fats	14%
Calcium	1.6%
Phosphorus	1%

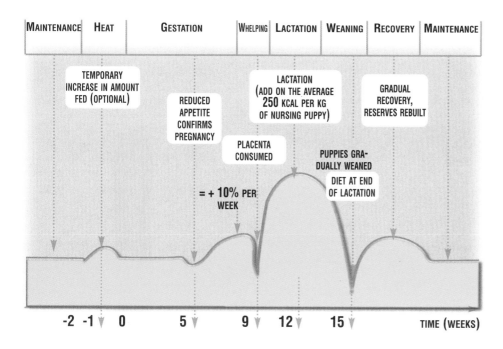

gestation are prone to eclampsia. Before whelping, eclampsia can cause premature whelping. After whelping, it can cause accidental crushing of the puppies.

In summary, a gestational diet should take the following points into account:

- An increase of about ten percent per week in the bitch's nutritional requirements after the fifth week of pregnancy means that dry food needs to be given (since homemade and canned foods contain about 80% more water and so are twice as bulky as dry foods in a stomach with reduced capacity).

- The food should have a high energy content (a metabolizable energy source of between 3800 and 4300 kcal per kilogram of food, depending on the fitness, activity level and temperament of the bitch). It should also be highly digestible, which can easily be ascertained by observing the volume and consistency of the stools.

- The protein content should be increased (about 25 to 36% proteins per kilogram food, depending on the number of puppies expected), since the "dry weight" of puppies at birth is about 70 to 80% protein.

- The mineralization of fetal skeletons at the end of gestation requires an increase in the minerals needed for this process, namely calcium and phosphorus. The amount of calcium should be calculated as a function of the food's energy content, which determines the amount eaten by the bitch. It should not exceed four grams of calcium per thousand kcal, to reduce the risk of shutdown of the parathyroid gland, which causes eclampsia (attacks of tetany) during whelping or lactation. Phosphorus content is usually calculated to ensure that the calcium/phosphorus ratio remains between 1.2 and 1.4, which is a physiological proportion with respect to bone composition.

- To reduce the risk of whelping difficulties due to excess fat in the birth canal, the mother's weight at the end of gestation should not exceed 120% of her maintenance weight (or 110% in giant breeds, 130% in miniature breeds).

Reproduction Pathology

False pregnancy and associated lactation

These conditions are not considered to be pathological, since they are observed more frequently in wild dogs than domestic dogs, disappear spontaneously in a few weeks without treatment, and usually have no after-effects.

Bitches with a false pregnancy display all the symptoms and hormonal changes of a true pregnancy, without being pregnant. This makes the diagnosis of pregnancy even more complicated in dogs, because it is impossible to distinguish between true and false pregnancy by means of behavioral changes (such as collecting various objects to make a "nest"), weight gain or even lactation.

The cause of false pregnancy is not yet known, but the condition tends to recur with each sexual cycle.

Breeding dogs are rarely affected. The condition occurs more often in house pets, which are often submissive and extremely attached to their owners. False pregnancy does not seem to arise from an unfulfilled wish for gestation, since pregnancy does not prevent recurrence.
Owners are even more likely to consult the veterinarian for lactation associated with false pregnancy than for the pregnancy itself. In this case, the bitch is excited and constantly licks her teats, which are swollen with milk. The licking causes lactation by the same neuro-hormonal mechanisms as the reflex associated with sucking.

Treatment of lactation arising during false pregnancy consists of administering anti-prolactin medication, restricting drinking water, and applying astringent ointments on the nipples. The owner should not massage the nipples while applying the ointment, and should attempt to prevent the bitch from licking herself (by having her wear a tether ring), in order to break the vicious circle of stimulation leading to lactation. Ovariectomy (removal of the ovaries) is the only effective way to prevent recurrence.

Metritis

Metritis is a uterine infection that generally affects bitches only during a very specific period in their reproductive cycle. Usually, the uterus is contaminated by entry of a pathogen while the cervix is open, either during estrus or after whelping. Certain types of metritis appear within one or two months after estrogen treatment designed to prevent implantation after a mismating.
With closure of the cervix and post-estrus progesterone saturation, metritis can develop into pyometra, an accumulation of pus in the uterus.

Pyometra

The symptoms of pyometra may not be obvious if there is no vaginal discharge (locked pyometra). This is the riskiest type, because the fluid will not drain spontaneously, for three reasons:
- The cervix is closed.
- Progesterone saturation maintains the uterus in a relaxed state as if it were pregnant.
- The horizontal position of the uterine horns does not facilitate spontaneous drainage.

Clinically speaking, pyometra often causes lethargy, increased thirst (polydipsia) and increased urine out-

LAPAROSCOPY IN DOMESTIC CARNIVORES

Laparoscopy, or celioscopy, is defined as the exploration of the abdominal cavity using an endoscope.

For a very long time, laparoscopy was used only to observe the abdominal viscera. Gradually, it became possible to perform biopsies on organs, then surgical procedures. Today, endoscopic surgery is common in humans. One of its most frequent indications is removal of the gall bladder (cholecystectomy).

Veterinary medicine has reaped great benefits from the technological advances in endoscopy equipment, and reproductive surgery on the dog was one of the first areas to benefit.

Ovariectomy in bitches, vasectomy in male dogs, and removal of ectopic testicles in the abdomen can all be performed by laparoscopy. Thanks to the unique approach used by the Animal Reproduction Department at the Ecole Nationale Vétérinaire veterinary college in Alfort, France, to perfect surgical techniques, laparoscopy can be put to practical use to treat domestic carnivores.

Professor Nicolas Nudelmann
Reproduction Department
Ecole Nationale Vétérinaire, Alfort, France

put (polyuria). This can be complicated by kidney dysfunction due to the toxins produced. The veterinarian can confirm the diagnosis by means of a vaginal smear, abdominal palpation, blood samples, X-rays or ultrasound.

A considerable amount of pus (several liters!) may accumulate.

Medical treatment relies on certain antibiotics and hormones (prostoglandins) that cause the uterus to contract and the cervix to open, thus facilitating drainage.

Unfortunately, this treatment is restricted to bitches that can tolerate it (depending on the seriousness of the disease) and whose owners wish to salvage their ability to breed. In other cases, surgery (removal of the uterus and the pus it contains) is usually indicated to give the best chance for a rapid and permanent recovery.

Ovarian and testicular tumors

In medical terms, a tumor is simply a mass of tissue, which says nothing about whether the tumor is benign or malignant (cancerous). The term excludes all cysts and fluid- or fat-filled abscesses.

Cancerous tumors of the ovary are rare in bitches (about 1% of cancers in dogs), but are more difficult to diagnose than testicular tumors, which are usually visible externally.

Most ovarian tumors secrete hormones that disrupt the sexual cycle and cause bilaterally symmetrical hair loss on the flanks or thighs. The clinical picture is complicated by abdominal distention due to ascites (collection of fluid in the abdominal cavity). Diagnosis is made by examination with a celioscope or cytological examination of the ascitic fluid. X-rays or ultrasound often detect these tumors too late, because the tumors are hidden at first by the ovarian bursa.

If the tumor has not metastasized to the peritoneum, ovariectomy is the best treatment against the cancer.

Testicular tumors in males are also infrequent. Even if there is no pain or swelling of the testicles, tumors should be suspected in old dogs with hormonal problems (testicular feminization syndrome), hypertrophy of the prostate, infertility or localized hair loss. Persistence of one or both testicles in the abdomen is a classic indicator that an old dog is prone to this type of tumor.

Monorchidism and cryptorchidism

Early in fetal life, the testicles and ovaries are found in the same location in the abdomen, behind the kidneys. Unlike the ovaries, which remain in this position, the testicles normally pass through the inguinal canal and descend into the scrotum under the influence of hormones and traction by a cord (the gubernaculum

testis). The external position of the testicles is necessary after puberty for the production of spermatozoa, which require a temperature below body temperature.

The testicles should descend within a few days after birth, because after this time the inguinal canal closes and becomes too narrow for them to pass. The resulting testicular ectopia (displacement) is called monorchidism if only one testicle is affected, or cryptorchidism if both testicles are affected. As an example, "inguinal cryptorchidism" means that both testicles have failed to descend but can be felt by the veterinarian when the inguinal region is palpated.

Definitive placement of the testicles in the scrotum happens later (at an average age of six months), and the testicles sometimes temporarily return through the inguinal canal when the puppy is exposed to cold or lies on its back. The veterinarian should look for this abnormality during the prepurchase examination so that a certificate of suspected defect can be completed early, if the abnormality has not been noted on the bill of sale.

Medical treatments designed to cause descent of the testicles generally have d.sappointing results if performed late (after the age of six weeks).

Testicular ectopia occurs frequently in dogs, to such an extent that it is listed as one of the redhibitory defects that can annul a sale when the abnormality is confirmed at the age of six months. Although monorchid dogs are perfectly capable of reproducing normally (unlike cryptorchids), they should not be allowed to mate because they may transmit this defect to their offspring. Furthermore, they do not conform to breed standards.

Finally, to reduce the risk of testicular tumors in ectopic testicles, it is recommended that these animals be surgically castrated before the age of six years.

Infectious diseases

Many infectious diseases, both bacterial and viral in origin, can affect reproduction by causing infertility, metritis, abortion or neonatal death.

Most bacterial diseases affecting the genital tract are difficult to diagnose with certainty because, while it is simple to isolate the organisms in samples (such as vaginal or preputial swabs), it is much more difficult to prove that they are responsible for the symptoms observed. Their presence may result from contamination of the sample by urine, vaginal mucus (in bitches) or prostatic fluid (in male dogs).

In all cases, any abnormally profuse discharges from the vulva or sheath should be analyzed by the veterinarian, who will treat them with the appropriate antiseptic or antibiotic agents. However, such medications are ineffective against some common viral infections such as canine herpes virus.

The Basics of Genetics

While we will not delve into complicated methods of genetic selection that are of interest mainly to breeders, it would seem useful to provide some basic knowledge so that anyone can understand the rather complicated field of genetics and be able to answer at least this basic question: "How are genetic traits transmitted?" In genetics, a trait is the visible or measurable expression of one or more genes. Coat color, a dog's ability to flush game, its height at the withers, and hip dysplasia are all examples of genetic traits in the broadest sense of the term.

The Underlying Genetics of Traits

A gene is a program module located at a precise position (locus) on a chromosome. Each of a dog's cells contains 39 pairs of chromosomes in its nucleus, except cells that lack a nucleus (e.g., red blood cells) and sex cells (spermatozoa and ova). Sex cells have only one copy of each of the 39 chromosomes.

The complete set of chromosomes contains the genes that make up an individual's genetic inheritance, or genome—the entire program that determines the individual's appearance and much of its behavior.

The reason that there are two copies of each chromosome (a pair) is that one copy is inherited from the father and one from the mother. Each "copy" is called an allele. When both copies are the same, and so give the same orders to the cell, the individual is said to be homozygotic for the trait under consideration. For example, the allele "b" (for "brown") codes for a brown coat in the puppy if two copies are present, one copy having been inherited from each parent. The puppy is said to by "homozygotic b/b."

Conversely, if the chromosome inherited from the father carries the "B" gene (for "black"), and the chromosome inherited from the mother carries the "b" gene, the dog is said to be "heterozygotic B/b", and its coat will be as black as its father's. The coat will be black in this case because the "B" gene (with a capital letter) is "dominant" with respect to the "b" gene (with a lower-case letter), which is said to be "recessive." A recessive gene cannot be expressed unless the individual is homozygotic for that gene.

How traits are passed on

When sex cells (gametes) are created, the thirty-nine pairs of chromosomes of the original cell are separated through a complex process known as meiosis. The chromosomes are mixed up, as if being shuffled like a deck of cards, and the new combinations are re-distributed as the 39 single chromosomes found in each gamete. The genetic diversity of the gametes ensures genetic variability within each breed of dog.

At fertilization, a spermatozoon and an ovum join to form an egg (zygote), in which the chromosomes inherited from the two parents are again joined into homologous pairs.

In this way, natural selection operates on two involuntary and uncontrolled levels:

- first, during meiosis, when different genetic information is passed to each gamete;

- second, at fertilization, since it is impossible to predict which spermatozoon will fertilize which ovum.

Furthermore, genes can mutate, which modifies the characteristics of whatever they encode. At the moment of conception, each individual has about one chance in ten of carrying a mutated gene.

Is appearance controlled by the genes?

As we have seen, both dominant and recessive traits exist, as in the example of coat color, where black (B) is dominant over brown (b). Given a brown dog, it is easy to deduce its genotype (which genes are present), which can only be b/b, since the recessive trait of brown coat color can be expressed only in a homozygous individual. For recessive genes, the phenotype (the characteristic seen in the animal) is a true reflection of the genotype.

However, the "black coat" phenotype could correspond to either of two different genotypes - either B/b (heterozygous) or BB (homozygous). In the first case, the dog is black but carries a "brown" allele that can be transmitted to its offspring. In the second case, the black homozygous parent can transmit only a black allele to its offspring, which will therefore all be black in the first generation, regardless of the other allele they carry.

NEW PERSPECTIVES FOR GENETIC IMPROVEMENT IN DOGS

Dogs are among the last of the important domestic-animal species to be affected by the revolution in methods and techniques for genetic improvement. It must be noted that humans' affection and respect for dogs does not predispose them to take an eminently scientific approach to selective breeding. This is unusual among the domestic animals.

From a genetic and phenotypic point of view, dogs are characterized by remarkably diverse morphologies and psychologies, motivated in part by aesthetic considerations and in part by utilitarian considerations. While traditional methods of selection have yielded good results in many breeds, they should be replaced or complemented in these modern times by more efficient (although also more complex) procedures. This could be done quickly by adapting and using knowledge acquired in other species.

The goal is to estimate the genetic value ("genetic index") of each dog, which indicates the intrinsic potential of the animal that can be transmitted to its progeny. Genetic indices will soon be calculated and used for the Malinois Sheepdog. The experience gained in this first effort will then only need to be generalized. This represents a true challenge for dog lovers, that will be met only through exemplary cooperation between breeders, competitors, racing officials, officials of the *Société Centrale Canine* and scientists.

Professor Jean-François Courreau
Head, Department of Genetics
Ecole Nationale Vétérinaire, Alfort, France

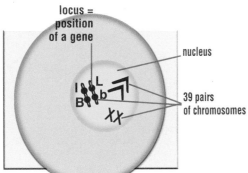

locus =
position
of a gene

nucleus

39 pairs
of chromosomes

Genetic Diseases in Dogs

Currently, there are no less than 250 genetic diseases (called hereditary or genetic defects) in dogs. It is known that among these, about ninety are caused by a recessive gene, fifteen by a dominant gene, and forty-five by combinations of several genes.

Diseases caused by recessive genes appear only if two copies of the gene are present (one each from the father and the mother). A heterozygous individual will not show signs of the disease, but will be able to transmit it to any offspring. This individual is called a healthy carrier.

Such diseases can be prevented by thorough knowledge of the family history of candidates for breeding, and the ultimate goal is to eliminate them (as with Collie eye anomaly).

When disease are caused by a dominant gene, healthy carriers cannot exist and it is easy to prevent the spread of the disease by excluding the affected animals from the breeding pool. However, some diseases, such as progressive retinal atrophy, can be expressed late in the dog's life, sometimes after it has reproduced, which explains why the disease persists in some breeds.

Other diseases, such as those linked to the "merle" coat (namely deafness) may never be expressed in some resistant individuals, which then transmit the disease to their offspring without the owner realizing it.

Still other diseases are caused by several genes together, as the action of any one of the genes alone is too weak to cause the disease. In this case, it is the synergistic and cumulative effects of several undesirable genes, along with unhealthy elements in the dog's lifestyle (unbalanced diet, too much exercise, etc.), that allow expression of the defect. Hip dysplasia, cryptorchidism and dental abnormalities are examples of this type of disease, which is understandably difficult to eradicate. The earliest possible detection is the most effective remedy.

These examples merely serve to demonstrate the complexity of canine genetics. A thorough knowledge of this science allows breeders to produce quality puppies for the general public.

EXAMPLE OF RANDOM
TRANSMISSION OF TWO TRAITS
DURING SPERMATOGENESIS
(MEIOSIS)

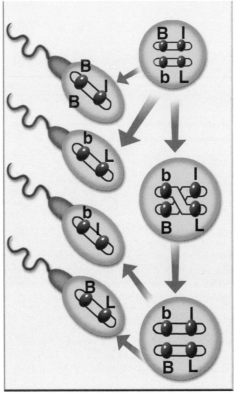

INBREEDING AND CROSSBREEDING

	ADVANTAGES	*DISADVANTAGES*
Inbreeding	Selection occurs on individuals of known genetic composition Fast, visible results Recessive defects are expressed visibly Can fix a characteristic (in the breed)	Genetic dead-end Defects and their carriers must be eliminated Reduced fertility
Crossbreeding	Allows "backward steps" Genetic enrichment	Slow rate of change Subjective evaluation of genetic value

A plan for genetic improvement of dogs through selective breeding involves study of breeders'notes and family histories, allowing crosses for improved recombination from time to time by means of inbreeding to fix the characteristics obtained.

Whelping

Perinatal supervision begins with the prenatal veterinary visit, which is essential for first-time or at-risk mothers. The visit should take place in the eighth week of gestation.

- A gynecological examination of the bitch will reveal any possible obstacles to whelping. The presence of fibrous bands in the vagina in primiparas (bitches carrying their first litter) can hinder expulsion of the puppies.

- One or more abdominal X-rays during this time will determine the number of fetuses more accurately than by ultrasound. This examination also reveals possible abnormalities that could cause dystocia, such as the small size of the pelvis, fetal mummification (shown by cloudy images, bone dislocations) or disproportion between the fetus and the mother. However, note that the positions of the fetuses as revealed by the X-ray are not good predictors of dystocia, because the position may change (rotate 180°) at the last minute.

- An ultrasound image of the uterus may help to evaluate the puppies' vitality by showing their heartbeats.

Preliminary Signs of Whelping

A bitch's behavior will usually change in the week before whelping. She will make off with various objects to use for her nest, search for a quiet spot or seek her owner's company. Reduced appetite, constipation and swollen nipples are not reliable signs, particularly in primiparas, whose milk sometimes does not come in until the day of whelping or even after the birth.

In the three days before whelping, the vulva becomes swollen and relaxed due to estrogen saturation, which sometimes causes symptoms of a false heat.

Rectal temperature falls by 1°C in the twenty-four hours before whelping. This indicator can be used if the temperature is taken morning and evening in the four days before the predicted whelping date. A fall of one degree relative to the four previous days indicates that whelping is imminent.

This temporary drop in temperature accompanies a fall in progesterone levels. These two examinations are signs of the fetuses' maturity and indicate that they can be born either naturally or by Cesarean section without a major risk to the newborns. Note that inducing labor by medical means is dangerous in dogs.

Finally, the appearance of the mucus plug from the cervix indicates that whelping is imminent, and precedes the first contractions by a matter of twenty-four to thirty-six hours.

Normal Whelping

Unless the prenatal visit revealed specific risks, it is not usually necessary to intervene during whelping.

The first signs of whelping appear within sixty-three days of fertilization, on average. A gestation period of sixty-five days may indicate problems, while a period of seventy days is definitely abnormal.

The first contractions are uterine contractions, which often cannot be detected except by the nervous behavior of the bitch, who looks repeatedly at her sides and usually seeks a quite place to be alone and make a bed, if she does not already have a nest. Loss of appetite (anorexia) is normal at this time, and can even extend to vomiting. This preparatory phase lasts an average of six to twelve hours, but can last up to thirty-six hours in a primipara. If the owner is worried, he should check vaginal dilatation using one or two gloved fingers, at the same time determining the presence and position of any puppy in the birth canal.

The entrance of the first puppy into the birth canal causes visible contractions of the abdominal muscles (Ferguson's reflex) that help the expulsive efforts of the uterus and should cause the first water sac (allantois) to break within less than three hours. The second water sac (amniotic sac), with the puppy inside, then appears at the vulva (a maximum of twelve hours after the water first breaks). If the amniotic sac is not broken by passage through the birth canal, the mother usually ruptures it within a minute of birth, breaks the umbilical cord, and licks the newborn puppy's torso, which stimulates the first breathing movements. At this stage, intervention is necessary only in the case of a breech presentation (about forty percent of births that are taking a long time) or if the puppy remains inert in spite of maternal stimulation. In the first case, help the mother by pulling lightly in time with the abdominal contractions. In the second, make sure the upper portion of the puppy's airway is not obstructed (which is frequently the case with breech births), and if necessary, clear it by means of an enema syringe or centrifugal motions, which also promote blood flow to the head. If these measures are ineffective, cold water or respiratory stimulants must be tried.

Each puppy is generally followed within about fifteen minutes (unless the contractions are intense) by its afterbirth, which is usually eaten by the mother. Puppies are born at intervals a few minutes to a half-hour. A delay greater than two hours between puppies is a sign of an abnormality such as primary uterine inertia (caused by fatigue, hypoglycemia or hypocalcemia) or secondary uterine inertia due to blockage (transverse

Size	Number of Puppies
Small Breed (less than 10 kg) (22 lb)	1 to 3
Medium Breed (10 to 25 kg) (22-55 lb)	4 to 6
Large and Giant Breed (more than 25 kg) (55 lb)	8 to 12

EXAMPLE OF RECTAL TEMPERATURE VARIATION AS A PREDICTOR OF WHELPING

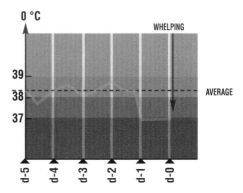

SUPERVISION OF WHELPING

Chronology	Event	Practical Consequences
Prenatal Examination		
Week 8 of gestation	Gynecological examination	Reveals possible obstacles to whelping (particularly in primiparas)
	Abdominal X-rays	Determine number of fetuses, reveal indications of fetal death, disproportion between fetus and mother, abnormal position
	Ultrasound of uterus	Evaluates the vitality of the puppies
Preliminary Signs		
-7 days to 0 days	Milk comes in (later in primiparas)	Plan whelping
-2 days	Relaxation of vulva	Isolate the mother, prepare her environment
-4 to 0 days	Rectal temperature falls by 1°C	
-1 to 0 days Before this date, premature puppies often suffer from respiratory failure.	Progesterone levels drop to less than 2 ng/ml	Plan for Cesarean if one may be necessary
0 days	Mucus plug is ejected	Whelping is imminent
Whelping		
6 to 12 hours (up to 30 hours in primiparas)	Preparatory phase—nervousness, uterine contractions	Check vaginal dilatation
A few minutes to 3 hours after the first contractions	Abdominal contractions Expulsion of first puppy Tearing of amniotic sac	Intervene if time intervals are abnormal or contractions are unproductive. In breech presentations, expulsion will take longer.
A few minutes to 4 hours between two expulsions fatigue	Rest Expulsion and ingestion of placenta	Intervene if there is uterine with no blockage (this occurs frequently in obese, old, or excitable dogs and susceptible breeds)

DECLARATION OF BIRTH (FRENCH SITUATION)

As soon as the Société Centrale Canine receives the certification of service, it sends the declaration of birth form to the breeder. This form should be filled out and returned to the SCC within two weeks following the birth.

As soon as the puppies are given identification (tattoos or ID chips), the breeder sends the SCC a request for temporary registration of the litter in the Livre des origines français (French stud book). The registration does not become final unless the puppies are judged to meet conformation standards when they reach adulthood.

---

presentation, presence of two fetuses in the birth canal at the same time, blockage of the birth canal). In these cases, medical and/or surgical intervention is necessary.

Medical Intervention

Systematic use of oxytocin (a hormone that stimulates uterine contractions and is naturally released by the posterior hypophysis) is discouraged. Unthinking use of this hormone in the absence of an exact diagnosis may

• cause uterine tears if the inertia is the result of a blockage,

• suffocate the puppies still waiting to be born by prematurely constricting the afferent vessels of the umbilical cord,

• have no effect whatsoever on the uterus, which has a natural refractory period with respect to oxytocin during the uterus' rest periods (for about a half-hour after each expulsion), and so causing only side effects (namely diarrhea).

• cause the posterior hypophysis to stop secreting it, which disturbs milk production later,

• cause secondary eclampsia.

Primary uterine inertia (i.e., when no anatomical obstacles are present) occurs frequently in certain bitches prone to it, such as:

• small-breed bitches (Yorkshire Terriers, Miniature Poodles, small hounds) or giant breeds (Bull Mastiff, Bordeaux Dog);

• bitches that are very calm (Basset Hounds) or too excitable (Cocker Spaniel) during labor;

• obese or elderly bitches;

• bitches with large litters.

In these cases, perfusion of calcium gluconate while monitoring the heart rate is usually sufficient to restart uterine contractions. Massaging the nipples can cause reflex secretion of endogenous oxytocin, which is preferable to giving it as a medication.

Surgical Intervention

Obstetrical manipulations are very limited in dogs. When medical treatments do not work, or there is obvious obstruction of the natural passages, episiotomy (incision of the superior commissure of the vulva) or Cesarean section are indicated. The main reason to perform a Cesarean is disproportion between the fetus and the mother, a frequently-encountered condition…

• in brachycephalic breeds: the large, flattened heads fit poorly through the pelvis and often cause lateral presentation with the head folded against the neck.

• when whelping is late or there are only one or two puppies in the litter. The puppies are then too large in relation to the diameter of the birth canal.

• in miniature breeds.

• when the bitch was mated with a much larger dog.

The viability of the puppies about to be born depends on their maturity (which can be verified by the progesterone level), the duration of unproductive contractions (which cause anoxia and pain in the puppy in the birth canal and also in the waiting puppies), the promptness of the intervention and the type of anesthesia used.

Postnatal Care

It is important to direct each newborn puppy to a teat if the mother does not push it in that direction herself, so that it can drink the colostrum (first milk), which contains protective antibodies that confer passive immunity on the puppy (in contrast to the active immunity gained through vaccination or infection).

When the number of puppies is less than the number predicted from the X-rays, a new abdominal X-ray should be taken in order to find any missing puppies and avoid an unnecessary Cesarean if they are found… in the mother's stomach. In fact, it is not uncommon for the mother to eat stillborn puppies along with the placentas.

Certain homeopathic herbal products aid the emptying and involution of the uterus. Some simple rules of hygiene help prevent the uterus from becoming infected during the expulsion of the lochia (greenish discharges during the three days following parturition). Systematic use of antibiotics is absurd in economical, medical and sanitary terms. Not only might the antibiotics pass into the milk and poison the puppies (sometimes causing malformation of the dental enamel), they also select for resistant organisms against which they are no longer effective.

Nursing

The end of diestrus (the period corresponding to pregnancy or false pregnancy) is indicated hormonally by a decrease in the level of progesterone in the blood, a temporary increase in estrogen that allows dilatation of the cervix, and an increase in prolactin, the hormone responsible for colostrum and milk production.

These hormone changes are the same whether the bitch is pregnant or not, which explains the frequency of "false-pregnancy lactation." This phenomenon is also observed in packs of wild dogs, mainly in bitches of lower rank in the hierarchy, who can then serve as nursemaids if a dominant bitch's milk supply should fail. It emphasizes the importance of the mind in triggering lactation, which is true of many mammals.

Lactation

Given this "mental factor", it is understandable that a bitch who is not comfortable with motherhood, whose choice of nest has been overruled, or who has been anesthetized for a Cesarean can show a clear delay in milk production. This condition can be treated by a change in environment, by homeopathic herbs or by administering certain antiemetics that stimulate secretion of prolactin by the central nervous system.

Once the first puppies have been born, milk secretion continues on its own by a neurohormonal reflex action. Nursing or massage of the teats stimulates the secretion of another hormone, oxytocin, which causes the milk to move into the milk ducts. This mechanism is proportional to the number of nursing puppies, and so allows milk production to adapt to the puppies' appetites, which in a sense take priority over the mother's health.

Milk production

The first milk, called colostrum, is secreted by the mother for two days after whelping. It has neither the appearance nor the composition of regular milk. In fact, it is so yellowish and translucent that it can easily be confused with pus.

Colostrum is much higher in proteins than milk. In addition to its nutritive value, it stimulates the first defecations by the puppies and provides ninety-five percent of the antibodies needed to protect them against infection. In this way, the mother passively transfers her immunologic memory to the puppies for a period of five to seven weeks, until they are able to actively defend themselves against infections.

Puppies are able to absorb these maternal defenses only during a period of less than forty-eight hours after birth. After this time, the antibodies are destroyed in

AVERAGE COMPOSITION OF BITCH MILK (Cloche, 1987)	
Dry matter (g/kg)	220 to 250
Proteins (g)	55 to 80
Fats (g)	50 to 90
Lactose (g)	30 to 40
Energy (kcal)	1200 to 1500
Minerals (g)	9 to 13
including calcium (g)	1.5 to 3
and phosphorus (g)	1 to 2.5

COMPARISON OF COW'S MILK AND BITCH MILK

Primary constituents	Whole milk (cow)		Bitch milk		Difference, bitch milk/cow milk
	(as % of crude prod.)	(as % of dry matter)	(as % of crude prod.)	(as % of dry matter)	(% of difference in relation dry matter)
Moisture Content	85.5	0	78	0	
Dry matter	12.5	100	22	100	
Proteins	3.33	26.64	7.5	34	- 7.4
Fats	3.78	30.24	9	41	+ 11
Minerals	0.75	6	1.2	5.45	- 0.55
Lactose	4.54	36.32	4	18.2	- 18.12
Calcium	0.12	0.96	0.25	1.14	+ 0.18
Phosphorus	0.092	0.74	0.19	0.86	+ 0.12
Sodium	0.048	0.38	0.05	0.23	- 0.15
Potassium	0.157	1.26	0.10	0.45	- 0.81
Magnesium	0.012	0.10	0.012 – 0.02	0.05 – 0.09	- 0.02
Zinc	0.38*	3.04*	0.9*	4.1*	+ 1

Amino Acids	(as % of crude prod.)	(as % of dry matter)	(as % of crude prod.)	(as % of dry matter)	Difference, bitch milk/cow milk (in relation to total proteins)
Lysine	0.26	7.81	0.35	4.38	- 3.43
Histidine	0.089	2.67	0.20	2.5	- 0.17
Arginine	0.12	6.01	0.44	5.5	- 0.5
Threonine	0.15	4.5	0.32	4	- 0.5
Cystine	0.026	0.78	0.11	1.38	+ 0.6
Valine	0.23	6.91	0.38	4.75	- 2.16
Methionine	0.084	2.52	0.14	1.75	- 0.77
Isoleucine	0.21	6.31	0.335	4.19	- 2.12
Leucine	0.35	10.51	0.93	11.63	+ 1.12
Tyrosine	0.17	5.11	0.27	3.38	- 1.73
Phenylalanine	0.17	5.11	0.33	4.13	- 0.98
Methionine + Cystine	0.11	3.3	0.35	4.38	+ 1.08

* in mg/100 g

Total Milk Production (kg) = W[C + 0.1 (N-4)]

W = Weight of the bitch in kg
C = A constant equal to...
    1.6 for small-breed bitches, adult weight of less than 8 kg (e.g., Dachshunds)
    1.8 for medium-breed bitches, adult weight between 10 and 25 kg (e.g., Brittany Spaniels)
    2 for large and giant breed bitches, adult weight exceeding 25 kg (e.g., Great Danes).
N = Number of nursing puppies

the stomach before they can be absorbed, and so lose their effectiveness. In this case, the puppies are protected only by the antibodies that were able to cross the placental barrier during gestation (not more than 5%).

Colostrum is replaced by milk in a few days. The composition of the milk depends on the size of the breed (large breeds have milk that is richer in proteins), individual genetics and which teat is producing it (the posterior teats are more productive).

On average, lactation lasts six weeks after whelping, with maximum production at about the third week. In the following weeks, decreasing milk production causes the mother to regurgitate her food to supplement the puppies' milk diet. The puppies also begin to take an interest in her dish. This period marks the beginning of gradual weaning, which ends at about the sixth week when the puppies begin eating growth-formula dog food.

The amount of milk a bitch produces can be evaluated by regularly weighing the puppies before and after they nurse. Such measurements allow us to determine a curve of milk production as a function of factors that influence it directly (weight and size of the mother, number of nursing puppies) and to formulate a predictive equation for estimating milk production:

So we can estimate that a Labrador Retriever bitch weighing 32 kg and nursing 8 puppies will produce 2.4 times her own weight in milk to feed her litter!

Of course, it is very presumptuous to try to "pin down" milk production using an equation that also ought to take into account parameters such as the temperature during the maternity period, the mother's water consumption, parity and stress level, to name a few.

Nevertheless, this equation allows us to obtain a relatively close estimate of the amount of milk produced when lactation peaks, namely, four percent of the total amount produced. This means that the bitch produces about three liters of milk per day at the height of lactation, which obviously requires a considerable nutritional adjustment to avoid excessive weight loss during this period, which can be considered as the most difficult and demanding period of her sexual cycle.

Feeding Lactating Bitches

Unlike gestation, lactation causes a considerable increase in the nutritional requirements of the bitch, given the exceptional richness (in calcium, energy and proteins) of the milk she produces. The energy content of the milk is between 1200 and 1500 kcal per kg, depending on the breed and the day of lactation.

If we assume an average energy content of 1350 kcal/kg of milk at 80% production, the increase in the bitch's energy needs can be estimated as 3 x 1350/0.8 = 5,000 additional kcal per day at peak lactation.

The primary goal during this period is to provide food for the bitch in adequate amounts and of sufficient quality so that she can provide for her puppies' growth needs without weakening herself. To accomplish this, it is important to control the balance between supply (lactation) and demand (the puppies' development).

In some very prolific breeds, such as the Irish Setter, it is very difficult to balance "intake" and "outgo", since the latter can represent up to four times the nutritional needs of a maintenance diet.

During lactation, the mother should be provided a highly appetizing food with a high energy content, allowing her to meet her nutritional needs without eating so much food that digestion is impaired. It is difficult to imagine that a bitch used to eating one kilogram of food per day on a maintenance diet could get used to eating four kg per day of the same food while nursing!

The food should be highly digestible and provide a minimum of 30% proteins (as a percentage of dry weight), 25% fats, and about 4500 kcal/kg of energy. Such a food should be adequate for most nursing bitches. It is also recommended that the bitch have free access to food during lactation, as long as the food will not spoil or be contaminated by excrement.

The nutritional profile of a food for lactating bitches is as follows (as a percentage of dry weight): 30-35% proteins, 20-30% fats, 1-2% crude fiber, 1.5-2% calcium, 0.9-1% phosphorus, 10,000 IU/kg vitamin A, energy content 4200-5000 kcal/kg, protein-to-energy ratio 75-85 g per 1000 kcal.

In summary, when choosing a food for a lactating bitch, the following points should be considered:

- the palatability of the food, which depends mainly on the quality and quantity of fats and animal proteins;

- the digestibility of the food, which should be very high and allow for good assimilation of the food in reasonable quantities (avoiding a distended stomach after the meal, reducing the volume of the stools and improving their consistency);

- the food's energy content, which should be high and suggests the choice of dry dog food;

- the amount and quality of proteins, which are essential for the skeletal and muscular development of the puppies.

- calcium, magnesium and vitamin D levels, which should be sufficient to limit the risks of eclampsia (convulsions during lactation), particularly in small bitches with large litters.

Of course, balanced growth of the litter provides an indirect source of information about the characteristics of the milk, and so about the mother's health.

It should be remembered that the essential goal is a nutritionally-balanced food, since addition of any supplement to correct a deficiency in one food constituent runs the risk of disrupting absorption of the other constituents. The most frequent examples of this are zinc deficiency and lactation tetany resulting from excessive calcium supplementation.

No matter what amount of food is given, the mother should not have lost more than ten percent of her "ideal weight" after one month of lactation, and any weight loss (which is often unavoidable) should be regained within a month after the puppies are weaned.

Supplementing with Milk Substitutes

When milk production is insufficient to meet the needs of each puppy during the first three weeks of lactation (which is often the case in primiparas), it is recommended that a milk substitute be given to the entire litter, rather than pulling out one or two puppies and feeding them exclusively on a substitute.

Temporary milk substitute

When the entire litter is deprived of the mother's milk, if the mother dies or her milk does not come in (agalactia), is not sufficient (hypogalactia) or is toxic (mastitis), use of a milk substitute adapted for dogs usually ensures the survival of the puppies, although there may be a slight slowdown (less than ten percent) in growth compared to the average of the breed, which is often regained later by spontaneous consumption of a weaning formula.

On their own, puppies will nurse more than twenty times per day. It would be difficult for the owner to keep up with such a feeding schedule! A schedule of feeding once every three hours for the first week should be adequate, as long as the feedings are regular and the sleep schedule is respected (puppies sleep more than ninety percent of the time during the first week) so the puppies get the rest so essential to bonding and imprinting.

While it is possible to adapt cow's milk for puppies, powdered puppy formulas are much better, especially since their lactose content is limited.

In addition to saving time and money, powdered puppy formulas are packaged dry. This limits the risk of diarrhea in the puppies, whose stomach acid is not yet strong enough to completely sterilize the digesting food.

After adding water and heating the formula to 37°C, the owner can feed the puppy either by means of a bottle, or by gavage, using a probe (urinary probe), if the puppy refuses to nurse. If the milk is given by mouth using a syringe, it should have the consistency

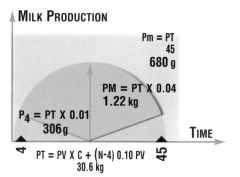
TYPICAL DAILY RATION FOR A LACTATING BITCH

Formula (g) for 1220 kcal metabolizable energy/kg

Lean Beef	450
Cooked Rice	400
Carrots	150
Green beans	50
Bone meal	20

COMPOSITION AS PERCENTAGE OF DRY MATTER

Crude Protein	31%
Fats	20%
Calcium	1.5%
Phosphorus	1%

HOW TO MAKE A MILK SUBSTITUTE

A household recipe that can be used temporarily as a substitute for bitch milk

Unsweetened evaporated milk	270 g
Fresh cream	70 g
9 eggs without shell	450 g
1 egg with shell	56 g
Mineral water	154 g
Total	1000 g

of rather thick baby cereal to trigger the swallowing reflex and limit the risk of food "going down the wrong way." If food enters the respiratory tract, bronchial pneumonia may result.

The following are a few points that will help decide how much milk to feed the puppies.

- One kilogram of bitch milk contains about 1350 kilocalories.
- A puppy needs three to four milliliters of milk per gram of weight gain.
- The caloric requirements of nursing puppies are more than two-and-a-half times greater than the maintenance requirements of an adult dog of the same weight.

For example, if a one-month-old puppy weighs three kilograms (adult weight twenty-two kilograms), its daily average weight gain is about six grams per kilogram of estimated adult weight, or 130 grams per day.

To gain this much weight, the puppy must eat 4 x 130 = 520 grams of milk per day, which is equal to 0.52 x 1350 = 600 kilocalories.

Adoption by a "wet nurse"

If another bitch at the same stage of lactation (or even false-pregnancy lactation) is available, it is preferable to avoid feeding the puppies a milk substitute and try to have them "adopted" by the lactating bitch.

If the orphan puppy is rubbed against the substitute mother's puppies, it will acquire a scent that may help it to be accepted. While the puppy is not yet particularly bonded with its mother in the two days after birth, the mother certainly recognizes her own offspring.

After three weeks, the puppies can gradually be introduced to a growth formula in the form of warm cereal as a supplement to the mother's milk. Milk production will begin dropping at this time. Some puppies will head for the mother's dish on their own and begin to lap and imitate her eating behavior.

Like baby birds, the puppies may begin to beg their mother to regurgitate food for them at this age.

All of these signs indicate that weaning can begin.

Weaning

As all changes in diet, weaning is gradual, which allows the puppy to change slowly from a milk diet to a growth food. The food should be adapted to the changing digestive ability of the puppy, and not vice versa.

The Puppy's Changing Digestive Ability

Many gradual changes occur as the puppy develops and its ability to digest foods changes. To cite only one example, the number of lactose-digesting enzymes gradually decreases, while the ability to digest cooked starch increases much more slowly. These variations explain why some puppies cannot tolerate cow's milk (which is three times richer in lactose than bitch milk), and why it is sometimes sufficient to limit the amount of cow's milk fed to stop diarrhea caused by exceeding the digestive ability of the lactases.

These changes are essentially genetically determined and depend very little on the eating habits imposed on the puppies.

Nutrition During Weaning

The beginning of weaning is naturally imposed when milk production by the bitch levels off. It is as though the mother, having reached maximum production, gives up and admits that she can no longer satisfy the increasing needs of her puppies.

In small-breed bitches, lactation covers the most intense growth period of the puppies, and meets their greatest needs. In medium- and large-breed dogs, however, the puppies are "abandoned" by the mother's milk at a critical period in their growth. So, while gestation and lactation are more taxing in small-breed bitches than in large-breed bitches, the opposite is true for the puppies.

No matter how the puppies get their milk, weaning should be a gradual change of diet beginning at about three weeks of age and ending at seven or eight weeks, at which time the mother will begin to distance herself from the puppies, mainly by asserting her precedence at the dog dish.

The puppies should not be completely separated from their mother before this time, so as to avoid adding any stress to a period that is already sensitive to any drastic change in routine. As an example, the puppies could be separated from their mother during the day, and reunited with her at night.

While the puppies are being weaned, their nutritional requirements are qualitatively comparable to those of their mother at the end of lactation (i.e., during the period when she is rebuilding her reserves), which makes the owner's job considerably easier.

DIFFERENTIAL GROWTH OF THE PUPPY AND PATHOLOGICAL RISKS
(**PARAGON AND GRANDJEAN, 1993**)

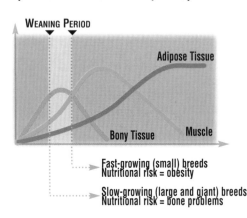

If no weaning formula is available, the owner can put out a little puppy kibble (growth formula) mixed with warm water or puppy formula. Gradually, less and less water will be added to this food, so that at the end of weaning it is given dry.

It should be emphasized here that the use of home-made food always requires correction of mineral levels in the base food by addition of a commercial supplement, ground eggshell, or bone meal; otherwise, mineralization of the skeleton might be hindered. The daily readjustment required with such supplementation makes the practice rare these days.

In contrast, the addition of a mineral supplement to an already-balanced (commercial) base food may lead to early and irreversible calcification, even in large breeds, thus seriously compromising the growth and the futures of the puppies.

Calcium requirements are calculated as a function of the puppy's weight, ranging from 400 mg/kg at the beginning of growth to 200 mg/kg, the estimated need of the adult, at the end of growth.

As an example, a growing puppy that weighs 30 kg will require six times more calcium than a 5-kg puppy at the same stage of development. However, its energy requirement will be only four times greater. This is why it is important to feed each puppy a food having a calcium/energy ratio adapted to its growth potential.

Feeding the litter dry food that is always available avoids any competition for food among the puppies, and so also any diarrhea related to overeating. When weaning, it is recommended that the puppies be fed three or four meals a day for a limited time (15 minutes) to avoid obesity.

After weaning, two meals per day are adequate for most puppies.

Any obesity appearing when fat cells are multiplying at full speed (known as hyperplastic obesity) would be much more difficult to treat than excess fat acquired in adulthood (hypertrophic obesity).

During the growth period, any nutritional imbalance affects the tissues that are forming. So small-breed puppies, weaned right in the middle of adipose tissue formation, are predisposed to obesity if they overeat. For this reason, slight under-feeding is less harmful in these dogs than overeeding, since slightly retarded weight gain can be compensated for afterwards, while obesity arising during the growth period is difficult to reverse once the dog reaches adulthood.

In large-breed puppies, on the other hand, weaning takes place during the period of skeletal growth. Any dietary deficiency of proteins or calcium will affect the formation of the bones (osteofibrosis). In contrast, consumption of excess energy accelerates growth, which makes the puppy vulnerable to many problems such as hypertrophic osteodystrophy and joint dysplasias.

Early Developmental Stages in the Puppy

Physical Development

Puppies grow thanks to the creation and maturation of many tissue types. The different kinds of tissues do not all grow at the same time or the same rate, which explains why the dietary needs of puppies change with respect to the amount and content of the food.

Physical development can be compared to a factory. Factory construction starts with a plan (the nervous system), then machines (the skeleton) are put into place. To make the machines work, workers (muscles) are needed, and the workers will demand benefits (fat).

While this image is too simplistic, since these stages naturally occur both gradually and simultaneously, it does emphasize the risks inherent in each stage of a puppy's growth and illustrates:
- why there is an insufficient energy reserve when the puppy is born. Fat is not deposited until late in development, although it is the main form of energy storage. The puppy has no energy source to turn to except its

small glycogen reserves (in the liver and muscles), which meet its needs for about a dozen hours after birth. It is therefore highly dependent on external temperature conditions until the appearance of the shivering reflex (after the sixth day of life), the deposit of adipose tissue (at the end of the third week) and the development of temperature-control mechanisms.
- variations in dietary requirements from one breed to another, and from one phase of life to another in the same individual. Body composition changes throughout the growth period: the water and protein contents decrease, and the proportion of fats and minerals increases.
- obesity, which affects small breeds much earlier than large breeds.
Most breed clubs have charts available showing average growth for males and females. Such charts allow the owner to keep an eye on the dog's weight from puppyhood through adulthood. Depending on the breed and sex, a puppy's weight can vary from seventy to seven hundred grams at birth. After a physiological loss of weight on the first day, which should

CHANGE IN MINIMUM BODY TEMPERATURE OF A PUPPY

Birth	35.5°C ± 0.5°C
Week 1	37°C
Week 3	36 to 38°C
Week 4	38.5°C
	(= adult body temperature)

not exceed ten percent, puppies normally grow very rapidly, gaining from five to ten percent per day during the first weeks. Weighing the puppies daily, always at the same time, will allow the owner to monitor their growth. Large-breed puppies, which can weigh one hundred times more as adults than as puppies, should be watched especially carefully.

In general, a puppy that fails to gain weight for two consecutive days should be carefully watched. The cause of any slowdown in growth should be sought. If the entire litter is affected, the mother may be the cause (insufficient or toxic milk), or there may be individual factors (hare lip, competition for food, etc.) if only one or a few puppies are affected.

The owner should also regularly listen to the puppies' cries, watch them nurse, observe the mother's behavior, evaluate the puppies' vitality, take the rectal temperature and check hydration during this period, when morbidity and death can appear very quickly.

Behavioral Development

Before weaning, the puppies' mother plays an active part in their physical and behavioral development - much more so than the father - and so plays a decisive role in their stability and eventual integration into their new social environment.

Although we will not study all of the developmental stages of the puppy here, especially since they occur at significantly different times in different breeds (small breeds develop faster), it should be noted that many errors and disappointments can easily be avoided simply by knowing which periods are favorable for training or susceptible to aversion.

A puppy's nerve development is incomplete at birth. Puppies are born blind, deaf, with a very limited sense of smell, and with a nervous system mostly lacking in myelin, which means that nerves are incapable of rapid conduction of nerve impulses. Knowledge of motor, psychological and sensory development is useful for early diagnosis of certain abnormalities, and also for directing the puppy's development along lines related to the use to which it will eventually be put. For example, it is possible to detect deafness in breeds prone to it (Dalmatians, Argentinian Mastiffs, dogs with merle coats or having a bare patch) as early as the fourth week.

During the first two weeks, it is usually sufficient to verify that the bitch's maternal instincts have kicked in (particularly with regard to cleaning the puppies, which is essential to their defecation and urination reflexes) and to observe nursing, taking care to place the weaker or subordinate puppies at the posterior teats, which have richer milk. The owner may sometimes need to make sure that the puppies' nails are not scratching the teats, which may cause the mother to refuse to nurse.

Behaviorists generally divide the maturation period of puppies into four successive stages.

The prenatal period

Fetuses in utero are not totally isolated from the outside world. Ultrasound techniques have allowed us to observe their reactions to abdominal palpation of the mother beginning with the fourth week of gestation. Their sense of touch develops very early, and they may very well be sensitive to all the petting received by the mother during gestation. Similarly, the mother's stress may well be felt by the puppies and lead to abortion, retarded growth in utero, learning difficulties after birth or even immune deficits.

NUMBER OF MEALS PER DAY FOR PUPPIES AS A FUNCTION OF AGE AND SIZE

	No. meals/day	Small breeds (<10 kg)	Medium breeds (10-25 kg)	Large and Giant Breeds (>25 kg)
Week 1	8	10-20 ml	20-30 ml	25-40 ml
Week 2	7	30 ml	50 ml	70 ml
Week 3	6	50 ml	70 ml	120 ml
Week 4	5	60 ml	70 ml	120 ml

Finally, even though the sense of smell does not develop until after birth, the sense of taste appears earlier: in fact, it seems that the food the mother eats during gestation can affect the later food preferences of the puppies she carries.

The neonatal period

The neonatal period begins at birth and ends when the eyes open. It has often been called the "vegetative phase", since the puppy's life appears to be dominated by sleeping and a few reflex activities. The puppy reacts only to tactile stimuli and crawls toward heat sources. Crawling is made possible by the development of the nervous system, as myelination occurs from the anterior to the posterior end of the dog, allowing the dog to move its front legs before its hind legs.

Also, excluding reflexes, the perception of pain is the last thing to appear in neurological development, which explains why some minor surgical operations can be performed without anesthesia during this time.

During the neonatal period, the mother and her litter should be confined in a warm, safe maternity area. If the mother seems to be lacking in maternal instincts, or the litter is small, the tactile stimulation of the puppies can be supplemented by checking their reflexes (urination, defecation, nursing, taste). Other stimuli sometimes found in breeding operations (music, toys, colors, etc.) have no effect at this age and merely disturb the litter's sleep.

The transition period

Also called the "awakening phase", the transition period begins when the puppies' eyes open (at an age of ten to fifteen days) and ends when the puppy begins to hear, i.e., react to sounds (at an age of about four weeks). While vision is not yet perfect at this stage, the persistence of behaviors such as burrowing and tactile exploration are an early indication of vision problems.
At this time, the puppies will normally risk a bit of exploration and begin to play, to bond to their mother and to recognize their fellows (the phenomenon of imprinting). The owner can take advantage of the puppies' waking hours to get them used to human presence and odor, to play with them and to gently handle them.

The socialization period

As indicated by its name, the socialization period represents a social learning period for the puppies, beginning with an attraction phase (they are afraid of nothing) and continuing through a period of aversion (they are afraid of anything new). The puppies gradually become capable of communicating and acquire a sense of hierarchy as they interpret maternal reprimands and olfactory and postural signals.
If, for one reason or another (lack of time or unawareness), the owner does not take advantage of a puppy's attraction phase (usually three to nine weeks) to help

it become accustomed to its future environment, it will be much more difficult to break the puppy of bad habits later.

The owner or breeder can take advantage of this extremely sensitive and malleable period to:

- facilitate contacts with the future owners (especially children), if the dog is to be a pet, and other creatures with which the puppy will come into contact and towards whom it must behave well (postmen, cats, sheep, etc.).
- accustom the puppy to the stimuli it will encounter (noises, the odors of clothing, cars, helicopters or gunfire - for a future hunting dog such as a pointer or setter).
- reinforce the hierarchy by imposing submissive postures (holding the puppy on its back or by the skin of the neck), if necessary. By the same method, it is possible to reinforce desired behaviors and eliminate undesired activities.
- provide opportunities for play between puppies and discipline those that do not yet control the strength of their bite.
- observe the behavior of the puppies so that future owners can be chosen as a function of each puppy's characteristics. Dominant tendencies can be discovered at this time by observing games, imitation of sexual behavior and precedence when feeding. In some breeds (namely the Cocker Spaniel and Golden Retriever), aggression has even become a disqualifying fault.

Many so-called "natural" talents can be acquired during this period, especially if the mother is already habituated to these stimuli and can have a calming effect on her litter during the aversion period.

For these reasons, the classic advice has been to sell puppies during the following two favorable periods:

- an early sale can be made during the seventh week, if the owner is an expert in early canine education and wishes to acquire a "malleable" puppy.
- a late sale can be made at the end of the aversion period (about twelve weeks of age), if a beginner is looking for a "turnkey puppy" that has already been socialized and whose training has been begun by a professional.

In all cases, it is useful to direct the future owner to a puppy that will meet his or her needs (cf. Campbell behavioral assessments) and to provide socialization advice, which should be reinforced by the veterinarian at the prepurchase examination. To prevent the dog from becoming too attached to its owner (which often results in serious damage to the home when the dog is left alone), it is wise to keep in mind the natural detachment that spontaneously occurs before puberty if the puppy is left with its mother.

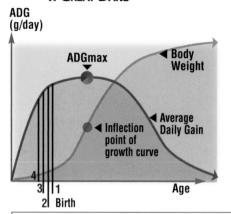

ADG at weaning*		
1 ▸ Small Breed	20 g/day	6 g/kg adult weight
2 ▸ Medium Breed	60 g/day	5 g/kg adult weight
3 ▸ Large Breed	150 g/day	4 g/kg adult weight
4 ▸ Giant Breed	160 g/day	3 g/kg adult weight

* Estimated ADG at weaning as a function of adult weight.
For example, for a Beagle puppy, the ADG after weaning
would be 5 g x 12 (predicted adult weight) = 60 g/day.

WEIGHT INCREASE CURVES FOR VARIOUS DOG BREEDS

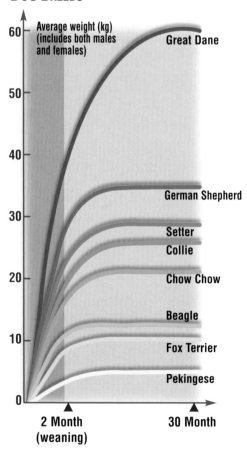

The Growing Puppy

Everyone agrees that the growth period is the most critical period for a dog, because it has such a great effect on the optimal course of the dog's life, and includes successive phases with high pathological risk - particularly the growth phase following weaning, which is the most intense. This is in fact a particularly delicate phase, because during this period several important, changing requirements must be met (nutritional requirements, first preventive vaccinations, behavioral development) that will affect:

- growth itself (weight gain, which determines the adult weight) and the rate of growth (weight gain per unit of time);

- development (acquisition of conformation and the various adult characteristics) in relation to the puppy's age (i.e., the rate of development, whether the dog becomes a physiological adult at a faster or slower rate).

At the beginning of this period, the puppy is also acquired by its owner and separated from its mother, which frequently leads to several changes in diet, lifestyle and bonding attachments.

Small, Medium, Large or Giant Breed Puppies do not Grow at the Same Rate

A puppy's growth is not linear with time. In other words, its daily weight gain changes over time. The daily weight gain increases after birth, then reaches a plateau of varying duration, then decreases as the animal approaches its adult weight and size. Mathematically speaking, the changing rate of growth (with growth in terms of ADG, average daily gain) corresponds to the derivative of the sigmoid function represented by the growth curve (change in weight as a function of time).

Studying the reference curves for various breeds reveals that small breeds, which grow slowly and reach adulthood quickly, are already relatively heavy with respect to their adult weight both at birth and at weaning. To state this more clearly, small-breed puppies are born "more finished" than medium- and large-breed puppies. Large-breed puppies have a relatively low birth weight and the ability to grow vigorously for an extended period of time.

It is important to understand such differences in rate of development and biological behavior, because they explain why it is advantageous to adapt a dog's food not only to its age, but also to its size.

In more concrete terms, the differences between dog breeds are visible beginning at birth. For example, a Poodle bitch has a litter of one to three puppies, each weighing 150 to 200 grams. In contrast, the birth weight of Newfoundland puppies (eight to ten puppies per litter) can vary from 600 to 700 grams. Even though an adult of a giant breed can weigh up to twenty-five times more than a small-breed dog, the birth weights differ only by a factor of from one to six. This means that the different breeds have very different growth

patterns, with the amount and duration of growth being proportional to the final weight of the dog.

- A small-breed puppy reaches half its adult weight by the age of three months, a large-breed puppy does not reach half its adult weight until the age of five or six months.

- A Poodle reaches its adult weight at an age of about eight months, at which time it has multiplied its birth weight by twenty. A Newfoundland continues to grow until the age of eighteen to twenty-four months, at which time it is about 100 times heavier than at birth.

Nutritional Requirements of Puppies as a Function of their Size

Generally speaking, puppy food should take into account

- the various breeds and growth curves, and
- the puppy's ability to properly digest foods - even food meeting the highest standards sometimes runs into the hurdle of digestive intolerance, even if the food is well balanced.

This said, it is true of all puppies, regardless of breed or type, that their energy needs (per kg of body weight) are much greater than an adult's. The puppy needs not only "maintenance" energy, but also energy for construction of the new tissues needed for growth. Its protein, mineral and vitamin requirements are also markedly higher than in the adult, which is why puppy food should have a high protein content (more than thirty percent of the dry weight for small breeds, thirty-seven to thirty-eight percent for large breeds) provided by high-quality proteins. Young dogs are much more sensitive than adults to protein deficiency, which

Puppy Growth Curves

The growth phase is a key stage in a puppy's life. It determines the characteristics of the future adult, as well as its morphology and balanced appearance. An animal that has "grown poorly" may have an abnormal size and weight for its breed, while the same puppy, under optimal conditions, could have met the height and weight standards.

To determine whether a puppy is growing normally, a veterinarian has a powerful tool: growth curves. There are two types of growth curves: weight curves, which are readily available in a number of reference works on dogs, and height curves, which are much more difficult to find. By comparing a puppy's measurements with a standard curve, it is easy to see whether it is keeping up with others of its breed, and to predict its adult size and weight. Thus, a German Shepherd puppy that weighs 14 kg at the age of 4 months and stands 45 cm tall at the withers will weigh 40 kg when it reaches adulthood, and will measure 70 cm at the withers. The adult size and weight of any puppy can be predicted after two visits to the veterinarian after the age of three months (e.g., a visit at three months and a visit at five months). Such measurements are very important because they are the best way to track the puppy's development and to quickly detect any abnormalities.

Professor Lucile Martin
Nutrition Laboratory
École Nationale Vétérinaire, Nantes, France

Prediction Of Growth In Puppies Of Different Sizes (Vétalim ND)

The weight for successuve months is read horizontally, beginning with the puppy's weight at three months. Example: a puppy weighs 4 kg at the age of 3 months. Reading across, it will weigh 5.3 kg at 4 months, 6.4 kg at 5 months, etc., and will reach its adult weight of 9.2 kg at the age of 12 months.

Age (mo.)	3	4	5	6	7	8	9	10	11	12	13	14	15	16	17	18	19
Weight (kg)* 1	1.3	1.6	1.8	1.9	2.0	2.1	2.2	2.2	2.2								
2	2.6	3.2	3.6	3.9	4.1	4.2	4.4	4.4	4.5	Adult weight							
3	4.0	4.8	5.4	5.9	6.2	6.4	6.6	6.7	6.8								
4	5.3	6.4	7.2	7.9	8.4	8.7	8.9	9.1	9.2								
5	6.6	8.0	9.1	9.9	10.6	11.0	11.3	11.5	11.7	11.8	11.8	Adult weight					
6	7.9	9.6	11.0	12.0	12.8	13.3	13.7	14.0	14.2	14.3	14.4						
7	9.3	11.3	12.9	14.1	15.1	15.7	16.2	16.6	16.8	17.0	17.1	17.2	17.3				
8	10.6	12.9	14.8	16.3	17.4	18.2	18.8	19.2	19.5	19.7	19.9	20.0	20.1				
9	11.9	14.5	16.7	18.4	19.7	20.7	21.4	21.9	22.3	22.5	22.7	22.9	23.0	Adult weight			
10	13.2	16.2	18.6	20.6	22.1	23.2	24.1	24.7	25.1	25.4	25.7	25.8	25.9				
11	14.6	17.8	20.5	22.7	24.5	25.8	26.8	27.5	28.0	28.4	28.7	28.9	29.0				
12	15.9	19.4	22.4	24.9	26.8	28.4	29.5	30.3	31.0	31.4	31.8	32.0	32.2				
13	17.2	21.0	24.3	27.0	29.2	30.9	32.2	33.2	34.0	34.5	34.9	35.2	35.4	35.6	35.7	35.8	
14	18.4	22.5	26.2	29.2	31.6	33.5	35.0	36.2	37.0	37.7	38.1	38.5	38.8	39.0	39.1	39.2	
15	19.7	24.1	28.0	31.2	33.9	36.1	37.8	39.1	40.1	40.8	41.4	41.8	42.1	42.4	42.6	42.7	
16	20.9	25.6	29.7	33.3	36.2	38.6	40.5	42.0	43.1	44.0	44.7	45.2	45.6	45.9	46.1	46.2	
17	22.1	27.0	31.4	35.2	38.4	41.0	43.2	44.8	46.1	47.1	47.9	48.5	49.0	49.4	49.6	49.8	
18	23.3	28.4	33.0	37.1	40.5	43.4	45.7	47.6	49.1	50.3	51.2	51.9	52.4	52.9	53.2	53.4	
19	24.5	29.7	34.6	38.9	42.6	45.6	48.2	50.3	51.9	53.3	54.3	55.2	55.8	56.3	56.7	57.0	
20	25.6	31.0	36.0	40.5	44.4	47.8	50.5	52.8	55.0	56.2	57.4	58.3	59.1	59.7	60.2	60.6	

* 1 kg = 2,2 lb

Daily Feeding for Growth and Maintenance, for Three Different-sized Breeds, Aged Three Months to Adult (Homemade Food)

YORKSHIRE TERRIER

	2/3 of full growth										Maintenance Diet
Age	3	4	5	6	7	8	9	10	11	12	There-after
Weight (W, in kg)	1	1.31	1.57	1.77	1.92	2.03	2.1	2.15	2.18	2.2	2.2
Growth ER (kcal ME/day)	286	296	295	290	284	279	275	272	271	269	264
Ration (g/day)											
Soy oil	1.6	1.6	1.6	1.6	1.6	1.5	1.5	1.5	1.5	1.5	1.5
Green beans	87	90	89	88	86	84	83	83	82	82	80
Minced meat (10% fat)	80	83	77	75	74	72	72	71	70	70	69
Completely cooked rice or noodles	97	101	109	107	105	103	102	101	100	100	98
VMS	s.q.	s.q.	s.q.	s.q.	s.q.	s.q.	s.q.	s.q.	s.q.	s.q.	s.q.
PCR (g protein/Mcal ME)	71	71	67	67	67	67	67	67	67	67	67
MER (kcal ME/kg)	156	187	211	228	241	250	256	260	262	264	264

POINTER

	2/3 of full growth														Maintenance Diet
Age	3	4	5	6	7	8	9	10	11	12	13	14	15	16	There-after
Weight (kg)	11.0	14.6	17.8		20.5	22.7	24.5	25.8	26.8	27.5	28.0	28.4	28.7	28.9	29.0
Growth ER (kcal ME/day)	1529	1627	1656	1649	1627	1601	1576	1556	1541	1528	1519	1513	1508	1504	1475
Ration (g/day)															
Soy oil	8.5	9.0	9.2	9.2	9.0	8.9	8.8	8.6	8.6	8.5	8.4	8.4	8.4	8.4	8.2
Green beans	463	493	502	500	493	485	478	472	467	463	460	458	457	456	447
Minced meat (10% fat)	459	488	497	462	455	448	441	436	431	428	425	424	422	361	354
Completely cooked rice or noodles	610	649	661	700	691	680	669	661	654	649	645	642	640	715	701
VMS	s.q.	s.q.	s.q.	s.q.	s.q.	s.q.	s.q.	s.q.	s.q.	s.q.	s.q.	s.q.	s.q.	s.q.	s.q.
PCR (g protein/Mcal ME)	76	76	76	73	73	73	73	73	73	73	73	73	73	73	66
MER (kcal ME/kg)	772	931	1064	1170	1253	1316	1363	1397	1422	1440	1453	1463	1470	1475	1475

BULL MASTIFF

	2/3 of full growth																	Maintenance Diet
Age	3	4	5	6	7	8	9	10	11	12	13	14	15	16	17	18	19	There-after
Weight (kg)	20	26	31	36	41	44	48	51	53	55	56	57	58	59	60	60	61	61
Growth ER (kcal ME/day)	2400	2578	2676	2716	2719	2700	2672	2640	2609	2577	2557	2537	2520	2506	2495	2486	2479	2409
Ration (g/day)																		
Soy oil	13.3	14.3	14.9	15.1	15.1	15.0	14.8	14.7	14.5	14.3	14.2	14.1	14.0	13.9	13.9	13.8	13.8	13.4
Green beans	727	781	811	823	824	818	810	800	791	781	775	769	764	759	756	753	751	730
Minced meat (10% fat)	768	825	856	869	816	810	801	792	783	773	767	761	756	752	749	746	744	626
Completely cooked rice or noodles	897	963	1000	1015	1085	1078	1066	1054	1042	1029	1021	1013	1006	1000	996	992	990	1084
VMS	s.q.	s.q.	s.q.	s.q.	s.q.	s.q.	s.q.	s.q.	s.q.	s.q.	s.q.	s.q.	s.q.	s.q.	s.q.	s.q.	s.q.	s.q.
PCR (g protein/Mcal ME)	79	79	79	79	76	76	76	76	76	76	76	76	76	76	76	76	76	69
MER (kcal ME/kg)	1151	1355	1541	1703	1842	1959	2056	2135	2199	2258	2291	2324	2350	2386	2399	2409	2409	2409

Growth ER = puppy's energy needs
ME = metabolizable energy
VMS = vitamin and mineral supplements
PCR = real protein/calorie ratio of the food
MER = maintenance energy requirement for weight W
s.q. = sufficient quantity

can slow growth, irreversibly damage conformation, or cause anemia, a drop in blood proteins, or a deficiency of antibodies leading to greater susceptibility to disease. Calcium and phosphorus intake should be monitored to prevent a serious bone disease (osteofibrosis) that occurs when there is no mineralization of the skeleton, a classic disease appearing in puppies fed exclusively on meat or homemade food without a mineral supplement. This is why a food should contain between 1.3 and 1.6% of calcium and 1 to 1.3% of phosphorus (as a proportion of dry weight), depending on its energy content and the size of the puppy.

There are thus a number of characteristics common to different puppy-food formulations, namely high energy content, high concentration of all essential nutrients and a limited amount of starch.

Special adaptations are required, however, for different-sized breeds. At the age of three months, a terrier puppy weighs two to three kilograms, while a giant-breed dog can weigh about twenty kilograms. Obviously, the jaw sizes of the two puppies will be different! As we will see later, dry food is incontestably the best for puppies, however, the terrier puppy will have a hard time picking up medium-sized kibble, while the larger puppy will waste it. It is therefore practical to offer different kibble sizes for small-, medium- and large-breed puppies. A large-or giant breed puppy requires more calcium than a small-breed puppy. A twenty-kilogram puppy eats only one-and-a-half times as much (in terms of energy) as a ten-kilogram puppy of the same age. If they eat the same food, the larger puppy may suffer from calcium deficiency. Puppy food for large-breed puppies should have a higher concentration of calcium.

Finally, the amount of time a growth-formula food should be used varies according to breed: eight to ten months for small breeds, ten to fourteen months for medium-sized breeds, fourteen to twenty months for large breeds, and sixteen to twenty-four months for giant breeds.

Feeding your Puppy Well

At the risk of repeating ourselves, we reiterate that to achieve balanced growth and avoid pathological problems, puppies must be properly fed. A puppy should not over- or undereat, and in no case should he be stuffed on the pretext of making him happy. Wet or homemade foods, in addition to their less precise nutritional balance, are more appetizing than dry foods, which is why they are not recommended. For best results, feed kibble or broth. The puppy will be better able to regulate its daily consumption, and the owner can more accurately determine the amount fed. The number of meals per day will change with age, beginning with four meals just after weaning, then reducing to three, then two halfway through the growth period. Ideally,

FEEDING LARGE OR GIANT BREED PUPPIES DURING THE GROWTH PERIOD

A large-breed puppy (adult weight greater than 25 kg) weighs 80 times more at the age of one year than at birth, and can grow for up to two years. A small-breed puppy (adult weight less than 10 kg) increases its weight by only twenty times, and its growth ends at about ten months of age. These differences explain why malformation of the skeleton is encountered almost exclusively in large-breed dogs, and why food is so important during a large dog's growth period.

Heredity is a major factor in the bone and joint diseases of large or giant breeds, such as hip dysplasia and osteochondrosis. Conscientious breeders eliminate any individuals carrying these genes from the breeding pool, however, such selection is difficult because the genes are not consistently expressed. In other words, a dog carrying the genes for hip dysplasia will not necessarily suffer from the disease, or transmit the gene to all of its progeny. Diet and exercise can also affect the expression of these unfavorable genes.

Owners and some breeders of large or giant dogs often believe that if they overfeed their dog, it will grow to be a larger adult. This is not true! The dog will simply reach its adult size more quickly. This accelerated growth is not desirable, because it subjects the dog's immature skeleton to excessive stress, which may lead to bone and joint deformities. This is why veterinarians recommend that large-dog owners limit the amount of food given and use foods with a lower calorie count, thus not as rich in fats, during the growth period. Such practices are the best way to control growth and ensure proper skeletal development.

It is not rare for owners of large or giant dogs to supplement their puppy's diet with calcium-rich supplements. This is justified only if the dog is receiving homemade food, i.e., food specially prepared for the dog with meat, vegetables and other starches as the base ingredients. If the puppy is eating a commercial growth formula, calcium supplementation is not only useless but dangerous as well. Research on the calcium needs of large breeds during growth has clearly shown that overconsumption of calcium can inhibit growth and cause bone and joint deformities. Commercial foods should not be supplemented with additional calcium.

Puppy foods are often high in proteins to ensure proper development of the muscles and the whole body, as well as the beauty of the coat. Contrary to popular opinion, the high levels of proteins in these foods have no adverse effects on growth or on the kidneys. Rather, they make the food more appetizing to the puppies and reduce the levels of starch (complex sugars present in grains and potatoes), which is not always well-tolerated by young puppies. Vitamin C supplements serve no purpose, and excessive consumption may adversely affect skeletal development.

A balanced exercise program is also very important for proper development in large-breed puppies. Lack of exercise (e.g., for puppies confined in cages that are too small) or too much exercise (e.g., intensive training of puppies that are too young, rough games with other puppies) can result in impaired skeletal development and serious injury.

In conclusion, since heredity is an important factor in the growth problems of large or giant breed dogs, buy puppies only from reputable breeders. Use a complete, balanced food specially formulated for large-breed puppies, and do not overfeed. Do not give calcium supplements. Ensure adequate exercise. And do not hesitate to ask your veterinarian's advice!

Vincent Biourge
Doctor in Veterinary Medicine
Royal Canin Research Center

the amount of food given should be based on the growth curves for the various breeds. Puppies should be weighed frequently to allow early detection of any abnormality.

It is recommended that at the end of the growth period, the puppy's food be changed to an adult diet. For most dogs, this should be a maintenance diet. Maintenance diets are lower in energy, fat, and proteins than puppy foods. They should also take the dog's size into account.

Growth-Related Diseases

During the growth period, the puppy is faced with a number of growth-related diseases, some of which are nutritional in origin. Once again we must state that the growth phase is the most physiologically difficult period of a dog's life, because tissue growth is so rapid and intense. This period requires implementation of preventive veterinary medicine bringing together a wide range of different fields, including nutrition. Nutritional imbalance can cause or be a factor in a number of specific diseases with immediate or delayed clinical symptoms. These diseases, caused by nutritional deficiencies, overconsumption, or even feeding errors, affect mainly the bones and joints.

Bone diseases

Growing bone is constantly being reworked. Not only is new bone continuously being constructed by specialized cells; old bone is constantly being broken down and renewed. A very precise hormonal balance protects the integrity of the bone and ensures homeostasis.

Dwarfism and retarded growth

Certain factors can permanently disrupt a puppy's growth, namely:
- chronic malnutrition,
- intestinal parasites,
- hormonal dysfunction (primordial dwarfism, caused by the hypophysis, or disproportionate dwarfism, caused by hypothyroidism), and
- genetic abnormalities in bone or cartilage synthesis.

Practically speaking, a slowdown in a puppy's growth should be evaluated immediately by a veterinarian, in order to discover the origin of the problem and correct it if possible.

Rickets

Rickets in dogs is similar to rickets in humans. As scientific knowledge advances, bone diseases such as rickets that are caused by nutritional deficiency have practically disappeared. Rickets results from a dietary deficiency of vitamin D and causes improper mineralization of the bony tissue. Only a few sporadic cases have been reported in the last decade.

Calcium deficiency

In puppies, calcium deficiency leads to juvenile osteofibrosis, a common bone disease. This is the most common deficiency disease in puppies, because it is associated with a diet of homemade food, wrongly considered as an ideal diet, which is too rich in meat, not supplemented with minerals (a mineral supplement with twice as much calcium as phosphorus is needed), and—even worse—is supplemented only with vitamin D. Calcium deficiency, which causes what veterinarians call "all-meat syndrome", lowers the level of calcium in the blood, which causes the animal to draw calcium from its bones, thus demineralizing them. Clinically speaking, this disease is associated with bone and ligament problems. The puppy's skeleton is deformed, palpation or pressure is painful, the knees and hocks are weak, and the gait becomes increasingly plantigrade. The weakening bones finally break with no apparent cause, leading to greenstick fractures that are very difficult to treat.

The treatment of osteofibrosis in puppies is simplest when begun as early as possible: it is sufficient simply to balance the ratio of phosphorus to calcium in the food. When the puppy is provided with a complete food formulated for its size, it will return to normal, as long as it is not older than six or seven months (for a large-breed puppy).

Other nutritional deficiencies

Deficiencies of certain nutrients having various functions in bone growth can lead to permanent disorders. Vitamin A, for example, is essential for skeletal development during growth. Deficiency causes shortened bones or even bone deformities. In contrast, although vitamin C is used by some breeders, it has no preventive role in bone diseases in growing puppies.

Vitamin D overdose

An overdose of vitamin D, which is also too frequent in puppies (in nutrition, more is not always better), causes hypertrophic osteopathy syndrome. This disease leads to uncontrolled bone growth. The bones "swell" and the dog has a pronounced limp. Unfortunately, calcium and vitamin D overdose are still too frequent, particularly in large-breed puppies, and owners should realize that this disease is essentially irreversible.

Vitamin A overdose

This disease is much less frequent in puppies than in cats, due to certain insalubrious dietary habits of the latter (consumption of too much liver). In dogs, vitamin A overdose is usually due to daily feeding of cod liver oil, which contains about 2000 International Units of vitamin A per gram! Excess vitamin A blocks bone formation and causes shortening of the long bones, as well as bone deformation. These effects are usually irreversible.

Joint diseases

Various joint diseases arising in growing puppies are grouped together under the general heading "osteochondroses." These diseases affect mainly large-breed puppies and are marked by hypertrophy of the joint cartilage, causing pain, joint deformities, carpus curvus, etc. Chronic, painful limping causes the joint cartilage to become fissured (the classic case of this is seen in the shoulder of the Labrador retriever).

In such cases, the main aggravating factor, other than extreme calcium overdose, is excess food, which causes early excess weight gain. Even a perfectly balanced food can quickly lead to excess weight if too much is given, and the mechanical effects on the still-growing joints and cartilaginous structures will not take long to appear. Such overfeeding may be unintentional on the part of the owner,

- if the food is too appetizing and the puppy begs continually (this is consistently true of moist commercial food, and generally true of foods that are too fat), or
- when the food's energy content is not properly evaluated. Since highly-digestible high-end dry foods have been put on the market, the traditional model for evaluation, "3.5-3.5-8.5" (3.5 kcal of metabolizable energy per gram of proteins and starch, and 8.5 kcal per gram of fat) has become a "4-4-9" model, since the nutrients are better used by the animal. Such food can cause a 20-kg puppy halfway through the growth stage to deposit 20 to 25 grams per day of useless and harmful body fat.

In such cases, and independently of any surgical treatment that might eventually become necessary, the puppy's feeding program should be revised. First, the type of food should be changed, respecting the nutritional balance defined elsewhere. By far the most effective solution appears to be the use of complete dry foods adapted for breed size. As far as quantity is concerned, a very strict program should be followed, including these steps:

- Stick strictly to the portion size prescribed by the veterinarian or suggested by the manufacturer. If the puppy is too large for its age, feed it 75% of this amount for three or four weeks.

- Do not feed the puppy anything else.

Obesity in puppies

While large-breed puppies are subject to the bone and joint problems just discussed, small-breed puppies are often at risk of early obesity (juvenile adipocyte hyperplasia). As a general rule, a small-breed puppy that eats too much will first make more fat cells, which are rather like small balloons that later fill with fat if overconsumption of food continues. Owners of small-breed dogs often have a very affectionate relationship with them, thus, a very anthropomorphic one. Unconsciously, the owner (and his children) easily give in when the puppy begs for food. Tidbits are more common than petting, stealing food from the table is a sign of the dog's intelligence, and many owners think begging is cute. While signs of obesity are readily visible in adult dogs, they are not as noticeable in puppies, because the little ball of fluff is so adorable. Again, the causes triggering obesity are overeating, often linked to food that is too appetizing (canned food) and that is overfed. Obesity is very difficult to treat once the dog becomes an adult.

In summary, we now understand how poor nutrition can be the major cause of specific growth diseases in puppies. Bone and joint problems are usually absent in small-breed puppies—which, however, are often subject to early obesity that shortens their life expectancy.

Aging and Its Effects

Aging is a gradual biological process that begins at birth and continuously intensifies until death. No matter what the species, aging causes cellular, metabolic, and organic changes. We are beginning to better understand these changes in dogs.

The most important change is probably that of increasing variability between members of a canine population that is already very heterogeneous, with individual size being one of the most important factors. We should therefore take a critical approach with regard to general trends based on averages because, while clinical examination reveals a slowdown in many biological processes in old dogs, such changes could also be caused by certain intercurrent diseases. Furthermore, the emergence of new physiological theories based on the concept of chaotic dynamics has sometimes caused us to rethink what medical wisdom has classically attributed to aging, namely, that aging is merely the consequence of disruption of an automatic, ordered, living system. It follows that random effects could appear that would change the organism's normal rhythms.

Paradoxically, however, a young and healthy heart may behave more chaotically than an old heart. Sometimes, although of course this is not a general rule, more regular function comes with old age. Before becoming old, however, the dog becomes "mature." In fact, we can consider that, biologically speaking, there are two successive stages in the life of an adult dog, with the second of these preceding old age.

Maturity Comes Before Old Age

In dogs, a mature phase precedes old age. This stage is a second stage of adulthood. (For simplicity's sake, we can speak of "adult", between the end of the growth period and maturity, and mature, the period preceeding old age.) Maturity is a time when the dog comes into its own, but also when cellular changes take place that are still invisible but which are the forerunners old age.

The Effects of Aging on the Body

While it is true that aging is irreversible, and that there are many theories about how it occurs, certain effects of aging at the cellular, organic, behavioral and sensory levels appear to be less well defined. The best possible knowledge of these effects will allow the owner to improve the dog's overall health environment, of which food adapted to the dog is an essential part, helping to reduce factors that exacerbate the normal aging processes. "Old age" begins at different times in different breeds. Small-breed dogs are old at about eight years of age, medium-breed dogs at seven years of age, and large-breed dogs at the age of six. The changes that appear with age gradually increase the dog's susceptibility to disease and stress. In old dogs, the risk of mortality is considered to double every one or two years. Physiological potential decreases with age, and the animal becomes more vulnerable to stress of all types, at the same time its immune protection from infectious diseases is decreasing.

In terms of the overall body composition, the following are seen in old dogs:

- an increase in fat deposits, as the dog is fatter and cannot mobilize lipids as well, and
- reduced hydration, or chronic dehydration, which is harmful to proper functioning of the body.

Some non-digestive functions are altered:

- reduction of immunity,
- reduced resistance to cold and heat,
- gradual reduction of kidney function,
- slow demineralization of the skeleton,
- destruction of cell membranes due to oxidative membrane stress,
- increase in cases of liver or heart failure,
- obvious increase in the frequency of both benign and malignant tumors,
- the hair turns gray and the skin becomes slack.

Digestive functions are also affected.

- Once old age has set in, the teeth may suddenly become a problem, with increased tartar formation (which should be treated) causing gum inflammations and infections leading to tooth loss.
- Less saliva is produced as soon as the dog becomes fat and adipose tissue invades the salivary glands.
- The passage of food through the intestinal tract slows, due to a decrease in intestinal muscle tone. This subjects the dog to bouts of constipation, often followed by diarrhea.
- The intestine becomes increasingly less able to adapt to changes in diet. For this reason, the diet must remain the same. Absorption of the food is also less efficient, requiring that the dog be fed a highly digestible food.

Finally, the dog's senses and behavior also change.

- Loss of visual acuity and hearing are common.
- The sense of smell may diminish.
- Being weaker and less hardy, the dog becomes apathetic , which means that it requires a food with a lower energy content.

An old dog is much more sensitive than a young dog to the amount of human contact each day. It will seek out its owner's company, and mealtimes become much more important to it.

Be that as it may, the dog's food should compensate for its increased susceptibility due to aging, and should help it keep its health as long as possible and live out its full life expectancy. Obviously, feeding errors at any age will accelerate the aging process: Food for old dogs should take the following rules into account.

- The overall amount fed should be reduced by ten to twenty percent, to prevent the risk of obesity due to reduced physical activity.
- The protein concentration of the food (at least twenty-five percent) should be increased slightly, or at least maintained, for optimal nutritional balance

and to help the dog fight stress and keep up its immunity. The reduction in protein content for older dogs recommended by some is very harmful and has no justification whatsoever as a preventive of chronic kidney failure.

- The dietary fiber content should be increased. This is necessary because fiber improves digestive health, guards against the frequent phenomenon of constipation, and allows the food's energy content to be decreased without any reduction in the size of the meals.
- The amount of vitamins and trace minerals should be increased, particularly the antioxidant vitamins (vitamin E and, in this case, vitamin C) to help the cells fight oxidative membrane stress, the age-linked destruction of cell membranes.

For all of the reasons mentioned above, it is preferable to change the aging dog's diet to a complete dry food (kibble or dehydrated broth) that is specially formulated for this type of dog. Naturally, it is possible to adapt the portion according to the type of food. A balanced daily ration of homemade food should include (per kg of food):

- Lean beef	270 grams
- Liver	80 grams
- Cooked rice	400 grams
- Wheat bran	160 grams
- Whole hard-boiled egg	80 grams
- 1 teaspoon sunflower oil	
- 1 teaspoon coconut butter	
- 2 capsules fish oil	
- Mineral and vitamin supplement.	

Taking the dog's size into account, as do some complete dry foods, is important for old dogs also. For example, proper kibble size will help the dog to eat at an age where its teeth are increasingly fragile; highly-digestible primary ingredients will prevent episodes of diarrhea; and a low phosphorus content will help the kidneys to continue functioning.

Because small-, medium-, and large-breed dogs do not

age at the same rate, the nutritional program should be organized by age brackets, with foods adapted for "Adult" dogs (the dog is in full possession of all its faculties), "Mature" dogs and "Senior" dogs (the dog is aging and its physical capacities are gradually declining).

Diseases of old age

Progress in veterinary medicine, in particular with regard to improved food and better daily health practices, has significantly increased the lifespan of dogs and cats in recent years. A new branch of veterinary science, geriatrics, has developed to better respond to the specific problems that arise. Changes in the body due to aging mean that an animal will be subject to fairly specific diseases. Below, we discuss the main diseases, and also certain abnormal behaviors that appear.

Behavioral problems

Behavioral specialists identify three main problems that appear with age.

First, old dogs can become hyperaggresive. With no apparent reason, the dog becomes increasingly aggressive, beginning to bite (including children and puppies). In seventy-five percent of cases, these dogs become bulimic. The only real treatment is by medication, although obedience training and agility exercises can be helpful.

Second, in involutional depression, the dog gradually loses its social skills, is no longer house-trained, does not respond to commands, or eats everything within reach (leading to ingestion of foreign bodies that may have to be removed surgically). It has difficulty sleeping and sometimes howls for no reason. Currently, medications exist that are sometimes successful in treating this condition.

Third, an old dog can be affected by dysthymia, which causes it to have difficulty judging the relationship between its own size and the size of the path it decides to take. A dysthymic dog tends to try to force its way through, and may become stuck for hours, growling and whining. Currently, only one medication seems to be effective in treating this condition.

Heart diseases

Old dogs are often said to suffer from heart failure, a disease actually related to the heart valves, sometimes with dilatation of the heart.

These age-related diseases cause the dog to run out of breath quickly, have a deep cough, and in their final stages, to "decompensate" by accumulating fluids (edema, often pulmonary edema, depending on what part of the heart is affected). While diagnosis (through ultrasound) and treatment (with converting-enzyme inhibitors) have improved greatly in recent years, it is important for the owner to be aware of the problem as early as possible.

Chronic kidney failure

Chronic kidney failure in dogs can be defined as progressive and irreversible loss of the kidney's excretory, regulatory, and hormonal functions. This disease becomes apparent when more than seventy-five percent of the weight of the nephrons (the functional units of the kidney) has been lost. Since the kidney has many functions, including the excretion of metabolic wastes in the urine, the clinical symptoms associated with this chronic disease are quite variable, ranging from polyuria (frequent urination) and polydipsia (the dog drinks large amounts), through chronic diarrhea, significant loss of appetite, and demineralization of the bones (the kidney and liver are the two organs that activate vitamin D), to anemia. These visible signs are associated with many changes in the blood, revealed by the necessary supplementary tests (urea, creatinine, proteins, ionogram, phosphates, calcium, cholesterol).

Although chronic kidney failure affects many old dogs, early detection and aggressive treatment can slow the inexorable progression toward the terminal stage.

Diet also plays an important role in improving the effectiveness of medical treatment for chronic kidney failure. Years of research and practical experience have shown that slightly restricted protein content (optimal protein content of the food = 17-18% of dry weight) in conjunction with high-quality protein sources improves clinical symptoms and decreases urea levels in the blood. The most important dietary consideration is restriction of phosphorus (the food should be no more than 0.4% phosphorus), which combats the harmful effects of this kidney disease on the bones. A slight restriction of sodium intake and the inclusion of omega 3 fatty acids should also be taken into account in the food. It is easy to understand why veterinarians recommend that owners feed dogs suffering from chronic kidney failure a complete food formulated for treatment of this disease.

Diseases of the digestive tract

Tartar and periodontal disease
As a dog ages, tartar tends to deposit on its teeth and cause inflammation or infection of the gums, bad breath, and tooth loss (periodontal disease). In fact, the consequences of this common disease can also be much more serious for the dog, since the "gateways" it creates for pathogens can lead to lung, heart, kidney, and joint diseases. While commercial food was wrongly blamed for years, many recent studies have debunked this myth and shown that dry kibble prevents dental plaque and tartar better than canned foods. Wet food particles are more likely to collect at the gumline, while kibble has an abrasive cleaning effect. Dry food, along with regular brushing (many products are now available through your veterinarian), can prevent this problem. Certain types of chew treats can also contribute to the dog's oral hygiene.

Treatment is by ultrasound removal of tartar by the veterinarian, frequently accompanied by specific antibiotic therapy.

Constipation
While not a true disease, constipation occurs frequently in old dogs as their intestines lose muscle tone. This problem can be prevented by choosing a well-formulated food as mentioned previously. The veterinarian may use paraffin oil or laxatives administered rectally to treat this problem.

Other diseases

Many other diseases increase in frequency as the dog ages. These can include eye and skin problems, as well as the development of both benign and malignant tumors. These diseases are discussed elsewhere, and no adjustment in treatment is necessary in a geriatric context.

As we have seen, an owner owes it to his old dog to take a specific approach both to preventive care (particularly with regard to food and daily health care) and to treatment of diseases (requiring regular geriatric veterinary examinations). Early detection of a disease can help the dog live longer.

Part 8

Dog's Nutrition

Nutrition and Feeding

"Proteins, Fats, Carbohydrates, Vitamins, Minerals, Trace Elements"

Each element in food plays a role in overall nutrition. Both excesses and deficiencies can have an adverse effect on the health of a dog. Therefore, it is important to fully understand the types and quantities of food that dogs require, since a dog's nutritional needs vary greatly from those of humans. Unfortunately, many people still believe that dogs biologically require a varied diet, and that dogs have a poor sense of taste and therefore essentially choose which foods to eat using their highly developed sense of smell. While owners may feel good about feeding lamb or chicken, those foods may not actually meet the nutritional requirements of the dog. Unintentionally, errors are sometimes made when preparing homemade dog food, and these errors can be dangerous to a dog's health. A trained nutritionist will consider a dog's specific needs (lactation, gestation, growth, maintenance, old age, sterilization) and consider foods in terms of their nutritional and biological value, digestibility and healthful properties, adapting the diet to the size and weight of the individual dog, rather than in terms of the ingredients, such as chicken, lamb, fish, liver, etc. Some diseases can be cured, or better yet, prevented, by feeding a special diet. However, the healthiest food in the world is useless if the dog will not eat it. Therefore, food must appeal to a dog's sense of taste. Today's modern commercial foods, particularly top-of-the-line nutritional dry foods, meet these various requirements.

Basic Nutrition for Dogs

Dogs are not people and it is not good for them to eat the same foods as their owners. A dog's ideal diet consists of proteins (meat, fish, eggs), fiber (vegetables), fats (vegetable and animal), minerals and vitamins. The relative proportion of each of these elements is determined by:
- the size of the dog (a two-kilogram Chihuahua is not likely to have the same diet as an eighty-kilogram Saint Bernard).
- the dog's physiological condition (growth, gestation, lactation, sporting activity and old age are all factors that change dietary needs).
- the dog's health (in many cases, diet has become an important aspect of medical treatment).

Whether you buy prepared food (dry or canned) or make your own dog food, it is essential to carefully choose the commercial food or feed a healthy balance of the foods that you prepare at home. Many people think it is a good idea to change a dog's diet often, but this is not the case, since changes in diet disturb the intestinal flora, which is more fragile than ours To ensure health and vitality throughout the dog's life, the dog's food must meet all its nutritional needs, without deficiency or overdose.

Fifty Essential Nutrients

Dogs, like people, are made up of hundreds of millions of cells that act as tiny power plants and provide energy for all life activities. These power plants, so necessary for life, constantly require fuel (food) and a combustion agent (oxygen) to produce the heat and energy that allow the dog to develop, grow and maintain a constant body temperature.

Feeding a dog well requires a thorough understanding of nutrition, which includes "all the processes involved in the exchange between an organism and its environment and which allow the living being to assimilate foreign substances and to produce energy".

• Nutrients and their roles

A nutrient is a simple component that must be present in a dog's food in the proper proportions required for good health. The dog needs to eat each of the 50 essential nutrients every day, because even though they cannot be made by the body, each has an important function in bodily processes.

• Water: the most essential nutrient of all

It may seem strange to call water a nutrient, but we can be certain that an animal will die after three days without it, although is able to go weeks without food. Water makes up two-thirds of a dog's body and all of the tissues are bathed in it. For example, eighty percent of a muscle's weight is water!
A dog can lose all of its fat and half of its protein and still survive, but the loss of only ten percent of its water leads to death. Water has so many important functions that it is the essential nutrient for dogs, as for all living creatures. Dogs require about sixty milliliters of water per day for each kilogram of body weight (although sometimes much more, depending on conditions such as hot weather, sporting activity, gestation and lactation).

• Proteins: the body's building blocks

The main function of proteins is to act as building blocks for the bones, muscles, nerve structures and all other living tissue. A protein molecule is made up of both essential and non-essential amino acids. Different proteins have different nutritional values where digestion is concerned. "Good" proteins (red or white meat, fish, eggs) are digestible, while "bad" proteins (tendons, connective tissue) are indigestible and will reappear in the stools. Even a highly digestible protein (one that is absorbed in the form of amino acids) will not necessarily be fully utilized (metabolized) by the dog. It may lack some of the essential amino acids, without which the dog cannot synthesize its own proteins. The "biological value" of a protein can be illustrated by a flag metaphor: The essential amino acids in a protein are like red, white and blue pieces of cloth. If there is enough of each color of cloth, you can make an American or an English flag, but if one of the colors is missing, you cannot. In the case of proteins, synthesis stops when one "color" runs out and the remaining amino acids are wasted. Remember that foods with a high protein content are not necessarily of high quality. It is important to look at the types of proteins used (their balance of essential amino acids).

Finally, if the food is deficient in energy content, the dog will "burn" its own proteins for energy instead of saving them for building. The energy/protein balance of a food is thus very important.

• Fats: more than just an energy source

The main function of fats in food is to provide energy. Dogs digest fats very well - much better than humans do, in fact - and like the smell and taste of fat (which means that they will eat too much fat if given the chance). However, this craving for fat should not be allowed to upset the nutritional balance of the food. Obesity can result, as in the United States, where about fifty percent of dogs are obese and France, where twenty-five to thirty percent of dogs are obese. (Medically speaking, "obesity" in dogs is defined as being overweight by twenty percent.)

Chemically speaking, dietary lipids are long-chain esters of fatty acids and glycerol, of varying lengths and saturated to varying degrees. A food's energy content is essentially a matter of the fats it contains. In fact, while glucide and protein exchange in dogs are essentially isocaloric, one extra percentage point of fat adds fifty extra kilocalories per kilogram of food. An increase in the amount of fat, thus of the energy content, also makes the food more palatable. The temptation is therefore to add

extra lipids to certain commercial or home-made foods, to make them more appetizing. The resulting possibility of overconsumption requires great vigilance in the matter of portion size.

While dogs tolerate high-fat foods very well, these should be given only to active dogs or dogs with very high energy requirements, such as lactating bitches.

Fats have very different fatty-acid contents, depending on their origins and thus do not all have the same nutritional value. In fact, fatty acids have two functions:

- **nonspecific,** as energy providers. All fatty acids have this function, but saturated fats from tallow (ruminant fat) or lard (pork fat) have only this function.

- **specific,** namely structural and functional roles. Fats are part of all cell membranes and are precursors of cellular transmitters and hormones.

Specific functions are carried out by so-called "essential" polyunsaturated fatty acids, which the dog cannot synthesize and so must obtain in its food. There are two types of essential fatty acids with which dog owners should be acquainted, in spite of their daunting names:

- **The omega 6 series,** which naturally occurs in vegetable oils more often than in animal fats (except poultry). A deficiency in these fatty acids leads to dry, flaky skin, alopecia (hair loss) and dull hair. This is one of the most important nutrients for a beautiful coat.

- **The omega 3 series,** found mainly in fish fats, which is very important to the integrity of cell membranes and the functioning of the nervous system and immune system. Nowadays, these fatty acids are also used for their anti-inflammatory properties (for treating many types of itchy skin) and oxygenating ability (they improve passage of oxygen into the cells and the deformability of red blood cells, properties that are of interest for sporting dogs and older dogs).

Fats are particularly volatile ingredients that can break down rapidly. Rancid fats make food less appetizing and can also lead to physiolog-

NUTRIENTS AND THEIR SOURCES

Nutrient	Dietary Source
Proteins	Meat (raw or slightly cooked) Cooked fish, cooked eggs, Milk (if the dog tolerates it), cheese Avoid scraps with many tendons, raw eggs, raw fish
Starch	Well-cooked grains (rice, noodles, corn, wheat) Avoid potatoes, bread, raw grains
Fiber	Vegetables (green beans, carrots, cooked greens), bran (in very small quantities) Avoid cabbage, onions, turnips
Fats	Animal fats (lard, tallow, poultry fat), vegetable oils (soy, corn, borage) Avoid rancid or overcooked fats
Minerals	Bone meal, calcium carbonate
Vitamins	Mineral supplements, Yeast (vitamins), Dairy products (calcium) Avoid excess supplements

ical problems for the dog, such as indigestion and pancreatic or liver problems. To prevent fats from becoming rancid, commercial dog food contains antioxidants. For homemade foods, avoid using cooked fats.

• Glucides (Carbohydrates)

Glucides are nutrients found almost exclusively in plants. The basic elements of glucides are simple sugars with names ending in –ose, the most common being glucose, the basic component of starch and cellulose. Other glucides, such as pectins and gums, are more complex molecules composed of uronic acids arising from oxidation of the simple sugars. Some of these glucides (such as starch and sugars) are digestible and can be assimilated by the dog, while the indigestible carbohydrates (also called fiber or cellulose) stimulate and regulate the passage of food through the intestine.

- **Digestible glucides** include lactose, which is important for puppies.
Like all animals, dogs have a metabolic requirement for glucose, which is both a source of energy needed for certain organs such as the brain and a component required for the synthesis of many other biological molecules. Unlike most other animals, dogs can maintain their blood-sugar levels even if no glucides are present in their diet. They are able to use certain amino acids found in proteins for glucose synthesis. Thus, there is no risk of glucose deficiency in a dog's diet.
Lactose aids digestion and absorption of nutrients. It also plays a role in synthesizing nutrients required for metabolism (ex. folic acid).
Bitch milk contains half as much lactose (the sugar found milk) as cow's milk. Puppies do use lactose, but they have a limited ability to digest it, so overconsumption always leads to digestive problems. When feeding puppies any milk other than bitch's milk, it is imperative to take this into account and ensure that the substitute does not contain too much lactose. Adult dogs have an even more limited ability to digest lactose, so consumption of milk can lead to diarrhea.
Starch is actually a complex of glucose polymers, which are branched to varying degrees depending on the plant from which they originate and are tangled into a lumpy ball called a starch grain.

Digestion of starch requires amylases, enzymes produced by the pancreas.

Starch can be made much more digestible by cooking it. It is found in grains (wheat, corn, rice, etc.) and potatoes and provides quick energy if well cooked. Rice added to dog food should be sticky so that it is digestible and will not cause diarrhea. Two cooking processes are used for complete dry dog foods: extrusion (kibble) and steam flaking (gravy). Both processes ensure that starch is completely cooked and so is digestible.

- **Dietary fiber** is not digested, but is a requirement for dogs. Fiber consists of all glucides that are still undigested after passing through the small intestine: cellulose, hemicellulose, lignin, pectic matter, etc.

Fiber regulates the passage of food through the digestive tract, causing it to slow down or speed up as needed. Since intestinal activity depends on the dog's stress level and physical activity, the amount of fiber supplements added to the food should depend on the ultimate purpose of the food. Fiber also provides a substrate for fermentation by the bacterial population in the large intestine and helps balance it. For this reason, an abrupt change in the source of fiber can cause a transient disruption of equilibrium, with uncontrolled fermentation leading to flatulence and diarrhea.

While fiber is necessary for digestive health, it also has some disadvantages. It decreases the digestibility of a food and can reduce the digestive availability of some minerals through complex substances known as phytates.

Reduced digestibility of food can be taken advantage of, however, in foods for inactive dogs or in low-calorie diet foods for obese dogs. In this case, what is desired is reduced assimilation of food and a "diluting effect" so that the volume of the digesta will not be reduced too drastically. Selecting particular types of fiber can optimize this effect while limiting the disadvantages. However, it is still necessary to add certain nutrients to the food to offset decreased digestibility.

CANINE NUTRITION IS A SPECIALTY IN ITS OWN RIGHT

The European Society of Veterinarian and Comparative Nutrition was created in 1995. This scientific organization is dedicated to improving knowledge in the area of nutrition for domestic animals. Its members include veterinary nutritionists from all over Europe and from the United States. Its principal areas of study and development include species and topics not studied in the fields of agronomy or human nutrition. Dogs are one of its main areas of interest. Studies range from food for the canine athlete to meeting basic nutritional needs during critical periods (as after surgery). The ESVCN's affiliation with the Société européenne de médecine vétérinaire interne (European Society of Internal Veterinary Medicine) shows the extent to which dietetics is now an integral part of medical treatment for many canine diseases. The ESVCN organizes an annual international conference that brings together several hundred veterinarians from all over the world.

Professor Elen Kienzle,
Doctor of Veterinary Medicine
University of Munich (Germany)

• Minerals are highly interactive

Minerals comprise only a small fraction of a dog's weight, however, their role is essential and their content in food must be carefully controlled. Furthermore, all minerals can affect the digestion or metabolism of other minerals, which means that it is essential both to ensure an adequate supply of each and to avoid any unbalance, which could be even more harmful to the dog than mere deficiency.

Nutritionally speaking, minerals are divided into two groups:

- **Macronutrients,** for which requirements are expressed in grams for an average dog. These include calcium, phosphorus, magnesium, sodium, potassium and chlorine.

MINERALS: THEIR FUNCTIONS AND SOURCES

Mineral	Functions	Sources
Calcium (Ca)	Component of skeleton Transmission of nerve signals	Bone meal Calcium carbonate Calcium phosphate
Phosphorus (P)	Component of skeleton Component of cell membranes Energy metabolism	Bone meal Phosphates
Sodium (Na) Potassium (K)	Cellular equilibria Regulation of water equilibria Energy metabolism	Kitchen salt Potassium salts
Magnesium (Mg)	Component of skeleton Nervous system Energy metabolism	Bone meal Magnesia Magnesium salts
Iron (Fe)	Component of red blood cells Cellular respiration Enzymes	Meat Iron salts
Copper (Cu)	Hemoglobin formation Cellular oxidation Copper salts	Bone formation Bone meal Meat
Cobalt (Co)	Hemoglobin formation Production of red blood corpuscles	Bone meal Yeasts
Manganese (Mn)	Enzymatic activation Cartilage formation	Manganese salts
Iodine (I)	Synthesis of thyroid hormones	Sea salt Fish
Zinc (Zn)	Enzymatic systems Integrity of the skin Reproduction	Zinc salts

- **Trace minerals,** for which requirements are expressed in milligrams (or less) per day. These include iron, copper, manganese, zinc, iodine, selenium, fluorine, cobalt, molybdenum, etc. Quantitatively speaking, calcium and phosphorus are the main minerals required. They are major components of the skeleton and also have other important metabolic functions, such as phosphorus' role in energy transfers within the cell. The skeleton is a very important buffer reserve. The dog draws on this reserve if there is a deficiency, which explains why bone diseases appear when the phosphorus/calcium content of the food is not balanced. Magnesium is also important in bone metabolism and, along with potassium, is present in the intracellular liquid that is so important for many reactions.

Trace minerals are also essential to the creation of red blood cells and oxygen transport, to the integrity and pigmentation of the skin, to the functioning of enzymatic systems, to the synthesis of thyroid hormones, etc. Each plays one or more roles in the functioning of the organism.

• Vitamins: not too many, not too few

Everyone has heard of vitamins, a category that actually includes a wide range of substances essential to life. If any vitamin is absent or deficient in the diet, clinical symptoms of deficiency immediately appear and may lead to serious diseases in the long term.

As a group, the vitamins are distinguished by two characteristics.

- Unlike trace minerals such as iron iodine or zinc, vitamins are organic substances.

- A dog's daily requirement for each vitamin is expressed in milligrams or micrograms.

Vitamins are found in food and can be fat soluble or water soluble.

Dogs need thirteen vitamins. Each has an important function, whether it be maintaining the skin's integrity; facilitating good vision, normal growth and proper utilization of fats; or repairing blood vessels and nerve tissue.

VITAMINS: THEIR FUNCTIONS AND SOURCES

Vitamin	Functions	Sources
Vitamin A (retinol)	Vision, growth, resistance to diseases	Fish-liver oil, liver, eggs
Vitamin D (calciferol)	Balanced metabolism of phosphorus and calcium, improved absorption of calcium	Sunlight (UV), fish-liver oil, eggs
Vitamin E (tocopherol)	Antioxidant, prevention muscular pathology (strain)	Milk, germ of various of grains, eggs
Vitamin K	Production of coagulants	Fish, liver, seeds
Vitamin B1 (thiamine)	Energy metabolism (glucides), proper functioning of the nervous system	Grains, bran, yeast
Vitamin B2 (riboflavin)	Metabolism of amino acids and fats	Grains, milk, yeast
Vitamin B6 (pyridoxine)	Metabolism of proteins, fats, glucides and iron	Grains, milk, fish, yeast
Niacin (nicotinic aci3d)	Tissue integrity (skin)	Grains, yeast, fish, eggs
Folic acid	Protein metabolism, hemoglobin synthesis	Yeast, liver
Vitamin B12 (cyanocobalamin)	Protein metabolism, hemoglobin synthesis	Iron, fish, dairy products
Pantothenic acid	Tissue integrity (skin)	Liver, fish, dairy products, rice
Biotin	Integrity of the skin, metabolism of glucides, lipids and proteins	Yeast, natural ingredients
Vitamin B4 (choline)	Fat metabolism, protection of liver	Natural ingredients

Overconsumption of certain vitamins (especially A and D) can be particularly dangerous. These vitamins are necessary and useful in the proper doses, but harmful and toxic at higher doses. In contrast, some vitamins, such as vitamin E, seem to be very well tolerated even at high doses. In fact, high doses seem to be useful for curing and preventing cell membrane problems. No sign of vitamin E overdose has ever been discovered, so vitamin E content in excess of the physiological requirement may be an indicator of a quality food.

Finally, it may be remembered that brewers'yeast is an excellent natural source of B vitamins and can greatly improve the appearance of the coat.

PREBIOTICS (FOS) IN DOG FOOD

Fructo-oligosaccharides (FOS) are a certain type of sugar classified as fermentable fibers. These non-digestible sugars are rapidly fermented by the bacterial flora in the intestines. They stimulate production of volatile fatty acids (acetate, propionate, and butyrate), which maintain and promote growth of the cells that form the lining of the large intestine.

FOS favors the establishment of a healthful bacterial flora (bifidobacterium and lactobacillus). The benefits to the digestive tract are well known:

- They inhibit the growth of pathogenic bacteria;
- Stimulate the immune system;
- Aid digestion and absorption of nutrients;
- And play a role in synthesizing nutrients required for metabolism (ex. folic acid).

Action of fructo-oligosaccharides

Stimulate growth of bifidobacteria and lactobacillus

Produce lactate (39%), acetate (36%), propionate (19%), and buyrate (6%)

Acidify the intestinal tract

Limit proliferation of potentially harmful bacteria. (Clostrides, E-coli, Salmonella)

Protect the digestive tract: "barrier effect"

(according to Reinhardt)

However, excess FOS leads to loose, or even runny, stools. They break down almost completely in the large intestine due to the fact that they promote proliferation of bacteria. To maintain firm stools, another source of fiber, for example beet pulp, which is not broken down as readily by bacteria, must be included with FOS.

Bibliographical reference
REINHART G.A. – Prebiotics in pets nutrition.
7th Annual Congress ESVIM,
Lyons 1997, 56-58.

Maintenance	1
Work, 1 hour	1.1
Greyhound, training	1.2
End of growth period	1.25
Work, 1 day	1.4
Maintenance, 0°C	1.5
Middle of growth period	1.6
End of gestation	1.4
Beginning of growth period	2
Puppy (not weaned)	2.5
Lactating bitch	2 to 4
Sled dog	2 to 4
Animal in hospitalization cage	0.8 to 0.9

ENERGY RECOMMENDATIONS FOR OLDER DOGS

(kcal of metabolizable energy per day)

Weight (kg)	Very Calm Dog	"Normal" Dog	Excitable Dog
2	140	165	190
4	240	280	320
6	325	380	430
8	400	470	530
10	475	555	630
12	545	640	725
14	610	720	810
16	675	790	900
18	740	870	980
20	800	940	1060
22	860	1005	1140
24	920	1080	1220
26	980	1140	1290
28	1030	1200	1360
30	1080	1270	1440
32	1140	1330	1510
34	1190	1390	1580
36	1240	1450	1650
38	1290	1515	1720
40	1350	1575	1785
50	1590	1860	2110

1kg = 2,2 lb

Basic Nutrition: The Maintenance Diet

A "maintenance" diet provides the minimum nutritional requirements for an adult dog living in an ambient temperature of approximately 20 degrees C. and maintaining an "average" activity level, with no increased energy needs due to illness or of physiological origin, such as gestation, lactation, or growth. The nutritional needs of this "average" medium-sized dog (weighing ten to twenty-five kilograms) serve as a point of reference from which other requirements (for active, pregnant, aging, or sick dogs) are calculated.

In fact, dogs rarely keep to a strict minimum of physical activity, so feeding a dog a maintenance diet does not imply simply "maintaining" it as it is, but rather maintaining optimal health while avoiding any tendency to obesity, which is so prevalent in dogs.

The Maintenance Diet

The main characteristics of a maintenance diet are that it will:

- maintain the dog's weight at a healthy level by providing highly digestible food without excess fat and

- contribute to the beauty of the coat and hair by providing sufficient fatty acids, amino acids and B complex vitamins.

The food should be nutritionally balanced as follows (optimal for a medium-sized adult dog):
- 25% proteins
- 12% fats
- 5 to 7% dietary fiber
- 1.1% calcium
- 0.8 to 0.9% phosphorus.

An adult dog needs a certain amount of energy to maintain its weight, but the greater the weight (in relation to the dog's size), the less energy per kilogram of body weight is needed. The base value is 132 kilocalories of metabolizable energy per kilogram of body weight raised to the power of 0.75. For this reason, small-breed dogs need food containing a higher concentration of energy (i.e., fat) than do medium-sized breeds. The increase in energy content also implies an increase in the protein, mineral and vitamin content of the food. In large-breed dogs, increasing the energy content of the food allows the amount of food given to be reduced, thus reducing the risk of poor digestion or even gastric torsion.

SEASONAL CHANGES IN THE MAINTENANCE ENERGY REQUIREMENT FOR DOGS LIVING OUTDOORS

Increase in caloric intake (%)	Climate Continental (Minneapolis)	Climate Coastal (Boston)	Climate Mediterranean (Los Angeles)
January	100	60	30
February	100	60	30
March	70	30	15
April	40	15	10
May	10	5	0
October	10	5	0
November	40	15	10
December	70	30	15

BASIC DIFFERENCES BETWEEN SMALL AND GIANT DOGS

Difference	Minimum (Chihuahua)	Factor of Variation	Maximum (St. Bernard)
Length of growth period	8 months	3 times shorter	24 months
Amount of growth	Birth weight x 20	5 times less	Birth weight x 100
Tooth size	Length of canine: 4-5 mm	3 times shorter	Length of canine: 15-16 mm
Energy requirement	132 kcal/kg body weight	3 times more per kg	45 kcal/kg body weight
Relative weight of digestive tract	7% of body weight	More than twice as great	2.8% of body weight
Life expectancy	>12 years	Nearly twice as long	7 years

Adapting Feeding to the Dog's Size and Age

The length of the growth period, amount of growth, size of the teeth, energy requirements, relative weight of the digestive tract and average life expectancy all depend on the size of the dog and must be accounted for when choosing the type of food. To best meet the dog's needs and keep it in good health, dietary adjustments will be needed at every stage of its life.

In order to thoroughly understand the key points of such a custom feeding program, the following points must be kept in mind.

Puppies have Special Nutritional Needs Arising from their Size

Differences between breeds are evident beginning at birth. For example, a Poodle bitch will have a litter of one to three puppies weighing from 150 to 200 grams each, whereas the birth weight of each of the eight to twelve puppies of a Newfoundland is between 600 and 700 grams. Even though a large-breed adult dog can weigh twenty-five times more than a small-breed dog, the ratio of their birth weights is only between one and six. This means that each breed has a very different path to follow as it grows. The length of the growth period and amount of growth are proportional to the dog's final weight.

• A small-breed dog reaches half of its adult weight by about three months after birth, while a large-breed dog does not reach half of its adult weight until five or six months after birth.
- A Poodle reaches its adult weight by the age of eight months, at which time it weighs twenty times more than at birth. A Newfoundland continues growing until the age of eighteen to twenty-four months, at which time it weighs 100 times more than at birth.

In every breed, puppies need more energy, proteins, minerals and vitamins than adults. Puppies do not digest starch as well as adult dogs. A certain number of characteristics are thus common to all puppy foods, namely a high energy content, high concentrations of all essential nutrients and a limited amount of starch. However, puppy foods must also be adapted for the size of the breed.

• At the age of three months, a terrier puppy weighs two to three kilograms, while a large-breed puppy weighs eighteen to twenty kilograms. Obviously, the jaw sizes of the two puppies will be different! The terrier puppy will have a hard time picking up medium-sized kibble, while the large puppy will waste it. It is therefore practical to offer different kibble sizes for small-, medium- and large-breed puppies.
- Large-breed puppies are particularly susceptible to growth problems: faulty stance, deformed bones, joint lesions, etc. These problems appear more frequently if too much energy is consumed, causing the puppy to gain weight too rapidly. Feeding large-breed puppies an appropriate amount of food with a limited energy content can help control the speed of growth and minimize the risk of such diseases.

• Large-breed puppies require more calcium than small-breed puppies. A twenty-kilogram puppy eats only one-and-a-half times as much as a ten-kilogram puppy of the same age. If they eat the same food, the larger puppy may suffer from calcium deficiency. Puppy food for large-breed puppies should have a higher concentration of calcium.

• The amount of time a growth-formula food should be used varies according to breed: eight to ten months for small breeds, ten to fourteen months for medium-sized breeds and fourteen to twenty-four months for large breeds.

Adult Dogs also Have Special Nutritional Needs Arising from their Size

Once the puppy has become an adult, it requires a certain amount of energy to maintain its weight. The heavier the dog, the less energy per kilogram it requires. Consequently, a small-

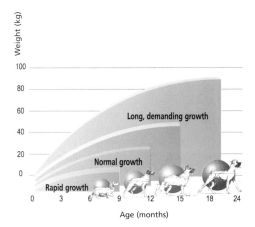
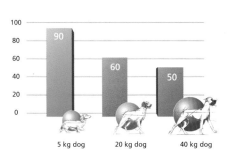
561

SMALL, MEDIUM, LARGE, AND GIANT BREEDS

The range of weights and sizes between the different breeds of dogs is one of the widest in the animal kingdom. For adult dogs, three groups can be distinguished: small breeds weighing less than 10 kg (22 lb.), medium breeds from 10 to 25 kg (22 to 77 lb.), large breeds from 25 to 45 kg and giant breeds from 45 to 90 Kg and more.

This range leads to differences in morphologies, physiologies, metabolisms and behaviours in the different breeds.

Thus, it is observed that:

The average lifetime goes from 15 years for the small breeds to 13 years for the medium and 10-11 years for the large breeds.

The growth factor and duration: when adult, a small breed puppy will have multiplied his birth weight by 20, compared to around 50 for a medium breed and 80 or more for a giant breed.
A small breed dog is adult at 8 months, while for a large breed dog this will be between 18 and 24 months.

The number of puppies and their weights at birth are different: a small breed dog will give birth to one to three puppies each weighing around 5% of her weight, while a large breed dog will have carried eight to twelve puppies each weighing scarcely 1% of her weight. The size of different organs is proportionally different: thus, e.g., the weight of the digestive tract in large breed dogs is one half that of small breed dogs.

The energy requirements of a 50-kg dog are not 5 times but 3.3 times higher than those of a 10-kg dog. Thus their metabolisms differ with their weight.
The temperament also differs with size: large breed dogs are, in general, more placid than the small breed dogs but contrary to the latter they need more living space.
Certain illnesses, such as dysplasia of the hip particularly afflict large breeds.

These differences between small, medium and large breeds have major consequences with respect to their health and feeding and the friendly relationships which should prevail between humans and dogs.

breed dog needs a food with a higher energy content (i.e., a higher fat content) than a medium-breed dog. Higher energy content also implies a higher protein, mineral and vitamin content. Foods with a higher fat content are more appetizing to dogs, which means that food cravings can become a problem for small dogs, especially since their owners often give in to their desires. Small dogs will eat small kibbles more readily than large kibbles.

In large-breed dogs, an increase in energy content allows smaller meals to be given, thus reducing the risk of poor digestion. This is also a preventive measure for gastric dilatation and torsion, a frequent problem in large-breed dogs. The form of the food is important as well: large, low-density kibble slows ingestion somewhat.

Small, Medium, Large and Giant Breeds, Maturity is not the Same as Old Age

In dogs, as in humans, maturity is not the same as old age. Advancing years do not automatically make a dog "old"; rather, the normal changes that occur during "middle age" could be called "the beginning of old age".

To keep a dog in good health, the owner should ensure that it has a healthy lifestyle. By continuing regular physical activity, the dog keeps its muscles and avoids excess weight. The teeth and coat should also be well looked after. Regular visits to the veterinarian are a must, allowing for early detection of any kidney, cardio-respiratory or joint failure. Aging is an insidious phenomenon. A dog can remain in good health until it reaches a ripe old age: Nevertheless, its body is invisibly degenerating little by little.

Dogs age at different rates, depending on their size. Large dogs tend to age much more rapidly than small dogs.

Dogs reach the equivalent of age fifty or fifty-five at about...

- age eight or nine in small-breed dogs. In spite of their sometimes rather sophisticated appearance, these dogs are fairly hardy, with above-average longevity.
- age seven in medium-breed dogs. These dogs are mostly hardy dogs - hunting dogs, herding dogs, etc. Selected for physical ability (speed and endurance), they have few health problems, in principle, until they reach an advanced age.
- age five or six in large-breed dogs, which have a relatively short lifespan (typically less than ten years), particularly in the largest breeds).

If there are no specific health problems, it is possible to reduce the effects of aging through a good diet.

"Human Years" and "Dog Years"

Age of dog	Small Breeds (less than 10 kg)	Medium-Sized Breeds (11 to 25 kg)	Large Breeds (more than 25 kg)
6 months	17 years	12 years	6 years
12 months	22 years	20 years	12 years
18 months	25 years	23 years	16 years
2 years	27 years	25 years	22 years
4 years	29 years	39 years	40 years
6 years	36 years	51 years	55 years
8 years	46 years	63 years	75 years
10 years	55 years	75 years	94 years
12 years	62 years	85 years	
14 years	68 years	95 years	
16 years	76 years		
18 years	87 years		
20 years	99 years		

562

In order to be effective, the change in diet should be made at age five for a large-breed dog, age seven for a medium-breed dog and age eight for a small-breed dog.

An appropriate food for this age group should be…

- enriched in vitamins C and E, to protect the dog's cells from the harmful effects of "oxidative stress" linked to aging.

- made with higher-quality proteins. Contrary to a widespread notion that has been taught for years, reducing the amount of protein in an aging dog's food serves no purpose. Since mature dogs do not use proteins as well as young dogs do, improving the quality of the protein is sufficient. The only restriction that is justified is restriction of dietary phosphorus in order to slow the progressive degradation of kidney function.

- high in trace minerals (iron, copper, zinc, manganese) to keep the skin and coat in good condition. Addition of trace minerals in their chelated form allows for improved metabolism in dogs with reduced digestive efficiency.

AGING VARIES WITH SIZE

The different stages of aging

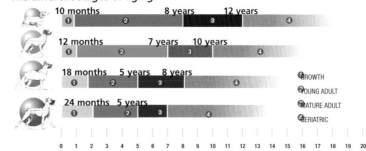

☞ *The larger a dog, the earlier the aging process begins. Large dogs, which have a short life expectancy, reach maturity early, at five years of age.*

- enriched in unsaturated fatty acids (soy or borage oil), to maintain a high-quality coat, even if there is a physiological weakness.

- somewhat high in fiber in order to furnish a bit more "bulk" This reduces the risk of constipation, which arises as the dog's level of activity decreases.

A "lite" diet is not necessary unless the dog is obviously overweight, which is true for only a minority of dogs.

For mature dogs, the rule for energy content is the same as for adult dogs: small breeds need special food
a higher energy content to meet their higher needs and large breeds need a higher energy content to compensate for their limited digestive capacity.

In dogs, mouth and tooth problems increase with age. To ensure that your dog continues to eat normally, help it chew up the food by serving a soft kibble appropriate to the size of the dog.

THE DIGESTIBILITY OF FOOD

The digestibility of a food is expressed by its digestive utilization (DU) ratio or digestibility. Digestibility is a very concrete expression of the way in which the dog's digestive tract uses the food. However, although both veterinary nutritionists and dog owners may regard digestibility as a fundamental criterion for nutritional quality, they differ somewhat in their practical approach.

To the nutritionist, food digestibility represents the relationship between what the dog retains (digests) and the food that was consumed.

To the owner, digestibility is reflected in the amount, frequency and characteristics of the dog's feces (excrement).

A dog's feces, which reflect its nutrition and fitness, are affected by two parameters:

- **the digestibility of the dry matter (DM) in the food**

DU of DM = (DMingested – DMexcreted)/DMingested.

Thus, in the case of a dog that consumes 100 grams of dry matter (what remains of the food when the water has been removed) and whose excrement weighs 20 grams, the digestibility of the food is 80%.

If the dog retained 85 grams instead of 80, the digestibility would be five percentage points higher, which would represent a reduction of dry matter excreted in the feces of 5/20 or 25%! This shows that a slight improvement (5%) in the digestibility of a food can result in a significant reduction (one quarter) in the amount of excrement produced each day, which explains the efforts of the better manufacturers along these lines.

- the moisture content of the feces is equally important. Stools are 65 to 75% water. If the water content is reduced, the volume of the stool will be reduced as well and it will hold together better.

Many other parameters also change the digestive utilization of a food, including the type of dog. For example, if a Beagle and a Fox Terrier are given the same food, the Fox Terrier digests it better, with a 5% improvement in digestibility. The amount of food eaten can greatly affect the digestibility: increasing the amount eaten at a single meal reduces digestibility, which is why it is often recommended that dogs with sensitive digestive tracts or dogs with high nutritional needs (sport dogs, lactating bitches, etc.) be given meals in small portions throughout the day.

In summary, digestibility is an important concept in dog nutrition and is a prime consideration determining the difference between a good food and a bad one.

PREVENTING THE ONSET OF ARTHROSIS

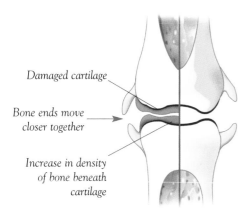

Damaged cartilage

Bone ends move
closer together

Increase in density
of bone beneath
cartilage

☞ **Chondroitin sulfate and glucosamine promote flexibility of the joints in older dogs.**

Chondroitin sulfate slows enzymatic breakdown of cartilage. Glucosamine stimulates production of cartilage (cellular regeneration).

REINFORCING THE BODY'S IMMUNE RESPONSE

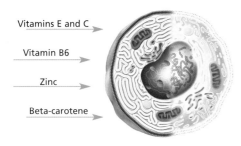

Vitamins E and C

Vitamin B6

Zinc

Beta-carotene

Cell damaged by oxidation caused by free radicals.

☞ **Vitamins E, C, and B6, zinc, and beta-carotene maintain and stimulate the weakened immune system of the older dog.**

PROTECTING THE NERVOUS/SENSORY SYSTEM

➤ Eye - Cross-section

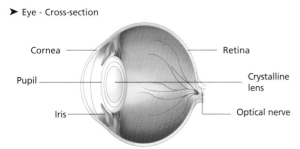

Cornea

Pupil

Iris

Retina

Crystalline lens

Optical nerve

Vitamin E plays a role in preventing degenerative disorders of the nervous system. Combined with Vitamin C and beta-carotene, it helps prevent the development of cataracts (clouding of the lens of the eye).

☞ **Vitamin B6 is appropriate for treating neuro-muscular deficiencies in older dogs.**

NUTRITION FOR THE OLDER DOG

A dog is said to have reached old age when it has lived 75-80% of his expected life span. Signs of aging become increasingly apparent and easily recognizable beginning around the age of:

Twelve years in small dogs
Ten years in medium dogs
Eight years in large dogs

When a dog reaches the "geriatric" stage, his diet must be adjusted to counter the effects of aging and maintain optimal health for as long as possible. The following is vital:

GOALS	CORRESPONDING NUTRITIONAL NEEDS
Promote healthy skin and coat	Essential fatty acids: fish oils and borage; zinc
Diminish cellular aging	Anti-oxidants; Vitamins E and C, beta-carotene
Decrease the effects of arthritis	Glucosamine and chondroitin sulphate, essential fatty acids
Strengthen the animal's immune system and increase resistance to infection	Vitamins E and C, beta-carotene, zinc, Vitamin B6
Inhibit the development of cataracts, degenerative diseases, tumors, etc.	Vitamins E and C, beta-carotene

Older dogs are not all alike. The diet of a healthy older dog will differ significantly from that of an ailing older dog. Regular visits to the veterinarian are vital in order to catch any health problems, such as kidney or heart problems, as early as possible. In many of the chronic conditions that appear with old age, nutrition can prevent the onset or limit the severity of clinical symptoms. A veterinarian can recommend the most effective diet for each dog's specific condition.

HEALTHY SKIN AND COAT

☞ **In order to maintain healthy, beautiful skin and coat, sufficient amounts of specific nutrients must be consumed on a regular basis.**

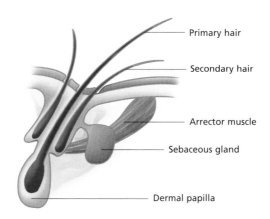

Primary hair

Secondary hair

Arrector muscle

Sebaceous gland

Dermal papilla

Borage oil *makes the coat shinier and skin more supple.*
Zinc *(chelated for better absorption) is recommended for older dogs with a coat in poor condition.*

PROTECTING THE DIGESTIVE SYSTEM: PREVENTIVE MEASURES

On an average, one in five visits to a veterinarian is prompted by a digestive disorder. In many cases, a change of diet can relieve symptoms. Your veterinarian is in the best position to prescribe a diet that takes the following into account:

- Use clay to protect the mucous membrane of the intestines
Two properties make clays particularly useful:
   - Protection: Clays reinforce the protective properties of parietal mucus;
   - Adsorption: Clays protect the digestive tract by adsorbing substances that may damage the mucous membrane.

- Control infectious agents by maintaining intestinal flora
Provide nutrients that promote growth of bacteria that aid digestion (for example, fructo-oligosaccharides, which promote reproduction of lactobacillus).

- Provide adequate fiber to regulate the movement of food through the intestinal tract
Beet pulp provides an excellent source of fiber for dogs with sensitive digestive systems. It slows the movement of food through the digestive tract slightly without reducing digestibility. In addition, the fact that it is only moderately fermentable means that it does not break down completely in the intestines and therefore provides the bulk which is vital to move food through the digestive tract.

- Limit protein fermentation
Some protein sources are gentler on the digestive system than others. Casein and fish meal are good sources of protein.

- Provide easily digestible starches
Rice is the most easily digested of all the grains used in dog foods. Even if the starch contained in the food is extremely digestible and very well cooked, it should never account for more than 25% of solids.

- Prevent overeating
A food with the appropriate calorie content must be selected to meet the needs of each dog, taking into account the dog's age and size. Size is a major consideration when choosing a food.

THE DIGESTIVE SYSTEM BECOMES MORE SENSITIVE WITH AGE

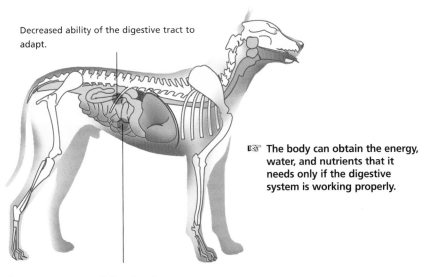

Decreased ability of the digestive tract to adapt.

☞ The body can obtain the energy, water, and nutrients that it needs only if the digestive system is working properly.

More frequent occurrence of digestive disorders.

LIMIT DIGESTIVE DISORDERS BY PROTECTING THE INTESTINAL LINING

Volatile fatty acids produced as fiber is utilized to nourish and promote reproduction of the cells of the intestines

☞ In order to maintain the integrity of the intestinal lining, food containing the appropriate nutrients must be consumed on a regular basis.

FIBER PROMOTES A HEALTHY DIGESTIVE SYSTEM

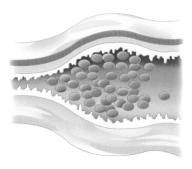

The five hundred individual species that make up the bacterial flora in the intestinal tract must maintain a healthy balance.

☞ The highly fermentable fructo-oligosaccharides (FOS) maintain the balance of the intestinal flora.

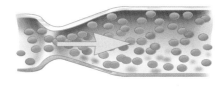

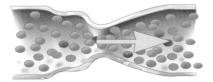

Food's passage through the digestive tract must be slow enough to allow nutrients to be absorbed, but fast enough to avoid constipation.

☞ Beet pulp (moderately fermentable) provides "bulk" which regulates the speed of passage through the digestive tract.

1. Good nutrition plays an important role
in optimizing physical performance, as
does genetic selection and training.

2. To maintain optimal weight in an active
dog, the number of calories consumed per
day must be adapted to the dogs needs.
A sled dog running a long-distance race
may need 8.5 times more calories than
normal to stay in peak condition.

3. Food rich in oils improves performance
for sprints as well as over long distances.
Feeding oil-rich food to provide energy
allows a dog to conserve the glycogen in
his muscles and delay the onset of
fatigue. However, the dog must be conditioned to the new diet for one month
prior to the beginning of training so that
his body and muscles can adapt and use
the oils most efficiently.

4. When feeding an active dog, some oils
are better than others:
- coconut oil provides fatty acids that are
quickly available to the muscles;
- fish oil provides fatty acids that reduce
inflammation often caused by strain and
physical effort.

5. Food containing carnitine promotes
efficient use of oils and conserves the
body's energy reserves. Vitamin E and C
supplements help protect a dog's body
against increased production of free radicals released during physical activity.

6. Intense physical activity and its associated stress increase a dog's need for protein. A protein-rich diet reduces the risk
of injury and improves performance by
promoting muscular oxygenation.

7. Not only working and sporting dogs
need high-calorie diets. Such a diet is
appropriate for dogs that live outdoors in
winter, lactating bitches, dogs preparing
for competition, those with sensitive
digestive systems, those recovering from
injury or illness, etc.

Large and Giant Breeds:
Nature has not Kept up with Selection,
so the Food must Compensate

Large-breed fanciers must acknowledge that while large and giant dogs are magnificent, nature often has not had time to catch up with selective breeding by humans;
thus, they have some natural weaknesses.

These dogs have a very long and intense growth period, are less precocious than
smaller dogs and have a relatively smaller digestive tract as well as a reduced life
expectancy, which means that old age sets in earlier.

**DIFFERENT
DIGESTIVE
CAPACITIES**

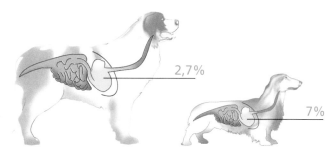

2,7 %

7 %

☞ The digestive tract of a large dog is smaller in proportion to its
overall size than that of a small dog. Therefore, proportionately, a
large dog has a lesser digestive capacity than a small dog.

Special Food

The fact that selection improves performance
and appearance while making an organism
more delicate and sensitive is also known from
other species, such as cattle and swine. The
organism is like a magnificent Formula 1 car,
which takes a long time to make, is sturdy and
offers high performance, but which can be
stopped by one tiny missing part or by low-qual-
ity fuel. While a dog cannot be compared to a
machine, this metaphor is nonetheless revealing, because like Formula 1 cars, large dogs
require very specific and carefully-formulated
"fuel" to function.

- It is important to closely watch a large-breed
puppy's growth rate to prevent development of
bone and joint problems, as well as hip dysplasia. To help control daily weight gain, the food
should not be too rich in fats and should be
served in moderate portions. Protein content,
however, has no effect on growth rate. Uncontrolled calcium supplementation is particularly dangerous in these puppies.

- An adult large-breed dog has relatively low
digestive tolerance and requires particularly
digestible food with sufficient energy content
so that the meals are not too large.

- Choosing a highly digestible food with a high
energy content can help prevent gastric dilatation and torsion.

- Adding natural antioxidants (vitamins C and
E) to the food and reducing the phosphorus
content (thus helping prevent kidney troubles
due to aging) are the first steps to take to help
a dog enter its mature years under the best possible conditions.

- After the age of six, large dogs become more
delicate. To keep them in good health, the
owner should offer a very appetizing, well-balanced food made with high-quality ingredients: milk, egg and fish proteins; borage oil;
chelated trace minerals; etc.

Such a diet, in conjunction with regular veterinary examinations, will improve the dog's
quality of life and increase its longevity.

The Eating Habits of Dogs

Knowing the factors that affect normal eating habits in dogs helps the owner to discover any unusual behavior and so to deduce whether the change arises from the dog itself (if it is ill, for example), from the food or from an environmental factor.

Basic Principles

The color of the food doubtless makes more of an impression on the owner than on the dog. (The same is true of kibbles shaped like bits of meat or tiny vegetables.) The odor of the food, however, is an entirely different story. Everyone has seen a dog sniff its dish before gobbling down the contents. It is common knowledge that a dog's sense of smell is much more developed than a human's (on the order of a thousand times more sensitive), so it is not surprising that odor plays a key role in the choice of food. Even a slight blockage of the nasal passages (if the dog has a cold, for example) will markedly reduce food consumption.

Two practical examples show the influence of smell on the dog's eating habits.

- A bitch's diet affects the olfactory preferences of her puppies. In fact, certain tastes from the bitch's food find their way into her milk and influence the puppies'later taste preferences. Beginning at the age of four days, puppies'olfactory imprinting is also affected by odors from the dog dish and later, the puppies spontaneously prefer foods having similar odors. Thus, puppies can be conditioned from a very early age to like the food they will eat once they are weaned.

- When a dog temporarily refuses a food, which sometimes happens with dry food, addition of warm water will improve the flavor. Warm water thus becomes a simple, economical and effective "condiment".

When a dog chews (which it barely does at all) and swallows, it blocks respiration and so cannot smell the food a second time. So as soon as a food is in the mouth, only the taste, texture and temperature count. Dogs seem to sense the same four basic tastes (sour, bitter, salty, sweet) as humans, but since their sense of smell is so much better, they naturally enlist the aid of their taste buds in smelling. So a dog sniffs, tastes and then swallows. This is a good time to point out that a dog can remember more than 4,000 different odors.

The Most Frequent Eating Problems

• The dog will not eat

There are many causes of anorexia in dogs. The most frequent are fever, sexual excitation (for a male near a bitch in heat) or competition for food when a dominant dog keeps another dog away from the dish. Lack of appetite also frequently results from food that has been improperly stored and has spoiled. A dog that refuses to eat for reasons other than the above should be taken to a veterinarian.

• The dog eats too much

Bulimia can be caused by the fear of "missing out" (competition between dogs for the food), a neuro-hormonal disorder, boredom, food that has insufficient energy content or problems assimilating the food during digestion. The owner can help the veterinarian with a diagnosis in this case by determining the amount of food consumed, the amount of excrement produced, changes in the dog's weight and careful observation of behavior.

• The dog eats everything

A dog that eats inedible substances suffers from pica. The occasional ingestion of grass, systematically followed by vomiting, is not caused by any psychological problem or dietary deficiency and even if the dog seems to vomit on purpose at times, it is merely a game. However, if this behavior becomes more frequent, it often signals the beginnings of gastritis (inflammation of the mucous membrane lining the stomach). In contrast, true pica is indicated if the dog licks walls or the ground or eats dirt and usually corresponds to a depressive syndrome. A dog suffering from pica should be treated and its living arrangements should be changed immediately, as they are often a cause.

• *The dog eats excrements*

Coprophagy is a condition in which a dog eats its own excrement or that of other dogs. Except in bitches with litters, who clean their puppies by licking away the fecal matter, coprophagy in dogs usually arises from the fact that the excrement consumed contains undigested nutrients that may still have some appetizing qualities. The most important thing to look for is thus a problem of digestive assimilation in the dog whose excrement was consumed (often the same dog that was eating it), by analyzing the stool to determine whether parasites or undigested fats or starch are present. This phenomenon can also result from overeating, which causes decreased digestibility because the digestive capacity is exceeded and the passage of the food through the intestinal tract is accelerated. In this case, a simple reduction in the amount of food given will suffice to bring things back to normal. Finally, note that certain breeds of dogs are predisposed to coprophagy. This is the case with large dogs such as the German Shepherd, which frequently suffer from pancreatic insufficiency.

Mistaken Ideas About Feeding

Dog owners are too often misled by a number of generally accepted ideas that have been handed down through the years. The following paragraphs should set the record straight.

• *"A dog should fast once a week"*

This may be convenient for the owner, but has nothing to do with the dog's health.

• *"A fasting dog works better"*

This idea persists in certain circles, although it is now widely recognized that for endurance activities (hunting, sledding), it is much better to feed a light meal at least two hours before the activity begins.

• *"My dog eats what I eat"*

Many owners anthropomorphize their dogs. They don't know or they pretend not to know, that dogs have different dietary habits than humans. Dogs are carnivores, although not strict carnivores; they are not omnivores. They digest high-quality vegetable proteins as well as animal proteins, but can also assimilate large quantities of fat, unlike humans. Dogs tolerate starch as an energy source only if it is completely cooked and in a proportion that takes their physiological limitations into account. A dog's vitamin and mineral needs are also very different from those of its owner (a puppy, for example, needs 400% less vitamin D than a human baby).

• *"A dog needs a varied diet"*

Ideally, a dog will eat the same food from the same dish every day at the same time and place—exactly the opposite of what its owner would enjoy! In fact, changing the food too frequently changes the habits that contribute to the dog's well-being, as well as exposes it to digestive problems. The intestinal microflora is adapted to a specific type of food and sudden changes do not allow these "targeted" microorganisms enough time to adapt to the new food. This can result in increased production of certain poorly-tolerated metabolites or toxins. For example, adding meat of indifferent quality to the diet increases the action of proteolytic microbes, which causes an alkaline pH, leading to flatulence and diarrhea of varying severity. Thus, variety in a dog's diet is tolerated only within a range of foods that are similar in composition. Otherwise, when changing foods, the change should be implemented gradually over a period of one week.

THE TEN COMMANDMENTS
OF PROPER FEEDING

In 1985, Professor R. Wolter of the École Nationale Vétérinaire of Alfort, France, formulated his "ten commandments" for feeding dogs. These ten rules, reproduced in part below, will help dog owners avoid the most common errors with regard to the practical aspects of feeding dogs.

1. Give the dog plenty of water to drink.

Cool, potable water should be available to the dog at all times and should be replaced frequently. Average water consumption is sixty milliliters per day per kilogram of body weight or higher in puppies, lactating bitches, working dogs or in hot weather.

2. Change food gradually.

Any change in a dog's diet should be gradual, over a period of one week, so the dog's taste, digestion and metabolism can adapt and so that its intestinal microflora, which is much more adapted to the type of food eaten than that of humans, can be reconstituted as a function of the new food.

3. Feed regularly.

A dog is happiest when it eats the same food every day, from the same dish and at the same time and place. The number of meals depends on the dog's physiological state, which should be frequently evaluated.

4. Control the amount of food consumed.

The size of the portions given is calculated as a function of the dog's daily energy needs and the number of calories the food contains. Portion size should be re-evaluated often to avoid any decline into obesity and should be changed as the dog's weight changes.

5. Give the dog a balanced diet.

Whether the food is homemade or commercial, it should contain all the nutrients the dog needs, in sufficient quantities and in proportions appropriate for the dog's size (small, medium or large breed), physiological condition (maintenance, breeding, sport), age (puppy, mature adult, old dog) and pathological state if need be.

6. Choose the dog's food carefully.

The choice of food is not insignificant. Nutritional balance should be the overriding consideration. There are three basic criteria for choosing the right food for a dog: its age (puppy, adult, mature adult or old dog), its level of physical or physiological activity (active dog, sporting dog, breeding dog) and its size (small, medium or large).

7. Use the food properly.

The manner in which the food is given is just as important as what is in the food. This is why, when feeding commercial food, it is essential to follow the manufacturer's instructions. When feeding homemade food, certain words should never be heard, namely "My dog eats what I eat", "My dog eats what he wants" and "My dog only eats". Finally, table scraps, sweets, sugar, cake and chocolate have no place in a dog's diet. (It would be better to give the dog bits of rind from cheese.)

8. Cleanliness is next to godliness.

Commercial foods offer the best guarantee of healthful cleanliness. Used properly, they present no risk of food poisoning. Open cans of dog food, fresh food or defrosted food should be kept cold and dry food should be kept in its re-closed bag in a dry place. If the dog does not finish its meal, the remaining food should be thrown away. The dog dish should be washed every day.

9. Keep track of individual results.

A diet's effectiveness and the effects of any changes, should be kept track of through such simple indicators as changes in weight, the health of the dog's hair, the characteristics of its excrement, its appetite and its day-to-day behavior.

10. Do not hesitate to consult the veterinarian.

By training, a veterinarian is also a dietitian for both sick and healthy dogs. Consult your veterinarian for persistent lack of appetite or bulimia, abnormal weight loss or gain, persistent diarrhea or constipation, worrisome physical or behavioral problems or any notable changes in thirst or appetite that might be signs of a general illness requiring a thorough examination.

- **"Complete foods should be supplemented with meat"**

Many breeders and owners are nervous when they cannot identify the meat used in a commercial complete food. Although some brands try to remedy this by adding "with chicken", "with beef" or "with lamb" to their labels, it is still difficult for the owner to concede that these really are the main ingredient in the formulation and are often of better quality than the "meat for animals" bought at the butcher's. Note that, since complete dry foods sold as kibble have been studied and formulated to be nutritionally balanced for particular physiological conditions (growth, breeding, sport activities) or sizes of dog (small, medium or large), any addition will unbalance the diet and negatively affect the dog's health.

- **"Proteins overwork the kidneys"**

Incorrect application of results from research studies on rats has led to the completely erroneous but widespread idea that, with time, high levels of dietary proteins can lead to premature aging of the kidneys and the loss of their purifying function, leading to chronic kidney failure. Studies on this point have been conducted in France since 1975 (Paquin and Pibot, in collaboration with the veterinary college in Alfort and the Royal Canin company, published in 1979 and 1986) and in the United States over the last 15 years (Churchill, in collaboration with the Hill's Company, published in 1997) and have now made it abundantly clear that this statement is false, although very persistent in some minds. In fact, the urea produced by protein catabolism is eliminated passively by the kidney and if the kidney loses its function, it is either simply as the normal result of aging or as the result of a specific or intercurrent disease. An early and drastic restriction of the protein content of the food, as advocated by some, will only weaken the dog's immune system and thus the whole dog. Since 1997, the scientific world has been unanimous on this point: Dietary protein has no ill effects on the kidneys.

- **"Calcium makes a puppy's ears stand up"**

In dogs with prick ears (in particular the German Shepherd), drooping ears and a slight change of stance can be observed between the ages of four and six months, when the milk teeth fall out. At that moment, the owner often hurries to supply nutritional supplements rich in calcium and vitamins and then notices that things return to normal in a few weeks. In fact, the calcium and extra vitamins have no effect, since the ears are composed of cartilage, which of course does not fix calcium or it would turn into bone. No scientific data have ever shown that diet affects the position of the ears and this practice can only harm the puppy when it throws the diet out of balance.

- **"All the vitamins are in the vegetables"**

Vegetables are not the only source of vitamins for a dog. In fact, the fat-soluble vitamins (A, D, E and K) are stored in animal fat or certain storage organs. The liver, for example, contains a great deal of vitamin A - so much, in fact, that it would be dangerous for a dog to eat liver every day. Water-soluble vitamins (B complex) occur in both animal and vegetable matter. There is as much vitamin B1 in powdered milk as there is in green beans. In any case, prepared foods contain vitamins added separately to balance the food. The dehydrated vegetables found in certain dry foods with multiple ingredients are never a significant source of vitamins.

- **"Vitamin D needs to be added to puppy food"**

Puppies require relatively little vitamin D, so their needs can easily be met by a balanced food. Vitamin D overdose caused by unnecessary or excessive nutritional supplementation can in fact be dangerous and cause serious bone problems.

Commercial or Homemade?

In our society, the dog's changing status - from a utilitarian to a social function, in most cases - has contributed to the development of a completely dog-oriented market: the dog-food market. With the rise of commercial food, disagreement has arisen between proponents of "traditional foods" and those of "modern foods". Artificially placing these two schools in opposition serves no purpose, however: The rationale for choosing a food should be based on the nutritional quality of the food. Oversimplifying the debate merely hides the fact that underlying both types of food are basic qualitative standards such as knowledge of the dog's real needs, choice of ingredients and processing and cooking procedures adapted to the ingredients in the food. As long as homemade or industrial foods meet these requirements, they each deserved to be considered solely on the basis of their nutritional merits.

This said, it seems that everyone has conceded that the exact content of homemade food will always be uncertain, due to the inclusion of ingredients of variable and uncertain composition and the fact that it is very difficult to achieve nutritional balance in the home kitchen, given that some fifty essential nutrients are involved. It must be admitted that a well-chosen commercial food often approaches an ideal nutritional balance according to the latest scientific knowledge in this area. Commercial producers also have more resources, in the form of research centers and cooperative arrangements with universities, so they can offer the owner a range of consistently high-quality foods adapted to dogs of different sizes, for all physiological conditions and recently even for sick dogs.

The History of Dog Food

Ever since they have been domesticated, dogs have gradually turned away from the strictly carnivorous diet of their wild ancestors and adopted the diet provided by humans. Dogs' environments and their diets, have differed through the years according to the day and age and to the uses to which the dogs were put.

Until the 19th century, hunting dogs were often fed essentially on bread made with various grains (barley, wheat or rye); meat (offal) was fed only rarely, when the quarry was given to the hounds or on a temporary basis to strengthen "weak" dogs.

Sheepdogs in poor areas (such as Anatolian Sheepdogs) were also happy with grain-based foods and dairy products. Their work performance was not much affected by this diet, but they had a short life expectancy.

Meat was long considered to be an "optional" part of the canine diet, with some exceptions (coursing dogs hunting large game and war dogs were readily given meat, which was said to give them strength; sled dogs were traditionally fed seal meat, walrus meat or pemmican). However, we can guess that the fairly independent lifestyle of dogs in rural environments allowed them to supplement their daily ration of moistened bread with various other sorts of prey.

As the human standard of living rose, meat was more frequently included in dogs' diets, replacing bread and grains (much as people switched from "earning their bread" to "bringing home the bacon").

By the 19th century, meat had become the symbol of high living and was thought to be a nutritional cure-all for dogs, which people had redefined as strict carnivores. This oversimplification unfortunately led people to forget the dog's ancestral habits, which were perfectly adapted to foods other than meat.

This change in attitudes occurred in the context of a large shift in the dog's status at this time. Departing from their exclusively functional role (hunting, guarding, defense), dogs assumed a more social, even sociological, role as they became incorporated into the family, which no longer considered them as utilitarian objects but as living beings worthy of love and respect.

Vetalim® is a program for MS-DOS, designed to measure and formulate food for carnivorous animals using either individual calculations or a diet plan. All of the default values used for the calculations can be changed by the user to reflect the animal's characteristics or more recent knowledge. The program has three modules (animal, food and calculation modules), each of which can be accessed at any time.

This program can be used by breeders who are not nutrition specialists, who will use the default values furnished by the program. It can also be used by nutrition specialists, who can change the number and values of parameters.

The animal module takes into account:

- the identification of the animal and the owner,
- a listing of species, physiological conditions (growth, maintenance, gestation, lactation, physical activity, etc.) and pathologies (renal, cardiac, hepatic or digestive insufficiencies, etc.),
- the characteristics of the animal (weight, age, etc.) and
- the nutritional constraints for each type of animal.

The food module is based on:

- an editable list of household foods,
- a blank list of commercial foods that the user can fill in,
- the food value of each food, which can be changed by changing the ingredients of the food and
- the ability to add rules for inclusion and price limits.

The calculation module yields:
- a daily portion, which can be changed and
- a table of limitations calculated based on the daily portion and allowing a comparison to the theoretical limitations to be observed.

Professor B. M. Paragon
Small Animals Clinical Nutrition
École nationale vétérinaire, Alfort, France

Commercial food appeared at the beginning of the 19th century, relying on the affection given to dogs to construct a very specific market. The industry adapted and diversified in the wake of increasing urbanization, changing lifestyles, higher owner expectations and the different directions taken by the dog food companies depending on whether they considered the dog as a member of the family and played to the owners' emotional side - an easy thing to do. Such segmentation may seem rather rigid, but nevertheless reflects two diametrically opposed attitudes of dog owners, for whom the fact of feeding a dog can represent a daily ritual loaded with affection or, more rationally, can be considered as looking out for its biological best interests.

Since that time, the essential problem faced by commercial manufacturers (particularly kibble manufacturers) has been to conquer (through scientific debate, no less) the psychological resistance demonstrated by many owners who do not want to "take the easy way out" by feeding their dog commercially-prepared food. Homemade food, which takes more time to prepare, is for many owners (especially the elderly) a concrete expression of the love they have for their pet. Shortening the "meal ceremony" gives rise to a sense of guilt, which can lead to refusal to feed a reasonable diet. This reaction is very clear in France, with its great culinary tradition, while in countries with Germanic roots (Great Britain, the United States, Holland and Scandinavia), an opposite reaction can be observed.

Homemade Food

The "homemade food" category includes a heterogeneous mixture of food types, ranging from a diet exclusively of table scraps to a diet of sophisticated food prepared by the owner, who takes into account all of the data that are indispensable for a proper nutritional balance. Veterinarians even have a very complete computer program available, created by researchers at the veterinary schools in Alfort and Toulouse, France, that allows them to prescribe foods that are perfectly adapted to their canine patients in all cases.

In the classic sense, the daily portion consists of a mixture of meat, rice and carrots, to which specific vitamin and mineral supplements are added. Of course, different ingredients can be substituted, as long as they have an equivalent nutritional value. It is important to be familiar with the ingredients to avoid errors.

In the simplest case of a maintenance diet, the general formula of meat product + source of starch + vegetables + supplements can take many different forms depending on the ingredients chosen and the proportions in which they are used.

Practically speaking, the following are two classic rules of thumb:
- one third meat, one third uncooked rice, one third vegetables, with a vitamin and mineral supplement (the "1/3 +1/3 +1/3" rule).
- four parts meat to three parts uncooked rice, two parts vegetables, one part supplement. The supplement consists of one third dietetic yeast, one third bone meal, one third salad oil (the "4-3-2-1" model).

These models are far too simplistic, however and should be rethought because they do not account for factors such as the size of the breed.

Furthermore, the energy content of this type of food can drop from 2000 kcal per serving (if fat meat is used) to 1250 kcal (if lean meat is used) per serving!

THE EUROPEAN DOG FOOD MARKET (36 MILLION DOGS)

	VOLUME (Metric Tons)	ANIMALS FED Thousands of Animals	Market Share
DOG FOODS	–	36,000	
moist:	1,200	3,044	8.5%
dry:	1,360	11,362	31.6%
homemade:	–	21,594	59.9%

COMPOSITION OF ONE-KILOGRAM DAILY PORTION OF FOUR HOMEMADE FOODS
(IN INCREASING ORDER OF COST)

Ingredient (grams)	Food 1 (1,330 kcal ME per kg)	Food 2 (1,700 kcal ME per kg)	Food 3 (1,950 kcal ME per kg)	Food 4 (2,120 kcal ME per kg)
Lean meat	310		450	
Fat meat		420		500
Uncooked rice			230	100
Cooked rice	470	250		
Vegetables	160	250	230	300
Vitamin and mineral supplement*	60	30	90	100

* 1/3 brewers' yeast, 1/3 sunflower oil, 1/3 mixture of calcium carbonate and dicalcium phosphate.

ROYAL CANIN

DAILY PORTION, HOMEMADE FOOD
(WITH THE ABOVE COMPOSITION)

Weight of Dog (kg)	Food 1 (grams)	Food 2 (grams)	Food 3 (grams)	Food 4 (grams)
5	330	250	230	210
6	380	290	260	240
7	430	320	290	270
8	470	360	320	300
9	510	390	350	320
10	560	420	380	350
11	600	450	410	380
12	640	480	440	400
13	680	510	460	430
14	720	540	490	450
15	760	570	510	470
16	790	600	540	500
17	830	630	570	520
18	870	650	590	540
19	900	680	620	570
20	940	710	640	590
21	970	730	660	610
22	1010	760	690	630
23	1040	790	710	650
24	1080	810	730	670
25	1110	840	760	700
26	1140	860	780	720
27	1170	890	800	740
28	1210	910	820	760
29	1240	940	840	780
30	1270	960	870	800
31	1300	980	890	820
32	1330	1010	910	840
33	1370	1030	930	860
34	1400	1060	950	880
35	1430	1080	970	890

The food with the lowest cost per kilogram is not necessarily the most cost-effective. The cost of the food must be calculated with respect to how much is fed.
1 kg = 2,2 lb

DAILY PORTION, COMMERCIAL FOOD (IN GRAMS)

Weight of Dog (kg)	Moist Food (canned)	Semimoist Food	Dry Food (kibble)
5	400	160	88
6	460	180	128
7	520	200	144
8	570	220	160
9	620	240	168
10	670	260	184
11	720	280	200
12	770	300	208
13	820	320	224
14	870	340	240
15	910	360	248
16	960	380	264
17	1000	390	272
18	1050	410	288
19	1090	430	296
20	1130	440	312
21	1180	460	320
22	1220	480	336
23	1260	490	344
24	1300	510	360
25	1340	530	368
26	1380	540	376
27	1420	560	392
28	1460	570	400
29	1500	590	408
30	1540	600	424
31	1580	620	432
32	1610	630	440
33	1630	650	456
34	1690	660	464
35	1730	680	472

Moist food (canned), average energy content (ME): 1100 kcal/kg food
Semimoist (pouch), ME: 2800 kcal/kg food
Dry food (kibble), ME: 3850 kcal/kg food

A balanced diet with an appropriate caloric content are the keys to providing your dog with proper nutrition. These tables list information to help you determine your dogs nutritional needs. The quantities listed are merely guidelines. Keep in mind that ambient temperature, activity level, and daily environment will affect the amount of food an individual dog requires. When feeding commercial dog foods, follow the manufacturers guidelines.

TYPES OF COMMERCIAL FOOD AND DISTRIBUTION METHODS

Standard Foods
This category includes all foods meeting the average requirements of a dog on a maintenance diet, without being intended to meet any specific needs. In some cases they are very digestible (80%) and appetizing.

Nutritional Foods (sometimes called "premium")
High-end, complete foods are designed to meet the specific needs of a dog depending on its weight and size, its age and its level of activity.

These types of food meet standards for high digestibility (85-87%) and offer optimal coverage of specific nutritional needs in a highly appetizing food. They are manufactured using selected high-quality ingredients and require perfect mastery of the manufacturing process. They are carefully packaged and the packaging material contains natural preservation systems. These foods are highly stable.

Dietetic foods are designed to improve health
Prescribed and/or sold by veterinarians, this type of complete food can be used to correct diseases such as obesity, diabetes mellitus, chronic diarrhea and kidney failure. These foods are highly appetizing, to appeal to dogs that lack an appetite due to their illness. Their digestibility varies depending on the illness they are designed to treat. They can prevent the appearance of certain clinical symptoms and improve the effectiveness of medical treatment.

Distribution
Physiological foods can be obtained in large grocery stores (supermarkets and warehouse markets), most commonly as standard moist dog food and also through specialized distributors (pet stores, garden and hardware stores, agricultural cooperatives, etc.), mainly as nutritional dry dog foods.

Dietetic foods are sold exclusively by veterinarians. In France, veterinarians may also sell physiological foods. Over 80% of the total volume of dog and cat food sold by veterinarians is premium dry food (source: Royal Canin).

The number of calories from protein, which is so important to dogs, in fact depends heavily on the type of meat product used (lean or fat fish, type of meat, etc.). It is expressed in grams of protein per megacalorie of energy. The lipid content in different meats can vary from 0.5 to 35%, the protein content between 10 and 20% and the water content from 45 to 80%! For homemade food, it is also important to specify whether the sources of starch being weighed are cooked or not when used in the food, as rice takes in three times its weight in water during cooking. Finally, in the context of traditional feeding, the mineral and vitamin content as calculated from added supplements does not include the vitamins and minerals from other ingredients and the uncertainty of the proportional amount may alter the overall nutritional balance of the mixture. If the owner chooses to feed homemade food, he should use a supplement with a Ca/P ratio (proportion of calcium content to phosphorus content) equal to 2.

Special physiological requirements (growth, gestation, lactation, intense activity, aging, etc.) require an even more delicate nutritional balance than a simple maintenance diet.

- The proportion of proteins in the food must be increased during growth or reproduction.
- The energy content should be reduced for an over-large dog or for a large-breed dog during the growth phase.

In these cases, the uncertainty that is acceptable in a maintenance diet cannot be tolerated. A precise definition of the various ingredients and amounts used is of paramount importance. An exact determination according to precise scientific methods requires long and careful calculations, as well as complete documentation on the food values of all the ingredients. This workload has been greatly reduced, however, thanks to computers and a highly-developed program available to veterinarians.

Commercial Foods

Commercial foods arose from the agricultural (human food) and commercial livestock industries. They are classified according to their water content:

Moist foods (70 to 85% water)
- Canned foods, meat and vegetables
- Precooked meats to keep refrigerated

Semimoist foods (25 to 60% water)
- Cooked foods stabilized by preservatives or refrigeration

Dry foods (less than 14% water)
- Kibble
- Biscuits
- Flakes of grains
- Noodles
- Puffed rice

These various types of food can be "complete" or "supplementary". The latter type must be fed along with other foods to ensure that all physiological requirements are met.

• *Manufacturing techniques*

Canned foods
Canned foods are sterilized during the canning process (for 90 minutes, including 55 minutes at 120°C) and packaged in waterproof, airtight containers that keep microorganisms out. The products are usually formulated with meat and offal (by-products of the butchering process not usually consumed by humans) that are processed as fresh or frozen ingredients. The canned-food industry began in 1923 in the United States and developed extensively beginning in the 1950s.

Semimoist foods
These products have not been sterilized, but are stabilized with sugar, salt and chemical preservatives (propylene glycol) or refrigeration. They are usually in the form of "dog sausages" or very soft kibble. Although they have existed for over thirty years, these products have a very small share of the world market.

Dry foods (kibble)
The technology used to produce kibble was taken directly from the human food preservation industry.

- Noodles are prepared from semolina that is crushed in a vacuum, compressed and steam-cooked.
- Biscuits were created in Great Britain in 1885, then made their first appearance in France in 1920. They are made of kneaded flour that is cut out and steam-cooked in a tunnel oven.
- Cereal flakes are prepared just like human breakfast cereal: the grain is steam-cooked, crushed and dried.

Noodles, biscuits and flakes are supplementary foods intended to be eaten with meat.

- Kibbles are an extruded food. The combined effects of the pressure and short-duration high temperature (90-150°C for 20-30 seconds) in the extruder and subsequent drying, change the mixture of ingredients into a homogeneous product, which may then be covered with fat depending on the physiological purpose of the food. This category of food thoroughly dominates the American market (80% dry food, 66% kibble), which is currently the most mature market. It is gradually taking over every other market as well thanks to its nutritious characteristics, as proven in every test performed by consumer associations and its advantageous cost and convenience. It is this type of food that is generally used by professional breeders and prescribed by veterinarians.

• Ingredients

The pet food industry's role is essentially to develop foods or ingredients of excellent nutritional quality, which can often be further developed for the human food industry. Naturally, ingredients are not used unless they conform to very strict criteria and regulations.

- Guaranteed absence of **harmful bacteria**. Systematic inspections are performed by veterinary services and by the manufacturing companies themselves.

- **Homogeneous composition.**

The food's formula is reliable only if the food (the mixture of ingredients to be created) is homogeneous. This requires systematic and continual supervision by the manufacturers of all ingredients used.

- **Availability.**

In order to ensure standard formulations and steady production throughout the year, manufacturers diversify their suppliers so that stocks never run out.

Advantages and Disadvantages of the Different Types of Food

• Choice of ingredients

Proteins

Even more than with commercial food, the quality of homemade food depends on the quality of the ingredients. Whether table scraps or specially-purchased ingredients are used, quality is usually inconsistent, unless the owner buys meat or fish intended for human consumption. Traditionally, meat sold by butchers "for animals" consists of low-grade suet, which is considered by the industry to

Dry food for a small dog (less than 10 kg) (22 lb). Top to botom: For an adult dog, for a mature dog and puppy.

Dry food for a medium dog (10 to 25 kg) (22-55 lb). Top tobottom: For an adult dog, for a mature dog and puppy.

Dry food for a large dog (25 to 45 kg) (55-100 lb). Top to botom: For an adult dog, for a mature dog and puppy.

Dry food for a giant dog (over 45 kg) (over 100 lb). Top to botom: For an adult dog, for a mature dog and puppy.

be one of the lowest-quality ingredients. Note that some commercial foods use brewers' yeast or eggs as part of the protein content, thus including some of the same ingredients as household food.

Lipids

The quality of the fats used in dog food is of the utmost importance to the dog's health, including liver function, healthy hair, reproduction, etc. Both homemade and commercial foods should contain fats that have been prevented from oxidizing (becoming rancid). This is especially true for the essential fatty acids. For good nutrition, it is important that the food contain at least the minimum amount of essential fatty acids.

In cases where the fat content of a dog's food must be reduced to combat a tendency toward obesity, homemade food becomes relatively more expensive, since lean meat, fish or low-fat white cheese must be substituted for meat intended "for animal use" (which is too fatty). On the other hand, finding a food with a low energy (fat) content among the complete dry dog foods is a simple matter.

EVOLUTION OF FEEDING METHODS IN EUROPE

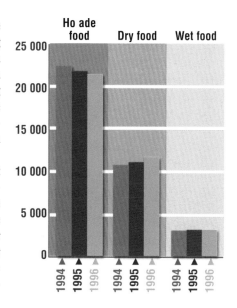

DRY FOOD (GRAMS OF KIBBLE PER DAY)

Weight of Dog (kg)	Living Indoors	Living Outdoors <2 hours exercise per day	Living Outdoors >2 hours exercise per day
Food for small breeds (food with energy content of 4,120 kcal/kg)			
1	25	30	35
2	50	55	60
3	65	70	80
4	80	90	95
5	95	105	115
6	105	120	130
7	120	135	145
8	130	145	160
9	145	160	175
10	155	170	190
Food for medium breeds (food with energy content of 3,920 kcal/kg)			
11	175	195	215
12	185	205	225
13	195	220	240
14	210	230	255
15	220	245	265
16	230	255	280
17	240	265	295
18	250	280	305
19	260	290	320
20	270	300	330
21	280	310	340
22	290	320	355
23	300	330	365
24	310	345	375
25	320	355	390
Food for large breeds (food with energy content of 4,140 kcal/kg)			
26	310	345	380
27	320	355	390
28	325	365	400
29	335	370	410
30	345	380	420
31	350	390	430
32	360	400	440
33	370	410	450
34	375	420	460
35	385	425	470
36	395	435	480
37	400	445	490
38	410	455	500
39	415	460	510
40	425	470	520
41	430	480	530
42	440	490	535
43	445	495	545
44	455	505	555
45	460	515	565
Food for giant breeds (food with energy content of 4,140 kcal/kg)			
46	470	520	575
47	475	530	585
48	485	540	590
49	490	545	600
50	500	555	610
55	535	595	655
60	570	635	695
65	605	670	740
70	640	710	780
75	670	745	820
80	705	780	860
85	735	815	900
90	765	850	935
95	795	885	975
100	830	920	1010

1 kg = 2,2 lb

Glucides

The main factor limiting inclusion of starch in homemade foods is the absolute requirement that the starch must be completely cooked. This is difficult unless the source of starch is derived from rice or noodles. Unless the starch is fully "gelatinized", digestive problems may result. Industrial cooking processes (extrusion, flaking, canning) meet this requirement and grains that are crushed and moistened before being cooked for a specific length of time become very digestible to dogs.

Fiber is provided by vegetables in most commercial foods. The fiber in dry food comes from a variety of sources, including bran and beet pulp. Replacing vegetables with other ingredients has no affect on the nutritional value of the food, since fiber content is what is important for moving food through the digestive system. But vegetables have such a good image among so many owners that some manufacturers try to take advantage of this in naming their products, whether dry or moist ("vegetable bits", "vegetable gravy", "vegetables and noodles"). In any case, vegetables do not affect the vitamin content of the product, as many people think, since the vitamins, along with the main minerals and trace elements, are added in a pre-mix containing them. These days, the vitamin content is adapted to the age, physiological condition and size of the dogs for which the food is intended.

Comparison shopping

While quality of ingredients, reliability and nutritional balance are all factors favoring commercial foods (as long as high-end products are chosen!), it is certainly possible to create homemade foods adapted to any situation. In this case, however, the advice and assistance of the veterinarian are indispensable.

THE DOG FOOD MARKET

Most foods on the market are intended for any dog, regardless of size. Even the most complete product lines take only the age of the dog into account. However, selective breeding by humans has created dogs with very different morphologies and lifestyles. In order to respect these differences, dog owners must be provided with products that are truly adapted to their dogs. Food that meets the dog's requirements as closely as possible, in conjunction with regular physical activity and periodic visits to the veterinarian, will contribute to improved well-being and a longer life expectancy.

ADVANTAGES AND DISADVANTAGES OF COMMERCIAL FOODS

Type of Food	Advantages	Disadvantages
Dry (kibble)	Does not spoil after opening More nutritious per unit of weight More economical than foods with a high water content	Requires addition of water Spoils if stored in a damp place
Semimoist	Very palatable Packaged in convenient daily portion sizes	Often requires a refrigerator or freezer Spoils after the package is opened Spoils if stored in a damp place Preserving food in this way is expensive Causes digestive problems in some dogs, contains preservatives
Moist (canned)	Durable packaging Very palatable	Preserving food in this way is expensive: the purchaser is paying for 75-82% water. Heavy to transport Heavy to store High fat content, increasing the risk of excess calorie intake Spoils after the can is opened

Owners should be wary of commercial foods that use meaningless phrases such as "visibly balanced", "with meat", "with shrimp", etc. When choosing a commercial food, the owner should weigh the advantages and disadvantages of dry food, semimoist food and moist food and not be influenced by anthropomorphic advertising that portrays dogs as customers in a gourmet restaurant.

The only true judge of a good dog food is the dog itself. The effectiveness of the diet and its adaptation to each individual dog can be ascertained by simple routine checks as dictated by common sense and observation, namely:

- Does the dog have a good appetite?
If the dog eats well, it probably is in good health and likes the odor, taste and consistency of its food.

- What are the characteristics of the dog's stool?
The volume, consistency, moisture content, color and odor of the stools are related to the digestibility of the food and proper digestive function, particularly of the large intestine.

- Has the dog's weight changed?
Regular weighing (weekly for young dogs and monthly for adults) will help keep the dog at its healthy weight, without excessive gain or loss.

COMPARISON OF DAILY COST OF DOG FOOD (EXAMPLE: FRANCE)

Daily Portion of Food (grams)	Average Retail Price (FF/kg)	Daily Budget per Dog (FF)	Comparison of Moist vs. Dry Food
Moist 1080 (canned)	8.60	9.29	x 2.9
Dry 330 (kibble)	9.90	3.25	

COST AS A FUNCTION OF PRODUCT FOR A 20-KG DOG

Example of product category	Average Price per kg (incl. tax)*	Annual Cost	
		Dry Food	Moist Food
Low-cost	between 4 and 6 FF	less than 600 FF	2,100 FF
Standard	between 8 and 10 FF	1,200 FF	3,400 FF
Premium	greater than 18 FF	2,000 FF	11,409 FF

For a 20-kg. dog, calculated from data provided by Nielsen sources
* Average prices per kg are essentially the same for dry and moist foods, within the same product category.

- What is the general condition of the hair and skin?
Healthy skin and a beautiful coat truly do reflect good health and can also reveal dietary imbalances or poor general health.

- How does the dog behave?
The dog should be happy and lively, depending on its normal personality.

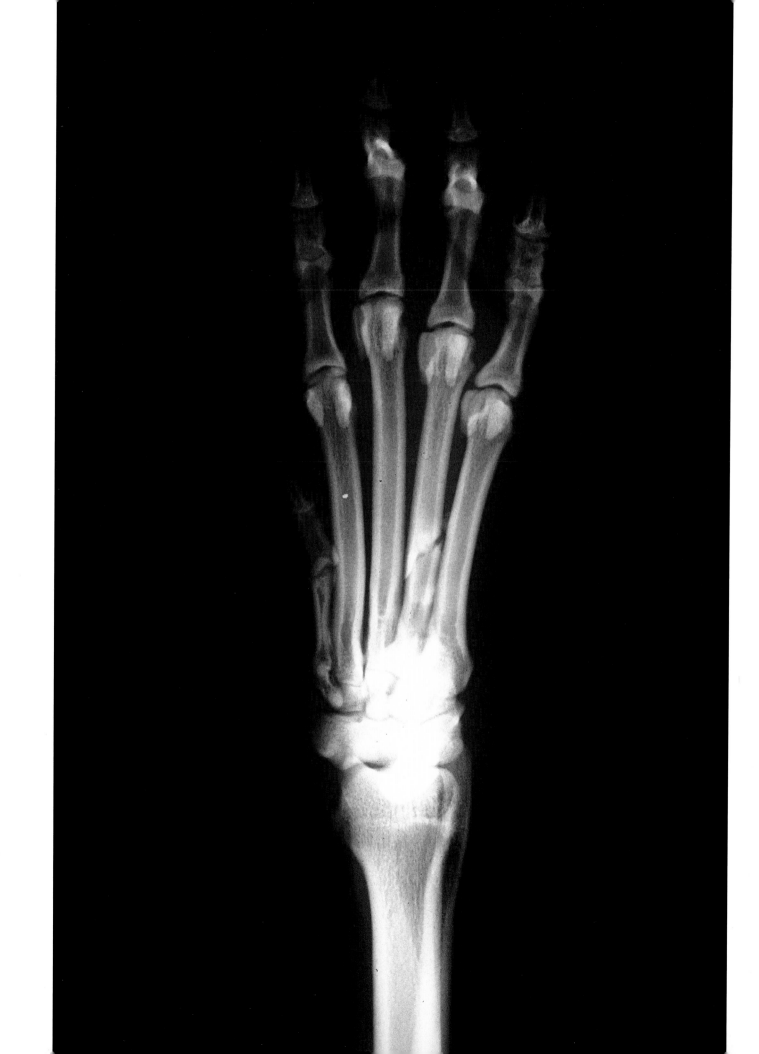

$Part\ 9$

Canine Medicine

Metacarpus fracture

Preventive Medicine

Parasitic Infestations

External parasite infestations affect mainly the skin and coat. They can cause eczema, pruritis or significant hair loss. Internal parasites are found mainly in the digestive tract (esophagus, stomach and intestines).

Many external parasites (ectoparasites) can drastically affect a dog's skin and coat. These parasites can be animal (fleas, ticks, lice, mites) or fungal (ringworm, mange) in origin. Internal endoparasitic infestations are often transmitted by fleas, ticks or mosquitoes. They can seriously impair a dog's health and cause contagious infectious diseases, some of which can now be prevented by vaccination. Vigilance and good daily hygiene can help prevent most of these sometimes fatal attacks on the dog's health.

Ectoparasites

Fleas

A flea is an insect with a wingless body that is flattened sideways. *Ctenocephalides canis* and *Ctenocephalides felis* are the fleas commonly found on dogs and only the adults are parasitic. They are usually found in areas frequented by the dog: it has been estimated that at any given time, only ten percent of the fleas present are in the dog's coat.

Fleas are quite prolific: the females lay many eggs (sometimes one or two thousand) within a few months. The eggs do not stick to the dog's coat, but fall to the ground and collect in rugs, wood floors, etc. Then they hatch and the larvae undergo metamorphosis, molt to become nymphs and when conditions are favorable, emerge as adults and become parasites on dogs, their definitive host. The adult flea pierces the dog's skin with its mouth parts and, after injecting some anticoagulant saliva, drinks the blood through its proboscis. The presence of fleas is revealed by their excrement: tiny black pellets found on the animal, particularly in the dorsal lumbar region. The pellets consist of blood eaten and digested by the fleas.

Fleas cause many diseases. First, they are a direct pathogen, although usually not a serious one, merely causing an itch. However, a dog can develop flea allergy dermatitis (FAD), causing significant pruritis that leads to hair loss and even sores from scratching, localized on the top of the body (especially in the lumbar region). This is less common in cold seasons when fleas are not as active.

Their indirect pathogenic role consists of transmitting pathogenic agents: bacteria (including the bacterium responsible for bubonic plague in humans) and digestive-tract parasites (transmitted when adult fleas are ingested).

Ticks

Ticks are very large acarids (from two to ten millimeters long) of the *Ixodidae* family. They display a significant sexual dimorphism: the female's abdomen can expand greatly, while the male's cannot. Their bodies are reddish-brown and flat, except after eating, when they are globular. They are intermittent parasites that live strictly on blood, except for the males of certain species, which do not eat at all. The main species that is parasitic on dogs is *Rhipicephalus sanguineus*, the kennel tick, which is highly specific to its host. It attaches preferentially to dogs and only dogs, at all stages of life (larva, nymph, adult).

Ticks attach to a dog's skin, preferring the most delicate areas. They use their mouth parts to pierce the skin and inject a special saliva, which solidifies into a very strong attachment point. The tick can then enjoy its meal of blood, after injecting more saliva with anticoagulant and vasodilating properties. Larvae, nymphs and unfertilized females take only small amount of blood, but fertilized females take large amounts (as much as several milliliters). While larvae, nymphs and adult females take only a single meal, the males eat very little but eat many times. Once the tick has finished its meal, another type of saliva is used to dissolve the attachment point so the tick can drop off.

A free-living stage can follow the parasitic phase, depending on outside conditions. This free-living stage of the tick's life cycle is much longer than the parasitic stage. The kennel tick usually reproduces on its host, then the female gorges on blood and drops to the ground. After a few weeks, the female lays several thousand eggs and dies. Depending on environmental conditions, the eggs incubate for several weeks and then hatch. A larva emerges from each egg, climbs a blade of grass and waits for its future canine host to pass by. It attaches to the host and takes its first meal, lasting several days, then drops to the ground again. After a time on the ground, the larva molts and becomes a nymph. The same process occurs again: the nymph attaches to the host and eats, drops to the ground and molts to become an adult male or female. The complete cycle is quite long, considering that the tick must attach to three hosts: under less-than-ideal conditions, it can last up to four years. Furthermore, not all eggs reach adulthood, because they may be ingested at any stage of development by various animals, particularly during the free-living stage.

Internal (Digestive) Parasites

Esophagus and stomach

Spirocerca lupi is the main parasite that infects the esophagus and stomach in dogs. *S. lupi* is a nematode usually found in the esophageal wall, more rarely in the stomach or even in the wall of the aorta. These parasites cause a serious disease that is endemic in tropical countries, northern Africa, and southern Europe. Dogs become infested by ingesting intermediate hosts, usually *Coleoptera* (beetles), or more commonly, small vertebrates.

Diseased animals show symptoms in the esophagus (regurgitation, sometimes inability to swallow) and stomach (repeated vomiting, increased thirst). Respiratory difficulties may be observed when the parasite is located in the wall of the aorta. Treatment is very difficult, involving injectable anthelminthics such as ivermectin. Given the wide variety of intermediate hosts (vectors) of the parasite that can infect dogs, it is practically impossible to design effective prophylaxis.

Stomach and intestine

Strongyloidosis, or hookworm infestation, is mainly due to *Uncinaria stenocephala*, the most common hookworm in France; to *Ancylostoma*

A dog and cat flea and its larva

A tick on a dog's skin

THE WHY AND HOW OF THE WAR AGAINST DOG AND CAT FLEAS

To effectively combat a parasite, the pet owner must know how it develops so he can intervene in the various stages of development. Larvae hide from the light. (In a house, this can be under rugs, cushions or skirting, between floorboards, in nooks and crannies, etc.) After one or two weeks of life, the larva changes to a cocoon, which is very resistant to flea treatments, and can survive this way for up to five months. The presence of animals or humans triggers the hatching of the adult from the cocoon. When a house has been inhabited for several months, a large number of cocoons can hatch all at once, leading to an infestation of fleas within a matter of hours.

The adult then jumps onto (usually) a cat or dog and bites the animal so that it can eat the blood. The females are the most ravenous, able to eat fifteen times their own weight in blood (seventy females can eat one milliliter of blood per day!). If nature calls while a female flea is eating, the flea deposits "flea dirts"—small black pellets that can be found in the coat and become deep red when placed on wet paper.

In addition to siphoning off blood, fleas frequently cause allergies and can also transmit a flatworm to dogs and cats, a phenomenon often found in adult carnivores.

Most flea treatments applied to the animal (collars, sprays, powders) do limit the number of fleas, but are not sufficient to eliminate all of them because there are often a large number still lurking in the environment. Two treatments are usually recommended.

The purpose of the first treatment, an insecticide, is to kill all the adult fleas on the dogs and cats living in the area to be treated. Antiparasitic

sprays (pyrethroids) or "spot on" applications (direct application of very concentrated spray solution that then diffuses throughout the animal's body and kills the fleas as they eat) are used for this purpose. This treatment must be repeated every month. Another method attempts to sterilize the fleas as they eat. This treatment is administered by giving the dog a pill once a month.

The second treatment attempts to kill the fleas (using an insecticide) or keep them from developing (by means of an insect growth regulator, or IGR) in the environment. Insect growth regulators have the advantage of being completely harmless to domestic animals and humans. Before applying this treatment, the entire area must be dusted and thoroughly cleaned (remember that the vacuum cleaner, as well as the cupboard where it is kept, can become a haven for fleas). Surfaces are then treated with an insecticide and/or insect growth regulator. In good weather, it is sometimes necessary to treat the yard as well (only the shady places where the dogs and cats lie down, and the products used must be resistant to ultraviolet radiation). Many effective insecticides and insect growth regulators are available, each with its own advantages and limitations.

The results obtained are usually good, but depend on the way the treatments are applied and how often they are used.

Bruno POLACK
Department of Parasitology, Mycology,
and Parasitic and Fungal Diseases
Ecole Nationale Vétérinaire, Alfort, France

caninum, particularly in torrid zones; and *Ancylostoma braziliense* in tropical countries. These parasites affect primarily animals living in groups, which is why in French an infestation is sometimes called "pack dog anemia," but other dogs may be infested as well. Hookworm larvae of the *Ancylostoma genus* penetrate through the skin or are ingested by puppies along with the bitch's milk. The infestation has several stages corresponding to larval migrations within the body. It begins with a cutaneous phase: small lesions appear on the dog's abdomen, then disappear spontaneously within about ten days.

The adults develop in the small intestine, which causes digestive symptoms such as alternating diarrhea and constipation, then the appearance of persistent diarrhea with a fetid odor. Finally, the dog's general health worsens due to anemia. In its severe forms, the disease may lead to death, while in more benign forms spontaneous recovery is possible.

The parasites take blood: the adult form attaches to the intestinal mucous membrane, eats a small amount of blood, and has the same effect as bleeding the dog. The parasites probably also have a toxic effect, and affect the immune system as well: As a result, there is a stronger skin reaction on reinfestation, which hinders larval migration. In this way, dogs can become fairly resistant to these hookworms. The primary means of prevention in areas with groups of dogs is to disinfect the area. Pregnant bitches can be given a preventive treatment of fenbendazole, which destroys the larvae. Puppies can also be treated once a week from the age of ten to forty-five days, then again at eight weeks and twelve weeks in areas where these parasites are prevalent.

Small intestine

Parasites of the small intestine include nematodes (roundworms) of the Ascaris family (*Toxascaris leonina*) and the Toxocara family (*Toxocara canis*). *T. canis* can be transmitted to humans. These parasites infest mainly young dogs less than a year old. The puppies ingest embryonic eggs in their drinking water or food, or the eggs are transmitted from the mother to the puppies either in utero or via the milk. Dogs that are in poor general health are more susceptible, particularly animals suffering from certain nutritional deficiencies. Massive infestation causes general symptoms such as slow growth, weight loss, and a high mortality rate in three- to seven-week-old puppies that were massively infested before birth.

Of course, the puppies display mainly digestive symptoms: diarrhea interspersed with periods of constipation, vomiting (to get rid of some of the parasites), and a distinctly pot-bellied appearance. Complications may also occur in the form of intestinal blockage (by a clump of worms) or even intestinal perforation leading to hemorrhage or peritonitis. In addition to causing these symptoms, the parasites ingest blood and some of the intestinal contents, which both contain constituents that are essential to the puppy's growth. Diagnosis is usually straightforward: the puppy's overall health is poor, its abdomen distended, and it sheds parasites in its stools or by vomiting. Analysis of a stool sample can sometimes help with the diagnosis. Many parasiticides are available, the most effective being pyrantel pamoate, nitroscanate, and ivermectin. Preventive measures include systematic treatment of young dogs and destruction of the adult worms present in the mother. It is extremely difficult to destroy eggs in the environment, as they are highly resistant.

Cestodes can also parasitize this portion of the digestive tract. These tapeworms, such as *Dipylidium caninum*, are transmitted when fleas are ingested. They affect dogs of all ages, leading to significant anal pruritis that causes the dog to rub its posterior on the ground. Associated digestive symptoms include the elimination of segments of the parasite (which look like grains of rice) in the stools, which may have the appearance of diarrhea. Reinfestation is common, facilitated by the fact that eggs can stick to the dog's hair and be ingested. The spoliatory effect is very slight: The parasites' main effect is to cause irritation and swelling of the anal glands.

Prophylaxis consists of first eliminating intermediate hosts, both fleas and, to a lesser extent, lice. Use of specific anti-cestode treatments such as praziquantel in the infested animals is then recommended. Multi-purpose anthelminthics such as nitroscanate can also be effective.

Large intestine

This portion of the digestive tract, namely the cecum and colon, is parasitized mainly by nematodes of the genus *Trichuris*. Dogs become infested by ingesting eggs present in the environment, with adults seeming to be affected more often. A massive infestation leads to symptoms such as diarrhea (which can be bloody), anemia, and obvious weight loss. These whipworms siphon off blood and cause lesions in which bacteria can develop. Diagnosis depends on a stool analysis, which reveals the presence of parasite eggs in the dog's feces.

Treatment is by administration of benzimidazoles such as flubendazole for three consecutive days, or of febantel for the same length of time. Reinfestation occurs very easily, however, so the owner must ensure that the facilities are clean and the food is sanitary.

Contagious Infectious Diseases

Contagious infectious diseases are caused by bacteria, viruses, or endoparasites and are often fatal. Vaccinations are available for most.

Leptospirosis

Leptospirosis results from infection with *Leptospira* microorganisms. It affects many species and can be transmitted to humans. In dogs, there are two main types (serovars): *Leptospira icterohaemorragiae* and *Leptospira canicola*. These diseases are endemic throughout the world and especially in humid areas and large populations of dogs.

Leptospirosis shows various clinical symptoms depending on the serovar present. At first, the dog may have hemorrhagic gastroenteritis, which can be caused by either of the serovars mentioned above. This is a severe form of gastroenteritis: After an incubation period of five days, the dog is exhausted and prostrate with anorexia and polydipsia (increased thirst). It will have a high fever for two or three days, followed by an abnormally low temperature. Palpation of the abdomen is extremely painful.

The clinical stage that follows is five to six days long. During this period, digestive symptoms appear (bloody vomit and diarrhea), as well as hemorrhagic patches on the mucous membranes and skin, inflammation of the oral mucosa (which smell extremely unpleasant), and acute kidney failure (reduced quantity of urine, sometimes tinged with blood). Nervous, visual, cardiac, and pulmonary symptoms may also be observed. This stage is followed by a coma, leading to death.

Gastroenteritis may be present in a superacute form leading to death within forty-eight hours, after a period of hypothermia accompanied by vomiting and diarrhea, followed by a coma. There is also a less acute form lasting about two weeks, in which the dog may recover after the gastroenteritis phase.

A second form of leptospirosis known as icteric leptospirosis (infectious jaundice) also exists. It is caused exclusively by Leptospira icterohaemorragiae. The incubation period lasts between five and eight days, giving way to hypothermia, exhaustion, and abdominal pain. The dog becomes anorexic. The clinical phase follows, during which the mucosa take on the reddish-orange color characteristic of jaundice. Associated digestive symptoms are diarrhea and vomiting. This form leads to death in five to fifteen days.

A third form of the disease, leptospiral nephritis, is caused by *Leptospira canicola*. There are two forms: a fast form in which gastroenteritis predominates, and a slow form, which is usually not discovered until its final stage, uremia (a large increase in the urea concentration in the blood). The dog dies after falling into a uremic coma.

Leptospirosis is diagnosed by examining the animal. The symptoms are fairly characteristic. Laboratory analysis can reveal leptospires in the blood before the eighth day of the disease, and in the urine after this date. Diagnosis by testing for antibodies is not possible until after the tenth day.

Dogs may contaminate themselves or each other by biting, licking, or coming into contact with dead animals. River or pond water and objects soiled by urine may lead to indirect contamination. Leptospires enter the body via the mucous membranes or through wounds in the skin. Sources include the excreta and secretions of diseased animals, blood at the beginning of the infection, and urine for several months after the eighth day. Dogs suffering from less acute and chronic forms of the disease can be treated with certain antibiotics. Preventive hygiene includes avoidance of water contamination, destruction of rodents (which are vectors), and disinfection of the premises. Vaccines do exist, and confer fairly good immunity with a maximum duration of six months, so they should be used in high-risk areas.

Leptospires can be transmitted from dogs to humans, who then develop jaundice similar to that seen in the dog.

Babesiosis

Babesiosis is caused by a protozoan (single-celled) parasite known as a piroplasmid, namely *Babesia canis*. During its life cycle, this parasite must pass through a vector host before transmitting the disease from one dog to another. The vector is the female tick.

Parasitic development in dogs has several stages corresponding to changes in the parasite. At first, the parasite is a very simple, circular organism known as a trophozoite. It enters the red blood cells and feeds on their hemoglobin, which it digests. The trophozoite undergoes asexual reproduction (simple cell division).

The nucleus of the cell divides first, then the membrane and cytoplasm (the liquid contained within the membrane). The division results in two droplet-shaped daughter cells, or merozoites, which are still inside the red blood cell. There may be more than two cells inside one red blood cell. Usually, the red blood cell is destroyed after division and the merozoites are released into the bloodstream. Each merozoite quickly attaches to another red blood cell, enters it, and forms a trophozoite. Some piroplasmids, called gamonts, stop dividing in the red blood cells.

The tick, an intermediate host, takes a meal on an infested dog. The red blood cells it ingests are destroyed in its intestine, as are the trophozoites and merozoites. Only the gamonts remain, which become gametes in the intestinal wall. Two gametes fuse, forming an egg, or zygote. The zygote produces a motile form that leaves the tick's intestine to enter its egg cells, where it multiplies and gives rise to motile spores. If a female tick in the next generation, i.e., one arising from an egg containing motile spores, bites a dog, the motile spores move into her salivary glands. Each motile spore becomes very large, and is then called a sporont. Inside the sporont, thousands of sporozoites form and infest the dog. Each sporozoite enters a red blood cell and becomes a trophozoite to complete the cycle.

Babesiosis is especially frequent in hot and temperate climates, in areas where ticks are abundant. It is more widespread during seasons in which ticks are active, and with certain lifestyles, as in hunting dogs. Highly-selected breeds such as Cocker Spaniels, spaniels, Yorkshire Terriers, and Dobermans are more susceptible than others. Puppies are more vulnerable than adults.

The incubation period, which corresponds to the period during which the parasites are multiplying in the dog's body, can last from two days to about two weeks. During this stage, no piroplasmids are present in the blood. After this stage, the parasites appear in the blood and symptoms appear almost simultaneously. In the acute form of this disease, the dog has a very high fever and is exhausted. The fever lasts an average of six to ten days. At the same time, anemia (pallor of the mucosa) is present due to the destruction of red blood cells as the parasites multiply inside of them. After several days of illness, hemoglobinuria arises and blood appears in the urine. Atypical clinical symptoms can be nervous, respiratory, digestive, cutaneous, or visual. The course of the disease is short: one week at the most. The dog becomes worse if untreated and falls into a coma leading to death. There is a chronic form of the disease, found mainly in adults, that can follow an acute form. The fever is not as high, or is absent, and the overall condition of the dog remains good. Anemia is always clearly present.

This is a slow form of babesiosis, and complications may occur. The disease may last several weeks and end with the dog's death.

Diagnosis is made based on the presence of fever and anemia. The dog's lifestyle should be taken into account. Microscopic examination of the blood can confirm the diagnosis. A blood sample is taken from a peripheral area - usually the ear - and examined for the presence of *Babesia* in the red blood cells. The parasites are more difficult to find in the chronic forms of the disease, since there are fewer in the blood.

There are treatments specific for *Babesia*, of which the most frequently-used is imidocarb. Sometimes two injections at an interval of forty-eight hours are necessary, since there is a risk of relapse. In addition to this specific treatment, the symptoms of the disease can be treated, particularly the anemia (by means of antianemic agents, or blood transfusions in the most serious cases).

Prevention is still the best cure. The disease can be prevented by destroying all ticks as early as possible, and by using acaricide (anti-tick) treatments.

There is a vaccine for babesiosis, but it is effective for a maximum of only six months. Furthermore, the vaccine is only about seventy percent effective, and can make diagnosis more difficult, for example, if the animal suffers from chronic babesiosis. Two injections are required, three weeks apart. The dog must be in good health and fast for twelve hours before receiving the vaccine.

Infectious Tracheobronchitis (Kennel Cough)

Kennel cough is a contagious respiratory disease characterized by a cough lasting up to several weeks. The syndrome is caused by bacterial and viral microorganisms, and is found mainly in large populations with dogs of various origins. It is also found in isolated animals, for example, after a dog show. The main bacterium responsible is *Bordetella bronchiseptica*, which often appears at the same time as a viral infection. The dog's general health is not affected. After an incubation period of about three days, the dog begins to cough and a purulent nasal discharge appears. Different viruses may cause the various symptoms. *Canine parainfluenza virus* may provoke a slight inflammation of the nasopharyngeal region and a cough lasting a few days. This virus is highly contagious and can be transmitted to nearby dogs. Finally, various *Mycoplasma* may increase the effects of other

microorganisms, although they alone do not cause symptoms.

The most common clinical symptom of kennel cough, tracheobronchitis, is uncomplicated. It causes a severe cough that is dry, harsh, nonproductive, and persistent. The symptoms may disappear in less than a week or last several weeks in more serious forms of the illness.
Associated symptoms are inflammation of the conjunctiva, sinuses, tonsils, and pharynx. Usually, the dog's overall health is not affected.

More rarely, in dogs with diminished immune response, a more serious form of the illness develops, leading to pneumonia and affecting general health (producing exhaustion, anorexia, and fever). This form develops slowly over several weeks.

Diagnosis is easier within a population than on a single animal. Kennel cough is usually suspected if a cough corresponding to the previous description is observed. Laboratory analysis of a sample of the nasal secretions can confirm which viruses or bacteria are responsible, thus indicating which treatment will be most effective. For isolated cases, other possible causes of the same symptoms should be investigated before concluding that the disease is kennel cough.

The value of laboratory analysis in implementing treatment is limited. The only effective medical treatment is an aerosolized antibiotic. If treatment is administered less than forty-eight hours after the appearance of the first symptoms, injection of serum specific for the principal pathogens may be effective. To make the dog more comfortable, antitussives are also given.

The risk of kennel cough can be reduced by taking proper sanitary measures. The facility's layout is important in this regard: an outside area and an area with a constant temperature should be available to the dogs. The facility should be easy to disinfect. A quarantine period allows the facility's operator to determine a dog's state of health before introducing it into a group, and vaccinations can be administered. A number of vaccines exist, although their effectiveness varies.

Infectious Canine Hepatitis

Infectious canine hepatitis is an infectious disease that is specific to carnivores and is caused by a virus that was isolated in dogs in 1933. The disease is found mainly in northern and central Europe and the U.S., affecting mostly young dogs between three and twelve months of age, and occasionally adult dogs as well.

The disease is caused by *canine adenovirus 1* (CAV1), which can live for about ten days in the environment, but is destroyed by heat and ultraviolet radiation. It has superacute, acute, and subacute forms.

The superacute form affects puppies, which die within a few hours without displaying any particular symptoms. The acute form consists of an invasion phase during which the dog is apathetic and has a fever for about forty-eight hours; and a clinical phase during which digestive symptoms appear (diarrhea, vomiting, gastroenteritis, anorexia, and increased water intake), the size of certain ganglia increases, and optical symptoms such as conjunctivitis and corneal clouding ("blue eye") are seen. The dog usually recovers in six to ten days. More rarely, the disease leads to a coma and then death. The subacute form has essentially the same symptoms, but they are less severe than in the acute form. The dog recovers within three or four weeks.

The prognosis is usually good, except in the superacute form. However, in some cases, corneal clouding may persist.

Infection results from contact between an infected dog and a healthy one, or by indirect contact (contact with contaminated objects or food). Nursing bitches can also transmit the virus to their puppies, which then develop the superacute form of the disease. The virus enters the body mainly via the digestive tract, but also via the respiratory tract. It affects only dogs and foxes, which can spread it through the environment by any blood or excreta deposited during the illness. Urine can spread the disease for several months after the animal recovers.

Once in the body, the virus first multiplies in the tonsils and various ganglia, then it may or may not spread. The fact that it can remain localized in certain areas explains why so many cases remain undetected. In the third phase of the disease, the viral particles multiply in targeted organs (the liver, kidneys, digestive tract, and eyes), giving rise to the symptoms discussed above.

Treatments do exist. A specific treatment for infectious canine hepatitis consists of serum therapy, which is effective when administered during the first forty-eight hours of the infection.

The second part of the treatment consists of treatment of the major symptoms: vomiting, diarrhea, and corneal clouding. Sanitary prophylaxis, would consist of isolation of animals introduced into a group, and a search for antibodies against the virus. Vaccines also exist, based on the CAV2 strain, which is related to CAV1 but does not cause infectious hepatitis.

Distemper

Distemper is a highly contagious disease affecting dogs and wild carnivores, and is caused by a paramyxovirus. It has been very rare since 1960, when a vaccine was developed, but there are periodic outbreaks. Distemper affects dogs of all ages, although different dogs have varying susceptibility. Dogs usually become infected by direct contact, inhaling the virus, which enters through the respiratory tract. After the virus enters the body, it multiplies in the tonsils and bronchi, then spreads throughout the body in about eight days. From this point, the disease can develop in three different ways. In about half of all dogs, the immune response developed after the infection is adequate and the virus disappears. These dogs recover after displaying only a few mild symptoms. In other dogs, however, the immune response is inadequate. These dogs have the characteristic symptoms of the disease. Finally, in a minority of dogs, apparent recovery takes place, but the dogs have nervous symptoms a month later.

The most classic form of this disease develops as follows. The incubation period lasts three to seven days, during which the dog displays no symptoms. Then the virus spreads through the dog's body and a fever of 40°C is observed, with a yellow discharge from the eyes and nose and sometimes small pustules on the abdomen. This stage lasts two to three days and is followed by a stage in which the dog seems to return to normal, except for persistent conjunctivitis. Next comes the clinical phase, during which occur most of the symptoms typical of canine distemper. The temperature remains high (about 39.5°C), the mucous membranes are inflamed, a discharge appears from the nose and eyes, the dog has diarrhea, and coughing reveals the presence of tracheobronchitis.

The virus may be localized in various places: rhinitis, conjunctivitis, bronchial pneumonia (revealed by coughing and respiratory problems), gastroenteritis (causing diarrhea and vomiting), and keratitis (inflammation of the cornea) with ulceration are symptoms of complications due to the presence of bacteria. Later on, two types of nervous symptoms caused by the immune system's reaction to the disease may appear. If the symptoms appear rapidly, paralysis, convulsions, involuntary muscle contractions, and coordination problems while walking may be observed. When the symptoms take longer to appear—up to several months—the dog will still have difficulty coordinating its movements, and this ataxia progressively becomes paralysis. Involuntary muscle contractions and vision problems also occur.

There are several courses the disease can take. The dog may recover completely, without going through the clinical phase; or it may recover incompletely and suffer nervous, respiratory, or dental after-effects.

Atypical forms of the disease also exist. There is a form that affects the skin and nerves, which causes a thickening of the nose and footpads, discharge from the nose and eyes, and persistent fever. This form progresses slowly. After a few weeks, encephalitis appears and leads to death. Another form of encephalitis (old-dog encephalitis) can affect old dogs, as the name implies.

At least four of the following six criteria must be met for a positive diagnosis of distemper: discharge from the nose and eyes, digestive symptoms, respiratory symptoms, nerve symptoms, and persistent fever, observed in a young dog. Laboratory tests will confirm the clinical diagnosis.

The disease is transmitted by direct contact between an infected animal and a healthy one. The virus is usually inhaled, and all body secretions contain virus particles. Treatments include a specific treatment, consisting of administration of high doses of serum, and a more general treatment allowing the dog to fight secondary infections, as well as the digestive and respiratory symptoms. Preventive measures are the most effective way to protect a dog against this disease. In large populations of dogs, it is preferable to quarantine animals being brought in. The facilities should also be disinfected. Vaccines exist, and can be used after the age of eight weeks. Dogs should be immunized as soon as possible.

Rabies

This infectious disease, which can be prevented by vaccination, is caused by a rhabdovirus that is sensitive to heat and is inactivated by visible or ultraviolet light. It is preserved by cold. The rabies virus has a very marked affinity for nerve tissues. Its virulence is due to the G glycoprotein, a molecule on the viral coat. The virus is usually transmitted to dogs through a wound (bite, scratch, etc.) and multiplies locally. After multiplying in the muscle, the virus spreads through the body and enters the nerves. Rabies infection leads to nervous symptoms that are always fatal in dogs.

Once the dog has been infected, the disease may take many courses. Infection may be asymptomatic. In very rare cases, symptoms may occur but be followed by complete or incomplete recovery. In practically one hundred percent of cases, normal infection results in death.

The disease has several stages. Incubation lasts between fifteen and sixty days, after which the dog excretes virus particles in its saliva for an average of three to ten days. Then symptoms appear, and the dog dies after a short time (from two to ten days). There are two categories of symptoms: furious rabies and paralytic rabies.

As the disease progresses, the dog at first merely displays a change in character. It becomes nervous and is constantly active. Eventually, it seeks a quiet spot, then there are alternating periods of apathy and excitation. The general health of the dog does not appear to be a cause for alarm.

Next follows a period of intense agitation, and general problems begin to appear, most notably difficulty in chewing food. The dog then becomes "mad" and attacks everything around it. Finally, paralysis gradually appears and inexorably leads to death in four or five days, on the average.

Another clinical form exists, called paralytic rabies or dumb rabies, because the first symptom observed is paralysis of the jaw. The first phase of the disease consists only of depression. Paralysis of the head makes eating impossible, and the dog does not try to bite. The paralysis spreads to the rest of the body, and the dog dies within two or three days.

The most dangerous animals are those in the last stage of the incubation period, when the virus is being shed in the saliva, and those showing clinical signs of the disease. Many tissues and organs can be sources of the rabies virus. Some contain the virus within the organism, while others excrete it, and so make the dog dangerous to other dogs. The virus is transmitted mainly by the saliva, in which the viral concentration is particularly high, which explains why biting endangers other animals. The bodies of animals that have died of rabies are also dangerous, because the virus can live longer in them than in the outside environment or on contaminated objects.

While contagion is mainly through bites, not all bites are contagious. Transmission depends on the depth of the bite and the area bitten (with areas rich in nerve structures being the most dangerous). Contamination can occur in other ways as well, although bites are the most frequent means. Contact with the mucous membranes can spread the disease if lesions are present (such lesions are sometimes difficult to see). Objects recently contaminated by saliva from an infected animal can also spread the disease. There have even been rare cases of contamination by inhalation or ingestion of the virus, as well as cases of transmission from a pregnant female to her young.

Rabies is difficult to diagnose clinically: a diagnosis can be confirmed only by a sample taken from the dead animal's body. Rabies is suspected when the dog changes behavior or shows other telling symptoms, particularly in areas where rabies is still endemic. The dog's lifestyle can also shed light on the likelihood that it may have come in contact with an infected animal (fox, cat, another dog, etc.).

There is no treatment for rabies, which is almost always fatal.

To keep dogs and other domestic carnivores from becoming infected, preventive measures must be implemented. First, animals from countries that are not rabies-free should not be allowed into other countries, as they may be infected with the rabies virus. Measures for excluding such animals can include denial of entry, requirement for a certificate of good health, and quarantine. Second, wild animals, particularly foxes, are known to carry rabies: accordingly, programs to vaccinate wild animals have begun.

Individual precautions can be taken to prevent infection of one dog by another. Dogs that bite and dogs suspected of carrying rabies are placed under health surveillance. In France, several categories of suspects are legally defined. Clinical suspects are animals that display symptoms typical of rabies. Biting suspects are dogs that have bitten a person or another animal for no apparent reason, in an area where rabies is endemic. There is also a category of non-suspect biting dogs that have bitten for no apparent reason, in a rabies-free area.

"Suspected carriers" are placed under veterinary surveillance at the veterinarian's office for the length of time needed to confirm a diagnosis of rabies. Biting animals are placed under "biting dog" surveillance consisting of a two-week period during which the dog is examined three times by the veterinarian. The first visit is within twenty-four hours of the bite, the second on the seventh day thereafter, and the third fifteen days after the bite. During each of these visits, if the dog is in good health, the veterinarian draws up a certificate stating that on the date of the examination, the dog had no symptoms of rabies. Giving a booster shot of rabies vaccine during this period is prohibited.

Of course, the dog may remain with its owner. If at any time during this period the dog shows symptoms of rabies, it is immediately taken to the veterinarian and placed under veterinary surveillance, as for a suspected carrier. The "biting dog" surveillance is then ended.

A dog that has come into contact with an animal known (by laboratory diagnosis) to carry rabies, or that has been bitten or scratched by such an animal, must be destroyed as soon as possible, unless the infected dog is under "biting dog" surveillance. It is possible to obtain an exception for vaccinated dogs identified by tattoo, by requesting it from veterinary services.

The best way to protect a dog against rabies is to vaccinate it. There are various types of vaccines. Those made from inactivated or live virus are the most common. The first vaccination cannot be given unless the dog is at least three months old and is in good health. It generally consists of a single inoculation. Booster shots must be given annually.

Finally, it is important to remember that rabies can be transmitted to humans through bites or scratches, and that without the earliest possible medical treatment, it is also deadly to us.

Parvovirus

Parvoviral infection is a contagious disease that appeared in the U.S. and Australia in 1978, and is now found throughout the world. It is caused by a member of the parvovirus family that is very resistant in the environment. Only canid species are affected.

This disease usually causes hemorrhagic gastroenteritis. After an incubation period of three to four days, the clinical phase begins. During this stage, the dog is at first prostrate and anorexic. Vomiting then occurs, followed shortly by bloody diarrhea. After four to five days, the stools become pinkish-gray in appearance, which is characteristic of this disease.

In the superacute form of this disease, the dog becomes extremely dehydrated and dies within two or three days. In the acute form, the reduction in blood volume caused by diarrhea and vomiting and secondary bacterial infections cause death within five to six days. Animals that have not died by the fifth day recover.

The disease is deadliest in young puppies aged six to twelve weeks, i.e., when the protection conferred by the mother's antibodies wears off. There is also a rare myocardial form of the disease that affects only one- to two-month old puppies that did not receive immunity from their mother. The disease usually leads to death after a short period of respiratory distress. Puppies that survive suffer cardiac after-effects.

Finally, many dogs can be infected and show no symptoms.

Dogs can be directly infected by contact with an infected dog. They can also be indirectly infected by contact with objects that have been contaminated by an infected dog's stools.

The virus enters through the nose or mouth, then multiplies in the ganglia before spreading through the body via the blood between the second and fifth day. It is eliminated in the feces between the fourth and ninth days. Once the virus has been disseminated in the blood, it multiplies in the digestive tract and destroys cells there, causing an intestinal infection. The virus is excreted mainly in the feces, but also to a lesser extent in the urine and saliva. Young and old dogs are most susceptible to infection.

Diagnosis is practically impossible in a single animal, but is fairly easy within a population. In this case, the disease is highly contagious, affecting dogs six through twelve weeks of age with a fifty-percent mortality rate. Some animals suffer from hemorrhagic gastroenteritis. Those that live beyond the fifth day recover rapidly. Laboratory examination can confirm the diagnosis, either by detecting the virus in the stools, or by identifying antibodies specific for the disease in the blood. (The antibodies are present as soon as diarrhea appears.) It is possible to treat the symptoms to stop the vomiting and diarrhea, rehydrate the dog for about four days, and avoid secondary bacterial infections entering through the lesions caused by

the multiplication of viruses in the cells of the digestive tract.

In breeding establishments, preventive measures are strongly recommended. Contaminated areas should be disinfected with bleach, and affected animals should be quarantined (although this is made less effective by the fact that the virus is so resistant in the outside environment, particularly on the coat). Puppies can be vaccinated against parvovirus beginning at the age of eight weeks.

Vaccinations

Vaccinations, some of which are required, can stop fatal contagious infectious diseases in their tracks. They cannot be effective unless administered at the proper time, according to a strict schedule.

Immunity

Puppies receive their first immunity from their mother via antibodies in the colostrum, which are transmitted in the first hours of the puppy's life (within a maximum of twenty-four hours) when it nurses, if the mother's immunity is good. These antibodies disappear sometime between the fourth and eighteenth week and the puppy then has no protection unless it is vaccinated.

The puppy's immune system is not completely developed at birth, and is not mature until about the sixth week. During the first weeks of its life, the puppy's only weapon against infection is the antibodies received from its mother.

It is important that the puppy's first vaccinations not interfere with the maternal antibodies, which may persist until the tenth or twelfth week. Vaccination programs can be started as soon as the puppy is eight to ten weeks old.

Dogs should be vaccinated against any infectious diseases that might be fatal to them. In addition to a rabies shot, which is required by law, dogs should be inoculated against distemper, infectious hepatitis, leptospirosis, and parvovirus.

Different Types of Vaccines

When a dog is vaccinated, it is inoculated with pathogenic microorganisms, or parts of them, so that it can produce and acquire an immunity against these viruses or bacteria.

Some vaccines, called "live vaccines," contain microorganisms that can multiply within the organism, without being pathogenic. These include:

• vaccines containing attenuated agents: microorganisms (viruses or bacteria) with reduced pathogenic capability due to mutations obtained, for viruses, by successive passage through cultures of cells from other animals (chicken, guinea pig, etc.). The ability of the virus to cause a reaction in the dog is thus attenuated. For bacteria, other procedures have a similar effect.

If the strain used for the vaccination is the same as the strain responsible for the disease, the vaccine is said to be homologous. If a different microorganism is used that is closely related to the wild pathogen but less virulent, the vaccines is said to be heterologous.

• vaccines containing a pathogen that has been genetically modified to eliminate its virulence. Vaccines containing inert agents that are incapable of multiplying in the host also exist:

• vaccines containing inactivated pathogens killed by chemical means.
• vaccines containing only the part of the microorganism responsible for the appearance of the disease.

Inactivated-virus vaccines are more innocuous than live vaccines, but not as effective.

For this reason, they are often associated with an adjuvant, which prolongs their contact with the body. If an adjuvant is used with the rabies vaccine, the second injection for the first vaccination becomes unnecessary.

To avoid the necessity for multiple injections, several vaccines are often given together (the dog is vaccinated against several infectious diseases at the same time). However, care should be taken not to mix vaccines from different manufacturers.

Rabies

Rabies is a fatal disease caused by a rhabdovirus and transmitted by contact with an infected animal. The most frequently used rabies vaccine contains inactivated rhabdovirus. The first vaccination is given to puppies at least three months of age, with only one injection required if the vaccine is given with an adjuvant. Annual booster shots are required.

Distemper

Distemper is caused by a virus and affects dogs of all ages. The mortality rate is fifty percent, and half of the dogs that recover suffer serious after-effects that impair the nervous system.

The vaccine is a live attenuated virus, and so is not pathogenic. The vaccination is given as two injections one month apart. The first is given at about eight weeks of age. If the puppy is older than three months, only one injection is needed. Booster shots are given one year after the first vaccination, then every two years thereafter.

Infectious hepatitis

Caused by an adenovirus (CAV1 strain), infectious hepatitis affects mainly young dogs between three and twelve months of age.

Puppies can be vaccinated after they are eight weeks old. The vaccine is made from an attenuated related strain (CAV2) and is given as two injections one month apart. If the puppy is older than three months, only one injection is needed. Booster shots are given one year after the first vaccination, then every two years thereafter.

Parvovirus

Vaccines for parvovirus are homologous, but the pathogen is attenuated. Three-month-old puppies are given two injections, one at the age of six to eight weeks, the other at the age of twelve weeks. If the puppy is older than three months, only one injection is needed. The first booster shot is given one year after the first vaccination, then every two years thereafter.

Breeding dogs in infected kennels are vaccinated every year.

Leptospirosis

Unlike the preceding infectious diseases, leptospirosis, also known as canine typhus, is caused by a bacterium, of the genus Leptospira.

Destroying rodents and disinfecting the premises are very helpful in eradicating the disease. Dogs can also be vaccinated with inactivated leptospirosis antigens. They receive two injections three to five weeks apart, at seven weeks of age. Booster shots are usually given annually, except in areas where the disease is endemic, where they are given twice a year.

Other vaccines

For the dog's comfort, or when it is at risk, vaccines for tetanus, babesiosis, and kennel cough can also be given.

• Tetanus

Tetanus toxin, secreted by tetanus bacilli, affects the nervous system. It is secreted at the point where the bacteria enter the body, which is often a very small wound. Tetanus is characterized by involuntary muscle contractions that eventually involve the animal's entire body. Vaccinations are mainly given to working dogs or dogs often in areas where they might easily be injured (wreckage, work sites, etc.). There is no specific antitetanus vaccine for the dog. The horse vaccine, made from purified tetanus anatoxin, is used instead. The first vaccination is given as two injections four weeks apart. Booster shots are given after one year, then every three years thereafter, and whenever there is a wound.

• Babesiosis

Dogs that often walk in the forest or other areas harboring large tick populations are at a high risk. The height of tick season is in the spring and fall. Dogs can be vaccinated with a vaccine containing parasitic proteins, which is effective for about six months. The first vaccination is given as two injections three to four weeks apart, with a booster every six months (preferably in summer and winter).

• Kennel cough

Animals that must stay in a kennel or that are going to a dog show should be vaccinated. The disease can be kept from spreading by placing animals in quarantine before introducing them into a group.

There are various vaccines on the market, consisting of inactivated viruses or bacteria (Parainfluenza, Bordatella bronchiseptica). These vaccines are injectable, but not always effective. The first vaccination is given as two injections three weeks apart, with an annual booster shot. A more recent program seems to give better results: a live attenuated virus is administered intranasally.

PLANNING YOUR DOG'S VACCINATIONS

Initial vaccinations

Between 7 and 9 weeks of age:	Distemper, infectious hepatitis, parvovirus (vaccination 1)
Between 11 and 13 weeks of age:	Distemper, infectious hepatitis, parvovirus (vaccination 2)
	Leptospirosis [vaccination 1]
	Rabies [vaccination 1]
Between 15 and 17 weeks of age:	Leptospirosis [vaccination 2]

Boosters
Rabies: annually, required
Leptospirosis: annually, required, possibly twice a year in high-risk areas
Distemper, infectious hepatitis, parvovirus: one year after first vaccination, then every two years.

Other vaccinations
Kennel cough: Two initial vaccinations plus annual booster
Babesiosis: Two initial vaccinations plus annual booster

When and How Should My Dog Be Vaccinated?

Vaccination for Babesiosis

Frequently-asked questions

Should I take any special precautions before the vaccination?

The dog to be vaccinated should be in the best possible physical health and should not have a large meal in the twelve hours preceding the vaccination. Be sure to tell your veterinarian if the dog has had any problems within the last twelve months.

Vaccination is a treatment that should be given only to patients in good health, so a thorough physical examination is justified, with checks for fever, anorexia, adynamia, and anemia. If necessary, the absence of early babesiosis can be confirmed by a blood sample.

Is vaccination effective?

No vaccine can protect all individuals. Some individuals are incapable of producing a sufficient number of antibodies, for various reasons (age, poor health, intercurrent infectious diseases, physiological condition, origin, some treatments, recurring babesiosis, etc.).

While not contraindicated, the babesiosis vaccine is not recommended for such dogs.

How long does it take for the vaccination to become effective?

The initial vaccination requires two injections, and immunity does not appear until a few days after the second. Between injections, the dog is completely susceptible to the disease, and so must be watched carefully during this period.

How old must the dog be to receive the vaccination?

Puppies less than three months old should not be vaccinated due to their immunological immaturity with regard to babesiosis. Immunological maturity is not complete until about five months of age.

How is the vaccination given?

The initial vaccination requires two subcutaneous injections three or four weeks apart. This interval should never be less than fifteen days nor more than six weeks. Boosters are given annually.

Should the vaccination be given at a certain time of the year?

The presence of canine babesiosis is related to the biology of its arthropod vector, the tick. As a general rule, ticks are less active during cold, dry winters than during the summer. However, depending on the area and the local climate, cases of canine babesiosis can occur year-round. Your veterinarian knows about the regional epidemiology of this disease, and can advise you on this point.

Does the vaccination have any side-effects?

In rare cases, there may be temporary fatigue (twenty-four hours), and possibly slight edema at the injection site, which should disappear within a few days. In the vast majority of cases, the vaccine is very well tolerated by dogs.

Nevertheless, it is recommended that the dog be allowed to rest for twenty-four hours after the vaccination, and that no great effort (hunting, long walk, training session, etc.) be required of it during this period.

Can the babesiosis vaccine cause the disease in my dog?

This is impossible, since the vaccine is made from dead proteins of the parasite's membrane. However, it occasionally happens that a dog receiving the vaccine is already incubating babesiosis and that the disease flares up within a few days of the vaccination. This is why the veterinarian will perform a thorough physical examination before administering the injection.

Can my dog be vaccinated for babesiosis and other diseases on the same day?

Currently, anti-rabies vaccine and leptospirosis vaccine can be given with the babesiosis vaccine.

My dog has had several babesiosis infections. Should I have the dog vaccinated?

Although not contraindicated, vaccination is not recommended for such dogs. These animals seem to be unable to protect themselves against this disease.

My dog just had babesiosis. When can it be vaccinated?

You must wait eight weeks after treatment before giving the initial injection.

Sciences administration,
Merial laboratory

Vaccination for Rabies

The initial vaccination at three months of age includes two injections at least fifteen but not more than thirty days apart for vaccines including the Rabiffa valence (Leptorab, Pentadog, Rabiffa). Alternatively, a single injection of Rabisin, Hexadog or Leptorabisin can be given.

To maintain protection, the booster shot (Rabiffa or Rabisin) should be given less than one year after the second injection of the initial vaccination or the previous booster shot. If this deadline is not met, the next vaccination must be considered as a new initial vaccination.
(To be valid, the certificate of vaccination must be signed by the veterinarian.)

Initial vaccination for distemper, infectious hepatitisI (Adenovirus type 2) and Parvovirus

First vaccination: between seven and nine weeks of age.
Second vaccination: between eleven and thirteen weeks of age.

Initial vaccination for Leptospirosis

Two injections one month apart. The first should be at about seven weeks of age if the dog lives in a contaminated area and ten to twelve weeks of age if the dog lives in an uncontaminated area.

Boosters

The first booster for distemper, hepatitis and parvovirus should be given one year after the initial vaccination. Subsequent boosters are given every two years.
Current French law requires that rabies boosters be given every year. Leptospirosis vaccinations also require an annual booster, or a semi-annual booster in areas where the disease is endemic.
Vaccines that can be given together make annual booster shots much more practical.

Important recommendations

1. It is better not to vaccinate dogs that are in poor general health, particularly those that are heavily infested with ecto- or endoparasites. The dog should be treated for parasites.
2. If the vaccination program cannot be followed beginning at the age of 7 to 9 months, it must be started over as soon as possible, no matter how old the dog is, with the same intervals between vaccinations.

Dog Diseases

Primary Dog Diseases

The disorders listed below are mostly problems that affect the integumentary system, the heart and circulatory system, respiration and the lungs, eyes and vision and the musculoskeletal system.

Skin Disorders

Skin allergies

Dogs may manifest various traumas or disorders depending on their breed, size, age and use. The information provided in this chapter should enable the owner to better understand the veterinarian's diagnosis and to provide better health care for his animal.

Allergies are hypersensitive skin reactions that occur in already sensitized animals. The allergen can penetrate the body in one of four ways: inhalation (which can cause atopic uticaria), ingestion (which causes an allergy to food or medicine, or uticaria), through the skin (which causes a contact allergy) or parenterally (as in the case of dermatoses from flea bite allergies, shots or uticaria).

Alopecia

Alopecia is defined as abnormal hair loss that causes the skin to be exposed. Hair loss can be localized, regional, widespread, bilateral and symmetrical or asymmetrical. There are several categories of alopecia depending on the origin:

• Acquired alopecia
This can be associated with gender-neutral endocrinopathies (hyperthyroidism, Cushing's Syndrome, iatrogenic Cushing's Syndrome, pituitary dwarfism) or gender-specific (endocrine disorders from ovarian and testicular hormonal imbalances, Sertoli cell tumors, feminization syndrome in male dogs). It may be due to bacterial (pyoderma) or fungal infections, or the result of parasitic infections: mange (sarcoptic), demodectic mange, Cheyletiella infection, trombiculidiasis, pulicosis, flea allergy dermatitis or leishmaniasis. It could also be of unknown origin: acanthosis nigricans, seborrhea or pyotraumatic dermatitis.

• Hereditary alopecia
This can be inherited: congenital alopecia, color mutant alopecia (dobermans, setters, chow-chows). It can be associated with a necrotizing process: physical and chemical agents, deep pyoderma, severe mycosis, systematic or discoid lupus erythematosus or toxic epidermic necrosis. Finally, it can be neoplastic in origin.

Cutaneous asthenia

This congenital defect is characterized by hyperextensible skin, which becomes excessively wrinkled and tears easily.
- **Symptoms:** skin tears, causing wide, gapping wounds and trauma-induced hypodermic hematoma. Healing can occur if the wound is sutured, if not a scar forms.
- **Treatment:** incurable. Avoid wounds and accidents.

Acathanosis nigricans

This is a chronic infection, which is a specific form of melanodermatitis that causes hyperpigmentation, thickening and lichenification of the skin and is often accompanied by alopecia in the axillary region, paws, flanks and chest. It is especially common in the Dachshund.
- **Symptoms:** at 6 months, brown spots begin to appear under both armpits and then turn black. The skin is thicker and covered with a seborrheic film

(rancid odor) on the paws, chest, flanks and around the folds of the neck, causing an unpleasant odor. Obesity is an aggravating factor.
- **Treatment:** a controlled diet and adequate exercise will help fight against obesity. Good skin hygiene is required to treat the seborrhea. A veterinarian should also be consulted. He will start medical treatment.

Calluses

Calluses are areas of hyperkeratosis (round or oval) that occur on the skin around the pressure points. -
- **Symptoms:** areas of chapped, gray, hairless skin, especially on the elbow and the point of the hocks. Occurs in dachshunds, doberman pinschers and pointers. They also occur in the sternal region. Calluses primarily affect large breeds that lay unprotected on hard surfaces.
- **Treatment:** Surgery is required when the lesions are particularly large or infected.

Nutritional dermatoses

Occurring very rarely in France, nutritional dermatoses are caused by deficiencies in essential fatty acids, proteins, certain minerals (zinc, copper) or vitamins A (deficiency or excess), B and E. Deficiencies in essential fatty acids are sometimes found in animals that eat spoiled canned food exclusively. The rancidity breaks down the fatty acids, vitamin D and E and the biotin. The same symptoms found in dogs with digestive problems, chronic pancreatitis or chronic hepatitis are observed.
- **Symptoms:** at the beginning, the coat is dull and dry, the skin thickens and scales appear. Then seborrhea sets in (greasy coat) resulting in pyoderma. These appear primarily in the interdigital spaces.
- **Treatment:** supplement the diet with vegetable or animal fats in measured quantities so as to avoid obesity. Visible improvement will occur in one to two months.

Canine atopic dermatitis

This is an allergic, pruritic dermatitis, with genetic predisposition, caused by inhalation of allergens (pollen, dust, scales, etc.). It occurs in animals between the ages of one and three years old in breeds such as terriers, dalmations, Irish setters, Pekinese, etc. It is seasonal in nature.
- **Symptoms:** severe pruritus and erythema accompanied by papules that are complicated by crusts and alopecia. Affected areas often include the face, anus, interdigital spaces and limbs.
- **Treatment:** difficult. Hyposensitization can be attempted, but it takes time (approximately two years).

Irritant contact dermatitis

Irritant contact dermatitis is an inflammation of the skin caused when the skin comes into direct contact with an irritating substance (soaps, floor cleaners, insecticides, acids, tar, gasoline, etc.) or an allergenic substance (following repeated contact, a local dermatitis appears at the contact points, e.g.: plants, wool, synthetic carpets, rubber, plastic, flea collars, blankets, etc.)
- **Symptoms:** at the onset, erythema with papules and pruritus that can cause fluid-filled vesicles.
- **Treatment:** identify the allergen causing the problem and keep the dog away from it.

Lick Granulomas

Licking of the dorsal aspect of the forelegs out of boredom. This is typical of large, highly active dogs left alone during the day.
- **Symptoms:** alopecia first, then ulceration with the formation of a characteristic nodular plaque.
- **Treatment:** psychological above all.

Demodectic mange

Demodectic mange is a rather inflammatory parasitic dermatosis caused by an infection of the hair follicles by a microscopic vermiform acarine (*Demodex canis*).
- **Symptoms:** limited or generalized alopecia, the skin becomes very scaly and there is a risk of secondary bacterial infection (pyoderma). Especially affects young dogs because of contamination during the first few months of life (puppy-mother contact) while nursing. A lot of dogs are carriers (approximately 85%) but only a few develop demodectic mange. Often occurs between three and twelve months. Moist skin and poor breeding conditions are favorable conditions for demodex.

• **Dry demodexia**
- **Localized form:** limited number of nummular lesions often localized around the face (small patches around the eyes) and the limbs.
- **Generalized form:** prognosis less optimistic. Irregular hair loss in more or less ovular patches, circumscribed hair loss, subsequent irregularity of the skin increases seborrhea, which causes a rancid odor.
- **Treatment:** long, treated with Amitraz, administered by a veterinarian.

• **Pyoderma secondary bacterial infection.**
The epidermis has a high level of keratosis, accompanied by crusts on the oozing skin. Dog appears gaunt. Death will result in a couple of weeks if left untreated.

Flea bite dermatitis

Flea bite dermatitis is caused by the presence of fleas in the coat. The animal's tegument is oversensitive to the flea saliva. The neck, dorsal-lumbar region, abdominal and tail are affected the most.

- **Symptoms:** intense and prolonged pruritus especially. Generalized erythema appears first. Itching then causes crusts, oozing skin and hair loss on practically all the affected regions.

- The more severe form is more or less seasonal.
- The chronic form appears after several months of evolution characterized by a thickening of and wrinkling of the skin and decreased pruritus.

- **Treatment:** rid the dog and more importantly, his environment, of the fleas.

Solar dermatosis

Solar dermatosis manifests itself through a nasal dermatitis caused by intense solar radiation, especially on the dog's nose and bridge of the nose. Predisposed breeds are collies, Shetlands and their crossbreeds.

- **Symptoms:** erythema with crusty and ulcerative alopecia on regions lacking sufficient pigment (from birth). Lesions appear when solar rays are strong. If there is sufficient shade, the lesions give way to a pinkish, fragile, hairless epithelium.
- **Treatment:** the dog should stay in the shade between 10:00 a.m. and 4:00 p.m. Apply total sun block, or even a tattoo to give pigment to the skin.

Sarcoptic mange

Sarcoptic mange is a parasitic dermatosis that is highly contagious to humans and characterized by intense pruritus.

- **Symptoms:** reddened, ponctiform skin around the limbs and lower part of the body, lower chest, groin and ears. Lesions appear first around the edges of the ears and the tip of the elbow. Intense pruritus (scratching) resulting in alopecia and spread of lesions with crusts covering ulcers.
- **Treatment:** isolation and anti-parasitic treatment.
- **In humans:** small, red papules similar to bug bites on the arms and waist. Very intense itching at night (heat from the bed).

Ichthyosis

- **Symptoms:** no particular predisposition. Sudden onset of general and cutaneous symptoms (fever, anorexia, physical exhaustion). Skin covered with vesicular and bulbous lesions, turning into ulcers. Often affects the mucous membrane of the mouth, junctures of cutaneous tissue and mucus membranes and footpads. The lesions are painful but not pruritic. Etiology is not fully understood.
- **Treatment:** identify the cause. The disease resembles an extensive second-degree burn. Prognosis is guarded.

Autoiommune skin diseases

Relatively rare, autoimmune skin diseases occur when an organism become immunized against one of its own "constituents".
• **Bullous pemphigoid**
Antibodies are directed specifically against skin cells. Although rare, erosive and ulcerative lesions can affect, in particular, the mucous membranes, the junctures of cutaneous tissue and mucus membranes and the skin.
• **Non-Bullous pemphigoid**
Antibodies are directed against parts of any cell nucleus, especially those of the skin. Discoid lupus is a factor. This is the most common among autoimmune skin diseases. It affects only the face, symmetrically attacking the bridge of the nose, the periorbital regions and the ears.
- **Symptoms:** depigmentation, erythema, alopecia and crusts. Photosensitive disease.
- **Treatment:** long, using potent products with side effects.

Phthiriasis

Phthiriasis is an infestation of mallophage lice. Lice are host-specific, permanent parasites. They cause severe skin irritation resulting in pruritic dermatitis with squamatization. The nits stuck to the base of the hair shaft are highly visible.
- **Symptoms:** especially affects the head (ears) and neck. Long-haired breeds are most receptive (cocker spaniels, spaniels). Puppies are the most sensitive.
- **Treatment:** with a specific insecticide.

"Sine matera" pruritus

Sine matera pruritus is a neurodermatosis, in other words, a pruritic dermatosis without specific cuta-

neous lesions. Pruritis is the only apparent symptom. It is often violent and can be generalized or localized. Affects high-strung breeds (dwarf breeds, terriers) dogs in certain living conditions (instability, confinement, boredom).
- **Treatment:** anti-itch cream and sedatives in the form of tranquilizers.

Pseudo-mange

• **Cheyletiella**
Highly pruritic dermatitis due to the presence of microscopic acarine.
- **Symptoms:** diffuse squamatization on the upper dorsal-lumbar region. Intense and incessant pruritis. Positive otopodal reflex (the animal shakes his hind leg when his ear is scratched). Hair loss on the scratched surfaces. Highly contagious in kennels. Can be transmitted to humans (papular prurigo on the arms and trunk).
- **Treatment:** an acaricide must be used.

• **Trombiculosis**
Caused by the larvae of microscopic acari called harvest mites. Localized in the head and limb extremities.
- **Symptoms:** powdery, orange-colored (saffron) clusters. Skin irritation: highly pruritic dermatitis.
- **Treatment:** acaricide.

Seborrhea

Seborrhea is a skin disease characterized by an abnormal flow of sebum by the sebaceous glands of the hair follicles and excessive squamatization. Seborrhea may be primary in cocker spaniels, spaniels, English terriers and German shepherds. There is often a hormonal imbalance (often genital in females) which is the decisive cause.
- **Symptoms:** skin appears greasy and scaly. Characteristic rancid odor. Moderate to no pruritis. Often becomes chronic and complications may include a bacterial or parasitic secondary infection.
- **Treatment:** depends on the cause. Must be specific to the cause.

Ringworm (Tinea)

Ringworms are cutaneous mycoses (fungal growth) of the skin and phalanx.
- **Symptoms:** localized or generalized hair loss. Erythema and more or less intense squamatization. Ringworm is not accompanied by pruritis and does not affect the overall health of the dog, but it is highly contagious from dogs to humans. It is transmitted by tineal animals or through soil.

• **Dry tinea**
Often localized. Characterized by presence of abundant tinea. Regular patches of alopecia formed (incisive). Tegument is erythematous especially around the edges and is covered with grayish scales that have a powdery appearance. Lesions appear on the entire body and on the upper and anterior regions.

• **Suppurative tinea:** localized or generalized forms.
- **Treatment:** good hygiene with specific and lengthy local and general treatments.

Uticaria

Uticaria is an allergic dermatosis that can be induced by ingestion or injection of an allergenic substance and is primarily localized around the head, neck, limbs and upper line. Occurs most frequently in young dogs.
- **Symptoms:** cutaneous edema causing visible blisters on shaved animals.
- **Treatment:** same as for allergies.

Heart Diseases

With the exception of congenital heart defects, most heart disease affects older animals. Aggravation of these diseases may be one cause of high mortality. Only the major diseases will be presented below.

Myocardial Dilation

Myocardial diseases affect the myocardium (heart muscle) and are often of unknown origin. Myocardial dilation is characterized by dilation of the ventricles coupled with diminished contractile capacity of the heart, resulting in obstructed blood flow. It is found especially in large breeds, particularly in doberman pinschers, boxers and cocker spaniels.
- **Primary symptoms:** onset may be rapid in relatively young dogs (around five years old). Indications include: coughing that worsens, especially at night, difficulty breathing (increase in respiratory frequency, discordance, i.e. thoracic and abdominal respiratory movements are not synchronized, etc.), cyanosis (tongue becomes blue) and weight loss.
- **Steps to take:** all these signs are serious and a veterinarian must absolutely be consulted. In the meantime, keep the dog calm and walk him on a leash without letting him run.

Mitral insufficiency

Mitral insufficiency is one of the cardiac insufficiencies that affects the left side of the heart. Cardiac insufficiencies are defined as diminished pumping ability of the heart that causes serious side effects. With mitral insufficiency, the mitral valve between the left atrium and the ventricle is ruptured.
- **Primary symptoms:** back flow of blood into the left atrium causes a pulmonary edema. Depending on the severity, the pulmonary edema is characterized by a primarily nocturnal cough that starts as minor and increases in severity, visible respiratory difficulties upon effort at first and then spontaneously, major fits of breathlessness indicating acute pulmonary edema, cyanosis upon effort and in the most severe cases, syncope.
- **Steps to take:** depending on the severity, the dog's exercise should be reduced, even limited to constitutive walks. If properly diagnosed at the onset, treatment administered by a veterinarian can slow the progression of the symptoms.

Pulmonary Diseases

Bronchopneumonia

This is a purulent inflammation of the bronchioles and the adjacent pulmonary alveoli. Toxins are produced, which destroys the bronchioles, preventing them from draining properly.
- **Primary symptoms:** labored breathing with increased respiratory frequency: labial breathing (the flews raise when the dog exhales); short bouts of painful, fitful coughing; fever with irregular hyperthermia and noticeable exhaustion; possible cardiac disease.
- **Steps to take:** the general state of the dog in this condition requires a visit to the veterinarian. It is best to avoid dry climates and sudden temperature changes, which aggravate respiratory difficulties. Furthermore, ration the dog's food. Increase the number of meals per day but decrease the quantity. This will help improve the general health of the dog. If the dog spends a lot of time lying down, turn him over from time to time to prevent liquids from stagnating in the same side of the lungs.

Laryngeal œdema and stenosis

Occurs when the larynx lumen becomes constricted and causes respiratory difficulty and loud breathing. The intensity of the symptoms depends on whether one side of the larynx is paralyzed (tied-up guard dog, surgery) or both sides (sheepdogs, bull terriers, older brachycephalic breeds, neurological origins). Steps to take. Only surgery will provide results in certain cases.

Eye Diseases

Eyes can be affected by either congenital or acquired defects, or by more periodic disorders.

Progressive retinal atrophy (congenital defect)

Retinal atrophy affects the retina, killing off the vessels and/or pigment cells. It can be generalized as in dwarf and miniature poodles (around three to five years old) and cocker spaniels (one to three years old), or it can be centralized, which mostly occurs in working dogs (labrador, shepherds, Briard shepherds) from a couple months old to two years.
- **Primary symptoms:** in generalized atrophy the first sign is deterioration of night and twilight vision. In later stages, mydriasis occurs (pupil remains dilated) along with extremely weak photopic adaptation (the pupil does not contract in bright light), progressing to complete blindness. In some cases, cataracts may develop simultaneously at the beginning. Central progressive retinal atrophy is characterized by good peripheral vision and poor vision of close objects.
- **Steps to take:** consult a veterinarian, who, after confirming the symptoms, will prescribe either a vascular or circulatory treatment.

Ectropion and entropion (congenital defect)

Ectropion is an eversion of the eyelid, in which the eyelid rolls out. Therefore, the eye is constantly exposed to air. This occurs frequently in Saint-Bernards, English and American cocker spaniels and breeds with heavy flews that hang low. Entropion is defined as an inversion of the lid margin towards the cornea. Affected breeds include the chow-chow, Saint-Bernard, small poodles, German mastiff, sharpei, etc.
- **Primary symptoms:** with entropion, localized irritation and inflammation of the cornea and conjunctiva cause redness in the conjunctiva and a clear discharge that can become mucopurulent. The irritation and pain cause severe squinting and itching that aggravate the clinical signs. In later stages, cornea erosion may be observed. Clinical indications of ectropion include conjunctivitis with a clear discharge that may become infected and turn mucopurulent. The complications are clearly less severe than those of entropion.
- **Steps to take:** only surgery may be beneficial. In the meantime, it is entirely possible to regularly clean the dog's eyes (several times a day) with an eyewash containing a small amount of antiseptic.

Cataracts (acquired defect)

A cataract refers to a loss of transparency of one or all of the lens structures of the eye, preventing light rays from reaching the retina.
- **Primary symptoms:** whiteness of the lens and limited vision are the only indications of a cataract. Depending on its origin, a cataract may be accompanied by other symptoms.
- **Steps to take:** the only way to improve the evolution of a cataract is to consult a veterinarian. Depending on its size, medical or surgical treatment will be given.

Glaucoma (acquired defect)

Glaucoma refers to an ensemble of disorders that cause increased intraocular pressure, compromising vision and the future of the eye.
- **Primary symptoms:** the eye appears enlarged, as though it were popping out of its socket, total mydriasis (extremely dilated pupil) accompanied by a loss of photopic adaptation (the pupil does not contract when exposed to light); severe congestion in the vascularization of the conjunctiva (eye is extremely red and the vessels are enlarged and sinuous).
- **Steps to take:** quickly consult a veterinarian; vision and the eye may be irreparably harmed.

Conjunctivitis

Conjunctivitis is an inflammation of the conjunctiva and the nictitating membranes. It may be caused by allergies, infections or parasites.
- **Primary symptoms:** redness, edema (sometimes) stinging and irritation, ocular discharge that may be fluid, mucous or mucopurulent.
- **Steps to take:** cleaning the eye thoroughly with a cleansing eyewash will sooth the inflammation.

However, the causes can only be completely eliminated through treatment prescribed by a veterinarian.

Corneal ulcers

Corneal ulcers refers to corneal abrasion that can affect the different layers of the cornea. Their origins are diverse.
- **Primary symptoms:** extremely painful (scratching or rubbing the eye on the ground). Pain accompanied by severe squinting and mucopurulent fluid discharge. The cornea loses its smooth, shiny appearance and becomes cloudy.
- **Steps to take:** cleaning the eye with a mildly-antiseptic eyewash will sooth the inflammation. Avoid using corticosteroid-based eyewashes or ointments. It is best to consult a veterinarian, who will be able to diagnose the ulcers with precision and prescribe appropriate treatment.

Anterior uveitis

Anterior uveitis is caused by an inflammation of the iris and the ciliary bodies. The cause is still unknown, however, it is a known fact that major viral and infectious diseases in dogs are accompanied by anterior uveitis (canine distemper, infectious canine hepatitis, tuberculosis).
- **Primary symptoms:** pain (and therefore rubbing, scratching and severe squinting); conjunctive inflammation evidenced by the redness of the conjunctiva and the nictitating membranes; fluid discharge and miosis (constant contraction of the pupil). In later stages, modifications of the iris appear: it becomes edematous, congested, looks dull and hazy, changes color and can become heavily pigmented.
- **Steps to take:** consult a veterinarian without delay because the aftereffects of anterior uveitis can be lethal to the dog's vision.

Keratitis

Keratitis is caused by an inflammation of the various layers of the cornea. The causes may be allergic, immunity-related, microbial, viral or mycotic in origin. They may be accompanied by ulcerations.
- **Primary symptoms:** inflammation of the cornea with neovascularization (appearance of blood vessels in the cornea); cornea becomes opaque; pain, rubbing and scratching; severe squinting; conjunctivitis.

Among German shepherds, there are three forms of keratitis: chronic keratitis, superficial (surface) keratitis and pigmentary keratitis. Lesions begin at the extreme outer corner of the eye with massive neovascularization and a whitening of the cornea. In later stages, melanic pigments are deposited on the cornea. A second type, limited surface keratitis, usually affects long-haired dachshunds. The eye is especially painful and is accompanied by severe squinting.
- **Steps to take:** only adequate treatment can relieve the symptoms.

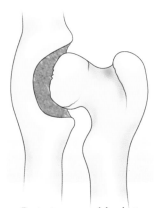

Normal hip - no sign of dysplasia

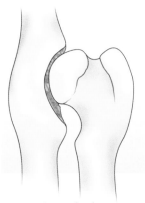

Beginning stage of dysplasia

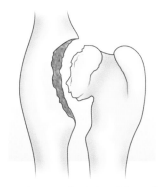

Severe dysplasia

Extremely severe dysplasia - dislocated joint

Diseases of the Musculoskeletal System

The only musculoskeletal diseases that should be treated are the ones that are not sustained as a result of a trauma.

Degenerative joint disease

This disease affects the joints and is characterized by the progressive breakdown of the articular cartilage associated with the formation of osteophytes (small bones) and a remodeling of the bone beneath the cartilage and the synovial membrane. It is the systematic degeneration of a painful joint.

- **Primary symptoms:** pain that is exacerbated by humidity and cold weather. Moderate exercise may lessen the pain, but exercise that is too strenuous will aggravate it. These symptoms represent stage 1. Stage 2 is marked by acute episodes: cries, lameness. It evolves into total joint block with a decrease in pain (stage 3).

- **Steps to take:** as the disease begins to progress, continue to make the dog exercise in order to prevent ankylosis. Depending on which stage the degeneration is in, the veterinarian will begin a treatment of analgesics or anti-imflammatories, or a medical treatment (glycosaminoglycans), or may even suggest surgery.

Arthritis

Arthritis is an inflammation of the joints. Its origins may be varied: septic with the presence of an infectious germ in the joint (the germ may be inoculated during a bite for example), or sterile because it is immunological (polyarthritis is the most common) or not.

- **Primary symptoms:** septic arthritis is characterized by inflammation (redness, heat, swelling, pain) with distinct swelling and possible lameness. It can affect one or several joints, mainly the larger, weight-bearing or intervertebral joints. The same symptoms occur in polyarthritis, but some are more specific to certain breeds.

- **Steps to take:** after additional testing, the veterinarian will be able to determine whether the arthritis is septic or polyarthritis and can therefore prescribe adequate treatment.

Hip dysplasia

Hip dysplasia is a congenital disorder, with a disputed hereditary factor that is characterized by a deformity of the coxofemoral joint, causing the femur to rub on the hip joint socket. It occurs frequently in large breeds and evolves very quickly (Newfoundland terrier, labrador, Pyrenean mountain dog, German shepherd, etc.).

- **Primary symptoms:** the first phase, which is dominated by pain, is observed in dogs reaching the end of their growth phase. The following signs may be indicators: abnormal or "swaying" gait of the hindquarters; hind legs resemble an "X" when seen from behind; refusal to run; "bunny-hop" run, i.e. the dog does not develop extension-flexion movement in the hind legs, giving him this characteristic gait; refusal to jump; constant lameness; and pain when extension-flexion movement is forced. The second phase intervenes at about age three. The same symptoms persist and are exacerbated by osteoarthritis.

Steps to take: radiography can confirm the presence of hip dysplasia. This test is performed at the end of the growth cycle (around twelve to eighteen months, depending on the breed). Other tests that can be performed earlier are currently being studied. Worldwide, an eradication program has been implemented to wipe out this defect.

Osteochondrosis

Osteochondrosis is a localized, nutritional disorder of the articular cartilage or relating to growth. It is triggered by excess weight, when the animal receives too much food during growth (the risk is greatly diminished when complete dry food is used). Cartilage fragments can break away from certain areas and become localized in the joint. Osteochondrosis is observed in certain, rapid-growth breeds and appears around the age of five to seven months. The joints most affected are the shoulder, neck and knee joints and the tibia-tarsal joint.

- **Primary symptoms:** lameness is observed, often limited to the above-mentioned joints. Forced manipulation is painful.

- **Steps to take:** most osteochondroses disappear with a lot of exercise (the cartilage fragments are resorbed) and the symptoms then disappear. Food portions should be monitored frequently to prevent excess weight gain. Pain may persist, however. Surgery to remove the cartilage fragments is required in this case.

Diseases of the Digestive System

The digestive system includes all the tissues and organs responsible for the digestion of food in the organism. Each one of these elements can be the source of a disorder or injury with either localized or generalized repercussions.

Oral cavity

A puppy has thirty-two teeth at birth and by the age of about four months, has a full complement of forty-two adult teeth. The adult teeth wear down rather quickly depending on the dog's eating and play habits. This is why dogs should not be given stones or hard toys. During growth spurts, a dog's teeth can be affected by various defects. First, baby teeth frequently do not fall out, especially in small breeds. These supernumerary teeth should be extracted if the dog shows signs of pain when eating. Conversely, several teeth may be missing but this will not cause problems in eating. Abnormal teeth position can also be observed, which among other things, prevent the mouth from closing properly. Some teeth may appear to be abnormally formed, with for example, poor quality enamel.

Dogs also suffer frequently from abscesses or fistula. Although rare, they may also develop tooth decay just like humans. In either case, only a veterinarian can determine whether the tooth needs to be extracted or whether dental treatment is required. However, the most frequently-encountered problem in dogs is and remains, tartar buildup. Tartar buildup causes the animal's mouth to emit a characteristic putrid odor known as halitosis. Moreover, the tartar causes severe lesions on the teeth and gums, which may result in loss of the teeth. This problem can evolve into gingival pyorrhea or parondotosis. The animal suffers immensely and can no longer feed itself. At this stage, the only relief for the dog is extraction of some, if not all of the teeth. This is why it is necessary to check the dog's teeth and if necessary, have them descaled regularly.

An examination of the oral cavity may also reveal the presence of stomatitis and small ulcers. These inflammations are either caused solely by a localized disease or they are the result of a generalized disease. They are generally benign, causing only increased salivation and irritation when food is grasped.

Among the more common lesions is ranula. This strange term, in fact, refers to the formation of a saliva pocket between the jawbone and the flews. It forms in response to an obstruction of the salivary gland ducts. Depending on the nature of the obstruction and the amount of liquid collected, the veterinarian may decide to remove the salivary glands. These lesions are sometimes observed on the neck, which indicates an obstruction high up in the salivary glands.

Dogs are often in the habit of playing with anything. Careful attention must be paid in particular to pieces of wood that can tear the palate. These tears are known as traumatic palatine fissures. Sometimes congenital palatine fissures can be observed. They bring the nasal and oral cavities into contact, causing vomiting and respiratory difficulty. Finally, some dog breeds with short noses, such as boxers and Pekinese, may suffer from a defect of the soft palate. In addition to the snoring that this defect may cause, it also gives rise to difficulty breathing, especially with effort.

Finally, the oral cavity is often injured as a result of traffic accidents or falls. The lower jaw may sustain fractures from the impact, which causes insufferable pain. Generally, these fractures can be repaired in a satisfactory manner.

Esophagus

Three types of disorders can affect this soft tissue. The first category is dilated esophagus, which is either generalized and corresponds to a megaesophagus, or localized in diverticulum and corresponds to an esophageal crop. A megaesophagus can be congenital or acquired. The precise origin is not yet known.

The esophageal crop indicates that the esophagus passage is blocked. Depending on the age of the animal, this is thought to be due either to a congenital defect, a foreign object or a tumor. The symptoms include difficulty swallowing and regurgitating food. Progressively, the dog loses weight and grows weaker. Radiography is used to diagnose this disorder and among other things, to give a prognosis.

The second type of esophagus disorder is inflammation. The origins of esophagitises are twofold: ingestion of caustic products and reflux of gastric juices. Certain harmful foreign objects may also be responsible. The dog shows signs of hypersalivation and difficulty swallowing and refuses to eat. Esophagitis is a secondary disorder. It is important to determine the cause through adequate testing.

Finally, the esophagus may be perforated by foreign objects, in particular chicken or rabbit bones. Depending on where the perforation is located, the consequences may vary from a simple wound to a lung puncture. In general, the dog shows signs of irritation and pain. He constantly tries to vomit or cough.

Stomach

The characteristic symptom of gastric disorder is vomiting within a few minutes, even up to one hour, after a meal. Among the most classic disorders are lesions of the gastric lining, gastric dysfunction and stomach tumors. The first category includes acute or chronic gastritis and ulcers. The origins of acute gastritis are varied. Unsuitable food, toxic substances, foreign bodies, parasitic or infectious diseases, or even hormone imbalances are all possible causes. Chronic gastritis, which is characterized by vomiting that is often resistant to classic treatments, is part of a complex syndrome. Inflammatory, allergic or even metabolic phenomena are often causes. The general health of the dog is affected fairly quickly. Gastric ulcers are characterized by vomiting blood, poor overall health and abdominal pain. They are sometimes the result of acute gastritis. Most often, however, they are caused by medicines such as aspirin or toxic products and more rarely, infectious or parasitic agents. The occurrence of psychosomatic ulcers has not been observed in dogs.

Problems with gastric functions result in either gastroesophageal reflux or food retention that leads to

vomiting undigested food several hours after the meal. The dog therefore loses weight very quickly. The cause is linked to a stenosis of the pylorus or a nerve anomaly in gastric motivity. Surgical treatment is sometimes necessary.

Finally, it is not possible to talk about gastric disorders without mentioning the gastric dilation-torsion complex. This particular disorder affects large dogs. It is characterized by abdominal bloating, episodes of vomiting that is rather violent but produces very little and rapid decline of the dog's general health. The dog goes into shock and will die if surgery is not performed as quickly as possible. To prevent the onset of this lethal disease, a few basic rules should be followed. Do not engage the dog in play after a meal and feed the dog digestible food, preferably in two meals per day.

Intestines

Intestinal disorders are dominated by enteritis. Enteritis is a rather severe inflammation of the intestinal lining that has various origins: infectious agents, unsuitable food, parasites, foreign objects, etc. Depending on the length of evolution, it can either be chronic or acute. The symptoms are extremely variable, ranging from constipation to diarrhea, hyperthermia and exhaustion. Sometimes it is associated with a gastric disorder and is then referred to as gastroenteritis. Because of the metabolic disorder it entails, it can lead to severe dehydration, which is sometimes lethal for weaker animals.

CRITERIA FOR ASSESSING THE PHYSICAL CONDITION OF A DOG

Parameters	Underweight (by 10-20%)	Ideal Weight (by 10-20%)	Overweight
Ribs, vertebrae and pelvic bone	visible	not visible, but easily felt	difficult to feel
Body fat	no fat, ribs can be felt	thin, palpable layer of fat tissue	massive on the thorax and the bulk of the tail

Intestinal occlusions or obstructions are among the cases that require surgery the most. They are generally caused by ingesting foreign objects such as pieces of string or plastic toys.

Special attention must be paid to intestinal parasites. Dogs may be infested by round worms (Ascaris, Trichuris, Ankylostoma) and/or flat worms (Taenia, Dipylidium, Echinococcus). They ingest worms either as they are digging up ground or through the intermediary of carrier insects such as fleas. These parasites cause weight loss, vomiting and diarrhea. The dog shows his pain by dragging his hindquarters on the ground in what is called "the dragnet sign". Animals of all ages can be infected but puppies seem to have the highest risk. The infection can also be transmitted from dogs to humans. A de-worming regime needs to be established each year with the veterinarian.

Chronic colonitis is a chronic inflammation that occurs in the large intestine or the colon. Again, the origins are diverse: food or allergy-related, parasitic or metabolic, inflammatory or simply unknown. It is characterized by mucous-like feces, pain during defecation and rather severe episodes of diarrhea.

Pancreas

In addition to being affected by inflammation and tumors, the pancreas can also malfunction, resulting in a pancreatic insufficiency. This is observed in young animals in the form of excessive weight loss accompanied by polyphagia. Periods of diarrhea alternate with periods of constipation. In fact, the pancreas is incapable of secreting the enzymes needed for digestion. Therefore, the dog does not properly digest the food he ingests. Enzyme supplements and an adapted diet of highly digestible food help treat this disorder.

The pancreas is also where insulin is produced and just as in humans, inadequate production can lead to diabetes. Diabetes is treated with daily insulin shots at fixed times.

Liver

In puppies, hepatitis is brought on by poisoning or infectious diseases such as infectious canine hepatitis. The liver becomes congested and it increases in size. Hepatitis can induce irreversible and lethal cirrhotic states. Symptoms include episodes of diarrhea with loose stools, followed by constipation. The abdomen is painful and the dog is exhausted.

Acute hepatic insufficiency is characterized by disorders of the digestive and nervous systems. Its etiology is varied: infections, toxins, medicines, metabolism and trauma. Urgent treatment is required given the sometimes lethal repercussions on the body.

Chronic hepatic insufficiency evolves more slowly, but in a manner that is just as dangerous. It causes weight loss, decline in overall health and digestive disorders. A veterinarian must run complementary tests in order to determine the cause.

Hernias

Congenital umbilical hernias occur frequently in puppies and are caused when the small opening of the umbilicus does not close at birth.
A small protrusion is observed, which is resorbed when pressure is placed on it. Although they pose no real danger to the animal, they can generally be corrected by surgery.
Diaphragmatic hernias occur as a result of a diaphragmatic trauma that allows part of the abdominal viscera to pass into the thoracic cavity. These hernias cause respiratory and digestive problems that require surgery.

Perineal hernias are found in certain breeds such as the German Shepherd. They are characterized by the formation of multiple fistulas around the anus, which converge into a circular mass that may or may not be ulcerated. A malodorous pus oozes from this mass, which leads to constant licking and difficulty defecating. These lesions are never resorbed and require surgical treatment.
In addition to all these disorders, benign or malignant tumors can develop in the digestive tract. As the dog ages, close attention must be paid to the slightest sign of a digestive disorder.

Vomiting

Carnivores in the wild are formidable predators who are perfectly adapted to the hunt. They are capable of eating phenomenal quantities of meat in a single meal. Upon their return, they can regurgitate this food without the slightest effort in order to feed their young. This ability requires not only a stomach that is capable of holding large quantities, but also a reflex mechanism that facilitates regurgitation of food and therefore vomit.
Dogs, who are domestic carnivores par excellence, have not lost any of this ability. How many dog owners in fact have witnessed their favorite animal regurgitate a meal that was a little too copious? Most of the time, there is nothing alarming in this behavior. Sometimes, however, vomiting is the first sign of an underlying disease.

Stages of vomiting

In general, a vomiting episode is preceded by a state of nausea in which the dog appears uncomfortable, turns in circles and sometimes tries to eat grass. It is almost as if the dog is trying to "purge" himself, though this term does not accurately reflect reality. The dog then vomits. Violent heaving of the flank and thorax is observed.
The dog lowers his head and appears to be smiling. Then after a final effort, the contents of the stomach are ejected. Given the violence of the phenomenon and the muscle fatigue that ensues, it may take the dog a few minutes to recuperate. In cases where only the contents of the esophagus are regurgitated, there is no noticeable effort. The food easily ejected by means of a simple reflex.

Physiological mechanisms in vomiting

Like any reflex, vomiting involves nerve mechanisms. They may originate in the central nervous system, in other words, directly from the brain (disruption of normal central nervous system functions, inflow of particle substances into the blood, even olfactory stimulus, cause the vomit center to react). The origin may also be peripheral, which involves receptors located in abdominal or thoracic organs. Information received is transmitted through a system of neurotransmitters to the vomit center in the brain. In both cases, this center responds by triggering the muscular action that causes vomiting.

Causes of vomiting

Vomiting is usually an indication of inflammation or excessive distension of organs, namely those of the digestive tract: esophagus, stomach, intestines and liver. The causes are numerous. Classic causes include poisoning, gastritis, ulcers, gastroenteritis, foreign objects, intestinal obstructions, gastric dilation-torsion or spoiled food. Vomiting may also be a symptom of an infectious or viral disease (canine distemper, canine parvovirus and leptospirosis are among the most notable, in addition to uterine infections, peritonitis, etc.). Absorbing excessive quantities of food, foreign objects or substances that prevent the stomach from emptying its contents into the small intestine also causes gastric distension and consequently, vomiting. Finally, vomiting can also be an indication of diseases that affect other organs, especially renal or hepatic insufficiencies or even nervous system disorders, such as motion sickness.

Evolution

Two types of evolution are observed with vomiting. It can either be acute or chronic. In the first case, the vomiting occurs suddenly and is temporary in nature. In the second instance, it builds progressively and is recurrent for over a month. Vomiting occurs more or less frequently during the day and may or may not be related to eating.

Consequences

Vomiting causes **dehydration** and rather severe **malnutrition**, as well as blood imbalances. Sooner or later, it will have repercussions on the general health of the dog. This is why vomiting must be treated quickly, especially in young animals.
In order to help the veterinarian establish a diagnosis, it is important to note the frequency of vomiting, the time when it occurs (after a meal? after drinking?) and its appearance. All this information will give the veterinarian indications about its origin and help him prescribe a treatment.

Diarrhea

The term diarrhea refers to an increase in the frequency of bowel movements, with rather loose, abundant stools. Diarrhea is one of the most common problems in dogs. It is important to note that stools vary greatly depending on the quality and quantity of the food given to the dog. Consequently, feeding the dog the wrong food is a major cause of diarrhea. As with vomiting, diarrhea can be either acute or chronic. The origins and symptoms of diarrhea are different. It can affect the small intestine or the colon.

Acute diarrhea

Acute diarrhea appears suddenly and is short in duration. In general, it has noticeable repercussions on the general health of the dog. There are multiple origins of this type of diarrhea.

Of course, improper food is the most frequent cause (changes in diet without a transition period destroys intestinal microflora, which is very fragile in dogs). Diarrhea can also be an indication of a viral infection such as canine distemper or parvovirus, or a bacterial infection where germs multiply on and in the intestinal lining. Intestinal parasites including worms and fungi often cause diarrhea symptoms as well, as do toxic substances or allergens. Finally, the list is completed by a certain number of metabolic disorders.

The mechanism that triggers acute diarrhea involves a disruption in the water exchange that occurs in the small intestine. Therefore, unsuitable foods require more water for digestion, which of course causes the stool to be more liquid. But water loss can also be attributed to the more or less consistent destruction of the cells in the intestinal lining that are responsible for the absorption of nutrients into the blood. The aforementioned agents are what cause these types of lesions. Finally and more rarely, diarrhea may be the result of changes in the digestive path, as is the case with stress-induced diarrhea.

Acute diarrhea is accompanied by various signs that are visible to the owner. First of all, the animal is run down, sometimes has a fever, refuses to eat and loses weight. There is often pain in the abdomen. Sometimes, diarrhea is accompanied by vomiting. In this case, the animal will quickly become dehydrated given the water loss with the bowel movement. In fact, quick action is required in order to prevent the dog from going into shock, especially with young and older animals.

Chronic diarrhea

Chronic diarrhea is diarrhea that lasts for over a month and tends to be recurrent. The causes are somewhat different from acute diarrhea. They include inflammations of the intestinal lining that are parasitic, allergic or autoimmune in origin, as well as malfunctions in the secretion of digestive enzymes or in the mechanisms involved in the absorption of nutrients by intestinal cells. Consequently, acute diarrhea that has caused severe destruction of the digestive tract lining may evolve into chronic diarrhea. Sometimes, chronic diarrhea indicates the presence of tumors in the body. Finally, as with the previous case, diarrhea may occur intermittently as a result of a particular, repeated stress.

With chronic diarrhea, the general health of the dog deteriorates slowly. The dog progressively loses weight in greater quantities than with acute diarrhea. However, the onset of dehydration is slower and often, abdominal pain is less severe.

As with vomiting, it is important to take the dog to the veterinarian as soon as possible. In fact, the health of the dog may deteriorate rapidly, especially with younger and older dogs. In order to help the veteri-narian determine the diagnosis, the owner should note the date when the symptoms first appeared and the frequency, consistency and color of the bowel movements (for example, there may be blood in the stool). Does the stool contain parasites or undigested food? Does the dog show signs of pain? etc.

All of this information will enable the veterinarian to determine the exact cause of the problem, decide which tests to run and prescribe a treatment.
As soon as diarrhea sets in, it is recommended that the dog be placed on a restricted diet and be taken to the veterinarian as quickly as possible.

Neonatal Disorders

Puppies are born blind and deaf, but this delay in development is not only limited to the sensory organs. It also affects thermal regulation, immunity, hydration and metabolism, in addition to which, there is a lack of hepatic and fatty reserves. All these handicaps make the puppy susceptible to numerous disorders of origins as diverse as trauma, infections, dehydration, hypoglycemia or low body temperature.

Risk Factors Related to the Mother

Age of mother

Neonatal mortality and morbidity rate increase as the litter size of the bitch increases. This phenomenon is most likely linked to the frequency of anoxia after-effects (lack of oxygen, which leads to lack of blood flow to the brain). These occur as a result of primary uterine inversion, which is often seen in older breeding bitches.

Consanguinity

An increase in the incidence of birth defects (cleft palate, megaesophagus, heart defects) within a litter can likely be traced to excessive inbreeding among the ascendants. In fact, since most of these defects are recessive traits, their occurrence necessarily means that two carrier genes of the disease were expressed simultaneously, one from the mother and one from the father. Excessive consanguinity (often more than four generations), therefore, increases the risks of recessive genes being expressed. At the same time, the degree of prolificacy decreases.

Mother's diet

The mother's diet during pregnancy is discussed in the chapter on nutrition. It should simply be noted that overeating during this period results in the deposit of fat in the pelvic region and thereby increases the risk of dystocia (abnormal birth). The risk is greatest during an episode of constipation in the final stages of gestation. Indeed, since the rectum is anatomically located above the vagina in dogs, a state of repletion reduces the size of the birth canal. This is why it is important to verify that the rectum is emptied the day before whelping and to give the breeding bitch an oral or rectal laxative if she is constipated.

Dystocia

Dystocia is a factor that obviously can cause neonatal mortality. Therefore, it is preferable to refrain from breeding a bitch that has experienced dystocia again, unless the cause of dystocia was clearly exceptional (temporary obesity, underdeveloped pelvic region, etc.).

Medication given during pregnancy

The most critical period for teratogenous action of certain medicines (which produces defects) is naturally during the embryonic phase when tissue is being differentiated (seventeen to twenty-one days). However, the fetus can also be exposed to risks later on that may cause defects in the late-forming organs such as the palate, cerebellum or the urinary tract.

Veterinarians are now familiar with the list of teratogenous products, their doses and period of maximal susceptibility for most species.

If possible, the simplest precaution is to refrain from administering drugs, anesthetics, hormones, external parasite treatments or even vaccinations during gestation, unless the health of the bitch depends on it and the veterinarian is completely sure that the treatment is innocuous.

Problems with lactation

While gestation and whelping are the most difficult hurdles to overcome for small breeds, it is lactation that can sap large breeding bitches and consequently, can impede the rapid growth of the litter.

In the canine species, mastitis is often caused by a trauma inflicted by the puppies' nails or an ascending infection transmitted through licking of the litter or resulting from a skin infection (pyoderma).

In addition to pathogenic germs in the milk that cause "toxic milk syndrome" (usually colibacillus, hemolytic streptococcus or staphylococcus), this form of mastitis frequently involves dilution of the milk, which alters the nutritional value of the milk. This is especially serious as this disorder generally occurs at the onset of lactation.

Prevention is simple in theory. It consists in identifying the germ that is causing the mastitis in order to eliminate the source. Although hygiene is usually easy to control during pregnancy, such is not the case with cutaneous staphylococci, which requires lengthy antibiotic treatment.

Observation and thorough palpation of the breasts will sometimes reveal malformations of the teats that contribute to ascending infections. These anatomical predispositions can sometimes warrant removing the mother from the litter, artificial nursing or giving the puppies to a foster mother.

While the ability to lactate is a trait that is largely considered to be predominantly heredity, hypogalactia (lack of milk), agalactia (absence of milk) or delays in the onset of lactation are generally difficult to predict, especially in primpara. Frequently these disorders are accompanied by maternal instinct problems, which are often associated with poor socialization or discomfort.

Since the passive immunization (immunoglobulin-G) of puppies is made possible almost exclusively through early ingestion of the colostrum, some breeders, as a precaution, either keep the colostrum of a donor bitch frozen or the mother's serum that they feed to the puppies to offset the absence of colostrum.

In the following days, the immunoglobulin A in the mother's milk serves to protect the puppy's intestinal epithelium and thereby naturally limits the occurrence of infectious diarrhea.

The onset of lactation can be stimulated through different treatments, including:

- Massaging the breasts or injecting oxytocin, which only stimulates ejection of the milk without producing any real action in terms of secretion (recommended only in cases of "lacteal retention");
- Herbal treatments (galega, malt, fennel, cumin, etc.) are often used in an empirical manner even though they have not yet been shown to produce any specific action!
- Certain anti-vomiting pills are used because they have a stimulating effect on prolactin secretion.

It should also be noted that, conversely, overproduction of milk may lead to excess consumption and saturation of the puppies' ability to digest lactose and

consequently, cause osmotic diarrhea. This generally occurs at the onset of lactation, but is rarely a contributing factor to mortality if care is taken to separate the gluttonous puppies from their mother's breast several times a day. This act is preferable to drying up the mother through medical means, unless the health of the mother so requires.

Viral infections transmitted by the mother

Canine herpes virus (CHV) is a cause of puppy mortality during the first week of life that is currently becoming an alarming problem among dogs.

In France, in fact, nearly 50% of breeders who are seeing a decline in the fertility rate of bitches and an increase in neonatal mortality are unknowingly harboring breeding bitches infected with canine herpes virus.

A herpes virus infection is often very discrete in adults. The virus grows in mucous membranes that are normally colder than the body temperature (genital, ocular and respiratory mucous membranes) owing to stress, secondary infection, immunodepression or a period of sexual activity.

In both males and females, this virus sometimes causes papules on the genital mucous membrane that are difficult to see without careful examination (total externalization of the bulbus penis in males and vaginal speculum in females) and are sometimes responsible for a refusal to cover.

The virus is essentially venereal. It is spread by infected external studs when they naturally mate while the virus is in an active stage.

Bacterial infections

The germs involved in most cases of neonatal septicemia or in toxic milk syndrome are generally found in the vaginal flora of all healthy bitches.
Simple, prepartum vaginal antisepsis is advised.

Digestive parasites

The most frequently observed parasites in puppies are helminths (Ascarids, Trichuris, Ankylostoma, Tenia) and protozoan (Giardia and Coccidia). The period of sexual activity of bitches is a factor that aggravates the risk of helminthic parasitism in puppies because the bitch provides a favorable environment for the breeding and not just the survival of parasites such as Toxocara canis, Uncinaria stenocephala and to a lesser degree, Ankylostoma caninum. Modifications of the bitch's hormone balance (and in particular, changes in progesterone levels) cause the larvae in hypobiosis (type of hibernation) to come out of hibernation and migrate towards the uterus and breasts. During this period, the fetus and then the puppies generally cannot escape infestation no matter what efforts are made to de-worm. The objective therefore is to attempt to reduce the parasitic pressure by working on the mothers, puppies and the environment at the same time.

Bucco-dental disorders

The mother's incisor teeth are rarely monitored before whelping whereas their importance should not be neglected given the role they play in cutting off the umbilical cord when the puppies are born. The quality of the joining edges of the dental arches is just as important as the presence of tartar or gingivitis. Brachycephalic or prognathic mothers will naturally encounter more problems in accomplishing this task and thereby expose their puppies to hemorrhaging of the cord (internal or external) and to umbilical infections that may be complicated by an umbilical hernia, abscess of the lining, peritonitis, even neonatal septicemia. In order to limit these risks of infection, it is possible to apply bioadhesive chlorhexidine patches to the mother in the peripartum phase. This procedure seems to be successful in limiting infection.

Risk Factors Linked to Puppies

A recent study showed that puppy mortality before weaning was 17.4% and fell to 4% after weaning. The highest losses occurred during the first week of life (55.6%). Weaning leads to another peak in mortality, which drops off around the twelfth week. These results indicate that prevention efforts must focus primarily on the first week.

Hypoxia

Parturition and the puppy's first respiratory movements are undeniably the most critical moments for the newborn.
Veterinarians now have several tools to prevent neonatal hypoxia on the first day:

- Estimating lung maturity of puppies by measuring progesterone levels and decreasing maternal pulmonary progesterone levels in the puppies by measuring progesterone, since maternal pulmonary progesterone levels are concomitant with the application of a lipoprotein surfactant, which is indispensable in deploying the pulmonary aveoli. This tool has considerably decreased neonatal mortality caused by premature caesarians, especially in brachycephalic breeds.
- If necessary, manual assistance during whelping in cases of listless parturition (especially during posterior presentation, which is an additional risk factor for still birth because the expulsion time is increased). Early medical assistance can also be given to reduce the risk of inhaling amniotic fluid, knowing that what stimulates the puppy's first breath does not seem to be separation from the placenta but rather the thoracic depression that follows pelvic compression (increase of the pCO_2 in the umbilical vessels);
- Monitoring anesthesia and palinesthesia during cesarean delivery;
- Clearing obstructions from the path of the puppy's upper airways by extracting amniotic fluids with a enema;
- Traditional emergency procedures (heating, rubbing, etc.) and treatments (in particular bulbar respiratory stimulants and oxygen masks) for puppies.

Hypoglycemia

As with piglets, puppies are not born with the brown adipose tissue that allows for thermogenesis without chills. Their hepatic and muscular glycogen stores are very limited (depleted within a few hours after birth). They are also difficult to mobilize, which traditionally makes the puppy predisposed to classic hypoglycemia during the first fifteen days. Whether a hypoglycemic attack occurs or not (convulsions, followed by listlessness), essentially depends on how quickly the colostrum is ingested and the surrounding temperature.

Thus, to prevent death from hypoglycemia in the first few hours, the puppies first need to be warmed up and put on the breast soon thereafter (glucose supplied from hydrolysis of the lactose). Finally, if these measures have not been successful, the puppies need to given a shot of isotonic glucose serum.

Hypothermia

Similar to an air conditioner, the evaporation of the amniotic fluid at birth causes the puppy's body surface to be proportionally cooled. This phenomenon explains why puppies of small breeds are more exposed to hypothermia than dogs of the same age from larger breeds.

As with glycemia, the puppy's body temperature is closely linked to how soon the first feeding occurs and how much colostrum is ingested.
No prevention tool for hypothermia is ideal:

- Infrared lamps sometimes cause dehydration in puppies (especially when hygrometry is less than 55%). They can also cause burns on the mother if they are placed too low.

- Heating pads and ground heaters have the disadvantage of heating the mother just as much as the puppies, which may impede lactation.

When extreme temperatures are needed, especially in the case of a CHV infection, incubators require that the puppies be separated from the mother.

Therefore, a few precautions are necessary:
- long before whelping begins, "test" the mother's ability to tolerate high temperatures while pregnant (accelerated breathing is a good indicator that her thermal regulation abilities have been saturated),
- in the case of hypothermia, do not separate the mother from her entire litter, but place the puppies an incubator on a rotating basis,
- allow the mother to see her puppy through the incubator glass.
- warm the puppies gradually in order to prevent cardio-respiratory failure,
- pay close attention to small litters in which it is difficult for puppies to warm themselves by huddling together,
- ensure that the temperature gradient is suitable for both puppies and mother.

Dehydration

The risk factors for dehydration in puppies during the first fifteen days of life depend on the weight/area ratio (which is lower in small breed puppies), how developed retinal filtration is, the surrounding temperature and hygrometry, how smoothly feeding occurs and possibly diarrhea. Diarrhea, however, can all too often go unnoticed because of the mother licking the puppies (often all that is left to see is the "wet bottom").

In order to prevent death from dehydration, it must first be diagnosed (skin fold indicators, regularly weighing the puppy for the first few days), the abovementioned parameters must be fully understood (usefulness of humidifiers) and if necessary, the puppy can be rehydrated orally or parenterally. Conversely, the risks of over-hydration in puppies are considerable if their bodies are unable to regulate renal filtration.

Lack of care at birth

Without dwelling on the well-known principles of intensive care (assisting with delivery, rupturing the amniotic sac, stimulating the first breath, etc), it is important to emphasize the usefulness of regular antisepsis of the umbilical cord until healing is complete. Remember that the both mother's mouth (especially from licking the puppies'lochia and the perianal region) and the litter are the main risk factors in terms of umbilical cord contamination.

Other causes of neonatal mortality

The are many diverse causes of neonatal mortality in puppies. However, the following should be mentioned:

• **Hemorrhagic syndrome,** when it is linked to the fact that the mother's food is not properly preserved, can be effectively prevented through prolonged doses of vitamin K1 given to the mother and the puppies.

• **Hemolytic syndrome,** which, if it occurs too frequently in a genetic line, would justify blood typing the parents before they are mated or at least, before any blood transfusion is performed on the mother.

• **"Swimmer Puppy" Syndrome** (hind legs in a "frog" position), which in less severe cases, leaves room for hope for accelerated recovery through sensory stimulation of the front footpads (with a toothbrush, for example). Chances are also good that the hindquarters will temporarily solidify by using elastoplast "handcuffs" and of course, by placing the puppy on a rougher surface. Vitamin E-based treatments and selenium have not produced results that are significantly different from the spontaneous recovery that is sometimes observed.

• **Iatrogenic neonatal mortality** (that is caused or at least precipitated when medical treatment is given without choosing the medication and dosage based on the fact that sensitivity and pharmacokineics are different in puppies than in adults). However, veterinarians are now sufficiently aware of the main contraindications and the recommended dosages that they can refer to them before making any treatment decision that affects the mother or the puppies.

• **Puppy Diarrhea** is all too often systematically medicated, whereas in most cases, all that needs be done is to adapt the quantity, quality or frequency of food intake (whether it be the mother's milk, substitute milk or weaning food). This should be done in order to adapt to the slow maturation of the puppy's enzymatic digestive tools (lactase and amylase, in particular).

• **Viral Infections** are prevented, whenever possible, by passive immunization (colostrum, seropathy) or active immunization (vaccination).

Bacterial infections

Many bacteria that cause neonatal septicemia or diarrhea in puppies are also found in clinically healthy animals. Therefore, whether puppies develop symptoms or not will generally depend on the number of bacteria involved. It also depends on the animal's immune system, which in turn depends on the immune status of the mother, as well as the amount of colostrum absorbed, the age of the puppy, the amount of microbes in the surrounding environment, stress and many other individual factors.

Thus it is clearly difficult to blame any one type of bacteria simply because it was found to be present during a bacteriological examination of the stool.

That being the case, the most common pathogenic bacteria in puppies are:

• the germs responsible for mastitis in the mother ("toxic milk syndrome") that can cause particularly severe gastroentritis in puppies. This can then lead to rapid dehydration and cause the anus to turn blue and to protrude in what is referred to a "cauliflower" shape. Withdrawing the puppies and feeding them artificially will protect the litter from the risks of embolization of intestinal germs (septicemia).

The presence of cutaneous abscesses (staphylococcic) in the mother can also cause neonatal septicemia in puppies. Septicemia can also be the result of umbilical infections, especially when the mother is suffering from a prognathism, because this malocclusion makes it difficult for her to cut the umbilical cords;

• Escherichia transmitted by feces, milk or the mother's coat.

Endocrinology

Endocrinology is the science of hormones - the study of their physiology and pathology. Hormones are secreted by the endocrine glands. They are the body's messengers, transmitting long-distance information from their point of origin. Therefore, they play an important role in body functions. Consequently, any disease that affects the endocrine system can lead to general disorders ranging from simple skin problems to cardiac irregularities.

Simply put, disorders that affect the endocrine system fall into two categories. The first is hyperfunctioning, which entails overproduction of hormones. This is often the case with endocrine gland tumors. At the other end of the spectrum is secondary hypofunctioning, caused either by a drop in hormonal secretion, or when the body becomes resistant to hormonal action. With the thyroid gland for example, there is hypothyroidism and hyperthyroidism.

Each endocrine gland will be briefly described, after which the related diseases will be presented for each gland. Emphasis will be placed on clinical symptoms, especially those that should catch the attention of the owner. Finally, after an overview of treatments, the predisposed breeds will be described wherever possible. The goal of this chapter is to provide an overview, which is hardly exhaustive, of the primary disorders that affect canine endocrines.

Pancreas

The pancreas is the organ that regulates glycemia, or blood sugar level, with an important hormone called insulin. Insulin is secreted by the pancreas after a meal. It enables blood sugar to enter the cells for use in cell functions. Insulin deficiency results in chronic hyperglycemia, which is called diabetes, whereas on the contrary, over secretion of insulin leads to hypoglycemia.

Diabetes

Diabetes is a frequent illness in dogs, especially in animals over five years old. Contrary to common thought, diabetes does not affect only animals that are obese or eat sugar. It may be due to a defect in insulin secretion. More frequently, however, it is a side effect of a defect in the activity of this hormone.

The warning signs are very significant and rarely go unnoticed: polyuria (increase in urine volume), polydipsia (drinking lots of water), polyphagia (increased appetite) and weight loss.

The owner finds himself with a dog that constantly wants food and water and yet is rapidly losing weight. In addition to these quasi-constant symptoms, other signs may complete the list of clinical signs: rapid onset of a cataract causing sudden blindness, digestive disorders (vomiting, diarrhea), or various infections (e.g. urinary tract infections or cystitis) that cannot be cured or are recurrent despite classic anti-infection treatments.

Diabetes is diagnosed by measuring the level of sugar in the blood and urine.

There are two stages of diabetes: non-ketoacidosis, for which the prognosis is good after treatment and ketoacidosis, which requires urgent hospitalization of the dog and which, left untreated, may cause the animal to fall into a coma and die.
Treatment entails administering shots of insulin under the skin.

Starting treatment requires that the animal be hospitalized so that a twenty-four hour glycemia curve can be established in order to adjust the dose of insulin needed. In females, the estrus cycle makes it difficult to stabilize the diabetes. Therefore, it is imperative to castrate diabetic bitches. The treatment of a diabetic then requires a lot of strict follow-up on the part of the owner (daily insulin shots, special diet, meals at fixed times and monitoring for recurrence of diabetes symptoms). The prognosis depends on the animal's state of health at the time of diagnosis. A dog with non-ketoacidosis, diabetes mellitus can live for more than two years.

Adult hypoglycemia

Hypoglycemia is the reverse phenomenon of diabetes. It is caused by over-secretion of insulin. In 80% of the cases, it is a side effect of pancreatic insulinoma. The clinical signs include convulsions (epileptic-like fits) that generally occur two to six hours after a meal. Giving the dog sugar will quickly quell these fits. Other than the convulsions, the dog may seem normal or may show symptoms of fatigue or inability to tolerate effort.

As with diabetes, hypoglycemia is diagnosed by measuring blood sugar levels. However, the blood sample must be taken during an attack and must register a glycemia level of below 0.7 g/l.
Insulinemia can also be measured.

Treatment entails administering hyperglycemic medications and surgery especially in the case of tumors. The prognosis is cautious since in most cases, the tumor is malignant and often, at the time of diagnosis, metastasis has already occurred since pancreas surgery is extremely delicate.

Adrenal Glands

The adrenal glands are responsible for the secretion (in fasciculate and reticulate zones of the medulloadrenal) of steroidal hormones called glucocorticoids. Glucocorticoids are molecules that perform many actions in the body. Synthetic molecules that are much more active than natural hormones are widely used in human and veterinarian medicine. Their most important properties are: a powerful anti-inflammatory action, allergy-fighting action, ability to maintain central venous pressure, shock absorber role, ability to decrease peripheral use of glucose (insulin resistance) and the ability to transform excess glucose into lipids and to redistribute fat masses.

The secretion of glucocorticoids is regulated by the hypothalamus-pituitary axis. The hypothalamus produces a hormone called CRH, which stimulates the pituitary gland to produce and release a hormone called ACTH. The ACTH then stimulates the adrenal glands to produce glucocorticoids. Furthermore, over stimulation of the adrenal glands by ACTH results in hypertrophy of the adrenal glands.

In addition to glucocorticoids, the adrenal glands (glomerural zone) produce another hormone called aldosterone. Aldosterone plays an important role in kidney functions. It stimulates the kidneys to reabsorb water and sodium and potassium ions and thereby contributes to maintaining the animal's hydration level.

Hyperadrenocorticism

This syndrome, which has numerous clinical outcomes, occurs frequently in dogs. It corresponds to a range of symptoms linked to an excess of endogenous or exogenous (caused by medicine) glucocorticoids in the body.

In this category are:

- Primary Cushing's syndrome, which is caused by excessive adrenal secretion and is a side effect of adrenal tumors (15% of hypercorticism cases);

- Secondary Cushing's disease, which is due to excessive stimulation of the adrenal glands by the pituitary gland (85% of the cases);

- Iatrogenic Cushing's syndrome, which is a side effect of chronic administration of exogenous corticoids.

Cushing's disease is generally seen in dogs older than six years and in certain breeds, especially poodles, dachshunds and boxers.

Clinical symptoms appear progressively and when there are many of them, they make for a most evocative clinical list:

- polyuria-polydipsia (increase in liquid consumption and urine volume). The dog may begin to drink more than 100 ml per kg in a 24-hour period;

- polyphagia: the dog constantly wants to eat;

- abdominal distension (barrel-like appearance);

- skin signs: diffuse hair loss on the flanks and abdomen, skin that becomes parchment thin, numerous blackheads and dermal infections (pyoderma);

- muscle fatigue with ligament anomalies that result in a dislocated patella or pulled hamstring. On the contrary, hypertonicity of muscles and limbs may appear in poodles.

The condition is diagnosed in a laboratory based on the observation of excessive cortisol levels in the blood. This requires that an ACTH stimulation test be performed on the adrenal glands. An etiological diagnosis can be made by using imaging techniques (scanner or echography), which reveal any possible tumor.

Treatment depends on the etiological diagnosis:

- surgery in the case of adrenal gland tumors;

- chemotherapy to destroy the adrenal glands in the case of Cushing's disease. The medication used is OP'-DDD. Since this treatment is dangerous, the dog must be carefully monitored once it begun. Other molecules may be used such as ketoconazole (which antagonizes the effects of corticosteroids without destroying the adrenal glands) or selegiline, which decreases ACTH secretion by the pituitary gland and therefore, decreases stimulation of the adrenal glands. They are not as effective, however, as Mitotane.

- radiation may be effective in cases of pituitary gland tumors.

The prognosis varies and the life expectancy of the animal ranges from a few days to seven years (average is two years). The disease recurs frequently and it is important to realize that the dog will have to continue treatment for the rest of his life.

Hypocorticism

Hypocorticism, or Addison's disease, is caused by a deficiency in mineralcorticoids and glucocorticoids due to the destruction of the adrenal glands (primary hypocorticism), or to a lack of ACTH stimulation (secondary hypocorticism). It may originate spontaneously (tumor, for example), or iatrogenically (side effect of chronic doses of corticoids or OP'-DDD).

The symptoms are not specific to this disease and may be encountered in many other pathogenic disorders, which makes rendering a diagnosis difficult. Symptoms include: anorexia, vomiting, weakness, lethargy, diarrhea, weight loss, polyuria-polydipsia, chills, shaking, abdominal pain, dehydration and brachycardia.

The diagnosis is essentially based on complementary tests, in particular, ionograms, which detect hyperkaliemia and measuring hormone levels (the same ACTH stimulation test is performed when hypercorticism is suspected).

The prognosis must remain cautious during the critical period. Once the critical period has passed, the prognosis improves greatly since the animal has survived this period. Treatment entails administering the deficient hormones: glucocorticoids (prednisone) and emergency treatment when an attack occurs (perfusion, etc).

No breeds have been shown to be predisposed.

Thyroid

The thyroid is where the thyroidal hormones T3 and T4 are produced. As with adrenal glands, thyroid activity is regulated by a control center. Using TRH, the hypothalamus stimulates the production of TSH by the pituitary gland, which in turn stimulates the thyroid. Thyroidal hormones exert negative feedback on the hypothalamus and the pituitary gland (elevated levels of thyroidal hormones causes a decrease in the production of TRH and TSH). The role of thyroidal hormones is essentially to activate metabolism. Thus at normal levels, they play a role in thermogenetics (the production of heat in the body in order to maintain a constant temperature) and in proteidic anabolism. At excessive levels, they develop catabolic activity associated with energy inefficiency.

Hyperthyroidism

Hyperthyroidism is rare in dogs, unlike cats in whom it is a disease frequently associated with age. Contrary to cats, it is caused by a thyroidal tumor (adenocarcinoma) in 90% of cases.
Clinical symptoms essentially include weight loss, polyphagia, which may or may not be accompanied by polyuria-polydipsia, digestive symptoms with diarrhea, behavioral problems with hyperactivity, increased heart rate and above all, a palpable mass in the thyroid region.

The diagnosis is based by feeling the abnormal mass in the thyroid region, measuring thyroidal hormone levels (T4) and possibly using scintigraphy.
The prognosis is cautious, in so far as metastasis is frequent.

Treatment essentially entails surgery that may or may not be accompanied by chemotherapy.

Hypothyroidism

This disorder occurs much more frequently in dogs. In 95% of the cases, it corresponds to impairment of the thyroid gland (immunity-related, idiopathic or tumoral primary hypothyroidism), but it can also be due to insufficient TSH secretion, which causes gland atrophy (secondary hypothyroidism, e.g. pituitary gland tumors).

The most affected breeds are: golden retrievers, doberman pinschers, dachshunds, Irish setters, dwarf schnauzers, Great danes, poodles, boxers and German shepherds.

The symptoms appear insidiously and often go unnoticed at the beginning. Symptoms include: weight gain without increase of food intake, sensitivity to cold (the dog seeks out warm places), skin disorders in 70% of cases (diffuse alopecia, dry skin, hyperkeratosis, myxedema, pyoderma, dry or oily seborrhea), reproductive problems (infertility), cardiac disorders (bradycardia or, decreased heart rate) and neuromuscular problems with fatigue.

The diagnosis is based on measuring T4 thyroidal hormone levels before and after indirect stimulation of the thyroid with TRH.

Treatment entails administering synthetic thyroidal hormones. Once the diagnosis is established, this treatment may have to be administered for life and must be regularly monitored to avoid overdoses.

Cancerology in Dogs

This section will simply take stock of the existing body of knowledge concerning cancer in dogs, in particular the epidemology and the main types of tumors encountered in the various dog breeds. It will also highlight the particularities in terms of diagnosing a cancerous process in dogs and will conclude by discussing possible treatments and the prognosis.

Epidemiology of Cancer in Dogs

As a result of major developments in canine veterinarian medicine and especially testing methods (scanners, echography, etc.), knowledge about animal oncology has made much progress in the last ten years so much so that is now equals oncology knowledge about humans. From an anatomy-pathology standpoint in particular, diagnostic techniques have been refined and laboratories are now able to establish the exact history of a tumor and determine how aggressive it is ("grading"). This enables the veterinarian to better adapt the choice of treatment and above all, to give the owner a prognosis.

The average age for the onset of cancer in dogs is between six and ten years old. More and more females are being affected (almost double the number). The elevated ratio is easily explained by the high incidence of breast cancer in dogs, particularly as these tumors are generally easy to operate on and surgery has become more commonplace.

Several breeds are predisposed, including poodles, German shepherds, boxers, cockers and dachshunds, followed by Breton spaniels, Yorkshire and fox terriers. Looking at all types of tumors, the percentage of benign tumors is significantly higher in dogs under three years of age and the opposite is true with dogs older than seven.

As for the types of cancer, breast cancer is by far dominant, followed by skin cancer, cancer of the mesenchymal tissue and finally, cancer of the male genitals, mouth and hemolymphocytopoiesis system.

Finally, certain breeds are predisposed to certain types of tumors. This is the case with dolicephalic breeds (predisposed to tumors in the nasal cavity), large breeds (predisposed to tumors of the skeleton), boxers (predisposed to skin tumors, especially mastocytomas) and breeds with pigmented mucous membranes (chow-chows and Scottish terriers), which are predisposed to melanoma tumors of the oral cavity.

Diagnostic Procedure in Veterinarian Cancerology

Identifying a cancerous process can be quite easy (as in the case of a visible skin tumor). Or, it may require advanced, complementary testing when the tumoral growth is not easily identified at first glance.

No matter what the case may be, in any cancerous process, it is necessary to locate the tumor growth, determine how far the cancer has spread, identify the histological nature of the tumor and determine the degree of aggressiveness. This is necessary in order to propose a treatment with full knowledge of the facts and especially, to give a prognosis that helps quantify the life expectancy of the dog if possible.

"Cancer" should be considered whenever rapidly-evolving lesions or skin lumps appear, when general symptoms do not respond to classic forms of treatment (vomiting, diarrhea, etc.), when there is rapid weight loss for no apparent reason and whenever any changes in the shape or size of a structure are noted.

Depending on the symptoms observed, the veterinarian will use different testing methods (pulmonary radiography for respiratory anomalies, abdominal echograms if a lump is felt on the abdomen, blood tests to explore metabolic disorders, etc.).

Once the cancer is located, the next step is to determine how far the cancer has spread locally (in relationship to the surrounding tissues and structures) and regionally (whether it has spread to the ganglions that drain the region involved) and how far it has spread in general (metastasis). The development and acquisition of new imaging techniques, such as scanners and scintigraphy for example, allows for extremely precise determinations to be made as to how far the cancer has spread. Consequently, tumors can be clinically classified just as they are for humans.

The last step in the process before considering possible treatment, is to understand the histological nature of the tumor. To this end, a needle can be used to puncture the tumor (whenever surgical ablation cannot be performed), in order to perform a cytological test or biopsy. Or, the tumor can even be surgically removed in order to study its histology.

Treatment

Once a diagnosis of cancer has been established, the decision of whether to treat it must be made in consultation with the owners, based on the prognosis and the how comfortable the animal's life will be. The

goal is to provide as much healing as possible and to be palliative if the desire is simply to prolong the animal's life in good conditions.

There are several means to treat cancer in dogs: surgery, radiation and chemotherapy. The choice of treatment depends on the histological nature of the tumor and where it is located (for example, radiation is recommended for inoperable brain tumors and chemotherapy is recommended for systematic cancer such as lymphosarcoma).

Chemotherapy entails administering substances that alter cell growth and functions and therefore, directly attack the tumor. However, these substances will also have side effects on replicating cells in the body (such as bone marrow, which produces red corpuscles for example. The resulting side effect is anemia).

Radiation relies on the physical effects of radiation on matter. These physical effects cause biological effects, which kill the cells. The goal of radiation is twofold: to kill cancerous cells and to protect surrounding healthy cells.

The different treatments may be combined for increased effectiveness.

Contrary to common thought, chemotherapy will not cause the dog to lose all its hair and will not systematically make him sick. In fact, dogs tolerate chemotherapy better than humans.

Veterinarian medicine is not ill-equipped to deal with cancer in dogs, especially since the fields of human and veterinarian medicine are working together in specialized centers to develop new treatments in the fight against cancer.

Dog Neurology

Below is a description of the main neurological symptoms as well as recommended treatment or steps for the owner to take.

Cerebral Vascular Accidents

The sudden onset of a neurological syndrome is observed. This is caused by a vascular hemorrhage, obstruction or spasm in the cerebral region.
- **Symptoms:** from the sudden onset, the following can be observed: brief loss of consciousness or beginning of a comma, dilated pupils, increased heart rate and convulsions. The location and extent of the resulting paralysis will vary.
- **Evolution:** progressive improvement is noted, sometimes with aftereffects such as a head refraction or a decrease in visual acuity.
- **Treatment:** administered by the veterinarian. It is necessary to fight against the cerebral edema, to keep the respiratory path open and to administer a cerebral vasodilator.

Vertebral Arthrosis

Vertebral arthrosis is a degenerative disease of the spinal column that causes the formation of bony extensions in the form of a "parrot's beak". These extensions can fuse several vertebrae together. In isolation, it can lead to a medullary syndrome, but it can also cause ankylosis and pain.
- **Treatment:** it is imperative to consult a veterinarian.

Ataxia

Ataxia refers to an inability to coordinate voluntary movements and balance problems when standing or walking.
- **Classification:** Medullary ataxia (lesions on the dorsal nerve cord of the spinal chord that correspond to deep sensitivity); cerebellar ataxia (degenerative or inflammatory disease of the cerebellum or a disease due to a congenital defect); vestibular ataxia (due to a peripheral attack – otitis, tumor, etc. – or a central attack – infection, tumor, cerebral poisoning – centers of balance).
- **Treatment:** consult a veterinarian.

Cerebral Compression

Cerebral compression refers to intracranial pressure created by a mass (tumor, abscess, etc.), an increase in cerebral volume (edema) or an abnormal build up of liquid (hemorrhage, hydrocephalia).
- **Symptoms:** the dog holds his head in an abnormal position, walks in circles, changes behavior, has convulsions, has visual problems, a cranial nerve deficit and ataxia or paresis.
- **Treatment:** administered by a veterinarian. Entails decreasing intracranial pressure, by means of surgery if necessary.

Convulsions (convulsive syndrome, epilepsy)

Convulsions are a neurological manifestation of cerebral pain associated with diminished consciousness, sensory disruption and loss of muscle tone, as well as salivation, urination and defecation.
- **Causes:** several are possible: deformity (hydrocephalia), encephalitis, metabolical disorders, poisoning, trauma or cerebral tumors.
- **Treatment:** administered by a veterinarian. Entails decreasing the frequency, duration and severity of attacks.

Heat Stroke (cerebral congestion)

Heat stroke is a cerebral edema caused by a deficiency in the thermoregulation mechanisms. It occurs more frequently in brachycephalic breeds when the climate is hot and humid with poor ventilation.
- **Symptoms:** hyperthermia (over 41∞ C), increased respiratory frequency, cyanosis (blue mucous membranes), shivering, convulsions and stupor.
- **Treatment:** it is necessary to lower the temperature by immersing the dog in very cold water and to prevent cerebral edema.

Fibro-Cartilaginous Embolism

This refers to an acute necrosis of the spinal chord caused by an obstruction of fibro-cartilaginous material in the arteriods. The origin could be a trauma to the intervertebral disks. This phenomenon occurs most frequently in the lumbar region.
- **Symptoms:** Unilateral or bilateral paralysis rapidly sets in but there is no pain to the spinal column (unlike a vertebral disk hernia).
- **Treatment:** consult a veterinarian.

Encephalitis/Encephalomyelitis

This is a disorder of viral, bacterial, parasitic or immunity-related origins characterized by multiple lesions disseminated in different parts of the central nervous system.
- **Symptoms:** extremely varied because they depend on the location of the lesions.
- **Evolution:** begins to evolve several days after a slow start.
- **Diagnosis:** determined by analyzing the cephalorachidian fluid.
- **Treatment:** consult a veterinarian. There is no effective treatment for viral encephalomyelitis.

Hepatic Encephalosis

Hepatic encephalosis is a complex neurological syndrome of metabolic origin. It occurs when the liver no longer provides detoxification of the different intestinal elements, including ammoniac.
- **Symptoms:** a visible neurological attack occurs one to three hours after a meal with ataxia, changes in consciousness and convulsions. In addition, there are a few variable symptoms depending on the nature of the initial hepatic disorder.
- **Treatment:** complex and administered by the veterinarian.

Hematomyelitis

Hematomyelitis is a complication of trauma to the spinal chord, especially following an acute vertebral disk hernia. It involves necrosis and hemorrhaging of the gray matter, which destroys an entire segment of the spine.
- **Treatment:** none.

Vertebral Disk Hernias

- **Henson Type I:** in chondrodystrophic breeds, this refers to a cartilaginous metaplasia of the vertebral disk in which the ring becomes brittle and discal matter is allowed to pass into the spinal canal, which can severely compress the spine.

- **Henson Type II:** in non-chondrodystrophic breeds, this involves a fibrous metaplasia of the nucleus without the ring becoming brittle. The ring progressively becomes deformed and discal matter does not pass through. Spinal compression, therefore, is slow.

Vertebral disk hernias are categorized according to their severity:

Degree	Symptoms	Prognosis	Treatment
1	pain	good	medical, unless it is a cervical hernia
2	lost of proprioception	fair	medical
3	paralysis	cautious	medical and surgical
4	loss of deep pain sensitivity	poor; if loss >48 hrs., extremely poor	emergency medical and surgical

Hydrocephalia

Hydrocephalia refers to an increase in the number of cerebral ventricles due to excess secretion, problems with resorption, or an obstacle blocking the flow of cephalo-rachidian fluid. The disorder may be congenital (especially with miniature breeds) or acquired.
- **Symptoms:** when it is congenital, hydrocephalia sets in between the ages of five weeks and six years (70% before age one). In young dogs: skull deformity, retarded growth, prostration of aggressiveness, convulsions and visual deficiency are observed. In adults: there is a predominance of convulsions, stupor, prostration and the head hangs down in a low position.
- **Treatment:** possible for congenital hydrocephalia, but the prognosis remains bleak if the disease is acquired.

Cervical Vertebrae Instability

Cervical vertebrae instability is a defect in the cervical vertebrae or their joints. It causes stenosis of the spinal canal and compression of the spinal chord.
- **Predisposed breeds:** mastiffs, dobermans and basset hounds.
- **Symptoms:** Ataxia of the hindquarters, which can result in paresis. In more advanced forms, the forequarters are also attacked. There is no cervical pain.
- **Treatment:** medical and surgical.

Degenerative Myelopathycana

This is a degenerative disorder of the spine beginning in the thorax-lumbar region and causing paresis and ataxia.

- **Predisposed breeds:** German shepherds and sheepdogs after age seven.
- **Treatment:** administered by a veterinarian.

Facial Paralysis

Facial paralysis is caused by an inflammation of the facial nerve, resulting from an otitis media or idiopathic otitis.
- **Symptoms:** A deviation in the healthy side of the face can be seen. On the injured side, the lip droops and there is hypersalivation.
- **Prognosis:** healed in three to four weeks.
- **Treatment:** administered by a veterinarian only.

Paralysis of the Jaw

Paralysis of the jaw occurs as a result of inflammation of the trigeminal nerve.
- **Symptoms:** rapid onset, paralysis of the jaw is observed with the mouth remaining open. Consequently, food intake becomes impossible and the dog has some difficulty drinking and swallowing.
- **Prognosis:** healed in two to three weeks.
- **Treatment:** administered by a veterinarian.

Paralysis of the Radial Nerve

Paralysis of the radial nerve involves a loss of motor functions of the extensor muscles in the shoulder, cuff and digits, as well as a loss of feeling in the dorsal side of the foreleg, which is caused by a lesion on the nerve path.
- **Symptoms:** paresis of the foreleg, nails are abnormally worn because they rub on the ground on the dorsal side of the paw.
- **Treatment:** lengthy, administered by a veterinarian, sometimes requires surgery.

Spondylodiscitis

This is an infection of the intervertebral disk and the vertebrae located on both sides. It may be a complication of a urinary or prostatic infection or be caused by migration of a foreign object (a thorn for example).
- **Symptoms:** - general - fever and anorexia;
- nervous system - paresis or paralysis, pain at the site of the lesion.
- **Treatment:** surgical.

Atlanto-Axial Sublaxation

Atlanto-axial sublaxation refers to cervical medullary compression caused by a discrete sublaxation of the axis (first cervical vertebra) in the spinal canal. There is a certain predisposition in dwarf breeds.
- **Symptoms:** if the compression is acute, a tetraplegia is observed. If it is chronic, there is cervical pain, paresis of the four limbs and ataxia. Pain associated with neck flexion is systematically observed.
- **Treatment:** dispensed by a veterinarian.

Cauda Equina Syndrome

Cauda equina syndrome refers to compression of the cauda equina nerve (lower end of the spinal chord), located between the last lumbar vertebra and the first sacral. It is caused by arthrosis. It is especially common in German shepherds.
- **Symptoms:** Pain is noted in the lumbar-sacral region, difficulty rising, paresis or ataxia of the hind limbs and sometimes urinary and fecal incontinence.
- **Treatment:** administered by a veterinarian, with possibility of surgery if necessary.

Alternative Medicine and Dogs

Some believe in it, others do not. No matter what the case may be, alternative medicine is practiced on dogs just like it is on humans, sometimes successfully, according to the specialists. To rule it out, therefore, could seem unfair or at the very least, subjective. Moreover, veterinarians who are interested and specialized in these different fields have come together to form national and international institutions that provide the appropriate training.

Homeopathy

The basic principle of homeopathic medicine ("simili similibus curant") is well known. It consists of treating the evil with an evil. A product or substance that causes a given disease is diluted to obtain an infinitesimally smaller dosage that then helps fight against the disease. In fact, the concept of "hahnemannian treatment" - named for its creator - has spread somewhat and although the substances and molecules in question are always diluted several hundred times, they are not always involved in the treated disease. Homeopathic medicines come in the form of drops or pills and are diluted in a centesimal (CH) or decimal (DH) manner. They are normally given at times other than mealtimes and are given several times per day. There are now several levels of homeopathic treatment available to the canine veterinarian.

Phytotherapy

Although not very developed in canine medicine, phytotherapy is beginning to take its place in alternative medicine especially as certain plants truly have medicinal qualities. Certain forms of quackery that have at times been developed or promoted by well-known personalities in the media or arts world, have led us to forget that most allopathic medicines have their origins in the plant kingdom. What could be more normal, as long as a rigorous, scientific approach is maintained and the underlying principle is not that plants can heal everything but that rather the healing properties of certain plants should be used to a benefit? These plants can be used as a whole (referred to as "simple"), in the form of essential oil extracts ("aromatherapy") or, certain parts of the plant that have higher concentrations of the active ingredient can be used (buds, roots, sprouts, etc. This is called "germinotherapy").

The same logic behind natural healing is seen in the use of certain clays such as smectite to treat simple diarrhea.

Acupuncture

Acupuncture is derived directly from traditional Chinese medicine. It is based on the use of needles placed on perfectly defined anatomical spots on the body. It is also used on dogs. Here again, some veterinarians have specialized in this field and have obtained good results, normally in relation to certain forms of chronic lameness. The veterinarian school in Beijing even offers a complete training program in this field for its students since in certain cases, surgical anesthesia is only performed in conjunction with acupuncture.

Osteopathy

The term osteopathy is undoubtedly not the best term to designate a medical practice, which is without a doubt highly effective when practiced by a person with an educational background in biology and medicine - a veterinarian in the case of a dog. The spinal column is the basic framework of the living organism. All nerves start here and radiate out to all points of the body. Intelligent manipulation of these vertebrae and sometimes the limbs will, in many cases (pain, lameness, neuralgia, etc.), help restore good order in cases where more traditional treatment has failed.

All these techniques, rightly or wrongly called "alternative medicine," are only of interest when they are practiced:

- by a person skilled in the art (veterinarian) and not by quacks who do not have a scientific education;

- as the perfect compliment to the more classic medical and surgical techniques;

- with a true sense of honesty as to their limitations (traumology, cancerology or infectious diseases cannot be treated with alternative medicine alone).

COMPARATIVE INTEREST OF ANIMAL PATHOLOGY FOR THE STUDY OF HUMAN MYOPATHIES

Studies of animal diseases have shown that some of them are very similar to human diseases, both in terms of symptoms and lesions and the causes. For instance, canine muscular pathology involves certain diseases that are similar to human myopathies. This observation provides hope that in-depth study of animal diseases will promote better understanding of the underlying mechanisms in human myopathies and will bring about more effective treatments. This is all the more true as dogs are large enough that it is easy to implement treatments that can ultimately be used on humans, whereas in smaller species, such as mice, transposing these treatments is much more difficult. Two examples will better illustrate the interest in comparative pathology in order to increase knowledge of human myopathies.

Duchenne-type muscular dystrophy is a rather common hereditary disease, affecting 1 out of every 3,500 boys. It is a dramatic disease because starting from age four or five, it causes progressive loss of muscular strength due to deterioration of all the muscles. The young patients are therefore confined to a wheelchair and often die before the age of twenty-one.

This disease is transmitted through a sex-related chromosome. It is caused by a defective gene that normally governs the production of a protein, dystrophine, which is necessary for stability of muscle cells and consequently, for repairing the intra and extra environment of the muscle cells. This complex disease, however, is not fully understood, nor treated effectively. In dogs, there is a myopathy that is caused by a lack of dystrophine and which is sex-related and a recessive trait. Therefore, this disease is very close to the human disease and needs to be studied further in order to better understand the human disease.

Experiments in treatments can be systematically given to canines, either by using certain medications, or by implementing genetic treatment. This would entail transferring the genes that are able to correct the dystrophine deficiency and consequently, reestablish normal membrane permeability in the muscle cells.

Another very interesting disease is myasthenia (Myasthenia gravis), which is characterized both in humans and in canines by the inability to properly transmit nerve impulses to neuromuscular functions. This is due to an insufficiency in, or the destruction of, receptors that carry acetylcholine, in other words, the neuromediator that is able to transmit nerve motor impulses to the muscle cells. Like the human version, the canine version of the disease can be congenital or acquired. Once again, experimental treatments carried out on canines could provide precious information for treating the human disease.

Examples like those from the field of myopathy can be found in most other medical disciplines. Spontaneous pathology is therefore a very important source for animal models that promote medical progress. There is no doubt that progress in veterinarian medicine will benefit human medicine, which in turn, increases our knowledge of animal diseases.

Professor Robert Moraillon
Dean
École Nationale Vétérinaire d'Alfort, France

Special Diets in Cases of Illness
The Basics of Palliative Dietetics

With dogs just as with humans, a healthy body essentially depends on food to keep its physical capacities intact and to be able to resist harmful elements in the environment. Therefore, preventing nutritional deficiencies and avoiding excessive food intake (both in terms of quantity and quality) is a basic and effective means of preventing many diseases. However, nutrition does not only play a role in ensuring balanced growth in puppies and in the growth and development of dogs in general; an appropriate diet in cases of disease or accident can help slow the clinical progression of the disease and contribute effectively to its treatment. Thus, nutrition is undoubtedly the best form of alternative medicine. Unfortunately, it is all too often neglected.

Underweight

According to existing studies, only 2 – 3% of the canine population is underweight, making it a rather rare disorder. It may have several causes:

- **malnutrition**, due to the fact that the dog is given a diet that is insufficient, unappetizing, indigestible or of very poor quality;

- **anorexia** (complete loss of appetite), which can be linked to the progression of a disease (fever, physical suffering, cancer, etc.) or to a psychological behavioral problem (over-excitability, insecurity, melancholy, etc.);

- **high metabolism**, which can occur when the dog is in critical condition following a serious trauma or major surgery;

- **weight loss despite a ferocious appetite**, which may be linked to massive parasitic-induced disorders or inability to digest food (pancreatic insufficiency, exocrine, chronic intestinal inflammation, etc.).
When a dog begins to lose weight, it is first of all important that a veterinarian diagnose the cause. Once the cause has been determined, the owner should place the dog on a high calorie "weight gain" diet that contains easily digestible raw materials. The amount of cellulose (plant fibers from vegetables) should be limited, excess minerals should be avoided and protein and fat intake should be increased. In reality, the ideal approach would be to use easy-to-digest, complete dry food that is formulated for stress-related situations and which contains more than 35% protein and approximately 25% fat. In extreme cases, it is also possible to feed the dog special liquid meals that can be obtained from the veterinarian, who can insert a feeding tube if necessary.

BREAKDOWN OF A HYPOCALORIC RATION (PER 1KG OF FOOD)

Maintenance Ration (in grams)

lean beef	420
cooked rice	430
carrots	130
sunflower oil	20

Obesity Ration (in grams)

white meat or lean fish	330
cooked rice	300
carrots	180
wheat bran	180
sunflower oil	10

COMPARATIVE DAILY INTAKE FOR NORMAL DOGS AND OBESE DOGS
normal dogs on a maintenance diet and dogs that are 20% overweight

Food	Daily Intake (in g per day), according to the weight of the dog in kg: I= ideal weight. O= obesity											
	I	O	I	O	I	O	I	O	I	O	I	O
Weight of Dog (in kg)	5	6	10	12	20	24	30	36	40	48	50	60
lean beef	120		210		350		480		590		700	
white meat or lean fish		70		110		180		250		310		370
well-cooked rice	130	60	220	100	370	170	500	230	620	290	730	370
carrots	30	30	50	60	90	100	120	130	150	160	180	190
wheat bran		30		60		90		130		160		190
water*		120		240		360		500		600		700
sunflower oil	10	5	10	10	15	10	20	10	30	10	30	10
vitamin-enriched mineral supplement	10	10	15	15	20	20	30	30	40	35	50	40

* Water makes the bran swell, multiplying its volume by seven and thereby filling the stomach.

Obesity

Obesity is defined as being overweight by more than 15% of the normal body weight of an adult dog. Surveys show that 25 – 35% of dogs are clinically overweight. In many cases, this disease concerns the owner as well since dog owners are notoriously ignorant of obesity. They regard it as merely "being a few pounds overweight" and they feel it is better to "satisfy the dog than to pity the dog". However, obesity is in fact a full-fledged disease that is also cause for concern since it:
- causes or aggravates other disorders (diabetes, cardio-respiratory deficiencies, etc.);
- increases the risks involved in surgery (anesthesia is more difficult to administer and more dangerous in obese dogs);
- leads to nutritional deficiencies;
- causes serious problems with locomotion (osteoarthritis, slipped disk, etc.);
- decreases reproductive capacity (diminished libido and sperm quality in dogs);
- creates serious skin problems.

• Origins of obesity

Clearly, the main cause of obesity in dogs is consuming more food than the body requires. The progression of this disease is twofold:
- in the initial phase, referred to as the dynamic phase, caloric intake is excessive and the animal gains weight;
- in the second phase, referred to as the static or stabilization phase, the dog reduces his intake on his own and his weight remains constant (it is often said that "the obese actually eat less").

Among the causes of obesity, diet is certainly a prominent factor, often along with a lack of exercise, especially in urban settings. However, certain breeds are genetically predisposed, such as Cocker Spaniels, Labradors and Collies, to name a few. In these cases, the puppy's diet plays a critical role during growth because an increase in the amount of fatty tissue in obese adults is the result of an increase in the size and especially, the number of fat cells (adipose cells). Overfed puppies will produce a lot of fat cells. Once the puppy becomes an adult, these little balloons need only be filled with fat. Therefore, it is important to provide the best possible diet for growing puppies. Avoid feeding puppies extremely appetizing food and instead use specially formulated complete dry food.

Gratifying the dog by stuffing him with sweets and cakes is another non-negligible factor in the development of obesity. Finally, obesity is also frequently associated with more serious endocrine diseases (hypothyroidism, Cushing's disease, etc.), or it may sometimes be the "result" of these diseases. This is all the more reason for overweight dogs to have full, regular medical checkups.

• What to do for obesity

Once the diagnosis has been made and the degree of obesity of the dog ascertained, the success rate of the weight loss regime will essentially depend on how informed the owner is and how determined he is to ensure that the dog stays on the diet. The owner will have to:
- weigh the dog every week in order to monitor changes in weight and to ensure that the dog is losing weight at the rate recommended by the veterinarian;
- be dogmatic about eliminating all foods that are high in sugar, starch or fats. If the dog begs for these foods, they could be strategically replaced with foods such as apple peels;
- reduce the quantity of food given to the dog (so that it covers only 60% of the dog's caloric needs as determined in relationship to the target weight);
- reduce the proportion of fat in the diet;
- add a small quantity of protein, mineral and vitamin supplements to the food.

Reducing the quantity of food the dog consumes per day, however, may cause problems because the dog will not willingly agree to have his food restricted. The objective of a well-planned diet therefore is to maintain the level of food intake, but increase the amount of essential nutrients. Once again, the best solution in reality is to use specially formulated complete food, which covers specific needs (the ideal being low calorie diet food either in the form of complete dry food or dehydrated broth, which can be purchased from most veterinarians). For those owners who prefer to prepare their dog's food themselves, it is always possible to use a home diet plan.
By following the guidelines above, the dog can be expected to lose 4 – 5% of his body weight every month, thereby allowing him to regain his health, vitality and life expectancy.

Diabetes

An increase of blood sugar level (glucose) and the presence of sugar in the urine characterize the form of diabetes known as "diabetes mellitus". In terms of clinical symptoms, the diabetic dog will drink and urinate more, eat a lot and sometimes suffer from cataracts of the eyes. As the disease progresses, the dog becomes very thin and his urine takes on the characteristic odor of pippin apples. If the diabetes is not treated, the dog will eventually go into a coma and die. This disease can be detected through a simple blood and urine analysis.

The causes of diabetes are both genetic and linked to external factors. They stem from a decrease in the secretion of insulin (a hypoglycemic hormone) by the pancreas. There is a form of juvenile diabetes that affects certain breeds more than others (Doberman Pinschers, German Shepherds and Poodles). However, this form only represents 1 – 2% of all cases of diabetes, since diabetes occurs more frequently in adults. The following elements influence this serious, chronic disease:
- breed of the dog (German Shepherd, Collie, Pekinese, Boxer, etc.);
- age (onset occurs between five and twelve years);
- sex (diabetes affects twice as many females);
- related factor of obesity.

Without providing all the details about the complex medical classification, suffice it to note that there are two main types of diabetes mellitus in adult dogs. The second stems from the progression of the first. The first type is called non-insulin dependant diabetes (which can be controlled by diet alone). The second type is called insulin dependant diabetes (in which case, the animal is given one or more insulin shots per day and the diet has to be adjusted according to the shots, especially in terms of meal times).

In the most simple form of insulin dependant diabetes (dietetically-speaking and not medically-speaking), a traditional diet that is low in fat will suffice. A diet of easily digested foods such as dehydrated food or dry food can be used in order to better spread out fat consumption over a longer period of time. Rapid-absorption sugars (saccharose) are not recommended. It is imperative to strictly observe the meal times that the veterinarian prescribes based on the type of insulin used and never to change the dog's diet once it is balanced.

In the case of non-insulin dependant diabetes, the dog is still able to control glycemia to a certain extent. It is important to ensure that blood sugar levels remain as low as possible after meals, so that the pancreas is not called upon to produce large quantities

SAMPLE HOME DIET FOR DIABETIC DOGS	
For 1 kg of food	
White meat and liver	250 g
Cooked rice	250 g
Green vegetables	420 g
Wheat bran	50 g
Sunflower oil	10 g
Special "diabetic" supplements	20 g
in addition, an apple may be given as a treat without providing too much sugar.	

of insulin. In order to do so, either low calorie dietetic dry food or dehydrated broth can be used, or a home diet can be used that contains:
- slow-absorption fats (rice, pasta);
- high quality proteins (lean red or white meat);
- fiber (various kind of lettuce, green beans or bran; carrots are rather high in sugar and should be avoided.).

The ideal is to break up the food intake as much as possible by feeding the dog three to four small meals spread out over the day in order to prevent what is referred to as "post-pardial hyperglycemic peaks" (increase in blood sugar observed following a meal).

Diarrheas

Diet can play two different roles in diarrhea:
- an inductive role if the diet is not balanced;
- a palliative role if it is used to help treat the diarrhea in question.

Food can cause diarrhea when:
- the dog's diet is changed too abruptly, from one day to the next, without allowing a week for the dog to adjust to the new diet;
- the quantity of food is too high, overwhelming the dog's ability to digest it;
- the diet is too high in hard-to-digest fats, which causes sour-smelling diarrhea. This is the case with certain dogs that cannot tolerate milk or that are no longer used to milk, or when the starch in rice or pasta is not cooked thoroughly. This is true for breeds that are the closest to wild dogs (Nordic dogs, German Shepherds) as they are particularly fragile in this respect.
- the diet is too high in hard-to-digest proteins (poor quality meats, tendons, fascia, raw grains and overheated meat), which are "fermented" by the time they reach the large intestine and which result in the production of various toxic substances that causes putrid-smelling diarrhea.

A balanced diet, however, can help prevent or treat diarrhea. In cases of acute diarrhea, the following measures should be adopted:
- the dog should be placed on a twenty-four hour liquid diet (nothing to eat and unlimited drinks) in order to prevent dehydration and to allow the intestines to rest;
- meals should be broken up (as soon as the fast is over, give the dog as many small meals as possible, in order to put the digestive system "back on track");
- large quantities of easily digested food should be fed to the dog.

Cases of chronic diarrhea (more than several weeks) are more complicated because the diet needs to be adapted differently depending on the cause. Diarrhea originating in the small intestine can be controlled by easily digested food, whereas diarrhea originating in the large intestine will require that the quantity of cellulosic fibers be increased so that their hygienic effects can be maximized. Treating chronic diarrhea is somewhat of an art, in fact and the veterinarian must also serve as "dietician".

Urinary Disorders

Because the subject of chronic renal failure a disease often associated with aging, has already been discussed elsewhere - it would be useful rather to consider canine urolithiasis, also known as urinary calculi. Urinary calculi are crystals that form and grow in the bladder. They may cause an obstruction or more frequently, they are associated with an inflammation of the bladder (cystitis). This is the case of the dog that squats every ten meters to urinate a few drops, or the dog that lifts his leg in vain during the entire walk. It is also seen in the case of the dog that loses a few drops of urine, often with blood in it, around the apartment for no apparent reason. It is currently estimated that 21% of dogs brought to the veterinarian are affected with cystitis. Certain breeds are more likely to be affected such as Chihuahuas, Yorkshires, Poodles, Dachshunds and especially Dalmatians. The latter are in fact genetically predisposed to certain calculi. That being the case, the question of diet would normally be relatively simple if there were only one type of calculi in dogs. Unfortunately, such is not the case: any number of calculi including struvite (ammoniomagnesuim phosphate), oxalate, urate (Dalmatians), cystine (Dachshunds), silicate and carbonate calculi, can all be the culprits. In making his diagnosis, therefore, the veterinarian needs to analyze the type of calculus in question before he can prescribe a special diet as part of the treatment. In any case, the goal of the special diet is to limit the supply of the element that is contributing to the growth of the calculus (less magnesium in the case of struvite, for example). The goal is also to create pH conditions in the bladder by means of the urine that will prevent the growth of calculi. Thus, the urine of a dog suffering from struvite would be rendered more acidic and inversely, the urine of a dog with cystine or oxalate calculi would be made more alkaline.

Therefore, it is necessary for the owner to have a precise diagnosis, with a specialized laboratory analysis, before discussing with the veterinarian what the most appropriate diet would be, based on the results of the analysis, in order to achieve the most effective results.

SAMPLE HOME DIET FOR CHRONIC KIDNEY INSUFFICIENT DOG

For 1 kg of food

White meat	250 g
Carrots	300 g
Tapioca starch	380 g
Sunflower oil	65 g
Purified salmon oil	5 g

Completed balanced dry or canned foods, especially adapted, are also available by veterinarians.

Other Disorders that Require a Special Diet

Numerous other disorders may require that the dog's diet be adjusted in order to assist in the healing process.

Constipation can be treated by increasing fiber in the dog's diet (by adding wheat bran, for example) or by choosing low calorie complete dry food. Skin diseases, which occur frequently in dogs, may be related to a poor diet, or in rare cases, linked to allergy problems. It is now known, however, that certain dietary supplements play an important role in dermatological treatments (vitamin B, sulfur amino acids and essential fatty acids). Omega 3 fatty acids (purified fish oil) even have an antipruritic effect (eliminates itching).

A special diet may be required following surgery:
- liquid diet, possibly fed through a tube, in cases of digestive surgery;
- high-calorie diet rich in nutrients during the convalescence phase;
- protein-rich diet during stressful periods (medical hospitalization).

All these examples highlight the importance diet now plays in veterinarian medicine in terms of medical treatment of a disease or surgery. Although the veterinarian advises the owner regarding the choice of food or the composition of a home diet, the responsibility for administering the diet still falls upon the owner. And owners will only make a concerted and ongoing effort in the interest of their dog if they are convinced of the importance of their role.

Location Of The Main Hereditary And Congenital Disorders
(Breed Predispositions) (Except for hip dysplasia)

The table below provides a summary of the weak points and presumed hereditary defects for dogs from the main large, medium and small breeds, based on the most recent data on hereditary and congenital canine diseases. Some definitions of canine diseases or anomalies are also provided in addition to those mentioned in the chapters on dog diseases. Hip dysplasia is not included in this table as it affects dogs of many breeds and almost every size, though large dogs are the most affected. Reference will be made to the chapter on diseases of the musculoskeletal system.

Small Breeds (less than 10 kg) (22 lb)

Breed / "Weak Point"	Presumed Hereditary Defects
Affenpinscher	
Face	Hare lip
Bedlington Terrier	
Liver	Hepatitis caused by a buildup of copper
Eye	Retina dysplasia
Bichon Frise	
Musculoskeletal system	Dislocation of the patella
Nervous system	Epilepsy
Border Terrier	
Jaw	Craniomandibular osteopathy
Boston Terrier	
Kidney	Renal diabetes insipidius
Eye	Microphthalmia, strabismus
Vertebral column	Hemivertebra
Cairn Terrier	
Nervous system	Paralysis related to an enzyme deficiency
Kidney	Juvenile renal disease
Jaw	Craniomandibular osteopathy
Cavalier King Charles Spaniel	
Eye	Microphthalmia
Chihuahua	
Nervous system	Hydrocephalus
Musculoskeletal system	Dislocation of the patella
Dwarf Poodle	
Kidney	Diabetes insipidus
Heart	Persistent ductus arteriosus
Dwarf Schnauzer	
Eye	Progressive retinal atrophy
Jack Russel Terrier	
Eye	Dislocation of the crystalline lens
Musculoskeletal	Ataxia, myasthenia system
Lhasa Apso	
Kidney	Renal diabetes insipidius, juvenile renal disease
Eye	Ectropion, progressive retinal atrophy
Long-Haired Dachshund	
Eye	Keratitis punctata
Vertebral column	Slipped disk
Papillon	
Eye	Entropion
Ear	Deafness
Pekinese	
Tongue	Macroglossia
Eye	Ectropion, dislocation of the eye

Breed / "Weak Point"	Presumed Hereditary Defects
Pomeranian	
Eye	Malformation of the eyelids
Pug	
Central nervous system	Loss of balance
Eye	Congenital cataract, extropion, malformation of the eyelids
Muscle	Myotonia
Scottish Terrier	
Muscles	Cramps
Sealyham Terrier	
Eye	Dislocation of the crystalline lens
Shetland Sheepdog	
Eye	Numerous disorders
Face	Cleft palate
Short Hair Fox Terrier	
Eye	Dislocation of the crystalline lens
Heart	Pulmonary stenosis
Shih Tzu	
Kidney	Renal diabetes insipidius, juvenile renal disease
Eye	Ectropion
Smooth Fox Terrier	
Musculoskeletal system	Myasthenia, ataxia
Tibetan Terrier	
Eye	Dislocation of the crystalline lens
Nervous system	Lipofusinosis
West Highland White Terrier	
Blood	Anemia related to enzyme disorders
Heart	Ventricular septal defect
Jaw	Craniomandibular osteopathy
Immune system	Numerous allergies
Wire Fox Terrier	
Central nervous system	Loss of balance
Eye	Dislocation of the crystalline lens
Digestive tract	Megaesophagus
Wiry Dachshund	
Skin	Keratitis punctata
Vertebral column	Slipped disk
Yorkshire Terrier	
Blood	Microphthalmia, keratitis sicca
Heart	Persistent ductus arteriosus
Vertebral column	Hemivertebra
Musculoskeletal system	Necrosis of the femoral head system

Medium Breeds
(10 – 25 kg)
(22-55 lb)

BREED / "WEAK POINT"	PRESUMED HEREDITARY DEFECTS
American Cocker Spaniel	
Eye	Numerous ocular disorders including entropion
Basenji	
Kidney	Junevile renal disease
Eye	Optical nerve disorder
	Persistent pupillary membrane
Intestine	Immunity enteritis
Blood	Enzymatic disorder-induced anemia
Basset Hound	
Immune system	Immune deficiency
Eye	Eversion of the third eyelid
Beagle	
Kidney	Junevile renal disease
Eye	Microphthalmia, cataract
Coagulation	Hemophilia A
Heart	Pulmonary stenosis
Face	Cleft palate
Border Collie	
Nervous system	Behavioral problems related to a buildup of pigments (lipofuscin) in the nervous system
Breton Spaniel	
Muscles	Muscular dystrophy
Bull Terrier	
Kidney	Junevile polycystic renal disease
Extremities	Lethal acrodermatitis (digits, nose, jaw)
Eye	Eyelid malformation
Cocker Spaniel	
Kidney	Juvenile renal disease
Behavior	Aggressiveness
Eye	Numerous ocular disorders including microphthalmia and ectropion
Face	Cleft palate
Dalmatian	
Central nervous system	Deafness, enzyme deficiencies
Kidney	Juvenile renal disease, urate calculus
English Bulldog	
Heart	Pulmonary stenosis, ventricular septal defect
Eye	Entropion
English Cocker Spaniel	
Eye	Numerous ocular disorders
English Setter	
Eye	Entropion
Behavior	Lipofuscinosis

BREED / "WEAK POINT"	PRESUMED HEREDITARY DEFECTS
English Springer Spaniel	
Eye	Numerous ocular disorder
Heart	Ventricular septal defect
Muscles	Myasthenia
Skin	Skin laxity
French Bulldog	
Eye	Entropion
Gordon Setter	
Central nervous system	Balance problems
Grey Collie	
Eye	Numerous ocular disorders
Bone marrow	Cyclical hematopoiesis
Irish Setter	
Central nervous system	Balance problems
Eye	Microphthalmia
Coagulation	Hemophilia
Digestion	Gluten intolerance
Keeshond	
Heart	Ventricular septal disorder
Kerry Blue Terrier	
Eye	Eyelid malformation
Nervous system	Cerebellum degeneration
Pointer	
Eye	Cataract, retinal atrophy
Nervous system	Epilepsy, deafness
Poodle	
Kidney	Juvenile renal disease
Eye	Cataract, defective eyelash placement
Shar Pei	
Skin	Cutaneous mastocytoma
Kidney	Renal amyloidosis
Eye	Numerous ocular disorders including strabismus
Endocrine system	Hypothyroidism
Siberian Husky	
Urinary tract	Ureteral ectopia
Heart	Ventricular septal disorder
Eye	Numerous ocular disorders
Skin	Zinc responsive dermatitis,
Larynx	Paralysis of the larynx
Standard Collie	
Eye	Collie eye anomaly, microphthalmia
Welsh Corgi	
Eye	Cataract
Urinary tract	Cystine calculus

Vocabulary

Amyloidosis
A disorder characterized by the deposit of an amorphous substance called amyloid in various organs, which then impedes organ functions.

Atresia of the Lacrimal Ducts
Occurs when the lacrimal ducts are absent at birth.

Cerebellar Hypoplasia
Underdevelopment of the cerebellum resulting in ataxia (lack of balance) and hypermetria (exaggerated movements).

Collie Eye Anomaly
A series of retinal lesions that can cause blindness. Affects Collies and related breeds.

Color Mutant Alopecia
Refers to a loss of hair that only affects certain colored regions of the body.

Corneal Dystrophy
Refers to a nutritional problem in the cornea.

Cortical Renal Hypoplasia
A defect in the formation of the outer layer of the kidney, causing polydipsia and polyuria (the dog drinks and eats too much).

Craniomandibular Osteopathy
A bone disease characterized by irregular proliferation of the mandible and tympanic bulla bones. This disease causes discomfort when eating and intermittent fever. Sometimes corrects itself spontaneously.

Cryptorchidism
Failure of the testes to descend into the scrotum.

Cushing's Disease
A malfunction of the adrenal glands which causes in particular, hair loss and obesity. May be linked to a malfunction of the adrenal glands themselves or to injections of anti-inflammatory steroids (cortisone).

Degenerative Myelopathy
A spinal cord disorder causing degeneration of the spinal cord, which then results in nerve and locomotive disorders

Distichiasis
The abnormal presence of two complete rows of eyelashes (or a few extra eyelashes).

Ectropion
An eversion of the eyelid.

Ectopic Ureter
Occurs when the ureter, the duct that links the kidney to the bladder, is in an abnormal position.

Ehlers Danlos Syndrome
A disorder of the sub-cutaneous connective tissues. The skin becomes fragile and is accompanied by overelasticity of the ligaments.

Entropion
An inversion of the eyelid.

Fallot's Tetralogy
A complex cardiac malformation characterized by a defect in the ventricular septum, pulmonary stenosis, misalignment of the aorta and hypertrophy of the right ventricle.

Glaucoma
An increase in intraocular pressure. May result in blindness.

Hemophilia A
A blood disease characterized by prolonged bleeding and spontaneous hemorrhages.

Hereditary Polyneuropathy
Nerve disorder that causes lameness and progressive muscular weakness.

Hydrocephalia
A buildup of fluids in the cerebral ventricles.

Hypoplastic Trachea
Abnormal development of the trachea resulting in chronic cough, dyspnea and inability to tolerate exercise.

Hypospadias
Abnormal placement of the urethra on the penis.

Hypothyroidism
Insufficient secretion of thyroid hormones.

Legg-Calvé-Perthes Disease or Aseptic Necrosis of the Femoral Head
Frequent anomaly in small breeds which results in lameness and destruction of the femoral head.

Breed / "Weak Point"	Presumed Hereditary Defects
Afghan Hound	
Spinal cord	Necrotizing myelopathy
Akita	
Eye	Retina disorders
Alaskan Malamute	
Nervous system	Polyneuropathy
Beauceron	
Skin	Necrotizing bullous dermatosis
Berger Picard	
Female genital tract	Vulva malformation
Eye	Photoreceptor dysplasia
Bernese Mountain Dog	
Eye	Entropion
Bobtail	
Eye	Microphthalmia
Bordeau Bulldog	
Eye	Entropion
Borzoi	
Eye - Disorders of the eye, retina and optical nerve	
Borzoi Sighthound	
Eye	Microphthalmia
Bouvier Des Flandres	
Larynx	Paralysis of the larynx
Boxer	
Heart	Numerous cardiac malformations (aortic stenosis, pulmonary stenosis, ventricular septal disorder)
Briard Sheepdog	
Urinary tract	Ureteral ectopia
Bullmastiff	
Eye	Entropion
Central nervous system	Cerebellum degeneration
Doberman	
Kidney	Juvenile renal disorder
Eye	Numerous ocular disorders including microphthalmia
Skin	Alopecia of coats that have been thinned
Nervous system	Trembling, cervical pain, deafness
Metabolism	Malignant hyperthermia
Cranium	Craniomandibular osteopathy
Heart	Dilated cardiomyopathy

Breed / "Weak Point"	Presumed Hereditary Defects
German Mastiff	
Eye	Numerous ocular disorders including ectropion
German Shepherd	
Heart	Aortic stenosis
Kidney	Nephrogenic diabetes insipidus
Coagulation	Hemophilia A
Eye	Chronic superficial keratitis Congenital cataract
Digestion	Pancreatic insufficiency
Spinal cord	Cauda equina syndrome
Other	Sudden puppy death
German Wolf-Spitz	
Heart	Ventricular septal disease
Golden Retriever	
Heart	Aortic stenosis
Eye	Numerous ocular disorders including microphthalmia and strabismus
Muscles	Dystrophic myopathy
Central nervous system	Essential epilepsy
Greyhound	
Metabolism	Malignant hyperthermia
Groenendael	
Muscles	Muscular dystrophy
Digestive tract	Stomach cancer
Labrador	
Urinary tract	Ureteral ectopia
Eye	Numerous ocular disorders including central retina atrophy and retinal dysphasia
Muscles	Myopathies
Central nervous system	Essential epilepsy
Malamute	
Eye	Corneal dystrophy
Coagulation	Hemophilia A
Cartilage	Chondrodysplasia
Mastiff	
Eye	Microphthalmia, persistent pupillary membrane
Newfoundland	
Heart	Aortic stenosis
Urinary tract	Cystine calculus
Eye	Ectropion
Norweigan Buhund	
Eye	Cataract
Norwegian Elkhound	
Eye	Entropion

BREED / "WEAK POINT"	PRESUMED HEREDITARY DEFECTS
Pyrenean Mountain Dog	
Eye	Entropion, cataract, distichiasis
Coagulation	Hemophilia
Rottweiler	
Muscles	Muscular dystrophy
Saint Bernard	
Eye	Numerous ocular disorders
Coagulation	Hemophilia
Heart	Cardiomyopathy
Saint Hubert	
Eye	Eyelid malformations
Samoyed	
Coagulation	Hemophilia
Kidney	Juvenile renal disease
Heart	Atrial septal defect
Muscles	Muscular dystrophy
Schnauzer	
Kidney	Renal diabetes insipidus
Eye	Microphthalmia
Face	Cleft palate
Tervuren	
Nervous system	Epilepsy
Tibetan Mastiff	
Eye	Entropion
Weimar Pointer	
Diaphragm	Diaphragmatic hernia
Muscles	Myotonia
Eye	Ectropion

Lethal Acrodermatitis
Refers to puppies with a lighter coat at birth, growth problems, difficulty chewing and swallowing, digits that spread, skin infections, otitis, diarrhea, nasal discharge, etc. It is generally fatal.

Lipofuscinosis
A buildup of pigments called lipofuscins in the nervous system, which can cause behavioral problems.

Mastocytoma
A tumor of the skin and blood cells (mast cells). Several degrees of malignancy are recognized.

Megaesophagus
An esophagus anomaly resulting in difficulty swallowing and false passage.

Microphthalmia
The abnormal development of the eyes (too small).

Myasthenia Gravis
Muscle degeneration causing muscular weakness.

Odontoid Process Hypoplasia
A vertebral malformation that can cause various symptoms ranging from pain to quadriplegia.

Pancreatic Insufficiency
An anomaly in pancreatic secretion resulting in weight loss and marlaceous stools.

Pemphigus Foliaceus
An immune system disease that essentially causes cutaneous symptoms (hair loss, lesions on the footpads).

Persistent Ductos Arterios
The incomplete closure of an artery between the aorta and the pulmonary artery.

Persistent Hyperplastic Primary Portosystemic Shunt
A developmental anomaly in certain, primarily hepatic veins that can cause nervous signs through blood "poisoning".

Persistent Pupillary Membrane
A congenital defect consisting in the persistence of a fetal membrane originating in the iris. It is characterized by the existence of thin membranes connecting the iris to the cornea and the iris to the crystalline lens and results in opacity at both levels.

Progressive Retinal Atrophy
A degeneration of night vision, followed by day vision, progressing into complete blindness. Dilated pupils, atrophy of the retinal vessels. Several distinct types of are recognized. This term designates the degeneration of various types of photoreceptors in the retina.

Prolapsed Intervertebral Disc
A prolapse of the intervertebral discs resulting in compression of the spinal cord followed by paresis, then paralysis.

Pulmonary Stenosis
A narrowing of the pulmonary artery at its point of origin.

Renal Hypoplasia
Underdevelopment of the kidneys (too small).

Retinal Dysplasia
A congenital defect of the retina characterized by abnormal differentiation and proliferation of certain layers of the retina.

Ventricular Septal Defect
A defect in the septum between the two cardiac ventricles.

Vitreous
A congenital anomaly caused by the persistence of the primary vitreous, which takes the form of an opaque mass on the posterior side of the crystalline lens.

Part 10

The Setting
of the Canine World

The Veterinarian and Related Professions

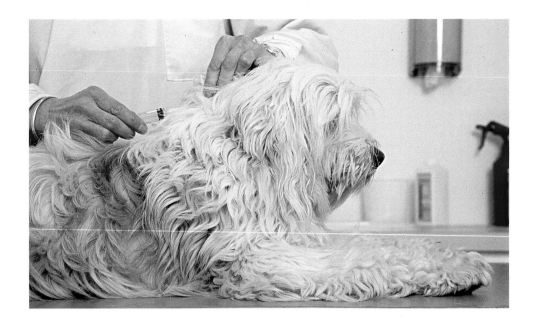

History of Veterinary Medicine

Veterinary and human medicine have evolved side by side ever since the beginning. The practitioners of these two disciplines were, in fact, generally the same.

From Egyptian Papyrus to Hippocrates

In ancient times, medicine was based on empirical knowledge and botany, both of which were fraught with mystical powers. No distinction was really made in the methodologies used to treat humans and animals. However, some evidence has been found of a specifically veterinary science among the Egyptians from a papyrus dating back to 1750 BC, which discusses animal ophthalmology. Also, the walls of tombs were sometimes painted with frescos depicting scenes of calving and the care of bovine hooves. It even appears that a special caste was established for animal doctors. Of course, sacred animals were the first to benefit from the latest advances in knowledge at the time.

The Greeks were the first to make significant advances in medical science. Around 400 BC, Hippocrates perfected pragmatic medicine by systematically questioning and examining the patient. The first medical prescriptions are also attributed to him. After Hippocrates came Plato, Herophilus and Galen. Each one devoted himself to the task of describing human diseases and sometimes animal diseases. Hippocrates was interested in cerebral disorders in cattle and sheep. But it was not until Aristotle that animal pathology began to be systematically studied. Aristotle described the most well known diseases: rabies, swine erysipelas and horse colic. He was even interested in elephants. His teachings were used at the famous medical school of Alexandria.

Throughout all antiquity, the desire to better comprehend animal medicine was largely dictated by the importance of the military cavalry, a necessary tool in the great conquests of the time. In addition, there were frequent epidemics that wiped out entire herds. Texts have been found on the subject of the cattle plague in Greece and the Byzantine Empire.

With the advent of the Middle Ages, science declined steadily and veterinary medicine was no longer an exception to the rule. The instruments and techniques remained practically unchanged. Bloodletting, enemas, cauterization, trocars and vinegar and salt were all prescribed. Only the Arabs continued to increase their knowledge based on the work of Hippocrates and Galen. They perfected different types of surgical scalpels and setting methods used on horses.

Horses – The Subject of All Treatment

At any rate, war horses received special attention and the blacksmith trade played a prominent role. The Crusades, the domestic wars and the tournaments of the Knights all required mounts and frequently after combat, horses were taken to surgeons or other medical apprentices. Moreover, the art of medicine was practiced by members of religious orders at the time. Early on, however, high-ranking church authorities forbade the monks from studying anatomy and the medical writings of Antiquity were tucked away. The Middle Ages were ravaged by epidemics, much more so than any other period. Superstition and the church leaders prevented a number of intellectuals from studying these epidemics. In the eyes of the Church, they symbolized divine punishment. Satanic practices on animals also began to appear during these dark times and it was not a good time to be treating cats and birds.

Reason finally won out and starting in the 12th century, the first medical schools began to open. Animal pathology, anatomy and physiology were often studied along with fields pertaining to humans. Veterinary medicine was divided into pastoral and equestrian medicine. An Italian, Giardono Rufo, was the first to write about the blacksmith trade and about horse medicine and surgery in 1250 AD.

New gains were made during the Renaissance. The study of anatomy seemed to be an obsession. The greatest scientific minds were interested in anatomy, with Leonard de Vinci leading the pack. Of course, horses were again the first to benefit from the most advanced studies. Dissection instruments were developed that were used until the 19th century.

In 1650, Marcello Malpighi invented the modern microscope and the study of cells and tissues contributed to the advancement medical science. During the same period, a Maltese knight, Ludwig Melzo, wrote the first book that listed all the horse diseases. Included in the book are illustrations of the instruments used in treatment: syringes, gags and forceps. This book served as a reference for several decades. Once again, horses occupied a predominant place vis-à-vis other animal species.

During the Enlightenment, scientific thought became more influential and during the 18th century, the idea of establishing an actual school for veterinary medicine began to form and ended up taking concrete shape in France.

The First Veterinary School

In 1761, Claude Bourgelat, one of the best riders in Europe, had been the director of the King's Academy in Lyons for twenty years. Horse-riding, weaponry, music and mathematics were all taught there. However, Bourgelat's interest in anatomy and equine diseases led him to think about the foundations of a veterinary teaching program that would be able to preserve and improve the equine species and to protect cattle from the epidemics that were destroying them. He succeeded in convincing Bertin, the General Comptroller of Finances, to grant him a subsidy in order to create the first veterinary medicine school in Lyons. The Guillotière school was thus founded in February 1762.

Unlike university teaching at the time, veterinary education focused more on reflection and observation, manual dexterity and visual memory. From the start, the students performed checkups and hospitalized animals. This first school quickly began to attract students from abroad and became the point of reference in veterinary medicine. It became the Royal Veterinary School in 1764.

In 1765, Bourgelat opened the Veterinary School of Alfort, which remains the oldest veterinarian school to date because it still stands on the original foundation. After Alfort, numerous other schools cropped up across Europe: Turin in 1769, Vienna in 1777, Hanover in 1778, Dresden in 1780 and London in 1792. Disciples and students of Bourgelat ensured the continued development of these schools.

Veterinary education evolved as scientific discoveries were made and its teaching mission was expanded to include research. Numerous diseases were wiped out thanks to cooperation between doctors and veterinarians. Among the most notable were: Henry Bouley and Pasteur and their work on the anti-anthrax vaccination, Camille Guérin and Doctor Albert Calmette, who developed the BCG vaccine against tuberculosis, and Auguste Ramon, who discovered anti-tetanic and anti-dipteric anatoxins.

Today, veterinary medicine enjoys the best medical and surgical techniques. Ultrasounds and endoscopy are performed daily and scanners are even sometimes used on animals. Current research tends to bring improvements in animal care and thereby contribute to progress in human medicine.

Canine Veterinarians

All veterinarians must treat canine pathologies, even if he or she practices in a rural setting: 43% of dogs live in rural areas, whereas 19% live in apartments, 69% live individual homes (65% of which have a yard) and 12% live on a farm. This has lead many veterinarians to treat only dogs and cats, either for general checkups or for specialized examinations.

General Practitioners

The majority of general practitioners are in the field of canine medicine. Their clientele is often limited to individual dog owners and perhaps to a handful of small breeders. Their role, just like a human doctor, is to ensure that the animals are in good health, no matter what their habitat is. This role may be:

• **preventive:** annual or biannual vaccinations, deworming, anti-parasite treatments, even shampoos and food. This category may include a few surgical acts such as descaling (before an agomphiasis of the teeth), elective ovariectomies (removal of the ovaries to prevent heat and mating). Other acts include making diagnoses and monitoring pregnancy in order to ensure that whelping occurs under the best possible conditions.

• **curative:** including all surgeries associated with disease, such as pyometra (infection of the uterus), castrating monorchidic dogs and traumas (fractures, bites, severe wounds, etc.). Also included is medical treatment and care for vomiting, diarrhea, infections, etc.

• **advisory:** more and more, veterinarians are being called upon to provide advice about training, diet, choice of breed, etc. Often the owner's most basic concern is the well-being of the animal and he or she is seeking a sort of partner for the dog.

As can be seen, the field of general veterinary medicine is vast. This is why veterinarians rarely work alone and their office is actually a small business with assistants (such as secretaries and veterinary assistants) and sometimes partners.

"Breeding" Veterinarians

Currently, many large dog-breeding operations are springing up. Veterinarians are of course called upon to provide health care, but they also oversee and pay close attention to all the various breeding parameters. This involves the installation of buildings and their level of hygiene (ventilation, nitrogen levels, surface area per dog, etc.) and the distribution of food to the various groups of animals (breeding bitches, lactating or pregnant bitches and puppies).

In order to obtain the best possible breeding results, the veterinarian sets up his or her office on site, provides detailed reports about the breeding progress and can also provide the breeder with guidelines about what approach to adopt with his or her animals.

Specialists

Just as in human medicine, certain fields of application are developed through research and progress. For this reason, some veterinary practitioners, such as veterinary school professors or established veterinarians, specialize in one particular field.

Cardiology
This field entails detecting one or more cardiac anomalies through clinical examination of the dog and also through the use of sophisticated equipment: radiography, ultrasound and electrocardiographs.

Neurology
In this field, the veterinarian is particularly interested in non-muscular locomotive problems and disorders of the nerve centers (spinal cord and brain). Here again, radiography can be helpful in making a diagnosis (for slipped disk, for example), as can electromyography.

Dermatology/Parasitology
This essentially involves treating skin diseases after examining the dog and taking samples that are stained

and studied under a microscope. Some diseases can be diagnosed immediately, while others require laboratory analysis.

Ophthalmology

As with humans, dogs may require ophthalmalic care, for example in cases of scratches. However, this field also includes ocular surgery for cataracts or bascule-ment of the crystalline lens.

Bone surgery

It is not unusual for dogs to break bones in an accident. The length of surgery and the amount of care required will depend on the severity of the fracture. Included in this field are dysplasia operations, bone growth deficiencies, etc.

For most areas of specialization, the equipment required is very costly. This is why generalists often do not have all the equipment and when a dog requires specific care, he or she refers the dog to a specialist.

Traveling veterinarians

These veterinarians travel the world over to accompany expedition dogs, during dog sled races for example. They monitor the physical health of the dogs so that they can continue the race. Often, this entails treating muscle problems (pulled muscles, aches, cramps, etc.) or tendon problems (sprains, etc.). They also monitor food intake, which has to be adapted to the exercise conditions of the dog. The veterinarians do not follow along with the race. Rather they set up posts to check the dogs at points where they will necessarily pass.

Specialized Veterinary Assistants

Specialized veterinary assistants are an invaluable source of help for professional veterinarians. They have not always been called by this name; this terminology was officially defined in France in 1992. In the past, they were called assistants, veterinary nurses or animal health assistants. This field is mostly composed of women (99%).

An invaluable help at the front desk...

Assistants help relieve the veterinarian of some of his tasks. They contribute to the image the clients have of the office through their professionalism and by how warmly they greet client. Their manner has to be adapted to the character of each client, according to whether the client is outgoing or reserved, in a hurry or not; the assistant needs to know how to behave in any situation. Moreover, the assistant must serve as a "filter" between the veterinarian and the client as well as answer phone calls, whether a simple request for information or an emergency. They also handle the client files. They can fill out vaccination cards and send reminder cards about vaccinations. They monitor the supply of medicines available at the office, place orders and store the medicine according to

instructions of the veterinarian. The assistant is also extremely helpful during the examination when a medical act needs to be performed and it is difficult to restrain the animal.

Although he or she is not a surface technician, the assistant does help maintain and disinfect the examining rooms, which implies an understanding of the risk of contamination. In general, the veterinarian also entrusts the assistant with the responsibility of monitoring the hospital kennels. He or she administers the day-to-day care under the guidance of the veterinarian. The assistant is also expected to inform the veterinarian of any problems so that the veterinarian may take immediate action.

... and in surgery

The veterinary assistant generally assists in surgery especially during the pre and post-operation stages. He or she sterilizes the surgical tools and prepares them before every operation. He or she also prepares the animal for surgery by shaving a large area of the body where the veterinarian will operate, disinfects this area with soaps and solutions and then places the patient on the operating table. During the operation, the veterinary assistant is responsible for ensuring that there are no problems with the anesthesia and may also be in charge of handing the surgeon the tools he or she needs. He or she monitors the animal as it awakens from the anesthesia and cleans the surgical wound, applying a bandage if necessary. If need be, he or she also monitors animals that are on drips. In addition to this care, the assistant may assist the veterinarian in conducting biological and paraclinical analyses. However, the veterinary assistant must be familiar with the techniques of radiography in order to take plates on his or her own. The assistant may also take various samples, such as blood or urine samples or skin scrapes.

An advisory role

When helping the client, the assistant needs to gather information about the reason for the client's visit. If the client only wants information or to purchase food or medicine, he or she should not be made to wait needlessly. The assistant can give practical advice to the client about vaccination protocols for pets, deworming, diet and even hygiene. He or she can sell medicines, but only non-prescription medicines and anti-parasite products, and can also renew prescriptions for certain medicines such as those taken for life. The veterinary assistant is also responsible for setting up the waiting area and the display area for the sale of food and medicines. Clients often form their opinion of the veterinarian's office on the basis on the appearance of the waiting room.

Veterinary assistant training programs in France

Veterinary assistants are trained in specialized centers that fall under ministerial responsibility. Training involves both theory, which is taught at the center,

and practical experience in the form of internships. The theory portion comprises only 25% of the program; most learning takes place "on the job", depending on the needs of the veterinarian with whom the veterinary assistant does his or her internship. The assistant is not systematically hired on after the internship; nonetheless obtaining employment is one of the goals of this type of training. Training at the center is divided into two parts. The first part consists in learning about office and client management including reception and communication, business relations, secretarial and computer skills, accounting and English. In the second part, the future veterinary assistants learn about animal maintenance and management and about caring for the animal. Thus, they learn all about sanitizing the rooms, animal biology relating to pets – anatomy, physiology, reproduction and diet -, identifying and approaching the animal, recognizing breeds, ethology, setting and tattooing. In addition, they take surgery foundation classes, in other words, the basics of surgery, the different techniques for caring for and examining animals, as well veterinarian pharmaceutics and legislation. The first training project was launched in 1979. In 1987, the first CNFA (National Veterinary Assistant Training Center) was founded, offering part time training.

Training abroad

There are similar training centers throughout the world. In Great Britain, for example, a training program that confers a "nursing" degree has been in place for about thirty years. Before receiving an education at these schools, the future nurses work first at a veterinarian's office. Training is a two-year program and the student receives a State-recognized diploma.
In Denmark, the program is three years and is not administered by a school, but by an association. Approximately thirty students are trained each year. Training is similar in Germany and the Netherlands. In the United States, the "veterinary technicians" follow a two-year curriculum at a school that is linked to a veterinary school. They then do an internship in the area of clientele, which allows them to apply the knowledge they gained in the training program. At the end of the program, they receive a national certificate and a certificate from the State in which the diploma was earned. In some States, continuing education is mandatory.

Becoming a Veterinarian in France

Many youth are attracted to the firmly-rooted image of veterinary medicine and decide to pursue this career very early on. In order to purse this career, however, the candidate must overcome two obstacles.

Two obstacles to overcome

The first obstacle is to gain admission to one of the preparation classes for the entrance examination for veterinary schools. These classes are reserved for students who have passed their baccalaureate in science, following examination of their student records. Once admitted, the students take one to two years to prepare for the entrance examination.

The second obstacle occurs in two phases. First, there is a written examination that the student must pass in order to take the oral examination. The applicant is tested on very different subjects, including biology, physics, mathematics and also foreign languages and French. Approximately one fourth of the applicants are admitted each year based on competitive examination and are then placed in one of the four national schools in France. Every year, a certain quota of slots are reserved for students who have completed a DEUG (two-year university degree) or a BSTA (vocational training degree).

The first year of veterinary medicine courses correspond in fact to the second year of a university program and the preparatory class corresponds to the first year. The next three years correspond to the last two years of a degree program and provide a common initial training. The students study the various fields in veterinary medicine. At the end of these four years, the students obtain a diploma in basic veterinary medicine studies. They then have one year to write a thesis, after which, they earn the title of veterinary doctor and are authorized to practice.

Those who so desire may undertake postgraduate studies with a specialization, working toward a university doctoral degree in three years.

By training, the veterinarian is polyvalent. He or she must be a generalist, surgeon, dentist, ophthalmologist, dermatologist and even a behavioral scientist at the same time. Therein lies the difference with their human medicine counterparts, who generally specialize in one given field.

On-site training
One of the unique aspects of veterinary training in France is that along with their theoretical classes, the students also perform checkups, participate in surgical operations and monitor hospitalized animals of all species. Of course, they are supervised and advised by their professors. The students work in pairs with the older students teaching the younger ones. This shadowing system provides an important practical approach. In other European countries, veterinary medicine is taught in schools and universities where the course format is essentially lectures for the most part. Practical experience is gained by doing internships with established veterinarians.

In the United States and Canada, the system is closer to the French system and leaves much to individual initiative.

Finally, being a veterinarian today no longer simply means being an animal doctor. Some veterinarians work in laboratories, others work in agribusiness and still others work in the government or consumer

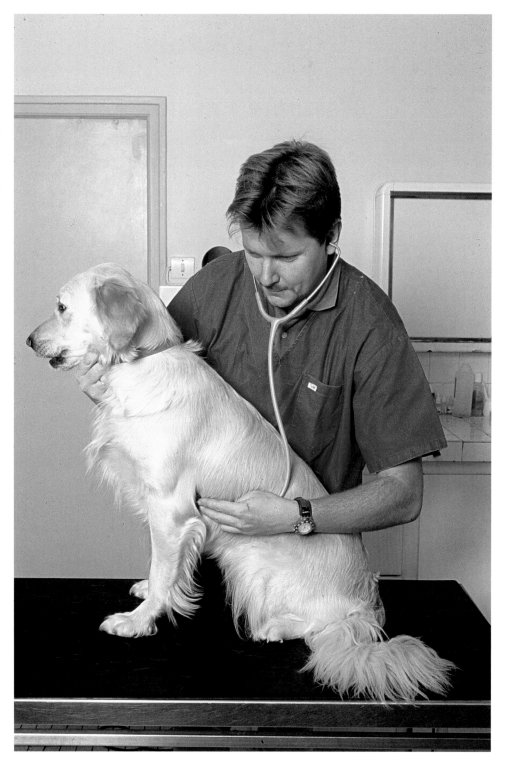

health sectors. Some specialize in particular fields such as sporting dogs or wild animals. They are not numerous, however, given the uncertain employment possibilities. Finally, others choose a military career and become veterinarians with the fire department for example, where they save animals in danger.
The field of veterinary medicine has evolved much over the past decades. On the one hand, it has evolved because the relationship between humans and animals has changed and on the other hand, it has evolved because this training opens doors to many other fields.

Raising Dogs

DESIGNING A KENNEL

EXAMPLE OF LOGICALLY LAID OUT FACILITY

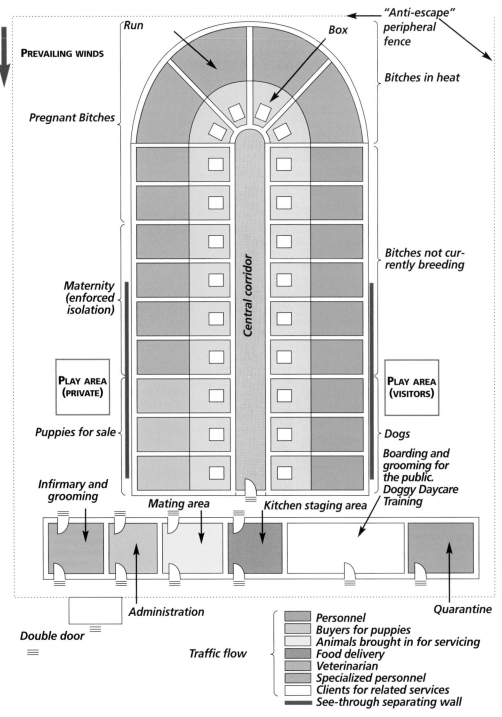

PREVAILING WINDS

Run — *Box* — "Anti-escape" peripheral fence

Bitches in heat

Pregnant Bitches

Bitches not currently breeding

Maternity (enforced isolation)

Central corridor

PLAY AREA (PRIVATE)

PLAY AREA (VISITORS)

Puppies for sale

Dogs

Boarding and grooming for the public. Doggy Daycare Training

Infirmary and grooming

Mating area — *Kitchen staging area*

Administration

Quarantine

Double door

Traffic flow

▉	Personnel
▉	Buyers for puppies
▉	Animals brought in for servicing
▉	Food delivery
▉	Veterinarian
▉	Specialized personnel
▢	Clients for related services
▬	See-through separating wall

Architecture of a Kennel

The design of a kennel must not only meet legal requirements, but must also be laid out in such a way so as to facilitate the daily care of a group of animals:

- There must be space for staff, dogs, delivery personnel, veterinarians and visitors to come and go while minimizing the risk of contamination from section to section;
- A contingency plan needs to be in place to respond to emergency situations, such as a parasitic or infectious outbreak;
- Prevailing winds should be taken into consideration;
- The facility must be easy to maintain and cost-effective;
- Disturbances must be kept to a minimum;
- Space may be added for other activities, such as boarding, training or grooming;
- The kennel must be able to expand in order to meet demand;
- Evacuation plans need to be in place in case of fire.

Before putting the design down on paper, it is helpful to think through the daily process of raising dogs. This form of "dynamic design" can be very useful. Priority must be given to preventing the spread of infection. Certain areas should be as far apart as possible. For example, the nursery should not be near the infirmary.

Areas designed specifically for dogs at different stages of life (birth, growth, adulthood, pregnancy, nursing, old age) and in varying degrees of health (suspected illness, sick dogs, contagious dogs, etc.) are required. The layout of these areas must be carefully planned to meet the daily requirements of each individual dog. The following guidelines apply:

- Areas likely to be contaminated by people or dogs entering the facility (areas housing dogs to be observed, boarded, trained or groomed) must be isolated and have separate entrances.
- Areas reserved for breeding, so-called "clean" areas, should be situated away from the areas where contamination may occur. The facility should be laid out in the following manner:

- The kitchen should be in a central area so that meals may be distributed quickly (and thus limit barking);
- Living areas should be assigned based on the risk of infection of the dog occupying that space.

For example, the cervix of whelping bitches and bitches in heat is open, making them particularly susceptible to uterine infections.

The immune system of newborn puppies is not fully developed. Therefore, newborns should be protected from possible infection introduced from the outside.

Layout of the various areas should take cleaning requirements into consideration. At risk areas (maternity) should be cleaned first, followed by living areas for adult dogs. Areas likely to be contaminated (infirmary, quarantine) should be cleaned last. In this way, germs are not spread from contaminated areas into the rest of the kennel.

The most susceptible dogs (pregnant dogs, puppies) should be lodged along the periphery, whereas potentially diseased dogs (dogs in quarantine or coming in from the outside) should be placed downwind from the rest of the kennel.

Another prudent step for preventing contamination is to set up two separate exercise areas, one for boarders and dogs brought in from the outside, and one for dogs being raised at the kennel.

A well laid-out kennel will resemble a puzzle, with each section, area or room representing a piece fitting logically into the greater whole.

When designing a kennel, the following questions should be asked:

- Do you have to walk through the entire kennel to show a puppy to a potential buyer?
- Will the prevailing winds carry germs brought in by outside visitors into the breeding area?
- Where will waste be eliminated?
- What daily circuits will be made by personnel—cleaning, distribution of meals, etc.?
- Where will noise and odors spread?
- Has the kennel been designed in such a way that the entire kennel can be viewed from one area?

Choice Of Materials

Many factors need to be considered when choosing the building materials for a kennel, including cost, durability (resistance to wear, rust, fire, regular disinfecting and vermin), danger to the animal if licked, touched or struck by the animal, insulating ability, waterproof characteristics and ease of disassembly. Buildings that must be regularly heated and disinfected (box, maternity area, central corridor, quarantine, infirmary) require insulating layers covered with waterproof materials.

Dog Runs

Floor

The floor of dog runs must be made of materials that will not retain urine or wash water. It must be non-slip, durable enough to resist detergents and daily scrubbing and disinfecting, and be as smooth as possible.

The dusty surface of plain cement can cause skin allergies wherever the dog comes into contact with the floor (pads, elbows, hocks, genitals, sternum).

Therefore, vibrated concrete is a better choice. It resists humidity better, is less likely to crumble or chip, and causes fewer allergies. Smooth concrete (with ridges draining toward gutters) is also a good choice. For ease of cleaning, the floor should be waterproofed with a resin epoxy.

Separating walls

Separating walls must be washable and solid, so that a dog standing up on his hind legs cannot come into direct contact with neighboring dogs. This decreases the possibility of spreading diseases such as kennel cough and warts (typically in the mouth) to the entire kennel.

Health authorities recommend that the junction of wall and floor be rounded rather than square (ninety-degree angle).

Gutters must never pass through the dog runs. Toxic products used to clean and sanitize the gutters must be kept away from the animals.

Cement blocks are not a good choice for this application, because they retain water and the lower portion of the blocks is an excellent environment for growing mold and mildew.

Smooth concrete may be used if covered with waterproof vinyl paint or chlorinated rubber. A mixture of lime and white cement spread over the concrete is also effective. The upper portion of the wall may be of welded mesh, which is easier to disinfect than woven mesh. The best choice is vertical stainless or galvanized steel bars.

Ideally, the walls of each individual run should be made of thick, unbreakable glass allowing dogs to see each other (and allowing staff to keep an eye on all dogs in the area at once) without risking contamination. Maintaining this type of wall is also much easier. However, this type of construction is expensive.

Use of mesh or bars for the entire separating wall is not acceptable unless empty space is left between the walls of each individual run to prevent direct contact and to limit the spread of air-borne elements. However, this type of wall is not as effective for preventing the spread of air-borne contaminants, nor does it protect the dogs from cold or drafts. Even in the absence of a breeze, just a simple cough or sneeze can spray secretions from the nose and throat up to 1.5 m.

Exterior wall

The exterior wall of each run should be made of stainless or galvanized steel bars with a door providing access for cleaning and allowing the dog access to play areas. Bars, though more expensive than other materials, can appear cagelike to uninformed visitors.

However, bars have fewer places for the dog to bite or paw than wire mesh, and therefore reduce the likelihood of injury.

Roof

A roof must cover at least a portion of the run in order to provide shade and protection from the elements. It also keeps the area between the box and the run dry.

Several different materials make good roofs:

- retractable blinds (expensive);
- aluminum roofing – not aesthetically pleasing, but reflects the heat and light of the sun in summer and reduces radiated heat;
- sheets of asbestos cement, which provide better insulation, cost less, and are more appealing to the eye, but can break down over time as a result of contact with water;
- fiberglass or plastic sheets.

Boxes

Boxes should be part of the heated central corridor. For this reason, they must be insulated.

Box floors

Cellular or no-fines concrete (rated at K = 0.8) improves insulation of the floor. The manufacturer lists the K rating on the product. The lower the K rating, the better its insulating qualities.

This type of flooring can be reinforced by pouring the concrete over a layer of compacted sand.

With this type of construction, the floor can be heated without significant heat loss.

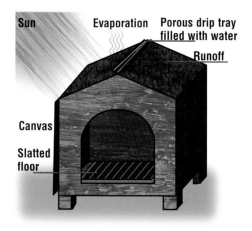

EXAMPLE OF IMPROVISED COOLING SYSTEM FOR HOT DAYS

Sun Evaporation Porous drip tray filled with water Runoff Canvas Slatted floor

Roof

Since the boxes are part of the heated central corridor, roofs are optional. If there is no roof on the box, it is easier to monitor dogs from the central corridor.

However, if a roof is installed, sandwich panels with an insulating layer in the middle effectively limit heat loss.

Fiberglass is likely to attract rodents and retain humidity and condensation. Better choices are expanded polystyrene, polyurethane foam or a combination of reflective films and insulating pads, such as those used in the aeronautics industry.

Walls

The wall separating the box from the run must provide not only heat insulation but also reduce noise levels. Sandwich panels with cork in the center are an excellent choice.

The opening from the box into the run must be as small as possible to limit heat loss. A galvanized steel doorframe will reduce damage caused by chewing. Since the walls must be washed and disinfected regularly, they must be waterproof. The sandwich panel should include a moisture barrier of kraft paper to limit condensation and keep out rodents.

Doghouse

The doghouse must be easy to disassemble for cleaning. For this reason, untreated wood is not recommended, despite its excellent insulation qualities. Moreover, an untreated wood construction typically lasts only three years or so.

Sleeping Area

Disposable bedding must be soft, absorbent, provide insulation, and not cause intestinal blockages if ingested.

Straw bedding can cause allergies when inhaled and can lead to mite (chigger) or insect infestation (darkling beetles reproduce at temperatures above 18 degrees C, fleas, etc.) Moreover, storing this type of bedding is a fire hazard.

Newsprint is a better option. Waste can be picked up more easily if this type of bedding is used, reducing the amount of water required for cleaning. Though the newsprint may slightly discolor light-coated dogs, newsprint is still an excellent choice of bedding.

Sawdust provides excellent insulating qualities, shines the coats of long-haired dogs, and can be easily burned.

Easy to disinfect, rubber mats are the most hygienic and economical choice.

Fire Safety

There are certain building regulations that apply to all public buildings: Fire extinguishers must be installed and inspected regularly; wiring must be inspected, etc. Other aspects of construction and layout are left to common sense. The kennel owner can work with the local fire department to determine what

fire safety measures should be taken, such as where to place water sources.

During construction of the kennel, the breeder and architect should select fire-resistant building materials and pay careful attention to their characteristics. They should consider whether the material is non-flammable, combustible and stable when heated by fire, and whether it is designed as a flame shield or firebreak.

Designing a Living Area

After a general plan has been drawn up and the legal conditions fulfilled, living areas can be built based on the following provisions:

- health and environmental requirements; and
- facilities for maintaining, heating, and supervising the kennel and distributing meals.

These provisions relate to French legislation but are of technical interest to breeders from any country.

The Double Pen/Run and Central Hallway System

The combination of an inside pen plus an outside run is currently the best system (except for pack dogs).
It is designed to accommodate two dogs who are hierarchically compatible.
Dogs kept alone in a run become bored and may develop tics and bad habits or exhibit stereotypical behaviors (constant pacing, paw licking, chewing, self mutilation) that harm not only their health but also their productivity (decreased fertility, weight loss, etc.).
Conversely, the more dogs kept in a single living area, the greater the risk of contamination and hierarchical conflict, and the lower the chances of reproduction for non-dominant males and bitches.
Therefore, the happy medium is generally two dogs per run.

There has been much debate over the ideal surface area for runs. Andersen's norms (3 m2 per 2.5 cm at the withers) are difficult to apply in dog breeding kennels since they correspond to 70 m2 for a medium-sized dog!
In addition, most dogs do not use this much space and develop inhibitions due to a lack of contact with the breeder and other dogs.
In fact, living space depends on each dog's temperament, since it is based on the dog's escape distance (the distance beyond which he will run from a stranger) and his critical zone (the distance beyond which he is forced to attack or submit).

It is possible to decrease run size when a private area (pen and doghouse) is provided in which the dog can

take shelter, hide and feel safe from attack. Modern doghouses are based on this idea, which is essential to the dog's comfort.
As a general rule, the length of the run must be at least twice its width.
The minimum surface area is 4 m2 for small-sized breeds, 6 m2 for medium-sized breeds, and 8 m2 for large-sized breeds.

Keeping Dogs Comfortable

Most dogs like to stand guard on the roof of their doghouse when it is level. The roof is an ideal observation point for satisfying their curiosity and eluding enemies.
It is a good idea to leave a few toys and easy-to-clean objects for canine residents, especially if they do not have regular access to a play area or agility course.
A retractable roof makes it possible to create a shady area in periods of intense heat by reflecting a portion of the sun's rays.

The surface area of the pen should be greater than 1.5 m2 for small-sized breeds and double that for large-sized breeds. Since hot air rises, most heat will be lost through the ceiling. For this reason, a fresh air vent should be located at the bottom of the pens, and stale warm air in the pens and common hallway should be forced upward (through exhaust vents).
The purpose of doghouses is to protect dogs from climatic variation (heat, cold, rain, freezes, wind, etc.). Entryway must be free of sharp angles and ringed with rust-free metal to prevent chewing. They must also be raised off the ground (20 to 30 cm) and separated from the walls and roof, in order to facilitate cleaning and prevent heat loss through conduction.

Convenience for the Breeder

With stable doors between the pens and central hallway, the breeder can simply open the upper doors to supervise the dogs and provide food and water without having to enter the pens.
With sectional overhead doors, the breeder can let dogs out into their runs in the morning by activating the doors from the hallway. Feeding, on the other hand, attracts the dogs back into their pens so the breeder can close the doors behind them and keep them inside for the night. This doorway system also makes it possible to evacuate animals rapidly in the case of a fire.

To facilitate cleaning, breeders should invest from the start in materials that resist corrosion, acid and alkaline disinfectants, freezes, heat and strong pressure (Karcher-type high-pressure pumps).
A slope of 2 to 4% from one side to the other toward the collecting gutters is generally sufficient for draining urine, rainwater and cleaning products.
With this setup, runs can be cleaned when the dogs are inside and pens can be cleaned when the dogs are outside.

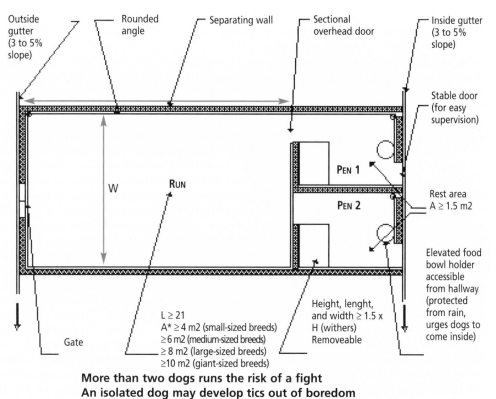

Outside gutter (3 to 5% slope)

Rounded angle

Separating wall

Sectional overhead door

Inside gutter (3 to 5% slope)

Stable door (for easy supervision)

W

RUN

PEN 1

PEN 2

Rest area A ≥ 1.5 m2

Gate

L ≥ 21
A* ≥ 4 m2 (small-sized breeds)
≥ 6 m2 (medium-sized breeds)
≥ 8 m2 (large-sized breeds)
≥10 m2 (giant-sized breeds)

Height, lenght, and width ≥ 1.5 x H (withers) Removeable

Elevated food bowl holder accessible from hallway (protected from rain, urges dogs to come inside)

L = length
W = width
H = height at the withers
A = surface area ≥ greater than or equal to
(*) Andersen's norms (3 m2 per 2.5 cm at the withers) are inapplicable in practice.

**More than two dogs runs the risk of a fight
An isolated dog may develop tics out of boredom**

It also gives the breeder peace of mind, since he can frequently observe the behavior and condition of all his residents without bothering them.

A panoramic kennel observation area is recommended so that the breeder can detect at a glance any signs of incompatibility between dogs, abnormal behavior, etc.

Controlling the Pen Environment

Ventilation

By adjusting ventilation, it is possible to maintain the quality of the ambient air by preventing the accumulation of irritating or foul-smelling gases, limiting the risk of airborne contamination and influencing air temperature.

Gases move based on their temperature and density in relation to the air. Ammonia (produced by the fermentation of excrement), which is lighter than air, tends to accumulate at higher layers, while carbon dioxide (about 15 liters per hour are exhaled by a dog weighing 20 kg), which is heavier than air, stagnates in lower layers. Ambient odors can therefore be used to detect and localize ventilation problems. Ideally, no odors or drafts should be detectable in dog breeding kennels. Dogs can tolerate a maximum of 3,500 ppm (3.5 l/m3) of carbon dioxide and 15 ppm of ammonia.

For this reason, ventilation must ensure air renewal

about five times per hour in winter and up to thirty times per hour in summer to eliminate odors.

Air speed can be evaluated very simply by using a candle. When a lighted candle is brought into the pen, the flame should vacillate slightly, indicating an air speed less than 30 centimeters per second or less than 1 km/h.

When animals are absent, air circulation can be evaluated by using fumigants, which show where air is entering and exiting so that air vents and the heating system can be adjusted.

To control air ventilation in the pens without expensive techniques, such as mechanical ventilation, it is most important to situate openings properly relative to dominant winds, ensure that joints are air-tight, and regulate the points of ventilation and exhaust.

Humidity

A lack of humidity in kennel air is very rare, since the air exhaled by dogs already contains water vapor. Ideally, a kennel should have about 65% humidity. Unfortunately, humidity is difficult to control, since it depends essentially on climatic conditions.

Still, humidity has little effect on canine health and heat regulation when the temperature is maintained at 15 to 20°C.

At higher temperatures, excessive humidity limits the effectiveness of pulmonary perspiration in dogs, the main factor regulating their body temperature. Conversely, if the temperature is too low, excessive humidity increases heat loss.

Without a hygrometer, breeders can at least check for the absence of odors and condensation on walls and windows. The presence of water droplets on these surfaces indicates excessive humidity that promotes the development of mildew and certain respiratory and skin diseases (mycosis, strawberry footrot).

In addition, the tiny water droplets that form fog are the main carriers of odors. Excessive use of the high-pressure pump can cause this.

To reduce these nuisances, limit the amount of cleaning water used (by first collecting or vacuuming out the largest pieces of waste), avoid wetting porous or permeable materials (this may cause a gradual graining out of moisture), and clean runs in sunny weather.

Temperature

After puppies are born, they slowly (in three weeks to a month) acquire the ability to regulate body temperature (homeothermy) and thus fight against cold or excessive heat by expending additional energy. Each dog has a neutral heat zone based on age and breed, that is, a range of ambient temperature in which the animal will not need to expend any extra energy to regulate body temperature. Therefore, to optimize a dog's performance and spare him from wasting energy, breeders should try to provide an average pen temperature between 15 to 20°C and keep daily fluctuations below 2°C, if possible. However, this temperature range must be adjusted based on the following subtleties:

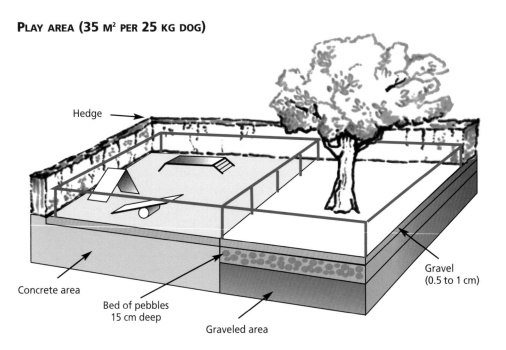

Hedge

Concrete area

Bed of pebbles
15 cm deep

Graveled area

Gravel
(0.5 to 1 cm)

- Since dogs have a very limited ability to perspire, they are better equipped to fight cold than heat. Panting is one sign of excessive heat.

- Certain breeds, including Nordic dogs, are naturally better adapted to fighting cold, given their thick layer of fur, their physical makeup (weight vs. surface area), their behavior and their energy efficiency.
- Most often, it is not the temperature itself, but rather extreme variations in temperature that cause respiratory disorders in dogs. Heat should therefore be turned up and down gradually in order to minimize thermal variation.

- Pen temperature should be measured not only with a thermometer but also with relation to humidity and air circulation. Once again, intense humidity magnifies the effects of excessive heat or cold. An increase in air speed will temper the effects of heat but aggravate the effects of cold: An acceleration of 10 cm/s or 0.4 km/h, equals a drop in temperature of about 1°C.

Therefore, and in contrast to the norms decreed by departmental health regulations, there is no ideal temperature for all dogs. For this reason, make sure that dogs always have a way to escape the consequences of cold or heat.

Lighting

The nyctohemeral period (the light-dark cycle) has proven effects on the onset and timing of heats in some female animals (cats, horses, sheep, etc.) and on psyche and mood (in humans). So far, no studies in this field have proven the effects on dogs. Still, one may logically extrapolate that dogs need a minimum of twelve to fourteen hours of light per day for their sexual and emotional well-being.
Of equal importance is the essential role of light in the development of vision in puppies. Complete, pro-

longed darkness in the stage when a puppy's eyes first open can lead to permanent blindness. Darkness also promotes the spread of many pests (germs, fungus, and most insects and rodents). For this reason the duration of natural light should be extended in winter by using electric lighting in pens for several hours after dusk.

Stress

Dogs need a rich, varied environment to keep them alert.

The absence of stimuli can lead to boredom and behavioral disorders such as dermatitis from licking (beginning most often on the left paw), bulimia (excessive eating followed by purging), and potomania (excessive drinking).

Conversely, excessive sensory stimulation from which dogs cannot escape can lead to disorders such as weight loss, diarrhea, behavioral and reproductive problems, poor socialization, etc.
It is therefore necessary to strike a balance between the total absence of stimuli and overstimulation.

This balance can be established through a regular schedule for feeding, visits, playtime and maintenance of the facility, as well as choosing certain auditory and visual stimuli.

Even though sound perception in dogs (65 to 15,000 Hz) and humans is very different, playing the radio is still useful in socializing puppies, drowning out external noise, and reducing stress in kennel personnel. With all reserves, we must mention studies by Dr. Diottalevi (an Italian veterinarian) which show that most dogs prefer opera and rhythmic folk music!

Understanding color perception in dogs is helpful in

choosing paint color. Even though it is now well-established that dogs perceive blue and green shades better than humans (as opposed to red), and that dogs see better than us in dim light, it has not been proven that paint color has any influence whatsoever on canine behavior in breeding kennels.

Reducing Kennel Nuisances

Declared or authorized breeding kennels are classified facilities, that is, potential sources of environmental nuisances. For this reason, kennel staff must work hard to limit the facility's impact on the neighborhood.

This is an area where what is good for the breeder is also good for the environment:

- Good sound insulation maintains calm both in the surrounding neighborhood and inside the kennel by reducing the factors that cause barking (hallway noise, alarms, other dogs barking, etc.).
- Meticulous hygiene both limits pollution and makes the kennel less attractive to insects and rodents.

Noise

Noise is the most common cause of lawsuits involving dog kennels. Barking is the source of nearly 20% of the complaints involving neighborhood problems.

These disputes set breeders against their neighbors but can also pit kennel staff against their employer if daily sound exposure is greater than 90 decibels.

From the start, the kennel building plans should take into account how the kennel's location and setup will affect how the noise of barking will carry.
Building a kennel at a higher altitude, far from any human residence, road or railway, will effectively curb most barking.

In addition, through good training dogs can be limited to a few necessary barks (for guarding, hunting, tracking, and searching through wreckage).

For this, it is necessary to:

- accustom dogs to a regular schedule of kennel maintenance, meals and customer visiting hours;
- always have visitors accompanied by a staff member to whom the dogs are accustomed;
- limit visual, auditory and scent stimuli from both outside and inside (such as the odors and noises of food preparation in the kitchen). Installing an impervious fence around the kennel is recommended for this purpose;
- keep confined dogs from seeing dogs in the play area (with a separating hedge);
- house dogs in compatible pairs and separate them in the case of repeated conflict;
- distribute meals individually and in sufficient quantities to prevent fighting over food, offering meals first

to the noisiest dogs who, consequently, should be housed near the kitchen;
- keep to a minimum the time necessary for meal preparation and distribution (using dry foods, distributing food using a rolling cart); and
- at night, confine dogs to a blind pen, with the opening of the doghouse facing the central hallway.

If, despite all these precautions, nuisance barking persists, unconditioning training can be used. Currently, there are two methods for stopping undesirable behavior:

- pain (use of a painful stimulus); and
- surprise (use of a so-called "disruptive" stimulus).

These two principles are the basis of various types of "anti-bark" collars that use ultrasound, electric shock and even citronella spray. It is best to beware of devices that use only electricity or ultrasound, since the punishment threshold for these sources is very close to the pain threshold. These devices are only moderately effective (reducing barking by 30 to 50%) and present many contraindications that have led them to be banned in a growing number of countries (Switzerland, Scandinavia, Italy, etc.), since such methods can aggravate pre-existing aggression or anxiety.

- Anti-bark collars with citronella spray punish barking by releasing an odor that is unpleasant to dogs. This sudden discharge is just as surprising to dogs in the form of auditory stimuli (ultrasound). With these devices, the dog must first make the connection between barking and unpleasant sensations and then learn to associate wearing a collar with not being allowed to bark. This takes only a few days for dogs of average ability.
The proven effectiveness of these devices is close to 80%. Failure tends to occur in dogs with behavioral disorders. For this reason, it is best to focus on the cause (aggression toward other dogs, separation anxiety) rather than trying to eliminate the consequences. Dogs who resist this type of collar may exhibit self-destructive behavior if trainers continue to punish them for barking without eliminating the cause.

These collars should not be worn all the time and should naturally be used first on canine "agitators".
- Some ingenious breeders have invented an automatic system consisting of a barking sensor (microphone) and a valve that causes punishment to rain down from the sky (a stream of water or any other surprising "punishment") on offenders.

Once unconditioning has been achieved, it is enough to replace all these systems with fake equipment (a collar that is not loaded, a showerhead without a valve) to maintain the results of training.

Odors
Odors are carried by tiny water droplets, evaporate with heat, and are dispersed by wind. Unpleasant ken-

nel odors can thus be controlled by maintaining adequate humidity, temperature, and ventilation while of course limiting the source of odors related to food and poor hygiene.

Preventing unpleasant odors
- Providing highly digestible foods facilitates elimination and limits the amount of excrement produced. It is not uncommon that switching to a highly digestible ("premium") food reduces excrement production by one half.
To prove this, the breeder need only observe the consistency of stools and weigh them: With an adapted food, 45 to 65 grams of stools are produced for every 100 grams of ingested food.

- Collecting or vacuuming out the largest pieces of excrement prior to cleaning reduces the amount of water used and thereby prevents unpleasant odors from evaporating into the air.
- Waterproofing materials limits leaks that cause a constant build-up of humidity.
- When possible, rely on the sun to dry runs faster, especially since the sun's ultraviolet rays have considerable health-promoting qualities. This is why it is preferable to design south-facing runs.
- Use a high-pressure steam pump to completely remove encrusted organic residue. This kind of pump destroys most infectious agents, even in the tightest corners (including parasite eggs and bacterial spores), and leaves surfaces nearly dry after use.
- Clean runs one to two hours after feeding, since dogs generally defecate in the hour just after a meal.
- Clean more frequently in humid or stormy weather (when odors stagnate).
- Include a collecting pit of adequate capacity (prefabricated pit or covered, buried cement form with a capacity of about 3,000 liters for forty dogs). Keep it separate from the water discharge circuit and have it drained regularly by a specialized company.
- Ensure the proper functioning of the upper-level exhaust system in covered parts of the kennel (pens, central hallway), since unpleasant odors (ammonia, methane, foul-smelling gases) tend to move upward.

The fight against unpleasant odors
Deodorizers are often sprays consisting of heavy droplets that trap odors as they fall downward. These products are therefore only temporarily effective.
It is preferable to use a thermal mister which, with its small diameter (1 to 5 microns) and use of tiny, heated droplets, diffuses antiseptic particles in suspension more widely at higher levels and is longer lasting.

Using essential oils in this kind of device can also help prevent respiratory illness and eliminate insects (given the insecticidal properties of terpenes). For example, an emulsion of 1% essential oils per 1 ml/m3 can be used in the presence of animals to effectively deodorize the air.

Thermal misters can also be used to disinfect closed-

off rooms (whelping area, quarantine room, infirmary) when animals are removed to clean and disinfect the facility. Devices can be shared with other breeders to save money.

Running away
Installing a peripheral fence around the kennel keeps dogs in and rodents out, as long as norms for ground depth and chain link size are obeyed.

An anti-escape scheme (elevation) is not really essential, except under prison-like conditions. Elevation may actually be more useful in keeping intruders from getting inside the kennel.

Insects and mites

Attracted by the presence of dogs, stored food, stagnant water and excrement and characterized by a life cycle linked closely to ambient temperature, these pests cause considerable problems, both for:

- the environment (flies, the transmission of zoonoses); and
- the kennel, as carriers of disease and parasites and through their own destructive habits (invasion of thermal insulation by beetles, tunneling through woodwork, etc.).

To the extent possible, openings to the central hallway, whelping area, quarantine room, infirmary and kitchen should be protected by mosquito nets with mesh no greater than 2 mm. Doors should be protected by strip curtains.
Avoid unintentionally creating areas that promote the development of insects or mites, such as:

- Needless sources of stagnant water (puddles, cast-off containers, etc.);
- Hot and humid areas: For insects, an average of 100 to 150 days separate egg laying from the appearance of adult forms at a constant temperature of 20°C. If

"ANTI-ESCAPE" PERIPHERAL FENCE

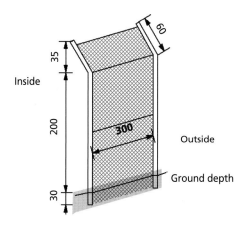

this temperature is raised 10°C, the cycle is reduced to a mere twenty-one days. Conversely, at temperatures below 12°C, most cycles are interrupted until the return of warm weather;
- straw;
- attics and false ceilings;
- food stored in excessive quantities or for too long, unless kept in air-tight containers. To the extent possible, separate the food storage area from the meal preparation area and avoid keeping any unnecessary items (baskets, cleaning implements, etc.). It is important to use stored food according to the "first in, first out" method.
- wastebaskets, which should be as small as possible so that they must be emptied frequently.

Actinic lamps that zap insects electrically are perfect for closed areas. However, they are insufficient outside, where it is often necessary to use chemical insecticides.

Insecticides should be chosen based on their effective period and non-toxicity to dogs through licking or contact. Some substances, including pyrethroids and carbamates, are safe to use around warm-blooded animals. Still, be careful to prevent these substances from coming into contact with bitches in the early stages of gestation (given the risk of fetal deformation associated with carbaryl).

These products can be used as a preventative (before the insect season, when animals are removed for cleaning and disinfecting specific areas) or as a curative during the summer as often as required, based on their effective period.

The insecticide should be released after the animals have been removed, beginning with the ceilings, then the walls, and finally the floors. It is important to thoroughly mist the following:

- woodwork, especially when worm-eaten;
- false ceilings and false floors, where darkness promotes larval development; and
- shelving made of open hollow tubing, which is perfect for insect nests. Dead insects should be vacuumed out before disinfecting, and the vacuum bag should be emptied regularly, unless a piece of insecticidal collar is always kept inside, a practice followed by many breeders.

The most commonly used products in breeding areas are paints containing insect repellent or insecticide. These paints, mixed with kaolin (a bleaching agent which increases the product's effective period) and a type of glue (to prevent bleaching the coat of dogs who rub against it), are applied with a brush or roller, especially to areas around openings and light sources.
It is helpful to vary the products used, in order to keep insects from developing resistance to a certain product.

Since all insecticides authorized in France are biodegradable, they are not effective for the long-term treatment of collecting pits. For this purpose, adding waste oil (one half liter for every 10 m3 of excrement) once every two months is generally sufficient to prevent eggs and larva from developing without excessively polluting the environment.

If these measures are insufficient, they can be supplemented with adhesive insect traps or traditional fly tape.

Nosing coated with insecticidal varnish and placed beneath doors keeps crawling insects out.
The geographic distribution of some diseases depends on where their carriers proliferate (biotope).

In enzootic disease zones, it is therefore prudent to take certain basic precautions adapted to regional risk factors:

- Avoid dark colors, which attract and camouflage insects;
- Bring dogs inside their pens at dusk (when carrier mosquitoes come out);
- Select elevated structures (sand flies, which carry Leishmania, fly at an altitude of less than one meter);
- Be doubly cautious during the reproductive season of carriers;
- Protect dogs from bites, especially around the nose-bridge, remembering that insecticidal collars rarely protect the entire body, especially in large-breed dogs. Still, certain acaricidal collars are very effective against ticks, scabies and chiggers; and
- As a last resource, keep in mind the possibility of antiparasitic vaccination (piroplasmosis) or primary chemoprophylaxis (piroplasmosis, Leishmania, dirofilariasis), although difficult, expensive, and only temporarily effective in dog breeding kennels.

Rodents
Rodents are potential carriers of disease through their bites, excrement, urine, fleas and even their flesh.

Of these diseases, only leptospirosis is still a problem for dogs.

Actually, the nuisances caused by rodents are centered around the depredation of:

- thermal insulation materials (roof garrets, etc.);
- electrical equipment (fire risk, etc.); and
- walls (cracks, etc.).

In addition, the amount of stolen food is far from negligible, given that rats consume their own weight in food each day, on average.
Naturally, cleanliness and the absence of leftovers are essential in effective prevention of infestation.
Next, identify local species (sewer rats, attic rats, mice, garden dormice, muskrats, etc.) in order to adapt prevention techniques to their way of life.

The depth at which peripheral fencing is set into the ground, the size of chain links and the approaches to food storage buildings should be adapted to rodents' size and digging habits.
Steps at least 30 cm high can effectively protect the entry to the kitchen.

It is helpful to seal or fence all openings (metal links smaller than 15 mm, sewage pipes, ridged roofing).
In addition, avoid letting climbing plants grow along walls, since rodents can use them as ladders, and they attract insects and birds.
Finally, consider a "sanitation contract" with a specialized company who can identify pests and set traps in their potential paths.
The best and simplest method is still, when possible, to use natural methods including cats, although this introduces the problem of contact between cats and dogs!

Most rodenticides are poisonous anticoagulants that cause fatal internal bleeding in animals that ingest them. Their delayed effect (sometimes over three days), which counters rodents' usual mistrust, explains why it is rare to find dead rodents near bait. Since these products are palatable and toxic to most species (including human children!), they must be used with extreme caution. Note that they are also indirectly toxic to cats who eat poisoned rodents. Consequently, they should not be used when cats are employed to eliminate rats.

Before using rodenticide, it is a good idea to take the following precautions:

• Identify the species being targeted, and adapt the bait to the feeding habits of the rodent being eliminated:

- wheat for black attic rats;
- oat groats for mice, which eat only the inside of grains;
- carrots or beets placed at burrow openings for muskrats, which usually eat roots; and
- fruit, dry cakes, nuts or gingerbread for garden dormice and dormice).

• Carefully follow the manufacturer's instructions.

• Do not handle these products without gloves, in order to avoid picking up suspicious odors.

• Refill bait stations every two to three days.

• Alternate products (risk of habituation).

• Place bait in dark places (light-sensitive products).

A final note: Every year, doctors and veterinarians treat cases of rodenticide poisoning. For obvious safety reasons, pest elimination is strictly regulated. To avoid error, it is obviously preferable to use the services of a professional.

Hygiene and Disinfection

Following basic rules of hygiene is still the best way to prevent most pests.

For this reason, kennel staff should first master the general principles of cleaning and disinfection and then learn how to select the most effective products for the purpose.

General principles of hygiene

Keeping a sanitary kennel is a constant struggle against the enemies (bacteria, viruses, mildew, parasites) that threaten dogs, food, drinking water and buildings.

These nuisances are transported by carriers (excrement, boots, wind, insects, rodents, etc.).

They can be combated through preventive or curative physical means (heat, ultraviolet light, high pressure, etc.) or chemical means (detergents, disinfectants). These methods provide many ways to prevent contamination.

Naturally, it is impossible to keep the kennel completely sterile at all times (the complete absence of germs). It is possible only to reach a balance between the germ level of the kennel and the natural defenses of dogs. This can be done by maintaining facilities that are unfavorable to the development of disease-causing agents. In a favorable environment, bacteria attach themselves to surfaces (adhesion factors) and multiply exponentially (every bacterium divides in two in each generation).

Cleaning involves removing encrusted organic matter using detergent and elbow grease.

Cleaning is followed by disinfection, aimed at limiting the development of remaining germs (bacteriostatic and virustatic effects, etc.) or destroying most of the sensitive germs (bactericidal and virucidal properties, etc.). A well-chosen disinfectant has a range of effectiveness that covers the germs in question; for example, it should destroy 99% of the germs on the first use and 99% of the remaining 1% in the second use before they can reproduce.

Simply omitting one cleaning sequence (such as during a weekend break) can lead to the development of dangerous levels of disease-causing germs.

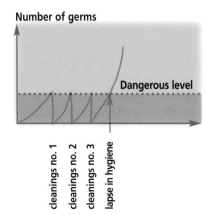

Number of germs

Dangerous level

cleanings no. 1
cleanings no. 2
cleanings no. 3
lapse in hygiene

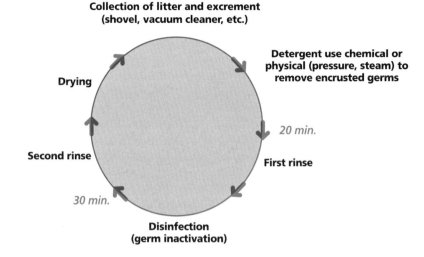

Collection of litter and excrement
(shovel, vacuum cleaner, etc.)

Detergent use chemical or physical (pressure, steam) to remove encrusted germs

Drying

20 min.

Second rinse

First rinse

30 min.

Disinfection
(germ inactivation)

Knowing the following principles can help readers to better plan their kennel hygiene:

- "An ounce of prevention is worth a pound of cure". There is no shortcut to good hygiene.
- Due to scratches and unevenness, an apparently smooth surface may have a much greater real surface area.

This explains why materials like stainless steel and tile are much easier to disinfect than rusted metal and wooden blocks, which give germs a much greater opportunity for shelter and adhesion.

• Some physical factors, such as temperature (both cold and heat), humidity and light (UV rays) can inhibit the spread of bacteria.

Remember as a general rule that warm temperatures, humidity and the lack of sun are unfavorable to good hygiene.

It is thus helpful, for example, to reinforce the activity of most disinfectants by diluting them in hot water and using them on runs during sunny periods.

• A good cleaning without disinfection is better than disinfection without cleaning. By making the water "more slippery", detergents (such as soap) help to remove organic matter and thereby expose germs to disinfectants. Conversely, many disinfectants lose their effectiveness in the presence of organic matter (excrement, dirt).

When organic matter comes into contact with disinfectants, it forms a crust that shelters and protects germs against the action of disinfectants.

For this reason, it is best to work in three separate steps (using detergent, rinsing, disinfecting) instead of using mixed products which, while they may save

time, are never as effective. Thus, simply soaking soiled implements in a bucket of water mixed with household bleach gives only a false sense of security, since household bleach has little effect on organic matter.

It is better to manually remove dirt from implements or soak them in a detergent.

Burning organic matter (using a gardener's flame gun, for example), produces effects comparable to the incrustation of surface proteins through coagulation. This method is therefore not recommended until all surface waste has been removed.

In sum, although it may seem illogical, it is impossible to properly disinfect surfaces unless they are already clean.

• Each disinfectant has a certain range of effectiveness, that is, a series of germs it can usually fight.

The most common resistant germs are bacterial spores (certain bacteria resist environments that become unfavorable), parasite eggs and mildew.

As we saw above for insecticides, the repeated use of the same disinfectant may eventually lead to resistant germs that can develop with impunity. Effective hygiene therefore means alternating the products used.

Of course, alternating products does not mean mixing them, because certain disinfectants are incompatible with each other.

It is recommended to use an alkaline disinfectant six days out of seven (effective on organic matter) and to complement it with an acid disinfectant on the seventh day (effective on most mineral matter).

• Some products, such as quaternary ammonium compounds, are not very effective in hard water.

The breeder can have water quality checked by public services or install a water softener which will also protect pipes and high-pressure pumps from scaling that will shorten their service life.

Other disinfectants, such as household bleach, can be used at different dilutions based on the purpose.

• Most disinfectants are more effective in hot water. Remember this when choosing products exposed to cold (foot baths).

As a general rule, the lower the temperature, the longer the product application time.

Some modern disinfectants have the added benefit of losing their color when they are no longer effective (visual check).

• Disinfectants often have a very short effective period (less than six hours). This depends mainly on the excipient.

• Others are sensitive to light. It is therefore necessary to check their manufacturing date and avoid trying to save money by storing them for a long period (household bleach, even in a sealed container, loses its effectiveness after only three months of storage).

Choosing products

Unlike with disinfectants, the breeder can select one or two detergents once and for all and should avoid making changes if they give satisfactory results.

If cleaning water flows into a septic tank, biodegradable detergents should be used, but not in conjunction with bacteriostatic products, which inhibit the natural decomposition of slurry.

All these criteria must be considered when choosing a detergent. In practice, most detergents are suitable for dog breeding kennels.

The criteria for choosing disinfectants involve characteristics related to the product (range of effectiveness, lack of toxicity, cost, effectiveness on organic matter), the object being cleaned (resistance to corrosion) and the breeder's purpose (disinfection of the air or floor, for example).

Unfortunately, there are no universal disinfectants capable of destroying all disease-causing germs (given their forms of resistance).

Just as there are no good or bad antiseptics for a wound, there are no good or bad disinfectants for treating a surface.

There are only bad matches (products poorly chosen for the purpose) and mistakes in usage when the product is too concentrated, too cold or not used according to the directions.

In the absence of infection, it is difficult for a breeder to check the effectiveness of a product, since products work at a microscopic level.

Nutritional hygiene

Although dogs are at low risk of toxi-infections caused by food (few types of bacteria can resist the high acidity level in a dog's stomach), certain hygiene precautions must be taken in the storage, preparation and distribution of food.

- Food should be stored in its original packaging away from light, humidity and air. Bags should thus have an air-tight seal to prevent oxidation and the rancidity of fats. Alternately, the contents can be transferred to air-tight stainless steel or plastic containers. Bags of food should be stored off the ground, away from the floor and walls and far from the source of water used to clean food bowls (due to the risk of spattering). The storage period must be limited to guarantee palatability (relating particularly to the degree of preservation of fats), nutritional quality and vitamin content.
- The entryway to the storage area should be equipped with a foot bath (in case the delivery person was just at another breeding kennel) and a step at the threshold to protect against crawling insects and rodents.
- The windows should be protected by mosquito nets, the walls covered with insect repellent paint and the room equipped with an actinic lamp in the warm season.
- Large frozen pieces of food should not be thawed at

room temperature, since thawing too slowly promotes the spread of bacteria. Similarly, leftover food should be taken away from dogs especially in warm, stormy weather.

Removing dogs for kennel cleaning

This technique, commonly used in the breeding of "production" animals, consists of taking advantage of the temporary absence of animals in a room to disinfect it and remove parasites as thoroughly as possible. The products available for this purpose are likely to be toxic to animals. Animals must be kept out for at least one week for a small room and two weeks for an entire building, based on the principle that the germs that survive disinfection will die from dessication, the lack of a living host or simply from age. Here is one technique that can be used in the whelping area or quarantine room of a dog breeding kennel:

1. Dismantle and remove all accessories and utensils (doghouses, food bowls, etc.).
2. Collect or vacuum out all waste.

3. Clean floors and walls with a high-pressure pump (30 to 150 kg/cm3, for a flow rate of about 800 liters per hour) or, better yet, with a steam sprayer if there are parasite problems in the kennel.
4. Scour manually, using a stiff brush and detergent.
5. Perform first disinfection.
6. Remove insects overnight (make sure to separate this step from the preceding one because of the incompatibility between disinfectants and insecticides).
7. Vacuum out dead insects.
8. Bleach walls and ceilings with an insecticidal paint containing glue and kaolin.
9. The following day, disinfect the air with disinfectant dispensed from a thermal mister.
10. Repeat misting forty-eight hours before bringing animals back in.

The above steps should be repeated two or three times a year.

REQUIRED WATER QUALITY FOR A DOG BREEDING KENNEL (EXCLUDING BACTERIA)	
pH (measure of acidity)	6.5 < pH > 8.5
Hardness (level of dissolved calcium salts)	< 30°F
Nitrates	< 50 mg/l
Iron	< 0.2 mg/l

EXAMPLES FOR USE OF BLEACH AT A STRENGTH OF 12 DEGREES OF CHLORINITY USE DILUTION

	Contact time	
Disinfecting food	2 drops per liter of water	5 minutes
Dishes	2 cl per 10-liter pail	5 min.
Smooth surfaces	20 cl per pail	5 min.
Rough surfaces	1 liter per pail	15 min.
Pipes	undiluted	15 min.
Weed killer	undiluted	spreading

UNIVERSAL DECLARATION OF ANIMAL RIGHTS

Preamble

Whereas all animal possess rights,

Whereas disregard and contempt of these rights has led and continues to lead humans to commit crimes against nature and against animals,

Whereas the recognition by humans of the right of other animal species to exist constitutes the foundation of coexistence of species throughout the world,

Whereas humans carry out genocide and likely will continue to do so,

Whereas respect for animals by humans is tied to the respect of humans for one another, Whereas education must begin at an early age, teaching children to observe, understand, respect, and love animals,

We now therefore proclaim

Article 1.

Every animal is born with an equal and has an equal right to life.

Article 2.

1) Every animal has the right to be respected.
2) Humans, as an animal species, cannot claim the right to exterminate other animals or to exploit them by violating this right: Humans have the obligation to use their knowledge to help animals.
3) Every animal has the right to attention, care, and protection by humans.

Article 3.

1) No animal shall be subjected to cruel or inhumane treatment.
2) If an animal must be put to death, the death must be instantaneous, painless, and free of suffering.

Article 4.

1) Every animal belonging to a wild species has the right to live freely in its own natural land, air, or aquatic environment, and has the right to reproduce.
2) Any deprivation of this freedom, even for education purposes, violates this right.

Article 5.

1) Every animal belonging to a species traditionally living in a human environment has the right to life and development at the rate and under the conditions of life and liberty specific to that species.
2) Any modification of this rate or these conditions imposed by humans for financial gain violates this right.

Article 6.

1) Every animal that a human chooses as a companion has the right to live a life equivalent to its natural lifespan.
2) Abandonment of an animal is a cruel and degrading act.

Article 7.

Every animal has the right to reasonable length and intensity of work, to healthful food, and to rest.

Article 8.

1) Animal experimentation, whether medical, commercial, or in any other form, causing physical or psychological suffering is incompatible with the rights of animals.
2) Alternative techniques must be used and developed.

Article 9.

When an animal is raised for consumption, it must be fed, sheltered, transported, and killed without causing anxiety or pain to the animal.

Article 10.

1) No animal may be exploited for human entertainment.
2) Shows and performances using animal are incompatible with the dignity of the animal.

Article 11.

1) Any act resulting in the unnecessary death of an animal is a biocide, and therefore a crime against the species.
2) Pollution and destruction of the natural environment lead to genocide.

Article 12.

1) Animals must be treated with respect.
2) Violent scenes showing animals as the victims must be banned in movies and on television, unless the purpose is to demonstrate a violation of animal rights.

Article 13.

1) Organizations for the protection and rescue of animals must be represented at the governmental level.
2) Animal rights must be protected by law in the same way as human rights.

Tips for Outings, Transporting and Traveling with Your Dog

If you would like your dog to accompany you as often as possible, it is wise to accustom your dog to your outings at an early age. You should also check to see if you are allowed to bring the dog into the places where you go. Below are some practical tips to help you avoid unpleasant surprises.

Before Leaving on Vacation

- One month prior departure, check that the vaccinations are up to date and if not, take the dog to the veterinarian for booster shots. In addition to the standard vaccinations (canine distemper, parvovirus, leptospirosis, infectious canine hepatitis and rabies), it is also possible to immunize the dog against babesiosis (piroplasmosis), a disease transmitted by certain ticks. This may be necessary at certain destinations. Specialized flea collars may help reduce infections from ticks and other external parasites. If the dog is not used to rocky terrain, coat his footpads with lotions made from picric acid in order to toughen them up.
- At least two weeks before: have the dog de-wormed and prepare an emergency medical kit. If traveling abroad, have the veterinarian prepare a certificate of good health.

The Day Before Departure

Feed the dog a light meal approximately ten hours before departure. To limit the risk of vomiting, do not give the dog anything to eat during the trip, unless the travel time is more than twelve hours.

Gather all the equipment needed to care for the dog on site: water and food bowls, sleeping mat and a brush (and/or comb).

The Day of Departure

If the dog becomes sick or anxious easily, give him an antinauseant or a sedative as prescribed by the veterinarian. This will prevent the dog from becoming agitated. Be aware, however that a sedated dog may sometimes have more difficulty walking, which is something to be particularly aware of with heavier dogs. To simply calm the dog somewhat, a few drops of cough syrup containing antihistamines will suffice.

Before departure, walk the dog. Bring enough plastic sacks and paper to clean up the excrement when stopping at rest areas while traveling.

Food During the Trip

There is no need to add extra stress to the dog by changing his diet. If a change in diet is required, the change should be made at least three weeks before departure. While on vacation, maintain the same meal times as normal: one to two meals per day as the case may be. The dog may refuse to eat at the beginning of the stay. Do not worry too much and do not give in to the dog by offering him treats to whet his appetite. The dog will quickly learn how to be spoiled on a regular basis. The quantity of food can be adjusted according to how active the dog is. Give him water frequently when the temperature is high.

Dogs and Hotels

At hotels, basic good manners dictate a few simple rules of behavior:
- alert the hotel manager to the presence of the dog when making reservations;
- do not leave the dog alone in the room and walk him at least three times per day;
- keep the dog on a leash while inside the hotel;
- prevent him from barking;
- show respect for the furniture: set up a sleeping area for the dog somewhere other than the bed or sofa.

Dogs and Restaurants

It is best to feed the dog before going out to eat so that he will not beg at the table. If dining at the hotel restaurant, it is best to tell the chef in advance what food to prepare for the dog if the dog is accustomed to a standard "meat-rice-vegetables" diet. Request a table off to the side to provide peace and quiet for the dog and those around you.

Dogs and Cars

Traveling in cars will not cause problems if the dog has been used to riding in cars since a very young age. In order to best prevent problems, however, (restlessness, agitation, barking, vomiting, etc.), remember the following:
- do not feed the dog ten hours prior to the trip, but do give him water. Give the dog an antinauseant or even a sedative prescribed by the veterinarian;
- do not allow the dog to stick his head out the window as this may cause irritation of the eyes or ears.

In cases of long trips, it is wise to stop every two hours to allow the dog to stretch his legs and attend to his needs if necessary.

Caution! Never leave the dog locked in a vehicle parked in the sun or he may suffer from heat stroke (the passenger side of a car can reach as high as 70° C!) (150°F). Finally, in cases of car accidents, any wounds suffered by the animal will normally be covered by the automobile insurance of the driver at fault.

Long distance trips call for maximum security.

The dog's place is on the back seat.

Inside the vehicle the dog should remain in your company. In a station wagon, arrange a comfortable place for him in the back of the car.

-It is not advisable to put the dog in the trunk of the car and strictly forbidden to shut him up in there completely. Emissions from the exhaust pipe can asphyxiate him. Openings for ventilation must be adapted to meet security standards. (According to a law adopted in 1982, it is illegal to shut an animal up in a trunk that does not meet certain criteria for ventilation.)

- If you still opt for the trunk, be aware that there is specially designed equipment to this purpose.

Dogs and Trains

This is the mode of transportation that our companions appreciate the most. Train travel generally does not cause any problems for dogs. If you have any doubts, it is advisable to avoid feeding the dog ten hours prior to departure.

In France, SCNF (French railways board) regulations are very precise: the mode of transportation depends of the weight of the dog.

Other countries: Germany, Austria, Belgium, Holland, Italy, Portugal and Switzerland. The rules in force are the same: the dog must be on a leash and muzzled and a half-fare ticket must be purchased. In Spain and Great Britain, animals are not allowed in passenger cars. They are placed in the baggage car and a tax must be paid.

Dogs in Airplanes

In order to enable the dog to travel comfortably without causing stress or vomiting, be sure to:
- refrain from feeding the dog ten hours before departure;

- give him an antinauseant thirty minutes before boarding, or even a sedative prescribed by a veterinarian for dogs with extreme anxiety;
- take him to relieve himself before placing him in his cage.
If all of the above is done, there should be no problems!
Can the dog travel in the passenger cabin, or must he travel in a cage in the hold? It is the weight of the dog that will determine how comfortable he is and where he will travel. In both cases, tell the airline about the dog when making your reservations.

In Boats

For all those contemplating a cruise, the main concern of cruise companies is to provide you with the largest array of fun and entertainment possible on board. However, you will have to forget about taking a "tour of the world" with your dog. International law forbids pets from boarding ships.

In Urban Transportation

In most of the neighboring countries, dogs are widely "tolerated." The same rules apply: the dog must be kept on a leash and muzzled, and you must purchase a half-price ticket for him.
Before deciding to travel with the dog, be sure that it is necessary to do so before subjecting the dog to these constraints.
As for taxis, the dog may only ride in the taxi if the driver agrees.

In Parks and Gardens

Dogs are not allowed in public gardens for reasons of hygiene and safety.
Some parks allow dogs both on or off a leash. In the woods, certain conditions must observed especially in terms of whether the dog can run freely.
Dogs are normally not allowed in national parks and preserves, even on a leash. They are usually allowed on beaches if they are on a leash, provided the owner cleans up and throws away any excrement the dog may leave and that the dog does not bother anyone: no inappropriate digging in the sand, no pushing over swimmers, etc.
Assistance dogs for disabled persons are an exception to the above-mentioned rules. They are allowed to follow their owner everywhere.

In Public Places

Dogs are allowed in most places except hospitals, save for hospitals equipped with special rooms to accommodate animals for psychological and healing purposes. Some retirement homes allow pets.
Of course, the animals have to be calm, clean and kept on a leash, or even muzzled if necessary or required.

Boarding Kennels

There are different types of boarding kennels depending on the number of dogs kept: inside the house or in cages. It is important to visit the establishment first to be sure that it is licensed, clean and has pleasant surroundings. Dogs adjust very well to kennel life even if they have never experienced it. The owner should not feel guilty if the dog whines when he or she leaves.

Whatever solution is chosen, the owner of the establishment should be informed of the dog's health. Leave the dog's health card with the number of the veterinarian. It is also a good idea to provide information about the dog's diet and habits in order to avoid needless disturbances. A few of the dog's personal objects can also be left (blanket, toys, etc.). In cases of marked separation anxiety, discuss the situation with the veterinarian, who will provide advice about what to do so that the owner may leave under good conditions.

Administrative Matters

Insurance

Before leaving, be sure that the dog is listed on your "head of household" or "multi-risk homeowners" policy. The mandatory "third-party liability" insurance will protect you against damages caused by your dog to other persons – from the accident he may cause if he strays or escapes, to the material damage at the hotel caused in your absence, to biting, etc.
- Read your policy carefully. Some risks are not necessarily covered and there may be a lot of exclusions.
- Purchase "dog" insurance (at least in France). The advantage of this insurance is that it covers the policyholder as well as any other person taking care of the dog, provided the person is watching the dog free of charge.

Assistance

Take out an international emergency assistance policy and request that the company make provisions to care for the dog in the event that you have to be medically evacuated.
- Always leave an address and telephone number of a relative or friend who can be contacted in case of an emergency.
- For lost or found animals, alert the closest police station and veterinarian immediately.

What to do if You Lose Your Dog's Papers While Traveling.

This situation is only serious in terms of the rabies vaccination card or the certificate of good health. To avoid problems, make a photocopy of all your documents before leaving. Contact the veterinarian who administered the vaccinations as soon as possible to request a second copy of the rabies card and file a report with the police in order to obtain a statement of loss. As for the certificate of good health, go to the closest veterinarian to obtain another one.

Customs Formalities

The laws of the European Union member countries governing the transit of pets have not been modified since January 1993. Two certificates are mandatory:
- The certificate of good health
A veterinarian must draw up this certificate less than one week before departure and between three and five days before crossing the border. Ask for an international health certificate. This is a form drafted in four languages (for Europe, for example, Germany requires that the certificate be translated).
- To cross the border, the health certificate must not be older than ten days. If you plan to travel for longer than ten days, bear in mind the return with your dog. You will need to have a new one drawn up on site.
- The rabies vaccination card
The dog may only cross the border if his last vaccinations were given at least thirty days, but not more than one year before (the thirty-day minimum does not apply to booster shots).

Quarantine

Quarantine is still in force in certain insular countries, which require six months of quarantine. The owner of course bears the kennel costs.
We would only advise you to contemplate taking your dog along with you if you are planning to stay for awhile!

No matter what form of transportation is used, certain rules must be respected. Ensure that the surrounding temperature is not too hot. If necessary, provide ventilation or wet the dog's head with a damp cloth. Heat stroke is a serious accident requiring emergency treatment by the veterinarian.
Stop and give the dog water frequently, at least every two hours in intense heat.

First Aid

Fever and Temperature

All too often, pet owners think that if their dog's nose is warm, it means he has a fever. This preconceived notion is unfounded, though it does contain partial truth.

What really happens?
Several notions are important:

1. Hyperthermia (increased body temperature):

There may be several causes:
• **External:**
This is essentially caused by heat stroke caused when dogs are left in a car in the sun.

• **Internal/psychological:**
This form of hyperthermia is linked to effort, emotion and excitation (as with a dog that pants a lot in extreme heat). In these cases, changes in body temperature will not alter the general state of the dog.

• **Internal/pathological:**
This occurs in cases of disease (infectious, viral, parasitic, etc.). In these cases, changes in the dog's general health are observed: fatigue exhaustion, loss of appetite.

2. Chills:

If the dog has chills, is this a sign of hyperthermia?
• Not always, because chills can also be psychological in origin such as when the dog is cold (which is rare nonetheless), frightened or anxious (during a visit to the veterinarian for example).

• It may also be pathological in cases of illness accompanied by increased or even decreased body temperature.

Coming back to so-called febrile excitation:
• **Psychological:**
Any time the dog makes an effort or becomes excited, his temperature increases, his breathing accelerates and he has his mouth open. All the mucous membranes become congested (tongue, eyes, nose, etc.). The dog perspires almost exclusively through panting; in other words, he "perspires" in order to regulate body temperature.

• **Pathological:**
Certain serious diseases can cause febrile excitation (poisoning, cerebral attack, certain viral diseases such as canine distemper, rabies and hypocalcemia in nursing bitches, which causes convulsions).

Taking the dog's temperature:
When you take the dog's temperature, bear in mind everything that has been stated above.
The normal body temperature of dogs and cats is from 38.5° to 39°C, which is a 1° difference from the average for humans. However, 40°C is just as serious in dogs as in humans, so the margin is slimmer.
If the owner is worried, it is best to check the dog's temperature when he is calm and resting, before consulting the veterinarian and certainly not after walking in the woods for an hour in extreme 35°C heat.

Notes about Body Temperature:
Although fleas on dogs and cats rarely bite humans, if they do have the choice between humans and house dogs, they tend to pick dogs simply because they prefer to feed off blood at 39°C. Blood at 37°C does not suit them at all.

Three ways to properly carry a wounded dog without harming him.

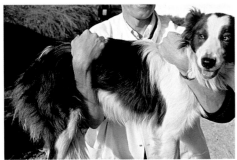

SERIOUS TRAUMA

The range of possible lesions in terms of wounds, contusions, hemorrhages and burns is great both in number and degree of severity. The following are the most severe:

WOUND WITH PROFUSE HEMORRHAGING: *Hemorrhaging can be venous (dark blood running out in patches) or arterial (light red blood running out in spurts) in origin. In both cases, clean compresses should be applied to the area that is bleeding. For arterial bleeding, apply pressure to the artery with your finger or fist in an uphill direction (tourniquets are not advised). An emergency visit to the veterinarian is required.*

CRANIAL OR OCULAR TRAUMA: *These traumas are often related to automobile or hunting accidents. The dog should be taken to the veterinarian as quickly as possible, taking care not to move him too much.*

SPINAL COLUMN TRAUMA: *Again, take the dog to the veterinarian as quickly as possible, keeping the dog in a position that allows his head, trunk and pelvis to stay in alignment during transportation.*

OPEN FRACTURES AND CONTUSIONS: *Although these are rarely a dire emergency, the risk of infection and the pain involved do make them a relatively serious emergency. It is important to immobilize the fracture with materials you have on hand (splint or piece of stick) while covering the wounded surface with damp compresses before taking the dog to the veterinarian.*

SNAKE BITES: *Whatever the type of snake, it is first of all important to avoid touching the wound (sucking, bloodletting). If possible, place an ice pack on the bite and keep the animal as calm as possible while taking him to the veterinarian.*

Frostbite

Frostbite occurs especially in sledding dogs or in the high mountains, on the most exposed areas of the body: testicles, penis and breasts. The consequences are the same as with burns except that the frostbitten areas should be slowly reheated (in 30°C (85°F) water) only as long as these areas will not be exposed to freezing temperatures again (e.g. if the dog has to go outside again). If you are not sure, it is better to try to maintain the frostbite.

Respiratory Distress

Respiratory distress occurs when there is a loss of respiratory reflexes (with partial loss of consciousness) or when the respiratory tract is obstructed. The obstruction may be of external origin (foreign object lodged in the throat, drowning, etc.) or internal (tracheal collapse, pulmonary hemorrhaging, etc.). The animal should be taken to the veterinarian immediately. In the case of an external obstruction, an attempt may be made to remove the water or the object by holding onto the dog's hind legs and shaking him downward. Mouth-to-nose may be administered by holding the dog's mouth shut and breathing air into his nose with a short breath approximately every five seconds.

Check to see if the dog is suffering from cardiac arrest by placing your hand on the thorax behind the left elbow. If so, mouth-to-nose should be combined with cardio-pulmonary resuscitation. Place the animal on his right side and stimulate the heart by applying chest compressions at the base of the thorax between the third and fifth rib. Give five compressions after every breath.

In this scenario, the chances of survival are uncertain and every minute counts in the rescue attempt.

Gastric Dilation-Torsion Complex

Gastric dilation-torsion complex is a disorder specific to giant and large breeds. The stomach dilates, rotates on its axis and puts pressure on important organs (such as the spleen and diaphragm) and the circulatory system. If you own a dog at risk, prevention is the best medicine: divide his daily food ration into several meals and avoid exercise before meals. It is also important to be able to recognize the early warning signs.

In the first stage, the dog begins to salivate, his abdomen becomes hard and painful (but not necessarily bloated at this point) and he constantly tries to vomits. In the next stage, he lies down, begins to swell very quickly and has difficulty breathing. If no action is taken at this point, the dog will soon die.

Take the dog to the veterinarian immediately. Keep him warm without preventing him from vomiting and transport him in a position that allows him to breathe easily. Even if immediate care is sought, the dog will remain in critical condition for at least forty-eight hours due to the digestive and cardiac complications that often accompany dilation-torsion complex.

SERIOUS BURNS

Burns are serious when they cover a large area and/or are deep. They are often lethal if they cover more than 2/3 of the body surface. They are frequently seen in three cases.

BURNS BY ELECTROCUTION: *These burns occur frequently with puppies that tend to chew on everything, including electrical wires. If the dog is still in contact with the wire, cut the power before trying to move the dog and revive him if necessary. Once the dog is out of danger, run cold water over the burn (rinse thoroughly for 20 minutes) before taking him to the veterinarian.*

CAUSTIC BURNS: *Rinse the burned area in the same manner. If the animal has ingested the poison, do not try to make him vomit or swallow anything. He should be taken to the veterinarian immediately.*

BURNS FROM FIRE OR HYPERTHERMIA: *Serious burns (3rd or 4th degree) are painless at first, then a sulcus forms around the wounded area and the center necrotizes. The animal may die of dehydration due to loss of fluids or secondary infections. The animal must of course be treated immediately, and you may also wash the wounded area thoroughly.*

GIVING AN INJECTION UNDER THE SKIN

1. Pinch the skin firmly behind the neck, between the shoulder blades in order to form a skin fold. Disinfect the area with a piece of alcohol-soaked cotton.

2. Pierce the skin with the needle at the base of the skin fold.

3. Hold the syringe perpendicular to the fold and inject the product.

 First Aid Kit

- Alcohol-based disinfectant
- Hydrogen peroxide
- Iodine-based disinfectant gel
- Gastric protection gel
- Anti-diarrhea clay (smectite)
- Balm made from hyperoxide fatty acids
- Flea spray
- Multi-purpose vermifuge
- Antinauseant
- Cough syrup
- 375 mg aspirins
- Ear cleaning solution
- Tanning spray for footpads
- Tweezers
- Round-tipped scissors
- Thermometer
- Cotton
- Compresses
- Bandages
- Medicated adhesive strips
- Swabs

LUXATIONS

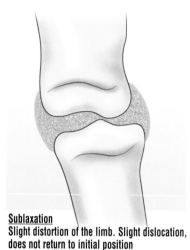

Sublaxation
Slight distortion of the limb. Slight dislocation, does not return to initial position

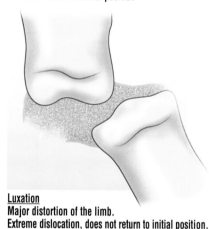

Luxation
Major distortion of the limb.
Extreme dislocation, does not return to initial position.

FRACTURES

Different Types of Fractures

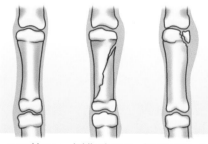

normal bone   hairline fracture   fragmented fracture

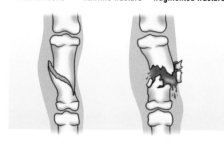

complete fracture   compound fracture

Questions / Answers

My dog's heart is beating rapidly:

What to do:
A dog whose heart is beating rapidly is suffering from tachycardia. Except in cases of stress, emotion or effort, an abnormal increase in the heart rate is always related to a serious disease. Therefore, the veterinarian should be consulted without delay.

What not to do:
Avoid confusing the effects of simple emotions with chronic problems.

Consult the veterinarian?
Definitely, given the seriousness of cardiac diseases.

My dog is limping:

What to do:
- Identify the lame leg and closely inspect the foot-pads and digits (for cuts, foreign objects, etc.).
- Check to see if the joints are warm and swollen.
- Do not attempt to mobilize the limb that the dog is not using.

What not to do:
- Force the dog to walk.
- Apply a splint without having a clear diagnosis.

Consult the veterinarian?
Yes, if the dog seems to be suffering and the problem is not simply a foreign object lodged in between the digits.
If the lameness persists for more than forty-eight hours, it is imperative to see the veterinarian.

My Dog is having convulsions:

What to do:
Cover the dog with a blanket and put him in a calm spot so that he will not hurt himself.

What not to do:
- Attempt to open the mouth.
- Handle the dog during an attack.
- Force the dog to swallow water.

Consult the veterinarian?
Yes, because convulsions require emergency treatment.

My dog has an earache:

What to do:
- Clean the ears regularly.
- Remove hair from the ears.
- Check to see if a thorn has gotten lodged in the ear canal.

What not to do:
Clean the ears with a cotton swab.

Consult the veterinarian?
Consulting the veterinarian is highly advisable given the risk of rather severe otitis or internal lesions caused by thorns.

My dog has cut himself:

What to do:
- Apply pressure to the wound to stop the bleeding.
- Clean the wound with hydrogen peroxide.
- Apply a bandage of compresses and gauze after having shaved the area around the wound.

What not to do:
Make a tourniquet.

Consult the veterinarian?
Not necessarily, if the cut is small (under a centimeter). If it is over one centimeter, the veterinarian will have to put in stitches.

My dog has broken a leg:

What to do:
Put the dog in his basket, keep him calm and take him to the veterinarian at once without making any abrupt movements.

What not to do:
Move the dog too much or try to make a splint.

Consult the veterinarian?
Yes, as a matter of urgency in all cases.

My dog is paralyzed:

What to do:
Look to see if he is moving his tail or his legs, or if he has feeling in his extremities. If he is completely paralyzed, wrap him with a blanket, place him in his basket and take him to the veterinarian.

What not to do:
Handle the dog or try to make him walk.

Consult the veterinarian?
Definitely, for diagnostic and treatment.

My dog is in stroke:

What to do:
If the dog goes into a coma as a result of heat stroke, it is necessary to bring down his body temperature with wet cloths or by putting him in a bath. Do not hesitate to perform "mouth-to-nose" resuscitation. Massage the extremities to increase circulation to the limbs.

What not to do:
- Feed the dog or make him drink.
- Close the dog up in a warm place.

Consult the veterinarian?
Definitely, in all cases.

My dog has sore eyes:

What to do:
Clean the eyes with normal saline solution or eye drops.

What not to do:
Use an all-purpose eyewash.

Consult the veterinarian?
If symptoms persist for more than twenty-four hours, consult the veterinarian. There are now veterinarians who are specialized in ophthalmology.

My dog is itching:

What to do:
- Look to see if the dog has external parasites or fleas (even though these are not constantly on the dog).
- Look for wounds.
- If the dog has fleas, it is important to treat the dog and his environment.
- Itching wounds are often recurrent.

What not to do:
- Use medicines that are indicated for eczema.
- Wash the dog, because some localized diseases can spread.

Consult the veterinarian?
In cases of a parasitic infection, a parasite treatment will suffice. But since certain types of itch have another origin, it is always helpful to consult the veterinarian.

My dog has been burned:

What to do:
- Clean the wounds with a .5% Cetavlon type solution and apply a sterile bandage.

- Change the bandage twice a day and give the dog an analgesic for the pain.

What not to do:
- Disinfect the wound with pure antiseptic.
- Apply a dry bandage directly to the wound.
- Use materials that are not sterilized.

Consult the veterinarian?
Yes, if the burns cover a large area, because there can be numerous and serious medical complications from burns.

My dog has swallowed a poisonous product:

What to do:
- Try to find the toxic product or plant in question.
- Contact a veterinarian immediately.

What not to do:
- Give the dog water, milk or anything to drink.
- Try to make him vomit.
- Give the dog a purgative.
- Clean or wash the coat.

Consult the veterinarian?
The veterinarian should be called urgently in all cases.

My dog has been stung by a wasp:

What to do:
- Try to remove the stinger with a pin.
- Disinfect.

What not to do:
Give the dog an antihistamine or any other medication.

Consult the veterinarian?
Urgently, if there is massive swelling or if the dog has been stung in the throat.

My dog has been bitten by a snake:

What to do:
- Disinfect the wound.

- Keep the dog as calm as possible.
- Apply ice to the bite wound.

What not to do:
- Make a tourniquet.
- Make an incision and suck the wound.

Consult the veterinarian?
Yes, within an hour of the bite if possible. Above all, avoid agitating the dog. Carry him so as not to increase his heart rate and thereby diffuse the poison.

My dog urinates frequently:

What to do:
- Measure the amount of water he drinks throughout the day.
- Observe his appetite (normal, increased, decreased).
- With bitches, check for puss on the vulva.
- Weigh the animal.

What not to do:
Reduce the amount of water given to the dog.

Consult the veterinarian?
Yes, in all cases since many serious diseases, starting with diabetes, can cause polyuria.

My dog has puss in his urine:

What to do:
If the dog has an infection of the sheath or the vulva, simply disinfect the area two to three times a day with a gynecological disinfectant.

What not to do
Disinfect the area with an irritating substance.

Consult the veterinarian?
Yes, a preliminary visit is always in order because it could be metritis (infection of the uterus) or a prostrate abscess.

My dog has blood in his urine:

What to do:
In the case of a bitch, check to see if she is simply in heat.
If the urine is light brown in color (piroplasmosis), inspect the coat for ticks.

What not to do:
Give the dog an antibiotic or a urinary antiseptic.

Consult the veterinarian?
Yes, in all cases, because dark-colored urine is always indicative of a serious disease.

My dog is not urinating normally:

What to do:
Take careful note of the manner in which the dog urinates (frequently, in small quantities, involuntarily, etc.)

What not to do:
Attempt to administer a treatment without first obtaining the opinion of the veterinarian.

Consult the veterinarian?
Yes, in all cases, given the seriousness of the diseases in question.

Many canine diseases need to be treated by a veterinarian as quickly as possible. There are also special situations that absolutely cannot wait. These are true emergencies, in which the dog's life, or at least his major body functions are altered. Specific treatment and rapid intervention by the veterinarian are the precious tools that will save the dog's life. Three rules should be observed: take the dog to the veterinarian as quickly as possible, protect the dog, and protect yourself as a wounded animal may act unpredictably. If the dog is conscious, he should be muzzled unless there is a chance he may vomit. Do not muzzle an unconscious animal but still pay close attention.

HEAT STROKE

All too often, dogs are seen left alone in vehicles parked in the sun or even in the shade with the window generously rolled down – by all of about 5 cm.

This attitude is mainly one of irresponsibility. Remember that unlike humans, dogs do not perspire through their skin.

Perspiration or sweating is an excellent system that allows human to conduct temperature exchanges with the outside air, thereby preventing body temperature from rising too quickly in extreme heat.
This system is also used artificially in cats. When they lick themselves, they deposit saliva on their coat, which thereby allows for a thermal exchange to take place.

With dogs, even though their skin does not produce the sweat that is necessary for thermal exchange, air blowing in an open space does help cool their body through radiation and conduction.

Dogs therefore, do not only breathe with their mouths, they perspire through their mouths.
What Happens in the Event of Heat Stroke?

If left in the heat in a vehicle that is almost entirely closed, the dog will begin to pant in order to perspire and to lower his rising body temperature. Moreover, he is unable to lower his temperature through his skin because there is no air circulating (closed vehicle).
Therefore, his body temperature rises to a dangerously high level. In addition, a panting dog quickly exhausts the amount of healthy air available in the vehicle and ends up breathing in exhaled air that is high in carbon dioxide and low in oxygen.
The combination of these factors makes the dog highly susceptible to fainting. It occurs suddenly. The dog is often standing, as though in a daze, his legs spread apart, gasping for air and breathing quickly. Often, he begins to

tremble or may even have convulsions.
If his temperature reaches 42°C, he will begin to vomit and will end up going into a state of shock, which may quickly become irreversible.

Rapid Action Must Be Taken Insofar as Possible:
The dog's temperature must be brought down as quickly as possible by placing him in lukewarm water that is progressively cooled, or in cool water that is in a well-ventilated, airy place.
Monitor the dog's temperature and general state.
Take the dog to the veterinarian as soon as possible.

Which Animals are At Risk?
- The larger the dog, the more quickly he will use up the air in the vehicle.
- Dogs with cardiac problems or respiratory difficulties run the risk of suffering heat stroke very rapidly since gaseous exchanges in their lungs are extremely limited.
- Breeds with short faces (Boxers, Pekinese) have more problems breathing than other breeds.
- Animals that are high-strung by nature may also be sensitive to heat stroke.
- Obese animals, since fat is good insulation.

Prevention:
- Never leave a dog in a vehicle parked in the hot sun.
- Remember that even if the vehicle is parked in a cool, shady spot, it may be in the sun a few hours later.
- Always leave the windows sufficiently open.
- Never leave puppies, older dogs or dogs with cardiac problems in a vehicle in the heat, even in the shade.

Doctor Marc HABIB, Veterinarian
Paris, France

Index